S0-AWY-786

Customer Support Information

Plunkett's Entertainment & Media Industry Almanac 2007

Please register your book immediately...

if you did not purchase it directly from Plunkett Research, Ltd. This will enable us to fulfill your replacement request if you have a damaged product, or your requests for assistance. Also it will enable us to notify you of future editions, so that you may purchase them from the source of your choice.

If you are an actual, original purchaser but did not receive a FREE CD-ROM version with your book...*

you may request it by returning this form.

_____ YES, please register me as a purchaser of the book.
I did not buy it directly from Plunkett Research, Ltd.

_____ YES, please send me a free CD-ROM version of the book.
I am an actual purchaser, but I did not receive one with my book.
(Proof of purchase may be required.)

Customer Name _____

Title_____

Organization _____

Address _____

City_____State_____Zip_____

Country (if other than USA) _____

Phone_____Fax _____

E-mail _____

Mail or Fax to: **Plunkett Research, Ltd.**

Attn: FREE CD-ROM and/or Registration
P.O. Drawer 541737, Houston, TX 77254-1737 USA
713.932.0000 · Fax 713.932.7080 · www.plunkettresearch.com

* Only the original purchaser of the book is eligible to register. Use of CD-ROMs is subject to the terms of their end user license agreements.

PLUNKETT'S ENTERTAINMENT & MEDIA INDUSTRY ALMANAC 2007

The Only Comprehensive Guide to the Entertainment & Media Industry

Jack W. Plunkett

Published by:
Plunkett Research, Ltd., Houston, Texas
www.plunkettresearch.com

PLUNKETT'S ENTERTAINMENT & MEDIA INDUSTRY ALMANAC 2007

Editor and Publisher:
Jack W. Plunkett

Executive Editor and Database Manager:
Martha Burgher Plunkett

Senior Editors and Researchers:
Andrew Frishman
Christie Manck
John Peterson

Editors, Researchers and Assistants:
Toby Beeny
Brandon Brison
Addie K. FryeWeaver
Jason Litton
Leslie Miller
Suzanne Zarosky

E-Commerce Managers:
Mark Cassells
Heather M. Cook
Brian J. Holsinger
Ian Markham

Information Technology Manager
Wenping Guo

Cover Design:
Kim Paxson, Just Graphics
Junction, TX

Special Thanks to:
Association of American Publishers
Book Industry Study Group
International Federation of the Phonographic
Industries (IFPI)
Kagan Research, LLC
Magazine Publishers of America
National Association of Theatre Owners
National Cable & Telecommunications Association
Nielsen Media Research
Newspaper Association of America
U.S. Bureau of Labor Statistics
U.S. Census Bureau
Universal McCann

Plunkett Research, Ltd.
P. O. Drawer 541737, Houston, Texas 77254, USA
Phone: 713.932.0000 Fax: 713.932.7080 www.plunkettresearch.com

Published by:
Plunkett Research, Ltd.
P.O. Drawer 541737
Houston, Texas 77254-1737

Phone: 713.932.0000
Fax: 713.932.7080
Internet: www.plunkettresearch.com

ISBN10 # 1-59392-066-0
ISBN13 # 978-1-59392-066-1

Disclaimer of liability
for use and results of use:

PLUNKETT'S ENTERTAINMENT & MEDIA INDUSTRY ALMANAC 2007

CONTENTS

Continued on the next page

Continued from the previous page

A Short Entertainment & Media Industry Glossary

1080p: A classification for high-definition video. 1080 refers to 1,080 lines of vertical resolution; p refers to progressive scan, meaning that the lines that comprise the video picture appear on the screen sequentially. This standard is used in the production of high definition film, high definition television (HDTV) and high definition digital video disc (HD DVD). 1080p is a superior technology to 1080i (i stands for interlaced) which delivers lines of video alternatively resulting in slight distortions in picture quality.

10-K (10K): An annual report filed by publicly held companies. It provides a comprehensive overview of the company's business and its finances. By law, it must contain specific information and follow a given form, the "Annual Report on Form 10-K." The U.S. Securities and Exchange Commission requires that it be filed within 90 days after fiscal year end. However, these reports are often filed late due to extenuating circumstances. Variations of a 10-K are often filed to indicate amendments and changes. Most publicly held companies also publish an "annual report" that is not on Form 10-K. These annual reports are more informal and are frequently used by a company to enhance its image with customers, investors and industry peers.

802.11a (Wi-Fi5): A faster wireless network standard than 802.11b ("Wi-Fi"). 802.11a operates in the 5-GHz band at speeds of 50 Mbps or more. This standard may be affected by weather and is not as suitable for outdoor use. 802.11 standards are set by the IEEE (Institute of Electrical and Electronics Engineers).

802.11b (Wi-Fi): An extremely popular, Wi-Fi short-range wireless connection standard created by the IEEE (Institute of Electrical and Electronics Engineers). It operates at 11 Mbps and can be used to connect computer devices to each other. 802.11b competes with the Bluetooth standard. Its range is up to 380 feet, but 150 feet or so may be more practical in some installations.

802.11g: A recent addition to the series of 802.11 specifications for Wi-Fi wireless networks, 802.11g provides data transfer at speeds of up to 54 Mbps in the 2.4-GHz band. It can easily exchange data with 802.11b-enabled devices, but at much higher speed. 802.11g equipment, such as wireless access points, will be able to provide simultaneous WLAN connectivity for both 802.11g and 802.11b equipment. The 802.11 standards are set by the IEEE (Institute of Electrical and Electronics Engineers).

802.11n (MIMO): Multiple Input Multiple Output antenna technology. The new standard in the series of 802.11 Wi-Fi specifications for wireless networks. It has the potential of providing data transfer speeds of 100 to perhaps as much as 500 Mbps. 802.11n also boasts better operating distances than current networks. MIMO uses spectrum more efficiently without any loss of reliability. The technology is based on several different antennas all tuned to the same channel, each transmitting a different signal.

802.15: See "Ultrawideband (UWB)." For 802.15.1, see "Bluetooth."

802.16 (WiMAX): An advanced wireless standard with significant speed and distance capabilities, WiMax is officially known as the 802.16 standard. Using microwave technologies, it has the potential to broadcast at distances up to 30 miles and speeds of up to 70 Mbps. The 802.XX standards are set by the IEEE (Institute of Electrical and Electronics Engineers).

Advertising-On-Demand: Television advertising that viewers can watch voluntarily, in contrast to traditional television advertising, which is shown on the air without viewer choice. See "Demand-Driven Advertising."

Affiliate: A broadcast radio or television station that is an "affiliate" of a national network, such as NBC or CBS, contracts with the national network, which provides programming to the affiliate for all or part of each day. In return, the affiliate provides the network with an agreed-upon number of minutes of advertising time, which the network then resells to advertisers.

AM (Amplitude Modulation): Radio broadcasts in the range of 535 kHz to 1705 kHz.

American Research Bureau (ARB): One of several national firms that conduct audience research. ARB is the founder of Arbitron ratings.

Analog: A form of transmitting information characterized by continuously variable quantities. Digital transmission, in contrast, is characterized by discrete bits of information in numerical steps. An analog signal responds to changes in light, sound, heat and pressure.

Area of Dominant Influence (ADI): A market area established by Arbitron that places cities and/or parts of counties into groupings that are reached by the same local radio or television stations. It is similar to Nielsen's "Designated Market Area." For example, advertising on radio stations in Boston will reach listeners far outside of Boston within the surrounding ADI.

ARPU (Average Revenue Per User): A measure of the average monthly billing revenue of a wireless company on a per user basis.

ATM (Asynchronous Transfer Mode): A digital switching and transmission technology based on high speed. ATM allows voice, video and data signals to be sent over a single telephone line at speeds from 25 million to 1 billion bits per second (bps). This digital ATM speed is much faster than traditional analog phone lines, which allow no more than 2 million bps. See "Broadband."

Baby Boomer: Generally refers to people born in the U.S. and Western Europe from 1946 to 1964. In the U.S., the total number of Baby Boomers is about 78 million--one of the largest and most affluent demographic groups. The term evolved to include the children of soldiers and war industry workers who were involved in World War II. When those veterans and workers returned to civilian life, they started or added to families in large numbers. As a result, the baby boom generation is one of the largest demographic segments in the U.S. Some baby boomers have already started reaching early retirement age. By 2011, millions will begin turning traditional retirement age (65), resulting in extremely rapid growth in the senior portion of the population.

Bandwidth: The data transmission capacity of a network, measured in the amount of data (in bits and bauds) it can transport in one second. A full page of text is about 15,000 to 20,000 bits. Full-motion, full-screen video requires about 10 million bits per second, depending on compression.

Basic Cable: Primary level or levels of cable service offered for subscription. Basic cable offerings may include retransmitted broadcast signals as well as local and access programming. In addition, regional and national cable network programming may be provided.

Blog (Web Log): A web site consisting of a personal journal, news coverage, special-interest content or other data that is posted on the Internet, frequently updated and intended for public viewing by anyone who might be interested in the author's thoughts. Short for "web log," blog content is frequently distributed via RSS (Real Simple Syndication). Blog content has evolved to include video files (VLOGs) and audio files (Podcasting) as well as text. See "RSS (Real Simple Syndication)," "VLOG (Video Blog)" and "Podcasting."

Bluetooth: An industry standard for a technology that enables wireless, short-distance infrared connections between devices such as cell phone headsets, Palm Pilots or PDAs, laptops, printers and Internet appliances. Compatible with the IEEE's 802.15.1 specification, Bluetooth is ideally suited for connecting devices that will remain close to each other (within 30 feet or less). Since its power consumption is very low, it is also ideally suited for battery-powered devices such as cell phones. See www.bluetooth.com. Data transmission speeds are up to 3 megabits per second, vastly slower than Ultrawideband. See "Ultrawideband (UWB)." Bluetooth 2.0 offers three times the speed of Bluetooth 1.0 plus lower power consumption. The succeeding version, code named "Lisbon" will offer enhanced encryption, better transmission of audio and video files and better "pairing" of Bluetooth devices for stronger connections. The future edition to follow Lisbon is currently code named "Seattle", which will likely incorporate UWB technology, enabling very fast data transfers.

Branding: A marketing strategy that places a focus on the brand name of a product, service or firm in order to increase the brand's market share, increase sales, establish credibility, improve satisfaction, raise the profile of the firm and increase profits.

Broadband: The high-speed transmission range for telecommunications and computer data. Broadband refers to any transmission at 2 million bps (bits per second) or higher (much higher than analog speed). A broadband network can carry voice, video and data all at the same time. Internet users enjoying broadband access typically connect to the Internet via DSL line, cable modem or T1 line. Several wireless methods now offer broadband as well.

Broadcast: Electronic transmission of media by radio or television; generally refers to wireless methods.

Browser: A program that allows a user to read Internet text or graphics and to navigate from one page to another. The most popular browsers are Microsoft Internet Explorer and Netscape Navigator. Firefox is an open source browser introduced in 2005 that is rapidly gaining popularity.

B-to-B, or B2B: See "Business-to-Business."

B-to-C, or B2C: See "Business-to-Consumer."

Business Process Outsourcing (BPO): The outsourcing of non-mission-critical business processes that may include call centers, basic accounting or human resources management, depending on the industry involved. Also, see "ITES (IT-Enabled Services)."

Business-to-Business: An organization focused on selling products, services or data to commercial customers rather than individual consumers. Also known as B2B.

Business-to-Consumer: An organization focused on selling products, services or data to individual consumers rather than commercial customers. Also known as B2C.

Cable Modem: An interface between a cable television system and a computer or router. Most cable modems are external devices that connect to the PC through a standard 10Base-T Ethernet card and twisted-pair wiring. External Universal Serial Bus (USB) modems and internal PCI modem cards are also available. The cable modem enables a computer to access the Internet via a TV cable. Cable modem access can be very high-speed and is much faster than traditional "dial-up" access via a standard telephone line. Cable modem speeds vary, depending on the cable modem system and current traffic load. From the Internet to the computer, the modem may connect at speeds as high as 1 to 3 Mbps. From the computer to network, speeds typically run between 500 Kbps

and 2.5 Mbps. Cable modem access competes with DSL access.

Cable TV: A television system consisting of a local television station that is equipped with an antenna or satellite dish. The antenna or dish receives signals from distant, central network stations and retransmits those signals via TV cable to the local subscriber.

Caching: A method of storing data in a temporary location closer to the user so that it can be retrieved quickly when requested.

Call Letters: Letters that identify a station, e.g., KTRU. Call letters are established by the Federal Communications Commission. Each broadcast station has unique letters. The letters may denote whether the station is in the eastern or western U.S.

Captive Offshoring: Used to describe a company-owned offshore operation. For example, Microsoft owns and operates significant captive offshore research and development centers in China and elsewhere that are offshore from Microsoft's U.S. home base. Also see "Offshoring."

CATV: Cable television.

CDF (Channel Definition Format): Used in Internet-based broadcasting. With this format, a channel serves as a web site that also sends an information file about that specific site. Users subscribe to a channel by downloading the file.

Circulation: The numerical distribution of print media such as magazines or newspapers. "Controlled circulation" refers to magazines that are generally sent to a defined subscriber base free-of-charge. "Audited circulation" refers to a subscription base that has been verified as to its size by an independent agency.

Click Through: In advertising on the Internet, click through refers to how often viewers respond to an ad by clicking on it. Also known as click rate.

Closed Circuit TV (CCTV): Programs or other material that limit the target audience to a specific group instead of the general public. For example, major retailers use such private TV systems, distributed via satellite, to provide training to employees at remote store locations.

Codec: Hardware or software that converts analog to digital and digital to analog (in both audio and video formats). Codecs can be found in digital telephones, set-top boxes, computers and videoconferencing equipment. The term is also used to refer to the compression of digital information into a smaller format.

Community Antenna Television: A community television system that is served through cable and is connected to a common set of antennae.

Compression: A technology in which a communications signal is squeezed so that it uses less bandwidth (or capacity) than it normally would. This saves storage space and shortens transfer time. The original data is decompressed when read back into memory.

Content Aggregator: A content aggregator collects content and distributes it to subscribers, network operators or other content companies.

Contract Manufacturer: A company that manufactures products that will be sold under the brand names of its client companies. For example, a large number of consumer electronics, such as laptop computers, are manufactured by contract manufacturers for leading brand-name computer companies such as Dell. Many other types of products are made under contract manufacturing, from apparel to pharmaceuticals. Also see "OEM (Original Equipment Manufacturer)" and "ODM (Original Design Manufacturer)."

Controlled Circulation: See "Circulation."

Cookie: A piece of information sent to a web browser from a web server that the browser software saves and then sends back to the server upon request. Cookies are used by web site operators to track the actions of users returning to the site.

Cost Per Click (CPC): Online advertising that is billed on a response basis. An advertiser sells a banner ad and is paid by the number of users who click on the ad.

Cost Per Thousand (CPM): A charge for advertising calculated on a fixed amount multiplied by the number of users who view an ad, computed in thousands.

CPC: See "Cost Per Click (CPC)."

CPM: See "Cost Per Thousand (CPM)."

CRM (Customer Relationship Management): The automation of integrated business processes involving customers, including sales (contact management, product configuration), marketing (campaign management, telemarketing) and customer service (call center, field service).

Cyberspace: Refers to the entire realm of information available through computer networks and the Internet.

DBA: Doing business as.

DBS (Direct Broadcast Satellite): A high-powered satellite authorized to broadcast television programming directly to homes. Home subscribers use a dish and a converter to receive and translate the TV signal. An example is the DirecTV service. DBS operates in the 11.70- to 12.40-GHz range.

Decompression: See "Compression."

Demand-Driven Advertising: Allows television viewers to choose which commercials to watch, how many to watch and when to watch them.

Demographics: The breakdown of the population into statistical categories such as age, income, education and sex.

Dendrimer: A type of molecule that can be used with small molecules to give them certain desirable characteristics. Dendrimers are utilized in technologies for electronic displays. See "OLED (Organic LED)."

Dial-Up Access: The connection of a computer or other device to a network through a modem and a public telephone network. The only difference between dial-up access and a telephone connection is that computers are at each end of the connection rather than people. Dial-up access is slower than DSL, cable modem and other advanced connections.

Digital: The transmission of a signal by reducing all of its information to ones and zeros and then regrouping them at the reception end. Digital transmission vastly improves the carrying capacity of the spectrum while reducing noise and distortion of the transmission.

Digital Subscriber Line (DSL): A broadband (high-speed) Internet connection provided via telecommunications systems. These lines are a cost-effective means of providing homes and small businesses with relatively fast Internet access. Common variations include ADSL and SDSL. DSL competes with cable modem access and wireless access.

Direct Marketing: A form of non-store retailing in which customers are exposed to merchandise through catalogs, direct-mail brochures, telemarketing or television. Direct marketing may be used to generate direct-response purchases, store traffic, sales leads or a combination thereof.

Direct Selling: A form of marketing, which involves manufacturing, and then selling merchandise or services through direct mail or through salespeople who contact consumers directly or by telephone at home or place of work (e.g., Mary Kay cosmetics).

Distributor: An individual or business involved in marketing, warehousing and/or shipping of products manufactured by others to a specific group of end users. Distributors do not sell to the general public. In order to develop a competitive advantage, distributors often focus on serving one industry or one set of niche clients. For example, within the medical industry, there are major distributors that focus on providing pharmaceuticals, surgical supplies or dental supplies to clinics and hospitals.

DMA (Designated Market Area): A television market as delineated by AC Nielsen.

DOCSIS (Data Over Cable Service Interface Specification): Standards for transferring data over cable television.

DRM (Digital Rights Management): Enables control and maintenance of publishers' rights by delivering encrypted information and, instead of providing the key (or using the recipient's public key for encryption), in effect permitting the recipient to borrow the decryption key in a highly controlled fashion.

DS-1: A digital transmission format that transmits and receives information at a rate of 1,544,000 bits per second.

DSL: See "Digital Subscriber Line (DSL)."

Dub: A recorded copy of a TV or radio appearance on video or audiotape.

DVD (Digital Video Disc): Similar to music CDs, these discs can store more than seven times as much data. (DVDs store 4.7 gigabytes of data, compared to 650 megabytes on a CD.) They are commonly used to store full-length motion pictures.

DVR (Digital Video Recorder): A device that records video files, typically television programming including movies, in digital format to be replayed at a later time. The most commonly known PVR is the TiVo. DVRs encode video as MPEG files and save them onto a hard drive. DVRs are also known as PVRs (Personal Video Recorders).

Dynamic HTML: Web content that changes with each individual viewing. For example, the same site could appear differently depending on geographic location of the reader, time of day, previous pages viewed or the user's profile.

EC (European Community): See "EU (European Union)."

Echo Boomers: See "Generation Y."

E-Commerce: The use of online, Internet-based sales methods. The phrase is used to describe both business-to-consumer and business-to-business sales.

EDI (Electronic Data Interchange): An accepted standard format for the exchange of data between various companies' networks. EDI allows for the transfer of e-mail as well as orders, invoices and other files from one company to another.

Electronic Book (e-Book): An electronic method of storing and accessing books online or in portable e-book viewing machines (readers), so that consumers can purchase and read a digital copy of a book instead of a traditional print copy. Advantages include the ability to search by key word and the ability to store dozens of books in digital form on one portable device.

Electronic Paper Displays (EPD): Electronic paper is a term used to describe a recently developed type of high contrast, flexible display. The displays use low amounts of power and can be viewed in bright sunlight and at any angle. They are well suited for use as screens on mobile devices and may have broad applications in outdoor advertising.

ENPS (Electronic News Production System): A content management software application designed by broadcasters for use in television newsrooms. Introduced in 1997, the application addresses nearly all newsroom activities, including scripting, messaging, archiving, news wire management and text searching of news feeds.

Enterprise Resource Planning (ERP): An integrated information system that helps manage all aspects of a business, including accounting, ordering and human resources, typically across all locations of a major corporation or organization. ERP is considered to be a critical tool for management of large organizations. Suppliers of ERP tools include SAP and Oracle.

EU (European Union): A consolidation of European countries (member states) functioning as one body to facilitate trade. Previously known as the European Community (EC), the EU expanded to include much of Eastern Europe in 2004, raising the total number of member states to 25. In 2002, the EU launched a unified currency, the Euro. See europa.eu.int.

EU Competence: The jurisdiction in which the EU can take legal action.

EV-DO (CDMA 2000 1xEV-DO): A 3G (third generation) cellular telephone service standard that is an improved version of 1xRTT. The EV-DO (Evolution Data Optimized) standard introduced in 2004 allows data download speeds of as much as 2.4 Mbps. A version slated for 2006 allows up to 3.1 Mbps data download speeds. EV-DO is also known as CDMA 2000 1xEV-DO. EV-DO's capabilities will be used by the entertainment industry to enable video via cell phone.

Extensible Markup Language: See "XML (Extensible Markup Language)."

Extranet: A computer network that is accessible in part to authorized outside persons, as opposed to an intranet, which uses a firewall to limit accessibility.

FCC (Federal Communications Commission): See "Federal Communications Commission (FCC)."

Federal Communications Commission (FCC): The U.S. Government agency that regulates broadcast television and radio, as well as satellite transmission, telephony and all uses of radio spectrum.

Field Emission Display (FED): A self-luminescent display that can be extremely thin, draw very low power, and be very bright from all angles and in all types of light. The latest FEDs are based on carbon nanotubes. Samsung is a leader in this field. Early applications include high-end television and computer monitors.

FM (Frequency Modulation): Radio broadcasts in the range of 88 MHz to 108 MHz.

Frequency: The number of times that an alternating current goes through its complete cycle in one second. One cycle per second is referred to as one hertz; 1,000 cycles per second, one kilohertz; 1 million cycles per second, one megahertz; and 1 billion cycles per second, one gigahertz.

Frequency Band: A term for designating a range of frequencies in the electromagnetic spectrum.

FTTH/FTTP (Fiber to the Home/Fiber to the Premises): Refers to the extension of a fiber-optic system through the last mile so that it touches the home or office where it will be used. This can provide Internet access at speeds of 10 to 20 Mbps, much faster than typical T1, DSL or cable modem access. FTTH is now commonly installed in new communities where telecom infrastructure is being built for the first time. Another phrase used to describe such installations is FTTP, or Fiber to the Premises.

FVOD (Free Video On Demand): VOD programming offered by a network operator free of charge. FVOD programming includes on-demand advertising and on-demand programming offered as part of a basic VOD package.

Gatekeeper: A person or persons controlling the flow of information. Individuals who allow information to pass through them to be disseminated to the public are referred to as gatekeepers. These include newspaper publishers, editors, reporters, television and radio producers, station owners and executives.

GDP (Gross Domestic Product): The total value of a nation's output, income and expenditures produced with a nation's physical borders.

General Magazines: Consumer magazines that are not aimed at special-interest audiences.

Generation Y: Refers to Americans born between 1977 and 1997, who number about 75 million. They are also known as Echo Boomers. These are children of the Baby Boomers are filling the U.S. work force as Baby Boomers retire.

Geostationary: A geosynchronous satellite angle with zero inclination, making a satellite appear to hover over one spot on the earth's equator.

GIF (Graphic Interchange Format): See "Graphic Interchange Format (GIF)."

Global Positioning System (GPS): A satellite system, originally designed by the U.S. Department of Defense for navigation purposes. Today, GPS is in wide use for consumer and business purposes, such as navigation for drivers, boaters and hikers. It utilizes satellites orbiting the earth at 10,900 miles to enable users to pinpoint precise locations using small, electronic wireless receivers.

Globalization: The increased mobility of goods, services, labor, technology and capital throughout the world. Although globalization is not a new development, its pace has increased with the advent of new technologies, especially in the areas of telecommunications, finance and shipping.

GNP (Gross National Product): A country's total output of goods and services from all forms of economic activity measured at market prices for one calendar year. It differs from GDP (Gross Domestic Product) in that GNP includes income from investments made in foreign nations.

GPS: See "Global Positioning System (GPS)."

Graphic Interchange Format (GIF): A widely used format for image files.

Gross Rating Points (GRPs): Measures the audience share of a television program's audience

delivery. GRPs are the sum of individual ratings for all programs in a particular time slot. See "Ratings/Ratings Points/Ratings Share."

HD Radio (High Definition Radio): A technology that enables station operators to slice existing radio spectrum into multiple, thin bands. Each band is capable of transmitting additional programming. One existing radio station's spectrum may be sliced into as many as eight channels.

HDMI (High-Definition Multi-Media Interface): HDMI is an industry-standard interface to conduct uncompressed, all-digital audio and video signals into high definition entertainment components including HDTV. The goal is to enable consumer entertainment devices to display high quality, high-definition content. HDMI is backward compatible with earlier DVI equipment, so that HDMI can HDMI equipment can display video received from DVI products.

Headend: A facility that originates and distributes cable service in a given geographic area. Depending on the size of the area it serves, a cable system may be comprised of more than one headend.

Hertz: A measure of frequency equal to one cycle per second. Most radio signals operate in ranges of megahertz or gigahertz.

High-Definition Television (HDTV): A type of television broadcasting that increases the resolution of the visual field contained by the image, making for a clearer and more movie-like viewing experience. HDTV requires advanced digital broadcasting and receiving equipment.

Homes Passed: Households that have the ability to receive cable service and may opt to subscribe.

Impressions: In Internet advertising, the total number of times an ad is displayed on a web page. Impressions are not the same as "hits," which count the number of times each page or element in a page is retrieved. Since a single complicated page on a web site could consist of five or more individual elements, including graphics and text, one viewer calling up that page would register multiple hits but just a single impression.

Impulse VOD: Affords television viewers the ability to order VOD programming without having to phone in an order to the content provider.

Infotainment: Programming which combines information with entertainment. It most often refers to television programming or web-based programming that informs the viewer while extolling the virtues of a product or service that is for sale.

Initial Public Offering (IPO): A company's first effort to sell its stock to investors (the public). Investors in an up-trending market eagerly seek stocks offered in many IPOs because the stocks of newly public companies that seem to have great promise may appreciate very rapidly in price, reaping great profits for those who were able to get the stock at the first offering. In the United States, IPOs are regulated by the SEC (U.S. Securities Exchange Commission) and by the state-level regulatory agencies of the states in which the IPO shares are offered.

Interactive: In entertainment, advertising and communications, interactive refers to systems that enable the viewer or user to interact via a response or two-way communication. For example, interactive television advertising may enable the viewer to respond via a set-top box, immediately purchasing the item being advertised.

Interactive TV (ITV): Allows two-way data flow between a viewer and the cable TV system. A user can exchange information with the cable system—for example, by ordering a product related to a show he/she is watching or by voting in an interactive survey.

Internet: A global computer network that provides an easily accessible way for hundreds of millions of users to send and receive data electronically when appropriately connected via computers or wireless devices. Access is generally through HTML-enabled sites on the World Wide Web. Also known as the Net.

Internet Appliance: A non-PC device that connects users to the Internet for specific or general purposes. A good example is an electronic game machine with a screen and Internet capabilities. It is anticipated that many types of Internet appliances will be of common use in homes in the near future.

Internet Sharing Programs: Internet networks that allow users to share files and programs, in spite of possible copyright restrictions (e.g., Napster, before the federal ruling that barred it from downloading music files free of charge).

Intranet: A network protected by a firewall for sharing data and e-mail within an organization or company. Usually, intranets are used by organizations for internal communication.

IP Number/IP Address: A number or address with four parts that are separated by dots. Each machine on the Internet has its own IP (Internet protocol) number, which serves as an identifier.

IP VOD: See "VOD-Over-IP."

IPTV: Internet Protocol Television. That is, television delivered by Internet-based means such as fiber to the home (FTTH) or a very high speed DSL. Microsoft is a leading provider of advanced IPTV software. SBC and BT are two leading telecom firms that are using Microsoft's new software to offer television services over high-speed Internet lines.

ISP (Internet Service Provider): A company that sells access to the Internet to individual subscribers. Leading examples are MSN and AOL.

ITES (IT-Enabled Services): The portion of the Information Technology industry focused on providing business services, such as call centers, insurance claims processing and medical records transcription, by utilizing the power of IT, especially the Internet. Most ITES functions are considered to be back-office procedures. Also, see "Business Process Outsourcing (BPO)."

ITV: See "Interactive TV (ITV)."

IVOD (Interactive Video On Demand): An extension of VOD that offers many of the functions typically provided by VCRs, such as pause, fast forward and fast rewind. Through a set-top box, the IVOD customer can browse, select and purchase products; avoid or select advertisements; and investigate additional details about news events.

Java: A programming language developed by Sun Microsystems that allows web pages to display interactive graphics. Any type of computer or operating systems can read Java.

JPEG (Joint Photographic Experts Group): A widely used format for digital image files.

LAN (Local Area Network): A computer network that is generally within one office or one building. A LAN can be very inexpensive and efficient to set up when small numbers of computers are involved. It may require a network administrator and a serious investment if hundreds of computers are hooked up to the LAN. A LAN enables all computers within the office to share files and printers, to access common databases and to send e-mail to others on the network.

LBA (Location Based Advertising): The ability for advertisers and information providers to push information to mobile consumers based on their locations. For example, GPS equipped cell phones have the potential to alert consumers on the go to nearby restaurants, entertainment attractions, and special sale events at retailers.

LED (Light Emitting Diode): A small tube containing material that emits light when exposed to electricity. The color of the light depends upon the type of material. The LED was first developed in 1962 at the University of Illinois at Urbana-Champaign. LEDs are important to a wide variety of industries, from wireless telephone handsets to signage to displays for medical equipment, because they provide a very high quality of light with very low power requirements. They also have a very long useful life and produce very low heat output when. All of these characteristics are great improvements over a conventional incandescent bulb. Several advancements have been made in LED technology. See "OLED (Organic LED)," "PLED (Polymer Light Emitting Diode)," "SMOLED (Small Molecule Organic Light Emitting Diode)" and "Dendrimer."

Linear Programming: See "Linear TV."

Linear TV: A type of television programming that is (1) standard non-PVR and non-VOD television service. (2) TV programming that the producers, broadcasters, etc. do not want the viewer leaving in any way, including visiting the program advertiser's website. (3) Programming that is dependent on programming that has already been presented. (4) Non-interactive TV.

Liquid Crystal Display (LCD): A digital screen composed of liquid crystal cells that change luminosity when exposed to an electric field. The newest LCDs have a higher resolution and use less power than conventional displays.

Local Area Network (LAN): See "LAN (Local Area Network)."

Location-Based Entertainment: The use of entertainment themes and attractions to draw consumers to specific locations, such as shopping malls, casinos and restaurants.

LOHAS: Lifestyles of Health and Sustainability. It is a marketing term that refers to consumers who choose to purchase and/or live with items that are natural, organic, less polluting, etc. Such consumers may also have a preference for products powered by alternative energy, such as hybrid cars.

Long Form Advertisement: Usually takes the form of a lengthy television commercial with entertaining and/or educational elements. These advertisements may be offered with other commercials or as links for viewers to click on for more information about the advertised product or service.

M2M (Machine-to-Machine): Refers to the transmission of data from one device to another, typically through wireless means such as Wi-Fi. For example, a Wi-Fi network might be employed to control several machines in a household from a central computer. Such machines might include air conditioning and entertainment systems. In logistics and retailing, M2M can refer to the use of RFID tags to transmit information. See "RFID (Radio Frequency Identification.)"

MAN (Metropolitan Area Network): A data and communications network that operates over metropolitan areas and recently has been expanded to nationwide and even worldwide connectivity of high-speed data networks. A MAN can carry video and data.

Market Segmentation: The division of a consumer market into specific groups of buyers based on demographic factors.

Marketing: Includes all planning and management activities and expenses associated with the promotion of a product or service. Marketing can encompass advertising, customer surveys, public relations and many other disciplines. Marketing is distinct from selling, which is the process of sell-through to the end user.

Mass Media: Refers to all media that disseminate information throughout the world, including television, radio, film, print, photography and electronic media.

Mbps (Megabits per second): 1 million bits transmitted per second.

M-Commerce: Mobile e-commerce over wireless devices.

Media: Used loosely to refer to the entire communications system of reporters, editors, producers, print publications, broadcast programs, magazines and online publications.

Media Literacy: Refers to an individual's ability to read, analyze and evaluate media. If one is media literate, that person can recognize the rhetorical arguments and techniques used by the media to persuade audiences.

Media Outlet: A broadcast or publication that brings news and features to the public through a distribution channel.

Mega-Theater: A movie theater with as many as 30 screens and more frequent show times. Some also offer luxury seating, with amenities such as restaurant-style food, a wait staff and reservations.

Merchandising: Any marketing method utilized to foster sales growth.

Metropolitan Area Network (MAN): See "MAN (Metropolitan Area Network)."

Miles of Plant: The number of cable plant miles laid or strung by a cable system; the cable miles in place.

Modem: A device that allows a computer to be connected to a phone line, which in turn enables the computer to receive and exchange data with other machines via the Internet.

MOS (Media Object Server): An XML-based protocol designed to transfer information between newsroom automation systems and other systems, including media servers. The MOS protocol allows various devices to be controlled from a central device or piece of software, which limits the need to have operators stationed at multiple locations throughout the news studio.

MOST (Media Oriented Systems Transport): A standard adopted in 2004 by the Consumer Electronics Association for the integration of or interface with consumer electronics (such as iPods) into entertainment systems in automobiles.

MP3: A subsystem of MPEG used to compress sound into digital files. It is the most commonly used format for downloading music and audio books. MP3 compresses music significantly while retaining CD-like quality. MP3 players are personal, portable devices used for listening to music and audio book files. See "MPEG."

MPEG, MPEG-1, MPEG-2, MPEG-3, MPEG-4: Moving Picture Experts Group. It is a digital standard for the compression of motion or still video for transmission or storage. MPEGs are used in digital cameras and for Internet-based viewing.

MSO (Multiple System Operator): An individual or company owning two or more cable systems.

Multicasting: Sending data, audio or video simultaneously to a number of clients. Also known as broadcasting.

Multimedia: Refers to a presentation using several different media at once. For example, an encyclopedia in CD-ROM format is generally multimedia because it features written text, video and sound in one package.

Multipoint Distribution System (MDS): A common carrier licensed by the FCC to operate a broadcast-like omni-directional microwave transmission facility within a given city. MDS carriers often pick up satellite pay-TV programming and distribute it, via their local MDS transmitter, to specially installed antennas and receivers.

NAND: NAND memory is an advanced type of flash memory chip. It is popular for use in consumer electronics such as MP3 players and digital cameras.

Network: In computing, a network is created when two or more computers are connected. Computers may be connected by wireless methods, using such technologies as 802.11b, or by a system of cables, switches and routers.

Network Numbers: The first portion of an IP address, which identifies the network to which hosts in the rest of the address are connected.

Network Storage: See "Network-Based VOD."

Network-Based VOD: Involves a television content provider storing either all or most of its programming content at its location, usually on its servers. Network-based VOD is more typical of cable TV than satellite TV.

New Media: A wide array of digital communication technologies, including Internet development tools and services, desktop and portable personal computers, workstations, servers, audio/video compression and editing equipment, graphics hardware and software, high-density storage services and video conferencing systems.

Newspaper Syndicate: A firm selling features, photos, columns, comic strips or other special material for publication in a large number of newspapers. For example, a typical fee charged by a syndicate to a daily newspaper for a popular comic strip is $10 per day. Generally, the syndicate splits the fee with the author.

Nielsen Ratings: Ratings created by ACNielsen, a company engaged in television audience ratings and other market research.

Nielsen Station Index (NSI): An index that rates individual television stations.

Nielsen Television Index (NTI): An index that rates national television network programming.

Non-Store Retailing: A form of retailing that is not store-based. Non-store retailing can be conducted through vending machines, direct-selling, direct-marketing, party-based selling, catalogs, television programming, telemarketing and Internet-based selling.

nPVR (Network Personal Video Recording): See "Server-Based SVOD Programming."

NVOD (Near Video On Demand): An alternative method of VOD television programming delivery. NVOD delivers only a small portion of the ordered programming to the customer before playback. This initial download serves as a buffer while the rest of the programming is viewed directly off the provider's server. In contrast, traditional VOD typically involves the delivery of the entire ordered programming to the customer for playback from the customer's hard drive.

ODM (Original Design Manufacturer): A contract manufacturer that offers complete, end-to-end design, engineering and manufacturing services. ODMs design and build products, such as consumer electronics, that client companies can then brand and sell as their own. For example, a large percentage of laptop computers, cell phones and PDAs are made by ODMs. Also see "OEM (Original Equipment Manufacturer)" and "Contract Manufacturer."

OEM (Original Equipment Manufacturer): A company that manufactures a product or component for sale to a customer that will integrate the component into a final product or assembly. The OEM's customer will distribute the end product or resell it to an end user. For example, a personal computer made under a brand name by a given company may contain various components, such as hard drives, graphics cards or speakers, manufactured by several different OEM "vendors," but the firm doing the final assembly/manufacturing process is the final manufacturer. Also see "ODM (Original Design Manufacturer)" and "Contract Manufacturer."

Offshoring: The rapidly growing tendency among U.S., Japanese and Western European firms to send knowledge-based and manufacturing work overseas. The intent is to take advantage of lower wages and operating costs in such nations as China, India, Hungary and Russia. The choice of a nation for offshore work may be influenced by such factors as language and education of the local workforce, transportation systems or natural resources. For example, China and India are graduating high numbers of skilled engineers and scientists from their universities. Also, some nations are noted for large numbers of workers skilled in the English language, such as the Philippines and India. Also see "Captive Offshoring" and "Outsourcing."

OLED (Organic LED): This is a type of electronic display based on the use of organic materials that produce light when stimulated by electricity. Also see "Organic Polymer," "PLED (Polymer Light Emitting Diode)," "SMOLED (Small Molecule Organic Light Emitting Diode)" and "Dendrimer."

On-Demand Advertising: See "Advertising-On-Demand."

On-Demand Video Magazines: Video clips concerning a variety of subjects offered by content providers as part of a VOD programming package.

Original Design Manufacturer: See "ODM (Original Design Manufacturer)."

Original Equipment Manufacturer: See "OEM (Original Equipment Manufacturer)."

Out-of-Home Advertising: Advertising in public places through billboards, signs on buses, etc. Also referred to as outdoor advertising.

Outsourcing: The hiring of an outside company to perform a task otherwise performed internally by the company, generally with the goal of lowering costs and/or streamlining work flow. Outsourcing contracts are generally several years in length. Companies that hire outsourced services providers often prefer to focus on their core strengths while sending more routine tasks outside for others to perform. Typical outsourced services include the running of human resources departments, telephone call centers and computer departments. When outsourcing is performed overseas, it may be referred to as offshoring. Also see "Offshoring."

P2P (Peer-to-Peer): Refers to a connection between computers that creates equal status between the computers. P2P can be used in an office or home to create a simple computer network. However, P2P more commonly refers to networks of computers that share information online. For example, peer-to-peer music sharing networks enable one member to search the hard drives of other members to locate music files and then download those files. These systems can be used for legal purposes. Nonetheless, they became notorious as systems that enable members to collect music and videos for free, circumventing copyright and other legal restrictions. At one time Napster was widely known as a P2P music system that enabled users to circumvent copyright.

Palm Pilot: A handheld device in which data is stored and may also be transmitted. Data usually consists of address books, calendar information and e-mail. These small personal computers are known as PDAs. See "PDA (Personal Digital Assistant)."

Parental Guidelines: A rating system established by the television industry in 1997, which gives parents information about the content and age-appropriateness of television programming.

Pay Cable: A network or service available for an added monthly fee. Also called premium cable. Some services, called mini-pay, are marketed at an average monthly rate below that of full-priced premium.

Pay Cable Unit: Each premium service to which a household subscribes.

Pay-Per-View (PPV): A service that enables television subscribers, including cable and satellite viewers, to order and view events or movies on an individual basis. PPV programming may include sporting events.

PDA (Personal Digital Assistant): A handheld or pocket-size device containing address and calendar information, as well as e-mail, games and other features. A Palm Pilot is a PDA.

Peer-to-Peer: See "P2P (Peer-to-Peer)."

Periodical: A publication that changes on a regular publishing schedule, such as weekly or monthly. (In contrast, a book that does not change on a regular basis is referred to as a monograph.)

Personal Television (PTV): Television programming that has been manipulated to a viewer's personal taste. For example, the TiVo service allows viewers to eliminate commercials, watch programming stored in memory or watch selected real-time moments in slow motion.

Personalized VOD Entertainment: A VOD service that automatically detects household television viewing interests by monitoring the channel-surfing behavior of residents. The system uses this viewing data to select programming relevant to the household. The service can also deliver custom VOD libraries to PVRs.

PLED (Polymer Light Emitting Diode): An advanced technology that utilizes plastics (polymers) for the creation of electronic displays (screens). It is based on the use of organic polymers which emit light when stimulated with electricity. They are solution processable, which means they can be applied to substrates via ink jet printing.

Podcasting: The creation of audio files as webcasts. The name comes from the ability of these files to be used on iPods and portable MP3 players. They can also be listened to on personal computers. Podcasts can be anything from unique radio-like programming to sales pitches to audio press releases. Audio RSS (Real Simple Syndication) enables the broadcast of these audio files to appropriate parties. Also see "RSS (Real Simple Syndication)," "VLOG (Video Blog)" and "Blog (Web Log)."

Portal: A comprehensive web site that is designed to be the first site seen when a computer logs on to the web. Portal sites are aimed at broad audiences with common interests and often have links to e-mail usage, a search engine and other features. Yahoo! and msn.com are portals.

Positioning: The design and implementation of a merchandising mix, price structure and style of selling to create an image of the retailer, relative to its competitors, in the customer's mind.

Powerline: A method of networking computers, peripherals and appliances together via the electrical wiring that is built in to a home or office. Powerline competes with 802.11b and other wireless networking methods.

PTV (Personal Television): See "Personal Television (PTV)."

Publication: A printed magazine or newspaper containing information, news or feature stories.

PVR (Personal Video Recorder): See "DVR (Digital Video Recorder)."

Ratings/Rating Points/Ratings Share: The rating of a medium is its audience size expressed as a percentage of the measured market, where one rating point is equivalent to 1% of the base. Ratings are often referred to as "percent coverage." A television show with a 22% share has 22 points, or 22% of the total TV audience within its market.

Reach: The geographic area inhabited by a potential audience. Also the number of readers, listeners or viewers that are able to access a given medium. A prime time television show on a national network such as ABC has nationwide reach.

Real Time: A system or software product specially designed to acquire, process, store and display large amounts of rapidly changing information almost instantaneously, with microsecond responses as changes occur.

Recommendation-Based VOD: See "Personalized VOD Entertainment."

Return on Investment (ROI): A measure of a company's profitability, expressed in percentage as net profit (after taxes) divided by total dollar investment.

RFID (Radio Frequency Identification): A technology that applies a special microchip-enabled tag to an individual item or piece of merchandise or inventory. RFID technology enables wireless, computerized tracking of that inventory item as it moves through the supply chain from factory to transport to warehouse to retail store or end user. Also known as radio tags.

RSS (Real Simple Syndication): Uses XML programming language to let web logs and other data be broadcast to appropriate web sites and users. Formerly referred to as RDF Site Summary or Rich Site Summary, RSS also enables the publisher to create a description of the content and its location in the form of an RSS document. Also useful for distributing audio files. See "Podcasting."

SACD (Super Audio Compact Disc): A technology that offers high-resolution digital audio.

Satellite Broadcasting: The use of Earth-orbiting satellites to transmit, over a wide area, TV, radio, telephony, video and other data in digitized format.

Server: A computer that performs and manages specific duties for a central network such as a LAN. It may include storage devices and other peripherals. Competition within the server manufacturing industry is intense among leaders Dell, IBM, HP and others.

Server-Based SVOD Programming: Programming that is delivered directly to the customer's TV from where it is stored on the content provider's servers. In contrast, non-server-based SVOD (satellite TV) needs a storage device at the customer's location (such as a PVR or DVR) to store and play VOD content for the viewer's TV. Server-based SVOD surpasses non-server-based SVOD in its ability to simultaneously send or receive more than one video stream to or from the customer.

Set-Top Box: Sits on top of a TV set and provides enhancement to cable TV or other television reception. Typically a cable modem, this box may enable interactive enhancements to television viewing. For example, a cable modem is a set-top box that enables Internet access via TV cable. See "Cable Modem."

Share: In broadcasting, the percentage of television households tuned into a particular program or category of programming. The higher the share, the larger the amount that can be charged for advertising on the program.

SMOLED (Small Molecule Organic Light Emitting Diode): A type of organic LED that relies on expensive manufacturing methods. Newer technologies are more promising. See "Organic Polymer" and "PLED (Polymer Light Emitting Diode."

Spam: A term used to refer to generally unwanted, solicitous, bulk-sent e-mail. In recent years, significant amounts of government legislation have been passed in an attempt to limit the use of spam. Also, many types of software filters have been introduced in an effort to block spam on the receiving end. In addition to use for general advertising purposes, spam may be used in an effort to spread computer viruses or to commit financial or commercial fraud.

Specialty Publication: A trade or professional magazine that is industry- or audience-specific (e.g., Shopping Center World magazine).

Spot Revenue: Revenue from advertising placed on a cable system by a local or national advertiser.

Streaming Media: One-way audio and/or video that is compressed and transmitted over a data network. The media is viewed or heard almost as soon as data is fed to the receiver; there is usually a buffer period of a few seconds.

Subscriber: A term used interchangeably with household in describing cable, Internet access or telephone customers.

Subsidiary, Wholly-Owned: A company that is wholly controlled by another company through stock ownership.

Superstation: A local television station with a signal that is retransmitted via satellite to distant cable systems that cannot be reached by over-the-air signals.

Superstore: A large specialty store, usually over 40,000 square feet and realizing at least 10% of its revenue from GM/HBC. Many superstores focus on a particular field of merchandise. For example, BestBuy is a consumer electronics superstore.

Supply Chain: The complete set of suppliers of goods and services required for a company to operate its business. For example, a manufacturer's supply chain may include providers of raw materials, components, custom-made parts and packaging materials.

SVOD (Subscription Video On Demand): Allows subscribers unlimited access to selected VOD television programming for a fixed monthly fee.

Syndicated: A report, story, television program, radio program or graphic that is sold to multiple media outlets simultaneously. For example, popular newspaper columns are commonly syndicated to various newspapers throughout the United States, but only one newspaper per market is allowed to participate.

System (Cable): A facility that provides cable television service in a given geographic area, consisting of one or more headends.

T1: A standard for broadband digital transmission over phone lines. Generally, it can transmit at least 24 voice channels at once over copper wires, at a high speed of 1.5 Mbps. Higher speed versions include T3 and OC3 lines.

T3: Transmission over phone lines that supports data rates of 45 Mbps. T3 lines consist of 672 channels, and such lines are generally used by Internet service providers. They are also referred to as DS3 lines.

Telecommunications: Systems of hardware and software used to carry voice, video and/or data between locations. This includes telephone wires, satellite signals, cellular links, coaxial cable and related devices.

Telemarketing: See "Non-Store Retailing."

Telescopic On-Demand PVR/VOD Advertising: Telescopic On-Demand PVR/VOD Advertising is a short television commercial that offers the viewer access to another longer, related commercial. The commercial is called telescopic because it can be made longer if the viewer so desires.

Third Screen: Refers to the cell phone as a viewing device that is beyond the two primary screens used by consumers--the TV and the computer monitor.

Time Shifting: Services that allow viewers to digitally record television programs for playback at a later, more convenient time. Such services include video-on-demand (VOD) and personal TV services. Time shifting will eventually make up a significant portion of all television viewing.

Time-And-Channel-Based TV: See "Linear TV."

TiVo: A digital recorder that allows customers to record television shows through a hard disk and computer schedule instead of a videotape or manual recording set-up.

Transactional VOD: Allows VOD customers to pay a single price for a single VOD program or a set of programs rather than paying a set fee for a set amount of VOD programming (as in SVOD services).

TV over IP: See "IPTV."

TVOD (True Video On Demand): Offers VOD customers seamless interaction with the VOD system. TVOD allows users to not only order programs, but perform VCR-like commands at VCR-like speeds on the VOD system.

UHF (Ultra High Frequency): The frequency band ranging from 300 MHz to 3,000 MHz, which includes TV channels 14 through 83.

Ultrawideband (UWB): A means of low-power, limited-range wireless data transmission that takes advantage of bandwidth set aside by the FCC in 2002. UWB encodes signals in a dramatically different way, sending digital pulses in a relatively secure manner that will not interfere with other wireless systems that may be operating nearby. It has the potential to deliver very large amounts of data to a distance of about 230 feet, even through doors and other obstacles, and requires very little power. Speeds are scalable from approximately 100 Mbps to 2Gbps. UWB works on the 802.15.3 IEEE specification.

UWB: See "Ultrawideband (UWB)."

V-Chip: A system built into TV sets that helps parents screen out programs with questionable parental guideline ratings. Consumers can purchase a special set-top box that performs the same function.

Very Small Aperture Terminal (VSAT): A small Earth station terminal, generally 0.6 to 2.4 meters in size, that is often portable and primarily designed to handle data transmission and private-line voice and video communications.

VHF (Very High Frequency): The frequency band ranging from 30 MHz to 300 MHz, which includes TV channels 2 through 13 and FM radio.

VLOG (Video Blog): The creation of video files as webcasts. VLOGs can be viewed on personal computers and wireless devices that are Internet-enabled. They can include anything from unique TV-like programming to sales pitches to music videos, news coverage or audio press releases. Online video is one of the fastest-growing segments in Internet usage. Leading e-commerce companies such as Microsoft, through its MSN service, Google and Yahoo!, as well as mainstream media firms such as Reuters, are making significant investments in online video services. RSS (Real Simple Syndication) enables the broadcasting of these files to appropriate parties. Also see "RSS (Real Simple Syndication)," "Podcasting" and "Blog (Web Log)."

VOD (Video On Demand): A system that allows customers to request programs or movies over cable or the Internet. Generally, the customer can select from an extensive list of titles. In some cases, a set-top device can be used to record digitally a broadcast for replay at a future date.

VOD-Over-IP: VOD (video on demand) television viewing that is distributed via the Internet.

WAP (Wireless Access Protocol): A technology that enables the delivery of World Wide Web pages in a smaller format readable by screens on cellular phones.

Web 2.0: Web 2.0 generally refers to the evolving system of advanced services available via the Internet. These services include collaborative sites that enable multiple users to create content such as wikis, sites such as photo-sharing services that share data among large or small groups and sites such as Friendster and MySpace that enable consumers to form groups of people with similar interests.

Web Page: A document on the World Wide Web that is identified by a URL.

Web Services: Self-contained modular applications that can be described, published, located and invoked over the World Wide Web or another network. Web services architecture evolved from object-oriented design and is geared toward e-business solutions. Microsoft Corporation is focusing on web services with its .NET initiative. Also see "XML (Extensible Markup Language)."

Web Site: A specific domain name location on the World Wide Web. Each site contains a homepage and usually consists of additional documents.

Weblog: See "Blog (Web Log)."

Webmaster: Any individual who runs a web site. Webmasters generally perform maintenance and upkeep.

Wi-Fi: A popular phrase that refers to 802.11b and other 802.11 specifications. See "802.11b (Wi-Fi)."

Wi-Fi5: A popular phrase that refers to 802.11a. See "802.11a (Wi-Fi5)."

Wiki: A web site that enables large or small groups of users to create and co-edit data. The best known example is Wikipedia, a high traffic web site that presents a public encyclopedia that is continuously written and edited by a vast number of volunteer contributors and editors who include both experts and enthusiasts in various subjects.

WiMAX (802.16): A wireless standard with exceptional speed and distance capabilities, officially known as the 802.16 standard. See "802.16 (WiMAX)." Wi-Fi stands for "World Interoperability for Microwave Access."

Wire Service: An organization that sends news stories, features and other types of information by direct line to subscribing or member newspapers, radio stations and television stations. The Associated Press (AP) is a well-known wire service.

Wireless: Transmission of voice, video or data by a cellular telephone or other wireless device, as opposed to landline, telephone line or cable. It includes Wi-Fi, WiMAX and other local or long-distance wireless methods.

Wireless Cable: A pay television service that delivers multiple programming services to subscribers equipped with special antennae and tuners. It is an alternative to traditional, wired cable TV systems.

World Wide Web: A computer system that provides enhanced access to various sites on the Internet through the use of hyperlinks. Clicking on a link displayed in one document takes you to a related document. The World Wide Web is governed by the World Wide Web Consortium, located at www.w3.org. Also known as the web.

XML (Extensible Markup Language): A programming language that enables designers to add extra functionality to documents that could not otherwise be utilized with standard HTML coding. XML was developed by the World Wide Web Consortium. It can communicate to various software programs the actual meanings contained in HTML documents. For example, it can enable the gathering and use of information from a large number of databases at once and place that information into one web site window. XML is an important protocol to web services. See "Web Services."

INTRODUCTION

PLUNKETT'S ENTERTAINMENT & MEDIA INDUSTRY ALMANAC, the seventh edition of our guide to the entertainment and media field, is designed as a general source for researchers of all types.

The data and areas of interest covered are intentionally broad, ranging from the most important trends in the entertainment and media industry, to emerging technologies, to an in-depth look at the 400 major firms (which we call "THE ENTERTAINMENT 400") within the many sectors that make up the entertainment and media industry, such as book, newspaper and magazine publishing; electronic games; gambling and casinos; retailers, such as bookstores, of entertainment and media products; radio; television, including broadcast, satellite and cable; movie production and distribution; movie theaters, publishers of databases and much more, including related services, hardware and software.

This reference book is designed to be a general source for researchers. It is especially intended to assist with market research, strategic planning, employment searches, contact or prospect list creation (be sure to see the export capabilities of the accompanying CD-ROM that is available to book and eBook buyers) and financial research, and as a data resource for executives and students of all types.

PLUNKETT'S ENTERTAINMENT & MEDIA INDUSTRY ALMANAC takes a rounded approach for the general reader. This book presents a complete overview of the entertainment and media field (see "How To Use This Book"). For example, the impact of the Internet upon entertainment is discussed in exacting detail, along with easy-to-use tables on all facets of entertainment and media in general, from the types of services involved to names and descriptions of the divisions and affiliates of the major firms within this industry.

THE ENTERTAINMENT 400 is our unique grouping of the biggest, most successful corporations in all segments of the entertainment and media industry. Tens of thousands of pieces of information, gathered from a wide variety of sources, have been researched and are presented in a unique form that can be easily understood. This section includes thorough indexes to THE ENTERTAINMENT 400, by geography, industry, sales, brand names, subsidiary names and many other topics. (See Chapter 4.)

Especially helpful is the way in which PLUNKETT'S ENTERTAINMENT & MEDIA INDUSTRY ALMANAC enables readers who have no business background to readily compare the financial records and growth plans of entertainment companies and major industry groups. You'll see the mid-term financial record of each firm, along with the impact of earnings, sales and strategic plans on each company's potential to fuel growth, to serve new markets and to provide investment and employment opportunities.

No other source provides this book's easy-to-understand comparisons of growth, expenditures, technologies, corporations and many other items of great importance to people of all types who may be studying this, one of the most rapidly evolving industries in the world today.

By scanning the data groups and the unique indexes, you can find the best information to fit your personal research needs. The major companies in entertainment are profiled and then ranked using several different groups of specific criteria. Which firms are the biggest employers? Which companies earn the most profits? These things and much more are easy to find.

In addition to individual company profiles, an overview of entertainment and media technology and its trends is provided. This book's job is to help you sort through easy-to-understand summaries of today's trends in a quick and effective manner.

Whatever your purpose for researching the entertainment and media field, you'll find this book to be a valuable guide. Nonetheless, as is true with all resources, this volume has limitations that the reader should be aware of:

- Financial data and other corporate information can change quickly. A book of this type can be no more current than the data that was available as of the time of editing. Consequently, the financial picture, management and ownership of the firm(s) you are studying may have changed since the date of this book. For example, this almanac includes the most up-to-date sales figures and profits available to the editors as of early 2007. That means that we have typically used corporate financial data as of mid-2006.

- Corporate mergers, acquisitions and downsizing are occurring at a very rapid rate. Such events may have created significant change, subsequent to the publishing of this book, within a company you are studying.

- Some of the companies in THE ENTERTAINMENT 400 are so large in scope and in variety of business endeavors conducted within a parent organization, that we have been unable to completely list all subsidiaries, affiliations, divisions and activities within a firm's corporate structure.

- This volume is intended to be a general guide to a vast industry. That means that researchers should look to this book for an overview and, when conducting in-depth research, should contact the specific corporations or industry associations in question for the very latest changes and data. Where possible, we have listed contact names, toll-free telephone numbers and World Wide Web site addresses for the companies, government agencies and industry associations involved so that the reader may get further details without unnecessary delay.

- Tables of industry data and statistics used in this book include the latest numbers available at the time of printing, generally through mid-2005. In a few cases, the only complete data available was for earlier years.

- We have used exhaustive efforts to locate and fairly present accurate and complete data. However, when using this book or any other source for business and industry information, the reader should use caution and diligence by conducting further research where it seems appropriate. We wish you success in your endeavors, and we trust that your experience with this book will be both satisfactory and productive.

Jack W. Plunkett
Houston, Texas
January 2007

HOW TO USE THIS BOOK

The two primary sections of this book are devoted first to the entertainment & media industry as a whole and then to the "Individual Data Listings" for THE ENTERTAINMENT 400. If time permits, you should begin your research in the front chapters of this book. Also, you will find lengthy indexes in Chapter 4 and in the back of the book.

THE ENTERTAINMENT & MEDIA INDUSTRY

Glossary: A short list of entertainment and media industry terms.

Chapter 1: Major Trends Affecting the Entertainment & Media Industry. This chapter presents an encapsulated view of the major trends that are creating rapid changes in the entertainment and media industry today, from mergers and acquisitions, to Internet delivery, to personal video recorders.

Chapter 2: Entertainment & Media Industry Statistics. This chapter presents in-depth statistics ranging from an industry overview, to sector-by-sector revenues, to the growing use of the Internet and much more.

Chapter 3: Important Entertainment & Media Industry Contacts – Addresses, Telephone Numbers and World Wide Web Sites. This chapter covers contacts for important government agencies, industry organizations and trade groups. Included are numerous important World Wide Web sites.

THE ENTERTAINMENT 400

Chapter 4: THE ENTERTAINMENT 400: Who They Are and How They Were Chosen. The companies compared in this book (the actual count is 393) were carefully selected from the entertainment and media industry, largely in the United States. 61 of the firms are based outside the U.S. For a complete description, see THE ENTERTAINMENT 400 indexes in this chapter.

Individual Data Listings:
Look at one of the companies in THE ENTERTAINMENT 400's Individual Data Listings. You'll find the following information fields:

Company Name:
The company profiles are in alphabetical order by company name. If you don't find the company you are seeking, it may be a subsidiary or division of one of the firms covered in this book. Try looking it up in the Index by Subsidiaries, Brand Names and Selected Affiliations in the back of the book.

Ranks:

Industry Group Code: An NAIC code used to group companies within like segments. (See Chapter 4 for a list of codes.)

Ranks Within This Company's Industry Group: Ranks, within this firm's segment only, for annual sales and annual profits, with 1 being the highest rank.

Business Activities:

A grid arranged into six major industry categories and several sub-categories. A "Y" indicates that the firm operates within the sub-category. A complete Index by Industry is included in the beginning of Chapter 4.

Types of Business:

A listing of the primary types of business specialties conducted by the firm.

Brands/Divisions/Affiliations:

Major brand names, operating divisions or subsidiaries of the firm, as well as major corporate affiliations—such as another firm that owns a significant portion of the company's stock. A complete Index by Subsidiaries, Brand Names and Selected Affiliations is in the back of the book.

Contacts:

The names and titles up to 27 top officers of the company are listed, including human resources contacts.

Address:

The firm's full headquarters address, the headquarters telephone, plus toll-free and fax numbers where available. Also provided is the World Wide Web site address.

Financials:

Annual Sales (2006 or the latest fiscal year available to the editors, plus up to four previous years): These are stated in thousands of dollars (add three zeros if you want the full number). This figure represents consolidated worldwide sales from all operations. 2006 figures may be estimates or may be for only part of the year—partial year figures are appropriately footnoted.

Annual Profits (2006 or the latest fiscal year available to the editors, plus up to four previous years): These are stated in thousands of dollars (add three zeros if you want the full number). This figure represents consolidated, after-tax net profit from all operations. 2006 figures may be estimates or may be for only part of the year—partial year figures are appropriately footnoted.

Stock Ticker, International Exchange, Parent Company: When available, the unique stock market symbol used to identify this firm's common stock for trading and tracking purposes is indicated. Where appropriate, this field may contain "private" or "subsidiary" rather than a ticker symbol. If the firm is a publicly-held company headquartered outside of the U.S., its international ticker and exchange are given. If the firm is a subsidiary, its parent company is listed.

Total Number of Employees: The approximate total number of employees, worldwide, as of the end of 2006 (or the latest data available to the editors).

Apparent Salaries/Benefits:

(The following descriptions generally apply to U.S. employers only.) A "Y" in appropriate fields indicates "Yes."

Due to wide variations in the manner in which corporations report benefits to the U.S. Government's regulatory bodies, not all plans will have been uncovered or correctly evaluated during our effort to research this data. Also, the availability to employees of such plans will vary according to the qualifications that employees must meet to become eligible. For example, some benefit plans may be available only to salaried workers—others only to employees who work more than 1,000 hours yearly. Benefits that are available to employees of the main or parent company may not be available to employees of the subsidiaries. In addition, employers frequently alter the nature and terms of plans offered.

NOTE: Generally, employees covered by wealth-building benefit plans do not *fully* own ("vest in") funds contributed on their behalf by the employer until as many as five years of service with that employer have passed. All pension plans are voluntary—that is, employers are not obligated to offer pensions.

Pension Plan: The firm offers a pension plan to qualified employees. In this case, in order for a "Y" to appear, the editors believe that the employer offers a defined benefit or cash balance pension plan (see discussions below).The type and generosity of these plans vary widely from firm to firm. Caution: Some employers refer to plans as "pension" or "retirement" plans when they are actually 401(k) savings plans that require a contribution by the employee.

- Defined Benefit Pension Plans: Pension plans that do not require a contribution from the employee are infrequently offered. However, a few companies, particularly larger employers in high-profit-margin industries, offer defined benefit pension plans where the employee is guaranteed to receive a set pension benefit upon retirement. The amount of the benefit is determined by the years of service with the company and the employee's salary during the later years of employment. The longer a person works for the employer, the higher the retirement benefit. These defined benefit plans are funded entirely by the employer. The benefits, up to a reasonable limit, are guaranteed by the Federal Government's Pension Benefit Guaranty Corporation. These plans are not portable—if you leave the company, you cannot transfer your benefits into a different plan. Instead, upon retirement you will receive the benefits that vested during your service with the company. If your employer offers a pension plan, it must give you a summary plan description within 90 days of the date you join the plan. You can also request a summary annual report of the plan, and once every 12 months you may request an individual benefit statement accounting of your interest in the plan.

- Defined Contribution Plans: These are quite different. They do not guarantee a certain amount of pension benefit. Instead, they set out circumstances under which the employer will make a contribution to a plan on your behalf. The most common example is the 401(k) savings plan. Pension benefits are not guaranteed under these plans.

- Cash Balance Pension Plans: These plans were recently invented. These are hybrid plans—part defined benefit and part defined contribution. Many employers have converted their older defined benefit plans into cash balance plans. The employer makes deposits (or credits a given amount of money) on the employee's behalf, usually based on a percentage of pay. Employee accounts grow based on a predetermined interest benchmark, such as the interest rate on Treasury Bonds. There are some advantages to these plans, particularly for younger workers: a) The benefits, up to a reasonable limit, are guaranteed by the Pension Benefit Guaranty Corporation. b) Benefits are portable—they can be moved to another plan when the employee changes companies. c) Younger workers and those who spend a shorter number of years with an employer may receive higher benefits than they would under a traditional defined benefit plan.

ESOP Stock Plan (Employees' Stock Ownership Plan): This type of plan is in wide use. Typically, the plan borrows money from a bank and uses those funds to purchase a large block of the corporation's stock. The corporation makes contributions to the plan over a period of time, and the stock purchase loan is eventually paid off. The value of the plan grows significantly as long as the market price of the stock holds up. Qualified employees are allocated a share of the plan based on their length of service and their level of salary. Under federal regulations, participants in ESOPs are allowed to diversify their account holdings in set percentages that rise as the employee ages and gains years of service with the company. In this manner, not all of the employee's assets are tied up in the employer's stock.

Savings Plan, 401(k): Under this type of plan, employees make a tax-deferred deposit into an account. In the best plans, the company makes annual matching donations to the employees' accounts, typically in some proportion to deposits made by the employees themselves. A good plan will match one-half of employee deposits of up to 6% of wages. For example, an employee earning $30,000 yearly might deposit $1,800 (6%) into the plan. The company will match one-half of the employee's deposit, or $900. The plan grows on a tax-deferred basis, similar to an IRA. A very generous plan will match 100% of employee deposits. However, some plans do not call for the employer to make a matching deposit at all. Other plans call for a matching contribution to be made at the discretion of the firm's board of directors. Actual terms of these plans vary widely from firm to firm. Generally, these savings plans allow employees to deposit as much as 15% of salary into the plan on a tax-deferred basis. However, the portion that the company uses to calculate its matching deposit is generally limited to a maximum of 6%. Employees should take care to diversify the holdings in their 401(k) accounts, and most people should seek professional guidance or investment management for their accounts.

Stock Purchase Plan: Qualified employees may purchase the company's common stock at a price below its market value under a specific plan. Typically, the employee is limited to investing a small percentage of wages in this plan. The discount may range from 5 to 15%. Some of these plans allow for deposits to be made through regular monthly payroll deductions. However, new accounting rules for corporations, along with other factors, are leading many companies to curtail these plans—dropping the discount allowed, cutting the maximum yearly stock purchase or otherwise making the plans less generous or appealing.

Profit Sharing: Qualified employees are awarded an annual amount equal to some portion of a company's profits. In a very generous plan, the pool of money awarded to employees would be 15% of profits. Typically, this money is deposited into a long-term retirement account. Caution: Some employers refer to plans as "profit sharing" when they are actually 401(k) savings plans. True profit sharing plans are rarely offered.

Highest Executive Salary: The highest executive salary paid, typically a 2006 amount (or the latest year available to the editors) and typically paid to the Chief Executive Officer.

Highest Executive Bonus: The apparent bonus, if any, paid to the above person.

Second Highest Executive Salary: The next-highest executive salary paid, typically a 2006 amount (or the latest year available to the editors) and typically paid to the President or Chief Operating Officer.

Second Highest Executive Bonus: The apparent bonus, if any, paid to the above person.

Other Thoughts:

Apparent Women Officers or Directors: It is difficult to obtain this information on an exact basis, and employers generally do not disclose the data in a public way. However, we have indicated what our best efforts reveal to be the apparent number of women who either are in the posts of corporate officers or sit on the board of directors. There is a wide variance from company to company.

Hot Spot for Advancement for Women/Minorities: A "Y" in appropriate fields indicates "Yes." These are firms that appear either to have posted a substantial number of women and/or minorities to high posts or that appear to have a good record of going out of their way to recruit, train, promote and retain women or minorities. (See the Index of Hot Spots For Women and Minorities in the back of the book.) This information may change frequently and can be difficult to obtain and verify. Consequently, the reader should use caution and conduct further investigation where appropriate.

Growth Plans/ Special Features:

Listed here are observations regarding the firm's strategy, hiring plans, plans for growth and product development, along with general information regarding a company's business and prospects.

Locations:

A "Y" in the appropriate field indicates "Yes."

Primary locations outside of the headquarters, categorized by regions of the United States and by international locations. A complete index by locations is also in the front of this chapter.

Chapter 1

MAJOR TRENDS AFFECTING THE ENTERTAINMENT & MEDIA INDUSTRY

Major Trends Affecting the Entertainment & Media Industry:

1) Introduction to the Entertainment & Media Industry
2) Multimedia Hub Homes Slowly Become a Reality
3) DVR Market Evolves; Time-Shifting Becomes Widespread
4) Apple's iPod Revitalizes the Music Industry
5) Internet Film Content Explodes
6) Netflix Soars/Blockbuster Suffers
7) Major Casino Expansion Continues in the U.S. and Macau
8) Reality TV Dominates Broadcast Programming/Networks Find New Ways to Distribute Content
9) New Platforms Revolutionize Electronic Games
10) "Cell" Chip Technology Sizzles in PS3
11) Satellite Radio Fails to Earn a Profit/Traditional Radio Faces Challenges
12) Radio Via IP Grows/The Era of Digital Radio Begins
13) Cable and Satellite TV Compete Fiercely for Market Share
14) Video-on-Demand (VOD) and Subscription Video-on-Demand (SVOD) Go Mass Market
15) TV over IP—Telecom Companies Enter the Television Market

16) TV over IP—TV Networks, Cable Companies and Web Sites Converge
17) High-Definition Grows—HDTV and HD-DVD
18) Movie Attendance Rallies/Film Companies Innovate with DVDs, IMAX and Big Budget Films
19) Last Mile Challenges Tumble; Mass Broadband Markets Emerge
20) Entertainment-Based Retailing, including Power Towns
21) Video Via Cell Phone Takes Off
22) Music Plays a Major Role in New Cell Phones
23) Rules for Digital TV Are Finalized

1)   Introduction to the Entertainment & Media Industry

Total spending (including advertising) in the U.S. on media of all types was about $900 billion in 2006. U.S. advertising spending alone was about $296 billion.

Broadly measured, the entertainment and media industry spans multiple sectors, from America's 9,042 FM radio stations, to the 1.4 billion movie tickets sold each year. The gambling sector with $57 billion in annual revenues, is often included when considering entertainment as a whole.

Today, new media of all types must be considered when considering the scope of the entertainment and media industry. The number of broadband Internet connections in the U.S. has reached true mass market in size, at about 50 million lines as 2006 ended. Comcast (the cable TV provider) alone has 11 million high-speed Internet subscribers. Advertising on the Internet is now a $16 billion industry. Most recently, the "Third Screen" (cell phone-based entertainment including video and music) is becoming a major factor in entertainment and media.

Meanwhile, revenues are mixed at traditional entertainment and media segments. Book sales were up about 10% in the U.S. for 2005, at $25 billion, after falling slightly in 2004. Movie theater attendance is up, reversing a sharp fall after 1999. The traditional, storefront video rental sector is suffering due to alternatives including Netflix, TiVo and video-on-demand services. Newspapers are finding it increasingly difficult to compete against Internet news and advertising delivery rivals. Recorded music sales on CD-ROM continue to suffer while sales of digital music files are soaring. Traditional radio broadcasting is suffering, finding it increasingly difficult to gather listeners for advertising-based radio programming due to such alternatives as satellite radio and digital MP3 players.

The burning issue affecting all sectors of the entertainment and media industry is maintaining control of content and audiences while taking advantage of myriad new electronic delivery venues. Competition in the entertainment sector is fierce. Gone are the days when television and radio programmers enjoyed captive audiences who happily sat through ad after ad, or planned their schedules around a favorite show. Consumers, especially consumers in younger demographics, now demand more and more control over what they watch, read and listen to.

Issues related to control include:

1) Pricing for content (including free-of-charge access; illegal downloads versus authorized downloads; and full ownership of a paid download versus pay-per-view).

2) Portability (including the ability for a consumer to download once, and then use a file on multiple platforms and devices including iPods and cell phones, or the ability to share a download with friends).

3) And delayed viewing or listening (such as viewing TV programming at the consumer's convenience via TiVo and similar personal video recorders).

The competition among entertainment delivery platforms has intensified; all sectors face daunting challenges from alternative delivery methods. For example, satellite radio delivery (XM and Sirius) of subscription-based music and talk programming has hit its stride multimillion subscriber counts for Sirius and its competitor XM. Another example: telecommunications companies such as AT&T (formerly known as SBC Communications) are now delivering television programming to the home via telephone wires, battling cable and satellite TV firms for market share.

Today, electronic offerings such as DVDs, personal video recorders (PVRs), video-on-demand (VOD) and MP3 players have vastly altered the way consumers enjoy entertainment. People watch and listen according to their own desires and whims. Miss the finale to a favorite television show? Rent or buy it on DVD or record it to watch later. Interested in only one track from a recording artist's new CD? Buy and download just the one song via the Internet. Love a prime-time drama on a major network but hate commercials? Record the show while skipping over the commercials with a PVR.

The implications of these changes are staggering. The business models upon which most entertainment companies have traditionally run are becoming obsolete. Revenue from traditional advertising is in jeopardy while revenue from subscription-based business models is soaring. Online advertising is growing at supersonic speed. Television programming schedules are losing relevance while electronic program guides are becoming more and more vital. Traditional media are losing share while new digital media are becoming the norm. Entertainment companies are being forced to radically change to deal with new technologies and new demands from consumers.

Rapid changes in viewing habits are already occurring. Network TV news, radio news and newspapers all find that they have to compete fiercely against Internet-based news content. A large portion of sports programming has migrated away from "free" broadcasts on TV and onto paid cable channels and pay-per-view systems.

Meanwhile, platforms and delivery are evolving quickly. Multipurpose cell phones are now used for more and more entertainment purposes, including video and TV-like programming. Game machines are going multipurpose with the ability to connect to the Internet and play DVDs. Broadband to the home has reached the mass-market tipping point, while wireless broadband systems such as Wi-Fi are enhancing the mobility of entertainment and media access. A serious evolution of access and delivery methods will continue at a rapid-fire pace, and media companies will be forced to be more nimble than ever.

Sony's new PlayStation 3 utilizes a supercomputer-like chip called "Cell" that has the potential to revolutionize the electronic games industry due to its ability to run highly realistic, advanced software at amazing speed.

Recommendation software that learns the habits and tastes of consumers will evolve and will do a better job of pushing appropriate entertainment choices toward audiences. Amazon.com has long been a leader in the use of such software. Netflix has created an admirable package of its own. Likewise, Apple's iTunes software is strong on recommending content to customers. Some interesting mergers might be driven by the potential to use extremely powerful recommendation software to attract and better serve consumers across multiple types of entertainment media.

The gambling sector remains strong, with massive new projects in Las Vegas and Macau, along with experienced operators rushing to rebuild the Gulf Coast casinos that were wiped out by 2005's hurricanes.

Advertising, long the main revenue source for much of the media industry, is rapidly moving to the Internet, as shown by the incredible financial success of Yahoo! and Google, among other search sites that offer advertising services.

You should count on continued, rapid changes: The revolution in new media continues, platforms will evolve quickly, consumers will obtain even greater control and competition will become even hotter.

2) Multimedia Hub Homes Slowly Become a Reality

Computer software and hardware companies have growing stakes in entertainment. Microsoft, after spending more than 10 years and billions of dollars on the development of its home entertainment empire, saw sales of more than 10 million of its Windows XP Media Centers in 2006. The software, combined with specially configured PCs, plays and records television shows, manages music video and personal photo files, plays music files and burns CDs and DVDs, all by remote control. Today's version, "Windows XP Media Center Edition 2005", includes Internet radio among its other entertainment features. The widely anticipated new operating system, Vista, will incorporate all of the above and more, but has

suffered some developmental setbacks and a delayed release set for 2007.

Designing computers to serve as electronic hubs of digital homes, routing music, movies, TV programming, e-mail and news between the web and PCs, television set-top boxes, stereo speakers and other gadgets, has long been the goal of Microsoft, as well as Sony, Gateway, HP, Apple and Digeo to name a few. Intel is also at the forefront of PC-controlled home entertainment, investing in ever-more-powerful chips capable of generating high-definition video images suitable for many video uses, including cutting-edge projection TVs. (Meanwhile, an amazing chip from IBM, utilizing "cell" technology, will make the electronic game machines manufactured by Sony an integral part of the home entertainment center. See "New Platforms Revolutionize Electronic Games" in this chapter.)

Home entertainment centers now connect components such as TVs, sound systems, cable or satellite set-top boxes and, increasingly, PCs. On the fixed end, a home network is tied to an Internet connection that runs at increasingly higher speeds. Internet access for advanced entertainment is delivered by the consumer's choice of DSL, cable modem or satellite dish. In an increasing number of new neighborhoods, access is achieved by true fiber to the home (FTTH) networks capable of delivery at blazing speeds, enabling such holy grail media as video-on-demand and interactive TV. In a few communities, consumers can log into widespread, public Wi-Fi wireless networks for access at home or on the go. Over the mid-term, longer-range WiMax wireless systems will enhance the portability of entertainment systems.

Within the home, there are two schools of thought as to the best way to connect all of the entertainment components. Since Ethernet wire is prohibitively expensive, many electronics, cable and satellite companies are looking towards using either existing electrical wiring or coaxial cable. On the electrical wiring side, a standard called HomePlug AV carries up to 150 megabits of data per second over home electrical wiring. Devices would simply be plugged into electrical outlets to be connected. Proponents of this idea are members of the HomePlug Powerline Alliance (HPPA www.homeplug.org) and include companies such as Intel, Comcast, RadioShack and Sony. Detractors claim that signal interference is a problem, but proponents say that many of the difficulties have been ironed out.

Coaxial cable has its own supporters who have organized the Multimedia Over Coax Alliance (MoCA, www.mocalliance.org). This system uses coaxial cable installed by cable television companies. Devices are connected to cable outlets for data and programming delivered at up to 100 megabits per second. Participating companies in MoCA include Echostar, Panasonic and Verizon. While signal interference is not a problem, most homes are not built with cable access in every room (although MoCA says that cable is easily installed).

Both systems can easily utilize ultrawideband (UWB) wireless to beam data at up to 480 megabits per second across distances of up to 30 feet. Wireless makes it possible to place that new plasma TV on a wall that doesn't have a cable outlet. UWB completes the multimedia home, making it possible to enjoy entertainment literally anywhere in the house—even in the backyard.

The HomePlug Powerline Alliance and MoCA have many of the same companies backing them. Comcast, Motorola and RadioShack are all members of both alliances, since making and selling electronics and services that cater to both systems is relatively cheap. Through the near term, products using these technologies will rely on small adapters that plug into electrical sockets or cable outlets.

Until recently, Microsoft's Media Center software claimed only a small percentage of the home computer market. Technical problems such as poor video quality plagued the software giant, and a hefty percentage of the home entertainment consumer base refused to watch video programming on computer monitors. The latest version of Windows XP Media Center offers significantly enhanced TV quality, as well as compatible hardware with multiple TV tuners that receive up to three signals. Viewers can watch one program while recording another. The greatest breakthrough, however, is the release of the Media Center Extender, utilizing home Wi-Fi systems, as the missing link that beams content from a PC to TVs in up to five other rooms. Microsoft projects that Media Center PCs equipped with its software will represent from 10% to 20% of the home computer market over the next few years. Microsoft founder Bill Gates announced that Media Center PCs made up 40% of all Windows sales in December 2005, and exceeded 10 million units in 2006.

Many computer industry giants such as Gateway, Dell Computer and Hewlett-Packard have been quick to join the party with their own versions of Media Center PCs. Prices start at about $1,400 and run up to about $3,000. Some, such as Alienware DHS 5,

are designed to be stacked in with other entertainment components and have sleek, living-room-worthy looks. The top-of-the-line Niveus Media Denali Edition operates silently thanks to a fanless system. Silence appears to be golden, since the Denali's price starts at $7,999.

Apple, Inc. (which changed its name from Apple Computer in 2007 to emphasize its focus on consumer electronics and entertainment as well as computers) has a secure place in the home media center arena. One of its most brilliant products is Apple TV. The moderately-priced ($299.00) Apple TV unit acts as an interface between a consumer's television, computer and iPod. For example, Apple TV will send digital entertainment that is stored on your computer directly to your TV. This is becoming increasingly important since widescreen home TVs are now standard equipment in many living rooms, and these widescreens are vastly superior to computer monitors for watching videos. Also, the Apple TV unit will send home videos, movies, TV shows, and photos from your video iPod to your TV.

Entertainment-Enabled Macs and PCs

In short, consumers now have the ability to manage virtually all of their home entertainment options via personal computer or Apple's Macintosh computers. For example, Microsoft's Windows Media Center running on a fully featured entertainment PC from makers such as Dell or Sony can offer:

- [ ] Television access, which can be connected to cable, antenna or satellite
- [ ] Electronic games
- [ ] Internet access
- [ ] Communication, including VoIP telephony and e-mail
- [ ] PVR (personal video recording of TV programs)
- [ ] Music recording, storage and management in MP3 or WMA format, as well as conversion of music CDs into MP3 files
- [ ] Recording and playing of CDs and DVDs
- [ ] Multiple picture frames on one screen
- [ ] Digital photography management, including editing of still and video
- [ ] Integration with a wireless home network
- [ ] Internet-based radio

---

3)   **DVR Market Evolves; Time-Shifting Becomes Widespread**

Digital Video Recorders (DVRs, also known as Personal Video Recorders or PVRs) allow viewers to download broadcast television, satellite television and cable programs for later viewing. Viewers are typically able to store between 80 and 810 hours of programming for playback at their discretion. Programming can also be viewed and manipulated to skip commercials almost in real-time. (Or, in some cases, viewers can fast-forward through commercials.) Viewers can also playback key moments or watch in slow motion. This is all accomplished via a hard drive connected to a television set (often in addition to a cable box, satellite receiver box and/or video game equipment). The fact that very large hard drives are available at modest prices is accelerating the acceptance of DVRs.

TiVo was the first DVR to attract any serious market share. Simple, elegant and easy to use, TiVo has attracted a limited but rabidly loyal subscriber base of 4.4 million, as of the beginning of 2007. However, it's facing tough competition from Motorola, Digeo, ReplayTV, THOMSON and Akimbo, to name but a few. Despite the fact that TiVo was first and has achieved brand recognition, it is far from having a lock on the DVR market.

Costs for the boxes when they debuted in 2001 ran between $250 and $400, depending on recording capacity, plus a monthly service fee. New players by a host of manufacturers have driven the price down as low as $70 after rebates.

DVRs have caught on in a big way. As of the beginning of 2007, there were an estimated 18 million homes with these devices in the U.S., according to Nielsen Media Research. By 2010, 39% of U.S. households are expected to have the devices. Within the television industry, recording and delayed viewing of programming is referred to as "time-shifting." Industry veterans expect time-shifting to account for 40% to 50% of all TV viewing over the long term.

The impact of these devices on the advertising industry, as well as ancillary businesses such as television networks and cable companies, is very great indeed. Television advertising has long been based on charging the most for ad time in and around the highest-rated shows. Fox's top-rated *American Idol*, for example, commands advertising rates of more than $1 million per 30-second spot for the season finale (30-second spots aired during the Super Bowl are expected to cost $2.6 million in 2007). It's not surprising then, that advertisers cry foul over DVR viewers' ability to skip or fast-forward through their extremely expensive ads. A CBS news study in 2005 found that 64% of PVR users skipped

commercials entirely, while and additional 26% fast-forwarded though most ads.

The ad-skipping phenomenon is forcing advertising agencies to become more creative. For example, in mid-2006, Sony Corporation began running ads for its Bravia flat-panel TVs that encouraged viewers to choose an ending of the ad from two on-screen choices (viewers choose the desired ending using their remote controls).

Other alternative ad approaches such as showcases and branded tags are available to DVR users. TiVo now offers a setup screen in which advertising videos as well as film and television program previews are "showcased." Viewers must choose to view the showcase. Branded tags are advertising icons that appear while fast-forwarding through commercials while watching TiVo. Viewers can select the icon with their remotes to learn more information about the product. In yet another attempt to get DVR accustomed to sitting through ads, KFC promoted an ad in 2006 in which a secret code word appeared in a single frame of a spot for its Buffalo Snacker sandwich. DVR users could slow or stop the ad to see the code and then go to the company's web site where that code could be entered for a free sandwich coupon. 103,000 viewers went to the KFC site and claimed the coupon. As an added dividend, news programs ran stories on the promotion and the fast food company enjoyed a 40% spike in traffic to its web site.

Cable companies, satellite services, electronics manufacturers and even entertainment PC manufacturers are building DVRs into their devices. For example, Time Warner offers a set-top cable box with DVR capabilities made by Scientific Atlanta. Comcast offers a similar set-top box DVR option through its partnership with Motorola. Many users would rather purchase DVR access as part of cable or satellite services to avoid stacking yet another box on or near their TV sets, a preference these companies are attempting to capitalize on.

TiVo finally succeeded in its attempts to partner with Comcast in March 2005. The cable giant now offers its digital customers (which amount to about 12.1 million of its 24.1 million cable customers) TiVo service. The two companies were able to agree upon payment and control issues, with Comcast paying the DVR company a monthly fee for each subscriber. Satellite system DirecTV has long been a major distributor of TiVo, but it pays the DVR firm a nominal fee per month per customer.

The real future of TiVo, and subsequently all DVR companies, lies in expanded services and more sophisticated technology. Portability of recorded programming will become standard. New services will include the ability to watch recorded programming on PCs or PDAs. To accomplish this, TiVo is partnering with Microsoft, Sonic and AMD to provide a service called TiVoToGo. Sonic Solutions has launched an enhanced version of its MyDVD Studio line that enables users to transfer TiVo programming to DVD for playback later on any DVD-equipped device. In 2005, TiVo signed licensing agreements to allow Internet content to be stored on its DVRs. In 2006, the company teamed with Verizon Wireless to launch TiVo Mobile, which allows Verizon customers to schedule recordings from their cell phones. Watch for further shifts in DVR technology as the ability to download video programming from the Internet becomes widespread.

4)   Apple's iPod Revitalizes the Music Industry

The sale of legal downloadable music via the Internet and Internet-enabled cell phones is finally gaining significant traction. This is due to several factors, including the growing clampdown on illegal downloads by court systems worldwide, the rising popularity of advanced features on cell phones, and the incredible popularity of Apple's iPod and the related iTunes music download site. Nielsen SoundScan reports that while album sales were down 4.9% in 2006 over the previous year, digital track sales increased by 65% with 582 million songs sold. Digital album sales more than doubled, reaching almost 33 million sold in 2006.

Since the advent of sites such as Napster.com in the late-90s, tens of millions of Internet surfers have downloaded unlimited free music. Although the original Napster.com site was shut down by the court system for aiding copyright violations, the ruling did not curtail the bootleg traffic of music and video files, which continue to proliferate in cyberspace. Peer-to-peer (P2P) Internet sharing programs such as KaZaA enable users to share files whether legal or not.

Consequently, global recorded music revenues declined significantly since 1998. Profit margins, once 15% to 20% in the 1980s, fell to 5% or so. Overall, music publishers lose $4 billion to piracy each year. The music companies are being forced to seek ways to safeguard digital music files against illegal download and distribution. At the same time, music makers are seeking ways in which to profit from music files downloaded by legal, authorized means from the Internet.

The saga continued in March 2005 when the U.S. Supreme Court found that file-sharing companies such as Grokster and Streamcast can be held liable for copyright infringement due to marketing and technical advice that induces customers to share files illegally. The ruling opens the door for further suits against file sharing sites by music producers. Courts in other nations have entered rulings against peer-to-peer software firms as well.

A big step forward for the music industry came in the form of the groundbreaking iTunes Music Store, a digital service provided by Apple Computer, Inc. Launched in April 2003, the service offers single track and album files for download from all five major U.S. music companies. Priced at $0.99 per song, with no subscription fees, Apple announced 2 million song downloads in the venture's first 16 days. The iTunes site as of early 2007 offers over 3.5 million songs as well as 20,000 audio books, plus 3,000 music videos and 200 television shows, and has strengthened its hold on the music download industry thanks to Apple's incredibly popular personal digital music player—the iPod. In early 2007, the iTunes Store topped 2 billion songs, 50 million TV episodes and over 1.3 million feature-length films sold since its launch.

The iPod started off slowly from a storage point of view; early models were limited to 5 gigabytes (GB) of storage (the equivalent of less than 1,000 high-quality song recordings). However, iPod sales really took off when the firm introduced a 10-GB unit in March 2002. Even more powerful units are common today, enabling the latest iPods to download and display video as well as audio content. The iPod is an astonishing success. In 2006, 39.4 million iPods were sold. Apple has added to the iPod experience by partnering with a broad spectrum of companies that make iPod carrying cases, speakers and adapters that integrate iPod files into home and car sound systems. Everything from snappy Kate Spade leather carrying cases to powerful and portable Altec Lansing and Bose speakers are keeping consumers closely tied to the iPod brand, which holds approximately 66% of the digital music player market.

In 2007, Apple offers the ability to store and play video as well as music on its 30 GB and 80 GB models. Priced starting at $249, the units hold up to 20,000 songs, full-color album cover art and up to 25,000 photos, in addition to up to 100 hours of video on a 2.5-inch color display. Music-only aficionados can choose the $199, 2 GB, 4 GB or 8 GB iPod nano.

Apple's online music service is simple to use and offers a truly broad selection of music. Users set up the iTunes "jukebox" with a quick download from the Apple site. Once installed, users merely click a button to view song selections. Thirty-second previews of any song may be heard for free, and purchases are made with one click. Once the songs are downloaded, users have virtually unlimited use of the purchased files. (The files are permanent and may be burnt onto CDs or downloaded onto MP3 players a total of 10 times, which limits mass reproduction.)

iTunes arrive in a format called AAC. The file format is relatively small (requiring minimal disk space), boasts sound quality superior to that of MP3 files and may be run on a standard computer or Apple's iPod. (The iTunes service was initially available only to Macintosh users, with a version for Windows-based computers available shortly after launch.) Apple is keeping its system proprietary, meaning that iTunes patrons can only listen to music on iPods. Competitors such as Microsoft's MSN Music, Yahoo!'s Musicmatch and the legally reborn Napster offer music than can be played on a variety of different devices by different manufacturers, with the exception of iPods. This is reminiscent of the VHS-Betamax format battle when videotapes were first introduced.

Listeners are happy with the iTunes system, as is evident from its continuing success. The music companies also stand to benefit, receiving about $0.65 in gross revenue per song. More importantly, the advent of iTunes is a watershed for the industry, enabling it for the first time to significantly limit music file piracy in a manner that is extremely popular with consumers.

Rival online music services, such as Rhapsody (offering 3 million songs) and the legal version of Napster.com (offering 3 million songs), are betting on subscription services as opposed to iTunes' single-song/album purchase store. Subscription services typically charge between $7.95 and $15 per month for listening to an unlimited number of songs on a computer. The business model is especially attractive to the subscription providers because they pay far less per song to the music companies than the $0.65 paid by online stores like iTunes for an outright sale. Gross margins for music sale services are 10% to 15%, while for subscription services, those margins can be 40% to 50%. However, until recently consumers have been limited to listening to subscription music on their computers. Subscribers now have the options of burning CDs or listening on MP3 players, and in some cases, iPods.

Consumers so far have firmly shown their preference for online music stores, largely because of the ability to listen to purchased music on iPods, MP3 players and CD players in addition to computers.

In an effort to remain competitive, many subscription services also offer song/album purchase as an additional service. However, subscription appears to be the service that most online music purveyors are backing. Thanks to the technology by Microsoft called Janus that allows devices such as MP3 players to play songs downloaded via subscription (songs are programmed to expire on a set date, but dates are automatically extended when users continue to subscribe), subscription services believe that consumer tastes will shift. Napster, Inc. introduced its Napster To Go subscription service in February 2005. This service utilizes the Microsoft software that makes it possible to listen to rented music on portable players in addition to PCs. RealNetworks and FYE.com are planning to offer similar services.

It will be interesting to see whether on not buyers will make that change from *a la carte* song purchases to monthly subscriptions, as well as how Apple will refine and expand its brand over the mid-term in an effort to retain its supremacy. (Meanwhile, satellite music delivery subscription services like XM and Sirius will create deep competition for online music subscription services.)

Plunkett's Law of Online Consumers:
    Online consumer usage grows exponentially as broadband access prices decline (both fixed and mobile) and wireless Internet devices are adopted. This creates increased demand from online consumers, and leads to increased offerings of enhanced online services, entertainment and telephony.

---

5)   Internet Film Content Explodes
    The music industry's plight over pirated music has proven a valuable lesson for filmmakers and distributors. Film files are far larger than music files, so film companies had the luxury of time, since it took several years for broadband access to penetrate a large segment of the U.S. home market, to determine how to a) battle illegal copies of movies in digital form, and b) offer movie downloads for sale. Since 2005, the number of films and videos available for sale on the Internet have increased dramatically, as

film studios, electronics manufacturers, broadband providers and even cable TV companies all try to get a piece of the action.

Unfortunately, illegal downloads of movies via the Internet are also commonplace. In May 2005, when the last installment of the "Star Wars" films hit movie theaters, an illegal online version was posted on file-sharing site Elite Torrents, which was shut down by federal agents several days later. According to the Motion Picture Association of America, the film industry loses $6.1 billion each year to piracy, and has therefore been keenly observing the effort made by the music industry to limit illegal downloads. Thanks to groundbreaking digital rights technology developed by Microsoft, video files can now be made more difficult to hack, and filmmakers have far greater control over how a file is shared and on how many devices.

The handful of web sites that currently offer legal movie downloads include Movielink (www.movielink.com) and CinemaNow (www.cinemanow.com) , which offer pay-per-view downloads (and some rentals) and Starz!Ticket on Real Movies (starz.real.com), which offers monthly subscription services. Users log onto a site, browse to find a movie, download it and then watch the film on their computer monitors, or, if they have connected their PC to a television (or taken the time to burn the movie file onto a CD), watch with far superior video quality in the comfort of a living room or bedroom. Users with fast broadband connections need between 500 and 800 megabytes (MB) of space available on their computers and anywhere from 20 to 90 minutes for the file to download. Movies must be watched within 24 to 48 hours after the download is complete. Costs for pay-per-view titles range from $1.99 to $5, and $10 to $30 per month for subscription service.

Walt Disney Co. and its ABC subsidiary initiated a bold video download program in 2006 by offering 10 TV shows for download from its web site free of charge. The company has sold brief advertising slots, alongside these programs, to companies including AT&T and Toyota Motor Corp. to pay for the venture.

The Yankee Group estimated that customers downloaded 5.8 million movies in 2005, generating revenues of $26.3 million for the companies that provide the films. Looking ahead to 2008, analysts project that downloads will exceed 37 million and generate $169.4 million in revenue.

For the time being, however, most users of movies legally downloaded from the Internet are tech-savvy college students or business travelers who want to watch a movie on their laptops while flying from meeting to meeting. (There is also a rapidly growing market for short film clips that are viewed on Internet-enabled cell phones.) For now, the selection of movies available remains low. In contrast, DVDs offer much greater depth of selection. Netflix, the online service that delivers DVDs through the mail, offers more than 70,000 titles. Blockbuster offers 65,000 titles through its stores and mail delivery service.

In order for the legitimate movie download business to become truly profitable, the number of titles available must be significantly larger, and viewers must have an easy way to watch downloaded files on their TVs instead of on their computers. Many companies are scrambling to provide new products and services to make this possible. Intel, for example, offers Viiv, a platform that easily connects PCs and TVs. Likewise, Cisco is promoting its DP 600, a DVD player that has a broadband connection to the Internet, Apple, Inc. has its new Apple TV unit, and Microsoft is pushing its Xbox 360 as a full media center in addition to a gaming console.

Apple's iTunes site began selling various types of videos at $1.99 each in 2005. Programming for sale included short films from Pixar and selected TV shows from Disney, NBC Universal, the SciFi Channel and the USA Network. More than 1 million videos were sold in the first 20 days of the new service.

Apple's big news in 2007 is the announcement of a further entry into the video industry with the debut of a new device that will make downloaded movies more useful and more portable. The $299 Apple TV unit acts as an interface between a consumer's television, computer and iPod. For example, Apple TV will send digital entertainment that is stored on your computer directly to your TV. Also, the Apple TV unit will send home videos, movies, TV shows, and photos from your video iPod to your TV.

As part of this Apple TV strategy, Apple is boosting the amount of video content available for sale at iTunes. Apple has a deal with Walt Disney Co. to offer more than 75 of the studio's full length titles, which will take approximately 30 minutes each to download (using a broadband connection) and cost between $9.99 and $12.99 each. One obstacle to the release of the new devices is the proposed pricing scale, since Wal-Mart sells the same titles on DVD for between $16 and $18 (approximately). Wal-Mart currently accounts for approximately 40% of DVD sales in the U.S. Apple, Disney and Wal-Mart are currently in negotiations.

Wal-Mart also attempted to enter the movie download arena with a special promotion launched in late 2006. Customers who purchased the film "Superman Returns" on DVD have a video download option that allows them to watch the film on portable devices (such as iPods) or PCs/laptops. The cost for the bundled package (DVD plus download option) is $14.87 for the DVD, plus $1.97 to download to portable devices or $3.97 to download to a computer.

Amazon.com is jumping on the download bandwagon as well. It launched its Unbox service in 2006. Unlike many of the other movie download options, Unbox movies are only viewable on computers and certain portable devices—there is currently no support for burning disks that will play in a DVD player.

A digital video recorder called Akimbo stores up to 100 hours of programming downloaded from the Internet. The hardware is a set-top box, very similar to TiVo, which connects to the Internet and to TVs via wired or wireless home networks. The cost for the box is $199.99, and monthly service is about $10. Its limitations are many. Users cannot watch programming until it is fully downloaded. Available content is a fraction of what is available to cable subscribers. The latest Akimbo equipment is compatible with Microsoft Media Center. Other companies, such as TiVo, are attempting to offer customers similar systems with many of the same limitations.

Both the music and film industries have learned that paid options must equal the ease and depth of selection available in free, illegal Internet files. Over the mid-term, music firms and moviemakers will have to evolve to find ways of harnessing the power of the Internet rather than becoming a victim of it. Film companies will seek ways to sell digital movie files directly to the consumer, bypassing the middleman. In addition, the Motion Picture Association of America is launching an all-out campaign to boost awareness of the consequences of film piracy and has filed hundreds of suits against individuals as well as companies who are involved in illegal movie downloads.

SPOTLIGHT: Brightcove, Inc.

Founded in 2004, Brightcove (www.brightcove.com) is an Internet TV system that facilitates the offering of video and other content for download from the Internet. Headquartered in Cambridge, Massachusetts, Brightcove is a private company headed by management culled from entertainment firms such as Comcast, Lycos, News Corp. and Discovery Networks. The firm helps content owners, web publishers and advertisers (among others) to create Internet TV channels, and also consults with existing channel operators to enhance their sites and increase revenue. Selected customers include MTV Networks, The New York Times, Reuters and SonyBMG. Not only is the company amassing an impressive clientele, it is backed by some of the biggest names in electronics and entertainment including AOL/Time Warner, InterActiveCorp/IAC, the Hearst Corporation and General Electric.

Major electronics companies including Sony, Sharp Corp., Toshiba Corp. and Hitachi Ltd. are banding together to establish standards for Internet-connected TVs in an attempt to compete with computer hardware makers. The electronics firms hope to standardize aspects of Internet TV such as the operating system, copyright protection, connectivity and security.

As the Internet provides more and more video entertainment, new issues arise regarding the rights of TV networks versus those of web sites, Internet providers and so forth. Take, for example, the broadcast of Major League Baseball (MLB) games. MLB has exclusive deals with local and regional TV stations for the broadcast of it games (each regional agreement earns MLB about $250 million per year). 2,400 games each season are also broadcast online to subscribers (which nets MLB another $265 million per year). In order to maintain the TV stations' exclusive airing rights, Internet subscribers' access to local games is blocked.

Meanwhile, video-on-demand and subscription-based video-on-demand, very rapidly growing services offered by cable and satellite TV systems, appears to be succeeding in a big way where Internet-based film services have found only modest results. For details, see "Video-on-Demand (VOD) and Subscription Video-on-Demand (SVOD) Go Mass Market."

6)   Netflix Soars/Blockbuster Suffers

Netflix.com, an online DVD rental service, was launched in 2002. Now the largest such service in the world, it offers its members access to more than 70,000 titles. For a typical monthly subscription fee of $17.99, users may keep up to three DVDs at any given time. A lower-level subscription plan at $9.99 monthly enables subscribers to have only one DVD on loan at a time (the company also offers several additional levels of membership). Users select the titles they wish to view, and the discs are mailed to them in paper envelopes. For return, subscribers tear off the top flap of the paper mailer, revealing a pre-addressed and postage-paid envelope ready for mailing back to Netflix. Users are encouraged to maintain a list, or queue, of desired DVDs. As soon as one is returned, the next selection in the list is shipped out. One of the best selling points is the company's policy of no late fees. Users keep their rentals as long as they like, since there are never due dates for returns.

Gauging by the number of subscribers, Netflix is catching on in a big way, with total membership exceeding 5.7 million as of late 2006. Its success has had a serious impact on rivals including Blockbuster and Wal-Mart. Total revenues nearly doubled in 2005 for Netflix, to $688 million, and profits more than doubled to $41.9 million.

Blockbuster has responded with both an in-store subscription program and an online service, which it has recently combined in a program called Total Access. Customers can select movies online, receive them by mail and then return by mail or in a Blockbuster store. Monthly subscription pricing runs between $9.99 and $17.99, depending on the number of movies rented at a time. If this model sounds familiar, it's only because Blockbuster had to totally redesign its business in order to stay competitive with Netflix, especially embracing the no late fee policy. Although Blockbuster's sales still exceed those of Netflix handily (2005 sales were $5.8 billion), it has consistently lost money since 2002 (2005 losses were $588.1 million).

Striking yet another blow to Blockbuster, Netflix took over Wal-Mart's DVD rental business in May 2005 in return for the promotion of Wal-Mart's movie sales business on the Netflix web site.

Watch for increased competition in online video rental markets as Netflix attempts to maintain its momentum. Netflix is said to be working on a partnership with TiVo to enter the video-on-demand arena. At the same time, Blockbuster is partnering with Microsoft's MSN Internet site to do the same.

Meanwhile, Netflix maintains significant competitive advantage due to the software that drives its online system. In a manner similar to the way that Amazon.com suggests book titles to customers, the Netflix system does a superb job of recommending movies to customers, based on their history on the site. Additionally, Netflix customers receive superior service, and they enjoy prompt, effortless delivery of movies thanks to the company's network of 41 distribution centers in strategic locations nationwide.

7)   Major Casino Expansion Continues in the U.S. and Macau

The U.S. gambling mecca of Las Vegas, along with other gambling outposts including Atlantic City and the rapidly growing Chinese enclave of Macau, are experiencing phenomenal growth. For 2005, gaming revenues in Las Vegas alone topped $7.6 billion (an 11.5% increase over 2004) while Macau's revenues reached $5.7 billion (a similar increase of 11% over 2004). Related firms are scrambling to capitalize on the boom with even more casinos, hotels and resorts of ever-larger sizes.

Industry analysts project between $25 billion to $30 billion in new building construction in Las Vegas by 2010. MGM Mirage is planning a 66-acre, $7-billion CityCenter complex that is expected to include 6,800 hotel rooms and condos, as well as a 4,000-room hotel-casino designed by world-famous architect Cesar Pelli and high-end shops and spas. Big developments continue in Las Vegas, with the opening of the $2.5-billion Wynn Las Vegas megaresort in 2005 and the addition of 8,800 new rooms at new and existing hotels by the end of 2007. Next door to the Wynn, the Las Vegas Sands (which owns the Venetian in Las Vegas and the Sands Macao in China) has broken ground on another mega-resort called the Palazzo. It will feature 3,025 new suites, including a series of huge suites on the top floors and around the pool, ranging up to 11,000 square feet each, plus a total of 450,000 square feet of meeting space, with an anticipated completion date in 2007.

In addition to acres of slot machines, black jack tables and roulette wheels, Las Vegas is teeming with new versions of famous restaurants, luxe shopping boutiques and world-class entertainment including internationally known singers, dancers and comedians and several different permanent shows by the Cirque du Soleil troupe of acrobats, clowns and musicians. Las Vegas hotels and casinos make roughly one-half their net profits through non-gambling activities.

Two mega-mergers that took place in 2005 significantly altered the gambling industry. Harrah's Entertainment, Inc. acquired Caesars Entertainment, Inc. in a $9.4-billion transaction, while MGM Mirage took over the Mandalay Resort Group in a $7.9-billion deal. The Harrah's acquisition positions the former riverboat and casino-hotel operator as a vast gambling company with operations throughout the U.S. In addition to a number of casinos in Las Vegas (including Caesars Palace, the Flamingo and Paris), Harrah's has smaller gambling centers across the country on riverboats and on Native American reservations and pueblos.

The MGM Mirage/Mandalay Resort deal entrenches the empire run by billionaire investor Kirk Kerkorian as the dominant force on the Las Vegas strip, with holdings of more than half of the famous street's 72,000 hotel rooms. Top properties include Bellagio, Mandalay Bay, Luxor and New York-New York.

Gambling is still one of today's major growth industries, grossing more than $50 billion per year in the U.S., as casino/hotels, riverboat casinos, Native American reservation casinos and bingo halls and slot machine parlors continue to attract visitors by the millions. Destinations such as Atlantic City and Biloxi, Mississippi are investing heavily in Las Vegas-style attractions such as luxe retailers, big name entertainment and swanky restaurants to lure customers. The Native American gaming industry has more than doubled since 2000, bringing in about $22 billion per year.

Meanwhile, online gambling is growing at a tremendous rate. Although illegal in the U.S., Internet gambling sites are expected to net $24.5 billion in 2010 after paying out winnings, up from 2004's $8.2 billion, according to Christiansen Capital Advisory. All of these businesses are based outside the U.S., and are therefore largely beyond the jurisdiction of the U.S. Department of Justice.

Part of what is spurring this online growth is peer-to-peer betting, or wagering directly against another player as opposed to betting against the house. Services popping up to enable peer-to-peer betting include BetBug (www.betbug.com), a file-sharing program similar to the music-sharing program Morpheus. BetBug was originally developed by 1X, Inc., a Toronto software company, which designed a downloadable application that builds a self-sustaining network of gamblers (BetBug was acquired by Trident Gaming in June 2005, which also owns Gamebookers). Any BetBug user who proposes a wager can find a taker on the network.

Wagered amounts are kept in escrow accounts, and BetBug makes sure that all parties have deposited agreed-upon amounts and deducts 5% of the winnings. It's simple and anonymous, which attracts users from around the world, including millions of gamblers in the U.S.

The next big thing in gambling may well be wireless hand-held gaming devices. In 2005, Nevada became the first state to allow the use of the devices, which afford gamblers the ability to play video poker, blackjack, roulette and other games on hand-held units in public areas of casinos such as bars, restaurants and pools. The devices are banned in hotel rooms and other private areas, and will require additional security and surveillance equipment in order for casinos to enforce the ban. Users rent the units from the casinos with proper identification and a deposit of funds into an electronic account. Cantor G&W, a subsidiary of financial services company Cantor Fitzgerald and the initiator of the Nevada bill to allow wireless gaming devices, is bidding to provide participating Las Vegas casinos with the hand-held units and the networks that run them. Legislation allowing the devices is possibly the first step toward legalized online gambling in the U.S.

8)   **Reality TV Dominates Broadcast Programming/Networks Find New Ways to Distribute Content**

Reality TV programming began with the comic *Candid Camera* in 1948. Host Allen Funt filmed unwitting people reacting to rigged situations such as talking mailboxes. Far less humorous but riveting television aired on PBS in 1973 when *An American Family* showed the unscripted breakdown of a marriage and the coming out of a homosexual son. The show attracted 10 million viewers. More recently, unscripted life has been caught on videotape in shows such as MTV's *Real World* and Fox's *America's Most Wanted*. Other reality formats, including *Big Brother*, were pioneered in Europe during the late 1990s.

Today, reality shows such as *Survivor* and *American Idol* are changing the landscape of broadcast television. In the fall of 2006, 13 reality shows were on the schedules of the four major U.S. broadcast networks (ABC, CBS, Fox and NBC). At the Fox network, as much as 60% of the primetime schedule is devoted to reality programs.

One reason why this kind of programming is so popular with viewers is that producers cash in on the suspense and drama inspired by challenges. Will the hopeful young singer, that viewers have come to know and love, win a record contract on *American Idol*? Which contestant will be voted off the *Survivor* program after hours of grueling competition?

As a business model, shows of this ilk are providing advertisers with new means of reaching viewers with implanted advertising. This is vital since, with the advent of DVRs, viewers are fast-forwarding through ads or skipping them altogether. *Survivor* reaches as many as 28 million viewers who watch contestants win a new Pontiac or guzzle Mountain Dew after scaling an arduous cliff. This style of advertising is called product placement and is generally believed to be a bit crass when used in scripted television. Other newly popular alternatives to classic 30- and 60-second commercials are advertiser sponsorships. For example, Ford, Coca-Cola and Cingular sponsor *American Idol*.

Industry analysts are reluctant to predict how long the reality TV craze will continue, but many question the proliferation and how it might kill off the genre by airing too much reality for viewers to swallow. The 12th season of *Survivor* aired in February 2006, a mere two months after the finale from the previous season. Another limitation to reality TV is that it does not go into syndication, since the current nature of the shows is part of the appeal. Syndication allows many other types of programs to be produced at a loss, and then generate profits when aired again.

Meanwhile, for the first time in more than a decade, Nielsen Media Research reported that viewership among the coveted 18 to 40 year old age bracket for the Big Four networks was up. Admittedly, the margin of just 17,000 new viewers was small, but the increase is significant. Analysts credit a rash of hip new programming such as ABC's *Grey's Anatomy* and *Desperate Housewives* and CBS' *CSI: Crime Scene Investigation* as the impetus.

Despite the increase, the major networks as well as cable networks are rightly concerned about keeping viewers tuned in. Production is hugely expensive, as a one-hour episode of a new series can cost between $1 million and $2 million or more. Advertising revenues and cable fees are often not enough to cover the costs, so the networks are looking for other avenues. Releasing programming on DVD, pay-per-view or internationally are several ways to raise additional cash, and more creative means are emerging as well. For example, *Desperate Housewives* reruns are now available for purchase by iPod users who have the new, video-enabled units. CBS is selling replays of its *CSI* series and *Survivor* to Comcast barely hours after their first run. Several

television programs are now available as pay-per-view on Internet-enabled cell phones.

Watch for more innovative ways in which television networks will attempt to stay profitable. NBC, ranked fourth overall behind ABC, CBS and Fox, is especially intent on offering digital content to beef up its ratings. New initiatives include the promotion of NBC shows on broadband comedy channel (www.dotcomedy.com); an online preview channel (www.nbc.com/NBC_First_Look); and 30 "webisodes" of the network's sitcom *The Office* available for viewing online on the NBC web site. See "TV over IP—TV Networks and Web Sites Converge" in this chapter for more on the online TV phenomenon.

In January 2007, the CBS television network announced several new initiatives to make its content available online and on multiple platforms. One of the most interesting developments at CBS is a test with technology provider Slingbox to enable Slingbox users to share clips of CBS programming with their friends by posting the clips to a CBS-branded website. (Slingbox is a technology firm that sells set-top boxes that enable users to watch TV programming on PCs or mobile devices.) Meanwhile, CBS extended its cooperation with YouTube (where users can already view CBS program clips) to include a contest where YouTube users can submit a 15-second video to be played during a SuperBowl 2007 TV ad.

9) New Platforms Revolutionize Electronic Games

Electronic games are king. U.S. revenues in 2005 for the video game industry topped $10.5 billion according to the NPD Group, a jump of 6% over 2004's $9.9 billion. PricewaterhouseCoopers expects worldwide sales to escalate to $55 billion by 2008. The big news is the release of ever-more-complex technology that not only combines games with MP3 and DVD players, but offers full Internet access and interactive TV as well. Game players can find online opponents, check e-mail, shop online and download music and video entertainment with a single system. The future of games lies in one word: online.

Sony's Play Station 2, released in the fall of 2001, was the first unit to play DVDs and audio CDs while offering top-of-the-line high-tech gaming. By mid-2005, Play Station 2 had sold 90 million units worldwide, and the company dropped its retail price from $179 to $149, thereby extending the sales life of the unit.

Microsoft was hoping to break Sony's dominance in the market with its Xbox, which was released in November 2001 (with a $500-million marketing budget). Xbox is a major step in the company's attempt to revolutionize the home in the same way that PCs revolutionized the office. The unit is a combination of some of the functions of a high-end PC, complete with high-speed Internet port and a powerful graphics chip; a video game console; and ultimately a headset that will allow players to talk to other players down the street or in another country via the Internet. Microsoft had sold more than 20 million units in North America by the middle of 2005.

Xbox Live, Microsoft's online gaming subscription service, was launched in November 2003 and is expected to exceed 6 million members by mid-2007. It provides gamers with the ability to play against each other using the Internet and is becoming a key component to the video gaming experience. Xbox Live's popularity places the software giant in contention for the first time with top-rated Sony, long the number-one video game company in the world.

More news in the Sony-versus-Microsoft video game war was Sony' release of the PlayStation Portable, or PSP. Launched in late 2004 in Japan, and in mid-2005 in the U.S., the PSP was Sony's first hand-held portable game player. It boasts cutting-edge graphics and the ability to play MP3 music files as well as movies on a 4.3-inch-wide screen. Users can also access the Internet via built-in Wi-Fi connectivity and web browser. (For details regarding "Cell" chip technology and the 2006 launch of PlayStation 3, see "Cell" Chip Technology Sizzles in PS3" in this chapter.)

The debut of Microsoft's $4-billion baby, the Xbox 360, was a major milestone in video gaming. Released for sale at midnight, November 22, 2005, Xbox 360 is a completely redesigned game console, which, not surprisingly, continues to focus on games as part of Microsoft's complete home entertainment concept. In addition to the game console, it has a wireless controller, cables for TV connection, a DVD player, a removable 20 GB hard disk, a headset and a complimentary pass to Xbox Live (this is the setup for the $400 premium version, there is also a more basic system for $300 that does not include the connecting cables or headset and has a wired controller). The console includes ports for attaching digital cameras, portable MP3 music players (including Apple's iPod) or Microsoft's Windows Media Center PC. The software giant hopes that sales of its new game systems will spur further sales of its other home products. The Xbox 360, with its three-core 3.2-gigahertz custom chip from IBM, has been a big hit so far, with about 3 million units selling in the first 90 days alone. Hundreds of thousands of would-be Xbox owners were forced to place their names on waiting lists as initial supplies sold out immediately. In January 2007, Microsoft announced that it shipped 10.4 million units worldwide by the end of 2006.

Nintendo, the third key player in video game sets, currently holds the number-one position in sales of hand-held game players with its Game Boy Micro. In a vigorous attempt to hold on to its top spot and to compete with Sony's PSP, Nintendo launched its super small player in 2005. At $100, it is barely four inches wide and two inches tall. It has a leg up over other portable devices because it is compatible with more than 700 games designed for earlier Game Boy models.

Nintendo released of its own new game system, Nintendo Wii (pronounced "we"), in 2006. Equipped with a state-of-the-art wireless controller and priced at $249, the system offers gamers new, sensory-enhanced playing. The controller communicates with sensors mounted near a television that respond to the player's hand and arm movements. A fishing game, for example, causes the controller to "tug" on the player's hand when a fish is hooked, and the player can then "jerk" on the controller like a fishing pole to reel the catch in. The new technology works with long-time game favorites including *Pokémon*, *Mario Bros.* and *The Legend of Zelda*.

Not surprisingly, because of its lengthy history of dominating certain software segments, Microsoft maintains complete control over the licensing of its Xbox consoles and the games that can be played on it. Conversely, Sony allows almost any game developer to design games that can be run on Play Station 2 and on PS3 as well. This allows online interaction between Sony players without subscribing to an additional service such as Xbox Live.

Spotlight: Electronic Arts

In the world of video games, developer Electronic Arts (EA) is the undisputed megastar. Although the delayed release of Sony's Playstation 3 posed some significant problems, EA still brought in almost $3 billion in 2006 revenues. It makes most of the top video games on the market, especially in genres such as sports, movies and action heroes. Top titles include *Madden NFL 07, NBA Live 07, Harry Potter and the Goblet of Fire* and *MVP 06: NCAA Baseball.*

EA partners with leading film studios, sports franchises, publishers and recording artists to design games with cutting-edge style. Movie producers looking to market their new films are quick to license content to EA. For example, legendary director Steven Spielberg is collaborating with EA to develop three new original games. Likewise, recording artists are eager to have tracks from not-yet-released CDs included in EA games. The firm maintains an in-house creative team that is largely culled from the film and music industries. EA is a powerhouse that has the creative, marketing and financial ability to enable it to enter into exclusive agreements with such organizations as the NFL for development of new games.

Firmly committed to expanding its online gaming, EA offers its own Sports Nation network. Betting on its top-rated sports games, the company is offering tournament play, leagues, rankings, stats and laddering systems, as well as sweetening the pot with offers of prizes or cash payments for winners.

As for online games, they have become one of the largest and fastest-growing sectors of the worldwide entertainment business. Online video games were expected to attract 40 million players in the U.S. alone by 2006, according to Jupiter Research.

Gaming has presented new ways of making money. Multi-player games (known as massively multiplayer online games or MMOGs) have sparked a new market in which players broker deals to buy and sell game currency, point-building online items and even winning players' online personas, which are called avatars. Many games, such as Sony Online Entertainment's EverQuest or Vivendi subsidiary Blizzard Entertainment's phenomenally popular World of Warcraft are designed so that players must conquer a large number of challenges to win points and proceed to higher levels. Game masters reach the pinnacle by performing all tasks, which can number as many as 60 or 70. Gamers looking to cash in on the booming popularity of these games (World of Warcraft has 7 million subscribers worldwide) are finding ways to buy and sell virtual assets for real currency.

For a time, winning player avatars and other assets were traded on eBay (the auction site has since ceased to allow these kinds of items on its site), and numerous private buying and selling sites have sprung up, such as IGE (www.ige.com) to handle the demand. Some game companies are setting up real money trade (RMT) services of their own. In July of 2005, Sony created Station Exchange, which hosted $540,000 in RMTs in its first three months, and charging a 10% commission on each transaction.

The potential for this new market is huge. IGE claims that the 2005 marketplace for virtual assets was as high as $900 million. The practice raises some sticky questions, however, about the true ownership of cyber-assets. Some game companies maintain that all currency, points, avatars and other assets are their property and not that of its players. Others disagree. As greater and greater sums are being made from virtual asset brokerage, the question becomes more important. Is a game company liable to its players for their cyber-assets should it discontinue the game or alter its rules? It is also possible that in the U.S., the Internal Revenue Service will begin taxing profits made selling these assets.

When most people think of video game enthusiasts, they picture kids and young men playing violent, action-packed titles such as *Counter-Strike* and *EverQuest*. However, 82.5 million people in the U.S. play "simple" online games such as checkers, mah jong and bridge, vastly larger than the number of people who play sophisticated titles. It's a market that earns $450 million per year for game companies, largely through advertising. Less than 2% of the players of these kinds of games pay to subscribe.

The average "simple" online player is female and between the ages of 35 and 54. Game playing is as much a social activity as a solitary pursuit, as many players connect online with opponents both known and unknown. Xfire (www.xfire.com), an advertiser-supported web site that tracks friends, browses servers, posts game statistics and provides instant messaging, is cashing in on the play-with-friends trend. It debuted in January 2004 with $5 million in venture funding and was acquired by Viacom in 2006. In late 2006, the site surpassed 5 million registered users.

Simple games such as hearts and pool not only attract more users, they are much cheaper and easier to produce. A major shoot 'em up action game can require dozens of computer coders and designers as well as budgets of between $5 million and $15 million. Simple games, such as Yahoo!'s hit pool game, take one developer and about $100,000 to put together. A typical Friday afternoon finds upwards of 36,000 people playing pool on Yahoo!'s gaming site.

Microsoft is capitalizing on the popularity of its video games as a way to gain a strong position in the entertainment industry. The firm's online gaming site, Zone.MSN.com, is extremely successful. However, it is facing tough competition from firms such as Electronic Arts, Yahoo! and Sony, who are all looking for the next smash (read simple) online game.

10) "Cell" Chip Technology Sizzles in PS3

By releasing Xbox 360 in November 2005, Microsoft beat Sony's widely anticipated release of its PlayStation 3 (PS3), which was released in the U.S. a year later. By the end of 2006, Sony had shipped 1 million of the consoles to U.S. retailers. Priced between $499 and $599, PS3 includes a high-definition DVD player using the Sony standard called Blu-ray. This is a bold move since the entertainment industry is still undecided as to which DVD technology will be embraced by the buying public, and stand-alone Blu-ray players are expected to command a $1,000 price tag. Sony is actually taking a loss on the DVD player included in PS3 in order to market the new technology and soften the blow for movie watchers who will have to buy high-definition versions of their favorite DVDs.

Cell, Xbox 360, Pentium 4-840 Processor Speeds Compared		
Chip:	*Transistors:*	*Speed in gigaflops:*
Cell, PlayStation 3 (November 2006 release)		
	234 million	230
Xbox 360 (November 2005 release)		
	165million	77
Pentium 4 (Extreme Edition 840, 3.2 GHz, 2005 release)		
	230 million	26

The biggest innovation for PS3 is an extremely powerful seven-core, 3.2-gigahertz "Cell" microprocessor developed by IBM and Toshiba. This Cell chip represents a true revolution in technology for consumer devices, since it essentially packs the processing speed of a supercomputer. The

PS3 can call on the Cell chip to crunch up to 2 trillion calculations per second. This means that game developers can create extremely realistic virtual characters and settings that move at blistering-fast speeds. To put the Cell chip into perspective, it runs at speeds nine-times as fast as a very high level Intel Pentium 4, dual-core chip.

While other firms are pursuing the Cell with high-speed chip designs of their own, the Cell's early lead will result in rapid adoption by game developers and by makers of other electronics devices. The fact that the Cell was forced to be created as a low-power consumption, lightweight, high-speed chip for use in a revolutionary game machine will lend it to creative use in other devices and multi-use platforms. Watch for the Cell to be used as an enabler for entertainment units of all kinds, with enriched media offerings such as real-time video chat and extremely evolved interactive TV on the go. Multi-use cell phones with vast numbers of entertainment offerings via fast wireless Internet access and high-definition color screens will become the biggest benefactors. Meanwhile, the games designed for PS3 will reach a new level of extreme virtual reality and virtual world immersion. Non-entertainment uses for Cell chip technology will evolve rapidly as well, including applications for engineering, research and aerospace.

11) Satellite Radio Fails to Earn a Profit/Traditional Radio Faces Challenges

Satellite broadcast radio provides yet another example of consumers seeking niche, often ad-free entertainment. There are two major players in this sector, XM Satellite Radio and Sirius. Each offers more than 130 themed radio channels in clear, CD-quality sound. Both firms have signed up multimillion subscriber bases, although they are below their initial goals, while racking up huge losses.

XM Satellite Radio has an important leg-up on Sirius because it hit the market almost a year ahead in September 2001. It broadcasts more than 170 music, information and entertainment channels through two satellites with a small amount of advertising (many channels are completely ad-free). As of the beginning of 2007, XM had 7.6 million subscribers (up from 3.2 million at the first of 2005) who pay $12.95 per month. The company had targeted 9 million users in 2006 but fell short.

Sirius, formerly known as CD Radio, was launched in July 2002. It transmits its more than 131 channels of news, information, entertainment and music from three satellites to any vehicle or home equipped with a Sirius receiver. Its early 2007 subscriber total reached 6 million, and monthly subscription fees are the same $12.95 charged by XM.

Both companies face fierce opposition from traditional radio stations (terra stations) which form a powerful lobby known as the National Association of Broadcasters (NAB). Throughout satellite radio's development, the NAB has pushed through legislation that severely limits satellite radio's activity. FCC regulations require satellite firms to have paying subscribers (free, advertising-supported stations are forbidden), and air space is limited to 25 megahertz. In addition, the Digital Performance Right in Sound Recordings Act of 1995 frees terra radio from paying royalties to recording artists, while requiring that satellite stations do so. XM paid almost $20 million in royalties in its first two years on the air (17% of total revenue for that period).

The most difficult regulation of all for satellite radio is that it is banned from broadcasting local programming. No local traffic, weather or sports reporting may be beamed into specific markets. However, in 2004, XM found a loophole in the requirement and began broadcasting 20 localized feeds via satellite to particular channels. These channels are broadcast nationally so listeners across the U.S. can tune into traffic reports for a city such as New York or Los Angeles, but the audience for the channels is more likely to be local. In a further development, XM acquired WCS Wireless LLC, a Nevada wireless company that owns part of the broadcasting spectrum that is right next to XM's in 15 of the top 20 metropolitan markets. The new spectrum enables XM to target local markets with local programming.

Traditional radio is attempting to fight back by tinkering with its programming and formats. Many stations, including those owned by industry leader Clear Channel Communications, Inc., are cutting commercials and playing more music. Viacom's Infinity Broadcasting offers an open source format on one of its San Francisco AM stations. Instead of its standard talk radio programs, KYOU is airing podcasts, which are submissions from its listeners with a wide variety of home-grown content. Clear Channel also offers podcasting channels as of mid-2005. Many traditional stations are also offering high-definition (HD) radio channels such as Clear Channel's Mother Trucker country and southern rock digital channel and Full Metal Racket heavy metal channel.

Meanwhile, satellite radio is scrambling to maintain its subscribership and cut costs. Many of the most expensive startup costs, such as the satellites and the design and manufacture of receivers, are behind the two companies, but both are facing unexpected new costs such as escalating contracts for on-air talent such as Sirius' $500-million, five-year contract with notorious disc jockey Howard Stern that began in January 2006.

Attempts to build subscriber revenue via agreements that each company has with various major automakers have created their own problems. Sirius has partnerships with a lengthy list of car makers, including Ford, DaimlerChrysler and BMW, allowing the car companies to equip new vehicles with their receivers. Part of the subscription revenue is paid as a royalty to the automaker during the full lifetime of the automobile. XM is partnering with GM and Honda (both automakers have stakes in XM), as well as with Toyota and Hyundai. These agreements do get the product in front of potential customers, but both XM and Sirius are finding that many drivers choose not to activate subscriptions. The firms countered by offering free trial access to car buyers starting in 2006, but are discovering that the rate of drivers who choose to keep the service once the trials run out is expected to be disappointingly low.

Satellite radio does offer an ever-increasing depth and variety of programming. XM has the rights to broadcast all Major League Baseball games. Sirius has the rights to broadcast National Football League games. With the plethora of channels available from both companies, coverage of sporting events can offer a dizzying variety of flavors. Take the 2006 Super Bowl, for example. XM covered the game on at least six different channels. One favored the Pittsburgh Steelers, while another offered a pro-Seattle Seahawk slant. Moreover, other channels broadcast the game in languages from Spanish to Chinese to German.

Satellite radio is also beamed into homes, offices and even offshore, with service for everything from the living room to the tractor to the pleasure boat. The receivers cost between $100 and $200 and can be purchased through most major electronics retailers, including Best Buy, Circuit City and Wal-Mart. Newer receivers such as Sirius' S50 and XM's Nexus have the ability to record up to 750 songs or other programming and organize that material in playlists similar to the Apple iPod. Cost for these receivers is around $180.

Satellite radio does have the ability to broadcast content other than audio entertainment and news. Real-time weather content is now being broadcast to the yachting and shipping market. Also, Sirius has launched a few channels of children's video entertainment, aimed at back-seat screens in automobiles.

However, XM and Sirius have their work cut out for them if they are to continue to build subscribership and manage to finally make a profit. Watch for possible cost-cutting measures over the mid-term and new ways of seeking those elusive new subscribers who may prefer to stick to their iPods.

The good news is that the firms are getting better control of subscriber acquisition costs (SAC). For example, Sirius reports that average costs for acquiring one new subscriber fell by 23% from September 2005 to September 2006, to $114 from $149. This is due primarily to a reduction in the firm's subsidy for each receiver thanks to reduced manufacturing and chip costs. Nonetheless, for the third quarter of 2006 the firm lost $162.9 million (compared to a $180.4 million loss in the same quarter of 2005), while revenues totaled $167.1 million (up 150% from the third quarter of 2005).

12) Radio Via IP Grows/The Era of Digital Radio Begins

It is now common for broadcast radio stations in markets across the U.S. to stream real-time programming on their web sites at the same time that the programming is on the air. This makes it possible for a listener to tune in via PC, even when thousands of miles away. It also enables the station to maintain a multimedia connection with the listener, since the web site can post ads, program schedules, DJ profiles and the like.

Peer-to-peer (P2P) web sites that operate in a radio-like manner (but are not part of traditional radio stations) are proliferating at a rapid rate as well. Generally, such sites enable a listener to request a constant stream of either popular genres or very specific niche music. For example, a listener could receive a constant stream of reggae music, or jazz or classical music. Hundreds of thousands of listeners are tuning in through this method. On the programming end, thousands of amateur enthusiasts are packaging their favorite music, or commentary, and playing it via the web. For example, AOL offers such a service called Shoutcast, a free streaming MP3 music file server.

Other sites use simple streaming technology that is not P2P. Companies attempting to create revenues by enabling online listening include Live365 (www.live365.com) and Mercora (search.mercora.com). Yahoo! is in the business with its Launchcast service, as is RealNetworks with its Rhapsody service.

In 2005, AOL reached an agreement with XM Satellite radio. AOL now offers 20 XM stations free of charge to its subscribers and for a $5 monthly fee to non-subscribers. The deal should help AOL retain some of its subscribers, while boosting XM's exposure.

The broadcast and satellite radio industry will watch these developments closely and may seek new ways to compete via IP delivery. These radio via IP services operate in a legal manner. Music is available for listening, but the files are streamed temporarily to listeners' PCs, not permanently downloaded.

A recent radio industry innovation, digital radio, refers to technology that improves radio signals while increasing the number of channels available. Approximately 1,000 U.S. stations broadcast digital signals by the beginning of 2006. However, since the signals require special digital receivers at the consumer end, few people are listening to these broadcasts at present. Nonetheless, digital broadcasting offers several advantages. To begin with, the reception is higher quality, with clearer tones and less interference.

Next, utilizing digital technology enables broadcasters to get create extra stations from the same bandwidth. In this manner, extra stations, typically called HD-2 and HD-3, can be broadcast that offer niche content. For example, a broadcaster that typically offers a wide variety of jazz on its main station could focus on Latin jazz on HD-2 and classic jazz of the 1940s on HD-3.

Currently, prices for digital receivers are high, with offerings on the market from Kenwood, Polk Audio and others. However, prices will plummet if the receivers become widely popular. Meanwhile, these receivers are already available in a handful of new cars.

While digital radio broadcasting is in its infancy, it could easily become the standard of the future. In the same way that the FCC is requiring that all TV broadcasts become digital by February 17, 2009, similar rulings may eventually be passed regarding radio.

13) Cable and Satellite TV Compete Fiercely for Market Share

In the race for home media customers, cable companies and satellite firms are battling to offer the most services, the greatest convenience and, more importantly in today's market, more consumer control over what to view. Nielsen Media Research estimates that, as of late 2006, approximately 73 million U.S. households currently subscribe to cable service while about 23 million homes have satellite service (up from only 1.6 million in late 1997). Based on subscribers alone, cable appears to have the lion's share of the market. However, changes in technology, viewer tastes and habits are profoundly changing, creating more and more room in the market for satellite and its many components.

Satellite companies took millions of customers away from cable firms in recent years, but cable companies are using new bundled services to fight back. The reasons for satellite TV's success include lower prices and the widely spreading availability of local channels via satellite. Monthly cable subscription prices were notorious for rising abruptly. U.S. cable leader Comcast Corporation raised its rates by an average of 5.9% in 2004, after a 5.7% hike in 2003. However, in 2005, many cable companies including Comcast began offering discounts, which continued through 2006, thereby cutting into satellite's long-held advantage on monthly rates.

Cable companies are faced with perhaps the toughest competition they've yet seen, and they are fighting back with new technology that may lure customers back from the satellite providers. Thanks to the approximately $100 billion spent by cable companies in the past decade on new high-speed fiber-optic lines and large numbers of localized servers that house movies and programs for fast download by nearby customers, new services offered today include Internet access, video-on-demand (VOD) and VOIP telephone service. Cable companies Time Warner, Inc. and Cablevision Systems Corp. are bundling these services together to entice customers with complete packages at discounted prices.

A newcomer to the cable-versus-satellite fray is AT&T, which launched a cable TV service called U-verse in 2005. The service, which offers up to 300+ channels and charges monthly fees of between $44 and $99, was first tested in San Antonio, Texas, and is expected in the San Francisco, New Haven and Hartford, Connecticut markets in early 2007. AT&T plans to make U-verse available to 19 million households by 2008.

Local programming is another significant issue in the battle between cable and satellite companies. Since 2001, the two major satellite companies, EchoStar and DirecTV have added enough satellite capacity to add local channels such as ABC, NBC, CBS, PBS and Fox affiliates to more than 92% of subscriber households. DirecTV, the leading satellite company in the U.S. with 15.7 million subscribers in 2006, is investing $1 billion to launch new satellites that offer local channels with high definition. Cable is quickly losing its local edge in most markets.

Now, cable providers face new competition from telephone companies such as AT&T, Inc. (formerly known as SBC Communications). Up until recently, cable's best competitive advantage over satellite was its ability to offer superior high-speed Internet connections and VOIP telephone service via cable. Comcast, the nation's largest cable company, is also the nation's largest provider of broadband Internet access, with 11 million Internet access subscribers as of the beginning of 2007. The competitive situation is changing, however, as major telecom companies, which have long been cable's competition in broadband access, now have the ability to deliver television programs through fiber-optic lines (see "TV over IP—Telecom Companies Enter the Television Market"). Phone companies including Verizon Communications and AT&T are offering television service in addition to phone service (landline or VOIP) and high-speed Internet access in some markets, with the hope to roll out these bundled services nationwide.

14) Video-on-Demand (VOD) and Subscription Video-on-Demand (SVOD) Go Mass Market

Cable companies such as Comcast, Time Warner Cable and Cablevision already have a presence in a vast number of U.S. homes. In a growing number of markets across the U.S., they offer video-on-demand (VOD), subscription video-on-demand (SVOD), high-speed Internet service and/or digital programming for HDTV. According to Leichtman Research Group, the percentage of cable subscribers who watch VOD almost doubled in 2006 to 65%.

With regard to VOD, there are two ways in which digital cable watchers can access paid programming. The first way is to select a film or television show for a per-unit price (usually about $3.95). It is transmitted from the hundreds of films and television shows stored on hard drives in the cable company's offices, and the viewer can watch it as many times as they wish during a 24-hour period. The second way is to subscribe to unlimited access to a particular set of shows, such as an entire season of a favorite television show or selected programming from a particular network such as HBO. The price for this option is around $6.95 per month.

Satellite companies such as DirecTV and EchoStar Communications so far control only a small part of the high-speed Internet access market, and satellite-based VOD is limited because the two-way communication necessary between subscriber and provider is limited to telephone lines (cable utilizes broadband lines much better suited to two-way communication). Satellites can beam programming to TVs, but cannot easily receive data. However, satellite companies do have a competitive offering with DVRs. These recorders, of which TiVo is a major brand, can be included in satellite converter boxes. This is a plus for viewers who are tired of the excess of receiver boxes and other electronic equipment stacked around their television sets. Satellite companies are gambling that the record-now, watch-later, skip-over-advertising features inherent in DVRs are more than a match for VOD. (For more on DVRs and their impact on the entertainment industry, see "DVR Market Evolves; Time-Shifting Becomes Widespread.") Another plus for satellite companies is a decisive lead in HDTV programming.

Meanwhile, huge enhancements to the cable experience were launched during 2006 as set-top boxes got an upgrade. Microsoft, with its Foundation software, Digeo and Liberate Technologies (owned in a joint venture between Comcast and Cox Communications called Double C Technologies, LLC) are all vying to sell their advanced technology software to the cable providers. This software, along with improved set-top box hardware, will enable cable firms to provide the latest in VOD, digital video recording (providing TiVo with even more competition) and interactive services such as on-screen shopping.

An excellent example of the use of VOD is Comcast's "ON DEMAND" service. ON DEMAND includes hundreds of movies, programming for children, fitness programs, lifestyle programs, music videos, concerts and sports such as NFL game highlights. While most of the ON DEMAND programming is free, the firm uses the system to build revenue by selling access to movies for $3.95 for new releases and $2.95 for other movies, as well as fees for access to special programming such as concerts. It also makes popular series available via

ON DEMAND, such as *CSI Crime Scene Investigation* and *Survivor*. Using On DEMAND, customers can play, fast-forward, rewind, pause and restart their selections as many times as they want during the 24 hours after they select the program. Comcast's customers watch more than 100 million ON DEMAND programs each month.

15)   TV over IP—Telecom Companies Enter the Television Market

The future of television may look something like this: From 2007 through 2010 or so, broadcasters, along with cable and satellite TV providers, will largely enjoy business as usual. At some point over the mid-term, however, TV over IP (IPTV) will become a serious threat. This is due to several reasons, including a) the cost and difficulty of digital production and distribution are plummeting, b) high-speed broadband access to the Internet in homes will become standard and c) the number of homes equipped with media PCs, capable of capturing TV programming from the web and sending it to high-tech monitors for display in the living room, will grow rapidly. Apple's exciting new Apple TV unit, introduced in 2007, will accelerate this trend.

Some of the implications include the possibility of thousands of new "channels" of TV over the Internet. Independent producers will have a plethora of new outlets. Online program guides will be absolutely essential so that consumers can determine what channels to watch. The TV audience is already fragmented because of the vast number of satellite and cable channels. IPTV will increase this fragmentation, creating both challenges and opportunities for advertisers, producers and delivery platforms. The potential for highly targeted, niche audience ads will be immense. The future may see viewers faced with hundreds of Martha Stewart look-alikes offering advice via Internet TV channels. At the same time, TV viewing will become much more portable, as mobile viewing platforms evolve and are made extremely useful via 3G cellular, WiMAX and other wireless networks. Broadcast, cable and satellite TV providers may compete by positioning themselves with value-added content and services, such as enhanced interactive TV and expensive programming such as made-for-TV movies and major league sports coverage. IPTV is already growing rapidly in Asian markets such as Japan.

Thanks to a technological breakthrough by Microsoft, telecom companies are now able to provide television programming in addition to phone service and high-speed Internet access. The software, called Microsoft TV Internet Protocol Television, digitally encodes and compresses TV signals so that they can be transmitted over phone lines. Customers have a set-top box that decodes and decompresses the signals for viewing. All programming is delivered as VOD (video-on-demand).

In June 2006, AT&T launched its Homezone service in San Antonio, Texas. The service provides video-on-demand over DSL along with satellite TV provided by EchoStar's Dish Network using a set-top box manufactured by 2Wire, Inc. Video-on-demand arrives via Movielink, an online video service. The monthly price for the package starts at about $59. While users may balk at the download time necessary to watch movies (cable companies provide movies on demand immediately) and at the currently limited selection, Homezone is a major breakthrough since it brings Internet content to the TV set instead of limiting it to viewing on computer monitors. AT&T launched a service called U-verse in 2006, which provides digital TV over its own proprietary network. The telecom giant hopes to sell the service to as many as 19 million homes in 13 states by mid-2008. Overall, AT&T is investing $4.6 billion in IPTV.

At the same time, Verizon tested a full menu of TV channels bundled with its high-speed Internet service in Keller, Texas. The service offers 150 channels for about $36.90 per month (which is substantially cheaper than many premium monthly cable packages). Based on the success of the Keller trial, Verizon introduced the service in other Texas towns, as well as some communities in Florida, California and New York in early 2006.

The prospect of IPTV is a boon to telecom companies, since it gives them a highly coveted entertainment service to add to their bundle of offerings. They will have the ability to bundle services that might include any or all of the following: Internet access, landline telephone, long-distance, VOIP telephony, cellular telephone and television via IP—all on one discounted bill. The major telephone service providers have been in a tough spot in the past few years, with revenues from landline customers declining as more consumers switch to cellular phones and VOIP as their standard methods of communication.

As for Microsoft, TV over IP technology is a long-awaited break into the television market. Over several years, the software giant has invested $20 billion in cable companies and other TV-related activities. Some of those investments, such as WebTV and UltimateTV, were not great successes. With IPTV, Microsoft technology has an additional entrée not only into living rooms, but also onto devices such as cell phones and PDAs, which are expected to be able to provide TV programming once wireless speeds become fast enough. In February 2006, Microsoft announced a partnership with British Telecom Group and Virgin Mobile to provide digital TV over mobile phone networks. Microsoft also provides software to Verizon, which began offering a service called V Cast TV in 2005.

16) TV over IP—TV Networks, Cable Companies and Web Sites Converge

Internet portals, web sites and television networks are acutely aware of the potential afforded should television audiences truly turn to their PCs for entertainment. Many popular Internet sites are already producing programming, while television networks are finding ways to air their content online on their own sites. America Online (AOL) offers a selection of free programming such as Live 8 concerts and business programs hosted by top analysts Stephen R. Covey and Tom Peters. The Live 8 web cast in July 2005 attracted an estimated 3 billion viewers worldwide, who clicked between footage of performances in London, Paris, Philadelphia, Toronto, Rome and Berlin.

Television stations such as CNN, MTV and Nickelodeon are airing programming on their web sites. CNN debuted its CNN Pipeline service (www.cnn.com/pipeline) in 2005, which offers users a choice of four live news video streams for $2.95 per month. MTV has an Internet video service called MTV Overdrive (www.mtv.com/overdrive) which offers dozens of music and celebrity related programs, including a daily web cast of music news and events. There is no fee for the service, which is funded by online advertising. Unlike DVR programming on television, in which viewers can fast forward or skip advertising altogether, the ads on MTV Overdrive bookend programming and also reside in separate windows that can't be closed. Lucrative online advertising is spurring many media companies to take hard looks at ways to diversify programming away from TV and toward the PC.

Portals such as Yahoo! are also getting into the IPTV act by providing video searches. Yahoo! Search (http://video.search.yahoo.com) offers a search engine for a wide variety of video on the web from an extensive list of sources including CBS, Warner Brothers, *BusinessWeek*, ESPN and many more. As programming proliferates, the need for efficient methods to search for content becomes critical.

Probably nowhere is the convergence of TV and the Internet better illustrated than by the 2005 acquisitions by media mogul Rupert Murdoch's News Corporation (which owns the Fox network) of the social networking site MySpace and a gaming site called IGN, as well a sports site Scout Media. Collectively, the acquisitions were worth about $1.3 billion, and firmly placed News Corporation in the thick of the Internet. In addition, the firm created Fox Interactive Media to manage its Internet assets.

Cable companies such as Comcast and Time Warner are also getting into the act by investing heavily in new technology that makes video content available on their web sites to all and sundry, not just to their subscribers. Subscribers may, however, route web site content to their TVs for high-quality viewing in comfort.

Search engine sites such as Yahoo! and Google have further expanded their businesses as well, including video content from a variety of sources. These sites enable movie studios, television networks and even sports associations such as Major League Baseball to sell content directly to consumers.

17) High-Definition Grows—HDTV and HD-DVD

High-definition TV (HDTV) is a part of the category of TV known as digital television or DTV. The Consumer Electronics Association (CEA) estimates that 11 million HDTV sets were sold in 2006, and that annual sales will rise to 27 million in 2008. These sets have a minimum of 720 progressive scanning lines; a 16:9 ratio for wide screens and 4:3 ratio for standard screens; and Dolby digital audio or an equivalent sound system. (DTV sets have a minimum of 480 progressive scanning lines.) This technology also uses a 1080p standard. 1080 refers to 1,080 lines of vertical resolution; p refers to progressive scan, meaning that the lines that comprise the video picture appear on the screen sequentially. What that really means is that the video quality provided by these systems is the sharpest, clearest and richest ever produced, as much as 10 times sharper than analog TV.

There are three categories of HDTV sets: rear-projection, plasma and liquid-crystal displays (LCDs). Rear-projection systems are the cheapest, at between $1,500 and $6,000, but are large, bulky units best watched in darkened rooms. Plasma screens have significantly dropped in price and can now be had at between $1,450 and $4,500 (prices fell 12% in the last quarter of 2006 alone). Screens of up to 102 inches in size are available, although they vary in picture quality (the best being enhanced definition, or EDTV, which has the highest resolution). At the 2007 Consumer Electronics Show in Las Vegas, Sharp Electronics unveiled a 108-inch LCD TV. Not all plasma screens can display high-definition content. LCD sets are among the most expensive at between $3,000 and $10,000. They are lighter than plasma screens and more energy-efficient; however, they do not offer screens as large as those available in plasma.

The catch to all this cutting-edge technology is that there are a limited number of TV channels that beam high-definition content. ABC, CBS and NBC each broadcast 14 high-definition programs in prime time, and a few cable and satellite channels such as HBO HD, Showtime HD and ESPN HD offer it.

HDTV reception is achieved via special antenna, cable or satellite. The antennae receive free broadcasts from the major networks over the airwaves in major urban areas. Most cable companies offer a handful of HTDV channels as do satellite providers EchoStar and DirecTV.

Meanwhile, consumers can get high-definition in their DVDs as well as in their TV reception thanks to HD DVDs that contain films and other recorded programming. The future for high-definition DVDs is bright. High-definition DVDs debuted in early 2003 in Japan. This new disc format holds five times as much data and features high-definition video of up to 1,080 lines of vertical resolution on screen (in comparison to the 480 lines of standard DVDs). The difference in color and clarity is noticeable, but there's a catch to using the new discs. They only play on high-definition DVD players (which also play standard DVDs). The discs and their players hit the U.S. market in 2006. State-of-the-art systems feature a re-writeable optical disc with both play and record capabilities.

There is currently an intense rivalry in the consumer electronics industry as to what the leading standard will be for this technology. Sony, Dell, HP and an extensive list of other companies are backing a standard known as Blu-ray, which has six times the capacity of traditional DVDs and awe-inspiring clarity. Toshiba, NEC and Sanyo are pushing one called HD-DVD that has less capacity but is cheaper, since existing DVD plants can produce it. The conflict between the two camps continues into 2007, even though industry analysts expected an agreement as to which format was to be globally adopted by the end of 2005. The point may be moot, however, since consumers are already enjoying many of the benefits afforded by cutting-edge DVDs by watching high-definition VOD and using DVRs.

As of the end of 2006, Blu-ray had a slight edge over HD-DVD due in part to the Playstation 3's incorporation of a Blu-ray player, and despite the endorsement of HD-DVD by Microsoft. However, HD-DVD got a boost when Pioneer Corp. delayed the release of its Blu-Ray player by several months due to production problems. Regardless of which format wins, the crystal-clear graphics and vivid color comes a high price. The players cost between $500 and $1,000, the disks go for $20 and up and title selection is currently limited (as of early 2007, only about 200 titles were available).

Internet Research Tip:
For general information and a list of web sites pertaining to HDTV, see www.hdtv.com.

---

18) Movie Attendance Rallies/Film Companies Innovate with DVDs, IMAX and Big Budget Films

U.S. box office ticket sales rallied in 2006, with receipts up 6.5% in 2006 over 2005, rising to a total of about $9.5 billion. (In contrast, sales were down by about 5% in 2005, to $9 billion, compared $9.4 billion in 2004. 2006 attendance was also up by almost 5%. Approximately 1.44 million movie theater tickets were sold in the U.S. during 2006, up about 3% from the previous year. Box office sales generally account for 25% of a film's revenues, plus 25% from pay television, cable and broadcast TV, while the remaining 50% comes from video rentals, DVD sales and VOD.

Studios are enjoying excellent response to late 2006 releases of a string of blockbusters including *Pirates of the Caribbean: Dead Man's Chest, The Da Vinci Code, Ice Age: Meltdown* and *Casino Royale*. With a total 2006 worldwide gross of $1.06 billion, *Pirates of the Caribbean: Dead Man's Chest* led the pack for the year, followed by *The Da Vinci Code* with $756.6 million. Several other 2006 films grossed more than $300 million each, including *Cars, X-Men: The Last Stand, Mission Impossible III* and *Superman Returns*. Industry analysts attribute the rise in profits and attendance to the production of a broader range of films that appeal to a wider range of tastes and ages.

Meanwhile, IMAX continues to grow in popularity, and many films are reformatted for IMAX viewing. *The Polar Express* earned about 30% of its revenues from its IMAX release in 2005.

DVDs, with U.S. sales and rentals revenues of about $23.4 billion in 2005, remain a vital source of revenue. However, the DVD market has matured to the point that sales have tapered off from the growth of previous years. Analysts estimate that DVD sales would grow only 2% in 2006 over 2005. Additional important income streams come from character licensing, international release, TV and cable release. To a growing extent, new formats such as video clips for iPod and cell phone will become very important as well.

Movie theater companies are investing heavily in a high-end new concept called Cinema De Lux (CDL) which outfits theaters with martini bars, Starbucks coffee counters, concierge desks, private party rooms, and theaters that boast luxurious leather reclining seats which are assigned (as opposed to open seating), live performances before showings and escorted seating service. National Amusements, a Massachusetts-based theater business chaired by media mogul Sumner Redstone, already has 11 CDLs, with plans to convert a large number of its existing theater complexes.

19) Last Mile Challenges Tumble; Mass Broadband Markets Emerge

A mass-market "tipping point" of consumer broadband access to the Internet occurred during the first quarter of 2004, when more than 26 million U.S. homes and businesses had broadband connections of one type or another. As high-speed Internet prices continue to fall, a large proportion of consumers accessing the Internet are choosing broadband methods over than dial-up. The Age of Convergence, between television, the Internet, telephones, entertainment systems and computers, has begun in earnest.

By the end of 2006, broadband connections in the U.S. reached more than 50 million homes and businesses. Fueling this growth has been intense price competition between cable and DSL providers, with monthly service now starting as low as $14.95 (for new customers for the first year) in some markets. Dial-up users by the millions will continue to convert to broadband at these low prices. If you add the number of wireless broadband users to the totals above, the Internet is now reaching a vast U.S. market.

What will widespread use of fast Internet access mean to consumers? Here's a great example: Apple's booming iTunes site is the convergence between recorded music, video, the Internet, personal computers and personal electronic devices.

Opportunities are endless, and the amount of entertainment, news and reference content repurposed to take advantage of broadband will grow rapidly. Likewise, more and more content, such as television news and sports coverage, is being reformatted to be viewed over state-of-the-art cell phones.

Faster adoption of broadband over the mid-term will be fueled by several factors: wider availability thanks to evolving technologies; reduced connection prices due to increased competition; and greatly improved content and web-based consumer services that will grow in relation to the number of people who have broadband.

By 2012 to 2015, Plunkett Research estimates that as many as 80 to 100 million U.S. homes and businesses will have high-speed, broadband Internet access. Broadband in the home will be essential for everyday activities ranging from children's homework to distance education for adults, from shopping to managing financial accounts, from renewing a driver's license to filing an insurance claim. Connections will be much faster. Online entertainment and information options will be vast. Some online services will seem indispensable, and always-on will become the accepted standard. The quality of streaming video and audio will be clear and reliable, making music and movie downloads possible in a matter of seconds, and allowing Internet telephone users to see their parties on the other end as if they were in the same room. Compression and caching techniques will have evolved, and distribution and storage costs will have plummeted. Consumers will accept pay-per-view or pay-per-use service offerings because of their convenience and moderate cost. A significant portion of today's radio, television and movie entertainment will migrate to the web.

Plunkett's Law of Convergence:
Online consumer usage grows exponentially as broadband access prices decline and more and more Internet devices are adopted—fixed and mobile. This increases demand for new online products and leads to increased offerings of high-value online services and entertainment at reasonable prices.

---

20) Entertainment-Based Retailing, including Power Towns

Since the earliest days of the marketplace, merchants have realized that entertainment draws crowds of people who linger and shop. Even during the Dark Ages, jugglers, storytellers and other entertainers were an integral part of public markets, helping to draw throngs of people who might purchase goods.

For the foreseeable future, entertainment's value as a drawing card for retail customers will be of paramount importance, especially for the retailing of goods beyond everyday staple items. In fact, the explosive growth of retailing over the Internet means that brick and mortar retailers must offer more than the mere availability of merchandise in order to lure shoppers out of their homes, away from their computer screens and web browsers and into the retail store. New shopping centers, especially those in urban areas, are devoting up to 40% of gross leaseable area (GLA) to entertainment, restaurants and movie theaters.

Yet consumers still want the convenience found in neighborhood centers. Consequently, many new shopping center developments will include the most desirable elements of both power centers and lifestyle centers, including dominant anchor tenants in large formats, dotted with smaller specialty retailers and a plethora of entertainment and dining facilities, all set in a pleasant outdoor environment with sidewalks, trees, lawns and ponds. In many ways, they will be the shopping center equivalent of the super-merchandiser stores.

Several of these new centers, sometimes called power towns, have already been built, including Desert Ridge in Scottsdale, Arizona; the Burbank Empire Center in Burbank, California; and Avon Common in Avon, Ohio. These centers sprawl over 80 to 100 acres and contain 600,000 to 1,000,000 square feet of retail space. Builders spent 25% to 30% more on these areas than on a comparable power center, sparing no expense to make the stores and surrounding areas as pleasant and attractive as possible. Though the costs of power towns might be intimidating, they have impressive drawing power for customers. Desert Ridge, for example, brings in shoppers from a 15-mile radius, with many people driving past other shopping centers just to go to there.

Beyond these initial projects, however, lies the potential for even more ambitious mixed-use projects. Developers are planning to make centers that not only provide entertainment but are also designed to be communities, with space for offices and residential areas. These projects may even include areas for post offices, day-care centers and community centers for performance theatres and galleries. An early form of this idea is found in the Easton Town Center, in Columbus, Ohio. Built for pedestrians instead of cars, the 1.5-million-square-foot center contains anchors such as Nordstrom, Barnes & Noble, a Virgin Megastore and an AMC theatre, mixed in with a spa and fitness center, a comedy club and a mammography center.

Another example is the massive $2-billion Meadowlands Xanadu center being built by Colony Capitol Acquisitions in New Jersey (the project was originally under the control of Mills Corp.). Beyond retail tenants, there will be a House of Blues, a fashion runway at the ELLE pavilion, a sports complex and a children's education district featuring Wannado City, an indoor, kid-size city promoting various careers. It will also include an extravagant Snow Dome, which will be America's first major indoor ski slope. Four 14-story office buildings and a 520-room hotel are also in the development plans. The planned opening date for the center is in 2008. Developers are betting that Xanadu's entertainment features will draw enough shoppers to justify steeper than usual rent averages of $67.50 per square foot for its non-anchor space.

21) Video Via Cell Phone Takes Off

Cell phones with advanced technology have great potential as entertainment platforms. There are challenges here as well, such as the small screens and the fact that consumers often face cellular service disruptions. Nonetheless, cell phones are too big a market for media and entertainment firms to ignore. In 2006, an estimated 800 million cell phones were sold worldwide—many of them having advanced 3G features. In fact, more cell phones are sold each year than any other type of consumer electronic. Of the 210 million mobile phone subscribers in the U.S., 1% of them pay for video as of early 2006. That is expected to increase to 26 million by 2009. According to market intelligence firm IDC, $3 billion in revenues will be generated by mobile-video subscriptions by 2009. Advertising and technology consulting firm Ovum predicts that there will be $1.26 billion in spending on cell-phone ads by 2009 as well.

Video via cell phone is rapidly becoming a major business. It is currently a $62 million market in the U.S., but is expected to swell to $500 million by 2010. Cell phone service provider Verizon already offers the V Cast video service on a subscription basis at about $15 monthly. V Cast uses Microsoft Windows Media software to stream short clips of entertainment, sports, news and weather to subscribers via their cell phone screens. Twentieth Century Fox Television is one of several companies producing one-minute entertainment episodes

designed for the small screen. Other programs creating "mobisodes" for cell phone viewing include *Sesame Street, The Daily Show, Fox Sports, 24* and several reality shows. The technology has quite a way to go, however, since it can take between 30 and 90 seconds to load a one- to two-minute video clip. An uncompressed video clip download requires about 50 times the bandwidth used by a typical song download.

Verizon may have solved many of its problems with the early 2007 release of V Cast Mobile TV. The service offers true broadcast quality television service for cell phones using a technology called MediaFLO from QUALCOMM. MediaFLO operates as a dedicated broadcast network delivering signals to devices equipped with compatible receivers. The picture has the quality of normal broadcast TV, delivering 30 frames per second. Sprint and T-Mobile are testing the technology.

Cell phone video is already very popular in Japan, Korea and parts of Europe. In the U.S., in addition to Verizon's offering, Alltel, Cingular and Sprint Nextel are in the business with MobiTV, a subscription service that costs $9.99 monthly.

Other video content providers such as News Corporation, MTV and CBS Corporation are bypassing wireless companies and selling content directly to users. News Corporation's Mobizzo is a mobile entertainment store backed by a production studio that focuses strictly on content for cell phones. Programming is available on a piecemeal basis for between $1.99 and $2.99, and there are also two subscription plans for $5.99 per month each. CBS News to Go is a similar service available for 99 cents per month and E.T. to Go, a service with programming from the television show *Entertainment Tonight,* is available for $3.99 per month.

22) Music Plays a Major Role in New Cell Phones

Many new cell phones on today's market come equipped with software to play MP3 music files and can utilize stereo headphones with outlets for each ear, such as Motorola's Bluetooth Stereo Headset HT820 (about $100). Many users are finding the sound quality to be similar to mobile devices such as iPods or portable CD players. After a few initial sour notes, when the early music phones read MP3 files but not popular alternatives such as music downloaded from Apple's iTunes or RealNetworks' Rhapsody, new models are compatible with a wider variety of formats. For example, Motorola's iTunes phone, the ROKR, plays songs downloaded from

Apple's iTunes jukebox with a somewhat limited storage capability of 100 songs. Nokia hopes to solve the storage problem with the introduction of its N91 phone, which boasts a 4-gigabyte hard drive (capable of storing up to 1,000 songs). The N91 debuted in late 2005.

The big news in cell phones is the debut of Apple's iPhone at the Macworld Conference & Expo in San Francisco in early 2007. The unit features a touch screen that combines some features from the iPod with those from a highly advanced cell phone. There is a 4-GB model that retails for $499 and a larger 8-GB unit that goes for $599. Included are a widescreen iPod and an Internet communications device with email, web browsing, maps and searching capabilities, in addition to a cell phone that offers the ability to dial a number by touching a listing in the unit's address book. The phone syncs with PCs, Macs and Internet services for names, phone numbers and addresses.

Radio is also part of the cell phone lexicon. Sprint Nextel offers a radio service from Sirius for $6.95 per month in addition to regular subscriber fees for commercial-free streaming music in a variety of genres. LM Ericsson and Napster, Inc. reached an agreement in June 2005 to provide a digital music service for cell phones, and began offering the service in early 2006. Cingular teamed with Napster and Yahoo! in 2006 also, and the company now offers a music service on its cell phone network

Verizon launched V Cast Music, a music service offering up to 1.4 million songs in early 2007 Songs are priced at $1.99 each and can be downloaded directly to Verizon cell phones and also to a PC (Spring Nextel offers a similar service for $2.50 per song). Verizon charges a $15 per month subscription fee for the service (which also includes video clips and e-mail), which generates revenue for the company even if subscribers do not purchase music. Phones equipped to play these music files start at $99 and have 1-gigabyte memory cards that can hold up to 700 songs. Many analysts were watching V Cast closely as a competitor to the widely successful Apple iPod, but the debut of Apple's new iPhone may mean that all bets are off.

Ringtones Making Sweet Music

Music performing rights organization BMI projected that U.S. ringtone sales for cellular phones in 2006 exceeded $600 million, up from $500 million in 2005 and $245 million in 2004. This is at a time when sales of CDs, cassettes and videos fell 7.6% from 2004 to 2005. The tones cost between $2.50 and $3.50 to download, and record companies are enthusiastic about the new sources of revenue as well as their value as marketing tools. Warner Music Group released "Hung Up" by Madonna as a ringtone a month before the song was released to radio stations or available for sale online or in music stores.

---

23) Rules for Digital TV are Finalized

The era of the digital TV in the U.S. is building momentum. Federal regulations will most likely require that all television broadcasts move to digital format by February 17, 2009. This has many implications. To begin with, older televisions based on analog technology will not receive broadcasts unless retrofitted with a converter. However, since the change is for broadcast TV only, households that rely entire on cable or satellite reception will see no effect, and this includes the vast majority of homes in the U.S.

The new rules are fueled by the Federal government's desire to open up vast amounts of spectrum currently reserved for analog television broadcast. The government will reap $10 billion or more by auctioning off this soon-to-be unused spectrum for other purposes. Meanwhile, all new television sets sold in the U.S. will eventually be required to be digital rather than analog. Watch for consumers to buy increasing numbers of very sophisticated, high-definition, digital-enabled TV sets as prices come down and volumes go up. Large, flat screens will become standard in the U.S. home. Upper income homes will purchase advanced HDTVs, with giant flat screens made from LEDs. These LEDs offer much richer colors and longer life than competitors, but they are significantly more expensive.

Chapter 2

ENTERTAINMENT & MEDIA INDUSTRY STATISTICS

U.S. Entertainment & Media Industry Overview

	Amount	Date	Source
Total U.S. Media Spending	$857.6 bil.	2005	Veronis Suhler Stevenson
Total U.S. Media Spending	$900.0 bil.	2006	PRE
Annual U.S. Advertising Spending	$296.3 bil.	2006	PRE
Total Consumer Media Spending*, U.S.	$199.3 bil.*	2005	Veronis Suhler Stevenson
RADIO			
Full Service FM Radio Stations, Including Educational, U.S.	9,042	Sep. 2006	FCC
Licensed AM Radio Stations, U.S.	4,751	Sep. 2006	FCC
Radio Stations Authorized to Broadcast Digitally, U.S.	994	Dec. 2006	FCC
PRINT MEDIA			
U.S. Magazine Revenues, PIB Measured Magazines	$23.1 bil.	2005	Publishers Information Bureau
Total Daily and Sunday Newspapers, U.S.	2,366	2005	Editor & Publisher
Annual Newspaper Advertising Expenditures, U.S.	$24.4 bil.	2005	Newspaper Association of America
Total Book Publishing Net Sales, U.S.	$27.0 bil.	2006	PRE
TELEVISION			
U.S. Households with Televisions	111.4 mil. (98.2%)	2007	Nielsen Media Research
Broadcast TV Stations, Including Class A, U.S.	2,890	Sep. 2006	FCC
Basic Cable TV Subscribers, U.S.	65.6 mil.	Sep. 2006	Kagan Research LLC
Digital Cable Subscribers, U.S.	31.4 mil.	Sep. 2006	Kagan Research LLC
Cable High Speed Data Subscribers, U.S.	29.9 mil.	Sep. 2006	Kagan Research LLC
Non-Cable Multichannel Video Program Subscribers, U.S.	31.9 mil.	Sep. 2006	Kagan Research LLC
Number of Mobile Phone TV Subscribers	3.4 mil.	2006	PRE
Mobile Phone TV Revenues	$350 mil.	2006	PRE
Number of TiVo Subscribers, U.S.	4.4 mil.	2006	PRE
MUSIC			
Album Sales, U.S.	619 mil. units**	2005	PRE
Global Downloaded Music Sales, incl. Internet and Cell Phone	$1.1 bil.	2005	IFPI
Satellite Radio Subscribers, U.S.	13.6 mil.	2006	PRE
Number of iPods Sold during the Year	39.4 mil.	2006	Apple Computer, Inc.
OTHER			
Cell Phone Subscribers, U.S.	235 mil.	2006	PRE
Gambling Revenues, U.S.	$57.6 bil.	2006	PRE
Internet Users, Worldwide	1.07 bil.	2006	Int'l Telecom. Union
FILM			
U.S. Box Office Revenues	$8.99 bil.	2005	NATO
Number of Movie Tickets Sold, U.S.	1.40 bil.	2005	NATO
Number of Movie Screens, U.S.	37,740	2005	NATO
Consumer Spending on VHS & DVD, Rental and Sell-Through	$24.9 bil.	2005	Adams Media Research
ELECTRONIC GAMES			
Total Video Game Industry Revenues, Worldwide	$30.0 bil.	2006	PRE

IFPI = International Federation of the Phonographic Industry   FCC = Federal Communications Commission

PRE = Plunkett Research estimate   NATO = National Organization of Theatre Owners

* Estimate. Includes consumer spending on cable and satellite TV access and services; consumer books; consumer internet access and content; consumer magazine subscriptions; entertainment (box office, home video, interactive television, recorded music and video games); newspaper subscriptions, satellite radio subscriptions.

** Includes downloaded music with 10 downloaded song tracks counted as one album.

Plunkett's Entertainment & Media Industry Almanac 2007

Estimated U.S. Information and Entertainment Sector Revenues by NAICS Code, 2005-2006

(In Millions of US$)

NAICS Code[1]	Kind of business	2006			2005		% of Total**
		3Q*	2Q	1Q	4Q	3Q	
51	Information	261,736	260,218	249,338	258,920	247,405	100.0
511	Publishing industries	73,510	71,450	67,996	74,116	69,866	28.1
51111	Newspaper publishers	11,862	12,650	12,144	13,227	12,446	4.5
51112	Periodical publishers	12,110	11,655	10,483	11,864	11,391	4.6
5111	Book, database and directory, and other publishers[2]	16,643	14,805	14,392	15,638	16,736	6.4
5112	Software publishers	32,895	32,340	30,977	33,387	29,293	12.6
512	Motion picture and sound recording industries	20,061	21,149	19,725	22,517	19,770	7.7
513	Broadcasting and telecommunications	139,738	139,245	135,360	135,905	132,308	53.4
5131	Radio and television broadcasting	12,348	13,443	12,969	13,614	11,654	4.7
5132	Cable networks and program distribution	32,071	32,496	30,357	30,104	29,102	12.3
5133	Telecommunications	95,319	93,306	92,034	92,187	91,552	36.4
51331	Wired telecommunications carriers	48,703	48,528	48,845	50,202	50,336	18.6
51332	Wireless telecom. carriers (except satellite)	40,710	39,171	37,969	37,195	36,570	15.6
5133	Other telecommunications[3]	5,906	5,607	5,220	4,790	4,646	2.3
514	Information services and data processing services	28,427	28,374	26,257	26,382	25,461	10.9
5141	Information services	11,214	11,421	10,426	10,357	9,920	4.3
5142	Data processing services	17,213	16,953	15,831	16,025	15,541	6.6

Estimates have not been adjusted for seasonal variation, holiday or trading-day differences, or price changes. Estimates are based on data from the Quarterly Services Survey and have been adjusted using results of the 2004 Service Annual Survey. Sector totals and subsector totals may include data for kinds of business not shown.

[1] For a full description of the NAICS codes used in this table, see www.census.gov/epcd/www/naics.html.

[2] Includes NAICS 51113 (book publishers), 51114 (database and directory publishers), and 51119 (other publishers).

[3] Includes NAICS 51333 (telecommunications resellers), 51334 (satellite telecommunications), and 51339 (other telecommunications).

* Preliminary estimate.

** Percent of total information sector revenue based on third quarter 2006.

Source: U.S. Census Bureau

Plunkett's Entertainment & Media Industry Almanac 2007

Estimated Annual U.S. Advertising Expenditures: 2000-2006

(In Millions of US$)

Advertising Medium	2000	2001	2002	2003	2004[e]	2005[e]	2006[P]
Newspapers	49,050	44,255	44,031	44,843	46,935	49,618	52,397
National	7,229	6,615	6,806	7,357	7,762	8,290	8,754
Local	41,821	37,640	37,225	37,486	39,173	41,328	43,642
Magazines	12,370	11,095	10,995	11,435	12,121	13,006	13,734
Broadcast TV	44,802	38,881	42,068	41,932	46,020	46,675	44,973
Network	15,888	14,300	15,000	15,030	16,458	16,787	17,727
Spot (National)	12,264	9,223	10,920	9,948	10,943	10,834	11,441
Spot (Local)	13,542	12,256	13,114	13,520	14,670	14,967	15,805
Syndication[1]	3,108	3,102	3,034	3,434	3,949	4,087	4,316
Cable	15,455	15,736	16,297	18,814	21,069	22,568	23,831
Cable Network	11,765	11,777	12,071	13,954	15,628	16,722	17,658
Spot (Local)	3,690	3,959	4,226	4,860	5,441	5,846	6,173
Radio	19,295	17,861	18,877	19,100	19,779	20,981	22,156
Network	780	711	775	798	852	924	976
Spot (National)	3,668	2,956	3,340	3,540	3,575	3,782	3,994
Spot (local)	14,847	14,194	14,762	14,762	15,352	16,275	17,186
Yellow Pages	13,228	13,592	13,776	13,896	14,035	14,499	15,311
National	2,093	2,087	2,087	2,114	2,135	2,242	2,368
Local	11,135	11,505	11,689	11,782	11,900	12,257	12,943
Direct Mail	44,591	44,725	46,067	48,370	52,240	57,203	60,406
Business Papers	4,915	4,468	3,976	4,004	4,094	4,252	4,490
Out of Home[2]	5,176	5,134	5,175	5,443	5,790	6,080	6,421
National	2,068	2,051	2,061	2,298	2,440	2,584	2,729
Local	3,108	3,083	3,114	3,145	3,350	3,496	3,692
Internet	6,507	5,645	4,883	5,650	7,062	8,828	9,322
Miscellaneous	32,083	29,895	30,730	31,990	34,554	36,907	38,974
National	24,418	23,042	23,414	24,550	26,735	28,713	30,321
Local	7,665	6,853	7,316	7,440	7,819	8,194	8,653
Total National	151,664	141,797	145,429	152,482	165,994	178,254	188,236
Total Local	95,808	89,490	91,446	92,995	97,705	102,363	108,095
Grand Total	247,472	231,287	236,875	245,477	263,699	280,617	296,332

[1] Syndication includes PAX, UPN & WB.

[2] Out Of Home replaces Billboards, to include billboards on buses, etc.

e = Estimate   P = Plunkett Research estimate.

Source: Prepared for Universal McCann by Robert J. Coen

Plunkett's Entertainment & Media Industry Almanac 2007

U.S. Magazine Advertising Revenue and Pages for PIB* Measured Magazines: 1960-2005

(Latest Year Available)

Year	Magazine Advertising Revenue	Magazine Advertising Pages	Number of Magazines Measured
1960	829,727,760	74,861	79
1965	1,048,765,191	80,147	86
1970	1,168,668,178	76,924	89
1975	1,336,313,425	80,735	94
1980	2,846,083,540	114,705	102
1985	4,919,948,386	152,566	142
1990	6,753,356,745	171,689	164
1991	6,538,195,541	156,650	170
1992	7,141,903,718	163,513	176
1993	7,625,491,794	176,973	179
1994	8,504,647,259	180,589	185
1995	10,114,898,726	208,378	201
1996	11,179,246,682	213,781	208
1997	12,754,950,695	231,371	216
1998	13,813,403,372	242,383	227
1999	15,508,357,011	255,383	238
2000	17,665,305,333	286,932	248
2001	16,213,541,737	237,612	250
2002	17,254,061,740	225,619	234
2003	19,216,085,358	225,831	228
2004	21,313,206,733	234,428	235
2005	23,068,182,388	243,305	244

* PIB = Publishers Information Bureau.

Sunday supplements excluded.

Source: www.magazine.org

Plunkett's Entertainment & Media Industry Almanac 2007

Number of U.S. Magazines*: 1988-2005

(Latest Year Available)

Year	National Directory of Magazines	SRDS	ABC	BPA Worldwide	PIB
1988	13,541	1,723	559	N/A	156
1989	12,797	1,795	585	196	166
1990	14,049	1,904	587	232	164
1991	14,256	2,000	600	244	170
1992	14,870	2,126	617	243	176
1993	14,302	2,256	631	245	179
1994	15,069	2,347	643	252	187
1995	15,996	2,428	668	273	201
1996	17,195	2,470	711	312	208
1997	18,047	2,513	751	311	216
1998	18,606	2,522	758	448	227
1999	17,970	2,520	750	485	238
2000	17,815	2,567	836	494	248
2001	17,694	2,600	817	505	250
2002	17,321	2,431	764	N/A	234
2003	17,254	2,509	703	N/A	228
2004	18,821	2,570	708	208	235
2005	18,267	2,640	718	N/A	239

*There are several sources that provide the number of consumer magazines available in the U.S., some more comprehensive than others. The chart cites five of these sources: the National Directory of Magazines, Standard Rate and Data Service (SRDS), Audit Bureau of Circulations (ABC), BPA Worldwide and the Publishers Information Bureau (PIB).

Source: www.magazine.org

Plunkett's Entertainment & Media Industry Almanac 2007

Average Circulation of the Top 25 U.S. ABC* Magazines, Through June 2006

Rank	Publication Name	Subscriptions	Single Copy	Total
1	AARP THE MAGAZINE**	23,065,890	1,822	23,067,712
2	AARP BULLETIN**	22,438,497		22,438,497
3	READER'S DIGEST	9,659,418	434,868	10,094,286
4	BETTER HOMES AND GARDENS	7,436,012	179,167	7,615,179
5	NATIONAL GEOGRAPHIC	4,893,962	179,860	5,073,822
6	GOOD HOUSEKEEPING	3,976,583	632,626	4,609,209
7	LADIES' HOME JOURNAL	3,843,980	259,500	4,103,480
8	TIME-THE WEEKLY NEWSMAGAZINE	3,980,116	119,466	4,099,582
9	FAMILY CIRCLE	3,227,246	827,624	4,054,870
10	WOMAN'S DAY	3,390,814	612,056	4,002,870
11	PEOPLE	2,300,496	1,523,108	3,823,604
12	AAA WESTWAYS**	3,731,611		3,731,611
13	TV GUIDE	3,417,944	300,231	3,718,175
14	PREVENTION	2,989,278	313,072	3,302,350
15	SPORTS ILLUSTRATED	3,113,344	99,066	3,212,410
16	NEWSWEEK	3,031,903	110,378	3,142,281
17	PLAYBOY	2,770,866	260,316	3,031,182
18	COSMOPOLITAN	978,788	1,930,073	2,908,861
19	SOUTHERN LIVING	2,619,968	201,011	2,820,979
20	VIA MAGAZINE**	2,790,115		2,790,115
21	MAXIM	2,088,966	490,150	2,579,116
22	AMERICAN LEGION MAGAZINE**	2,531,506		2,531,506
23	AAA GOING PLACES**	2,515,154		2,515,154
24	AAA LIVING**	2,390,073		2,390,073
25	REDBOOK	2,089,889	280,816	2,370,705

* ABC = Audit Bureau of Circulations.

** High proportion of titles' circulation attributed to membership benefits.

Source: www.magazine.org

Plunkett's Entertainment & Media Industry Almanac 2007

U.S. Periodical Publishing Revenues 2001-2005

(In Millions of US$; Latest Year Available)

	2005*	2004	2003	2002	2001
Sources of Revenue					
Total Revenue	44,000	41,760	39,560	39,757	40,189
Periodicals, print, total	N/A	31,020	29,931	31,119	31,763
Subscriptions and sales	N/A	12,231	12,126	13,276	13,381
Advertising	N/A	18,788	17,805	17,844	18,382
Periodicals, internet, total	N/A	1,528	1,446	1,329	1,312
Subscriptions and sales	N/A	994	1,071	915	888
Advertising	N/A	S	374	S	S
Periodicals, other media, total	N/A	2,932	2,647	2,405	2,209
Subscriptions and sales	N/A	2,863	2,573	2,329	2,119
Advertising	N/A	S	73	76	S
Contract printing services	N/A	700	643	706	944
Distribution of flyers, inserts, samples, etc	N/A	S	S	121	108
Graphic design services	N/A	S	S	S	S
Sale or licensing of rights to content	N/A	S	300	281	247
Rental or sale of mailing lists	N/A	170	168	172	164
Publishing services for others	N/A	S	321	S	347
Other services revenue	N/A	4,485	3,906	3,215	3,035
Break Down of Revenue	N/A				
General interest periodicals	N/A	16,812	16,396	16,693	17,004
Special interest periodicals	N/A	17,169	16,051	16,695	18,280
Other periodicals	N/A	S	1,576	S	S
Inventories at the End of the Year					
Total	N/A	1,708	1,578	1,711	1,672
Finished goods and work-in-process	N/A	1,243	1,183	1,282	1,251
Materials, supplies, fuel, etc	N/A	466	S	429	421

S = Data do not meet publication standards because of high sampling variability.

* Plunkett Research estimate.

Source: U.S. Census Bureau

Plunkett's Entertainment & Media Industry Almanac 2007

U.S. Newspaper Publishing Revenue: 2001-2005

(In Millions of US$; Latest Year Available)

	2005*	2004	2003	2002	2001
Sources of Revenue					
Total Revenue	50,400	48,599	47,443	46,402	46,039
Newspapers, print, total	N/A	42,670	41,756	41,105	41,139
Subscriptions and sales	N/A	9,149	9,383	9,213	9,094
Advertising	N/A	33,521	32,372	31,892	32,045
Newspapers, internet, total	N/A	902	718	583	401
Subscriptions and sales	N/A	S	S	S	S
Advertising	N/A	716	554	455	296
Newspapers, other media, total	N/A	103	149	161	150
Subscriptions and sales	N/A	S	S	60	52
Advertising	N/A	67	94	101	99
Contract printing services	N/A	1,622	1,628	1,708	1,728
Distribution of flyers, inserts, samples, etc.	N/A	1,251	1,163	996	908
Graphic design services	N/A	S	S	S	S
Market research	N/A	4	S	2	2
Archival sales services	N/A	26	25	22	24
Sale or licensing of rights to content	N/A	77	73	44	67
Rental or sale of mailing lists	N/A	7	7	S	13
Non-newspaper publishing	N/A	200	361	298	252
Publishing services for others	N/A	21	19	12	11
Other services revenue	N/A	1,705	1,536	1,450	1,335
Breakdown of Revenue					
General newspapers	N/A	41,461	40,926	40,272	40,553
Specialized newspapers	N/A	90	106	78	62
Other newspapers	N/A	S	S	S	S

S = Data do not meet publication standards because of high sampling variability.

* Plunkett Research estimate.

Source: U.S. Census Bureau

Plunkett's Entertainment & Media Industry Almanac 2007

Annual U.S. Newspaper Advertising Expenditures, 1990-2006

(In Millions of US$)

Year	NATIONAL $	% Change	RETAIL $	% Change	CLASSIFIED $	% Change	PRINT TOTAL $	% Change
1990	$4,122	4.40%	$16,652	0.90%	$11,506	-3.50%	$32,280	-0.30%
1991	$3,924	-4.80%	$15,839	-4.90%	$10,587	-8.00%	$30,349	-6.00%
1992	$3,834	-2.30%	$16,041	1.30%	$10,764	1.70%	$30,639	1.00%
1993	$3,853	0.50%	$16,859	5.10%	$11,157	3.70%	$31,869	4.00%
1994	$4,149	7.70%	$17,496	3.80%	$12,464	11.70%	$34,109	7.00%
1995	$4,251	2.50%	$18,099	3.40%	$13,742	10.30%	$36,092	5.80%
1996	$4,667	9.80%	$18,344	1.40%	$15,065	9.60%	$38,075	5.50%
1997	$5,315	13.90%	$19,242	4.90%	$16,773	11.30%	$41,330	8.50%
1998	$5,721	7.70%	$20,331	5.70%	$17,873	6.60%	$43,925	6.30%
1999	$6,732	17.70%	$20,907	2.80%	$18,650	4.30%	$46,289	5.40%
2000	$7,653	13.70%	$21,409	2.40%	$19,608	5.10%	$48,670	5.10%
2001	$7,004	-8.50%	$20,679	-3.40%	$16,622	-15.20%	$44,305	-9.00%
2002	$7,210	2.90%	$20,994	1.50%	$15,898	-4.30%	$44,102	-0.50%
2003	$7,797	8.10%	$21,341	1.70%	$15,801	-0.60%	$44,939	1.90%
2004	$8,083	3.70%	$22,012	3.10%	$16,608	5.10%	$46,703	3.90%
2005	$7,910	-2.15%	$22,187	0.79%	$17,312	4.24%	$47,408	1.51%
2006 1Q	$1,737	-4.82%	$4,880	-1.00%	$3,893	4.68%	$10,509	0.35%
2006 2Q	$1,988	-3.84%	$5,601	1.00%	$4,106	0.00%	$11,705	-0.20%
2006 3Q	$1,713	-8.30%	$5,324	-0.30%	$4,116	-3.00%	$11,153	-2.60%

	ONLINE TOTAL $	% Change	PRINT AND ONLINE TOTAL $	% Change
2003	$1,216	N/A	$46,156	N/A
2004	$1,541	26.70%	$48,244	4.50%
2005	$2,027	31.48%	$49,435	2.47%
2006 1Q	$613	34.90%	$11,122	1.80%
2006 2Q	$667	33.20%	$12,372	1.10%
2006 3Q	$638	23.00%	$11,791	-1.50%

Source: Newspaper Association of America
Plunkett's Entertainment & Media Industry Almanac 2007

Daily & Sunday Newspaper Readership,
Total U.S. Adults: 1998-2006

(In Thousands)

Total Adults				Average Sunday Readership					
Year	Total Adults	Men	Women	Total Adults	% of Adults	Men	% of Men	Women	% of Women
1998	134,992	64,972	70,021	92,039	68.2%	44,324	68.2%	47,715	68.1%
1999	136,575	65,785	70,790	91,415	66.9%	43,996	66.9%	47,420	67.0%
2000	138,937	66,922	72,014	90,450	65.1%	43,506	65.0%	46,944	65.2%
2001	140,609	67,763	72,846	89,506	63.7%	42,591	62.9%	46,915	64.4%
2002	143,668	69,245	74,423	91,378	63.6%	43,347	62.6%	48,031	64.5%
2003	146,323	70,486	75,837	91,500	62.5%	43,463	61.7%	48,037	63.3%
2004	148,340	71,534	76,807	90,795	61.2%	43,234	60.4%	47,561	61.9%
2005	150,674	72,874	77,799	89,819	59.6%	42,687	58.6%	47,132	60.6%
2006	152,515	73,941	78,574	87,263	57.2%	41,363	55.9%	45,900	58.4%

Average Daily Readership						
Year	Total Adults	% of Adults	Men	% of Men	Women	% of Women
1998	79,046	58.6%	40,442	62.2%	38,624	55.2%
1999	77,680	56.9%	39,860	60.6%	37,821	53.4%
2000	76,596	55.1%	39,330	58.8%	37,267	51.7%
2001	76,367	54.3%	38,998	57.5%	37,369	51.3%
2002	79,638	55.4%	40,318	58.2%	39,321	52.8%
2003	79,094	54.1%	40,030	56.8%	39,064	51.5%
2004	78,285	52.8%	39,727	55.5%	38,558	50.2%
2005	77,673	51.6%	39,428	54.1%	38,245	49.2%
2006	76,088	49.9%	38,693	52.3%	37,395	47.6%

Note: Beginning in 1998, readership data is based on the top 50 markets measured by Scarborough Research. Projections are not comparable to previous years.

Sources: Scarborough Research; Newspaper Association of America

Plunkett's Entertainment & Media Industry Almanac 2007

Estimated U.S. Book Publishing Industry Net Sales, 2002-2005

(In Thousands of US$; Latest Year Available)

	2002 Census	2003 $	2003 % Change	2004 $	2004 % Change	2005 $	2005 % Change	Compound Growth Rate 2002-2005
Trade (Total)	6,027,658	6,534,828	8.4%	6,267,199	-4.1%	7,828,050	24.9%	9.1%
Adult Hardbound	2,111,628	2,060,949	-2.4%	2,190,788	6.3%	2,221,700	1.4%	1.7%
Adult Paperbound	1,020,015	1,013,895	-0.6%	1,042,284	2.8%	1,140,989	9.5%	3.8%
Juvenile Hardbound	2,114,091	2,718,721	28.6%	2,264,695	-16.7%	3,614,748	59.6%	19.6%
Juvenile Paperbound	781,924	741,264	-5.2%	769,432	3.8%	850,613	10.6%	2.8%
Book Clubs & Mail Order	1,946,640	1,771,443	-9.0%	1,613,784	-8.9%	1,505,661	-6.7%	-8.2%
Mass Market Paperback	1,207,630	1,187,100	-1.7%	1,081,448	-8.9%	1,083,611	0.2%	-3.5%
Audiobooks	143,410	161,049	12.3%	159,922	-0.7%	206,299	29.0%	12.9%
Religious	588,153	883,406	50.2%	932,877	5.6%	875,971	-6.1%	14.2%
E-books	29,979	80,793	169.5%	123,695	53.1%	179,110	44.8%	81.5%
Professional	3,155,191	3,628,778	3.6%	3,334,153	2.0%	3,300,812	-1.0%	1.5%
El-Hi (K-12 Education)	5,795,044	5,939,920	2.5%	5,945,860	0.1%	6,570,175	10.5%	4.3%
Higher Education	3,025,029	3,133,930	3.6%	3,190,340	1.8%	3,359,428	5.3%	3.6%
All Other	136,488	153,932	12.8%	161,629	5.0%	158,558	-1.9%	5.1%
Total	22,055,222	23,115,180	4.8%	22,810,907	-1.3%	25,067,676	9.9%	4.4%

Source: Association of American Publishers

Plunkett's Entertainment & Media Industry Almanac 2007

Quantity of Books Sold, U.S.: 2004-2009

(In Millions)

Type of publication	2004	2005	2006[P]	2007[P]	2008[P]	2009[P]
Total	2966.2	3078.9	3150.1	3171.2	3183.0	3228.2
Trade	1613.1	1689.8	1747.3	1748.1	1747.5	1776.1
Adult	785.8	810.4	828.3	841.8	848.3	861.0
Hardback	396.9	406.4	413.8	419.2	421.0	424.7
Paperback	388.9	404.0	414.5	422.6	427.2	436.3
Juvenile	827.3	879.4	919.0	906.2	899.3	915.1
Hardback	253.4	273.0	274.7	277.4	302.8	279.5
Paperback	574.0	606.4	644.4	628.9	596.5	635.7

Mass market paperbacks, rack sized

	2004	2005	2006	2007	2008	2009
Religious	241.1	255.5	266.9	278.0	288.9	300.0
Hardback	85.3	91.0	97.1	101.2	105.2	109.2
Paperback	155.8	164.5	169.8	176.9	183.7	190.8
Professional	274.0	278.9	282.7	286.7	290.9	295.9
Hardback	97.8	99.2	100.0	101.0	96.9	96.2
Paperback	176.1	179.8	182.7	185.8	194.0	199.7

	2004	2005	2006	2007	2008	2009
University press	24.7	24.5	24.6	24.7	24.6	24.7
Hardback	9.3	9.1	9.2	9.3	9.3	9.3
Paperback	15.4	15.5	15.3	15.4	15.4	15.4
Elementary/High school text	159.5	179.8	181.6	189.6	194.2	199.0
Hardback	56.1	63.2	64.9	67.7	69.4	71.1
Paperback	103.4	116.6	116.8	121.9	124.9	127.9
College text	77.1	76.5	75.9	75.4	74.4	73.8
Hardback	34.2	33.8	33.5	33.3	32.8	32.6
Paperback	42.9	42.7	42.4	42.2	41.6	41.3

Represents net publishers' shipments after returns. Includes all titles released by publishers in the United States and imports which appear under the imprints of American publishers. Multivolume sets, such as encyclopedias, are counted as one unit. Due to changes in methodology and scope, these data are not comparable to those previously published.

P = Projected

Source: Book Industry Study Group, Inc.

Plunkett's Entertainment & Media Industry Almanac 2007

Books Sold—Value of U.S. Domestic Consumer Expenditures: 2004-2009

(In Millions of US$)

Type of publication	2004	2005	2006[P]	2007[P]	2008[P]	2009[P]
Total	**49146.6**	**51919.8**	**53723.8**	**55546.9**	**57194.3**	**58875.2**
Trade	23394.4	24571.1	25362.6	25992.3	26553.2	27086.2
Adult	14952.1	15532.4	15937.2	16370.1	16670.0	16985.4
Hardback	9036.3	9387.6	9631.4	9904.1	10095.2	10330.8
Paperback	5915.8	6144.8	6305.8	6466.0	6574.8	6654.6
Juvenile	5369.3	5883.0	6185.9	6298.4	6500.5	6643.7
Hardback	2489.0	2727.1	2755.3	2831.4	3122.1	2927.4
Paperback	2880.3	3155.9	3430.6	3467.0	3378.4	3716.3
Mass market paperbacks, rack sized	3,073.00	3,155.70	3,239.50	3,323.80	3,382.70	3,457.10
Religious	4104.0	4436.7	4725.7	5013.5	5322.2	5628.5
Hardback	2436.6	2634.1	2847.8	3018.2	3207.2	3391.7
Paperback	1667.4	1802.6	1877.9	1995.3	2115.0	2236.8
Professional	10275.3	10680.4	11046.6	11415.8	11798.1	12192.4
Hardback	6428.0	6695.8	6923.4	7175.8	7428.8	7553.5
Paperback	2791.9	2908.5	3017.5	3112.2	3218.9	3465.5
Subscription reference	1055.4	1076.1	1105.7	1127.8	1150.4	1173.4
University press	547.1	582.3	639.9	655.8	667.4	682.0
Hardback	267.4	279.5	305.8	310.9	315.7	320.5
Paperback	279.7	302.8	334.1	344.9	351.7	361.5
Elementary/High school text	4622.0	5320.0	5507.6	5892.9	6187.6	6493.7
Hardback	2307.3	2654.6	2793.4	2989.0	3138.5	3295.4
Paperback	2314.7	2665.4	2714.2	2903.9	3049.1	3198.3
College text	6203.8	6329.3	6441.4	6576.6	6665.8	6792.4
Hardback	4156.6	4221.5	4289.8	4379.9	4439.3	4523.7
Paperback	2047.2	2107.8	2151.6	2196.7	2226.5	2268.7

Includes all titles released by publishers in the United States and imports which appear under the imprints of American publishers. Due to changes in methodology and scope, these data are not comparable to those previously published.

P = Projected

Source: Book Industry Study Group, Inc.

Plunkett's Entertainment & Media Industry Almanac 2007

Number and Percent of U.S. Households (HH) with TV, Wired Cable, Pay Cable & VCRs: 1975-2007

(In Thousands)

Year	TV Households	% of Total HH	Wired Cable HH	% of TV HH	Pay Cable HH	% of TV HH	VCR HH	% of TV HH
1975	68,500	97.1	8,600	12.6%	140	0.2%	-	-
1976	69,600	97.4	10,100	14.5%	470	0.7%	-	-
1977	71,200	97.4	11,300	15.9%	980	1.4%	-	-
1978	72,900	97.6	12,500	17.1%	1,600	2.2%	200	0.3%
1979	74,500	97.7	13,600	18.3%	3,100	4.2%	400	0.5%
1980	76,300	97.9	15,200	19.9%	5,200	6.8%	840	1.1%
1981	79,900	98.1	17,830	22.3%	8,100	10.1%	1,440	1.8%
1982	81,500	98.1	24,290	29.8%	12,600	15.5%	2,530	3.1%
1983	83,300	98.1	28,320	34.0%	16,100	19.4%	4,580	5.5%
1984	83,800	98.1	32,930	39.3%	19,820	23.7%	8,967	10.7%
1985	84,900	98.1	36,340	42.8%	21,840	25.7%	17,744	20.9%
1986	85,900	98.1	39,160	45.6%	22,840	26.6%	30,924	36.0%
1987	87,400	98.1	41,690	47.7%	22,850	26.1%	42,564	48.7%
1988	88,600	98.1	43,790	49.4%	24,290	27.4%	51,388	58.1%
1989	90,400	98.2	47,770	52.8%	26,100	28.9%	58,398	64.6%
1990	92,100	98.2	51,900	56.4%	27,120	29.4%	63,181	68.6%
1991	93,100	98.2	54,860	58.9%	27,040	29.0%	66,939	71.9%
1992*	92,100	98.3	55,490	60.2%	25,990	28.2%	69,075	75.0%
1993	93,100	98.3	57,200	61.4%	25,850	27.8%	71,780	77.1%
1994	94,200	98.3	58,750	62.4%	26,070	27.7%	74,420	79.0%
1995	95,400	98.3	60,460	63.4%	27,100	28.4%	77,270	81.0%
1996	95,900	98.3	62,580	65.3%	30,360	31.7%	78,830	82.2%
1997	97,000	98.4	64,470	66.5%	31,620	32.6%	81,670	84.2%
1998	98,000	98.3	65,810	67.2%	34,090	34.8%	82,910	84.6%
1999	99,400	98.2	67,120	67.5%	39,100	39.3%	84,140	84.6%
2000	100,800	98.2	68,550	68.0%	31,760**	31.5%	85,810	85.1%
2001	102,200	98.2	69,490	68.0%	34,100	33.4%	88,120	86.2%
2002	105,500	98.2	73,230	69.4%	41,900	39.7%	96,190	91.2%
2003	106,700	98.2	74,430	69.8%	40,760	38.2%	97,630	91.5%
2004	108,400	98.2	73,860	68.1%	39,950	36.9%	98,400	90.8%
2005	109,600	98.2	73,930	67.5%	35,120	32.0%	98,860	90.2%
2006	110,200	98.2	73,210	66.4%	34,040	30.9%	97,690	88.6%
2007	111,400	98.2	71,390	64.1%	35,580	31.9%	95,210	85.5%

Note: Cable HH data is based on Wired Cable Homes only, and does not include alternative delivery systems (ADS).

* Reflects adjustments to conform to the 1990 census.

** Decline due to reclassification of the Disney channel.

Source: Nielsen Media Research

Plunkett's Entertainment & Media Industry Almanac 2007

Percent of U.S. Households with Alternative Broadcast Delivery Systems: 1997-2006

Year	Quarter	SMATV	MMDS	Satellite Dish	DBS	Total ADS
1997	1st	0.9	1.1	1.5	2.7	6.1
	2nd	0.9	1.1	1.7	2.9	6.5
	3rd	0.9	1.2	1.7	3.4	7.2
	4th	1.0	1.2	1.6	3.9	7.7
1998	1st	1.1	1.0	1.5	4.7	8.3
	2nd	0.8	1.1	1.4	5.3	8.7
	3rd	0.7	1.1	1.4	5.7	8.8
	4th	0.8	1.0	1.6	5.9	9.1
1999	1st	0.9	0.8	1.4	6.2	9.2
	2nd	0.7	0.9	1.3	6.6	9.5
	3rd	0.7	0.9	1.1	6.7	9.3
	4th	0.7	0.8	0.9	6.9	9.3
2000	1st	0.8	0.7	1.0	7.4	9.9
	2nd	0.8	0.6	1.1	7.8	10.3
	3rd	0.8	0.6	1.2	9.1	11.5
	4th	0.8	0.6	1.0	9.2	11.4
2001	1st	0.8	0.6	0.8	9.8	11.8
	2nd	0.7	0.5	0.7	11.0	12.8
	3rd	0.6	0.5	0.7	12.0	13.6
	4th	0.6	0.4	0.7	12.4	14.1
2002	1st	0.7	0.4	0.5	13.2	14.8
	2nd	0.6	0.3	0.5	13.7	15.0
	3rd	0.6	0.3	0.5	14.2	15.4
	4th	0.6	0.3	0.5	15.1	16.3
2003	1st	0.6	0.3	0.4	15.6	16.7
	2nd	0.7	0.2	0.5	15.8	17.0
	3rd	0.5	0.2	0.3	16.4	17.3
	4th	0.5	0.2	0.4	17.3	18.2
2004	1st	0.5	0.1	0.5	17.6	18.6
	2nd	0.5	0.1	0.4	18.0	18.9
	3rd	0.5	0.1	0.3	18.0	18.8
	4th	0.5	0.0	0.3	18.6	19.3
2005	1st	0.4	0.0	0.2	19.1	19.6
	2nd	0.4	0.0	0.2	19.9	20.4
	3rd	0.4	0.0	0.2	19.9	20.4
	4th	0.5	0.1	0.2	20.2	20.8
2006	1st	0.5	0.1	0.1	20.9	21.5
	2nd	0.5	0.1	0.1	22.0	22.6
	3rd	0.5	0.1	0.1	22.9	23.5

SMATV = Satellite Master Antenna: In complexes or hotels, signals received via satellite, and distributed by coaxial cable.

MMDS = Microwave Multi Distribution System, "Wireless Cable": Distributes signals by microwave. Home receiver picks up signal, then distributes via internal wiring.

Satellite Dish (C-Band/KU Band), "Big Dish": Household receives transmissions from satellite, via a 1 to 3 meter dish.

DBS = Direct Broadcast Satellite: Satellite service delivers directly via household's own small (usually 18") dish.

Source: Nielsen Media Research

Plunkett's Entertainment & Media Industry Almanac 2007

U.S. Cable Network Statistics, 1986-2007

Average Monthly Price for Expanded Basic Programming Packages		Revenue From Advertising				Revenue From Customers		
		Cable Network Revenue	Local/Spot Revenue	Regional Sports Revenue	Total Ad Revenue	Basic Cable	Premium Cable	Total Customer Revenue
Year	Basic Price	*(In Millions of US$)*						
2007[e]	42.76	20,731	4,752	789	26,939	33,608	6,467[e]	74,716
2006	41.17	18,210	4,296	724	23,757	32,274	6,414	68,233
2005	39.96	15,865	3,978	659	20,968	31,075	6,389	62,267
2004	38.23	13,873	3,807	588	18,602	30,336	5,871	57,600
2003	36.59	12,288	3,354	530	16,406	28,960	5,190	51,300
2002	34.52	10,790	3,294	490	14,718	28,492	5,533	49,427
2001	31.58	10,325	2,860	443	13,715	27,031	5,259	43,518
2000	30.08	10,444	2,879	425	13,802	24,445	4,949	40,855
1999	28.92	8,874	2,667	426	11,976	23,146	4,930	36,919
1998	27.81	7,188	2,233	317	9,738	21,830	4,857	33,503
1997	26.48	5,901	1,925	261	8,087	20,405	4,823	30,493
1996	24.41	4,911	1,662	225	6,799	18,395	4,757	27,706
1995	23.07	3,999	1,433	201	5,633	16,860	4,607	25,421
1994	21.62	3,293	1,204	169	4,666	15,170	4,394	23,134
1993	19.39	2,835	978	164	3,977	13,528	4,810	22,843
1992	19.08	2,426	818	140	3,384	12,433	5,108	21,079
1991	18.10	2,100	710	118	2,928	11,418	4,968	19,426
1990	16.78	1,821	634	103	2,557	10,174	4,882	17,582
1989	15.21	1,397	496	74	1,967	8,671	4,663	15,378
1988	13.86	1,135	374	52	1,561	7,345	4,308	13,409
1987	12.18	891	268	33	1,192	6,016	3,959	11,563
1986	10.67	748	195	22	965	4,887	3,767	9,955

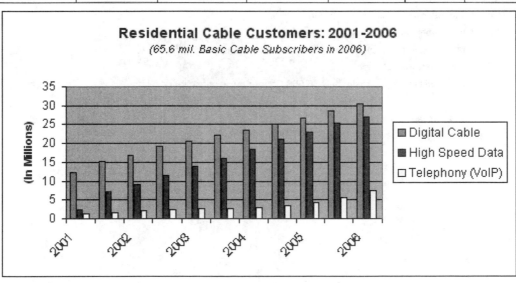

Residential Cable Customers: 2001-2006
(65.6 mil. Basic Cable Subscribers in 2006)

e = Estimates

Sources: Kagan Research, LLC; Telephony data: National Cable & Telecommunications Association (NCTA)

Plunkett's Entertainment & Media Industry Almanac 2007

Top 25 U.S. Cable MSOs* As of September 2006

Rank	MSO	Subscribers
1	Comcast Cable Communications[1]	24,051,000
2	Time Warner Cable[1]	13,471,000
3	Charter Communications[&]	5,476,600
4	Cox Communications[e]	5,400,000
5	Cablevision Systems	3,110,800
6	Bright House Networks[e]	2,294,000
7	Suddenlink Communications[2,e]	1,516,600
8	Mediacom LLC	1,394,000
9	Insight Communications	1,318,800
10	CableOne	689,981
11	RCN Corp.[3]	372,000
12	WideOpenWest[e]	361,200
13	Bresnan Communications[e]	293,500
14	Service Electric[e]	287,800
15	Atlantic Broadband[&]	265,164
16	Armstrong Group of Cos.	232,354
17	Midcontinent Communications	196,313
18	Pencor Services[e]	183,700
19	Knology Holdings	177,708
20	NewWave Communications[4,e]	164,400
21	Millennium Digital Media[e]	157,800
22	MetroCast Cablevision[&]	147,023
23	Northland Communications Corporation	146,940
24	Buckeye CableSystem	146,446
25	MidOcean Ptnrs. & Crestview Ptnrs.[e]	139,000

Note: Unless otherwise noted, counts include owned and managed subscribers.

* MSO = Multi-System Operator   e = Estimate

& Counts include recent sale or acquisition.

[1] Pro forma Adelphia acquisitions.

[2] Pro forma acquisition of approximately 240,000 Charter basic subscribers.

[3] Includes commercial customers.

[4] Pro forma acquisition of approximately 76,000 Charter basic subscribers.

Source: Kagan Research, LLC

Plunkett's Entertainment & Media Industry Almanac 2007

Number of High Speed Internet Lines, U.S.: 2000-2006

Types of Technology[1]	June-00	June-01	June-02	June-03	June-04	June-05	June-06*
ADSL	951,583	2,693,834	5,101,493	7,675,114	13,817,280	16,182,076	18,000,000
Other Wireline	758,594	1,088,066	1,186,680	1,215,713	1,468,566	905,648	543,000
Coaxial Cable	2,284,491	5,184,141	9,172,895	13,684,225	21,357,400	23,938,908	25,000,000
Fiber	307,151	455,593	520,884	575,613	697,779	864,831	1,036,800
Satellite or Wireless	65,615	194,707	220,588	309,006	549,621	970,133	1,513,000
Total Lines	**4,367,434**	**9,616,341**	**16,202,540**	**23,459,671**	**37,890,646**	**42,866,469**	**46,092,800**

[1] The mutually exclusive types of technology are, respectively: Asymmetrical digital subscriber line (ADSL) technologies, which provide speeds in one direction greater than speeds in the other direction; wireline technologies other than ADSL, including traditional telephone company high speed service and symmetric DSL services that provide equivalent functionality; coaxial cable, including the typical hybrid fiber-coax (HFC) architecture of upgraded cable TV systems; optical fiber to the subscriber's premises (e.g., Fiber-to-the-Home or FTTH); and satellite and terrestrial wireless systems, which use radio spectrum to communicate with a radio transmitter.

Note: A high speed line is a connection to an end-user customer that is faster than 200 kbps in at least one direction. Advanced services lines, which are a subset of high speed lines, are connections to end-user customers that are faster than 200 kbps in both directions. The speed of the purchased service varies among end user customers. For example, a high speed service delivered to the end-user customer over other traditional wireline technology, such as DS1 or DS3 services, or over optical fiber to the end user's premises may be much faster than ADSL or cable modem service purchased by a different or by the same, end user. Numbers of lines report here are not adjusted for the speed of the service delivered over the line or the number of end users able to utilize the lines.

* Plunkett Research Estimate

Source: U.S. Federal Communications Bureau (FCC)

Plunkett's Entertainment & Media Industry Almanac 2007

Number of U.S. Movie Screens and Total Admissions: 1987-2006

Year	Indoor Screens	Drive-In Screens	Total Screens	Admissions (In Billions)
1987	20,595	2,084	22,679	1.09
1988	21,632	1,497	23,129	1.08
1989	21,907	1,014	22,921	1.26
1990	22,904	910	23,814	1.19
1991	23,740	899	24,639	1.14
1992	24,344	870	25,214	1.17
1993	24,789	837	25,626	1.24
1994	25,830	859	26,689	1.29
1995	26,995	848	27,843	1.26
1996	28,905	826	29,731	1.34
1997	31,050	815	31,865	1.39
1998	33,418	750	34,168	1.48
1999	36,448	683	37,131	1.47
2000	35,567	683	36,280	1.42
2001	34,490	683	35,173	1.49
2002	35,170	666	35,836	1.63
2003	35,361	634	35,995	1.57
2004	36,012	640	36,652	1.53
2005	37,092	648	37,740	1.40
2006	N/A	N/A	38,000*	1.40*

Indoor screen counts are for the last day of each year. Because many drive-ins are closed for the winter on Dec. 31, drive-in screen counts for each year are tallied the previous summer.

Figures do not include Puerto Rico screens.

* Plunkett Research estimate.

Source: National Association of Theater Owners (NATO)
Plunkett's Entertainment & Media Industry Almanac 2007

Global Recording Industry Trade Revenues by Format, 2004-2005

(In Billions of US$; Latest Year Available)

	2004	2005	Growth
CD	18.109	17.019	-6%
DVD	1.610	1.540	-4%
Digital sales	0.397	1.143	188%
Singles	0.821	0.721	-12%
Other physical*	0.531	0.372	-30%

* Includes cassettes, LPs, VHS and other.

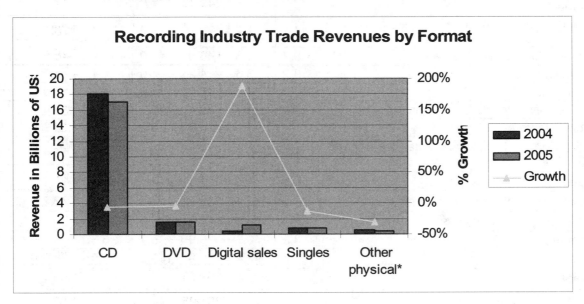

Source: International Federation of the Phonographic Industry (IFPI)

Plunkett's Entertainment & Media Industry Almanac 2007

U.S. Personal Consumption Expenditures for Recreation: 1990-2005

(In Billions of US$; Latest Year Available)

Type of product or service	1990	1995	2000	2001	2002	2003	2004	2005
Total recreation expenditures	290.2	418.1	585.7	604.0	629.9	659.9	708.4	756.3
Percent of total personal consumption	7.6	8.4	8.7	8.6	8.6	8.6	8.6	8.7
Books and maps	16.2	23.2	33.7	34.6	37.1	38.7	40.6	42.2
Magazines, newspapers, and sheet music	21.6	27.5	35.0	35.0	35.1	36.3	39.6	43.8
Nondurable toys and sport supplies	32.8	44.4	56.6	57.6	59.2	60.6	63.5	67.2
Wheel goods, sports and photographic equipment[1]	29.7	39.7	57.6	59.2	61.4	65.6	71.4	81.5
Video and audio products, computer equipment, and musical instruments	53.0	81.5	116.6	115.5	120.0	123.1	133.4	141.2
Video and audio goods, including musical instruments	44.1	57.2	72.8	73.6	75.4	76.5	81.8	85.8
Computers, peripherals, and software	8.9	24.3	43.8	42.0	44.6	46.6	51.6	55.4
Radio and television repair	3.2	3.6	4.2	4.0	4.1	4.1	4.6	4.8
Flowers, seeds, and potted plants	10.9	14.0	18.0	18.0	18.0	17.9	18.3	19.7
Admissions to specified spectator amusements	15.1	21.1	30.4	32.2	34.8	36.0	37.4	38.3
Motion picture theaters	5.1	5.6	8.6	9.0	9.6	9.9	9.9	9.7
Legitimate theaters and opera, and entertainments of nonprofit institutions[2]	5.2	8.1	10.3	10.9	11.7	11.9	12.4	12.7
Spectator sports[3]	4.8	7.4	11.5	12.4	13.5	14.3	15.1	15.9
Clubs and fraternal organizations except insurance[4]	13.5	17.4	19.0	20.0	21.1	22.2	22.3	23.5
Commercial participant amusements[5]	25.2	48.8	75.8	79.6	83.7	91.2	100.7	107.3
Pari-mutuel net receipts	3.5	3.7	5.0	5.1	5.3	5.2	5.6	6.2
Other[6]	65.4	93.4	133.9	143.2	150.0	158.9	170.9	180.0

[1] Includes boats and pleasure aircraft.

[2] Except athletic.

[3] Consists of admissions to professional and amateur athletic events and to racetracks, including horse, dog, and auto.

[4] Consists of current expenditures (including consumption of fixed capital) of nonprofit clubs and fraternal organizations and dues and fees paid to proprietary clubs.

[5] Consists of billiard parlors; bowling alleys; dancing, riding, shooting, skating, and swimming places; amusement devices and parks; golf courses; sightseeing buses and guides; private flying operations; casino gambling; and other commercial participant amusements.

[6] Consists of net receipts of lotteries and expenditures for purchases of pets and pet care services, cable TV, film processing, photographic studios, sporting and recreation camps, video cassette rentals, and recreational services, not elsewhere classified.

Source: Bureau of Economic Analysis

Plunkett's Entertainment & Media Industry Almanac 2007

U.S. Employment in Entertainment and Media Occupations, May 2005

(Latest Year Available)

Occupation Title	Number Employed[1]	Median Hourly	Mean Hourly	Mean Annual[2]	Mean RSE[3]
Art Directors	29,350	$30.75	$35.48	$73,790	1.0%
Multi-Media Artists and Animators	23,790	$24.18	$27.53	$57,270	3.8%
Fashion Designers	12,980	$29.26	$32.39	$67,370	4.6%
Set and Exhibit Designers	8,380	$17.98	$20.15	$41,920	1.7%
Actors	59,590	$13.60	$23.73	N/A	4.4%
Producers and Directors	59,070	$25.89	$33.16	$68,970	3.1%
Dancers	16,240	$8.92	$13.22	N/A	3.5%
Choreographers	16,150	$15.84	$18.26	$37,970	3.2%
Music Directors and Composers	8,610	$16.74	$20.90	$43,470	3.6%
Musicians and Singers	50,410	$17.90	$25.16	N/A	3.8%
Radio and Television Announcers	41,090	$11.60	$17.11	$35,600	2.1%
Broadcast News Analysts	6,680	$20.58	$30.73	$63,920	2.5%
Reporters and Correspondents	52,920	$15.52	$19.41	$40,370	1.5%
Editors	96,270	$21.88	$24.88	$51,750	0.9%
Technical Writers	46,250	$26.52	$27.75	$57,720	0.8%
Writers and Authors	43,020	$22.32	$25.89	$53,850	1.5%
Interpreters and Translators	29,240	$16.73	$18.41	$38,300	1.6%
Audio and Video Equipment Technicians	40,390	$15.84	$17.48	$36,350	1.3%
Broadcast Technicians	30,730	$14.62	$17.00	$35,350	1.5%
Radio Operators	1,190	$17.42	$18.21	$37,880	2.3%
Sound Engineering Technicians	12,680	$18.46	$22.98	$47,790	2.6%
Photographers	58,260	$12.55	$15.10	$31,410	2.0%
Camera Operators, Television, Video, and Motion Picture	22,530	$20.01	$22.13	$46,040	3.8%
Film and Video Editors	15,200	$22.56	$26.31	$54,730	2.5%

[1] Estimates do not include self-employed workers.

[2] Annual wages have been calculated by multiplying the hourly mean wage by a "year-round, full-time" hours figure of 2,080 hours; for those occupations where there is not an hourly mean wage published, the annual wage has been directly calculated from the reported survey data.

[3] The relative standard error (RSE) is a measure of the reliability of a survey statistic. The smaller the relative standard error, the more precise the estimate.

N/A = There is wide variation in the number of hours worked by those employed as actors, dancers, musicians, and singers. It is extremely rare for a performer to have guaranteed employment for a period that exceeds 3 to 6 months.

Source: U.S. Bureau of Labor Statistics

Plunkett's Entertainment & Media Industry Almanac 2007

Chapter 3

IMPORTANT ENTERTAINMENT & MEDIA INDUSTRY CONTACTS

Contents:

I. Advertising/Marketing Associations

Advertising Club, The
235 Park Ave. S., 6th Fl.
New York, NY 10003-1450 US
Phone: 212-533-8080
Fax: 212-533-1929
Web Address: www.theadvertisingclub.org
The Advertising Club strives to elevate the understanding of marketing and advertising communications in New York by providing a forum for members of the industry to address common interests.

Advertising Research Foundation (ARF)
641 Lexington Ave.
New York, NY 10022 US
Phone: 212-751-5656
E-mail Address: *info@thearf.org*
Web Address: www.thearf.org

The Advertising Research Foundation (ARF), a nonprofit corporate-membership association, is a leading professional organization in the fields of advertising, marketing and media research.

Advertising Women of New York (AWNY)
25 W. 45th St., Ste. 1001
New York, NY 10036 US
Phone: 212-221-7969
Fax: 212-221-8296
E-mail Address: *awny@awny.org*
Web Address: www.awny.org
Advertising Women of New York (AWNY) provides a forum for personal and professional growth, serves as a catalyst for the advancement of women in the communications field and promotes and supports philanthropic endeavors through the AWNY Foundation.

American Advertising Federation, Inc. (AAF)
1101 Vermont Ave. NW, Ste. 500
Washington, DC 20005-6306 US
Phone: 202-898-0089
Fax: 202-898-0159
E-mail Address: *aaf@aaf.org*
Web Address: www.aaf.org
The American Advertising Federation, Inc. (AAF) protects and promotes the well-being of advertising through a nationally coordinated network of advertisers, agencies, media companies, local advertising clubs and college chapters.

American Association of Advertising Agencies (AAAA)
405 Lexington Ave., 18th Fl.
New York, NY 10174-1801 US
Phone: 212-682-2500
Fax: 212-682-8391
Web Address: www.aaaa.org
The American Association of Advertising Agencies (AAAA) is the national trade association representing the advertising agency industry in the United States.

American Business Media (ABM)
675 3rd Ave.
New York, NY 10017-5704 US
Phone: 212-661-6360
Fax: 212-370-0736
E-mail Address: *info@abmmail.com*
Web Address: www.americanbusinessmedia.com
American Business Media (ABM) is the industry association for business-to-business information providers, including producers of magazines, CD-ROMS, web sites, trade shows and other ancillary products that build upon the printed product.

American Institute of Graphic Arts (AIGA)
164 5th Ave.
New York, NY 10010 US
Phone: 212-807-1990
Fax: 212-807-1799
Web Address: www.aiga.org
The purpose of the American Institute of Graphic Arts (AIGA) is to further excellence in communication design, both as a strategic tool for business and as a cultural force.

American Marketing Association (AMA)
311 S. Wacker Dr., Ste. 5800
Chicago, IL 60606 US
Phone: 312-542-9000
Fax: 312-542-9001
Toll Free: 800-262-1150
Web Address: www.marketingpower.com
The American Marketing Association (AMA) serves marketing professionals in both business and education and serves all levels of marketing practitioners, educators and students.

Arbitron
Web Address: www.arbitron.com
Arbitron is the leading radio broadcasting market-research company.

Art Directors Club, Inc.(ADC)
106 W. 29th St.
New York, NY 10001 US
Phone: 212-643-1440
Fax: 212-643-4266
E-mail Address: *info@adcglobal.org*
Web Address: www.adcglobal.org
The Art Directors Club (ADC) is an international not-for-profit organization of creative leaders in advertising, graphic design, interactive media, broadcast design, typography, packaging, environmental design, photography, illustration and related disciplines.

Association for Women In Communications (AWC)
3337 Duke St.
Alexandria, VA 22314 US
Phone: 703-370-7436
Fax: 703-370-7437
E-mail Address: *info@womcom.org*
Web Address: www.womcom.org

The Association for Women In Communications (AWC) is a professional organization that champions the advancement of women across all communications disciplines by recognizing excellence, promoting leadership and positioning its members at the forefront of the communications industry.

Association of Canadian Advertisers, Inc. (ACA)
175 Bloor St. E., S. Tower, Ste. 307
Toronto, ON M4W 3R8 Canada
Phone: 416-964-3805
Fax: 416-964-0771
Toll Free: 800-565-0109
E-mail Address: *rscotland@acaweb.ca*
Web Address: www.aca-online.com
The Association of Canadian Advertisers (ACA) is the only organization expressly dedicated to representing the interests of companies that market and advertise their products in Canada.

Association of Independent Commercial Producers (AICP)
3 W. 18th St., 5th Fl.
New York, NY 10011 US
Phone: 212-929-3000
E-mail Address: *info@aicp.com*
Web Address: www.aicp.com
The Association of Independent Commercial Producers (AICP) represents the interests of U.S. companies that specialize in producing commercials in various media for advertisers and agencies.

Association of Independent Creative Editors (AICE)
300 E. 40th St., Ste. 16T
New York, NY 10016 US
Phone: 212-972-3556
Fax: 212-681-9481
E-mail Address: *info@aice.org*
Web Address: www.aice.org
The Association of Independent Creative Editors (AICE) is a national association serving the needs and interests of independent creative editorial companies.

Audit Bureau of Circulations (ABC)
900 N. Meacham Rd.
Schaumburg, IL 60173-4968 US
Phone: 847-605-0909
Fax: 847-605-0483
Web Address: www.accessabc.com

The Audit Bureau of Circulations (ABC) is the leading third-party auditing trade organization in the U.S. and strives to conduct audits that set the industry standard for integrity, objectivity and accuracy.

BPA Worldwide
2 Corporate Dr., Ste. 900
Shelton, CT 06484 US
Phone: 203-447-2800
E-mail Address: *info@bpaww.com*
Web Address: www.bpaww.com
BPA Worldwide is a global provider of audited data to the marketing, media and information industries.

Business Marketing Association (BMA)
400 N. Michigan Ave., 15th Fl.
Chicago, IL 60611 US
Fax: 312-822-0054
Toll Free: 800-664-4262
Web Address: www.marketing.org
The Business Marketing Association (BMA) serves the professional, educational and career development needs of business-to-business marketers and their partner suppliers.

Cabletelevision Advertising Bureau (CAB)
830 3rd Ave., 2nd Fl.
New York, NY 10022 US
Phone: 212-508-1200
Fax: 212-832-3268
Web Address: www.onetvworld.org
The Cabletelevision Advertising Bureau (CAB) provides information and resources to the advertising community to support marketing and media planning; assists its industry members in maximizing advertising revenues; and promotes the use of cable as an advertising medium locally, regionally and nationally.

Direct Marketing Association (DMA)
1120 Ave. of the Americas
New York, NY 10036-6700 US
Phone: 212-768-7277
Fax: 212-302-6714
Web Address: www.the-dma.org
The Direct Marketing Association (DMA) is the oldest and largest trade association for users and suppliers in the direct, database and interactive marketing fields.

Intermarket Agency Network (IAN)
5307 S. 92nd St.
Hales Corners, WI 53130 US

Phone: 414-425-8800
Fax: 414-425-0021
E-mail Address: *bille@nonbox.com*
Web Address: www.intermarketnetwork.com
The Intermarket Agency Network (IAN) is a network
of independent, full-service advertising agencies.

International Advertising Association (IAA)
521 5th Ave., Ste. 1807
New York, NY 10175 US
Phone: 212-557-1133
Fax: 212-983-0455
E-mail Address: *iaa@iaaglobal.org*
Web Address: www.iaaglobal.org
The International Advertising Association (IAA) is a
strategic partnership that champions the common
interests of disciplines across the full spectrum of the
marketing communications industry.

International Association of Business Communicators (IABC)
One Hallidie Plaza, Ste. 600
San Francisco, CA 94102 US
Phone: 415-544-4700
Fax: 415-544-4747
Toll Free: 800-776-4222
E-mail Address: *service_centre@iabc.com*
Web Address: www.iabc.com
The International Association of Business
Communicators (IABC) is the leading resource for
effective business communication practices.

International Public Relations Association (IPRA)
One Dunley Hill Ct.
Ranmore Common
Dorking, Surrey RH5 6SX UK
Phone: 44-1483-280-130
Fax: 44-1483-280-131
E-mail Address: *iprasec@btconnect.com*
Web Address: www.ipra.org
The International Public Relations Association
(IPRA) is an international group of public relations
practitioners that promotes the exchange of
information and cooperation in the profession and
creates development opportunities aimed at
enhancing the role of public relations in management
and international affairs.

Mailing & Fulfillment Service Association (MFSA)
1421 Prince St., Ste. 410
Alexandria, VA 22314-2806 US
Phone: 703-836-9200

Fax: 703-548-8204
E-mail Address: *kkight@mfsanet.org*
Web Address: www.mfsanet.org
The Mailing & Fulfillment Service Association
(MFSA), the national trade association for the
mailing and fulfillment services industry, works to
improve the business environment for mailing and
fulfillment companies and to provide opportunities
for the learning and professional development of the
managers of these companies.

Marketing Agencies Association Worldwide (MAA)
460 Summer St., 4th Fl.
Stamford, CT 06901 US
Phone: 203-978-1590
Fax: 203-969-1499
E-mail Address: *maaw_jl@yahoo.com*
Web Address: www.maaw.org
Marketing Agencies Association Worldwide (MAA)
exists to help clients select, manage and evaluate
promotion marketing agencies and to provide its
members with professional support, management
development, research and an open forum for the
exchange of ideas that will build their businesses
profitably.

Media Credit Association (MCA)
810 7th Ave., 24th Fl.
New York, NY 10019 US
Phone: 212- 872-3700
E-mail Address: *mpa@magazine.org*
Web Address:
www.magazine.org/finance_and_operations/media_c
redit_association
The Media Credit Association (MCA) is the credit
information gathering service of the Magazine
Publishers of America. It assists credit professionals
in the assessment of risk associated with selling ad
pages to advertising agencies and direct accounts.

National Advertising Division of the Council of Better Business Bureaus, Inc. (NAD)
70 W. 36th St., 13th Fl.
New York, NY 10018 US
E-mail Address: *sharris@nad.bbb.org*
Web Address: www.nadreview.org
The National Advertising Division of the Council of
Better Business Bureaus, Inc. (NAD) provides the
advertising community with a system of self-
regulation, minimizes government intervention and
fosters public confidence in the credibility of
advertising.

National Agri-Marketing Association (NAMA)
11020 King St., Ste. 205
Overland Park, KS 66210 US
Phone: 913-491-6500
Fax: 913-491-6502
E-mail Address: *agrimktg@nama.org*
Web Address: www.nama.org
The National Agri-Marketing Association (NAMA)
unites those involved in marketing communications,
public relations, products management and sales in
the agribusiness industry.

New York American Marketing Association (NYAMA)
60 E. 42nd St., Ste. 1765
New York, NY 10165 US
Phone: 212-687-3280
Fax: 212-557-9242
E-mail Address: *info@nyama.org*
Web Address: www.nyama.org
The New York American Marketing Association
(NYAMA) exists to advance the practice and
understanding of effective marketing through
international directories, awards, publications,
conferences, web sites and career development
resources.

Outdoor Advertising Association of America, Inc. (OAAA)
1850 M St. NW, Ste. 1040
Washington, DC 20036 US
Phone: 202-833-5566
Fax: 202-833-1522
Web Address: www.oaaa.org
The Outdoor Advertising Association of America,
Inc. (OAAA) is a leading trade association
representing the outdoor advertising industry.

Point-of-Purchase Advertising Institute (POPAI)
1600 Duke St., Ste. 400
Alexandria, VA 22314 US
Phone: 703-373-8800
E-mail Address: *info@popai.org*
Web Address: www.popai.com
The Point-of-Purchase Advertising Institute (POPAI)
is an international nonprofit trade association
dedicated to serving the interests of advertisers,
retailers, producers and suppliers of point-of-
purchase products and services. POPAI has over
1,700 member companies.

Public Relations Society of America, Inc. (PRSA)
33 Maiden Ln., 11th Fl.

New York, NY 10038-5150 US
Phone: 212-460-1400
Fax: 212-995-0757
E-mail Address: *pr@pras.org*
Web Address: www.prsa.org
The Public Relations Society of America (PRSA)
exists to unify, strengthen and advance the profession
of public relations.

Television Bureau of Advertising (TVB)
3 E. 54th St.
New York, NY 10022-3108 US
Phone: 212-486-1111
Fax: 212-935-5631
E-mail Address: *info@tvb.org*
Web Address: www.tvb.org
The Television Bureau of Advertising (TVB) is the
not-for-profit trade association of America's
broadcast television industry, providing resources
that enable advertisers to make the best use of local
television.

Women Executives in Public Relations, Inc. (WEPR)
FDR Station, P.O. Box 7657
New York, NY 10150-7657 US
Phone: 212-859-7375
Fax: 212-859-7375
Web Address: www.wepr.org
Women Executives in Public Relations, Inc.
(WEPR), a Special Sector of Advertising Women of
New York, is the premier public relations
organization for senior-level women in the field. It
works to support career advancement of female
practitioners and to foster the use of public relations
to benefit the goals of business and society.

Women in Direct Marketing International (WDMI)
WDMI/NY c/o Wunderman
285 Madison Ave., 14th Fl.
New York, NY 10017 US
Phone: 732-469-5900 ext. 307
E-mail Address: *bladden@directmaildepot.com*
Web Address: www.wdmi.org
Women in Direct Marketing International (WDMI) is
a network of direct marketers dedicated to connecting
women in the field and to promoting excellence in
direct marketing.

II.   Advertising/Marketing Resources

USA TODAY ADTRACK
Web Address:
www.usatoday.com/money/advertising/adtrack/index
.htm
USA TODAY ADTRACK is a web site that delivers
the results of a weekly poll conducted by USA
TODAY and Harris Interactive to determine the
effectiveness of major advertising campaigns.

III.   Booksellers Associations

American Booksellers Association, Inc.
200 White Plains Rd.
Tarrytown, NY 10591 US
Fax: 914-591-2720
Toll Free: 800-637-0037
E-mail Address: *info@bookweb.org*
Web Address: www.bookweb.org
The American Booksellers Association is a nonprofit
association representing independent bookstores in
the United States.

Midwest Booksellers Association (MBA)
3407 W. 44th St.
Minneapolis, MN 55410 US
Phone: 612-926-5868
Fax: 612-926-6657
Toll Free: 800-784-7522
E-mail Address: *info@midwestbooksellers.org*
Web Address: www.midwestbooksellers.org
The Upper Midwest Booksellers Association (MBA)
is an organization representing independent
booksellers in the upper Midwest.

National Association of College Stores (NACS)
500 E. Lorain St.
Oberlin, OH 44074 US
Fax: 440-775-4769
Toll Free: 800-622-7498
E-mail Address: *webteam@nacs.org*
Web Address: www.nacs.org
The National Association of College Stores (NACS)
is the professional trade association representing
college retailers and associate members who supply
books and other products to college stores.

IV.   Broadcasting, Cable, Radio & TV Associations

Academy of Television Arts and Sciences
5220 Lankershim Blvd.
North Hollywood, CA 91601-3109 US
Phone: 818-754-2800
Fax: 818-761-2827
E-mail Address: *webmaster@emmys.org*
Web Address: www.emmys.org
The Academy of Television Arts and Sciences is a
nonprofit corporation devoted to the advancement of
telecommunications arts and sciences and to fostering
creative leadership in the telecommunications
industry.

Advanced Television Systems Committee (ATSC)
1750 K St. NW, Ste. 1200
Washington, DC 20006 US
Phone: 202-872-9160
Fax: 202-872-9161
E-mail Address: *mricher@atsc.org*
Web Address: www.atsc.org
The Advanced Television Systems Committee
(ATSC) is an international nonprofit membership
organization that develops voluntary standards for the
entire spectrum of advanced television systems.

Alliance for Community Media (ACM)
666 11th St. NW, Ste. 740
Washington, DC 20001-4542 US
Phone: 202-393-2650
Fax: 202-393-2653
E-mail Address: *acmwebmaster@cinci.rr.com*
Web Address: www.alliancecm.org
The Alliance for Community Media (ACM) is a
group committed to assuring universal access to
electronic media.

**American Federation of Television and Radio
Artists (AFTRA)**
260 Madison Ave.
New York, NY 10016-2401 US
Phone: 212-532-0800
Fax: 212-532-2242
E-mail Address: *info@aftra.com*
Web Address: www.aftra.org
The American Federation of Television and Radio
Artists (AFTRA) represents actors and other
professional performers and broadcasters in
television, radio, sound recordings, non-
broadcast/industrial programming and new

technologies such as interactive programming and CD-ROMs.

American Sportscasters Association (ASA)
225 Broadway, Ste. 2030
New York, NY 10007 US
Phone: 212-227-8080
Fax: 212-571-0556
E-mail Address: *lschwa8918@aol.com*
Web Address: www.americansportscasters.com
The American Sportscasters Association (ASA) is a professional organization for the promotion and support of sports broadcasters.

American Women in Radio and Television, Inc. (AWRT)
8405 Greensboro Dr., Ste. 800
McLean, VA 22102 US
Phone: 703-506-3290
Fax: 703-506-3266
E-mail Address: *info@awrt.org*
Web Address: www.awrt.org
American Women in Radio and Television (AWRT) is a national nonprofit organization dedicated to advancing the role of women in electronic media and related fields.

Association for International Broadcasting (AIB)
P.O. Box 141
Cranbrook, TN17 9AJ UK
Phone: 44-0-20-7993-2557
Fax: 44-0-20-7993-8043
E-mail Address: *info@aib.org.uk*
Web Address: www.aib.org.uk
The Association for International Broadcasting (AIB) aims to increase the scope and effectiveness of international broadcasting, working on a global, co-operative basis.

Association for Maximum Service Television, Inc. (MSTV)
4100 Wisconsin Ave., NW
Washington, DC 20016 US
Phone: 202-966-1956
Fax: 202-966-9617
E-mail Address: *sbaurenfeind@mstv.org*
Web Address: www.mstv.org
Association for Maximum Service Television (MSTV) is a national association of local television stations dedicated to preserving and improving the technical quality of free, universal, community-based television service to the American public.

Association of America's Public Television Stations (APTS)
666 11th St. NW, Ste. 1100
Washington, DC 20001 US
Phone: 202-654-4200
Fax: 202-654-4236
E-mail Address: *jeffrey@apts.org*
Web Address: www.apts.org
The Association of America's Public Television Stations (APTS) is a nonprofit membership organization formed to support the continued growth and development of strong and financially sound noncommercial television service for the American public.

Broadcast Cable Credit Association, Inc. (BCCA)
550 W. Frontage Rd., Ste. 3600
Northfield, IL 60093 US
Phone: 847-881-8757
Fax: 847-784-8059
E-mail Address: *info@bccacredit.com*
Web Address: www.bccacredit.com
The Broadcast Cable Credit Association (BCCA) exists to provide tools and services that allow its members to perform their functions to the best of their abilities and achieve a profitable bottom line.

Broadcast Cable Financial Management Association (BCFM)
550 W. Frontage Rd., Ste. 3600
Northfield, IL 60093 US
Phone: 847-716-7000
Fax: 847-716-7004
E-mail Address: *mcollins@bcfm.com*
Web Address: www.bcfm.com
The Broadcast Cable Financial Management Association (BCFM) exists to provide and maintain open, intellectual exchange and create opportunities to help its members grow professionally and personally.

Broadcast Designers' Association, Inc. (BDA)
Promax & BDA
9000 W. Sunset Blvd., Ste. 900
Los Angeles, CA 90069 US
Phone: 310-788-7600
Fax: 310-788-7616
E-mail Address: *anush@promax.tv*
Web Address: www.promax.tv
Broadcast Designers' Association (BDA) is the world's foremost organization working on behalf of those involved in the promotion, marketing and design of all electronic media.

Broadcast Education Association (BEA)
1771 N St. NW
Washington, DC 20036-2891 US
Phone: 202-429-3935
Toll Free: 888-380-7222
E-mail Address: *beainfo@beaweb.org*
Web Address: www.beaweb.org
The Broadcast Education Association (BEA) is the professional association for professors, industry professionals and graduate students interested in teaching and research related to electronic media and multimedia enterprises.

Broadcast Pioneers Library of American Broadcasting (LAB)
3210 Hornbake Library
University of Maryland
College Park, MD 20742 US
Phone: 301-405-9160
Fax: 301-314-2634
E-mail Address: *labcast@umd.edu*
Web Address: www.lib.umd.edu/lab/
The Broadcast Pioneers Library of American Broadcasting (LAB) holds a wide-ranging collection of audio and video recordings, books, pamphlets, periodicals, personal collections, oral histories, photographs, scripts and vertical files devoted exclusively to the history of broadcasting.

Broadcasters' Foundation, Inc.
7 Lincoln Ave.
Greenwich, CT 06830 US
Phone: 203-862-8577
Fax: 203-629-5739
E-mail Address:
ghastings@broadcastersfoundation.org
Web Address: www.broadcastersfoundation.org
The Broadcasters' Foundation is the only organization in radio and television that provides anonymous financial assistance to fellow broadcasters in acute need.

Cable & Telecommunications Association for Marketing (CTAM)
201 N. Union St., Ste. 440
Alexandria, VA 22314 US
Phone: 703-549-4200
E-mail Address: *info@ctam.com*
Web Address: www.ctamnetforum.com/eweb
The Cable & Telecommunications Association for Marketing (CTAM) is dedicated to the discipline and development of consumer marketing excellence in

cable television, new media and telecommunications services.

Cable in the Classroom (CIC)
1724 Massachusetts Ave. NW
Washington, DC 20036 US
Phone: 202-775-1040
Fax: 202-775-1047
Web Address: www.ciconline.com
The Cable in the Classroom (CIC) program provides schools across the U.S. with free cable service and over 540 hours per month of commercial-free educational programming.

Cable Television Laboratories, Inc. (CableLabs)
858 Coal Creek Cir.
Louisville, CO 80027-9750 US
Phone: 303-661-9100
Fax: 303-661-9199
Web Address: www.cablelabs.com
Cable Television Laboratories (CableLabs) is a nonprofit research and development consortium dedicated to pursuing new cable telecommunications technologies and to helping its cable operator members integrate those technical advancements into their business objectives.

Cable TV Public Affairs Association (CTPAA)
P.O. Box 33697
Washington, DC 20033 US
Fax: 202-775-1083
Web Address: www.ctpaa.org
The Cable TV Public Affairs Association (CTPAA) is the only national professional organization specifically addressing the issues, needs and interests of the cable industry's public affairs professionals.

Canadian Association of Broadcasters (CAB)
350 Sparks St., Ste. 306
Ottawa, ON K1R 7S8 Canada
Phone: 613-233-4035
Fax: 613-233-6961
E-mail Address: *mforget@cab-acr.ca*
Web Address: www.cab-acr.ca
The Canadian Association of Broadcasters (CAB) is the collective voice of the majority of Canada's private radio and television stations, networks and specialty services.

Community Broadcasters Association (CBA)
3605 Sandy Plains Rd., Ste. 240462
Marietta, GA 30066 US
Toll Free: 800-215-7655

E-mail Address:
webmaster@communitybroadcasters.com
Web Address: www.communitybroadcasters.com
The Community Broadcasters Association (CBA) is a national organization dedicated to enhancing and representing the diversity, vitality, localism, community service and economic survival of Class A and low-power television stations in the U.S.

Country Radio Broadcasters, Inc. (CRB)
819 18th Ave. S.
Nashville, TN 37203 US
Phone: 615-327-4487
Fax: 615-329-4492
Web Address: www.crb.org
Country Radio Broadcasters (CRB) brings together country radio broadcasters from around the world for the purpose of assuring the continued vitality of the country radio format.

Hollywood Radio & Television Society (HRTS)
13701 Riverside Dr., Ste. 205
Sherman Oaks, CA 91423 US
Phone: 818-789-1182
Fax: 818-789-1210
E-mail Address: *info@hrts.org*
Web Address: www.hrts.org
The Hollywood Radio & Television (HRTS) is an organization of executives from west coast networks, stations, studios, production companies, advertisers, ad agencies, cable companies, media companies, legal firms, publicity agencies, talent and management agencies, performers, services, suppliers and allied fields.

International Federation of Television Archives (IFTA)
E-mail Address: *office@fiatifta.org*
Web Address: www.fiatifta.org
International Federation of Television Archives (IFTA) is an association of broadcast and national audiovisual archives and libraries involved in the collection and preservation of film and television images.

National Association of Black Owned Broadcasters, Inc. (NABOB)
1155 Connecticut Ave. NW, Ste. 600
Washington, DC 20036 US
Phone: 202-463-8970
Fax: 202-429-0657
E-mail Address: *info@nabob.org*
Web Address: www.nabob.org

The National Association of Black Owned Broadcasters (NABOB) seeks to improve and increase the opportunities for success for black and minority owners in the broadcast industry.

National Association of Broadcasters (NAB)
1771 N St. NW
Washington, DC 20036 US
Phone: 202-429-5300
Fax: 202-429-4199
E-mail Address: *nab@nab.org*
Web Address: www.nab.org
The National Association of Broadcasters (NAB) represents broadcasters for radio and television. The organization also provides benefits to employees of member companies and to indivuduals and companies that provide products and services to the electronic media industries.

National Association of Television Program Executives (NATPE)
5757 Wilshire Blvd., Penthouse 10
Los Angeles, CA 90036-3681 US
Phone: 310-453-4440
Fax: 310-453-5258
E-mail Address: *info@natpe.org*
Web Address: www.natpe.org
The National Association of Television Program Executives (NATPE) is the leading association for content professionals in the global television industry.

National Broadcasting Society (NBS)
Millersville University
Attn. Dr. Bill Dorman, Dept. of Comm. And Theatre
Millersville, PA 17551 US
Phone: 717-872-3236
Fax: 717-871-2051
E-mail Address: *bill.dorman@millersville.edu*
Web Address: www.nbs-aerho.org
The National Broadcasting Society (NBS), also known as Alpha Epsilon Rho, exists to enhance the development of college and university students involved in broadcasting, cable, telecommunications and other electronic media.

National Cable and Telecommunications Association (NCTA)
1724 Massachusetts Ave. NW
Washington, DC 20036 US
Phone: 202-775-3550
E-mail Address: *webmaster@ncta.com*
Web Address: www.ncta.com

The National Cable and Telecommunications
Association (NCTA) is the principal trade association
of the cable television industry in the United States.

National Cable Television Institute (NCTI)
Jones/NCTI
9697 E. Mineral Ave.
Centennial, CO 80112 US
Phone: 303-797-9393
Web Address: www.ncti.com
The National Cable Television Institute (NCTI) is the
largest independent provider of broadband
communications training in the world.

National Captioning Institute (NCI)
1900 Gallows Rd., Ste. 3000
Vienna, VA 22182 US
Phone: 703-917-7600
Fax: 703-917-9853
E-mail Address: *mail@ncicap.org*
Web Address: www.ncicap.org
The National Captioning Institute (NCI) is a
nonprofit corporation that promotes and provides
closed captioning technology and services to make
television programming accessible to people who are
deaf or hard of hearing.

National Religious Broadcasters (NRB)
9510 Technology Dr.
Manassas, VA 20110 US
Phone: 703-330-7000
Fax: 703-330-7100
E-mail Address: *info@nrb.org*
Web Address: www.nrb.org
National Religious Broadcasters (NRB) is an
association representing evangelical Christian radio
and television stations, program producers,
multimedia developers and related organizations
around the world.

National Television Academy (NTA)
111 W. 57th St., Ste. 600
New York, NY 10019 US
Phone: 212-586-8424
Fax: 212-246-8129
E-mail Address: *hq@natasonline.com*
Web Address: www.emmyonline.org
The National Television Academy (NTA) is
dedicated to the advancement of the arts and sciences
of television and the promotion of creative leadership
for artistic, educational and technical achievements
within the television industry.

**New York State Broadcasters Association
(NYSBA)**
1805 Western Ave.
Albany, NY 12203 US
Phone: 518-456-8888
Fax: 518-456-8943
E-mail Address: *info@nysbroadcastersassn.org*
Web Address: www.nysbroadcastersassn.org
New York State Broadcasters Association (NYSBA)
serves as the primary advocate and active
representative for New York State's broadcast
industry in state and national issues.

Parents Television Council (PTC)
707 Wilshire Blvd., Ste. 2075
Los Angeles, CA 90017 US
Phone: 213-629-9255
Fax: 213-629-9254
Toll Free: 800-882-6868
E-mail Address: *editor@parentstv.org*
Web Address: www.parentstv.org
The Parents Television Council (PTC) provides
reviews of television shows, screening for violence,
sexuality and language.

Public Radio News Directors, Inc. (PRNDI)
WUNC FM
120 Friday Ctr. Dr.
Chapel Hill, NC 27517 US
Phone: 919-966-5454 ext. 291
E-mail Address: *cwalker@wunc.org*
Web Address: www.prndi.org
Public Radio News Directors (PRNDI) is a nonprofit
national service organization that encourages the
professional development and training of public radio
journalists.

Radio Advertising Bureau (RAB)
1320 Greenway Dr., Ste. 500
Irving, TX 75038-2510 US
Toll Free: 800-232-3131
Web Address: www.rab.com
The mission of the Radio Advertising Bureau (RAB)
is to increase the awareness, credibility and salability
of radio by designing, developing and implementing
appropriate programs, research, tools and activities
for member stations.

Radio Marketing Bureau (RMB)
175 Bloor St. E., Ste. 316, N. Tower
Toronto, ON M4W 3R8 Canada
Phone: 416-922-5757
Fax: 416-922-6542

Toll Free: 800-667-2346
E-mail Address: *info@rmb.ca*
Web Address: www.rmb.ca
The Radio Marketing Bureau (RMB) is a marketing source for radio advertising in Canada, representing stations generating over 80% of all Canadian radio revenue.

Radio Television News Directors Association (RTNDA Canada)
2175 Sheppard Ave. E., Ste. 310
Toronto, ON M2J 1W8 Canada
Phone: 416-756-2213
Fax: 416-491-1670
Toll Free: 877-257-8632
E-mail Address: *info@rtndacanada.com*
Web Address: www.rtndacanada.com
Radio Television News Directors Association (RTNDA Canada) offers a forum for open discussion and action in the broadcast news industry in Canada.

Radio Television News Directors Association (RTNDA)
1600 K St. NW, Ste. 700
Washington, DC 20006-2838 US
Phone: 202-659-6510
Fax: 202-223-4007
Toll Free: 800-807-8632
E-mail Address: *rtnda@rtnda.org*
Web Address: www.rtnda.org
The Radio Television News Directors Association (RTNDA) is the world's largest professional organization exclusively committed to professionals in electronic journalism.

Satellite Broadcasting & Communications Association of America (SBCA)
1730 M St. NW, Ste. 600
Washington, DC 20036 US
Phone: 202-349-3620
Fax: 202-349-3621
Toll Free: 800-541-5981
E-mail Address: *info@sbca.org*
Web Address: www.sbca.com
The Satellite Broadcasting & Communications Association of America (SBCA) is the national trade organization representing all segments of the satellite consumer services industry.

Syndication Network Television Association (SNTA)
630 5th Ave., Ste. 2320
New York, NY 10111 US

Phone: 212-259-3740
Fax: 212-259-3770
E-mail Address: *mburg@snta.com*
Web Address: www.snta.com
The Syndication Network Television Association (SNTA) is an organization of national and independent television stations that syndicate television shows.

Television Bureau of Canada (TVB)
160 Bloor St. E., Ste. 1005
Toronto, ON M4W 1B9 Canada
Phone: 416-923-8813
Fax: 416-413-3879
E-mail Address: *tvb@tvb.ca*
Web Address: www.tvb.ca
The Television Bureau of Canada (TVB) is a resource center for television stations, networks and their sales representatives.

The Cable Center
2000 Buchtel Blvd.
Denver, CO 80210 US
Phone: 303-871-4885
Fax: 303-871-4514
Web Address: www.cablecenter.org
The Cable Center supports communication in the business, technology and programming of cable telecommunications and provides education, training and research for all aspects of the industry.

Women in Cable & Telecommunications (WICT)
14555 Avion Pkwy., Ste. 250
Chantilly, VA 20151 US
Phone: 703-234-9810
Fax: 703-817-1595
E-mail Address: *mnorthern@wict.org*
Web Address: www.wict.org
Women in Cable & Telecommunications (WICT) exists to advance the position and influence of women in media through leadership programs and services at both the national and local level.

V.   Careers-First Time Jobs/New Grads

Black Collegian Home Page
140 Carondelet St.
New Orleans, LA 70130 US
Phone: 832-615-8871
E-mail Address: *stewart@imdiversity.com*
Web Address: www.black-collegian.com
Black Collegian Home Page features listings for job and internship opportunities. The site includes a list

of the top 100 minority corporate employers and an assessment of job opportunities.

Collegegrad.com
576 N. Washington Ave.
Cedarburg, WI 53012 US
Phone: 262-375-6700
Web Address: www.collegegrad.com
Collegegrad.com offers in-depth resources for new grads seeking entry-level jobs.

Job Web
62 Highland Ave.
Bethlehem, PA 18017-9085 US
Phone: 610-868-1421
Fax: 610-868-0208
Toll Free: 800-544-5272
Web Address: www.jobweb.com
Job Web, provided by the National Association of Colleges and Employers (NACE), includes job openings and employer descriptions. The site also offers a database of career fairs, searchable by state or keyword, with contact information.

MBAjobs.net
Fax: 413-556-8849
E-mail Address: *contact@mbajobs.net*
Web Address: www.mbajobs.net
MBAjobs.net is a unique international service for MBA students and graduates, employers, recruiters and business schools.

MonsterTrak
11845 W. Olympic Blvd., Ste. 500
Los Angeles, CA 90064 US
Toll Free: 800-999-8725
Web Address: www.monstertrak.monster.com
MonsterTrak features links to hundreds of university and college career centers across the U.S. with entry-level job listings categorized by industry. Major companies can also utilize MonsterTrak.

National Association of Colleges and Employers (NACE)
62 Highland Ave.
Bethlehem, PA 18017-9085 US
Phone: 610-868-1421
Fax: 610-868-0208
Toll Free: 800-544-5272
Web Address: www.naceweb.org
The National Association of Colleges and Employers (NACE) is a premier U.S. organization representing college placement offices and corporate recruiters

who focus on hiring new grads. The site offers in-depth resources.

VI.   Careers-General Job Listings

America's Job Bank
Toll Free: 877-348-0502
E-mail Address: *info@careeronestop.org*
Web Address: www.jobsearch.org
America's Job Bank was developed by the U.S. Department of Labor as part of an array of web-based job tools. It offers an extensive list of searchable employment vacancies as well as other job resources.

Career Exposure, Inc.
805 SW Broadway, Ste. 2250
Portland, OR 97205 US
Phone: 503-221-7779
Fax: 503-221-7780
E-mail Address: *info@careerexposure.com*
Web Address: www.careerexposure.com
Career Exposure is an online career center and job placement service, with resources for employers, recruiters and job seekers.

CareerBuilder
200 N. LaSalle St.
Chicago, IL 60601 US
Phone: 773-527-3600
Toll Free: 800-638-4212
Web Address: www.careerbuilder.com
CareerBuilder focuses on the needs of companies and also provides a database of job openings, called the Mega Job Search. Hundreds of thousands of job openings are posted. Resumes are sent directly to the company, and applicants can set up a special e-mail account for job-seeking purposes. CareerBuilder, Inc. is a joint venture of three newspaper giants: Knight Ridder, Gannett and Tribune Company.

Careers.wsj.com from the Publishers of the Wall Street Journal
P.O. Box 300
Princeton, NJ 08543-0300 US
Web Address: www.careers.wsj.com
The Wall Street Journal's interactive job search and career-management site posts job opportunities with employers worldwide. It provides a weekly career column and a range of articles about topics including promotion, career crisis and negotiation for higher wages.

HotJobs
44 W. 18th St.
New York, NY 10011 US
Phone: 646-351-5300
Fax: 212-944-8962
Web Address: hotjobs.yahoo.com
HotJobs, designed for experienced professionals, is a Yahoo-owned site that provides company profiles, a resume posting service and a resume workshop. The site allows posters to block resumes from being viewed by certain companies and provides a notification service of new jobs.

HRS Federal Job Search
Web Address: www.hrsjobs.com
HRS Federal Job Search features a database of federal jobs available across the U.S. The job seeker creates a profile with desired job type, salary and location to receive applicable postings by e-mail.

JobCentral
DirectEmployers Association, Inc.
9002 N. Purdue Rd., Quad III, Ste. 100
Indianapolis, IN 46268 US
Phone: 317-874-9000
Fax: 317-874-9100
Toll Free: 866-268-6206
E-mail Address: info@jobcentral.com
Web Address: www.jobcentral.com
JobCentral, operated by the nonprofit DirectEmployers Association, links users directly to hundreds of thousands of job opportunities posted on the sites of participating employers, thus bypassing the usual job search sites. This saves employers money and allows job seekers to access many more job opportunities.

LaborMarketInfo
7000 Franklin Blvd., Ste. 1100
Sacramento, CA 95823 US
Phone: 916-262-2162
Fax: 916-262-2352
Web Address: www.labormarketinfo.edd.ca.gov
LaborMarketInfo, formerly the California Cooperative Occupational Information System, is sponsored by California's Economic Development Office. The web site is geared to providing job seekers and employers a wide range of resources. It provides demographical statistics for employment on both a local and regional level, as well as career searching tools for California residents.

Mediabistro.com
494 Broadway, 4th Fl.
New York, NY 10012 US
Phone: 212-929-2588
Fax: 212-966-8984
E-mail Address: wecare@mediabistro.com
Web Address: www.mediabistro.com
Mediabistro.com offers an array of employment resources, including job listings in the media industry.

Monster
Toll Free: 800-666-7837
Web Address: www.monster.com
Monster is an electronic career center that hosts more than 8,000 employers and serves more than 18 million job seekers each month. Job seekers can build and store a resume online and find job listings that match their profiles. Monster e-mails the results once per week.

Recruiters Online Network
Web Address: www.recruitersonline.com
The Recruiters Online Network provides job postings from thousands of recruiters, Careers Online Magazine and a resume database, as well as other career resources.

TrueCareers, Inc.
Web Address: www.truecareers.com
TrueCareers, Inc. offers job listings and provides an array of career resources. The company also offers a search of over 2 million scholarship.

VII.   Careers-Job Reference Tools

Newspaperlinks.com
E-mail Address: sally.clarke@naa.org
Web Address: www.newspaperlinks.com
Newspaperlinks.com, a service of the Newspaper Association of America, links individuals to local, national and international newspapers. Job seekers can search through thousands of classified sections.

Vault.com
150 W. 22nd St.
New York, NY 10011 US
Phone: 212-366-4212
Web Address: www.vault.com
Vault.com is a comprehensive career web site for employers and employees, with job postings and valuable information on a wide variety of industries, although many of its features are geared toward

MBAs. The site focuses on helping the user understand what it's really like to work at a particular firm. The site offers a wide variety of industry guides for sale.

VIII.   Computer & Electronics Industry Associations

HomePlug Powerline Alliance
Web Address: www.homeplug.org
The HomePlug Powerline Alliance's goal is to promote standards-based home networks that utilize existing electrical wiring to carry signals between personal computers, entertainment systems and other home devices.

Multimedia Over Coax Alliance (MoCA)
Web Address: www.mocalliance.org
Multimedia Over Coax Alliance (MoCA)'s goal is to promote standards-based home networks that utilize coaxial cable to carry signals between personal computers, entertainment systems and other home devices. Membership consists of major electronics firms.

IX.   Corporate Information

bizjournals.com
120 W. Morehead St., Ste. 400
Charlotte, NC 28202 US
Phone: 704-973-1000
Fax: 704-973-1001
E-mail Address: *info@bizjournals.com*
Web Address: www.bizjournals.com
bizjournals.com is the online media division of American City Business Journals, the publisher of dozens of leading city business journals nationwide. It provides access to research into the latest news regarding companies small and large.

Business Wire
44 Montgomery St., 39th Fl.
San Francisco, CA 94104 US
Phone: 415-986-4422
Fax: 415-788-5335
Toll Free: 888-381-9473
Web Address: www.businesswire.com
Business Wire offers news releases, industry- and company-specific news, top headlines, conference calls, IPOs on the Internet, media services and access to tradeshownews.com and BW Connect On-line

through its informative and continuously updated web site.

Edgar Online
50 Washington St., 9th Fl.
Norwalk, CT 06854 US
Phone: 203-852-5666
Fax: 203-852-5667
Toll Free: 800-416-6651
Web Address: www.edgar-online.com
Edgar Online is a gateway and search tool for viewing corporate documents, such as annual reports on Form 10-K, filed with the U.S. Securities and Exchange Commission.

PRNewswire
810 7th Ave., 32nd Fl.
New York, NY 10019 US
Phone: 212-596-1500
Toll Free: 800-832-5522
E-mail Address: *information@prnewswire.com*
Web Address: www.prnewswire.com
PRNewswire provides comprehensive communications services for public relations and investor relations professionals ranging from information distribution and market intelligence to the creation of online multimedia content and investor relations web sites. Users can also view recent corporate press releases.

Silicon Investor
Web Address: www.siliconinvestor.com
Silicon Investor is focused on technology companies. The site serves as a financial discussion forum and offers quotes, profiles and charts.

X.   Economic Data & Research

STAT-USA
U.S. Department of Commerce
HCHB, Rm. 4885
Washington, DC 20230 US
Phone: 202-482-1986
Fax: 202-482-2164
E-mail Address: *statmail@esa.doc.gov*
Web Address: www.stat-usa.gov
STAT-USA is an agency in the Economics and Statistics Administration of the U.S. Department of Commerce. The site offers daily economic news, statistical releases, and databases relating to export and trade, as well as the domestic economy.

XI. Engineering, Research & Scientific Associations

Association of Federal Communications Consulting Engineers (AFCCE)
Cohen, Dippell and Everist, P.C.
1300 L St. NW, Ste. 1100
Washington, DC 20005 US
Web Address: www.afcce.org
The Association of Federal Communications Consulting Engineers (AFCCE) is a professional organization of individuals who regularly assist clients on technical issues before the Federal Communications Commission (FCC).

Audio Engineering Society, Inc. (AES)
60 E. 42nd St., Rm. 2520
New York, NY 10165-2520 US
Phone: 212-661-8528
Fax: 212-682-0477
Web Address: www.aes.org
The Audio Engineering Society (AES) provides information on educational and career opportunities in audio engineering.

Broadcast Technological Society (BTS) of the Institute of Electrical & Electronics Engineers, Inc.
445 Hoes Ln.
Piscataway, NJ 08854 US
Phone: 732-739-0282
E-mail Address: *a.monroe@ieee.org*
Web Address:
www.ieee.org/organizations/society/bt/index.html
The Broadcast Technological Society (BTS) is the arm of the Institute of Electrical & Electronics Engineers (IEEE) devoted to devices, equipment, techniques and systems related to broadcast technology.

Society of Broadcast Engineers, Inc. (SBE)
9247 N. Meridian St., Ste. 305
Indianapolis, IN 46260 US
Phone: 317-846-9000
Fax: 317-846-9120
E-mail Address: *mclappe@sbe.org*
Web Address: www.sbe.org
The Society of Broadcast Engineers (SBE) exists to increase knowledge of broadcast engineering and promote its interests, as well as to continue the education of professionals in the industry.

Society of Cable Telecommunications Engineers (SCTE)
140 Philips Rd.
Exton, PA 19341-1318 US
Phone: 610-363-6888
Fax: 610-363-5898
Toll Free: 800-542-5040
E-mail Address: *scte@scte.org*
Web Address: www.scte.org
The Society of Cable Telecommunications Engineers (SCTE) is a nonprofit professional association dedicated to advancing the careers and serving the industry of telecommunications professionals by providing technical training, certification and standards.

Society of Motion Picture and Television Engineers (SMPTE)
3 Barker Ave.
White Plains, NY 10601 US
Phone: 914-761-1100 ext. 4965
E-mail Address: *sdamato@smpte.org*
Web Address: www.smpte.org
The Society of Motion Picture and Television Engineers (SMPTE) is the leading technical society for the motion imaging industry.

XII. Entertainment & Amusement Associations

American Amusement Machine Association (AAMA)
450 E. Higgins Rd., Ste. 201
Elk Grove Village, IL 60007 US
Phone: 847-290-9088
Fax: 847-290-9121
Toll Free: 866-372-5190
E-mail Address: *information@coin-op.org*
Web Address: www.coin-op.org
The American Amusement Machine Association (AAMA) is an international nonprofit trade organization representing the manufacturers, distributors and suppliers of the coin-operated amusement industry.

Amusement and Music Operators Association (AMOA)
33 W. Higgins Rd., Ste. 830
S. Barrington, IL 60010 US
Phone: 847-428-7699
Fax: 847-428-7719
E-mail Address: *amoa@amoa.com*
Web Address: www.amoa.com

The Amusement and Music Operators Association
(AMOA) serves the global amusement, music,
entertainment and vending industries.

**Amusement Industry Manufacturers and
Suppliers, International (AIMS)**
1250 SE Port St. Lucie Blvd., Ste. C
Port St. Lucie, FL 34952 US
Phone: 772-398-6701
Fax: 772-398-6702
E-mail Address: *info@aimsintl.org*
Web Address: www.aimsintl.org
Amusement Industry Manufacturers and Suppliers
International (AIMS) is a nonprofit organization that
represents amusement industry manufacturers and
suppliers worldwide.

Entertainment Technology Center (ETC)
734 W. Adams Blvd., 3rd Fl.
Los Angeles, CA 90089-7725 US
Phone: 213-743-1600
Fax: 213-743-1803
E-mail Address: *info@etcenter.org*
Web Address: www.etcenter.org
The Entertainment Technology Center (ETC) exists
to discover, research, develop and accelerate
entertainment technology.

Game Manufacturers Association (GAMA)
280 N. High St., Ste. 230
Columbus, OH 43215 US
Phone: 614-255-4500
Fax: 614-255-4499
E-mail Address: *ops@gama.org*
Web Address: www.gama.org
The Game Manufacturers Association (GAMA) is an
international nonprofit trade association serving the
hobby games industry.

**Information Display and Entertainment
Association (IDEA)**
1990 E. Lohman Ave., Ste. 126
Las Cruces, NM 88001-3116 US
Toll Free: 888-832-4332
E-mail Address: *liz.brown@ideaontheweb.org*
Web Address: www.ideaontheweb.org
The Information Display and Entertainment
Association (IDEA) is a worldwide association of
electronic display system and scoreboard operators.

**International Association of Amusement Parks
and Attractions (IAAPA)**
1448 Duke St.

Alexandria, VA 22314 US
Phone: 703-836-4800
Fax: 703-836-9678
E-mail Address: *communications@iaapa.org*
Web Address: www.iaapa.org
The International Association of Amusement Parks
and Attractions (IAAPA) is dedicated to the
preservation and prosperity of the amusement
industry.

**International Association of Assembly Managers
(IAAM)**
635 Fritz Dr., Ste. 100
Coppell, TX 75019-4442 US
Phone: 972-906-7441
Fax: 972-906-7418
E-mail Address: *mike.meyers@iaam.org*
Web Address: www.iaam.org
The International Association of Assembly Managers
(IAAM) is an international trade organization
representing managers and suppliers of public
assembly facilities, such as arenas, amphitheaters,
auditoriums, convention centers/exhibit halls,
performing arts venues, stadiums and university
complexes.

International Laser Display Association (ILDA)
3721 SE Henry St.
Portland, OR 97202 US
Phone: 503-407-0289
E-mail Address: *david@laserist.org*
Web Address: www.ilda.wa.org
The International Laser Display Association (ILDA)
is a nonprofit organization dedicated to advancing the
use of laser displays in art, entertainment and
education.

International Special Events Society (ISES)
401 N. Michigan Ave.
Chicago, IL 60611-4267 US
Phone: 312-321-6853
Fax: 312-673-6953
Toll Free: 800-688-4737
E-mail Address: *info@ises.com*
Web Address: www.ises.com
The International Special Events Society (ISES) is a
society of special events professionals representing
the industry's diverse disciplines.

International Ticketing Association (INTIX)
330 W. 38th St., Ste. 605
New York, NY 10018 US
Phone: 212-629-4036

Fax: 212-629-8532
E-mail Address: *info@intix.org*
Web Address: www.intix.org
The International Ticketing Association (INTIX) is a nonprofit trade and professional organization for the admission services industry, representing professionals in the performing arts, theater, entertainment, professional sports and college and university athletics.

International Ticketing Association (ITA)
330 W. 38th St., Ste. 605
New York, NY 10018 US
Phone: 212-581-0600
Fax: 212-581-0885
E-mail Address: *info@intix.org*
Web Address: www.intix.org
The International Ticketing Association (ITA) advances the success of the admission service industry and its members.

National Association of Theater Owners (NATO)
750 First St. NE, Ste. 1130
Washington, DC 20002 US
Phone: 202-962-0054
Fax: 202-962-0370
E-mail Address: *nato@natodc.com*
Web Address: www.natoonline.org
The National Association of Theater Owners (NATO) represents 26,000 movie screens in all 50 U.S. states and 20 countries.

National Association of Ticket Brokers (NATB)
214 N. Hale St.
Wheaton, IL 60187 US
Phone: 630-510-4594
Fax: 630-510-4501
E-mail Address: *gadler@oconnorhannan.com*
Web Address: www.natb.org
The National Association of Ticket Brokers (NATB) is a nonprofit trade organization representing the ticket broker industry.

World Waterpark Association (WWA)
8826 Santa Fe Dr., Ste. 310
Overland Park, KS 66212 US
Phone: 913-599-0300
Fax: 913-599-0520
E-mail Address: *memberservices@waterparks.org*
Web Address: www.waterparks.org
The World Waterpark Association (WWA) is an international not-for-profit partnership of private and public water leisure facility owners, managers, suppliers and developers.

XIII.   Film & Television Resources

Baseline, Inc.
520 Broadway St., Ste. 230
Santa Monica, CA 90401 US
Phone: 310-393-9999
Fax: 310-393-7799
Toll Free: 800-858-3669
Web Address: www.baseline.hollywood.com
Baseline, Inc. offers baseline.hollywood.com, a B2B informational tool, serving and supporting those in the film, television, media and financial sectors of the entertainment industry.

Directors World
creativePLANET Communities
865 S. Figueroa St., Ste. 2330
Los Angeles, CA 90017 US
Phone: 213-228-0381
E-mail Address: *news@creativeplanet.com*
Web Address:
www.uemedia.com/CPC/directorsworld/
DirectorsWorld is an Internet community for film and video professionals providing daily information on the art, technology and business of directing.

IFILM
1024 N. Orange Dr.
Hollywood, CA 90038 US
Phone: 323-308-3400
E-mail Address: *feedback@ifilm.com*
Web Address: www.ifilm.com
IFILM is a leading broadband entertainment content network for consumers and marketers.

Independent Feature Project (IFP)
104 W. 29th St., 12th Fl.
New York, NY 10001-5310 US
Phone: 212-465-8200
Fax: 212-465-8525
E-mail Address: *webmaster@ifp.org*
Web Address: www.ifp.org
The Independent Feature Project (IFP) exists to facilitate the professional development and exhibition of new work from a diverse community of American filmmakers.

Internet Movie Database (IMDB)
Web Address: www.imdb.com

The Internet Movie Database (IMDB) provides excellent information on such topics as which movies grossed the highest box office revenues, in addition to production and cast details on thousands of movies and television shows. It is a unit of Amazon.com.

Kidon Media-Link
E-mail Address: *media-link@kidon.com*
Web Address: www.kidon.com/media-link
Kidon Media-Link provides newspapers, film, television, radio and other related media links divided by section and country.

Movieweb
E-mail Address: *support@movieweb.com*
Web Address: www.movieweb.com
Movieweb features links to studio web sites and tracks box office results.

Museum of Broadcast Communications (MBC)
400 N. State St., Ste. 240
Chicago, IL 60610 US
Phone: 312-245-8200
Fax: 312-245-8207
E-mail Address: *archives@museum.tv*
Web Address: www.museum.tv
The Museum of Broadcast Communications (MBC) is one of only two broadcast museums in America and offers visitors interactive exhibits on the history of radio and television.

Museum of Television and Radio (MT&R)
25 W. 52nd St.
New York, NY 10019 US
Phone: 212-621-6800
E-mail Address: *publicrelations@mtr.org*
Web Address: www.mtr.org
The Museum of Television and Radio (MT&R), with locations in both New York and Los Angeles, provides a historical look at the broadcasting industry.

Samuel French Theater and Film Bookshops
45 W. 25th St.
New York, NY 10010 US
Phone: 212-206-8990
Fax: 212-206-1429
E-mail Address: *info@samuelfrench.com*
Web Address: www.samuelfrench.com
Samuel French seeks out the world's best plays and makes them available to a wide range of producing groups.

SCREENSite
E-mail Address: *webmaster@screensite.org*
Web Address: www.screensite.org
SCREENSite is a resource center for film and TV scholarship with an archive of course syllabi, e-mail listings of media scholars, conference information, school listings and job list.

Screenwriters Online
E-mail Address: *tonyg12345@aol.com*
Web Address: www.screenwriter.com
Screenwriters Online is a web site offering information on screenwriting, scriptwriting and creative writing software, books, supplies and contests.

XIV. Film & Theater Associations

Academy of Interactive Arts & Sciences (AIAS)
23622 Calabasas Rd., Ste. 220
Calabasas, CA 91302 US
Fax: 818-876-0850
Toll Free: 818-876-0826 ext. 201
E-mail Address: *info@interactive.org*
Web Address: www.interactive.org
The Academy of Interactive Arts & Sciences (AIAS) is a nonprofit membership organization serving the interactive entertainment development community.

Academy of Motion Picture Arts and Sciences (AMPAS)
8949 Wilshire Blvd.
Beverly Hills, CA 90211-1972 US
Phone: 310-247-3000
Fax: 310-859-9619
Web Address: www.oscars.org
The Academy of Motion Picture Arts and Sciences (AMPAS) is a professional honorary organization, founded to advance the arts and sciences of motion pictures.

Alliance of Motion Picture and Television Producers (AMPTP)
15503 Ventura Blvd.
Encino, CA 91436 US
Toll Free: 818-995-3600
Web Address: www.amptp.org
The Alliance of Motion Picture and Television Producers (AMPTP) is the primary trade association with respect to labor issues in the motion picture and television industry.

American Cinema Editors (ACE)
100 Universal City Plaza
Verna Fields Bldg. 2282, Rm. 190
Universal City, CA 91608 US
Phone: 818-777-2900
Fax: 818-733-5023
Web Address: www.ace-filmeditors.org
American Cinema Editors (ACE) is an honorary
society of motion picture editors that seeks to
advance the art and science of the editing profession.

American Society of Cinematographers (ASC)
1782 N. Orange Dr.
Hollywood, CA 90028 US
Phone: 323-969-4333
Fax: 323-882-6391
Toll Free: 800-448-0145
E-mail Address: *office@theasc.com*
Web Address: www.theasc.com
The American Society of Cinematographers (ASC) is
a trade association for cinematographers in the
motion picture industry.

Art Directors Guild (ADG)
11969 Ventura Blvd., Ste. 200
Studio City, CA 91604 US
Phone: 818-762-9995
Fax: 818-762-9997
E-mail Address: *lydia@artdirectors.org*
Web Address: www.artdirectors.org
The Art Directors Guild (ADG) represents the
creative talents that conceive and manage the
background and settings for most films and television
projects.

**Association of Cinema and Video Laboratories
(ACVL)**
Web Address: www.acvl.org
The Association of Cinema and Video Laboratories
(ACVL) is an international organization whose
members are pledged to the highest possible
standards of service to the film and video industries.

**Association of Film Commissioners International
(AFCI)**
314 N. Main St.
Helena, MT 59601 US
Phone: 406-495-8040
Fax: 406-495-8039
E-mail Address: *info@afci.org*
Web Address: www.afci.org

The Association of Film Commissioners International
(AFCI) is an association of government film contacts
worldwide.

**Canadian Film and Television Production
Association (CFTPA)**
160 John St., 5th Fl.
Toronto, ON M5V 2E5 Canada
Phone: 416-304-0280
Fax: 416-304-0499
Toll Free: 800-267-8208
E-mail Address: *toronto@cftpa.ca*
Web Address: www.cftpa.ca
The mission of the Canadian Film and Television
Production Association (CFTPA) is to create a
favorable national and international environment for
the film industry and culture to prosper.

Casting Society of America (CSA)
606 N. Larchmont Blvd., Ste. 4-B
Los Angeles, CA 90004-1309 US
Phone: 323-463-1925
Fax: 323-463-5753
E-mail Address: *info@castingsociety.com*
Web Address: www.castingsociety.com
Casting Society of America (CSA) is an association
of casting professionals in film, television and
theater.

**Directors Guild of America, Inc. (Los Angeles
DGA)**
7920 Sunset Blvd.
Los Angeles, CA 90046 US
Phone: 310-289-2000
Fax: 310-289-2029
Toll Free: 800-421-4173
E-mail Address: *darrellh@dga.org*
Web Address: www.dga.org
The Directors Guild of America (DGA) seeks to
protect directorial teams' legal and artistic rights,
contend for their creative freedom and strengthen
their ability to develop meaningful and credible
careers.

Directors Guild of America, Inc. (New York DGA)
110 W. 57th St.
New York, NY 10019 US
Phone: 212-581-0370
Fax: 212-581-1441
Toll Free: 800-356-3754
E-mail Address: *darrellh@dga.org*
Web Address: www.dga.org

The Directors Guild of America (DGA) seeks to protect directorial teams' legal and artistic rights, contend for their creative freedom and strengthen their ability to develop meaningful and credible careers.

DirectorsNet
E-mail Address: *info@directorsnet.com*
Web Address: www.directorsnet.com
DirectorsNet is the home of creative professionals focused on motion picture, television, music videos, corporate video and commercial production.

Film Arts Foundation (FAF)
145 9th St., Ste. 101
San Francisco, CA 94103 US
Phone: 415-552-8760
Fax: 415-552-0882
E-mail Address: *info@filmarts.org*
Web Address: www.filmarts.org
The Film Arts Foundation (FAF) is a nonprofit leader in the media arts field, providing comprehensive training, equipment, information, consultations and exhibition opportunities to independent filmmakers.

Hollywood Post Alliance (HPA)
225 E. 9th St., Ste. 299
Los Angeles, CA 90015 US
Phone: 213-614-0860
Fax: 213-614-0890
E-mail Address: *ekramer@hpaonline.com*
Web Address: www.hpaonline.com
The Hollywood Post Alliance (HPA) is an organization dedicated to serving the entertainment technology industry by bringing together the post-production community.

Independent Film & Television Alliance (IFTA)
10850 Wilshire Blvd., 9th Fl.
Los Angeles, CA 90024-4321 US
Phone: 310-446-1000
Fax: 310-446-1600
E-mail Address: *info@ifta-online.org*
Web Address: www.ifta-online.org
The Independent Film & Television Alliance (IFTA), formerly the American Film Marketing Association (AFMA), is a trade association whose mission is to provide the independent film and television industry with high-quality, market-oriented services and worldwide representation.

International Alliance of Theatrical Stage Employees (IATSE)
1430 Broadway, 20th Fl.
New York, NY 10018 US
Phone: 212-730-1770
Fax: 212-730-7809
E-mail Address: *webmaster@iatse-intl.org*
Web Address: www.iatse-intl.org
The International Alliance of Theatrical Stage Employees (IATSE) is the labor union representing technicians, artisans and crafts workers in the entertainment industry, including live theater, film and television production and trade shows.

International Animated Film Society (ASIFA-Hollywood)
2114 Burbank Blvd.
Burbank, CA 91506 US
Phone: 818-842-8330
Fax: 818-842-5645
E-mail Address: *info@asifa-hollywood.org*
Web Address: www.asifa-hollywood.org
International Animated Film Society (ASIFA-Hollywood) is a nonprofit organization dedicated to the advancement of the art of animation.

International Documentary Association (IDA)
1201 W. 5th St., Ste. M320
Los Angeles, CA 90017 US
Phone: 213-534-3600
Fax: 213-534-3610
E-mail Address: *sandra@documentary.org*
Web Address: www.documentary.org
The International Documentary Association (IDA) is a nonprofit member service organization, providing publications, benefits and a public forum to its members for issues regarding nonfiction film, video and multimedia.

International Quorum of Motion Picture Producers
E-mail Address: *simona@playground-media.com*
Web Address: www.iqfilm.org
The International Quorum of Motion Picture Producers is a select group of filmmakers and video producers, representing 36 countries on six continents.

Motion Picture Association of America (MPAA)
15503 Ventura Blvd.
Encino, CA 91436 US
Phone: 818-995-6600
Web Address: www.mpaa.org

The Motion Picture Association of America (MPAA) serves as the voice and advocate of the U.S. motion picture, home video and television industries.

Motion Picture Editors Guild (MPEG)
7715 Sunset Blvd., Ste. 200
Hollywood, CA 90046 US
Phone: 323-876-4770
Fax: 323-876-0861
Toll Free: 800-705-8700
E-mail Address: *mail@editorsguild.com*
Web Address: www.editorsguild.com
The Motion Picture Editors Guild's (MPEG) web site provides an online directory of editors, a discussion forum and links to related magazines and other organizations that serve the motion picture industry.

National Film Board of Canada (NFB)
P.O. Box 6100
Station Centre-ville
Montreal, QC H3C 3H5 Canada
Phone: 514-283-9000
Fax: 514-283-7564
Toll Free: 800-542-2164
E-mail Address:
Web Address: www.nfb.ca
The National Film Board (NFB) of Canada is a public agency that produces and distributes films and other audiovisual works that reflect Canada to Canadians and the rest of the world.

National Film Preservation Board (NFPB)
Library of Congress (4690)
101 Independence Ave. SE
Washington, DC 20540 US
E-mail Address: *sleg@loc.gov*
Web Address: lcweb.loc.gov/film
The federally charted National Film Preservation Board (NFPB) seeks to preserve national film treasures.

National Film Preservation Foundation (NFPF)
870 Market St., Ste. 1113
San Francisco, CA 94102 US
Phone: 415-392-7291
Fax: 415-392-7293
E-mail Address: *info@filmpreservation.org*
Web Address: www.filmpreservation.org
The National Film Preservation Foundation (NFPF) is the nonprofit organization created by the U.S. Congress to save America's film heritage.

New York Screen Actors Guild (SAG New York)
360 Madison Ave. 12th Fl.
New York, NY 10017 US
Phone: 212-944-1030
Web Address: www.sag.org
The New York Screen Actors Guild (SAG New York) represents guild members in New York and serves as the east coast national headquarters.

Producers Guild of America (PGA)
8530 Wilshire Blvd., Ste. 450
Beverly Hills, CA 90211 US
Phone: 310-358-9020
Fax: 310-358-9520
E-mail Address: *info@producersguild.org*
Web Address: www.producersguild.org
The Producers Guild of America (PGA) is a nonprofit organization for career professionals who initiate, create, coordinate, supervise and control all aspects of the motion picture and television production processes.

Screen Actors Guild (SAG)
5757 Wilshire Blvd.
Los Angeles, CA 90036-3600 US
Phone: 323-954-1600
Fax: 323-549-6603
Toll Free: 800-724-0767
Web Address: www.sag.org
The Screen Actors Guild (SAG) represents its members through negotiation and enforcement of collective bargaining agreements that establish equitable levels of compensation, benefits and working conditions for performers.

Stuntmen's Association of Motion Pictures (SAMP)
10660 Riverside Dr., 2nd Fl., Ste. E
Toluca Lake, CA 91602 US
Phone: 818-766-4334
Fax: 818-766-5943
E-mail Address: *info@stuntmen.com*
Web Address: www.stuntmen.com
The Stuntmen's Association of Motion Pictures (SAMP) is a nonprofit organization of top stuntmen in the motion picture and television industries.

Sundance Institute
P.O. Box 3630
Salt Lake City, UT 84110-3630 US
Phone: 801-328-3456
Fax: 801-575-5175
E-mail Address: *press@sundance.org*

Web Address: www.sundance.org
The Sundance Institute is dedicated to the
development of artists involved in independent film
and the exhibition of their work.

Women In Film (WIF)
8857 W. Olympic Blvd., Ste. 201
Beverly Hills, CA 90211 US
Phone: 310-657-5144
E-mail Address: *info@wif.org*
Web Address: www.wif.org
Women In Film (WIF) strives to empower, promote
and mentor women in the entertainment,
communication and media industries through a
network of contacts, educational programs and
events.

XV.   Graphic Artists Associations

Graphic Arts Technical Foundation (GATF)
200 Deer Run Rd.
Sewickley, PA 15143 US
Phone: 412-741-6861
Fax: 412-741-2311
Toll Free: 800-910-4283
E-mail Address: *piagatf@piagatf.org*
Web Address: www.gain.net
Graphic Arts Technical Foundation (GATF) seeks to
reposition print media as an integral part of the
information technology sector.

Society of Illustrators (SI)
128 E. 63rd St.
New York, NY 10021-7303 US
Phone: 212-838-2560
Fax: 212-838-2561
E-mail Address: *info@societyillustrators.org*
Web Address: www.societyillustrators.org
The Society of Illustrators (SI) espouses concern and
support for its members and the well-being of the
illustration industry.

XVI.   Human Resources Industry Associations

Society of Human Resource Management (SHRM)
1800 Duke St.
Alexandria, VA 22314 US
Phone: 703-548-3440
Fax: 703-535-6490
Toll Free: 800-283-7476
Web Address: www.shrm.org

The Society of Human Resource Management
(SHRM) addresses the interests and needs of HR
professionals through its resource materials.

XVII.   Industry Research/Market Research

ACNielsen
770 Broadway
New York, NY 10003 US
Phone: 646-654-5000
Fax: 646-654-5002
E-mail Address: *globalc@acnielsen.com*
Web Address: www.acnielsen.com
ACNielsen provides market research, information
and analysis for a number of industries.

ACNielsen EDI
6255 Sunset Blvd., 19th Fl.
Hollywood, CA 90028 US
Phone: 323-860-4600
Fax: 323-860-4610
E-mail Address: *mike.marcell@nielsenedi.com*
Web Address: www.entdata.com
ACNielsen EDI provides the film industry with
instantaneous and comprehensive box office results.

Adams Media Research
27865 Berwick Dr.
Carmel, CA 93923 US
Phone: 831-624-0303
Fax: 813-624-2190
E-mail Address: *info@adamsmediaresearch.com*
Web Address: www.adamsmediaresearch.com
Adams Media Research is a media industry source of
market data and financial analysis in the filmed
entertainment and interactive media markets.

Forrester Research
400 Technology Sq.
Cambridge, MA 02139 US
Phone: 617-613-6000
Fax: 617-613-5200
Web Address: www.forrester.com
Forrester Research identifies and analyzes emerging
trends in technology and their impact on business.
Among the firm's specialties are the financial
services, retail, health care, entertainment,
automotive and information technology industries.

Marketresearch.com
38 E. 29th St.
New York, NY 10016 US
Phone: 212-807-2600

Fax: 212-807-2676
Toll Free: 800-298-5699
E-mail Address:
customerservice@marketresearch.com
Web Address: www.marketresearch.com
Marketresearch.com is a leading broker for
professional market research and industry analysis.
Users are able to search the company's database of
research publications including data on global
industries, companies, products and trends.

Plunkett Research, Ltd.
P.O. Drawer 541737
Houston, TX 77254-1737 US
Phone: 713-932-0000
Fax: 713-932-7080
E-mail Address: *info@plunkettresearch.com*
Web Address: www.plunkettresearch.com
Plunkett Research, Ltd. is a leading provider of
market research, industry trends analysis and
business statistics. Since 1985, it has served clients
worldwide, including corporations, universities,
libraries, consultants and government agencies. At
the firm's web site, visitors can view product
information and pricing and access a great deal of
basic market information on industries such as
financial services, InfoTech, e-commerce, health care
and biotech.

Reuters Investor
Web Address: www.investor.reuters.com
Reuters Investor is an excellent source for industry
and company reports written by professional stock
and business analysts. It also offers news and advice
on stocks, funds and personal finance, and allows
users to screen a database of major corporations and
view pertinent financial and business data on selected
firms.

Simba Information
60 Long Ridge Rd., Ste. 300
Stamford, CT 06902 US
Phone: 203-325-8193
Fax: 203-325-8915
E-mail Address: *info@simbanet.com*
Web Address: www.simbanet.com
Simba Information is a leading authority for market
intelligence and forecasts in all aspects of the media
industry.

XVIII. Internet Business/Technology

Association for Interactive Media
1430 Broadway, 8th Fl.
New York, NY 10018 US
Fax: 212-391-9233
Toll Free: 888-337-0008
Web Address: www.imarketing.org
The Association for Interactive Media is a nonprofit
association geared toward those using the Internet for
business purposes.

World Teleport Association (WTA)
55 Broad St., 14th Fl.
New York, NY 10004 US
Phone: 212-825-0218
Fax: 212-825-0075
E-mail Address: *wta@worldteleport.org*
Web Address: www.worldteleport.org
The World Teleport Association (WTA) is a
nonprofit trade association representing the key
commercial players in broadband.

XIX.   Internet Industry Associations

International Academy of Digital Arts and Sciences (IADAS)
41 Union Square W., Ste. 1131
New York, NY 10003 US
Phone: 212-675-3555
E-mail Address: *dmdavies@iadas.net*
Web Address: www.iadas.net
The International Academy of Digital Arts and
Sciences (IADAS) is dedicated to the progress of
new media worldwide.

World Wide Web Consortium (W3C)
Laboratory for Computer Science
32 Vassar St., Rm. 32-G515
Cambridge, MA 02139 US
Phone: 617-253-2613
Fax: 617-258-5999
Web Address: www.w3.org
The World Wide Web Consortium (W3C), housed at
the Laboratory for Computer Science on the MIT
campus, develops technologies and standards to
enhance the performance and utility of the World
Wide Web.

XX.   MBA Resources

MBA Association
E-mail Address: *info@mbaassociation.org*
Web Address: www.mbaassociation.org
The MBA Association aims to develop an exclusive
and unmatched online resource for the estimated 5
million MBA professionals around the world.

MBA Depot
1781 Spyglass Ln., Ste. 198
Austin, TX 78746 US
Phone: 512-499-8728
Fax: 847-556-0608
Toll Free: 888-858-8806
Web Address: www.mbadepot.com
MBA Depot is an online community for MBA
professionals.

XXI.   Media Associations-Educational

Center for Communication, Inc.
561 Broadway, Ste. 12-B
New York, NY 10012 US
Phone: 212-686-5005
Fax: 212-504-2632
E-mail Address: *info@cencom.org*
Web Address: www.cencom.org
The Center for Communication is a nonprofit
organization that encourages university students to
meet professionals in communications industries.

XXII.   Media Industry Information

BIA Financial Network, Inc.
15120 Enterprise Ct., Ste. 100
Chantilly, VA 20151 US
Phone: 703-818-2425
Fax: 703-803-3299
E-mail Address: *info@bia.com*
Web Address: www.bia.com
The BIA Financial Network offers merchant banking
and financial and strategic advisory services for
media, telecommunications and related industries.

Caslon Analytics Pty Ltd.
GPO Box 3239
Canberra, ACT 2601 Australia
Phone: 02-6262-5445
Fax: 02-6230-6265
E-mail Address: *info@caslon.com.au*
Web Address: www.caslon.com.au

Caslon Analytics Pty Ltd. Is a research firm with a
web site that offers a wealth of information on such
sectors as publishing, intellectual property and media
regulatory issues.

Ketupa.net
Caslon Analytics Pty Ltd
GPO Box 3239
Canberra, ACT 2601 Australia
Web Address: www.ketupa.net
Operated by research firm Caslon Analytics Pty Ltd.,
ketupa.net offers an abundance of historical research
data and timelines on major media sectors and
corporations.

SRDS Media Solutions
1700 Higgins Rd.
Des Plaines, IL 60018-5605 US
Phone: 847-375-5000
Fax: 847-375-5001
Toll Free: 800-851-7737
Web Address: www.srds.com
SRDS Media Solutions creates publications and
directories that unite the buyers and sellers of media
coverage throughout the nation.

Veronis Suhler Stevenson (VSS)
350 Park Ave.
New York, NY 10022 US
Phone: 212-935-4990
Fax: 212-381-8168
E-mail Address: *stevensonj@vss.com*
Web Address: www.vss.com
Veronis Suhler Stevenson (VSS) is a leading
independent merchant bank solely dedicated to the
media, communications and information industries.
Its web site offers a wealth of information about the
media industry.

XXIII. News Organizations

Associated Press (AP)
450 W. 33rd St.
New York, NY 10001 US
Phone: 212-621-1500
E-mail Address: *info@ap.org*
Web Address: www.ap.org
The Associated Press (AP) is the leading provider of
news services to newspapers, radio, television and the
World Wide Web.

XXIV. Printers & Publishers Associations

AcqWeb's Internet Directory of Specialty Publishers and Vendors
E-mail Address: *orkiszewskip@appstate.edu*
Web Address:
acqweb.library.vanderbilt.edu/pubr.html
This portion of AcqWeb, the directory of web resources for book buying professionals, provides an international directory of publishers and vendors used by libraries.

American Book Producers Association (ABPA)
160 5th Ave.
New York, NY 10010 US
Phone: 212-645-2368
Fax: 212-242-6799
Toll Free: 800-209-4575
E-mail Address: *office@abpaonline.org*
Web Address: www.abpaonline.org
The American Book Producers Association (ABPA) is the trade association for independent book producers in the U.S. and Canada.

Associated Collegiate Press (ACP)
2221 University Ave. SE, Ste. 121
Minneapolis, MN 55414 US
Phone: 612-625-8335
Fax: 612-626-0720
E-mail Address: *info@studentpress.org*
Web Address: www.studentpress.org/acp
The Associated Collegiate Press (ACP) is an organization of college media outlets, offering a forum for discussion, networking and awards for publications through different categories.

Association for Suppliers of Printing, Publishing and Converting Technologies (NPES)
1899 Preston White Dr.
Reston, VA 20191-4367 US
Phone: 703-264-7200
Fax: 703-620-0994
E-mail Address: *npes@npes.org*
Web Address: www.npes.org
The Association for Suppliers of Printing, Publishing and Converting Technologies (NPES) is a trade association for companies that manufacture and distribute equipment, systems, software and supplies used in printing, publishing and converting printed material.

Association of Alternative Newsweeklies (AAN)
1250 Eye St. NW, Ste. 804
Washington, DC 20005 US
Phone: 202-289-8484
Fax: 202-289-2004
E-mail Address: *web@aan.org*
Web Address: www.aan.org
The Association of Alternative Newsweeklies (AAN) is the trade organization for the alternative newspaper industry.

Association of American Publishers, Inc. (AAP)
71 5th Ave., 2nd Fl.
New York, NY 10003-3004 US
Phone: 212-255-0200
Fax: 212-255-7007
E-mail Address: *dhuntington@publishers.org.*
Web Address: www.publishers.org
The Association of American Publishers (AAP) is the principal trade association of the book publishing industry.

Printers & Publishers Associations
71 W. 23rd St.
New York, NY 10010 US
Phone: 212-989-1010
Fax: 212-989-0275
E-mail Address: *info@aaupnet.org*
Web Address: www.aaupnet.org
The Association of American University Presses (AAUP) is a nonprofit group of scholarly publishers.

Association of Education Publishers (AEP)
510 Heron Dr., Ste. 201
Logan Township, NJ 08085 US
Phone: 856-241-7772
Fax: 856-241-0709
E-mail Address: *mail@edpress.org*
Web Address: www.edpress.org
The Association of Education Publishers (AEP) supports the growth of educational publishing and its positive impact on learning and teaching. It tracks education and industry information and trends, provides professional development and promotes quality supplemental materials as essential learning resources.

Association of Free Community Papers (AFCP)
1630 Miner St., Ste. 204
Box 1989
Idaho Springs, CO 80452 US
Fax: 781-459-7770
Toll Free: 877-203-2327
Web Address: www.afcp.org

The Association of Free Community Papers (AFCP) represents publishers of more than 2,000 free-circulation community papers, reaching nearly 40 million homes weekly.

Book & Periodical Council (BPC)
192 Spadina Ave., Ste. 107
Toronto, ON M5T 2C2 Canada
Phone: 416-975-9366
Fax: 416-975-1839
E-mail Address: *info@freedomtoread.ca*
Web Address: www.freedomtoread.ca
The Book & Periodical Council (BPC) is the umbrella organization for associations involved in the writing, editing, publishing manufacturing, distribution, selling and lending of books and periodicals in Canada.

Book Industry Study Group, Inc. (BISG)
19 W. 21st St., Ste. 905
New York, NY 10010 US
Phone: 646-336-7141
Fax: 646-336-6214
E-mail Address: *info@bisg.org*
Web Address: www.bisg.org
Book Industry Study Group (BISG) is a nonprofit corporation examining the business of print and electronic media.

Book Manufacturers' Institute, Inc. (BMI)
2 Armand Beach Dr., Ste. 1B
Palm Coast, FL 32137-2612 US
Phone: 386-986-4552
Fax: 386-986-4553
E-mail Address: *info@bmibook.com*
Web Address: www.bmibook.com
The Book Manufacturers' Institute (BMI) is the leading nationally recognized trade association of the book manufacturing industry.

BookWire
R.R. Bowker
630 Central Ave.
New Providence, NJ 07974 US
Fax: 908-219-0073
Toll Free: 888-269-5372 ext. 0072
E-mail Address: *alex.stamatellos@bowker.com*
Web Address: www.bookwire.com
BookWire provides information on thousands of titles, authors and publishers, as well as offering news and bestseller lists.

Bowker
630 Central Ave.
New Providence, NJ 07974 US
Phone: 908-286-1090
Toll Free: 800-526-9537
E-mail Address:
Web Address: www.bowker.com
Bowker is a leading source for book, serial and publishing data serving library, publishing and bookselling professionals and their patrons worldwide. The company is also the steward of the U.S. International Standard Book Numbering (ISBN) Agency.

Center for Book Arts, Inc.
28 W. 27th St., 3rd Fl.
New York, NY 10001 US
Phone: 212-481-0295
E-mail Address: *info@centerforbookarts.org*
Web Address: www.centerforbookarts.org
The Center for Book Arts is dedicated to preserving the traditional crafts of book-making, as well as exploring and encouraging contemporary interpretations of the book as an art object.

City & Regional Magazine Association (CRMA)
4929 Wilshire Blvd., Ste. 428
Los Angeles, CA 90010 US
Phone: 323-937-5514
Fax: 323-937-0959
E-mail Address: *jdowden@prodigy.net*
Web Address: www.citymag.org
The City & Regional Magazine Association (CRMA) is dedicated exclusively to the interests and concerns of city and regional magazines.

Council of Literary Magazines & Presses (CLMP)
154 Christopher St., Ste. 3C
New York, NY 10014-9110 US
Phone: 212-741-9110
Fax: 212-741-9112
E-mail Address: *info@clmp.org*
Web Address: www.clmp.org
The Council of Literary Magazines & Presses (CLMP) serves the independent publishers of fiction, poetry and prose.

Evangelical Christian Publishers Association (ECPA)
9633 S. 48th St., Ste. 140
Phoenix, AZ 85044 US
Phone: 480-966-3998
Fax: 480-966-1944

E-mail Address: *info@ecpa.org*
Web Address: www.ecpa.org
The Evangelical Christian Publishers Association (ECPA) is an international, not-for-profit trade organization serving the Christian publishing industry by promoting excellence and professionalism, sharing relevant data, raising the effectiveness of member houses and equipping them to meet the needs of the changing marketplace.

Evangelical Press Association (EPA)
P.O. Box 28129
Crystal, MN 55428 US
Phone: 763-535-4793
Fax: 763-535-4794
E-mail Address: *director@epassoc.org*
Web Address: www.epassoc.org
The Evangelical Press Association (EPA) is a religious and educational nonprofit corporation that seeks to promote the cause of evangelical Christianity and enhance the influence of Christian journalism.

International Digital Enterprise Alliance (IDEAlliance)
1421 Prince St., Ste. 230
Alexandria, VA 22314-2805 US
Phone: 703-837-1070
Fax: 703-837-1072
E-mail Address: *info@idealliance.org*
Web Address: www.idealliance.org
The International Digital Enterprise Alliance (IDEAlliance) is a not-for-profit membership organization striving to advance user-driven, cross-industry solutions for all publishing and content-related processes by developing standards, fostering business alliances and identifying best practices.

International Newspaper Financial Executives (INFE)
21525 Ridgetop Cir., Ste. 200
Sterling, VA 20166 US
Phone: 703-421-4060
Fax: 703-421-4068
E-mail Address: *webmaster@infe.org*
Web Address: www.infe.org
International Newspaper Financial Executives (INFE) is a professional association serving the newspaper financial management community.

International Newspaper Marketing Association (INMA)
10300 N. Central Expy., Ste. 467
Dallas, TX 75231 US

Phone: 214-373-9111
Fax: 214-373-9112
Web Address: www.inma.org
The International Newspaper Marketing Association (INMA) is dedicated to strengthening the marketing of newspaper companies' products and approaching all activities with a global perspective.

International Prepress Association (IPA)
7200 France Ave. S, Ste. 223
Edina, MN 55435 US
Fax: 952-896-0181
Toll Free: 800-255-8141
E-mail Address: *info@ipa.org*
Web Address: www.ipa.org
The International Prepress Association (IPA) is a trade association consisting of the world's leading graphic communications and graphic arts supplier companies.

International Publishers Association (IPA)
Av. de Miremont 3
Geneva, 1206 Switzerland
Phone: 41-22-346-3018
Fax: 41-22-347-5717
E-mail Address: *info@ipa-uie.org*
Web Address: www.ipa-uie.org
The International Publishers Association (IPA) represents the publishing industry world-wide through 78 national, regional and specialized publishers associations in 65 countries.

International Publishing Management Association (IPMA)
710 Regency Dr., Ste. 6
Kearney, MO 64060 US
Phone: 816-902-4762
Fax: 816-902-4766
E-mail Address: *ipmainfo@ipma.org*
Web Address: www.ipma.org
The International Publishing Management Association (IPMA) is an exclusive not-for-profit organization dedicated to assisting in-house corporate publishing and distribution professionals.

International Regional Magazine Association, Inc. (IRMA)
E-mail Address: *us002848@mindspring.com*
Web Address: www.regionalmagazines.org
The International Regional Magazine Association (IRMA) exists to provide free and open communication among the publishers of North American regional publications.

Jewish Book Council (JBC)
15 E. 26th St.
New York, NY 10010 US
Phone: 212-532-4949 ext. 297
Fax: 212-481-4174
Web Address: www.jewishbookcouncil.org
The Jewish Book Council (JBC) publishes reviews
on books covering various topics of Jewish religion
and culture. Many reviews are available online.

Magazine Publishers of America, Inc.
810 7th Ave., 24th Fl.
New York, NY 10019 US
Phone: 212-872-3700
E-mail Address: *mpa@magazine.org*
Web Address: www.magazine.org
Magazine Publishers of America is the industry
association for consumer magazines.

Media Coalition, Inc.
139 Fulton St., Ste. 302
New York, NY 10038 US
Phone: 212-587-4025
Fax: 212-587-2436
E-mail Address: *info@mediacoalition.org*
Web Address: www.mediacoalition.org
Media Coalition is an association that defends First
Amendment rights to produce and sell books,
magazines, recordings, videotapes and videogames,
as well as to have access to the broadest possible
range of opinion and entertainment.

**National Association of Independent Publishers
Representatives (NAIPR)**
111 E. 14th St., PMB 157
Zeckendorf Towers
New York, NY 10003 US
Fax: 800-416-2586
Toll Free: 888-624-7779
E-mail Address: *greatblue2@rcn.com*
Web Address: www.naipr.org
The National Association of Independent Publishers
Representatives (NAIPR) is a trade association of
book publishers' commission representatives, book
publishers and other associate members.

**National Association of Printers & Lithographers
(NAPL)**
75 W. Century Rd.
Paramus, NJ 07652-1408 US
Phone: 201-634-9600
Fax: 201-986-2976
Toll Free: 800-642-6275

E-mail Address: *information@napl.org*
Web Address: www.napl.org
The National Association of Printers & Lithographers
(NAPL) focuses on helping graphic arts professionals
increase their expertise.

National Newspaper Association (NNA)
127-129 Neff Annex
University of Missouri-Columbia
Columbia, MO 65211-1200 US
Phone: 573-882-5800
Fax: 573-884-5490
Toll Free: 800-829-4662
E-mail Address: *briansteffens@nna.org*
Web Address: www.nna.org
The National Newspaper Association (NNA)
represents the owners, publishers and editors of
America's community newspapers.

National Press Foundation (NPF)
1211 Connecticut Ave. NW, Ste. 310
Washington, DC 20036 US
Phone: 202-663-7280
Fax: 202-530-2855
E-mail Address: *npf@nationalpress.org*
Web Address: www.nationalpress.org
The National Press Foundation (NPF) is an
organization offering issue-oriented professional
development programs and awards for journalists.

National Scholastic Press Association (NSPA)
2221 University Ave. SE, Ste. 121
Minneapolis, MN 55414 US
Phone: 612-625-8335
Fax: 612-626-0720
E-mail Address: *info@studentpress.org*
Web Address: www.studentpress.org/nspa
The National Scholastic Press Association (NSPA) is
an organization of student media outlets, offering a
forum for discussion, networking and awards for
publications through different categories.

Newspaper Association of America (NAA)
1921 Gallows Rd., Ste. 600
Vienna, VA 22182-3900 US
Phone: 703-902-1600
Fax: 703-917-0636
E-mail Address: *webmaster@naa.org*
Web Address: www.naa.org
The Newspaper Association of America (NAA) is a
nonprofit organization representing the newspaper
industry.

Newspaper Guild (The)
501 3rd St. NW, 6th Fl.
Washington, DC 20001 US
Phone: 202-434-7177
Fax: 202-434-1472
E-mail Address: *guild@cwa-union.org*
Web Address: www.newsguild.org
The Newspaper Guild exists to advance the economic
interests and improve the working conditions of its
members, raise the standards of journalism and ethics
in the industry and promote industrial unity.

**Organization for the Advancement of Structured
Information Standards (OASIS)**
630 Boston Rd., Ste. M-102
Billerica, MA 01821 US
Phone: 978-667-5115
Fax: 978-667-5114
Toll Free:
E-mail Address: *info@oasis-open.org*
Web Address: www.oasis-open.org
The Organization for the Advancement of Structured
Information Standards (OASIS) is a consortium
which drives the development and adoption of e-
business standards.

**Periodical & Book Association of America, Inc.
(PBAA)**
481 8th Ave., Ste. 826
New York, NY 10001 US
Phone: 212-563-6502
Fax: 212-563-4098
E-mail Address: *lscott@pbaa.net*
Web Address: www.pbaa.net
The Periodical & Book Association of America
(PBAA) is an organization that represents newsstand
publications to the retail community.

**Protestant Church-Owned Publishers Association
(PCPA)**
2850 Kalamazoo Ave. SE
Grand Rapids, MI 49560 US
Phone: 616-224-0795
E-mail Address: *mulder@pcpaonline.org*
Web Address: www.pcpanews.org
The Protestant Church-Owned Publishers
Association (PCPA) is an association of publishers
directly connected to their respective church
denominations and is devoted to the welfare of
official church-owned publishing houses.

Publishers Marketing Association (PMA)
627 Aviation Way

Manhattan Beach, CA 90266 US
Phone: 310-372-2732
Fax: 310-374-3342
E-mail Address: *info@pma-online.org*
Web Address: www.pma-online.org
The Publishers Marketing Association (PMA) is a
trade association of independent publishers.

Small Press Center (SPC)
20 W. 44th St.
New York, NY 10036 US
Phone: 212-764-7021
Fax: 212-354-5365
E-mail Address: *info@smallpress.org*
Web Address: www.smallpress.org
The Small Press Center (SPC) provides information
and draws public awareness to the offerings of
smaller, independent publishers.

Society for Scholarly Publishing (SSP)
10200 W. 44th Ave., Ste. 304
Wheat Ridge, CO 80033-2840 US
Phone: 303-422-3914
Fax: 303-422-8894
Web Address: www.sspnet.org
The mission of the Society for Scholarly Publishing
(SSP) is to facilitate learning, communication and the
advancement of appropriate technologies among
those involved in scholarly communication.

**Southern Newspaper Publishers Association
(SNPA)**
5775 Peachtree-Dunwoody Rd.
Bld. G, Ste. 100
Atlanta, GA 30342 US
Phone: 404-256-0444
Fax: 404-252-9135
E-mail Address: *edward@snpa.org*
Web Address: www.snpa.org
The Southern Newspaper Publishers Association
(SNPA) is a regional trade association representing
daily newspaper owners and publishers.

**Women's National Book Association, Inc.
(WNBA)**
2166 Broadway, Ste. 9-E
New York, NY 10024 US
Phone: 212-208-4629
Fax: 212-208-4629
E-mail Address: *publicity@bookbuzz.com*
Web Address: www.wnba-books.org

The Women's National Book Association (WNBA) is the oldest organization open to women and men in all occupations allied to the publishing industry.

World Association of Newspapers (WAN)
7 Rue Geoffroy St. Hilaire
Paris, 75005 France
Phone: 33-1-47-42-85-00
Fax: 33-1-47-42-49-48
E-mail Address: *contact_us@wan.asso.fr*
Web Address: www.wan-press.org
The World Association of Newspapers (WAN) groups 72 national newspaper associations, individual newspaper executives in 100 nations, 13 national and international news agencies, a media foundation and seven affiliated regional and worldwide press organizations.

Yellow Pages Association (YPA)
2 Connell Dr., 1st Fl.
Berkeley Heights, NJ 07922-2747 US
Phone: 908-286-2380
Fax: 908-286-0620
E-mail Address: *neg.norton@ypassociation.org*
Web Address: www.yppa.org
The Yellow Pages Association (YPA) leads, serves and helps to foster the global print and electronic media industry.

XXV. Recording & Music Associations

American Composers Alliance (ACA)
648 Broadway, Rm. 803
New York, NY 10012 US
Phone: 212-362-8900
Fax: 212-925-6798
E-mail Address: *info@composers.com*
Web Address: www.composers.com
The American Composers Alliance (ACA) is a membership organization serving professional composers of concert music in America.

American Federation of Musicians
1501 Broadway, Ste. 600
New York, NY 10036 US
Phone: 212-869-1330
Fax: 212-764-6134
Web Address: www.afm.org
The American Federation of Musicians (AFM) is the largest union in the world for music professionals.

American Society of Composers, Authors & Publishers (ASCAP)
1 Lincoln Plaza
New York, NY 10023 US
Phone: 212-621-6000
Fax: 212-724-9064
E-mail Address: *info@ascap.com*
Web Address: www.ascap.com
American Society of Composers, Authors & Publishers (ASCAP) is a membership association of U.S. composers, songwriters and publishers of every kind of music with hundreds of thousands of members worldwide.

Broadcast Music, Inc. (BMI)
320 W. 57th St.
New York, NY 10019-3790 US
Phone: 212-586-2000
Web Address: www.bmi.com
Broadcast Music, Inc. (BMI) is an American performing rights organization that represents songwriters, composers and music publishers in all genres of music.

Country Music Association, Inc. (CMA)
One Music Cir. S.
Nashville, TN 37203 US
Phone: 615-244-2840
Fax: 615-726-0314
Web Address: www.cmaworld.com
The Country Music Association (CMA) is a trade association dedicated to promoting and guiding the development of country music throughout the world.

International Association of Audio Information Services (IAAIS)
Toll Free: 800-280-5325
Web Address: www.iaais.org
International Association of Audio Information Services (IAAIS) is an organization that provides audio access to information for people who are print-disabled.

International Federation of the Phonographic Industry (IFPI)
54 Regent Street
London, W1B 5RE UK
Phone: 44 (0)20 7878 7900
Fax: 44 (0)20 7878 7950
E-mail Address: *info@ifpi.org*
Web Address: www.ifpi.org
The IFPI represents recorded music publishers worldwide in 75 countries. Its goals include the fight

against music piracy and the promotion of fair market access and adequate copyright laws. The IFPI publishes extensive studies yearly regarding its industry.

International Recording Media Association
182 Nassau St., Ste. 204
Princeton, NJ 08542 US
Phone: 609-279-1700
Fax: 609-279-1999
E-mail Address: *info@recordingmedia.org*
Web Address: www.recordingmedia.org
The International Recording Media Association is a worldwide trade association encompassing organizations involved in every facet of recording media.

Music Publisher's Association of the United States (MPA)
243 5th Ave., Ste. 236
New York, NY 10016 US
Phone: 212-327-4044
E-mail Address: *mpa-admin@mpa.org*
Web Address: www.mpa.org
The Music Publisher's Association of the United States (MPA) serves as a forum for publishers to deal with the music industry's vital issues and is actively involved in supporting and advancing compliance with copyright law, combating copyright infringement and exploring the need for further reform.

National Association of Recording Merchandisers (NARM)
9 Eves Dr., Ste. 120
Marlton, NJ 08053 US
Phone: 856-596-2221
Fax: 856-596-3268
Web Address: www.narm.com
The National Association of Recording Merchandisers (NARM) is a not-for-profit trade association whose member companies represent the retailers, wholesalers and distributors of prerecorded music in the U.S.

National Music Publisher's Association (NMPA)
711 3rd Ave.
New York, NY 10017 US
Phone: 212-834-0100
Fax: 646-487-6779
Web Address: www.nmpa.org
The National Music Publisher's Association (NMPA) works to interpret copyright law, educate the public

about licensing and safeguard the interests of its members.

Recording Academy (The)
3402 Pico Blvd.
Santa Monica, CA 90405 US
Phone: 310-392-3777
Fax: 310-399-3090
Web Address: www.grammy.com
The Recording Academy is the premier outlet for honoring achievements in the recording arts and supporting the music community. It is internationally known for the Grammy awards.

Recording Industry Association of America (RIAA)
E-mail Address: *webmaster@riaa.com*
Web Address: www.riaa.com
The Recording Industry Association of America (RIAA) is the trade group that represents the U.S. recording industry.

Society of Professional Audio Recording Services (SPARS)
9 Music Sq. S., Ste. 222
Nashville, TN 37203 US
Fax: 616-296-0386
Toll Free: 800-771-7727
E-mail Address: *spars@spars.com*
Web Address: www.spars.com
The Society of Professional Audio Recording Services (SPARS) is an organization for members of the recording industry to share practical business information about audio and multimedia facility ownership, management and operations.

Songwriters Guild of America
1500 Harbor Blvd.
Weehawken, NJ 07086 US
Phone: 201-867-7603
Fax: 201-867-7535
Web Address: www.songwriters.com
The Songwriters Guild of America is the nation's largest and oldest songwriters' organization, serving its members with information and programs to further their careers and understanding of the music industry.

XXVI. Retail Industry Associations

Video Software Dealer Association (VSDA)
16530 Ventura Blvd., Ste. 400
Encino, CA 91436-4551 US
Fax: 818-385-0567

Toll Free: 800-955-8732
E-mail Address: *vsdaoffice@vsda.org*
Web Address:
www.idealink.org/resource.phx/public/aboutvsda.htx
The Video Software Dealer Association (VSDA) is
the trade organization that represents the home video
entertainment industry.

XXVII.   Software Industry Associations

Entertainment Software Association (ESA)
575 7th St. NW, Ste. 300
Washington, DC 20036 US
E-mail Address: *esa@theesa.com*
Web Address: www.theesa.com
The Entertainment Software Association (ESA)
represents the entertainment software industry on
legislative issues.

XXVIII.   Sports Industry Resources

American Bar Association (ABA) Forum on the Entertainment & Sports Industries
321 N. Clark St.
Chicago, IL 60610 US
Phone: 312-988-5000
Web Address:
www.abanet.org/forums/entsports/home.html
The American Bar Association (ABA) Forum on the
Entertainment & Sports Industries, formed in 1977,
seeks to educate attorneys in the transactional and
legal principles of sports and entertainment law. The
forum's quarterly newsletter is directed toward
lawyers practicing entertainment, sports, arts and
intellectual property law.

XXIX.   U.S. Government Agencies

Bureau of Economic Analysis (BEA)
1441 L St. NW
Washington, DC 20230 US
Phone: 202-606-9900
E-mail Address: *customerservice@bea.gov*
Web Address: www.bea.gov/beahome.html
The Bureau of Economic Analysis (BEA), an agency
of the U.S. Department of Commerce, is the nation's
economic accountant, preparing estimates that
illuminate key national, international and regional
aspects of the U.S. economy.

Bureau of Labor Statistics (BLS)
2 Massachusetts Ave. NE

Washington, DC 20212-0001 US
Phone: 202-691-5200
Fax: 202-691-6325
Web Address: stats.bls.gov
The Bureau of Labor Statistics (BLS) is the principal
fact-finding agency for the Federal Government in
the field of labor economics and statistics. It is an
independent national statistical agency that collects,
processes, analyzes and disseminates statistical data
to the American public, U.S. Congress, other federal
agencies, state and local governments, business and
labor. The BLS also serves as a statistical resource to
the Department of Labor.

FCC-Common Carrier Bureau (CCB)
445 12th St. SW
Washington, DC 20554 US
Phone: 202-418-1500
Fax: 202-418-2825
Web Address: www.fcc.gov/wcb
The Common Carrier Bureau (CCB) is a unit of the
Federal Communications Commission (FCC). It is
responsible for administering the FCC's policies
concerning companies that provide wireline
telecommunications.

FCC-Mass Media Bureau
445 12th St. SW
Washington, DC 20554 US
Fax: 202-418-0232
Toll Free: 888-225-5322
E-mail Address: *mbinfo@fcc.gov*
Web Address: www.fcc.gov/mb
The Mass Media Bureau of the Federal
Communications Commission (FCC) regulates
broadcast television and radio stations in the United
States for the FCC.

Federal Ccommunications Commission (FCC)-Wireless Bureau
445 12th St. SW
Washington, DC 20554 US
Fax: 202-418-0710
Toll Free: 888-225-5322
Web Address: wireless.fcc.gov
The Wireless Bureau of the Federal Communications
Commission (FCC) handles nearly all FCC domestic
wireless telecommunications programs and policies.

Federal Communications Commission (FCC)
445 12th St. SW
Washington, DC 20554 US
Fax: 866-418-0232

Toll Free: 888-225-5322
E-mail Address: *fccinfo@fcc.gov*
Web Address: www.fcc.gov
The Federal Communications Commission (FCC) is an independent U.S. government agency established by the Communications Act of 1934, and charged with regulating interstate and international communications by radio, television, wire, satellite and cable.

Federal Communications Commission (FCC)-International Bureau
445 12th St. SW
Washington, DC 20554 US
Fax: 202-418-0232
Toll Free: 888-225-5322
Web Address: www.fcc.gov/ib
The International Bureau of the Federal Communications Commission (FCC) exists to administer the FCC's international telecommunications policies and obligations.

Federal Communications Commission (FCC)-Office of Engineering & Technology (OET)
445 12th St. SW
Washington, DC 20554 US
Fax: 202-418-0232
Toll Free: 888-225-5322
Web Address: www.fcc.gov/oet
The Office of Engineering & Technology (OET) unit of the Federal Communications Commission (FCC) evaluates technologies and equipment.

FedWorld
5285 Port Royal Rd.
Springfield, VA 22161 US
Phone: 703-605-6000
Web Address: www.fedworld.gov/jobs/jobsearch.html
FedWorld, a program of the U.S. Department of Commerce, provides an annotated index of links to job-, labor- and management-related U.S. government web sites. Employment opportunities, labor statistics and links to other government information sites are also offered.

Government Printing Office (GPO)
732 N. Capitol St. NW
Washington, DC 20401 US
Phone: 202-512-0000
Fax: 202-512-2104
E-mail Address: *contactcenter@gpo.gov*
Web Address: www.gpo.gov
The U.S. Government Printing Office (GPO) is the primary information source concerning the activities of Federal agencies.

U.S. Business Advisor
Web Address: www.business.gov
U.S. Business Advisor offers a searchable directory of business-specific government information. Topics include taxes, regulations, international trade, financial assistance and business development. U.S. Business Advisor was created by the Small Business Administration and an interagency task force.

U.S. Census Bureau
4700 Silver Hill Rd.
Washington, DC 20233 US
E-mail Address: *pio@census.gov*
Web Address: www.census.gov
The U.S. Census Bureau is the official collector of data about the people and economy of the U.S. It provides official social, demographic and economic information.

U.S. Copyright Office
101 Independence Ave. SE
Washington, DC 20559-6000 US
Phone: 202-707-3000
Web Address: www.copyright.gov
The U.S. Copyright Office promotes the progress of the arts and protection for the works of authors.

U.S. Department of Commerce (DOC)
1401 Constitution Ave. NW
Washington, DC 20230 US
Phone: 202-482-2000
Web Address: www.doc.gov
The U.S. Department of Commerce (DOC) regulates trade and provides valuable economic analysis of the economy.

U.S. Department of Labor (DOL)
Frances Perkins Building
200 Constitution Ave. NW
Washington, DC 20210 US
Toll Free: 866-487-2365
Web Address: www.dol.gov
The U.S. Department of Labor (DOL) is the government agency responsible for labor regulations. This site provides tools to help citizens find out whether companies are complying with family and medical-leave requirements.

U.S. Patent and Trademark Office (PTO)
Public Search Facility
Dulany St., 1st Fl.
Alexandria, VA 22314 US
Phone: 571-272-1000
Toll Free: 800-786-9199
Web Address: www.uspto.gov
The U.S. Patent and Trademark Office (PTO) administers patent and trademark laws for the U.S. and enables registration of patents and trademarks.

U.S. Securities and Exchange Commission (SEC)
100 F St. NE
Washington, DC 20549 US
Phone: 202-551-6551
E-mail Address: *help@sec.gov*
Web Address: www.sec.gov
The U.S. Securities and Exchange Commission (SEC) is a nonpartisan, quasi-judicial regulatory agency responsible for administering federal securities laws. These laws are designed to protect investors in securities markets and ensure that they have access to disclosure of all material information concerning publicly traded securities. Visitors to the web site can access the EDGAR database of corporate financial and business information.

White House (The)
1600 Pennsylvania Ave.
Washington, DC 20500 US
Phone: 202-456-1414
Fax: 202-456-2461
Web Address: www.whitehouse.gov
The White House site was designed for communication between the Federal Government and the American people. It provides access to all government information and services that are available on the Internet.

XXX. Wireless & Cellular Industry Associations

UWB Forum
c/o IEEE-ISTO
445 Hoes Lane
Piscataway, NJ 08854 US
Phone: 913-980-8781
E-mail Address: *info@uwbforum.org*
Web Address: www.uwbforum.org
The UWB Forum is comprised of over 100 companies committed to making ultrawideband technology a reality. The group is dedicated to ensuring that standards-based ultrawideband products from multiple vendors are interoperable. The Forum also facilitates the worldwide regulatory approval process for ultrawideband systems.

WiMedia Alliance
2400 Camino Ramon, Ste. 375
San Ramon, CA 948583 US
Phone: 925-275-6604
Fax: 925-275-6691
E-mail Address: *help@wimedia.org*
Web Address: www.wimedia.org
The WiMedia Alliance is an open, nonprofit wireless industry association that promotes the adoption and standardization of ultrawideband (UWB) worldwide.

XXXI. Writers, Photographers & Editors Associations

American Association of Sunday and Feature Editors (AASFE)
College of Journalism
1117 Journalism Bldg., University of Maryland
College Park, MD 20742-7111 US
Phone: 301-314-2631
Web Address: www.aasfe.org
The American Association of Sunday and Feature Editors (AASFE) is an international organization and a network of creative editors dedicated to the quality of features in newspapers and to the craft of feature writing.

American Medical Writers Association (AMWA)
40 W. Gude Dr., Ste. 101
Rockville, MD 20850 US
Phone: 301-294-5303
Fax: 301-294-9006
E-mail Address: *amwa@amwa.org*
Web Address: www.amwa.org
The American Medical Writers Association (AMWA) seeks to promote excellence in writing, editing and producing printed and electronic biomedical communications.

American Society of Journalists and Authors, Inc. (ASJA)
1501 Broadway, Ste. 302
New York, NY 10036 US
Phone: 212-997-0947
Fax: 212-937-2315
Web Address: www.asja.org
The American Society of Journalists and Authors (ASJA) is of the nation's leading organizations of independent nonfiction writers.

American Society of Magazine Editors (ASME)
810 7th Ave., 24th Fl.
New York, NY 10019 US
Phone: 212-872-3700
E-mail Address: *asme@magazine.org*
Web Address: www.magazine.org/editorial
The American Society of Magazine Editors (ASME)
is a professional organization for editors of print and
online magazines.

**American Society of Media Photographers
(ASMP)**
150 N. 2nd St.
Philadelphia, PA 19106 US
Phone: 215-451-2767
Fax: 215-451-0880
Web Address: www.asmp.org
The American Society of Media Photographers
(ASMP) is a trade organization that promotes
photographers' rights, educates photographers in
better business practices and produces business
publications for photographers.

American Society of Newspaper Editors (ASNE)
11690B Sunrise Valley Dr.
Reston, VA 20191-1409 US
Phone: 703-453-1122
Fax: 703-453-1133
E-mail Address: *asne@asne.org*
Web Address: www.asne.org
The American Society of Newspaper Editors (ASNE)
is an association that brings together editors of daily
newspapers and people directly involved with
developing content for daily newspapers.

Associated Press Sports Editors (APSE)
E-mail Address: *cgrimes@dallasnews.com*
Web Address: apse.dallasnews.com
Associated Press Sports Editors (APSE) is a trade
organization for professional sports reporters, editors,
copy editors and designers.

Association for Women in Sports Media (AWSM)
P.O. Box F
Bayville, NJ 08721 US
E-mail Address: *info@awsmonline.org*
Web Address: www.awsmonline.org
The Association for Women in Sports Media
(AWSM) is a global organization of over 600 women
and men employed in sports writing, editing,
broadcast and production, public relations and sports
information.

**Association of Writers & Writing Programs
(AWP)**
George Mason University, Mailstop 1E3
Fairfax, VA 22030-4444 US
Phone: 703-993-4301
Fax: 703-993-4302
Web Address: www.awpwriter.org
The Association of Writers & Writing Programs
(AWP) exists to foster literary talent and
achievement, to advance the art of writing as
essential to a good education and to serve the makers,
teachers, students and readers of contemporary
writing.

Authors Guild
31 E. 28th St., 10th Fl.
New York, NY 10016 US
Phone: 212-563-5904
Fax: 212-564-5363
E-mail Address: *staff@authorsguild.org*
Web Address: www.authorsguild.org
The Authors Guild is a society of published authors
and a leading advocate for fair compensation, free
speech and copyright protection.

Authors Registry, Inc.
31 E. 28th St., 10th Fl.
New York, NY 10016 US
Phone: 212-563-6920
Fax: 212-564-5363
E-mail Address: *staff@authorsregistry.org*
Web Address: www.authorsregistry.org
The Authors Registry is a nonprofit organization
formed to help expedite the flow of royalty payments
and small re-use fees to authors, particularly for new-
media uses.

Editorial Freelancers Association (EFA)
71 W. 23rd St., Ste. 1910
New York, NY 10010 US
Phone: 212-929-5400
Fax: 212-929-5439
Toll Free: 866-929-5400
E-mail Address: *info@the-efa.org*
Web Address: www.the-efa.org
The Editorial Freelancers Association (EFA) is a
national, nonprofit, professional organization of self-
employed workers in the publishing and
communications industries.

Education Writers Association (EWA)
2122 P St. NW, Ste. 201
Washington, DC 20037 US

Phone: 202-452-9830
Fax: 202-452-9837
E-mail Address: *ewa@ewa.org*
Web Address: www.ewa.org
The Education Writers Association (EWA) is the
national professional organization of education
reporters, offering seminars, fellowships, publications
and contests.

Football Writers Association of America (FWAA)
18652 Vista del Sol
Dallas, TX 75287 US
E-mail Address: *webmaster@sportswriters.net*
Web Address: www.footballwriters.com
The Football Writers Association of America
(FWAA) consists of North American journalists,
broadcasters and publishers who cover college
football. The FWAA also includes executives in all
areas that involve the game.

Garden Writers Association of America (GWAA)
10210 Leatherleaf Ct.
Manassas, VA 20111 US
Phone: 703-257-1032
Fax: 703-257-0213
Web Address: www.gwaa.org
The Garden Writers Association of America
(GWAA) is an organization of over 1,800
professional communicators in the lawn and garden
industry.

Horror Writers Association (HWA)
P.O. Box 50577
Palo Alto, CA 94303 US
E-mail Address: *hwa@horror.org*
Web Address: www.horror.org
The Horror Writers Association (HWA) is a
worldwide organization of writers and publishing
professionals dedicated to promoting the interests of
writers of horror and dark fantasy.

International Journalists' Network (IJNet)
International Center for Journalists
1616 H St. NW, 3rd Fl.
Washington, DC 20006 US
Phone: 202-737-3700
Fax: 202-737-0530
E-mail Address: *editor@icfj.org*
Web Address: www.ijnet.org
International Journalists' Network (IJNet) is an online
source for media news, journalism training
opportunities, reports on the state of media around
the world and media directories.

International Women's Writing Guild (IWWG)
Box 810, Gracie Station
New York, NY 10028-0082 US
Phone: 212-737-7536
Fax: 212-737-9469
E-mail Address: *dirhahn@aol.com*
Web Address: www.iwwg.com
The International Women's Writing Guild (IWWG)
is a network for the personal and professional
empowerment of women through writing.

Investigative Reporters & Editors (IRE)
138 Neff Annex, UMC School of Journalism
Columbia, MO 65211 US
Phone: 573-882-2042
Fax: 573-882-5431
E-mail Address: *info@ire.org*
Web Address: www.ire.org
Investigative Reporters & Editors (IRE) provides
educational services to reporters, editors and others
interested in investigative journalism.

**Media Communications Association International
(MCAI)**
2810 Crossroads Dr., Ste. 3800
Madison, WI 53718 US
Phone: 608-443-2464
Fax: 608-443-2474
E-mail Address: *info@mca-i.org*
Web Address: www.mca-i.org
The Media Communications Association
International (MCAI) is the leading global
community for media communications professionals
seeking to drive the convergence of communications
and technology for the growth of the profession.

Mystery Writers of America, Inc. (MWA)
17 E. 47 St., 6th Fl.
New York, NY 10017 US
Phone: 212-888-8171
Fax: 212-888-8107
E-mail Address: *mwa@mysterywriters.org*
Web Address: www.mysterywriters.org
Mystery Writers of America (MWA) is the premier
organization for mystery writers and other
professionals in the mystery field.

National Association of Black Journalists (NABJ)
8701 A Adelphi Rd.
Adelphi, MD 20783-1716 US
Phone: 301-445-7100
Fax: 301-445-7101
E-mail Address: *nabj@nabj.org*

Web Address: www.nabj.org
The National Association of Black Journalists
(NABJ) is an organization of journalists, students and
media-related professionals that provides quality
programs and services to and advocates on behalf of
black journalists worldwide.

**National Association of Hispanic Journalists
(NAHJ)**
1000 National Press Bldg.
529 14th St. NW
Washington, DC 20045-2001 US
Phone: 202-662-7145
Fax: 202-662-7144
Toll Free: 888-346-6245
E-mail Address: *nahj@nahj.org*
Web Address: www.nahj.org
The National Association of Hispanic Journalists
(NAHJ) is dedicated to the recognition and
professional advancement of Hispanics in the news
industry.

**National Association of Science Writers, Inc.
(NASW)**
P.O. Box 890
Hedgesville, WV 25427 US
Phone: 304-754-5077
Fax: 304-754-5076
E-mail Address: *info@nasw.org*
Web Address: www.nasw.org
The National Association of Science Writers
(NASW) exists to foster the dissemination of
accurate information regarding science through all
media devoted to informing the public.

**National Collegiate Baseball Writers Association
(NCBWA)**
5201 N. O'Connor, Ste. 300
Irving, TX 75039 US
E-mail Address: *rdanderson@c-usa.org*
Web Address: www.ncbwa.com
The National Collegiate Baseball Writers Association
(NCBWA) consists of writers, broadcasters and
publicists of college baseball in the U.S.

National Conference of Editorial Writers (NCEW)
3899 N. Front St.
Harrisburg, PA 17110 US
Phone: 717-703-3015
Fax: 717-703-3014
E-mail Address: *ncew@pa-news.org*
Web Address: www.ncew.org

The National Conference of Editorial Writers
(NCEW) strives to stimulate the conscience and
quality of editorial writing.

**National Federation of Abstracting & Information
Services (NFAIS)**
1518 Walnut St., Ste. 1004
Philadelphia, PA 19102-3403 US
Phone: 215-893-1561
Fax: 215-893-1564
E-mail Address: *nfais@nfais.org*
Web Address: www.nfais.org
The National Federation of Abstracting &
Information Services (NFAIS) serves groups that
aggregate, organize and facilitate access to
information and provides a forum for its members to
address common interests through education and
advocacy.

National Federation of Press Women (NFPW)
P.O. Box 5556
Arlington, VA 22205 US
Fax: 703-534-5751
Toll Free: 800-780-2715
E-mail Address: *presswomen@aol.com*
Web Address: www.nfpw.org
The National Federation of Press Women (NFPW) is
an organization of professional journalists and
communicators.

National Press Club (NPC)
529 14th St. NW
Washington, DC 20045 US
Phone: 202-662-7500
Web Address: npc.press.org
The National Press Club (NPC) provides people who
gather and disseminate news with a center for the
advancement of their professional standards and
skills, the promotion of free expression, mutual
support and social fellowship.

National Press Club of Canada
150 Wellington St.
Ottawa, ON KIP 5A4 Canada
Phone: 613-233-5641
Fax: 613-233-3511
E-mail Address: *manager@pressclub.on.ca*
Web Address: www.pressclub.on.ca
The National Press Club of Canada provides a
location for growth and discussion and a social home
for reporters, editors and others involved in the news
industry.

**National Press Photographers Association, Inc.
(NPPA)**
3200 Croasdaile Dr., Ste. 306
Durham, NC 27705 US
Phone: 919-383-7246
Fax: 919-383-7261
E-mail Address: *info@nppa.org*
Web Address: www.nppa.org
The National Press Photographers Association
(NPPA) is dedicated to the advancement, creation,
editing and distribution of photojournalism in all
news media.

**National Society of Newspaper Columnists
(NSNC)**
1345 Fillmore St., Ste. 507
San Francisco, CA 94115 US
Phone: 415-563-5403
Web Address: www.columnists.com
The National Society of Newspaper Columnists
(NSNC) provides a forum for newspaper columnists
to discuss the industry and common interests.

National Writers Union (NWU)
113 University Pl., 6th Fl.
New York, NY 10003 US
Phone: 212-254-0279
Fax: 212-254-0673
E-mail Address: *nwu@nwu.org*
Web Address: www.nwu.org
The National Writers Union (NWU) is a labor union
that represents freelance writers in all genres, formats
and media. It is committed to improving the
economic and working conditions of freelance
writers.

Outdoor Writers Association of America (OWAA)
121 Hickory St., Ste. 1
Missoula, MT 59801 US
Phone: 406-728-7434
Fax: 406-728-7445
Web Address: www.owaa.org
The Outdoor Writers Association of America
(OWAA) exists to improve the professional skills of
its members, set the highest ethical and
communications standards, encourage public
enjoyment and conservation of natural resources and
be mentors for the next generation of professional
outdoor communicators.

Overseas Press Club of America (OPCA)
40 W. 45th St.
New York, NY 10036 US

Phone: 212-626-9220
Fax: 212-626-9210
Web Address: www.opcofamerica.org
The Overseas Press Club of America (OPCA) is an
international association of journalists working in the
United States and abroad.

Poetry Society of America
15 Gramercy Park
New York, NY 10003 US
Phone: 212-254-9628
Web Address: www.poetrysociety.org
The Poetry Society of America provides a local
meeting place for poets and information regarding
readings, seminars, competitions, and other
resources.

**Reporters Committee for Freedom of the Press
(RCFP)**
1101 Wilson Blvd., Ste. 1100
Arlington, VA 22209 US
Phone: 703-807-2100
Toll Free: 888-336-4243
E-mail Address: *rcfp@rcfp.org*
Web Address: www.rcfp.org
The Reporters Committee for Freedom of the Press
(RCFP) is a nonprofit organization dedicated to
providing free legal help to journalists and news
organizations.

Romance Writers of America (RWA)
16000 Stuebner Airline Rd., Ste. 140
Spring, TX 77379 US
Phone: 832-717-5200
Fax: 832-717-5201
E-mail Address: *info@rwanational.org*
Web Address: www.rwanational.com
Romance Writers of America (RWA) is the
professional association for published and aspiring
romance writers.

**Science Fiction & Fantasy Writers of America,
Inc. (SFWA)**
P.O. Box 877
Chestertown, MD 21620 US
Web Address: www.sfwa.org
Science Fiction & Fantasy Writers of America
(SFWA) is an organization for writers in the science
fiction and fantasy genres, promoting dialogue and
furthering the rights of its members.

Society for Technical Communication (STC)
901 N. Stuart St., Ste. 904

Arlington, VA 22203 US
Phone: 703-522-4114
Fax: 703-522-2075
E-mail Address: *stc@stc.org*
Web Address: www.stc.org
Society for Technical Communication (STC) is a
membership organization dedicated to advancing the
art and science of technical writing.

**Society of American Business Editors & Writers
(SABEW)**
Missouri School of Journalism
134 Neff Annex
Columbia, MO 65211 US
Phone: 573-882-7862
Fax: 573-884-1372
E-mail Address: *sabew@missouri.edu*
Web Address: www.sabew.org
The Society of American Business Editors & Writers
(SABEW) is a not-for-profit organization of business
journalists in North America that promotes business
journalism through education.

Society of American Travel Writers (SATW)
1500 Sunday Dr., Ste. 102
Raleigh, NC 27607 US
Phone: 919-861-5586
Fax: 919-787-4916
E-mail Address: *satw@satw.org*
Web Address: www.satw.org
The Society of American Travel Writers (SATW)
promotes responsible journalism, provides
professional support and development for members
and encourages the conservation and preservation of
travel resources worldwide.

**Society of Children's Book Writers and
Illustrators (SCBWI)**
8271 Beverly Blvd.
Los Angeles, CA 90048 US
Phone: 323-782-1010
Fax: 323-782-1892
E-mail Address: *scbwi@scbwi.org*
Web Address: www.scbwi.org
The Society of Children's Book Writers and
Illustrators (SCBWI) serves people who write,
illustrate or share a vital interest in children's
literature.

Society of Environmental Journalists (SEJ)
P.O. Box 2492
Jenkintown, PA 19046 US
Phone: 215-884-8174

Fax: 215-884-8175
E-mail Address: *sej@sej.org*
Web Address: www.sej.org
The Society of Environmental Journalists (SEJ) seeks
to advance public understanding of environmental
issues by improving the quality, accuracy and
visibility of environmental reporting.

Society of Professional Journalists (SPJ)
3909 N. Meridian St.
Indianapolis, IN 46208 US
Phone: 317-927-8000
Fax: 317-920-4789
E-mail Address: *questions@spj.org*
Web Address: www.spj.org
The Society of Professional Journalists (SPJ) is
dedicated to the perpetuation of a free press.

**United States Basketball Writers Association
(USBWA)**
1818 Chouteau Ave.
St. Louis, MO 63103 US
E-mail Address: *webmaster@sportswriters.net*
Web Address: www.sportswriters.net/usbwa/
The United States Basketball Writers Association
(USBWA) is an organization representing writers
who follow college and high school basketball in the
U.S.

Western Writers of America, Inc.
1012 Fair St.
Franklin, TN 37064 US
Web Address: www.westernwriters.org
Western Writers of America, Inc. exists to promote
the literature of the American West.

Writers Guild of America East, Inc. (WGAE)
555 W. 57th St., Ste. 1230
New York, NY 10019 US
Phone: 212-767-7800
Fax: 212-582-1909
Web Address: www.wgaeast.org
The Writers Guild of America East (WGAE) is the
east coast branch of WGA, a labor union that protects
and defends the rights of television, radio and film
writers.

Writers Guild of America West, Inc. (WGAW)
7000 W. 3rd St.
Los Angeles, CA 90048 US
Phone: 323-951-4000
Fax: 323- 782-4800
Toll Free: 800-548-4532

Web Address: www.wga.org
The Writers Guild of America West (WGAW) is the
west coast branch of the WGA, a labor union that
protects and defends the rights of television and film
writers.

Chapter 4

THE ENTERTAINMENT 400: WHO THEY ARE AND HOW THEY WERE CHOSEN

Includes Indexes by Company Name, Industry & Location, And a Complete Table of Sales, Profits and Ranks

The companies chosen to be listed in PLUNKETT'S ENTERTAINMENT & MEDIA INDUSTRY ALMANAC comprise a unique list. THE ENTERTAINMENT 400 (the actual count is 393 companies) were chosen specifically for their dominance in the many facets of the entertainment and media industry in which they operate. Complete information about each firm can be found in the "Individual Profiles," beginning at the end of this chapter. These profiles are in alphabetical order by company name.

THE ENTERTAINMENT 400 companies are from all parts of the United States, Canada, Europe and beyond. Essentially, THE ENTERTAINMENT 400 includes companies that are deeply involved in the technologies, services and products that keep the entire industry forging ahead.

Simply stated, THE ENTERTAINMENT 400 contains 393 of the largest, most successful, fastest growing firms in entertainment and related industries in the world. To be included in our list, the firms had to meet the following criteria:

1) Generally, these are corporations based in the U.S., however, the headquarters of 61 firms are located in other nations.

2) Prominence, or a significant presence, in entertainment, media services and supporting fields. (See the following Industry Codes section for a complete list of types of businesses that are covered).

3) The companies in THE ENTERTAINMENT 400 do not have to be exclusively in the entertainment and media field.

4) Financial data and vital statistics must have been available to the editors of this book, either directly from the company being written about or from outside sources deemed reliable and accurate by the editors. A small number of companies that we would like to have included are not listed because of a lack of sufficient, objective data.

INDUSTRY LIST, WITH CODES

This book refers to the following list of unique industry codes, based on the 1997 NAIC code system (NAIC is used by many analysts as a replacement for older SIC codes because NAIC is more specific to today's industry sectors). Companies profiled in this book are given a primary NAIC code, reflecting the main line of business of each firm.

Entertainment & Hospitality

Toys, Sporting Goods & Miscellaneous Manufacturing
339000   Miscellaneous Manufacturing
Book & Magazine Distribution
422920   Books or Magazines Distribution
422921   Videos/Games/Software/Recorded Music Distribution
Publishing
511000   Publishing, General
511110   Newspapers, Publishing
511120   Magazines Publishing
511130   Books, Publishing
511140   Databases & Directories, Publishing
511191   Greeting Cards, Publishing
Film, Video & Music Recording
512110   TV/Video/Theatrical, Production
512131   Movie Theaters
512191   Film and Video Post-Production
512230   Music, Publishing
532230   Video Rental
Broadcasting
513111   Radio Broadcasting
513111A   Radio Broadcasting via Satellite
513120   Television Broadcasting
513210   Cable TV Networks
513220   Cable & Satellite TV & Data Service
Hotels & Accommodations
721110   Hotels/Resorts/Motels
721120   Casino Resorts
Entertainment Events & Sports
711211   Stadiums/Sports Teams
711310   Entertainment Events
Gambling & Recreation
713110   Theme Parks/Rides/Game Centers
713210   Casinos/Horse Racing, Gambling
713290   Gambling Equipment
713910   Golf Courses & Country Clubs
713920   Snow Skiing Facilities
713940   Fitness Centers/Health Clubs
713950   Bowling Facilities
713990   Games/Auto Racing/Misc. Recreation

	Food Service
722110	Restaurants

Financial Services

Financial Data
514100 Financial Data Publishing- Print & Online
Banking, Credit & Finance
522210 Credit **Card** Issuing
522220A Financing--Business
Credit Bureau
561450 Credit Bureau

InfoTech

Computers & Electronics Manufacturing
334110 Computer Networking & Related Equipment, Manufacturing
334310 Audio & Video Equipment, Consumer Electronics
Software
511202 Computer Software, Content & Document Management
511204 Computer Software, Operating Systems, Languages & Development Tools
511208 Computer Software, Games & Entertainment
511209 Computer Software, Multimedia, Graphics & Publishing
Information & Data Processing Services
514199 Online Publishing, Services & Niche Portals
514199B Search Engine Portals
514199C Recruiting & Job Services Online

Manufacturing

Food Products Manufacturing
311330 Chocolate & Confectionery Manufacturing
Beverage & Tobacco Manufacturing
312120 Beverages--Breweries
Printing Services
323000 Printing

Retailing

Computers & Electronics Stores
443110 Electronics, Audio & Appliance Stores
443110E Electronics, Audio & Appliance Stores-Online
Sporting Goods, Hobbies, Books & Music Stores
451120 Toys/Hobbies/Games Stores
451211 Book Stores
451211E Book Stores-Online
451220 Music Stores
451220E Music Stores-Online

Miscellaneous Retailers
453220 Gift/Sundry Stores
453990 Other Retailers, Misc. Retailers
Nonstore Retailers
454110A Direct Selling, Including Mail Order & Misc. Online
454110B TV Shopping

Services

Real Estate
525930 Real Estate Investment Trusts - REITs
Consulting & Professional Services
541800 Marketing Agencies & Related Services
541810 Advertising Services/Agencies
541810A Advertising/Marketing--Online
541850 Advertising, Display & Billboards
541870 Advertising Material Distribution Services
541910 Market Research
Management
551110 Management of Companies & Enterprises

Telecommunications

Telecommunications
513300A Telephone Service-Local Exchange Carrier & Diversified
Telecommunications
514191 Internet Access Provider

INDEX OF RANKINGS WITHIN INDUSTRY GROUPS

Company	Industry Code	2005 Sales (U.S. $ thousands)	Sales Rank	2005 Profits (U.S. $ thousands)	Profits Rank
Advertising Material Distribution Services					
DG FASTCHANNEL	541870	58,352	1	-1,216	1
Advertising Services/Agencies					
CLEAR CHANNEL OUTDOOR	541810	2,666,078	4	61,573	3
INTERPUBLIC GROUP OF COMPANIES INC	541810	6,270,000	3	-262,900	4
OMNICOM GROUP INC	541810	10,481,100	1	790,700	1
WPP GROUP PLC	541810	9,244,400	2	684,700	2
Advertising, Display & Billboards					
LAMAR ADVERTISING CO	541850	1,021,656	1	41,779	1
Advertising/Marketing--Online					
24/7 REAL MEDIA INC	541810A	139,794	1	38	2
DOUBLECLICK INC	541810A				
TRAFFIX INC	541810A	62,856	2	2,428	1
YAHOO! SEARCH MARKETING GROUP	541810A				
Agents, Performers, Models, Athletes					
CREATIVE ARTISTS AGENCY	711410				
ENDEAVOR AGENCY	711410				
FORD MODELS INC	711410				
IMG WORLDWIDE INC	711410				
INTERNATIONAL CREATIVE MANAGEMENT (ICM)	711410	140,000	1		
UNITED TALENT AGENCY INC	711410				
WILLIAM MORRIS AGENCY INC	711410				
Audio & Video Equipment, Consumer Electronics					
BOSE CORPORATION	334310	1,800,000	7		
CLARION CO LTD	334310	1,660,537	8	47,597	7
DIGEO INC	334310				
DIGITAL VIDEO SYSTEMS INC	334310				
DOLBY LABORATORIES INC	334310	327,967	10	52,293	6
DTS INC	334310	75,252	13	7,908	8
LOUD TECHNOLOGIES INC	334310	204,328	11	3,757	9
MATSUSHITA ELECTRIC INDUSTRIAL CO LTD	334310	81,298,000	1	546,000	4
OMNIVISION TECHNOLOGIES	334310	388,062	9	76,387	5
PIONEER CORPORATION	334310	6,906,476	6	-82,140	13
SAMSUNG ELECTRONICS CO	334310	56,720,306	3	7,542,165	1
SANYO ELECTRIC COMPANY	334310	24,173,700	4	-1,603,200	14
SHARP CORPORATION	334310	23,960,934	5	724,953	3
SONY CORPORATION	334310	66,912,000	2	1,531,000	2
SRS LABS INC	334310	23,228	15	-1,424	10
TIVO INC	334310	172,055	12	-79,842	12
TRANS-LUX CORPORATION	334310	54,368	14	-1,793	11
Beverages--Breweries					
ANHEUSER BUSCH COS INC	312120	15,035,700	1	1,839,200	1

Company	Industry Code	2005 Sales (U.S. $ thousands)	Sales Rank	2005 Profits (U.S. $ thousands)	Profits Rank
Book Stores					
BARNES & NOBLE INC	451211	4,873,595	1	143,376	1
BOOKS A MILLION INC	451211	474,099	3	10,199	3
BORDERS GROUP INC	451211	3,879,500	2	131,900	2
Book Stores-Online					
AMAZON.COM INC	451211E	8,490,000	1	359,000	1
BARNESANDNOBLE.COM INC	451211E	419,800	2		
Books or Magazines Distribution					
ADVANCED MARKETING SERVICES INC	422920	915,000	2		
ANDERSON NEWS LLC	422920	2,696,000	1		
EBSCO INDUSTRIES INC	422920				
Books, Publishing					
EDUCATIONAL DEVELOPMENT	511130	31,651	9	2,406	6
HARPERCOLLINS PUBLISHERS	511130				
HOUGHTON MIFFLIN CO	511130	1,282,100	5	-56,300	7
JOHN WILEY & SONS INC	511130	974,048	6	83,841	3
LERNER PUBLISHING GROUP	511130				
MARVEL ENTERTAINMENT INC	511130	390,507	7	102,819	2
MCGRAW HILL COS INC	511130	6,003,642	2	844,306	1
PEARSON PLC	511130	7,045,000	1		
RANDOM HOUSE INC	511130	2,185,200	3		
SCHOLASTIC CORP	511130	2,079,900	4	64,300	4
SIMON & SCHUSTER INC	511130				
THOMAS NELSON INC	511130	237,817	8	19,817	5
Bowling Facilities					
AMF BOWLING WORLDWIDE	713950	569,578	1	-10,698	1
Cable & Satellite TV & Data Service					
BRITISH SKY BROADCASTING	513220	7,526,750	6	1,132,340	3
CABLEVISION SYSTEMS CORP	513220	5,175,911	10	94,300	10
CHARTER COMMUNICATIONS	513220	5,254,000	9	-967,000	22
COMCAST CORP	513220	22,300,000	2	928,000	4
COX COMMUNICATIONS INC	513220	6,722,300	7	-230,700	20
DIRECTV GROUP INC	513220	13,164,500	3	335,900	8
ECHOSTAR COMMUNICATIONS	513220	8,425,501	5	1,514,540	2
I-CABLE COMMUNICATIONS	513220	314,799	20	67,988	12
INSIGHT COMMUNICATIONS	513220	1,117,681	16	-84,929	18
ITV PLC	513220	3,796,687	12	394,144	7
KNOLOGY INC	513220	230,857	22	-55,402	16
LIBERTY GLOBAL	513220	5,151,332	11	-80,097	17
LODGENET ENTERTAINMENT	513220	275,771	21	-6,959	14
MATAV-CABLE SYSTEMS MEDIA	513220				
MEDIACOM COMMUNICATIONS	513220	1,098,822	17	-222,228	19
NASPERS LIMITED	513220	2,243,200	14	417,800	6
NTL INCORPORATED	513220	3,402,304	13	735,411	5
ON COMMAND CORP	513220				
PANAMSAT CORP	513220	861,003	18	72,729	11
PRIMACOM AG	513220	156,060	23	-316,700	21
ROGERS COMMUNICATIONS	513220	6,389,571	8	-38,136	15

Company	Industry Code	2005 Sales (U.S. $ thousands)	Sales Rank	2005 Profits (U.S. $ thousands)	Profits Rank
SHAW COMMUNICATIONS INC	513220	1,861,800	15	135,300	9
SKY NETWORK TELEVISION	513220	347,306	19	56,002	13
SUDDENLINK COMMUNICATIONS	513220				
TELEWEST GLOBAL INC	513220				
TIME WARNER CABLE	513220	9,498,000	4		
TIME WARNER INC	513220	43,652,000	1	2,905,000	1
Cable TV Networks					
A&E TELEVISION NETWORKS	513210	625,000	9		
CABLE NEWS NETWORK LP	513210	794,000	8		
CROWN MEDIA HOLDINGS INC	513210	197,384	10	-232,758	4
CW NETWORK	513210				
DISCOVERY COMMUNICATIONS	513210	2,700,000	6		
ESPN INC	513210	4,031,000	5		
FOX BROADCASTING COMPANY	513210	2,624,000	7		
FOX SPORTS NET INC	513210				
MTV NETWORKS	513210				
NBC UNIVERSAL	513210	14,689,000	2	3,092,000	1
RAINBOW MEDIA HOLDINGS	513210				
TURNER BROADCASTING SYSTEM	513210	9,611,000	3		
UNITED PARAMOUNT NETWORK (UPN)	513210				
VIACOM INC	513210	9,609,600	4	1,256,900	3
WALT DISNEY COMPANY	513210	31,944,000	1	2,533,000	2
Casino Resorts					
AMERISTAR CASINOS INC	721120	961,358	7	66,285	7
AZTAR CORP	721120	915,442	8	55,960	8
BOYD GAMING CORP	721120	2,471,003	3	144,610	6
CAESARS ENTERTAINMENT	721120				
DIAMONDHEAD CASINO CORP	721120			-642	14
HARRAH'S ENTERTAINMENT	721120	7,111,000	1	236,400	4
KERZNER INTERNATIONAL LIMITED	721120	721,524	11	50,648	9
LAS VEGAS SANDS CORP (THE VENETIAN)	721120	1,824,225	4	283,686	2
MGM MIRAGE	721120	6,481,967	2	443,256	1
MONARCH CASINO & RESORT	721120	139,785	14	21,035	10
MTR GAMING GROUP INC	721120	358,295	12	7,769	11
PINNACLE ENTERTAINMENT	721120	725,900	9	6,125	12
RIVIERA HOLDINGS CORP	721120	202,227	13	-3,999	15
SANDS REGENT	721120	81,132	15	3,831	13
STATION CASINOS INC	721120	1,108,833	5	161,886	5
TRUMP ENTERTAINMENT RESORTS INC	721120	992,221	6	251,856	3
WYNN RESORTS LIMITED	721120	721,981	10	-90,836	16
Casinos/Horse Racing, Gambling					
CANTERBURY PARK HOLDING	713210	55,223	8	3,053	7
CENTURY CASINOS INC	713210	37,445	9	4,481	6
CHURCHILL DOWNS INC	713210	408,801	5	78,908	2
DOVER DOWNS GAMING & ENTERTAINMENT INC	713210	216,852	6	26,040	3
ISLE OF CAPRI CASINOS INC	713210	947,572	3	18,038	4

Company	Industry Code	2005 Sales (U.S. $ thousands)	Sales Rank	2005 Profits (U.S. $ thousands)	Profits Rank
LAKES ENTERTAINMENT INC	713210	18,222	11	-11,870	9
MAGNA ENTERTAINMENT	713210	624,655	4	-105,293	10
PENN NATIONAL GAMING INC	713210	1,412,466	1	120,930	1
RANK GROUP PLC	713210	1,408,887	2	-362,519	11
TRANS WORLD CORP	713210	23,249	10	79	8
YOUBET.COM INC	713210	88,837	7	5,691	5
Chocolate & Confectionery Manufacturing					
HERSHEY CO	311330	4,836,000	1	493,200	1
Computer Hardware, Manufacturing					
APPLE INC	334111	13,931,000	1	1,328,000	1
CONCURRENT COMPUTER	334111	78,685	3	-7,729	3
NINTENDO CO LTD	334111	4,788,400	2	812,800	2
Computer Software, Content & Document Management					
MACROVISION CORP	511202	203,230	1	22,115	1
Computer Software, Electronic Games & Entertainment					
ACTIVISION INC	511208	1,405,857	3	138,335	3
BIOWARE CORP	511208				
CONCRETE SOFTWARE INC	511208				
DIGITAL BRIDGES LIMITED	511208				
ELECTRONIC ARTS INC	511208	3,129,000	2	504,000	1
GLU MOBILE	511208				
HANDS-ON MOBILE	511208				
LUCASARTS ENTERTAINMENT COMPANY LLC	511208				
MIDWAY GAMES INC	511208	150,078	8	-112,487	9
NTN BUZZTIME INC	511208	40,759	9	-2,019	8
SEGA SAMMY HOLDINGS INC	511208	4,340,090	1	425,650	2
SHANDA INTERACTIVE ENTERTAINMENT LIMITED	511208	235,014	7	20,480	7
TAKE-TWO INTERACTIVE SOFTWARE INC	511208	1,202,595	4	37,475	6
THQ INC	511208	756,731	6	62,790	4
VINDIGO INC	511208				
VIVENDI GAMES	511208	770,688	5	49,295	5
Computer Software, Multimedia, Graphics & Publishing					
AVID TECHNOLOGY INC	511209	775,400	1	34,000	2
INTERVIDEO INC	511209	109,229	3	3,583	3
REALNETWORKS INC	511209	325,059	2	312,345	1
Computer Software, Operating Systems, Languages & Development Tools					
MICROSOFT CORP	511204	39,788,000	1	12,254,000	1
Credit Bureau					
DUN & BRADSTREET CORP (THE, D&B)	561450	1,443,600	2	242,000	2
MOODY'S CORPORATION	561450	1,731,600	1	560,800	1
Credit Card Issuing					
AMERICAN EXPRESS CO	522210	24,300,000	1	3,734,000	1
Databases & Directories, Publishing					
DAG MEDIA INC	511140	4,447	3	-511	3
PROQUEST COMPANY	511140				
REED ELSEVIER GROUP PLC	511140	8,982,132	1	806,719	2

Company	Industry Code	2005 Sales (U.S. $ thousands)	Sales Rank	2005 Profits (U.S. $ thousands)	Profits Rank
THOMSON CORPORATION	511140	8,703,000	2	934,000	1
Direct Selling, Including Mail Order & Misc. Online					
TICKETMASTER	454110A	950,200	1		
Electronics, Audio & Appliance Stores					
BEST BUY CO INC	443110	27,433,000	1	984,000	1
CIRCUIT CITY STORES INC	443110	10,472,364	2	61,658	3
HARVEY ELECTRONICS INC	443110	40,400	7	-800	5
INTERTAN CANADA LTD	443110	454,900	5		
RADIOSHACK CORPORATION	443110	5,081,700	3	267,000	2
REX STORES CORP	443110	379,023	6	27,549	4
TWEETER HOME ENTERTAINMENT GROUP INC	443110	795,090	4	-74,353	6
Electronics, Audio & Appliance Stores-Online					
BUY.COM INC	443110E				
Entertainment Events					
LIVE NATION INC	711310	2,936,845	1	-130,619	1
RENAISSANCE ENTERTAINMENT	711310				
Film & Video Post-Production					
ASCENT MEDIA GROUP INC	512191	697,700	1		
LASERPACIFIC MEDIA CORP	512191				
Financial Data Publishing-Print & Online					
BLOOMBERG LP	514100	4,100,000	2		
INTERACTIVE DATA CORP	514100	542,867	3	93,864	2
MARKETWATCH INC	514100	50,000	5		
REUTERS GROUP PLC	514100	4,189,700	1	838,391	1
VALUE LINE INC	514100	84,478	4	21,318	3
Financing--Business					
GENERAL ELECTRIC CO (GE)	522220A	149,702,000	1	18,275,000	1
Fitness Centers/Health Clubs					
24 HOUR FITNESS USA	713940				
BALLY TOTAL FITNESS HOLDING CORPORATION	713940	1,071,033	1	-9,614	1
CURVES INTERNATIONAL INC	713940				
GOLD'S GYM INTERNATIONAL	713940				
Gambling Equipment					
AMERICAN WAGERING INC	713290	11,108	12	-1,128	10
ARISTOCRAT LEISURE LTD	713290	920,683	3	173,523	3
BALLY TECHNOLOGIES INC	713290	484,030	5	-20,317	13
GAMETECH INTERNATIONAL	713290	49,651	11	1,336	9
GAMING PARTNERS INTERNATIONAL CORP	713290	57,121	10	4,328	8
GTECH HOLDINGS CORP	713290	1,257,235	2	196,394	2
INTERNATIONAL GAME TECHNOLOGY	713290	2,379,400	1	436,500	1
INTERNATIONAL LOTTERY & TOTALIZATOR SYSTEMS	713290	9,666	13	-1,762	11
MULTIMEDIA GAMES INC	713290	153,216	7	17,643	7
PROGRESSIVE GAMING INTERNATIONAL CORP	713290	78,221	9	-5,983	12
SCIENTIFIC GAMES CORP	713290	781,683	4	75,319	4

Company	Industry Code	2005 Sales (U.S. $ thousands)	Sales Rank	2005 Profits (U.S. $ thousands)	Profits Rank
SHUFFLE MASTER INC	713290	112,860	8	29,180	5
WMS INDUSTRIES INC	713290	388,400	6	21,200	6
Games/Misc. Recreation Items					
AMERICAN COIN MERCHANDISING INC	713990				
Gift/Sundry Stores					
DELAWARE NORTH COMPANIES	453220	2,000,000	1		
Golf Courses & Country Clubs					
AMERICAN GOLF INC	713910				
CLUBCORP INC	713910	1,028,088	1	70,754	1
Greeting Cards, Publishing					
AMERICAN GREETINGS CORP	511191	1,883,367	2	95,279	1
HALLMARK CARDS INC	511191	4,200,000	1		
Hotels/Resorts/Motels					
GAYLORD ENTERTAINMENT	721110	868,789	1	21,033	1
Internet Access Provider					
AOL LLC	514191	8,300,000	1		
UNITED ONLINE INC	514191	525,100	2	47,100	1
Magazines, Publishing					
ADVANCE PUBLICATIONS INC	511120	7,315,000	1		
CONDE NAST PUBLICATIONS	511120				
DENNIS PUBLISHING LTD	511120	106,100	16	-300	6
EMAP PLC	511120	2,006,500	4	103,300	4
FORBES INC	511120	450,000	10		
JOHNSON PUBLISHING COMPANY INC	511120	495,700	9		
LAGARDERE ACTIVE MEDIA	511120				
MARTHA STEWART LIVING OMNIMEDIA INC	511120	209,462	13	-75,789	9
MEREDITH CORP	511120	1,221,289	5	129,042	3
PENTON MEDIA INC	511120	192,847	14	-8,422	8
PLAYBOY ENTERPRISES INC	511120	338,153	12	-735	7
PRIMEDIA INC	511120	990,500	7	564,600	2
READER'S DIGEST ASSOCIATION INC	511120	2,389,700	3	-90,900	10
RODALE INC	511120	500,000	8		
TIME INC	511120	5,846,000	2		
TRADER CLASSIFIED MEDIA NV	511120	372,323	11	15,277	5
UNITED BUSINESS MEDIA PLC	511120	1,172,006	6	824,641	1
US NEWS AND WORLD REPORT	511120				
WENNER MEDIA LLC	511120				
ZIFF DAVIS MEDIA INC	511120	187,611	15	-118,075	11
Management of Companies & Enterprises					
BERKSHIRE HATHAWAY INC	551110	81,663,000	1	8,528,000	1
VULCAN INC	551110				
Market Research					
ARBITRON INC	541910	309,995	3	67,308	3
HARRIS INTERACTIVE INC	541910	196,965	4	1,583	4
NETRATINGS INC	541910	68,017	5	-8,395	5
TAYLOR NELSON SOFRES (TNS)	541910	1,725,450	2	94,600	2
VNU NV	541910	4,180,121	1	307,738	1

Company	Industry Code	2005 Sales (U.S. $ thousands)	Sales Rank	2005 Profits (U.S. $ thousands)	Profits Rank
Marketing Agencies & Related Services					
MDI ENTERTAINMENT INC	541800				
Miscellaneous Manufacturing					
AMERICAN EDUCATIONAL PRODUCTS LLC	339000				
Movie Theaters					
AMC ENTERTAINMENT INC	512131	1,806,600	2	-70,600	5
CARMIKE CINEMAS INC	512131	468,900	4	200	4
CINEMARK INC	512131	1,020,600	3	22,400	2
CINEMASTAR LUXURY THEATERS INC	512131				
IMAX CORPORATION	512131	144,930	5	16,598	3
NATIONAL AMUSEMENTS INC	512131				
REGAL ENTERTAINMENT GROUP	512131	2,516,700	1	91,800	1
SIMEX-IWERKS	512131				
Music Stores					
CD WAREHOUSE INC	451220				
TRANS WORLD ENTERTAINMENT CORP	451220	1,365,133	1	41,841	1
WHEREHOUSE ENTERTAINMENT (RECORD TOWN INC)	451220				
Music Stores-Online					
AUDIBLE INC	451220E	63,237	1	221	1
LIQUID DIGITAL MEDIA	451220E				
MP3.COM INC	451220E				
NAPSTER INC	451220E	46,729	2	-29,506	2
Music, Publishing					
EMI GROUP PLC	512230	3,937,820	4	194,400	2
INTEGRITY MEDIA INC	512230				
SONY BMG MUSIC ENTERTAINMENT	512230	5,000,000	3		
UNIVERSAL MUSIC GROUP	512230	5,794,800	2		
VIVENDI SA	512230	23,059,000	1	3,733,000	1
WARNER MUSIC GROUP	512230	3,502,000	5	-169,000	3
Newspapers, Publishing					
BELO CORP	511110	1,521,234	10	127,688	7
COMMUNITY NEWSPAPER HOLDINGS INC	511110				
COX ENTERPRISES INC	511110	12,000,000	1		
DAILY JOURNAL CORP	511110	33,272	22	4,287	15
DOW JONES & COMPANY INC	511110	1,769,690	8	81,820	9
E W SCRIPPS CO	511110	2,513,890	7	249,153	5
FREEDOM COMMUNICATIONS	511110	103,500	21		
GANNETT CO INC	511110	7,598,939	2	1,244,654	1
HARTE-HANKS INC	511110	1,134,993	12	114,458	8
HEARST CORPORATION	511110	4,550,000	4		
HOLLINGER INC	511110	457,889	19	-11,969	17
JOURNAL COMMUNICATIONS	511110	764,461	16	66,243	11
JOURNAL REGISTER CO	511110	556,629	17	46,868	12
LANDMARK COMMUNICATIONS	511110	1,719,000	9		
LEE ENTERPRISES INC	511110	818,890	14	76,878	10
MCCLATCHY COMPANY	511110	1,186,115	11	160,519	6

Company	Industry Code	2005 Sales (U.S. $ thousands)	Sales Rank	2005 Profits (U.S. $ thousands)	Profits Rank
MEDIA GENERAL INC	511110	917,937	13	-243,042	18
MEDIANEWS GROUP INC	511110	779,300	15	39,900	13
METRO INTERNATIONAL SA	511110	359,700	20	-6,971	16
MORRIS COMMUNICATIONS COMPANY LLC	511110	465,100	18	31,300	14
NEW YORK TIMES CO	511110	3,372,800	6	259,700	4
NEWS WORLD COMMUNICATIONS INC	511110				
TRIBUNE CO	511110	5,595,617	3	534,689	2
WASHINGTON POST CO	511110	3,553,887	5	314,344	3
Online Publishing, Services & Niche Portals					
CNET NETWORKS INC	514199	352,951	2	27,693	3
DIALOG NEWSEDGE	514199				
GEMSTAR-TV GUIDE INTERNATIONAL INC	514199	604,192	1	54,815	2
HOLLYWOOD MEDIA CORP	514199	95,614	4	-8,913	6
HOOVER'S INC	514199	70,000	6		
IGN ENTERTAINMENT	514199				
IVILLAGE INC	514199	91,061	5	9,456	4
JUPITERMEDIA CORP	514199	124,577	3	78,399	1
SALON MEDIA GROUP INC	514199	6,628	7	-518	5
Other Retailers, Misc. Retailers					
GETTY IMAGES INC	453990	733,729	1	149,703	1
Printing					
BANTA CORPORATION	323000	1,523,252	2	68,005	2
COURIER CORP	323000	227,039	3	22,134	3
R R DONNELLEY & SONS CO	323000	8,430,200	1	137,100	1
Publishing, General					
BERRY COMPANY	511000				
Radio Broadcasting					
BEASLEY BROADCAST GROUP	513111	124,294	12	10,705	8
CBS RADIO	513111	2,114,800	2		
CITADEL BROADCASTING CORP	513111	419,907	7	69,757	3
CLEAR CHANNEL COMMUNICATIONS INC	513111	6,610,418	1	935,662	1
CORUS ENTERTAINMENT INC	513111	575,500	4	59,900	5
COX RADIO INC	513111	437,930	5	61,273	4
CUMULUS MEDIA INC	513111	327,756	9	-213,367	12
EMMIS COMMUNICATIONS	513111	618,460	3	-304,368	13
ENTERCOM COMMUNICATIONS	513111	432,520	6	78,361	2
GRUPO RADIO CENTRO SA DE CV	513111	55,619	14	6,107	9
RADIO ONE	513111	371,134	8	50,530	6
REGENT COMMUNICATIONS	513111	85,600	13	-6,639	10
SALEM COMMUNICATIONS	513111	211,839	10	12,980	7
SPANISH BROADCASTING SYSTEM INC	513111	169,832	11	-35,270	11
Radio Broadcasting via Satellite					
SIRIUS SATELLITE RADIO	513111A	242,245	2	-862,997	2
XM SATELLITE RADIO HOLDINGS INC	513111A	558,266	1	-666,715	1
Real Estate Investment Trusts - REITs					
ENTERTAINMENT PROPERTIES TRUST	525930	148,744	1	57,707	1

Company	Industry Code	2005 Sales (U.S. $ thousands)	Sales Rank	2005 Profits (U.S. $ thousands)	Profits Rank
Recruiting & Job Services Online					
MONSTER WORLDWIDE	514199C	986,900	1	107,500	1
Restaurants					
LANDRY'S RESTAURANTS INC	722110	1,254,806	1	44,815	1
Search Engine Portals					
GOOGLE INC	514199B	6,138,560	1	1,465,397	2
YAHOO! INC	514199B	5,258,000	2	1,896,000	1
Snow Skiing Facilities					
AMERICAN SKIING COMPANY	713920	276,477	2	-73,315	2
BOOTH CREEK SKI HOLDINGS	713920				
BOYNE USA RESORTS	713920				
VAIL RESORTS INC	713920	809,987	1	23,138	1
Stadiums/Sports Teams					
ANSCHUTZ ENTERTAINMENT GROUP	711211				
Telephone Service--Local Exchange Carrier & Diversified					
AT&T INC	513300A	43,862,000	2	4,786,000	2
RCN CORP	513300A	560,964	3	-136,112	3
VERIZON COMMUNICATIONS	513300A	75,112,000	1	7,397,000	1
Television Broadcasting					
ABC INC	513120	13,207,000	4		
ACME COMMUNICATIONS INC	513120	40,934	24	-15,945	15
BERTELSMANN AG	513120	21,415,000	2	1,246,090	2
BRITISH BROADCASTING CORPORATION (BBC)	513120	7,205,400	5	-353,600	22
CANWEST GLOBAL COMMUNICATIONS	513120	2,588,600	8	8,700	11
CBS CORP	513120	14,536,400	3	-7,089,100	23
ENTRAVISION COMMUNICATIONS CORP	513120	280,964	15	-9,657	14
FISHER COMMUNICATIONS INC	513120	144,471	21	-5,072	13
FOX ENTERTAINMENT GROUP	513120				
GRANITE BROADCASTING	513120	86,160	23	-98,926	19
GRAY TELEVISION INC	513120	261,553	16	3,362	12
GRUPO TELEVISA SA	513120	2,968,180	7	559,747	4
HEARST-ARGYLE TELEVISION	513120	706,883	12	100,217	9
ION MEDIA NETWORKS	513120	254,176	17	-235,670	20
ION MEDIA NETWORKS INC	513120	254,176	18	-235,670	21
LIN TV CORP	513120	380,400	14	-24,200	16
MODERN TIMES GROUP MTG	513120	1,036,941	10	160,099	7
NEWS CORPORATION LIMITED	513120	23,859,000	1	2,128,000	1
NEXSTAR BROADCASTING GROUP INC	513120	226,053	19	-48,730	18
RAYCOM MEDIA INC	513120				
RTL GROUP SA	513120	6,207,333	6	747,621	3
SAGA COMMUNICATIONS INC	513120	140,790	22	10,566	10
SHANGHAI MEDIA GROUP (SMG)	513120				
SINCLAIR BROADCAST GROUP	513120	692,067	13	187,310	5
TV AZTECA SA DE CV	513120	797,000	11	114,000	8
UNIVISION COMMUNICATIONS	513120	1,952,531	9	187,179	6
YOUNG BROADCASTING INC	513120	225,524	20	-44,276	17

Company	Industry Code	2005 Sales (U.S. $ thousands)	Sales Rank	2005 Profits (U.S. $ thousands)	Profits Rank
Television Broadcasting via the Intenet or Wireless					
JUMPTV INC	513120A				
MOBITV INC	513120A				
Theme Parks/Rides/Game Centers					
CEDAR FAIR LP	713110	568,707	3	160,852	1
EURO DISNEY SCA	713110	1,295,800	1	-114,300	3
PALACE ENTERTAINMENT	713110				
SIX FLAGS INC	713110	1,089,682	2	-110,938	2
Toys/Hobbies/Games Stores					
GAMESTOP CORP	451120	1,842,806	1	60,926	1
TV Shopping					
IAC/INTERACTIVECORP	454110B	5,753,700	1	868,200	1
SHOP AT HOME NETWORK LLC	454110B				
VALUEVISION MEDIA INC	454110B	623,634	2	-57,886	2
TV/Video/Theatrical, Production					
2929 ENTERTAINMENT	512110				
ALLIANCE ATLANTIS COMMUNICATIONS INC	512110	893,970	9	60,725	4
CENTRAL EUROPEAN MEDIA ENTERPRISES LTD	512110	400,978	13	42,495	5
CIRQUE DU SOLEIL INC	512110				
COLUMBIA TRISTAR MOTION PICTURE GROUP	512110				
DICK CLARK PRODUCTIONS INC	512110				
DREAMWORKS ANIMATION SKG	512110	462,316	12	104,585	2
DREAMWORKS LLC	512110				
FIRST LOOK STUDIOS INC	512110				
FOX FILMED ENTERTAINMENT	512110	5,919,000	5		
HARPO INC	512110	290,000	15		
LIBERTY MEDIA CORP	512110	7,960,000	2	-33,000	9
LIONS GATE ENTERTAINMENT	512110	842,586	10	20,336	7
LUCASFILM LTD	512110	1,483,000	7		
METRO-GOLDWYN-MAYER INC (MGM)	512110	1,430,000	8		
MGM PICTURES	512110				
MIRAMAX FILM CORP	512110				
NEW LINE CINEMA	512110				
ON STAGE ENTERTAINMENT	512110				
PARAMOUNT PICTURES CORP	512110	2,898,700	6		
PIXAR ANIMATION STUDIOS	512110	289,116	16	152,938	1
RENTRAK CORPORATION	512110	98,538	17	5,242	8
SONY PICTURES ENTERTAINMENT	512110	6,857,000	4		
UNITED ARTISTS CORP	512110				
UNIVERSAL PICTURES	512110				
WALT DISNEY STUDIOS	512110	7,587,000	3		
WARNER BROS ENTERTAINMENT INC	512110	11,850,000	1		
WESTWOOD ONE INC	512110	557,830	11	84,683	3
WORLD WRESTLING ENTERTAINMENT INC (WWF)	512110	366,431	14	39,147	6

Company	Industry Code	2005 Sales (U.S. $ thousands)	Sales Rank	2005 Profits (U.S. $ thousands)	Profits Rank
Video Rental					
BLOCKBUSTER INC	532230	5,864,400	1	-588,100	4
HASTINGS ENTERTAINMENT	532230	542,016	5	5,809	2
HOLLYWOOD ENTERTAINMENT	532230	933,100	3		
MOVIE GALLERY INC	532230	1,987,327	2	-552,740	3
NETFLIX	532230	688,000	4	41,900	1
Videos/Games/Software/Recorded Music Distribution					
ALLIANCE ENTERTAINMENT	422921				
INGRAM ENTERTAINMENT HOLDINGS INC	422921	839,000	1		

ALPHABETICAL INDEX

DREAMWORKS ANIMATION SKG INC
DREAMWORKS LLC
DTS INC
DUN & BRADSTREET CORP (THE, D&B)
E W SCRIPPS CO
EBSCO INDUSTRIES INC
ECHOSTAR COMMUNICATIONS CORP
EDUCATIONAL DEVELOPMENT CORP
ELECTRONIC ARTS INC
EMAP PLC
EMI GROUP PLC
EMMIS COMMUNICATIONS CORP
ENDEAVOR AGENCY (THE)
ENTERCOM COMMUNICATIONS CORP
ENTERTAINMENT PROPERTIES TRUST
ENTRAVISION COMMUNICATIONS CORPORATION
ESPN INC
EURO DISNEY SCA
FIRST LOOK STUDIOS INC
FISHER COMMUNICATIONS INC
FORBES INC
FORD MODELS INC
FOX BROADCASTING COMPANY
FOX ENTERTAINMENT GROUP INC
FOX FILMED ENTERTAINMENT
FOX SPORTS NET INC
FREEDOM COMMUNICATIONS INC
GAMESTOP CORP
GAMETECH INTERNATIONAL INC
GAMING PARTNERS INTERNATIONAL CORP
GANNETT CO INC
GAYLORD ENTERTAINMENT CO
GEMSTAR-TV GUIDE INTERNATIONAL INC
GENERAL ELECTRIC CO (GE)
GETTY IMAGES INC
GLU MOBILE
GOLD'S GYM INTERNATIONAL
GOOGLE INC
GRANITE BROADCASTING CORP
GRAY TELEVISION INC
GRUPO RADIO CENTRO SA DE CV
GRUPO TELEVISA SA
GTECH HOLDINGS CORP
HALLMARK CARDS INC
HANDS-ON MOBILE
HARPERCOLLINS PUBLISHERS INC
HARPO INC
HARRAH'S ENTERTAINMENT INC
HARRIS INTERACTIVE INC
HARTE-HANKS INC
HARVEY ELECTRONICS INC
HASTINGS ENTERTAINMENT INC
HEARST CORPORATION (THE)
HEARST-ARGYLE TELEVISION INC
HERSHEY CO
HOLLINGER INC
HOLLYWOOD ENTERTAINMENT CORP
HOLLYWOOD MEDIA CORP

HOOVER'S INC
HOUGHTON MIFFLIN CO
IAC/INTERACTIVECORP
I-CABLE COMMUNICATIONS
IGN ENTERTAINMENT
IMAX CORPORATION
IMG WORLDWIDE INC
INGRAM ENTERTAINMENT HOLDINGS INC
INSIGHT COMMUNICATIONS COMPANY INC
INTEGRITY MEDIA INC
INTERACTIVE DATA CORPORATION
INTERNATIONAL CREATIVE MANAGEMENT (ICM)
INTERNATIONAL GAME TECHNOLOGY
INTERNATIONAL LOTTERY & TOTALIZATOR
SYSTEMS
INTERPUBLIC GROUP OF COMPANIES INC
INTERTAN CANADA LTD
INTERVIDEO INC
ION MEDIA NETWORKS
ION MEDIA NETWORKS INC
ISLE OF CAPRI CASINOS INC
ITV PLC
IVILLAGE INC
JOHN WILEY & SONS INC
JOHNSON PUBLISHING COMPANY INC
JOURNAL COMMUNICATIONS INC
JOURNAL REGISTER CO
JUMPTV INC
JUPITERMEDIA CORP
KERZNER INTERNATIONAL LIMITED
KNOLOGY INC
LAGARDERE ACTIVE MEDIA
LAKES ENTERTAINMENT INC
LAMAR ADVERTISING CO
LANDMARK COMMUNICATIONS INC
LANDRY'S RESTAURANTS INC
LAS VEGAS SANDS CORP (THE VENETIAN)
LASERPACIFIC MEDIA CORP
LEE ENTERPRISES INC
LERNER PUBLISHING GROUP
LIBERTY GLOBAL
LIBERTY MEDIA CORP
LIN TV CORP
LIONS GATE ENTERTAINMENT CORP
LIQUID DIGITAL MEDIA
LIVE NATION INC
LODGENET ENTERTAINMENT CORP
LOUD TECHNOLOGIES INC
LUCASARTS ENTERTAINMENT COMPANY LLC
LUCASFILM LTD
MACROVISION CORP
MAGNA ENTERTAINMENT CORP
MARKETWATCH INC
MARTHA STEWART LIVING OMNIMEDIA INC
MARVEL ENTERTAINMENT INC
MATAV-CABLE SYSTEMS MEDIA LTD
MATSUSHITA ELECTRIC INDUSTRIAL CO LTD
MCCLATCHY COMPANY (THE)

MCGRAW HILL COS INC
MDI ENTERTAINMENT INC
MEDIA GENERAL INC
MEDIACOM COMMUNICATIONS CORP
MEDIANEWS GROUP INC
MEREDITH CORP
METRO INTERNATIONAL SA
METRO-GOLDWYN-MAYER INC (MGM)
MGM MIRAGE
MGM PICTURES
MICROSOFT CORP
MIDWAY GAMES INC
MIRAMAX FILM CORP
MOBITV INC
MODERN TIMES GROUP MTG AB
MONARCH CASINO & RESORT INC
MONSTER WORLDWIDE
MOODY'S CORPORATION
MORRIS COMMUNICATIONS COMPANY LLC
MOVIE GALLERY INC
MP3.COM INC
MTR GAMING GROUP INC
MTV NETWORKS
MULTIMEDIA GAMES INC
NAPSTER INC
NASPERS LIMITED
NATIONAL AMUSEMENTS INC
NBC UNIVERSAL
NETFLIX
NETRATINGS INC
NEW LINE CINEMA
NEW YORK TIMES CO (THE)
NEWS CORPORATION LIMITED (THE)
NEWS WORLD COMMUNICATIONS INC
NEXSTAR BROADCASTING GROUP INC
NINTENDO CO LTD
NTL INCORPORATED
NTN BUZZTIME INC
OMNICOM GROUP INC
OMNIVISION TECHNOLOGIES INC
ON COMMAND CORP
ON STAGE ENTERTAINMENT
PALACE ENTERTAINMENT
PANAMSAT CORP
PARAMOUNT PICTURES CORP
PEARSON PLC
PENN NATIONAL GAMING INC
PENTON MEDIA INC
PINNACLE ENTERTAINMENT INC
PIONEER CORPORATION
PIXAR ANIMATION STUDIOS
PLAYBOY ENTERPRISES INC
PRIMACOM AG
PRIMEDIA INC
PROGRESSIVE GAMING INTERNATIONAL CORP
PROQUEST COMPANY
R R DONNELLEY & SONS CO
RADIO ONE

RADIOSHACK CORPORATION
RAINBOW MEDIA HOLDINGS LLC
RANDOM HOUSE INC
RANK GROUP PLC (THE)
RAYCOM MEDIA INC
RCN CORP
READER'S DIGEST ASSOCIATION INC
REALNETWORKS INC
REED ELSEVIER GROUP PLC
REGAL ENTERTAINMENT GROUP
REGENT COMMUNICATIONS
RENAISSANCE ENTERTAINMENT CORP
RENTRAK CORPORATION
REUTERS GROUP PLC
REX STORES CORP
RIVIERA HOLDINGS CORP
RODALE INC
ROGERS COMMUNICATIONS INC
RTL GROUP SA
SAGA COMMUNICATIONS INC
SALEM COMMUNICATIONS CORP
SALON MEDIA GROUP INC
SAMSUNG ELECTRONICS CO LTD
SANDS REGENT
SANYO ELECTRIC COMPANY LTD
SCHOLASTIC CORP
SCIENTIFIC GAMES CORPORATION
SEGA SAMMY HOLDINGS INC
SHANDA INTERACTIVE ENTERTAINMENT
LIMITED
SHANGHAI MEDIA GROUP (SMG)
SHARP CORPORATION
SHAW COMMUNICATIONS INC
SHOP AT HOME NETWORK LLC
SHUFFLE MASTER INC
SIMEX-IWERKS
SIMON & SCHUSTER INC
SINCLAIR BROADCAST GROUP INC
SIRIUS SATELLITE RADIO
SIX FLAGS INC
SKY NETWORK TELEVISION LIMITED
SONY BMG MUSIC ENTERTAINMENT
SONY CORPORATION
SONY PICTURES ENTERTAINMENT
SPANISH BROADCASTING SYSTEM INC
SRS LABS INC
STATION CASINOS INC
SUDDENLINK COMMUNICATIONS
TAKE-TWO INTERACTIVE SOFTWARE INC
TAYLOR NELSON SOFRES PLC (TNS)
TELEWEST GLOBAL INC
THOMAS NELSON INC
THOMSON CORPORATION (THE)
THQ INC
TICKETMASTER
TIME INC
TIME WARNER CABLE
TIME WARNER INC

TIVO INC
TRADER CLASSIFIED MEDIA NV
TRAFFIX INC
TRANS WORLD CORP
TRANS WORLD ENTERTAINMENT CORP
TRANS-LUX CORPORATION
TRIBUNE CO
TRUMP ENTERTAINMENT RESORTS INC
TURNER BROADCASTING SYSTEM
TV AZTECA SA DE CV
TWEETER HOME ENTERTAINMENT GROUP INC
UNITED ARTISTS CORPORATION
UNITED BUSINESS MEDIA PLC
UNITED ONLINE INC
UNITED PARAMOUNT NETWORK (UPN)
UNITED TALENT AGENCY INC
UNIVERSAL MUSIC GROUP
UNIVERSAL PICTURES
UNIVISION COMMUNICATIONS INC
US NEWS AND WORLD REPORT LP
VAIL RESORTS INC
VALUE LINE INC
VALUEVISION MEDIA INC
VERIZON COMMUNICATIONS
VIACOM INC
VINDIGO INC
VIVENDI GAMES
VIVENDI SA
VNU NV
VULCAN INC
WALT DISNEY COMPANY (THE)
WALT DISNEY STUDIOS
WARNER BROS ENTERTAINMENT INC
WARNER MUSIC GROUP
WASHINGTON POST CO
WENNER MEDIA LLC
WESTWOOD ONE INC
WHEREHOUSE ENTERTAINMENT (RECORD TOWN INC)
WILLIAM MORRIS AGENCY INC
WMS INDUSTRIES INC
WORLD WRESTLING ENTERTAINMENT INC (WWF)
WPP GROUP PLC
WYNN RESORTS LIMITED
XM SATELLITE RADIO HOLDINGS INC
YAHOO! INC
YAHOO! SEARCH MARKETING GROUP
YOUBET.COM INC
YOUNG BROADCASTING INC
ZIFF DAVIS MEDIA INC

INDEX OF HEADQUARTERS LOCATION BY U.S. STATE

To help you locate members of the Firms geographically, the city and state of the headquarters of each company are in the following index.

ALABAMA
BOOKS A MILLION INC; Birmingham
COMMUNITY NEWSPAPER HOLDINGS INC; Birmingham
EBSCO INDUSTRIES INC; Birmingham
INTEGRITY MEDIA INC; Mobile
MOVIE GALLERY INC; Dothan
RAYCOM MEDIA INC; Montgomery

ARIZONA
AZTAR CORP; Phoenix
CLEAR CHANNEL OUTDOOR; Phoenix

CALIFORNIA
24 HOUR FITNESS USA; San Ramon
2929 ENTERTAINMENT; Santa Monica
ACME COMMUNICATIONS INC; Santa Ana
ACTIVISION INC; Santa Monica
ADVANCED MARKETING SERVICES INC; San Diego
AMERICAN GOLF CORP; Santa Monica
ANSCHUTZ ENTERTAINMENT GROUP; Los Angeles
APPLE INC; Cupertino
ASCENT MEDIA GROUP INC; Santa Monica
BOOTH CREEK SKI HOLDINGS INC; Truckee
BUY.COM INC; Aliso Viejo
CINEMASTAR LUXURY THEATERS INC; Oceanside
CNET NETWORKS INC; San Francisco
COLUMBIA TRISTAR MOTION PICTURE GROUP; Culver City
CREATIVE ARTISTS AGENCY INC; Beverly Hills
CROWN MEDIA HOLDINGS INC; Studio City
CW NETWORK (THE); Burbank
DAILY JOURNAL CORP; Los Angeles
DICK CLARK PRODUCTIONS INC; Burbank
DIGITAL VIDEO SYSTEMS INC; Mountain View
DIRECTV GROUP INC (THE); El Segundo
DOLBY LABORATORIES INC; San Francisco
DREAMWORKS ANIMATION SKG INC; Glendale
DREAMWORKS LLC; Glendale
DTS INC; Agoura Hills
ELECTRONIC ARTS INC; Redwood City
ENDEAVOR AGENCY (THE); Beverly Hills
ENTRAVISION COMMUNICATIONS CORPORATION; Santa Monica
FIRST LOOK STUDIOS INC; Los Angeles
FOX BROADCASTING COMPANY; Los Angeles
FOX FILMED ENTERTAINMENT; Los Angeles
FOX SPORTS NET INC; Los Angeles
FREEDOM COMMUNICATIONS INC; Irvine

GEMSTAR-TV GUIDE INTERNATIONAL INC; Los Angeles
GLU MOBILE; San Mateo
GOOGLE INC; Mountain View
HANDS-ON MOBILE; San Francisco
IGN ENTERTAINMENT; Brisbane
INTERNATIONAL CREATIVE MANAGEMENT (ICM); Beverly Hills
INTERNATIONAL LOTTERY & TOTALIZATOR SYSTEMS; Carlsbad
INTERVIDEO INC; Fremont
LASERPACIFIC MEDIA CORP; Hollywood
LIQUID DIGITAL MEDIA; Redwood City
LIVE NATION INC; Beverly Hills
LUCASARTS ENTERTAINMENT COMPANY LLC; San Francisco
LUCASFILM LTD; San Francisco
MACROVISION CORP; Santa Clara
MARKETWATCH INC; San Francisco
MCCLATCHY COMPANY (THE); Sacramento
METRO-GOLDWYN-MAYER INC (MGM); Los Angeles
MGM PICTURES; Los Angeles
MOBITV INC; Emeryville
MP3.COM INC; San Francisco
NAPSTER INC; Los Angeles
NETFLIX; Los Gatos
NTN BUZZTIME INC; Carlsbad
OMNIVISION TECHNOLOGIES INC; Sunnyvale
PALACE ENTERTAINMENT; Newport Beach
PARAMOUNT PICTURES CORP; Hollywood
PIXAR ANIMATION STUDIOS; Emeryville
SALEM COMMUNICATIONS CORP; Camarillo
SALON MEDIA GROUP INC; San Francisco
SIMEX-IWERKS; Burbank
SONY PICTURES ENTERTAINMENT; Culver City
SRS LABS INC; Santa Ana
THQ INC; Aguora Hills
TICKETMASTER; Los Angeles
TIVO INC; Alviso
UNITED ARTISTS CORPORATION; Los Angeles
UNITED ONLINE INC; Woodland Hills
UNITED PARAMOUNT NETWORK (UPN); Los Angeles
UNITED TALENT AGENCY INC; Beverly Hills
UNIVERSAL MUSIC GROUP; Santa Monica
UNIVERSAL PICTURES; Universal City
UNIVISION COMMUNICATIONS INC; Los Angeles
VIVENDI GAMES; Los Angeles
WALT DISNEY COMPANY (THE); Burbank
WALT DISNEY STUDIOS; Burbank
WARNER BROS ENTERTAINMENT INC; Burbank
WILLIAM MORRIS AGENCY INC; Beverly Hills
YAHOO! INC; Sunnyvale
YAHOO! SEARCH MARKETING GROUP; Burbank
YOUBET.COM INC; Woodland Hills

COLORADO
AMERICAN COIN MERCHANDISING INC; Louisville
AMERICAN EDUCATIONAL PRODUCTS LLC; Fort Collins
CENTURY CASINOS INC; Colorado Springs
ECHOSTAR COMMUNICATIONS CORP; Englewood
LIBERTY GLOBAL; Englewood
LIBERTY MEDIA CORP; Englewood
MEDIANEWS GROUP INC; Denver
ON COMMAND CORP; Denver
RENAISSANCE ENTERTAINMENT CORP; Louisville
VAIL RESORTS INC; Avon

CONNECTICUT
ESPN INC; Bristol
GENERAL ELECTRIC CO (GE); Fairfield
JUPITERMEDIA CORP; Darien
PANAMSAT CORP; Wilton
TIME WARNER CABLE; Stamford
TRANS-LUX CORPORATION; Norwalk
WORLD WRESTLING ENTERTAINMENT INC (WWF); Stamford

DELAWARE
DOVER DOWNS GAMING & ENTERTAINMENT INC; Dover

DISTRICT OF COLUMBIA
NEWS WORLD COMMUNICATIONS INC; Washington
US NEWS AND WORLD REPORT LP; Washington
WASHINGTON POST CO; Washington
XM SATELLITE RADIO HOLDINGS INC; Washington

FLORIDA
ALLIANCE ENTERTAINMENT CORP; Coral Springs
BEASLEY BROADCAST GROUP INC; Naples
DIAMONDHEAD CASINO CORPORATION; Madeira Beach
HOLLYWOOD MEDIA CORP; Boca Raton
ION MEDIA NETWORKS; West Palm Beach
ION MEDIA NETWORKS INC; West Palm Beach
SPANISH BROADCASTING SYSTEM INC; Coconut Grove

GEORGIA
CABLE NEWS NETWORK LP LLLP; Atlanta
CARMIKE CINEMAS INC; Columbus
CONCURRENT COMPUTER CORP; Duluth
COX COMMUNICATIONS INC; Atlanta
COX ENTERPRISES INC; Atlanta
COX RADIO INC; Atlanta
CUMULUS MEDIA INC; Atlanta
GRAY TELEVISION INC; Atlanta
KNOLOGY INC; West Point
MDI ENTERTAINMENT INC; Alpharetta
MORRIS COMMUNICATIONS COMPANY LLC; Augusta

TURNER BROADCASTING SYSTEM; Atlanta

ILLINOIS
BALLY TOTAL FITNESS HOLDING CORPORATION; Chicago
HARPO INC; Chicago
JOHNSON PUBLISHING COMPANY INC; Chicago
MIDWAY GAMES INC; Chicago
PLAYBOY ENTERPRISES INC; Chicago
R R DONNELLEY & SONS CO; Chicago
TRIBUNE CO; Chicago
WMS INDUSTRIES INC; Waukegan

INDIANA
EMMIS COMMUNICATIONS CORP; Indianapolis

IOWA
LEE ENTERPRISES INC; Davenport
MEREDITH CORP; Des Moines

KENTUCKY
CHURCHILL DOWNS INC; Louisville

LOUISIANA
LAMAR ADVERTISING CO; Baton Rouge

MARYLAND
DISCOVERY COMMUNICATIONS INC; Silver Spring
RADIO ONE; Lanham
SINCLAIR BROADCAST GROUP INC; Hunt Valley

MASSACHUSETTS
AVID TECHNOLOGY INC; Tewksbury
BOSE CORPORATION; Framingham
COURIER CORP; North Chelmsford
DIALOG NEWSEDGE; Burlington
HOUGHTON MIFFLIN CO; Boston
INTERACTIVE DATA CORPORATION; Bedford
NATIONAL AMUSEMENTS INC; Dedham
TWEETER HOME ENTERTAINMENT GROUP INC; Canton

MICHIGAN
BORDERS GROUP INC; Ann Arbor
BOYNE USA RESORTS; Boyne Falls
PROQUEST COMPANY; Ann Arbor
SAGA COMMUNICATIONS INC; Grosse Pointe Farms

MINNESOTA
BEST BUY CO INC; Richfield
CANTERBURY PARK HOLDING CORP; Shakopee
CONCRETE SOFTWARE INC; Chanhassen
LAKES ENTERTAINMENT INC; Minnetonka
LERNER PUBLISHING GROUP; Minneapolis
VALUEVISION MEDIA INC; Eden Prairie

MISSISSIPPI

ISLE OF CAPRI CASINOS INC; Biloxi

MISSOURI
AMC ENTERTAINMENT INC; Kansas City
ANHEUSER BUSCH COS INC; St. Louis
CHARTER COMMUNICATIONS; St. Louis
ENTERTAINMENT PROPERTIES TRUST; Kansas City
HALLMARK CARDS INC; Kansas City
SUDDENLINK COMMUNICATIONS; St. Louis

NEBRASKA
BERKSHIRE HATHAWAY INC; Omaha

NEVADA
AMERICAN WAGERING INC; Las Vegas
AMERISTAR CASINOS INC; Las Vegas
BALLY TECHNOLOGIES INC; Las Vegas
BOYD GAMING CORP; Las Vegas
CAESARS ENTERTAINMENT INC; Las Vegas
CITADEL BROADCASTING CORP; Las Vegas
GAMETECH INTERNATIONAL INC; Reno
GAMING PARTNERS INTERNATIONAL CORP; Las Vegas
HARRAH'S ENTERTAINMENT INC; Las Vegas
INTERNATIONAL GAME TECHNOLOGY; Reno
LAS VEGAS SANDS CORP (THE VENETIAN); Las Vegas
MGM MIRAGE; Las Vegas
MONARCH CASINO & RESORT INC; Reno
ON STAGE ENTERTAINMENT; Las Vegas
PINNACLE ENTERTAINMENT INC; Las Vegas
PROGRESSIVE GAMING INTERNATIONAL CORP; Las Vegas
RIVIERA HOLDINGS CORP; Las Vegas
SANDS REGENT; Reno
SHUFFLE MASTER INC; Las Vegas
STATION CASINOS INC; Las Vegas
WYNN RESORTS LIMITED; Las Vegas

NEW JERSEY
AUDIBLE INC; Wayne
DUN & BRADSTREET CORP (THE, D&B); Short Hills
HARVEY ELECTRONICS INC; Lyndhurst
JOHN WILEY & SONS INC; Hoboken
TRUMP ENTERTAINMENT RESORTS INC; Atlantic City

NEW YORK
24/7 REAL MEDIA INC; New York
A&E TELEVISION NETWORKS; New York
ABC INC; New York
ADVANCE PUBLICATIONS INC; Staten Island
AMERICAN EXPRESS CO; New York
ARBITRON INC; New York
BARNES & NOBLE INC; New York
BARNESANDNOBLE.COM INC; New York
BLOOMBERG LP; New York

CABLEVISION SYSTEMS CORP; Bethpage
CBS CORP; New York
CBS RADIO; New York
CONDE NAST PUBLICATIONS INC; New York City
DAG MEDIA INC; Kew Gardens
DELAWARE NORTH COMPANIES; Buffalo
DOUBLECLICK INC; New York
DOW JONES & COMPANY INC; New York
FORBES INC; New York
FORD MODELS INC; New York
FOX ENTERTAINMENT GROUP INC; New York
GRANITE BROADCASTING CORP; New York
HARPERCOLLINS PUBLISHERS INC; New York
HARRIS INTERACTIVE INC; Rochester
HEARST CORPORATION (THE); New York
HEARST-ARGYLE TELEVISION INC; New York
IAC/INTERACTIVECORP; New York
INSIGHT COMMUNICATIONS COMPANY INC; New York
INTERPUBLIC GROUP OF COMPANIES INC; New York
IVILLAGE INC; New York
MARTHA STEWART LIVING OMNIMEDIA INC; New York
MARVEL ENTERTAINMENT INC; New York
MCGRAW HILL COS INC; New York
MEDIACOM COMMUNICATIONS CORP; Middletown
MIRAMAX FILM CORP; New York
MONSTER WORLDWIDE; New York
MOODY'S CORPORATION; New York
MTV NETWORKS; New York
NBC UNIVERSAL; New York
NETRATINGS INC; New York
NEW LINE CINEMA; New York
NEW YORK TIMES CO (THE); New York
NEWS CORPORATION LIMITED (THE); New York
OMNICOM GROUP INC; New York
PRIMEDIA INC; New York
RAINBOW MEDIA HOLDINGS LLC; Jericho
RANDOM HOUSE INC; New York
READER'S DIGEST ASSOCIATION INC; Pleasantville
SCHOLASTIC CORP; New York
SCIENTIFIC GAMES CORPORATION; New York
SIMON & SCHUSTER INC; New York
SIRIUS SATELLITE RADIO; New York
SONY BMG MUSIC ENTERTAINMENT; New York
TAKE-TWO INTERACTIVE SOFTWARE INC; New York
TIME INC; New York
TIME WARNER INC; New York
TRAFFIX INC; Pearl River
TRANS WORLD CORP; New York
TRANS WORLD ENTERTAINMENT CORP; Albany
VALUE LINE INC; New York
VERIZON COMMUNICATIONS; New York
VIACOM INC; New York
VINDIGO INC; New York
WARNER MUSIC GROUP; New York

WENNER MEDIA LLC; New York
WESTWOOD ONE INC; New York
WHEREHOUSE ENTERTAINMENT (RECORD TOWN INC); Albany
YOUNG BROADCASTING INC; New York
ZIFF DAVIS MEDIA INC; New York

OHIO
AMERICAN GREETINGS CORP; Cleveland
BERRY COMPANY (THE); Dayton
CEDAR FAIR LP; Sandusky
E W SCRIPPS CO; Cincinnati
IMG WORLDWIDE INC; Cleveland
PENTON MEDIA INC; Cleveland
REGENT COMMUNICATIONS; Cincinnati
REX STORES CORP; Dayton

OKLAHOMA
CD WAREHOUSE INC; Oklahoma City
EDUCATIONAL DEVELOPMENT CORP; Tulsa
SIX FLAGS INC; Oklahoma City

OREGON
HOLLYWOOD ENTERTAINMENT CORP; Wilsonville
RENTRAK CORPORATION; Portland

PENNSYLVANIA
COMCAST CORP; Philadelphia
ENTERCOM COMMUNICATIONS CORP; Bala Cynwyd
HERSHEY CO; Hershey
JOURNAL REGISTER CO; Yardley
PENN NATIONAL GAMING INC; Wyomissing
RODALE INC; Emmaus

RHODE ISLAND
GTECH HOLDINGS CORP; West Greenwich
LIN TV CORP; Providence

SOUTH DAKOTA
LODGENET ENTERTAINMENT CORP; Sioux Falls

TENNESSEE
ANDERSON NEWS LLC; Knoxville
GAYLORD ENTERTAINMENT CO; Nashville
INGRAM ENTERTAINMENT HOLDINGS INC; La Vergne
REGAL ENTERTAINMENT GROUP; Knoxville
SHOP AT HOME NETWORK LLC; Nashville
THOMAS NELSON INC; Nashville

TEXAS
AT&T INC; San Antonio
BELO CORP; Dallas
BLOCKBUSTER INC; Dallas
CINEMARK INC; Plano

CLEAR CHANNEL COMMUNICATIONS INC; San Antonio
CLUBCORP INC; Dallas
CURVES INTERNATIONAL INC; Waco
DG FASTCHANNEL; Irving
GAMESTOP CORP; Grapevine
GOLD'S GYM INTERNATIONAL; Irving
HARTE-HANKS INC; San Antonio
HASTINGS ENTERTAINMENT INC; Amarillo
HOOVER'S INC; Austin
LANDRY'S RESTAURANTS INC; Houston
MULTIMEDIA GAMES INC; Austin
NEXSTAR BROADCASTING GROUP INC; Irving
RADIOSHACK CORPORATION; Fort Worth

UTAH
AMERICAN SKIING COMPANY; Park City

VIRGINIA
AMF BOWLING WORLDWIDE INC; Richmond
AOL LLC; Dulles
CIRCUIT CITY STORES INC; Richmond
GANNETT CO INC; McLean
LANDMARK COMMUNICATIONS INC; Norfolk
MEDIA GENERAL INC; Richmond
RCN CORP; Herndon

WASHINGTON
AMAZON.COM INC; Seattle
DIGEO INC; Kirkland
FISHER COMMUNICATIONS INC; Seattle
GETTY IMAGES INC; Seattle
LOUD TECHNOLOGIES INC; Woodinville
MICROSOFT CORP; Redmond
REALNETWORKS INC; Seattle
VULCAN INC; Seattle

WEST VIRGINIA
MTR GAMING GROUP INC; Chester

WISCONSIN
BANTA CORPORATION; Menasha
JOURNAL COMMUNICATIONS INC; Milwaukee

INDEX OF NON-U.S. HEADQUARTERS LOCATION BY COUNTRY

AUSTRALIA
ARISTOCRAT LEISURE LTD; Lane Cove

BAHAMAS
KERZNER INTERNATIONAL LIMITED; Paradise Island

BERMUDA
CENTRAL EUROPEAN MEDIA ENTERPRISES LTD; Hamilton

CANADA
ALLIANCE ATLANTIS COMMUNICATIONS INC; Toronto
BIOWARE CORP; Edmonton
CANWEST GLOBAL COMMUNICATIONS; Winnipeg
CIRQUE DU SOLEIL INC; Montreal
CORUS ENTERTAINMENT INC; Toronto
HOLLINGER INC; Toronto
IMAX CORPORATION; Mississauga
INTERTAN CANADA LTD; Barrie
JUMPTV INC; Toronto
LIONS GATE ENTERTAINMENT CORP; North Vancouver
MAGNA ENTERTAINMENT CORP; Aurora
ROGERS COMMUNICATIONS INC; Toronto
SHAW COMMUNICATIONS INC; Calgary
THOMSON CORPORATION (THE); Toronto

CHINA
I-CABLE COMMUNICATIONS; Hong Kong
SHANDA INTERACTIVE ENTERTAINMENT LIMITED; Shanghai
SHANGHAI MEDIA GROUP (SMG); Shanghai

FRANCE
EURO DISNEY SCA; Marne-la-Vallee Cedex 4
LAGARDERE ACTIVE MEDIA; Levallois-Perret
VIVENDI SA; Paris

GERMANY
BERTELSMANN AG; Gutersloh
PRIMACOM AG; Mainz

ISRAEL
MATAV-CABLE SYSTEMS MEDIA LTD; Netanya

JAPAN
CLARION CO LTD; Toda
MATSUSHITA ELECTRIC INDUSTRIAL CO LTD; Osaka
NINTENDO CO LTD; Kyoto
PIONEER CORPORATION; Tokyo

SANYO ELECTRIC COMPANY LTD; Osaka
SEGA SAMMY HOLDINGS INC; Tokyo
SHARP CORPORATION; Osaka
SONY CORPORATION; Tokyo

LUXEMBOURG
RTL GROUP SA; Luxembourg

MEXICO
GRUPO RADIO CENTRO SA DE CV; Mexico City
GRUPO TELEVISA SA; Colonia Santa Fe
TV AZTECA SA DE CV; Mexico City

NEW ZEALAND
SKY NETWORK TELEVISION LIMITED; Auckland

SOUTH AFRICA
NASPERS LIMITED; Cape Town

SOUTH KOREA
SAMSUNG ELECTRONICS CO LTD; Seoul

SWEDEN
MODERN TIMES GROUP MTG AB; Stockholm

THE NETHERLANDS
TRADER CLASSIFIED MEDIA NV; Amsterdam
VNU NV; Haarlem

UNITED KINGDOM
BRITISH BROADCASTING CORPORATION (BBC); London
BRITISH SKY BROADCASTING PLC; Isleworth
DENNIS PUBLISHING LTD; London
DIGITAL BRIDGES LIMITED; London
EMAP PLC; Peterborough
EMI GROUP PLC; London
ITV PLC; London
METRO INTERNATIONAL SA; London
NTL INCORPORATED; Hook
PEARSON PLC; London
RANK GROUP PLC (THE); London
REED ELSEVIER GROUP PLC; London
REUTERS GROUP PLC; London
TAYLOR NELSON SOFRES PLC (TNS); London
TELEWEST GLOBAL INC; London
UNITED BUSINESS MEDIA PLC; London
WPP GROUP PLC; London

INDEX BY REGIONS OF THE U.S. WHERE THE ENTERTAINMENT 400 FIRMS HAVE LOCATIONS

WEST
24 HOUR FITNESS USA
24/7 REAL MEDIA INC
2929 ENTERTAINMENT
A&E TELEVISION NETWORKS
ABC INC
ACME COMMUNICATIONS INC
ACTIVISION INC
ADVANCE PUBLICATIONS INC
ADVANCED MARKETING SERVICES INC
ALLIANCE ATLANTIS COMMUNICATIONS INC
ALLIANCE ENTERTAINMENT CORP
AMAZON.COM INC
AMC ENTERTAINMENT INC
AMERICAN COIN MERCHANDISING INC
AMERICAN EDUCATIONAL PRODUCTS LLC
AMERICAN EXPRESS CO
AMERICAN GOLF CORP
AMERICAN GREETINGS CORP
AMERICAN SKIING COMPANY
AMERICAN WAGERING INC
AMERISTAR CASINOS INC
AMF BOWLING WORLDWIDE INC
ANHEUSER BUSCH COS INC
ANSCHUTZ ENTERTAINMENT GROUP
APPLE INC
ARBITRON INC
ARISTOCRAT LEISURE LTD
ASCENT MEDIA GROUP INC
AT&T INC
AVID TECHNOLOGY INC
AZTAR CORP
BALLY TECHNOLOGIES INC
BALLY TOTAL FITNESS HOLDING CORPORATION
BANTA CORPORATION
BARNES & NOBLE INC
BEASLEY BROADCAST GROUP INC
BELO CORP
BERKSHIRE HATHAWAY INC
BERRY COMPANY (THE)
BERTELSMANN AG
BEST BUY CO INC
BLOCKBUSTER INC
BLOOMBERG LP
BOOTH CREEK SKI HOLDINGS INC
BORDERS GROUP INC
BOSE CORPORATION
BOYD GAMING CORP
BOYNE USA RESORTS
BRITISH BROADCASTING CORPORATION (BBC)
BUY.COM INC
CABLE NEWS NETWORK LP LLLP
CAESARS ENTERTAINMENT INC

CARMIKE CINEMAS INC
CBS CORP
CBS RADIO
CD WAREHOUSE INC
CEDAR FAIR LP
CENTURY CASINOS INC
CHARTER COMMUNICATIONS
CINEMARK INC
CINEMASTAR LUXURY THEATERS INC
CIRCUIT CITY STORES INC
CIRQUE DU SOLEIL INC
CITADEL BROADCASTING CORP
CLARION CO LTD
CLEAR CHANNEL COMMUNICATIONS INC
CLEAR CHANNEL OUTDOOR
CLUBCORP INC
CNET NETWORKS INC
COLUMBIA TRISTAR MOTION PICTURE GROUP
COMCAST CORP
COMMUNITY NEWSPAPER HOLDINGS INC
CONDE NAST PUBLICATIONS INC
COURIER CORP
COX COMMUNICATIONS INC
COX ENTERPRISES INC
COX RADIO INC
CREATIVE ARTISTS AGENCY INC
CROWN MEDIA HOLDINGS INC
CUMULUS MEDIA INC
CURVES INTERNATIONAL INC
CW NETWORK (THE)
DAILY JOURNAL CORP
DELAWARE NORTH COMPANIES
DG FASTCHANNEL
DIALOG NEWSEDGE
DICK CLARK PRODUCTIONS INC
DIGEO INC
DIGITAL BRIDGES LIMITED
DIGITAL VIDEO SYSTEMS INC
DIRECTV GROUP INC (THE)
DISCOVERY COMMUNICATIONS INC
DOLBY LABORATORIES INC
DOUBLECLICK INC
DOW JONES & COMPANY INC
DREAMWORKS ANIMATION SKG INC
DREAMWORKS LLC
DTS INC
DUN & BRADSTREET CORP (THE, D&B)
E W SCRIPPS CO
ECHOSTAR COMMUNICATIONS CORP
ELECTRONIC ARTS INC
EMAP PLC
EMI GROUP PLC
EMMIS COMMUNICATIONS CORP
ENDEAVOR AGENCY (THE)
ENTERCOM COMMUNICATIONS CORP
ENTERTAINMENT PROPERTIES TRUST
ENTRAVISION COMMUNICATIONS CORPORATION
FIRST LOOK STUDIOS INC

FISHER COMMUNICATIONS INC
FORD MODELS INC
FOX BROADCASTING COMPANY
FOX ENTERTAINMENT GROUP INC
FOX FILMED ENTERTAINMENT
FOX SPORTS NET INC
FREEDOM COMMUNICATIONS INC
GAMESTOP CORP
GAMETECH INTERNATIONAL INC
GAMING PARTNERS INTERNATIONAL CORP
GANNETT CO INC
GAYLORD ENTERTAINMENT CO
GEMSTAR-TV GUIDE INTERNATIONAL INC
GENERAL ELECTRIC CO (GE)
GETTY IMAGES INC
GLU MOBILE
GOLD'S GYM INTERNATIONAL
GOOGLE INC
GRANITE BROADCASTING CORP
GRAY TELEVISION INC
HALLMARK CARDS INC
HANDS-ON MOBILE
HARRAH'S ENTERTAINMENT INC
HARRIS INTERACTIVE INC
HARTE-HANKS INC
HASTINGS ENTERTAINMENT INC
HEARST CORPORATION (THE)
HEARST-ARGYLE TELEVISION INC
HERSHEY CO
HOLLYWOOD ENTERTAINMENT CORP
HOLLYWOOD MEDIA CORP
HOUGHTON MIFFLIN CO
IAC/INTERACTIVECORP
IGN ENTERTAINMENT
IMAX CORPORATION
IMG WORLDWIDE INC
INGRAM ENTERTAINMENT HOLDINGS INC
INTERACTIVE DATA CORPORATION
INTERNATIONAL CREATIVE MANAGEMENT (ICM)
INTERNATIONAL GAME TECHNOLOGY
INTERNATIONAL LOTTERY & TOTALIZATOR
SYSTEMS
INTERPUBLIC GROUP OF COMPANIES INC
INTERVIDEO INC
ION MEDIA NETWORKS
ION MEDIA NETWORKS INC
ISLE OF CAPRI CASINOS INC
JOHN WILEY & SONS INC
JOHNSON PUBLISHING COMPANY INC
JOURNAL COMMUNICATIONS INC
JUPITERMEDIA CORP
LAKES ENTERTAINMENT INC
LAMAR ADVERTISING CO
LANDMARK COMMUNICATIONS INC
LANDRY'S RESTAURANTS INC
LAS VEGAS SANDS CORP (THE VENETIAN)
LASERPACIFIC MEDIA CORP
LEE ENTERPRISES INC

LIBERTY GLOBAL
LIBERTY MEDIA CORP
LIN TV CORP
LIONS GATE ENTERTAINMENT CORP
LIQUID DIGITAL MEDIA
LIVE NATION INC
LODGENET ENTERTAINMENT CORP
LOUD TECHNOLOGIES INC
LUCASARTS ENTERTAINMENT COMPANY LLC
LUCASFILM LTD
MACROVISION CORP
MAGNA ENTERTAINMENT CORP
MARKETWATCH INC
MARVEL ENTERTAINMENT INC
MATSUSHITA ELECTRIC INDUSTRIAL CO LTD
MCCLATCHY COMPANY (THE)
MCGRAW HILL COS INC
MEDIACOM COMMUNICATIONS CORP
MEDIANEWS GROUP INC
MEREDITH CORP
METRO-GOLDWYN-MAYER INC (MGM)
MGM MIRAGE
MGM PICTURES
MICROSOFT CORP
MIDWAY GAMES INC
MOBITV INC
MONARCH CASINO & RESORT INC
MONSTER WORLDWIDE
MOODY'S CORPORATION
MORRIS COMMUNICATIONS COMPANY LLC
MOVIE GALLERY INC
MP3.COM INC
MTR GAMING GROUP INC
MTV NETWORKS
MULTIMEDIA GAMES INC
NAPSTER INC
NATIONAL AMUSEMENTS INC
NBC UNIVERSAL
NETFLIX
NETRATINGS INC
NEW YORK TIMES CO (THE)
NEWS CORPORATION LIMITED (THE)
NEXSTAR BROADCASTING GROUP INC
NINTENDO CO LTD
NTN BUZZTIME INC
OMNICOM GROUP INC
OMNIVISION TECHNOLOGIES INC
ON COMMAND CORP
ON STAGE ENTERTAINMENT
PALACE ENTERTAINMENT
PANAMSAT CORP
PARAMOUNT PICTURES CORP
PEARSON PLC
PENN NATIONAL GAMING INC
PENTON MEDIA INC
PINNACLE ENTERTAINMENT INC
PIONEER CORPORATION
PIXAR ANIMATION STUDIOS

PLAYBOY ENTERPRISES INC
PRIMEDIA INC
PROGRESSIVE GAMING INTERNATIONAL CORP
PROQUEST COMPANY
R R DONNELLEY & SONS CO
RADIO ONE
RADIOSHACK CORPORATION
RAINBOW MEDIA HOLDINGS LLC
RANDOM HOUSE INC
RAYCOM MEDIA INC
RCN CORP
READER'S DIGEST ASSOCIATION INC
REALNETWORKS INC
REGAL ENTERTAINMENT GROUP
REGENT COMMUNICATIONS
RENAISSANCE ENTERTAINMENT CORP
RENTRAK CORPORATION
REX STORES CORP
RIVIERA HOLDINGS CORP
SAGA COMMUNICATIONS INC
SALEM COMMUNICATIONS CORP
SALON MEDIA GROUP INC
SAMSUNG ELECTRONICS CO LTD
SANDS REGENT
SANYO ELECTRIC COMPANY LTD
SCHOLASTIC CORP
SCIENTIFIC GAMES CORPORATION
SEGA SAMMY HOLDINGS INC
SHARP CORPORATION
SHOP AT HOME NETWORK LLC
SHUFFLE MASTER INC
SIMEX-IWERKS
SINCLAIR BROADCAST GROUP INC
SIX FLAGS INC
SONY CORPORATION
SONY PICTURES ENTERTAINMENT
SPANISH BROADCASTING SYSTEM INC
SRS LABS INC
STATION CASINOS INC
SUDDENLINK COMMUNICATIONS
THOMAS NELSON INC
THOMSON CORPORATION (THE)
THQ INC
TICKETMASTER
TIME INC
TIME WARNER CABLE
TIME WARNER INC
TIVO INC
TRANS WORLD ENTERTAINMENT CORP
TRANS-LUX CORPORATION
TRIBUNE CO
TWEETER HOME ENTERTAINMENT GROUP INC
UNITED ARTISTS CORPORATION
UNITED BUSINESS MEDIA PLC
UNITED ONLINE INC
UNITED PARAMOUNT NETWORK (UPN)
UNITED TALENT AGENCY INC
UNIVERSAL MUSIC GROUP

UNIVERSAL PICTURES
UNIVISION COMMUNICATIONS INC
VAIL RESORTS INC
VERIZON COMMUNICATIONS
VIACOM INC
VIVENDI GAMES
VIVENDI SA
VNU NV
VULCAN INC
WALT DISNEY COMPANY (THE)
WALT DISNEY STUDIOS
WARNER BROS ENTERTAINMENT INC
WARNER MUSIC GROUP
WASHINGTON POST CO
WENNER MEDIA LLC
WESTWOOD ONE INC
WHEREHOUSE ENTERTAINMENT (RECORD TOWN INC)
WILLIAM MORRIS AGENCY INC
WORLD WRESTLING ENTERTAINMENT INC (WWF)
WPP GROUP PLC
WYNN RESORTS LIMITED
YAHOO! INC
YAHOO! SEARCH MARKETING GROUP
YOUBET.COM INC
YOUNG BROADCASTING INC
ZIFF DAVIS MEDIA INC

SOUTHWEST
24 HOUR FITNESS USA
2929 ENTERTAINMENT
ACME COMMUNICATIONS INC
ADVANCE PUBLICATIONS INC
ADVANCED MARKETING SERVICES INC
AMAZON.COM INC
AMC ENTERTAINMENT INC
AMERICAN EXPRESS CO
AMERICAN GOLF CORP
AMERICAN GREETINGS CORP
AMF BOWLING WORLDWIDE INC
ANDERSON NEWS LLC
ANHEUSER BUSCH COS INC
ANSCHUTZ ENTERTAINMENT GROUP
APPLE INC
ARBITRON INC
AT&T INC
BALLY TECHNOLOGIES INC
BALLY TOTAL FITNESS HOLDING CORPORATION
BANTA CORPORATION
BARNES & NOBLE INC
BELO CORP
BERKSHIRE HATHAWAY INC
BEST BUY CO INC
BLOCKBUSTER INC
BLOOMBERG LP
BOOKS A MILLION INC
BOOTH CREEK SKI HOLDINGS INC
BORDERS GROUP INC

BOSE CORPORATION
CABLE NEWS NETWORK LP LLLP
CARMIKE CINEMAS INC
CBS CORP
CBS RADIO
CD WAREHOUSE INC
CHARTER COMMUNICATIONS
CINEMARK INC
CIRCUIT CITY STORES INC
CITADEL BROADCASTING CORP
CLEAR CHANNEL COMMUNICATIONS INC
CLEAR CHANNEL OUTDOOR
CLUBCORP INC
CNET NETWORKS INC
COMCAST CORP
COMMUNITY NEWSPAPER HOLDINGS INC
COX COMMUNICATIONS INC
COX ENTERPRISES INC
COX RADIO INC
CUMULUS MEDIA INC
CURVES INTERNATIONAL INC
DAILY JOURNAL CORP
DELAWARE NORTH COMPANIES
DG FASTCHANNEL
DIALOG NEWSEDGE
DICK CLARK PRODUCTIONS INC
DIRECTV GROUP INC (THE)
DOW JONES & COMPANY INC
DUN & BRADSTREET CORP (THE, D&B)
E W SCRIPPS CO
ECHOSTAR COMMUNICATIONS CORP
EDUCATIONAL DEVELOPMENT CORP
ELECTRONIC ARTS INC
EMMIS COMMUNICATIONS CORP
ENTERCOM COMMUNICATIONS CORP
ENTERTAINMENT PROPERTIES TRUST
ENTRAVISION COMMUNICATIONS CORPORATION
FORD MODELS INC
FOX ENTERTAINMENT GROUP INC
FOX SPORTS NET INC
FREEDOM COMMUNICATIONS INC
GAMESTOP CORP
GAMETECH INTERNATIONAL INC
GANNETT CO INC
GAYLORD ENTERTAINMENT CO
GEMSTAR-TV GUIDE INTERNATIONAL INC
GENERAL ELECTRIC CO (GE)
GOLD'S GYM INTERNATIONAL
GOOGLE INC
GRAY TELEVISION INC
HALLMARK CARDS INC
HARRAH'S ENTERTAINMENT INC
HARTE-HANKS INC
HASTINGS ENTERTAINMENT INC
HEARST CORPORATION (THE)
HEARST-ARGYLE TELEVISION INC
HERSHEY CO
HOLLYWOOD ENTERTAINMENT CORP

HOOVER'S INC
HOUGHTON MIFFLIN CO
IAC/INTERACTIVECORP
IMAX CORPORATION
INGRAM ENTERTAINMENT HOLDINGS INC
INSIGHT COMMUNICATIONS COMPANY INC
INTERPUBLIC GROUP OF COMPANIES INC
ION MEDIA NETWORKS
ION MEDIA NETWORKS INC
JOURNAL COMMUNICATIONS INC
LAKES ENTERTAINMENT INC
LAMAR ADVERTISING CO
LANDMARK COMMUNICATIONS INC
LANDRY'S RESTAURANTS INC
LEE ENTERPRISES INC
LIBERTY MEDIA CORP
LIN TV CORP
LIVE NATION INC
LODGENET ENTERTAINMENT CORP
MAGNA ENTERTAINMENT CORP
MATSUSHITA ELECTRIC INDUSTRIAL CO LTD
MCGRAW HILL COS INC
MEDIANEWS GROUP INC
MEREDITH CORP
MICROSOFT CORP
MIDWAY GAMES INC
MONSTER WORLDWIDE
MOODY'S CORPORATION
MORRIS COMMUNICATIONS COMPANY LLC
MOVIE GALLERY INC
MULTIMEDIA GAMES INC
NETFLIX
NEW YORK TIMES CO (THE)
NEWS CORPORATION LIMITED (THE)
NEXSTAR BROADCASTING GROUP INC
NTN BUZZTIME INC
OMNICOM GROUP INC
ON COMMAND CORP
PALACE ENTERTAINMENT
PEARSON PLC
PRIMEDIA INC
PROGRESSIVE GAMING INTERNATIONAL CORP
PROQUEST COMPANY
R R DONNELLEY & SONS CO
RADIO ONE
RADIOSHACK CORPORATION
RAYCOM MEDIA INC
READER'S DIGEST ASSOCIATION INC
REALNETWORKS INC
REED ELSEVIER GROUP PLC
REGAL ENTERTAINMENT GROUP
REGENT COMMUNICATIONS
REX STORES CORP
SAGA COMMUNICATIONS INC
SALEM COMMUNICATIONS CORP
SAMSUNG ELECTRONICS CO LTD
SCHOLASTIC CORP
SCIENTIFIC GAMES CORPORATION

SEGA SAMMY HOLDINGS INC
SINCLAIR BROADCAST GROUP INC
SIX FLAGS INC
SONY CORPORATION
SPANISH BROADCASTING SYSTEM INC
STATION CASINOS INC
SUDDENLINK COMMUNICATIONS
THOMAS NELSON INC
THOMSON CORPORATION (THE)
THQ INC
TICKETMASTER
TIME INC
TIME WARNER CABLE
TIME WARNER INC
TRANS WORLD ENTERTAINMENT CORP
TRANS-LUX CORPORATION
TRIBUNE CO
TWEETER HOME ENTERTAINMENT GROUP INC
UNIVERSAL MUSIC GROUP
UNIVISION COMMUNICATIONS INC
VAIL RESORTS INC
VERIZON COMMUNICATIONS
VIVENDI GAMES
VIVENDI SA
VNU NV
WALT DISNEY COMPANY (THE)
WASHINGTON POST CO
WENNER MEDIA LLC
WHEREHOUSE ENTERTAINMENT (RECORD TOWN INC)
WPP GROUP PLC
YAHOO! INC

MIDWEST
24 HOUR FITNESS USA
24/7 REAL MEDIA INC
A&E TELEVISION NETWORKS
ACME COMMUNICATIONS INC
ACTIVISION INC
ADVANCE PUBLICATIONS INC
ADVANCED MARKETING SERVICES INC
ALLIANCE ENTERTAINMENT CORP
AMAZON.COM INC
AMC ENTERTAINMENT INC
AMERICAN EXPRESS CO
AMERICAN GOLF CORP
AMERICAN GREETINGS CORP
AMERISTAR CASINOS INC
AMF BOWLING WORLDWIDE INC
ANHEUSER BUSCH COS INC
ANSCHUTZ ENTERTAINMENT GROUP
APPLE INC
ARBITRON INC
ARISTOCRAT LEISURE LTD
ASCENT MEDIA GROUP INC
AT&T INC
AVID TECHNOLOGY INC
AZTAR CORP

BALLY TOTAL FITNESS HOLDING CORPORATION
BANTA CORPORATION
BARNES & NOBLE INC
BELO CORP
BERKSHIRE HATHAWAY INC
BERRY COMPANY (THE)
BERTELSMANN AG
BEST BUY CO INC
BLOCKBUSTER INC
BLOOMBERG LP
BOOKS A MILLION INC
BORDERS GROUP INC
BOSE CORPORATION
BOYD GAMING CORP
BOYNE USA RESORTS
CABLE NEWS NETWORK LP LLLP
CAESARS ENTERTAINMENT INC
CANTERBURY PARK HOLDING CORP
CANWEST GLOBAL COMMUNICATIONS
CARMIKE CINEMAS INC
CBS CORP
CBS RADIO
CD WAREHOUSE INC
CEDAR FAIR LP
CHARTER COMMUNICATIONS
CHURCHILL DOWNS INC
CINEMARK INC
CIRCUIT CITY STORES INC
CITADEL BROADCASTING CORP
CLEAR CHANNEL COMMUNICATIONS INC
CLEAR CHANNEL OUTDOOR
CLUBCORP INC
CNET NETWORKS INC
COMCAST CORP
COMMUNITY NEWSPAPER HOLDINGS INC
CONCRETE SOFTWARE INC
CONCURRENT COMPUTER CORP
CONDE NAST PUBLICATIONS INC
COURIER CORP
COX COMMUNICATIONS INC
COX ENTERPRISES INC
COX RADIO INC
CUMULUS MEDIA INC
CURVES INTERNATIONAL INC
DELAWARE NORTH COMPANIES
DG FASTCHANNEL
DIALOG NEWSEDGE
DICK CLARK PRODUCTIONS INC
DIRECTV GROUP INC (THE)
DISCOVERY COMMUNICATIONS INC
DOUBLECLICK INC
DOW JONES & COMPANY INC
DUN & BRADSTREET CORP (THE, D&B)
E W SCRIPPS CO
ECHOSTAR COMMUNICATIONS CORP
ELECTRONIC ARTS INC
EMAP PLC
EMMIS COMMUNICATIONS CORP

ENTERCOM COMMUNICATIONS CORP
ENTERTAINMENT PROPERTIES TRUST
FORD MODELS INC
FOX ENTERTAINMENT GROUP INC
FOX SPORTS NET INC
FREEDOM COMMUNICATIONS INC
GAMESTOP CORP
GAMETECH INTERNATIONAL INC
GANNETT CO INC
GEMSTAR-TV GUIDE INTERNATIONAL INC
GENERAL ELECTRIC CO (GE)
GETTY IMAGES INC
GOLD'S GYM INTERNATIONAL
GOOGLE INC
GRANITE BROADCASTING CORP
GRAY TELEVISION INC
HALLMARK CARDS INC
HARPERCOLLINS PUBLISHERS INC
HARPO INC
HARRAH'S ENTERTAINMENT INC
HARRIS INTERACTIVE INC
HARTE-HANKS INC
HASTINGS ENTERTAINMENT INC
HEARST CORPORATION (THE)
HEARST-ARGYLE TELEVISION INC
HERSHEY CO
HOLLINGER INC
HOLLYWOOD ENTERTAINMENT CORP
HOUGHTON MIFFLIN CO
IAC/INTERACTIVECORP
IGN ENTERTAINMENT
IMAX CORPORATION
IMG WORLDWIDE INC
INGRAM ENTERTAINMENT HOLDINGS INC
INSIGHT COMMUNICATIONS COMPANY INC
INTERACTIVE DATA CORPORATION
INTERNATIONAL GAME TECHNOLOGY
INTERPUBLIC GROUP OF COMPANIES INC
ION MEDIA NETWORKS
ION MEDIA NETWORKS INC
ISLE OF CAPRI CASINOS INC
JOHN WILEY & SONS INC
JOHNSON PUBLISHING COMPANY INC
JOURNAL COMMUNICATIONS INC
JOURNAL REGISTER CO
LAKES ENTERTAINMENT INC
LAMAR ADVERTISING CO
LANDMARK COMMUNICATIONS INC
LANDRY'S RESTAURANTS INC
LEE ENTERPRISES INC
LERNER PUBLISHING GROUP
LIBERTY MEDIA CORP
LIN TV CORP
LIVE NATION INC
LODGENET ENTERTAINMENT CORP
LOUD TECHNOLOGIES INC
MACROVISION CORP
MAGNA ENTERTAINMENT CORP

MATSUSHITA ELECTRIC INDUSTRIAL CO LTD
MCCLATCHY COMPANY (THE)
MCGRAW HILL COS INC
MEDIA GENERAL INC
MEDIACOM COMMUNICATIONS CORP
MEDIANEWS GROUP INC
MEREDITH CORP
MGM MIRAGE
MICROSOFT CORP
MIDWAY GAMES INC
MONSTER WORLDWIDE
MOODY'S CORPORATION
MORRIS COMMUNICATIONS COMPANY LLC
MOVIE GALLERY INC
MTR GAMING GROUP INC
MULTIMEDIA GAMES INC
NATIONAL AMUSEMENTS INC
NBC UNIVERSAL
NETFLIX
NEW YORK TIMES CO (THE)
NEWS CORPORATION LIMITED (THE)
NEXSTAR BROADCASTING GROUP INC
OMNICOM GROUP INC
OMNIVISION TECHNOLOGIES INC
ON COMMAND CORP
ON STAGE ENTERTAINMENT
PALACE ENTERTAINMENT
PEARSON PLC
PENN NATIONAL GAMING INC
PENTON MEDIA INC
PINNACLE ENTERTAINMENT INC
PLAYBOY ENTERPRISES INC
PRIMEDIA INC
PROGRESSIVE GAMING INTERNATIONAL CORP
PROQUEST COMPANY
R R DONNELLEY & SONS CO
RADIO ONE
RADIOSHACK CORPORATION
RAINBOW MEDIA HOLDINGS LLC
RAYCOM MEDIA INC
RCN CORP
READER'S DIGEST ASSOCIATION INC
REED ELSEVIER GROUP PLC
REGAL ENTERTAINMENT GROUP
REGENT COMMUNICATIONS
RENAISSANCE ENTERTAINMENT CORP
REX STORES CORP
SAGA COMMUNICATIONS INC
SALEM COMMUNICATIONS CORP
SAMSUNG ELECTRONICS CO LTD
SCHOLASTIC CORP
SCIENTIFIC GAMES CORPORATION
SEGA SAMMY HOLDINGS INC
SHARP CORPORATION
SHOP AT HOME NETWORK LLC
SHUFFLE MASTER INC
SINCLAIR BROADCAST GROUP INC
SIX FLAGS INC

SONY CORPORATION
SPANISH BROADCASTING SYSTEM INC
SUDDENLINK COMMUNICATIONS
THOMAS NELSON INC
THOMSON CORPORATION (THE)
THQ INC
TICKETMASTER
TIME INC
TIME WARNER CABLE
TIME WARNER INC
TRANS WORLD ENTERTAINMENT CORP
TRANS-LUX CORPORATION
TRIBUNE CO
TRUMP ENTERTAINMENT RESORTS INC
TWEETER HOME ENTERTAINMENT GROUP INC
UNITED BUSINESS MEDIA PLC
UNIVERSAL MUSIC GROUP
UNIVISION COMMUNICATIONS INC
VALUEVISION MEDIA INC
VERIZON COMMUNICATIONS
VIACOM INC
VIVENDI GAMES
VIVENDI SA
VNU NV
WALT DISNEY COMPANY (THE)
WASHINGTON POST CO
WENNER MEDIA LLC
WHEREHOUSE ENTERTAINMENT (RECORD TOWN INC)
WMS INDUSTRIES INC
WORLD WRESTLING ENTERTAINMENT INC (WWF)
WPP GROUP PLC
XM SATELLITE RADIO HOLDINGS INC
YAHOO! INC
YAHOO! SEARCH MARKETING GROUP
YOUNG BROADCASTING INC

SOUTHEAST
24 HOUR FITNESS USA
A&E TELEVISION NETWORKS
ACME COMMUNICATIONS INC
ACTIVISION INC
ADVANCE PUBLICATIONS INC
ALLIANCE ENTERTAINMENT CORP
AMC ENTERTAINMENT INC
AMERICAN EXPRESS CO
AMERICAN GOLF CORP
AMERICAN GREETINGS CORP
AMERISTAR CASINOS INC
AMF BOWLING WORLDWIDE INC
ANDERSON NEWS LLC
ANHEUSER BUSCH COS INC
ANSCHUTZ ENTERTAINMENT GROUP
APPLE INC
ARBITRON INC
ARISTOCRAT LEISURE LTD
ASCENT MEDIA GROUP INC
AT&T INC

AVID TECHNOLOGY INC
BALLY TECHNOLOGIES INC
BALLY TOTAL FITNESS HOLDING CORPORATION
BANTA CORPORATION
BARNES & NOBLE INC
BARNESANDNOBLE.COM INC
BEASLEY BROADCAST GROUP INC
BELO CORP
BERKSHIRE HATHAWAY INC
BERRY COMPANY (THE)
BERTELSMANN AG
BEST BUY CO INC
BLOCKBUSTER INC
BLOOMBERG LP
BOOKS A MILLION INC
BORDERS GROUP INC
BOSE CORPORATION
BOYD GAMING CORP
BOYNE USA RESORTS
CABLE NEWS NETWORK LP LLLP
CAESARS ENTERTAINMENT INC
CARMIKE CINEMAS INC
CBS CORP
CBS RADIO
CD WAREHOUSE INC
CHARTER COMMUNICATIONS
CHURCHILL DOWNS INC
CINEMARK INC
CIRCUIT CITY STORES INC
CITADEL BROADCASTING CORP
CLEAR CHANNEL COMMUNICATIONS INC
CLEAR CHANNEL OUTDOOR
CLUBCORP INC
CNET NETWORKS INC
COMCAST CORP
COMMUNITY NEWSPAPER HOLDINGS INC
CONCURRENT COMPUTER CORP
COX COMMUNICATIONS INC
COX ENTERPRISES INC
COX RADIO INC
CUMULUS MEDIA INC
CURVES INTERNATIONAL INC
DELAWARE NORTH COMPANIES
DG FASTCHANNEL
DIALOG NEWSEDGE
DIAMONDHEAD CASINO CORPORATION
DIRECTV GROUP INC (THE)
DISCOVERY COMMUNICATIONS INC
DOW JONES & COMPANY INC
DREAMWORKS LLC
DUN & BRADSTREET CORP (THE, D&B)
E W SCRIPPS CO
EBSCO INDUSTRIES INC
ECHOSTAR COMMUNICATIONS CORP
ELECTRONIC ARTS INC
EMMIS COMMUNICATIONS CORP
ENTERCOM COMMUNICATIONS CORP
ENTERTAINMENT PROPERTIES TRUST

ENTRAVISION COMMUNICATIONS CORPORATION
FORD MODELS INC
FOX ENTERTAINMENT GROUP INC
FOX SPORTS NET INC
FREEDOM COMMUNICATIONS INC
GAMESTOP CORP
GANNETT CO INC
GAYLORD ENTERTAINMENT CO
GENERAL ELECTRIC CO (GE)
GOLD'S GYM INTERNATIONAL
GOOGLE INC
GRAY TELEVISION INC
HALLMARK CARDS INC
HARRAH'S ENTERTAINMENT INC
HARTE-HANKS INC
HASTINGS ENTERTAINMENT INC
HEARST CORPORATION (THE)
HEARST-ARGYLE TELEVISION INC
HERSHEY CO
HOLLYWOOD ENTERTAINMENT CORP
HOLLYWOOD MEDIA CORP
HOUGHTON MIFFLIN CO
IAC/INTERACTIVECORP
IMAX CORPORATION
IMG WORLDWIDE INC
INGRAM ENTERTAINMENT HOLDINGS INC
INTEGRITY MEDIA INC
INTERPUBLIC GROUP OF COMPANIES INC
ION MEDIA NETWORKS
ION MEDIA NETWORKS INC
ISLE OF CAPRI CASINOS INC
JOURNAL COMMUNICATIONS INC
KNOLOGY INC
LAKES ENTERTAINMENT INC
LAMAR ADVERTISING CO
LANDMARK COMMUNICATIONS INC
LANDRY'S RESTAURANTS INC
LEE ENTERPRISES INC
LIBERTY MEDIA CORP
LIN TV CORP
LIVE NATION INC
LODGENET ENTERTAINMENT CORP
MAGNA ENTERTAINMENT CORP
MATSUSHITA ELECTRIC INDUSTRIAL CO LTD
MCCLATCHY COMPANY (THE)
MDI ENTERTAINMENT INC
MEDIA GENERAL INC
MEDIACOM COMMUNICATIONS CORP
MEREDITH CORP
MGM MIRAGE
MICROSOFT CORP
MONSTER WORLDWIDE
MOODY'S CORPORATION
MORRIS COMMUNICATIONS COMPANY LLC
MOVIE GALLERY INC
NETFLIX
NEW YORK TIMES CO (THE)
NEWS CORPORATION LIMITED (THE)

NEXSTAR BROADCASTING GROUP INC
NTN BUZZTIME INC
OMNICOM GROUP INC
ON COMMAND CORP
ON STAGE ENTERTAINMENT
PALACE ENTERTAINMENT
PENN NATIONAL GAMING INC
PINNACLE ENTERTAINMENT INC
PRIMEDIA INC
PROGRESSIVE GAMING INTERNATIONAL CORP
PROQUEST COMPANY
R R DONNELLEY & SONS CO
RADIO ONE
RADIOSHACK CORPORATION
RAYCOM MEDIA INC
READER'S DIGEST ASSOCIATION INC
REED ELSEVIER GROUP PLC
REGAL ENTERTAINMENT GROUP
REGENT COMMUNICATIONS
REX STORES CORP
SAGA COMMUNICATIONS INC
SALEM COMMUNICATIONS CORP
SAMSUNG ELECTRONICS CO LTD
SCHOLASTIC CORP
SCIENTIFIC GAMES CORPORATION
SEGA SAMMY HOLDINGS INC
SHARP CORPORATION
SHOP AT HOME NETWORK LLC
SIMEX-IWERKS
SINCLAIR BROADCAST GROUP INC
SIX FLAGS INC
SONY CORPORATION
SPANISH BROADCASTING SYSTEM INC
SUDDENLINK COMMUNICATIONS
THOMAS NELSON INC
THOMSON CORPORATION (THE)
TICKETMASTER
TIME INC
TIME WARNER CABLE
TIME WARNER INC
TRANS WORLD ENTERTAINMENT CORP
TRIBUNE CO
TURNER BROADCASTING SYSTEM
TWEETER HOME ENTERTAINMENT GROUP INC
UNIVERSAL MUSIC GROUP
UNIVERSAL PICTURES
UNIVISION COMMUNICATIONS INC
VERIZON COMMUNICATIONS
VIVENDI SA
VNU NV
WALT DISNEY COMPANY (THE)
WARNER MUSIC GROUP
WASHINGTON POST CO
WENNER MEDIA LLC
WHEREHOUSE ENTERTAINMENT (RECORD TOWN INC)
WILLIAM MORRIS AGENCY INC
WPP GROUP PLC

XM SATELLITE RADIO HOLDINGS INC
YAHOO! INC
YOUNG BROADCASTING INC

NORTHEAST
24/7 REAL MEDIA INC
A&E TELEVISION NETWORKS
ABC INC
ACTIVISION INC
ADVANCE PUBLICATIONS INC
ADVANCED MARKETING SERVICES INC
ALLIANCE ATLANTIS COMMUNICATIONS INC
ALLIANCE ENTERTAINMENT CORP
AMAZON.COM INC
AMC ENTERTAINMENT INC
AMERICAN COIN MERCHANDISING INC
AMERICAN EXPRESS CO
AMERICAN GOLF CORP
AMERICAN GREETINGS CORP
AMERICAN SKIING COMPANY
AMF BOWLING WORLDWIDE INC
ANHEUSER BUSCH COS INC
ANSCHUTZ ENTERTAINMENT GROUP
AOL LLC
APPLE INC
ARBITRON INC
ARISTOCRAT LEISURE LTD
ASCENT MEDIA GROUP INC
AT&T INC
AUDIBLE INC
AVID TECHNOLOGY INC
AZTAR CORP
BALLY TECHNOLOGIES INC
BALLY TOTAL FITNESS HOLDING CORPORATION
BANTA CORPORATION
BARNES & NOBLE INC
BARNESANDNOBLE.COM INC
BEASLEY BROADCAST GROUP INC
BELO CORP
BERKSHIRE HATHAWAY INC
BERRY COMPANY (THE)
BERTELSMANN AG
BEST BUY CO INC
BLOCKBUSTER INC
BLOOMBERG LP
BOOKS A MILLION INC
BOOTH CREEK SKI HOLDINGS INC
BORDERS GROUP INC
BOSE CORPORATION
BOYD GAMING CORP
BRITISH BROADCASTING CORPORATION (BBC)
CABLE NEWS NETWORK LP LLLP
CABLEVISION SYSTEMS CORP
CAESARS ENTERTAINMENT INC
CARMIKE CINEMAS INC
CBS CORP
CBS RADIO
CD WAREHOUSE INC

CEDAR FAIR LP
CHARTER COMMUNICATIONS
CINEMARK INC
CIRCUIT CITY STORES INC
CIRQUE DU SOLEIL INC
CITADEL BROADCASTING CORP
CLEAR CHANNEL COMMUNICATIONS INC
CLEAR CHANNEL OUTDOOR
CLUBCORP INC
CNET NETWORKS INC
COMCAST CORP
COMMUNITY NEWSPAPER HOLDINGS INC
CONCURRENT COMPUTER CORP
CONDE NAST PUBLICATIONS INC
COURIER CORP
COX COMMUNICATIONS INC
COX ENTERPRISES INC
COX RADIO INC
CUMULUS MEDIA INC
CURVES INTERNATIONAL INC
DAG MEDIA INC
DAILY JOURNAL CORP
DELAWARE NORTH COMPANIES
DENNIS PUBLISHING LTD
DG FASTCHANNEL
DIALOG NEWSEDGE
DICK CLARK PRODUCTIONS INC
DIGITAL BRIDGES LIMITED
DISCOVERY COMMUNICATIONS INC
DOLBY LABORATORIES INC
DOUBLECLICK INC
DOVER DOWNS GAMING & ENTERTAINMENT INC
DOW JONES & COMPANY INC
DREAMWORKS LLC
DUN & BRADSTREET CORP (THE, D&B)
E W SCRIPPS CO
ECHOSTAR COMMUNICATIONS CORP
ELECTRONIC ARTS INC
EMAP PLC
EMI GROUP PLC
EMMIS COMMUNICATIONS CORP
ENDEAVOR AGENCY (THE)
ENTERCOM COMMUNICATIONS CORP
ENTERTAINMENT PROPERTIES TRUST
ENTRAVISION COMMUNICATIONS CORPORATION
ESPN INC
FIRST LOOK STUDIOS INC
FORBES INC
FORD MODELS INC
FOX ENTERTAINMENT GROUP INC
FOX SPORTS NET INC
FREEDOM COMMUNICATIONS INC
GAMESTOP CORP
GANNETT CO INC
GEMSTAR-TV GUIDE INTERNATIONAL INC
GENERAL ELECTRIC CO (GE)
GETTY IMAGES INC
GOLD'S GYM INTERNATIONAL

GOOGLE INC
GRANITE BROADCASTING CORP
GRAY TELEVISION INC
GTECH HOLDINGS CORP
HALLMARK CARDS INC
HARPERCOLLINS PUBLISHERS INC
HARRAH'S ENTERTAINMENT INC
HARRIS INTERACTIVE INC
HARTE-HANKS INC
HARVEY ELECTRONICS INC
HEARST CORPORATION (THE)
HEARST-ARGYLE TELEVISION INC
HERSHEY CO
HOLLINGER INC
HOLLYWOOD ENTERTAINMENT CORP
HOLLYWOOD MEDIA CORP
HOOVER'S INC
HOUGHTON MIFFLIN CO
IAC/INTERACTIVECORP
IGN ENTERTAINMENT
IMAX CORPORATION
IMG WORLDWIDE INC
INGRAM ENTERTAINMENT HOLDINGS INC
INSIGHT COMMUNICATIONS COMPANY INC
INTERACTIVE DATA CORPORATION
INTERNATIONAL CREATIVE MANAGEMENT (ICM)
INTERPUBLIC GROUP OF COMPANIES INC
ION MEDIA NETWORKS
ION MEDIA NETWORKS INC
IVILLAGE INC
JOHN WILEY & SONS INC
JOHNSON PUBLISHING COMPANY INC
JOURNAL COMMUNICATIONS INC
JOURNAL REGISTER CO
JUMPTV INC
JUPITERMEDIA CORP
KERZNER INTERNATIONAL LIMITED
LAGARDERE ACTIVE MEDIA
LAMAR ADVERTISING CO
LANDMARK COMMUNICATIONS INC
LANDRY'S RESTAURANTS INC
LEE ENTERPRISES INC
LIBERTY MEDIA CORP
LIN TV CORP
LIONS GATE ENTERTAINMENT CORP
LIVE NATION INC
LODGENET ENTERTAINMENT CORP
LOUD TECHNOLOGIES INC
MACROVISION CORP
MAGNA ENTERTAINMENT CORP
MARTHA STEWART LIVING OMNIMEDIA INC
MARVEL ENTERTAINMENT INC
MATSUSHITA ELECTRIC INDUSTRIAL CO LTD
MCCLATCHY COMPANY (THE)
MCGRAW HILL COS INC
MEDIA GENERAL INC
MEDIACOM COMMUNICATIONS CORP
MEDIANEWS GROUP INC

MEREDITH CORP
METRO INTERNATIONAL SA
METRO-GOLDWYN-MAYER INC (MGM)
MGM MIRAGE
MICROSOFT CORP
MIRAMAX FILM CORP
MOBITV INC
MONSTER WORLDWIDE
MOODY'S CORPORATION
MORRIS COMMUNICATIONS COMPANY LLC
MOVIE GALLERY INC
MTR GAMING GROUP INC
MTV NETWORKS
MULTIMEDIA GAMES INC
NAPSTER INC
NATIONAL AMUSEMENTS INC
NBC UNIVERSAL
NETFLIX
NETRATINGS INC
NEW LINE CINEMA
NEW YORK TIMES CO (THE)
NEWS CORPORATION LIMITED (THE)
NEWS WORLD COMMUNICATIONS INC
NEXSTAR BROADCASTING GROUP INC
NTL INCORPORATED
OMNICOM GROUP INC
OMNIVISION TECHNOLOGIES INC
ON COMMAND CORP
ON STAGE ENTERTAINMENT
PALACE ENTERTAINMENT
PANAMSAT CORP
PEARSON PLC
PENN NATIONAL GAMING INC
PENTON MEDIA INC
PINNACLE ENTERTAINMENT INC
PLAYBOY ENTERPRISES INC
PRIMEDIA INC
PROGRESSIVE GAMING INTERNATIONAL CORP
PROQUEST COMPANY
R R DONNELLEY & SONS CO
RADIO ONE
RADIOSHACK CORPORATION
RAINBOW MEDIA HOLDINGS LLC
RANDOM HOUSE INC
RCN CORP
READER'S DIGEST ASSOCIATION INC
REED ELSEVIER GROUP PLC
REGAL ENTERTAINMENT GROUP
REGENT COMMUNICATIONS
RENAISSANCE ENTERTAINMENT CORP
REUTERS GROUP PLC
REX STORES CORP
RODALE INC
SAGA COMMUNICATIONS INC
SALEM COMMUNICATIONS CORP
SALON MEDIA GROUP INC
SAMSUNG ELECTRONICS CO LTD
SCHOLASTIC CORP

SCIENTIFIC GAMES CORPORATION
SEGA SAMMY HOLDINGS INC
SHARP CORPORATION
SHOP AT HOME NETWORK LLC
SIMON & SCHUSTER INC
SINCLAIR BROADCAST GROUP INC
SIRIUS SATELLITE RADIO
SIX FLAGS INC
SONY BMG MUSIC ENTERTAINMENT
SONY CORPORATION
SPANISH BROADCASTING SYSTEM INC
SUDDENLINK COMMUNICATIONS
TAKE-TWO INTERACTIVE SOFTWARE INC
TAYLOR NELSON SOFRES PLC (TNS)
THOMAS NELSON INC
THOMSON CORPORATION (THE)
THQ INC
TICKETMASTER
TIME INC
TIME WARNER CABLE
TIME WARNER INC
TRAFFIX INC
TRANS WORLD CORP
TRANS WORLD ENTERTAINMENT CORP
TRANS-LUX CORPORATION
TRIBUNE CO
TRUMP ENTERTAINMENT RESORTS INC
TURNER BROADCASTING SYSTEM
TWEETER HOME ENTERTAINMENT GROUP INC
UNITED BUSINESS MEDIA PLC
UNITED ONLINE INC
UNITED TALENT AGENCY INC
UNIVERSAL MUSIC GROUP
UNIVISION COMMUNICATIONS INC
US NEWS AND WORLD REPORT LP
VAIL RESORTS INC
VALUE LINE INC
VALUEVISION MEDIA INC
VERIZON COMMUNICATIONS
VIACOM INC
VINDIGO INC
VIVENDI GAMES
VIVENDI SA
VNU NV
WALT DISNEY COMPANY (THE)
WARNER MUSIC GROUP
WASHINGTON POST CO
WENNER MEDIA LLC
WESTWOOD ONE INC
WHEREHOUSE ENTERTAINMENT (RECORD TOWN INC)
WILLIAM MORRIS AGENCY INC
WORLD WRESTLING ENTERTAINMENT INC (WWF)
WPP GROUP PLC
XM SATELLITE RADIO HOLDINGS INC
YAHOO! INC
YAHOO! SEARCH MARKETING GROUP
YOUNG BROADCASTING INC

ZIFF DAVIS MEDIA INC

INDEX OF FIRMS WITH OPERATIONS
OUTSIDE THE U.S.

24 HOUR FITNESS USA
24/7 REAL MEDIA INC
A&E TELEVISION NETWORKS
ACTIVISION INC
ADVANCED MARKETING SERVICES INC
ALLIANCE ATLANTIS COMMUNICATIONS INC
AMAZON.COM INC
AMC ENTERTAINMENT INC
AMERICAN EXPRESS CO
AMERICAN GREETINGS CORP
AMF BOWLING WORLDWIDE INC
ANHEUSER BUSCH COS INC
ANSCHUTZ ENTERTAINMENT GROUP
AOL LLC
APPLE INC
ARBITRON INC
ARISTOCRAT LEISURE LTD
ASCENT MEDIA GROUP INC
AT&T INC
AUDIBLE INC
AVID TECHNOLOGY INC
BALLY TECHNOLOGIES INC
BALLY TOTAL FITNESS HOLDING CORPORATION
BANTA CORPORATION
BARNES & NOBLE INC
BERKSHIRE HATHAWAY INC
BERRY COMPANY (THE)
BERTELSMANN AG
BEST BUY CO INC
BIOWARE CORP
BLOCKBUSTER INC
BLOOMBERG LP
BORDERS GROUP INC
BOSE CORPORATION
BOYNE USA RESORTS
BRITISH BROADCASTING CORPORATION (BBC)
BRITISH SKY BROADCASTING PLC
BUY.COM INC
CABLE NEWS NETWORK LP LLLP
CAESARS ENTERTAINMENT INC
CANWEST GLOBAL COMMUNICATIONS
CBS CORP
CD WAREHOUSE INC
CENTRAL EUROPEAN MEDIA ENTERPRISES LTD
CENTURY CASINOS INC
CINEMARK INC
CINEMASTAR LUXURY THEATERS INC
CIRCUIT CITY STORES INC
CIRQUE DU SOLEIL INC
CLARION CO LTD
CLEAR CHANNEL COMMUNICATIONS INC
CLEAR CHANNEL OUTDOOR
CLUBCORP INC
CNET NETWORKS INC
COLUMBIA TRISTAR MOTION PICTURE GROUP

COMCAST CORP
CONCURRENT COMPUTER CORP
CONDE NAST PUBLICATIONS INC
CORUS ENTERTAINMENT INC
COX ENTERPRISES INC
CREATIVE ARTISTS AGENCY INC
CUMULUS MEDIA INC
CURVES INTERNATIONAL INC
DELAWARE NORTH COMPANIES
DENNIS PUBLISHING LTD
DIALOG NEWSEDGE
DIGITAL BRIDGES LIMITED
DIGITAL VIDEO SYSTEMS INC
DIRECTV GROUP INC (THE)
DISCOVERY COMMUNICATIONS INC
DOLBY LABORATORIES INC
DOUBLECLICK INC
DOW JONES & COMPANY INC
DREAMWORKS LLC
DTS INC
DUN & BRADSTREET CORP (THE, D&B)
E W SCRIPPS CO
ECHOSTAR COMMUNICATIONS CORP
ELECTRONIC ARTS INC
EMAP PLC
EMI GROUP PLC
EMMIS COMMUNICATIONS CORP
ENTERTAINMENT PROPERTIES TRUST
EURO DISNEY SCA
FIRST LOOK STUDIOS INC
FORBES INC
FORD MODELS INC
FOX ENTERTAINMENT GROUP INC
GAMESTOP CORP
GAMING PARTNERS INTERNATIONAL CORP
GANNETT CO INC
GEMSTAR-TV GUIDE INTERNATIONAL INC
GENERAL ELECTRIC CO (GE)
GETTY IMAGES INC
GLU MOBILE
GOLD'S GYM INTERNATIONAL
GOOGLE INC
GRUPO RADIO CENTRO SA DE CV
GRUPO TELEVISA SA
GTECH HOLDINGS CORP
HALLMARK CARDS INC
HANDS-ON MOBILE
HARPERCOLLINS PUBLISHERS INC
HARRAH'S ENTERTAINMENT INC
HARRIS INTERACTIVE INC
HARTE-HANKS INC
HEARST CORPORATION (THE)
HERSHEY CO
HOLLINGER INC
HOUGHTON MIFFLIN CO
IAC/INTERACTIVECORP
I-CABLE COMMUNICATIONS
IGN ENTERTAINMENT

IMAX CORPORATION
IMG WORLDWIDE INC
INTEGRITY MEDIA INC
INTERACTIVE DATA CORPORATION
INTERNATIONAL CREATIVE MANAGEMENT (ICM)
INTERNATIONAL GAME TECHNOLOGY
INTERNATIONAL LOTTERY & TOTALIZATOR
SYSTEMS
INTERPUBLIC GROUP OF COMPANIES INC
INTERTAN CANADA LTD
INTERVIDEO INC
ISLE OF CAPRI CASINOS INC
ITV PLC
JOHN WILEY & SONS INC
JOHNSON PUBLISHING COMPANY INC
JUMPTV INC
JUPITERMEDIA CORP
KERZNER INTERNATIONAL LIMITED
LAGARDERE ACTIVE MEDIA
LAMAR ADVERTISING CO
LANDMARK COMMUNICATIONS INC
LANDRY'S RESTAURANTS INC
LAS VEGAS SANDS CORP (THE VENETIAN)
LIBERTY GLOBAL
LIBERTY MEDIA CORP
LIONS GATE ENTERTAINMENT CORP
LIVE NATION INC
LODGENET ENTERTAINMENT CORP
LOUD TECHNOLOGIES INC
MACROVISION CORP
MAGNA ENTERTAINMENT CORP
MARVEL ENTERTAINMENT INC
MATAV-CABLE SYSTEMS MEDIA LTD
MATSUSHITA ELECTRIC INDUSTRIAL CO LTD
MCGRAW HILL COS INC
METRO INTERNATIONAL SA
METRO-GOLDWYN-MAYER INC (MGM)
MGM MIRAGE
MICROSOFT CORP
MIDWAY GAMES INC
MOBITV INC
MODERN TIMES GROUP MTG AB
MONSTER WORLDWIDE
MOODY'S CORPORATION
MORRIS COMMUNICATIONS COMPANY LLC
MOVIE GALLERY INC
MP3.COM INC
MTV NETWORKS
MULTIMEDIA GAMES INC
NAPSTER INC
NASPERS LIMITED
NATIONAL AMUSEMENTS INC
NBC UNIVERSAL
NETRATINGS INC
NEW YORK TIMES CO (THE)
NEWS CORPORATION LIMITED (THE)
NEWS WORLD COMMUNICATIONS INC
NINTENDO CO LTD

NTL INCORPORATED
OMNICOM GROUP INC
OMNIVISION TECHNOLOGIES INC
ON COMMAND CORP
PANAMSAT CORP
PEARSON PLC
PENN NATIONAL GAMING INC
PENTON MEDIA INC
PINNACLE ENTERTAINMENT INC
PIONEER CORPORATION
PLAYBOY ENTERPRISES INC
PRIMACOM AG
PROGRESSIVE GAMING INTERNATIONAL CORP
PROQUEST COMPANY
R R DONNELLEY & SONS CO
RADIOSHACK CORPORATION
RANDOM HOUSE INC
RANK GROUP PLC (THE)
READER'S DIGEST ASSOCIATION INC
REALNETWORKS INC
REED ELSEVIER GROUP PLC
REGAL ENTERTAINMENT GROUP
RENTRAK CORPORATION
REUTERS GROUP PLC
RODALE INC
ROGERS COMMUNICATIONS INC
RTL GROUP SA
SAGA COMMUNICATIONS INC
SAMSUNG ELECTRONICS CO LTD
SANYO ELECTRIC COMPANY LTD
SCHOLASTIC CORP
SCIENTIFIC GAMES CORPORATION
SEGA SAMMY HOLDINGS INC
SHANDA INTERACTIVE ENTERTAINMENT
LIMITED
SHANGHAI MEDIA GROUP (SMG)
SHARP CORPORATION
SHAW COMMUNICATIONS INC
SHUFFLE MASTER INC
SIMEX-IWERKS
SIMON & SCHUSTER INC
SIX FLAGS INC
SKY NETWORK TELEVISION LIMITED
SONY BMG MUSIC ENTERTAINMENT
SONY CORPORATION
SONY PICTURES ENTERTAINMENT
SPANISH BROADCASTING SYSTEM INC
SRS LABS INC
TAKE-TWO INTERACTIVE SOFTWARE INC
TAYLOR NELSON SOFRES PLC (TNS)
TELEWEST GLOBAL INC
THOMSON CORPORATION (THE)
THQ INC
TICKETMASTER
TIME INC
TIME WARNER INC
TIVO INC
TRADER CLASSIFIED MEDIA NV

TRAFFIX INC
TRANS WORLD CORP
TRANS WORLD ENTERTAINMENT CORP
TRANS-LUX CORPORATION
TRIBUNE CO
TV AZTECA SA DE CV
UNITED BUSINESS MEDIA PLC
UNITED ONLINE INC
UNIVERSAL MUSIC GROUP
UNIVISION COMMUNICATIONS INC
VERIZON COMMUNICATIONS
VIACOM INC
VIVENDI GAMES
VIVENDI SA
VNU NV
WALT DISNEY COMPANY (THE)
WARNER MUSIC GROUP
WASHINGTON POST CO
WILLIAM MORRIS AGENCY INC
WMS INDUSTRIES INC
WORLD WRESTLING ENTERTAINMENT INC (WWF)
WPP GROUP PLC
WYNN RESORTS LIMITED
XM SATELLITE RADIO HOLDINGS INC
YAHOO! INC
YAHOO! SEARCH MARKETING GROUP
ZIFF DAVIS MEDIA INC

Individual Profiles
On Each Of
THE ENTERTAINMENT 400

24 HOUR FITNESS USA

www.24hourfitness.com

Industry Group Code: 713940 Ranks within this company's industry group: Sales: Profits:

Print Media/Publishing:	Movies:	Equipment/Supplies:	Broadcast/Cable:	Music/Audio:	Sports/Games:	
Newspapers:	Movie Theaters:	Equipment/Supplies:	Broadcast TV:	Music Production:	Games/Sports:	Y
Magazines:	Movie Production:	Gambling Equipment:	Cable TV:	Retail Music:	Retail Games Stores:	
Books:	TV/Video Production:	Special Services:	Satellite Broadcast:	Retail Audio Equip.:	Stadiums/Teams:	
Book Stores:	Video Rental:	Advertising Services:	Radio:	Music Print./Dist.:	Gambling/Casinos:	
Distribution/Printing:	Video Distribution:	Info. Sys. Software:	Online Information:	Multimedia:	Rides/Theme Parks:	

TYPES OF BUSINESS:

Fitness Centers
Online Nutrition Information
Day Spa

BRANDS/DIVISIONS/AFFILIATES:

Forstmann Little & Company
California Fitness
24 Hour Fitness Active
24 Hour Fitness Sports
24 Hour Fitness Super-Sport
24 Hour Fitness Ultra-Sport
Re:fresh
Fit:perks

CONTACTS: Note: Officers with more than one job title may be intentionally listed here more than once.

Mark S. Mastrov, CEO
Colin Heggie, Exec. VP/CFO
Kevin D. Steele, VP-Sports Mktg.
Mark S. Mastrov, Chmn.

Phone: 925-543-3100	Fax: 925-543-3200
Toll-Free: 800-432-6348	
Address: 12647 Alcosta Blvd., 5th Fl., San Ramon, CA 94583 US	

GROWTH PLANS/SPECIAL FEATURES:

24 Hour Fitness USA is one of the world's largest privately owned and operated fitness center chains. The firm, a subsidiary of private equity company Forstmann Little and Co., has more than 3 million members and over 330 clubs in 16 states and four countries in Asia. The company operates several types of clubs, including the 24 Hour Fitness Active club, Fitness EXPRESS, the Sports club, the Super-Sport club and the Ultra-Sport club. The 24 Hour Fitness Active clubs are approximately 25,000 square feet and may include free weights, cardio equipment, group exercise, personal training, locker rooms, sauna, steam room and a children' play area. 24 Hour Fitness EXPRESS clubs are anywhere from 6,000-10,000 square feet and offer only limited strength and cardio equipment and some exercise classes. The company's Sports clubs range from 35,000 to 50,000 square feet and include all of the Active clubs' amenities as well as basketball courts and pools. The Super-Sport clubs, generally over 50,000 square feet, have all of the Sports club offerings as well as tanning beds and massage therapy. The Ultra-Sport clubs are generally over 100,000 square feet and may also include a volleyball court, racquetball, squash, rock climbing, an indoor running track and executive locker rooms. The company has international locations in Malaysia, Singapore, Hong Kong and Taiwan, all under the name California Fitness. Re:fresh is the company's free-standing day spa located in San Francisco. The Fit:perks program offers discounts and benefits to all 24 Hour Fitness members. The company is the exclusive official fitness center of the U.S. Olympic Team through the 2008 Olympic Games in Beijing.

24 Hour Fitness sponsors several charitable events and organizations, including the American Cancer Society, the Magic Johnson Foundation, the Lance Armstrong Foundation and the Andre Agassi Charitable Foundation.

FINANCIALS: Sales and profits are in thousands of dollars—add 000 to get the full amount. 2006 Note: Financial information for 2006 was not available for all companies at press time.

2006 Sales: $	2006 Profits: $	U.S. Stock Ticker: Private
2005 Sales: $	2005 Profits: $	Int'l Ticker: Int'l Exchange:
2004 Sales: $1,004,000	2004 Profits: $	Employees: 16,000
2003 Sales: $1,000,000	2003 Profits: $	Fiscal Year Ends: 12/31
2002 Sales: $1,000,000	2002 Profits: $	Parent Company:

SALARIES/BENEFITS:

Pension Plan:	ESOP Stock Plan:	Profit Sharing:	Top Exec. Salary: $	Bonus: $
Savings Plan:	Stock Purch. Plan:		Second Exec. Salary: $	Bonus: $

OTHER THOUGHTS:

Apparent Women Officers or Directors:
Hot Spot for Advancement for Women/Minorities:

LOCATIONS: ("Y" = Yes)

West:	Southwest:	Midwest:	Southeast:	Northeast:	International:
Y	Y	Y	Y		Y

24/7 REAL MEDIA INC

www.247realmedia.com

Industry Group Code: 541810A **Ranks within this company's industry group:** Sales: 1 Profits: 2

Print Media/Publishing:	Movies:	Equipment/Supplies:		Broadcast/Cable:	Music/Audio:	Sports/Games:
Newspapers:	Movie Theaters:	Equipment/Supplies:		Broadcast TV:	Music Production:	Games/Sports:
Magazines:	Movie Production:	Gambling Equipment:		Cable TV:	Retail Music:	Retail Games Stores:
Books:	TV/Video Production:	Special Services:	Y	Satellite Broadcast:	Retail Audio Equip.:	Stadiums/Teams:
Book Stores:	Video Rental:	Advertising Services:	Y	Radio:	Music Print./Dist.:	Gambling/Casinos:
Distribution/Printing:	Video Distribution:	Info. Sys. Software:	Y	Online Information:	Multimedia:	Rides/Theme Parks:

TYPES OF BUSINESS:

Internet Advertising
Web Design
Software
Direct Marketing
Promotions
Data Analysis

BRANDS/DIVISIONS/AFFILIATES:

24/7 Web Alliance
24/7 Web Results
24/7 Search
Open AdStream 6 Network Edition
Decide DNA 6
Dentsu 24/7 Search Holdings
Rich Media Foundry
K.K. 24-7 Search

CONTACTS:
Note: Officers with more than one job title may be intentionally listed here more than once.

David J. Moore, CEO
Jonathan K. Hsu, COO
Jonathan Hsu, CFO/Exec. VP
Ari Bluman, Sr. VP-US Sales
Jeff Marcus, Chief Tech. Officer
Mark E. Moran, General Counsel/Sr. VP
Matt Kain, VP-Corp. Dev.
Sushene Leitch, Dir.-Investor Relations
Rob Wilson, Dir.-Europe
Douglas C. Wagner, Pres., 24/7 Search
David J. Moore, Chmn.
Jae Woo Chung, Pres., TFSM Asia

Phone: 212-231-7100	**Fax:** 212-760-1774
Toll-Free: 877-247-2477	
Address: 132 W. 31st St., New York, NY 10001 US	

GROWTH PLANS/SPECIAL FEATURES:

24/7 Real Media, Inc. is a global provider of interactive technology and marketing solutions for web publishers, online advertisers, advertising agencies and e-marketers. The firm's services include advertising and direct marketing sales, search engine marketing services, online advertisement serving, web advertising, site representation and web analytics. The company sells its products and services from 20 locations in 12 countries in North America, Europe and Asia. 24/7 Real Media is organized into three principal divisions: Technology Solutions, Media Solutions and Search Solutions. The Technology Solutions group, through its Open AdSystem platform, is composed of service and software solutions designed for three customer segments: advertisers and agencies, web publishers and e-commerce merchants. The Media Solutions division consists of 24/7 Web Alliance, an alliance of web sites through which client advertisers can place targeted ad campaigns; and 24/7 Web Results, a subsidiary that provides performance-based marketing services for the Internet. The Search Solutions division, with its flagship product 24/7 Search, provides performance-based search marketing services for the Internet. In 2006, the firm introduced the Open AdStream 6 Network Edition, which manages over 850 billion web sites with over 12 billion impressions per month and over 117 million users. In July 2006, 24/7 Real Media unveiled Decide DNA 6, a flexible search engine-marketing platform. In November 2006, 24/7 Real Media teamed with Dentsu, Inc. to create new company Dentsu 24/7 Search Holdings. This venture will target markets throughout Asia and the Pacific Rim. 24/7 Real Media also recently announced the Rich Media Foundry, a new tool to streamline the creation and distribution rich media advertising including audio, mobile, DTV and video.

FINANCIALS: Sales and profits are in thousands of dollars—add 000 to get the full amount. 2006 Note: Financial information for 2006 was not available for all companies at press time.

2006 Sales: $	2006 Profits: $	**U.S. Stock Ticker: TFSM**
2005 Sales: $139,794	2005 Profits: $ 38	**Int'l Ticker:** Int'l Exchange:
2004 Sales: $85,255	2004 Profits: $-3,155	Employees: 368
2003 Sales: $49,181	2003 Profits: $-12,016	Fiscal Year Ends: 11/27
2002 Sales: $42,558	2002 Profits: $-17,499	Parent Company:

SALARIES/BENEFITS:

Pension Plan:	ESOP Stock Plan: Y	Profit Sharing:	Top Exec. Salary: $270,450	Bonus: $436,025
Savings Plan:	Stock Purch. Plan:		Second Exec. Salary: $200,000	Bonus: $167,702

OTHER THOUGHTS:

Apparent Women Officers or Directors: 1
Hot Spot for Advancement for Women/Minorities:

LOCATIONS: ("Y" = Yes)

West:	Southwest:	Midwest:	Southeast:	Northeast:	International:
Y		Y		Y	Y

Note: Financial information, benefits and other data can change quickly and may vary from those stated here.

2929 ENTERTAINMENT   www.2929entertainment.com

Industry Group Code: 512110 Ranks within this company's industry group: Sales: Profits:

Print Media/Publishing:	Movies:		Equipment/Supplies:	Broadcast/Cable:		Music/Audio:	Sports/Games:
Newspapers:	Movie Theaters:	Y	Equipment/Supplies:	Broadcast TV:		Music Production:	Games/Sports:
Magazines:	Movie Production:	Y	Gambling Equipment:	Cable TV:	Y	Retail Music:	Retail Games Stores:
Books:	TV/Video Production:	Y	Special Services:	Satellite Broadcast:		Retail Audio Equip.:	Stadiums/Teams:
Book Stores:	Video Rental:		Advertising Services:	Radio:		Music Print./Dist.:	Gambling/Casinos:
Distribution/Printing:	Video Distribution:		Info. Sys. Software:	Online Information:		Multimedia:	Rides/Theme Parks:

TYPES OF BUSINESS:

Movie & TV Production & Distribution
Movie Theaters
Cable Television Networks

BRANDS/DIVISIONS/AFFILIATES:

Rysher Entertainment
Magnolia Pictures Distribution
Landmark Theatre Corp.
Lions Gate Entertainment
2929 Productions
HDNet Films
HDNet Movies
Magnolia Home Entertainment

CONTACTS: *Note: Officers with more than one job title may be intentionally listed here more than once.*

Todd R. Wagner, CEO/Co-Owner
Sherry Yeaman, Press Contact
Marc Cuban, Co-Owner
Kevin Parke, COO/Pres., Landmark Theaters
Marc Butan, Pres., 2929 Productions
Kevin Parke, Sr. VP-Film Dev., Distrib. & Exhibition
Shebnem Askin, Head-Int'l

Phone: 310-309-5701	Fax: 310-309-5716
Toll-Free:	
Address: 2425 Olympic Blvd., Ste. 6040W, Santa Monica, CA 90404 US	

GROWTH PLANS/SPECIAL FEATURES:

2929 Entertainment has ownership stakes in movie and TV distribution and exhibition companies. The company owns Rysher Entertainment, Magnolia Pictures Distribution and Landmark Theatre Corp. It also owns an interest in Lions Gate Entertainment. Through Rysher, the firm owns syndication rights to television shows such as Lifestyles of the Rich and Famous, Hogan's Heroes and Star Search; while Magnolia is an independent distribution company. Landmark is the nation's largest art-house theater chain, with 59 theaters in 23 markets across the U.S. 2929 produces and finances movies through two production companies: 2929 Productions, which produces films in the $10- to $40-million budget range; and HDNet Films, which produces smaller-budget movies shot exclusively in high definition. Another subsidiary, 2929 International, handles the worldwide distribution rights of theatrical feature films produced by the company's production subsidiaries. 2929 is owned by partners Mark Cuban (the owner of the Dallas Mavericks) and Todd Wagner. Wagner and Cuban are also partnered in two general entertainment high-definition television show networks, HDNet and HDNet Movies, which are available through most major cable and satellite providers. In an effort to boost the market for HDNet Movies, 2929 recently signed a contract with Academy Award-winning director Steven Soderburgh for the production of six HD films to be released simultaneously in the theater, TV and home video. Past releases of 2929 include Good Night and Good Luck, Akeelah and the Bee, Turistas and Black Christmas. In 2006, Magnolia Home Entertainment released its first wave of titles on HD-DVD including Bubble, Enron: The Smartest Guys in The Room and The War Within.

FINANCIALS: Sales and profits are in thousands of dollars—add 000 to get the full amount. 2006 Note: Financial information for 2006 was not available for all companies at press time.

2006 Sales: $	2006 Profits: $	**U.S. Stock Ticker: Private**
2005 Sales: $	2005 Profits: $	**Int'l Ticker:** Int'l Exchange:
2004 Sales: $	2004 Profits: $	Employees:
2003 Sales: $	2003 Profits: $	Fiscal Year Ends:
2002 Sales: $	2002 Profits: $	Parent Company:

SALARIES/BENEFITS:

Pension Plan:	ESOP Stock Plan:	Profit Sharing:	Top Exec. Salary: $	Bonus: $
Savings Plan:	Stock Purch. Plan:		Second Exec. Salary: $	Bonus: $

OTHER THOUGHTS:

Apparent Women Officers or Directors: 3
Hot Spot for Advancement for Women/Minorities: Y

LOCATIONS: ("Y" = Yes)

West:	Southwest:	Midwest:	Southeast:	Northeast:	International:
Y	Y				

A&E TELEVISION NETWORKS
www.aetn.com

Industry Group Code: 513210 Ranks within this company's industry group: Sales: 9 Profits:

Print Media/Publishing:		Movies:		Equipment/Supplies:	Broadcast/Cable:		Music/Audio:		Sports/Games:	
Newspapers:		Movie Theaters:		Equipment/Supplies:	Broadcast TV:		Music Production:	Y	Games/Sports:	
Magazines:	Y	Movie Production:		Gambling Equipment:	Cable TV:	Y	Retail Music:		Retail Games Stores:	
Books:		TV/Video Production:	Y	Special Services:	Satellite Broadcast:		Retail Audio Equip.:		Stadiums/Teams:	
Book Stores:		Video Rental:		Advertising Services:	Radio:		Music Print./Dist.:		Gambling/Casinos:	
Distribution/Printing:		Video Distribution:		Info. Sys. Software:	Online Information:		Multimedia:		Rides/Theme Parks:	

TYPES OF BUSINESS:

Television Production
Cable Television
Magazine Publishing
Web Sites
CDs, DVDs & Videos

BRANDS/DIVISIONS/AFFILIATES:

Hearst
Disney ABC Cable
NBC Universal Cable
A&E
Biography Channel (The)
History Channel (The)
History Channel en Espanol (The)
History Channel International (The)

CONTACTS: *Note: Officers with more than one job title may be intentionally listed here more than once.*

Abbe Raven, CEO
Abbe Raven, Pres.
Gerard Gruosso, CFO/Exec. VP
Whitney Goit II, Exec. VP-Mktg. & Sales

Phone: 212-210-1400	**Fax:** 212-850-9370
Toll-Free:	
Address: 235 E. 45th St., New York, NY 10017 US	

GROWTH PLANS/SPECIAL FEATURES:

A&E Television Networks is an international media company with operations in television programming, magazine publishing, web sites, soundtrack CDs, and home videos and DVDs of their television programs. The company is a joint venture of media giants Hearst, Walt Disney's Disney ABC Cable and NBC Universal Cable, itself a subsidiary of General Electric. A&E is primarily a cable television group that focuses its programming in history, the arts, current events, popular culture, reality and nature. The firm works through two main cable networks, A&E and The History Channel; and three digital cable channels: The Biography Channel, The History Channel International and The History Channel en Espanol. The History Channel, with more than 87 million subscribers, offers historical dramas and documentaries. The Biography Channel offers biographical programming in more than 30 million homes. The History Channel International looks at international culture and history with 24-hour English broadcasting and limited broadcasting in French and Italian. The History Channel en Espanol provides 24-hour continual broadcasting in Spanish with features that focus on Latino heritage and achievements. The company's channels reach about 130 countries with more than 230 million subscribers.

A&E offers an employee benefits package that includes an employee assistance program, a 401(k) tax deferred savings plan, a non-contributory pension plan, tuition assistance, flexible spending accounts and adoption assistance.

FINANCIALS: Sales and profits are In thousands of dollars—add 000 to get the full amount. 2006 Note: Financial information for 2006 was not available for all companies at press time.

2006 Sales: $	2006 Profits: $	**U.S. Stock Ticker:** Joint Venture
2005 Sales: $625,000	2005 Profits: $	**Int'l Ticker:** Int'l Exchange:
2004 Sales: $	2004 Profits: $	Employees: 600
2003 Sales: $885,800	2003 Profits: $	Fiscal Year Ends: 12/31
2002 Sales: $813,700	2002 Profits: $	Parent Company:

SALARIES/BENEFITS:

Pension Plan: Y	ESOP Stock Plan:	Profit Sharing:	Top Exec. Salary: $	Bonus: $
Savings Plan: Y	Stock Purch. Plan:		Second Exec. Salary: $	Bonus: $

OTHER THOUGHTS:

Apparent Women Officers or Directors:
Hot Spot for Advancement for Women/Minorities:

LOCATIONS: ("Y" = Yes)

West:	Southwest:	Midwest:	Southeast:	Northeast:	International:
Y		Y	Y	Y	Y

ABC INC

www.abc.com

Industry Group Code: 513120 Ranks within this company's industry group: Sales: 4 Profits:

Print Media/Publishing:	Movies:		Equipment/Supplies:	Broadcast/Cable:		Music/Audio:	Sports/Games:
Newspapers:	Movie Theaters:		Equipment/Supplies:	Broadcast TV:	Y	Music Production:	Games/Sports:
Magazines:	Movie Production:		Gambling Equipment:	Cable TV:	Y	Retail Music:	Retail Games Stores:
Books:	TV/Video Production:	Y	Special Services:	Satellite Broadcast:		Retail Audio Equip.:	Stadiums/Teams:
Book Stores:	Video Rental:		Advertising Services:	Radio:		Music Print./Dist.:	Gambling/Casinos:
Distribution/Printing:	Video Distribution:		Info. Sys. Software:	Online Information:		Multimedia:	Rides/Theme Parks:

TYPES OF BUSINESS:

Broadcast TV
Cable Networks
Television Production
Online Television

BRANDS/DIVISIONS/AFFILIATES:

Walt Disney Company (The)
Touchstone Television
Buena Vista Television
A&E Television
ESPN
Monday Night Football
Lost
Desperate Housewives

CONTACTS: *Note: Officers with more than one job title may be intentionally listed here more than once.*

Anne M. Sweeney, Pres., Disney-ABC Television Group
Mike Shaw, Pres., Sales & Mktg., ABC Television Network
Jeffrey Rosen, Sr. VP-Human Resources
Preston A. Davis, Pres., Eng., ABC Television Network
Preston A. Davis, Pres., Broadcast Oper., ABC Television Network
Kate Nelson, VP-Bus. Oper. Daytime Disney/ABC Group

Phone: 212-456-7777	Fax: 212-456-1424
Toll-Free:	
Address: 77 W. 66th St., New York, NY 10023-6298 US	

GROWTH PLANS/SPECIAL FEATURES:

ABC, Inc., a subsidiary of The Walt Disney Company, operates the ABC Television Network. The network includes 10 owned stations that supplement approximately 228 affiliated stations operating under long-term agreements, reaching 99.9% of all U.S. households. The company broadcasts a variety of television programming including news, sports, family-focused and entertainment programs. ABC produces many of the programs it broadcasts through its Touchstone Television subsidiary. In addition, the Buena Vista Television unit syndicates and distributes Disney products (both films and television shows) for broadcast. The firm recently spun off ABC Radio, merging it with Citadel Broadcasting Corporations to form a new company called Citadel Communications. ABC, Inc. holds an interest in the ESPN, Lifetime and A&E cable networks. The company's Monday Night Football program is a long-standing leader in the prime-time lineup and the network also carries the NBA finals. In 2006, ABC.com was the first web site to make its full-length episodes of its most popular shows (Lost, Grey's Anatomy, Desperate Housewives, Ugly Betty, Six Degrees and Daybreak) available on the Internet for a small fee. In recent news, Yahoo! News and ABC News announced an agreement wherein ABC News will double the amount of content it contributes to Yahoo! News, providing ad-supported video free to Yahoo! users. Also in 2006, the firm sold its 39.5% ownership stake in E! Networks to Comcast for $1.23 billion. In addition, both companies extended their current broadcast agreement for ten years; ABC will broadcast its cable network shows and Disney movies to Comcasts's ON DEMAND service, marking the first time ABC programs will be made available on video on demand by any cable company.

The firm offers complimentary passes to Disney theme parks, educational reimbursement, a company scholarship program, an employee stock purchase plan, credit union membership, educational matching gifts and childcare centers.

FINANCIALS: Sales and profits are in thousands of dollars—add 000 to get the full amount. 2006 Note: Financial information for 2006 was not available for all companies at press time.

2006 Sales: $	2006 Profits: $	U.S. Stock Ticker: Subsidiary
2005 Sales: $13,207,000	2005 Profits: $	Int'l Ticker: Int'l Exchange:
2004 Sales: $11,780,000	2004 Profits: $	Employees:
2003 Sales: $10,941,000	2003 Profits: $	Fiscal Year Ends: 9/30
2002 Sales: $9,763,000	2002 Profits: $	Parent Company: WALT DISNEY COMPANY (THE)

SALARIES/BENEFITS:

Pension Plan:	ESOP Stock Plan:	Profit Sharing:	Top Exec. Salary: $	Bonus: $
Savings Plan:	Stock Purch. Plan: Y		Second Exec. Salary: $	Bonus: $

OTHER THOUGHTS:

Apparent Women Officers or Directors: 2
Hot Spot for Advancement for Women/Minorities:

LOCATIONS: ("Y" = Yes)

West:	Southwest:	Midwest:	Southeast:	Northeast:	International:
Y				Y	

ACME COMMUNICATIONS INC www.acmecommunications.com

Industry Group Code: 513120 Ranks within this company's industry group: Sales: 24 Profits: 15

Print Media/Publishing:	Movies:		Equipment/Supplies:	Broadcast/Cable:		Music/Audio:	Sports/Games:
Newspapers:	Movie Theaters:		Equipment/Supplies:	Broadcast TV:	Y	Music Production:	Games/Sports:
Magazines:	Movie Production:		Gambling Equipment:	Cable TV:		Retail Music:	Retail Games Stores:
Books:	TV/Video Production:	Y	Special Services:	Satellite Broadcast:		Retail Audio Equip.:	Stadiums/Teams:
Book Stores:	Video Rental:		Advertising Services:	Radio:		Music Print./Dist.:	Gambling/Casinos:
Distribution/Printing:	Video Distribution:		Info. Sys. Software:	Online Information:		Multimedia:	Rides/Theme Parks:

TYPES OF BUSINESS:
Broadcast Television
Television Production

BRANDS/DIVISIONS/AFFILIATES:
ACME Televisions, LLC
Daily Buzz (The)

CONTACTS: Note: Officers with more than one job title may be intentionally listed here more than once.
Jamie Kellner, CEO
Doug Gealy, COO
Doug Gealy, Pres.
Tom Allen, CFO/Exec. VP
Sharon Weiler, VP-Sales
Brent Stephenson, VP-Eng.
Ed Danduran, Controller/VP
Steve Bailey, VP-Promotion
Bob Shaw, VP-Programming
Mike Mingroni, VP-Graphics
Brent Stephenson, VP-FCC Compliance
Jamie Kellner, Chmn.

Phone: 714-245-9499	Fax: 714-245-9494

Toll-Free:

Address: 2101 E. 4th St., Ste. 202, Santa Ana, CA 92705 US

GROWTH PLANS/SPECIAL FEATURES:
ACME Communications, Inc. is a holding company with no independent operations other than through its indirect wholly-owned subsidiary, ACME Television, LLC. ACME Television, through its subsidiaries, owns and operates eight commercially licensed, full-power, broadcast television stations located throughout the U.S.: KWBQ, KASY, and KWBR in Albuquerque-Santa Fe, New Mexico; WBXX in Knoxville Tennessee; WBDT in Dayton, Ohio; WIWB in Green Bay-Appleton, Wisconsin; WBUI in Champaign-Springfield-Decatur, Illinois; and WBUW in Madison, Wisconsin. All but one of these stations are affiliates of The CW, a joint venture between CBS and Warner Brothers. The CW combines programming from the former UPN and WB networks. The remaining station, KASY-TV in Albuquerque-Santa Fe is an affiliate of MyNetworkTV, a Fox subsidiary. ACME broadcasts in markets that cover approximately 3% of all U.S. television households. ACME operates in medium sized markets due to lower operating costs and less competition than in larger markets. Its programming is targeted at young adults, teens and kids. In addition, the company provides local and regional sports programming as well as local news and weather updates. The firm also owns The Daily Buzz, a three hour morning news show that is produced jointly with Emmis Communications. In 2006, ACME completed the sale of KUWB-TV in Salt Lake City, Utah to Clear Channel Communications for $18.5 million; and entered into a definitive agreement for the sale of its television station WTVK in Ft. Myers-Naples, Florida to Sun Broadcasting for $45 million.

FINANCIALS: Sales and profits are in thousands of dollars—add 000 to get the full amount. 2006 Note: Financial information for 2006 was not available for all companies at press time.

2006 Sales: $	2006 Profits: $	U.S. Stock Ticker: ACME
2005 Sales: $40,934	2005 Profits: $-15,945	Int'l Ticker: Int'l Exchange:
2004 Sales: $39,257	2004 Profits: $-17,547	Employees: 195
2003 Sales: $35,722	2003 Profits: $74,968	Fiscal Year Ends: 12/31
2002 Sales: $36,000	2002 Profits: $-56,000	Parent Company:

SALARIES/BENEFITS:

Pension Plan:	ESOP Stock Plan:	Profit Sharing:	Top Exec. Salary: $387,750	Bonus: $
Savings Plan:	Stock Purch. Plan:		Second Exec. Salary: $387,750	Bonus: $

OTHER THOUGHTS:
Apparent Women Officers or Directors: 1
Hot Spot for Advancement for Women/Minorities:

LOCATIONS: ("Y" = Yes)

West:	Southwest:	Midwest:	Southeast:	Northeast:	International:
Y	Y	Y	Y		

Note: Financial information, benefits and other data can change quickly and may vary from those stated here.

ACTIVISION INC   www.activision.com

Industry Group Code: 511208 Ranks within this company's industry group: Sales: 3   Profits: 3

Print Media/Publishing:	Movies:	Equipment/Supplies:		Broadcast/Cable:	Music/Audio:	Sports/Games:	
Newspapers:	Movie Theaters:	Equipment/Supplies:		Broadcast TV:	Music Production:	Games/Sports:	Y
Magazines:	Movie Production:	Gambling Equipment:		Cable TV:	Retail Music:	Retail Games Stores:	
Books:	TV/Video Production:	Special Services:	Y	Satellite Broadcast:	Retail Audio Equip.:	Stadiums/Teams:	
Book Stores:	Video Rental:	Advertising Services:		Radio:	Music Print./Dist.:	Gambling/Casinos:	
Distribution/Printing:	Video Distribution:	Info. Sys. Software:		Online Information:	Multimedia:	Rides/Theme Parks:	

TYPES OF BUSINESS:

Video Games
Logistics Services

BRANDS/DIVISIONS/AFFILIATES:

Activision Publishing, Inc.
Vicarious Visions
Tony Hawk's Pro Skater
Marvel: Ultimate Alliance
Quake
Doom
Toys for Bob, Inc.
Beenox, Inc.

CONTACTS: *Note: Officers with more than one job title may be intentionally listed here more than once.*

Robert A. Kotick, CEO
William Chardavoyne, CFO/Exec. VP
Brian Hodous, Chief Customer Officer-Activision Publishing
Michael Rowe, Exec. VP-Human Resources
George Rose, General Counsel/Sr. VP/Corp. Sec.
Brian Kelly, Co-Chmn.
Ron Doornink, Senior Advisor-Activision Publishing, Inc.
Michael Griffith, CEO/Pres., Activision Publishing, Inc.
Robin Kaminsky, Exec. VP-Publishing
Robert A. Kotick, Chmn.

Phone: 310-255-2000	Fax: 310-255-2100
Toll-Free:	
Address: 3100 Ocean Park Blvd., Santa Monica, CA 90405 US	

GROWTH PLANS/SPECIAL FEATURES:

Activision, Inc., which operates solely through its subsidiary Activision Publishing, is a leading international publisher and distributor of interactive entertainment software for the action, adventure, action-sports, racing, role-playing, simulation and strategy game genres. The company maintains a number of strategic relationships with intellectual property owners and has acquired the rights to publish products based on properties such as Hasbro's Transformers and Pro-skater Tony Hawk. In 2006, the company entered into a distribution agreement with MTV Networks Kids and Family Group's Nickelodeon under which Activision will be the exclusive distributor of three new Nick Jr. PC CD-ROM titles, based on Dora The Explorer, The Backyardigans, and Go, Diego, Go! Activision develops products for the Sony PlayStation 2, Nintendo GameCube, Microsoft Xbox, Nintendo Game Boy and PC. The firm released four titles concurrently with the launches of the Sony Playstation 3, the Nintendo Wii, and Microsoft's Xbox360 including game title Call of Duty 3 for all three platforms. In addition, Activision published titles Marvel: Ultimate Alliance and new games in the Tony Hawk franchise for the Playstation 3 and Nintendo Wii consoles. Accompanying its publishing, the company maintains distribution operations in Europe that provide logistics and sales services to third-party publishers of interactive entertainment software, its own publishing operations and manufacturers of interactive entertainment hardware. In 2006, Activision acquired game developers Toys for Bob, Inc., and Beenox, Inc. Additionally, it has entered into an agreement to acquire video game publisher RedOctane, Inc., publisher of the popular Guitar Hero franchise. The firm recently opened a publishing office in Seoul, South Korea to improve the company's presence in the Asia Pacific region.

Activision offers an employee benefits package that includes a 401(k) plan, employee stock purchase plan, an employee assistance program, gym membership discounts and credit union membership.

FINANCIALS: Sales and profits are in thousands of dollars—add 000 to get the full amount. 2006 Note: Financial information for 2006 was not available for all companies at press time.

2006 Sales: $1,468,000	2006 Profits: $41,899	**U.S. Stock Ticker:** ATVI
2005 Sales: $1,405,857	2005 Profits: $138,335	**Int'l Ticker:** Int'l Exchange:
2004 Sales: $947,656	2004 Profits: $77,715	Employees: 2,149
2003 Sales: $864,100	2003 Profits: $66,200	Fiscal Year Ends: 3/31
2002 Sales: $786,400	2002 Profits: $52,200	Parent Company:

SALARIES/BENEFITS:

Pension Plan:	ESOP Stock Plan:	Profit Sharing:	Top Exec. Salary: $724,730	Bonus: $
Savings Plan: Y	Stock Purch. Plan: Y		Second Exec. Salary: $724,730	Bonus: $

OTHER THOUGHTS:

Apparent Women Officers or Directors: 2
Hot Spot for Advancement for Women/Minorities:

LOCATIONS: ("Y" = Yes)

West:	Southwest:	Midwest:	Southeast:	Northeast:	International:
Y		Y	Y	Y	Y

ADVANCE PUBLICATIONS INC
www.advance.net

Industry Group Code: 511120 Ranks within this company's industry group: Sales: 1 Profits:

Print Media/Publishing:		Movies:		Equipment/Supplies:		Broadcast/Cable:		Music/Audio:		Sports/Games:	
Newspapers:	Y	Movie Theaters:		Equipment/Supplies:		Broadcast TV:	Y	Music Production:		Games/Sports:	
Magazines:	Y	Movie Production:		Gambling Equipment:		Cable TV:		Retail Music:		Retail Games Stores:	
Books:		TV/Video Production:		Special Services:	Y	Satellite Broadcast:		Retail Audio Equip.:		Stadiums/Teams:	
Book Stores:		Video Rental:		Advertising Services:		Radio:		Music Print./Dist.:		Gambling/Casinos:	
Distribution/Printing:		Video Distribution:		Info. Sys. Software:		Online Information:		Multimedia:		Rides/Theme Parks:	

TYPES OF BUSINESS:

Magazine Publishing
Online Publications
Newspaper Publishing
Newspaper Industry Consulting & Technology
Internet Service Provider
Broadcast Television

BRANDS/DIVISIONS/AFFILIATES:

Conde Nast Publications
American City Business Journals
Parade Publications
Advance Internet, Inc.
Vogue
GQ
New Yorker (The)
Wired

CONTACTS: Note: Officers with more than one job title may be intentionally listed here more than once.

Samuel I. Newhouse, Jr., CEO
Charles H. Townsend, COO
Donald E. Newhouse, Pres.
Arthur Silverstein, CFO
Peter Weinberger, Pres., Advance Internet
Charles H. Townsend, CEO-Conde Nast
Steve Newhouse, Chmn.-Advance Internet
Samuel I. Newhouse, Jr., Chmn.

Phone: 212-286-2860	Fax: 718-981-1456
Toll-Free:	
Address: 950 Fingerboard Rd., Staten Island, NY 10305 US	

GROWTH PLANS/SPECIAL FEATURES:

Advance Publications, Inc. publishes a variety of magazines, newspapers and business weeklies. Its publishing subsidiaries include Conde Nast Publications, Parade Publications, Fairchild Publications, American City Business Journals and the Golf Digest Companies. Advance daily newspapers, including the Cleveland Plain Dealer and the New Orleans Times-Picayune, cover over 20 local markets, with more than 28 newspapers. Conde Nast publishes a well-known portfolio of magazines, including Glamour, Vogue, GQ, The New Yorker, Wired and Vanity Fair. The company's advance.net media unit maintains an Internet presence through subsidiaries CondeNet and Advance Internet. Advance Internet, Inc. deals in sites that cater to the local needs and interests of various municipalities and states, as well as web sites for local newspapers; as of May 2006, it reaches 5.6 million visitors, with 287 million page views every month. Affiliated local sites include: al.com, Everything Alabama; Clevland.com; masslive.com, dedicated to Massachusetts; mlive.com, Everything Michigan; Nj.com, Everything New Jersey; Nola.com, Everything New Orleans; Oregonlive.com; Pennlive.com; silive.com, Everything Staten Island; and Syracuse.com. Advance Internet has affiliated newspapers in nine states: Alabama (3 affiliates), Ohio (2), Massachusetts (1), Michigan (11), New Jersey (14), Louisiana (1), Oregon (2), Pennsylvania (3) and New York (2). The subsidiary also maintains special-interest web sites dealing with careers, online car buying and selling and weather information. Advance Publications, in partnership with four other media groups, recently purchased AdOne Classified Network, which merged with PowerAdz to form PowerOne Media, Inc, a provider of consulting and technology to the newspaper industry. Advance/Newhouse manages Bright House Networks, an Internet service provider with approximately 2.2 million subscribers located in Florida, Alabama, California, Indiana and Michigan. Bright House also owns and operates two 24 hour television stations. The company has a significant interest in Discovery Communications, Inc.

FINANCIALS: Sales and profits are in thousands of dollars—add 000 to get the full amount. 2006 Note: Financial information for 2006 was not available for all companies at press time.

2006 Sales: $	2006 Profits: $	U.S. Stock Ticker: Private
2005 Sales: $7,315,000	2005 Profits: $	Int'l Ticker: Int'l Exchange:
2004 Sales: $	2004 Profits: $	Employees: 30,000
2003 Sales: $5,909,000	2003 Profits: $	Fiscal Year Ends: 12/31
2002 Sales: $5,565,000	2002 Profits: $	Parent Company:

SALARIES/BENEFITS:

Pension Plan: Y	ESOP Stock Plan:	Profit Sharing:	Top Exec. Salary: $	Bonus: $
Savings Plan: Y	Stock Purch. Plan:		Second Exec. Salary: $	Bonus: $

OTHER THOUGHTS:

Apparent Women Officers or Directors:
Hot Spot for Advancement for Women/Minorities:

LOCATIONS: ("Y" = Yes)

West:	Southwest:	Midwest:	Southeast:	Northeast:	International:
Y	Y	Y	Y	Y	

Note: Financial information, benefits and other data can change quickly and may vary from those stated here.

ADVANCED MARKETING SERVICES INC   www.advmkt.com

Industry Group Code: 422920 Ranks within this company's industry group: Sales: 2 Profits:

Print Media/Publishing:		Movies:	Equipment/Supplies:		Broadcast/Cable:	Music/Audio:	Sports/Games:
Newspapers:		Movie Theaters:	Equipment/Supplies:		Broadcast TV:	Music Production:	Games/Sports:
Magazines:		Movie Production:	Gambling Equipment:		Cable TV:	Retail Music:	Retail Games Stores:
Books:	Y	TV/Video Production:	Special Services:	Y	Satellite Broadcast:	Retail Audio Equip.:	Stadiums/Teams:
Book Stores:		Video Rental:	Advertising Services:	Y	Radio:	Music Print./Dist.:	Gambling/Casinos:
Distribution/Printing:		Video Distribution:	Info. Sys. Software:		Online Information:	Multimedia:	Rides/Theme Parks:

TYPES OF BUSINESS:

Book Distribution
Product Development, Handling & Merchandising Services
CD-ROM & Video Distribution
Merchandising Services
Book Publishing

BRANDS/DIVISIONS/AFFILIATES:

Thunder Bay
Laurel Glen
Silver Dolphin
Advantage Publishers Group
Portable Press
Publishers Group West
Advanced Global Distribution

CONTACTS: Note: Officers with more than one job title may be intentionally listed here more than once.

Bruce C. Meyers, CEO
Jack Dollard, COO/Exec. VP
Michael M. Nicita, Pres.
Curtis Smith, CFO
Adam R. Zoldan, Exec. VP-Mktg.
Micheal D. Molina, Exec. VP-Human Resources
Eric W. Januszko, CIO/Exec. VP
Gary Lloyd, General Counsel
Michael J. Focht, VP-Oper.
Loren C. Paulsen, VP-Facility Dev. & Special Projects
Robert F. Bartlett, Chmn.

Phone: 858-457-2500	Fax: 858-452-2237
Toll-Free: 800-695-3580	
Address: 5880 Oberlin Dr., Ste. 400, San Diego, CA 92121 US	

GROWTH PLANS/SPECIAL FEATURES:

Advanced Marketing Services, Inc. (AMS) distributes general-interest books, bestsellers, reference books, paperbacks, CD-ROMS, computer and business books and books on tape to the membership warehouse club industry and other specialty retailers. It also sells CD-ROM titles and videocassettes, provides selection advice, specialized merchandising services, product development services and distribution and handling services to more than 800 membership warehouse clubs throughout the U.S., Canada, Mexico, the U.K. and certain Pacific-Rim countries. Sam's Club and Costco are the company's largest clients and represent about three-quarters of sales. AMS provides weekly recommendations of new books tailored to each customer's marketing priorities and develops specially packaged books and book-related products for its customers. Subsidiary Advantage Publishers Group publishes books under the Silver Dolphin, Thunder Bay, Portable Press and Laurel Glen names. AMS also supplies an assortment of primarily business and computer titles to companies in the office product superstore industry, as well as other markets such as drugstores, children's education, and book specialty retailers and chain bookstores. In addition, AMS owns Publishers Group West, North America's largest distributor of independent publishers, and operates Advanced Global Distribution, the first global book distribution network targeting small and medium-sized publishers. The company filed for bankruptcy in January 2007.

FINANCIALS: Sales and profits are in thousands of dollars—add 000 to get the full amount. 2006 Note: Financial information for 2006 was not available for all companies at press time.

2006 Sales: $	2006 Profits: $	**U.S. Stock Ticker: MKTS.PK**
2005 Sales: $915,000	2005 Profits: $	**Int'l Ticker:** Int'l Exchange:
2004 Sales: $1,036,000	2004 Profits: $	Employees: 1,400
2003 Sales: $895,000	2003 Profits: $11,200	Fiscal Year Ends: 3/31
2002 Sales: $756,100	2002 Profits: $23,100	Parent Company:

SALARIES/BENEFITS:

Pension Plan:	ESOP Stock Plan:	Profit Sharing: Y	Top Exec. Salary: $444,468	Bonus: $163,500
Savings Plan: Y	Stock Purch. Plan:		Second Exec. Salary: $284,923	Bonus: $62,500

OTHER THOUGHTS:

Apparent Women Officers or Directors:
Hot Spot for Advancement for Women/Minorities:

LOCATIONS: ("Y" = Yes)

West:	Southwest:	Midwest:	Southeast:	Northeast:	International:
Y	Y	Y		Y	Y

ALLIANCE ATLANTIS COMMUNICATIONS INC
www.allianceatlantis.com
Industry Group Code: 512110 Ranks within this company's industry group: Sales: 9 Profits: 4

Print Media/Publishing:	Movies:		Equipment/Supplies:	Broadcast/Cable:		Music/Audio:	Sports/Games:
Newspapers:	Movie Theaters:	Y	Equipment/Supplies:	Broadcast TV:	Y	Music Production:	Games/Sports:
Magazines:	Movie Production:	Y	Gambling Equipment:	Cable TV:	Y	Retail Music:	Retail Games Stores:
Books:	TV/Video Production:	Y	Special Services:	Satellite Broadcast:		Retail Audio Equip.:	Stadiums/Teams:
Book Stores:	Video Rental:		Advertising Services:	Radio:		Music Print./Dist.:	Gambling/Casinos:
Distribution/Printing:	Video Distribution:		Info. Sys. Software:	Online Information:		Multimedia:	Rides/Theme Parks:

TYPES OF BUSINESS:
Television Production
Motion Picture Production & Distribution
Cable Television Networks
Movie Theaters

BRANDS/DIVISIONS/AFFILIATES:
Motion Picture Distribution, LP
Momentum Pictures
Aurom Producciones, S.A.
CSI: Crime Scene Investigation
Showcase Action
Alliance Atlantis International, Ltd.
Alliance Atlantis Productions, Ltd.
Southill Strategy, Inc.

CONTACTS: Note: Officers with more than one job title may be intentionally listed here more than once.
Phyllis N. Yaffe, CEO
David Lazzarato, CFO/Exec. VP
Brad Alles, Exec. VP-Sales
Jacquelyn Saad, Sr. VP-Human Resources
Rita Middleton, Sr. VP-IT Services
Andrea Wood, General Counsel/Exec. VP
Andrew Callum, Sr. VP-Strategy
Jennifer Bell, Dir.-Public Affairs & Comm.
Andrew Akman, VP-Investor Rel.
Rita Middleton, Sr. VP-Finance
Norm Bolen, Exec. VP-Content Group
Angela Young, Sr. VP-Internal Audit
Heather Conway, Exec. VP-Mktg., Creative Services & Public Affairs
Andrew Akman, VP-Corp. Dev.
Michael I. M. MacMillan, Chmn.
Edward A. Riley, Exec. Managing Dir.-International Content Dist.

Phone: 416-967-1174	Fax: 416-960-0971

Toll-Free:

Address: 121 Bloor St. E., Ste. 1500, Toronto, ON M4W 3M5 Canada

GROWTH PLANS/SPECIAL FEATURES:
Alliance Atlantis Communications, Inc. has three principal business activities: broadcasting, entertainment and motion picture distribution. Through its broadcasting arm, it offers 13 specialty channels in Canada boasting targeted, high quality programming. The Company also indirectly holds a 51% limited partnership interest in Motion Picture Distribution LP, a leading distributor of motion pictures in Canada, with a presence in motion picture distribution in the U.K. through its subsidiary Momentum Pictures, and in Spain through its subsidiary Aurom Producciones S.A. In addition, the company co-produces and internationally distributes (outside the US) the popular CSI: Crime Scene Investigation franchise. Alliance Atlantis internationally licenses its library of approximately 1,000 titles of programming. A part of the company's television lineup, Showcase Action, is consistently ranked the number one channel in Canada for the 25- to 54-year-old age demographic. In addition, five of its eight specialty channels, Showcase Action, Showcase Diva, BBC CANADA, National Geographic and IFC, ranked in the top ten for the same age group. Six of the eight digital channels have over 1 million subscribers. The company has output agreements for film distribution in Canada with New Line Cinema and Focus Features through 2008. In late 2006, Alliance Atlantis held a strategic review of its motion picture distribution holding. As a result of this review, the company will be exploring ownership alternatives for Motion Picture Distribution LP. The company was delisted from the NASDAQ in 2005, and filed with the SEC to terminate its registration in the U.S. Southhill Strategy, Inc. owns a 66.7% controlling interest in Alliance Atlantis.

FINANCIALS: Sales and profits are in thousands of dollars—add 000 to get the full amount. 2006 Note: Financial information for 2006 was not available for all companies at press time.

2006 Sales: $	2006 Profits: $	U.S. Stock Ticker: Private
2005 Sales: $893,970	2005 Profits: $60,725	Int'l Ticker: AAC Int'l Exchange: Toronto-TSX
2004 Sales: $848,000	2004 Profits: $24,800	Employees: 850
2003 Sales: $605,600	2003 Profits: $-12,800	Fiscal Year Ends: 12/31
2002 Sales: $602,400	2002 Profits: $29,700	Parent Company:

SALARIES/BENEFITS:
Pension Plan:	ESOP Stock Plan:	Profit Sharing:	Top Exec. Salary: $564,583	Bonus: $739,583
Savings Plan: Y	Stock Purch. Plan:		Second Exec. Salary: $500,000	Bonus: $250,000

OTHER THOUGHTS:
Apparent Women Officers or Directors: 7
Hot Spot for Advancement for Women/Minorities: Y

LOCATIONS: ("Y" = Yes)
West:	Southwest:	Midwest:	Southeast:	Northeast:	International:
Y				Y	Y

Note: Financial information, benefits and other data can change quickly and may vary from those stated here.

ALLIANCE ENTERTAINMENT CORP   www.aent.com

Industry Group Code: 422921 Ranks within this company's industry group: Sales: Profits:

Print Media/Publishing:	Movies:	Equipment/Supplies:	Broadcast/Cable:	Music/Audio:	Sports/Games:	
Newspapers:	Movie Theaters:	Equipment/Supplies:	Broadcast TV:	Music Production:	Games/Sports:	Y
Magazines:	Movie Production:	Gambling Equipment:	Cable TV:	Retail Music:	Retail Games Stores:	
Books:	TV/Video Production:	Special Services:	Satellite Broadcast:	Retail Audio Equip.:	Stadiums/Teams:	
Book Stores:	Video Rental:	Advertising Services:	Radio:	Music Print./Dist.: Y	Gambling/Casinos:	
Distribution/Printing:	Video Distribution:	Info. Sys. Software:	Online Information:	Multimedia:	Rides/Theme Parks:	

TYPES OF BUSINESS:

Entertainment Products Distribution
E-Commerce Software
Online Entertainment Portal

BRANDS/DIVISIONS/AFFILIATES:

Yucaipa Companies
Source Interlink
Innovation Distribution Network (IDN)
Matrix Software
Interlink Companies
One Way Records
AEC One Stop

CONTACTS: *Note: Officers with more than one job title may be intentionally listed here more than once.*

Alan Tuchman, COO
Alan Tuchman, Pres.
George Campagna, CFO
Lou DeBiase, General Mngr.-IDN
David Fritz, Pres., IDN
Tony Schnug, Chmn.

Phone: 954-255-4000	**Fax:** 954-255-4078
Toll-Free: 800-329-7664	
Address: 4250 Coral Ridge Dr., Coral Springs, FL 33065 US	

GROWTH PLANS/SPECIAL FEATURES:

Alliance Entertainment Corp. (AEC) provides 30,000 storefronts and more than three million individual customers with entertainment products such as music, video games, DVDs and related home entertainment products. The company is divided into two branches: the distribution and fulfillment services group (DFS) and the information services group (IS). Through DFS, AEC operates two distribution centers of over 400,000 square feet with state-of-the-art material handling automation, located in Coral Springs, Florida and Louisville, Kentucky, from which it distributes more than 265,000 products. Firm sales offices are based in California, Georgia, Pennsylvania and Vermont. The IS group, operated under AEC Direct, develops and provides support services, including e-commerce software, real-time inventory query, advanced checkout technology and flexible merchandising, which the company provides to its retailers. AEC is integrated with All Media Guide, a comprehensive database for the music, movie and video game industries, which provides much of the company's informational resources. Other companies operating under AEC include Innovation Distribution Network (IDN), which brings retailers products from independent manufactures of music and games; and Matrix Software, a developer and publisher of specialty astrological software. The firm's clients include Barnes and Noble, Blockbuster, Walgreens, Toys R' Us, Sears, Kmart, Meijer, Musicland, Trans World Music, Circuit City, Best Buy, AOL, BJ's Wholesale Club, Tower Records, Borders and Hastings Entertainment. The company's trading partners include the manufacturers of intellectual property, consumer goods and services companies and media companies. In March 2005, Alliance Entertainment merged with Source Interlink; Source Interlink controls 50% of the company, with the rest held by Yucaipa Companies, a private investment firm and the largest shareholder of Source Interlink. In late 2006, AEC received three year digital rights to titles in DIC Entertainment Holdings, Inc.'s animated and live-action library. The first releases in the multi-million dollar deal are due in early 2007.

FINANCIALS: Sales and profits are in thousands of dollars—add 000 to get the full amount. 2006 Note: Financial information for 2006 was not available for all companies at press time.

2006 Sales: $	2006 Profits: $	**U.S. Stock Ticker: Subsidiary**
2005 Sales: $	2005 Profits: $	**Int'l Ticker:** Int'l Exchange:
2004 Sales: $	2004 Profits: $	Employees: 1,400
2003 Sales: $870,000	2003 Profits: $	Fiscal Year Ends: 12/31
2002 Sales: $808,000	2002 Profits: $	Parent Company: SOURCE INTERLINK COMPANIES INC

SALARIES/BENEFITS:

Pension Plan:	ESOP Stock Plan:	Profit Sharing:	Top Exec. Salary: $	Bonus: $
Savings Plan:	Stock Purch. Plan:		Second Exec. Salary: $	Bonus: $

OTHER THOUGHTS:

Apparent Women Officers or Directors:
Hot Spot for Advancement for Women/Minorities:

LOCATIONS: ("Y" = Yes)

West:	Southwest:	Midwest:	Southeast:	Northeast:	International:
Y		Y	Y	Y	

AMAZON.COM INC
www.amazon.com

Industry Group Code: 451211E **Ranks within this company's industry group:** Sales: 1 Profits: 1

Print Media/Publishing:		Movies:		Equipment/Supplies:		Broadcast/Cable:		Music/Audio:		Sports/Games:	
Newspapers:		Movie Theaters:		Equipment/Supplies:		Broadcast TV:		Music Production:		Games/Sports:	
Magazines:		Movie Production:		Gambling Equipment:		Cable TV:		Retail Music:	Y	Retail Games Stores:	
Books:	Y	TV/Video Production:		Special Services:		Satellite Broadcast:		Retail Audio Equip.:	Y	Stadiums/Teams:	
Book Stores:		Video Rental:		Advertising Services:		Radio:		Music Print./Dist.:		Gambling/Casinos:	
Distribution/Printing:		Video Distribution:		Info. Sys. Software:		Online Information:		Multimedia:		Rides/Theme Parks:	

TYPES OF BUSINESS:
Online Retail
Online Books & Music Retail
Online Videos/DVDs Retail
Online Electronics Retail
Online Auctions
Online Household Goods Retail
E-Commerce Support & Hosting
Search Engine Technology

BRANDS/DIVISIONS/AFFILIATES:
Amazon Services, Inc.
Amazon Marketplace
Merchants@
A9.com, Inc.
Shopbop.com

CONTACTS: Note: Officers with more than one job title may be intentionally listed here more than once.
Jeffrey P. Bezos, CEO
Jeffrey P. Bezos, Pres.
Thomas J. Szkutak, CFO/Sr. VP
Diego Piacentini, VP-Worldwide Retail & Mktg.
Rick Dalzell, CIO/Sr. VP-Worldwide Arch. & Platform Software
Michelle Wilson, General Counsel/Sr. VP/Corp. Sec.
Jeff Wilke, Sr. VP-Worldwide Oper.
Mark S. Peek, VP/Chief Acct. Officer
Kal Raman, Sr. VP-Worldwide Hardlines Retail
Jeffrey P. Bezos, Chmn.

Phone: 206-266-1000	Fax: 206-266-1821
Toll-Free:	
Address: 1200 12th Ave. S., Ste. 1200, Seattle, WA 98144-2734 US	

GROWTH PLANS/SPECIAL FEATURES:

Amazon.com, Inc. is one of the leading Internet consumer-shopping sites. It offers millions of new, used, refurbished and collectible items in categories such as apparel, shoes, personal accessories, consumer electronics, DVDs, videos, gourmet food, office products, tools, hardware and books. The company operates several international web sites including amazon.co.uk, amazon.de and amazon.co.jp, which serve the U.K., Germany and Japan respectively. A large part of the firm's revenue comes from enabling e-commerce for others. For example, Amazon manages online sales for Office Depot and Target. The Amazon Marketplace and Merchants@ programs allow third parties to integrate their products on Amazon web sites, allow customers to shop for products owned by third parties using Amazon's features and technologies and allow individuals to complete transactions that include multiple sellers in a single checkout process. Amazon Marketplace generally serves individuals and small businesses, while the Merchants@ program serves larger companies and is primarily concentrated on expanding the selection of new products available on Amazon's web sites. Amazon also provides technology services and other marketing and promotional services, especially through subsidiary, A9.com. This unique site focuses on cutting-edge open search technology, which scours the web for image search results in addition to .html findings. In February 2006, the company acquired Shopbop.com, a women's fashion, shoes, apparel and accessories retailer. In June 2006, the firm launched an emergency preparedness store within its existing Tools & Hardware Store, to offer tools, communication devices, first aid supplies and safety equipment for the hurricane season. In addition, in July 2006, Amazon announced the launch of its grocery store, which offers over 14,000 dry grocery products.

Amazon.com offers employees flexible spending accounts, relocation assistance, an employee assistance program and several discount programs. Full-time employees also receive units of restricted stock.

FINANCIALS: Sales and profits are in thousands of dollars—add 000 to get the full amount. 2006 Note: Financial information for 2006 was not available for all companies at press time.

2006 Sales: $	2006 Profits: $	U.S. Stock Ticker: AMZN
2005 Sales: $8,490,000	2005 Profits: $359,000	Int'l Ticker: Int'l Exchange:
2004 Sales: $6,921,124	2004 Profits: $588,000	Employees: 12,000
2003 Sales: $5,263,699	2003 Profits: $35,282	Fiscal Year Ends: 12/31
2002 Sales: $3,932,900	2002 Profits: $-149,100	Parent Company:

SALARIES/BENEFITS:

Pension Plan:	ESOP Stock Plan:	Profit Sharing:	Top Exec. Salary: $175,000	Bonus: $
Savings Plan: Y	Stock Purch. Plan: Y		Second Exec. Salary: $160,343	Bonus: $

OTHER THOUGHTS:
Apparent Women Officers or Directors: 3
Hot Spot for Advancement for Women/Minorities: Y

LOCATIONS: ("Y" = Yes)

West:	Southwest:	Midwest:	Southeast:	Northeast:	International:
Y	Y	Y		Y	Y

Note: Financial information, benefits and other data can change quickly and may vary from those stated here.

AMC ENTERTAINMENT INC   www.amctheatres.com

Industry Group Code: 512131 Ranks within this company's industry group: Sales: 2   Profits: 5

Print Media/Publishing:	Movies:		Equipment/Supplies:	Broadcast/Cable:	Music/Audio:	Sports/Games:
Newspapers:	Movie Theaters:	Y	Equipment/Supplies:	Broadcast TV:	Music Production:	Games/Sports:
Magazines:	Movie Production:		Gambling Equipment:	Cable TV:	Retail Music:	Retail Games Stores:
Books:	TV/Video Production:		Special Services:	Satellite Broadcast:	Retail Audio Equip.:	Stadiums/Teams:
Book Stores:	Video Rental:		Advertising Services:	Radio:	Music Print./Dist.:	Gambling/Casinos:
Distribution/Printing:	Video Distribution:		Info. Sys. Software:	Online Information:	Multimedia:	Rides/Theme Parks:

TYPES OF BUSINESS:
Movie Theaters
Online Movie Ticket Sales

GROWTH PLANS/SPECIAL FEATURES:

AMC Entertainment, Inc. is one of the leading operators of movie theaters in North America. It currently operates 411 movie theaters with nearly 5,635 screens located in the U.S., Canada, France, Hong Kong, Japan, Portugal, Spain and the U.K. The firm is an industry leader in the development and operation of megaplex theaters, or theaters with 14 screens or more, primarily in large metropolitan markets. AMC's megaplexes have consistently ranked among its top grossing facilities on a per-screen basis and are among the top grossing theaters in North America. The megaplex theater format, now adopted by many of AMC's competitors, has led to consolidation in the industry. AMC currently operates the world's top grossing movie theater, Empire 25, located in Times Square in New York City. New AMC theaters often include amenities such as digital sound, advanced curved screens, AMC LoveSeat-style seating, restaurants, and refreshment and merchandise kiosks. The movietickets.com web site, operated in conjunction with several partners, is dedicated to the sale of movie tickets and additional content that assists users with their movie-going plans. In January 2006, AMC Entertainment merged with Loews Cineplex Entertainment Corp., completely integrating Loews's operations with its own. In May 2006, the company sold its interests in AMC Entertainment Espana S.A., which owned and operated four theatres with 86 screens in Spain; and its interests in Actividades Multi-Cinemas E Espectáculos, LDA, which owned and operated one theatre with 20 screens in Portugal. The company filed paperwork to go public in late 2006.

AMC offers its employees management training programs as well as various incentive programs, health benefits, life insurance, educational assistance and complimentary movie passes.

BRANDS/DIVISIONS/AFFILIATES:
American Multi-Cinema, Inc.
AMC Entertainment International, Inc.
movietickets.com
Loews Cineplex Entertainment Corp.

CONTACTS: Note: Officers with more than one job title may be intentionally listed here more than once.
Peter C. Brown, CEO
Philip M. Singleton, Exec. VP/COO
Peter C. Brown, Pres.
Craig R. Ramsey, CFO
Kevin M. Connor, General Counsel/Sr. VP
John D. McDonald, Exec. VP-North American Oper.
Terry W. Crawford, VP/Treas.
Richard T. Walsh, Exec. VP/Film Chmn.
Peter C. Brown, Chmn.

Phone: 816-221-4000	Fax: 816-480-4617
Toll-Free:	
Address: 920 Main St., Kansas City, MO 64105 US	

FINANCIALS: Sales and profits are in thousands of dollars—add 000 to get the full amount. 2006 Note: Financial information for 2006 was not available for all companies at press time.

2006 Sales: $1,730,450	2006 Profits: $-188,762	U.S. Stock Ticker: Private
2005 Sales: $1,806,600	2005 Profits: $-70,600	Int'l Ticker: Int'l Exchange:
2004 Sales: $1,782,820	2004 Profits: $-16,623	Employees: 21,400
2003 Sales: $1,791,600	2003 Profits: $-20,300	Fiscal Year Ends: 3/02
2002 Sales: $1,341,500	2002 Profits: $-11,500	Parent Company:

SALARIES/BENEFITS:

Pension Plan: Y	ESOP Stock Plan:	Profit Sharing:	Top Exec. Salary: $750,000	Bonus: $25,550
Savings Plan: Y	Stock Purch. Plan:		Second Exec. Salary: $482,000	Bonus: $16,250

OTHER THOUGHTS:
Apparent Women Officers or Directors: 1
Hot Spot for Advancement for Women/Minorities:

LOCATIONS: ("Y" = Yes)

West:	Southwest:	Midwest:	Southeast:	Northeast:	International:
Y	Y	Y	Y	Y	Y

AMERICAN COIN MERCHANDISING INC www.sugarloaf-usa.com

Industry Group Code: 713990 **Ranks within this company's industry group:** Sales: Profits:

Print Media/Publishing:	Movies:	Equipment/Supplies:		Broadcast/Cable:	Music/Audio:	Sports/Games:	
Newspapers:	Movie Theaters:	Equipment/Supplies:	Y	Broadcast TV:	Music Production:	Games/Sports:	Y
Magazines:	Movie Production:	Gambling Equipment:		Cable TV:	Retail Music:	Retail Games Stores:	
Books:	TV/Video Production:	Special Services:		Satellite Broadcast:	Retail Audio Equip.:	Stadiums/Teams:	
Book Stores:	Video Rental:	Advertising Services:		Radio:	Music Print./Dist.:	Gambling/Casinos:	
Distribution/Printing:	Video Distribution:	Info. Sys. Software:		Online Information:	Multimedia:	Rides/Theme Parks:	Y

TYPES OF BUSINESS:
Skill-Crane Game Machines
Simulators, Video Games & Rides
Plush Toy Manufacturing
Vending Machines

BRANDS/DIVISIONS/AFFILIATES:
Coinstar, Inc.
SugarLoaf Creations, Inc.
Folz Vending Company
Kiddie World
Rainbow Crane
SugarLoaf Toy Shoppe
SugarLoaf Bean Bag Shoppe
SugarLoaf Stop Shoppe

CONTACTS: Note: Officers with more than one job title may be intentionally listed here more than once.
Randall J. Fagundo, CEO
Randall J. Fagundo, Pres.
Steven Thompson, Controller
Judy Cochrane, Mgr.-Sales Support
David Cole, CEO-Coinstar, Inc.
William F. Dawson Jr., Chmn.

Phone: 303-444-2559	**Fax:** 303-247-0480
Toll-Free: 800-735-2559	
Address: 397 S. Taylor Ave., Louisville, CO 80027 US	

GROWTH PLANS/SPECIAL FEATURES:
American Coin Merchandising, Inc. (ACMI), and its franchises own and manage more than 320,000 coin-operated pieces of equipment including: skill-crane machines that dispense stuffed animals, plush toys, watches, jewelry and other items; bulk vending machines; children's ride machines; and video game machines. These are installed in more than 33,000 retail locations. The firm operates under the names SugarLoaf Creations, Inc. and Folz Vending Company, and is a subsidiary of Coinstar, Inc., which operates 44,000 automated coin sorters primarily in supermarkets. Through its subsidiary, Kiddie World, the company is the only U.S. supplier of Disney licensed rides. ACMI/SugarLoaf manufactures all of the plush toys that are placed inside the skill crane machines. These machines are manufactured by subsidiary Rainbow Crane and are placed in supermarkets, mass merchandisers, bowling centers, bingo halls, bars, restaurants, warehouse clubs and similar locations, including Wal-Mart, Denny's and Kmart. The machines come in a variety of shapes and sizes and offer different vending methods. Examples of machine names include the SugarLoaf Toy Shoppe, SugarLoaf Treasure Shoppe, SugarLoaf Bean Bag Shoppe and the SugarLoaf Stop Shoppe. The Folz Vending subsidiary is responsible for the bulk vending business, which primarily offers gum, candy and small novelties. Wal-Mart locations account for the largest share, 25.3%, of ACMI's total revenue. The company gives about one-third of machine revenue to host retailers for space rental. In 2007, Disney branded kiddie rides will be expanded to include characters from the movies Aladdin, Pirates of the Caribbean and Lilo & Stitch.

ACMI's employees receive a full range of health benefits, which include a prescription plan, life and accident insurance and paid vacations.

FINANCIALS: Sales and profits are in thousands of dollars—add 000 to get the full amount. 2006 Note: Financial information for 2006 was not available for all companies at press time.

2006 Sales: $	2006 Profits: $	**U.S. Stock Ticker:** Subsidiary
2005 Sales: $	2005 Profits: $	**Int'l Ticker:** Int'l Exchange:
2004 Sales: $	2004 Profits: $	Employees: 800
2003 Sales: $201,400	2003 Profits: $-2,000	Fiscal Year Ends: 12/31
2002 Sales: $144,400	2002 Profits: $-2,800	Parent Company: COINSTAR INC

SALARIES/BENEFITS:
Pension Plan:	ESOP Stock Plan:	Profit Sharing:	Top Exec. Salary: $325,000	Bonus: $
Savings Plan: Y	Stock Purch. Plan:		Second Exec. Salary: $145,222	Bonus: $

OTHER THOUGHTS:
Apparent Women Officers or Directors: 1
Hot Spot for Advancement for Women/Minorities:

LOCATIONS: ("Y" = Yes)
West:	Southwest:	Midwest:	Southeast:	Northeast:	International:
Y				Y	

AMERICAN EDUCATIONAL PRODUCTS LLC   www.amep.com

Industry Group Code: 339000   Ranks within this company's industry group: Sales: Profits:

Print Media/Publishing:	Movies:	Equipment/Supplies:	Broadcast/Cable:	Music/Audio:	Sports/Games:
Newspapers:	Movie Theaters:	Equipment/Supplies: Y	Broadcast TV:	Music Production:	Games/Sports:
Magazines:	Movie Production:	Gambling Equipment:	Cable TV:	Retail Music:	Retail Games Stores:
Books: Y	TV/Video Production: Y	Special Services:	Satellite Broadcast:	Retail Audio Equip.:	Stadiums/Teams:
Book Stores:	Video Rental:	Advertising Services:	Radio:	Music Print./Dist.:	Gambling/Casinos:
Distribution/Printing:	Video Distribution:	Info. Sys. Software:	Online Information:	Multimedia:	Rides/Theme Parks:

TYPES OF BUSINESS:

Manufacturing-Educational Products
Educational Video Production
Map Manufacturing

BRANDS/DIVISIONS/AFFILIATES:

Aristotle Corporation (The)
Scott Resources, Inc.
Hubbard Scientific, Inc.
National Teaching Aids
NTA Microslide
Gonge Creative Learning
Morphun Systems
Ginsberg Scientific Company

CONTACTS: *Note: Officers with more than one job title may be intentionally listed here more than once.*

Michael Anderson, Pres.
Dean Johnson, CFO/VP
Crystal Salas, Head-Sales
Tom Halblieb, Head-Product Dev.

Phone: 970-484-7445	Fax: 970-484-1198
Toll-Free: 800-289-9299	
Address: 401 W. Hickory St., Fort Collins, CO 80522 US	

GROWTH PLANS/SPECIAL FEATURES:

American Educational Products, LLC (AEP) develops, manufactures and distributes educational products to parents, teachers, principals, public and private schools and school districts throughout the U.S. and in some international locations. The firm is an indirect subsidiary of The Aristotle Corporation, which manufactures medical teaching aids such as CPR mannequins and computer-based teaching aids. AEP's products are supplemental instructional aids for elementary to high school mathematics and science courses. The products attempt to present educational content in a format different than traditional textbooks. AEP serves as an Original Equipment Manufactuerer (OEM); its products are manufactured through three primary subsidiaries. Scott Resources, Inc. produces math videos, manuals, teachers' guides and math curriculum programs. AEP is widely recognized for its line of earth science products (rock and mineral collections) and videos manufactured through Hubbard Scientific. The Hubbard subsidiary is also the largest U.S. producer of high-quality raised relief maps, with approximately 300 different maps. Subsidiary National Teaching Aids produces science products such as the NTA Microslide system, which functions similarly to a microscope. AEP also markets products from Gonge Creative Learning, which offers equipment, such as trampolines, balancing eggs and labyrinth games that stimulate the development of motor skills; Morphun Systems, a producer of plastic construction blocks; and fellow Aristotle subsidiary Ginsberg Scientific Company, a manufacturer that specializes in labware for chemistry, physics and the earth sciences. AEP's OEM customers include Ray-O-Vac Batteries, Princess Cruise Lines, Meade Instruments, Scholastic, Rand McNally and Boy Scouts of America.

FINANCIALS: Sales and profits are in thousands of dollars—add 000 to get the full amount. 2006 Note: Financial information for 2006 was not available for all companies at press time.

2006 Sales: $	2006 Profits: $	U.S. Stock Ticker: Subsidiary
2005 Sales: $	2005 Profits: $	Int'l Ticker: Int'l Exchange:
2004 Sales: $	2004 Profits: $	Employees: 95
2003 Sales: $	2003 Profits: $	Fiscal Year Ends: 12/31
2002 Sales: $	2002 Profits: $	Parent Company: ARISTOTLE CORPORATION

SALARIES/BENEFITS:

Pension Plan:	ESOP Stock Plan:	Profit Sharing:	Top Exec. Salary: $	Bonus: $
Savings Plan:	Stock Purch. Plan:		Second Exec. Salary: $	Bonus: $

OTHER THOUGHTS:

Apparent Women Officers or Directors: 1
Hot Spot for Advancement for Women/Minorities:

LOCATIONS: ("Y" = Yes)

West:	Southwest:	Midwest:	Southeast:	Northeast:	International:
Y					

AMERICAN EXPRESS CO   www.americanexpress.com

Industry Group Code: 522210 Ranks within this company's industry group: Sales: 1   Profits: 1

Print Media/Publishing:	Movies:	Equipment/Supplies:	Broadcast/Cable:	Music/Audio:	Sports/Games:
Newspapers:	Movie Theaters:	Equipment/Supplies:	Broadcast TV:	Music Production:	Games/Sports:
Magazines: Y	Movie Production:	Gambling Equipment:	Cable TV:	Retail Music:	Retail Games Stores:
Books:	TV/Video Production:	Special Services: Y	Satellite Broadcast:	Retail Audio Equip.:	Stadiums/Teams:
Book Stores:	Video Rental:	Advertising Services: Y	Radio:	Music Print./Dist.:	Gambling/Casinos:
Distribution/Printing:	Video Distribution:	Info. Sys. Software:	Online Information:	Multimedia:	Rides/Theme Parks:

TYPES OF BUSINESS:

Credit Card Issuing
Travel-Related Services
Lending & Financing
Transaction Services
Point-of-Sale Systems
International Banking Services
Expense Management
Magazine Publishing

BRANDS/DIVISIONS/AFFILIATES:

American Express Travel Related Services Company
American Express Publishing Corporation
Food & Wine
Travel+Leisure
OPEN: The Small Business Network

CONTACTS: Note: Officers with more than one job title may be intentionally listed here more than once.

Kenneth I. Chenault, CEO
Gary L. Crittenden, CFO/Exec. VP
John D. Hayes, Exec. VP-Global Advertising & Brand Mgmt.
L. Kevin Cox, Exec. VP-Human Resources & Quality
Stephen Squeri, CIO/Exec. VP
Louise M. Parent, General Counsel/Exec. VP
Thomas Schick, Exec. VP-Corp. Affairs & Comm.
Edward P. Gilligan, Group Pres., Global Corp. Svcs. & Intl. Payments
Alfred F. Kelly, Jr., Group Pres., U.S. Consumer & Small Bus. Svcs.
Kenneth I. Chenault, Chmn.

Phone: 212-640-2000	Fax: 212-619-9802
Toll-Free:	
Address: World Financial Ctr., 200 Vesey St., New York, NY 10285 US	

GROWTH PLANS/SPECIAL FEATURES:

American Express Co. (Amex), founded in 1850, provides travel-related services, credit cards and international banking services. The company generates revenue from credit cards, traveler's checks and banking as well as airline, hotel and rental car reservations. Some other significant services include consumer and small business lending, merchant acquiring and transaction processing, point-of-sale systems, international banking and expense management. American Express cards, its most notable product, are issued in 45 currencies and enable card members to purchase goods and services worldwide. American Express Travel Related Services (TRS) includes in-depth travel arrangement and reservations services. Another division, American Express Publishing, operates several leading magazines for affluent readers, including Food & Wine and Travel+Leisure. Amex has noted expertise in selling to the small business market and to the corporate travel and purchasing market. Recently, the firm introduced OPEN: The Small Business Network from American Express, which provides products, services, online account management tools and partnerships for small businesses. American Express Financial Advisors (AEFA), a $400 billion financial planning company that included more than 10,000 financial advisors, was spun off as a free-standing company called Ameriprise Financial, Inc. in September 2005. In December 2005, Amex launched its first cards issued in Russia. In the first part of 2006, business was initiated, enhanced or resumed in Brazil, Cambodia and Bosnia and Herzegovina.

American Express is one of the largest American corporations to have an African-American CEO. It is committed to maintaining diversity throughout the organization. For its U.S. employees, Amex provides health care plans, a life and disability insurance plan, travel discounts and assistance programs covering legal advice, adoption, education and personal issues.

FINANCIALS: Sales and profits are in thousands of dollars—add 000 to get the full amount. 2006 Note: Financial information for 2006 was not available for all companies at press time.

2006 Sales: $	2006 Profits: $	**U.S. Stock Ticker: AXP**
2005 Sales: $24,300,000	2005 Profits: $3,734,000	**Int'l Ticker:** Int'l Exchange:
2004 Sales: $22,000,000	2004 Profits: $3,445,000	Employees: 65,800
2003 Sales: $25,866,000	2003 Profits: $2,987,000	Fiscal Year Ends: 12/31
2002 Sales: $23,807,000	2002 Profits: $2,671,000	Parent Company:

SALARIES/BENEFITS:

Pension Plan: Y	ESOP Stock Plan:	Profit Sharing:	Top Exec. Salary: $1,092,308	Bonus: $6,000,000
Savings Plan: Y	Stock Purch. Plan:		Second Exec. Salary: $569,231	Bonus: $1,660,000

OTHER THOUGHTS:

Apparent Women Officers or Directors: 3
Hot Spot for Advancement for Women/Minorities: Y

LOCATIONS: ("Y" = Yes)

West:	Southwest:	Midwest:	Southeast:	Northeast:	International:
Y	Y	Y	Y	Y	Y

Note: Financial information, benefits and other data can change quickly and may vary from those stated here.

AMERICAN GOLF CORP   www.americangolf.com

Industry Group Code: 713910 Ranks within this company's industry group: Sales: Profits:

Print Media/Publishing:	Movies:	Equipment/Supplies:	Broadcast/Cable:	Music/Audio:	Sports/Games:	
Newspapers:	Movie Theaters:	Equipment/Supplies:	Broadcast TV:	Music Production:	Games/Sports:	Y
Magazines:	Movie Production:	Gambling Equipment:	Cable TV:	Retail Music:	Retail Games Stores:	
Books:	TV/Video Production:	Special Services: Y	Satellite Broadcast:	Retail Audio Equip.:	Stadiums/Teams:	
Book Stores:	Video Rental:	Advertising Services:	Radio:	Music Print./Dist.:	Gambling/Casinos:	
Distribution/Printing:	Video Distribution:	Info. Sys. Software:	Online Information:	Multimedia:	Rides/Theme Parks:	

TYPES OF BUSINESS:

Golf Courses
Resorts
Golf Promotion
Real Estate

BRANDS/DIVISIONS/AFFILIATES:

American Golf Foundation
Adopt-A-Charity

GROWTH PLANS/SPECIAL FEATURES:

American Golf Corporation (AGC) is a premier manager of golf courses and resorts, owning and operating more than 160 private, resort and daily fee golf courses in the U.S. The company also sells real estate connected with its golf resorts and communities. Its ownerships are combined with a stated philosophy of developing the quality of life within these communities. American Golf's portfolio includes courses in 29 states, with its largest holdings in Arizona and California. American Golf established the American Golf Foundation, a nonprofit organization devoted to promoting golf. It has also formed an alliance with the Tiger Woods Foundation to increase golf exposure to disadvantaged youth and has introduced 50,000 new golfers to the game through demonstration and instruction. The firm's Adopt-A-Charity program has raised more than $32 million over the last 10 years.

CONTACTS: Note: Officers with more than one job title may be intentionally listed here more than once.

Tom Ferguson, CEO
Paul Major, Pres.
Bob Riesbeck, CFO/Sr. VP
Mark Friedman, General Counsel/Sr. VP
Keith Brown, Sr. VP/COO-West
Steve Paris, Sr. VP/COO-East
Craig Kniffen, Sr. VP-Maintenance

Phone: 310-664-4000	Fax: 310-664-6160
Toll-Free:	
Address: 2951 28th St., Santa Monica, CA 90405 US	

FINANCIALS: Sales and profits are in thousands of dollars—add 000 to get the full amount. 2006 Note: Financial information for 2006 was not available for all companies at press time.

2006 Sales: $	2006 Profits: $	U.S. Stock Ticker: Private
2005 Sales: $	2005 Profits: $	Int'l Ticker: Int'l Exchange:
2004 Sales: $	2004 Profits: $	Employees: 10,000
2003 Sales: $700,000	2003 Profits: $	Fiscal Year Ends: 12/31
2002 Sales: $715,000	2002 Profits: $	Parent Company:

SALARIES/BENEFITS:

Pension Plan:	ESOP Stock Plan:	Profit Sharing:	Top Exec. Salary: $	Bonus: $
Savings Plan: Y	Stock Purch. Plan:		Second Exec. Salary: $	Bonus: $

OTHER THOUGHTS:

Apparent Women Officers or Directors:
Hot Spot for Advancement for Women/Minorities:

LOCATIONS: ("Y" = Yes)

West:	Southwest:	Midwest:	Southeast:	Northeast:	International:
Y	Y	Y	Y	Y	

AMERICAN GREETINGS CORP
www.corporate.americangreetings.com

Industry Group Code: 511191 Ranks within this company's industry group: Sales: 2 Profits: 1

Print Media/Publishing:	Movies:	Equipment/Supplies:		Broadcast/Cable:	Music/Audio:	Sports/Games:
Newspapers:	Movie Theaters:	Equipment/Supplies:	Y	Broadcast TV:	Music Production:	Games/Sports:
Magazines:	Movie Production:	Gambling Equipment:		Cable TV:	Retail Music:	Retail Games Stores:
Books:	TV/Video Production:	Special Services:	Y	Satellite Broadcast:	Retail Audio Equip.:	Stadiums/Teams:
Book Stores:	Video Rental:	Advertising Services:		Radio:	Music Print./Dist.:	Gambling/Casinos:
Distribution/Printing:	Video Distribution:	Info. Sys. Software:		Online Information:	Multimedia:	Rides/Theme Parks:

TYPES OF BUSINESS:
Greeting Cards
Gift Wrap
Party Supplies
Candles
Stationery
Digital Media
Online Greetings Services
Educational Products

BRANDS/DIVISIONS/AFFILIATES:
Carlton Cards
Guildhouse
DateWorks
DesignWare
AGI Shutz Merchandising
Learning Horizons
AG Interactive
bluemountain.com

CONTACTS: Note: Officers with more than one job title may be intentionally listed here more than once.
Zev Weiss, CEO
Jeffery M. Weiss, COO
Jeffery M. Weiss, Pres.
Michael J. Merriman, CFO/Sr. VP
William R. Mason, Sr. VP-Mktg.
Rajiv Jain, CTO
George A. Wenz, VP-Mass Merch. Channel
Catherine M. Kilbane, General Counsel
Paul J. Conley, VP-Digital Media
Stephen J. Smith, VP-Investor Rel.
Stephen J. Smith, Treas.
Steven Willensky, Sr. VP-Sales & Mktg.
Thomas H. Johnson, Sr. VP-Creative
William R. Mason, Sr. VP-Wal-Mart Team
Tamra Seldin, Sr. VP/Consumer Products
Morry Weiss, Chmn.
John S.N. Charlton, Sr. VP-Int'l Oper.
Michael L. Goulder, Sr. VP-Exec. Supply Chain Officer

Phone: 216-252-7300	Fax: 216-252-6778
Toll-Free:	
Address: One American Rd., Cleveland, OH 44144-3298 US	

GROWTH PLANS/SPECIAL FEATURES:
American Greetings Corp. is engaged in the design, manufacture and sale of everyday and seasonal greeting cards and other social expression products. The firm's products are sold across the U.S. and in countries around the world, including Canada, the U.K., Australia and China, under a variety of names, including AG Interactive, a new subsidiary focusing on the digital media market. Besides greeting cards, the company's product lines also include gift wrap, party goods, candles, stationery, calendars, ornaments, ringtones, wallpapers, avatars and emoticons. The firm owns intellectual properties including Strawberry Shortcake, Care Bears, Holly Hobbie and Twisted Whiskers. The company also owns 92% of americangreetings.com, which markets e-mail greetings, personalized printable greeting cards and other products through its web sites, including bluemountain.com and egreetings.com. This subsidiary also offers design and verse content services for use in CD-ROM software products. Another subsidiary, Learning Horizons, distributes supplemental education products. American Greetings' largest customers include mass merchandisers and major drug stores. In 2005, the AG Interactive division announced several partnerships, including one with Concord Music Group and one with SI Mobile, Sports Illustrated's wireless media group, aimed at the development and distribution of content through online, mobile and Instant Messaging channels. Also in 2005, the company expanded its global presence by acquiring a European manufacturer of high quality gift-wrap products. In September 2006, American Greetings relaunched the bluemountain.com web site following a nine-month review and redesign process.

FINANCIALS: Sales and profits are in thousands of dollars—add 000 to get the full amount. 2006 Note: Financial information for 2006 was not available for all companies at press time.

2006 Sales: $1,885,701	2006 Profits: $84,376	U.S. Stock Ticker: AM
2005 Sales: $1,883,367	2005 Profits: $95,279	Int'l Ticker: Int'l Exchange:
2004 Sales: $1,937,540	2004 Profits: $104,670	Employees: 29,500
2003 Sales: $1,995,900	2003 Profits: $121,100	Fiscal Year Ends: 2/28
2002 Sales: $2,355,700	2002 Profits: $122,300	Parent Company:

SALARIES/BENEFITS:

Pension Plan: Y	ESOP Stock Plan:	Profit Sharing: Y	Top Exec. Salary: $675,000	Bonus: $1,166,693
Savings Plan: Y	Stock Purch. Plan:		Second Exec. Salary: $556,250	Bonus: $817,279

OTHER THOUGHTS:
Apparent Women Officers or Directors: 2
Hot Spot for Advancement for Women/Minorities: Y

LOCATIONS: ("Y" = Yes)

West:	Southwest:	Midwest:	Southeast:	Northeast:	International:
Y	Y	Y	Y	Y	Y

Note: Financial information, benefits and other data can change quickly and may vary from those stated here.

AMERICAN SKIING COMPANY   www.peaks.com

Industry Group Code: 713920 Ranks within this company's industry group: Sales: 2 Profits: 2

Print Media/Publishing:	Movies:	Equipment/Supplies:	Broadcast/Cable:	Music/Audio:	Sports/Games:	
Newspapers:	Movie Theaters:	Equipment/Supplies:	Broadcast TV:	Music Production:	Games/Sports:	Y
Magazines:	Movie Production:	Gambling Equipment:	Cable TV:	Retail Music:	Retail Games Stores:	
Books:	TV/Video Production:	Special Services:	Satellite Broadcast:	Retail Audio Equip.:	Stadiums/Teams:	
Book Stores:	Video Rental:	Advertising Services:	Radio:	Music Print./Dist.:	Gambling/Casinos:	
Distribution/Printing:	Video Distribution:	Info. Sys. Software:	Online Information:	Multimedia:	Rides/Theme Parks:	

TYPES OF BUSINESS:

Ski Resorts
Real Estate Development
Alpine Resort Villages

BRANDS/DIVISIONS/AFFILIATES:

Canyons (The)
Steamboat
Sugarloaf/USA
Killington
Attitash Bear Peak
Mount Snow
Grand Summit Resort Properties, Inc.
Steamboat Grand Resort Hotel & Condominiums

CONTACTS: *Note: Officers with more than one job title may be intentionally listed here more than once.*

William J. Fair, CEO
Hernan R. Martinez, COO
William J. Fair, Pres.
Betsy Wallace, Sr. VP/CFO
Franklin Carey, Jr., Sr. VP-Mktg. & Sales
Foster A. Stewart, Jr., Sr. VP/General Counsel
Helen E. Wallace, Treas.
Foster A. Stewart, Jr., Corp. Sec.
Stan Hansen, Sr. VP-Real Estate & Planning

Phone: 435-615-0340	Fax: 435-615-4780
Toll-Free:	
Address: 136 Heber Ave., Ste. 303, Park City, UT 84060 US	

GROWTH PLANS/SPECIAL FEATURES:

American Skiing Company (ASC) owns and operates eight major ski resorts in New England and the Rockies. The resorts include Pico Mountain, Mount Snow and Killington in Vermont; Sugarloaf/USA and Sunday River in Maine; Attitash Bear Peak in New Hampshire; Steamboat in Steamboat Springs, Colorado; and the Canyons in Park City, Utah. The Canyons and Steamboat are rated among the best ski resorts in North America, and three of ASC's other resorts are ranked in the top 10 eastern resorts. As well as operating alpine resorts, the company develops mountainside condominiums and vacation timeshares. ASC operates alpine villages at prime locations within Sunday River, Mount Snow, Steamboat and Sugarloaf/USA, with new buildings currently under construction at Sugarloaf/USA. Recently, Mount Snow agreed to sell its separately operated Haystack Ski Resort in Wilmington, Vermont. Additionally, the company's Grand Summit Resort Properties, Inc. subsidiary completed an auction of units in its Steamboat Grand Resort Hotel & Condominiums complex in March 2006.

FINANCIALS: Sales and profits are in thousands of dollars—add 000 to get the full amount. 2006 Note: Financial information for 2006 was not available for all companies at press time.

2006 Sales: $307,810	2006 Profits: $-65,653	**U.S. Stock Ticker: AESK**
2005 Sales: $276,477	2005 Profits: $-73,315	**Int'l Ticker:** Int'l Exchange:
2004 Sales: $284,111	2004 Profits: $-28,502	Employees: 1,300
2003 Sales: $264,500	2003 Profits: $-44,374	Fiscal Year Ends: 7/31
2002 Sales: $272,100	2002 Profits: $173,900	Parent Company:

SALARIES/BENEFITS:

Pension Plan:	ESOP Stock Plan:	Profit Sharing:	Top Exec. Salary: $407,692	Bonus: $28,800
Savings Plan: Y	Stock Purch. Plan:		Second Exec. Salary: $269,300	Bonus: $

OTHER THOUGHTS:

Apparent Women Officers or Directors: 1
Hot Spot for Advancement for Women/Minorities:

LOCATIONS: ("Y" = Yes)

West:	Southwest:	Midwest:	Southeast:	Northeast:	International:
Y				Y	

Note: Financial information, benefits and other data can change quickly and may vary from those stated here.

AMERICAN WAGERING INC   www.americanwagering.com

Industry Group Code: 713290 Ranks within this company's industry group: Sales: 12   Profits: 10

Print Media/Publishing:	Movies:	Equipment/Supplies:		Broadcast/Cable:	Music/Audio:	Sports/Games:	
Newspapers:	Movie Theaters:	Equipment/Supplies:		Broadcast TV:	Music Production:	Games/Sports:	
Magazines:	Movie Production:	Gambling Equipment:	Y	Cable TV:	Retail Music:	Retail Games Stores:	
Books:	TV/Video Production:	Special Services:	Y	Satellite Broadcast:	Retail Audio Equip.:	Stadiums/Teams:	
Book Stores:	Video Rental:	Advertising Services:		Radio:	Music Print./Dist.:	Gambling/Casinos:	Y
Distribution/Printing:	Video Distribution:	Info. Sys. Software:		Online Information:	Multimedia:	Rides/Theme Parks:	

TYPES OF BUSINESS:

Gambling Equipment
Sports Book Facilities
Race Book Computer Systems
Casino-Hotel

BRANDS/DIVISIONS/AFFILIATES:

Leroy's Horse and Sports Place, Inc.
AWI Manufacturing, Inc.
AWI Gaming, Inc.
Sturgeon's, LLC
Sturgeon's Inn & Casino
Computerized Bookmaking Systems, Inc.
Contest Sports Systems, Inc.

CONTACTS: *Note: Officers with more than one job title may be intentionally listed here more than once.*

Victor J. Salerno, CEO
Victor J. Salerno, COO
Victor J. Salerno, Pres.
Timothy Lockinger, CFO
Timothy Lockinger, Treas.
Timothy Lockinger, Corp. Sec.

Phone: 702-735-5529	Fax: 702-735-0142
Toll-Free:	
Address: 675 Grier Dr., Las Vegas, NV 89119 US	

GROWTH PLANS/SPECIAL FEATURES:

American Wagering, Inc. was originally formed in 1995 as a holding company for Leroy's Horse and Sports Place. The company operates through three segments: wagering, hotel/casino and systems. The wagering segment comprises Leroy's Horse & Sports Place, Inc. and AWI Manufacturing, Inc. (AWIM). Leroy's owns and operates race and sports books in the state of Nevada. AWIM leases self-service race and sports wagering kiosks. At the present time, Leroy's accounts for the bulk of AWIM's revenues. The hotel/casino segment is comprised of AWI Gaming, Inc. (AWIG) and Sturgeon's, LLC, a company acquired in March 2006. AWIG is the sole member of Sturgeon's, the operator of Sturgeon's Inn & Casino in Lovelock, Nevada. The systems segment includes Computerized Bookmaking Systems, Inc. (CBS) and Contest Sports Systems, Inc. (CSS). CBS designs, sells, installs and maintains computerized race and sports book systems for the Nevada gaming industry. CSS leases contest-related self-service kiosks.

FINANCIALS: Sales and profits are in thousands of dollars—add 000 to get the full amount. 2006 Note: Financial information for 2006 was not available for all companies at press time.

2006 Sales: $12,524	2006 Profits: $ 419	U.S. Stock Ticker: BETM
2005 Sales: $11,108	2005 Profits: $-1,128	Int'l Ticker: Int'l Exchange:
2004 Sales: $10,891	2004 Profits: $- 487	Employees: 198
2003 Sales: $11,600	2003 Profits: $ 400	Fiscal Year Ends: 1/31
2002 Sales: $12,000	2002 Profits: $ 900	Parent Company:

SALARIES/BENEFITS:

Pension Plan:	ESOP Stock Plan:	Profit Sharing:	Top Exec. Salary: $240,000	Bonus: $
Savings Plan: Y	Stock Purch. Plan:		Second Exec. Salary: $120,000	Bonus: $

OTHER THOUGHTS:

Apparent Women Officers or Directors:
Hot Spot for Advancement for Women/Minorities:

LOCATIONS: ("Y" = Yes)

West:	Southwest:	Midwest:	Southeast:	Northeast:	International:
Y					

AMERISTAR CASINOS INC   www.ameristarcasinos.com

Industry Group Code: 721120 Ranks within this company's industry group: Sales: 7 Profits: 7

Print Media/Publishing:	Movies:	Equipment/Supplies:	Broadcast/Cable:	Music/Audio:	Sports/Games:	
Newspapers:	Movie Theaters:	Equipment/Supplies:	Broadcast TV:	Music Production:	Games/Sports:	
Magazines:	Movie Production:	Gambling Equipment:	Cable TV:	Retail Music:	Retail Games Stores:	
Books:	TV/Video Production:	Special Services:	Satellite Broadcast:	Retail Audio Equip.:	Stadiums/Teams:	Y
Book Stores:	Video Rental:	Advertising Services:	Radio:	Music Print./Dist.:	Gambling/Casinos:	
Distribution/Printing:	Video Distribution:	Info. Sys. Software:	Online Information:	Multimedia:	Rides/Theme Parks:	

TYPES OF BUSINESS:

Casino Resorts
Casino Management

BRANDS/DIVISIONS/AFFILIATES:

Cactus Pete's Resort Casino
Ameristar Casino Hotel Kansas City
Ameristar Casino St. Charles
Ameristar Casino Hotel Council Bluffs
Ameristar Casino Hotel Vicksburg
Horseshu Hotel & Casino
Mountain High Casino

CONTACTS: *Note: Officers with more than one job title may be intentionally listed here more than once.*

Craig H. Neilsen, CEO
John M. Boushy, Pres.
Thomas M. Steinbauer, CFO/Exec. VP-Finance
Paul Eagleton, Chief Mktg. Officer
Ursula Conway, CIO
Mary Siero, VP-IT
Peter C. Walsh, General Counsel/Sr. VP
Angela R. Frost, Sr. VP-Oper.
Gordon R. Kanofsky, Exec. VP-Corp. Dev., Gov't & Legal Affairs
Thomas Malone, VP-Finance/Controller
Richard deFlon, Sr. VP-Design
Alan Rose, Sr. VP-Construction
Ray Neilsen, Corp. VP-Oper. & Special Projects
Adrian Caldwell, Sr. VP/General Mgr.-Ameristar Vicksburg
Craig H. Neilsen, Chmn.

Phone: 702-567-7000	Fax: 702-369-8860
Toll-Free:	
Address: 3773 Howard Hughes Pkwy., Ste. 490 S., Las Vegas, NV 89109 US	

GROWTH PLANS/SPECIAL FEATURES:

Ameristar Casinos, Inc. is a multi-jurisdictional gaming company that owns and operates casinos located in Colorado, Nevada, Missouri, Mississippi and Iowa. The company's subsidiaries include Cactus Pete's Resort Casino, the Horseshu Hotel & Casino, Mountain High Casino, Ameristar Casino Hotel Vicksburg, Ameristar Casino Hotel Council Bluffs, Ameristar Casino Hotel Kansas City and Ameristar Casino St. Charles. Cactus Pete's Resort Casino and the Horseshu Hotel & Casino are both located in Jackpot, Nevada. Ameristar Casino Hotel Vicksburg is a permanently docked riverboat casino located on the Mississippi River. Ameristar Casino Hotel Council Bluffs is the largest cruising riverboat casino on the Missouri River. The firm emphasizes slot machine play at its properties and continually invests in new slot equipment and technology to promote customer satisfaction and loyalty. Ameristar leads the industry in implementing cashless slot technology and new-generation multi-coin (nickel and penny denomination) slot machines. All of its properties also offer table games such as blackjack, craps and roulette. In addition, Ameristar St. Charles, Ameristar Kansas City and Cactus Pete's offer poker, keno and sports book wagering. The company generally emphasizes competitive minimum and maximum betting limits based on each market. Ameristar is currently in the process of developing a new casino location in Philadelphia on the Delaware waterfront.

Ameristar offers its employees a benefits package that includes a 401(k) retirement plan with company match, flexible spending accounts, employee assistance program and tuition reimbursement. People of more than 25 different nationalities are employed by the firm.

FINANCIALS: Sales and profits are in thousands of dollars—add 000 to get the full amount. 2006 Note: Financial information for 2006 was not available for all companies at press time.

2006 Sales: $	2006 Profits: $	U.S. Stock Ticker: ASCA
2005 Sales: $961,358	2005 Profits: $66,285	Int'l Ticker: Int'l Exchange:
2004 Sales: $854,700	2004 Profits: $61,979	Employees: 7,560
2003 Sales: $782,000	2003 Profits: $47,600	Fiscal Year Ends: 12/31
2002 Sales: $698,000	2002 Profits: $40,500	Parent Company:

SALARIES/BENEFITS:

Pension Plan:	ESOP Stock Plan:	Profit Sharing:	Top Exec. Salary: $930,288	Bonus: $740,324
Savings Plan: Y	Stock Purch. Plan:		Second Exec. Salary: $407,404	Bonus: $342,682

OTHER THOUGHTS:

Apparent Women Officers or Directors: 4
Hot Spot for Advancement for Women/Minorities: Y

LOCATIONS: ("Y" = Yes)

West:	Southwest:	Midwest:	Southeast:	Northeast:	International:
Y		Y	Y		

AMF BOWLING WORLDWIDE INC

www.amf.com

Industry Group Code: 713950 Ranks within this company's industry group: Sales: 1 Profits: 1

Print Media/Publishing:	Movies:	Equipment/Supplies:		Broadcast/Cable:	Music/Audio:	Sports/Games:	
Newspapers:	Movie Theaters:	Equipment/Supplies:	Y	Broadcast TV:	Music Production:	Games/Sports:	Y
Magazines:	Movie Production:	Gambling Equipment:		Cable TV:	Retail Music:	Retail Games Stores:	
Books:	TV/Video Production:	Special Services:		Satellite Broadcast:	Retail Audio Equip.:	Stadiums/Teams:	
Book Stores:	Video Rental:	Advertising Services:		Radio:	Music Print./Dist.:	Gambling/Casinos:	
Distribution/Printing:	Video Distribution:	Info. Sys. Software:	Y	Online Information:	Multimedia:	Rides/Theme Parks:	

TYPES OF BUSINESS:

Bowling Equipment
Bowling Centers
Billiards Tables
Bowling Software

BRANDS/DIVISIONS/AFFILIATES:

QubicaAMF
AMF Bowling UK
300 Centers
Code Hennessy & Simmons, LLC
QubicaAMF Worldwide
Bowland X
Conqueror Pro
Mad Lanes

CONTACTS: *Note: Officers with more than one job title may be intentionally listed here more than once.*

Frederick R. Hipp, CEO
Frederick R. Hipp, Pres.
William McDonnell, CFO/VP
Paul Barkley, Sr. VP-New Center Dev.
Merrell Wreden, Public Affairs
Christopher F. Caesar, Sr. VP/Treas.

Phone: 804-730-4000	**Fax:** 804-559-6276
Toll-Free: 800-342-5263	
Address: 8100 AMF Dr., Richmond, VA 23111 US	

GROWTH PLANS/SPECIAL FEATURES:

AMF Bowling Worldwide, Inc. is one of the largest owners and operators of commercial bowling centers in the U.S., with 348 bowling centers nationwide and 13 internationally. In fiscal 2006, bowling centers contributed roughly 93% of consolidated revenue. AMF operates through two business segments: the operation of bowling centers; and Holdings, which includes its joint venture QubicaAMF and a U.K. service company that provides services to QubicaAMF. Through QubicaAMF, the company is one of the world's leading manufacturers of bowling center equipment, such as automatic pinspotters, scoring equipment, bowling center furniture, bowling pins, high-performance lanes, ball returns and spare parts, as well as bowling products such as shoes, shirts, balls and ball bags. Until December 2005, AMF manufactured and sold the PlayMaster, Highland and Renaissance brands of billiards tables through AMF Billiards. This segment was sold for approximately $4.5 million. The firm recently began developing so-called new concept bowling centers, which will feature enhanced facilities, services and food and beverages. These new centers will be called 300 Centers and will first be implemented in the Richmond, Atlanta, Dallas, San Jose, Austin and Long Island markets; as of December 2006, the centers have not been implemented. AMF is owned by private investment firm Code Hennessy & Simmons, LLC. AMF has a new 50/50 joint venture, QubicaAMF Worldwide, with Qubica Worldwide. QubicaAMF manufactures bowling and amusement products including Bowland X and BES scoring systems; Conqueror Pro bowling management software, Mad Lanes, Quest Furniture and Highway 66 miniature bowling.

The company offers its employees benefits including flexible spending accounts, incentive programs, a 401(k) plan, tuition assistance, scholarships and education programs, and employee discounts on bowling, food and bowling products. AMF also sponsors the Dick Weber Scholarship League, which awards $350,000 worth of scholarship funds to young bowlers annually.

FINANCIALS: Sales and profits are in thousands of dollars—add 000 to get the full amount. 2006 Note: Financial information for 2006 was not available for all companies at press time.

2006 Sales: $499,149	2006 Profits: $-15,885	**U.S. Stock Ticker:** Private
2005 Sales: $569,578	2005 Profits: $-10,698	**Int'l Ticker:** Int'l Exchange:
2004 Sales: $678,800	2004 Profits: $-66,800	Employees: 9,362
2003 Sales: $667,600	2003 Profits: $3,400	Fiscal Year Ends: 6/30
2002 Sales: $341,900	2002 Profits: $-34,600	Parent Company:

SALARIES/BENEFITS:

Pension Plan:	ESOP Stock Plan:	Profit Sharing:	Top Exec. Salary: $600,000	Bonus: $
Savings Plan: Y	Stock Purch. Plan:		Second Exec. Salary: $288,555	Bonus: $28,800

OTHER THOUGHTS:

Apparent Women Officers or Directors:
Hot Spot for Advancement for Women/Minorities:

LOCATIONS: ("Y" = Yes)

West:	Southwest:	Midwest:	Southeast:	Northeast:	International:
Y	Y	Y	Y	Y	Y

Note: Financial information, benefits and other data can change quickly and may vary from those stated here.

ANDERSON NEWS LLC

www.andersonnews.com

Industry Group Code: 422920 Ranks within this company's industry group: Sales: 1   Profits:

Print Media/Publishing:	Movies:	Equipment/Supplies:		Broadcast/Cable:	Music/Audio:		Sports/Games:
Newspapers:	Movie Theaters:	Equipment/Supplies:		Broadcast TV:	Music Production:		Games/Sports:
Magazines:	Movie Production:	Gambling Equipment:		Cable TV:	Retail Music:		Retail Games Stores:
Books:	TV/Video Production:	Special Services:	Y	Satellite Broadcast:	Retail Audio Equip.:		Stadiums/Teams:
Book Stores:	Video Rental:	Advertising Services:		Radio:	Music Print./Dist.:	Y	Gambling/Casinos:
Distribution/Printing:	Video Distribution:	Info. Sys. Software:		Online Information:	Multimedia:		Rides/Theme Parks:

TYPES OF BUSINESS:
Book & Magazine Distributor
Music Distribution
Online Music Distribution

BRANDS/DIVISIONS/AFFILIATES:
Anderson Merchandisers LP
Geneva Media LLC
Liquid Digital Media

CONTACTS: Note: Officers with more than one job title may be intentionally listed here more than once.
Charles Anderson, CEO
Charles Anderson, Pres.
John Campbell, Sr. VP-Finance
Joel R. Anderson, Chmn.

Phone: 865-584-9765	Fax: 865-584-3498
Toll-Free:	
Address: 6016 Brookvale Ln., Ste. 151, Knoxville, TN 37919 US	

GROWTH PLANS/SPECIAL FEATURES:
Anderson News, LLC is a book and magazine distributor. It manages the shipping, distribution, merchandising and promotion of products produced by outside publishers and manufacturers. Anderson News markets thousands of books and magazines to retailers. Currently, approximately 40,000 retailers in the U.S in 45 states are serviced by the company. The firm serves retailers including bookstores, mass merchants, discount retailers and grocery stores. Its product lines include books, magazines, maps, comics and collectibles. Anderson News employs Mosaic Category Management, a proprietary software program, to increase store sales and efficiencies. The company also offers an online data-analysis tool for Anderson News clients. Magazines Anderson News distributes include Meredith Wedding Series, Better Homes and Gardens Creative Collection Series and All Recipes.com. The books that Anderson News distributes include such titles as The House by Danielle Steel; Irish Dreams by Nora Roberts; Angels All Over Town by Luanne Rice; The Templar Legacy by Steve Berry; McKettrick's Luck by Linda Lael Miller; and All Night Long by Jayne Ann Krentz. The company also runs Point-of-Purchase display promotions. Anderson News, LLC is the parent company of Geneva Media LLC through which it owns Liquid Digital Media. Liquid Digital Media is the online music distributor for Wal-Mart. Anderson Merchandisers, LP is an affiliate of the company based in Amarillo, Texas that distributes CDs to Wal-Mart.

FINANCIALS: Sales and profits are in thousands of dollars—add 000 to get the full amount. 2006 Note: Financial information for 2006 was not available for all companies at press time.

2006 Sales: $	2006 Profits: $	U.S. Stock Ticker: Private
2005 Sales: $2,696,000	2005 Profits: $	Int'l Ticker: Int'l Exchange:
2004 Sales: $	2004 Profits: $	Employees: 12,100
2003 Sales: $	2003 Profits: $	Fiscal Year Ends: 12/31
2002 Sales: $	2002 Profits: $	Parent Company:

SALARIES/BENEFITS:
Pension Plan:	ESOP Stock Plan:	Profit Sharing:	Top Exec. Salary: $	Bonus: $
Savings Plan:	Stock Purch. Plan:		Second Exec. Salary: $	Bonus: $

OTHER THOUGHTS:
Apparent Women Officers or Directors:
Hot Spot for Advancement for Women/Minorities:

LOCATIONS: ("Y" = Yes)

West:	Southwest:	Midwest:	Southeast:	Northeast:	International:
	Y		Y		

ANHEUSER BUSCH COS INC   www.anheuser-busch.com

Industry Group Code: 312120 Ranks within this company's industry group: Sales: 1   Profits: 1

Print Media/Publishing:	Movies:	Equipment/Supplies:		Broadcast/Cable:	Music/Audio:	Sports/Games:	
Newspapers:	Movie Theaters:	Equipment/Supplies:		Broadcast TV:	Music Production:	Games/Sports:	
Magazines:	Movie Production:	Gambling Equipment:		Cable TV:	Retail Music:	Retail Games Stores:	
Books:	TV/Video Production:	Special Services:	Y	Satellite Broadcast:	Retail Audio Equip.:	Stadiums/Teams:	
Book Stores:	Video Rental:	Advertising Services:		Radio:	Music Print./Dist.:	Gambling/Casinos:	
Distribution/Printing:	Video Distribution:	Info. Sys. Software:		Online Information:	Multimedia:	Rides/Theme Parks:	Y

TYPES OF BUSINESS:

Breweries
Agriculture-Grain Processing
Packaging
Recycling
Rail Shipping
Transportation
Theme Parks
Resort & Spa

BRANDS/DIVISIONS/AFFILIATES:

Anheuser-Busch, Inc. (ABI)
Budweiser
Michelob
Busch Agricultural Resources, Inc.
Metal Container Corp.
Busch Gardens
SeaWorld
Rolling Rock

CONTACTS: Note: Officers with more than one job title may be intentionally listed here more than once.

Michael S. Harding, CEO
Michael S. Harding, Pres.
W. Randolph Baker, CFO/VP
Michael J. Owens, VP-Mktg. & Sales, ABI
Joseph P. Castellano, VP-Human Resources
Douglas J. Muhleman, VP-Brewing Tech.
Mark T. Bobak, Chief Legal Officer/VP
Peter J. Kraemer, VP-Oper.
Thomas W. Santel, VP-Corp. Dev.
John E. Jacob, Exec. VP-Global Comm.
John F. Kelly, VP/Controller
August A. Busch, IV, Pres., ABI
Joseph P. Sellinger, Chmn./CEO/Pres., Packaging Bus.
Keith M. Kasen, Chmn./Pres., Busch Entertainment
Anthony T. Ponturo, VP-Global Media & Sports Mktg., ABI
August A. Busch, III, Chmn.
Stephen J. Burrows, VP-Int'l Oper.
Timothy E. Armstrong, VP-Transportation, Logistics

Phone: 314-577-2000	Fax: 314-577-2900
Toll-Free: 800-342-5283	
Address: One Busch Pl., St. Louis, MO 63118 US	

GROWTH PLANS/SPECIAL FEATURES:

Anheuser-Busch Companies, Inc. (ABC) runs Anheuser-Busch, Inc. (ABI), the world's largest brewer of beer. ABC is also the parent company of Busch Entertainment Corporation, as well as several packaging and real estate companies. ABI produces beer through its 12 breweries, marketing it under brand names including Budweiser, Michelob, Busch, Natural Ice, King Cobra and Tequiza. ABI also brews Kirin beer in cooperation with Japan's Kirin Brewing Company and owns interest in Seattle-based Redhook Ale Brewery and Portland's Widmer Brothers Brewing Co. ABC's Busch Agricultural Resources, Inc. operates rice-milling facilities, grain elevators, barley processing plants and research facilities. The company's packaging business operates through Metal Container Corp., Anheuser-Busch Recycling Corp., Precision Printing and Packaging and Eagle Packaging. ABC also owns and operates Manufacturers Railway Co., a transportation service business. Busch Entertainment Corp. owns and operates nine theme parks. Busch Gardens in Tampa Bay, Florida is an African-themed park featuring an 80-acre setting of the Serengeti Plain, thrill-rides and live entertainment. Busch Gardens in Williamsburg, Virginia, features European themed attractions, rides and shows. Water Country USA in Williamsburg is the mid-Atlantic's largest water park. SeaWorld parks in Orlando, Florida; San Diego, California; and San Antonio, Texas and Discovery Cove in Orlando offer marine-life entertainment and education. Sesame Place, outside of Philadelphia is a Sesame Street-themed park with water attractions and live shows. Busch Properties, Inc. operates the Kingsmill resort and spa in Williamsburg. The firm has recently been investing in Chinese beer, and it increased its interest in Tsingtao Brewing Co. to 27%. In May 2006, Anheuser-Busch agreed to buy the Rolling Rock brand from InBev $82 million.

Anheuser-Busch offers tuition reimbursement and employee assistance. Anheuser-Busch Entertainment also offers adoption benefits, free admission and family passes to Anheuser-Busch parks, complimentary event tickets and complimentary beer for employees over age 21.

FINANCIALS: Sales and profits are in thousands of dollars—add 000 to get the full amount. 2006 Note: Financial information for 2006 was not available for all companies at press time.

2006 Sales: $	2006 Profits: $	U.S. Stock Ticker: BUD
2005 Sales: $15,035,700	2005 Profits: $1,839,200	Int'l Ticker: Int'l Exchange:
2004 Sales: $14,934,200	2004 Profits: $2,240,300	Employees: 31,485
2003 Sales: $14,147,000	2003 Profits: $2,076,000	Fiscal Year Ends: 12/31
2002 Sales: $13,566,000	2002 Profits: $1,934,000	Parent Company:

SALARIES/BENEFITS:

Pension Plan: Y	ESOP Stock Plan:	Profit Sharing:	Top Exec. Salary: $1,526,745	Bonus: $
Savings Plan: Y	Stock Purch. Plan:		Second Exec. Salary: $950,000	Bonus: $

OTHER THOUGHTS:

Apparent Women Officers or Directors: 3
Hot Spot for Advancement for Women/Minorities: Y

LOCATIONS: ("Y" = Yes)

West:	Southwest:	Midwest:	Southeast:	Northeast:	International:
Y	Y	Y	Y	Y	Y

Note: Financial information, benefits and other data can change quickly and may vary from those stated here.

ANSCHUTZ ENTERTAINMENT GROUPwww.aegworldwide.com

Industry Group Code: 711211 Ranks within this company's industry group: Sales: Profits:

Print Media/Publishing:	Movies:		Equipment/Supplies:		Broadcast/Cable:	Music/Audio:	Sports/Games:	
Newspapers:	Movie Theaters:		Equipment/Supplies:		Broadcast TV:	Music Production:	Games/Sports:	Y
Magazines:	Movie Production:	Y	Gambling Equipment:		Cable TV:	Retail Music:	Retail Games Stores:	
Books:	TV/Video Production:	Y	Special Services:	Y	Satellite Broadcast:	Retail Audio Equip.:	Stadiums/Teams:	Y
Book Stores:	Video Rental:		Advertising Services:	Y	Radio:	Music Print./Dist.:	Gambling/Casinos:	
Distribution/Printing:	Video Distribution:		Info. Sys. Software:		Online Information:	Multimedia:	Rides/Theme Parks:	

TYPES OF BUSINESS:

Stadiums & Sports Teams
Sports Team Franchises
Sports Facilities Management & Development
Entertainment Complexes
Entertainment Investments
Concerts & Live Entertainment Events
Filmed Entertainment
Marketing & Consulting Services

BRANDS/DIVISIONS/AFFILIATES:

Anschutz Corporation
STAPLES Center
Regal Entertainment Group
Los Angeles Kings
AEG Ehrlich Ventures, LLC
L.A. Live
Home Depot Center
Walden Media

CONTACTS: Note: Officers with more than one job title may be intentionally listed here more than once.

Timothy J. Leiweke, CEO
Timothy J. Leiweke, Pres.
Randy Phillips, Pres./CEO-AEG Live
Philip Anschutz, Chmn./CEO-The Anschutz Company
David Weil, CEO-Anschutz Film Group
Cary Granat, CEO-Walden Media

Phone: 213-763-7700	**Fax:** 303-298-8881
Toll-Free:	
Address: 1100 South Flower St., Los Angeles, CA 90015 US	

GROWTH PLANS/SPECIAL FEATURES:

Anschutz Entertainment Group, Inc. (AEG) is a subsidiary of Anschutz Corporation and a leading sports and entertainment investment, development and management company.   The firm owns the STAPLES Center, Toyota Sports Center, Toyota Park, NOKIA Theatre Times Square, The Forum and the Nokia Theater at Grand Prairie. Furthermore, the company cooperated with Home Depot to build the Home Depot National Training Center in Carson, California, which is an official U.S. Olympic training site. The company recently designed the Nokia Theater Times Square a 2,100 person capacity theater. The company also controls a number of domestic sports franchises, including the Los Angeles Kings, Los Angeles Riptide, Chicago Fire, Reading Royals, Houston Dynamo and the Manchester Monarchs. The firm's subsidiary AEG Marketing is a sponsorship, consulting and sales company.   AEG Creative is a full service marketing and advertising agency.   Parent firm Anschutz Corporation is an investment company that also has a 79% stake in the Regal Entertainment Group.   Other interests of Anschutz Corp. include stakes in film and television production companies Crusader Entertainment and Walden Media. Currently, the firm is investing $600 million to renovate London's Millennium Dome as a modern entertainment complex.   Walden Media is a subsidiary of Anschutz Film Group. In 2005, it released The Chronicles of Narnia: The Lion, the Witch and the Wardrobe, which it co-produced with Disney. Anschutz Film Group is focused on making high-quality family entertainment, especially films with a positive message. In 2006, AEG acquired a 49% stake in Marshall Arts, an international talent agent. In 2007, AEG will open L.A. Live, a 4 million-square-foot mixed-use development in downtown Los Angeles.   In 2006, AEG acquired Ken Ehrlich Productions, producer of the Grammy Awards, and formed the joint venture, AEG Ehrlich Ventures, LLC. Also in 2006, the company purchased the Champions on Ice figure skating tour.

FINANCIALS: Sales and profits are in thousands of dollars—add 000 to get the full amount. 2006 Note: Financial information for 2006 was not available for all companies at press time.

2006 Sales: $	2006 Profits: $	**U.S. Stock Ticker: Private**
2005 Sales: $	2005 Profits: $	**Int'l Ticker:** Int'l Exchange:
2004 Sales: $	2004 Profits: $	Employees:
2003 Sales: $	2003 Profits: $	Fiscal Year Ends: 12/31
2002 Sales: $	2002 Profits: $	Parent Company:

SALARIES/BENEFITS:

Pension Plan:	ESOP Stock Plan:	Profit Sharing:	Top Exec. Salary: $	Bonus: $
Savings Plan:	Stock Purch. Plan:		Second Exec. Salary: $	Bonus: $

OTHER THOUGHTS:

Apparent Women Officers or Directors:
Hot Spot for Advancement for Women/Minorities:

LOCATIONS: ("Y" = Yes)

West:	Southwest:	Midwest:	Southeast:	Northeast:	International:
Y	Y	Y	Y	Y	Y

AOL LLC

www.corp.aol.com

Industry Group Code: 514191 **Ranks within this company's industry group:** Sales: 1 Profits:

Print Media/Publishing:	Movies:	Equipment/Supplies:		Broadcast/Cable:	Music/Audio:	Sports/Games:
Newspapers:	Movie Theaters:	Equipment/Supplies:		Broadcast TV:	Music Production:	Games/Sports:
Magazines:	Movie Production:	Gambling Equipment:		Cable TV:	Retail Music:	Retail Games Stores:
Books:	TV/Video Production:	Special Services:	Y	Satellite Broadcast:	Retail Audio Equip.:	Stadiums/Teams:
Book Stores:	Video Rental:	Advertising Services:	Y	Radio:	Music Print./Dist.:	Gambling/Casinos:
Distribution/Printing:	Video Distribution:	Info. Sys. Software:		Online Information:	Multimedia:	Rides/Theme Parks:

TYPES OF BUSINESS:

Online Content Provider
Online Music Services
Online Communities
Entertainment & Information Offerings
Instant Messaging
E-Mail
VoIP Telephony
Internet Service Provider

BRANDS/DIVISIONS/AFFILIATES:

Time Warner, Inc.
America Online, Inc.
Netscape
MusicNet@AOL
AOL Instant Messenger
ICQ
Moviefone
MapQuest

CONTACTS: *Note: Officers with more than one job title may be intentionally listed here more than once.*

Randy Falco, CEO
Ron Grant, COO
Ron Grant, Pres.
Stephen Swad, CFO/Exec. VP
Lance Miyamoto, Exec. VP-Human Resources
Ira Parker, General Counsel/Exec. VP
Tricia P. Wallace, Exec. VP-Corp. Comm.
Randy Falco, Chmn.

Phone: 703-265-1000	**Fax:** 703-265-1101
Toll-Free:	
Address: 22000 AOL Way, Dulles, VA 20166 US	

GROWTH PLANS/SPECIAL FEATURES:

AOL LLC, formerly America Online, a subsidiary of Time Warner, Inc., is a provider of online content including streaming video, Voice over Internet Protocol (VoIP) phone service, anti-virus software and parental controls. Though AOL had traditionally acquired revenue as a subscription Internet Service Provider (ISP), the company underwent a massive corporate restructuring in 2006 which de-emphasized the ISP aspects of the business and began offering services free to the general public that had formerly only been available to subscribers. As part of this restructuring, the company officially changed its name from America Online, Inc. to AOL LLC. Additionally, it began offering its suites of anti-virus software and Internet parental controls under the names Active Virus Shield and AOL Parental Controls, respectively. AOL has launched several new services including: My eAddress, which allows users to create their own custom e-mail address for free; In2TV, a broadband television network offering streaming and downloadable television shows from Time Warner's library; Gold Rush, an interactive treasure hunt game; and True Stories, a website that offers documentary films in both free streaming and low cost downloadable formats. The company owns several highly recognized brands such as Mapquest, an online map and directions provider; Winamp, a music player program; instant messaging programs ICQ and AOL Instant Messenger, which became an open source program in 2006; and the Netscape search engine. In 2006, AOL acquired Relegence Corporation, a financial news and information search technology company; Userplane, a developer and marketer of community networking software including chat and instant messaging tools; and Lightningcast, Inc. a broadband video advertising company.

FINANCIALS: Sales and profits are in thousands of dollars—add 000 to get the full amount. 2006 Note: Financial information for 2006 was not available for all companies at press time.

2006 Sales: $	2006 Profits: $	**U.S. Stock Ticker: Subsidiary**
2005 Sales: $8,300,000	2005 Profits: $	**Int'l Ticker:** Int'l Exchange:
2004 Sales: $8,692,000	2004 Profits: $	Employees: 19,000
2003 Sales: $6,428,000	2003 Profits: $	Fiscal Year Ends: 12/31
2002 Sales: $7,148,000	2002 Profits: $	Parent Company: TIME WARNER INC

SALARIES/BENEFITS:

Pension Plan:	ESOP Stock Plan:	Profit Sharing:	Top Exec. Salary: $	Bonus: $
Savings Plan:	Stock Purch. Plan:		Second Exec. Salary: $	Bonus: $

OTHER THOUGHTS:

Apparent Women Officers or Directors: 1
Hot Spot for Advancement for Women/Minorities:

LOCATIONS: ("Y" = Yes)

West:	Southwest:	Midwest:	Southeast:	Northeast:	International:
				Y	Y

APPLE INC   www.apple.com

Industry Group Code: 334111 Ranks within this company's industry group: Sales: 1 Profits: 1

Print Media/Publishing:	Movies:	Equipment/Supplies:		Broadcast/Cable:		Music/Audio:		Sports/Games:	
Newspapers:	Movie Theaters:	Equipment/Supplies:	Y	Broadcast TV:	Y	Music Production:		Games/Sports:	
Magazines:	Movie Production:	Gambling Equipment:		Cable TV:		Retail Music:	Y	Retail Games Stores:	
Books:	TV/Video Production:	Special Services:		Satellite Broadcast:		Retail Audio Equip.:		Stadiums/Teams:	
Book Stores:	Video Rental:	Advertising Services:	Y	Radio:		Music Print./Dist.:	Y	Gambling/Casinos:	
Distribution/Printing:	Video Distribution:	Info. Sys. Software:	Y	Online Information:		Multimedia:		Rides/Theme Parks:	

TYPES OF BUSINESS:
Computer Hardware-PCs
Software
Computer Accessories
Retail Stores
Portable Music Players
Online Music Sales
Cellular Phones
Home Entertainment Software & Systems

BRANDS/DIVISIONS/AFFILIATES:
Power Mac
QuickTime
Mac OS
iTunes
iBook
iMac
iPod
iPhone

CONTACTS: *Note: Officers with more than one job title may be intentionally listed here more than once.*
Steve P. Jobs, CEO
Timothy D. Cook, COO
Peter Oppenheimer, CFO/Sr. VP
Avadis Tevanian, Jr., Sr. VP/CTO-Software
Bertrand Serlet, Sr. VP-Software Eng.
Donald J. Rosenberg, General Counsel/Sr. VP
Ronald B. Johnson, Sr. VP-Retail
Philip W. Schiller, Sr. VP-Worldwide Prod. Mktg.
Sina Tamaddon, Sr. VP-Applications
Tony Fadell, Sr. VP-iPod Div.
Bill Campbell, Chmn.

Phone: 408-996-1010	Fax: 408-974-2113
Toll-Free: 800-275-2273	
Address: One Infinite Loop, Cupertino, CA 95014 US	

GROWTH PLANS/SPECIAL FEATURES:

Apple, Inc., formerly Apple Computer, Inc., is a world leader in the design and manufacture of microprocessor-based personal computers, hardware and software. Apple's hardware products include basic iMac PCs, eMac PCs, Power Mac PCs, Xserve and Xserve RAID Storage System, Power Book and iBook notebook computers and AirPort Extreme Base Stations. Additional products include iPod portable music players, iSight digital video cameras and various LCD flat-panel displays. In addition, Apple's software includes the Mac OS X operating system, the QuickTime 6 suite of multimedia applications and iTunes, the company's fully integrated music store and player, which allows users to access MP3s to purchase, preview, download, share, organize and transfer to the iPod. The common thread among all Apple products is eye-catching designs and colors coupled with ease of use. The Macintosh-type computer has a devoted following that believes the Mac has significant advantages over PCs, especially for graphics and artistic endeavors. While Apple's share of the global PC market is low (at a bit more than 2%), the firm is evolving into an entertainment device company. In early 2005, Apple introduced a breakthrough home version of the Mac, the Mac mini, which sells for only $499, as well as a $99 version of the iPod, the iPod shuffle. The iPod accounts for a significant portion of the company's revenues, with 70 million units sold at the end of 2006. The firm's retail stores account for about 15% of revenues and Apple is expanding the chain with a new boutique format in high traffic spots like airports. Stores are now in the U.K., Japan and Canada, in addition to the U.S. In 2006, Apple began selling hardware products with Intel microprocessors, intending to complete the transition of all its hardware to Intel microprocessors by the end of 2007. The company unveiled the iPhone in early 2007.

Apple offers employee benefits including fitness plans, flex dollars, a good savings plan, health education, preventive care, product discounts and tuition assistance. Part-time employees also receive certain benefits.

FINANCIALS: Sales and profits are in thousands of dollars—add 000 to get the full amount. 2006 Note: Financial information for 2006 was not available for all companies at press time.

2006 Sales: $19,315,000	2006 Profits: $1,989,000	U.S. Stock Ticker: AAPL
2005 Sales: $13,931,000	2005 Profits: $1,328,000	Int'l Ticker: Int'l Exchange:
2004 Sales: $8,279,000	2004 Profits: $266,000	Employees: 14,800
2003 Sales: $6,207,000	2003 Profits: $69,000	Fiscal Year Ends: 9/30
2002 Sales: $5,742,000	2002 Profits: $65,000	Parent Company:

SALARIES/BENEFITS:

Pension Plan:	ESOP Stock Plan:	Profit Sharing:	Top Exec. Salary: $602,434	Bonus: $600,239
Savings Plan: Y	Stock Purch. Plan: Y		Second Exec. Salary: $552,795	Bonus: $551,239

OTHER THOUGHTS:
Apparent Women Officers or Directors:
Hot Spot for Advancement for Women/Minorities:

LOCATIONS: ("Y" = Yes)

West:	Southwest:	Midwest:	Southeast:	Northeast:	International:
Y	Y	Y	Y	Y	Y

ARBITRON INC

www.arbitron.com

Industry Group Code: 541910 Ranks within this company's industry group: Sales: 3 Profits: 3

Print Media/Publishing:	Movies:	Equipment/Supplies:		Broadcast/Cable:	Music/Audio:	Sports/Games:
Newspapers:	Movie Theaters:	Equipment/Supplies:		Broadcast TV:	Music Production:	Games/Sports:
Magazines:	Movie Production:	Gambling Equipment:		Cable TV:	Retail Music:	Retail Games Stores:
Books:	TV/Video Production:	Special Services:	Y	Satellite Broadcast:	Retail Audio Equip.:	Stadiums/Teams:
Book Stores:	Video Rental:	Advertising Services:	Y	Radio:	Music Print./Dist.:	Gambling/Casinos:
Distribution/Printing:	Video Distribution:	Info. Sys. Software:	Y	Online Information:	Multimedia:	Rides/Theme Parks:

TYPES OF BUSINESS:

Radio Audience Ratings
Market Research
Market Research Software & Technology

BRANDS/DIVISIONS/AFFILIATES:

Portable People Meter
Continental Research

CONTACTS: Note: Officers with more than one job title may be intentionally listed here more than once.

Stephen B. Morris, CEO
Stephen B. Morris, Pres.
Sean Creamer, CFO
Pierre C. Bouvard, Pres., Sales & Mktg.
V. Scott Henry, CIO/Exec. VP
Linda Dupree, Exec. VP-New Prod. Dev.
Claire L. Kummer, Exec. VP-Oper., Integration & Manufacturing
Kathleen T. Ross, Chief Admin. Officer/Exec. VP
Tim Smith, Chief Legal Officer/Exec. VP
Owen Charlebois, Pres., Oper.
Sean Creamer, Exec. VP-Planning
Thom Mocarsky, Sr. VP-Press
Thom Mocarsky, Sr. VP-Investor Rel.
Sean Creamer, Exec. VP-Finance
Al Tupek, Chief Statistical Officer
Carol Hanley, Sr. VP-US Sales
Bill Rose, Sr. VP-Mktg.
Scott Musgrave, Sr. VP-Client Software Business
Brad Bedford, VP-Intl. Sales

Phone: 212-887-1300	Fax: 212-887-1390
Toll-Free:	
Address: 142 W. 57th St., New York, NY 10019-3300 US	

GROWTH PLANS/SPECIAL FEATURES:

Arbitron, Inc. is an international media and marketing research firm serving radio broadcasters, cable companies, advertisers, advertising agencies, outdoor media companies, retailers, cable television and online industries in the U.S., Mexico and Europe. Through its Scarborough joint venture, Arbitron also serves television broadcasters and print media. Arbitron's core businesses are measuring network and local market radio audiences; measuring national radio audiences; providing application software for accessing and analyzing media audience data; and providing consumer, shopping and media usage information. The company utilizes two main methods for data acquisition: using diary methodology and the Portable People Meter. In the former case, willing participants are sent a small diary and asked to keep track of what kind of media they use and when for seven days. A typical survey period is 12 weeks and the firm processes more than 1.4 million diaries a year. The Portable People Meter is a small device carried or worn by the participants, which picks up on code signals embedded in the audio portion of a client company's broadcast using encoders provided by Arbitron. The Portable People Meter can detect codes in radio, television, Internet and cable broadcasts, as well as satellite radio and satellite television. The Portable People Meter automatically sends all of its recorded codes to Arbitron for tabulation. In addition to quantitative data, Arbitron provides qualitative information about media usage, retail and shopping habits, demographics and lifestyles in 75 U.S. markets. Arbitron also owns Continental Research, located in London. Continental conducts market research in the media, advertising, financial and telecommunications arenas in the U.K. and Europe.

Arbitron employees are offered tuition reimbursement, flexible spending accounts, a 401(k) savings plan and a casual dress code. In 2005, Arbitron was listed in Fortune magazine's 100 Best Companies To Work For.

FINANCIALS: Sales and profits are in thousands of dollars—add 000 to get the full amount. 2006 Note: Financial information for 2006 was not available for all companies at press time.

2006 Sales: $	2006 Profits: $	U.S. Stock Ticker: ARB
2005 Sales: $309,995	2005 Profits: $67,308	Int'l Ticker: Int'l Exchange:
2004 Sales: $296,553	2004 Profits: $60,565	Employees: 1,742
2003 Sales: $273,550	2003 Profits: $49,873	Fiscal Year Ends: 12/31
2002 Sales: $249,757	2002 Profits: $42,755	Parent Company:

SALARIES/BENEFITS:

Pension Plan:	ESOP Stock Plan:	Profit Sharing:	Top Exec. Salary: $563,538	Bonus: $563,548
Savings Plan: Y	Stock Purch. Plan: Y		Second Exec. Salary: $333,399	Bonus: $236,187

OTHER THOUGHTS:

Apparent Women Officers or Directors: 13
Hot Spot for Advancement for Women/Minorities: Y

LOCATIONS: ("Y" = Yes)

West:	Southwest:	Midwest:	Southeast:	Northeast:	International:
Y	Y	Y	Y	Y	Y

Note: Financial information, benefits and other data can change quickly and may vary from those stated here.

ARISTOCRAT LEISURE LTD

www.aristocrat.com.au

Industry Group Code: 713290 Ranks within this company's industry group: Sales: 3 Profits: 3

Print Media/Publishing:	Movies:	Equipment/Supplies:		Broadcast/Cable:	Music/Audio:	Sports/Games:
Newspapers:	Movie Theaters:	Equipment/Supplies:		Broadcast TV:	Music Production:	Games/Sports:
Magazines:	Movie Production:	Gambling Equipment:	Y	Cable TV:	Retail Music:	Retail Games Stores:
Books:	TV/Video Production:	Special Services:	Y	Satellite Broadcast:	Retail Audio Equip.:	Stadiums/Teams:
Book Stores:	Video Rental:	Advertising Services:		Radio:	Music Print./Dist.:	Gambling/Casinos:
Distribution/Printing:	Video Distribution:	Info. Sys. Software:	Y	Online Information:	Multimedia:	Rides/Theme Parks:

TYPES OF BUSINESS:

Gaming Machines Manufacturing
Gaming Consulting & Services
Gaming Management Systems & Software
Gaming Accessories

BRANDS/DIVISIONS/AFFILIATES:

Aristocrat Technologies, Inc.
Casino Data Systems
ReelPower
Bonus Bank
Lucky Devil
System Account Play
Hyperlink
ACE Interactive

CONTACTS: *Note: Officers with more than one job title may be intentionally listed here more than once.*

Paul Oneile, CEO/Mng. Dir.
Simon Kelly, CFO
Steve Parker, Group Gen. Mgr.-Sales & Mktg.
Paul Cavanagh-Downs, CIO
Gareth Phillips, Chief Tech. Officer
Bruce Yahl, Group Mgr.-Legal & Commercial/Corp. Sec.
Ian Timmis, Group Gen. Mgr.-Bus. & Strategic Dev.
Warren Jowett, Exec. Gen. Mgr.-Australasia & Asia Pacific
Tim Parrott, CEO/Pres., Aristocrat Technologies, Americas
Julian Stanford, Gen. Mgr.-Europe
Robert McLoughlin, Exec. Chmn.
David J. Simpson, Chmn.

Phone: 61-2-9413-6300	Fax: 61-2-9420-1352
Toll-Free:	
Address: 71 Longueville Rd., Lane Cove, NSW 2066 Australia	

GROWTH PLANS/SPECIAL FEATURES:

Aristocrat Leisure, Ltd. is a major manufacturer of gaming machines and their components. The firm supplies clubs, hotels, casinos and bars in more than 55 countries with its gaming machines and systems. Aristocrat operates in the U.S. through Casino Data Systems. In addition to its gaming products, the firm provides gaming services, including technical support, training and documentation, sales support and gaming analysis. Aristocrat also offers consulting services that include venue analysis, commercialized project management and specialized gaming training. The company produces three types of gaming machines: line games, the most traditional form of video reel games; ReelPower games, which allow players to purchase reels rather than lines; and specialty games, which consist of the Bonus Bank product Line (Mr. Cashman, Aristocrat Technologies, Inc., Lucky Devil, Lady Luck and Zorro). The firm's gaming systems include System 5000 (a slot machine management and promotion system for the club industry), System 6000 (a casino slot machine management solution), System Account Play (which allows members to set up a player account that they can transfer money directly to gaming machines by using a member card), Cashless Gaming (which allows players to move around the gaming area at a venue and play machines using their membership cards), System Analyst (a slot machine management reporting solution), Ticket Out Auto Redemption (which allows gaming machines to issue a barcoded payout ticket) and System Xpress (a systems upgrade that offers easy navigation and touch screen capabilities). Aristocrat's accessories include stools, signage and LCD displays. Hyperlink is the company's patented bonusing product, which links all electronic gaming machines to its progressive gaming platform. In May 2006, Aristocrat acquired ACE Interactive products line, a server based lottery technology. In January, 2006, the firm acquired a 50% interest in the Elektroncek group of companies.

Aristocrat offers its employees health insurance, educational assistance, online training programs, and membership in a social club. The firm also offers a graduate development program in marketing, finance, game design and engineering. Employees have access to a 24/7 Internet training program called 'evolve. In addition, the firm provides a nine-month management training program called Lead On.

FINANCIALS: Sales and profits are in thousands of dollars—add 000 to get the full amount. 2006 Note: Financial information for 2006 was not available for all companies at press time.

2006 Sales: $	2006 Profits: $	**U.S. Stock Ticker: ARLUF**
2005 Sales: $920,683	2005 Profits: $173,523	**Int'l Ticker: ALL** Int'l Exchange: Sydney-ASX
2004 Sales: $804,583	2004 Profits: $100,974	Employees: 2,080
2003 Sales: $735,000	2003 Profits: $-79,400	Fiscal Year Ends: 12/31
2002 Sales: $499,200	2002 Profits: $45,200	Parent Company:

SALARIES/BENEFITS:

Pension Plan:	ESOP Stock Plan:	Profit Sharing:	Top Exec. Salary: $	Bonus: $
Savings Plan: Y	Stock Purch. Plan: Y		Second Exec. Salary: $	Bonus: $

OTHER THOUGHTS:

Apparent Women Officers or Directors: 3
Hot Spot for Advancement for Women/Minorities: Y

LOCATIONS: ("Y" = Yes)

West:	Southwest:	Midwest:	Southeast:	Northeast:	International:
Y		Y	Y	Y	Y

Note: Financial information, benefits and other data can change quickly and may vary from those stated here.

ASCENT MEDIA GROUP INC

www.ascentmedia.com

Industry Group Code: 512191 Ranks within this company's industry group: Sales: 1   Profits:

Print Media/Publishing:	Movies:		Equipment/Supplies:		Broadcast/Cable:	Music/Audio:	Sports/Games:
Newspapers:	Movie Theaters:		Equipment/Supplies:		Broadcast TV:	Music Production:	Games/Sports:
Magazines:	Movie Production:	Y	Gambling Equipment:		Cable TV:	Retail Music:	Retail Games Stores:
Books:	TV/Video Production:	Y	Special Services:	Y	Satellite Broadcast:	Retail Audio Equip.:	Stadiums/Teams:
Book Stores:	Video Rental:		Advertising Services:		Radio:	Music Print./Dist.:	Gambling/Casinos:
Distribution/Printing:	Video Distribution:		Info. Sys. Software:		Online Information:	Multimedia:	Rides/Theme Parks:

TYPES OF BUSINESS:

Motion Picture Post-Production & Distribution
Audio Post-Production Services
Creative Services
Network Services
Engineering & Consulting Services
Movie Restoration & Preservation

BRANDS/DIVISIONS/AFFILIATES:

Discovery Holding Company
AMG Creative Services
AMG Creative Sound Services
AMG Management Services
AMG Network Services
Ascent Media Systems & Technology Services
Cinetech, Inc.

CONTACTS: Note: Officers with more than one job title may be intentionally listed here more than once.

Scott Davis, Pres., Network Svcs.
George C. Platisa, Exec. VP/CFO
Stephen McKenna, Sr. VP-Strategic Mktg. & Sales
Dustin K. Finer, Sr. VP-Global Human Resources & Legal Affairs
William E. Niles, General Counsel/Exec. VP/Corp. Sec.
Richard C. Fickle, Exec. VP-Strategic Dev.
Dayna McCallum, Public Relations
Robert Solomon, Pres., Creative Services
Margret Craig, COO-Network Services
Richard Buchanan, COO-Mgmt. Services
Robert C. Rosenthal, COO-Creative Sound Services
William (Bill) R. Fitzgerald, Chmn.
Brenda Smith, Group Managing Dir.-U.K.

Phone: 310-434-7000	Fax: 310-434-7001

Toll-Free:

Address: 520 Broadway, 5th Fl., Santa Monica, CA 90401 US

GROWTH PLANS/SPECIAL FEATURES:

Ascent Media Group, Inc., a wholly-owned subsidiary of the Discovery Holding Company, provides creative and technical services to the media and entertainment industries. Its customers include major motion picture studios, independent producers, broadcast networks, cable channels, advertising agencies and other companies that produce, own and distribute entertainment, news, sports, corporate, educational, industrial and advertising content. Recently, the company was organized into two global operating divisions: creative services and network services. The creative services group develops content for films, television series, miniseries, commercials, music videos, advertising campaigns and corporate communications programming. The creative sound services group, now part of creative services, provides audio post-production services for feature films, TV series and movies, commercials, documentaries, independent films and interactive games. Ascent Media's management services group, which optimizes, archives, manages and repurposes media assets for global distribution, has been folded into the two main divisions. The network services group provides outsourced solutions for media management, content distribution, and connectivity. Systems integration and consulting capabilities round out the division's comprehensive service offering. Ascent Media Systems and Technology Services, a subsidiary of the network services group, provides engineering, consultation and turnkey systems solutions for the broadcast, cable, entertainment, satellite, production/post-production and corporate video industries. In recent years, Ascent has acquired Cinetech, Inc., a leader in the motion picture restoration, protection and preservation services market; and the assets of Sony's System Integration Center.

Ascent Media offers its employees benefits including medical, dental and vision coverage; vacation and sick leave; a 401(k) plan; and company health screenings.

FINANCIALS: Sales and profits are in thousands of dollars—add 000 to get the full amount. 2006 Note: Financial information for 2006 was not available for all companies at press time.

2006 Sales: $	2006 Profits: $	U.S. Stock Ticker: Subsidiary
2005 Sales: $697,700	2005 Profits: $	Int'l Ticker: Int'l Exchange:
2004 Sales: $631,200	2004 Profits: $	Employees: 4,000
2003 Sales: $506,100	2003 Profits: $	Fiscal Year Ends: 12/31
2002 Sales: $539,300	2002 Profits: $-135,200	Parent Company: DISCOVERY HOLDING COMPANY

SALARIES/BENEFITS:

Pension Plan:	ESOP Stock Plan:	Profit Sharing:	Top Exec. Salary: $753,846	Bonus: $
Savings Plan: Y	Stock Purch. Plan:		Second Exec. Salary: $451,620	Bonus: $

OTHER THOUGHTS:

Apparent Women Officers or Directors: 1
Hot Spot for Advancement for Women/Minorities:

LOCATIONS: ("Y" = Yes)

West:	Southwest:	Midwest:	Southeast:	Northeast:	International:
Y		Y	Y	Y	Y

AT&T INC   www.att.com

Industry Group Code: 513300A Ranks within this company's industry group: Sales: 2 Profits: 2

Print Media/Publishing:	Movies:	Equipment/Supplies:	Broadcast/Cable:	Music/Audio:	Sports/Games:
Newspapers:	Movie Theaters:	Equipment/Supplies:	Broadcast TV:	Music Production:	Games/Sports:
Magazines:	Movie Production:	Gambling Equipment:	Cable TV: Y	Retail Music:	Retail Games Stores:
Books: Y	TV/Video Production:	Special Services: Y	Satellite Broadcast:	Retail Audio Equip.:	Stadiums/Teams:
Book Stores:	Video Rental:	Advertising Services:	Radio:	Music Print./Dist.:	Gambling/Casinos:
Distribution/Printing:	Video Distribution:	Info. Sys. Software:	Online Information:	Multimedia:	Rides/Theme Parks:

TYPES OF BUSINESS:

Local Telephone Service
Wireless Telecommunications
Long-Distance Telephone Service
Corporate Telecom, Backbone & Wholesale Services
Directory Publishing
Entertainment & Television via Internet
International Telephone Services
Internet Access via DSL

BRANDS/DIVISIONS/AFFILIATES:

Cingular Wireless
SBC Communications
Southwestern Bell
BellSouth
AT&T Corp.
Pacific Bell
Cellular One
SBC Yahoo! DSL

CONTACTS: Note: Officers with more than one job title may be intentionally listed here more than once.

Edward E. Whitacre, Jr., CEO
Randall L. Stephenson, COO
David Dorman, Pres.
Richard G. Lindner, CFO/Sr. Exec. VP
Karen E. Jennings, Sr. Exec. VP-Advertising
Forest Miller, Group Pres.-Human Resources & Strategic Initiative
John Stankey, CTO/Sr. Exec. VP
James D. Ellis, General Counsel/Sr. Exec. VP
James S. Kahan, Sr. Exec. VP-Corp. Dev.
Karen E. Jennings, Sr. Exec. VP-Corp. Comm.
James W. Cicconi, Sr. Exec. VP-External & Legislative Affairs
Ray Wilkins, Group Pres.
Stan Sigman, Pres./CEO-Wireless
Rod Odom, Pres./CEO-AT&T Southeast
Edward E. Whitacre, Jr., Chmn.
Rayford Wilkins, Jr., Group Pres., Int'l, Directory & Sterling Commerce

Phone: 210-821-4105	Fax: 210-351-2071
Toll-Free:	
Address: 175 E. Houston, San Antonio, TX 78205 US	

GROWTH PLANS/SPECIAL FEATURES:

AT&T, Inc., the result of the November 2005 merger between SBC Communications and AT&T Corp, is one of the world's largest providers of diversified telecommunications services. The company and its subsidiaries delivers an extensive portfolio of traditional and IP-based voice, broadband Internet, data transport, entertainment, networking, wireless and video services, advertising and transport and termination of wholesale traffic services. AT&T offers Virtual Private Network (VPN), Voice Over IP (VOIP), security and support services and provides interoperability with the world's five leading IP PBX vendors as well as being a top provider of broadband DSL and Wi-Fi. AT&T is positioning itself for the future as an aggressive provider of bundled telephone, wireless, Internet service and entertainment services. Entertainment offerings focus on video-on-demand and television via Internet. It is investing in a massive, multi billion dollar network improvement to be able to offer very high speed Internet offerings of up to 25 Mbps to 18 million homes by the end of 2008. The company co-markets its DSL Internet service with Yahoo! In January 2007, AT&T completed its acquisition of BellSouth for $86 billion. The merger created a company with 67.5 million local lines in 22 states, 100% ownership of Cingular Wireless with 58.7 million subscribers, and 12 million broadband subscribers. In addition, the firm has 35,000 Wi-Fi hotspots in 70 nations, is America's largest directory publisher, delivering 178 million phone directories yearly, and is one of the world's largest providers of telecom backbone services, wholesale services and corporate services to Global 1000 corporations. Growth over the mid term will be focused on wireless subscriptions, the sale of advertising on its cellphone, TV and Internet services, Internet-based TV subscriptions and global corporate telecom services.

Employees have access to adoption assistance, tuition aid and a service discount program. Women make up 42% of the firm's U.S. managers and 45% of the workforce.

FINANCIALS: Sales and profits are in thousands of dollars—add 000 to get the full amount. 2006 Note: Financial information for 2006 was not available for all companies at press time.

2006 Sales: $	2006 Profits: $	**U.S. Stock Ticker: T**
2005 Sales: $43,862,000	2005 Profits: $4,786,000	**Int'l Ticker:** Int'l Exchange:
2004 Sales: $40,787,000	2004 Profits: $5,953,000	Employees: 301,000
2003 Sales: $40,498,000	2003 Profits: $8,505,000	Fiscal Year Ends: 12/31
2002 Sales: $43,138,000	2002 Profits: $5,653,000	Parent Company:

SALARIES/BENEFITS:

Pension Plan: Y	ESOP Stock Plan:	Profit Sharing:	Top Exec. Salary: $2,124,000	Bonus: $7,125,000
Savings Plan: Y	Stock Purch. Plan:		Second Exec. Salary: $934,500	Bonus: $1,975,000

OTHER THOUGHTS:

Apparent Women Officers or Directors: 1
Hot Spot for Advancement for Women/Minorities:

LOCATIONS: ("Y" = Yes)

West:	Southwest:	Midwest:	Southeast:	Northeast:	International:
Y	Y	Y	Y	Y	Y

Note: Financial information, benefits and other data can change quickly and may vary from those stated here.

AUDIBLE INC

www.audible.com

Industry Group Code: 451220E Ranks within this company's industry group: Sales: 1 Profits: 1

Print Media/Publishing:	Movies:	Equipment/Supplies:		Broadcast/Cable:	Music/Audio:		Sports/Games:	
Newspapers:	Movie Theaters:	Equipment/Supplies:		Broadcast TV:	Music Production:		Games/Sports:	
Magazines:	Movie Production:	Gambling Equipment:		Cable TV:	Retail Music:		Retail Games Stores:	
Books:	TV/Video Production:	Special Services:	Y	Satellite Broadcast:	Retail Audio Equip.:		Stadiums/Teams:	
Book Stores:	Video Rental:	Advertising Services:		Radio:	Music Print./Dist.:	Y	Gambling/Casinos:	
Distribution/Printing:	Video Distribution:	Info. Sys. Software:	Y	Online Information:	Multimedia:		Rides/Theme Parks:	

TYPES OF BUSINESS:

Audio Books-Online Sales
Audio Programming Software
Time-Shifted Radio Programming
Digital Audio Players
Educational Audio Materials

BRANDS/DIVISIONS/AFFILIATES:

audible.com
AudibleListener
Otis
Orb Networks, Inc.
Audible UK
Audible.fr
VangoNotes

CONTACTS: *Note: Officers with more than one job title may be intentionally listed here more than once.*

Donald R. Katz, CEO
Glenn M. Rogers, COO
William H. Mitchell, CFO
Guy Story, Jr., Chief Scientist
Brian M. Fielding, Exec. VP-Content & Legal Affairs
Guy Story, Jr., Sr. VP-Bus. Dev.
Beth Anderson, Sr. VP/Publisher
Will Lopes, VP-Customer Experience
Foy C. Sperring, Jr., VP-Customer Acquisition
Donald R. Katz, Chmn.

Phone: 973-837-2700	**Fax:** 973-890-2442
Toll-Free: 888-283-5051	
Address: 65 Willowbrook Blvd., Wayne, NJ 07470-7056 US	

GROWTH PLANS/SPECIAL FEATURES:

Audible, Inc. provides Internet-delivered premium spoken audio content for playback on personal computers and mobile devices. The company offers a variety of software systems and audio programming software designed to download, store and play between two and 28 hours of content from its online store, audible.com. Audible sells a wide array of audio content, including educational materials, humor, periodicals, fiction, nonfiction and time-shifted radio programming making up more than 115,000 hours worth of programming from more than 360 sources. The firm also offers customers the opportunity to subscribe to AudibleListener, a monthly audio service. AudibleListener customers can download their choice of programs from the company's web site. The company also has partnerships with leading audiobook, magazine and newspaper publishers, as well as broadcasters, business information providers and educational and cultural institutions. Audible.com features daily selected audio content from The Wall Street Journal and The New York Times, both available on a subscription basis in time for the morning drive to work each day. Other publications offered include Fast Company, Forbes, Harvard Business Review and Scientific American. In addition, the site offers a large collection of audiobook bestsellers and classics by authors such as Stephen King, James Patterson, William Shakespeare and Jane Austen, as well as speeches, lectures and on-demand radio programs. The company, in collaboration with textbook publisher Pearson Education, launched its new VangoNotes service in 2006, offering audio study aids in the fields of history, psychology and marketing, among others.

FINANCIALS: Sales and profits are in thousands of dollars—add 000 to get the full amount. 2006 Note: Financial information for 2006 was not available for all companies at press time.

2006 Sales: $	2006 Profits: $	**U.S. Stock Ticker: ADBL**
2005 Sales: $63,237	2005 Profits: $ 221	**Int'l Ticker:** Int'l Exchange:
2004 Sales: $34,319	2004 Profits: $2,077	Employees: 193
2003 Sales: $19,324	2003 Profits: $-3,560	Fiscal Year Ends: 12/31
2002 Sales: $12,400	2002 Profits: $-17,200	Parent Company:

SALARIES/BENEFITS:

Pension Plan:	ESOP Stock Plan:	Profit Sharing:	Top Exec. Salary: $250,000	Bonus: $
Savings Plan: Y	Stock Purch. Plan:		Second Exec. Salary: $225,000	Bonus: $

OTHER THOUGHTS:

Apparent Women Officers or Directors: 2
Hot Spot for Advancement for Women/Minorities:

LOCATIONS: ("Y" = Yes)

West:	Southwest:	Midwest:	Southeast:	Northeast:	International:
				Y	Y

AVID TECHNOLOGY INC

www.avid.com

Industry Group Code: 511209 **Ranks within this company's industry group:** Sales: 1 Profits: 2

Print Media/Publishing:	Movies:	Equipment/Supplies:		Broadcast/Cable:	Music/Audio:	Sports/Games:
Newspapers:	Movie Theaters:	Equipment/Supplies:	Y	Broadcast TV:	Music Production:	Games/Sports:
Magazines:	Movie Production:	Gambling Equipment:		Cable TV:	Retail Music:	Retail Games Stores:
Books:	TV/Video Production:	Special Services:		Satellite Broadcast:	Retail Audio Equip.:	Stadiums/Teams:
Book Stores:	Video Rental:	Advertising Services:		Radio:	Music Print./Dist.:	Gambling/Casinos:
Distribution/Printing:	Video Distribution:	Info. Sys. Software:	Y	Online Information:	Multimedia:	Rides/Theme Parks:

TYPES OF BUSINESS:

Film Editing Systems
Digital Audio Equipment
Image Manipulation Products
Network & Storage Products
Special Effects Software

BRANDS/DIVISIONS/AFFILIATES:

Softimage
Digidesign
Unity MediaNet
Avid AlienBrain
Avid Unity MediaNet
M-Audio
Pinnacle Systems
Sibelius Software Ltd.

CONTACTS: *Note: Officers with more than one job title may be intentionally listed here more than once.*

David Krall, CEO
David Krall, Pres.
Paul J. Milbury, CFO/VP
Patricia A. Baker, VP-Human Resources
Michael J. Rockwell, CTO
Sharad Rastogi, VP-Corp. Dev.
David M. Lebolt, VP/General Mgr.-Digidesign
Joseph Bentivegna, COO/VP-Avid Video
Charles L. Smith, VP/General Mgr.-Avid
Robert M. Halperin, Chmn.

Phone: 978-640-6789	Fax: 978-640-1366
Toll-Free:	
Address: Avid Technology Park, One Park W., Tewksbury, MA 01876 US	

GROWTH PLANS/SPECIAL FEATURES:

Avid Technology, Inc. sells products for creating, manipulating and marketing digital media content. Avid's nonlinear video and film editing systems are designed to improve the productivity of video and film editors by enabling them to edit moving pictures and sound. The company also develops and sells a range of image manipulation products that allow users to create graphics and special effects for use in feature films, television shows, advertising and news programs. These products include 3D and special effects software products developed by its Softimage subsidiary. Through its Digidesign division, Avid develops and sells digital audio systems used in music, film, television, video, broadcast, streaming media and web development. These systems are based upon proprietary Digidesign/Avid audio hardware, software and control surfaces and permit users to record, edit, mix, process and master audio in an integrated manner. The firm also markets Avid AlienBrain products, which help develop computer graphics-based video games, 3D simulation products and animated films. Avid provides complete network, storage and database solutions with its Avid Unity MediaNet technology. This technology enables users to share and manage media assets throughout a project or organization. Other divisions include M-Audio, a provider of electronic recording equipment for both musicians and audio professionals; and Pinnacle Systems, acquired in 2005, which is a supplier of video creation and distribution products. In 2006, Avid acquired Sibelius Software Ltd., a music applications software developer, as well as Sundance Digital, Inc., a developer of automation and device control software for broadcast video servers, tape transports, graphics systems and other broadcast station equipment.

The company offers employees a health package, life and disability insurance, stock options, tuition reimbursement and operates an on-site fitness center at its corporate headquarters.

FINANCIALS: Sales and profits are in thousands of dollars—add 000 to get the full amount. 2006 Note: Financial information for 2006 was not available for all companies at press time.

2006 Sales: $	2006 Profits: $	U.S. Stock Ticker: AVID
2005 Sales: $775,400	2005 Profits: $34,000	Int'l Ticker: Int'l Exchange:
2004 Sales: $589,600	2004 Profits: $71,700	Employees: 2,613
2003 Sales: $471,912	2003 Profits: $40,889	Fiscal Year Ends: 12/31
2002 Sales: $418,700	2002 Profits: $3,000	Parent Company:

SALARIES/BENEFITS:

Pension Plan:	ESOP Stock Plan:	Profit Sharing:	Top Exec. Salary: $530,000	Bonus: $430,360
Savings Plan: Y	Stock Purch. Plan: Y		Second Exec. Salary: $320,000	Bonus: $144,768

OTHER THOUGHTS:

Apparent Women Officers or Directors: 5
Hot Spot for Advancement for Women/Minorities: Y

LOCATIONS: ("Y" = Yes)

West:	Southwest:	Midwest:	Southeast:	Northeast:	International:
Y		Y	Y	Y	Y

AZTAR CORP

www.aztar.com

Industry Group Code: 721120 Ranks within this company's industry group: Sales: 8 Profits: 8

Print Media/Publishing:	Movies:	Equipment/Supplies:	Broadcast/Cable:	Music/Audio:	Sports/Games:	
Newspapers:	Movie Theaters:	Equipment/Supplies:	Broadcast TV:	Music Production:	Games/Sports:	
Magazines:	Movie Production:	Gambling Equipment:	Cable TV:	Retail Music:	Retail Games Stores:	
Books:	TV/Video Production:	Special Services:	Satellite Broadcast:	Retail Audio Equip.:	Stadiums/Teams:	Y
Book Stores:	Video Rental:	Advertising Services:	Radio:	Music Print./Dist.:	Gambling/Casinos:	
Distribution/Printing:	Video Distribution:	Info. Sys. Software:	Online Information:	Multimedia:	Rides/Theme Parks:	

TYPES OF BUSINESS:

Casino Hotel
Riverboat Casinos

BRANDS/DIVISIONS/AFFILIATES:

Tropicana Atlantic City
Tropicana Las Vegas
Casino Aztar Evansville
Casino Aztar Caruthersville
Ramada Express Hotel and Casino
Folies Bergere
Tropicana Lehigh Valley
Columbia Sussex Corp.

CONTACTS: Note: Officers with more than one job title may be intentionally listed here more than once.

Robert M. Haddock, CEO
Robert M. Haddock, Pres.
Neil A. Ciarfalia, CFO
Nelson W. Armstrong, Jr., VP-Admin.
Joe C. Cole, VP-Corp. Comm.
Neil A. Ciarfalia, VP/Treas.
Nelson W. Armstrong, Jr., Corp. Sec.
Meredith P. Sipek, Controller
Robert M. Haddock, Chmn.

Phone: 602-381-4100	Fax: 602-381-4108

Toll-Free:

Address: 2390 E. Camelback Rd., Ste. 400, Phoenix, AZ 85016-3452 US

GROWTH PLANS/SPECIAL FEATURES:

Aztar Corporation operates casino hotels in Atlantic City, New Jersey and Las Vegas and Laughlin, Nevada and riverboat casinos in Caruthersville, Missouri and Evansville, Indiana. Each of the company's land-based casinos is designed and themed for the tastes of its particular target-market. The riverboat casinos share a common theme and brand, Casino Aztar. Casino Aztar Evansville is the larger of the company's two riverboat casinos and operates on the Ohio River, while Casino Aztar Caruthersville operates on a 37-acre site on the Mississippi River. The 14-acre Tropicana Atlantic City has beach frontage of 220 yards and its 148,000-square-foot casino contains 4,300 slot machines and 80 table games. It recently added a new expansion called the Quarter at Tropicana, consisting of a 200,000-square-foot dining, entertainment and retail center modeled after Old Havana. Tropicana Las Vegas boasts a similar tropical island theme and one of the world's largest indoor/outdoor swimming pools, as well as a five-acre water park and a tropical garden. It also houses the Folies Bergere, the longest-running show in Las Vegas. The 61,000-foot casino runs 1,333 slots machines, 35 table games and offers 110,000 square feet of convention/exhibition space. The Ramada Express Hotel and Casino in Laughlin, Nevada is located on the Colorado River and is colored by various Victorian-era railroad themed designs and attractions, such as a train that carries guests between parking areas and the hotel. Aztar is currently formulating plans to develop a new Tropicana Hotel and Casino in Lehigh Valley, Pennsylvania. In May 2006, Columbia Sussex Corp. agreed to acquire Aztar for $1.94 billion.

Employees of Aztar receive benefits that vary by location. They may include pharmaceutical assistance, educational assistance, credit union services, local discounts and multiple employee events during the year.

FINANCIALS: Sales and profits are in thousands of dollars—add 000 to get the full amount. 2006 Note: Financial information for 2006 was not available for all companies at press time.

2006 Sales: $	2006 Profits: $	**U.S. Stock Ticker: Subsidiary**
2005 Sales: $915,442	2005 Profits: $55,960	**Int'l Ticker:** Int'l Exchange:
2004 Sales: $789,993	2004 Profits: $28,500	Employees: 9,800
2003 Sales: $789,024	2003 Profits: $60,930	Fiscal Year Ends: 12/31
2002 Sales: $834,300	2002 Profits: $58,900	Parent Company: COLUMBIA ENTERTAINMENT

SALARIES/BENEFITS:

Pension Plan:	ESOP Stock Plan:	Profit Sharing:	Top Exec. Salary: $904,938	Bonus: $806,885
Savings Plan: Y	Stock Purch. Plan:		Second Exec. Salary: $606,496	Bonus: $538,286

OTHER THOUGHTS:

Apparent Women Officers or Directors: 1
Hot Spot for Advancement for Women/Minorities:

LOCATIONS: ("Y" = Yes)

West:	Southwest:	Midwest:	Southeast:	Northeast:	International:
Y		Y		Y	

Note: Financial information, benefits and other data can change quickly and may vary from those stated here.

BALLY TECHNOLOGIES INC

www.bally.com

Industry Group Code: 713290 Ranks within this company's industry group: Sales: 5   Profits: 13

Print Media/Publishing:	Movies:	Equipment/Supplies:		Broadcast/Cable:	Music/Audio:	Sports/Games:	
Newspapers:	Movie Theaters:	Equipment/Supplies:		Broadcast TV:	Music Production:	Games/Sports:	
Magazines:	Movie Production:	Gambling Equipment:	Y	Cable TV:	Retail Music:	Retail Games Stores:	
Books:	TV/Video Production:	Special Services:	Y	Satellite Broadcast:	Retail Audio Equip.:	Stadiums/Teams:	
Book Stores:	Video Rental:	Advertising Services:		Radio:	Music Print./Dist.:	Gambling/Casinos:	Y
Distribution/Printing:	Video Distribution:	Info. Sys. Software:		Online Information:	Multimedia:	Rides/Theme Parks:	

TYPES OF BUSINESS:

Gaming Machines
Electronic Slot & Video Gaming Machines
Gaming Software
Slot Monitoring & Casino Management Systems
Casino Hotel
Progressive Gaming Operations

BRANDS/DIVISIONS/AFFILIATES:

Alliance Gaming Corporation
Bally Gaming and Systems
Alpha Game Engine
Blazing 7s
Blues Brothers
Rainbow Hotel Casino

CONTACTS: Note: Officers with more than one job title may be intentionally listed here more than once.

Richard Haddrill, CEO
Gavin Isaacs, COO
Richard Haddrill, Pres.
Robert C. Caller, Exec. VP/CFO
Robert Luciano, CTO
Mark Lerner, General Counsel/Corp. Sec.
Mark Lipparelli, Exec. VP-Oper.
Paul A. Lofgren, Exec. VP-New Bus. Dev.
Robert C. Caller, Treas.
Robert L. Saxton, Exec. VP-Gaming/Treas.
Mark Lerner, Sr. VP-Law & Gov.
Ramesh Srinivasan, Exec. VP-Bally Systems Division
Steven Des Champs, Sr. VP-Bus. Analysis

Phone: 702-270-7600	Fax: 702-270-7696
Toll-Free: 877-462-2559	
Address: 6601 S. Bermuda Rd., Las Vegas, NV 89119 US	

GROWTH PLANS/SPECIAL FEATURES:

Bally Technologies, Inc., formerly Alliance Gaming Corporation, is a leading global designer, manufacturer and distributor of advanced gaming devices and systems. Operating under the name Bally Gaming and Systems, the firm has marketed over 100,000 gaming machines in the last five years, and also sells used gaming machines and spare parts. The company's gaming equipment includes electronic slot and video gaming machines. The Linux-based Alpha Game Engine operating system is approved in all major jurisdictions, including Nevada, Mississippi, New Jersey, Missouri, Washington, New York, Rhode Island and Native American jurisdictions. The firm has launched game themes such as Blazing 7s and Blues Brothers on the Alpha Game Engine, as well as titles developed by other companies. Bally also designs, integrates and sells specialized computer monitoring systems that provide casinos with networked accounting and security services, including slot monitoring systems, casino management systems and systems facilitating cashless play. In addition, the company owns and operates the Rainbow Hotel Casino, a dockside casino in Vicksburg, Mississippi with approximately 12 table games and 890 gaming devices. The firm's Gaming Operations division operates Wide- and Near-Area Progressive gaming systems, such as Thrillions, which allow players to compete for shared progressive jackpots via separate machines; as well as non-linked daily fee games. In fiscal 2005, Bally spent approximately $43.4 million on research and product development. In February 2006, Bally opened an office in Macau, China to serve the Asian gaming market. Alliance gaming changed its name to Bally Technologies in March 2006. In April 2006, the firm contracted with Boyd Gaming Corp. to provide casino management, slot accounting and bonusing solutions across all Boyd's 19 Casino properties, covering approximately 30,000 slot machines.

The company offers a comprehensive medical insurance, life and disability, travel accident benefits, credit union membership, a CollegeBound fund and educational reimbursement.

FINANCIALS: Sales and profits are in thousands of dollars—add 000 to get the full amount. 2006 Note: Financial information for 2006 was not available for all companies at press time.

2006 Sales: $	2006 Profits: $	**U.S. Stock Ticker: AGI**
2005 Sales: $484,030	2005 Profits: $-20,317	**Int'l Ticker:** Int'l Exchange:
2004 Sales: $480,408	2004 Profits: $80,636	Employees: 1,640
2003 Sales: $407,600	2003 Profits: $19,500	Fiscal Year Ends: 6/30
2002 Sales: $594,100	2002 Profits: $63,800	Parent Company:

SALARIES/BENEFITS:

Pension Plan:	ESOP Stock Plan:	Profit Sharing:	Top Exec. Salary: $701,077	Bonus: $
Savings Plan: Y	Stock Purch. Plan:		Second Exec. Salary: $370,000	Bonus: $

OTHER THOUGHTS:

Apparent Women Officers or Directors:
Hot Spot for Advancement for Women/Minorities:

LOCATIONS: ("Y" = Yes)

West:	Southwest:	Midwest:	Southeast:	Northeast:	International:
Y	Y		Y	Y	Y

Note: Financial information, benefits and other data can change quickly and may vary from those stated here.

BALLY TOTAL FITNESS HOLDING CORPORATION
www.ballyfitness.com

Industry Group Code: 713940 Ranks within this company's industry group: Sales: 1   Profits: 1

Print Media/Publishing:	Movies:	Equipment/Supplies:		Broadcast/Cable:	Music/Audio:	Sports/Games:	
Newspapers:	Movie Theaters:	Equipment/Supplies:	Y	Broadcast TV:	Music Production:	Games/Sports:	Y
Magazines:	Movie Production:	Gambling Equipment:		Cable TV:	Retail Music:	Retail Games Stores:	
Books:	TV/Video Production:	Special Services:	Y	Satellite Broadcast:	Retail Audio Equip.:	Stadiums/Teams:	
Book Stores:	Video Rental:	Advertising Services:		Radio:	Music Print./Dist.:	Gambling/Casinos:	
Distribution/Printing:	Video Distribution:	Info. Sys. Software:		Online Information:	Multimedia:	Rides/Theme Parks:	

TYPES OF BUSINESS:
Fitness Clubs
Nutritional Supplements
Personal Training Services
Fitness Classes
Fitness Equipment
Martial Arts Training

BRANDS/DIVISIONS/AFFILIATES:
Bally Sports Clubs
Sports Clubs of Canada (The)
Build Your Own Membership (BYOM)
ballystore.com
Bally Total Martial Arts
Pinnacle Fitness

CONTACTS: Note: Officers with more than one job title may be intentionally listed here more than once.
Barry R. Elson, Acting CEO
John H. Wildman, COO/Sr. VP
Ronald G. Eidell, CFO/Sr. VP
James A. McDonald, Chief Mktg. Officer/ Sr. VP
Gail Holmberg, CIO/ Sr. VP
Harold Morgan, Chief Admin. Officer/Sr. VP
Marc D. Bassewitz, General Counsel/Sr. VP/Corp. Sec.
Thomas Massimino, Sr. VP-Oper.
William G. Fanelli, Sr. VP-Planning & Dev.
Katherine L. Abbott, Treas./VP
Cary A. Gaan, Sr. VP/Special Counsel to the Pres.
Julie Adams, Sr. VP-Membership Services
David S. Reynolds, Controller
Don R. Kornstein, Interim Chmn.

Phone: 773-380-3000	Fax: 773-693-2982
Toll-Free: 800-515-2582	
Address: 8700 W. Bryn Mawr Ave., Chicago, IL 60631 US	

GROWTH PLANS/SPECIAL FEATURES:
Bally Total Fitness Holding Corp. is one of North America's largest commercial operators of fitness centers. The firm operates nearly 390 fitness centers and 30 franchises with approximately 3.5 million members, concentrated in major metropolitan areas in 27 states. The company has international locations in Mexico, Canada, South Korea, China and the Caribbean. The majority of the centers use the Bally Total Fitness or Bally Sports Clubs brands, with other facilities operating under brands such as The Sports Clubs of Canada. Bally provides state-of-the-art gyms featuring a broad selection of cardiovascular, conditioning and strength equipment, with extensive aerobic and group training programs. Many locations also include pools, racquet courts and other athletic facilities. Bally target's customers aged 18 to 54 with mid-level income. The firm offers various membership options and payment plans (such as the Build Your Own Membership program), ranging from single-club memberships to premium plans, which provide access to all centers nationwide. Other products and services include personal training and private-label nutritional products, such as meal replacement shakes and drinks, energy and snack bars and multi-vitamins, which are sold in 7,000 retail outlets. Bally's licensed portable exercise equipment is sold in more than 90,000 retail outlets. Recently, the company expanded its martial arts programming to include on-on-one instruction with master teachers; and opened its fourth franchise in Seoul, South Korea. In 2006, the company announced the sale of Crunch Business, including the Gorilla Sports brand, for $45 million to an investor group formed by Angelo, Gordon, & Company. As part of its strategy for growth, Bally is cross training all employees in customer service, fitness, nutrition and sales.

Bally Total Fitness offers its employees a 401(k) plan, training programs, tuition reimbursement, and medical and dental insurance.

FINANCIALS: Sales and profits are in thousands of dollars—add 000 to get the full amount. 2006 Note: Financial information for 2006 was not available for all companies at press time.

2006 Sales: $	2006 Profits: $	U.S. Stock Ticker: BFT
2005 Sales: $1,071,033	2005 Profits: $-9,614	Int'l Ticker: Int'l Exchange:
2004 Sales: $1,047,988	2004 Profits: $-30,256	Employees: 21,600
2003 Sales: $953,500	2003 Profits: $-646,000	Fiscal Year Ends: 12/31
2002 Sales: $968,100	2002 Profits: $3,500	Parent Company:

SALARIES/BENEFITS:

Pension Plan: Y	ESOP Stock Plan:	Profit Sharing:	Top Exec. Salary: $575,000	Bonus: $900,000
Savings Plan: Y	Stock Purch. Plan:		Second Exec. Salary: $350,000	Bonus: $225,000

OTHER THOUGHTS:
Apparent Women Officers or Directors: 3
Hot Spot for Advancement for Women/Minorities: Y

LOCATIONS: ("Y" = Yes)

West:	Southwest:	Midwest:	Southeast:	Northeast:	International:
Y	Y	Y	Y	Y	Y

Note: Financial information, benefits and other data can change quickly and may vary from those stated here.

BANTA CORPORATION   www.banta.com

Industry Group Code: 323000 Ranks within this company's industry group: Sales: 2   Profits: 2

Print Media/Publishing:	Movies:	Equipment/Supplies:	Broadcast/Cable:	Music/Audio:	Sports/Games:
Newspapers:	Movie Theaters:	Equipment/Supplies:	Broadcast TV:	Music Production:	Games/Sports:
Magazines:	Movie Production:	Gambling Equipment:	Cable TV:	Retail Music:	Retail Games Stores:
Books: Y	TV/Video Production:	Special Services: Y	Satellite Broadcast:	Retail Audio Equip.:	Stadiums/Teams:
Book Stores:	Video Rental:	Advertising Services:	Radio:	Music Print./Dist.:	Gambling/Casinos:
Distribution/Printing:	Video Distribution:	Info. Sys. Software: Y	Online Information:	Multimedia:	Rides/Theme Parks:

TYPES OF BUSINESS:

Printing Services
Digital Imaging Services
Digital Content Management
e-Business Web Development
Supply Chain Management
CD-ROM Printing

BRANDS/DIVISIONS/AFFILIATES:

Banta Global Turnkey Group
Banta Corporation Foundation, Inc.
Banta Publications Group

CONTACTS: Note: Officers with more than one job title may be intentionally listed here more than once.

Stephanie A. Streeter, CEO
Stephanie A. Streeter, Pres.
Geoffrey J. Hibner, CFO
Dennis J. Meyer, VP-Mktg.
Frank W. Rudolph, VP-Human Resources
Damani Short, CIO/VP
Ronald D. Kneezel, General Counsel/Corp. Sec./VP
Sara Armbuster, VP-Bus. Dev.
Mark Fleming, Dir.-Corp. Comm.
Mark Fleming, Dir.-Investor Rel.
Ginger M. Jones, Corp. Controller
Padraic Allen, Pres., Supply-Chain Management Group
Michael Allen, Pres., Banta Print Sector
Dennis J. Meyer, VP-Planning
Stephanie A. Streeter, Chmn.
David Engelkemeyer, VP-Worldwide Oper.

Phone: 920-751-7777	Fax: 920-751-7790
Toll-Free: 800-291-1171	
Address: 225 Main St., Menasha, WI 54952-8003 US	

GROWTH PLANS/SPECIAL FEATURES:

Banta Corporation operates in two business segments: printing services and supply chain management. The company provides a complete range of printing and digital imaging services to leading publishers and direct marketers that manage, produce and distribute clients' information, from printed materials to Internet-based electronic media. Products in this segment include books, catalogs, publications, product brochures, literature management services and educational materials. Its primary print products fall into four niche markets (soft cover trade books, special-interest magazines, catalogs and direct marketing materials), while its electronic media offerings include digital content management, e-business web site development and CD-ROMs. The firm's supply chain management section operates through Banta Global Turnkey, providing global supply chain management services to companies in the computer hardware, software, networking, medical device manufacturer and telecommunications sectors. Its services include component procurement, product assembly and packaging, product tracking, order fulfillment and worldwide distribution. The company currently has operations in approximately 40 locations in North America, Europe and Asia. The company also owns Banta Corporation Foundation, Inc., a company that provides support to charitable, educational and literary scholarship organizations. In spring 2006, Banta partnered with Geoscope International to target Hispanic markets via Geoscape's HomeBase and BizBase databases. Using these tools, Banta will have direct access to 215 million individuals in 110 million households for target marketing. In summer 2006, the firm opened a multi-million dollar, state-of-the-art distribution center in Bolingbrook, Illinois. The new facility will focus on providing low postage rates for magazines. In November 2006, the company agreed to be acquired by R. R. Donnelley & Sons for about $1.3 billion.

FINANCIALS: Sales and profits are in thousands of dollars—add 000 to get the full amount. 2006 Note: Financial information for 2006 was not available for all companies at press time.

2006 Sales: $	2006 Profits: $	U.S. Stock Ticker: Subsidiary
2005 Sales: $1,523,252	2005 Profits: $68,005	Int'l Ticker: Int'l Exchange:
2004 Sales: $1,523,300	2004 Profits: $68,000	Employees: 8,500
2003 Sales: $1,418,500	2003 Profits: $46,600	Fiscal Year Ends: 1/03
2002 Sales: $303,489	2002 Profits: $43,799	Parent Company: R R DONNELLEY & SONS CO

SALARIES/BENEFITS:

Pension Plan: Y	ESOP Stock Plan:	Profit Sharing:	Top Exec. Salary: $724,500	Bonus: $762,682
Savings Plan: Y	Stock Purch. Plan:		Second Exec. Salary: $364,000	Bonus: $230,265

OTHER THOUGHTS:

Apparent Women Officers or Directors: 6
Hot Spot for Advancement for Women/Minorities: Y

LOCATIONS: ("Y" = Yes)

West:	Southwest:	Midwest:	Southeast:	Northeast:	International:
Y	Y	Y	Y	Y	Y

BARNES & NOBLE INC
www.barnesandnobleinc.com

Industry Group Code: 451211 Ranks within this company's industry group: Sales: 1 Profits: 1

Print Media/Publishing:		Movies:		Equipment/Supplies:		Broadcast/Cable:		Music/Audio:		Sports/Games:	
Newspapers:		Movie Theaters:		Equipment/Supplies:		Broadcast TV:		Music Production:		Games/Sports:	
Magazines:		Movie Production:		Gambling Equipment:		Cable TV:		Retail Music:	Y	Retail Games Stores:	Y
Books:	Y	TV/Video Production:		Special Services:		Satellite Broadcast:		Retail Audio Equip.:		Stadiums/Teams:	
Book Stores:	Y	Video Rental:		Advertising Services:		Radio:		Music Print./Dist.:		Gambling/Casinos:	
Distribution/Printing:		Video Distribution:		Info. Sys. Software:		Online Information:		Multimedia:		Rides/Theme Parks:	

TYPES OF BUSINESS:
Book Stores
Music & Software Sales
In-Store Cafes
Online Sales
Book Publishing
Book Distribution

BRANDS/DIVISIONS/AFFILIATES:
B. Dalton Bookseller
Barnes & Noble Bookseller
Sterling Publishing, Inc.
barnesandnoble.com, LLC

CONTACTS: Note: Officers with more than one job title may be intentionally listed here more than once.
Stephen Riggio, CEO
Mitchell S. Klipper, COO
Joseph J. Lombardi, CFO
Michelle Smith, VP-Human Resources
Chris Troia, CIO
Mary Ellen Keating, Sr. VP-Corp. Comm. & Public Affairs
Andy Milevoj, Mgr.-Investor Rel.
David Deason, VP-Barnes & Noble Dev.
Mark Bottini, VP/Dir.-Stores
J. Alan Kahn, Pres., Barnes & Noble Publishing Group
Marie Toulantis, CEO-Barnes & Noble.com
Leonard S. Riggio, Chmn.
William F. Duffy, Exec. VP-Logistics & Dist.

Phone: 212-633-3300	Fax: 212-675-0413
Toll-Free: 800-422-7717	
Address: 122 5th Ave., New York, NY 10011 US	

GROWTH PLANS/SPECIAL FEATURES:
Barnes and Noble, Inc. is one of the nation's largest booksellers. It operates approximately 800 book stores in 50 states and the District of Columbia, including 681 stores operating under the Barnes & Noble Bookseller trade name and 118 stores operating under the B. Dalton Bookseller trade name. These stores are designed to be reminiscent of old-world libraries, with wood fixtures, antique-style chairs and tables, ample public space, a cafe serving sandwiches and Starbucks coffee, a children's area, music, DVD, video and game sections and public restrooms. An in-store music department, which might range in size between 1,700 and 7,800 square feet, provides over 40,000 titles in classical music, opera, jazz, blues and pop rock, marketed to the company's core customers between 35 and 45 years of age. The stores principally sell trade books, mass-market paperbacks, children's books, off-price bargain books and magazines. While stores average 25,000 square feet each, the largest are 60,000-square-foot giants stocking up to 200,000 titles. Typical stores stock approximately 60,000 core titles within a variety of popular subject categories reflecting local interests, which are supplemented by new releases and bestsellers. The company has comparatively recently entered the book publishing business in a dramatic way, publishing its own line of classics and acquiring Sterling Publishing, Inc. In total, B&N has publishing or distribution rights to nearly 10,000 titles.

Barnes and Noble provides employees with a 30% discount on books as well as tuition assistance, a baby care program, a book loan program, transit benefits and a 401(k) savings plan. In addition, it is one of the few companies to offer health benefits to part-time employees.

FINANCIALS: Sales and profits are in thousands of dollars—add 000 to get the full amount. 2006 Note: Financial information for 2006 was not available for all companies at press time.
2006 Sales: $5,103,004	2006 Profits: $146,681	U.S. Stock Ticker: BKS
2005 Sales: $4,873,595	2005 Profits: $143,376	Int'l Ticker: Int'l Exchange:
2004 Sales: $4,372,177	2004 Profits: $151,775	Employees: 39,000
2003 Sales: $	2003 Profits: $	Fiscal Year Ends: 1/31
2002 Sales: $	2002 Profits: $	Parent Company:

SALARIES/BENEFITS:
Pension Plan:	ESOP Stock Plan:	Profit Sharing:	Top Exec. Salary: $750,000	Bonus: $656,250
Savings Plan: Y	Stock Purch. Plan:		Second Exec. Salary: $750,000	Bonus: $656,250

OTHER THOUGHTS:
Apparent Women Officers or Directors: 7
Hot Spot for Advancement for Women/Minorities: Y

LOCATIONS: ("Y" = Yes)
West:	Southwest:	Midwest:	Southeast:	Northeast:	International:
Y	Y	Y	Y	Y	Y

Note: Financial information, benefits and other data can change quickly and may vary from those stated here.

BARNESANDNOBLE.COM INC

www.bn.com

Industry Group Code: 451211E Ranks within this company's industry group: Sales: 2   Profits:

Print Media/Publishing:		Movies:		Equipment/Supplies:		Broadcast/Cable:		Music/Audio:		Sports/Games:	
Newspapers:		Movie Theaters:		Equipment/Supplies:		Broadcast TV:		Music Production:		Games/Sports:	
Magazines:		Movie Production:		Gambling Equipment:		Cable TV:		Retail Music:		Retail Games Stores:	
Books:		TV/Video Production:		Special Services:	Y	Satellite Broadcast:		Retail Audio Equip.:		Stadiums/Teams:	
Book Stores:	Y	Video Rental:		Advertising Services:		Radio:		Music Print./Dist.:		Gambling/Casinos:	
Distribution/Printing:		Video Distribution:		Info. Sys. Software:		Online Information:		Multimedia:		Rides/Theme Parks:	

TYPES OF BUSINESS:

Books, Online Retail
Online Publishing
Distance Learning
Music Sales
Affiliate Purchase Program

BRANDS/DIVISIONS/AFFILIATES:

Barnes and Noble, Inc.
Barnes & Noble University
What America's Reading
Meet the Writers
Barnes & Noble, Jr.
B&N Screening Room

CONTACTS: *Note: Officers with more than one job title may be intentionally listed here more than once.*

Marie J. Toulantis, CEO
Kevin M. Frain, CFO
Kevin M. Frain, VP-Oper.
Leonard S. Riggio, Chmn.

Phone: 212-414-6000	Fax: 212-414-6140
Toll-Free:	
Address: 76 9th Ave., 9th Fl., New York, NY 10011-4962 US	

GROWTH PLANS/SPECIAL FEATURES:

Barnesandnoble.com is an online retailer of books, magazines, software, DVDs, videos, music and other items, as well as a provider of online courses through Barnes and Noble University, serving customers in 230 countries. The firm is a holding company and wholly-owned subsidiary of Barnes and Noble, Inc. The online store's database of more than 1 million titles offers bestsellers, diverse books from small presses and university publishers and access to approximately 30 million listings for out-of-print, used and rare books. The web site contains book descriptions, reviews and excerpts, as well as a section that features recommendations from other readers, called What America's Reading. In addition, the Meet the Writers section contains profiles, biographies, audio and video interviews of authors. The online music store sells classical, jazz, rock and world music, and offers exclusive interviews, free downloads, over 1 million sample audio clips, nearly 100,000 music reviews and a roster of 40,000 artist biographies. The company's PC Games and Video Store carries thousands of new and used titles, consoles, accessories and strategy guides. The Prints and Posters section carries magazine subscriptions and color reproductions on paper and canvas. Barnes & Noble, Jr. is an online section devoted to children. B&N Screening Room is a web page where browsers can view and order more than 10,000 full length previews. Online classes are offered in technology and computer skills, literature, writing, foreign languages, history, business and life improvement. Barnes and Noble owns and operates two facilities, in New Jersey and Tennessee, dedicated to distribution, fulfillment operations and customer service for the company's web site. In addition, the firm offers a membership to Affiliate.net, an affiliate network alliance (including AOL, Yahoo and MSN) with an 8.5% quarterly check for direct link referral purchases. Shipping costs are free if purchases are $25 or more.

FINANCIALS: Sales and profits are in thousands of dollars—add 000 to get the full amount. 2006 Note: Financial information for 2006 was not available for all companies at press time.

			U.S. Stock Ticker: Subsidiary
2006 Sales: $	2006 Profits: $		
2005 Sales: $419,800	2005 Profits: $	Int'l Ticker: Int'l Exchange:	
2004 Sales: $	2004 Profits: $	Employees: 1,001	
2003 Sales: $424,800	2003 Profits: $-11,300	Fiscal Year Ends: 1/31	
2002 Sales: $422,800	2002 Profits: $-73,700	Parent Company: BARNES & NOBLE INC	

SALARIES/BENEFITS:

Pension Plan:	ESOP Stock Plan:	Profit Sharing:	Top Exec. Salary: $596,153	Bonus: $273,000
Savings Plan:	Stock Purch. Plan:		Second Exec. Salary: $293,269	Bonus: $63,000

OTHER THOUGHTS:

Apparent Women Officers or Directors: 1
Hot Spot for Advancement for Women/Minorities:

LOCATIONS: ("Y" = Yes)

West:	Southwest:	Midwest:	Southeast:	Northeast:	International:
			Y	Y	

BEASLEY BROADCAST GROUP INC
www.beasleybroadcasting.com

Industry Group Code: 513111 Ranks within this company's industry group: Sales: 12 Profits: 8

Print Media/Publishing:	Movies:	Equipment/Supplies:		Broadcast/Cable:	Music/Audio:	Sports/Games:
Newspapers:	Movie Theaters:	Equipment/Supplies:		Broadcast TV:	Music Production:	Games/Sports:
Magazines:	Movie Production:	Gambling Equipment:		Cable TV:	Retail Music:	Retail Games Stores:
Books:	TV/Video Production:	Special Services:		Satellite Broadcast:	Retail Audio Equip.:	Stadiums/Teams:
Book Stores:	Video Rental:	Advertising Services:	Y	Radio:	Music Print./Dist.:	Gambling/Casinos:
Distribution/Printing:	Video Distribution:	Info. Sys. Software:		Online Information:	Multimedia:	Rides/Theme Parks:

TYPES OF BUSINESS:
Radio Station Owner/Operator
Radio Broadcasting
Online Media
Web Development

BRANDS/DIVISIONS/AFFILIATES:
Beasley Interactive
iBiquity
HD Radio Technology

CONTACTS: *Note: Officers with more than one job title may be intentionally listed here more than once.*
George G. Beasley, CEO
Bruce G. Beasley, COO
Bruce G. Beasley, Pres.
B. Caroline Beasley, CFO/Exec. VP
Patricia Russell, Dir.-Human Resources
Robert L. Demuth, CTO/VP
Joyce N. Fitch, General Counsel
Brian E. Beasley, VP-Oper.
Kathleen MacCarten-Bricketto, VP-Interactive Div.
Denyse S. Mesnik, Dir.-Corp. Comm.
Marie Tedesco, VP-Finance
Allen B. Shaw, Vice Chmn./Board of Dir.
Shaun P. Greening, VP-Financial Reporting
George G. Beasley, Chmn.

Phone: 239-263-5000	Fax: 239-263-8191
Toll-Free:	
Address: 3033 Riviera Dr., Ste. 200, Naples, FL 34103 US	

GROWTH PLANS/SPECIAL FEATURES:
Beasley Broadcasting Group (BBG) is a U.S. radio broadcasting company. The company owns and operates 42 stations (26 FM and 16 AM) which broadcast to over 3.5 million listeners. Of these stations, 19 are located in seven of the top 50 U.S. radio markets: Atlanta, Philadelphia, Boston, Miami-Ft. Lauderdale, Las Vegas, and West Palm Beach. BBG seeks to acquire clusters of stations in high-growth large and mid-sized markets located primarily in the eastern U.S., with a special focus on markets including Atlanta, Las Vegas, Philadelphia, Miami and Jacksonville. The company's radio stations program a variety of formats, including rock, country, contemporary hit radio and talk. The firm also has an Internet presence through its Beasley Interactive division and is working to generate sales from advertising, e-commerce and web development. The company's CEO, George Beasley, controls nearly 80% of the firm. When ranked by revenue, BBG is the 18th largest radio broadcaster in the nation, transmitting simultaneous digital and analog broadcasts using HD Radio. The firm holds interest in iBiquity, the developer of HD Radio Technology, and is a member of the HD Digital Radio Alliance Association. In August 2006, the firm purchased the Las Vegas station KDWN-AM from Radio Nevada Corp for $17 million with plans to enhance its talk radio programming. In addition, BBG purchased 27 acres of land from Radio Nevada Corp. for $5 million. The firm plans to purchase WJBR-FM in Wilmington, Delaware from NextMedia Group, Inc. for $42 million, pending FCC approval. In November 2006, the company unveiled a new Interactive Division. This new aspect of the firm will streamline online initiatives and create revenue through database and web development.

The firm's community initiatives include participation in the National Moment of Remembrance, holiday food and clothing bank drives, and co-sponsoring Special Olympic awareness races.

FINANCIALS: Sales and profits are in thousands of dollars—add 000 to get the full amount. 2006 Note: Financial information for 2006 was not available for all companies at press time.

2006 Sales: $	2006 Profits: $	**U.S. Stock Ticker:** BBGI
2005 Sales: $124,294	2005 Profits: $10,705	**Int'l Ticker:** Int'l Exchange:
2004 Sales: $122,205	2004 Profits: $12,031	**Employees:** 662
2003 Sales: $114,482	2003 Profits: $12,771	**Fiscal Year Ends:** 12/31
2002 Sales: $114,700	2002 Profits: $-3,700	**Parent Company:**

SALARIES/BENEFITS:

Pension Plan:	ESOP Stock Plan:	Profit Sharing:	Top Exec. Salary: $633,046	Bonus: $200,000
Savings Plan: Y	Stock Purch. Plan:		Second Exec. Salary: $411,951	Bonus: $100,000

OTHER THOUGHTS:
Apparent Women Officers or Directors: 6
Hot Spot for Advancement for Women/Minorities: Y

LOCATIONS: ("Y" = Yes)

West:	Southwest:	Midwest:	Southeast:	Northeast:	International:
Y			Y	Y	

Note: Financial information, benefits and other data can change quickly and may vary from those stated here.

BELO CORP

www.belo.com

Industry Group Code: 511110 **Ranks within this company's industry group:** Sales: 10　Profits: 7

Print Media/Publishing:		Movies:		Equipment/Supplies:		Broadcast/Cable:		Music/Audio:		Sports/Games:	
Newspapers:	Y	Movie Theaters:		Equipment/Supplies:		Broadcast TV:	Y	Music Production:		Games/Sports:	
Magazines:		Movie Production:		Gambling Equipment:		Cable TV:	Y	Retail Music:		Retail Games Stores:	
Books:		TV/Video Production:	Y	Special Services:		Satellite Broadcast:		Retail Audio Equip.:		Stadiums/Teams:	
Book Stores:		Video Rental:		Advertising Services:		Radio:		Music Print./Dist.:		Gambling/Casinos:	
Distribution/Printing:		Video Distribution:		Info. Sys. Software:		Online Information:		Multimedia:		Rides/Theme Parks:	

TYPES OF BUSINESS:

Newspaper Publishing
Broadcast Television
Cable News Channels
Online Media

BRANDS/DIVISIONS/AFFILIATES:

Dallas Morning News (The)
Providence Journal (The)
Press-Enterprise (The)
Denton Record-Chronicle
Northwest Cable News
Texas Cable News
Belo Interactive, Inc.
WUPL-TV

CONTACTS: Note: Officers with more than one job title may be intentionally listed here more than once.

Robert W. Decherd, CEO
Robert W. Decherd, Pres.
Dennis A. Williamson, CFO/Sr. Corp. VP
Marian Spitzberg, Sr. VP-Human Resources
Guy H. Kerr, Sr. VP-Law & Gov't
Dunia A. Shive, Pres., Media Oper.
Carey Hendrickson, VP-Corp. Comm.
Alison K. Engel, VP/Corp. Controller
James M. Moroney III, Publisher/CEO-The Dallas Morning News
Robert W. Decherd, Chmn.

Phone: 214-977-6606	Fax: 214-977-6603
Toll-Free:	
Address: 400 S. Record St., Dallas, TX 75202-4841 US	

GROWTH PLANS/SPECIAL FEATURES:

Belo Corp., one of the largest media companies in the U.S., operates a diversified group of broadcast television stations, newspapers, cable news networks and web sites. Founded as a Texas newspaper company in 1842, the company publishes four daily newspapers with a combined readership of 2.1 million, including The Dallas Morning News, which has the country's ninth-largest daily circulation. Belo also publishes The Providence Journal, The Press-Enterprise in Riverside, California and the Denton Record-Chronicle in Denton, Texas. The firm's group of 19 television stations reaches 13.8% of U.S. television-watching households in ten states. Six of Belo's television stations operate in the top 16 television markets. It owns four ABC affiliates, five CBS affiliates, four NBC affiliates, two WB affiliates, one FOX affiliate, one UPN affiliate and two independent stations, as well as seven 24-hour cable news channels including Texas Cable News and Northwest Cable News. Four of its cable news channels are operated in partnership with Cox Communications. Its Internet subsidiary, Belo Interactive, Inc., manages over 30 web sites, several interactive alliances and a broad range of Internet-based products and services.

Belo offers an employee benefits package that includes flexible spending accounts, a 401(k) savings plan, adoption assistance, tuition assistance, credit union membership, employee assistance and subsidized public transportation. The firm also administers the Belo Foundation, which has given more than $20 million in grants for the creation of urban public parks and green spaces and the funding of college-level journalism programs. In addition, Belo has raised more than $20 million to aid in the relief of victims of Hurricane Katrina.

FINANCIALS: Sales and profits are in thousands of dollars—add 000 to get the full amount. 2006 Note: Financial information for 2006 was not available for all companies at press time.

2006 Sales: $	2006 Profits: $	U.S. Stock Ticker: BLC
2005 Sales: $1,521,234	2005 Profits: $127,688	Int'l Ticker:　Int'l Exchange:
2004 Sales: $1,515,752	2004 Profits: $132,496	Employees: 7,800
2003 Sales: $1,436,011	2003 Profits: $128,525	Fiscal Year Ends: 12/31
2002 Sales: $1,427,800	2002 Profits: $131,100	Parent Company:

SALARIES/BENEFITS:

Pension Plan: Y	ESOP Stock Plan:	Profit Sharing: Y	Top Exec. Salary: $880,000	Bonus: $475,000
Savings Plan: Y	Stock Purch. Plan:		Second Exec. Salary: $600,000	Bonus: $250,000

OTHER THOUGHTS:

Apparent Women Officers or Directors: 5
Hot Spot for Advancement for Women/Minorities: Y

LOCATIONS: ("Y" = Yes)

West:	Southwest:	Midwest:	Southeast:	Northeast:	International:
Y	Y	Y	Y	Y	

BERKSHIRE HATHAWAY INC   www.berkshirehathaway.com

Industry Group Code: 551110 Ranks within this company's industry group: Sales: 1 Profits: 1

Print Media/Publishing:	Movies:	Equipment/Supplies:	Broadcast/Cable:	Music/Audio:	Sports/Games:
Newspapers: Y	Movie Theaters:	Equipment/Supplies:	Broadcast TV:	Music Production:	Games/Sports:
Magazines:	Movie Production:	Gambling Equipment:	Cable TV:	Retail Music:	Retail Games Stores:
Books: Y	TV/Video Production:	Special Services:	Satellite Broadcast:	Retail Audio Equip.:	Stadiums/Teams:
Book Stores:	Video Rental:	Advertising Services:	Radio:	Music Print./Dist.:	Gambling/Casinos:
Distribution/Printing:	Video Distribution:	Info. Sys. Software:	Online Information:	Multimedia:	Rides/Theme Parks:

TYPES OF BUSINESS:

Direct Property & Casualty Insurance & Reinsurance
Retail Operations
Foodservice Operations
Building Products & Services
Apparel & Footwear
Technology Training
Manufactured Housing & RVs
Business Jet Flexible Ownership Services

BRANDS/DIVISIONS/AFFILIATES:

General Re
GEICO
International Dairy Queen
Benjamin Moore & Co.
FlightSafety International, Inc.
Dexter Shoe Company
Borsheim's Jewelry Corp.
Acme Building Brands, Inc.

CONTACTS: Note: Officers with more than one job title may be intentionally listed here more than once.

Warren E. Buffet, CEO
Marc D. Hamburg, Treas./VP
Charles T. Munger, Vice Chmn.
Jo Ellen Rieck, Dir.-Taxes
Mark D. Millard, Dir.-Financial Assets
Daniel J. Jakisch, Controller
Warren E. Buffet, Chmn.

Phone: 402-346-1400	Fax: 402-346-3375
Toll-Free:	
Address: 1440 Kiewit Plaza, Omaha, NE 68131 US	

GROWTH PLANS/SPECIAL FEATURES:

Berkshire Hathaway, Inc. is a holding company that owns subsidiaries engaged in diverse business activities, most importantly insurance and reinsurance. Berkshire provides property and casualty insurance and reinsurance, and life accident and health reinsurance through approximately 60 U.S. and foreign businesses. General Re Corp., through its subsidiaries, conducts global reinsurance business in 62 cities and provides reinsurance worldwide. GEICO mainly provides auto insurance and is the fifth-largest private-passenger auto insurer in the U.S. The company's financial subsidiaries include Clayton Homes, a manufactured housing company; XTRA, a provider of transportation equipment leases; furniture rental company CORT Business Services Corp.; and General Re Securities. Berkshire's apparel and footwear businesses include Fruit of the Loom, Garan, Fechheimer Brothers, H.H. Brown Shoe Group and Justin Brands. The firm manufactures and distributes building products through Acme Building Brands, Benjamin Moore & Co., Johns Manville and MiTek. Subsidiary FlightSafety International, Inc. provides training to aircraft and ship pilots; while NetJets, Inc. offers fractional ownership programs for aircraft. Subsidiary International Dairy Queen services approximately 5,900 Dairy Queen, Orange Julius and Karmelkorn stores. Other non-insurance operations include grocery and foodservice distribution, furniture retail, jewelry retail, carpet manufacturing, utilities and energy, newspapers, cleaning products, confectioneries, agricultural equipment, kitchen tools and recreational vehicles. Berkshire's 2006 acquisitions include Iscar Metalworking Companies, a maker of metalworking tools; Applied Underwriters, a leader in workers' compensation; and Business Wire, a leading global distributor of corporate news and regulatory filings. The firm has recently made an agreement to acquire sporting goods company Russell Corporation.

Berkshire Hathaway's CEO, Warren Buffett, is world-famous for his business and investment expertise.

FINANCIALS: Sales and profits are in thousands of dollars—add 000 to get the full amount. 2006 Note: Financial information for 2006 was not available for all companies at press time.

2006 Sales: $	2006 Profits: $	U.S. Stock Ticker: BRK
2005 Sales: $81,663,000	2005 Profits: $8,528,000	Int'l Ticker: Int'l Exchange:
2004 Sales: $74,382,000	2004 Profits: $7,308,000	Employees: 192,000
2003 Sales: $64,288,000	2003 Profits: $8,151,000	Fiscal Year Ends: 12/31
2002 Sales: $42,670,000	2002 Profits: $4,286,000	Parent Company:

SALARIES/BENEFITS:

| Pension Plan: Y | ESOP Stock Plan: Y | Profit Sharing: | Top Exec. Salary: $612,500 | Bonus: $ |
| Savings Plan: | Stock Purch. Plan: | | Second Exec. Salary: $100,000 | Bonus: $ |

OTHER THOUGHTS:

Apparent Women Officers or Directors: 1
Hot Spot for Advancement for Women/Minorities:

LOCATIONS: ("Y" = Yes)

West:	Southwest:	Midwest:	Southeast:	Northeast:	International:
Y	Y	Y	Y	Y	Y

Note: Financial information, benefits and other data can change quickly and may vary from those stated here.

BERRY COMPANY (THE)
www.lmberry.com

Industry Group Code: 511000 Ranks within this company's industry group: Sales:　Profits:

Print Media/Publishing:		Movies:		Equipment/Supplies:		Broadcast/Cable:		Music/Audio:		Sports/Games:	
Newspapers:		Movie Theaters:		Equipment/Supplies:		Broadcast TV:		Music Production:		Games/Sports:	
Magazines:		Movie Production:		Gambling Equipment:		Cable TV:		Retail Music:		Retail Games Stores:	
Books:	Y	TV/Video Production:		Special Services:	Y	Satellite Broadcast:		Retail Audio Equip.:		Stadiums/Teams:	
Book Stores:		Video Rental:		Advertising Services:	Y	Radio:		Music Print./Dist.:		Gambling/Casinos:	
Distribution/Printing:		Video Distribution:		Info. Sys. Software:		Online Information:		Multimedia:		Rides/Theme Parks:	

TYPES OF BUSINESS:

Yellow Pages Advertising
Marketing
Sales
Management Training
Publishing
Strategic Planning
Investment Research

BRANDS/DIVISIONS/AFFILIATES:

BellSouth Corporation
South Central Area
Berry Network, Inc.
Berry Sales & Marketing Solutions
Real Yellow Pages (The)

CONTACTS: Note: Officers with more than one job title may be intentionally listed here more than once.

Dan Graham, CEO
Dan Graham, Pres.
Karen Payne, Dir.-Mktg.
Anita Moore, VP-Human Resources
Barb Bertrams, VP-IT & Publishing
Mark Schindler, Dir.-IT
Joe Armanini, General Counsel/VP
Carol Warner, VP-Finance
Kathy Geiger-Schwab, Exec. Dir.-Berry Sales & Mktg. Solutions/Pres.,BNI
Kevin Payne, Group VP-Berry Network, Inc.
Greg Meineke, Group VP-South Central Area
John Snyder, Group VP-Independents

Phone: 937-296-2121	Fax: 937-296-2011
Toll-Free: 800-366-2379	
Address: 3170 Kettering Blvd., Dayton, OH 45439 US	

GROWTH PLANS/SPECIAL FEATURES:

The Berry Company (Berry), a wholly owned subsidiary of the BellSouth Corporation, is one of the largest yellow pages advertising sales agencies in the U.S. It provides yellow page directory services including electronic ad design; sales; marketing and sales support; and composition pagination, compilation, printing, billing and delivery. The company is organized into four operating units: Independent Line of Business (ILOB), which consists of seven units that serve independent yellow page publishers in over 500 markets for over 100 telephone companies; South Central Area (SCA), which operates in nine divisions across five states and is dedicated to publishing print and Internet yellow pages for BellSouth; Berry Network, Inc. (BNI), which provides domestic clients with full-service marketing, research and strategic planning for investments for over 600 clients; and Berry Sales & Marketing Solutions, a domestic and international consulting service that helps clients reach their growth potential through sales, marketing and management training and solutions. Berry has 41 offices located in 38 states; in total, the company covers over 700 markets. In 2006, BNI was selected as Kawasaki Motors Corp., U.S.A.'s national yellow pages advertising agency. As such, BNI will conduct a full-service ad campaign for more than 1,500 Kawasaki dealers, which will include directory selection, advertising placement, and billing and research services. The SCA division publishes The Real Yellow Pages for BellSouth.

Employees of Berry receive benefits including paid holidays, medical and dental plans, a 401(k) plan, a pension plan, access to the BellSouth retirement savings plan, tuition reimbursement, a scholarship program, personal time, short- and long-term disability, life insurance, floating holidays and child care discounts.

FINANCIALS: Sales and profits are in thousands of dollars—add 000 to get the full amount. 2006 Note: Financial information for 2006 was not available for all companies at press time.

2006 Sales: $	2006 Profits: $	U.S. Stock Ticker: Subsidiary
2005 Sales: $	2005 Profits: $	Int'l Ticker:　Int'l Exchange:
2004 Sales: $	2004 Profits: $	Employees:
2003 Sales: $	2003 Profits: $	Fiscal Year Ends: 12/31
2002 Sales: $	2002 Profits: $	Parent Company: BELLSOUTH CORP

SALARIES/BENEFITS:

Pension Plan: Y	ESOP Stock Plan:	Profit Sharing:	Top Exec. Salary: $	Bonus: $
Savings Plan: Y	Stock Purch. Plan:		Second Exec. Salary: $	Bonus: $

OTHER THOUGHTS:

Apparent Women Officers or Directors: 7
Hot Spot for Advancement for Women/Minorities: Y

LOCATIONS: ("Y" = Yes)

West:	Southwest:	Midwest:	Southeast:	Northeast:	International:
Y		Y	Y	Y	Y

BERTELSMANN AG
www.bertelsmann.com

Industry Group Code: 513120 Ranks within this company's industry group: Sales: 2 Profits: 2

Print Media/Publishing:		Movies:		Equipment/Supplies:		Broadcast/Cable:		Music/Audio:		Sports/Games:	
Newspapers:	Y	Movie Theaters:		Equipment/Supplies:		Broadcast TV:	Y	Music Production:	Y	Games/Sports:	
Magazines:	Y	Movie Production:		Gambling Equipment:		Cable TV:	Y	Retail Music:		Retail Games Stores:	
Books:	Y	TV/Video Production:		Special Services:		Satellite Broadcast:		Retail Audio Equip.:		Stadiums/Teams:	
Book Stores:	Y	Video Rental:		Advertising Services:	Y	Radio:	Y	Music Print./Dist.:	Y	Gambling/Casinos:	
Distribution/Printing:		Video Distribution:		Info. Sys. Software:	Y	Online Information:		Multimedia:		Rides/Theme Parks:	

TYPES OF BUSINESS:
Television Broadcasting
Radio Broadcasting
Magazine & Newspaper Publishing
Book Publishing
e-Commerce
Music Publishing
Print & Media Services
Book & Music Clubs

BRANDS/DIVISIONS/AFFILIATES:
RTL Group
Random House
Gruner + Jahr
Sonopress
Bertelsmann Arvato
DirectGroup Bertelsmann
BMG
Bertelsmann Digital Media Investments

CONTACTS: Note: Officers with more than one job title may be intentionally listed here more than once.
Gunter Thielen, CEO
Thomas Rabe, CFO
Ulrich Koch, Dir.-Legal Dept.
Guenter Grueger, Dir.-Controlling & Strategic Planning
Jasmine Borhan, Exec. VP-Corp. Comm.
Shobhna Mohn, VP-Investor Rel.
Verena Volpert, Exec. VP-Finance/Treas.
Hartmut Ostrowski, CEO-Bertelsmann Arvato
Peter Olson, CEO/Chmn.-Random House
Bernd Kundrun, Chmn./CEO-Gruner + Jahr
Ewald Walgenbach, CEO-DirectGroup Bertelsmann
Gunter Thielen, Chmn.

Phone: 49-5241-80-0	Fax: 49-5241-80-9662

Toll-Free:

Address: Carl-Bertelsmann-Strasse 270, Gutersloh, D-33311 Germany

GROWTH PLANS/SPECIAL FEATURES:

Bertelsmann AG, based in Germany, is a private media company that dominates its markets worldwide. With operations in 63 countries, the company's global reach encompasses television and radio; magazines and newspapers; music labels; book publishers; professional information; print and media services; book and music clubs; and e-commerce media. Each of the company's primary subsidiaries handles a different aspect of media. Major subsidiaries include the RTL Group, the largest broadcasting and production company in Europe, operating approximately 30 television stations and more than 30 radio stations in nine countries; Random House, the world's largest book publishing group; Gruner + Jahr, a magazine and newspaper publisher with more than 120 print titles and professional web sites in nine countries; and BMG, a leading company in the global markets for music and trade information with more than 200 labels including Arista, RCA and Ariola. BMG Music Publishing, a subsidiary of BMG, is the world's third-largest music publisher. Bertelsmann Arvato, another subsidiary, provides various media services, from conventional printing to modern services such as financial clearinghouses and data centers. Sonopress, an Arvato subsidiary, is a giant in the production of CDs and CD-ROMs. It also manufactures more than 160 million DVDs each year. Subsidiary DirectGroup Bertelsmann is a leader in media distribution through an assortment of book clubs and the Internet. In September 2006, Bertelsmann signed a definitive agreement to sell BMG Music Publishing Group to Vivendi Universal for $2.09 billion. The company also recently established a venture capital fund called Bertelsmann Digital Media Investments.

Bertelsmann offers international internships in the media business to recent graduates and undergraduates.

FINANCIALS: Sales and profits are in thousands of dollars—add 000 to get the full amount. 2006 Note: Financial information for 2006 was not available for all companies at press time.

2006 Sales: $	2006 Profits: $	U.S. Stock Ticker: Foreign	
2005 Sales: $21,415,000	2005 Profits: $1,246,090	Int'l Ticker: BTG4 Int'l Exchange: Frankfurt	
2004 Sales: $20,368,400	2004 Profits: $1,402,980	Employees: 88,516	
2003 Sales: $	2003 Profits: $	Fiscal Year Ends: 12/31	
2002 Sales: $	2002 Profits: $	Parent Company:	

SALARIES/BENEFITS:

Pension Plan:	ESOP Stock Plan:	Profit Sharing:	Top Exec. Salary: $	Bonus: $
Savings Plan: Y	Stock Purch. Plan:		Second Exec. Salary: $	Bonus: $

OTHER THOUGHTS:
Apparent Women Officers or Directors: 3
Hot Spot for Advancement for Women/Minorities: Y

LOCATIONS: ("Y" = Yes)

West:	Southwest:	Midwest:	Southeast:	Northeast:	International:
Y		Y	Y	Y	Y

Note: Financial information, benefits and other data can change quickly and may vary from those stated here.

BEST BUY CO INC

www.bestbuy.com

Industry Group Code: 443110 Ranks within this company's industry group: Sales: 1   Profits: 1

Print Media/Publishing:	Movies:	Equipment/Supplies:	Broadcast/Cable:	Music/Audio:	Sports/Games:
Newspapers:	Movie Theaters:	Equipment/Supplies:	Broadcast TV:	Music Production:	Games/Sports:
Magazines:	Movie Production:	Gambling Equipment:	Cable TV:	Retail Music: Y	Retail Games Stores:
Books:	TV/Video Production:	Special Services:	Satellite Broadcast:	Retail Audio Equip.:	Stadiums/Teams:
Book Stores:	Video Rental:	Advertising Services: Y	Radio:	Music Print./Dist.:	Gambling/Casinos:
Distribution/Printing:	Video Distribution:	Info. Sys. Software: Y	Online Information:	Multimedia:	Rides/Theme Parks:

TYPES OF BUSINESS:

Consumer Electronics Stores
Retail Music & Video Sales
Personal Computers
Office Supplies
Furniture
Appliances
Cameras
Consumer Electronics Installation & Service

BRANDS/DIVISIONS/AFFILIATES:

Magnolia Audio Video
Future Shop
Geek Squad
Studio D

CONTACTS: *Note: Officers with more than one job title may be intentionally listed here more than once.*

Bradbury H. Anderson, CEO
Brian Dunn, COO
Brian Dunn, Pres.
Darren Jackson, CFO/Exec. VP
Michael Linton, Exec. VP/Chief Mktg. Officer
Shari Ballard, Exec. VP-Human Resources
Ron Boire, Exec. VP/Global Merch. Mgr.
Joe Joyce, Sr. VP/General Counsel
Allen Lenzmeier, Vice Chmn.-Corp. Strategy & Svcs.
Susan Hoff, Sr. VP/Chief Comm. Officer
Sue Grafton, Chief Acc. Officer
Ron Biore, Exec. VP-Gen. Merch. Manager
Richard Schulze, Chmn.
Robert Willett, CEO-Best Buy Int'l
Michael London, Exec. VP-Global Sourcing

Phone: 612-291-1000	**Fax:** 612-292-4001
Toll-Free: 888-237-8289	
Address: 7601 Penn Ave. S., Richfield, MN 55423 US	

GROWTH PLANS/SPECIAL FEATURES:

Best Buy Co., Inc. is one of the nation's largest specialty retailers of name-brand consumer electronics, entertainment software and appliances; it also offers home office products, cameras, computer and audio/video equipment furniture, computer upgrades, and car audio and security system installation. Best Buy also offers product service and repair; its Geek Squad computer support services are available in 12 stand-alone Geek Squad stores and all U.S. and Canadian Best Buy stores, employing over 12,000 Geek Squad agents. The company operates 742 retail Best Buy stores in 49 states and the District of Columbia and 118 Future Shop stores and 44 Best Buy stores in Canada. In 2005, the company announced plans to open 20 to 50 stand-alone Geek Squad stores in the next 12 to 18 months, aspiring to make the subsidiary North America's largest provider of in-home computer repair and installation services. The firm's 20 Magnolia Audio Video stores, located in Washington, Oregon and California, serve the more upscale home electronics market. The firm's expansion strategy has been to enter major metropolitan areas with the simultaneous opening of several stores and then to expand into smaller markets. Sales per square foot per year average about $940. Best Buy expects to open about 60 U.S.-based and 15 Canadian stores per year. The eventual goal is about 1,000 Best Buy stores in the U.S. and 200 Best Buy and Future Shop stores in Canada. In addition, Best Buy will open several consumer electronics stores in China. The firm is experimenting with a boutique store format called Studio D in Naperville, Illinois. During the first half of 2006, Best Buy opened 29 new stores in the U.S.

Qualified employees enjoy savings and stock purchase plans, a variety of insurance coverage, employee discounts and tuition assistance.

FINANCIALS: Sales and profits are in thousands of dollars—add 000 to get the full amount. 2006 Note: Financial information for 2006 was not available for all companies at press time.

2006 Sales: $30,848,000	2006 Profits: $1,140,000	**U.S. Stock Ticker: BBY**
2005 Sales: $27,433,000	2005 Profits: $984,000	**Int'l Ticker:** Int'l Exchange:
2004 Sales: $24,547,000	2004 Profits: $704,000	Employees: 128,000
2003 Sales: $20,946,000	2003 Profits: $99,000	Fiscal Year Ends: 2/28
2002 Sales: $19,597,000	2002 Profits: $570,000	Parent Company:

SALARIES/BENEFITS:

Pension Plan:	ESOP Stock Plan:	Profit Sharing:	Top Exec. Salary: $1,164,283	Bonus: $
Savings Plan: Y	Stock Purch. Plan: Y		Second Exec. Salary: $738,044	Bonus: $1,189,401

OTHER THOUGHTS:

Apparent Women Officers or Directors: 5
Hot Spot for Advancement for Women/Minorities: Y

LOCATIONS: ("Y" = Yes)

West:	Southwest:	Midwest:	Southeast:	Northeast:	International:
Y	Y	Y	Y	Y	Y

Note: Financial information, benefits and other data can change quickly and may vary from those stated here.

BIOWARE CORP
www.bioware.com

Industry Group Code: 511208 **Ranks within this company's industry group:** Sales: Profits:

Print Media/Publishing:	Movies:	Equipment/Supplies:		Broadcast/Cable:	Music/Audio:	Sports/Games:	
Newspapers:	Movie Theaters:	Equipment/Supplies:		Broadcast TV:	Music Production:	Games/Sports:	Y
Magazines:	Movie Production:	Gambling Equipment:		Cable TV:	Retail Music:	Retail Games Stores:	
Books:	TV/Video Production:	Special Services:		Satellite Broadcast:	Retail Audio Equip.:	Stadiums/Teams:	
Book Stores:	Video Rental:	Advertising Services:		Radio:	Music Print./Dist.:	Gambling/Casinos:	
Distribution/Printing:	Video Distribution:	Info. Sys. Software:	Y	Online Information:	Multimedia:	Rides/Theme Parks:	

TYPES OF BUSINESS:
Computer Software/Games

BRANDS/DIVISIONS/AFFILIATES:
Baldur's Gate
Infinity Engine
BioWare Odyssey Engine
Star Wars: Knights of the Old Republic
Neverwinter Nights
Pandemic Studios, LLC
Elevation Partners
VG Holdings

CONTACTS: Note: Officers with more than one job title may be intentionally listed here more than once.
Greg Zeschuk, Joint CEO
Richard Iwaniuk, Dir.-Finance
Richard Iwaniuk, Dir.-Info. Systems
Ray Muzyka, Joint CEO

Phone: 780-430-0164	Fax: 780-439-6374
Toll-Free:	
Address: 200, 4445 Calgary Trail, Edmonton, AB T6H 5R7 Canada	

GROWTH PLANS/SPECIAL FEATURES:
BioWare Corp. is an electronic entertainment company specializing in creating computer and console video games. The Canadian firm is one of the most successful game developers in the world, selling hundreds of thousands, sometimes millions of units per title. Its first title, Shattered Steel, was released in 1996 and sold nearly 200,000 units. In 1998, BioWare unveiled its best-selling game, Baldur's Gate, which has sold over 2 million units for the PC. This title was followed by Baldur's Gate: Tales of the Sword Coast, Baldur's Gate II: Shadows of Amn and Baldur's Gate II: Throne of Bhaal. Together the Baldur's Gate series of titles have sold almost 5 million copies. Other titles the company has released include Neverwinter Nights and Star Wars: Knights of the Old Republic. BioWare also licenses its game engine technology; a number of popular games, including Planescape: Torment and the Icewind Dale series have been developed using BioWare's Infinity Engine. The Bioware Aurora Engine will be used to power the upcoming Neverwinter Nights 2 from Obsidian Entertatinment and Atari, and the BioWare Odyssey Engine will be used to make Star Wars: Knights of the Old Republic 2: The Sith Lords. Major ownership interests in the company were recently bought by a private equity firm called Elevation Partners. Simultaneously, Elevation Partners bought ownership interests in another major game developer, Pandemic Studios, LLC. Bioware and Pandemic have been brought together in a joint venture under the temporary name VG Holdings. Under the terms of the deal, Bioware and Pandemic will have separate creative operations, but will engage in some business operations together. The company began a new handheld game development group in 2006, producing games for the Nintendo DS system.

FINANCIALS: Sales and profits are in thousands of dollars—add 000 to get the full amount. 2006 Note: Financial information for 2006 was not available for all companies at press time.

2006 Sales: $	2006 Profits: $	U.S. Stock Ticker: Private
2005 Sales: $	2005 Profits: $	Int'l Ticker: Int'l Exchange:
2004 Sales: $18,400	2004 Profits: $	Employees:
2003 Sales: $	2003 Profits: $	Fiscal Year Ends: 12/31
2002 Sales: $	2002 Profits: $	Parent Company:

SALARIES/BENEFITS:

Pension Plan:	ESOP Stock Plan:	Profit Sharing:	Top Exec. Salary: $	Bonus: $
Savings Plan:	Stock Purch. Plan:		Second Exec. Salary: $	Bonus: $

OTHER THOUGHTS:
Apparent Women Officers or Directors:
Hot Spot for Advancement for Women/Minorities:

LOCATIONS: ("Y" = Yes)

West:	Southwest:	Midwest:	Southeast:	Northeast:	International:
					Y

Note: Financial information, benefits and other data can change quickly and may vary from those stated here.

BLOCKBUSTER INC   www.blockbuster.com

Industry Group Code: 532230 Ranks within this company's industry group: Sales: 1   Profits: 4

Print Media/Publishing:	Movies:		Equipment/Supplies:	Broadcast/Cable:	Music/Audio:	Sports/Games:	
Newspapers:	Movie Theaters:		Equipment/Supplies:	Broadcast TV:	Music Production:	Games/Sports:	Y
Magazines:	Movie Production:		Gambling Equipment:	Cable TV:	Retail Music:	Retail Games Stores:	Y
Books:	TV/Video Production:		Special Services:	Satellite Broadcast:	Retail Audio Equip.:	Stadiums/Teams:	
Book Stores:	Video Rental:	Y	Advertising Services:	Radio:	Music Print./Dist.:	Gambling/Casinos:	
Distribution/Printing:	Video Distribution:		Info. Sys. Software:	Online Information:	Multimedia:	Rides/Theme Parks:	

TYPES OF BUSINESS:

Videocassette Rental Stores
DVD Rentals
Video Game Rentals & Sales
DVD & VHS Sales
Consumer Electronics Sales
Online Video Rental Service

BRANDS/DIVISIONS/AFFILIATES:

Xtra-Vision
Rhino Video Games
Games Station, Ltd.
Gamestation
Blockbuster Online
Game Rush
Rent it! Like it! Buy it!

CONTACTS: *Note: Officers with more than one job title may be intentionally listed here more than once.*

John F. Antioco, CEO
Larry Zine, CFO/Exec. VP
Frank G. Paci, Exec. VP-Finance, Strategic Planning & Dev.
Nick Shepherd, Pres., U.S. Store Oper.
John F. Antioco, Chmn.

Phone: 214-854-3000	Fax: 214-854-4848
Toll-Free:	
Address: 1201 Elm St., Dallas, TX 75270 US	

GROWTH PLANS/SPECIAL FEATURES:

Blockbuster, Inc. is one of the world's leading providers of rentable home movies and video games, with approximately 8,700 owned and franchised stores, including more than 2,600 located throughout 24 other countries. The firm also rents DVD players, VCRs and video game consoles. In the Republic of Ireland and Northern Ireland, the company operates under the Xtra-Vision brand name; in Australia, the firm operates a freestanding game store chain called Game Rush; and Blockbuster also owns Games Station, Ltd., the second-largest games retailer in the U.K., which operates under the brand name Gamestation. In the U.S., the firm owns and runs a specialty game store by the name of Rhino Video Games. Blockbuster stores feature Rent it! Like it! Buy it!, a program designed to increase customer satisfaction with their purchases by offering a low-cost alternative to view a movie prior to making a purchasing decision. Viacom spun off its 81.5% stake in Blockbuster during late 2004. Blockbuster has been engaged in an ongoing price war with Netflix, the highly successful pioneer company offering unlimited online DVD rentals for a flat monthly fee with no late charges. In an effort to compete, the company launched Blockbuster Online, which has a similar operating model to that of Netflix, with 40,000 titles to choose from, no late fees and free shipping. Blockbuster hopes to expand its in-store video game boutiques, giving customers new reasons to come into stores. In late 2006, the firm offered free DVD rentals at Blockbuster stores in exchange for Netflix mailing labels.

Blockbuster offers its eligible employees tuition reimbursement, free video rentals and discounts on store merchandise, flexible schedules, credit union affiliation, auto and homeowners insurance programs, pet insurance, an employee assistance program, a business casual environment, a 401(k) savings plan and other company-sponsored discount programs.

FINANCIALS: Sales and profits are in thousands of dollars—add 000 to get the full amount. 2006 Note: Financial information for 2006 was not available for all companies at press time.

2006 Sales: $	2006 Profits: $	U.S. Stock Ticker: BBI
2005 Sales: $5,864,400	2005 Profits: $-588,100	Int'l Ticker: Int'l Exchange:
2004 Sales: $6,053,200	2004 Profits: $-1,248,800	Employees: 72,600
2003 Sales: $5,911,700	2003 Profits: $-983,900	Fiscal Year Ends: 12/31
2002 Sales: $5,566,000	2002 Profits: $-1,628,000	Parent Company:

SALARIES/BENEFITS:

Pension Plan:	ESOP Stock Plan:	Profit Sharing:	Top Exec. Salary: $1,633,333	Bonus: $
Savings Plan: Y	Stock Purch. Plan:		Second Exec. Salary: $624,615	Bonus: $

OTHER THOUGHTS:

Apparent Women Officers or Directors: 1
Hot Spot for Advancement for Women/Minorities:

LOCATIONS: ("Y" = Yes)

West:	Southwest:	Midwest:	Southeast:	Northeast:	International:
Y	Y	Y	Y	Y	Y

BLOOMBERG LP
www.bloomberg.com

Industry Group Code: 514100 Ranks within this company's industry group: Sales: 2   Profits:

Print Media/Publishing:		Movies:		Equipment/Supplies:		Broadcast/Cable:		Music/Audio:		Sports/Games:	
Newspapers:		Movie Theaters:		Equipment/Supplies:		Broadcast TV:	Y	Music Production:		Games/Sports:	
Magazines:	Y	Movie Production:		Gambling Equipment:		Cable TV:		Retail Music:		Retail Games Stores:	
Books:		TV/Video Production:		Special Services:		Satellite Broadcast:		Retail Audio Equip.:		Stadiums/Teams:	
Book Stores:		Video Rental:		Advertising Services:	Y	Radio:		Music Print./Dist.:	Y	Gambling/Casinos:	
Distribution/Printing:		Video Distribution:		Info. Sys. Software:	Y	Online Information:		Multimedia:		Rides/Theme Parks:	

TYPES OF BUSINESS:
Financial Data Publishing-Print & Online
Magazine Publishing
Management Software
Multimedia Presentation Services
Broadcast Television
Radio Broadcasting
Electronic Exchange Systems
Software

BRANDS/DIVISIONS/AFFILIATES:
Bloomberg Professional
Bloomberg Television
Bloomberg Radio
Bloomberg Tradebook
Bloomberg Markets Magazine
Bloomberg Money Magazine
Bloomberg Tradebook
Bloomberg Data License

CONTACTS: Note: Officers with more than one job title may be intentionally listed here more than once.
Lex Fenwick, CEO
Tom Secunda, Dir.-Worldwide Sales
Peter T. Grauer, Chmn.

Phone: 212-318-2000	Fax: 917-369-5000
Toll-Free:	
Address: 731 Lexington Ave., New York, NY 10022 US	

GROWTH PLANS/SPECIAL FEATURES:
Bloomberg, LP is one of the world's largest information services, news and media companies, serving the financial services industry as well as government offices and agencies, corporations and news organizations in 125 countries. The firm's core business, the Bloomberg Professional service, is delivered online to Bloomberg terminals that are rented by subscribers. The terminals provide traders and asset managers a combination of real-time, around-the-clock financial news, market data, analysis, electronic trading, multimedia report capabilities and e-mail on a single platform at an average monthly fee of about $1,425 per month per terminal. There are four primary services included with Bloomberg Professional. Bloomberg Tradebook is an electronic global agency trader offering customers the ability to trade on 65 markets in 54 countries. The Bloomberg Order Management System allows the firm's professional services to work in conjunction with outside infrastructure and includes a global risk-management software solution (Bloomberg Trade Order Management System) and a portfolio management system. Bloomberg Data License provides access to the Bloomberg financial database and to more than 4 million financial instruments. Finally, Bloomberg Roadshows is a multimedia presentation service featuring synchronized slides, audio, streaming video and live video technology. Issuers and underwriters use it to target buy-side clients directly through distribution of presentations on all types of debt, equity, structured finance issues and research. Over 300,000 Bloomberg terminals are in use around the world. Bloomberg also includes a global news service, encompassing Bloomberg Television, Bloomberg Radio, Bloomberg.com and the Bloomberg Magazine Group, which publishes Bloomberg Markets magazine in the U.S. and Bloomberg Money in the U.K. Bloomberg News, the company's financial newswire service, is comprised of 1,600 reporters in 94 bureaus worldwide, writing more than 4,000 news stories daily.

FINANCIALS: Sales and profits are in thousands of dollars—add 000 to get the full amount. 2006 Note: Financial information for 2006 was not available for all companies at press time.

		U.S. Stock Ticker: Private
2006 Sales: $	2006 Profits: $	Int'l Ticker: Int'l Exchange:
2005 Sales: $4,100,000	2005 Profits: $	Employees: 8,200
2004 Sales: $3,100,000	2004 Profits: $	Fiscal Year Ends: 12/31
2003 Sales: $3,000,000	2003 Profits: $	Parent Company:
2002 Sales: $2,800,000	2002 Profits: $	

SALARIES/BENEFITS:

Pension Plan:	ESOP Stock Plan:	Profit Sharing:	Top Exec. Salary: $	Bonus: $
Savings Plan:	Stock Purch. Plan:		Second Exec. Salary: $	Bonus: $

OTHER THOUGHTS:
Apparent Women Officers or Directors:
Hot Spot for Advancement for Women/Minorities:

LOCATIONS: ("Y" = Yes)

West:	Southwest:	Midwest:	Southeast:	Northeast:	International:
Y	Y	Y	Y	Y	Y

BOOKS A MILLION INC   www.booksamillioninc.com

Industry Group Code: 451211 Ranks within this company's industry group: Sales: 3   Profits: 3

Print Media/Publishing:		Movies:	Equipment/Supplies:	Broadcast/Cable:	Music/Audio:	Sports/Games:
Newspapers:		Movie Theaters:	Equipment/Supplies:	Broadcast TV:	Music Production:	Games/Sports:
Magazines:		Movie Production:	Gambling Equipment:	Cable TV:	Retail Music:	Retail Games Stores:
Books:		TV/Video Production:	Special Services:	Satellite Broadcast:	Retail Audio Equip.:	Stadiums/Teams:
Book Stores:	Y	Video Rental:	Advertising Services:	Radio:	Music Print./Dist.:	Gambling/Casinos:
Distribution/Printing:		Video Distribution:	Info. Sys. Software:	Online Information:	Multimedia:	Rides/Theme Parks:

TYPES OF BUSINESS:

Book Stores
Newsstands
Coffee Bars
Wholesale Distribution
Online Sales
Internet Development & Services

BRANDS/DIVISIONS/AFFILIATES:

Books & Co.
Bookland
Joe Muggs
American Internet Services, Inc.
bamm.com
American Wholesale Book Company
Book$mart, Inc.
NetCentral

CONTACTS: *Note: Officers with more than one job title may be intentionally listed here more than once.*

Sandra B. Cochran, CEO
Sandra B. Cochran, Pres.
Douglas G. Markham, CFO
Sandra B. Cochran, Corp. Sec.
Terrance G. Finley, Pres., Merch. Group
Clyde B. Anderson, Chmn.

Phone: 205-942-3737	Fax: 205-942-6601
Toll-Free:	
Address: 402 Industrial Ln., Birmingham, AL 35211 US	

GROWTH PLANS/SPECIAL FEATURES:

Books-A-Million, Inc. is one of the leading book retailers in the southeastern United States. Books-A-Million currently operates more than 200 stores in 19 states and the District of Columbia. The company has two business operating segments: retail trade, which consists of its retail stores and distribution centers, and electronic commerce, which handles its online business. The company has developed three distinct store formats to address the various market areas it serves. The Books-A-Million Superstores average approximately 20,000 square feet and operate under the names Books-A-Million and Books & Co. The firm also operates Bookland and Books-A-Million stores, primarily mall-based stores located in small markets and averaging 4,000 square feet. Joe Muggs newsstands are concentrated in business and entertainment districts and are tailored to the demographics of the particular market area. Each newsstand carries an extensive selection of magazines and newspapers, along with hardcover and paperback books and also offers an espresso and coffee bar. All store formats offer a variety of bestsellers and other hardcover and paperback books, magazines, newspapers, cards and gifts. Many of the stores feature a coffee shop and a selection of merchandise under the Joe Muggs brand name. In addition to retail store formats, Books-A-Million, through its subsidiary American Internet Services, Inc. (AIS), offers its products over the Internet on its Booksamillion.com and Joemuggs.com web sites. The company also owns a book wholesale distribution subsidiary, American Wholesale Book Company, which markets primarily to other book stores, wholesale clubs, supermarkets, department stores and mass merchandisers, as well as Book$mart, Inc., a bargain book distributor. In addition, through AIS, Books-A-Million owns an Internet development and services company called NetCentral, based in Nashville, Tennessee.

Books-A-Million offers opportunities as booksellers or managers in its local stores, clerk positions in its warehouses as well as positions for corporate professionals.

FINANCIALS: Sales and profits are in thousands of dollars—add 000 to get the full amount. 2006 Note: Financial information for 2006 was not available for all companies at press time.

2006 Sales: $503,751	2006 Profits: $13,067	**U.S. Stock Ticker:** BAMM
2005 Sales: $474,099	2005 Profits: $10,199	**Int'l Ticker:** Int'l Exchange:
2004 Sales: $457,234	2004 Profits: $7,201	Employees: 5,000
2003 Sales: $442,700	2003 Profits: $1,400	Fiscal Year Ends: 1/31
2002 Sales: $442,900	2002 Profits: $4,000	Parent Company:

SALARIES/BENEFITS:

Pension Plan:	ESOP Stock Plan:	Profit Sharing:	Top Exec. Salary: $420,000	Bonus: $385,000
Savings Plan:	Stock Purch. Plan:		Second Exec. Salary: $325,000	Bonus: $253,854

OTHER THOUGHTS:

Apparent Women Officers or Directors: 1
Hot Spot for Advancement for Women/Minorities:

LOCATIONS: ("Y" = Yes)

West:	Southwest:	Midwest:	Southeast:	Northeast:	International:
	Y	Y	Y	Y	

BOOTH CREEK SKI HOLDINGS INC   www.boothcreek.com

Industry Group Code: 713920 Ranks within this company's industry group: Sales: Profits:

Print Media/Publishing:	Movies:	Equipment/Supplies:	Broadcast/Cable:	Music/Audio:	Sports/Games:	
Newspapers:	Movie Theaters:	Equipment/Supplies:	Broadcast TV:	Music Production:	Games/Sports:	Y
Magazines:	Movie Production:	Gambling Equipment:	Cable TV:	Retail Music:	Retail Games Stores:	
Books:	TV/Video Production:	Special Services:	Satellite Broadcast:	Retail Audio Equip.:	Stadiums/Teams:	
Book Stores:	Video Rental:	Advertising Services:	Radio:	Music Print./Dist.:	Gambling/Casinos:	
Distribution/Printing:	Video Distribution:	Info. Sys. Software:	Online Information:	Multimedia:	Rides/Theme Parks:	

TYPES OF BUSINESS:

Ski Resorts
Golf Courses
Event Hosting
Summer Recreation

BRANDS/DIVISIONS/AFFILIATES:

Northstar-at-Tahoe
Sierra-at-Tahoe
Summit at Snoqualmie (The)
Waterville Valley
Cranmore Mountain Resort
Loon Mountain
Booth Creek Resorts

CONTACTS: Note: Officers with more than one job title may be intentionally listed here more than once.

Chris Ryman, CEO
Chris Ryman, Pres.
Betsy Cole, Exec. VP/CFO
Julie Maurer, VP-Mktg. & Sales
Laura Moriarty, VP-Human Resources
Frank Richey, IT Mgr.
Susie Tjossem, VP-Prod. Dev.
Ross Agre, VP/General Counsel
Heath Nielsen, VP-Oper.
Tim Beck, Exec. VP-Planning
Julie Maurer, VP-Public Rel.
Brian Pope, VP-Finance & Acct.
Susie Tjossem, VP-Guest Experience
Mark Petrozzi, VP-Risk Mgmt.
Heath Neilsen, VP-Commercial Property
Jim Mandel, Special Counsel

Phone: 530-550-7112	Fax: 530-550-9455
Toll-Free:	
Address: 12257 Business Park Dr., Ste.8, Truckee, CA 96161 US	

GROWTH PLANS/SPECIAL FEATURES:

Booth Creek Ski Holdings, operating as Booth Creek Resorts, is one of the largest ski resort operators in North America, with over 2 million visitors per year. The company's six resorts are located in California, New Hampshire and Washington, and are each within 200 miles of major skiing markets such as Boston, Seattle and the San Francisco Bay Area. Booth Creek's resorts feature over 6,500 acres of skiable terrain, 353 trails and 87 lifts, including 14 high-speed lifts and two gondolas. The firm's resorts are Northstar-at-Tahoe, Sierra-at-Tahoe, Waterville Valley, Cranmore Mountain Resort, Loon Mountain and The Summit at Snoqualmie. These resorts provide a full range of services, such as equipment rentals, skiing lessons and restaurants. In addition to alpine skiing and snowboarding, Booth Creek's resorts offer opportunities for cross-country skiing, telemarking, tubing, snowmobiling, snowshoeing and snowbiking. In the summer months, several Booth Creek properties are open for events and activities including golf, mountain biking, fly fishing, horseback riding, ATV tours and hiking, and also have event facilities. At its California resorts, the company offers the Vertical Plus program. Through this program, frequent skiers and snowboarders can track the number of vertical feet that they ski via a personal wristband, which is scanned at participating lifts. These guests also receive discounts and gain access to special lift lines. Booth Creek recently finished a project to build a beginners' snowboard park at Loon Mountain and is extensively developing Northstar-at-Tahoe, adding condominiums, shopping facilities, a spa and other developments.

Booth Creek's various resorts offer employees perks such as skiing privileges, including reciprocal privileges at other resorts; guest vouchers; free lessons; food, gift shop and equipment rental discounts; pro-purchase programs; ride sharing programs; housing assistance; supplemental insurance; and employee assistance. The resorts employ a number of international workers. Many resort jobs are seasonal.

FINANCIALS: Sales and profits are in thousands of dollars—add 000 to get the full amount. 2006 Note: Financial information for 2006 was not available for all companies at press time.

2006 Sales: $	2006 Profits: $	U.S. Stock Ticker: Private
2005 Sales: $	2005 Profits: $	Int'l Ticker: Int'l Exchange:
2004 Sales: $115,400	2004 Profits: $-1,800	Employees: 4,109
2003 Sales: $115,047	2003 Profits: $-5,361	Fiscal Year Ends: 10/31
2002 Sales: $120,500	2002 Profits: $-1,900	Parent Company:

SALARIES/BENEFITS:

Pension Plan:	ESOP Stock Plan:	Profit Sharing:	Top Exec. Salary: $335,000	Bonus: $175,000
Savings Plan:	Stock Purch. Plan:		Second Exec. Salary: $275,000	Bonus: $175,000

OTHER THOUGHTS:

Apparent Women Officers or Directors: 4
Hot Spot for Advancement for Women/Minorities: Y

LOCATIONS: ("Y" = Yes)

West:	Southwest:	Midwest:	Southeast:	Northeast:	International:
Y	Y			Y	

Note: Financial information, benefits and other data can change quickly and may vary from those stated here.

BORDERS GROUP INC
www.bordersgroupinc.com

Industry Group Code: 451211 Ranks within this company's industry group: Sales: 2 Profits: 2

Print Media/Publishing:		Movies:		Equipment/Supplies:		Broadcast/Cable:		Music/Audio:		Sports/Games:	
Newspapers:		Movie Theaters:		Equipment/Supplies:		Broadcast TV:		Music Production:		Games/Sports:	
Magazines:		Movie Production:		Gambling Equipment:		Cable TV:		Retail Music:	Y	Retail Games Stores:	
Books:		TV/Video Production:		Special Services:	Y	Satellite Broadcast:		Retail Audio Equip.:		Stadiums/Teams:	
Book Stores:	Y	Video Rental:		Advertising Services:		Radio:		Music Print./Dist.:		Gambling/Casinos:	
Distribution/Printing:		Video Distribution:		Info. Sys. Software:		Online Information:		Multimedia:		Rides/Theme Parks:	

TYPES OF BUSINESS:
Book Stores
Music & Movie Retailing
Specialty Coffee
Online Sales

BRANDS/DIVISIONS/AFFILIATES:
Books, etc.
Waldenbooks
Paperchase Products, Ltd.
BordersExpress
Borders Outlet

CONTACTS: *Note: Officers with more than one job title may be intentionally listed here more than once.*
George L. Jones, CEO
George L. Jones, Pres.
Edward W. Wilheim, CFO
Daniel T. Smith, Sr. VP-Human Resources
Cedric J. Vanzura, Pres., Tech.
Thomas D. Carney, Sr. VP/General Counsel
Steve Davis, Sr. VP-Borders Group Oper.
Cedric J. Vanzura, Pres., Strategy
Vincent E. Altruda, Pres., Borders Worldwide
Cedric J. Vanzura, Pres., Emerging Bus.
Gregory Josefowicz, Chmn.

Phone: 734-477-1100	Fax: 734-477-1965
Toll-Free:	
Address: 100 Phoenix Dr., Ann Arbor, MI 48108 US	

GROWTH PLANS/SPECIAL FEATURES:

Borders Group, Inc. is the second-largest operator of book, music and movie superstores (and the largest operator of mall-based bookstores) in the world based on sales and number of stores. Borders Group's retail operations are carried out by its subsidiaries: Borders, Inc.; Walden Book Company, Inc.; Borders UK Limited; Borders Australia Pty Limited; and others. Borders group operates 528 superstores under the Borders name, including 473 in the U.S., 35 in the U.K., 14 in Australia, three in Puerto Rico, two in New Zealand and one in Singapore. The company also operates 678 mall-based and other bookstores primarily under the Waldenbooks name in the U.S. and 33 bookstores under the Books etc. name in the U.K. In addition, Borders Group owns and operates U.K.-based Paperchase Products Limited, a designer and retailer of stationery, cards and gifts. Paperchase operates 90 stores, primarily in the U.K.; and Paperchase shops are present in nearly 100 domestic Borders superstores. In 2005, Borders Group opened 15 new Borders superstores, which averaged sales of $5.8 million per superstore. Borders superstores carry an average of 93,500 book titles across numerous categories, including many hard-to-find titles. 461 of the 473 domestic Borders superstores are in a book, music and movie format, which also features an extensive selection of pre-recorded music, with a broad assortment in categories such as jazz, classical and world music, and a broad assortment of DVDs, focusing on new release and catalog movies. A typical Borders superstore carries approximately 14,000 titles of music and over 10,000 titles of movies. Borders superstores average 25,000 square feet in size, including approximately 12,900 square feet devoted to books, 3,500 square feet devoted to music, 800 square feet devoted to newsstand and 700 square feet devoted to movies. The company remodeled 100 Borders superstores during 2005.

Borders offers employees numerous benefits including flexible spending accounts, adoption assistance, flexible schedules, domestic partner benefits, emergency assistance, scholarship assistance, training and development opportunities, a casual dress code and discounts on insurance, tickets and merchandise.

FINANCIALS: Sales and profits are in thousands of dollars—add 000 to get the full amount. 2006 Note: Financial information for 2006 was not available for all companies at press time.

2006 Sales: $4,030,700	2006 Profits: $101,000	**U.S. Stock Ticker: BGP**	
2005 Sales: $3,879,500	2005 Profits: $131,900	**Int'l Ticker:** Int'l Exchange:	
2004 Sales: $3,698,600	2004 Profits: $115,200	Employees: 35,500	
2003 Sales: $3,486,100	2003 Profits: $115,200	Fiscal Year Ends: 1/31	
2002 Sales: $3,387,900	2002 Profits: $87,400	Parent Company:	

SALARIES/BENEFITS:

Pension Plan:	ESOP Stock Plan:	Profit Sharing:	Top Exec. Salary: $723,654	Bonus: $
Savings Plan: Y	Stock Purch. Plan:		Second Exec. Salary: $332,885	Bonus: $

OTHER THOUGHTS:
Apparent Women Officers or Directors:
Hot Spot for Advancement for Women/Minorities:

LOCATIONS: ("Y" = Yes)

West:	Southwest:	Midwest:	Southeast:	Northeast:	International:
Y	Y	Y	Y	Y	Y

BOSE CORPORATION

www.bose.com

Industry Group Code: 334310 Ranks within this company's industry group: Sales: 7 Profits:

Print Media/Publishing:	Movies:	Equipment/Supplies:		Broadcast/Cable:	Music/Audio:		Sports/Games:
Newspapers:	Movie Theaters:	Equipment/Supplies:	Y	Broadcast TV:	Music Production:		Games/Sports:
Magazines:	Movie Production:	Gambling Equipment:		Cable TV:	Retail Music:		Retail Games Stores:
Books:	TV/Video Production:	Special Services:		Satellite Broadcast:	Retail Audio Equip.:	Y	Stadiums/Teams:
Book Stores:	Video Rental:	Advertising Services:		Radio:	Music Print./Dist.:		Gambling/Casinos:
Distribution/Printing:	Video Distribution:	Info. Sys. Software:		Online Information:	Multimedia:		Rides/Theme Parks:

TYPES OF BUSINESS:

Audio Equipment-Manufacturing & Retailing
Speaker Technology
Home & Automobile Sound Systems
Professional Sound Systems
Noise Reduction Headsets
Materials Testing Equipment

BRANDS/DIVISIONS/AFFILIATES:

Wave
Acoustimass
Lifestyle
3-2-1 DVD
Acoustic Noise Canceling
Aviation Headset X
Triport Tactical
Auditioner

CONTACTS: Note: Officers with more than one job title may be intentionally listed here more than once.

Amar G. Bose, CEO
Bob Maresca, Pres.
Daniel A. Grady, CFO
Thomas Froschle, Dir.-Research
Joanne Berthiume, Spokeswoman
Amar G. Bose, Chmn.

Phone: 508-879-7330	Fax: 508-766-7543
Toll-Free: 800-278-8029	
Address: The Mountain, Framingham, MA 01701 US	

GROWTH PLANS/SPECIAL FEATURES:

Bose Corporation is a leading global manufacturer of audio products, with over 100 stores nationwide. It is best known for the development of its acoustic waveguide speaker technology found in Wave radio, Wave radio/CD and Acoustic Wave music systems. Acoustimass, another speaker technology, allows Bose to create speakers small enough to fit in the palm of a person's hand that produce sound quality previously thought impossible from small speakers. Nearly 60% of Bose`s annual sales are generated by their professional system division. The remaining 40% is generated by the company's home and personal audio segment. Bose manufactures sound systems for homes and automobiles, as well as professional audio products for large venues and stage performers. Its home product brands include Wave systems, Lifestyle home entertainment systems, 3-2-1 DVD systems, Acoustic Noise Canceling headphones/headsets, Acoustimass speaker systems and Direct/Reflecting speakers. Bose's automotive systems division designs customized systems for the manufacturers of certain makes and models of luxury cars. The company's professional products include custom-designed Bose professional sound systems for auditoriums, hotels, performance centers, places of worship, restaurants, retail locations, schools and stadiums. Each system includes a variety of professional component parts (speaker systems, loudspeakers, amplifiers, controllers, cards and accessories). Bose's Auditioner, an audio demonstration technology, allows builders, architects and facility managers to hear what a Bose system will sound like in their building, before any equipment is installed. In addition, Bose produces professional noise reduction headsets, such as the Aviation Headset X for commercial pilots, and Combat Vehicle Crewman and Triport Tactical headsets for the military. Bose's ElectroForce Systems Group, formerly EnduraTEC, provides materials testing equipment to research institutions, universities, medical device companies and engineering companies worldwide. In late 2006, the firm announced that Bose Corporation India (BCIPL) plans to open 12 new stores by mid-2008.

FINANCIALS: Sales and profits are in thousands of dollars—add 000 to get the full amount. 2006 Note: Financial information for 2006 was not available for all companies at press time.

2006 Sales: $	2006 Profits: $	U.S. Stock Ticker: Private
2005 Sales: $1,800,000	2005 Profits: $	Int'l Ticker: Int'l Exchange:
2004 Sales: $1,700,000	2004 Profits: $	Employees: 8,000
2003 Sales: $1,600,000	2003 Profits: $	Fiscal Year Ends: 3/31
2002 Sales: $1,300,000	2002 Profits: $	Parent Company:

SALARIES/BENEFITS:

Pension Plan:	ESOP Stock Plan:	Profit Sharing:	Top Exec. Salary: $	Bonus: $
Savings Plan: Y	Stock Purch. Plan:		Second Exec. Salary: $	Bonus: $

OTHER THOUGHTS:

Apparent Women Officers or Directors: 1
Hot Spot for Advancement for Women/Minorities:

LOCATIONS: ("Y" = Yes)

West:	Southwest:	Midwest:	Southeast:	Northeast:	International:
Y	Y	Y	Y	Y	Y

BOYD GAMING CORP
www.boydgaming.com

Industry Group Code: 721120 Ranks within this company's industry group: Sales: 3 Profits: 6

Print Media/Publishing:	Movies:	Equipment/Supplies:	Broadcast/Cable:	Music/Audio:	Sports/Games:	
Newspapers:	Movie Theaters:	Equipment/Supplies:	Broadcast TV:	Music Production:	Games/Sports:	
Magazines:	Movie Production:	Gambling Equipment:	Cable TV:	Retail Music:	Retail Games Stores:	
Books:	TV/Video Production:	Special Services:	Satellite Broadcast:	Retail Audio Equip.:	Stadiums/Teams:	Y
Book Stores:	Video Rental:	Advertising Services:	Radio:	Music Print./Dist.:	Gambling/Casinos:	
Distribution/Printing:	Video Distribution:	Info. Sys. Software:	Online Information:	Multimedia:	Rides/Theme Parks:	

TYPES OF BUSINESS:
Casinos & Hotels
Casino Management

BRANDS/DIVISIONS/AFFILIATES:
California Hotel & Casino
Borgata Hotel & Casino
Blue Chip Hotel & Casino
Delta Downs Racetrack & Casino
Stardust Resort & Casino
Par-A-Dice Gaming Corp.
Sam's Town Hotel & Casino
Coast Casinos

CONTACTS:
Note: Officers with more than one job title may be intentionally listed here more than once.
William S. Boyd, CEO
Keith E. Smith, COO
Keith E. Smith, Pres.
Ellis Landau, CFO/Exec. VP
Ellis Landau, Treas.
Marianne Boyd Johnson, Sr. VP
William R. Boyd, VP
Michael Gaughan, CEO, Coast Casinos
Robert Boughner, CEO, Borgata Hotel Casino & Spa
William S. Boyd, Chmn.

Phone: 702-792-7200   Fax: 702-792-7313
Toll-Free:
Address: 2950 Industrial Rd., Las Vegas, NV 89109 US

GROWTH PLANS/SPECIAL FEATURES:
Boyd Gaming Corp. is a multi-jurisdictional gaming company and one of the country's leading casino operators. Boyd is committed to providing high-quality entertainment to its primarily middle-income customers at an affordable price, focusing on slot machines and traditional gaming tables. The company currently owns and operates 18 casinos. In Nevada, these include the Stardust Resort and Casino, Sam's Town Hotel & Gambling Hall, El Dorado Casino, Joker's Wild Casino, California Hotel and Casino, Main Street Station Casino, Brewery and Hotel and the Fremont Hotel and Casino. In Mississippi, Boyd owns and operates a second Sam's Town Hotel & Gambling Hall in Tunica. In Louisiana, Boyd owns the Delta Downs Racetrack & Casino and the Treasure Chest Casino. In Illinois, the company owns the Par-a-Dice Hotel and Casino. In Indiana, its holdings consist of the Blue Chip Hotel and Casino. In conjunction with MGM Mirage, and as part of string of recent expansion moves, Boyd opened Borgata, a billion-dollar, 2,000-room resort in Atlantic City, New Jersey. More recently, the company also acquired Harrah's Shreveport Hotel and Casino, now known as Sam's Town Hotel and Casino; as well as Coast Casinos, Inc. for $1.3 billion. The latter merger brings with it Coast Casinos' Gold Coast, Suncoast, Orleans and Barbary Coast casinos. In February 2006, the company purchased a 40-acre plot of land in the northwest part of Las Vegas for about $35 million, with the intention of constructing another casino in the near future.

FINANCIALS:
Sales and profits are in thousands of dollars—add 000 to get the full amount. 2006 Note: Financial information for 2006 was not available for all companies at press time.

2006 Sales: $	2006 Profits: $	U.S. Stock Ticker: BYD
2005 Sales: $2,471,003	2005 Profits: $144,610	Int'l Ticker: Int'l Exchange:
2004 Sales: $1,932,091	2004 Profits: $111,454	Employees: 23,400
2003 Sales: $1,394,529	2003 Profits: $40,933	Fiscal Year Ends: 12/31
2002 Sales: $1,228,900	2002 Profits: $40,000	Parent Company:

SALARIES/BENEFITS:

Pension Plan:	ESOP Stock Plan:	Profit Sharing: Y	Top Exec. Salary: $1,166,667	Bonus: $2,000,000
Savings Plan: Y	Stock Purch. Plan:		Second Exec. Salary: $725,000	Bonus: $406,327

OTHER THOUGHTS:
Apparent Women Officers or Directors: 1
Hot Spot for Advancement for Women/Minorities:

LOCATIONS: ("Y" = Yes)

West:	Southwest:	Midwest:	Southeast:	Northeast:	International:
Y		Y	Y	Y	

BOYNE USA RESORTS

www.boyne.com

Industry Group Code: 713920 **Ranks within this company's industry group:** Sales: Profits:

Print Media/Publishing:	Movies:	Equipment/Supplies:	Broadcast/Cable:	Music/Audio:	Sports/Games:	
Newspapers:	Movie Theaters:	Equipment/Supplies:	Broadcast TV:	Music Production:	Games/Sports:	Y
Magazines:	Movie Production:	Gambling Equipment:	Cable TV:	Retail Music:	Retail Games Stores:	
Books:	TV/Video Production:	Special Services:	Satellite Broadcast:	Retail Audio Equip.:	Stadiums/Teams:	
Book Stores:	Video Rental:	Advertising Services:	Radio:	Music Print./Dist.:	Gambling/Casinos:	
Distribution/Printing:	Video Distribution:	Info. Sys. Software:	Online Information:	Multimedia:	Rides/Theme Parks:	

TYPES OF BUSINESS:

Ski Resorts
Golf Courses
Real Estate Development
Retail Operations
Indoor Waterpark

BRANDS/DIVISIONS/AFFILIATES:

Big Sky Resort
Brighton Resort
Crystal Mountain
Cypress Mountain
Boyne Mountain
Boyne Highlands
Boyne Realty
Avalanche Bay

CONTACTS: Note: Officers with more than one job title may be intentionally listed here more than once.

Stephen Kircher, Pres.
Julie Ard, Mgr.-Public Rel.
Ed Dembek, Comptroller
Stephen Kircher, Pres., Eastern Oper.
John Kircher, Pres., Western Oper.

Phone: 231-549-6060	Fax: 231-549-6896
Toll-Free: 800-462-6963	
Address: One Boyne Mountain Rd., Boyne Falls, MI 49713 US	

GROWTH PLANS/SPECIAL FEATURES:

Boyne USA Resorts, one of America's largest privately owned resort companies, owns and operates ski and golf resorts located in the western and midwestern U.S. The company's ski resorts include Big Sky Resort, Montana; Brighton, Utah; Crystal Mountain, Washington; Cypress Mountain, British Columbia; and Boyne Highlands and Boyne Mountain in Michigan. Boyne also operates the Gatlinburg Sky Lift in Gatlinburg, Tennessee, a scenic, year-round chairlift offering views of Great Smoky Mountain National Park. The resorts in Montana and Michigan run golf courses during the summer, as do Michigan's Country Club of Boyne, Crooked Tree Golf Club and another full-service resort, the Inn at Bay Harbor, which only offers golf and other non-ski activities. The company operates most of its resorts year-round, with winter snow sports and golf complemented by other activities, such as tennis, swimming, fly fishing, mountain biking, hiking and kayaking. Through subsidiary Boyne Realty, Boyne also markets condominiums, cottages, homes and acreage at its Boyne Highlands Harbor Springs, Bay Harbor Petoskey, Boyne Mountain, Boyne City and Big Sky Resorts. The company has retail operations under the name Boyne Country Sports and offers online ski, golf and travel shopping. Boyne USA's most recent ventures are two additions to the Boyne Mountain property: Avalanche Bay, an indoor water park, and Mountain Grand Lodge, an alpine-themed condominium hotel and spa.

Boyne USA offers its employees partial tuition reimbursement, as well as discounts on skiing, golfing and other purchases.

FINANCIALS: Sales and profits are in thousands of dollars—add 000 to get the full amount. 2006 Note: Financial information for 2006 was not available for all companies at press time.

2006 Sales: $	2006 Profits: $	**U.S. Stock Ticker: Private**	
2005 Sales: $	2005 Profits: $	**Int'l Ticker:** Int'l Exchange:	
2004 Sales: $	2004 Profits: $	Employees:	
2003 Sales: $	2003 Profits: $	Fiscal Year Ends: 12/31	
2002 Sales: $	2002 Profits: $	Parent Company:	

SALARIES/BENEFITS:

Pension Plan:	ESOP Stock Plan:	Profit Sharing:	Top Exec. Salary: $	Bonus: $
Savings Plan: Y	Stock Purch. Plan:		Second Exec. Salary: $	Bonus: $

OTHER THOUGHTS:

Apparent Women Officers or Directors: 1
Hot Spot for Advancement for Women/Minorities:

LOCATIONS: ("Y" = Yes)

West:	Southwest:	Midwest:	Southeast:	Northeast:	International:
Y		Y	Y		Y

BRITISH BROADCASTING CORPORATION (BBC)

www.bbc.co.uk

Industry Group Code: 513120 Ranks within this company's industry group: Sales: 5 Profits: 22

Print Media/Publishing:	Movies:	Equipment/Supplies:	Broadcast/Cable:		Music/Audio:	Sports/Games:
Newspapers:	Movie Theaters:	Equipment/Supplies:	Broadcast TV:	Y	Music Production:	Games/Sports:
Magazines:	Movie Production:	Gambling Equipment:	Cable TV:	Y	Retail Music:	Retail Games Stores:
Books:	TV/Video Production: Y	Special Services: Y	Satellite Broadcast:		Retail Audio Equip.:	Stadiums/Teams:
Book Stores:	Video Rental:	Advertising Services:	Radio:		Music Print./Dist.:	Gambling/Casinos:
Distribution/Printing:	Video Distribution:	Info. Sys. Software:	Online Information:		Multimedia:	Rides/Theme Parks:

TYPES OF BUSINESS:

Television Broadcasting
Television Production
News Agency
Radio Broadcasting
Online Publishing
Media Distribution & Services

BRANDS/DIVISIONS/AFFILIATES:

BBC
BBC One
BBC Two
CBBC Channel
Cbeebies
BBC Online
BBC World Service
BBC Trust

CONTACTS: Note: Officers with more than one job title may be intentionally listed here more than once.

Mark Thompson, Dir.-General
Tim Davie, Dir.-Mktg.
Stephen Kelly, Dir.-BBC People
Ashley Highfield, Dir.-New Media & Tech.
Caroline Thomson, Dir.-Policy & Legal
Caroline Thompson, Dir.-Strategy & Distribution
Tim Davie, Dir.-Comm. & Audiences
Zarin Patel, Dir.-Finance
Jenny Abramsky, Dir.-Radio & Music
Jana Bennett, Dir.-Television
Mark Byford, Deputy Dir.-General
John Smith, CEO-BBC Worldwide, Ltd.

Phone: 44-20-7580-4468	Fax: 44-20-7765-1181
Toll-Free:	
Address: Broadcasting House, Portland Pl., London, W1A 1AA UK	

GROWTH PLANS/SPECIAL FEATURES:

The British Broadcasting Corporation (BBC) is one of the most far-reaching news sources in the world. BBC One and Two are the company's two main public television stations. BBC One sees itself as the U.K.'s most valued channel, as it offers the broadest range of programming of any U.K. mainstream network, covering national and international sports events and issues. BBC Two is a mixed-genre channel that combines factual and specialist subjects with comedy and drama in an attempt to bring intelligent television to a wide audience. BBC Three is aimed primarily at younger viewers and contains a mixed schedule of news, current affairs, education, music, arts, science and coverage of international issues, as well as offering drama, comedy, and entertainment. BBC Four prides itself on offering more intellectually stimulating and culturally enriching programming, as compared to the mainstream line-up. Other smaller television services include: the CBBC Channel, Cbeebies, BBC Parliament and BBC News 24. BBC Interactive allows programmers to maximize coverage by providing viewers with increasing interactivity. BBC Online provides millions of users with a web portal operational in 33 languages, and BBC Radio offers listeners over 10 channels of programming. One of the company's major subsidiaries is BBC Worldwide, which offers international television programming such as BBC Prime and BBC America. Other ventures include business and media services, such as media distribution and management, production and technology solutions. The BBC's Royal Charter expired at the end of 2006, a development that will eventually lead to the replacement of the current Board of Governors with a unit called the BBC Trust. The transition is designed to make BBC administrators more accountable to its patrons, which support the company through television fees.

BBC offers its employees benefits including maternity/paternity leave, subsidized child care and flexible working arrangements, including a job-share scheme.

FINANCIALS: Sales and profits are in thousands of dollars—add 000 to get the full amount. 2006 Note: Financial information for 2006 was not available for all companies at press time.

2006 Sales: $6,966,700	2006 Profits: $6,300	U.S. Stock Ticker: Government-Owned
2005 Sales: $7,205,400	2005 Profits: $-353,600	Int'l Ticker: Int'l Exchange:
2004 Sales: $6,766,200	2004 Profits: $-454,400	Employees: 25,377
2003 Sales: $5,559,000	2003 Profits: $-495,100	Fiscal Year Ends: 3/31
2002 Sales: $4,822,700	2002 Profits: $-22,700	Parent Company:

SALARIES/BENEFITS:

Pension Plan: Y	ESOP Stock Plan:	Profit Sharing:	Top Exec. Salary: $448,003	Bonus: $107,000
Savings Plan:	Stock Purch. Plan:		Second Exec. Salary: $338,409	Bonus: $75,497

OTHER THOUGHTS:

Apparent Women Officers or Directors: 6
Hot Spot for Advancement for Women/Minorities: Y

LOCATIONS: ("Y" = Yes)

West:	Southwest:	Midwest:	Southeast:	Northeast:	International:
Y				Y	Y

Note: Financial information, benefits and other data can change quickly and may vary from those stated here.

BRITISH SKY BROADCASTING PLC

www.sky.com

Industry Group Code: 513220 Ranks within this company's industry group: Sales: 6 Profits: 3

Print Media/Publishing:	Movies:	Equipment/Supplies:	Broadcast/Cable:		Music/Audio:	Sports/Games:
Newspapers:	Movie Theaters:	Equipment/Supplies:	Broadcast TV:	Y	Music Production:	Games/Sports:
Magazines:	Movie Production:	Gambling Equipment:	Cable TV:	Y	Retail Music:	Retail Games Stores:
Books:	TV/Video Production:	Special Services:	Satellite Broadcast:		Retail Audio Equip.:	Stadiums/Teams:
Book Stores:	Video Rental:	Advertising Services:	Radio:		Music Print./Dist.:	Gambling/Casinos:
Distribution/Printing:	Video Distribution:	Info. Sys. Software:	Online Information:		Multimedia:	Rides/Theme Parks:

TYPES OF BUSINESS:

Satellite TV Broadcasting
Digital TV
Broadcast TV
Mobile Phone TV
Interactive Television
Broadband Service

BRANDS/DIVISIONS/AFFILIATES:

Sky One
Sky Travel
Sky News
Sky Sports
Sky Movies
Sky Broadband
Sky Active
News Corporation

CONTACTS: Note: Officers with more than one job title may be intentionally listed here more than once.

James R. Murdoch, CEO
Richard Freudenstein, COO
Jeremy Darroch, CFO
Jon Florsheim, Chief Mktg. Officer
Beryl Cook, Dir.-People & Organizational Dev.
Jeff Hughes, Group Dir.-IT
Robin Crossley, Strategic Adviser-Tech.
Alun Webber, Group Dir.-Eng.
James Conyers, General Counsel
Mike Darcey, Dir.-Group Comm. & Strategy
Julian Eccles, Dir.-Comm. & Corp. Affairs
Nick Milligan, Managing Dir.-Sky Media
Robert Fraser, Mgr.-Corp. Comm.
Jon Florsheim, Managing Dir.-Customer Group
Dawn Airey, Managing Dir.-Channels & Svcs.
K. Rupert Murdoch, Chmn.

Phone: 44-20-7705-3000	Fax: 44-20-7705-3453
Toll-Free:	
Address: Grant Way, Isleworth, Middlesex TW7 5QD UK	

GROWTH PLANS/SPECIAL FEATURES:

British Sky Broadcasting plc (BSkyB) is the U.K.'s premier pay television service. It distributes entertainment, news and sports programming to more than 8.2 million subscribers through cable and satellite. The firm offers over 100 channels and operates 28 on its own, including Sky One, Sky Travel, Sky News, Sky Sports and Sky Movies. BSkyB also owns the broadcast rights to England's professional soccer league and domestic cricket matches, as well as certain other sports events in the U.K. and Ireland, including rugby, motorsports, golf and boxing. In addition, the firm is marketing a digital video recorder similar to TiVo, called Sky+, and has developed an interactive television network, called Sky Active, allowing viewers to interact through contests, quizzes, voting events, shopping or wagering, all through an electronic fixture connected to the television set and a modem. International media mogul Rupert Murdoch, the current chairman, is the owner of News Corporation, which owns a 36% controlling interest in BSkyB. In July 2006, the company began offering free broadband service to many of its customers via Sky Broadband.

FINANCIALS: Sales and profits are in thousands of dollars—add 000 to get the full amount. 2006 Note: Financial information for 2006 was not available for all companies at press time.

2006 Sales: $8,126,220	2006 Profits: $1,079,450	U.S. Stock Ticker: BSY
2005 Sales: $7,526,750	2005 Profits: $1,132,340	Int'l Ticker: BSY Int'l Exchange: London-LSE
2004 Sales: $6,607,900	2004 Profits: $784,400	Employees: 11,216
2003 Sales: $5,252,800	2003 Profits: $313,700	Fiscal Year Ends: 6/30
2002 Sales: $4,251,000	2002 Profits: $-2,117,100	Parent Company:

SALARIES/BENEFITS:

Pension Plan:	ESOP Stock Plan:	Profit Sharing:	Top Exec. Salary: $1,314,084	Bonus: $2,102,427
Savings Plan: Y	Stock Purch. Plan:		Second Exec. Salary: $770,889	Bonus: $1,121,294

OTHER THOUGHTS:

Apparent Women Officers or Directors: 2
Hot Spot for Advancement for Women/Minorities:

LOCATIONS: ("Y" = Yes)

West:	Southwest:	Midwest:	Southeast:	Northeast:	International: Y

Note: Financial information, benefits and other data can change quickly and may vary from those stated here.

BUY.COM INC

www.buy.com

Industry Group Code: 443110E Ranks within this company's industry group: Sales: Profits:

Print Media/Publishing:		Movies:		Equipment/Supplies:		Broadcast/Cable:		Music/Audio:		Sports/Games:	
Newspapers:		Movie Theaters:		Equipment/Supplies:	Y	Broadcast TV:		Music Production:		Games/Sports:	
Magazines:	Y	Movie Production:		Gambling Equipment:		Cable TV:		Retail Music:	Y	Retail Games Stores:	Y
Books:	Y	TV/Video Production:		Special Services:	Y	Satellite Broadcast:		Retail Audio Equip.:	Y	Stadiums/Teams:	
Book Stores:		Video Rental:		Advertising Services:		Radio:		Music Print./Dist.:		Gambling/Casinos:	
Distribution/Printing:		Video Distribution:		Info. Sys. Software:		Online Information:		Multimedia:		Rides/Theme Parks:	

TYPES OF BUSINESS:

Consumer Electronics, Online Retail
Book, Game, DVD, VHS & Music Sales
Software & Accessories Sales
Music Downloads
Social Networking Web Site

BRANDS/DIVISIONS/AFFILIATES:

Internet Superstore (The)
BuyMagazine
metails.com
buymusic.com
BuyTV.com
Yub.com

CONTACTS: Note: Officers with more than one job title may be intentionally listed here more than once.

Neel Grover, CEO
Neel Grover, Pres.
Roger Andelin, CIO
Robb Brock, CTO
Eoin Matthews, VP-Bus. Dev.
Scott Blum, Chmn.

Phone: 949-389-2000	Fax: 949-389-2800
Toll-Free: 888-880-1030	
Address: 85 Enterprise, Ste. 100, Aliso Viejo, CA 92656 US	

GROWTH PLANS/SPECIAL FEATURES:

Buy.com, Inc. is an online retailer that sells a wide variety of items, including computer hardware, computer accessories and software, electronics, cellular products and services, books, bags, games, toys, DVDs, CDs and music downloads. Under its trademarked moniker The Internet Superstore, the company offers more than 2 million products to over 8.4 million customers through the various online channels on the buy.com web site. Buy.com's computer products include computers, printers, monitors, modems and peripherals, and computer software titles from leading manufacturers including Microsoft, Adobe and Corel. The firm also stocks hardback, paperback and audio book titles, enabling customers to read the first chapter of many books, submit their own book reviews and read professional and customer reviews. In addition, the company retails DVD and VHS titles from a range of categories. Buy.com distributes BuyMagazine, a monthly digital publication that lists products for sale and contains editorial columns that help customers understand the features of the products offered. The company also owns metails.com, a social networking web site that allows users to create pages that outline specific interests, favorite products and other facts about themselves. Users can then search the Metails database for other individuals with common interests. They can also share specific product information and reviews with other users. Metails enables the purchasing of these products through partner e-retail sites, whereby the users themselves are rewarded for becoming referrers of products. In 2006, Buy.com launched a Canadian website, as well as BuyTV.com, which focuses on entertainment-based retailing. After having been taken private for several years, the firm has filed with the SEC for a proposed initial public offering.

FINANCIALS: Sales and profits are in thousands of dollars—add 000 to get the full amount. 2006 Note: Financial information for 2006 was not available for all companies at press time.

2006 Sales: $	2006 Profits: $	U.S. Stock Ticker: BUYY
2005 Sales: $	2005 Profits: $	Int'l Ticker: Int'l Exchange:
2004 Sales: $290,800	2004 Profits: $-15,400	Employees: 121
2003 Sales: $238,200	2003 Profits: $-25,600	Fiscal Year Ends: 12/31
2002 Sales: $301,700	2002 Profits: $-22,700	Parent Company:

SALARIES/BENEFITS:

Pension Plan:	ESOP Stock Plan:	Profit Sharing:	Top Exec. Salary: $217,755	Bonus: $
Savings Plan:	Stock Purch. Plan:		Second Exec. Salary: $184,462	Bonus: $10,000

OTHER THOUGHTS:

Apparent Women Officers or Directors:
Hot Spot for Advancement for Women/Minorities:

LOCATIONS: ("Y" = Yes)

West:	Southwest:	Midwest:	Southeast:	Northeast:	International:
Y					Y

CABLE NEWS NETWORK LP LLLP   www.cnn.com

Industry Group Code: 513210 Ranks within this company's industry group: Sales: 8   Profits:

Print Media/Publishing:	Movies:		Equipment/Supplies:		Broadcast/Cable:		Music/Audio:		Sports/Games:	
Newspapers:	Movie Theaters:		Equipment/Supplies:		Broadcast TV:		Music Production:		Games/Sports:	
Magazines:	Movie Production:		Gambling Equipment:		Cable TV:	Y	Retail Music:		Retail Games Stores:	
Books:	TV/Video Production:	Y	Special Services:	Y	Satellite Broadcast:		Retail Audio Equip.:		Stadiums/Teams:	
Book Stores:	Video Rental:		Advertising Services:		Radio:		Music Print./Dist.:		Gambling/Casinos:	
Distribution/Printing:	Video Distribution:		Info. Sys. Software:		Online Information:		Multimedia:		Rides/Theme Parks:	

TYPES OF BUSINESS:

TV News Production
News Radio Broadcasting
Satellite Networks
Online News Information
Syndicated News Service

BRANDS/DIVISIONS/AFFILIATES:

Turner Broadcasting
Time Warner
CNN Money
CNN Headline News
CNN International
CNN Radio
CNN Mobile
CNN Newsource

CONTACTS: *Note: Officers with more than one job title may be intentionally listed here more than once.*

Jim Walton, Pres., CNN Worldwide
Greg D'Alba, Exec. VP/COO-Advertising Sales & Mktg.
Jack Womack, Exec. VP-Admin., CNN/U.S.
David Payne, General Mgr.-CNN.com/Sr. VP
Susan Bunda, Sr. VP-News, CNN
Chris Cramer, Mng. Dir.-CNN Int'l
Mitch Gelman, Sr. VP/Exec. Producer-CNN.com
Jonathan Klein, Pres., CNN/U.S.

Phone: 404-827-1700	Fax: 404-827-1099
Toll-Free:	
Address: One CNN Center, Atlanta, GA 30303 US	

GROWTH PLANS/SPECIAL FEATURES:

Cable News Network LP, LLLP, more commonly known as CNN, is a unit of Turner Broadcasting, which is owned by Time Warner. It operates 42 news bureaus around the world, including 11 in the U.S. The company operates 15 cable and satellite television networks, including CNN Money, CNN Airport Network and CNN en Espanol; two private, place-based networks (CNN Headline News and CNN International); two radio networks (CNN Radio and CNN en Espanol Radio); 12 network-affiliated web sites; CNN Mobile, which sends news reports and other information to members' wireless devices; and CNN Newsource, one of the world's most extensively syndicated news services. The firm's TV news programs include American Morning, House Call, Anderson Cooper 360, Paula Zahn Now, Lou Dobbs Tonight, CNN Presents, CNN Live Forum, CNN Live Today and The Situation Room. It also features the popular interview program, Larry King Live. CNN News Services, the administration business unit of CNN News Group, consists of six divisions: CNN Business Operations, cnn.com, CNN Content Sales/Business Development, CNN Newsource Sales, CNNRadio and Turner Learning. CNN recently launched CNN Pipeline, an on-demand broadband video service which gives subscribers access to over 50,000 videos. In 2006, CNN won two Emmy awards for Business and Financial Reporting. Also in 2006, CNN introduced I-Report, which allows individual viewers to send their original content to CNN.com. Content is vetted before being released on the air or Internet.

FINANCIALS: Sales and profits are in thousands of dollars—add 000 to get the full amount. 2006 Note: Financial information for 2006 was not available for all companies at press time.

2006 Sales: $	2006 Profits: $	**U.S. Stock Ticker: Subsidiary**
2005 Sales: $794,000	2005 Profits: $	**Int'l Ticker:** Int'l Exchange:
2004 Sales: $	2004 Profits: $	Employees: 4,000
2003 Sales: $	2003 Profits: $	Fiscal Year Ends: 12/31
2002 Sales: $	2002 Profits: $	Parent Company: TURNER BROADCASTING SYSTEM

SALARIES/BENEFITS:

Pension Plan:	ESOP Stock Plan:	Profit Sharing:	Top Exec. Salary: $	Bonus: $
Savings Plan:	Stock Purch. Plan:		Second Exec. Salary: $	Bonus: $

OTHER THOUGHTS:

Apparent Women Officers or Directors: 1
Hot Spot for Advancement for Women/Minorities:

LOCATIONS: ("Y" = Yes)

West:	Southwest:	Midwest:	Southeast:	Northeast:	International:
Y	Y	Y	Y	Y	Y

CABLEVISION SYSTEMS CORP
www.cablevision.com

Industry Group Code: 513220 Ranks within this company's industry group: Sales: 10 Profits: 10

Print Media/Publishing:	Movies:		Equipment/Supplies:		Broadcast/Cable:		Music/Audio:		Sports/Games:	
Newspapers:	Movie Theaters:	Y	Equipment/Supplies:		Broadcast TV:	Y	Music Production:		Games/Sports:	
Magazines:	Movie Production:		Gambling Equipment:	Y	Cable TV:	Y	Retail Music:		Retail Games Stores:	
Books:	TV/Video Production:		Special Services:	Y	Satellite Broadcast:		Retail Audio Equip.:		Stadiums/Teams:	
Book Stores:	Video Rental:		Advertising Services:		Radio:		Music Print./Dist.:	Y	Gambling/Casinos:	
Distribution/Printing:	Video Distribution:		Info. Sys. Software:		Online Information:		Multimedia:		Rides/Theme Parks:	

TYPES OF BUSINESS:

Cable Television Service
Professional Sports Teams
Television Programming
Communications Services
Sports & Music Venues
Voice-Over-Cable Service
Movie Theaters
High-Speed Internet Service

BRANDS/DIVISIONS/AFFILIATES:

Rainbow Media Holdings, Inc.
Clearview Cinemas
Radio City Entertainment
Optimum Voice
Madison Square Garden
New York Knicks
iO Games
Optimum Online

CONTACTS: Note: Officers with more than one job title may be intentionally listed here more than once.

James L. Dolan, CEO
Tom Rutledge, COO
James L. Dolan, Pres.
Michael Huseby, CFO/Exec. VP
Wilt Hildenbrand, Exec. VP-Tech.
Wilt Hildenbrand, Exec. VP-Eng.
Jonathan D. Schwartz, General Counsel/Exec. VP
Patricia Armstrong, Sr. VP-Investor Rel.
Kevin F. Watson, Sr. VP/Treas.
Hank J. Ratner, Vice Chmn.
John Bickham, Pres., Cable & Comm.
Joshua Sapan, CEO/Pres., Rainbow Media Holdings LLC
Dave Pistacchio, Exec. VP/General Mgr., Lightpath
Charles F. Dolan, Chmn.

Phone: 516-803-2300	Fax: 516-803-3134
Toll-Free:	
Address: 1111 Stewart Ave., Bethpage, NY 11714 US	

GROWTH PLANS/SPECIAL FEATURES:

Cablevision Systems Corp. is one of the largest cable operators in the U.S. The company also has investments in cable programming networks, entertainment businesses and telecommunications companies. Cablevision serves nearly 3 million subscribers, primarily in and around the New York City metropolitan area. The firm owns the American Movie Classics channel, the Independent Film Channel, the WE: Women's Entertainment Channel, Fox Sports Net for multiple states and Radio City Entertainment (which operates Radio City Music Hall in New York City under a long-term lease). Through its wholly-owned subsidiary, Rainbow Media Holdings, Inc., Cablevision owns 60% of Madison Square Garden and the adjoining Theater at Madison Square Garden, the New York Knickerbockers professional basketball team, the New York Rangers professional hockey team, the New York Liberty professional women's basketball team, the Hartford Wolf Pack professional hockey team and the Madison Square Garden Network. Telecommunications offerings include its iO: Interactive Optimum digital television offering, Optimum Online high-speed Internet service, Optimum Voice digital voice-over-cable service and Lightpath integrated business communication services, which provide switched telephone services and high-speed Internet access to the business market. The company also owns or has interests in Clearview Cinemas (a chain of 57 movie theaters) and Northcoast Communications, LLC (a wireless personal communications services business). Optimum Voice, Cablevision's new telephone service offering, is a voice-over-cable system enabled by installing a special adapter in the home. In November 2005, Cablevision rolled out a new suite of premium Internet products, titled Optimum Online, which allow for high-speed Internet access at speeds up to 50 Mbps. In October 2006, the company announced that it has received a $27 per share offer from the Dolan family (which owns 22.5% of the company's shares and 74% of the voting power) to convert Cablevision into a privately held firm.

FINANCIALS: Sales and profits are in thousands of dollars—add 000 to get the full amount. 2006 Note: Financial information for 2006 was not available for all companies at press time.

2006 Sales: $	2006 Profits: $	U.S. Stock Ticker: CVC
2005 Sales: $5,175,911	2005 Profits: $94,300	Int'l Ticker: Int'l Exchange:
2004 Sales: $4,750,037	2004 Profits: $-676,092	Employees: 20,425
2003 Sales: $4,177,148	2003 Profits: $-297,311	Fiscal Year Ends: 12/31
2002 Sales: $4,003,407	2002 Profits: $90,112	Parent Company:

SALARIES/BENEFITS:

Pension Plan: Y	ESOP Stock Plan:	Profit Sharing:	Top Exec. Salary: $1,600,000	Bonus: $7,092,000
Savings Plan: Y	Stock Purch. Plan: Y		Second Exec. Salary: $1,600,000	Bonus: $3,492,000

OTHER THOUGHTS:

Apparent Women Officers or Directors:
Hot Spot for Advancement for Women/Minorities:

LOCATIONS: ("Y" = Yes)

West:	Southwest:	Midwest:	Southeast:	Northeast:	International:
				Y	

CAESARS ENTERTAINMENT INC
www.caesars.com

Industry Group Code: 721120 Ranks within this company's industry group: Sales: Profits:

Print Media/Publishing:	Movies:	Equipment/Supplies:	Broadcast/Cable:	Music/Audio:		Sports/Games:	
Newspapers:	Movie Theaters:	Equipment/Supplies:	Broadcast TV:	Music Production:	Y	Games/Sports:	
Magazines:	Movie Production:	Gambling Equipment:	Cable TV:	Retail Music:		Retail Games Stores:	
Books:	TV/Video Production:	Special Services:	Satellite Broadcast:	Retail Audio Equip.:		Stadiums/Teams:	Y
Book Stores:	Video Rental:	Advertising Services:	Radio:	Music Print./Dist.:		Gambling/Casinos:	
Distribution/Printing:	Video Distribution:	Info. Sys. Software:	Online Information:	Multimedia:		Rides/Theme Parks:	

TYPES OF BUSINESS:
Casino Resorts
Restaurants
Hotels
Shopping Centers
Cruise Ships

BRANDS/DIVISIONS/AFFILIATES:
Park Place Entertainment Corp.
Bally's Las Vegas
Caesars Palace
Caesars Palace at Sea
Flamingo (The)
Las Vegas Hilton
Caesars Tahoe
Harrah's Entertainment

CONTACTS: *Note: Officers with more than one job title may be intentionally listed here more than once.*
Gary Loveman, Chmn./CEO/Pres., Harrah's Entertainment, Inc.
Tim Wilmott, COO, Harrah's Entertainment, Inc.
Charles L. Atwood, CFO, Harrah's Entertainment, Inc.
Tim Stanley, CIO/Sr. VP-Harrah's Entertainment, Inc.

Phone: 702-699-5093	Fax: 702-699-5202
Toll-Free:	
Address: 3930 Howard Hughes Pkwy., Las Vegas, NV 89109 US	

GROWTH PLANS/SPECIAL FEATURES:

Caesars Entertainment, Inc., a subsidiary of Harrah's Entertainment, Inc., is one of the world's foremost gaming and resort brand names. Caesar's holds 21 properties in three countries, representing 25,000 hotel rooms and 2 million square feet of casino space, maintaining its four original brand names: Caesars World, Bally's, Grand Casinos and Hilton gaming. In June 2005, Caesar's merged with Harrah's Entertainment, Inc., creating the world's largest gaming company, with more than 40 casinos in three countries. The merged company is based in Las Vegas, where it operates the famed Caesar's Palace and five other major casino resorts. The total merged portfolio now includes Caesar's Palace, Bally's Las Vegas, Flamingo Las Vegas, Caesar's Atlantic City, Bally's Atlantic City, Harrah's New Orleans, the Grand Casino Biloxi, Casino Windsor and Conrad Resort & Casio in Punta Del Este, Uruguay, among others. In addition, the merged company owns and operates Bluegrass Downs, a harness racetrack in Paducah, Kentucky, two Caesar's Palace at Sea casinos on cruise ships owned by Crystal Cruises, Inc. and operates the World Series of Poker tournament circuit and license trademarks for merchandise related to this brand. Recently, Harrah's announced the reopening of its New Orleans and Biloxi casinos, sold the assets of its Grand Casino Gulfport and reported several major additions to the growing entertainment support staff for its Caesars Singapore, including a deal with Hollywood icon James Cameron and an agreement with STAR, Asia's leading media and entertainment company.

Caesars Entertainment offers its workers flexible spending accounts, tuition reimbursement, parking, dining privileges and employee discounts.

FINANCIALS: Sales and profits are in thousands of dollars—add 000 to get the full amount. 2006 Note: Financial information for 2006 was not available for all companies at press time.

2006 Sales: $	2006 Profits: $	U.S. Stock Ticker: Subsidiary
2005 Sales: $	2005 Profits: $	Int'l Ticker: Int'l Exchange:
2004 Sales: $4,206,000	2004 Profits: $297,000	Employees: 50,000
2003 Sales: $4,455,000	2003 Profits: $46,000	Fiscal Year Ends: 12/31
2002 Sales: $4,652,000	2002 Profits: $-824,000	Parent Company: HARRAH'S ENTERTAINMENT INC

SALARIES/BENEFITS:

Pension Plan: Y	ESOP Stock Plan:	Profit Sharing:	Top Exec. Salary: $998,462	Bonus: $1,225,000
Savings Plan: Y	Stock Purch. Plan:		Second Exec. Salary: $692,308	Bonus: $588,750

OTHER THOUGHTS:
Apparent Women Officers or Directors:
Hot Spot for Advancement for Women/Minorities:

LOCATIONS: ("Y" = Yes)

West:	Southwest:	Midwest:	Southeast:	Northeast:	International:
Y		Y	Y	Y	Y

Note: Financial information, benefits and other data can change quickly and may vary from those stated here.

CANTERBURY PARK HOLDING CORP

www.canterburypark.com

Industry Group Code: 713210 Ranks within this company's industry group: Sales: 8   Profits: 7

Print Media/Publishing:	Movies:	Equipment/Supplies:	Broadcast/Cable:	Music/Audio:	Sports/Games:	
Newspapers:	Movie Theaters:	Equipment/Supplies:	Broadcast TV:	Music Production:	Games/Sports:	Y
Magazines:	Movie Production:	Gambling Equipment:	Cable TV:	Retail Music:	Retail Games Stores:	
Books:	TV/Video Production:	Special Services:	Satellite Broadcast:	Retail Audio Equip.:	Stadiums/Teams:	
Book Stores:	Video Rental:	Advertising Services:	Radio:	Music Print./Dist.:	Gambling/Casinos:	Y
Distribution/Printing:	Video Distribution:	Info. Sys. Software:	Online Information:	Multimedia:	Rides/Theme Parks:	

TYPES OF BUSINESS:

Gambling-Horse Races
Simulcasting
Card Club
Event Hosting

BRANDS/DIVISIONS/AFFILIATES:

Canterbury Card Club
The Racino at Canterbury Park

CONTACTS: *Note: Officers with more than one job title may be intentionally listed here more than once.*

Randall D. Sampson, CEO/Gen. Mgr.
Randall D. Sampson, Pres.
David C. Hansen, CFO
John R. Harty, VP-Mktg.
Jerry Fuller, VP-Club Card Oper.
Kip Rakos, Mgr.-Corp. Comm.
Judy Dahlke, VP-Investor Rel.
David C. Hansen, VP-Finance/Sec.
Mark E. Erickson, VP-Facilities
Michael J. Garin, VP-Hospitality/Asst. Sec.
Eric Halstrom, VP-Racing & Simulcasting
Dale H. Schenian, Vice Chmn.
Curtis A. Sampson, Chmn.

Phone: 952-445-7223	**Fax:** 952-496-6400
Toll-Free: 800-340-6361	
Address: 1100 Canterbury Rd., Shakopee, MN 55379 US	

GROWTH PLANS/SPECIAL FEATURES:

Canterbury Park Holding Corp. hosts seasonal pari-mutuel wagering on live thoroughbred and quarter horse racing at its facilities in Shakopee, Minnesota from May through September. In addition, the firm offers simulcast racing from 20 different racetracks per day, seven days a week, 364 days per year. The firm's revenues are principally derived from pari-mutuel wagering and card club operations. In the most recent fiscal year, Card Club operations generated 53.6% of total revenues. Canterbury Park derives further revenues from related services and activities such as concessions, parking, admissions and programs and from other entertainment events held at the racetrack. When not conducting horse races, the firm hosts events such as snowmobile racing, arts and crafts shows, fundraisers, automobile shows and competitions and private parties. Canterbury Park also runs the Canterbury Card Club, in which patrons compete against each other in various unbanked card games, wagering against each other instead of the house. The card club is open 24 hours a day, seven days a week and offers poker and table games on up to 50 authorized tables. In 2007, the firm plans to introduce banked card games and electronic gaming devices if approved by the Minnesota Legislature. This concept, called the Racino at Canterbury Park, would include approximately 40 table games, 3,000 gaming devices, an Olympic scale horse park, additional restaurant venues, and a 250-room hotel. In 2006, the firm announced a program to repurchase up to 100,000 shares of its stock in order to increase long-term value. In late 2006, the company announced that it hoped to develop a new entertainment complex including a stadium for the Minnesota Vikings football team.

Canterbury Park offers its employees a referral bonus program and employee discounts. The firm gives 5% of pre-tax profits to charity annually.

FINANCIALS: Sales and profits are in thousands of dollars—add 000 to get the full amount. 2006 Note: Financial information for 2006 was not available for all companies at press time.

2006 Sales: $	2006 Profits: $	**U.S. Stock Ticker:** ECP
2005 Sales: $55,223	2005 Profits: $3,053	**Int'l Ticker:** Int'l Exchange:
2004 Sales: $54,899	2004 Profits: $3,862	Employees: 711
2003 Sales: $47,846	2003 Profits: $2,870	Fiscal Year Ends: 12/31
2002 Sales: $41,700	2002 Profits: $2,300	Parent Company:

SALARIES/BENEFITS:

Pension Plan:	ESOP Stock Plan: Y	Profit Sharing:	Top Exec. Salary: $200,054	Bonus: $50,014
Savings Plan: Y	Stock Purch. Plan: Y		Second Exec. Salary: $129,443	Bonus: $32,861

OTHER THOUGHTS:

Apparent Women Officers or Directors: 1
Hot Spot for Advancement for Women/Minorities:

LOCATIONS: ("Y" = Yes)

West:	Southwest:	Midwest:	Southeast:	Northeast:	International:
		Y			

Note: Financial information, benefits and other data can change quickly and may vary from those stated here.

CANWEST GLOBAL COMMUNICATIONS

www.canwestglobal.com

Industry Group Code: 513120 Ranks within this company's industry group: Sales: 8   Profits: 11

Print Media/Publishing:		Movies:		Equipment/Supplies:		Broadcast/Cable:		Music/Audio:		Sports/Games:	
Newspapers:	Y	Movie Theaters:		Equipment/Supplies:		Broadcast TV:	Y	Music Production:		Games/Sports:	
Magazines:		Movie Production:		Gambling Equipment:		Cable TV:	Y	Retail Music:		Retail Games Stores:	
Books:		TV/Video Production:	Y	Special Services:	Y	Satellite Broadcast:		Retail Audio Equip.:		Stadiums/Teams:	
Book Stores:		Video Rental:		Advertising Services:		Radio:		Music Print./Dist.:		Gambling/Casinos:	
Distribution/Printing:		Video Distribution:		Info. Sys. Software:		Online Information:		Multimedia:		Rides/Theme Parks:	

TYPES OF BUSINESS:

Television Broadcasting
Newspaper Publishing
Cable Broadcasting
Television Production & Distribution
Specialty TV Channels
Online Information
Web Site Development

BRANDS/DIVISIONS/AFFILIATES:

Global Television Network
CH
CanWest Entertainment
CanWest Interactive
Western International Communications
National Post
canada.com
Internet Broadcasting Systems

CONTACTS: *Note: Officers with more than one job title may be intentionally listed here more than once.*

Leonard J. Asper, CEO
Leonard J. Asper, Pres.
John E. Maguire, CFO
Grace Palombo, VP-Human Resources
Richard M. Leipsic, General Counsel/VP
David A. Asper, Exec. VP/Chmn., National Post
Gail S. Asper, Corp. Sec.
Derek H. Burney, Chmn.
Thomas C. Strike, Pres., CanWest MediaWorks Int'l

Phone: 204-956-2025	**Fax:** 204-947-9841
Toll-Free:	
Address: 3100 CanWest Global, 201 Portage Ave., 31st Fl., Winnipeg, MB R3B 3L7 Canada	

GROWTH PLANS/SPECIAL FEATURES:

CanWest Global Communications is the largest television broadcasting and diversified media company in Canada, reaching about 94% of the country's English-speaking population. Its holdings include the Global Television Network; CH, a second network located in Montreal, Hamilton and Victoria; CanWest Entertainment, a leading film and television production and distribution operation; CanWest Interactive, a growing Interactive media business with operations in consumer web sites (such as canada.com), as well as the creation and sale of financial data, text, photographs and video; eight specialty channels that offer niche programming (including Prime TV, a station targeted at those 50 years and older; Men TV; Mystery; DejaView, a television classics channel; Lonestar, a western genre channel; and Cool TV, a jazz music channel); and a significant international television and radio broadcasting presence in Australia (Network Ten) and New Zealand (TV3 and C4). The firm's television stations offer a line-up of popular shows from the U.S., such as Survivor, The Apprentice, Will & Grace and The Simpsons. CanWest is also Canada's largest newspaper publisher, with ownership of the National Post, 13 major metropolitan dailies and 23 smaller daily, weekly and community papers in communities throughout British Columbia. CanWest Interactive has a foothold in the rapidly expanding American telecommunications industry, with a major stake in Minnesota-based Internet Broadcasting Systems, which develops web sites for local television stations. The company has been concentrating on improving its Canadian operations for the past few years. In 2006, the company sold its Canadian radio stations to Corus Entertainment Inc. and its Irish television network, TV3, to funds managed by Doughty Hanson & Co.

FINANCIALS: Sales and profits are in thousands of dollars—add 000 to get the full amount. 2006 Note: Financial information for 2006 was not available for all companies at press time.

2006 Sales: $2,484,570	2006 Profits: $154,210	**U.S. Stock Ticker: CWG**	
2005 Sales: $2,588,600	2005 Profits: $8,700	**Int'l Ticker: CGS.A** Int'l Exchange: Toronto-TSX	
2004 Sales: $1,611,000	2004 Profits: $-10,300	Employees: 10,470	
2003 Sales: $1,643,300	2003 Profits: $33,200	Fiscal Year Ends: 8/31	
2002 Sales: $1,458,000	2002 Profits: $8,400	Parent Company:	

SALARIES/BENEFITS:

Pension Plan:	ESOP Stock Plan:	Profit Sharing:	Top Exec. Salary: $503,954	Bonus: $526,365
Savings Plan:	Stock Purch. Plan:		Second Exec. Salary: $465,188	Bonus: $279,113

OTHER THOUGHTS:

Apparent Women Officers or Directors: 2
Hot Spot for Advancement for Women/Minorities:

LOCATIONS: ("Y" = Yes)

West:	Southwest:	Midwest:	Southeast:	Northeast:	International:
		Y			Y

CARMIKE CINEMAS INC   www.carmike.com

Industry Group Code: 512131 Ranks within this company's industry group: Sales: 4   Profits: 4

Print Media/Publishing:	Movies:		Equipment/Supplies:	Broadcast/Cable:	Music/Audio:	Sports/Games:
Newspapers:	Movie Theaters:	Y	Equipment/Supplies:	Broadcast TV:	Music Production:	Games/Sports:
Magazines:	Movie Production:		Gambling Equipment:	Cable TV:	Retail Music:	Retail Games Stores:
Books:	TV/Video Production:		Special Services:	Satellite Broadcast:	Retail Audio Equip.:	Stadiums/Teams:
Book Stores:	Video Rental:		Advertising Services:	Radio:	Music Print./Dist.:	Gambling/Casinos:
Distribution/Printing:	Video Distribution:		Info. Sys. Software:	Online Information:	Multimedia:	Rides/Theme Parks:

TYPES OF BUSINESS:
Movie Theaters

BRANDS/DIVISIONS/AFFILIATES:
Hollywood Connection
Eastwynn Theatres, Inc.
Wooden Nickel Pub, Inc.
Military Services, Inc.
IQ 2000
IQ Zero
George G. Kerasotes Corporation

CONTACTS: Note: Officers with more than one job title may be intentionally listed here more than once.
Michael W. Patrick, CEO
Fred W. Van Noy, COO/Sr. VP
Michael W. Patrick, Pres.
Richard B. Hare, CFO
Lee Champion, General Counsel/Sr. VP/Corp. Sec.
Gary F. Krannacker, VP-Oper.
Richard B. Hare, Sr. VP-Finance/Treas.
Anthony J. Rhead, Sr. VP-Entertainment/Digital Cinema
H. Madison Shirley, Sr. VP-Concessions/Asst. Sec.
Larry B. Collins, VP-Film
Jeffery A. Cole, Asst. VP/Controller/Chief Acc. Officer
Michael W. Patrick, Chmn.

Phone: 706-576-3400	Fax: 706-576-2812
Toll-Free:	
Address: 1301 First Ave., Columbus, GA 31901 US	

GROWTH PLANS/SPECIAL FEATURES:
Carmike Cinemas, Inc. is a major chain of movie theaters in the U.S. The company operates 301 theatres and 2,475 screens in 37 states, primarily in the southeastern, northeastern and midwestern regions of the U.S. In addition, the company operates two family entertainment centers under the name Hollywood Connection. Carmike targets small to mid-sized communities; more than 80% of the company's theaters are located in towns with fewer than 100,000 residents. A Carmike theater typically includes a smaller number of screens than is usual in modern construction. These theaters, known as econoplexes, are intended for markets that are too small to host a megaplex (defined as a theater with more than 12 screens). Carmike Cinemas maintain low operating costs due to I.Q. 2000 and I.Q. Zero, information technology systems that instantly transmit all information to the corporate headquarters where executive management coordinates the administrative functions. Carmike's growth strategy centers on the development of new theaters and the addition of screens and other improvements to existing theaters, as well as selective acquisitions of theaters as available. The company recently entered into a licensing agreement with Christie/AIX for the instillation and licensing of 2,300 digital cinema projection systems. Carmike Cinemas emerged from chapter 11 bankruptcy in 2005. The firm also recently acquired 100% of the stock in the George G. Kerasotes Corporation, which operates 30 theatres with 263 screens in the Midwest.

FINANCIALS: Sales and profits are in thousands of dollars—add 000 to get the full amount. 2006 Note: Financial information for 2006 was not available for all companies at press time.

2006 Sales: $	2006 Profits: $	U.S. Stock Ticker: CKEC
2005 Sales: $468,900	2005 Profits: $ 200	Int'l Ticker: Int'l Exchange:
2004 Sales: $495,300	2004 Profits: $27,900	Employees: 7,908
2003 Sales: $493,085	2003 Profits: $107,378	Fiscal Year Ends: 12/31
2002 Sales: $507,200	2002 Profits: $-39,800	Parent Company:

SALARIES/BENEFITS:
Pension Plan:	ESOP Stock Plan:	Profit Sharing:	Top Exec. Salary: $1,934,923	Bonus: $667,238
Savings Plan: Y	Stock Purch. Plan:		Second Exec. Salary: $471,391	Bonus: $79,375

OTHER THOUGHTS:
Apparent Women Officers or Directors: 1
Hot Spot for Advancement for Women/Minorities:

LOCATIONS: ("Y" = Yes)
West:	Southwest:	Midwest:	Southeast:	Northeast:	International:
Y	Y	Y	Y	Y	

CBS CORP

www.cbs.com

Industry Group Code: 513120 Ranks within this company's industry group: Sales: 3 Profits: 23

Print Media/Publishing:		Movies:		Equipment/Supplies:		Broadcast/Cable:		Music/Audio:		Sports/Games:	
Newspapers:		Movie Theaters:		Equipment/Supplies:		Broadcast TV:	Y	Music Production:		Games/Sports:	
Magazines:		Movie Production:		Gambling Equipment:		Cable TV:	Y	Retail Music:		Retail Games Stores:	
Books:	Y	TV/Video Production:	Y	Special Services:	Y	Satellite Broadcast:		Retail Audio Equip.:		Stadiums/Teams:	
Book Stores:		Video Rental:		Advertising Services:	Y	Radio:		Music Print./Dist.:		Gambling/Casinos:	
Distribution/Printing:		Video Distribution:		Info. Sys. Software:		Online Information:		Multimedia:		Rides/Theme Parks:	Y

TYPES OF BUSINESS:

Broadcast Television
News Organization
Outdoor Advertising
Radio Networks & Programming
Television Production
Cable TV Networks
Book Publishing

BRANDS/DIVISIONS/AFFILIATES:

CBS News
CBS Sports
60 Minutes
Showtime Network
Movie Channel (The)
UPN Television Networks
Infinity Radio
Simon & Schuster

CONTACTS: *Note: Officers with more than one job title may be intentionally listed here more than once.*

Leslie Moonves, CEO
Leslie Moonves, Pres.
Fredric G. Reynolds, CFO
Anthony G. Ambrosio, VP-Human Resources
Amy Berkowitz, CIO/Sr. VP
Louis J. Briskman, General Counsel
Martin D. Franks, Exec. VP-Planning, Policy, Gvt. Rel.
Gil Schwartz, Exec. VP-Corp. Comm.
Martin M. Shea, Exec. VP-Investor Rel.
Susan C. Gordon, Chief Acct. Officer/Sr. VP
John Orlando, Sr. VP-Government Affairs
Angeline C. Straka, Sr. VP/Corp. Sec./Deputy Counsel
Carl D. Folta, Exec. VP-Office of the Chmn.
Joseph R. Ianniello, Sr. VP-Finance/Treas.
Sumner M. Redstone, Chmn.

Phone: 212-975-4321	Fax: 212-975-4516
Toll-Free:	
Address: 51 W. 52nd St., New York, NY 10019 US	

GROWTH PLANS/SPECIAL FEATURES:

CBS Corp., spun-off from Viacom in January 2006, is one of the largest radio and television broadcasters in the U.S. The company has four segments: Television networks and programming; Radio; Outdoor advertising; and Book publishing. CBS Television Networks operates through CBS News, CBS Sports and CBS Entertainment. CBS News operates a worldwide news organization including 60 Minutes, 48 Hours, The Early Show and Face the Nation. CBS Sports broadcasts NFL games, the PGA tour, the U.S. Open Tennis Championships and NCAA football and basketball. CBS Entertainment broadcasts a wide variety of programming including soap operas, dramas, comedies and late night programming. Showtime Network owns and operates three subscription television program services: Showtime, offering recently released feature films, original series and motion pictures, documentaries, boxing and concerts; The Movie Channel, offering recently released feature films and related programming; and Flix, offering older feature films. UPN Television Networks provides 13 hours of television programming to its 182 affiliate stations. The firm's in-house production studios include Paramount Television, King World and CBS Enterprises. CBS Radio operates through Infinity Radio, which owns and operates 183 stations. Infinity also owns 17% of Westwood One, Inc., which provides programming for 7,000 radio stations. Viacom Outdoor sell advertising space on billboards, transit shelters, buses, rail systems, mall kiosks and stadium signage. Additionally, Viacom Outdoor has exclusive rights to manage advertising space within the London Underground. The subsidiary also manages advertising displays in the Netherlands, France, Italy, Spain, Finland and Puerto Rico. Simon & Schuster publishes and distributes adult and children's consumer books in the U.S. and internationally. The company holds minority investments in CBS SportsLine.com and CBS MarketWatch.com. CBS is majority owned by National Amusements, Inc., which is owned by the Redstone family.

CBS offers a large number of internships to college students each year.

FINANCIALS: Sales and profits are in thousands of dollars—add 000 to get the full amount. 2006 Note: Financial information for 2006 was not available for all companies at press time.

2006 Sales: $	2006 Profits: $	U.S. Stock Ticker: CBS
2005 Sales: $14,536,400	2005 Profits: $-7,089,100	Int'l Ticker: Int'l Exchange:
2004 Sales: $14,547,300	2004 Profits: $-17,462,200	Employees: 28,900
2003 Sales: $26,585,300	2003 Profits: $1,416,900	Fiscal Year Ends: 12/31
2002 Sales: $7,490,000	2002 Profits: $	Parent Company:

SALARIES/BENEFITS:

Pension Plan:	ESOP Stock Plan:	Profit Sharing:	Top Exec. Salary: $5,806,651	Bonus: $7,125,000
Savings Plan: Y	Stock Purch. Plan:		Second Exec. Salary: $5,306,651	Bonus: $13,000,000

OTHER THOUGHTS:

Apparent Women Officers or Directors: 3
Hot Spot for Advancement for Women/Minorities: Y

LOCATIONS: ("Y" = Yes)

West:	Southwest:	Midwest:	Southeast:	Northeast:	International:
Y	Y	Y	Y	Y	Y

CBS RADIO
www.cbsradio.com

Industry Group Code: 513111 Ranks within this company's industry group: Sales: 2 Profits:

Print Media/Publishing:	Movies:	Equipment/Supplies:	Broadcast/Cable:	Music/Audio:	Sports/Games:
Newspapers:	Movie Theaters:	Equipment/Supplies:	Broadcast TV:	Music Production:	Games/Sports:
Magazines:	Movie Production:	Gambling Equipment:	Cable TV:	Retail Music:	Retail Games Stores:
Books:	TV/Video Production:	Special Services:	Satellite Broadcast:	Retail Audio Equip.:	Stadiums/Teams:
Book Stores:	Video Rental:	Advertising Services: Y	Radio:	Music Print./Dist.:	Gambling/Casinos:
Distribution/Printing:	Video Distribution:	Info. Sys. Software:	Online Information:	Multimedia:	Rides/Theme Parks:

TYPES OF BUSINESS:

Radio Broadcasting
Online Streaming Music
Podcasting

GROWTH PLANS/SPECIAL FEATURES:

CBS Radio, a subsidiary of CBS Corporation, is a large radio broadcasting firm operating out of New York City. The company was formerly known as Infinity Broadcasting, but the name changed after CBS's recent split from Viacom. CBS Radio's network consists of 179 stations, the majority of which are located in the top 50 radio markets in the country. A total of more than 76 million listeners tune in each week for a variety of programming ranging from adult contemporary music to news broadcasts and personality shows. Popular radio personalities broadcasting through the company include Howard Stern, Adam Carolla and Penn Jillette. CBS Radio is home to the live broadcasts of 29 professional sports teams. The company has an alliance with Westwood One, a firm that provides stations with news, sports, weather and music content. Additionally, the company owns CBS Radio Network, which provides hourly newscasts. CBS Radio has partnered with America Online to launch whfs.com, an online streaming music source based in Washington, D.C. The company has also partnered with six other stations to form the HD Digital Radio Alliance, which intends to facilitate the rollout of high definition digital radio; launched the world's first podcasting radio station, KYOURADIO; and has begun the process of selling up to 65 of its radio stations located in smaller markets.

BRANDS/DIVISIONS/AFFILIATES:

Viacom, Inc.
CBS Radio Network
whfs.com
CBS Corporation
HD Digital Radio Alliance
KYOURADIO
Infinity Broadcasting

CONTACTS: Note: Officers with more than one job title may be intentionally listed here more than once.

Joel Hollander, CEO
Walter Berger, CFO
David Goodman, Pres., Mktg.
Glynn Walden, VP-Eng.
Karen L. Mateo, VP-Corp. Comm.
Rob Barnett, Pres., Programming
Matt Timothy, VP-Streaming Media
Richard Lobel, Exec. VP-Integrated Solutions
Scott Herman, Exec. VP-Eastern Region
Joel Hollander, Chmn.

Phone: 212-846-3939	Fax: 212-314-9228
Toll-Free:	
Address: 1515 Broadway, 46th Fl., New York, NY 10036 US	

FINANCIALS: Sales and profits are in thousands of dollars—add 000 to get the full amount. 2006 Note: Financial information for 2006 was not available for all companies at press time.

2006 Sales: $	2006 Profits: $	U.S. Stock Ticker: Subsidiary
2005 Sales: $2,114,800	2005 Profits: $	Int'l Ticker: Int'l Exchange:
2004 Sales: $2,096,100	2004 Profits: $	Employees: 8,287
2003 Sales: $	2003 Profits: $	Fiscal Year Ends: 12/31
2002 Sales: $3,754,600	2002 Profits: $	Parent Company: CBS CORP

SALARIES/BENEFITS:

Pension Plan:	ESOP Stock Plan:	Profit Sharing:	Top Exec. Salary: $	Bonus: $
Savings Plan:	Stock Purch. Plan:		Second Exec. Salary: $	Bonus: $

OTHER THOUGHTS:

Apparent Women Officers or Directors: 3
Hot Spot for Advancement for Women/Minorities: Y

LOCATIONS: ("Y" = Yes)

West:	Southwest:	Midwest:	Southeast:	Northeast:	International:
Y	Y	Y	Y	Y	

CD WAREHOUSE INC

www.cdwarehouse.com

Industry Group Code: 451220 Ranks within this company's industry group: Sales: Profits:

Print Media/Publishing:	Movies:	Equipment/Supplies:	Broadcast/Cable:	Music/Audio:		Sports/Games:
Newspapers:	Movie Theaters:	Equipment/Supplies:	Broadcast TV:	Music Production:		Games/Sports:
Magazines:	Movie Production:	Gambling Equipment:	Cable TV:	Retail Music:	Y	Retail Games Stores:
Books:	TV/Video Production:	Special Services:	Satellite Broadcast:	Retail Audio Equip.:		Stadiums/Teams:
Book Stores:	Video Rental:	Advertising Services:	Radio:	Music Print./Dist.:		Gambling/Casinos:
Distribution/Printing:	Video Distribution:	Info. Sys. Software:	Online Information:	Multimedia:		Rides/Theme Parks:

TYPES OF BUSINESS:

Music Stores
Pre-Owned CD & DVD Sales
Franchising

BRANDS/DIVISIONS/AFFILIATES:

Music Trader
Disc Go Round
CD Exchange
Magnolia Entertainment, LLC

CONTACTS: *Note: Officers with more than one job title may be intentionally listed here more than once.*

Christopher M. Salyer, CEO
Christopher M. Salyer, Pres.
Wiley Carlile, VP-Company Store Oper.
Amy Mitchell, Mgr.-Franchise Dev.
Amy Mitchell, Mgr.-Comm.

Phone: 405-236-8742	**Fax:** 405-949-2566
Toll-Free: 800-641-2566	
Address: 900 N. Broadway, Oklahoma City, OK 73102 US	

GROWTH PLANS/SPECIAL FEATURES:

CD Warehouse, Inc. operates and franchises music stores specializing in used CDs. The company also sells new and used DVDs, t-shirts and related music memorabilia. CD The company does business through 155 stores, which offer between 10,000 and 16,000 CDs. CD Warehouse operates in 24 states and the District of Columbia and internationally, with 15 stores in Canada, the U.K., Guatemala, Venezuela and Thailand. The firm's stores operate under the names CD Warehouse, Music Trader, Disc Go Round and CD Exchange and are generally located in strip shopping centers, generating the majority of their revenues from used CD sales. Customers can trade CDs or sell them for cash or store credit. Typically, each store carries the majority of Billboard Top 100 music hits, in addition to a selection of pre-owned CDs, which are purchased for $1 to $5 and remarketed for $6 to $9. Increasingly, CD Warehouse's stores are engaged in the buying, selling and trading of DVDs, as the company sees this as a huge growth market. Franchise managers are given the company's proprietary software that helps decide whether the customer's used CDs should be accepted or rejected. The software indicates how much money the CD is worth and how many units the store should have in its inventory. CD Warehouse is owned by Magnolia Entertainment, LLC.

All CD Warehouse franchisees attend a corporate training program and are provided with comprehensive information packets. Support staff, who assist in everything from site selection to equipment and inventory ordering, are also provided to franchisees if requested.

FINANCIALS: Sales and profits are in thousands of dollars—add 000 to get the full amount. 2006 Note: Financial information for 2006 was not available for all companies at press time.

2006 Sales: $	2006 Profits: $	**U.S. Stock Ticker: Subsidiary**	
2005 Sales: $	2005 Profits: $	**Int'l Ticker:** Int'l Exchange:	
2004 Sales: $	2004 Profits: $	Employees: 293	
2003 Sales: $	2003 Profits: $	Fiscal Year Ends: 12/31	
2002 Sales: $	2002 Profits: $	Parent Company: MAGNOLIA ENTERTAINMENT LLC	

SALARIES/BENEFITS:

Pension Plan:	ESOP Stock Plan:	Profit Sharing:	Top Exec. Salary: $200,000	Bonus: $25,000
Savings Plan: Y	Stock Purch. Plan:		Second Exec. Salary: $120,000	Bonus: $25,000

OTHER THOUGHTS:

Apparent Women Officers or Directors: 1
Hot Spot for Advancement for Women/Minorities:

LOCATIONS: ("Y" = Yes)

West:	Southwest:	Midwest:	Southeast:	Northeast:	International:
Y	Y	Y	Y	Y	Y

Note: Financial information, benefits and other data can change quickly and may vary from those stated here.

CEDAR FAIR LP   www.cedarfair.com

Industry Group Code: 713110 Ranks within this company's industry group: Sales: 3 Profits: 1

Print Media/Publishing:	Movies:	Equipment/Supplies:	Broadcast/Cable:	Music/Audio:	Sports/Games:
Newspapers:	Movie Theaters:	Equipment/Supplies:	Broadcast TV:	Music Production:	Games/Sports:
Magazines:	Movie Production:	Gambling Equipment:	Cable TV:	Retail Music:	Retail Games Stores:
Books:	TV/Video Production:	Special Services:	Satellite Broadcast:	Retail Audio Equip.:	Stadiums/Teams:
Book Stores:	Video Rental:	Advertising Services:	Radio:	Music Print./Dist.:	Gambling/Casinos: Y
Distribution/Printing:	Video Distribution:	Info. Sys. Software:	Online Information:	Multimedia:	Rides/Theme Parks:

TYPES OF BUSINESS:

Amusement Parks
Water Parks
Hotels

BRANDS/DIVISIONS/AFFILIATES:

Castaway Bay
Valleyfair
Dorney Park
Wildwater Kingdom
Worlds of Fun
Knott's Berry Farm
Michigan's Adventure
Paramount Parks

CONTACTS: *Note: Officers with more than one job title may be intentionally listed here more than once.*

Richard L. Kinzel, CEO
Jacob T. Falfas, COO
Richard L. Kinzel, Pres.
Peter J. Crage, CFO/VP-Finance
Craig J. Freeman, VP-Admin.
Gregory Picon, VP/Gen. Mgr.-West Coast Oper.
Robert A. Decker, VP-Planning & Design
Stacy Frole, Dir.-Investor Rel.
Peter J. Crage, VP-Finance
H. John Hildebrandt, VP/Gen. Mgr.-Cedar Point
H. Philip Bender, VP/Gen. Mgr.-Worlds of Fun & Oceans of Fun
Camille Jourden-Mark, VP/Gen. Mgr.-Michigan's Adventure
William G. Spehn, VP/Gen. Mgr.-Geauga Lake & Wildwater Kingdom
Richard L. Kinzel, Chmn.

Phone: 419-627-2233	Fax: 419-627-2260
Toll-Free:	
Address: One Cedar Point Dr., Sandusky, OH 44870-5259 US	

GROWTH PLANS/SPECIAL FEATURES:

Cedar Fair, L.P., and its affiliates own and operate seven amusement parks: Cedar Point, located on Lake Erie in Sandusky, Ohio; Knott's Berry Farm, located near Los Angeles, California; Dorney Park & Wildwater Kingdom, in South Whitehall Township, Pennsylvania; Valleyfair, in Shakopee, Minnesota; Worlds of Fun in Kansas City, Missouri; Geauga Lake & Wildwater Kingdom, in Aurora, Ohio; and Michigan's Adventure near Muskegon, Michigan. The company also owns and operates the Castaway Bay Indoor Waterpark Resort in Sandusky, Ohio, and five separate-gated outdoor water parks. Three of the outdoor water parks are located adjacent to Cedar Point, Knott's Berry Farm and Worlds of Fun, the fourth is located near San Diego, and the fifth is in Palm Springs, California. In addition to parks, Cedar Point owns and operates four hotel facilities. The park's only year-round hotel is Castaway Bay, an indoor water park resort, which is located at the Causeway entrance to the park. Castaway Bay features a tropical Caribbean theme with 237 hotel rooms centered around a 38,000-square-foot indoor water park. The resort offers a state-of-the-art arcade, various dining and merchandising facilities, and a TGI Friday's restaurant. The park's largest hotel, the Hotel Breakers, has more than 600 guest rooms, including 230 in the 10-story Breakers Tower. Breakers Tower has 18 tower suites with spectacular views, an indoor pool, and a TGI Friday's restaurant. Located near the Causeway entrance to the park is Breakers Express, a 350-room, limited-service seasonal hotel. Cedar Point also features the Suites Hotel, which features 187 suites, a courtyard pool, tennis courts and the Breakwater Cafe, a contemporary waterfront restaurant. In May 2006, Cedar Fair announced the acquisition of the Paramount Parks, a wholly owned subsidiary of CBS Corp., for a cash purchase of $1.24 billion.

FINANCIALS: Sales and profits are in thousands of dollars—add 000 to get the full amount. 2006 Note: Financial information for 2006 was not available for all companies at press time.

2006 Sales: $	2006 Profits: $	**U.S. Stock Ticker: FUN**
2005 Sales: $568,707	2005 Profits: $160,852	**Int'l Ticker:** Int'l Exchange:
2004 Sales: $541,972	2004 Profits: $78,315	Employees: 16,200
2003 Sales: $509,976	2003 Profits: $85,888	Fiscal Year Ends: 12/31
2002 Sales: $502,900	2002 Profits: $71,400	Parent Company:

SALARIES/BENEFITS:

Pension Plan: Y	ESOP Stock Plan:	Profit Sharing:	Top Exec. Salary: $930,000	Bonus: $465,000
Savings Plan:	Stock Purch. Plan:		Second Exec. Salary: $398,822	Bonus: $205,000

OTHER THOUGHTS:

Apparent Women Officers or Directors: 2
Hot Spot for Advancement for Women/Minorities:

LOCATIONS: ("Y" = Yes)

West:	Southwest:	Midwest:	Southeast:	Northeast:	International:
Y		Y		Y	

CENTRAL EUROPEAN MEDIA ENTERPRISES LTD www.cetv-net.com

Industry Group Code: 512110 Ranks within this company's industry group: Sales: 13 Profits: 5

Print Media/Publishing:	Movies:		Equipment/Supplies:	Broadcast/Cable:		Music/Audio:	Sports/Games:
Newspapers:	Movie Theaters:		Equipment/Supplies:	Broadcast TV:	Y	Music Production:	Games/Sports:
Magazines:	Movie Production:		Gambling Equipment:	Cable TV:		Retail Music:	Retail Games Stores:
Books:	TV/Video Production:	Y	Special Services:	Satellite Broadcast:		Retail Audio Equip.:	Stadiums/Teams:
Book Stores:	Video Rental:		Advertising Services:	Radio:		Music Print./Dist.:	Gambling/Casinos:
Distribution/Printing:	Video Distribution:		Info. Sys. Software:	Online Information:		Multimedia:	Rides/Theme Parks:

TYPES OF BUSINESS:

Television Broadcasting
Television Production

BRANDS/DIVISIONS/AFFILIATES:

Apax Partners
TV Markiza
Pro TV
Acasa
TV Nova
Pop TV
Galaxie Sport
Studio 1+1

CONTACTS: *Note: Officers with more than one job title may be intentionally listed here more than once.*

Michael N. Garin, CEO
Wallace MacMillan, CFO
Daniel Penn, General Counsel
Romana Tomasova, Dir.-Corp. Comm.
Mark Wyllie, VP-Finance
Marina Williams, Exec. VP
Adrian Sarbu, General Dir.-Pro TV & Acasa
Marijan Jurenec, Regional Dir.
Ronald S. Lauder, Chmn.

Phone: 441-296-1431	Fax:
Toll-Free:	
Address: P.O. Box HM66, Clarendon House 2, Church St., Hamilton, Bermuda	

GROWTH PLANS/SPECIAL FEATURES:

Central European Media Enterprises, Ltd. (CEME) is an international television broadcasting company with administrative offices in Bermuda, the Netherlands and the U.K. and operations in Croatia, the Czech Republic, Slovakia, Romania, Slovenia and Ukraine. Founded on the idea that the newly democratized nations of the former Soviet Bloc could support independent television broadcasting, CEME began operating in 1994 and quickly grew into a large and successful enterprise. The group invests in, develops and operates a collection of national and regional commercial television stations and networks across Central and Eastern Europe, reaching about 91 million viewers. Operating 14 stations in six countries with market leadership in each of them, the company annually produces thousands of hours of original programming to support its broadcasting operations. Most of the stations affiliated with CEME air a variety of programs designed to appeal to a wide audience, including sporting events, news shows, game shows and locally produced programs. Advertising is the primary source of revenue for these stations, with Procter & Gamble, Wrigley, Unilever and Coca-Cola among the largest advertisers. CEME has a number of exclusive broadcast rights granted by American and Western European corporations to air foreign news programs and popular films from abroad. In 2006, Apax Partners purchased a 49.7% stake in the company for approximately $190 million, following CEME's acquisition of TV Markiza, a television broadcaster in the Slovak Republic, earlier in the year.

FINANCIALS: Sales and profits are in thousands of dollars—add 000 to get the full amount. 2006 Note: Financial information for 2006 was not available for all companies at press time.

2006 Sales: $	2006 Profits: $	U.S. Stock Ticker: CETV
2005 Sales: $400,978	2005 Profits: $42,495	Int'l Ticker: CETV Int'l Exchange: Prague-PX
2004 Sales: $182,339	2004 Profits: $18,531	Employees: 2,800
2003 Sales: $118,526	2003 Profits: $346,012	Fiscal Year Ends: 12/31
2002 Sales: $92,602	2002 Profits: $13,409	Parent Company:

SALARIES/BENEFITS:

Pension Plan:	ESOP Stock Plan: Y	Profit Sharing:	Top Exec. Salary: $625,000	Bonus: $950,000
Savings Plan:	Stock Purch. Plan:		Second Exec. Salary: $364,933	Bonus: $167,674

OTHER THOUGHTS:

Apparent Women Officers or Directors: 2
Hot Spot for Advancement for Women/Minorities: Y

LOCATIONS: ("Y" = Yes)

West:	Southwest:	Midwest:	Southeast:	Northeast:	International: Y

Note: Financial information, benefits and other data can change quickly and may vary from those stated here.

CENTURY CASINOS INC　　　　　www.cnty.com

Industry Group Code: 713210 Ranks within this company's industry group: Sales: 9　Profits: 6

Print Media/Publishing:	Movies:	Equipment/Supplies:	Broadcast/Cable:	Music/Audio:	Sports/Games:	
Newspapers:	Movie Theaters:	Equipment/Supplies:	Broadcast TV:	Music Production:	Games/Sports:	
Magazines:	Movie Production:	Gambling Equipment:	Cable TV:	Retail Music:	Retail Games Stores:	
Books:	TV/Video Production:	Special Services:	Satellite Broadcast:	Retail Audio Equip.:	Stadiums/Teams:	
Book Stores:	Video Rental:	Advertising Services:	Radio:	Music Print./Dist.:	Gambling/Casinos:	Y
Distribution/Printing:	Video Distribution:	Info. Sys. Software:	Online Information:	Multimedia:	Rides/Theme Parks:	

TYPES OF BUSINESS:

Casinos
Cruise Ship Casinos
Hotels & Restaurants

BRANDS/DIVISIONS/AFFILIATES:

Womacks/Legends Casino
Century Casinos Management
Silverstar Development
Century Casino & Hotel
Millenium Casino
Century Casinos Africa (Pty) Limited
Caledon Casino, Hotel & Spa
G5 Sp. z o.o.

CONTACTS: Note: Officers with more than one job title may be intentionally listed here more than once.

Erwin Haitzmann, Co-CEO
Christian Gernert, COO
Peter Hoetzinger, Pres./Co-CEO
Andreas Terler, CIO
Niclas Schmiedmaier, Senior Legal Counsel
Ray Sienko, Chief Acct. Officer
Larry J. Hannapel, Corp. Sec.
Erwin Haitzmann, Chmn.

Phone: 719-527-8300	**Fax:** 719-527-8301
Toll-Free:	
Address: 1263 Lake Plaza Dr., Ste. A, Colorado Springs, CO 80906 US	

GROWTH PLANS/SPECIAL FEATURES:

Century Casinos, Inc. is an international casino entertainment company that operates more than 100 casinos in 20 different countries. The company's major projects include the Womacks Casino and Hotel in Cripple Creek, Colorado; and the Casino Millennium in the Marriott Hotel in Prague, Czech Republic. Century also operates casinos aboard the Silver Wind, Silver Cloud and World of ResidenSea cruise ships, and aboard three of the vessels of Oceania Cruises. The company owns a 65% interest in, and has a management contract for, the Century Casino & Hotel in Central City, Colorado and has begun construction on a casino and hotel development in Edmonton, Alberta. Through its subsidiary Century Casinos Africa (Pty) Limited, Century owns and operates The Caledon Hotel, Spa & Casino near Cape Town, South Africa and owns 60% of, and provides technical casino services to, Century Casino Newcastle located in Newcastle, South Africa. The company continues to pursue other international projects in various stages of development. In recent news, the company entered into an agreement to acquire 100% of the issued and outstanding shares of Polish gaming firm G5 Sp. z o.o. for approximately $3.7 million.

FINANCIALS: Sales and profits are in thousands of dollars—add 000 to get the full amount. 2006 Note: Financial information for 2006 was not available for all companies at press time.

2006 Sales: $	2006 Profits: $	**U.S. Stock Ticker:** CNTY
2005 Sales: $37,445	2005 Profits: $4,481	**Int'l Ticker:**　Int'l Exchange:
2004 Sales: $35,765	2004 Profits: $4,738	Employees:　517
2003 Sales: $31,430	2003 Profits: $3,246	Fiscal Year Ends: 12/31
2002 Sales: $29,300	2002 Profits: $3,100	Parent Company:

SALARIES/BENEFITS:

Pension Plan:	ESOP Stock Plan:	Profit Sharing:	Top Exec. Salary: $303,866	Bonus: $236,149
Savings Plan: Y	Stock Purch. Plan:		Second Exec. Salary: $303,866	Bonus: $236,149

OTHER THOUGHTS:

Apparent Women Officers or Directors:
Hot Spot for Advancement for Women/Minorities:

LOCATIONS: ("Y" = Yes)

West:	Southwest:	Midwest:	Southeast:	Northeast:	International:
Y					Y

CHARTER COMMUNICATIONS

www.charter.com

Industry Group Code: 513220 Ranks within this company's industry group: Sales: 9   Profits: 22

Print Media/Publishing:	Movies:	Equipment/Supplies:		Broadcast/Cable:		Music/Audio:	Sports/Games:
Newspapers:	Movie Theaters:	Equipment/Supplies:		Broadcast TV:		Music Production:	Games/Sports:
Magazines:	Movie Production:	Gambling Equipment:	Y	Cable TV:	Y	Retail Music:	Retail Games Stores:
Books:	TV/Video Production:	Special Services:	Y	Satellite Broadcast:		Retail Audio Equip.:	Stadiums/Teams:
Book Stores:	Video Rental:	Advertising Services:		Radio:		Music Print./Dist.:	Gambling/Casinos:
Distribution/Printing:	Video Distribution:	Info. Sys. Software:		Online Information:		Multimedia:	Rides/Theme Parks:

TYPES OF BUSINESS:

Cable TV Service
Internet Access
Video-on-Demand
VOIP

BRANDS/DIVISIONS/AFFILIATES:

Charter Digital
Charter High-Speed Internet
Charter Cable TV
Charter DVR
Charter HDTV
Charter iTV
Charter OnDemand
Charter Latino Digital

CONTACTS: Note: Officers with more than one job title may be intentionally listed here more than once.

Neil Smit, CEO
Michael J. Lovett, Exec. VP/COO
Neil Smit, Pres.
Jeffrey T. Fisher, Exec. VP/CFO
Robert A. Quigley, Exec. VP/Chief Mktg. Officer
Lynne F. Ramsey, Sr. VP-Human Resources
Edward Machek, CIO/Sr. VP
Wayne H. Davis, Exec. VP/CTO
Grier C. Raclin, Exec. VP/General Counsel
Sue Ann R. Hamilton, Exec. VP-Programming
Grier C. Raclin, Corporate Secretary
Eric P. Brown, Sr. VP-Western Div. Oper.
Joshua L. Jamison, Sr. VP-Northeast Div. Oper.
Paul G. Allen, Chmn.

Phone: 314-965-0555	Fax: 314-965-9745

Toll-Free: 888-213-0965

Address: 12405 Powerscourt Dr., Ste. 100, St. Louis, MO 63131-3660 US

GROWTH PLANS/SPECIAL FEATURES:

Charter Communications Inc. is a broadband communications company that services approximately 6.16 million customers. The firm operates a broadband network consisting of coaxial and fiber optic cable, through which it offers traditional cable video programming (both analog and digital), high-speed Internet access, advanced broadband cable services such as video on demand, high definition television service and telephone service. Charter has approximately 5.88 million analog video customers, of which approximately 2.8 million are also digital video customers; further, the company services approximately 2.2 million high-speed Internet customers, of which approximately 253,400 receive only high-speed Internet services. Its traditional cable service package, Charter Cable TV, includes 70 standard channels. Charter Digital's advanced broadband services include Charter DVR (digital video recording), Charter HDTV (high-definition TV), Charter iTV (interactive television), Charter OnDemand, pay-per-view and a sports package. The company also provides business-to-business video, data and IP solutions through Charter Business, while advertising sales and production services are sold under the Charter Media brand. In addition, the Charter Telephone service provides telephone service via VOIP over the firm's broadband network. Charter's principal shareholder is billionaire Paul G. Allen, who is also a co-founder of Microsoft Corporation. In June 2005, Charter reached an agreement with GolTV to carry the full-time soccer network on both its Charter Latino Digital package and on the Digital Sports tier.

Employees of Charter receive cable services for free. The company also supports several charitable organizations and often takes part in functions for the YMCA, centers for the arts and the United Way.

FINANCIALS: Sales and profits are in thousands of dollars—add 000 to get the full amount. 2006 Note: Financial information for 2006 was not available for all companies at press time.

2006 Sales: $	2006 Profits: $	U.S. Stock Ticker: CHTR
2005 Sales: $5,254,000	2005 Profits: $-967,000	Int'l Ticker: Int'l Exchange:
2004 Sales: $4,977,000	2004 Profits: $-4,341,000	Employees: 17,200
2003 Sales: $4,819,000	2003 Profits: $-238,000	Fiscal Year Ends: 12/31
2002 Sales: $4,566,000	2002 Profits: $-2,514,000	Parent Company:

SALARIES/BENEFITS:

Pension Plan:	ESOP Stock Plan:	Profit Sharing:	Top Exec. Salary: $516,153	Bonus: $1,200,000
Savings Plan: Y	Stock Purch. Plan:		Second Exec. Salary: $415,385	Bonus: $838,900

OTHER THOUGHTS:

Apparent Women Officers or Directors: 3
Hot Spot for Advancement for Women/Minorities: Y

LOCATIONS: ("Y" = Yes)

West:	Southwest:	Midwest:	Southeast:	Northeast:	International:
Y	Y	Y	Y	Y	

CHURCHILL DOWNS INC
www.churchilldownsincorporated.com
Industry Group Code: 713210 Ranks within this company's industry group: Sales: 5   Profits: 2

Print Media/Publishing:	Movies:	Equipment/Supplies:		Broadcast/Cable:	Music/Audio:	Sports/Games:	
Newspapers:	Movie Theaters:	Equipment/Supplies:		Broadcast TV:	Music Production:	Games/Sports:	Y
Magazines:	Movie Production:	Gambling Equipment:		Cable TV:	Retail Music:	Retail Games Stores:	
Books:	TV/Video Production:	Special Services:	Y	Satellite Broadcast:	Retail Audio Equip.:	Stadiums/Teams:	Y
Book Stores:	Video Rental:	Advertising Services:		Radio:	Music Print./Dist.:	Gambling/Casinos:	Y
Distribution/Printing:	Video Distribution:	Info. Sys. Software:	Y	Online Information:	Multimedia:	Rides/Theme Parks:	

TYPES OF BUSINESS:
Horse Racing
Pari-Mutual Wagering
Simulcasting
Video Poker
Computer Graphics & Gambling Software
Online Retail

BRANDS/DIVISIONS/AFFILIATES:
Churchill Downs Management Company
Arlington Park Racecourse, LLC
Churchill Downs Investment Company
Calder Race Course
Fair Grounds Race Course
Hoosier Park, LP
Video Services, Inc.
Churchill Downs Simulcast Productions

CONTACTS:
Note: Officers with more than one job title may be intentionally listed here more than once.
Robert L. Evans, CEO
Robert L. Evans, Pres.
Michael E. Miller, CFO/Chief Acc. Officer/Exec. VP
Tim Scott, Sr. VP-Sales & Mktg.
Chuck Kenyon, VP-Human Resources
Atique R. Shah, VP-Cust. Rel. Mgmt. &Tech. Solutions
William C. Carstanjen, General Counsel/Exec. VP
William C. Carstanjen, Chief Dev. Officer
Alexander M. Waldrop, Sr. VP-Public Affairs
Michael W. Anderson, Treas./VP-Corp. Finance
Rebecca C. Reed, Sr. VP/General Counsel/Corp. Sec.
Steven Sexton, Pres., Churchill Downs Racetrack
C. Kenneth Dunn, Pres., Calder Race Course, Inc./Sr. VP
Clifford C. Goodrich, Pres., Arlington Park Racecourse, LLC
Carl F. Pollard, Chmn.

Phone: 502-636-4400	Fax: 502-636-4430
Toll-Free:	
Address: 700 Central Ave., Louisville, KY 40208 US	

GROWTH PLANS/SPECIAL FEATURES:
Churchill Downs, Inc. (CDI) is principally a racing company that conducts pari-mutuel wagering on live Thoroughbred, Quarter Horse and Standard bred horse racing and simulcasts signals of races. Additionally, they offer racing services and video poker operations. All operations are managed by Churchill Downs Management Company. CDI owns five racing tracks: Churchill Downs, Arlington Park, Calder Race Course, Fair Grounds Race Course and Hoosier Park. Additionally, the company operates off-track betting facilities. Churchill Downs Management Company manages the firm's racing operations and Video Services, Inc., a video poker machine operator associated with Fair Grounds in Louisiana. The company also owns Churchill Downs Investment Company and has a 100% interest in Churchill Downs Simulcast Productions which provides computer graphics software for the display of betting statistics and other racing related information to the racing industry. In addition to traditional racing and betting, the company conducts simulcast wagering on horse racing year-round through the Churchill Downs Simulcast Network to both proprietary and external betting facilities. Sources of income include gambling, admissions and seating, concession commissions and license, rights, broadcast and sponsorship fees and the sale of Kentucky Derby merchandise through its web site. In addition, the firm has a 50% interest in Kentucky Off-Track Betting, Inc., an alliance between Churchill Downs, Ellis Park Race Course and Kentucky's other thoroughbred racetracks, which operates off-track betting facilities in the Kentucky cities of Maysville, Jamestown, Pineville and Corbin. In 2006, CDI began developing a six to eight person technology team located in Silicon Valley. In late 2006, CDI completed the sale of the Ellis Park racetrack in Henderson, Kentucky.

FINANCIALS:
Sales and profits are in thousands of dollars—add 000 to get the full amount. 2006 Note: Financial information for 2006 was not available for all companies at press time.

2006 Sales: $	2006 Profits: $	U.S. Stock Ticker: CHDN
2005 Sales: $408,801	2005 Profits: $78,908	Int'l Ticker: Int'l Exchange:
2004 Sales: $361,187	2004 Profits: $8,915	Employees: 2,550
2003 Sales: $348,505	2003 Profits: $23,379	Fiscal Year Ends: 12/31
2002 Sales: $439,200	2002 Profits: $21,000	Parent Company:

SALARIES/BENEFITS:
Pension Plan: Y	ESOP Stock Plan:	Profit Sharing: Y	Top Exec. Salary: $499,021	Bonus: $240,914
Savings Plan:	Stock Purch. Plan: Y		Second Exec. Salary: $277,836	Bonus: $68,319

OTHER THOUGHTS:
Apparent Women Officers or Directors: 4
Hot Spot for Advancement for Women/Minorities: Y

LOCATIONS: ("Y" = Yes)
West:	Southwest:	Midwest:	Southeast:	Northeast:	International:
		Y	Y		

CINEMARK INC

www.cinemark.com

Industry Group Code: 512131 Ranks within this company's industry group: Sales: 3 Profits: 2

Print Media/Publishing:	Movies:		Equipment/Supplies:	Broadcast/Cable:	Music/Audio:	Sports/Games:
Newspapers:	Movie Theaters:	Y	Equipment/Supplies:	Broadcast TV:	Music Production:	Games/Sports:
Magazines:	Movie Production:		Gambling Equipment:	Cable TV:	Retail Music:	Retail Games Stores:
Books:	TV/Video Production:		Special Services:	Satellite Broadcast:	Retail Audio Equip.:	Stadiums/Teams:
Book Stores:	Video Rental:		Advertising Services:	Radio:	Music Print./Dist.:	Gambling/Casinos:
Distribution/Printing:	Video Distribution:		Info. Sys. Software:	Online Information:	Multimedia:	Rides/Theme Parks:

TYPES OF BUSINESS:

Movie Theaters

BRANDS/DIVISIONS/AFFILIATES:

Cinemark Holdings, Inc.
Cinemark USA, Inc.
Cinemark Properties, Inc.
CNMK Investments, Inc.
Cinemark Investments Corporation
Brasil Holdings, LLC
Cinemark Mexico (USA), Inc.
Century Theaters, Inc.

CONTACTS: Note: Officers with more than one job title may be intentionally listed here more than once.

Alan Stock, CEO
Tim Warner, COO
Tim Warner, Pres.
Robert Copple, CFO
Terrell Falk, VP-Mktg.
Michael D. Cavalier, General Counsel/Sr. VP
Terrell Falk, VP-Comm.
Robert Copple, Chief Acct. Officer/Treas.
Alan W. Stock, Pres., Cinemark USA, Inc.
Lee Roy Mitchell, Chmn.
Valmir Fernandes, Pres., Cinemark Int'l

Phone: 972-665-1000	Fax: 972-665-1004

Toll-Free: 800-246-3627

Address: 3900 Dallas Parkway,Ste. 500, Plano, TX 75093-7865 US

GROWTH PLANS/SPECIAL FEATURES:

Cinemark, Inc., a subsidiary of newly formed Cinemark Holdings, Inc., is a multinational theater corporation that conducts all of its business through Cinemark USA, Inc. and its subsidiaries. The company operates over 395 theatres and over 4,479 screens in 37 states in the U.S. and internationally in 13 countries, primarily in Mexico and South and Central America. Cinemark International, a subsidiary, operates over 956 screens. Most of the company's domestic theaters are first run, while roughly 40 operate as discount theaters. The company's largest market in terms of revenue after the U.S. is Brazil, with Mexico a close second. It also has operations in Argentina, Chile, Ecuador, Peru, Honduras, El Salvador, Costa Rica, Panama, Columbia and Nicaragua. Each region has its own management office. Cinemark opened ten new domestic theaters with 121 screens and acquired one theatre with 12 screens in the first nine months of 2006. In October 2006, the company acquired Century Theaters, Inc., a national theater chain with 77 theaters in 12 states for approximately $681 million and assumption of $360 million in debt. Approximately $150 million of the purchase price was issued as stock in Cinemark Holdings, Inc. NationalCineMedia, which Cinemark jointly holds with Regal Crown Entertainment Group and AMC Entertainment, Inc., filed for a proposed IPO in late 2006. NationalCineMedia is focused on marketing, sale and distribution of cinema advertising and promotional products; it is one of the world's largest digital distribution networks.

FINANCIALS: Sales and profits are in thousands of dollars—add 000 to get the full amount. 2006 Note: Financial information for 2006 was not available for all companies at press time.

2006 Sales: $	2006 Profits: $	U.S. Stock Ticker: Subsidiary
2005 Sales: $1,020,600	2005 Profits: $22,400	Int'l Ticker: Int'l Exchange:
2004 Sales: $	2004 Profits: $	Employees: 8,100
2003 Sales: $	2003 Profits: $	Fiscal Year Ends: 12/31
2002 Sales: $	2002 Profits: $	Parent Company: CINEMARK HOLDINGS INC

SALARIES/BENEFITS:

Pension Plan:	ESOP Stock Plan:	Profit Sharing:	Top Exec. Salary: $	Bonus: $
Savings Plan: Y	Stock Purch. Plan:		Second Exec. Salary: $	Bonus: $

OTHER THOUGHTS:

Apparent Women Officers or Directors:
Hot Spot for Advancement for Women/Minorities:

LOCATIONS: ("Y" = Yes)

West:	Southwest:	Midwest:	Southeast:	Northeast:	International:
Y	Y	Y	Y	Y	Y

Note: Financial information, benefits and other data can change quickly and may vary from those stated here.

CINEMASTAR LUXURY THEATERS INC www.cinemastar.com

Industry Group Code: 512131 Ranks within this company's industry group: Sales: Profits:

Print Media/Publishing:	Movies:		Equipment/Supplies:	Broadcast/Cable:	Music/Audio:	Sports/Games:
Newspapers:	Movie Theaters:	Y	Equipment/Supplies:	Broadcast TV:	Music Production:	Games/Sports:
Magazines:	Movie Production:		Gambling Equipment:	Cable TV:	Retail Music:	Retail Games Stores:
Books:	TV/Video Production:		Special Services:	Satellite Broadcast:	Retail Audio Equip.:	Stadiums/Teams:
Book Stores:	Video Rental:		Advertising Services:	Radio:	Music Print./Dist.:	Gambling/Casinos:
Distribution/Printing:	Video Distribution:		Info. Sys. Software:	Online Information:	Multimedia:	Rides/Theme Parks:

TYPES OF BUSINESS:
Movie Theaters

BRANDS/DIVISIONS/AFFILIATES:
CinemaStar Luxury Theaters, S.A. de C.V.
SCP Private Equity Partners, LP
Reel Rewards

CONTACTS: *Note: Officers with more than one job title may be intentionally listed here more than once.*
Jack R. Crosby, CEO
Kim Zolna, COO
Kim Zolna, Pres.
John Becker, CFO
Dan Cahill, Group Movie Ticket Sales
Wayne Weisman, Chmn.
John D. Prock, Pres., CinemaStar Luxury Theaters S.A. de C.V.

Phone: 760-945-2500   **Fax:** 760-945-2510
Toll-Free:
Address: 1949 Avenida Del Oro, Ste. 100, Oceanside, CA 92056 US

GROWTH PLANS/SPECIAL FEATURES:
CinemaStar Luxury Theaters, Inc. develops, leases and operates multi-screen, first-run movie theater locations in southern California and northern Mexico. The company currently operates 40 screens in four theater complexes in San Bernardino, Oceanside, Riverside and Perris, California. It also operates in Mexico as CinemaStar Luxury Theaters S.A. de C.V., with a total of 41 screens in Tijuana, Ensenada and Ciudad Obregon. The company's theater complexes typically contain multiple auditoriums, each having 120 to 500 seats, allowing the company flexibility to adjust screening schedules by shifting films among the larger and smaller auditoriums within the same complex in response to audience demand. All theaters feature digital THX sound systems, top-quality projection and screen systems, high-quality seats and premium concession selections. CinemaStar emphasizes a high standard of customer service and experience. Promotional offerings include discounted group tickets, gift certificates and the Reel Rewards program, which awards repeat customers with free popcorn and movie tickets. The firm operates a Spanish-language web site dedicated to its Mexican theaters at cinemaster.net. The majority of the firm is owned by SCP Private Equity Partners.

FINANCIALS: Sales and profits are in thousands of dollars—add 000 to get the full amount. 2006 Note: Financial information for 2006 was not available for all companies at press time.

2006 Sales: $	2006 Profits: $	U.S. Stock Ticker: Private
2005 Sales: $	2005 Profits: $	Int'l Ticker: Int'l Exchange:
2004 Sales: $	2004 Profits: $	Employees: 400
2003 Sales: $	2003 Profits: $	Fiscal Year Ends: 3/31
2002 Sales: $24,000	2002 Profits: $	Parent Company:

SALARIES/BENEFITS:
Pension Plan:	ESOP Stock Plan:	Profit Sharing:	Top Exec. Salary: $254,806	Bonus: $20,000
Savings Plan:	Stock Purch. Plan:		Second Exec. Salary: $161,538	Bonus: $

OTHER THOUGHTS:
Apparent Women Officers or Directors: 1
Hot Spot for Advancement for Women/Minorities:

LOCATIONS: ("Y" = Yes)
West:	Southwest:	Midwest:	Southeast:	Northeast:	International:
Y					Y

Note: Financial information, benefits and other data can change quickly and may vary from those stated here.

CIRCUIT CITY STORES INC
www.circuitcity.com

Industry Group Code: 443110 Ranks within this company's industry group: Sales: 2   Profits: 3

Print Media/Publishing:	Movies:	Equipment/Supplies:		Broadcast/Cable:	Music/Audio:		Sports/Games:
Newspapers:	Movie Theaters:	Equipment/Supplies:		Broadcast TV:	Music Production:		Games/Sports:
Magazines:	Movie Production:	Gambling Equipment:		Cable TV:	Retail Music:		Retail Games Stores:
Books:	TV/Video Production:	Special Services:		Satellite Broadcast:	Retail Audio Equip.:	Y	Stadiums/Teams:
Book Stores:	Video Rental:	Advertising Services:		Radio:	Music Print./Dist.:		Gambling/Casinos:
Distribution/Printing:	Video Distribution:	Info. Sys. Software:	Y	Online Information:	Multimedia:		Rides/Theme Parks:

TYPES OF BUSINESS:

Consumer Electronics Stores
Computers & Accessories
Home Office Products
Entertainment Software
Online Sales
Technical Services

BRANDS/DIVISIONS/AFFILIATES:

Circuit City Superstores
Circuit City Express
The Source By Circuit City
Circuit City Direct
Battery Plus
InterTAN, Inc.
Rogers Plus
firedog

CONTACTS: *Note: Officers with more than one job title may be intentionally listed here more than once.*

Phillip J. Schoonover, CEO
Phillip J. Schoonover, Pres.
Michael E. Foss, Exec. VP/CFO
Eric A. Jonas, Jr., Sr. VP-Human Resources
Michael L. Jones, Sr. VP/CIO
Philip J. Dunn, Controller
Douglas T. Moore, Exec. VP/Chief Merch. Officer
Marshall J. Whaling, Sr. VP-Retail Oper.
Reginald D. Hedgebeth, Sr. VP/General Counsel/Corp. Sec.
Philip J. Dunn, Sr. VP/Treas.
Marc J. Sieger, Sr. VP/General Merch. Mgr.
John J. Kelly, Sr. VP-General Merch. Mgr.-Tech.
Peter C. Weedfald, Sr. VP/General Merch. Mgr.
Steven P. Pappas, Sr. VP/Pres., Small Stores
W. Alan McCollough, Chmn.
Ronald G. Cuthbertson, Sr. VP-Supply Chain & Inventory Mgmt.

Phone: 804-527-4000	Fax: 804-527-4164
Toll-Free: 800-843-2489	
Address: 9950 Mayland Dr., Richmond, VA 23233-1464 US	

GROWTH PLANS/SPECIAL FEATURES:

Circuit City Stores, Inc. is on of the nation's largest retailers of consumer electronics, selling personal computers, home office products and entertainment software from 632 Superstores and five other locations in 158 U.S. markets. The company has more than 950 retail stores and dealer outlets in Canada through InterTAN, Inc. These stores consist of 540 small company-owned stores located in malls and shopping centers, mostly called The Source by Circuit City; 300 dealer outlets operating under their own names; 93 Rogers Plus stores, primarily wireless service retailers; and 21 Battery Plus stores, which sell batteries and other consumer electronics. InterTAN's stores were formerly licensed under the Radio Shack name, but this has been discontinued due to litigation. Retail operations in the U.S. consist of Circuit City Superstores and mall-based Circuit City Express stores. Circuit City distinguishes its stores from the competition by offering a broad merchandise selection along with excellent customer service. For each major product category, the company balances mid-priced items with high-end technology products that carry higher prices. The firm's web site, circuitcity.com, provides shoppers with extensive product information, direct shipment of purchases, real-time inventory status of products in stores and the ability to order online and pick up at a store. The company maintains a partnership with Amazon that increases selection and convenience for Amazon's consumer electronics shoppers. Circuit City recently introduced firedog, a technical support service brand under which the company will have vehicles, uniformed personnel and remote technical assistance through firedog.com and over a toll-free phone line.

The company offers its employees a comprehensive benefits package including educational scholarships, a gift matching program, credit union membership, an employee assistance program, discounts on merchandise and a 401(k) savings plan.

FINANCIALS: Sales and profits are in thousands of dollars—add 000 to get the full amount. 2006 Note: Financial information for 2006 was not available for all companies at press time.

2006 Sales: $11,598,000	2006 Profits: $139,746	U.S. Stock Ticker: CC
2005 Sales: $10,472,364	2005 Profits: $61,658	Int'l Ticker: Int'l Exchange:
2004 Sales: $9,745,400	2004 Profits: $-89,300	Employees: 46,007
2003 Sales: $9,953,500	2003 Profits: $106,100	Fiscal Year Ends: 2/28
2002 Sales: $12,792,000	2002 Profits: $219,000	Parent Company:

SALARIES/BENEFITS:

Pension Plan:	ESOP Stock Plan:	Profit Sharing:	Top Exec. Salary: $975,000	Bonus: $1,053,000
Savings Plan: Y	Stock Purch. Plan: Y		Second Exec. Salary: $716,346	Bonus: $704,700

OTHER THOUGHTS:

Apparent Women Officers or Directors: 4
Hot Spot for Advancement for Women/Minorities: Y

LOCATIONS: ("Y" = Yes)

West:	Southwest:	Midwest:	Southeast:	Northeast:	International:
Y	Y	Y	Y	Y	Y

Note: Financial information, benefits and other data can change quickly and may vary from those stated here.

CIRQUE DU SOLEIL INC   www.cirquedusoleil.com

Industry Group Code: 512110 Ranks within this company's industry group: Sales: Profits:

Print Media/Publishing:	Movies:	Equipment/Supplies:	Broadcast/Cable:	Music/Audio:	Sports/Games:	
Newspapers:	Movie Theaters:	Equipment/Supplies:	Broadcast TV:	Music Production:	Games/Sports:	
Magazines:	Movie Production:	Gambling Equipment:	Cable TV:	Retail Music:	Retail Games Stores:	
Books:	TV/Video Production:	Special Services:	Satellite Broadcast:	Retail Audio Equip.:	Stadiums/Teams:	
Book Stores:	Video Rental:	Advertising Services:	Radio:	Music Print./Dist.:	Gambling/Casinos:	
Distribution/Printing:	Video Distribution:	Info. Sys. Software:	Online Information:	Multimedia:	Rides/Theme Parks:	Y

TYPES OF BUSINESS:

Theatrical Entertainment
Hotels & Restaurants
Merchandising

BRANDS/DIVISIONS/AFFILIATES:

La Nouba
O
Mystere
Zumanity
Ka
LOVE
Club Cirque
Varekai

CONTACTS: *Note: Officers with more than one job title may be intentionally listed here more than once.*

Guy Laliberte, CEO
Daniel Lamarre, Pres.
Robert Blain, Sr. VP/CFO
Marc Gagnon, Exec. VP-Bus. Dev. & Services

Phone: 514-722-2324	Fax: 514-722-3692
Toll-Free: 800-678-2119	
Address: 8400 2nd Ave., Montreal, QC H1Z 4M6 Canada	

GROWTH PLANS/SPECIAL FEATURES:

Cirque du Soleil, Inc., French for Circus of the Sun, is a circus production company that blends street entertainment, exotic costumes and cabaret. The firm has preformed for more than 50 million spectators in more than 100 cities on four continents. In 2006, Cirque had 13 shows touring around the world. The company has six permanent productions including: La Nouba in Walt Disney World; O, an aquatic show at the Bellagio; Mystere at Treasure Island; Zumanity, an adult-focused show at New York-New York; Ka, at the MGM Grand hotel in Las Vegas; and Cirque's newest show, LOVE, a Beatles tribute show presented in a custom theater at the Mirage Hotel. The troupe's touring shows include Saltimbanco, Quidam, Corteo, Alegria, Dralion and Varekai. The MGM Grand recently built an elaborate $135-million theater for Ka and has now added LOVE at a cost of $140 million. The two firms split the shows' profits. Cirque sells merchandise including music, DVDs, books, apparel, collectables and souvenirs, through the company's web site and at shows. The company also plans to enter into hotels and restaurants, with a nightclub called Club Cirque and a Cirque Resort in Las Vegas currently in development. In January 2007, Cirque du Soleil opened its show Quidam in Dubai, United Arab Emirates. The company has announced that beginning in November 2007, it will present a new ten-week holiday show at the Theater at Madison Square Garden. The show is contracted with Cablevision Systems Corp. for a minimum of four years. Cirque is in the planning stages of a new permanent Elvis-themed show in Las Vegas. It's expected to open at the MGM Mirage CityCenter in November 2009.

Cirque du Soleil helps young people in difficult situations by allocating 1% of revenues each year to outreach programs.

FINANCIALS: Sales and profits are in thousands of dollars—add 000 to get the full amount. 2006 Note: Financial information for 2006 was not available for all companies at press time.

2006 Sales: $	2006 Profits: $	U.S. Stock Ticker: Private
2005 Sales: $	2005 Profits: $	Int'l Ticker: Int'l Exchange:
2004 Sales: $700,000	2004 Profits: $	Employees: 2,400
2003 Sales: $600,000	2003 Profits: $	Fiscal Year Ends: 12/31
2002 Sales: $	2002 Profits: $	Parent Company:

SALARIES/BENEFITS:

Pension Plan:	ESOP Stock Plan:	Profit Sharing:	Top Exec. Salary: $	Bonus: $
Savings Plan:	Stock Purch. Plan:		Second Exec. Salary: $	Bonus: $

OTHER THOUGHTS:

Apparent Women Officers or Directors:
Hot Spot for Advancement for Women/Minorities:

LOCATIONS: ("Y" = Yes)

West:	Southwest:	Midwest:	Southeast:	Northeast:	International:
Y				Y	Y

CITADEL BROADCASTING CORP
www.citadelcommunications.com

Industry Group Code: 513111 Ranks within this company's industry group: Sales: 7 Profits: 3

Print Media/Publishing:	Movies:	Equipment/Supplies:	Broadcast/Cable:	Music/Audio:	Sports/Games:
Newspapers:	Movie Theaters:	Equipment/Supplies:	Broadcast TV:	Music Production:	Games/Sports:
Magazines:	Movie Production:	Gambling Equipment:	Cable TV:	Retail Music:	Retail Games Stores:
Books:	TV/Video Production:	Special Services:	Satellite Broadcast:	Retail Audio Equip.:	Stadiums/Teams:
Book Stores:	Video Rental:	Advertising Services:	Radio:	Music Print./Dist.:	Gambling/Casinos:
Distribution/Printing:	Video Distribution:	Info. Sys. Software:	Online Information:	Multimedia:	Rides/Theme Parks:

TYPES OF BUSINESS:
Radio Station Owner/Operator

BRANDS/DIVISIONS/AFFILIATES:
Forstmann, Little and Co.
Citadel License, Inc.
Citadel Broadcasting Company
FLCC Holdings, Inc.

CONTACTS:
Note: Officers with more than one job title may be intentionally listed here more than once.
Farid Suleman, CEO
Judy Ellis, COO
Robert Freedline, CFO
Matt Hanlon, Regional Pres.
Wayne Leland, Regional VP
Farid Suleman, Chmn.

Phone: 702-804-5200	Fax: 702-804-5936

Toll-Free:

Address: 7201 W. Lake Mead Blvd., Ste. 400, Las Vegas, NV 89128 US

GROWTH PLANS/SPECIAL FEATURES:
Citadel Broadcasting Corp. acquires, develops and operates radio stations in mid-sized markets across the U.S. The company currently owns and operates 155 FM and 58 AM radio stations in 47 markets located in 24 states across the country. Citadel targets mid-sized markets due to less direct format competition and lower purchase prices. The company also considers mid-sized markets (defined as those ranked 30 to 150 by market revenue) attractive because they derive a significant portion of their revenue from local advertisers and there are more opportunities for consolidation in mid-sized markets than in larger markets. The company seeks to build station clusters through acquisitions in its existing and additional markets. Programming formats, geographic regions, audience demographics and advertising clients diversify the company's radio station portfolio. Citadel currently owns stations in cities including Providence, Rhode Island; Albuquerque, New Mexico; Baton Rouge, Louisiana; Salt Lake City, Utah; Little Rock, Arkansas; and Colorado Springs, Colorado. The firm's top 25 markets account for approximately 75% of its revenue. Citadel is 70% owned by Forstmann, Little and Co. In February 2006, Citadel Broadcasting Corp. agreed to acquire Walt Disney's radio broadcasting segment for $2.7 billion. Also in the course of 2006, the company completed acquisitions of six radio stations for a total purchase price of approximately $18.4 million.

FINANCIALS:
Sales and profits are in thousands of dollars—add 000 to get the full amount. 2006 Note: Financial information for 2006 was not available for all companies at press time.

2006 Sales: $	2006 Profits: $	**U.S. Stock Ticker: CDL**
2005 Sales: $419,907	2005 Profits: $69,757	**Int'l Ticker:** Int'l Exchange:
2004 Sales: $411,495	2004 Profits: $74,568	Employees: 3,428
2003 Sales: $371,500	2003 Profits: $-89,600	Fiscal Year Ends: 12/31
2002 Sales: $348,900	2002 Profits: $-89,200	Parent Company:

SALARIES/BENEFITS:

Pension Plan:	ESOP Stock Plan:	Profit Sharing:	Top Exec. Salary: $1,074,375	Bonus: $681,000
Savings Plan: Y	Stock Purch. Plan:		Second Exec. Salary: $494,583	Bonus: $158,333

OTHER THOUGHTS:
Apparent Women Officers or Directors: 2
Hot Spot for Advancement for Women/Minorities:

LOCATIONS: ("Y" = Yes)

West:	Southwest:	Midwest:	Southeast:	Northeast:	International:
Y	Y	Y	Y	Y	

CLARION CO LTD

www.clarion.com

Industry Group Code: 334310 **Ranks within this company's industry group:** Sales: 8   Profits: 7

Print Media/Publishing:	Movies:	Equipment/Supplies:	Broadcast/Cable:	Music/Audio:		Sports/Games:
Newspapers:	Movie Theaters:	Equipment/Supplies:	Broadcast TV:	Music Production:		Games/Sports:
Magazines:	Movie Production:	Gambling Equipment:	Cable TV:	Retail Music:		Retail Games Stores:
Books:	TV/Video Production:	Special Services:	Satellite Broadcast:	Retail Audio Equip.:	Y	Stadiums/Teams:
Book Stores:	Video Rental:	Advertising Services:	Radio:	Music Print./Dist.:		Gambling/Casinos:
Distribution/Printing:	Video Distribution:	Info. Sys. Software:	Online Information:	Multimedia:		Rides/Theme Parks:

TYPES OF BUSINESS:

Audio & Video Equipment, Manufacturing
Navigation Systems
Security Systems
Satellite Radios

BRANDS/DIVISIONS/AFFILIATES:

Clarion Corp. of America
Clarion Sales Co., Ltd.
Clarion Devices Co., Ltd.
Nissan Motor
HCX
Joyride
N.I.C.E. (Navigation In-Car Entertainment)
Sirius

CONTACTS: Note: Officers with more than one job title may be intentionally listed here more than once.

Tatsuhiko Izumi, Pres.
Tetsuro Yoshimine, Chief Dir.-Sales & Mktg.
Matt Matsuda, Pres., Clarion Corp. of America
Yasuhiko Wada, Chief Dir.-Bus. Promotion

Phone: 81-48-443-1111	**Fax:** 81-48-445-3810
Toll-Free: 800-462-5274	
Address: 50 Kami-Toda, Toda, Saitama 335-8511 Japan	

GROWTH PLANS/SPECIAL FEATURES:

Clarion Co., Ltd., headquartered in Japan, develops cutting-edge audio technology for automobiles and recreational vehicles. The company has three operating segments: automobile equipment, special equipment and other equipment. Clarion's automobile equipment segment manufactures and sells car audio, navigation and multi-media equipment; it also sells peripheral devices, such as cassettes, compact discs, mini discs, DVDs, radio tuners, monitors, audio speakers, audiovisual car navigation systems and car computing systems. The special equipment segment provides audiovisual products, driving control systems and others, such as auto-guide systems, multi-media, navigation systems, as well as cameras and television checking systems for buses and other vehicles. The other equipment segment offers communications equipment such as spread spectrum wireless equipment and cellular phones. The company also produces Sirius satellite radios. The firm's most successful product, the Joyride multimedia system, combines many of its other products and contains an AM/FM tuner, a DVD player, a CD player, an MP3 decoder, built-in Dolby Digital and DTS audio decoders, an address book function, an optional navigation package powered by an Intel Pentium MMX processor and a satellite radio connection. Clarion's largest customers are carmakers who integrate the products into the vehicles during manufacturing, including Nissan Motor, which is also its largest shareholder, with an approximate 10% interest in the firm.

FINANCIALS: Sales and profits are in thousands of dollars—add 000 to get the full amount. 2006 Note: Financial information for 2006 was not available for all companies at press time.

2006 Sales: $1,567,896	2006 Profits: $49,910	**U.S. Stock Ticker:**
2005 Sales: $1,660,537	2005 Profits: $47,597	**Int'l Ticker: 6796** Int'l Exchange: Tokyo-TSE
2004 Sales: $1,599,300	2004 Profits: $59,700	Employees: 9,211
2003 Sales: $1,548,100	2003 Profits: $13,000	Fiscal Year Ends: 3/31
2002 Sales: $1,417,000	2002 Profits: $-54,800	Parent Company:

SALARIES/BENEFITS:

Pension Plan:	ESOP Stock Plan:	Profit Sharing:	Top Exec. Salary: $	Bonus: $
Savings Plan:	Stock Purch. Plan:		Second Exec. Salary: $	Bonus: $

OTHER THOUGHTS:

Apparent Women Officers or Directors:
Hot Spot for Advancement for Women/Minorities:

LOCATIONS: ("Y" = Yes)

West:	Southwest:	Midwest:	Southeast:	Northeast:	International:
Y					Y

CLEAR CHANNEL COMMUNICATIONS INC
www.clearchannel.com

Industry Group Code: 513111 Ranks within this company's industry group: Sales: 1 Profits: 1

Print Media/Publishing:	Movies:	Equipment/Supplies:	Broadcast/Cable:	Music/Audio:	Sports/Games:	
Newspapers:	Movie Theaters:	Equipment/Supplies:	Broadcast TV:	Music Production:	Games/Sports:	
Magazines:	Movie Production:	Gambling Equipment:	Cable TV:	Retail Music:	Retail Games Stores:	
Books:	TV/Video Production:	Special Services:	Satellite Broadcast:	Retail Audio Equip.:	Stadiums/Teams:	
Book Stores:	Video Rental:	Advertising Services: Y	Radio:	Music Print./Dist.:	Gambling/Casinos:	
Distribution/Printing:	Video Distribution:	Info. Sys. Software:	Online Information:	Multimedia:	Rides/Theme Parks:	

TYPES OF BUSINESS:
Radio Station Owner/Operator
Outdoor Advertising

BRANDS/DIVISIONS/AFFILIATES:
Clear Channel Entertainment
Clear Channel Outdoor Holdings
Clear Channel Satellite Services

CONTACTS: Note: Officers with more than one job title may be intentionally listed here more than once.
Mark P. Mays, CEO
Randall T. Mays, Pres.
Randall T. Mays, CFO/Exec. VP
Bill Hamersly, Sr. VP-Human Resources
David Wilson, CIO/Sr. VP
Joe Shannon, CTO/VP
Andrew W. Levin, Chief Legal Officer/Exec. VP
Mike McGee, VP-Oper.
John T. Tippit, Sr. VP-Strategic Dev.
Lisa Dollinger, Chief Comm. Officer
Randy Palmer, Sr. VP-Investor Rel.
Julie Hill, Sr. VP-Finance
Jessica Marventano, Sr. VP-Gov't Affairs
Brian Coleman, VP/Treas.
Kathryn Johnson, Sr. VP-Corp. Rel.
Herb Hill, Sr. VP/Chief Acct. Officer
L. Lowry Mays, Chmn.

Phone: 210-822-2828	Fax: 210-822-2299
Toll-Free:	
Address: 200 E. Basse Rd., San Antonio, TX 78209 US	

GROWTH PLANS/SPECIAL FEATURES:

Clear Channel Communications, Inc. is a diversified media company with operations in radio broadcasting, domestic outdoor advertising and international outdoor advertising. In late 2006, Clear Channel announced it was selling all of its 42 TV stations and 448 of its radio stations. The company now owns, programs and sells airtime for 700 domestic radio stations. Clear Channel also has interests in various domestic and international radio broadcasting companies. The firm recently launched its Less-is-More initiative, an effort to enhance the value of its radio advertising by lowering the amount of commercial minutes by 15-20% across its stations. Clear Channel owns Katz Media Group, a full-service media representation firm that sells national spot advertising time for clients in the radio and television industries throughout the U.S., representing over 2,800 radio stations and 390 television stations. In 2005, Clear Channel spun off its Entertainment Group businesses into an independent firm called Live Nation, removing Clear Channel from the tour and concert production business. Also in 2005, it created a new, publicly held firm, Clear Channel Outdoor Holdings (CCO), as the owner of its outdoor advertising business. However, Clear Channel remains the majority owner of the stock of CCO. CCO is the world's largest outdoor media company, with annual sales of about $2.5 billion and over 823,500 advertising display faces in 49 domestic markets and 63 foreign countries. The display faces include billboards of various sizes, wallscapes, transit displays and street furniture displays. In November 2006, Clear Channel announced that it has agreed to be acquired by a group of private equity firms led by Thomas H. Lee Partners and Bain Capital for about $18.7 billion and $8 billion in acquired debt.

Clear Channel's employees receive benefits including flex spending, a 401(k) savings plan and a stock purchase plan.

FINANCIALS: Sales and profits are in thousands of dollars—add 000 to get the full amount. 2006 Note: Financial information for 2006 was not available for all companies at press time.

2006 Sales: $	2006 Profits: $	U.S. Stock Ticker: Private
2005 Sales: $6,610,418	2005 Profits: $935,662	Int'l Ticker: Int'l Exchange:
2004 Sales: $6,634,890	2004 Profits: $-4,038,169	Employees: 31,800
2003 Sales: $8,930,899	2003 Profits: $1,145,591	Fiscal Year Ends: 12/31
2002 Sales: $8,421,000	2002 Profits: $-16,054,000	Parent Company:

SALARIES/BENEFITS:

Pension Plan:	ESOP Stock Plan:	Profit Sharing:	Top Exec. Salary: $879,101	Bonus: $
Savings Plan: Y	Stock Purch. Plan: Y		Second Exec. Salary: $818,641	Bonus: $444,949

OTHER THOUGHTS:
Apparent Women Officers or Directors: 9
Hot Spot for Advancement for Women/Minorities: Y

LOCATIONS: ("Y" = Yes)

West:	Southwest:	Midwest:	Southeast:	Northeast:	International:
Y	Y	Y	Y	Y	Y

CLEAR CHANNEL OUTDOOR www.clearchanneloutdoor.com

Industry Group Code: 541810 Ranks within this company's industry group: Sales: 4 Profits: 3

Print Media/Publishing:	Movies:	Equipment/Supplies:		Broadcast/Cable:	Music/Audio:	Sports/Games:
Newspapers:	Movie Theaters:	Equipment/Supplies:		Broadcast TV:	Music Production:	Games/Sports:
Magazines:	Movie Production:	Gambling Equipment:		Cable TV:	Retail Music:	Retail Games Stores:
Books:	TV/Video Production:	Special Services:	Y	Satellite Broadcast:	Retail Audio Equip.:	Stadiums/Teams:
Book Stores:	Video Rental:	Advertising Services:	Y	Radio:	Music Print./Dist.:	Gambling/Casinos:
Distribution/Printing:	Video Distribution:	Info. Sys. Software:		Online Information:	Multimedia:	Rides/Theme Parks:

TYPES OF BUSINESS:

Outdoor Advertising
Mall & Airline Advertising
Outdoor Furniture Advertising
Live Event Advertising

BRANDS/DIVISIONS/AFFILIATES:

Clear Channel Adshel
Clear Channel Airports
Clear Channel Imaging
Clear Channel Malls
Clear Channel Spectacolor
Clear Channel Taxi Media

CONTACTS: *Note: Officers with more than one job title may be intentionally listed here more than once.*

Mark Mays, CEO
Paul Meyer, COO
Paul Meyer, Pres.
Randall Mays, CFO
Rocky Sisson, Dir.-Global Sales & Mktg.
Laura Toncheff, Exec. VP-Legal Affairs & Real Estate
Mike Deeds, Exec. VP-Oper., Americas
Michael Hudes, Exec. VP-Corp. Dev.
Kurt Tingey, CFO/Exec. VP-Americas
Michael Hudes, Global Dir.-Digital Media
Jonathan Bevan, CFO, Europe, Asia-Pacific, Africa
Coline McConville, CEO, Europe
Rickard Hedlund, CEO, Northern Europe
Augusto Claux, Regional Pres., Latin America

Phone: 602-381-5700	Fax:
Toll-Free:	
Address: 2850 E. Camelback Rd. Ste. 300, Phoenix, AZ 85016 US	

GROWTH PLANS/SPECIAL FEATURES:

Clear Channel Outdoor, a subsidiary of Clear Channel Communications, is a leading outdoor advertiser with over 800,000 out-of-home displays worldwide. The company is organized into six divisions: Clear Channel Adshel, Clear Channel Airports, Clear Channel Imaging, Clear Channel Malls, Clear Channel Spectacolor and Clear Channel Taxi Media. The Adshel division advertises through street furniture, operating over 6,000 municipal and transit contracts in 45 countries. The airports division is a top U.S. airport advertising company with over 1 billion targeted advertising messages to airline passengers during 2005. In imaging, the company offers large format UV digital printing for both indoor and outdoor advertising. Specialties include transit shelters, 30-sheets, mobile panels, bus vinyls, mall kiosks, car cards, illuminated street displays and airport dioramas. Clear Channel Malls organizes marketing and advertising campaigns focused on the environment, demographics and mindset of mall shoppers. The Spectacolor division works with clients to create one-of-a-kind events such as living billboards, live events, rooftop signage and wallscapes using the latest screens, fiber optics and lighting technologies. Through more than 23,000 Taxi panels operating nationwide, the Taxi Media division targets customers all day, all year in 12 major markets. Clear Channel Outdoor has recently launched a multicultural sales and marketing initiative in the U.S. to focus on the growing U.S. Hispanic and African American populations. During 2005, the company mounted a global HIV/AIDS awareness campaign in conjunction with UNICEF; was awarded a five-year contract in France to advertise in 29 bus networks; donated space to The African Wildlife Foundation at 8 U.S. airports for 50 displays to promote conservation programs; was awarded a contract for displays at the Sydney airport; and was awarded a 20-year contract with Washington D.C. to upgrade and expand the districts street furniture program. The company completed its IPO in November 2005.

FINANCIALS: Sales and profits are in thousands of dollars—add 000 to get the full amount. 2006 Note: Financial information for 2006 was not available for all companies at press time.

2006 Sales: $	2006 Profits: $	U.S. Stock Ticker: CCO
2005 Sales: $2,666,078	2005 Profits: $61,573	Int'l Ticker: Int'l Exchange:
2004 Sales: $2,447,040	2004 Profits: $-155,380	Employees: 7,600
2003 Sales: $2,174,597	2003 Profits: $-34,993	Fiscal Year Ends: 12/31
2002 Sales: $	2002 Profits: $	Parent Company:

SALARIES/BENEFITS:

Pension Plan:	ESOP Stock Plan:	Profit Sharing:	Top Exec. Salary: $	Bonus: $
Savings Plan:	Stock Purch. Plan:		Second Exec. Salary: $	Bonus: $

OTHER THOUGHTS:

Apparent Women Officers or Directors: 2
Hot Spot for Advancement for Women/Minorities:

LOCATIONS: ("Y" = Yes)

West:	Southwest:	Midwest:	Southeast:	Northeast:	International:
Y	Y	Y	Y	Y	Y

Note: Financial information, benefits and other data can change quickly and may vary from those stated here.

CLUBCORP INC   www.clubcorp.com

Industry Group Code: 713910 Ranks within this company's industry group: Sales: 1   Profits: 1

Print Media/Publishing:	Movies:	Equipment/Supplies:	Broadcast/Cable:	Music/Audio:	Sports/Games:	
Newspapers:	Movie Theaters:	Equipment/Supplies:	Broadcast TV:	Music Production:	Games/Sports:	Y
Magazines:	Movie Production:	Gambling Equipment:	Cable TV:	Retail Music:	Retail Games Stores:	
Books:	TV/Video Production:	Special Services:	Satellite Broadcast:	Retail Audio Equip.:	Stadiums/Teams:	
Book Stores:	Video Rental:	Advertising Services:	Radio:	Music Print./Dist.:	Gambling/Casinos:	
Distribution/Printing:	Video Distribution:	Info. Sys. Software:	Online Information:	Multimedia:	Rides/Theme Parks:	

TYPES OF BUSINESS:

Golf Courses & Country Clubs
Business/Sports Clubs
Resorts

BRANDS/DIVISIONS/AFFILIATES:

Pinehurst
Firestone Country Club
Indian Wells Country Club
Homestead (The)
Mission Hills Country Club
Boston College Club
Metropolitan Club
Barton Creek Resort and Spa

CONTACTS: Note: Officers with more than one job title may be intentionally listed here more than once.

John A. Beckert, CEO
John A. Beckert, COO
John A. Beckert, Pres.
Jeffrey P. Mayer, CFO
Frank C. Gore, Exec. VP-Sales
John H. Longstreet, Sr. VP-People Strategy
Thomas T. Henslee, Exec. VP/General Counsel/Corp. Sec.
Richard N. Beckert, Exec. VP-Oper. & Resorts
Murray S. Siegel, Exec. VP-Strategic Oper.
Angela A. Stephens, Sr. VP/Controller/Chief Acct. Officer
Lisa H. Kislak, Sr. VP-Mktg.
Douglas T. Howe, Exec. VP-Growth & Dev.
David B. Woodyard, Sr. VP-Bus. & Sports Div.
James P. McTeigue, Sr. VP-Golf Div.
Robert H. Dedman, Jr., Chmn.
William T. Walden, Sr. VP-Purchasing

Phone: 972-243-6191	Fax: 972-888-7700
Toll-Free:	
Address: 3030 LBJ Fwy., Ste. 600, Dallas, TX 75234 US	

GROWTH PLANS/SPECIAL FEATURES:

ClubCorp, Inc. is a leading owner and operator of golf courses, country clubs, private clubs and golf resorts in the U.S., with additional operations in Australia, Europe and Asia. The company has approximately 190,000 memberships and 170 operations in 29 states and three foreign countries (Australia, China and Mexico), including 71 private country clubs, 13 semi-private golf clubs, ten public golf facilities, four destination golf resorts (Pinehurst, The Homestead and Barton Creek Resort and Spa) and 61 business/sports clubs (including 44 business clubs, 13 business/sports clubs and four sports clubs). The firm's operations include nationally recognized golf courses and country clubs such as Pinehurst in Pinehurst, North Carolina, the largest golf resort in North America; the Firestone Country Club in Akron, Ohio; the Indian Wells Country Club in Indian Wells, California; The Homestead in Hot Springs, Virginia, the oldest resort in America; and the Mission Hills Country Club in Rancho Mirage, California. Additionally, the company's business and sports clubs can be found in major metropolitan areas, including the City Club on Bunker Hill in Los Angeles; the Citrus Club in Orlando, Florida; the Columbia Tower Club in Seattle; the Metropolitan Club in Chicago; the Tower Club in Dallas; the Boston College Club; and the City Club in Washington, D.C. In early 2006, the company added a fourth resort to its portfolio. The Ocean Edge Resort & Golf Club in Cape Cod, Massachusetts will be operated by ClubCorp, whose ownership includes plans of a $20 million upgrade to facilities.

The company offers internship programs for training in the areas of kitchen and catering, golf course operations and maintenance, accounting and member relations.

FINANCIALS: Sales and profits are in thousands of dollars—add 000 to get the full amount. 2006 Note: Financial information for 2006 was not available for all companies at press time.

2006 Sales: $	2006 Profits: $	U.S. Stock Ticker: Private
2005 Sales: $1,028,088	2005 Profits: $70,754	Int'l Ticker: Int'l Exchange:
2004 Sales: $938,802	2004 Profits: $-6,242	Employees: 18,300
2003 Sales: $892,709	2003 Profits: $-105,246	Fiscal Year Ends: 12/31
2002 Sales: $947,000	2002 Profits: $-61,600	Parent Company:

SALARIES/BENEFITS:

Pension Plan:	ESOP Stock Plan:	Profit Sharing:	Top Exec. Salary: $500,000	Bonus: $281,250
Savings Plan:	Stock Purch. Plan:		Second Exec. Salary: $500,000	Bonus: $235,000

OTHER THOUGHTS:

Apparent Women Officers or Directors: 2
Hot Spot for Advancement for Women/Minorities:

LOCATIONS: ("Y" = Yes)

West:	Southwest:	Midwest:	Southeast:	Northeast:	International:
Y	Y	Y	Y	Y	Y

CNET NETWORKS INC

www.cnet.com

Industry Group Code: 514199 Ranks within this company's industry group: Sales: 2 Profits: 3

Print Media/Publishing:		Movies:		Equipment/Supplies:		Broadcast/Cable:		Music/Audio:		Sports/Games:	
Newspapers:		Movie Theaters:		Equipment/Supplies:		Broadcast TV:		Music Production:		Games/Sports:	
Magazines:	Y	Movie Production:		Gambling Equipment:		Cable TV:		Retail Music:		Retail Games Stores:	
Books:		TV/Video Production:		Special Services:		Satellite Broadcast:		Retail Audio Equip.:		Stadiums/Teams:	
Book Stores:		Video Rental:		Advertising Services:		Radio:		Music Print./Dist.:		Gambling/Casinos:	
Distribution/Printing:		Video Distribution:		Info. Sys. Software:	Y	Online Information:		Multimedia:		Rides/Theme Parks:	

TYPES OF BUSINESS:

Online Publishing
Technology Web Sites
Internet Search & Navigation Services
Online News
Music
Information Collection & Delivery

BRANDS/DIVISIONS/AFFILIATES:

ZDNet
CNET TV
Webshots
MP3.com
CNET Download.com
CNET News.com
mySimon
GameSpot

CONTACTS: Note: Officers with more than one job title may be intentionally listed here more than once.

Neil M. Ashe, CEO
George E. Mazzotta, CFO
Joseph Gillispie, Chief Mktg. Officer
Martha Papalia, VP-Corp. Comm.
Gloria Lee, Investor Rel.
David Bernstein, Sr. VP-Finance/Chief Acc. Officer
Sam Parker, Sr. VP-Network
Shelby Bonnie, Co-Founder/Former CEO
Martin Green, Sr. VP-Community
Greg Mason, Sr. VP-Bus. Media & Channel
Jarl Mohn, Chmn.
Adam Power, Pres., Intl. Media

Phone: 415-344-2000	Fax: 415-395-9207
Toll-Free:	
Address: 235 2nd St., San Francisco, CA 94105 US	

GROWTH PLANS/SPECIAL FEATURES:

CNET Networks is a major global media company specializing in branding and operating web sites. The company distributes information to 13 countries via the Internet. Its online brands consist of four content categories: Business (ZDNet, Tech Republic and News.com); games and entertainment (TV.com, GameSpot, Chow.com); technology (CNET, CNET News.com, Download.com); and community (Webshots, MP3.com). ZDNet, TechRepublic and News.com anchor the company's business technology brands. ZDNet provides technology customers with information about computers and high-tech products. TechRepublic serves professionals representing the IT industry by providing information and tools for IT decision support and professional advice by job function. News.com focuses on the latest breaking news and in-depth coverage of industries such as technology, games and entertainment. CNET's games and entertainment brands consist mainly of GameSpot, an online downloadable music store. Complemented by GameFaqs and gamerankings.com, it gives users access to game reviews, previews, downloads, guides and hints. The firm's CNET.com site provides advice on technology and consumer electronics products and services through detailed reviews and recommendations. Download.com provides information to buyers and sellers of try-before-you-buy software, which allows customers to evaluate a software product before they purchase it. In 2006, the firm had an average of 116 million unique users per month, generating almost 104 million web pages per day. Recently, the firm sold its only magazine, Computer Shopper, to SX2 Media Labs, LLC. The firm also partnered with Cox Communications, TiVo, Inc. and TVN Entertainment to launch CNET TV, which distributes video footage on television and online. It launched CNET Podcast Central, featuring the following free podcasts: Gadget Girls, Studio C, MP3 Insider and The Real Deal. In addition, CNET's subsidiary, Webshots, launched AllYouCanUpload.com, a free photo uploading and hosting service. Also in 2006, the firm unveiled Chow.com, an online forum for food enthusiasts.

CNET provides employees with: medical; dental and vision coverage; tuition reimbursement; on-site massage therapy; and tai chi/yoga classes.

FINANCIALS: Sales and profits are in thousands of dollars—add 000 to get the full amount. 2006 Note: Financial information for 2006 was not available for all companies at press time.

2006 Sales: $	2006 Profits: $	U.S. Stock Ticker: CNET
2005 Sales: $352,951	2005 Profits: $27,693	Int'l Ticker: Int'l Exchange:
2004 Sales: $291,200	2004 Profits: $11,700	Employees: 2,340
2003 Sales: $246,200	2003 Profits: $-26,300	Fiscal Year Ends: 12/31
2002 Sales: $237,000	2002 Profits: $-360,600	Parent Company:

SALARIES/BENEFITS:

Pension Plan:	ESOP Stock Plan:	Profit Sharing:	Top Exec. Salary: $383,750	Bonus: $466,500
Savings Plan: Y	Stock Purch. Plan: Y		Second Exec. Salary: $357,962	Bonus: $375,533

OTHER THOUGHTS:

Apparent Women Officers or Directors: 2
Hot Spot for Advancement for Women/Minorities:

LOCATIONS: ("Y" = Yes)

West:	Southwest:	Midwest:	Southeast:	Northeast:	International:
Y	Y	Y	Y	Y	Y

COLUMBIA TRISTAR MOTION PICTURE GROUP
www.sonypictures.com/movies

Industry Group Code: 512110 Ranks within this company's industry group: Sales: Profits:

Print Media/Publishing:	Movies:		Equipment/Supplies:	Broadcast/Cable:	Music/Audio:	Sports/Games:
Newspapers:	Movie Theaters:		Equipment/Supplies:	Broadcast TV:	Music Production:	Games/Sports:
Magazines:	Movie Production:	Y	Gambling Equipment:	Cable TV:	Retail Music:	Retail Games Stores:
Books:	TV/Video Production:		Special Services:	Satellite Broadcast:	Retail Audio Equip.:	Stadiums/Teams:
Book Stores:	Video Rental:		Advertising Services:	Radio:	Music Print./Dist.:	Gambling/Casinos:
Distribution/Printing:	Video Distribution:		Info. Sys. Software:	Online Information:	Multimedia:	Rides/Theme Parks:

TYPES OF BUSINESS:
Film Production & Distribution

BRANDS/DIVISIONS/AFFILIATES:
Sony Pictures Entertainment
Sony Corporation of America
Columbia Pictures
Sony Pictures Classics
Screen Gems
TriStar Pictures
Sony Pictures Releasing
Columbia Pictures Film Production Asia

CONTACTS: Note: Officers with more than one job title may be intentionally listed here more than once.
Bob Osher, COO
Valeria Van Galder, Pres., Mktg. Group
Paul Smith, Pres., Worldwide Oper.
Richard Natale, Dir.-Media Rel.
Peter Iacono, Sr. Exec. VP-Local Language Productions
Doug Belgrad, Pres., Columbia Pictures
Gigi Semone, Exec. VP-Publicity
Andre Caraco, Exec. VP-Publicity
Amy Pascal, Chmn.-Sony Motion Picture Group
Jeff Blake, Chmn.-Worldwide Mktg. & Distribution

Phone: 310-244-4000	Fax: 310-244-2626
Toll-Free:	
Address: 10202 W. Washington Blvd., Culver City, CA 90232 US	

GROWTH PLANS/SPECIAL FEATURES:
Columbia TriStar Motion Picture Group (CTMPG) is the movie production, marketing, distribution and promotion subsidiary of Sony Pictures Entertainment, which is a subsidiary of Sony Corporation of America. The company releases roughly 25 films per year in the U.S. CTMPG produces its U.S. films through the Columbia Pictures production studio and produces international films through Columbia Pictures Film Production Asia, Columbia Films Producciones Espanolas and Columbia Pictures Producciones Mexico, as well as through operations in the U.K., Brazil and Japan. CTMPG produces and distributes its movies under four labels: Columbia Pictures, which produces wide-release movies such as Spider-Man; Sony Pictures Classics, which acquires, markets and distributes prestigious foreign and American independent films such as House of Flying Daggers; Screen Gems, which produces lower-budget films than Columbia Pictures; and TriStar Pictures, a marketing and acquisition unit focused on genre films. Recent releases include The Da Vinci Code, Marie Antoinette, The Pursuit of Happiness, The Holiday, Casino Royal and Stranger Than Fiction. In 2007, the company will release Spiderman 3. Columbia Pictures frequently partners with Revolution Studios to produce films such as Click and Zoom. TriStar oversees a library of more than 3,500 films, including 12 Best Picture Academy Award winners. CTMPG releases its films through two subsidiaries: Sony Pictures Releasing (U.S.) and Sony Pictures Releasing International. Combined, they are responsible for the sale, distribution and marketing of all TriStar films in 67 countries. In 2006, Columbia Pictures entered into a two-year first-look deal with Outlaw Productions.

Sony Pictures Entertainment offers its employees paid vacation, school credit, summer and academic year internships, and offers tuition reimbursement, a variety of insurance plans, a 401(k) plan, flexible spending accounts and an employee stock purchase plan. Benefits are extended to same-sex partners.

FINANCIALS: Sales and profits are in thousands of dollars—add 000 to get the full amount. 2006 Note: Financial information for 2006 was not available for all companies at press time.

2006 Sales: $	2006 Profits: $	U.S. Stock Ticker: Subsidiary
2005 Sales: $	2005 Profits: $	Int'l Ticker: Int'l Exchange:
2004 Sales: $	2004 Profits: $	Employees:
2003 Sales: $	2003 Profits: $	Fiscal Year Ends: 3/31
2002 Sales: $	2002 Profits: $	Parent Company: SONY CORPORATION

SALARIES/BENEFITS:

Pension Plan:	ESOP Stock Plan:	Profit Sharing:	Top Exec. Salary: $	Bonus: $
Savings Plan:	Stock Purch. Plan:		Second Exec. Salary: $	Bonus: $

OTHER THOUGHTS:
Apparent Women Officers or Directors: 3
Hot Spot for Advancement for Women/Minorities: Y

LOCATIONS: ("Y" = Yes)

West:	Southwest:	Midwest:	Southeast:	Northeast:	International:
Y					Y

Note: Financial information, benefits and other data can change quickly and may vary from those stated here.

COMCAST CORP

www.comcast.com

Industry Group Code: 513220 Ranks within this company's industry group: Sales: 2 Profits: 4

Print Media/Publishing:	Movies:		Equipment/Supplies:		Broadcast/Cable:		Music/Audio:	Sports/Games:
Newspapers:	Movie Theaters:		Equipment/Supplies:		Broadcast TV:		Music Production:	Games/Sports:
Magazines:	Movie Production:		Gambling Equipment:		Cable TV:	Y	Retail Music:	Retail Games Stores:
Books:	TV/Video Production:	Y	Special Services:	Y	Satellite Broadcast:		Retail Audio Equip.:	Stadiums/Teams:
Book Stores:	Video Rental:		Advertising Services:	Y	Radio:		Music Print./Dist.:	Gambling/Casinos:
Distribution/Printing:	Video Distribution:		Info. Sys. Software:		Online Information:		Multimedia:	Rides/Theme Parks:

TYPES OF BUSINESS:

Cable Television
VoIP Service
Cable Network Programming
High-Speed Internet Service
Video-on-Demand
Advertising Services
Interactive Program Schedules
Wireless Services

BRANDS/DIVISIONS/AFFILIATES:

AT&T Comcast
AOL Time Warner
Philadelphia 76ers
E! Entertainment
Golf Channel (The)
Outdoor Life Network
Metro-Goldwyn-Mayer

CONTACTS: Note: Officers with more than one job title may be intentionally listed here more than once.

Brian L. Roberts, CEO
Stephen B. Burke, COO
John R. Alchin, Co-CFO/Exec. VP
Charisse Lillie, VP-Human Resources
Karen D. Buchholz, VP-Admin.
Arthur R. Block, Esq., General Counsel/Sr. VP
Robert S. Pick, Sr. VP-Corp. Dev.
Mark A. Coblitz, Sr. VP-Strategic Planning
D'Arcy F. Rudnay, VP-Corp. Comm.
Marlene S. Dooner, VP-Investor Rel.
William E. Dordelman, VP-Finance
Stephen B. Burke, Pres., Comcast Cable Comm.
Lawrence S. Smith, Exec. VP/Co-CFO
Robert S. Pick, Sr. VP-Corp. Dev.
Lawrence J. Salva, Chief Acct. Officer/Sr. VP/Controller
Brian L. Roberts, Chmn.

Phone: 215-665-1700   Fax: 215-981-7790
Toll-Free: 800-266-2278
Address: 1500 Market St., Philadelphia, PA 19102-2148 US

GROWTH PLANS/SPECIAL FEATURES:

Comcast Corp. is principally engaged in developing and operating hybrid fiber-coaxial broadband cable communications networks and providing programming content. Comcast is one of the largest cable operators in the U.S., with 24.1 million subscribers in 27 states. Comcast offers enhanced digital video, high-speed Internet, cable telephone services and video-on-demand. The other significant portion of the company's business is cable network content. Comcast companies include E! Entertainment Television, Philadelphia 76ers, The Golf Channel, Outdoor Life Network and G4 Media. In 2005, Comcast, as part of a consortium led by Sony America, acquired Metro-Goldwyn-Mayer, including thousands of MGM movies. Comcast will develop new cable channels featuring movies from the MGM and Sony libraries, totaling 7,500 films along with 42,000 television programs. This development will greatly enhance Comcast's video-on-demand (VOD) strategy. It has a system of massive computer servers at local cable system offices that enable subscribers to play movies, television programming and news at any time. With over 11 million customers signed up for high speed Internet access, Comcast is one of America's largest providers of broadband access services, offering speeds of up to 8 Mbps. The company is also a major seller of advertising, generating about $1.4 billion yearly in advertising fees. Cable telephone service (VoIP) is available to all Comcast customers. In July 2006, the company announced that it and Time Warner Cable have completed the acquisition of substantially all of the assets of Adelphia Communication Corporation. Additionally, the company redeemed its ownership interest in Time Warner Cable.

Employees of Comcast are offered benefits including an employee referral program, educational reimbursement, an employee assistance program, a 401(k) savings plan and an employee stock purchase plan, as well as pre-paid legal services, pet insurance and courtesy on-line and cable services.

FINANCIALS: Sales and profits are in thousands of dollars—add 000 to get the full amount. 2006 Note: Financial information for 2006 was not available for all companies at press time.

2006 Sales: $	2006 Profits: $	U.S. Stock Ticker: CMCSA
2005 Sales: $22,300,000	2005 Profits: $928,000	Int'l Ticker: Int'l Exchange:
2004 Sales: $20,307,000	2004 Profits: $970,000	Employees: 80,000
2003 Sales: $18,348,000	2003 Profits: $3,240,000	Fiscal Year Ends: 12/31
2002 Sales: $12,460,000	2002 Profits: $-274,000	Parent Company:

SALARIES/BENEFITS:

Pension Plan:	ESOP Stock Plan:	Profit Sharing:	Top Exec. Salary: $2,368,250	Bonus: $7,714,500
Savings Plan: Y	Stock Purch. Plan: Y		Second Exec. Salary: $1,765,000	Bonus: $2,250,864

OTHER THOUGHTS:

Apparent Women Officers or Directors: 6
Hot Spot for Advancement for Women/Minorities: Y

LOCATIONS: ("Y" = Yes)

West:	Southwest:	Midwest:	Southeast:	Northeast:	International:
Y	Y	Y	Y	Y	Y

Note: Financial information, benefits and other data can change quickly and may vary from those stated here.

COMMUNITY NEWSPAPER HOLDINGS INC   www.cnhi.com

Industry Group Code: 511110 Ranks within this company's industry group: Sales: Profits:

Print Media/Publishing:		Movies:	Equipment/Supplies:	Broadcast/Cable:	Music/Audio:	Sports/Games:
Newspapers:	Y	Movie Theaters:	Equipment/Supplies:	Broadcast TV:	Music Production:	Games/Sports:
Magazines:		Movie Production:	Gambling Equipment:	Cable TV:	Retail Music:	Retail Games Stores:
Books:		TV/Video Production:	Special Services:	Satellite Broadcast:	Retail Audio Equip.:	Stadiums/Teams:
Book Stores:		Video Rental:	Advertising Services: Y	Radio:	Music Print./Dist.:	Gambling/Casinos:
Distribution/Printing:		Video Distribution:	Info. Sys. Software:	Online Information:	Multimedia:	Rides/Theme Parks:

TYPES OF BUSINESS:

Newspaper Publishing
Marketing Agencies
Online Publishing

BRANDS/DIVISIONS/AFFILIATES:

Eagle-Tribune Publishing Company
Eagle Marketing
XL Marketing

CONTACTS: Note: Officers with more than one job title may be intentionally listed here more than once.

Donna Barrett, CEO
Kevin Kampman, COO
Donna Barrett, Pres.
Lynn Pearson, CFO
Brenda Cole, VP-IT
Brenda Cole, CTO
Chris Muldrow, VP-Internet Operations
William B. Ketter, VP-News, Editorial Oper.
F. Steve McPhaul, Sr. VP-Newspaper Oper.
Frank Baker, Dir.-Eagle Marketing
George Wakefield, Chmn.

Phone: 205-298-7100	Fax: 205-298-7108
Toll-Free:	
Address: 3500 Colonnade Pkwy., Ste. 600, Birmingham, AL 35243 US	

GROWTH PLANS/SPECIAL FEATURES:

Community Newspaper Holdings, Inc. (CNHI) was founded to acquire community newspapers. The company seeks out newspapers in small markets with growth potential. For operational efficiency and in order to provide additional services to its readers, the firm attempts to buy newspapers in geographic proximity to each other. CNHI also has interests in a variety of ancillary publications and services that complement its newspapers. The company currently owns more than 100 daily, semiweekly and weekly publications in 22 states, with a combined circulation of more than 1 million. Oklahoma- and Texas-based newspapers make up approximately 30% of the firm's publications. Most of CNHI's papers have circulation ranging from 13,000 to 25,000. CNHI recently acquired the Eagle-Tribune Publishing Company, a newspaper company serving over 340,000 readers in Massachusetts and New Hampshire. The acquisition added 105,958 units to CNHI's daily circulation. CNHI also runs two marketing agencies: Eagle Marketing, a full-service advertising agency which offers its clients high quality printed materials, design services, web site design and multimedia development, special event marketing, sales and targeted marketing options; and XL Marketing which focuses on brand development. In 2006, CNHI bought six newspapers from Dow Jones for a reported price of $281.5 million. The purchase brings the total number of daily papers owned operated by CNHI to 94; this is in addition to the 49 non-daily papers the company runs. Each of the company's properties has an associated web site, plus a website dedicated to employees of the company at cnhireadership.com.

FINANCIALS: Sales and profits are in thousands of dollars—add 000 to get the full amount. 2006 Note: Financial information for 2006 was not available for all companies at press time.

2006 Sales: $	2006 Profits: $	U.S. Stock Ticker: Private
2005 Sales: $	2005 Profits: $	Int'l Ticker: Int'l Exchange:
2004 Sales: $	2004 Profits: $	Employees:
2003 Sales: $410,000	2003 Profits: $	Fiscal Year Ends: 12/31
2002 Sales: $390,000	2002 Profits: $	Parent Company:

SALARIES/BENEFITS:

Pension Plan:	ESOP Stock Plan:	Profit Sharing:	Top Exec. Salary: $	Bonus: $
Savings Plan:	Stock Purch. Plan:		Second Exec. Salary: $	Bonus: $

OTHER THOUGHTS:

Apparent Women Officers or Directors: 2
Hot Spot for Advancement for Women/Minorities:

LOCATIONS: ("Y" = Yes)

West:	Southwest:	Midwest:	Southeast:	Northeast:	International:
Y	Y	Y	Y	Y	

CONCRETE SOFTWARE INC   www.concretesoftware.com

Industry Group Code: 511208 Ranks within this company's industry group: Sales: Profits:

Print Media/Publishing:	Movies:	Equipment/Supplies:	Broadcast/Cable:	Music/Audio:	Sports/Games:	
Newspapers:	Movie Theaters:	Equipment/Supplies:	Broadcast TV:	Music Production:	Games/Sports:	Y
Magazines:	Movie Production:	Gambling Equipment:	Cable TV:	Retail Music:	Retail Games Stores:	
Books:	TV/Video Production:	Special Services:	Satellite Broadcast:	Retail Audio Equip.:	Stadiums/Teams:	
Book Stores:	Video Rental:	Advertising Services:	Radio:	Music Print./Dist.:	Gambling/Casinos:	
Distribution/Printing:	Video Distribution:	Info. Sys. Software:	Online Information:	Multimedia:	Rides/Theme Parks:	

TYPES OF BUSINESS:

Mobile Gaming Software

BRANDS/DIVISIONS/AFFILIATES:

Aces Omaha
Aces Texas Hold'em
Shoot Stuff
2020 Special Ops
Driving Log
Links Scorecard

GROWTH PLANS/SPECIAL FEATURES:

Concrete Software designs and produces software for mobile devices. The company provides software for mobile telephones manufactured by Nokia, Motorola, Sony Ericsson, Samsung, Siemens, NEC and LG; in addition, it produces software for other types of mobile devices made by BlackBerry, Palm, Pocket PC, TREO, and Microsoft. Concrete's product line includes games such as Aces Texas Hold'em-No Limit, Aces Blackjack, Aces Omaha-No Limit, Shoot Stuff and 2020 Special Ops. The company also offers non-gaming applications such as Links Scorecard and Driving Log, a program that keeps track of the distance one has driven with the help of a secure online synchronized database and GPS support. The company offers a paid update service for all of its software.

CONTACTS: *Note: Officers with more than one job title may be intentionally listed here more than once.*

Keith Pichelman, CEO

Phone:	Fax: 952-556-8734
Toll-Free:	
Address: 8531 Merganser Ct., Chanhassen, MN 55317 US	

FINANCIALS: Sales and profits are in thousands of dollars—add 000 to get the full amount. 2006 Note: Financial information for 2006 was not available for all companies at press time.

2006 Sales: $	2006 Profits: $	U.S. Stock Ticker: Private
2005 Sales: $	2005 Profits: $	Int'l Ticker: Int'l Exchange:
2004 Sales: $	2004 Profits: $	Employees:
2003 Sales: $	2003 Profits: $	Fiscal Year Ends:
2002 Sales: $	2002 Profits: $	Parent Company:

SALARIES/BENEFITS:

Pension Plan:	ESOP Stock Plan:	Profit Sharing:	Top Exec. Salary: $	Bonus: $
Savings Plan:	Stock Purch. Plan:		Second Exec. Salary: $	Bonus: $

OTHER THOUGHTS:

Apparent Women Officers or Directors:
Hot Spot for Advancement for Women/Minorities:

LOCATIONS: ("Y" = Yes)

West:	Southwest:	Midwest:	Southeast:	Northeast:	International:
		Y			

CONCURRENT COMPUTER CORP   www.ccur.com

Industry Group Code: 334111 Ranks within this company's industry group: Sales: 3   Profits: 3

Print Media/Publishing:	Movies:	Equipment/Supplies:		Broadcast/Cable:	Music/Audio:	Sports/Games:
Newspapers:	Movie Theaters:	Equipment/Supplies:	Y	Broadcast TV:	Music Production:	Games/Sports:
Magazines:	Movie Production:	Gambling Equipment:		Cable TV:	Retail Music:	Retail Games Stores:
Books:	TV/Video Production:	Special Services:	Y	Satellite Broadcast:	Retail Audio Equip.:	Stadiums/Teams:
Book Stores:	Video Rental:	Advertising Services:		Radio:	Music Print./Dist.:	Gambling/Casinos:
Distribution/Printing:	Video Distribution:	Info. Sys. Software:	Y	Online Information:	Multimedia:	Rides/Theme Parks:

TYPES OF BUSINESS:

Software-Real-Time & Video-on-Demand
Networking Systems Architecture
Operating Systems Software
Government Technology Services

BRANDS/DIVISIONS/AFFILIATES:

Everstream Holdings, Inc.
SUSE Linux Enterprise-Real Time
iHawk
ImaGen
PowerMAX Operating System
RedHawk Linux

CONTACTS: *Note: Officers with more than one job title may be intentionally listed here more than once.*

T. Gary Trimm, CEO
Warren K. Neuburger, COO
T. Gary Trimm, Pres.
Gregory S. Wilson, CFO
Gary Brust, VP-Worldwide Sales & Mktg. On-Demand
Suzanne Smith, VP-Worldwide Human Resources
Robert E. Chism, CTO
Fred R. Langston, VP-Mfg.
Suzanne Smith, VP- Admin. Services
Kirk L. Somers, General Counsel
Kirk L. Somers, VP-Investor Rel.
Scott Stroh, VP-Worldwide Sales & Mktg. Real-Time
Kenrick R. Jackson, VP-Concurrent Special Systems
Dave Mooney, VP-Quality Assurance
Steve G. Nussrallah, Chmn.
Del Kunert, VP-Int'l On-Demand

Phone: 678-258-4000	**Fax:** 678-258-4300
Toll-Free: 877-978-7363	
Address: 4375 River Green Pkwy., Ste. 100, Duluth, GA 30096 US	

GROWTH PLANS/SPECIAL FEATURES:

Concurrent Computer Corporation (CCC) provides computer systems for the video-on-demand market and real-time applications. The on-demand products consist of servers and related software, and are sold primarily to residential cable television operators that have upgraded their networks to support interactive digital services and are operated through subsidiary company Everstream Holdings, Inc. The firm's on-demand systems enable broadband telecommunication providers to streamline networks to customers. The customers are then able to control the video stream with familiar operations like pause, fast-forward and rewind. The company's real-time products consist of operating systems and diagnostic software tools combined with off-the-shelf hardware and services. These products provide a wide variety of companies with real-time computer systems for use in applications that require low latency response times such as simulation, image generation and data acquisition. These products are specifically designed for use with applications that acquire, process, store, analyze and display large amounts of rapidly changing data with microsecond response times. The company's real-time products include SUSE Linux Enterprise-Real Time, a version of the Novell open source Linux operating system, provided in partnership with Novell; iHawk servers; ImaGen imaging platform; PowerMAX, a UNIX based operating system; and RedHawk Linux, an operating system compatible with the popular Red Hat Linux. The company derived 21% of its 2006 revenues from the supply of products to U.S. government prime contractors and agencies of the U.S. government. This included selling computer systems, equipment, spare parts, and consulting services to government contractors such as Boeing, Lockheed-Martin and Raytheon. In late 2006, Concurrent Computer Corporation was nominated for an Emmy for Outstanding Innovation and Achievement in Advanced Media Technology for the Best Use of On Demand Technology Over Private (Closed) Networks.

FINANCIALS: Sales and profits are in thousands of dollars—add 000 to get the full amount. 2006 Note: Financial information for 2006 was not available for all companies at press time.

2006 Sales: $71,612	2006 Profits: $-9,345	**U.S. Stock Ticker:** CCUR
2005 Sales: $78,685	2005 Profits: $-7,729	**Int'l Ticker:** Int'l Exchange:
2004 Sales: $79,235	2004 Profits: $-5,725	Employees: 399
2003 Sales: $75,453	2003 Profits: $-24,552	Fiscal Year Ends: 6/30
2002 Sales: $89,400	2002 Profits: $4,400	Parent Company:

SALARIES/BENEFITS:

Pension Plan:	ESOP Stock Plan:	Profit Sharing:	Top Exec. Salary: $350,000	Bonus: $
Savings Plan: Y	Stock Purch. Plan:		Second Exec. Salary: $290,000	Bonus: $

OTHER THOUGHTS:

Apparent Women Officers or Directors: 1
Hot Spot for Advancement for Women/Minorities:

LOCATIONS: ("Y" = Yes)

West:	Southwest:	Midwest:	Southeast:	Northeast:	International:
		Y	Y	Y	Y

CONDE NAST PUBLICATIONS INC   www.condenast.com

Industry Group Code: 511120 Ranks within this company's industry group: Sales: Profits:

Print Media/Publishing:		Movies:	Equipment/Supplies:	Broadcast/Cable:	Music/Audio:	Sports/Games:
Newspapers:		Movie Theaters:	Equipment/Supplies:	Broadcast TV:	Music Production:	Games/Sports:
Magazines:	Y	Movie Production:	Gambling Equipment:	Cable TV:	Retail Music:	Retail Games Stores:
Books:	Y	TV/Video Production:	Special Services:	Satellite Broadcast:	Retail Audio Equip.:	Stadiums/Teams:
Book Stores:		Video Rental:	Advertising Services:	Radio:	Music Print./Dist.:	Gambling/Casinos:
Distribution/Printing:		Video Distribution:	Info. Sys. Software:	Online Information:	Multimedia:	Rides/Theme Parks:

TYPES OF BUSINESS:

Magazine Publishing
Internet Publishing

BRANDS/DIVISIONS/AFFILIATES:

Vogue
Fairchild Publications, Inc.
Details
Glamour
New Yorker (The)
Wired
Vanity Fair
CondeNet

CONTACTS: Note: Officers with more than one job title may be intentionally listed here more than once.

Charles H. Townsend, CEO
John Bellando, COO
Charles H. Townsend, Pres.
Debi Chirichella, CFO
Richard D. Beckman, Chief Mktg. Officer/Pres., Conde Nast Media Group
Maurie Perl, Chief Comm. Officer/Sr. VP
Mitchell Fox, Group Pres.
Thomas J. Wallace, Editorial Dir.
David Carey, Group Pres.
Sarah Chubb, Pres., CondeNet
Samuel I. (Si) Newhouse, Jr., Chmn.

Phone: 212-286-2860	Fax:
Toll-Free:	
Address: 4 Times Sq. Ste. 17, New York City, NY 10036 US	

GROWTH PLANS/SPECIAL FEATURES:

Conde Nast Publications, Inc., a subsidiary of Advance Publications, Inc., is a publisher of magazines and their affiliated websites. It operates in three major divisions: Conde Nast Media Group; Fairchild Publications; and CondeNet. Comag Marketing Group LLC (CMG), is a joint venture of The HearstCorporation and Condé Nast Publications, Inc. Conde Nast Media Group handles the company's well known magazine portfolio including: Vogue; W, Glamour; Allure; Self; GQ; Jane; Details; Architectural Digest; House & Garden; Brides; Lucky; Vanity Fair; Golf Digest; Conde Nast Traveler; Wired; The New Yorker; and the soon to be launched Conde Nast Portfolio, a monthly magazine focused on business. In 2007, Conde plans launch Vogue India and expand its Chinese offerings with GQ. In a recent reorganization, the 27 individual web sites associated with such titles as Glamour and Vanity Fair have been moved to the main Conde Nast group. CondeNet continues to operate the destination sites including: Concierge.com; Epicurious.com; and Style.com. CondeNet also controls the online ad sale functions of the company. Recently, Conde Nast estimated that only 1% of its revenue is generated online. Fairchild Publications operates: DNR; MensWeaer; Footwear News; and WWD. The company also runs Conde Nast Art, which sells art and photographs featured in Conde Nast publications through catalog and e-commerce. In late 2006, Fairchild Publications sold Home Furnishings News to Macfadden Communications Group. In November 2006, CondeNet acquired Reddit.com, a social book marking site. In 2007, the company is launching Stylefinder.com, a women's fashion web site targeting 15- to 45-year olds in the U.K. Also in 2007, the company will begin testing technology that will allow readers to purchase products through mobile phone text messages.

Conde Nast's employee benefits include: A company-funded pension plan; Tuition Reimbursement; Medical and Dental Plans; A legal plan; and a Health and Fitness Allowance.

FINANCIALS: Sales and profits are in thousands of dollars—add 000 to get the full amount. 2006 Note: Financial information for 2006 was not available for all companies at press time.

2006 Sales: $	2006 Profits: $	U.S. Stock Ticker: Subsidiary
2005 Sales: $	2005 Profits: $	Int'l Ticker: Int'l Exchange:
2004 Sales: $	2004 Profits: $	Employees:
2003 Sales: $	2003 Profits: $	Fiscal Year Ends: 12/31
2002 Sales: $	2002 Profits: $	Parent Company:

SALARIES/BENEFITS:

Pension Plan: Y	ESOP Stock Plan:	Profit Sharing:	Top Exec. Salary: $	Bonus: $
Savings Plan: Y	Stock Purch. Plan:		Second Exec. Salary: $	Bonus: $

OTHER THOUGHTS:

Apparent Women Officers or Directors: 32
Hot Spot for Advancement for Women/Minorities: Y

LOCATIONS: ("Y" = Yes)

West:	Southwest:	Midwest:	Southeast:	Northeast:	International:
Y		Y		Y	Y

CORUS ENTERTAINMENT INC
www.corusent.com

Industry Group Code: 513111 Ranks within this company's industry group: Sales: 4 Profits: 5

Print Media/Publishing:	Movies:	Equipment/Supplies:	Broadcast/Cable:	Music/Audio:	Sports/Games:
Newspapers:	Movie Theaters:	Equipment/Supplies:	Broadcast TV: Y	Music Production:	Games/Sports:
Magazines:	Movie Production:	Gambling Equipment:	Cable TV: Y	Retail Music:	Retail Games Stores:
Books: Y	TV/Video Production: Y	Special Services: Y	Satellite Broadcast:	Retail Audio Equip.:	Stadiums/Teams:
Book Stores:	Video Rental:	Advertising Services: Y	Radio:	Music Print./Dist.:	Gambling/Casinos:
Distribution/Printing:	Video Distribution:	Info. Sys. Software:	Online Information:	Multimedia:	Rides/Theme Parks:

TYPES OF BUSINESS:
Radio Broadcasting
Television Broadcast & Cable
Animated Children's Programming
Children's Book Publishing
Digital Music Services
Radio Marketing Services
Online Media
Advertising Services

BRANDS/DIVISIONS/AFFILIATES:
YTV
Treehouse TV
W
Movie Central
Max Trax
Deep Sky
Nelvana
Kids Can Press

CONTACTS: Note: Officers with more than one job title may be intentionally listed here more than once.
John M. Cassaday, CEO
John M. Cassaday, Pres.
Thomas C. Peddie, CFO/Sr. VP
Hal Blackadar, VP-Human Resources
Gary Maavara, General Counsel/VP
Sally Tindall, Dir. Media Rel./Publicity
David Spence, Controller/VP
Doug Murphy, Pres., Nelvana Enterprises
John P. Hayes, Pres., Corus Radio
Paul W. Robertson, Pres., Corus Television
John R. Perraton, Corp. Sec.
Heather A. Shaw, Exec. Chair

Phone: 416-642-3770	Fax: 416-642-3779
Toll-Free:	
Address: 181 Bay St., Ste. 1630, Toronto, ON M5J 2T3 Canada	

GROWTH PLANS/SPECIAL FEATURES:
Corus Entertainment, Inc. is a leading content producer and distributor working within Canada's entertainment industry. The company runs Canada's largest private radio operation and operates a variety of pay and specialty television networks and conventional broadcast channels in Canadian markets. The company's brands include YTV (Canada's leading youth network reaching more than 8.2 million households), Treehouse TV (designed for preschool children), W (designed for women ages 25 to 54) and Movie Central (a pay-per-view network with six channels). The company's Max Trax unit offers music content through digital cable providers in Canada. Corus operates Deep Sky, a radio marketing services division. The company's Nelvana subsidiary is a leading developer, producer and distributor of media content (mostly animation) for children worldwide. It airs on over 360 broadcast outlets internationally, in over 50 different languages. Corus also operates Kids Can Press, a publisher of children's literature. The company runs ytv.com, formerly Yabber.net, an online community designed for eight- to 15-year-olds, and owns 50% of TELETOON. Pending regulatory approval, the firm and CBC/Radio Canada have reached an agreement to have CBC/Radio Canada purchase Corus' 53% ownership stake in the digital service The Documentary Channel. Recently, Nelvana announced it would begin offering video-on-demand in the U.K. through an agreement with British Telecommunications. The firm announced the launch of its Digital Signage Division (TV screens featuring information and advertising in public places) through its subsidiary, Corus Custom Networks. The firm will also offer TV content from its W Network and CMT to retail clients. In 2006, the firm announced a new portfolio structure for its Content and Television including Nelvana Enterprises (focuses on international leverage of Corus' intellectual property) and a new Lifestyle, Movies, and Drama portfolio for television (the amalgamation of Movie Central, W Network, CMT and Scream).

FINANCIALS: Sales and profits are in thousands of dollars—add 000 to get the full amount. 2006 Note: Financial information for 2006 was not available for all companies at press time.

2006 Sales: $630,060	2006 Profits: $30,770	**U.S. Stock Ticker: CJR**
2005 Sales: $575,500	2005 Profits: $59,900	**Int'l Ticker: CJR.B** Int'l Exchange: Toronto-TSX
2004 Sales: $508,400	2004 Profits: $-17,600	Employees: 3,000
2003 Sales: $464,500	2003 Profits: $28,900	Fiscal Year Ends: 8/31
2002 Sales: $418,800	2002 Profits: $-106,500	Parent Company:

SALARIES/BENEFITS:

Pension Plan: Y	ESOP Stock Plan:	Profit Sharing:	Top Exec. Salary: $	Bonus: $
Savings Plan:	Stock Purch. Plan: Y		Second Exec. Salary: $	Bonus: $

OTHER THOUGHTS:
Apparent Women Officers or Directors: 5
Hot Spot for Advancement for Women/Minorities: Y

LOCATIONS: ("Y" = Yes)

West:	Southwest:	Midwest:	Southeast:	Northeast:	International:
					Y

Note: Financial information, benefits and other data can change quickly and may vary from those stated here.

COURIER CORP

www.courier.com

Industry Group Code: 323000 Ranks within this company's industry group: Sales: 3 Profits: 3

Print Media/Publishing:	Movies:	Equipment/Supplies:	Broadcast/Cable:	Music/Audio:	Sports/Games:
Newspapers:	Movie Theaters:	Equipment/Supplies:	Broadcast TV:	Music Production:	Games/Sports:
Magazines:	Movie Production:	Gambling Equipment:	Cable TV:	Retail Music:	Retail Games Stores:
Books: Y	TV/Video Production:	Special Services: Y	Satellite Broadcast:	Retail Audio Equip.:	Stadiums/Teams:
Book Stores:	Video Rental:	Advertising Services: Y	Radio:	Music Print./Dist.: Y	Gambling/Casinos:
Distribution/Printing:	Video Distribution:	Info. Sys. Software: Y	Online Information:	Multimedia:	Rides/Theme Parks:

TYPES OF BUSINESS:

Book Printing
Software Services
Intellectual Property Management
Multimedia Development
Commercial Printing
Prepress Services
Niche Book Publishing
Fulfillment Services

BRANDS/DIVISIONS/AFFILIATES:

Creative Homeowner
Dover Publications
Research & Education Association
Courier Company, Inc.
Moore-Langen Publishing Company, Inc.
Research and Education Association, Inc. (REA)

CONTACTS: Note: Officers with more than one job title may be intentionally listed here more than once.

James F. Conway, III, CEO
Robert P. Story, Jr., Exec. VP/COO
James F. Conway, III, Pres.
Peter Folger, Sr. VP/CFO
Lee E. Cochrane, Treas./VP
Peter Clifford, VP-Courier Corporation
Kathleen Leon, Corp. Controller
Peter D. Tobin, Exec. VP-National Publishing Co.
F. Beirne Lovely, Jr., Sec./Clerk
James F. Conway, III, Chmn.

Phone: 978-251-6000	Fax: 978-251-8228
Toll-Free:	
Address: 15 Wellman Ave., North Chelmsford, MA 01863 US	

GROWTH PLANS/SPECIAL FEATURES:

Courier Corporation publishes, prints and sells books. The company has two lines of business: full-service book manufacturing and specialty publishing. It also manufactures manuals, diskettes and CD-ROMs for publishers, software developers and other information providers. Courier also offers services from content management, prepress and production through storage and distribution. Courier's principal markets are religious, educational and specialty trade books with products including Bibles, educational texts and consumer books. Courier also provides related services involved in managing the process of creating and distributing these products. The company's book manufacturing operations consist of both electronic and conventional film processing, platemaking, printing and binding of soft- and hard-bound books. Through its seven printing facilities, Courier serves the needs of certain market niches, such as short-run book manufacturing, printing on lightweight paper and four-color book manufacturing. Specialty publishing subsidiary Dover Publications, Inc. publishes over 9,000 titles in more than 30 specialty categories ranging from literature and poetry classics to paper dolls. Through its subsidiary Courier New Media, Inc., an information management services company, the company works with publishers and other information developers to create products from new and existing intellectual properties. Another subsidiary, REA, publishes over 900 Test preparation and study guides including Problem Solvers, Essentials, Super Reviews and Test Preparation books. In 2006, the firm acquired Federal Marketing Corporation (d.b.a. Creative Homeowner) for $37 million in cash. Creative Homeowner's titles include the following subjects: home decoration; home arts; hunting and fishing; design and improvement; and gardening and landscaping.

The Printing Industry of America has named Courier a Best Workplace in the Americas for the sixth consecutive year.

FINANCIALS: Sales and profits are in thousands of dollars—add 000 to get the full amount. 2006 Note: Financial information for 2006 was not available for all companies at press time.

2006 Sales: $269,051	2006 Profits: $28,380	**U.S. Stock Ticker: CRRC**
2005 Sales: $227,039	2005 Profits: $22,134	**Int'l Ticker:** Int'l Exchange:
2004 Sales: $211,179	2004 Profits: $20,540	Employees: 1,724
2003 Sales: $202,000	2003 Profits: $20,100	Fiscal Year Ends: 9/30
2002 Sales: $202,200	2002 Profits: $16,200	Parent Company:

SALARIES/BENEFITS:

Pension Plan: Y	ESOP Stock Plan: Y	Profit Sharing: Y	Top Exec. Salary: $458,500	Bonus: $358,797
Savings Plan: Y	Stock Purch. Plan: Y		Second Exec. Salary: $375,100	Bonus: $315,000

OTHER THOUGHTS:

Apparent Women Officers or Directors: 3
Hot Spot for Advancement for Women/Minorities: Y

LOCATIONS: ("Y" = Yes)

West:	Southwest:	Midwest:	Southeast:	Northeast:	International:
Y		Y		Y	

COX COMMUNICATIONS INC

www.cox.com

Industry Group Code: 513220 Ranks within this company's industry group: Sales: 7 Profits: 20

Print Media/Publishing:	Movies:		Equipment/Supplies:	Broadcast/Cable:		Music/Audio:	Sports/Games:
Newspapers:	Movie Theaters:		Equipment/Supplies:	Broadcast TV:		Music Production:	Games/Sports:
Magazines:	Movie Production:		Gambling Equipment:	Cable TV:	Y	Retail Music:	Retail Games Stores:
Books:	TV/Video Production:	Y	Special Services:	Satellite Broadcast:		Retail Audio Equip.:	Stadiums/Teams:
Book Stores:	Video Rental:		Advertising Services:	Radio:		Music Print./Dist.:	Gambling/Casinos:
Distribution/Printing:	Video Distribution:		Info. Sys. Software:	Online Information:		Multimedia:	Rides/Theme Parks:

TYPES OF BUSINESS:

Cable TV Service
Digital Cable TV Service
Cable-Based Internet Access
Local Phone Service
Long-Distance Phone Service
Business Services

BRANDS/DIVISIONS/AFFILIATES:

Cox Enterprises, Inc.
Cox Digital Cable
Cox Cable
Cox High Speed Internet
Cox Express
Cox Digital Telephone
Cox Business Services
Cox Media

CONTACTS: *Note: Officers with more than one job title may be intentionally listed here more than once.*

James O. Robbins, CEO
Patrick J. Esser, Pres.
John M. Dyer, CFO/Sr. VP
Mae A. Douglas, Chief People Officer/Sr. VP
Scott A. Hatfield, CIO/Sr. VP
Christopher J. Bowick, CTO
Christopher J. Bowick, Sr. VP-Eng.
James A. Hatcher, Sr. VP-Legal & Regulatory Affairs
Jill Campbell, Sr. VP-Oper.
Dallas S. Clement, Sr. VP-Strategy & Dev.
Ellen M. East, VP-Corp. Comm.
J. Lacey Lewis, VP-Investor Rel.
Susan W. Coker, Treas./VP
Claus F. Kroger, Sr. VP-Oper.
William J. Fitzsimmons, Chief Acct. Officer/VP-Financial Planning
James Cox Kennedy, Chmn.

Phone: 404-843-5000	**Fax:** 404-843-5975
Toll-Free:	
Address: 1400 Lake Hearn Dr. NE, Atlanta, GA 30319 US	

GROWTH PLANS/SPECIAL FEATURES:

Cox Communications, Inc., owned by Cox Enterprises, is the U.S.'s third-largest cable broadband communications company, with cable systems in 20 states serving approximately 6.7 million customers nationwide. Cox also offers a variety of residential services through its subsidiaries, including cable television under the Cox Cable brand; advanced digital video programming services under the Cox Digital Cable brand; high-speed Internet access via Cox High Speed; local and long-distance telephone services under the Cox Digital Telephone brand; and commercial voice, video and data services via Cox Business Services. Cox invests in telecommunications companies such as Sprint PCS, as well as programming networks, including the Discovery Channel and TV Works, a provider of software for digital cable systems. Cable television services include the basic cable, expanded cable, pay-per-view and entertainment-on-demand packages. In November 2005, the company sold 940,000 basic cable subscriptions to Cebridge Connections for an estimated $2.3 billion dollars. The company also announced a joint venture with Sprint, Time Warner, Comcast, Nextel and Andvance/Newhouse to offer a combined package of cable TV, high-speed Internet access, VOIP and cellular service for a single price.

Cox employees receive discounted cable television, health club discounts and free tickets to cultural and sporting events. The firm also offers tuition reimbursement, 150 free online courses and discounts through Dell, Sprint, GM, Ford and Phillips Electronics. Other benefits include adoption assistance and an employee assistance program, as well as a pension plan, a 401(k) savings plan and an employee stock purchase plan.

FINANCIALS: Sales and profits are in thousands of dollars—add 000 to get the full amount. 2006 Note: Financial information for 2006 was not available for all companies at press time.

2006 Sales: $	2006 Profits: $	**U.S. Stock Ticker: Subsidiary**
2005 Sales: $6,722,300	2005 Profits: $-230,700	**Int'l Ticker:** Int'l Exchange:
2004 Sales: $6,106,100	2004 Profits: $-2,375,300	Employees: 22,530
2003 Sales: $5,458,800	2003 Profits: $-137,801	Fiscal Year Ends: 12/31
2002 Sales: $5,039,000	2002 Profits: $-274,000	Parent Company: COX ENTERPRISES INC

SALARIES/BENEFITS:

Pension Plan: Y	ESOP Stock Plan:	Profit Sharing:	Top Exec. Salary: $1,322,900	Bonus: $1,166,798
Savings Plan: Y	Stock Purch. Plan: Y		Second Exec. Salary: $760,000	Bonus: $574,560

OTHER THOUGHTS:

Apparent Women Officers or Directors: 4
Hot Spot for Advancement for Women/Minorities: Y

LOCATIONS: ("Y" = Yes)

West:	Southwest:	Midwest:	Southeast:	Northeast:	International:
Y	Y	Y	Y	Y	

Note: Financial information, benefits and other data can change quickly and may vary from those stated here.

COX ENTERPRISES INC   www.coxenterprises.com

Industry Group Code: 511110 Ranks within this company's industry group: Sales: 1 Profits:

Print Media/Publishing:		Movies:	Equipment/Supplies:		Broadcast/Cable:		Music/Audio:	Sports/Games:
Newspapers:	Y	Movie Theaters:	Equipment/Supplies:		Broadcast TV:	Y	Music Production:	Games/Sports:
Magazines:		Movie Production:	Gambling Equipment:		Cable TV:	Y	Retail Music:	Retail Games Stores:
Books:		TV/Video Production:	Special Services:	Y	Satellite Broadcast:		Retail Audio Equip.:	Stadiums/Teams:
Book Stores:		Video Rental:	Advertising Services:	Y	Radio:		Music Print./Dist.:	Gambling/Casinos:
Distribution/Printing:		Video Distribution:	Info. Sys. Software:		Online Information:		Multimedia:	Rides/Theme Parks:

TYPES OF BUSINESS:

Newspaper Publishing
Television Broadcasting
Cable Television
Radio Stations
Online Information
Vehicle Auctions
Automotive E-Commerce
Technology Products

BRANDS/DIVISIONS/AFFILIATES:

Cox Television, Inc.
Manheim Auctions, Inc.
Cox Communications, Inc.
Cox Radio, Inc.
AutoTrader.com
Atlanta Journal-Constitution (The)
Austin American Statesman (The)
accessatlanta.com

CONTACTS: Note: Officers with more than one job title may be intentionally listed here more than once.

James Cox Kennedy, CEO
Jimmy W. Hayes, COO
Jimmy W. Hayes, Pres.
Robert C. O'Leary, CFO/Exec. VP
Deborah E. Ruth, VP-Mktg.
Marybeth H. Leamer, VP-Human Resources
Robert N. Redella, VP-Dev.
Gregory B. Morrison, CIO/VP
Timothy W. Hughes, Sr. VP-Admin.
Andrew A. Merdek, General Counsel/VP-Legal Affairs/Corp. Sec.
J. Lacey Lewis, VP-Bus. Dev.
Roberto I. Jimenez, VP-Corp. Comm. & Pub. Affairs
Richard J. Jacobson, Sr. VP-Finance/Treas.
Patrick J. Eser, Pres., Cox Communications, Inc.
John G. Boyette, Sr. VP-Investments & Admin.
Alexander V. Netchvolodoff, Sr. VP-Pub. Policy
Preston B. Barnett, General Tax Counsel/VP
James Cox Kennedy, Chmn.
Michael J. Mannheimer, VP-Supply Chain Services/Chief Procurement Officer

Phone: 678-645-0000	Fax: 678-645-1079
Toll-Free:	
Address: 6205 Peachtree Dunwoody Rd., Atlanta, GA 30328 US	

GROWTH PLANS/SPECIAL FEATURES:

Cox Enterprises, Inc. maintains a diverse array of operations, ranging from television to automobile sales. Its major subsidiaries include: Cox Communications; Cox Newspapers; Cox Television; Cox Radio; Manheim Auctions, Inc.; and AutoTrader.com. Cox Communication, a broadband communications company, delivers cable TV, high-speed Internet and telecommunications services to 6.7 million customers in 22 states. Cox Television operates 15 network affiliated stations and two local cable channels in 11 markets, reaching roughly 30 million viewers. It owns three advertising sales rep firms (TeleRep, Harrinton, MMT Sales and Righter & Parson). Cox Newspapers publishes 17 daily papers and 25 non-dailies. The division also operates a direct mail business; and Cox Custom Media, a commercial newsletter publishing company. The firm's newspapers include The Atlanta Journal-Constitution and The Austin American Statesman. Through these newspaper subsidiaries Cox also operates approximately 20 online U.S. city guides, including accessatlanta.com, accesslasvegas.com, realpittsburgh.com and sanantonio360.com, which are among the highest-ranked web sites of their kind in the country. Cox Radio, Inc., a majority owned subsidiary, is publicly traded on the NYSE under CXE. It operates 79 stations, 66 FM and 13 AM, in 18 markets to over 13 million listeners each week; and operates Internet venture CoxRadio Interactive. Through Manheim Auctions, the firm is a global remarketing organization that registers 10 million vehicles for sales events at its 135 locations worldwide and online annually. The division announced the opening of offices and business initiatives in China in 2006. It is the leader in automotive Internet commerce through AutoTrader.com, which aggregates in a single location an average of 2.8 million vehicle listings from approximately 37,000 dealers and 200,000 private owners, averaging 10 million shoppers each week.

Benefits offered at the Cox companies include medical, dental and prescription drug coverage, flexible spending accounts and long-term care insurance.

FINANCIALS: Sales and profits are in thousands of dollars—add 000 to get the full amount. 2006 Note: Financial information for 2006 was not available for all companies at press time.

2006 Sales: $	2006 Profits: $	U.S. Stock Ticker: Private
2005 Sales: $12,000,000	2005 Profits: $	Int'l Ticker: Int'l Exchange:
2004 Sales: $15,522,000	2004 Profits: $	Employees: 77,000
2003 Sales: $10,700,000	2003 Profits: $	Fiscal Year Ends: 12/31
2002 Sales: $9,900,000	2002 Profits: $	Parent Company:

SALARIES/BENEFITS:

Pension Plan: Y	ESOP Stock Plan:	Profit Sharing:	Top Exec. Salary: $	Bonus: $
Savings Plan: Y	Stock Purch. Plan:		Second Exec. Salary: $	Bonus: $

OTHER THOUGHTS:

Apparent Women Officers or Directors: 6
Hot Spot for Advancement for Women/Minorities: Y

LOCATIONS: ("Y" = Yes)

West:	Southwest:	Midwest:	Southeast:	Northeast:	International:
Y	Y	Y	Y	Y	Y

COX RADIO INC

www.coxradio.com

Industry Group Code: 513111 **Ranks within this company's industry group:** Sales: 5 Profits: 4

Print Media/Publishing:	Movies:	Equipment/Supplies:		Broadcast/Cable:	Music/Audio:	Sports/Games:
Newspapers:	Movie Theaters:	Equipment/Supplies:		Broadcast TV:	Music Production:	Games/Sports:
Magazines:	Movie Production:	Gambling Equipment:		Cable TV:	Retail Music:	Retail Games Stores:
Books:	TV/Video Production:	Special Services:		Satellite Broadcast:	Retail Audio Equip.:	Stadiums/Teams:
Book Stores:	Video Rental:	Advertising Services:	Y	Radio:	Music Print./Dist.:	Gambling/Casinos:
Distribution/Printing:	Video Distribution:	Info. Sys. Software:		Online Information:	Multimedia:	Rides/Theme Parks:

TYPES OF BUSINESS:

Radio Broadcasting
Radio Station Web Sites
Sales & Marketing Services

BRANDS/DIVISIONS/AFFILIATES:

Cox Enterprises, Inc.
Cox Radio Interactive

CONTACTS: Note: Officers with more than one job title may be intentionally listed here more than once.

Robert F. Neil, CEO
Marc W. Morgan, COO/Exec. VP
Robert F. Neil, Pres.
Neil O. Johnston, CFO/VP
Roxann L. Miller, VP-Research
Robert B. Reed, Regional VP
Richard A. Reis, Group VP
Gregg A. Lindahl, VP-Cox Radio Interactive
Caroline J. Devine, Regional VP
James C. Kennedy, Chmn.

Phone: 678-645-0000	Fax: 404-645-5294
Toll-Free:	
Address: 6205 Peachtree Dunwoody Rd., Atlanta, GA 30328 US	

GROWTH PLANS/SPECIAL FEATURES:

Cox Radio, Inc. is one of the largest radio broadcasting companies in the U.S., as well as one of the largest pure-play radio station groups. Cox Radio owns, operates or provides sales and marketing services for 80 radio stations (67 FM and 13 AM) in 18 markets. The firm operates three or more stations in 15 of its 18 markets. Moreover, it operates a wide range of programming formats in geographically diverse markets nationwide. The company is an indirect majority-owned subsidiary of Cox Enterprises, Inc., a newspaper and cable company headquartered in Atlanta, Georgia. Cox Enterprises is one of the largest media companies in the U.S. The business was operated as part of Cox Enterprises prior to its initial public offering, when Cox Enterprises transferred all of its U.S. radio operations to Cox Radio. Cox Radio, as part of Cox Enterprises, was a pioneer in radio broadcasting, building its first station in 1934. Cox Radio's business strategy seeks to maximize the revenues and broadcast cash flow of its radio stations by operating and developing clusters of stations in demographically attractive and rapidly growing markets, including Atlanta, Birmingham, Houston, Jacksonville, Miami, Orlando, San Antonio and Tampa. The company has a history of acquiring, repositioning and improving the performance of under-performing stations. Cox Radio's program formats span genres such as alternative, adult contemporary, oldies, news/talk, country, soul and gospel. The firm's newest division is Cox Radio Interactive (CXRi), whose purpose is to design, develop and assist Cox Radio's stations with their station web sites. CXRi also conducts research to determine what station listeners want from radio web sites.

Cox Radio offers its employees benefits including tax-sheltered spending accounts and an employee assistance program. Cox Radio believes in hiring from within the company.

FINANCIALS: Sales and profits are in thousands of dollars—add 000 to get the full amount. 2006 Note: Financial information for 2006 was not available for all companies at press time.

2006 Sales: $	2006 Profits: $	U.S. Stock Ticker: CXR
2005 Sales: $437,930	2005 Profits: $61,273	Int'l Ticker: Int'l Exchange:
2004 Sales: $438,213	2004 Profits: $67,966	Employees: 2,136
2003 Sales: $425,873	2003 Profits: $66,625	Fiscal Year Ends: 12/31
2002 Sales: $420,600	2002 Profits: $46,000	Parent Company:

SALARIES/BENEFITS:

Pension Plan: Y	ESOP Stock Plan:	Profit Sharing:	Top Exec. Salary: $624,000	Bonus: $354,432
Savings Plan: Y	Stock Purch. Plan: Y		Second Exec. Salary: $456,287	Bonus: $194,378

OTHER THOUGHTS:

Apparent Women Officers or Directors: 4
Hot Spot for Advancement for Women/Minorities: Y

LOCATIONS: ("Y" = Yes)

West:	Southwest:	Midwest:	Southeast:	Northeast:	International:
Y	Y	Y	Y	Y	

Note: Financial information, benefits and other data can change quickly and may vary from those stated here.

CREATIVE ARTISTS AGENCY INC | www.caa.com

Industry Group Code: 711410 Ranks within this company's industry group: Sales: Profits:

Print Media/Publishing:	Movies:	Equipment/Supplies:		Broadcast/Cable:	Music/Audio:	Sports/Games:
Newspapers:	Movie Theaters:	Equipment/Supplies:		Broadcast TV:	Music Production:	Games/Sports:
Magazines:	Movie Production:	Gambling Equipment:		Cable TV:	Retail Music:	Retail Games Stores:
Books:	TV/Video Production:	Special Services:	Y	Satellite Broadcast:	Retail Audio Equip.:	Stadiums/Teams:
Book Stores:	Video Rental:	Advertising Services:	Y	Radio:	Music Print./Dist.:	Gambling/Casinos:
Distribution/Printing:	Video Distribution:	Info. Sys. Software:		Online Information:	Multimedia:	Rides/Theme Parks:

TYPES OF BUSINESS:

Talent Agency

BRANDS/DIVISIONS/AFFILIATES:

Creative Artists Agency College Events
Creative Artists Agency Contemporary Christian

CONTACTS: *Note: Officers with more than one job title may be intentionally listed here more than once.*

Scott Clayton, Comm. Affairs
Rob Light, Partner
Lee Gabler, Partner-Television
Richard Lovett, Partner
Bryan Lourd, Partner

Phone: 310-288-4545	Fax: 310-288-4800
Toll-Free:	
Address: 9830 Wilshire Blv., Beverly Hills, CA 90212-1825 US	

GROWTH PLANS/SPECIAL FEATURES:

Creative Artists Agency, Inc. (CAA) is one of the most prestigious talent agencies in the U.S. The firm represents talent of all kinds, including actors, athletes, writers, directors, and companies and their products. CAA's sports division is a major player in college football with a track record of signing premier prospects. The firm maintains a college events department that coordinates events for musicians, comedians and speakers. The college events department has a website (college.caa.com), which features talent biographies and availability, agent contact information and a promoter area for interested parties. CAA also has a division dedicated to contemporary Christian music. Some of the artists represented by the division include Amy Grant, Jars of Clay, Michael W. Smith, Relient K, Third Day, Steven Curtis Chapman and TobyMac. This division also has a website (ccm.caa.com) with similar content to the college events website. CAA's most famous division is the one working with Hollywood talent. Hilary Swank, Christian Slater, Tom Cruise, Angelina Jolie and Julia Roberts are on the firm's roster. CAA's final division is dedicated to corporate clients, including Coca-Cola and Proctor & Gamble. The firm is planning to move out of their Beverly Hills headquarters into a new location in Century City in 2007. The firm also has an office in Beijing, China.

FINANCIALS: Sales and profits are in thousands of dollars—add 000 to get the full amount. 2006 Note: Financial information for 2006 was not available for all companies at press time.

2006 Sales: $	2006 Profits: $	**U.S. Stock Ticker: Private**
2005 Sales: $	2005 Profits: $	**Int'l Ticker:** Int'l Exchange:
2004 Sales: $	2004 Profits: $	Employees:
2003 Sales: $	2003 Profits: $	Fiscal Year Ends: 12/31
2002 Sales: $	2002 Profits: $	Parent Company:

SALARIES/BENEFITS:

Pension Plan:	ESOP Stock Plan:	Profit Sharing:	Top Exec. Salary: $	Bonus: $
Savings Plan:	Stock Purch. Plan:		Second Exec. Salary: $	Bonus: $

OTHER THOUGHTS:

Apparent Women Officers or Directors:
Hot Spot for Advancement for Women/Minorities:

LOCATIONS: ("Y" = Yes)

West:	Southwest:	Midwest:	Southeast:	Northeast:	International:
Y					Y

CROWN MEDIA HOLDINGS INC
www.crownmedia.net

Industry Group Code: 513210 Ranks within this company's industry group: Sales: 10   Profits: 4

Print Media/Publishing:	Movies:		Equipment/Supplies:		Broadcast/Cable:		Music/Audio:		Sports/Games:	
Newspapers:	Movie Theaters:		Equipment/Supplies:		Broadcast TV:		Music Production:		Games/Sports:	
Magazines:	Movie Production:		Gambling Equipment:		Cable TV:	Y	Retail Music:		Retail Games Stores:	
Books:	TV/Video Production:	Y	Special Services:		Satellite Broadcast:		Retail Audio Equip.:		Stadiums/Teams:	
Book Stores:	Video Rental:		Advertising Services:		Radio:		Music Print./Dist.:		Gambling/Casinos:	
Distribution/Printing:	Video Distribution:		Info. Sys. Software:		Online Information:		Multimedia:		Rides/Theme Parks:	

TYPES OF BUSINESS:
Cable Television
Film Distribution
Television Production

BRANDS/DIVISIONS/AFFILIATES:
Hallmark Channel (The)
Hallmark Movie Channel (The)
Hallmark Entertainment, Inc.
Crown Media Distribution

CONTACTS: *Note: Officers with more than one job title may be intentionally listed here more than once.*
Henry Schleiff, CEO
Henry Schleiff, Pres.
Brian Stewart, CFO
William Abbott, VP-Advertising Sales
Charles L. Stanford, VP-Legal Bus. Affairs & General Counsel
David Kenin, Exec. VP-Programming
Donald J. Hall, Jr., Co-Chmn.
Herbert A. Granath, Co-Chmn.

Phone: 818-755-2400	**Fax:** 303-220-7660
Toll-Free:	
Address: 12700 Ventura Blvd., Studio City, CA 91604 US	

GROWTH PLANS/SPECIAL FEATURES:
Crown Media Holdings, Inc. owns and operates two television channels, The Hallmark Channel and The Hallmark movie channel. These channels are available in the U.S. and over 110 international markets, reaching 75 million subscribers through more than 5,300 cable systems. Hallmark Entertainment, Inc. holds approximately 91% of the voting power for Crown Media Holdings. The firm focuses on family-friendly television; its primary target demographic is women aged 25-54. Crown Media also has approximately 600 television and movie programs in its library, which it distributes through Crown Media Distribution. Crown Media's program library includes Larry McMurtry's Lonesome Dove, 10th Kingdom, Sabrina the Teenage Witch, Dog of the Yukon: Call of the Wild, William Faulkner's Old Man, Rose Hill, Sarah Plain and Tall, and What the Deaf Man Heard. Examples of third-party programming shown on the company's domestic channel include the popular series M*A*S*H, Magnum P.I., Matlock, Touched By An Angel, Rawhide, Bonanza and Perry Mason. Other examples of its third-party programming include acquired movies and miniseries such as Roots, North and South, The Thorn Birds and Shogun. Crown Media Holdings has a number of distribution agreements with leading cable television distributors, including AOL Time Warner, DirecTV, Adelphia, EchoStar and Sky Network. In November 2006, the corporation entered into an agreement to sell its Media Film Library to RHI Enterprises, LLC. This sale transfers ownership in the U.S. of more than 600 series, mini-series, and television movies. Crown Media retains rights to broadcast certain titles from the film library on the Hallmark Movie Channel for two years. In addition, the firm contracted RHI Entertainment Distribution (previously Hallmark Entertainment Division before being sold by Hallmark Cards in early 2006) to produce 31 original movies and 6 original mini-series in 2006, and 18 original movies and 3 original mini-series in 2007.

FINANCIALS: Sales and profits are in thousands of dollars—add 000 to get the full amount. 2006 Note: Financial information for 2006 was not available for all companies at press time.

2006 Sales: $	2006 Profits: $	**U.S. Stock Ticker:** CRWN
2005 Sales: $197,384	2005 Profits: $-232,758	**Int'l Ticker:** Int'l Exchange:
2004 Sales: $138,236	2004 Profits: $-316,806	Employees: 186
2003 Sales: $99,433	2003 Profits: $-205,153	Fiscal Year Ends: 12/31
2002 Sales: $161,000	2002 Profits: $-311,700	Parent Company:

SALARIES/BENEFITS:

Pension Plan:	ESOP Stock Plan:	Profit Sharing:	Top Exec. Salary: $1,312,500	Bonus: $377,568
Savings Plan: Y	Stock Purch. Plan:		Second Exec. Salary: $714,142	Bonus: $178,750

OTHER THOUGHTS:
Apparent Women Officers or Directors: 1
Hot Spot for Advancement for Women/Minorities:

LOCATIONS: ("Y" = Yes)

West:	Southwest:	Midwest:	Southeast:	Northeast:	International:
Y					

Note: Financial information, benefits and other data can change quickly and may vary from those stated here.

CUMULUS MEDIA INC   www.cumulus.com

Industry Group Code: 513111 Ranks within this company's industry group: Sales: 9   Profits: 12

Print Media/Publishing:	Movies:	Equipment/Supplies:		Broadcast/Cable:	Music/Audio:	Sports/Games:
Newspapers:	Movie Theaters:	Equipment/Supplies:		Broadcast TV:	Music Production:	Games/Sports:
Magazines:	Movie Production:	Gambling Equipment:		Cable TV:	Retail Music:	Retail Games Stores:
Books:	TV/Video Production:	Special Services:		Satellite Broadcast:	Retail Audio Equip.:	Stadiums/Teams:
Book Stores:	Video Rental:	Advertising Services:	Y	Radio:	Music Print./Dist.:	Gambling/Casinos:
Distribution/Printing:	Video Distribution:	Info. Sys. Software:	Y	Online Information:	Multimedia:	Rides/Theme Parks:

TYPES OF BUSINESS:

Radio Station Operator
Sales & Marketing Services
Media Operations Software

BRANDS/DIVISIONS/AFFILIATES:

Aurora Communications, LLC
DBBC, LLC
Broadcast Software International, Inc.
Cumulus Broadcasting
AdVisory Board, Inc.
Cumulus Media Partners
Susquehanna Pfaltzgraff Radio

CONTACTS: Note: Officers with more than one job title may be intentionally listed here more than once.

Lewis W. Dickey, Jr., CEO
Jonathan Pinch, COO/Exec. VP
Lewis W. Dickey, Jr., Pres.
Martin R. Gausvik, CFO/Exec. VP
John W. Dickey, VP-Mktg. & Promotion
Richard Denning, General Counsel/VP
Martin R. Gausvik, Treas.
John W. Dickey, Exec. VP
Lewis W. Dickey, Jr., Chmn.

Phone: 404-949-0700	Fax: 404-443-0743
Toll-Free:	
Address: 14 Piedmont Center, Ste. 1400, Atlanta, GA 30305 US	

GROWTH PLANS/SPECIAL FEATURES:

Cumulus Media, Inc., the country's second-largest operator of FM and AM radio broadcasters, acquires and develops radio stations and clusters in regional mid-size markets. In 2006, the firm joined with Bain Capital, Blackstone Group, and Thomas Lee Partners to form Cumulus Media Partners, LLC and acquire Susquehanna Pfaltzgraff Radio (broadcasting company) for $1.2 billion. Cumulus now owns over 345 stations in 67 U.S. markets. These stations are located in the U.S. with an additional network of five radio stations serving the English-language Caribbean market, including Barbados. Through Cumulus Media Partners, LLC, the company also operates in Tortola. The firm also provides sales and marketing services under local marketing, management and consulting agreements. Cumulus has diversified radio formats and target audiences within each market to attract larger and broader listener audiences and thereby interest a wider range of advertisers. The company owns DBBC, LLC, a broadcasting company operating 18 stations in Connecticut and New York and, Aurora Communications, LLC, which owns and operates three stations in Nashville, Tennessee. It also owns Broadcast Software International, Inc., a media operations software and systems company. Cumulus uses Internet-based software applications enabling the company to monitor daily sales performance by station and market compared with each station's respective budget. This system also provides each station with the ability to exchange ideas and views regarding station operations and ways to increase advertising revenues. Stations within each market share infrastructure in terms of office space, support personnel and certain senior management However, each station is developed and marketed as an individual brand with its own identity, programming, programming personnel, inventory of time slots and sales force. Company revenues are generated from the sale of local, regional and national advertising time. Local sales represent, on average, four-fifths of the company's advertising revenues.

FINANCIALS: Sales and profits are in thousands of dollars—add 000 to get the full amount. 2006 Note: Financial information for 2006 was not available for all companies at press time.

2006 Sales: $	2006 Profits: $	U.S. Stock Ticker: CMLS
2005 Sales: $327,756	2005 Profits: $-213,367	Int'l Ticker: Int'l Exchange:
2004 Sales: $320,132	2004 Profits: $30,369	Employees: 3,392
2003 Sales: $309,459	2003 Profits: $5,041	Fiscal Year Ends: 12/31
2002 Sales: $252,600	2002 Profits: $-92,800	Parent Company:

SALARIES/BENEFITS:

Pension Plan: Y	ESOP Stock Plan:	Profit Sharing:	Top Exec. Salary: $774,830	Bonus: $700,000
Savings Plan: Y	Stock Purch. Plan: Y		Second Exec. Salary: $532,400	Bonus: $225,000

OTHER THOUGHTS:

Apparent Women Officers or Directors:
Hot Spot for Advancement for Women/Minorities:

LOCATIONS: ("Y" = Yes)

West:	Southwest:	Midwest:	Southeast:	Northeast:	International:
Y	Y	Y	Y	Y	Y

CURVES INTERNATIONAL INC   www.curvesinternational.com

Industry Group Code: 713940 Ranks within this company's industry group: Sales: Profits:

Print Media/Publishing:		Movies:		Equipment/Supplies:		Broadcast/Cable:		Music/Audio:		Sports/Games:	
Newspapers:		Movie Theaters:		Equipment/Supplies:		Broadcast TV:		Music Production:		Games/Sports:	Y
Magazines:	Y	Movie Production:		Gambling Equipment:		Cable TV:		Retail Music:		Retail Games Stores:	
Books:		TV/Video Production:		Special Services:	Y	Satellite Broadcast:		Retail Audio Equip.:		Stadiums/Teams:	
Book Stores:		Video Rental:		Advertising Services:		Radio:		Music Print./Dist.:		Gambling/Casinos:	
Distribution/Printing:		Video Distribution:		Info. Sys. Software:		Online Information:		Multimedia:		Rides/Theme Parks:	

TYPES OF BUSINESS:

Fitness Centers
Magazine Publishing
Health Products
Travel Services
Online Information

BRANDS/DIVISIONS/AFFILIATES:

diane Magazine
Curves Heart Rate Monitor Watch
Curves Fitness Pedometer
Curves Flexibilty Mat
Curves Free Foods On the Go Lunchbox
Curves Travel
curvestravel.com

CONTACTS: *Note: Officers with more than one job title may be intentionally listed here more than once.*

Gary Heavin, CEO/Founder
Michael Raymond, Pres.
Becky Frusher, Comm. Specialist
Diane Heavin, Founder

Phone: 254-399-9285	Fax: 254-399-9731
Toll-Free: 800-848-1096	
Address: 100 Ritchie Rd., Waco, TX 76712 US	

GROWTH PLANS/SPECIAL FEATURES:

Curves International is one of the largest fitness franchises in the world, with approximately 10,000 franchised locations in 42 countries including the U.S., Canada, Mexico, Central America, The Caribbean, Australia, New Zealand and the U.K. The company provides fitness and weight-loss facilities specifically designed for women. Curves currently helps over 4 million women with their exercise and nutritional guidance needs. Its program provides a 30-minute circuit training workout session where all of the machines are arranged in a circle and clients can talk to each other as they move through the circuit. In addition to 30-minute workout sessions at Curves fitness facilities, the company provides a comprehensive program to educate and train women in healthy eating patterns. This program includes books, meal planners, tracking charts, weekly progress reports and other information geared toward helping women eat healthily. Through its web site, Curves provides links to other sites dedicated to educating women about the dangers of obesity and other serious diseases related to unhealthy living. The company recently launched diane magazine, and formed a partnership with Avon to create an exclusive line of Curves products for women, including the Curves Heart Rate Monitor Watch, Curves Fitness Pedometer, Curves Flexibility Mat and Curves Free Foods On the Go Lunchbox. Curves also recently launched its first franchise in Japan, with 2,000 more planned to open by 2010. Subsidiary Curves Travel operates mainly from curvestravel.com and offers deals and free booking and planning services to Curves members.

FINANCIALS: Sales and profits are in thousands of dollars—add 000 to get the full amount. 2006 Note: Financial information for 2006 was not available for all companies at press time.

2006 Sales: $	2006 Profits: $	U.S. Stock Ticker: Private
2005 Sales: $	2005 Profits: $	Int'l Ticker: Int'l Exchange:
2004 Sales: $	2004 Profits: $	Employees:
2003 Sales: $	2003 Profits: $	Fiscal Year Ends: 12/31
2002 Sales: $750,000	2002 Profits: $	Parent Company:

SALARIES/BENEFITS:

Pension Plan:	ESOP Stock Plan:	Profit Sharing:	Top Exec. Salary: $	Bonus: $
Savings Plan:	Stock Purch. Plan:		Second Exec. Salary: $	Bonus: $

OTHER THOUGHTS:

Apparent Women Officers or Directors: 2
Hot Spot for Advancement for Women/Minorities:

LOCATIONS: ("Y" = Yes)

West:	Southwest:	Midwest:	Southeast:	Northeast:	International:
Y	Y	Y	Y	Y	Y

Note: Financial information, benefits and other data can change quickly and may vary from those stated here.

CW NETWORK (THE)   www.cwtv.com

Industry Group Code: 513210 Ranks within this company's industry group: Sales: Profits:

Print Media/Publishing:	Movies:	Equipment/Supplies:	Broadcast/Cable:		Music/Audio:		Sports/Games:
Newspapers:	Movie Theaters:	Equipment/Supplies:	Broadcast TV:	Y	Music Production:	Y	Games/Sports:
Magazines:	Movie Production:	Gambling Equipment:	Cable TV:		Retail Music:		Retail Games Stores:
Books:	TV/Video Production: Y	Special Services:	Satellite Broadcast:		Retail Audio Equip.:		Stadiums/Teams:
Book Stores:	Video Rental:	Advertising Services:	Radio:		Music Print./Dist.:	Y	Gambling/Casinos:
Distribution/Printing:	Video Distribution:	Info. Sys. Software:	Online Information:		Multimedia:		Rides/Theme Parks:

TYPES OF BUSINESS:

Television Broadcasting
Television Production
Soundtrack Recordings
DVD Distribution

BRANDS/DIVISIONS/AFFILIATES:

CBS Corp.
Time Warner, Inc.
WB
UPN
Gilmore Girls
Beauty and the Geek
Everybody Hates Chris
Smallville

CONTACTS: Note: Officers with more than one job title may be intentionally listed here more than once.

John Maatta, COO
Dawn Ostroff, Pres.
Rich Haskins, Exec. VP-Mktg.
Eric Cardinal, Sr. VP-Research
Elizabeth Tumulty, Sr. VP-Network Distribution
Mitch Nedick, Exec. VP-Oper.
Rich Haskins, Exec. VP-Brand Strategy
Paul McGuire, Sr. VP-Network Comm.
Mitch Nedick, Exec. VP-Finance
Kim Fleary, Exec. VP-Comedy Dev.
Betsy Mc Gowen, Sr. VP/Gen. Mgr.-Kids WB! on The CW
Jennifer Bresnan, Sr. VP-Alternative Programming
Rick Mater, Sr. VP-Broadcast Standards

Phone: 818-977-5000	Fax: 818-977-6771
Toll-Free:	
Address: 4000 Warner Blvd., Bldg. 34R, Burbank, CA 91522 US	

GROWTH PLANS/SPECIAL FEATURES:

The CW Network is a 50-50 joint venture between CBS Corp. and Warner Bros. Entertainment (subsidiary of Time Warner), formed after the merger of the fledgling WB (owned by Time Warner) and UPN (owned by CBS) networks in 2006. The company provides proprietary television programming during prime-time hours for six nights a week, as well as a five-day-a-week afternoon lineup and a five-hour Saturday morning animation block. The CW's television shows include Smallville, Charmed and Gilmore Girls for teenagers and college students; family-oriented shows such as 7th Heaven, Beauty and the Geek, and Supernatural; and other popular programming, including Reba (the top rated sitcom on the network), Everybody Hates Chris, One Tree Hill, WWE Smackdown! The firm also offers show soundtracks, DVD sets and related merchandise. During Saturday mornings, the CW provides children's programming, including the Pokemon cartoon series. The CW reaches approximately 48% of households in the U.S., aiming for 95%. The company is in the process of changing programming to suit an older audience and producing original movies in an attempt to reverse low broadcasting ratings. The network began broadcasting in 2006, at which time the UPN and WB networks ceased operations. Tribune Co., which held a 22.5% stake in the WB, and CBS's UPN affiliates have signed a 10-year agreement to carry the CW network. In 2006, the firm launched a new version of its website, featuring a link to Kids WB, in-depth information on CW shows, as well as online chat forum for viewers. In 2007, the firm plans on introducing two new shows to its lineup, including The Search for the Next Pussycat Doll and Hidden Palms.

FINANCIALS: Sales and profits are in thousands of dollars—add 000 to get the full amount. 2006 Note: Financial information for 2006 was not available for all companies at press time.

2006 Sales: $	2006 Profits: $	U.S. Stock Ticker: Joint Venture
2005 Sales: $	2005 Profits: $	Int'l Ticker: Int'l Exchange:
2004 Sales: $700,000	2004 Profits: $	Employees:
2003 Sales: $660,000	2003 Profits: $	Fiscal Year Ends: 12/31
2002 Sales: $589,000	2002 Profits: $	Parent Company:

SALARIES/BENEFITS:

Pension Plan:	ESOP Stock Plan:	Profit Sharing:	Top Exec. Salary: $	Bonus: $
Savings Plan:	Stock Purch. Plan:		Second Exec. Salary: $	Bonus: $

OTHER THOUGHTS:

Apparent Women Officers or Directors: 5
Hot Spot for Advancement for Women/Minorities: Y

LOCATIONS: ("Y" = Yes)

West:	Southwest:	Midwest:	Southeast:	Northeast:	International:
Y					

DAG MEDIA INC

www.newyellow.com

Industry Group Code: 511140 Ranks within this company's industry group: Sales: 3 Profits: 3

Print Media/Publishing:	Movies:	Equipment/Supplies:		Broadcast/Cable:	Music/Audio:	Sports/Games:
Newspapers:	Movie Theaters:	Equipment/Supplies:		Broadcast TV:	Music Production:	Games/Sports:
Magazines:	Movie Production:	Gambling Equipment:		Cable TV:	Retail Music:	Retail Games Stores:
Books:	TV/Video Production:	Special Services:	Y	Satellite Broadcast:	Retail Audio Equip.:	Stadiums/Teams:
Book Stores:	Video Rental:	Advertising Services:	Y	Radio:	Music Print./Dist.:	Gambling/Casinos:
Distribution/Printing:	Video Distribution:	Info. Sys. Software:		Online Information:	Multimedia:	Rides/Theme Parks:

TYPES OF BUSINESS:

Directory Publishing
Yellow Pages Publications
Internet Portals
Hebrew-Language Publishing

BRANDS/DIVISIONS/AFFILIATES:

Jewish Israeli Yellow Pages (The)
Jewish Master Guide (The)
Kosher Yellow Pages
JewishYellow.com
JewishMasterguide.com
theonlykosherdirectory.com
Next Yellow (The)
Shopila Corporation

CONTACTS: Note: Officers with more than one job title may be intentionally listed here more than once.

Assaf N. Ran, CEO
Assaf N. Ran, Pres.
Inbar Evron-Yogev, CFO
Mark Alhadeff, CTO
Hagit Evenhaim, General Counsel
Assaf N. Ran, Chmn.

Phone: 718-520-1000	Fax: 718-793-2522
Toll-Free: 800-261-2799	
Address: 125-10 Queens Blvd., Ste. 14, Kew Gardens, NY 11415 US	

GROWTH PLANS/SPECIAL FEATURES:

DAG Media, Inc. is a publisher and distributor of business directories, both online and in print, for niche markets, particularly aimed at the Jewish communities in the U.S. The firm's primary source of revenue is derived from the sales of advertising space in these directories. Its primary directories are the Jewish Israeli Yellow Pages and the Jewish Master Guide. The Jewish Israeli Yellow Pages is a bilingual directory using both English and Hebrew. All advertisements are published in both languages, unless the advertiser specifically requests English-only. Quebecor World, Inc. prints the book in the U.S. and transports the finished product to DAG Media's New York office for distribution. The Jewish Master Guide, also known as the Kosher Yellow Pages, is a yellow page directory targeting the specific needs of the Hasidic and Orthodox Jewish communities in the greater New York City area. Unlike the Jewish Israeli book, the Jewish Master Guide is printed in English only and does not include any advertisements for services or products that might be offensive to the Orthodox Jewish and Hasidic communities. This directory is distributed by placing copies in synagogues and businesses located in Orthodox Jewish and Hasidic neighborhoods. In addition to printed publications, DAG also operates Internet portals including JewishYellow.com, JewishMasterGuide.com and theonlykosherdirectory.com. As a service to both the directory users and the advertisers in the books, the company provides a referral service. Recent news includes the launch of The Next Yellow website in June 2006, and the acquisition of 80% of the stock of Shopila Corporation in October 2006.

FINANCIALS: Sales and profits are in thousands of dollars—add 000 to get the full amount. 2006 Note: Financial information for 2006 was not available for all companies at press time.

2006 Sales: $	2006 Profits: $	U.S. Stock Ticker: DAGM
2005 Sales: $4,447	2005 Profits: $- 511	Int'l Ticker: Int'l Exchange:
2004 Sales: $5,949	2004 Profits: $1,035	Employees: 19
2003 Sales: $9,086	2003 Profits: $1,599	Fiscal Year Ends: 12/31
2002 Sales: $6,500	2002 Profits: $-1,100	Parent Company:

SALARIES/BENEFITS:

Pension Plan:	ESOP Stock Plan:	Profit Sharing:	Top Exec. Salary: $225,000	Bonus: $
Savings Plan:	Stock Purch. Plan:		Second Exec. Salary: $112,115	Bonus: $

OTHER THOUGHTS:

Apparent Women Officers or Directors: 1
Hot Spot for Advancement for Women/Minorities:

LOCATIONS: ("Y" = Yes)

West:	Southwest:	Midwest:	Southeast:	Northeast:	International:
				Y	

DAILY JOURNAL CORP   www.dailyjournal.com

Industry Group Code: 511110 Ranks within this company's industry group: Sales: 22 Profits: 15

Print Media/Publishing:		Movies:		Equipment/Supplies:		Broadcast/Cable:		Music/Audio:		Sports/Games:	
Newspapers:	Y	Movie Theaters:		Equipment/Supplies:		Broadcast TV:		Music Production:		Games/Sports:	
Magazines:	Y	Movie Production:		Gambling Equipment:		Cable TV:		Retail Music:		Retail Games Stores:	
Books:		TV/Video Production:		Special Services:	Y	Satellite Broadcast:		Retail Audio Equip.:		Stadiums/Teams:	
Book Stores:		Video Rental:		Advertising Services:	Y	Radio:		Music Print./Dist.:		Gambling/Casinos:	
Distribution/Printing:		Video Distribution:		Info. Sys. Software:		Online Information:		Multimedia:		Rides/Theme Parks:	

TYPES OF BUSINESS:

Newspaper Publishing
Online Publishing
Information Services
Judicial Publishing Technology

BRANDS/DIVISIONS/AFFILIATES:

Los Angeles Daily Journal
San Francisco Daily Journal
Nevada Journal (The)
California Real Estate Journal
Daily Recorder (The)
San Jose Post (The)
Business Journal
SUSTAIN Technologies, Inc.

CONTACTS: Note: Officers with more than one job title may be intentionally listed here more than once.

Gerald L. Salzman, CEO
Gerald L. Salzman, Pres.
Peter Daum, CTO
Gerald L. Salzman, Treas.
Ira A. Marshall, Corp. Sec.
Charles Munger, Chmn.

Phone: 213-229-5300	Fax: 213-680-3682
Toll-Free:	
Address: 915 E. First St., Los Angeles, CA 90012 US	

GROWTH PLANS/SPECIAL FEATURES:

Daily Journal Corporation operates web sites and publishes newspapers in California, Arizona and Nevada. The company also serves as a newspaper representative, specializing in public notice advertising. Its publications, which total 19 in general circulation, include the Los Angeles Daily Journal, San Francisco Daily Journal, The Daily Recorder, The San Jose Post, Business Journal, The Nevada Journal and California Real Estate Journal. These publications operate predominately on a subscription basis, and many of them cover issues concerning business, legal and real estate matters. Additionally, the company produces various information services, in print and online, including court rules, judicial profiles, bankruptcy notices and real estate services. Daily Journal's subsidiary SUSTAIN Technologies, Inc. provides technologies and applications to enable justice agencies to automate their operations, to allow users to file cases electronically and to allow courts to publish information online. Specialized information services include Judicial Profiles services, which contain biographical and professional information concerning nearly all judges in California; several court rules services, which reproduce court rules for certain state and federal courts in California; and online foreclosure information.

FINANCIALS: Sales and profits are in thousands of dollars—add 000 to get the full amount. 2006 Note: Financial information for 2006 was not available for all companies at press time.

2006 Sales: $32,369	2006 Profits: $2,438	**U.S. Stock Ticker: DJCO**
2005 Sales: $33,272	2005 Profits: $4,287	**Int'l Ticker:** Int'l Exchange:
2004 Sales: $33,862	2004 Profits: $3,731	Employees: 275
2003 Sales: $34,229	2003 Profits: $2,403	Fiscal Year Ends: 9/30
2002 Sales: $34,000	2002 Profits: $1,200	Parent Company:

SALARIES/BENEFITS:

Pension Plan:	ESOP Stock Plan:	Profit Sharing:	Top Exec. Salary: $250,000	Bonus: $250,000
Savings Plan: Y	Stock Purch. Plan:		Second Exec. Salary: $	Bonus: $

OTHER THOUGHTS:

Apparent Women Officers or Directors:
Hot Spot for Advancement for Women/Minorities:

LOCATIONS: ("Y" = Yes)

West:	Southwest:	Midwest:	Southeast:	Northeast:	International:
Y	Y			Y	

DELAWARE NORTH COMPANIES   www.delawarenorth.com

Industry Group Code: 453220 Ranks within this company's industry group: Sales: 1   Profits:

Print Media/Publishing:	Movies:	Equipment/Supplies:		Broadcast/Cable:	Music/Audio:	Sports/Games:	
Newspapers:	Movie Theaters:	Equipment/Supplies:		Broadcast TV:	Music Production:	Games/Sports:	
Magazines:	Movie Production:	Gambling Equipment:	Y	Cable TV:	Retail Music:	Retail Games Stores:	
Books:	TV/Video Production:	Special Services:	Y	Satellite Broadcast:	Retail Audio Equip.:	Stadiums/Teams:	Y
Book Stores:	Video Rental:	Advertising Services:		Radio:	Music Print./Dist.:	Gambling/Casinos:	
Distribution/Printing:	Video Distribution:	Info. Sys. Software:		Online Information:	Multimedia:	Rides/Theme Parks:	

TYPES OF BUSINESS:
Concession Stands
Catering & Food Services
Park & Resort Visitor Services
Professional Hockey Team
Event Centers
Pari-Mutuel Wagering

BRANDS/DIVISIONS/AFFILIATES:
Sportservice Corp.
DNC Travel Hospitality Services
DNC Parks & Resorts
Boston Bruins
American Park 'n Swap
DNC International
TD BankNorth Garden

CONTACTS: *Note: Officers with more than one job title may be intentionally listed here more than once.*
Jeremy M. Jacobs, Sr., CEO
Charles Moran, Jr., COO
Charles Moran, Jr., Pres.
Karen L. Kemp, CFO
Eileen Morgan, VP-Human Resources
Molly M. Fine, VP-IT
Gregory J. Lesperance, VP-Tech. & Bus. Process Solutions
Bryan J. Keller, General Counsel
Stephen Nowaczyk, VP-Financial Planning & Analysis
Wendy A. Watkins, VP-Corp. Comm. & Public Rel.
Daniel J. Zimmer, Treas./VP
William J. Bissett, VP-External Affairs
Ronald A. Sultemeier, Pres., Gaming & Entertainment Corp.
John A. Wentzell, Pres., Boston & TD BankNorth Garden
Dennis J. Szefel, Pres., Hospitality Group
Jeremy M. Jacobs, Sr., Chmn.
Johnathan Tribe, Mgr.-Delaware North Int'l

Phone: 716-858-5000   **Fax:** 716-858-5479
Toll-Free:
Address: 40 Fountain Plaza, Buffalo, NY 14202-2200 US

GROWTH PLANS/SPECIAL FEATURES:
Delaware North Companies, Inc. (DNC), one of the largest private companies in America, is a holding company for seven subsidiaries that operate in food service, hospitality and recreation: DNC Gaming and Entertainment, Sportservice Corp., DNC Parks and Resorts, DNC Travel Hospitality Services, American Park 'n Swap, DNC International and TD BankNorth Garden. DNC Gaming and Entertainment is one of the largest and most successful operators of pari-mutuel facilities in the U.S., with gaming and racing properties in Arizona, Arkansas, Florida, New York and West Virginia, featuring wagering on greyhound and horse racing, video slot gaming and fine dining. Sportservice Corp., the oldest of the firm's subsidiaries, is one of the largest food service companies in the country, providing food, beverage and retail services at high-profile events and over 50 ballparks, arenas and stadiums in the U.S. and Canada. DNC Parks and Resorts provides recreational visitor services at national attractions including Yosemite, Grand Canyon, Niagara Falls and Kennedy Space Center. DNC Travel Hospitality Services operates food service and retail facilities in 30 airports across the country. Another subsidiary, American Park 'n Swap, turns idle buildings and empty parking lots into destination events with musical entertainment, an array of foods and flea-market-style retail merchandise ranging from jewelry to tools and furniture. DNC International brings the company's food and hospitality services to Australia. In addition, DNC owns the Boston Bruins professional hockey team and operates the TD BankNorth Garden, a $160-million facility that houses the Bruins, the Boston Celtics and other entertainment events. In April 2006, the company agreed to sell the Delta Queen Steamboat Company to Ambassadors International, Inc.

FINANCIALS: Sales and profits are in thousands of dollars—add 000 to get the full amount. 2006 Note: Financial information for 2006 was not available for all companies at press time.
2006 Sales: $	2006 Profits: $	**U.S. Stock Ticker:** Private
2005 Sales: $2,000,000	2005 Profits: $	**Int'l Ticker:** Int'l Exchange:
2004 Sales: $1,700,000	2004 Profits: $	Employees: 30,000
2003 Sales: $1,600,000	2003 Profits: $	Fiscal Year Ends: 12/31
2002 Sales: $1,300,000	2002 Profits: $	Parent Company:

SALARIES/BENEFITS:
Pension Plan:	ESOP Stock Plan:	Profit Sharing:	Top Exec. Salary: $	Bonus: $
Savings Plan:	Stock Purch. Plan:		Second Exec. Salary: $	Bonus: $

OTHER THOUGHTS:
Apparent Women Officers or Directors: 4
Hot Spot for Advancement for Women/Minorities: Y

LOCATIONS: ("Y" = Yes)
West:	Southwest:	Midwest:	Southeast:	Northeast:	International:
Y	Y	Y	Y	Y	Y

Note: Financial information, benefits and other data can change quickly and may vary from those stated here.

DENNIS PUBLISHING LTD

www.theden.co.uk

Industry Group Code: 511120 Ranks within this company's industry group: Sales: 16   Profits: 6

Print Media/Publishing:	Movies:	Equipment/Supplies:	Broadcast/Cable:	Music/Audio:	Sports/Games:
Newspapers:	Movie Theaters:	Equipment/Supplies:	Broadcast TV:	Music Production:	Games/Sports:
Magazines: Y	Movie Production:	Gambling Equipment:	Cable TV:	Retail Music:	Retail Games Stores:
Books:	TV/Video Production:	Special Services: Y	Satellite Broadcast:	Retail Audio Equip.:	Stadiums/Teams:
Book Stores:	Video Rental:	Advertising Services: Y	Radio:	Music Print./Dist.:	Gambling/Casinos:
Distribution/Printing:	Video Distribution:	Info. Sys. Software:	Online Information:	Multimedia:	Rides/Theme Parks:

TYPES OF BUSINESS:

Magazine Publishing
Mailing Lists
Interactive Media
Mail Order & Fulfillment Services

BRANDS/DIVISIONS/AFFILIATES:

Maxim
Men's Fitness
Mac User
PC Pro
The Week
Fortean Times
Seymour Distribution Ltd.
Dennis Direct

CONTACTS: Note: Officers with more than one job title may be intentionally listed here more than once.

James Tye, CEO
Brett W. Reynolds, COO
Ian Leggett, Group Dir.-Finance
Julian Lloyd-Evans, Group Dir.-Advertising
Isabel Forbes, Human Resources Advisor
Guy Sneesby, Mng. Dir.-Dennis Interactive
Guy Sneesby, Mng. Dir.-Dennis Interactive
Pete Wootton, Dir.-Oper.
Guy Sneesby, Mng. Dir.-Dennis Interactive
Enfys Roberts, PR Mgr.
John Garewell, Publishing Dir.-Computer Div.
Bruce Sandell, Managing Dir.-Consumer Div.
Steven Colvin, Pres./CEO-Dennis Publishing U.S.
Felix Dennis, Chmn.
Richard Bean, Head-Int'l Licensing

Phone: 44-207-907-6000	**Fax:** 44-207-907-6020
Toll-Free:	
Address: 30 Cleveland St., London, W1T 4JD UK	

GROWTH PLANS/SPECIAL FEATURES:

Dennis Publishing, Ltd. is a leading independent publisher of periodicals based in London. Operating through multiple subsidiaries in the U.K. and the U.S., it is one of the world's fastest-growing independently owned media companies. Dennis publishes 25 magazines in the U.K. and four titles in the U.S. These include: Maxim, a popular men's magazine aimed at affluent men aged 18 to 34, with a circulation of over 3.8 million copies a month in 21 editions in 32 countries; Men's Fitness; Evo; Computer Shopper; MacUser; PC Pro; The Week, the company's most profitable U.K. magazine; Custom PC; Stuff; Bizarre; Fortean Times; and Viz. 12 of the firm's magazines are made available online through Dennis Interactive (DI), the company's new media division. The web sites for these magazines attract over 1.75 million unique users per month, with over 40 million page views. Moreover, through Dennis List Solutions, the company offers direct mailing lists to advertisers. American subsidiary Dennis Publishing, Inc. handles the U.S. versions of its magazines out of its New York offices. Dennis Direct, another subsidiary, offers mail order and fulfillment services for the group's magazines, as well as for third party clients. In recent news, DI launched a full-service games portal, covering all game formats, including online multiplayer games. Recently, Dennis launched a new mobile version of Maxim (mobile.maxim.com), which is designed to work with all types of web-enabled mobile phones. In late 2006, the firm launched Monkey, a weekly digital men's magazine with no print counterpart. Dennis acquired Micro Mart magazine from Trinity Mirror in 2006. The company jointly owns Seymour Distribution Ltd., a major independent distributor of magazine titles, with Frontline.

Dennis offers benefits including five weeks paid vacation, discounted gym membership, transportation reimbursement, 26 weeks paid maternity leave and various development opportunities.

FINANCIALS: Sales and profits are in thousands of dollars—add 000 to get the full amount. 2006 Note: Financial information for 2006 was not available for all companies at press time.

2006 Sales: $	2006 Profits: $	**U.S. Stock Ticker:** Private
2005 Sales: $106,100	2005 Profits: $- 300	**Int'l Ticker:** Int'l Exchange:
2004 Sales: $	2004 Profits: $	Employees: 640
2003 Sales: $358,987	2003 Profits: $- 300	Fiscal Year Ends: 12/31
2002 Sales: $	2002 Profits: $	Parent Company:

SALARIES/BENEFITS:

Pension Plan: Y	ESOP Stock Plan:	Profit Sharing:	Top Exec. Salary: $	Bonus: $
Savings Plan:	Stock Purch. Plan:		Second Exec. Salary: $	Bonus: $

OTHER THOUGHTS:

Apparent Women Officers or Directors: 2
Hot Spot for Advancement for Women/Minorities:

LOCATIONS: ("Y" = Yes)

West:	Southwest:	Midwest:	Southeast:	Northeast:	International:
				Y	Y

DG FASTCHANNEL
www.dgsystems.com

Industry Group Code: 541870 Ranks within this company's industry group: Sales: 1 Profits: 1

Print Media/Publishing:	Movies:	Equipment/Supplies:		Broadcast/Cable:	Music/Audio:	Sports/Games:
Newspapers:	Movie Theaters:	Equipment/Supplies:	Y	Broadcast TV:	Music Production:	Games/Sports:
Magazines:	Movie Production:	Gambling Equipment:		Cable TV:	Retail Music:	Retail Games Stores:
Books:	TV/Video Production:	Special Services:	Y	Satellite Broadcast:	Retail Audio Equip.:	Stadiums/Teams:
Book Stores:	Video Rental:	Advertising Services:	Y	Radio:	Music Print./Dist.:	Gambling/Casinos:
Distribution/Printing:	Video Distribution:	Info. Sys. Software:	Y	Online Information:	Multimedia:	Rides/Theme Parks:

TYPES OF BUSINESS:

Advertising Distribution Services
Digital Content Distribution
Software
Digital Transmission Equipment
Engineering Consulting
Online Database-TV Commercials

BRANDS/DIVISIONS/AFFILIATES:

Digital Generation Systems
StarGuide Digital Networks, Inc.
Source TV
Media DVX
DGConnect
FastChannel Network

CONTACTS: *Note: Officers with more than one job title may be intentionally listed here more than once.*

Scott K. Ginsberg, CEO
Omar A. Choucair, CFO
Tom Cox, VP-Sales
Scott K. Ginsberg, Chmn.

Phone: 972-581-2000	**Fax:** 972-581-2001
Toll-Free: 800-324-5672	
Address: 750 W. John Carpenter Fwy., Ste. 700, Irving, TX 75039 US	

GROWTH PLANS/SPECIAL FEATURES:

DG FastChannel, formerly Digital Generation Systems, operates a nationwide digital network that links more than 5,000 advertisers and advertising agencies to over 3,800 broadcast television and cable stations and over 10,000 radio stations across the U.S. and Canada. The company's network operation center in San Francisco delivers audio, video, image and data content between the advertising and broadcast industries. Revenues derive largely from advertising agencies, advertisers, tape duplication vendors and dealers, syndicated programmers and music companies. DG FastChannel delivers over 4 million commercials annually. The firm's services allow advertisers to have content distributed to radio and television stations in as little as one hour and at times when physical delivery services are not available. DG FastChannel also operates a fault-tolerant client/server online transaction system using relational databases and UNIX servers from Sun Microsystems. In addition, the firm develops software applications with operational capabilities including transaction management and system security. Subsidiary StarGuide Digital Networks, Inc. designs and sells high-speed digital information transmission and distribution systems, including bandwidth satellite receivers, audio compression codes and software. StarGuide also offers engineering consulting services. Subsidiary Source TV offers a searchable database of more than 350,000 U.S. television commercials, with information on commercials' content and credits. In 2005, DG FastChannel acquired the assets of Media DVX, which operates a news and programming distribution network, for $10 million. In May 2006, Digital Generation Systems merged with FastChannel Network, a major provider of technological products and services for the advertising industry, changing the company's name to DG FastChannel.

FINANCIALS: Sales and profits are in thousands of dollars—add 000 to get the full amount. 2006 Note: Financial information for 2006 was not available for all companies at press time.

2006 Sales: $	2006 Profits: $	**U.S. Stock Ticker:** DGIT
2005 Sales: $58,352	2005 Profits: $-1,216	**Int'l Ticker:** Int'l Exchange:
2004 Sales: $62,366	2004 Profits: $3,204	Employees: 317
2003 Sales: $57,687	2003 Profits: $4,199	Fiscal Year Ends: 12/31
2002 Sales: $66,300	2002 Profits: $-126,600	Parent Company:

SALARIES/BENEFITS:

Pension Plan:	ESOP Stock Plan:	Profit Sharing:	Top Exec. Salary: $250,000	Bonus: $20,000
Savings Plan: Y	Stock Purch. Plan:		Second Exec. Salary: $190,000	Bonus: $20,000

OTHER THOUGHTS:

Apparent Women Officers or Directors:
Hot Spot for Advancement for Women/Minorities:

LOCATIONS: ("Y" = Yes)

West:	Southwest:	Midwest:	Southeast:	Northeast:	International:
Y	Y	Y	Y	Y	

DIALOG NEWSEDGE
www.thomsonbusinessintelligence.com/products/newsEdge.s html

Industry Group Code: 514199 Ranks within this company's industry group: Sales: Profits:

Print Media/Publishing:	Movies:	Equipment/Supplies:		Broadcast/Cable:	Music/Audio:	Sports/Games:
Newspapers:	Movie Theaters:	Equipment/Supplies:		Broadcast TV:	Music Production:	Games/Sports:
Magazines:	Movie Production:	Gambling Equipment:		Cable TV:	Retail Music:	Retail Games Stores:
Books:	TV/Video Production:	Special Services:	Y	Satellite Broadcast:	Retail Audio Equip.:	Stadiums/Teams:
Book Stores:	Video Rental:	Advertising Services:		Radio:	Music Print./Dist.:	Gambling/Casinos:
Distribution/Printing:	Video Distribution:	Info. Sys. Software:	Y	Online Information:	Multimedia:	Rides/Theme Parks:

TYPES OF BUSINESS:
Syndicated Online News Content
Business News & Information
Online Publishing Technologies

BRANDS/DIVISIONS/AFFILIATES:
Thomson Corporation
Dialog
Dialog DataStar
Dialog Profound
Dialog NewsEdge
Dialog Intelliscope
My Live News

CONTACTS: Note: Officers with more than one job title may be intentionally listed here more than once.
Ciaran Morton, General Mgr.
Ciaran Morton, Exec. VP-Int'l Sales
Alton Zink, VP-Human Resources
Craig Lathrop, CTO
Thomas Karanian, VP-Client Services & Oper.
Sandy Scherer, VP-Corp. Comm.
Jim Colantino, Sr. VP-Sales
David Brown, Sr. VP-Strategic Accounts Group
Cheryl Curran, Sr. VP-Inside Sales
Libby Trudell, Sr. VP-Info. Professional Market Dev.

Phone: 781-229-3000	Fax: 781-229-3030
Toll-Free: 800-255-3343	
Address: 80 Blanchard Rd., Burlington, MA 01803 US	

GROWTH PLANS/SPECIAL FEATURES:
Dialog NewsEdge, a subsidiary of the Thomson Corporation, is a leading supplier of syndicated content services and electronic business publishing technologies. The company's services allow customers to create content for millions of users through a variety of high-technology media, such as intranets, web sites, extranets, desktop applications and distribution channels. Products such as Dialog, Dialog DataStar, Dialog Profound and Dialog NewsEdge, deployed as part of the infrastructure of large organizations, help companies convey news and information to large numbers of employees over intranets and local area networks. One of the firm's premier products is the My Live News feature that streams breaking headlines from over 2,300 sources 24 hours a day, seven days a week based on user-defined parameters. The firm uses editors to assist in winnowing out the less pertinent stories for its industry-specific readership. End users can be split into two groups: employees of large organizations that depend on news for competitive advantage; and visitors to web sites that content providers compete to retain. The company has over 1,400 customers, including more than 80% of Business Week's 100 largest global companies. Working side by side with its corporate clientele, the company's services and content are designed to appeal to specialized audiences, encourage return visits and result in increased purchases and business traffic.

FINANCIALS: Sales and profits are in thousands of dollars—add 000 to get the full amount. 2006 Note: Financial information for 2006 was not available for all companies at press time.

2006 Sales: $	2006 Profits: $	U.S. Stock Ticker: Subsidiary
2005 Sales: $	2005 Profits: $	Int'l Ticker: Int'l Exchange:
2004 Sales: $	2004 Profits: $	Employees: 309
2003 Sales: $	2003 Profits: $	Fiscal Year Ends: 12/31
2002 Sales: $	2002 Profits: $	Parent Company: THOMSON CORPORATION (THE)

SALARIES/BENEFITS:

Pension Plan:	ESOP Stock Plan:	Profit Sharing:	Top Exec. Salary: $232,496	Bonus: $89,780
Savings Plan:	Stock Purch. Plan:		Second Exec. Salary: $182,313	Bonus: $65,000

OTHER THOUGHTS:
Apparent Women Officers or Directors: 4
Hot Spot for Advancement for Women/Minorities: Y

LOCATIONS: ("Y" = Yes)

West:	Southwest:	Midwest:	Southeast:	Northeast:	International:
Y	Y	Y	Y	Y	Y

DIAMONDHEAD CASINO CORPORATION

Industry Group Code: 721120 Ranks within this company's industry group: Sales: Profits: 14

Print Media/Publishing:	Movies:	Equipment/Supplies:	Broadcast/Cable:	Music/Audio:	Sports/Games:	
Newspapers:	Movie Theaters:	Equipment/Supplies:	Broadcast TV:	Music Production:	Games/Sports:	
Magazines:	Movie Production:	Gambling Equipment:	Cable TV:	Retail Music:	Retail Games Stores:	
Books:	TV/Video Production:	Special Services:	Satellite Broadcast:	Retail Audio Equip.:	Stadiums/Teams:	
Book Stores:	Video Rental:	Advertising Services:	Radio:	Music Print./Dist.:	Gambling/Casinos:	Y
Distribution/Printing:	Video Distribution:	Info. Sys. Software:	Online Information:	Multimedia:	Rides/Theme Parks:	

TYPES OF BUSINESS:
Casino

BRANDS/DIVISIONS/AFFILIATES:
Casino World, Inc.
Mississippi Gaming Corp.

GROWTH PLANS/SPECIAL FEATURES:

Diamondhead Casino Corporation, through its wholly-owned subsidiary, Casino World, Inc., intends to develop a themed, destination casino resort and hotel at its 404-acre site on the Bay of St. Louis in Diamondhead, Mississippi.   Due to Hurricane Katrina, the company postponed any activity in 2005 until such time as the effects of Hurricane Katrina on the Gulf economy and the laws of Mississippi pertaining to the future of land-based casinos are more clearly understood.   Hurricane Katrina's direct effects on the company were limited to water damage in the office space leased in Diamondhead, Mississippi and piles of debris on the proposed casino site that will have to be removed. As the Mississippi legislature voted to allow casinos to be land-based in late 2005, the company intends to again revise its engineering and site plans to take advantage of the opportunity.

CONTACTS: Note: Officers with more than one job title may be intentionally listed here more than once.
Deborah A. Vitale, CEO
Deborah A. Vitale, Pres.
Robert A. Zimmerman, CFO
Deborah A. Vitale, Treas.
Gregory A. Harrison, VP/Corp. Sec.
Deborah A. Vitale, Chmn.

Phone: 727-393-2885	Fax: 727-391-9200
Toll-Free:	
Address: 150-153rd Ave. E., Ste. 201, Madeira Beach, FL 33708 US	

FINANCIALS: Sales and profits are in thousands of dollars—add 000 to get the full amount. 2006 Note: Financial information for 2006 was not available for all companies at press time.

2006 Sales: $	2006 Profits: $	U.S. Stock Ticker: DHCC.OB
2005 Sales: $	2005 Profits: $- 642	Int'l Ticker: Int'l Exchange:
2004 Sales: $ 168	2004 Profits: $- 640	Employees: 4
2003 Sales: $ 357	2003 Profits: $- 421	Fiscal Year Ends: 12/31
2002 Sales: $ 300	2002 Profits: $- 800	Parent Company:

SALARIES/BENEFITS:

Pension Plan:	ESOP Stock Plan: Y	Profit Sharing:	Top Exec. Salary: $133,654	Bonus: $
Savings Plan: Y	Stock Purch. Plan:		Second Exec. Salary: $	Bonus: $

OTHER THOUGHTS:
Apparent Women Officers or Directors: 1
Hot Spot for Advancement for Women/Minorities:

LOCATIONS: ("Y" = Yes)

West:	Southwest:	Midwest:	Southeast:	Northeast:	International:
			Y		

DICK CLARK PRODUCTIONS INC
www.dickclarkproductions.com

Industry Group Code: 512110 Ranks within this company's industry group: Sales: Profits:

Print Media/Publishing:	Movies:		Equipment/Supplies:		Broadcast/Cable:	Music/Audio:	Sports/Games:
Newspapers:	Movie Theaters:		Equipment/Supplies:		Broadcast TV:	Music Production:	Games/Sports:
Magazines:	Movie Production:	Y	Gambling Equipment:		Cable TV:	Retail Music:	Retail Games Stores:
Books:	TV/Video Production:	Y	Special Services:	Y	Satellite Broadcast:	Retail Audio Equip.:	Stadiums/Teams:
Book Stores:	Video Rental:		Advertising Services:	Y	Radio:	Music Print./Dist.:	Gambling/Casinos:
Distribution/Printing:	Video Distribution:		Info. Sys. Software:		Online Information:	Multimedia:	Rides/Theme Parks:

TYPES OF BUSINESS:
Television Production
Film Production
Restaurants
Publicity Services

BRANDS/DIVISIONS/AFFILIATES:
Dick Clark Restaurants
Dick Clark Corporate Productions
Dick Clark Communications
Dick Clark's American Bandstand Grill
Dick Clark's American Bandstand Theater
Dick Clark's AB Grill
Dick Clark's AB Diner
Dick Clark's Bandstand-Food, Spirits & Fun

CONTACTS: *Note: Officers with more than one job title may be intentionally listed here more than once.*
Richard W. Clark, CEO
Francis C. La Maina, COO
Francis C. La Maina, Pres.
William S. Simon, CFO
Michael Mahan, Sr. VP-Corp. Dev.
Brian Pope, VP-Bus. Affairs
Martin E. Weisberg, Corp. Sec.
Richard W. Clark, Chmn.

Phone: 818-841-3003	**Fax:** 818-954-8609
Toll-Free:	
Address: 3003 W. Olive Ave., Burbank, CA 91505-4590 US	

GROWTH PLANS/SPECIAL FEATURES:
Dick Clark Productions, Inc. (DCPI) is a diversified entertainment company with a variety of television, communications and restaurant businesses. The company develops and produces a wide range of television programming for television networks, first-run domestic syndicators, cable networks and advertisers. DCPI has been a significant supplier of television programming and has produced shows such as American Dreams, the Golden Globe Awards, the American Music Awards, the Academy of Country Music Awards, the Family Television Awards, the Daytime Emmy Awards, Bloopers and Beyond Belief: Fact or Fiction. Programming includes awards shows, comedy specials, children's programming, talk and game show series and dramatic series. The market for this programming is mainly composed of ABC, CBS, NBC, Fox and the new CW network. The company also licenses the rebroadcast rights to some of its programs, licenses certain segments of its programming to third parties, produces home videos and develops and produces theatrical motion pictures, generally in conjunction with third parties who provide the financing. DCPI operates a chain of five entertainment-themed restaurants named Dick Clark's American Bandstand Grill, located in Indianapolis, Newark, Kansas City, Phoenix and Salt Lake City. In addition, the firm offers television and entertainment-related publicity consulting services through Dick Clark Communications. DCPI planned to open two new restaurant locations in 2006 in New Jersey and Branson, Missouri, as well as Dick Clark's American Bandstand Theater, also in Branson.

FINANCIALS: Sales and profits are in thousands of dollars—add 000 to get the full amount. 2006 Note: Financial information for 2006 was not available for all companies at press time.

2006 Sales: $	2006 Profits: $	**U.S. Stock Ticker:** Private
2005 Sales: $	2005 Profits: $	**Int'l Ticker:** Int'l Exchange:
2004 Sales: $	2004 Profits: $	Employees: 710
2003 Sales: $	2003 Profits: $	Fiscal Year Ends: 6/30
2002 Sales: $	2002 Profits: $	Parent Company:

SALARIES/BENEFITS:

Pension Plan:	ESOP Stock Plan:	Profit Sharing:	Top Exec. Salary: $975,000	Bonus: $444,740
Savings Plan:	Stock Purch. Plan:		Second Exec. Salary: $577,059	Bonus: $308,546

OTHER THOUGHTS:
Apparent Women Officers or Directors:
Hot Spot for Advancement for Women/Minorities: Y

LOCATIONS: ("Y" = Yes)

West:	Southwest:	Midwest:	Southeast:	Northeast:	International:
Y	Y	Y		Y	

DIGEO INC
www.digeo.com

Industry Group Code: 334310 **Ranks within this company's industry group:** Sales: Profits:

Print Media/Publishing:	Movies:	Equipment/Supplies:		Broadcast/Cable:		Music/Audio:	Sports/Games:
Newspapers:	Movie Theaters:	Equipment/Supplies:	Y	Broadcast TV:		Music Production:	Games/Sports:
Magazines:	Movie Production:	Gambling Equipment:		Cable TV:	Y	Retail Music:	Retail Games Stores:
Books:	TV/Video Production:	Special Services:		Satellite Broadcast:		Retail Audio Equip.:	Stadiums/Teams:
Book Stores:	Video Rental:	Advertising Services:		Radio:		Music Print./Dist.:	Gambling/Casinos:
Distribution/Printing:	Video Distribution:	Info. Sys. Software:		Online Information:		Multimedia:	Rides/Theme Parks:

TYPES OF BUSINESS:
Cable TV Services
Interactive TV Services
Set-Top Boxes

BRANDS/DIVISIONS/AFFILIATES:
Moxi Digital, Inc.
Moxi Media Center
i-Games
Digeo iTV

CONTACTS:
Note: Officers with more than one job title may be intentionally listed here more than once.
Mike Fidler, CEO
Greg Gudorf, COO
Greg Gudorf, Pres.
Tom Grina, CFO
Allison Cornia, VP-Mktg.
Chauncey Gammage, Dir.-Human Resources
Chuck Broadus, VP-Eng.
Byron Springer, Jr., VP/General Counsel
Steve Martino, VP-Bus. Oper.
Allison Cornia, VP-Corp. Comm.
Bert Kolde, Sr. VP
Andy Saenz, Dir.-Program Mngmt.
Paul G. Allen, Chmn.

Phone: 425-896-6000 **Fax:** 425-896-6062
Toll-Free:
Address: 8815 122nd Ave. NE, Kirkland, WA 98033 US

GROWTH PLANS/SPECIAL FEATURES:
Digeo, Inc. is a cable television services company that focuses on interactive TV (iTV). The firm's merger with Moxi Digital, Inc. made it the industry's leading provider of advanced media center platforms and iTV services. Through its Emmy award-winning Moxi Media Center service, deployed in conjunction with several cable service providers, the company offers such popular features as high-definition TV and interactive viewing systems, in addition to music, photos and games. The service requires a specially designed set-top cable box that often includes a DVD player. Digeo's basic iTV service provides cable subscribers with eight information and commerce channels, including weather, local movie listings, news, sports, money, shopping and games. Also offered is a series of advanced services for the various needs of Moxi subscribers, including enhanced TV, digital video recording, telephone monitoring, advanced communication services, photos, music, games and wireless home networking. Digeo has designed its advanced platforms to work with partners including Charter, Motorola, Scientific Atlanta and Sony. In late 2006, Digeo released a software upgrade for the Moxi allowing it to support external hard drives.

FINANCIALS:
Sales and profits are in thousands of dollars—add 000 to get the full amount. 2006 Note: Financial information for 2006 was not available for all companies at press time.

2006 Sales: $	2006 Profits: $	**U.S. Stock Ticker:** Private
2005 Sales: $	2005 Profits: $	**Int'l Ticker:** Int'l Exchange:
2004 Sales: $	2004 Profits: $	Employees: 250
2003 Sales: $	2003 Profits: $	Fiscal Year Ends: 12/31
2002 Sales: $	2002 Profits: $	Parent Company:

SALARIES/BENEFITS:
Pension Plan:	ESOP Stock Plan:	Profit Sharing:	Top Exec. Salary: $	Bonus: $
Savings Plan:	Stock Purch. Plan:		Second Exec. Salary: $	Bonus: $

OTHER THOUGHTS:
Apparent Women Officers or Directors: 1
Hot Spot for Advancement for Women/Minorities:

LOCATIONS: ("Y" = Yes)
West:	Southwest:	Midwest:	Southeast:	Northeast:	International:
Y					

Note: Financial information, benefits and other data can change quickly and may vary from those stated here.

DIGITAL BRIDGES LIMITED

www.iplay.com

Industry Group Code: 511208 Ranks within this company's industry group: Sales: Profits:

Print Media/Publishing:	Movies:	Equipment/Supplies:	Broadcast/Cable:	Music/Audio:	Sports/Games:	
Newspapers:	Movie Theaters:	Equipment/Supplies:	Broadcast TV:	Music Production:	Games/Sports:	Y
Magazines:	Movie Production:	Gambling Equipment:	Cable TV:	Retail Music:	Retail Games Stores:	
Books:	TV/Video Production:	Special Services:	Satellite Broadcast:	Retail Audio Equip.:	Stadiums/Teams:	
Book Stores:	Video Rental:	Advertising Services:	Radio:	Music Print./Dist.:	Gambling/Casinos:	
Distribution/Printing:	Video Distribution:	Info. Sys. Software:	Online Information:	Multimedia:	Rides/Theme Parks:	

TYPES OF BUSINESS:
Mobile Entertainment Software

BRANDS/DIVISIONS/AFFILIATES:
I-Play
Jewel Quest
3D Pool Urban Hustle
Maria Sharapovna Tennis
2Fast 2Furious
3D Pool
2005 SI Football Trivia
Ditto Studios

CONTACTS: *Note: Officers with more than one job title may be intentionally listed here more than once.*
David Gosen, CEO
Colin Grant, CFO
Phil Cooke, Chief Tech. Officer
Chris Wright, Head-Game Dev.
Krishna Gidwani, VP-Corp. Dev.
Anders Evju, General Mgr.-Americas
Stephane Labrunie, VP-Sales, Europe
Daniel Gan, VP-Asia Pacific
Euan Stillie, Head-QA & Deployment

Phone: 44-207-901-1760	Fax: 44-207-901-1761
Toll-Free:	
Address: 1C Greencoat House, Francis St., London, SW1P 1DH UK	

GROWTH PLANS/SPECIAL FEATURES:
Digital Bridges, Ltd. develops and publishes downloadable and built-in entertainment software for cellular phones and other mobile devices. The company does business under the brand I-Play and markets its products to mobile networks, such as Orange, O2 and Vodafone, as well as through mobile retailers and distribution partners. The firm partners with entertainment companies and developers, network carriers, online portals and retailers. In return for its partners' services, Digital Bridges provides them with access to more than half a billion cell phone users worldwide. Other financial backing for Digital Bridges comes from leading investment and venture capital firms Apax Partners and Argo Global Capital. The games offered by the company include Jewel Quest, 2Fast 2Furious, 3D Pool Urban Hustle, Maria Sharapovna Tennis, Boulder Dash, Moto-X II and 2005 SI Football Trivia. In June 2005, the company acquired Ditto Studios, a mobile game porting specialist and developer. This acquisition greatly accelerates Digital Bridge's delivery time through the use of Ditto's proprietary technology designed to provide mobile games to hundreds of different handsets simultaneously. Additionally, in April 2006, the company entered into a licensing agreement with iWin, a San Francisco-based developer and publisher of online games. The agreement will allow the company to provide three new puzzle games to its customers.

FINANCIALS: Sales and profits are in thousands of dollars—add 000 to get the full amount. 2006 Note: Financial information for 2006 was not available for all companies at press time.

2006 Sales: $	2006 Profits: $	U.S. Stock Ticker: Private
2005 Sales: $	2005 Profits: $	Int'l Ticker: Int'l Exchange:
2004 Sales: $	2004 Profits: $	Employees:
2003 Sales: $	2003 Profits: $	Fiscal Year Ends: 12/31
2002 Sales: $	2002 Profits: $	Parent Company:

SALARIES/BENEFITS:

Pension Plan:	ESOP Stock Plan:	Profit Sharing:	Top Exec. Salary: $	Bonus: $
Savings Plan:	Stock Purch. Plan:		Second Exec. Salary: $	Bonus: $

OTHER THOUGHTS:

Apparent Women Officers or Directors:
Hot Spot for Advancement for Women/Minorities:

LOCATIONS: ("Y" = Yes)

West:	Southwest:	Midwest:	Southeast:	Northeast:	International:
Y				Y	Y

DIGITAL VIDEO SYSTEMS INC
www.dvsystems.com

Industry Group Code: 334310 Ranks within this company's industry group: Sales: Profits:

Print Media/Publishing:	Movies:	Equipment/Supplies:		Broadcast/Cable:	Music/Audio:		Sports/Games:
Newspapers:	Movie Theaters:	Equipment/Supplies:	Y	Broadcast TV:	Music Production:		Games/Sports:
Magazines:	Movie Production:	Gambling Equipment:		Cable TV:	Retail Music:		Retail Games Stores:
Books:	TV/Video Production:	Special Services:		Satellite Broadcast:	Retail Audio Equip.:	Y	Stadiums/Teams:
Book Stores:	Video Rental:	Advertising Services:		Radio:	Music Print./Dist.:		Gambling/Casinos:
Distribution/Printing:	Video Distribution:	Info. Sys. Software:		Online Information:	Multimedia:		Rides/Theme Parks:

TYPES OF BUSINESS:

Electronic Equipment-DVD Products

BRANDS/DIVISIONS/AFFILIATES:

DVS Korea, Ltd.
DVS Electronics (India) Ltd.

CONTACTS: Note: Officers with more than one job title may be intentionally listed here more than once.

Mali Kuo, CEO
Douglas T. Watson, COO
Shaun Kang, Pres.
Dean C. Seniff, CFO
Mali Kuo, Chmn./Co-CEO-DVS Korea
Shaun Kang, Co-CEO-DVS Korea
Mali Kuo, Chmn.

Phone: 650-938-8815	Fax: 650-938-8829

Toll-Free:

Address: 357 Castro St., Ste. 5, Mountain View, CA 94041 US

GROWTH PLANS/SPECIAL FEATURES:

Digital Video Systems, Inc. (DVS) specializes in developing digital video and optical disc technologies. The company has developed or acquired technologies for applications including automatic ad-insertion systems, network video servers, video CD players and commercial video kiosks. DVS owns the rights to over 100 patents for DVD-related technologies. The firm currently develops and markets primarily DVD-ROM drives and DVD loaders for consumer, commercial and computer peripherals markets. DVS' and its customers' finished products include home and portable DVD players, home theater systems, DVD recorders and automotive DVD players. The company also owns the DVD operations, patents and licenses to the DVD-related intellectual properties of Hyundai Electronics. The firm's production facility in China provides lower costs for labor and standard components, lower duties and taxes and shorter delivery lead-time to major customers. DVS operates a production facility near Seoul, South Korea through its subsidiary DVS Korea, Ltd. In response to declining revenues due to the commoditization of the home DVD market, DVS has narrowed its focus to automotive and recordable DVD products and consumer digital entertainment products in India. DVS Electronics (India) Ltd., the firm's division in India, has established a dealer and distribution network of approximately 500 retailers in 20 metropolitan areas; it is also pursuing exclusive digital content distribution agreements with Bollywood producers.

FINANCIALS: Sales and profits are in thousands of dollars—add 000 to get the full amount. 2006 Note: Financial information for 2006 was not available for all companies at press time.

2006 Sales: $	2006 Profits: $	U.S. Stock Ticker: DVID	
2005 Sales: $	2005 Profits: $	Int'l Ticker: Int'l Exchange:	
2004 Sales: $87,200	2004 Profits: $-13,070	Employees: 225	
2003 Sales: $89,133	2003 Profits: $-8,345	Fiscal Year Ends: 12/31	
2002 Sales: $157,200	2002 Profits: $-3,000	Parent Company:	

SALARIES/BENEFITS:

Pension Plan:	ESOP Stock Plan:	Profit Sharing:	Top Exec. Salary: $139,231	Bonus: $
Savings Plan:	Stock Purch. Plan:		Second Exec. Salary: $125,813	Bonus: $14,710

OTHER THOUGHTS:

Apparent Women Officers or Directors: 1
Hot Spot for Advancement for Women/Minorities:

LOCATIONS: ("Y" = Yes)

West:	Southwest:	Midwest:	Southeast:	Northeast:	International:
Y					Y

Note: Financial information, benefits and other data can change quickly and may vary from those stated here.

DIRECTV GROUP INC (THE)   www.directv.com

Industry Group Code: 513220 Ranks within this company's industry group: Sales: 3 Profits: 8

Print Media/Publishing:	Movies:	Equipment/Supplies:		Broadcast/Cable:	Music/Audio:	Sports/Games:
Newspapers:	Movie Theaters:	Equipment/Supplies:	Y	Broadcast TV:	Music Production:	Games/Sports:
Magazines:	Movie Production:	Gambling Equipment:		Cable TV:	Retail Music:	Retail Games Stores:
Books:	TV/Video Production:	Special Services:		Satellite Broadcast:	Retail Audio Equip.:	Stadiums/Teams:
Book Stores:	Video Rental:	Advertising Services:		Radio:	Music Print./Dist.:	Gambling/Casinos:
Distribution/Printing:	Video Distribution:	Info. Sys. Software:		Online Information:	Multimedia:	Rides/Theme Parks:

TYPES OF BUSINESS:

Satellite Broadcasting
Commercial Satellite Fleet
Satellite-Based Internet Services
Digital Television

BRANDS/DIVISIONS/AFFILIATES:

DIRECTV Holdings, LLC
Hughes Electronics Corporation
Fox Entertainment Group
Liberty Media Corp.
DIRECTV U.S.
DIRECTV Latin America
PanAmericana
Sky Brasil Servicos Ltda.

CONTACTS: *Note: Officers with more than one job title may be intentionally listed here more than once.*

Chase Carey, CEO
Chase Carey, Pres.
Michael W. Palkovic, CFO/Exec. VP
Romulo G. Pontual, CTO/Exec. VP
Larry D. Hunter, General Counsel/Exec. VP/Corp. Sec.
Patrick T. Doyle, Chief Acct. Officer/Sr. VP/Treas./Controller
Bruce B. Churchill, CEO/Pres., Latin America & New Enterprises
K. Rupert Murdoch, Chmn.

Phone: 310-964-0808	Fax: 310-535-5225
Toll-Free:	
Address: 2230 E. Imperial Hwy., El Segundo, CA 90245-0956 US	

GROWTH PLANS/SPECIAL FEATURES:

The DIRECTV Group, Inc., formerly Hughes Electronics Corporation, is one of the world's top providers of digital television entertainment and wireless systems. The company's two business segments, DIRECTV U.S. and DIRECTV Latin America, are engaged in acquiring, promoting, selling and distributing digital entertainment programming via satellite to residential and commercial subscribers. DIRECTV U.S. is the largest provider of direct-to-home digital television services and the second largest provider in the multi-channel video programming distribution industry in the U.S., with approximately 15.7 million subscribers. DIRECTV U.S. currently broadcasts its service from nine geosynchronous satellites. An additional satellite, DIRECTV 9S, was launched in October 2006. DIRECTV U.S. has three more satellites under construction, and plans to launch two, DIRECTV 10 and DIRECTV 11, in 2007. These two satellites will provide DIRECTV U.S. with increased capability for local and national high-definition channels, as well as capacity for new interactive and enhanced services and standard-definition programming. DIRECTV Latin America comprises PanAmericana, a group of companies that primarily includes the approximately 86% owned subsidiary DIRECTV Latin America, LLC and its local operating companies that provide services in countries other than Brazil and Mexico. DIRECTV Latin America also includes 74% of Sky Brasil Servicos Ltda. and 41% of Innova, S. de R.L. de C.V., or Sky Mexico. PanAmericana has approximately 1.3 million subscribers in 28 countries throughout the region and Sky Brazil has approximately 1.3 million subscribers. In August 2006, the company completed the merger of Galaxy Brasil Ltda. into Sky Brazil, and purchased News Corporation's and Liberty's interests in Sky Brazil. The firm is considering the launch of a massive, wireless voice and data network, probably based on WiMax, which would offer bundled services including TV, phone and Internet access. In December 2006, Liberty Media Corp. acquired sufficient DirecTV stock from News Corp. to give Liberty Media a controlling stake in DirecTV.

FINANCIALS: Sales and profits are in thousands of dollars—add 000 to get the full amount. 2006 Note: Financial information for 2006 was not available for all companies at press time.

2006 Sales: $	2006 Profits: $	U.S. Stock Ticker: DTV
2005 Sales: $13,164,500	2005 Profits: $335,900	Int'l Ticker: Int'l Exchange:
2004 Sales: $11,360,000	2004 Profits: $-1,944,000	Employees: 9,200
2003 Sales: $10,121,200	2003 Profits: $-361,800	Fiscal Year Ends: 12/31
2002 Sales: $8,934,900	2002 Profits: $-891,100	Parent Company:

SALARIES/BENEFITS:

Pension Plan: Y	ESOP Stock Plan:	Profit Sharing:	Top Exec. Salary: $2,076,000	Bonus: $2,958,000
Savings Plan: Y	Stock Purch. Plan:		Second Exec. Salary: $985,434	Bonus: $950,000

OTHER THOUGHTS:

Apparent Women Officers or Directors: 1
Hot Spot for Advancement for Women/Minorities:

LOCATIONS: ("Y" = Yes)

West:	Southwest:	Midwest:	Southeast:	Northeast:	International:
Y	Y	Y	Y		Y

Note: Financial information, benefits and other data can change quickly and may vary from those stated here.

DISCOVERY COMMUNICATIONS INC   www.discovery.com

Industry Group Code: 513210 Ranks within this company's industry group: Sales: 6   Profits:

Print Media/Publishing:	Movies:		Equipment/Supplies:	Broadcast/Cable:		Music/Audio:	Sports/Games:
Newspapers:	Movie Theaters:		Equipment/Supplies:	Broadcast TV:		Music Production:	Games/Sports:
Magazines:	Movie Production:		Gambling Equipment:	Cable TV:	Y	Retail Music:	Retail Games Stores:
Books:	TV/Video Production:	Y	Special Services:	Satellite Broadcast:		Retail Audio Equip.:	Stadiums/Teams:
Book Stores:	Video Rental:		Advertising Services:	Radio:		Music Print./Dist.:	Gambling/Casinos:
Distribution/Printing:	Video Distribution:		Info. Sys. Software:	Online Information:		Multimedia:	Rides/Theme Parks:

TYPES OF BUSINESS:

Cable TV Networks
Retail Stores
Catalog & Online Sales
Educational Products
Television Programming

BRANDS/DIVISIONS/AFFILIATES:

Discovery Channel
TLC
Animal Planet
Travel Channel
Discovery Kids
BBC America
Discovery Channel Stores
Discovery Channel Catalog (The)

CONTACTS: *Note: Officers with more than one job title may be intentionally listed here more than once.*

David Zaslav, CEO
David Zaslav, Pres.
Roger F. Millay, CFO/Sr. Exec. VP
Pandit F. Wright, Sr. Exec. VP-Human Resources
Mark Hollinger, General Counsel
Mark Hollinger, Sr. Exec. VP-Corp. Oper.
Donald Baer, Sr. VP-Dev. & Strategy
Frank Rosales, Pres., Discovery Commerce
William M. Campbell, III, Pres., U.S. Networks
John S. Hendricks, Chmn.
Dawn L. McCall, Pres., Int'l Networks

Phone: 240-662-2000	Fax: 240-662-1868
Toll-Free:	
Address: One Discovery Pl., Silver Spring, MD 20910 US	

GROWTH PLANS/SPECIAL FEATURES:

Discovery Communications, Inc. is a leading global media and entertainment company headquartered in Silver Spring, Maryland. The firm operates through three main divisions: U.S. networks, international networks and consumer products. Its U.S. networks division is a provider of real-world media and entertainment through several TV channels, including the Discovery Channel, TLC, Animal Planet, Discovery Health, FitTV, Travel Channel, Discovery Times, Discovery Kids, BBC America, Discovery en Espanol and Discovery HD Theater. With 17 offices outside of the U.S., the firm's international networks division serves over 160 countries and territories in 35 languages. International programming offers viewers both global perspectives and local stories. Local content includes such productions as the Asian Masterpiece series; Universo Discovery programming for Latin America; and the U.K. production Virtual History. The firm's consumer products division extends the company's television brands to consumers through an array of educational products and services. The division encompasses Discovery's retail operations, including a nationwide chain of 120 Discovery Channel Stores, The Discovery Channel Catalog and Discovery.com; Discovery Channel School, a supplementary education business, which provides Discovery content to 1.5 million teachers and students in 90,000 K-12 schools around the country; and global licensing and strategic partnerships that bring branded products to a larger global audience. The company recently launched Discovery Broadband in Germany.

FINANCIALS: Sales and profits are in thousands of dollars—add 000 to get the full amount. 2006 Note: Financial information for 2006 was not available for all companies at press time.

2006 Sales: $	2006 Profits: $	**U.S. Stock Ticker: Joint Venture**
2005 Sales: $2,700,000	2005 Profits: $	**Int'l Ticker:** Int'l Exchange:
2004 Sales: $2,365,000	2004 Profits: $	Employees: 6,000
2003 Sales: $1,717,000	2003 Profits: $	Fiscal Year Ends: 12/31
2002 Sales: $1,710,000	2002 Profits: $	Parent Company:

SALARIES/BENEFITS:

Pension Plan:	ESOP Stock Plan:	Profit Sharing:	Top Exec. Salary: $	Bonus: $
Savings Plan: Y	Stock Purch. Plan:		Second Exec. Salary: $	Bonus: $

OTHER THOUGHTS:

Apparent Women Officers or Directors: 4
Hot Spot for Advancement for Women/Minorities: Y

LOCATIONS: ("Y" = Yes)

West:	Southwest:	Midwest:	Southeast:	Northeast:	International:
Y		Y	Y	Y	Y

Note: Financial information, benefits and other data can change quickly and may vary from those stated here.

DOLBY LABORATORIES INC   www.dolby.com

Industry Group Code: 334310 Ranks within this company's industry group: Sales: 10 Profits: 6

Print Media/Publishing:	Movies:	Equipment/Supplies:		Broadcast/Cable:	Music/Audio:	Sports/Games:
Newspapers:	Movie Theaters:	Equipment/Supplies:	Y	Broadcast TV:	Music Production:	Games/Sports:
Magazines:	Movie Production:	Gambling Equipment:		Cable TV:	Retail Music:	Retail Games Stores:
Books:	TV/Video Production:	Special Services:	Y	Satellite Broadcast:	Retail Audio Equip.:	Stadiums/Teams:
Book Stores:	Video Rental:	Advertising Services:		Radio:	Music Print./Dist.:	Gambling/Casinos:
Distribution/Printing:	Video Distribution:	Info. Sys. Software:		Online Information:	Multimedia:	Rides/Theme Parks:

TYPES OF BUSINESS:
Audio & Video Equipment, Manufacturing
Audio Signal Processing Systems
Digital Audio Coding Technology
Technology Licensing

BRANDS/DIVISIONS/AFFILIATES:
Dolby Digital Surround DX
Dolby Stereo
DMA8 Digital Media
Dolby E
LM100
Dolby Pro Logic II
Dolby Digital 5.1
Dolby Digital 5.1 Creator

CONTACTS: *Note: Officers with more than one job title may be intentionally listed here more than once.*
N. W. Jasper, Jr., CEO
N. W. Jasper, Jr., Pres.
Kevin Yeaman, Sr. VP/CFO
Francois Modaresse, VP-Worldwide Mktg.
Steve E. Forshay, Sr. VP-Research
Craig Todd, VP-Tech. Strategy
Steve Jacobs, VP-Eng., Professional Div.
Jeff Griffith, VP-Manufacturing
Mark Anderson, General Counsel/Sr. VP
R. Richard Bell, VP-Oper.
David Watts, VP/Managing Dir.-U.K.
Tim Partridge, Sr. VP/General Mgr.-Professional Div.
Ramzi Haidamus, Sr. VP/General Mgr.-Consumer Div.
Marty A. Jaffe, Exec. VP-Bus. Affairs
Ray Dolby, Chmn.
See Weng Chan, VP-China

Phone: 415-558-0200   **Fax:** 415-863-1373
Toll-Free:
Address: 100 Potrero Ave., San Francisco, CA 94103-4813 US

GROWTH PLANS/SPECIAL FEATURES:
Dolby Laboratories develops, manufactures and markets audio signal processing systems and digital audio coding technology for cinemas, broadcasting, home audio systems, cars, DVDs, headphones, games, televisions and personal computers. Dolby also licenses these technologies to other companies, which incorporate them into a wide range of products, especially home entertainment equipment and speaker setups. The firm has over 900 issued patents and over 1,000 applications pending worldwide. The company's DMA8 Digital Media solution allows theater-quality digital sound in a home theater. Dolby has been an industry leader in motion picture audio systems since the early 1970s. The company provides its products, such as Dolby Stereo and Dolby Digital Surround EX, to both theaters and film production studios. Dolby's broadcasting segment provides digital and analog sound for HDTV, DTV, TV and radio broadcasters. Products include Dolby Digital, Dolby Pro Logic II, Dolby E and LM100 systems. Dolby Pro Logic II provides surround sound for television broadcasters. Dolby E is optimized for two-channel postproduction and broadcast transmissions. Dolby's LM100 is a revolutionary new device that allows broadcasters to automatically control the loudness of their audio broadcasts. The computer games segment incorporates Dolby Digital or Dolby Pro Logic II audio engines into video game software. Dolby enjoys a 20% to 40% profit margin and receives approximately $.75 for every TV, stereo, computer game or other product that is sold using its technology. The company operates licensing offices in London, Shanghai, Hong Kong and Tokyo; and manufacturing facilities in Brisbane, California and Wootton Basset, England. In September 2006, Dolby announced that the Nintendo Wii gaming console will incorporate Pro Logic II technology.

Dolby offers U.S. employees health benefits, a 401(k), educational assistance, flexible scheduling, equipment discounts and use of a company ski cabin. U.K. employees receive a pension plan.

FINANCIALS: Sales and profits are in thousands of dollars—add 000 to get the full amount. 2006 Note: Financial information for 2006 was not available for all companies at press time.

2006 Sales: $391,542	2006 Profits: $89,549	U.S. Stock Ticker: DLB
2005 Sales: $327,967	2005 Profits: $52,293	Int'l Ticker: Int'l Exchange:
2004 Sales: $289,000	2004 Profits: $34,600	Employees: 864
2003 Sales: $217,500	2003 Profits: $31,000	Fiscal Year Ends: 9/30
2002 Sales: $161,900	2002 Profits: $- 100	Parent Company:

SALARIES/BENEFITS:
Pension Plan:	ESOP Stock Plan:	Profit Sharing:	Top Exec. Salary: $611,539	Bonus: $383,078
Savings Plan: Y	Stock Purch. Plan:		Second Exec. Salary: $357,287	Bonus: $173,218

OTHER THOUGHTS:
Apparent Women Officers or Directors:
Hot Spot for Advancement for Women/Minorities:

LOCATIONS: ("Y" = Yes)
West:	Southwest:	Midwest:	Southeast:	Northeast:	International:
Y				Y	Y

Note: Financial information, benefits and other data can change quickly and may vary from those stated here.

DOUBLECLICK INC

www.doubleclick.com

Industry Group Code: 541810A Ranks within this company's industry group: Sales: Profits:

Print Media/Publishing:	Movies:	Equipment/Supplies:		Broadcast/Cable:	Music/Audio:	Sports/Games:
Newspapers:	Movie Theaters:	Equipment/Supplies:		Broadcast TV:	Music Production:	Games/Sports:
Magazines:	Movie Production:	Gambling Equipment:		Cable TV:	Retail Music:	Retail Games Stores:
Books:	TV/Video Production:	Special Services:		Satellite Broadcast:	Retail Audio Equip.:	Stadiums/Teams:
Book Stores:	Video Rental:	Advertising Services:	Y	Radio:	Music Print./Dist.:	Gambling/Casinos:
Distribution/Printing:	Video Distribution:	Info. Sys. Software:		Online Information:	Multimedia:	Rides/Theme Parks:

TYPES OF BUSINESS:

Online Advertising Services
Outsourcing Services
Advertising Software
Consumer Database Analysis

BRANDS/DIVISIONS/AFFILIATES:

MediaVisor
DART for Advertisers
Klipmart
DART Enterprise
DART Motif
Performics Search
Hellman & Friedman LLC
Falk eSolutions AG

CONTACTS: Note: Officers with more than one job title may be intentionally listed here more than once.

David S. Rosenblatt, CEO
Marianne Caponnetto, Chief Sales & Mktg. Officer
John M. Rehl, Sr. VP-Global Tech. Svcs.
Stephanie Abramson, General Counsel/Exec. VP
Stuart Frankel, Sr. VP/Pres., Performics
Chris Young, Exec. VP-Rich Media
Jason Bigler, VP-DoubleClick Product Management
Thomas Falk, Pres., DoubleClick Europe, Middle East, Africa
Ben Regensburger, Pres., DoubleClick Int'l

Phone: 212-683-0001	**Fax:** 212-287-1203
Toll-Free: 866-459-7606	
Address: 111 8th Ave., 10th Fl., New York, NY 10011 US	

GROWTH PLANS/SPECIAL FEATURES:

DoubleClick, Inc. is a leading provider of products and services that enable direct marketers, publishers and advertisers to market to consumers on the Internet. Products include MediaVisor, a software application for advertising campaign management; DART for Advertisers, a web-based ad management tool; DART for Publishers, a web-based tool for monetizing a publisher's advertising inventory; DART Sales Manager, a proposal and finance management tool; DART Enterprise, an ad management tool offering relatively detailed business management features, such as inventory management, traffic pattern analysis and real-time campaign result reporting; and DART Motif, a rich media advertising resource that has Flash-in-Flash capabilities as well as In-Stream, a differentiated Streaming video inventory. In 2006, the firm acquired Klipmart, which provides online video advertising and management solutions. The Performics division, responsible for performance-based marketing, includes Performics Search, which makes use of online search engines, and the Performics Affiliate Marketing program, which has a partnership with Yahoo! These products are designed to help companies target potential customers using online advertising and manage existing ones using various software applications. DoubleClick, in addition to its product packages, provides consulting services and technical support to its clients. Much of the company's recent growth has been focused on developing better streaming video for use as advertisements. DoubleClick manages online advertising for companies such as MySpace, Ford Motors, MTV, and CBS Sports. In 2005, the company was acquired by Hellman & Friedman LLC for $1.1 billion. The most significant structural change after the acquisition was the transition of Abacus-Direct, the customer data company, from a subsidiary of DoubleClick to an independent enterprise. In late 2006, DoubleClick agreed to sell the Abacus division to Alliance Data Systems Corp.'s Epsilon unit for $435 million. In 2006, the company acquired Falk eSolutions AG, a global online advertising delivery and marketing management solutions agency.

FINANCIALS: Sales and profits are in thousands of dollars—add 000 to get the full amount. 2006 Note: Financial information for 2006 was not available for all companies at press time.

2006 Sales: $	2006 Profits: $	**U.S. Stock Ticker:** Private
2005 Sales: $	2005 Profits: $	**Int'l Ticker:** Int'l Exchange:
2004 Sales: $301,600	2004 Profits: $37,500	**Employees:** 1,223
2003 Sales: $271,337	2003 Profits: $16,918	**Fiscal Year Ends:** 12/31
2002 Sales: $300,200	2002 Profits: $-117,900	**Parent Company:**

SALARIES/BENEFITS:

Pension Plan:	ESOP Stock Plan:	Profit Sharing:	Top Exec. Salary: $360,000	Bonus: $444,600
Savings Plan: Y	Stock Purch. Plan:		Second Exec. Salary: $300,000	Bonus: $240,000

OTHER THOUGHTS:

Apparent Women Officers or Directors: 2
Hot Spot for Advancement for Women/Minorities:

LOCATIONS: ("Y" = Yes)

West:	Southwest:	Midwest:	Southeast:	Northeast:	International:
Y		Y		Y	Y

DOVER DOWNS GAMING & ENTERTAINMENT INC

www.doverdowns.com

Industry Group Code: 713210 Ranks within this company's industry group: Sales: 6   Profits: 3

Print Media/Publishing:	Movies:	Equipment/Supplies:	Broadcast/Cable:	Music/Audio:	Sports/Games:	
Newspapers:	Movie Theaters:	Equipment/Supplies:	Broadcast TV:	Music Production:	Games/Sports:	Y
Magazines:	Movie Production:	Gambling Equipment:	Cable TV:	Retail Music:	Retail Games Stores:	
Books:	TV/Video Production:	Special Services:	Satellite Broadcast:	Retail Audio Equip.:	Stadiums/Teams:	
Book Stores:	Video Rental:	Advertising Services:	Radio:	Music Print./Dist.:	Gambling/Casinos:	Y
Distribution/Printing:	Video Distribution:	Info. Sys. Software:	Online Information:	Multimedia:	Rides/Theme Parks:	

TYPES OF BUSINESS:

Casinos & Gaming Facilities
Slot Machine Casino
Hotel & Conference Center
Horse Racing
Live Events

BRANDS/DIVISIONS/AFFILIATES:

Dover Downs Slots
Dover Downs Hotel & Conference Center
Dover Downs Raceway

CONTACTS: Note: Officers with more than one job title may be intentionally listed here more than once.

Denis McGlynn, CEO
Edward J. Sutor, COO/Exec. VP
Denis McGlynn, Pres.
Timothy R. Horne, CFO
Klaus M. Belohoubek, General Counsel/Sr. VP/Corp. Sec.
Timothy R. Horne, VP-Finance/Treas.
Henry B. Tippie, Chmn.

Phone: 302-674-4600	Fax: 302-857-3253
Toll-Free: 800-711-5882	
Address: 1131 N. DuPont Hwy., Dover, DE 19901 US	

GROWTH PLANS/SPECIAL FEATURES:

Dover Downs Gaming & Entertainment, Inc. is a gaming and entertainment company with operations in Delaware, consisting of Dover Downs Slots, a 97,000-square-foot slot machine casino complex; the Dover Downs Hotel & Conference Center, sporting conference, banquet, dining, ballroom and concert hall facilities; and the Dover Downs Raceway, a harness racing track that includes pari-mutuel wagering on live and simulcast horse races on numerous tracks across North America. The casino operates 2,700 slot machines ranging from a penny to $100 to play. The hotel and conference center includes 232 rooms, a multi-purpose ballroom/concert hall, five dining areas, a swimming pool and a health spa. The hotel also offers entertainment to its guests, such as music concerts and live boxing. Dover Downs Raceway conducts live harness races between November and April, and all are simulcast to tracks and other off-track betting locations across North America on each of the company's more than 140 live race dates. Recent renovations of the complex resulted in an enclosed harness racing grandstand with state-of-the-art broadcasting facilities. Dover Motorsports, the former auto racing division of Dover Downs, is now a separate company traded on the New York Stock Exchange.

Dover Downs offers its employees a health and dental package, life insurance, discounted entertainment tickets, credit union membership, free NASCAR tickets and leadership awards.

FINANCIALS: Sales and profits are in thousands of dollars—add 000 to get the full amount. 2006 Note: Financial information for 2006 was not available for all companies at press time.

2006 Sales: $	2006 Profits: $	**U.S. Stock Ticker:** DDE
2005 Sales: $216,852	2005 Profits: $26,040	**Int'l Ticker:** Int'l Exchange:
2004 Sales: $207,300	2004 Profits: $16,400	Employees: 922
2003 Sales: $207,499	2003 Profits: $17,237	Fiscal Year Ends: 12/31
2002 Sales: $219,806	2002 Profits: $21,442	Parent Company:

SALARIES/BENEFITS:

Pension Plan: Y	ESOP Stock Plan:	Profit Sharing:	Top Exec. Salary: $250,000	Bonus: $423,700
Savings Plan: Y	Stock Purch. Plan:		Second Exec. Salary: $220,000	Bonus: $95,539

OTHER THOUGHTS:

Apparent Women Officers or Directors:
Hot Spot for Advancement for Women/Minorities:

LOCATIONS: ("Y" = Yes)

West:	Southwest:	Midwest:	Southeast:	Northeast:	International:
				Y	

DOW JONES & COMPANY INC

www.dj.com

Industry Group Code: 511110 Ranks within this company's industry group: Sales: 8   Profits: 9

Print Media/Publishing:		Movies:		Equipment/Supplies:		Broadcast/Cable:		Music/Audio:		Sports/Games:	
Newspapers:	Y	Movie Theaters:		Equipment/Supplies:		Broadcast TV:		Music Production:		Games/Sports:	
Magazines:	Y	Movie Production:		Gambling Equipment:		Cable TV:		Retail Music:		Retail Games Stores:	
Books:		TV/Video Production:		Special Services:		Satellite Broadcast:		Retail Audio Equip.:		Stadiums/Teams:	
Book Stores:		Video Rental:		Advertising Services:	Y	Radio:		Music Print./Dist.:		Gambling/Casinos:	
Distribution/Printing:		Video Distribution:		Info. Sys. Software:	Y	Online Information:		Multimedia:		Rides/Theme Parks:	

TYPES OF BUSINESS:

Newspaper Publishing-Financial News
Business Publishing
Community Newspapers
Electronic & Online Publishing
Financial Indices
Financial Information Services

BRANDS/DIVISIONS/AFFILIATES:

Wall Street Journal (The)
Barron's
Dow Jones Newswires
Factiva
wsj.com
opinionjournal.com
Dow Jones Industrial Averages
Ottaway Newspapers, Inc.

CONTACTS: *Note: Officers with more than one job title may be intentionally listed here more than once.*

Richard F. Zannino, CEO
Todd H. Larsen, COO
William B. Plummer, Exec. VP/CFO
Ann Marks, Chief Corp. Mktg. Officer/VP
James A. Scaduto, VP-Human Resources
William A. Godfrey, III, CIO/VP
Joseph A. Stern, General Counsel/VP/Corp. Sec.
Thomas W. McGuirl, VP-Tax
Clare Hart, Pres., Enterprise Media group/Exec. VP
John N. Wilcox, Pres., Community Media group/ Sr. VP
L. Gordon Crovitz, Pres., Dow Jones Consumer Media/Pub. Wall Street J
Michael A. Petronella, Pres., Dow Jones Indexes/Ventures
Peter R. Kann, Chmn.

Phone: 212-416-2000	Fax: 212-416-4348
Toll-Free:	
Address: 200 Liberty St., New York, NY 10281 US	

GROWTH PLANS/SPECIAL FEATURES:

Dow Jones & Company, Inc. (DJ) is a global provider of business and financial news and information through newspapers, newswires, magazines, the Internet, television and radio stations. In addition, the firm owns certain general-interest community newspapers throughout the U.S. DJ operates through three business segments: print publishing, electronic publishing and community newspapers. The print segment, which is largely comprised of the operations of The Wall Street Journal, produces business and financial content worldwide. The Wall Street Journal is one of the largest daily newspapers in the U.S. and the firm's flagship publication. This segment also publishes Barron's, a weekly magazine that caters to financial professionals and investors, as well as international publications including The Wall Street Journal Europe and The Asian Wall Street Journal. The firm's electronic segment includes the operations of Dow Jones Newswires, consumer electronic publishing operations, Dow Jones Wealth Manager Web Services (launched 2006) and Dow Jones Indexes/Ventures. Dow Jones Newswires is a premier provider of real-time business and financial news displayed on almost 300,000 terminals around the world. Consumer electronic publications include The Wall Street Journal Online (wsj.com), a paid subscription site offering coverage of business news; opinionjournal.com; startupjournal.com; collegejournal.com; and careerjournal.com. Through Dow Jones Indexes, the company licenses the Dow Jones Industrial Averages and other indexes as the basis for trading options, futures, annuities and other products. Dow Jones Ventures handles the firm's reprints and permissions. DJ also publishes community newspapers through subsidiary Ottaway Newspapers, Inc. The company is constantly adapting its operations to changing trends. In 2006, DJ purchased Reuter's 50% share in Factiva, making DJ the sole owner. In 2006, the company agreed to sell six Ottaway community newspapers to Community Newspaper Holdings, Inc. for $282.5 million.

Dow Jones provides employees with tuition reimbursement, adoption assistance and a dependent care program.

FINANCIALS: Sales and profits are in thousands of dollars—add 000 to get the full amount. 2006 Note: Financial information for 2006 was not available for all companies at press time.

2006 Sales: $	2006 Profits: $	U.S. Stock Ticker: DJ
2005 Sales: $1,769,690	2005 Profits: $81,820	Int'l Ticker: Int'l Exchange:
2004 Sales: $1,671,500	2004 Profits: $99,500	Employees: 7,501
2003 Sales: $1,548,500	2003 Profits: $170,600	Fiscal Year Ends: 12/31
2002 Sales: $1,559,200	2002 Profits: $201,500	Parent Company:

SALARIES/BENEFITS:

Pension Plan: Y	ESOP Stock Plan:	Profit Sharing:	Top Exec. Salary: $990,315	Bonus: $918,500
Savings Plan: Y	Stock Purch. Plan: Y		Second Exec. Salary: $756,653	Bonus: $638,000

OTHER THOUGHTS:

Apparent Women Officers or Directors: 6
Hot Spot for Advancement for Women/Minorities: Y

LOCATIONS: ("Y" = Yes)

West:	Southwest:	Midwest:	Southeast:	Northeast:	International:
Y	Y	Y	Y	Y	Y

Note: Financial information, benefits and other data can change quickly and may vary from those stated here.

DREAMWORKS ANIMATION SKG INC
www.dreamworksanimation.com

Industry Group Code: 512110 Ranks within this company's industry group: Sales: 12   Profits: 2

Print Media/Publishing:	Movies:		Equipment/Supplies:		Broadcast/Cable:	Music/Audio:	Sports/Games:
Newspapers:	Movie Theaters:		Equipment/Supplies:		Broadcast TV:	Music Production:	Games/Sports:
Magazines:	Movie Production:	Y	Gambling Equipment:		Cable TV:	Retail Music:	Retail Games Stores:
Books:	TV/Video Production:		Special Services:		Satellite Broadcast:	Retail Audio Equip.:	Stadiums/Teams:
Book Stores:	Video Rental:		Advertising Services:		Radio:	Music Print./Dist.:	Gambling/Casinos:
Distribution/Printing:	Video Distribution:		Info. Sys. Software:	Y	Online Information:	Multimedia:	Rides/Theme Parks:

TYPES OF BUSINESS:
Animated Film Production
Animation Software

BRANDS/DIVISIONS/AFFILIATES:
DreamWorks Studios
EMOtion
Nile
Virtual Studio Collaboration
Wallace & Gromit: Curse of the Were-Rabbit
Shrek
Over the Hedge
Flushed Away

CONTACTS: Note: Officers with more than one job title may be intentionally listed here more than once.
Jeffrey Katzenberg, CEO
Ann Daly, COO
Lew Coleman, Pres.
Terry Press, Head-Worldwide Mktg.
Ed Leonard, CTO
Kristine Belson, Head-Dev.
Katherine Kendrick, General Counsel/Sec.
Derek Chan, Head-Digital Oper.
Fumi Kitahara, Media Contact
Bill Damaschke, Head-Creative Production & Dev.
Jane Hartwell, Head-Global Production
Nancy Bernstein, Head-Production, Dreamworks Animation, Glendale
Gloria Borders, Head-PDI/Dreamworks
Roger A. Enrico, Chmn.

Phone: 818-695-5000	Fax: 818-695-9944
Toll-Free:	
Address: Grandview Bldg., 1000 Flower St., Glendale, CA 91201 US	

GROWTH PLANS/SPECIAL FEATURES:
DreamWorks Animation SKG, Inc. develops and produces computer-generated (CG) animated feature films that are distributed and marketed by Paramount. The firm uses proprietary software to produce its films, such as EMOtion, Nile and Virtual Studio Collaboration. Operations take place at two facilities in Glendale and Redwood City, California. The company has released a total of nine animated films, including four that were CG-only and one direct-to-video title. Its films include such box office hits as Antz, Shrek and Shrek 2 (the third highest grossing film of all time, as of 2006). The firm has also collaborated with Aardman Animations to release Chicken Run and Wallace & Gromit: Curse of the Were-Rabbit. DreamWorks Animation's recent films include Shark Tale (its second highest-grossing film) and Madagascar. Over the Hedge, released in May 2006, was a modest hit grossing approximately $155 million domestically. Flushed Away, a film about sewer rats produced in conjunction with Aardman Animations, was released in November 2006. Dream Works has several films in production, including: Shrek 3, due May 2007; Bees, fall 2007; Kung Fu Panda, 2008; and Madagascar 2, 2008. The studio has four movies in pre-production: How to Train Your Dragon; Rex Havoc; It Came From Earth; and Route 66. In addition the firm has rights to Punk Farm and Mr. Peabody & Sherman. In October 2004, DreamWorks, LLC spun off DreamWorks Animation in an initial public offering, with net proceeds of $635.5 million. The firm has a multi-picture, multi-year promotional alliance with Kellogg Company that began with the release of Flushed Away. Dream Works' distribution agreement with Paramount runs through 2012.

DreamWorks Animation offers paid 10-12 week animation and engineering internships in the spring, summer and fall, as well as an entry-level outreach program for recent graduates.

FINANCIALS: Sales and profits are in thousands of dollars—add 000 to get the full amount. 2006 Note: Financial information for 2006 was not available for all companies at press time.

2006 Sales: $	2006 Profits: $	U.S. Stock Ticker: DWA
2005 Sales: $462,316	2005 Profits: $104,585	Int'l Ticker: Int'l Exchange:
2004 Sales: $1,078,160	2004 Profits: $333,000	Employees: 1,280
2003 Sales: $301,000	2003 Profits: $-187,100	Fiscal Year Ends: 12/31
2002 Sales: $434,300	2002 Profits: $-25,100	Parent Company:

SALARIES/BENEFITS:

Pension Plan:	ESOP Stock Plan:	Profit Sharing:	Top Exec. Salary: $1,000,000	Bonus: $
Savings Plan:	Stock Purch. Plan:		Second Exec. Salary: $579,039	Bonus: $

OTHER THOUGHTS:
Apparent Women Officers or Directors: 8
Hot Spot for Advancement for Women/Minorities: Y

LOCATIONS: ("Y" = Yes)

West:	Southwest:	Midwest:	Southeast:	Northeast:	International:
Y					

DREAMWORKS LLC

www.dreamworks.com

Industry Group Code: 512110 Ranks within this company's industry group: Sales: Profits:

Print Media/Publishing:	Movies:		Equipment/Supplies:	Broadcast/Cable:	Music/Audio:	Sports/Games:
Newspapers:	Movie Theaters:		Equipment/Supplies:	Broadcast TV:	Music Production:	Games/Sports:
Magazines:	Movie Production:	Y	Gambling Equipment:	Cable TV:	Retail Music:	Retail Games Stores:
Books:	TV/Video Production:	Y	Special Services:	Satellite Broadcast:	Retail Audio Equip.:	Stadiums/Teams:
Book Stores:	Video Rental:		Advertising Services:	Radio:	Music Print./Dist.:	Gambling/Casinos:
Distribution/Printing:	Video Distribution:		Info. Sys. Software:	Online Information:	Multimedia:	Rides/Theme Parks:

TYPES OF BUSINESS:

Film Production & Distribution
Animated Films
Foreign Film Distribution
Television Production

BRANDS/DIVISIONS/AFFILIATES:

DreamWorks Movies
DreamWorks TV
Go Fish Pictures
Viacom
Dreamworks SKG
Paramount

CONTACTS: Note: Officers with more than one job title may be intentionally listed here more than once.

Steven Spielberg, Principal/Co-founder
David Geffen, Principal/Co-founder
Jeffrey Katzenberg, Principal/Co-founder

Phone: 818-733-7000	**Fax:** 818-695-7574
Toll-Free:	
Address: 1000 Flower St., Glendale, CA 91201 US	

GROWTH PLANS/SPECIAL FEATURES:

DreamWorks, LLC, a subsidiary of Viacom operating under the name DreamWorks SKG, is a leading producer of live-action motion pictures, animated feature films, network and cable television programming, home video and DVD entertainment and consumer products. It was formed with the intention to create an artist-friendly studio to develop, produce and distribute film and music entertainment. DreamWorks was founded by Steven Spielberg, film director and producer; Jeffrey Katzenberg, a former Disney film executive and animation guru; and David Geffen, a recording industry executive. Together they own approximately 66% of the company. The firm has major offices in Glendale, Beverly Hills and Universal City, California; New York, New York; Nashville, Tennessee; London, England; and Toronto, Canada. DreamWorks has divisions that are involved in animation, the movie industry, TV programming production and video/DVD distribution. DreamWorks Movies produces feature films, including Oscar-winners American Beauty and Gladiator. DreamWorks TV produces network and cable television programs, for example, Las Vegas and Spin City. Go Fish Pictures is the new distribution arm of DreamWorks, focusing largely on releasing foreign films, especially Japanese anime, in the U.S. DreamWorks recently spun off DreamWorks Animation, which produces all of the company's animated works, including such hits as Shrek and Chicken Run, in an initial public offering. The company is further streamlining operations, having sold its record label and video game business and dramatically reducing television production.

Dreamworks offers both paid and unpaid internships for college students, with opportunities in almost all divisions of the film production business.

FINANCIALS: Sales and profits are in thousands of dollars—add 000 to get the full amount. 2006 Note: Financial information for 2006 was not available for all companies at press time.

2006 Sales: $	2006 Profits: $	**U.S. Stock Ticker: Subsidiary**
2005 Sales: $	2005 Profits: $	**Int'l Ticker:** Int'l Exchange:
2004 Sales: $1,110,000	2004 Profits: $	Employees: 1,100
2003 Sales: $1,250,000	2003 Profits: $	Fiscal Year Ends: 12/31
2002 Sales: $1,813,000	2002 Profits: $	Parent Company: VIACOM INC

SALARIES/BENEFITS:

Pension Plan:	ESOP Stock Plan:	Profit Sharing:	Top Exec. Salary: $	Bonus: $
Savings Plan:	Stock Purch. Plan:		Second Exec. Salary: $	Bonus: $

OTHER THOUGHTS:

Apparent Women Officers or Directors:
Hot Spot for Advancement for Women/Minorities: Y

LOCATIONS: ("Y" = Yes)

West:	Southwest:	Midwest:	Southeast:	Northeast:	International:
Y			Y	Y	Y

Note: Financial information, benefits and other data can change quickly and may vary from those stated here.

DTS INC

www.dtsonline.com

Industry Group Code: 334310 Ranks within this company's industry group: Sales: 13 Profits: 8

Print Media/Publishing:	Movies:	Equipment/Supplies:		Broadcast/Cable:	Music/Audio:	Sports/Games:
Newspapers:	Movie Theaters:	Equipment/Supplies:	Y	Broadcast TV:	Music Production:	Games/Sports:
Magazines:	Movie Production:	Gambling Equipment:		Cable TV:	Retail Music:	Retail Games Stores:
Books:	TV/Video Production:	Special Services:	Y	Satellite Broadcast:	Retail Audio Equip.:	Stadiums/Teams:
Book Stores:	Video Rental:	Advertising Services:		Radio:	Music Print./Dist.:	Gambling/Casinos:
Distribution/Printing:	Video Distribution:	Info. Sys. Software:		Online Information:	Multimedia:	Rides/Theme Parks:

TYPES OF BUSINESS:

Audio & Video Equipment, Manufacturing
Digital Multi-Channel (Surround Sound) Audio Technology
Digital Remastering
Video Restoration & Enhancement

BRANDS/DIVISIONS/AFFILIATES:

Digital Theater Systems
DTS Digital Images
Lowry Digital Images, Inc.

CONTACTS: Note: Officers with more than one job title may be intentionally listed here more than once.

Jon Kirchner, CEO
Jon Kirchner, Pres.
Mel Flanigan, CFO
Sharon K. Faltemier, Sr. VP-Human Resources
Paul Smith, Sr. VP-Research & Dev.
Jan Wissmuller, Sr. VP-Prod. Dev.
Jan Wissmuller, Sr. VP-Eng.
Blake Welcher, Exec. VP/General Counsel/Corp. Sec.
Andrea Nee, Exec. VP-Oper.
Patrick Watson, Sr. VP-Strategy & Bus. Dev.
Mel Flanigan, Exec. VP-Finance
Don Bird, Sr. VP-Cinema Div.
Kin Chan, Managing Dir.-Greater China
Brian Towne, Sr. VP-Consumer/Pro Div.
Nao Ohtake, Dir.-Oper., DTS Japan
Dan Slusser, Chmn.
Tony Nowak, Managing Dir.-DTS Europe

Phone: 818-706-3525	Fax: 818-706-1868
Toll-Free:	
Address: 5171 Clareton Dr., Agoura Hills, CA 91301 US	

GROWTH PLANS/SPECIAL FEATURES:

DTS, Inc., formerly Digital Theater Systems, is a leading provider of high-quality digital multi-channel audio technology, products and services for entertainment markets worldwide. The company provides products and services to film studios, production companies and movie theaters to produce and play back digital surround-sound soundtracks for films. The first movie to use the firm's technology was Steven Spielberg's Jurassic Park in 1993. The company licenses its sound technology to all major film distributors in the U.S., including 20th Century Fox, Buena Vista Pictures, Warner Bros. Pictures and many international distributors. The firm's playback systems for DTS-formatted soundtracks have been installed in over 27,000 movie theaters worldwide. DTS also licenses its technology to consumer electronics manufacturers for inclusion in products such as audio/video receivers, DVD players and home theater systems. Its technology enables consumers to enjoy movies, video games and music in DTS multi-channel format. The company's consumer business has grown to become its largest business segment. To date, DTS has entered into licensing agreements with substantially all of the major consumer audio electronics manufacturers, including Pioneer, Sony and Yamaha. The company's technology is also found in over 115 music titles in various genres and DVDs for the consumer retail market. DTS licenses titles by well-known recording artists, then re-mixes and releases these titles in its digital multi-channel format. The company's subsidiary, DTS Digital Images, provides restoration and enhancement services on film and digital movies. These services allow archive material to be presented in high quality, high definition formats.

DTS offers employee benefits including a 401(k) savings plan, flexible spending accounts, a cafeteria plan, health club discounts and an employee assistance program.

FINANCIALS: Sales and profits are in thousands of dollars—add 000 to get the full amount. 2006 Note: Financial information for 2006 was not available for all companies at press time.

2006 Sales: $	2006 Profits: $	U.S. Stock Ticker: DTSI
2005 Sales: $75,252	2005 Profits: $7,908	Int'l Ticker: Int'l Exchange:
2004 Sales: $61,431	2004 Profits: $9,976	Employees: 314
2003 Sales: $51,700	2003 Profits: $8,700	Fiscal Year Ends: 12/31
2002 Sales: $41,100	2002 Profits: $6,300	Parent Company:

SALARIES/BENEFITS:

Pension Plan:	ESOP Stock Plan:	Profit Sharing:	Top Exec. Salary: $320,306	Bonus: $160,000
Savings Plan: Y	Stock Purch. Plan:		Second Exec. Salary: $233,262	Bonus: $80,000

OTHER THOUGHTS:

Apparent Women Officers or Directors: 1
Hot Spot for Advancement for Women/Minorities:

LOCATIONS: ("Y" = Yes)

West:	Southwest:	Midwest:	Southeast:	Northeast:	International:
Y					Y

DUN & BRADSTREET CORP (THE, D&B)   www.dnb.com

Industry Group Code: 561450 Ranks within this company's industry group: Sales: 2   Profits: 2

Print Media/Publishing:		Movies:		Equipment/Supplies:		Broadcast/Cable:		Music/Audio:		Sports/Games:	
Newspapers:		Movie Theaters:		Equipment/Supplies:		Broadcast TV:		Music Production:		Games/Sports:	
Magazines:		Movie Production:		Gambling Equipment:		Cable TV:		Retail Music:		Retail Games Stores:	
Books:	Y	TV/Video Production:		Special Services:		Satellite Broadcast:		Retail Audio Equip.:		Stadiums/Teams:	
Book Stores:		Video Rental:		Advertising Services:		Radio:		Music Print./Dist.:		Gambling/Casinos:	
Distribution/Printing:		Video Distribution:		Info. Sys. Software:		Online Information:		Multimedia:		Rides/Theme Parks:	

TYPES OF BUSINESS:

Global Business Credit Bureau
Credit Risk Management Support
Purchasing & Supply Chain Intelligence
Account Collection Support
Online Business Information
Decision Support Services

BRANDS/DIVISIONS/AFFILIATES:

D&B
DUNSRight
D-U-N-S Number System
D&B Risk Management Solutions
D&B Sales & Marketing Solutions
D&B Supply Management Solutions
D&B E-Business Solutions
Hoover's, Inc.

CONTACTS: Note: Officers with more than one job title may be intentionally listed here more than once.

Steven W. Alesio, CEO
Steven W. Alesio, Pres.
Sara Mathew, CFO/Dir.-Strategy
James P. Burke, Chief Mktg. Officer
Patricia A. Clifford, Sr. VP-Human Resources
Byron C. Vielehr, CIO
Byron C. Vielehr, Sr. VP-Tech.
Lee A. Spirer, Sr. VP-Reengineering
David J. Lewinter, General Counsel/Corp. Sec.
Lee A. Spirer, Sr. VP-Strategy & Bus. Dev.
Jim Delaney, Sr. VP-Global Sales & Mktg.
Sara Mathew, Pres., U.S.
Lawrence M. Kutscher, Sr. VP-Small Bus. Solutions
Steven W. Alesio, Chmn.
Jim Howland, Pres., Int'l

Phone: 973-921-5500	Fax: 512-794-7670
Toll-Free: 800-234-3867	
Address: 103 JFK Pkwy., Short Hills, NJ 07078 US	

GROWTH PLANS/SPECIAL FEATURES:

The Dun & Bradstreet Corporation (D&B) is a worldwide provider of business information and related decision support services. The company has aggressively taken advantage of the Internet to the extent that about 80% of its data is now delivered online. D&B's proprietary DUNSRight process provides customers with comprehensive business information on demand. The firm's database contains statistics on more than 80 million companies in over 200 countries. This information is the foundation of D&B's four core software product lines: D&B Risk Management Solutions, which manages credit exposure; D&B Sales & Marketing Solutions, which enables clients to better acquire and manage customers; D&B Supply Management Solutions, which provides tools for the management of supplier relationships; and D&B E-Business Solutions, which help customers convert prospects into clients. Another product, the widely accepted D-U-N-S Number system, is used to identify and track a business globally through every phase of its life, including bankruptcy. The company also provides credit information solutions to help its customers extend commercial credit, approve loans and leases, underwrite insurance, evaluate clients and make other financial and risk assessment decisions. Hoover's, Inc., a firm subsidiary, is an Internet-based provider of industry and market intelligence on public and private companies. D&B's purchasing information solutions help clients understand their supplier base and evaluate new sources of supply. In addition, the company offers its clients a full range of accounts receivable management services, including third-party collection of accounts, demand letter-writing services and receivable outsourcing programs. In March 2006, D&B acquired Open Ratings, a provider of web-based supply risk management solutions.

D&B provides its employees with tuition reimbursement, personal and domestic partner insurance coverage, adoption assistance, a matching gifts program and merit scholarships. It is also known for its promotion of women to managerial positions.

FINANCIALS: Sales and profits are in thousands of dollars—add 000 to get the full amount. 2006 Note: Financial information for 2006 was not available for all companies at press time.

2006 Sales: $	2006 Profits: $	**U.S. Stock Ticker: DNB**
2005 Sales: $1,443,600	2005 Profits: $242,000	**Int'l Ticker:** Int'l Exchange:
2004 Sales: $1,414,000	2004 Profits: $211,800	Employees: 4,350
2003 Sales: $982,000	2003 Profits: $101,000	Fiscal Year Ends: 12/31
2002 Sales: $1,386,400	2002 Profits: $174,500	Parent Company:

SALARIES/BENEFITS:

Pension Plan: Y	ESOP Stock Plan:	Profit Sharing:	Top Exec. Salary: $750,000	Bonus: $1,200,000
Savings Plan: Y	Stock Purch. Plan: Y		Second Exec. Salary: $450,000	Bonus: $486,000

OTHER THOUGHTS:

Apparent Women Officers or Directors: 3
Hot Spot for Advancement for Women/Minorities: Y

LOCATIONS: ("Y" = Yes)

West:	Southwest:	Midwest:	Southeast:	Northeast:	International:
Y	Y	Y	Y	Y	Y

Note: Financial information, benefits and other data can change quickly and may vary from those stated here.

E W SCRIPPS CO

www.scripps.com

Industry Group Code: 511110 Ranks within this company's industry group: Sales: 7 Profits: 5

Print Media/Publishing:		Movies:		Equipment/Supplies:		Broadcast/Cable:		Music/Audio:		Sports/Games:	
Newspapers:	Y	Movie Theaters:		Equipment/Supplies:		Broadcast TV:	Y	Music Production:		Games/Sports:	
Magazines:	Y	Movie Production:		Gambling Equipment:		Cable TV:	Y	Retail Music:		Retail Games Stores:	
Books:		TV/Video Production:	Y	Special Services:	Y	Satellite Broadcast:		Retail Audio Equip.:		Stadiums/Teams:	
Book Stores:		Video Rental:		Advertising Services:		Radio:		Music Print./Dist.:		Gambling/Casinos:	
Distribution/Printing:		Video Distribution:		Info. Sys. Software:		Online Information:		Multimedia:		Rides/Theme Parks:	

TYPES OF BUSINESS:

Newspaper Publishing
Broadcast Television Stations
Television & Online Retail
Online Media
Newswire Service
Venture Capital
Newspapers

BRANDS/DIVISIONS/AFFILIATES:

Scripps Howard News Service
Home & Garden Television
Do It Yourself Network
Food Network
Fine Living
Shop At Home Network, LLC
Scripps Ventures
uSwitch.com

CONTACTS: *Note: Officers with more than one job title may be intentionally listed here more than once.*

Kenneth W. Lowe, CEO
Richard A. Boehne, COO
Kenneth W. Lowe, Pres.
Joseph G. NeCastro, CFO
Jennifer L. Weber, Sr. VP-Human Resources
B. Jeff Craig, CTO/VP
Mark Hale, Sr. VP-Tech. Oper.
Joseph G. NeCastro, Sr. VP-Finance & Admin.
A. B. Cruz, III, General Counsel/Sr. VP
Richard A. Boehne, Exec. VP-Oper.
Kenneth W. Lowe, Exec. VP-Corp. Dev.
Timothy E. Strautberg, VP-Comm.
Timothy E. Strautberg, VP-Investor Rel.
Lori A. Hickock, VP-Controller
Tim Peterman, Sr. VP-Interactive Media
William B. Peterson, Sr. VP-Television
Douglas F. Lyons, VP-Finance & Admin.-Interactive Media
Mark G. Contreras, Sr. VP-Newspapers
William R. Burleigh, Chmn.

Phone: 513-977-3000	Fax: 513-977-3721
Toll-Free:	
Address: 312 Walnut St., 2800 Scripps Center, Cincinnati, OH 45202 US	

GROWTH PLANS/SPECIAL FEATURES:

The E.W. Scripps Company (Scripps) operates in five segments: newspapers, broadcast television, national television networks, interactive media and television retailing. The company operates 21 daily newspapers in the U.S. with a combined circulation of 1.4 million daily subscribers. The firm also publishes several weekly and semiweekly community newspapers and operates the Scripps Howard News Service, the second-largest supplemental wire service in the U.S., covering stories in Washington, D.C., the U.S. and abroad. The company's newspapers each operate Internet sites featuring content included in their publications. Scripps Networks includes five national TV networks distributed by cable and satellite systems, including Home & Garden Television (HGTV); the Do It Yourself Network (DIY); the Food Network; and Fine Living and Great American Country (GAC). The Scripps Network stations also operate three web sites: FoodTV.com, HGTV.com and DIYnet.com. Shop At Home Network, LLC, Scripps' home shopping subsidiary, retails consumer goods directly to 73 million households via television and through its web site, ShopAtHomeTV.com. The broadcast television group includes 10 TV stations, nine of which are affiliated with national networks. The segment's stations derive revenue from local and national advertising. Additionally, Scripps syndicates over 150 comic strips, including Peanuts (which provides 95% of the firm's licensing revenues) and Dilbert through United Media and news features through United Feature Syndicate. Through Scripps Ventures, the company invests in new businesses, centered on early-stage Internet companies. In 2006, the firm announced plans for Jewelry Television to acquire the IT systems, real estate, call center, production studios and web site of the Shop At Home network for $17 million. Recently, Scripps acquired uSwitch.com, a U.K online comparison (for essential home services and finance) website for $366 million. The Scripps family owns approximately 87% of the company.

The firm manages a corporate foundation (Scripps Howard Foundation) that awards journalism scholarships.

FINANCIALS: Sales and profits are in thousands of dollars—add 000 to get the full amount. 2006 Note: Financial information for 2006 was not available for all companies at press time.

2006 Sales: $	2006 Profits: $	**U.S. Stock Ticker: SSP**
2005 Sales: $2,513,890	2005 Profits: $249,153	**Int'l Ticker:** Int'l Exchange:
2004 Sales: $2,167,500	2004 Profits: $303,800	Employees: 9,600
2003 Sales: $1,874,845	2003 Profits: $270,815	Fiscal Year Ends: 12/31
2002 Sales: $1,535,700	2002 Profits: $188,300	Parent Company:

SALARIES/BENEFITS:

Pension Plan: Y	ESOP Stock Plan: Y	Profit Sharing:	Top Exec. Salary: $1,050,000	Bonus: $1,105,398
Savings Plan:	Stock Purch. Plan:		Second Exec. Salary: $585,000	Bonus: $359,979

OTHER THOUGHTS:

Apparent Women Officers or Directors: 5
Hot Spot for Advancement for Women/Minorities: Y

LOCATIONS: ("Y" = Yes)

West:	Southwest:	Midwest:	Southeast:	Northeast:	International:
Y	Y	Y	Y	Y	Y

EBSCO INDUSTRIES INC

www.ebscoind.com

Industry Group Code: 422920 **Ranks within this company's industry group:** Sales: Profits:

Print Media/Publishing:		Movies:		Equipment/Supplies:		Broadcast/Cable:		Music/Audio:		Sports/Games:	
Newspapers:		Movie Theaters:		Equipment/Supplies:		Broadcast TV:		Music Production:		Games/Sports:	
Magazines:	Y	Movie Production:		Gambling Equipment:		Cable TV:		Retail Music:		Retail Games Stores:	
Books:	Y	TV/Video Production:	Y	Special Services:	Y	Satellite Broadcast:		Retail Audio Equip.:		Stadiums/Teams:	
Book Stores:		Video Rental:		Advertising Services:		Radio:		Music Print./Dist.:		Gambling/Casinos:	
Distribution/Printing:		Video Distribution:		Info. Sys. Software:	Y	Online Information:		Multimedia:		Rides/Theme Parks:	

TYPES OF BUSINESS:

Online Information Publishing
Publishing & Printing Services
Subscription Services
Online Bookstores
Information Services & Databases
Manufacturing-Sporting Goods & Firearms
Manufacturing-Furniture
Marketing Services

BRANDS/DIVISIONS/AFFILIATES:

EBSCO Information Services
EBSCO Magazine Express
Grand View Media Group
EBSCO Reception Room Subscription Services
Vulcan Service
EBSCO Subscription Services
EBSCO Publishing
Bowhunting World

CONTACTS: Note: Officers with more than one job title may be intentionally listed here more than once.

F. Dixon Brooke, Jr., CEO
F. Dixon Brooke, Jr., Pres.
Richard L. Bozzelli, CFO/VP
John C. Thompson, VP/General Mngr.-Human Resources
John Fitts, VP/General Mngr.-Information Systems & Svcs.
Becky Caldarello, VP/General Mngr.-Admin Svcs.
Joe K. Weed, VP/General Mngr.-Corp. Com.
Carol M. Johnson, Chief Accounting Officer/VP
Matt Carrington, Dir.-Acquisitions
Brooks Knapp, VP/General Mngr.-EBSCO Realty
James T. Stephens, Chmn.

Phone: 205-991-6600	Fax: 205-995-1636
Toll-Free:	
Address: 5724 Hwy. 280 E., Birmingham, AL 35242 US	

GROWTH PLANS/SPECIAL FEATURES:

EBSCO Industries, Inc. competes in a wide variety of markets including furniture and gun manufacturing, commercial insurance, publishing, fishing lures, online bookstores, and nursing and allied health databases. However, publishing is EBSCO's main focus. The firm operates through six divisions: information services, manufacturing, general services, publishing services, outdoor products, real estate and corporate services. The information services segment provides books, databases, subscriptions and e-resource management to libraries and other organizations through EBSCO Information Services, EBSCO Subscription Services and EBSCO Publishing. The Publishing Services division provides publishing and related services as well as specialty marketing services. It offers magazine publishing services though Grand View Media Group and magazine subscription services through EBSCO Magazine Express, EBSCO Reception Room Subscription Services and Vulcan Service. Publications tend to focus on outdoors and hunting topics. Among other offerings, the General Services division provides insurance, military products and services, textbook distribution and promotional merchandise. The Real Estate division has interests in two planned communities, Mt. Laurel and Alys Beach. The firm's Manufacturing Division includes companies that develop a variety of products including wild game decoys, cameras and accessories, steel joists and specialty furniture. The Outdoor Products division manufactures a variety of sporting goods including rifle barrels, fishing lures and treestands. Commonwealth Productions, a television production company falls under Outdoor Products division. The Corporate Services division is responsible for all corporate functions within EBSCO Industries as a whole.

EBSCO provides its employees with comprehensive benefits including profit sharing; medical, dental, vision and life insurance; credit union membership; tuition reimbursement; on-the-job training; employee discounts on EBSCO products; and college scholarships.

FINANCIALS: Sales and profits are in thousands of dollars—add 000 to get the full amount. 2006 Note: Financial information for 2006 was not available for all companies at press time.

2006 Sales: $	2006 Profits: $	U.S. Stock Ticker: Private
2005 Sales: $	2005 Profits: $	Int'l Ticker: Int'l Exchange:
2004 Sales: $1,800,000	2004 Profits: $	Employees: 4,900
2003 Sales: $1,400,000	2003 Profits: $	Fiscal Year Ends: 6/30
2002 Sales: $1,400,000	2002 Profits: $	Parent Company:

SALARIES/BENEFITS:

Pension Plan:	ESOP Stock Plan:	Profit Sharing: Y	Top Exec. Salary: $	Bonus: $
Savings Plan:	Stock Purch. Plan:		Second Exec. Salary: $	Bonus: $

OTHER THOUGHTS:

Apparent Women Officers or Directors: 2
Hot Spot for Advancement for Women/Minorities:

LOCATIONS: ("Y" = Yes)

West:	Southwest:	Midwest:	Southeast:	Northeast:	International:
			Y		

Note: Financial information, benefits and other data can change quickly and may vary from those stated here.

ECHOSTAR COMMUNICATIONS CORP www.dishnetwork.com

Industry Group Code: 513220 Ranks within this company's industry group: Sales: 5 Profits: 2

Print Media/Publishing:	Movies:	Equipment/Supplies:		Broadcast/Cable:	Music/Audio:	Sports/Games:
Newspapers:	Movie Theaters:	Equipment/Supplies:	Y	Broadcast TV:	Music Production:	Games/Sports:
Magazines:	Movie Production:	Gambling Equipment:		Cable TV:	Retail Music:	Retail Games Stores:
Books:	TV/Video Production:	Special Services:		Satellite Broadcast:	Retail Audio Equip.:	Stadiums/Teams:
Book Stores:	Video Rental:	Advertising Services:		Radio:	Music Print./Dist.:	Gambling/Casinos:
Distribution/Printing:	Video Distribution:	Info. Sys. Software:		Online Information:	Multimedia:	Rides/Theme Parks:

TYPES OF BUSINESS:
Satellite Broadcasting
Satellite Receivers

BRANDS/DIVISIONS/AFFILIATES:
DISH Network Services Corp.
EchoStar Technologies Corp.
Oxygen
Abu Dhabi
ABN-America

CONTACTS: *Note: Officers with more than one job title may be intentionally listed here more than once.*
Charles W. Ergen, CEO
Carl Vogel, Pres.
Bernie Han, CFO
James DeFranco, Exec. VP-Sales
Stephen Wood, VP-Human Resources
David K. Moskowitz, General Counsel/Exec. VP/Corp. Sec.
Nolan Daines, VP-Strategic Initiatives
Charles W. Ergen, Chmn.
Steven B. Schaver, Pres., Int'l
James DeFranco, Exec. VP-Dist.

Phone: 303-723-1000	Fax: 303-723-1399
Toll-Free: 800-333-3474	
Address: 9601 S. Meridian Blvd., Englewood, CO 80112 US	

GROWTH PLANS/SPECIAL FEATURES:
EchoStar Communications Corporation and its subsidiaries deliver satellite television products and services to over 12 million subscribers. The company operates out of two units: DISH Network Services Corp. and EchoStar Technologies Corp. DISH Network offers direct broadcast satellite (DBS) subscription television service throughout the U.S. DBS employs frequency allocation and wide spacing between satellites, which permits higher-powered transmissions than other satellite services and allows for reception with a small dish. DISH Network's nine owned and three leased satellites enable it to provide over 2,000 channels of video and audio services to subscribers throughout the U.S. and worldwide, including extensive Spanish-language programming and over 100 channels in foreign languages including Arabic, Chinese, Greek, Hindi and Russian. EchoStar Technologies, the firm's engineering division, focuses on the design of satellite receivers, which are necessary for consumers to receive DISH Network programming, and the sale of set-top boxes to international satellite operators in the consumer market. Satellite services provide video, audio and data services to business television customers and other satellite users. The company intends to enhance consumer awareness by continuing to form alliances with nationally recognized distributors of other consumer electronics products. For the past four years, Echostar has partnered with SBC Communications, Inc. to package its satellite TV services together with the partner's high-speed Internet and telephone offerings. In January 2005, the company purchased a 13-transponder satellite, ground facilities in South Dakota and related assets from Rainbow DBS Co. EchoStar currently has contracts with Lockheed Martin and Space Systems/Loral to construct four new satellites and plans to lease two others, which are scheduled for deployment by 2008. The company is continually adding new channels to its portfolio, some of the most recent being Oxygen, a channel devoted to women's interests; Abu Dhabi, an Arabic-language channel; and ABN-America, featuring shows produced in Africa.

FINANCIALS: Sales and profits are in thousands of dollars—add 000 to get the full amount. 2006 Note: Financial information for 2006 was not available for all companies at press time.

2006 Sales: $	2006 Profits: $	**U.S. Stock Ticker: DISH**
2005 Sales: $8,425,501	2005 Profits: $1,514,540	**Int'l Ticker:** Int'l Exchange:
2004 Sales: $7,151,216	2004 Profits: $214,769	Employees: 21,000
2003 Sales: $5,739,296	2003 Profits: $707,548	Fiscal Year Ends: 12/31
2002 Sales: $4,820,800	2002 Profits: $-881,700	Parent Company:

SALARIES/BENEFITS:

Pension Plan:	ESOP Stock Plan:	Profit Sharing:	Top Exec. Salary: $411,538	Bonus: $
Savings Plan: Y	Stock Purch. Plan: Y		Second Exec. Salary: $294,230	Bonus: $

OTHER THOUGHTS:
Apparent Women Officers or Directors: 1
Hot Spot for Advancement for Women/Minorities:

LOCATIONS: ("Y" = Yes)

West:	Southwest:	Midwest:	Southeast:	Northeast:	International:
Y	Y	Y	Y	Y	Y

Note: Financial information, benefits and other data can change quickly and may vary from those stated here.

EDUCATIONAL DEVELOPMENT CORP   www.edcpub.com

Industry Group Code: 511130 Ranks within this company's industry group: Sales: 9   Profits: 6

Print Media/Publishing:		Movies:		Equipment/Supplies:		Broadcast/Cable:		Music/Audio:		Sports/Games:	
Newspapers:		Movie Theaters:		Equipment/Supplies:		Broadcast TV:		Music Production:		Games/Sports:	
Magazines:		Movie Production:		Gambling Equipment:		Cable TV:		Retail Music:		Retail Games Stores:	
Books:	Y	TV/Video Production:		Special Services:		Satellite Broadcast:		Retail Audio Equip.:		Stadiums/Teams:	
Book Stores:		Video Rental:		Advertising Services:		Radio:		Music Print./Dist.:		Gambling/Casinos:	
Distribution/Printing:		Video Distribution:		Info. Sys. Software:		Online Information:		Multimedia:		Rides/Theme Parks:	

TYPES OF BUSINESS:

Children's Book Publishing
Book Distribution

BRANDS/DIVISIONS/AFFILIATES:

Usborne Publishing Limited
Usborne Kid Kits

CONTACTS: *Note: Officers with more than one job title may be intentionally listed here more than once.*

Randall W. White, CEO
Randall W. White, Pres.
W. Curtis Fossett, Principal Financial & Acct. Officer
Craig M. White, VP-Info. Systems
Randall W. White, Treas.
Ronald T. McDaniel, VP-Publishing Div.
W. Curtis Fossett, Corp. Sec./Controller
Randall W. White, Chmn.

Phone: 918-622-4522	**Fax:** 918-665-7919
Toll-Free: 800-475-4522	
Address: 10302 E. 55th Pl., Tulsa, OK 74146-6515 US	

GROWTH PLANS/SPECIAL FEATURES:

Educational Development Corp. (EDC) is the sole U.S. trade publisher and distributor of a line of children's books produced in the U.K. by Usborne Publishing Limited. The company operates two divisions, the home business division and the publishing division. The home business division distributes books through independent consultants who hold book showings in individual homes, as well as through book fairs, direct sales and Internet sales. The division also distributes these titles to schools and public libraries. The division has approximately 6,000 consultants in all 50 states. The publishing division markets books to approximately 12,000 bookstores, toy stores, specialty stores and other retail outlets including museums and schools. EDC currently carries over 2,000 different book titles. EDC also distributes a product called Usborne Kid Kits. These Kid Kits take an Usborne book and combine it with specially selected items and/or toys that complement the information contained in the book. The kits are packaged in a reusable vinyl bag, with some kits also available in a box package. Currently, 60 different Kid Kits are available. The company operates out of its 105,000-square-foot office and warehouse facilities in Tulsa, Oklahoma.

FINANCIALS: Sales and profits are in thousands of dollars—add 000 to get the full amount. 2006 Note: Financial information for 2006 was not available for all companies at press time.

2006 Sales: $31,789	2006 Profits: $2,398	**U.S. Stock Ticker:** EDUC
2005 Sales: $31,651	2005 Profits: $2,406	**Int'l Ticker:** Int'l Exchange:
2004 Sales: $30,362	2004 Profits: $2,373	Employees: 76
2003 Sales: $24,880	2003 Profits: $2,038	Fiscal Year Ends: 2/28
2002 Sales: $20,554	2002 Profits: $1,531	Parent Company:

SALARIES/BENEFITS:

Pension Plan:	ESOP Stock Plan:	Profit Sharing:	Top Exec. Salary: $150,000	Bonus: $22,000
Savings Plan: Y	Stock Purch. Plan:		Second Exec. Salary: $	Bonus: $

OTHER THOUGHTS:

Apparent Women Officers or Directors:
Hot Spot for Advancement for Women/Minorities:

LOCATIONS: ("Y" = Yes)

West:	Southwest:	Midwest:	Southeast:	Northeast:	International:
	Y				

ELECTRONIC ARTS INC

www.ea.com

Industry Group Code: 511208 Ranks within this company's industry group: Sales: 2 Profits: 1

Print Media/Publishing:	Movies:	Equipment/Supplies:	Broadcast/Cable:	Music/Audio:	Sports/Games:	
Newspapers:	Movie Theaters:	Equipment/Supplies:	Broadcast TV:	Music Production:	Games/Sports:	Y
Magazines:	Movie Production:	Gambling Equipment:	Cable TV:	Retail Music:	Retail Games Stores:	
Books:	TV/Video Production:	Special Services:	Satellite Broadcast:	Retail Audio Equip.:	Stadiums/Teams:	
Book Stores:	Video Rental:	Advertising Services:	Radio:	Music Print./Dist.:	Gambling/Casinos:	
Distribution/Printing:	Video Distribution:	Info. Sys. Software:	Online Information:	Multimedia:	Rides/Theme Parks:	

TYPES OF BUSINESS:

Computer Software-Video Games
Online Interactive Games
E-Commerce Sales
Mobile Games

BRANDS/DIVISIONS/AFFILIATES:

ea.com
Need for Speed
Sims (The)
Highstakes Pool
All-Star Football
EA SPORTS
Pogo
EA GAMES

CONTACTS: *Note: Officers with more than one job title may be intentionally listed here more than once.*

Lawrence Probst, CEO
Warren Jenson, CFO/Exec. VP
Gabrielle Toledano, Exec. VP-Human Resources
Warren Jenson, Chief Admin. Officer
Steve Bene, Acting General Counsel/VP
Joel Linzner, Sr. VP-Bus.
David Gardner, COO, Worldwide Studios
V. Paul Lee, Pres., Worldwide Studios
Nancy Smith, Exec. VP-The Sims
William Gordon, Chief Creative Officer/Exec. VP
Lawrence Probst, Chmn.

Phone: 650-628-1500	Fax: 650-628-1415
Toll-Free:	
Address: 209 Redwood Shores Pkwy., Redwood City, CA 94065 US	

GROWTH PLANS/SPECIAL FEATURES:

Electronic Arts (EA) creates, markets and distributes entertainment software. The company currently develops software for 10 different hardware platforms: Sony PlayStation, PlayStation 2, PlayStation 3 PSP; Nintendo Wii, DS, Game Boy and GameCube; Microsoft Xbox and Xbox 360; Nokia N-Gage; PCs; and the Internet. Approximately 43% of 2005 company revenue was derived from sales of EA Studio games for PlayStation 2. The products produced by the EA Studios fall under the EA GAMES, EA SPORTS and EA SPORTS BIG categories. EA GAMES includes Highstakes Pool, Command and Conquer and Need for Speed; recent EA SPORTS tittles are Pebble Beach Golf, Top Down Baseball and All-Star Football; and EA SPORTS BIG includes SSX Snowdreams. EA also distributes a number of co-published titles and titles developed by affiliated labels. The company's designers regularly work with celebrities and organizations in sports, entertainment and other areas to develop gaming products. EA has contracts with FIFA, NASCAR, PGA TOUR, Tiger Woods, Warner Bros. and the NFL, among others. The firm's second business segment, ea.com, is its online and e-commerce division, which develops, publishes and distributes online interactive games, such as Pogo. Operations include subscription revenue collected for play on its web sites, web site advertising, sales of packaged goods for Internet-only games and sales of EA games sold through the firm's web store. The company recently announced plans to bring the Sims 2 franchise to consoles and mobile phones, as well as an expanded lineup of free games on its pogo.com web site. In December 2005, Electronic Arts agreed to acquire Jamdat, a leading mobile phone gaming company, for $680 million.

EA offers its employees on-site fitness facilities and performance bonuses. In addition, the company offers extensive training programs, discounts on game systems, education reimbursement and a company store. Full-time employees receive a paid week off at Christmas.

FINANCIALS: Sales and profits are in thousands of dollars—add 000 to get the full amount. 2006 Note: Financial information for 2006 was not available for all companies at press time.

2006 Sales: $2,951,000	2006 Profits: $236,000	U.S. Stock Ticker: ERTS
2005 Sales: $3,129,000	2005 Profits: $504,000	Int'l Ticker: Int'l Exchange:
2004 Sales: $2,957,141	2004 Profits: $577,292	Employees: 7,200
2003 Sales: $2,482,200	2003 Profits: $317,100	Fiscal Year Ends: 3/31
2002 Sales: $1,724,700	2002 Profits: $101,500	Parent Company:

SALARIES/BENEFITS:

Pension Plan:	ESOP Stock Plan:	Profit Sharing:	Top Exec. Salary: $680,012	Bonus: $
Savings Plan: Y	Stock Purch. Plan: Y		Second Exec. Salary: $674,080	Bonus: $

OTHER THOUGHTS:

Apparent Women Officers or Directors: 2
Hot Spot for Advancement for Women/Minorities:

LOCATIONS: ("Y" = Yes)

West:	Southwest:	Midwest:	Southeast:	Northeast:	International:
Y	Y	Y	Y	Y	Y

EMAP PLC

www.emap.com

Industry Group Code: 511120 Ranks within this company's industry group: Sales: 4   Profits: 4

Print Media/Publishing:		Movies:		Equipment/Supplies:		Broadcast/Cable:		Music/Audio:		Sports/Games:	
Newspapers:		Movie Theaters:		Equipment/Supplies:		Broadcast TV:		Music Production:		Games/Sports:	
Magazines:	Y	Movie Production:		Gambling Equipment:		Cable TV:	Y	Retail Music:		Retail Games Stores:	
Books:		TV/Video Production:		Special Services:	Y	Satellite Broadcast:		Retail Audio Equip.:		Stadiums/Teams:	
Book Stores:		Video Rental:		Advertising Services:	Y	Radio:		Music Print./Dist.:		Gambling/Casinos:	
Distribution/Printing:		Video Distribution:		Info. Sys. Software:		Online Information:		Multimedia:		Rides/Theme Parks:	

TYPES OF BUSINESS:

Magazine Publishing
Music Television Channels
Radio Broadcasting
Exhibitions, Trade Shows & Conventions
Mobile Phone Media Content
Ticket Sales

BRANDS/DIVISIONS/AFFILIATES:

Digital Photo
Golf Weekly
Classic Bike
Top Sante
Arena
Heat
Mother & Baby
FHM

CONTACTS: *Note: Officers with more than one job title may be intentionally listed here more than once.*

Tom Moloney, CEO
Ian Griffiths, Group Dir.-Finance
Nick Folland, General Counsel
Derek Carter, CEO-Comm.
Derek Carter, CEO-Emap Communications
Paul Keenan, CEO-Consumer Media
Alun Cathcart, Chmn.

Phone: 44-1733-213-700   **Fax:** 44-1733-312-115

Toll-Free:

Address: Wentworth House, Wentworth St., Peterborough, PE1 1DS UK

GROWTH PLANS/SPECIAL FEATURES:

Emap plc is a leading media conglomerate in the U.K. with over 150 consumer magazines; 200 business-to-business events, exhibitions and magazines; 19 radio stations; and eight digital music television stations. Emap's consumer magazine segment publishes more than 150 magazines, including publications in the automotive, young women, entertainment, lifestyle and celebrity gossip categories. Titles include Digital Photo, Golf World, Classic Bike, Top Sante, Arena, Heat, Mother & Baby and FHM. FHM, one of the world's top-selling men's magazines, has 30 international editions and over 1 million subscribers in the U.S. The company's communication division publishes business-to-business magazines covering international business, retail business, broadcasting and media, construction, health care and government. This segment also produces dozens of exhibitions and events for each business segment. Emap also owns four radio networks with 19 stations in the U.K. The television segment offers eight 24/7 music channels that provide programmed and on-demand music. Other businesses include offering magazine and radio content to third-generation mobile phone users and ticket sales to concerts and shows.

Emap offers its employees life and medical insurance, health club membership, dental plans, childcare and extensive incentive programs. The company prefers to promote from within.

FINANCIALS: Sales and profits are in thousands of dollars—add 000 to get the full amount. 2006 Note: Financial information for 2006 was not available for all companies at press time.

2006 Sales: $1,485,500	2006 Profits: $219,200	**U.S. Stock Ticker: EMAPF**
2005 Sales: $2,006,500	2005 Profits: $103,300	**Int'l Ticker: EMA** Int'l Exchange: London-LSE
2004 Sales: $1,917,100	2004 Profits: $169,800	Employees: 6,277
2003 Sales: $1,522,000	2003 Profits: $135,400	Fiscal Year Ends: 3/31
2002 Sales: $1,466,900	2002 Profits: $156,800	Parent Company:

SALARIES/BENEFITS:

Pension Plan: Y	ESOP Stock Plan:	Profit Sharing: Y	Top Exec. Salary: $921,518	Bonus: $153,013
Savings Plan:	Stock Purch. Plan:		Second Exec. Salary: $584,548	Bonus: $63,612

OTHER THOUGHTS:

Apparent Women Officers or Directors: 3
Hot Spot for Advancement for Women/Minorities: Y

LOCATIONS: ("Y" = Yes)

West:	Southwest:	Midwest:	Southeast:	Northeast:	International:
Y		Y		Y	Y

EMI GROUP PLC

www.emigroup.com

Industry Group Code: 512230 Ranks within this company's industry group: Sales: 4 Profits: 2

Print Media/Publishing:	Movies:	Equipment/Supplies:	Broadcast/Cable:	Music/Audio:		Sports/Games:
Newspapers:	Movie Theaters:	Equipment/Supplies:	Broadcast TV:	Music Production:	Y	Games/Sports:
Magazines:	Movie Production:	Gambling Equipment:	Cable TV:	Retail Music:		Retail Games Stores:
Books:	TV/Video Production:	Special Services:	Satellite Broadcast:	Retail Audio Equip.:		Stadiums/Teams:
Book Stores:	Video Rental:	Advertising Services:	Radio:	Music Print./Dist.:	Y	Gambling/Casinos:
Distribution/Printing:	Video Distribution:	Info. Sys. Software:	Online Information:	Multimedia:		Rides/Theme Parks:

TYPES OF BUSINESS:

Music Production
Music Publishing
Recording Studios
Licensing
Digital Music Licensing

BRANDS/DIVISIONS/AFFILIATES:

EMI Music
EMI Music Publishing
Angel
Blue Note
Capitol
EMI Classics
Virgin
Abbey Road Studios

CONTACTS: Note: Officers with more than one job title may be intentionally listed here more than once.

Eric Nicoli, CEO/Chmn.-EMI Music
Stuart Ells, COO-EMI Music
Martin Stewart, CFO
Roger Faxon, CEO-EMI Music Publishing
Tony Wadsworth, Chmn./CEO-EMI Music UK & Ireland
Jean-Francois Cecillon, Chmn./CEO-EMI Music Continental Europe
Normal Cheng, Chmn./CEO-EMI Music Asia
Eric Nicoli, Chmn.
David Munns, CEO-EMI Music North America

Phone: 44-20-7795-7000	Fax: 44-20-7795-7296
Toll-Free:	
Address: 27 Wrights Ln., London, W8 5SW UK	

GROWTH PLANS/SPECIAL FEATURES:

EMI Group plc is a leading global music company, with operations in 50 countries and licensees in another 20. The firm operates through two divisions: EMI Music and EMI Music Publishing (EMP). EMI Music represents more than 1,300 recording artists and owns a catalog of over 3 million recorded tracks. The firm's artists include classic stars such as The Beatles, The Beach Boys, The Rolling Stones and Pink Floyd; contemporary performers such as Norah Jones, The Beastie Boys and Janet Jackson; a wide collection of emerging stars in countries around the world; and classical and jazz performers including Maria Callas, Mtislav Rostropovich, Simon Rattle, Itzhak Perlman, Angela Gheorghiu and Cassandra Wilson. The subsidiary's record labels include Angel, Astralworks, Blue Note, Capitol, Capitol Nashville, EMI, EMI Classics, EMI CMG, EMI Televisa Music, Mute, Parlophone and Virgin. EMI Music also operates the renowned Abbey Road Studios in London and Capitol Studios in Los Angeles. EMP owns a catalog constaining over 1 million songs. Best-selling songs include Bohemian Rhapsody, Over The Rainbow, Singin' In The Rain, the James Bond theme, Wild Thing and Santa Claus Is Coming To Town. EMP's signed writer/performers include Eminem, Enya, Jewel and Sting. EMI has been an innovator in digital music: it released the first ever digital album and was the first label to offer a video single online. The firm has license agreements with over 400 partners for digital distribution of its content. Fiscal 2006 saw the company's revenues from digital music grow by 135%, and it estimates that digital could account for 25% of music revenues by 2010. In January 2006, EMP signed and agreement that takes steps toward a pan-European system for licensing online music rights. In August 2006, EMP licensed its catalog to Qtrax, the world's first legal, ad-supported peer-to-peer music download service.

FINANCIALS: Sales and profits are in thousands of dollars—add 000 to get the full amount. 2006 Note: Financial information for 2006 was not available for all companies at press time.

2006 Sales: $4,092,680	2006 Profits: $232,390	**U.S. Stock Ticker: EMIPY**
2005 Sales: $3,937,820	2005 Profits: $194,400	**Int'l Ticker: EMI** Int'l Exchange: London-LSE
2004 Sales: $	2004 Profits: $	Employees: 6,312
2003 Sales: $	2003 Profits: $	Fiscal Year Ends: 3/31
2002 Sales: $	2002 Profits: $	Parent Company:

SALARIES/BENEFITS:

Pension Plan:	ESOP Stock Plan:	Profit Sharing:	Top Exec. Salary: $	Bonus: $
Savings Plan:	Stock Purch. Plan:		Second Exec. Salary: $	Bonus: $

OTHER THOUGHTS:

Apparent Women Officers or Directors: 1
Hot Spot for Advancement for Women/Minorities:

LOCATIONS: ("Y" = Yes)

West:	Southwest:	Midwest:	Southeast:	Northeast:	International:
Y				Y	Y

EMMIS COMMUNICATIONS CORP   www.emmis.com

Industry Group Code: 513111 Ranks within this company's industry group: Sales: 3 Profits: 13

Print Media/Publishing:		Movies:		Equipment/Supplies:		Broadcast/Cable:		Music/Audio:		Sports/Games:	
Newspapers:		Movie Theaters:		Equipment/Supplies:		Broadcast TV:	Y	Music Production:		Games/Sports:	
Magazines:	Y	Movie Production:		Gambling Equipment:		Cable TV:		Retail Music:		Retail Games Stores:	
Books:	Y	TV/Video Production:		Special Services:		Satellite Broadcast:		Retail Audio Equip.:		Stadiums/Teams:	
Book Stores:		Video Rental:		Advertising Services:	Y	Radio:		Music Print./Dist.:		Gambling/Casinos:	
Distribution/Printing:		Video Distribution:		Info. Sys. Software:		Online Information:		Multimedia:		Rides/Theme Parks:	

TYPES OF BUSINESS:

Radio Broadcasting
Television Broadcasting
Magazine Publishing
Book Publishing

BRANDS/DIVISIONS/AFFILIATES:

Emmis Broadcasting Corp.
HOT 97 FM
Power 106 FM
Texas Monthly Magazine
Atlanta Magazine
Cincinnati Magazine
Indianapolis Monthly Magazine
Country Sampler

CONTACTS: *Note: Officers with more than one job title may be intentionally listed here more than once.*

Jeffrey H. Smulyan, CEO
Jeffrey H. Smulyan, Pres.
Patrick Walsh, CFO
Michael Levitan, Exec. VP-Human Resources
Gary Kaseff, General Counsel/Exec. VP
Richard F. Cummings, Pres., Radio
Gary Thoe, Pres., Publishing
Randy Bongarten, Pres., Television
Richard Hunt, Publisher-Emmis Books
Jeffrey H. Smulyan, Chmn.
Paul W. Fiddick, Pres., Int'l

Phone: 317-266-0100	**Fax:** 317-631-3750
Toll-Free:	
Address: One Emmis Plaza, 40 Monument Cir., Ste. 700, Indianapolis, IN 46204 US	

GROWTH PLANS/SPECIAL FEATURES:

Emmis Communications Corporation is a diversified media company with radio broadcasting, regional book and magazine publishing and television broadcasting operations. The company owns or operates 21 FM radio stations and two AM radio stations, with interests in the U.S.'s three largest radio markets of New York City, Los Angeles and Chicago. Among its FM stations are the highly influential hip-hop stations Power 106 in Los Angeles and HOT 97 in New York City. The firm has additional stations in Austin, Texas; St. Louis, Missouri; Terra Haute and Indianapolis, Indiana; and overseas interests in radio stations in Hungary, Belgium, Bulgaria and Slovakia. Emmis formerly owned 16 television stations across the country, but has sold all but two, in Honolulu, Hawaii and New Orleans, Louisiana. The company also publishes six city and local interest magazines including Atlanta Magazine, Country Sampler, Indianapolis Monthly, Los Angeles Magazine, Cincinnati Magazine and Texas Monthly. Emmis also publishes book titles targeted to Midwestern audiences. The firm's business strategy is to acquire underdeveloped or under-performing media properties in growing markets and modify their operations to increase their cash flow. In recent news, the company sold radio stations in Phoenix and Orlando and opened a new rhythmic contemporary station, Movin 93.9, in Los Angeles.

Emmis offers stock options to employees at every level of the company. The company provides a Diversity Fellowship Program designed to attract college students. The students are then matched with a mentor to help them work towards their career goals, and at the end of 18 months to two years, the student may be placed in a permanent position with the company. Emmis was named one of Fortune's 100 Best Companies to Work For in 2005.

FINANCIALS: Sales and profits are in thousands of dollars—add 000 to get the full amount. 2006 Note: Financial information for 2006 was not available for all companies at press time.

2006 Sales: $	2006 Profits: $	**U.S. Stock Ticker: EMMS**
2005 Sales: $618,460	2005 Profits: $-304,368	**Int'l Ticker:** Int'l Exchange:
2004 Sales: $679,927	2004 Profits: $2,256	Employees: 3,002
2003 Sales: $562,400	2003 Profits: $-164,500	Fiscal Year Ends: 12/31
2002 Sales: $533,800	2002 Profits: $-61,900	Parent Company:

SALARIES/BENEFITS:

Pension Plan:	ESOP Stock Plan:	Profit Sharing: Y	Top Exec. Salary: $664,000	Bonus: $1,084,561
Savings Plan: Y	Stock Purch. Plan: Y		Second Exec. Salary: $391,500	Bonus: $277,014

OTHER THOUGHTS:

Apparent Women Officers or Directors: 1
Hot Spot for Advancement for Women/Minorities:

LOCATIONS: ("Y" = Yes)

West:	Southwest:	Midwest:	Southeast:	Northeast:	International:
Y	Y	Y	Y	Y	Y

Note: Financial information, benefits and other data can change quickly and may vary from those stated here.

ENDEAVOR AGENCY (THE)

Industry Group Code: 711410 Ranks within this company's industry group: Sales: Profits:

Print Media/Publishing:	Movies:	Equipment/Supplies:		Broadcast/Cable:	Music/Audio:	Sports/Games:
Newspapers:	Movie Theaters:	Equipment/Supplies:		Broadcast TV:	Music Production:	Games/Sports:
Magazines:	Movie Production:	Gambling Equipment:		Cable TV:	Retail Music:	Retail Games Stores:
Books:	TV/Video Production:	Special Services:	Y	Satellite Broadcast:	Retail Audio Equip.:	Stadiums/Teams:
Book Stores:	Video Rental:	Advertising Services:		Radio:	Music Print./Dist.:	Gambling/Casinos:
Distribution/Printing:	Video Distribution:	Info. Sys. Software:		Online Information:	Multimedia:	Rides/Theme Parks:

TYPES OF BUSINESS:
Talent Agency

BRANDS/DIVISIONS/AFFILIATES:

GROWTH PLANS/SPECIAL FEATURES:

The Endeavor Agency was formed when a group of agents left International Creative Management, Inc. in 1995. It is a talent and literary agency based in Beverly Hills, California. It represents writers, directors and actors. In addition, its marketing division, partially owned by Interpublic, readies third party content for distribution. The firm does not maintain a web site. Endeavor maintains a flat management structure and an incentive-based compensation plan, which have helped it lure top talent recruiters from other agencies. In early 2007, Robert Newman, formerly of International Creative Management, left to join Endeavor, bringing with him directors Baz Luhrmann (Moulin Rouge) and Guillerom del Toro (Pan's Labyrinth).

CONTACTS:
Note: Officers with more than one job title may be intentionally listed here more than once.
Ari Emanuel, Founding Partner
Sean Perry, Partner
Matt Solo, Partner
Robert Newman, Partner

Phone: 310-248-2000	**Fax:** 310-248-2020
Toll-Free:	
Address: 9601 Wilshire Blvd. Fl. 10, Beverly Hills, CA 90212 US	

FINANCIALS:
Sales and profits are in thousands of dollars—add 000 to get the full amount. 2006 Note: Financial information for 2006 was not available for all companies at press time.

2006 Sales: $	2006 Profits: $	**U.S. Stock Ticker: Private**
2005 Sales: $	2005 Profits: $	**Int'l Ticker:** Int'l Exchange:
2004 Sales: $	2004 Profits: $	Employees:
2003 Sales: $	2003 Profits: $	Fiscal Year Ends:
2002 Sales: $	2002 Profits: $	Parent Company:

SALARIES/BENEFITS:

Pension Plan:	ESOP Stock Plan:	Profit Sharing:	Top Exec. Salary: $	Bonus: $
Savings Plan:	Stock Purch. Plan:		Second Exec. Salary: $	Bonus: $

OTHER THOUGHTS:
Apparent Women Officers or Directors:
Hot Spot for Advancement for Women/Minorities:

LOCATIONS: ("Y" = Yes)

West:	Southwest:	Midwest:	Southeast:	Northeast:	International:
Y				Y	

Note: Financial information, benefits and other data can change quickly and may vary from those stated here.

ENTERCOM COMMUNICATIONS CORP   www.entercom.com

Industry Group Code: 513111 Ranks within this company's industry group: Sales: 6 Profits: 2

Print Media/Publishing:	Movies:	Equipment/Supplies:		Broadcast/Cable:	Music/Audio:	Sports/Games:
Newspapers:	Movie Theaters:	Equipment/Supplies:		Broadcast TV:	Music Production:	Games/Sports:
Magazines:	Movie Production:	Gambling Equipment:		Cable TV:	Retail Music:	Retail Games Stores:
Books:	TV/Video Production:	Special Services:		Satellite Broadcast:	Retail Audio Equip.:	Stadiums/Teams:
Book Stores:	Video Rental:	Advertising Services:	Y	Radio:	Music Print./Dist.:	Gambling/Casinos:
Distribution/Printing:	Video Distribution:	Info. Sys. Software:		Online Information:	Multimedia:	Rides/Theme Parks:

TYPES OF BUSINESS:
Radio Broadcasting
Radio Advertising
Digital Radio

BRANDS/DIVISIONS/AFFILIATES:
iBiquity Digital Corporation

CONTACTS: *Note: Officers with more than one job title may be intentionally listed here more than once.*
David J. Field, CEO
David J. Field, Pres.
Stephen F. Fisher, CFO/Exec. VP
Noreen McCormack, VP-Human Resources
John Graefe, Dir.-IT
Martin D. Hadfield, VP-Eng.
John C. Donlevie, General Counsel/Exec. VP
Marijane Milton, VP-Training & Dev.
Sandy Smallens, Sr. VP-Digital
Eugene D. Levin, Treas./Controller
Melissa Forrest, VP/Market Mgr.-Austin
Steve Oshin, VP/Gen.Mgr.-Seattle
Ken Beck, VP-News/Talk Programming
Pat Paxton, Sr. VP-Programming

Phone: 610-660-5610	Fax: 610-660-5620
Toll-Free:	
Address: 401 City Ave., Ste. 809, Bala Cynwyd, PA 19004 US	

GROWTH PLANS/SPECIAL FEATURES:
Entercom Communications Corp. is one of the nation's largest radio broadcasting companies. It owns and runs multi-station operations in 23 markets: Boston, Seattle, Denver, Sacramento, Cincinnati, Portland, Kansas City, Indianapolis, Milwaukee, Austin, Norfolk, Buffalo, New Orleans, Providence, Memphis, Greensboro, Rochester, Greenville/Spartanburg, Madison, Wichita, Wilkes-Barre/Scranton, Springfield and Gainesville/Ocala. The majority of each station's local and regional advertising sales are generated through direct solicitations of local advertising agencies and businesses. Entercom retains a national representative firm to sell national spot commercial airtime on its stations to advertisers outside of its local markets. This advertising accounts for almost 20% of each radio station's revenues on average. Entercom builds station clusters in large growth markets and acquires underdeveloped properties that offer potential for significant improvements in revenues, with a principal focus on the top 50 markets. Entercom's stations feature oldies, rock, news and talk, country, smooth jazz and sports. In addition, the company is the exclusive radio broadcaster of the Boston Celtics, Seattle Mariners, Buffalo Sabres, Seattle Seahawks, Kansas City Chiefs and a number of major college sports teams. The firm also broadcasts HD Radio (digital radio), owns a stake in iBiquity Digital Corporation, and is a founding member of the HD Digital Radio Alliance Association. In 2006, Entercom exchanged radio stations in Cincinnati with Cumulus Media Partners. The firm exchanged its Oldies 103.5 WGGR-FM for Cumulus' Country WYGY-FM. In addition, the firm plans to acquire, pending FCC approval, WBEC-105.5 FM (Springfield) from Great Northern Radio, LLC. for $5.75 million. Also in 2006, the firm and the Boston Red Sox signed a ten-year agreement to return the club's games to WRKO Radio 680 AM. In addition, Entercom announced a sister station to WWI 870 in New Orleans to further cater to those living in the city with time-shifted talk radio programming.

FINANCIALS: Sales and profits are in thousands of dollars—add 000 to get the full amount. 2006 Note: Financial information for 2006 was not available for all companies at press time.

2006 Sales: $	2006 Profits: $	U.S. Stock Ticker: ETM
2005 Sales: $432,520	2005 Profits: $78,361	Int'l Ticker: Int'l Exchange:
2004 Sales: $423,455	2004 Profits: $75,634	Employees: 2,380
2003 Sales: $401,056	2003 Profits: $71,780	Fiscal Year Ends: 12/31
2002 Sales: $391,300	2002 Profits: $-83,100	Parent Company:

SALARIES/BENEFITS:
Pension Plan: Y	ESOP Stock Plan:	Profit Sharing:	Top Exec. Salary: $693,201	Bonus: $575,000
Savings Plan: Y	Stock Purch. Plan: Y		Second Exec. Salary: $533,232	Bonus: $

OTHER THOUGHTS:
Apparent Women Officers or Directors: 6
Hot Spot for Advancement for Women/Minorities: Y

LOCATIONS: ("Y" = Yes)
West:	Southwest:	Midwest:	Southeast:	Northeast:	International:
Y	Y	Y	Y	Y	

Note: Financial information, benefits and other data can change quickly and may vary from those stated here.

ENTERTAINMENT PROPERTIES TRUST   www.eprkc.com

Industry Group Code: 525930 Ranks within this company's industry group: Sales: 1 Profits: 1

Print Media/Publishing:	Movies:		Equipment/Supplies:	Broadcast/Cable:	Music/Audio:	Sports/Games:
Newspapers:	Movie Theaters:	Y	Equipment/Supplies:	Broadcast TV:	Music Production:	Games/Sports:
Magazines:	Movie Production:		Gambling Equipment:	Cable TV:	Retail Music:	Retail Games Stores:
Books:	TV/Video Production:		Special Services:	Satellite Broadcast:	Retail Audio Equip.:	Stadiums/Teams:
Book Stores:	Video Rental:		Advertising Services:	Radio:	Music Print./Dist.:	Gambling/Casinos:
Distribution/Printing:	Video Distribution:		Info. Sys. Software:	Online Information:	Multimedia:	Rides/Theme Parks:

TYPES OF BUSINESS:

REIT-Entertainment Properties
Megaplex Movie Theaters
Entertainment Retail Centers
Ski Resort

BRANDS/DIVISIONS/AFFILIATES:

Mad River Ski Resort

CONTACTS: *Note: Officers with more than one job title may be intentionally listed here more than once.*

David M. Brain, CEO
David M. Brain, Pres.
Fred L. Kennon, CFO/VP
Gregory K. Silvers, General Counsel/VP/Corp. Sec.
Gregory K. Silvers, Chief Dev. Officer
Jonathan B. Weis, Dir.-Corp. Comm.
Fred L. Kennon, Treas./Controller
Robert J. Druten, Chmn.

Phone: 816-472-1700	Fax: 816-472-5794
Toll-Free: 888-377-7348	
Address: 30 Pershing Rd., Ste. 201, Kansas City, MO 64108 US	

GROWTH PLANS/SPECIAL FEATURES:

Entertainment Properties Trust (EPT) is a self-administered real estate investment trust and one of the largest owners of entertainment-related real estate in North America. The company owns mostly megaplex movie theaters, which typically have at least 14 screens with stadium-style seating and are equipped with enhanced audio and visual amenities. EPT's portfolio is composed of 7.1 million square feet of properties, including 54 movie megaplexes (of which three are joint ventures) in 22 U.S. states and Ontario, Canada with a total of approximately 1,660 screens and 140,660 seats. The firm also has ten entertainment retail centers (including one joint venture property) located in Westminster, Colorado; New Rochelle, New York; and Ontario, Canada, as well as other specialty properties and land parcels leased to restaurant and retail operators adjacent to several of its theater properties. EPT leases its theater properties to leading theater operations, including AMC Theatres, Loews Cineplex, Wallace Theaters, Rave Motion Pictures, Consolidated Theatres, Muvico Theatres, AmStar Entertainment, Crown Theatres, Regal Entertainment, Southern Theaters and Kerasotes ShowPlace Theatres. Approximately 61% of the company's megaplex properties are leased to AMC. In June 2005, EPT announced that it would supply $48.9 million in financing to construct the Metropolis retail entertainment development in Toronto, Ontario. This was followed in December 2005 by the acquisition of four megaplex properties leased to Regal Cinemas in California and the acquisition of the Mad River Ski Resort in Ohio in an agreement valued at $52 million.

FINANCIALS: Sales and profits are in thousands of dollars—add 000 to get the full amount. 2006 Note: Financial information for 2006 was not available for all companies at press time.

2006 Sales: $	2006 Profits: $	U.S. Stock Ticker: EPR
2005 Sales: $148,744	2005 Profits: $57,707	Int'l Ticker: Int'l Exchange:
2004 Sales: $124,980	2004 Profits: $48,250	Employees: 13
2003 Sales: $91,160	2003 Profits: $32,131	Fiscal Year Ends: 12/31
2002 Sales: $71,610	2002 Profits: $31,159	Parent Company:

SALARIES/BENEFITS:

Pension Plan:	ESOP Stock Plan:	Profit Sharing:	Top Exec. Salary: $385,688	Bonus: $462,825
Savings Plan:	Stock Purch. Plan:		Second Exec. Salary: $243,280	Bonus: $218,952

OTHER THOUGHTS:

Apparent Women Officers or Directors:
Hot Spot for Advancement for Women/Minorities:

LOCATIONS: ("Y" = Yes)

West:	Southwest:	Midwest:	Southeast:	Northeast:	International:
Y	Y	Y	Y	Y	Y

ENTRAVISION COMMUNICATIONS CORPORATION
www.entravision.com

Industry Group Code: 513120 Ranks within this company's industry group: Sales: 15   Profits: 14

Print Media/Publishing:	Movies:	Equipment/Supplies:	Broadcast/Cable:		Music/Audio:	Sports/Games:
Newspapers:	Movie Theaters:	Equipment/Supplies:	Broadcast TV:	Y	Music Production:	Games/Sports:
Magazines:	Movie Production:	Gambling Equipment:	Cable TV:		Retail Music:	Retail Games Stores:
Books:	TV/Video Production:	Special Services:	Satellite Broadcast:		Retail Audio Equip.:	Stadiums/Teams:
Book Stores:	Video Rental:	Advertising Services: Y	Radio:		Music Print./Dist.:	Gambling/Casinos:
Distribution/Printing:	Video Distribution:	Info. Sys. Software:	Online Information:		Multimedia:	Rides/Theme Parks:

TYPES OF BUSINESS:
Television Broadcasting
Spanish-Language Broadcasting
Radio Broadcasting
Outdoor Advertising

BRANDS/DIVISIONS/AFFILIATES:

CONTACTS: Note: Officers with more than one job title may be intentionally listed here more than once.
Walter F. Ulloa, CEO
Philip C. Wilkinson, COO
Philip C. Wilkinson, Pres.
John F. DeLorenzo, CFO/Exec. VP
Brian Reed, VP-Sales
Susan Knoll, VP-Research
Michael G. Rowles, General Counsel/Sr. VP
John F. DeLorenzo, Treas.
Larry A. Safir, Exec. VP
Jeffery A. Liberman, Pres., Radio Div.
Christopher T. Young, Pres., Outdoor Div.
Walter F. Ulloa, Chmn.

Phone: 310-447-3870	Fax: 310-447-3899

Toll-Free:

Address: 2425 Olympic Blvd., Ste. 6000 W., Santa Monica, CA 90404 US

GROWTH PLANS/SPECIAL FEATURES:

Entravision Communications Corporation, along with its subsidiaries, is a diversified Spanish-language media company with a unique portfolio of television, radio and outdoor advertising assets, reaching approximately 70% of all Hispanics in the U.S. The company owns and/or operates 48 primary television stations, the majority of which are located in the southwestern U.S., including the U.S./Mexican border markets. The television stations consist primarily of affiliates of Univision, serving 20 of the top 50 U.S. Hispanic markets. The company's television assets are primarily made up of the largest affiliate groups for Univision and TeleFutura, the two television networks of Univision Communications, Inc. The firm also owns and operates one of the largest groups of Spanish-language radio stations in the country, with 52 stations in 50 U.S. markets, including Spanish-language stations in Los Angeles, San Francisco, Phoenix and Dallas-Ft. Worth. Entravision's outdoor advertising operations consist of approximately 11,100 advertising billboards located primarily in high-density Hispanic communities in Los Angeles and New York. The company generates its revenue from sales of national and local advertising time on television and radio stations as well as advertising on the firm's billboards. In recent news, the company sold its Dallas radio stations to Liberman Broadcasting of Dallas, Inc. for $92.5 million.

FINANCIALS: Sales and profits are in thousands of dollars—add 000 to get the full amount. 2006 Note: Financial information for 2006 was not available for all companies at press time.

2006 Sales: $	2006 Profits: $	U.S. Stock Ticker: EVC
2005 Sales: $280,964	2005 Profits: $-9,657	Int'l Ticker: Int'l Exchange:
2004 Sales: $259,100	2004 Profits: $6,100	Employees: 1,148
2003 Sales: $237,956	2003 Profits: $2,267	Fiscal Year Ends: 12/31
2002 Sales: $238,469	2002 Profits: $-10,645	Parent Company:

SALARIES/BENEFITS:

Pension Plan:	ESOP Stock Plan:	Profit Sharing:	Top Exec. Salary: $770,833	Bonus: $450,000
Savings Plan: Y	Stock Purch. Plan:		Second Exec. Salary: $770,833	Bonus: $450,000

OTHER THOUGHTS:
Apparent Women Officers or Directors: 1
Hot Spot for Advancement for Women/Minorities:

LOCATIONS: ("Y" = Yes)

West:	Southwest:	Midwest:	Southeast:	Northeast:	International:
Y	Y		Y	Y	

Note: Financial information, benefits and other data can change quickly and may vary from those stated here.

ESPN INC

www.espn.go.com

Industry Group Code: 513210 Ranks within this company's industry group: Sales: 5 Profits:

Print Media/Publishing:		Movies:		Equipment/Supplies:		Broadcast/Cable:		Music/Audio:		Sports/Games:	
Newspapers:		Movie Theaters:		Equipment/Supplies:		Broadcast TV:		Music Production:		Games/Sports:	
Magazines:	Y	Movie Production:		Gambling Equipment:		Cable TV:	Y	Retail Music:		Retail Games Stores:	
Books:	Y	TV/Video Production:	Y	Special Services:		Satellite Broadcast:		Retail Audio Equip.:		Stadiums/Teams:	
Book Stores:		Video Rental:		Advertising Services:		Radio:		Music Print./Dist.:		Gambling/Casinos:	
Distribution/Printing:		Video Distribution:		Info. Sys. Software:		Online Information:		Multimedia:		Rides/Theme Parks:	

TYPES OF BUSINESS:

Sports Television Broadcasting
Sports Radio Broadcasting
Online Sports Information
Magazine & Book Publishing
Sports Websites

BRANDS/DIVISIONS/AFFILIATES:

ESPN
ESPN2
ESPNEWS
ESPN Deportes
ESPN Regional Television
ESPN Interactive
ESPN Radio
Bassmaster Magazine

CONTACTS: *Note: Officers with more than one job title may be intentionally listed here more than once.*

George W. Bodenheimer, Pres.
Christine Driessen, CFO/Exec. VP
Sean H. R. Bratches, Exec. VP-Mktg. & Sales
Mike Fox, Worldwide Advertising
George W. Bodenheimer, Chmn.
Russell Wolff, Mng. Dir.-ESPN Int'l

Phone: 860-766-2000	**Fax:** 860-766-2213
Toll-Free:	
Address: ESPN Plaza, 935 Middle St., Bristol, CT 06010 US	

GROWTH PLANS/SPECIAL FEATURES:

ESPN, Inc. is 80%-owned by Walt Disney through Disney ABC Cable; the other 20% is owned by Hearst. It is a leading cable sports broadcaster with seven domestic television networks: ESPN, ESPN 2, ESPN Classic (archived sports footage), ESPN Deportes (Spanish-language sports network), ESPNU (college sports network), ESPN Today (interactive sports channel) and ESPNEWS. It also operates ESPN HD and ESPN2 HD, which provide high-definition simulcast services. The company's other television subsidiaries include ESPN Regional Television, ESPN PPV, ESPN 360, ESPN On Demand, ESPN Interactive and ESPN International, which encompasses 30 international networks. The firm's radio subsidiaries include ESPN Radio in the U.S. and ESPN Deportes Radio, which is syndicated in 13 international countries. Its affiliated web sites include espn.com, espndeportes.com, espnradio.com, espnsoccernet.com and expn.com. The company's publishing division includes ESPN The Magazine, Bassmaster Magazine, BASS Times, Fishing Tackle & Retailer and ESPN Books, publisher of the SportsCentury almanac. SportsTicker covers real-time sports news and statistics broadcasts. Through ESPN Enterprises, the firm has developed new products and businesses using the ESPN brand and assets, including the ESPN Zones sports-themed restaurant chain, a variety of consumer products (ESPN Videogames, DVDs, CDs, ESPN25, ESPN Golf Schools and ESPN Russell Racing Schools), the ESPN Sports Poll research polling service and the ESPN Club at Disney World Orlando. The firm also improves its brand awareness by hosting and managing various sporting events, including the X Games, ESPN Outdoors & BASS, the ESPY Awards, bowl games and Jimmy V Men's and Women's Basketball Classics. Mobile ESPN was discontinued in late 2006. In Australia in early 2007, ESPN acquired a minority stake in a 19-team arena soccer league along with its broadcast rights. In late 2006, ESPN agreed to acquire American Sports Network from Setanta Sport Holdings Ltd. and Benchmark Capital Europe.

FINANCIALS: Sales and profits are in thousands of dollars—add 000 to get the full amount. 2006 Note: Financial information for 2006 was not available for all companies at press time.

2006 Sales: $	2006 Profits: $	**U.S. Stock Ticker: Subsidiary**
2005 Sales: $4,031,000	2005 Profits: $	**Int'l Ticker:** Int'l Exchange:
2004 Sales: $3,223,000	2004 Profits: $	Employees: 3,400
2003 Sales: $2,869,000	2003 Profits: $	Fiscal Year Ends: 9/30
2002 Sales: $2,120,000	2002 Profits: $	Parent Company: WALT DISNEY COMPANY (THE)

SALARIES/BENEFITS:

Pension Plan: Y	ESOP Stock Plan:	Profit Sharing:	Top Exec. Salary: $	Bonus: $
Savings Plan:	Stock Purch. Plan: Y		Second Exec. Salary: $	Bonus: $

OTHER THOUGHTS:

Apparent Women Officers or Directors: 1
Hot Spot for Advancement for Women/Minorities:

LOCATIONS: ("Y" = Yes)

West:	Southwest:	Midwest:	Southeast:	Northeast:	International:
				Y	

EURO DISNEY SCA
www.eurodisney.com

Industry Group Code: 713110 Ranks within this company's industry group: Sales: 1 Profits: 3

Print Media/Publishing:	Movies:	Equipment/Supplies:	Broadcast/Cable:	Music/Audio:	Sports/Games:	
Newspapers:	Movie Theaters:	Equipment/Supplies:	Broadcast TV:	Music Production:	Games/Sports:	
Magazines:	Movie Production:	Gambling Equipment:	Cable TV:	Retail Music:	Retail Games Stores:	
Books:	TV/Video Production:	Special Services:	Satellite Broadcast:	Retail Audio Equip.:	Stadiums/Teams:	
Book Stores:	Video Rental:	Advertising Services:	Radio:	Music Print./Dist.:	Gambling/Casinos:	
Distribution/Printing:	Video Distribution:	Info. Sys. Software:	Online Information:	Multimedia:	Rides/Theme Parks:	Y

TYPES OF BUSINESS:
Theme Park
Resorts
Hotels
Golf
Property Developments

BRANDS/DIVISIONS/AFFILIATES:
Disneyland Paris
Walt Disney Studios
Disney Village
Val d'Europe
Village d'Ile-de-France
Walt Disney Company (The)
Space Mountain: Mission 2
EDL Hotels

CONTACTS:
Note: Officers with more than one job title may be intentionally listed here more than once.

Karl Holz, CEO
Ignace Lahoud, Sr.VP/CFO
Federico J. Gonzalez, VP-Mktg.
Wendy Crudele, VP-Human Resources
Francois Pinon, General Counsel/VP-Legal Affairs
Dominique Cocquet, Sr. VP-Dev. & External Affairs
Beatrice M. de Lacharriere, VP-Corp. Comm.
Andrew de Csillery, VP-Strategic Planning & Pricing
Norbert Stiekema, VP-Sale & Distribution
Christian Perdrier, Sr. VP-Parks, Disney Village & Security
Patrick Avice, VP-Hotels & Convention Centers
Karl Holz, Chmn.

Phone: 33-1-64-74-4000	Fax: 33-1-64-74-5636

Toll-Free:

Address: Le Club Actionnaires, BP 100, Marne-la-Vallee Cedex 4, 77777 France

GROWTH PLANS/SPECIAL FEATURES:
Euro Disney S.C.A. is a holding company that owns Euro Disney Associes (EDA), which in turn operates Disneyland Paris, a top European vacation destination. EDA is a segment that is 18%-owned by a subsidiary of The Walt Disney Company. The park receives over 12 million annual visits, with 60% of visitors coming from outside France. Disneyland Paris features a Walt Disney Studios theme park, a Disney Village entertainment district, two convention centers, 68 dining outlets, 54 boutiques and a 27-hole golf course. The subsidiary EDL Hotels is wholly owned by EDA, and operates host of Disney themed hotels, which include the majority of Disneyland's 13 hotels. These include: Disney's Newport Bay Club, Sequoia Lodge, Hotel Santa Fe and Hotel Cheyenne. The Newport Bay Club offers one of the largest conference centers in France, and included with Disneyland Paris' other conference center, amounts to about 17,000 square meters of space. Euro Disney has a large stake in Val d'Europe, an urban development project featuring a shopping center, an international business center, offices, apartments, homes and hotels. In February 2005, Euro Disney announced the official completion of its legal and financial restructuring. The firm recently opened the Space Mountain: Mission 2 attraction, and plans to launch Buzz Lightyear's Laser Blast in 2006.

Euro Disney offers employees language and professional training, a 35-hour work week, a multinational work environment and student internships. It also offers Hote d'Acceuil Touristique, a training program resulting in a diploma recognized as preparing participants for various tourism-related fields.

FINANCIALS:
Sales and profits are in thousands of dollars—add 000 to get the full amount. 2006 Note: Financial information for 2006 was not available for all companies at press time.

2006 Sales: $1,441,190	2006 Profits: $-117,390	**U.S. Stock Ticker:** ERDBF
2005 Sales: $1,295,800	2005 Profits: $-114,300	**Int'l Ticker:** EDL Int'l Exchange: Paris-Euronext
2004 Sales: $1,291,700	2004 Profits: $-179,000	Employees: 12,162
2003 Sales: $1,221,000	2003 Profits: $-64,900	Fiscal Year Ends: 9/30
2002 Sales: $1,055,600	2002 Profits: $32,500	Parent Company:

SALARIES/BENEFITS:

Pension Plan:	ESOP Stock Plan:	Profit Sharing:	Top Exec. Salary: $	Bonus: $
Savings Plan:	Stock Purch. Plan:		Second Exec. Salary: $	Bonus: $

OTHER THOUGHTS:
Apparent Women Officers or Directors: 2
Hot Spot for Advancement for Women/Minorities:

LOCATIONS: ("Y" = Yes)

West:	Southwest:	Midwest:	Southeast:	Northeast:	International:
					Y

Note: Financial information, benefits and other data can change quickly and may vary from those stated here.

FIRST LOOK STUDIOS INC   www.firstlookmedia.com

Industry Group Code: 512110 Ranks within this company's industry group: Sales: Profits:

Print Media/Publishing:	Movies:		Equipment/Supplies:	Broadcast/Cable:	Music/Audio:	Sports/Games:
Newspapers:	Movie Theaters:		Equipment/Supplies:	Broadcast TV:	Music Production:	Games/Sports:
Magazines:	Movie Production:	Y	Gambling Equipment:	Cable TV:	Retail Music:	Retail Games Stores:
Books:	TV/Video Production:	Y	Special Services:	Satellite Broadcast:	Retail Audio Equip.:	Stadiums/Teams:
Book Stores:	Video Rental:		Advertising Services: Y	Radio:	Music Print./Dist.:	Gambling/Casinos:
Distribution/Printing:	Video Distribution:		Info. Sys. Software:	Online Information:	Multimedia:	Rides/Theme Parks:

TYPES OF BUSINESS:

Independent Film Distribution
Film Production
Film Licensing
Television Production

BRANDS/DIVISIONS/AFFILIATES:

First Look International
First Look Pictures
First Look Home Entertainment
First Look Media
First Look Studios
First Look SPV LLC
Ventura Home Entertainment
DEJ Productions

CONTACTS: Note: Officers with more than one job title may be intentionally listed here more than once.

Henry Winterstern, CEO
William Lischak, COO
William Lischak, Pres.
William Lischak, CFO
Michael McLeod, Sr. VP- Sales
Richard Shore, General Counsel/Sec.
Irving Der, Dir.-Publicity
Kenneth Lynch, Sr. VP/Controller
Christopher J. Cooney, Pres., Branded Entertainment
Bill Bromiley, Pres., First Look Home Entertainment
Amir Khoury, VP-Oper., First Look Home Entertainment
Gordon Prend, Sr. VP-Mktg.
Liz Mackiewicz, Sr. VP-Worldwide Sales

Phone: 323-337-1000	Fax: 323-337-1037
Toll-Free:	

Address: 8000 Sunset Blvd., E. Penthouse, Los Angeles, CA 90046 US

GROWTH PLANS/SPECIAL FEATURES:

First Look Studios, Inc. serves as a producer and distributor for independently produced movies. The company is one of the founding members of the American Film Marketing Association (AFMA). The firm conducts its business through four operating segments: First Look International, the international sales division; First Look Pictures, the U.S. theatrical releasing division; First Look Home Entertainment (FLHE), the U.S. video and DVD distribution operation; and First Look Media, the branded content segment. The firm produces independent and artistic films such as A Map of the World, Titus, The Runner and The Secret Life of Girls. Some of the best-known productions in its library of over 350 films include Antonia's Line, The Secret of Roan Inish, Waking Ned Devine and The Prophecy. The company also engages in licensing theatrical, video, pay television (HBO, Showtime and Encore), free television (USA, Sci-Fi and Lifetime), satellite and other distribution rights to foreign sub-distributors in major international territories and regions. In addition, the company distributes films domestically, licensing them for videocassette transference, DVD and pay-per-view through First Look Home Entertainment. The firm is currently expanding the FLHE division. First Look Studios owns and operates two studio facilities, one in New York and one in North Carolina, where the Dawson's Creek series was produced. In 2006, First Look acquired Ventura Home Entertainment for $20 million. In 2006, the company transferred all of its affiliate's assets to its subsidiary, First Look SPV LLC, in connection with obtaining an $80 million revolving credit facility from Merrill Lynch Commercial Financial Corporation. In exchange, First Look SPV LLC paid the company $18.8 million in cash and a subordinated demand promissory note for $28.3 million.

FINANCIALS: Sales and profits are in thousands of dollars—add 000 to get the full amount. 2006 Note: Financial information for 2006 was not available for all companies at press time.

2006 Sales: $	2006 Profits: $	U.S. Stock Ticker: FRST.PK
2005 Sales: $	2005 Profits: $	Int'l Ticker: Int'l Exchange:
2004 Sales: $	2004 Profits: $	Employees: 47
2003 Sales: $	2003 Profits: $	Fiscal Year Ends: 12/31
2002 Sales: $26,700	2002 Profits: $-9,400	Parent Company:

SALARIES/BENEFITS:

Pension Plan:	ESOP Stock Plan:	Profit Sharing:	Top Exec. Salary: $295,200	Bonus: $212,500
Savings Plan:	Stock Purch. Plan:		Second Exec. Salary: $194,808	Bonus: $

OTHER THOUGHTS:

Apparent Women Officers or Directors:
Hot Spot for Advancement for Women/Minorities:

LOCATIONS: ("Y" = Yes)

West:	Southwest:	Midwest:	Southeast:	Northeast:	International:
Y				Y	Y

Note: Financial information, benefits and other data can change quickly and may vary from those stated here.

FISHER COMMUNICATIONS INC
www.fsci.com

Industry Group Code: 513120 Ranks within this company's industry group: Sales: 21   Profits: 13

Print Media/Publishing:	Movies:	Equipment/Supplies:	Broadcast/Cable:	Music/Audio:	Sports/Games:
Newspapers:	Movie Theaters:	Equipment/Supplies:	Broadcast TV: Y	Music Production:	Games/Sports:
Magazines:	Movie Production:	Gambling Equipment:	Cable TV:	Retail Music:	Retail Games Stores:
Books:	TV/Video Production:	Special Services: Y	Satellite Broadcast:	Retail Audio Equip.:	Stadiums/Teams: Y
Book Stores:	Video Rental:	Advertising Services: Y	Radio:	Music Print./Dist.:	Gambling/Casinos:
Distribution/Printing:	Video Distribution:	Info. Sys. Software:	Online Information:	Multimedia:	Rides/Theme Parks:

TYPES OF BUSINESS:

Television Broadcasting
Radio Broadcasting
Media Content Distribution
Special Events Center

BRANDS/DIVISIONS/AFFILIATES:

Fisher Media Services Company
Fisher Broadcasting Company
Fisher Plaza
Fisher Pavilion
Fisher Pathways

CONTACTS: Note: Officers with more than one job title may be intentionally listed here more than once.

Colleen B. Brown, CEO
Warren J. Spector, COO
Colleen B. Brown, Pres.
Mae Numata, CFO/Sr. VP
Laura J. Boyd, VP-Human Resources
Mel L. Martin, Chief Research Officer
Judith A. Endejan, General Counsel/Sr. VP
Benjamin W. Tucker, Pres., Fisher Broadcasting Co.
Mark A. Weed, Pres., Fisher Properties, Inc.
Kirk G. Anderson, Pres., Fisher Media Services Co.
Sharon J. Johnston, Corp. Sec.
Phelps K. Fisher, Chmn.

Phone: 206-404-7000	Fax: 206-404-7050
Toll-Free:	
Address: 100 4th Ave. N., Ste. 510, Seattle, WA 98109 US	

GROWTH PLANS/SPECIAL FEATURES:

Fisher Communications, Inc. is a communications and media company focused primarily on broadcasting. The company is divided into two subsidiaries: Fisher Broadcasting Company and Fisher Media Services Company. Fisher owns and operates 19 network-affiliated television stations and owns a 50% interest in a company with another television station, as well as owning and operating nine radio stations. The company's broadcasting operations provided approximately 97% of consolidated revenue from continuing operations, with television broadcasting accounting for approximately 68% and radio broadcasting accounting for approximately 32% in 2005. The television and radio stations are located in Washington, Oregon, Idaho and Montana and reach 3.6 million households. The firm also sells advertising for an FM station under a joint sales agreement. Fisher Plaza, located in Seattle, Washington, is the company's communications center. The center is designed to enable the distribution of analog and digital media content through broadcast, satellite, cable, Internet, broadband and wireless distribution channels. Fisher Pavilion hosts a range of events including festivals, trade shows, concerts and other special events. Fisher recently purchased a variety of television stations, expanding its total from 9 to 19. The company also divested itself of twenty-four small-market radio stations located in Montana and eastern Washington.

FINANCIALS: Sales and profits are in thousands of dollars—add 000 to get the full amount. 2006 Note: Financial information for 2006 was not available for all companies at press time.

2006 Sales: $	2006 Profits: $	U.S. Stock Ticker: FSCI
2005 Sales: $144,471	2005 Profits: $-5,072	Int'l Ticker: Int'l Exchange:
2004 Sales: $153,866	2004 Profits: $-11,953	Employees: 931
2003 Sales: $138,387	2003 Profits: $8,228	Fiscal Year Ends: 12/31
2002 Sales: $154,088	2002 Profits: $-66,746	Parent Company:

SALARIES/BENEFITS:

Pension Plan:	ESOP Stock Plan:	Profit Sharing:	Top Exec. Salary: $500,000	Bonus: $523,333
Savings Plan: Y	Stock Purch. Plan:		Second Exec. Salary: $318,958	Bonus: $437,778

OTHER THOUGHTS:

Apparent Women Officers or Directors: 5
Hot Spot for Advancement for Women/Minorities: Y

LOCATIONS: ("Y" = Yes)

West:	Southwest:	Midwest:	Southeast:	Northeast:	International:
Y					

FORBES INC

www.forbesinc.com

Industry Group Code: 511120   Ranks within this company's industry group: Sales: 10   Profits:

Print Media/Publishing:		Movies:		Equipment/Supplies:		Broadcast/Cable:		Music/Audio:		Sports/Games:	
Newspapers:		Movie Theaters:		Equipment/Supplies:		Broadcast TV:		Music Production:		Games/Sports:	
Magazines:	Y	Movie Production:		Gambling Equipment:		Cable TV:	Y	Retail Music:		Retail Games Stores:	
Books:	Y	TV/Video Production:	Y	Special Services:	Y	Satellite Broadcast:		Retail Audio Equip.:		Stadiums/Teams:	
Book Stores:		Video Rental:		Advertising Services:		Radio:		Music Print./Dist.:		Gambling/Casinos:	
Distribution/Printing:		Video Distribution:		Info. Sys. Software:		Online Information:		Multimedia:		Rides/Theme Parks:	

TYPES OF BUSINESS:

Magazine Publishing
Online Publishing & Forums
Seminars
Newsletters
Conferences
Television & Radio Production

BRANDS/DIVISIONS/AFFILIATES:

Forbes Magazine
Forbes.com
Forbes Television
ForbesLife
Forbes Asia
American Heritage
Social Register Association
Forbes Media LLC

CONTACTS: Note: Officers with more than one job title may be intentionally listed here more than once.

Steve Forbes, CEO
Timothy C. Forbes, COO
Steve Forbes, Pres.
Sean P. Hegarty, CFO/Exec. VP
Raymond Ouellette, CIO
Jim Spanfeller, Pres./CEO-Forbes.com
James Berrien, Pres./Publisher-Forbes Magazine Group
Steve Forbes, Editor-in-Chief-Forbes Magazine
Kendall Crolius, VP/General Mng.-Forbes Conference Group
Scott Masterson, Pres., American Heritage
Christopher Forbes, Vice Chmn.

Phone: 212-620-2200	Fax: 212-620-2245
Toll-Free:	
Address: 60 5th Ave., New York, NY 10011 US	

GROWTH PLANS/SPECIAL FEATURES:

Forbes, Inc., a privately held publishing and new media company, is the publisher of Forbes Magazine which celebrates its 90th anniversary in 2007. The company also includes: Forbes.com, a leading business web site with over 1,500 articles published daily; Forbes Conference Group, a producer of peer-driven forums for senior executives such as the Forbes CEO Forum; Forbes Newsletter Group, which publishes ten specialty newsletters and has marketing, content and distribution relationships with 35 outside newsletters; Forbes Investors Advisory Institute; Forbes Television, responsible for the co-branded show Forbes on Fox; Forbes Radio, which is responsible for a weekly three-hour radio show, Forbes on Radio; Forbes Custom Media, which provides clients with customized print and electronic publication services in areas such as financial services, business-to-business markets and technology; The Forbes Collection, a showcase of historical artifacts; ForbesLife (formerly Forbes FYI), is a bi-monthly lifestyle magazine with a humorous bent; Forbes Asia, an English language bi-weekly with a circulation of 80,000 in the Asia/Pacific region; and American Heritage, a magazine which looks to the past to explain the present. The American Heritage division also publishes: American Heritage of Invention & Technology, a quarterly magazine dedicated to the history of American innovations; American Legacy, a quarterly magazine dedicated to African-American history and culture; and AmericanHeritage.com, branded as History's Homepage. Forbes Magazine is published bi-weekly with over 60 concise articles. Including the magazine's eight local-language editions (Hebrew, Arabic, Russian, Polish, Japanese, Korean, Chinese and Turkish) and Forbes Asia, the magazine has a worldwide audience of over 5 million readers. Forbes, Inc. is also behind the Social Register Association which lists approximately 25,000 people in its twice yearly publication. In late 2006, private-equity firm Elevation Partners acquired a 40% interest in the newly formed company, Forbes Media LLC.

FINANCIALS: Sales and profits are in thousands of dollars—add 000 to get the full amount. 2006 Note: Financial information for 2006 was not available for all companies at press time.

2006 Sales: $	2006 Profits: $	U.S. Stock Ticker: Private	
2005 Sales: $450,000	2005 Profits: $	Int'l Ticker: Int'l Exchange:	
2004 Sales: $	2004 Profits: $	Employees:	
2003 Sales: $	2003 Profits: $	Fiscal Year Ends: 12/31	
2002 Sales: $	2002 Profits: $	Parent Company:	

SALARIES/BENEFITS:

Pension Plan:	ESOP Stock Plan:	Profit Sharing:	Top Exec. Salary: $	Bonus: $
Savings Plan:	Stock Purch. Plan:		Second Exec. Salary: $	Bonus: $

OTHER THOUGHTS:

Apparent Women Officers or Directors: 7
Hot Spot for Advancement for Women/Minorities: Y

LOCATIONS: ("Y" = Yes)

West:	Southwest:	Midwest:	Southeast:	Northeast:	International:
				Y	Y

FORD MODELS INC

www.fordmodels.com

Industry Group Code: 711410 Ranks within this company's industry group: Sales: Profits:

Print Media/Publishing:	Movies:	Equipment/Supplies:		Broadcast/Cable:	Music/Audio:	Sports/Games:
Newspapers:	Movie Theaters:	Equipment/Supplies:		Broadcast TV:	Music Production:	Games/Sports:
Magazines:	Movie Production:	Gambling Equipment:		Cable TV:	Retail Music:	Retail Games Stores:
Books:	TV/Video Production:	Special Services:	Y	Satellite Broadcast:	Retail Audio Equip.:	Stadiums/Teams:
Book Stores:	Video Rental:	Advertising Services:	Y	Radio:	Music Print./Dist.:	Gambling/Casinos:
Distribution/Printing:	Video Distribution:	Info. Sys. Software:		Online Information:	Multimedia:	Rides/Theme Parks:

TYPES OF BUSINESS:

Modeling Agency

BRANDS/DIVISIONS/AFFILIATES:

CONTACTS: Note: Officers with more than one job title may be intentionally listed here more than once.

Katie Ford, CEO
John Caplin, COO
Katie Ford, Pres.
John Caplin, CFO

Phone: 212-219-6500	Fax: 212-966-5028
Toll-Free:	
Address: 111 5th Ave., New York, NY 10003 US	

GROWTH PLANS/SPECIAL FEATURES:

Ford Models, Inc. is one of the top fashion model representation agencies in the world. Based out of New York City, it also has offices in: Los Angeles; Miami; Chicago; Scottsdale, Arizona; Toronto; Paris; and Sao Paulo and Rio de Janeiro, Brazil. The company operates through several divisions representing different categories of models. The children's division works with children aged six months and older that live within 100 miles of New York City, Chicago or Los Angeles. During the summer, the division also works with out-of-town models staying temporarily in the area. The men's division looks for men between the heights of 6 feet and 6-foot-2 and 18 to 25 years old. The plus-sized women's division works with women between the heights of 5-foot-8 and 5-foot-11, sizes 12 to 18 and between the ages of 15 and 30. The women's division works with women between the heights of 5-foot-8 and 5-foot-11, sizes 2 to 8 and between the ages of 18 and 21. Ford also has divisions specializing in mature models, classics and in models who display specific body parts, such as hands or feet. The company holds open casting at many of their locations throughout the year. In November 2006, the firm opened a new office in San Francisco, California.

FINANCIALS: Sales and profits are in thousands of dollars—add 000 to get the full amount. 2006 Note: Financial information for 2006 was not available for all companies at press time.

2006 Sales: $	2006 Profits: $	U.S. Stock Ticker: Private
2005 Sales: $	2005 Profits: $	Int'l Ticker: Int'l Exchange:
2004 Sales: $	2004 Profits: $	Employees:
2003 Sales: $	2003 Profits: $	Fiscal Year Ends:
2002 Sales: $	2002 Profits: $	Parent Company:

SALARIES/BENEFITS:

Pension Plan:	ESOP Stock Plan:	Profit Sharing:	Top Exec. Salary: $	Bonus: $
Savings Plan:	Stock Purch. Plan:		Second Exec. Salary: $	Bonus: $

OTHER THOUGHTS:

Apparent Women Officers or Directors: 1
Hot Spot for Advancement for Women/Minorities:

LOCATIONS: ("Y" = Yes)

West:	Southwest:	Midwest:	Southeast:	Northeast:	International:
Y	Y	Y	Y	Y	Y

Note: Financial information, benefits and other data can change quickly and may vary from those stated here.

FOX BROADCASTING COMPANY   www.fox.com

Industry Group Code: 513210 **Ranks within this company's industry group:** Sales: 7   Profits:

Print Media/Publishing:	Movies:	Equipment/Supplies:	Broadcast/Cable:		Music/Audio:	Sports/Games:
Newspapers:	Movie Theaters:	Equipment/Supplies:	Broadcast TV:	Y	Music Production:	Games/Sports:
Magazines:	Movie Production:	Gambling Equipment:	Cable TV:		Retail Music:	Retail Games Stores:
Books:	TV/Video Production:	Special Services:	Satellite Broadcast:		Retail Audio Equip.:	Stadiums/Teams:
Book Stores:	Video Rental:	Advertising Services:	Radio:		Music Print./Dist.:	Gambling/Casinos:
Distribution/Printing:	Video Distribution:	Info. Sys. Software:	Online Information:		Multimedia:	Rides/Theme Parks:

TYPES OF BUSINESS:

Television Broadcasting
Television Stations

BRANDS/DIVISIONS/AFFILIATES:

Fox Entertainment Group, Inc.
News Corporation
FOX Television Network
Simpsons (The)
American Idol
House
24
COPS

CONTACTS: *Note: Officers with more than one job title may be intentionally listed here more than once.*

Andrew Setos, Pres., Engineering
Del Mayberry, Exec. VP-Admin.
Del Mayberry, Exec. VP-Finance
Ed Wilson, Pres., FOX Television Network

Phone: 310-369-1000	**Fax:** 310-369-1283
Toll-Free:	
Address: 10201 W. Pico Blvd., Los Angeles, CA 90035 US	

GROWTH PLANS/SPECIAL FEATURES:

Fox Broadcasting Company (FOX), a subsidiary of Fox Entertainment Group, Inc., itself a subsidiary of News Corporation, operates the FOX Television Network. The company owns and operates 35 full-power stations located in 9 of the 10 largest designated market areas. Its television broadcast network consists of over 200 affiliated stations, including the full-power television stations that are owned by subsidiaries of FOX, which reach approximately 98% of all U.S. television households. The firm broadcasts approximately 15 hours of primetime, sports events and Sunday morning news television programming created by other Fox Entertainment subsidiaries, including Twentieth Century Fox Television, Fox Television Studios, Fox News Channel, Fox Sports Networks, FX Network and several foreign subsidiaries. The company principally derives its revenues from the sale of advertising time sold to national advertisers. FOX's most prominent primetime programs include The Simpsons, American Idol, House, 24, COPS, and America's Most Wanted. The firm licenses sports programming from organizations such as the NFL, MLB and NASCAR.

The company offers benefits including flexible spending accounts, employee assistance, education reimbursement, credit union membership, company paid parking and discounts on local attractions and merchandise. FOX also offers both paid and academic credit internships.

FINANCIALS: Sales and profits are in thousands of dollars—add 000 to get the full amount. 2006 Note: Financial information for 2006 was not available for all companies at press time.

2006 Sales: $	2006 Profits: $	**U.S. Stock Ticker: Subsidiary**	
2005 Sales: $2,624,000	2005 Profits: $	**Int'l Ticker:** Int'l Exchange:	
2004 Sales: $4,556,000	2004 Profits: $	Employees: 425	
2003 Sales: $4,359,000	2003 Profits: $	Fiscal Year Ends: 6/30	
2002 Sales: $3,923,000	2002 Profits: $	Parent Company: NEWS CORPORATION LIMITED (THE)	

SALARIES/BENEFITS:

Pension Plan: Y	ESOP Stock Plan:	Profit Sharing:	Top Exec. Salary: $	Bonus: $
Savings Plan: Y	Stock Purch. Plan:		Second Exec. Salary: $	Bonus: $

OTHER THOUGHTS:

Apparent Women Officers or Directors:
Hot Spot for Advancement for Women/Minorities:

LOCATIONS: ("Y" = Yes)

West:	Southwest:	Midwest:	Southeast:	Northeast:	International:
Y					

FOX ENTERTAINMENT GROUP INC

www.fox.com

Industry Group Code: 513120 Ranks within this company's industry group: Sales: Profits:

Print Media/Publishing:		Movies:		Equipment/Supplies:		Broadcast/Cable:		Music/Audio:		Sports/Games:	
Newspapers:		Movie Theaters:		Equipment/Supplies:		Broadcast TV:	Y	Music Production:	Y	Games/Sports:	Y
Magazines:		Movie Production:	Y	Gambling Equipment:		Cable TV:	Y	Retail Music:		Retail Games Stores:	
Books:		TV/Video Production:	Y	Special Services:		Satellite Broadcast:		Retail Audio Equip.:		Stadiums/Teams:	Y
Book Stores:		Video Rental:		Advertising Services:	Y	Radio:		Music Print./Dist.:		Gambling/Casinos:	
Distribution/Printing:		Video Distribution:		Info. Sys. Software:		Online Information:		Multimedia:		Rides/Theme Parks:	

TYPES OF BUSINESS:

Broadcast Television
Film Distribution and Production
Television Programming
Online Communities and Game Sites
Professional Sports
Electronic Games
Cable TV Programming
Online Entertainment

BRANDS/DIVISIONS/AFFILIATES:

News Corporation
Fox Filmed Entertainment
Twentieth Century Fox Television
Fox Television Studios
Fox Interactive Media
MySpace.com
National Geographic Channel

CONTACTS: Note: Officers with more than one job title may be intentionally listed here more than once.

K. Rupert Murdoch, CEO
Peter Chernin, COO
Peter Chernin, Pres.
David F. DeVoe, CFO/Sr. Exec. VP
Arthur M. Siskind, General Counsel/Sr. VP
Ross Levinsohn, Pres., Fox Interactive Media
Lachlan K. Murdoch, Pres., Fox Television Stations
Anthony J. Vinciquerra, CEO/Pres., Fox Networks Group
Roger Ailes, Chmn./CEO-Fox News Channel
K. Rupert Murdoch, Chmn.

Phone: 212-852-7017	Fax: 212-852-7145
Toll-Free:	
Address: 1211 Ave. of the Americas, New York, NY 10036 US	

GROWTH PLANS/SPECIAL FEATURES:

Fox Entertainment Group, Inc. (FEG), a unit of News Corporation, is an entertainment conglomerate that operates through four business segments: filmed entertainment, television stations, television broadcast network and cable network programming. The company engages in feature film and television production and distribution principally through the following businesses: Fox Filmed Entertainment, a leading producer and distributor of feature films; Twentieth Century Fox Television, a producer of network television programming; Fox Television Studios, a leading producer of U.S. broadcast, cable and international programming; and Fox Interactive Media, a network of integrated Internet sites including Myspace.com, which has more than 60 million users worldwide. Twentieth Century Fox Home Entertainment, Inc. distributes motion pictures and other programming produced by units of Fox Entertainment and its affiliates in all home media formats, including digital media available for download from Apple's iTunes Music Store. The company's motion picture and television library consists of varying rights to well over 3,000 previously released motion pictures and many television programs. In television, Fox Television Stations owns and operates 35 full-power stations located in nine of the 10 largest designated market areas, reaching 98% of all U.S. television households. Its television broadcast network consists of approximately 200 affiliated stations, including the full-power stations that are owned by subsidiaries of Fox. The company produces television programs through Twentieth Century Fox Television, Fox Television Studios, Fox News Channel, Fox Sports Networks, FX Network, SPEED Channel, FUEL, National Geographic Channel, Fox Movie Channel and several foreign subsidiaries. The company also owns a 14.6% limited partnership interest in the Colorado Rockies, the baseball franchise in Denver, Colorado. In December 2006, Liberty Media Corp. acquired the firm's interest in DirecTV.

Fox provides its employees with an employee assistance program, education reimbursement and merchandise discounts.

FINANCIALS: Sales and profits are in thousands of dollars—add 000 to get the full amount. 2006 Note: Financial information for 2006 was not available for all companies at press time.

2006 Sales: $	2006 Profits: $	U.S. Stock Ticker: Subsidiary
2005 Sales: $	2005 Profits: $	Int'l Ticker: Int'l Exchange:
2004 Sales: $12,175,000	2004 Profits: $1,353,000	Employees: 12,500
2003 Sales: $11,002,000	2003 Profits: $1,031,000	Fiscal Year Ends: 6/30
2002 Sales: $9,725,000	2002 Profits: $581,000	Parent Company: NEWS CORPORATION LIMITED (THE)

SALARIES/BENEFITS:

Pension Plan: Y	ESOP Stock Plan:	Profit Sharing:	Top Exec. Salary: $4,508,694	Bonus: $21,175,000
Savings Plan: Y	Stock Purch. Plan:		Second Exec. Salary: $8,100,008	Bonus: $21,175,000

OTHER THOUGHTS:

Apparent Women Officers or Directors:
Hot Spot for Advancement for Women/Minorities:

LOCATIONS: ("Y" = Yes)

West:	Southwest:	Midwest:	Southeast:	Northeast:	International:
Y	Y	Y	Y	Y	Y

Note: Financial information, benefits and other data can change quickly and may vary from those stated here.

FOX FILMED ENTERTAINMENT   www.foxmovies.com

Industry Group Code: 512110 Ranks within this company's industry group: Sales: 5   Profits:

Print Media/Publishing:	Movies:		Equipment/Supplies:	Broadcast/Cable:	Music/Audio:	Sports/Games:
Newspapers:	Movie Theaters:		Equipment/Supplies:	Broadcast TV:	Music Production:	Games/Sports:
Magazines:	Movie Production:	Y	Gambling Equipment:	Cable TV:	Retail Music:	Retail Games Stores:
Books:	TV/Video Production:	Y	Special Services:	Satellite Broadcast:	Retail Audio Equip.:	Stadiums/Teams:
Book Stores:	Video Rental:		Advertising Services:	Radio:	Music Print./Dist.:	Gambling/Casinos:
Distribution/Printing:	Video Distribution:		Info. Sys. Software:	Online Information:	Multimedia:	Rides/Theme Parks:

TYPES OF BUSINESS:

Movie Production & Distribution
Animated Films
Television Production & Distribution
Video & DVD Distribution

BRANDS/DIVISIONS/AFFILIATES:

Fox Entertainment Group, Inc.
Twentieth Century Fox
Fox 2000
Fox Searchlight
Twentieth Century Fox Animation
Twentieth Century Fox Home Entertainment
Twentieth Century Fox Television
Fox Atomic

CONTACTS: *Note: Officers with more than one job title may be intentionally listed here more than once.*

Dean Hallett, CFO/Exec. VP
David Lux, Sr. VP-Corp. Publicity
Dean Hallett, Exec. VP-Finance
Thomas E. Rothman, Co-Chmn.
James N. Gianopulos, Co-Chmn.

Phone: 310-369-1000	**Fax:** 310-203-1558
Toll-Free:	
Address: 10201 W. Pico Blvd., Los Angeles, CA 90035 US	

GROWTH PLANS/SPECIAL FEATURES:

Fox Filmed Entertainment (FFE), a subsidiary of Fox Entertainment Group, Inc., is one of the world's major producers and distributors of feature films and a leader in U.S. television programming. FFE produces films through four studios: Twentieth Century Fox, Fox 2000, Fox Searchlight and Twentieth Century Fox Animation. The company's Twentieth Century Fox and Fox 2000 subsidiaries produce big-budget movies such as Titanic, Fight Club, Moulin Rouge, X-Men and the Star Wars series. Another subsidiary, Fox Searchlight, produces or funds smaller art-house film such as The Dancer Upstairs. Twentieth Century Fox Animation produces animated films such as Ice Age and the upcoming The Simpsons Movie. Through Twentieth Century Fox Home Entertainment, the firm distributes motion pictures on video and DVD for sale and rental. Twentieth Century Fox Television produces and distributes programming for a variety of U.S. networks. Prominent shows have included Boston Legal, Judging Amy and The Simpsons. In addition, FFE has certain distribution agreements with Regency Entertainment, Inc., a film company in which the firm holds a 20% interest. In 2006, the company released smash-hit comedy Borat: Cultural Learnings of America for Make Benefit Glorious Nation of Kazakhstan. Seven movies are currently scheduled for release in 2007: Epic Movie, Reno 911: Miami, Pathfinder, Firehouse Dog, Fantastic Four: Rise of the Silver Surfer, Live Free or Die Hard and The Simpsons Movie. In late 2006, Twentieth Century Fox Home Entertainment signed an exclusive deal with Zoke Culture Group to distribute DVDs in China. Also in 2006, FFE launched a new theatrical movie studio, Fox Atomic. The studio targets 17-24 year olds with films, comics and digital content. In 2007, the studio will release three films: The Hills Have Eyes II, The Comebacks and 28 Weeks Later.

FINANCIALS: Sales and profits are in thousands of dollars—add 000 to get the full amount. 2006 Note: Financial information for 2006 was not available for all companies at press time.

2006 Sales: $	2006 Profits: $	**U.S. Stock Ticker: Subsidiary**
2005 Sales: $5,919,000	2005 Profits: $	**Int'l Ticker:** Int'l Exchange:
2004 Sales: $	2004 Profits: $	Employees:
2003 Sales: $	2003 Profits: $	Fiscal Year Ends: 6/30
2002 Sales: $	2002 Profits: $	Parent Company: FOX ENTERTAINMENT GROUP INC

SALARIES/BENEFITS:

Pension Plan:	ESOP Stock Plan:	Profit Sharing:	Top Exec. Salary: $	Bonus: $
Savings Plan:	Stock Purch. Plan:		Second Exec. Salary: $	Bonus: $

OTHER THOUGHTS:

Apparent Women Officers or Directors:
Hot Spot for Advancement for Women/Minorities:

LOCATIONS: ("Y" = Yes)

West:	Southwest:	Midwest:	Southeast:	Northeast:	International:
Y					

FOX SPORTS NET INC

msn.foxsports.com

Industry Group Code: 513210 Ranks within this company's industry group: Sales: Profits:

Print Media/Publishing:	Movies:		Equipment/Supplies:		Broadcast/Cable:		Music/Audio:	Sports/Games:
Newspapers:	Movie Theaters:		Equipment/Supplies:		Broadcast TV:	Y	Music Production:	Games/Sports:
Magazines:	Movie Production:	Y	Gambling Equipment:		Cable TV:	Y	Retail Music:	Retail Games Stores:
Books:	TV/Video Production:	Y	Special Services:	Y	Satellite Broadcast:		Retail Audio Equip.:	Stadiums/Teams:
Book Stores:	Video Rental:		Advertising Services:		Radio:		Music Print./Dist.:	Gambling/Casinos:
Distribution/Printing:	Video Distribution:		Info. Sys. Software:		Online Information:		Multimedia:	Rides/Theme Parks:

TYPES OF BUSINESS:

Sports Broadcasting
Film & TV Production & Distribution
Online Sports Broadcasting
Regional Sports Networks

BRANDS/DIVISIONS/AFFILIATES:

Fox Sports Net
Fox Entertainment Group
News Corporation Limited (The)
National Sports Partners
National Advertising Partners

CONTACTS: Note: Officers with more than one job title may be intentionally listed here more than once.

Robert Thompson, Pres.
Lou D'Ermilio, Sr. VP-Media Relations
David Rone, Exec. VP-Rights Acquisitions
Dan Bell, VP-Communications
David Hill, Chmn.

Phone: 310-369-6000	**Fax:** 212-354-6902
Toll-Free:	
Address: 10201 W. Pico Blvd., Bldg. 101, 5th Fl., Los Angeles, CA 90035 US	

GROWTH PLANS/SPECIAL FEATURES:

Fox Sports Net (FSN), Inc., owned by Fox Entertainment Group, itself a majority-owned subsidiary of The News Corporation Limited, produces and distributes films and television programs. The company provides professional and collegiate sports programming through interests in 15 regional sports networks (RSNs), as well as through Fox Sports Net, a national sports news program that operates through six additional RSNs. FSN's programming, which is received by 85 million households, combines the content of RSNs with national programming that is consistent throughout all regions. The company has the rights to broadcast the live events of 66 NBA, NHL, MLB teams, as well as several high school and collegiate teams. In addition, the firm hosts the ACC, Big 12 and Pac 10 conferences. Most of the company's revenue is culled through advertising time slots. The company has various partnerships with Rainbow Media Sports, with the result that the two companies have owned different stakes in various regional Fox Sports Net operations. Recently, the firm announced that it will digitally distribute the five full-length NFL games from the 2007 Tostitos Bowl Bash (including preview shows and highlights), marking the first time FOX Sports has made downloadable content available for sports fans on the Internet.

Fox Sports Net offers its employees medical, dental, and vision plans; life insurance; child care on the studio lot; an employee assistance program; Credit union membership; advance movie screenings; and paid vacation.

FINANCIALS: Sales and profits are in thousands of dollars—add 000 to get the full amount. 2006 Note: Financial information for 2006 was not available for all companies at press time.

2006 Sales: $	2006 Profits: $	**U.S. Stock Ticker: Subsidiary**
2005 Sales: $	2005 Profits: $	**Int'l Ticker:** Int'l Exchange:
2004 Sales: $	2004 Profits: $	Employees:
2003 Sales: $	2003 Profits: $	Fiscal Year Ends: 6/30
2002 Sales: $	2002 Profits: $	Parent Company: FOX ENTERTAINMENT GROUP INC

SALARIES/BENEFITS:

Pension Plan: Y	ESOP Stock Plan:	Profit Sharing:	Top Exec. Salary: $	Bonus: $
Savings Plan: Y	Stock Purch. Plan:		Second Exec. Salary: $	Bonus: $

OTHER THOUGHTS:

Apparent Women Officers or Directors:
Hot Spot for Advancement for Women/Minorities:

LOCATIONS: ("Y" = Yes)

West:	Southwest:	Midwest:	Southeast:	Northeast:	International:
Y	Y	Y	Y	Y	

Note: Financial information, benefits and other data can change quickly and may vary from those stated here.

FREEDOM COMMUNICATIONS INC
www.freedom.com

Industry Group Code: 511110 Ranks within this company's industry group: Sales: 21 Profits:

Print Media/Publishing:		Movies:		Equipment/Supplies:		Broadcast/Cable:		Music/Audio:		Sports/Games:	
Newspapers:	Y	Movie Theaters:		Equipment/Supplies:		Broadcast TV:	Y	Music Production:		Games/Sports:	
Magazines:	Y	Movie Production:		Gambling Equipment:		Cable TV:		Retail Music:		Retail Games Stores:	
Books:	Y	TV/Video Production:		Special Services:		Satellite Broadcast:		Retail Audio Equip.:		Stadiums/Teams:	
Book Stores:		Video Rental:		Advertising Services:		Radio:		Music Print./Dist.:		Gambling/Casinos:	
Distribution/Printing:		Video Distribution:		Info. Sys. Software:		Online Information:		Multimedia:		Rides/Theme Parks:	

TYPES OF BUSINESS:

Newspaper Publishing
Magazine Publishing
Television Broadcasting
Online Publishing
Books & Calendars

BRANDS/DIVISIONS/AFFILIATES:

Community Newspapers, Inc.
East Valley/Scottsdale Tribune
Orange County Register
EmeraldCoast.com
HighDesert.com
MyRGV.com
PanamaCity.com
fresh!nk

CONTACTS: *Note: Officers with more than one job title may be intentionally listed here more than once.*

Scott N. Flanders, CEO
Scott N. Flanders, Pres.
Douglas S. Bennett, CFO/Sr. VP
Marcy Bruskin, VP-Human Resources
Mike Brown, CIO
Rachel Sagan, General Counsel/VP
Marcy Bruskin, VP-Organizational Dev.
Stephanie Miclot, Media Contact
JoAnne Norton, VP-Shareholder Rel.
Nancy Trillo, VP/Controller
Michael J. Mathieu, Pres., Freedom Interactive
Chris Anderson, Pres., Freedom Orange County Information
Jonathan Segal, Pres., Freedom Newspapers, Inc.
Doreen Wade, Pres., Freedom Broadcasting, Inc.
Thomas W. Bassett, Chmn.

Phone: 949-253-2300	**Fax:** 949-474-7675
Toll-Free:	
Address: 17666 Fitch Ave., Irvine, CA 92614-6022 US	

GROWTH PLANS/SPECIAL FEATURES:

Freedom Communications, Inc. is a media conglomerate that has interests in newspaper publishing, television broadcasting and Internet web sites. The company's newspaper division is divided into two parts: Community Newspapers, Inc. and Metro Newspapers. Together, these divisions publish over 70 newspapers and nearly 240 niche publications. Community Newspapers is made up of 25 daily and 12 weekly publications in 10 states, including Arizona, California, Florida, New Mexico, North Carolina, Illinois, Indiana, Missouri, Texas and Ohio. The Metro division includes the East Valley/Scottsdale Tribune and the Orange County Register. The combined circulation of Freedom's newspapers is more than 1.2 million. The company launched 239 new niche products in 2005, including history books, pet calendars and worship guides. The company's television broadcasting segment consists of five CBS affiliates, three ABC affiliates and one CW affiliate acquired in December 2006. These stations are located in New York, Texas, Tennessee, Oregon, Rhode Island, Florida and Michigan. Using digital broadcast technology, three of the CBS affiliates and one ABC affiliate air the CW Network through a single digital signal. The company's Internet businesses, run by Freedom Interactive, are primarily community-oriented news and information sites including Coloradosprings.com, EmeraldCoast.com, HighDesert.com, MyRGV.com and PanamaCity.com. The interactive division has 33 websites and Internet portals, which have roughly 25 million page views monthly. In 2006, Freedom paired with Monster Worldwide, Inc. to provide recruitment services to all of Freedom's newspaper, television and online brands. Also in 2006, the company launched fresh!nk, a weekly tabloid targeting the teen population. It is availably for free at over 80 locations and is supported by its website, freshinkonline.com.

All of Freedom Communications' interests are run on a Libertarian philosophy stressing Individual Freedom, Self-Responsibility and Integrity.

FINANCIALS: Sales and profits are in thousands of dollars—add 000 to get the full amount. 2006 Note: Financial information for 2006 was not available for all companies at press time.

2006 Sales: $	2006 Profits: $	**U.S. Stock Ticker: Private**
2005 Sales: $103,500	2005 Profits: $	**Int'l Ticker:** Int'l Exchange:
2004 Sales: $	2004 Profits: $	Employees: 7,000
2003 Sales: $824,000	2003 Profits: $	Fiscal Year Ends: 12/31
2002 Sales: $	2002 Profits: $	Parent Company:

SALARIES/BENEFITS:

Pension Plan:	ESOP Stock Plan:	Profit Sharing:	Top Exec. Salary: $	Bonus: $
Savings Plan:	Stock Purch. Plan:		Second Exec. Salary: $	Bonus: $

OTHER THOUGHTS:

Apparent Women Officers or Directors: 7
Hot Spot for Advancement for Women/Minorities: Y

LOCATIONS: ("Y" = Yes)

West:	Southwest:	Midwest:	Southeast:	Northeast:	International:
Y	Y	Y	Y	Y	

Note: Financial information, benefits and other data can change quickly and may vary from those stated here.

GAMESTOP CORP

www.gamestop.com

Industry Group Code: 451120 **Ranks within this company's industry group:** Sales: 2 Profits: 1

Print Media/Publishing:		Movies:		Equipment/Supplies:		Broadcast/Cable:		Music/Audio:		Sports/Games:	
Newspapers:		Movie Theaters:		Equipment/Supplies:		Broadcast TV:		Music Production:		Games/Sports:	
Magazines:	Y	Movie Production:		Gambling Equipment:		Cable TV:		Retail Music:		Retail Games Stores:	Y
Books:		TV/Video Production:		Special Services:		Satellite Broadcast:		Retail Audio Equip.:		Stadiums/Teams:	
Book Stores:		Video Rental:		Advertising Services:		Radio:		Music Print./Dist.:		Gambling/Casinos:	
Distribution/Printing:		Video Distribution:		Info. Sys. Software:		Online Information:		Multimedia:		Rides/Theme Parks:	

TYPES OF BUSINESS:

Video Games-Retail
PC Software Sales
Game Accessories
Online Sales

BRANDS/DIVISIONS/AFFILIATES:

Game Informer Magazine
GameStop.com
EB Games
Electronics Boutique Holdings Corp.
GameStop Holdings Corp.
ebgames.com

CONTACTS: Note: Officers with more than one job title may be intentionally listed here more than once.

R. Richard Fontaine, CEO
Daniel A. DeMatteo, COO
Steven R. Morgan, Pres.
David W. Carlson, CFO/Exec. VP
R. Richard Fontaine, Chmn.
Ronald Freeman, Exec. VP-Dist.

Phone: 817-424-2000	**Fax:** 817-424-2062
Toll-Free: 800-883-8895	
Address: 625 Westport Pkwy., Grapevine, TX 76051 US	

GROWTH PLANS/SPECIAL FEATURES:

GameStop Corp. is one of the largest U.S. retailers of new and used video games and PC entertainment software. The company operates 4,490 retail stores in throughout the U.S., Australia, Canada and Europe, primarily under the GameStop and EB Games brands. Additionally, the company operates gamestop.com and ebgames.com, as well as publishes Game Informer, one of the largest video game magazines in the U.S. with 1.9 million subscribers. Of the 4,490 stores, the majority are located in the U.S., with only 866 stores located overseas. The stores are generally located in power strip centers and average approximately 1,500 square feet, carry a balanced mix of new and used video game hardware, video game software and accessories, as well as PC entertainment software in selected stores. The mall stores, which average approximately 1,200 square feet, carry primarily new video game products, as well as PC entertainment software and a limited selection of used video game products. The firm's used video game products provide a unique value proposition to the stores' customers, and its purchasing of video game products provides its customers with an opportunity to trade in their used video game products for store credits and apply those credits towards other merchandise, which, in turn, drives more sales. In late 2005, several Gamestop subsidiaries were merged with and into GameStop Holdings Corp. and Electronics Boutique Holdings Corp., pursuant to which these two holding companies became separate subsidiaries of GameStop Corp. All GameStop's operations are through these two companies. As a result of the merger, the number of stores operated by GameStop nearly tripled from early to late 2005.

Full-time employees receive benefits including flexible spending accounts, flexible schedules and product discounts at GameStop stores, in addition to a 401(k) savings plan, sick pay and job security.

FINANCIALS: Sales and profits are in thousands of dollars—add 000 to get the full amount. 2006 Note: Financial information for 2006 was not available for all companies at press time.

2006 Sales: $3,091,783	2006 Profits: $100,784	**U.S. Stock Ticker:** GME	
2005 Sales: $1,842,806	2005 Profits: $60,926	**Int'l Ticker:** Int'l Exchange:	
2004 Sales: $1,578,838	2004 Profits: $63,467	Employees: 32,000	
2003 Sales: $1,352,800	2003 Profits: $52,400	Fiscal Year Ends: 1/31	
2002 Sales: $1,121,100	2002 Profits: $7,000	Parent Company:	

SALARIES/BENEFITS:

Pension Plan:	ESOP Stock Plan:	Profit Sharing:	Top Exec. Salary: $643,846	Bonus: $1,110,000
Savings Plan: Y	Stock Purch. Plan:		Second Exec. Salary: $530,000	Bonus: $949,000

OTHER THOUGHTS:

Apparent Women Officers or Directors: 1
Hot Spot for Advancement for Women/Minorities:

LOCATIONS: ("Y" = Yes)

West:	Southwest:	Midwest:	Southeast:	Northeast:	International:
Y	Y	Y	Y	Y	Y

GAMETECH INTERNATIONAL INC   www.gametech-inc.com

Industry Group Code: 713290 Ranks within this company's industry group: Sales: 10 Profits: 9

Print Media/Publishing:	Movies:	Equipment/Supplies:		Broadcast/Cable:	Music/Audio:	Sports/Games:
Newspapers:	Movie Theaters:	Equipment/Supplies:		Broadcast TV:	Music Production:	Games/Sports:
Magazines:	Movie Production:	Gambling Equipment:	Y	Cable TV:	Retail Music:	Retail Games Stores:
Books:	TV/Video Production:	Special Services:	Y	Satellite Broadcast:	Retail Audio Equip.:	Stadiums/Teams:
Book Stores:	Video Rental:	Advertising Services:		Radio:	Music Print./Dist.:	Gambling/Casinos:
Distribution/Printing:	Video Distribution:	Info. Sys. Software:	Y	Online Information:	Multimedia:	Rides/Theme Parks:

TYPES OF BUSINESS:

Electronic Bingo Game Systems
Bingo Software

BRANDS/DIVISIONS/AFFILIATES:

AllTrack
AllTrack 2
Diamond
Summit Amusement & Distributing, Ltd.

CONTACTS: Note: Officers with more than one job title may be intentionally listed here more than once.

Jay Meilstrup, CEO
Jay Meilstrup, Pres.
Tracy Pearson, CFO
John McCafferty, VP-Product Mktg.
Justin K. Goodman, VP-R&D
Cole B. Wilson, General Counsel/VP
Keith P. Larkin, VP-Government Affairs
Richard T. Fedor, Chmn.

Phone: 775-850-6000	Fax: 775-850-6090
Toll-Free:	
Address: 900 Sandhill Rd., Reno, NV 89521 US	

GROWTH PLANS/SPECIAL FEATURES:

GameTech International, Inc. designs, develops and markets interactive electronic bingo terminals and systems for charitable, Native American and commercial bingo operators. The company installs both portable and fixed-base units in bingo halls in 25 out of the 47 states that allow electronic bingo. GameTech also has international operations in four countries. The company's electronic bingo units enable players to play substantially more bingo cards than possible on paper cards, typically leading to more spending per player and higher profits per session for the operator. The firm installs the electronic bingo systems, typically at no cost to the operator, and charges either a fixed fee per use per session, a fixed weekly fee per unit or a percentage of the revenue generated by each unit. GameTech typically enters into one- to three-year contracts with bingo operators. The firm has exclusive licensing rights to bingo software packages called AllTrack and AllTrack2. The AllTrack systems provide bingo operators with a package of accounting and marketing information. In addition, GameTech offers its proprietary operating system known as the Diamond system. Diamond allows bingo operators to verify when a player has legitimately won a game and whether the game was won on a card sold for the session being played. The Diamond and AllTrack systems can operate together, significantly enhancing management of a bingo hall. In 2006, the company entered into a definitive agreement to acquire Summit Amusement & Distributing, Ltd. a privately held developer and manufacturer of entertainment driven gaming devices. The company was also recently granted a license to manufacture and distribute gaming devices by the Nevada Gaming Commission.

GameTech offers its employees a range of benefits including employee assistance plans, dependent care spending accounts, educational assistance and a 401(k) savings plan.

FINANCIALS: Sales and profits are in thousands of dollars—add 000 to get the full amount. 2006 Note: Financial information for 2006 was not available for all companies at press time.

2006 Sales: $	2006 Profits: $	U.S. Stock Ticker: GMTC
2005 Sales: $49,651	2005 Profits: $1,336	Int'l Ticker: Int'l Exchange:
2004 Sales: $51,490	2004 Profits: $-9,906	Employees: 200
2003 Sales: $52,329	2003 Profits: $1,191	Fiscal Year Ends: 10/31
2002 Sales: $48,900	2002 Profits: $2,700	Parent Company:

SALARIES/BENEFITS:

Pension Plan:	ESOP Stock Plan:	Profit Sharing:	Top Exec. Salary: $193,910	Bonus: $
Savings Plan: Y	Stock Purch. Plan:		Second Exec. Salary: $155,833	Bonus: $

OTHER THOUGHTS:

Apparent Women Officers or Directors: 1
Hot Spot for Advancement for Women/Minorities:

LOCATIONS: ("Y" = Yes)

West:	Southwest:	Midwest:	Southeast:	Northeast:	International:
Y	Y	Y			

GAMING PARTNERS INTERNATIONAL CORP

www.gpigaming.com

Industry Group Code: 713290 Ranks within this company's industry group: Sales: 11   Profits: 8

Print Media/Publishing:	Movies:	Equipment/Supplies:		Broadcast/Cable:	Music/Audio:	Sports/Games:
Newspapers:	Movie Theaters:	Equipment/Supplies:		Broadcast TV:	Music Production:	Games/Sports:
Magazines:	Movie Production:	Gambling Equipment:	Y	Cable TV:	Retail Music:	Retail Games Stores:
Books:	TV/Video Production:	Special Services:	Y	Satellite Broadcast:	Retail Audio Equip.:	Stadiums/Teams:
Book Stores:	Video Rental:	Advertising Services:		Radio:	Music Print./Dist.:	Gambling/Casinos:
Distribution/Printing:	Video Distribution:	Info. Sys. Software:		Online Information:	Multimedia:	Rides/Theme Parks:

TYPES OF BUSINESS:

Casino Table Game Equipment
Gaming Furniture
Cards, Dice, Chips & Roulette Wheels
RFID-Equipped Devices

BRANDS/DIVISIONS/AFFILIATES:

Paul-Son Gaming Supplies, Inc.
Bourgogne et Grasset
Bud Jones Company (The)
GPI USA
GPI SAS
GPI Mexicana S.A. de C.V.
Air-Rail

CONTACTS: Note: Officers with more than one job title may be intentionally listed here more than once.

Gerard P. Charlier, CEO
Gerard P. Charlier, Pres.
David W. Grimes, CFO
Laura M. Cox, Chief Legal & Gaming Compliance Officer
David W. Grimes, CFO-Gaming Partners Int'l U.S.A, Inc.

Phone: 702-384-2425	Fax: 702-384-1965
Toll-Free:	
Address: 1700 Industrial Rd., Las Vegas, NV 89102 US	

GROWTH PLANS/SPECIAL FEATURES:

Gaming Partners International Corporation (GPI) manufactures gambling equipment, focusing on products such as dice, gaming chips, playing cards, layouts, plaques, roulette wheels and gaming furniture for casinos worldwide. GPI, with its headquarters in Las Vegas, was formed from the merger of Bourgogne et Grasset, The Bud Jones Company and Paul-Son Gaming Supplies, Inc. It is currently organized into two divisions, GPI USA and GPI SAS, the latter of which handles the company's international operations. The company still offers its products under the Paul-Son, Bud Jones and Bourgogne et Grasset name brands and continually tests them to ensure durability, ease of use and security. The highest-security option the company offers is an anti-counterfeiting feature for casino gaming chips using radio frequency identification devices (RFIDs). An RFID microchip is embedded in a gaming chip, allowing casinos to efficiently and securely identify each chip, its location and denomination. Since a given casino will generally purchase all of its chips from one supplier, the company focuses on acquiring contracts with newly built casinos. In addition to tables and layouts, the firm also offers table accessories such as the Air-Rail system. The Air-Rail system provides a positive flow of air at the table blowing cigar and cigarette smoke away from the dealer and helps non-smokers to contend with second-hand smoke. Small air vent devices underneath the table draw the smoke in and disperse it wherever the casino's primary ventilation systems can distribute it.

FINANCIALS: Sales and profits are in thousands of dollars—add 000 to get the full amount. 2006 Note: Financial information for 2006 was not available for all companies at press time.

2006 Sales: $	2006 Profits: $	U.S. Stock Ticker: GPIC
2005 Sales: $57,121	2005 Profits: $4,328	Int'l Ticker: Int'l Exchange:
2004 Sales: $44,585	2004 Profits: $2,614	Employees: 870
2003 Sales: $36,171	2003 Profits: $1,233	Fiscal Year Ends: 5/31
2002 Sales: $21,900	2002 Profits: $-2,200	Parent Company:

SALARIES/BENEFITS:

Pension Plan: Y	ESOP Stock Plan:	Profit Sharing:	Top Exec. Salary: $250,246	Bonus: $
Savings Plan: Y	Stock Purch. Plan:		Second Exec. Salary: $185,000	Bonus: $7,743

OTHER THOUGHTS:

Apparent Women Officers or Directors: 3
Hot Spot for Advancement for Women/Minorities: Y

LOCATIONS: ("Y" = Yes)

West:	Southwest:	Midwest:	Southeast:	Northeast:	International:
Y					Y

Note: Financial information, benefits and other data can change quickly and may vary from those stated here.

GANNETT CO INC

www.gannett.com

Industry Group Code: 511110 Ranks within this company's industry group: Sales: 2 Profits: 1

Print Media/Publishing:		Movies:		Equipment/Supplies:		Broadcast/Cable:		Music/Audio:		Sports/Games:	
Newspapers:	Y	Movie Theaters:		Equipment/Supplies:		Broadcast TV:	Y	Music Production:		Games/Sports:	
Magazines:	Y	Movie Production:		Gambling Equipment:		Cable TV:	Y	Retail Music:		Retail Games Stores:	
Books:		TV/Video Production:		Special Services:	Y	Satellite Broadcast:		Retail Audio Equip.:		Stadiums/Teams:	
Book Stores:		Video Rental:		Advertising Services:	Y	Radio:		Music Print./Dist.:		Gambling/Casinos:	
Distribution/Printing:		Video Distribution:		Info. Sys. Software:		Online Information:		Multimedia:		Rides/Theme Parks:	

TYPES OF BUSINESS:

Newspaper Publishing
Broadcast & Cable Television
Radio Broadcasting
Electronic Information Services
Magazine Publishing
Online Publishing
Direct Marketing

BRANDS/DIVISIONS/AFFILIATES:

USA TODAY
USA WEEKEND
Newsquest
Gannett News Service
Gannett Offset
Clipper
Captivate
PointRoll, Inc.

CONTACTS: *Note: Officers with more than one job title may be intentionally listed here more than once.*

Craig A. Dubow, CEO
Craig A. Dubow, Pres.
Gracia C. Martore, CFO/Sr. VP
Roxanne V. Horning, VP-Human Resources
Thomas L. Chapple, Chief Admin. Officer/Sr. VP
Kurt Wimmer, Sr. VP/General Counsel
Daniel S. Ehrman, Jr., VP-Planning & Dev.
Tara J. Connell, VP-Corp. Comm.
John B. Jaske, Sr. VP-Labor Rel.
George R. Gavagan, VP/Treas.
Michael A. Hart, VP/Treas.
Craig A. Moon, Publisher/Pres., USA TODAY
Robert B. Oliver,, VP-Compensation & Benefits
Sue Clark-Johnson, Pres., Newspaper Div.
Craig A. Dubow, Chmn.

Phone: 703-854-6000	Fax: 703-364-0855
Toll-Free: 800-778-3299	
Address: 7950 Jones Branch Dr., McLean, VA 22107 US	

GROWTH PLANS/SPECIAL FEATURES:

Gannett Co., Inc. is a diversified news and information company that serves audiences through publishing, television and the Internet. As the largest newspaper group in the U.S., the company publishes 99 daily newspapers including USA TODAY, the nation's largest-selling daily, combining for an average daily U.S. circulation of 7.6 million. Gannett also owns hundreds of non-daily and specialty U.S. publications, chief among them being USA WEEKEND, a weekly newspaper magazine with a circulation of 22.7 million delivered in nearly 600 Gannett and non-Gannett Sunday newspapers. Based in Virginia, Gannett's operations encompass 41 States, the District of Columbia, the U.K., Guam, Belgium, Germany and Hong Kong. Gannett additionally owns and operates 22 television stations, covering over 17% of the U.S., and operates over 130 web sites in the U.S. and U.K., including USATODAY.com. Other company operations include Gannett News Service and Captivate, which delivers advertising and program content via television screens installed in elevators in premier American office complexes. The company additionally utilizes its resources for extended services through divisions including Gannett Retail Advertising Group, Gannett Direct Marketing Services, Gannett Offset commercial printing, Gannett Media Technologies, Clipper direct-mail advertising and database marketing company Telematch. In 2005, Gannett acquired HomeTown Communications Network, Inc., a community publishing company with publications in Michigan, Ohio and Kentucky; and purchased The Detroit Free Press from Knight Ridder. The company also recently acquired the stock of PointRoll, Inc. and a 25% stake of Topix.net. Specialty publications include coupon-filled shoppers, Spanish-language papers and free, weekly community tabloids. Combined with the firm's powerful web sites, these publications give the firm deep advertising penetration into consumers who are not frequent readers of traditional daily newspapers.

FINANCIALS: Sales and profits are in thousands of dollars—add 000 to get the full amount. 2006 Note: Financial information for 2006 was not available for all companies at press time.

2006 Sales: $	2006 Profits: $	U.S. Stock Ticker: GCI
2005 Sales: $7,598,939	2005 Profits: $1,244,654	Int'l Ticker: Int'l Exchange:
2004 Sales: $7,283,662	2004 Profits: $1,317,186	Employees: 52,600
2003 Sales: $6,711,115	2003 Profits: $1,211,213	Fiscal Year Ends: 12/31
2002 Sales: $6,422,000	2002 Profits: $1,160,000	Parent Company:

SALARIES/BENEFITS:

Pension Plan:	ESOP Stock Plan:	Profit Sharing:	Top Exec. Salary: $1,600,000	Bonus: $2,350,000
Savings Plan: Y	Stock Purch. Plan:		Second Exec. Salary: $780,625	Bonus: $1,200,000

OTHER THOUGHTS:

Apparent Women Officers or Directors: 4
Hot Spot for Advancement for Women/Minorities: Y

LOCATIONS: ("Y" = Yes)

West:	Southwest:	Midwest:	Southeast:	Northeast:	International:
Y	Y	Y	Y	Y	Y

Note: Financial information, benefits and other data can change quickly and may vary from those stated here.

GAYLORD ENTERTAINMENT CO
www.gaylordentertainment.com

Industry Group Code: 721110 Ranks within this company's industry group: Sales: 1 Profits: 1

Print Media/Publishing:	Movies:	Equipment/Supplies:		Broadcast/Cable:	Music/Audio:	Sports/Games:	
Newspapers:	Movie Theaters:	Equipment/Supplies:		Broadcast TV:	Music Production:	Games/Sports:	
Magazines:	Movie Production:	Gambling Equipment:		Cable TV:	Retail Music:	Retail Games Stores:	
Books:	TV/Video Production:	Special Services:	Y	Satellite Broadcast:	Retail Audio Equip.:	Stadiums/Teams:	Y
Book Stores:	Video Rental:	Advertising Services:		Radio:	Music Print./Dist.:	Gambling/Casinos:	Y
Distribution/Printing:	Video Distribution:	Info. Sys. Software:		Online Information:	Multimedia:	Rides/Theme Parks:	

TYPES OF BUSINESS:

Hotels & Convention Centers
Vacation Property Management
Live Entertainment Venues
Online Vacation Rental Booking
Radio Station Operation
Golf Courses
Theme Parks

BRANDS/DIVISIONS/AFFILIATES:

ResortQuest International
Grand Ole Opry
Ryman Auditorium
General Jackson Showboat
Wildhorse Saloon
Gaylord Opryland Resort & Convention Center
Gaylord Palms Resort & Convention Center
Gaylord Texan Resort & Convention Center

CONTACTS: Note: Officers with more than one job title may be intentionally listed here more than once.

Colin V. Reed, CEO
Colin V. Reed, Pres.
David C. Kloeppel, Exec. VP/CFO
Melissa J. Buffington, Sr. VP-Human Resources
Rich Maradik, CIO
Carter R. Todd, General Counsel
Melissa J. Buffington, Sr. VP-Comm.
Mark Fioravanti, Pres., ResortQuest/Exec. VP
John Caparella, COO-Gaylord Hotels
John Imaizumi, Sr. VP/General Mgr.-Gaylord Texan Resort
Stephen Buchanan, Sr. VP-Media & Entertainment
Colin V. Reed, Chmn.

Phone: 615-316-6000	Fax: 615-316-6555
Toll-Free:	
Address: One Gaylord Dr., Nashville, TN 37214 US	

GROWTH PLANS/SPECIAL FEATURES:

Gaylord Entertainment Company owns and operates diversified hospitality businesses and attractions in four principal business segments: hospitality, ResortQuest, Opry and attractions and corporate. The hotel segment creates 90% of the firm's revenues, and manages the company's hotels including the Gaylord Opryland Resort in Nashville; the Gaylord Palms Resort in Kissimmee, Florida; the Gaylord Texan Resort in Grapevine, Texas; and the Gaylord National Resort in Prince George's County, Maryland. Each of the firm's resorts is designed to accommodate corporate meetings and events. The ResortQuest division is the one of the U.S.'s leading vacation property management companies and a major online provider of reservations for vacation home rentals, providing management services to around 16,000 properties. The majority of these homes are second or vacation homes open to rental during off-seasons. The firm's Opry and attractions group operates country radio station WSM-AM radio; the General Jackson Showboat; the Gaylord Springs Golf Links, a championship golf course; and live music venues such as the Grand Ole Opry, the Ryman Auditorium and the Wildhorse Saloon. These attractions are located on the firm's Opry Complex property in Nashville, Tennessee. Gaylord's corporate segment includes a minority ownership interest the Bass Pro Shops' Outdoor World retail chain and an investment in Viacom and the Nashville Predators hockey team. In April 2005, the company announced its agreement to purchase the Aston Waikiki Beach Hotel in Honolulu, Hawaii. The firm said that it expected to bring in a partner that will own the majority interest in the property. To that end, the company announced in May 2005 that it would sell 80.1% of the ownership interest in the hotel to DB Real Estate Opportunities Group, while also entering into a long-term management agreement calling for ResortQuest to manage the property.

Gaylord Entertainment Company believes in promoting from within the company and provides training through its Gaylord University.

FINANCIALS: Sales and profits are in thousands of dollars—add 000 to get the full amount. 2006 Note: Financial information for 2006 was not available for all companies at press time.

2006 Sales: $	2006 Profits: $	U.S. Stock Ticker: GET
2005 Sales: $868,789	2005 Profits: $21,033	Int'l Ticker: Int'l Exchange:
2004 Sales: $730,827	2004 Profits: $-13,932	Employees: 8,649
2003 Sales: $448,800	2003 Profits: $ 900	Fiscal Year Ends: 12/31
2002 Sales: $414,400	2002 Profits: $95,200	Parent Company:

SALARIES/BENEFITS:

Pension Plan: Y	ESOP Stock Plan:	Profit Sharing:	Top Exec. Salary: $715,705	Bonus: $780,457
Savings Plan:	Stock Purch. Plan: Y		Second Exec. Salary: $460,160	Bonus: $333,542

OTHER THOUGHTS:

Apparent Women Officers or Directors: 1
Hot Spot for Advancement for Women/Minorities:

LOCATIONS: ("Y" = Yes)

West:	Southwest:	Midwest:	Southeast:	Northeast:	International:
Y	Y		Y		

Note: Financial information, benefits and other data can change quickly and may vary from those stated here.

GEMSTAR-TV GUIDE INTERNATIONAL INC

www.gemstartvguide.com

Industry Group Code: 514199 Ranks within this company's industry group: Sales: 1 Profits: 2

Print Media/Publishing:		Movies:		Equipment/Supplies:		Broadcast/Cable:		Music/Audio:		Sports/Games:	
Newspapers:		Movie Theaters:		Equipment/Supplies:		Broadcast TV:		Music Production:		Games/Sports:	
Magazines:	Y	Movie Production:		Gambling Equipment:		Cable TV:		Retail Music:		Retail Games Stores:	
Books:		TV/Video Production:		Special Services:	Y	Satellite Broadcast:		Retail Audio Equip.:		Stadiums/Teams:	
Book Stores:		Video Rental:		Advertising Services:	Y	Radio:		Music Print./Dist.:		Gambling/Casinos:	
Distribution/Printing:		Video Distribution:		Info. Sys. Software:		Online Information:		Multimedia:		Rides/Theme Parks:	

TYPES OF BUSINESS:

Online Information Service-TV Listings
Magazine & Catalog Publishing
Online Publishing
Electronic Book Publishing
Satellite Broadcast Services
Program Promotion & Guide Services
Interactive Information Delivery Services

BRANDS/DIVISIONS/AFFILIATES:

TV Guide
Gemstar International Group, Ltd.
TV Guide Magazine
TV Guide Channel
TVG Network
TV Guide Online
TV Guide Interactive
jumptheshark.com

CONTACTS: *Note: Officers with more than one job title may be intentionally listed here more than once.*

Richard Battista, CEO
Mike McKee, COO
Bedi A. Singh, CFO
Alan Cohen, Chief Mktg. Officer/Exec. VP
Dustin Finer, Sr. VP-Human Resources
Steve Shannon, Exec. VP-Product Dev.
Stephen H. Kay, General Counsel/Exec. VP
Sanjay Reddy, Sr. VP-Bus. Dev. & Strategic Planning
Peter Halt, Chief Acct. Officer
J. Scott Crystal, Pres., TV Guide Publishing Group
Ryan O'Hara, Pres., TV Guide Channel & TV Guide SPOT
Richard Cusik, Sr. VP/Gen. Mgr.-Digital Media
Mike McKee, Pres., Interactive Program Guides
Anthea Disney, Chmn.

Phone: 323-817-4600	Fax: 323-817-4673
Toll-Free:	
Address: 6922 Hollywood Blvd., 12th Fl., Los Angeles, CA 90028 US	

GROWTH PLANS/SPECIAL FEATURES:

Gemstar-TV Guide International, Inc. is a media, entertainment and technology company that develops, licenses, markets and distributes technologies and services for television guidance to meet the needs of television viewers worldwide. The best-known brand of the company is the TV Guide brand. Through TV Guide Magazine, TV Guide Channel, TV Guide Online and North American TV Guide IPG, the company reaches more than 70 million viewers per week. The company is organized into four business segments: publishing, cable and satellite, consumer electronic licensing and corporate. The publishing segment consists of TV Guide Magazine, TV Guide Online, TV Guide Merchandise Licensing and the TV Guide Data Solutions. TV Guide Magazine's weekly circulation tops 4.5 million copies and TV Guide Online reaches more than 3 million users per month with 14 day customizable television program listings. The cable and satellite segment consists primarily of TV Guide Channel, TV Guide Interactive, TV Guide International and TVG Network. TV Guide Channel offers information on programs, celebrities and trends in television as well as program listings and descriptions. TV Guide Interactive licenses technologies and services to cable ad satellite service providers primarily in the U.S. and provides them with operational support, content and data. The TVG Network provides localized listings to the firm's data licensees in all 210 U.S. media markets. The consumer electronics licensing division licenses the firm's proprietary technologies to various consumer electronics manufacturers. The corporate segment represents all centralized functions such as corporate management, corporate legal and corporate finance. The company's SkyMall business was sold in late 2005, and in June 2006 the company acquired entertainment website jumptheshark.com and related assets from Jump the Shark, Inc.

FINANCIALS: Sales and profits are in thousands of dollars—add 000 to get the full amount. 2006 Note: Financial information for 2006 was not available for all companies at press time.

2006 Sales: $	2006 Profits: $	U.S. Stock Ticker: GMST
2005 Sales: $604,192	2005 Profits: $54,815	Int'l Ticker: Int'l Exchange:
2004 Sales: $676,369	2004 Profits: $-94,461	Employees: 1,780
2003 Sales: $878,700	2003 Profits: $-577,400	Fiscal Year Ends: 12/31
2002 Sales: $1,001,391	2002 Profits: $-6,423,175	Parent Company:

SALARIES/BENEFITS:

Pension Plan:	ESOP Stock Plan:	Profit Sharing:	Top Exec. Salary: $850,000	Bonus: $496,496
Savings Plan: Y	Stock Purch. Plan: Y		Second Exec. Salary: $624,318	Bonus: $281,279

OTHER THOUGHTS:

Apparent Women Officers or Directors: 4
Hot Spot for Advancement for Women/Minorities: Y

LOCATIONS: ("Y" = Yes)

West:	Southwest:	Midwest:	Southeast:	Northeast:	International:
Y	Y	Y		Y	Y

GENERAL ELECTRIC CO (GE)

www.ge.com

Industry Group Code: 522220A Ranks within this company's industry group: Sales: 1 Profits: 1

Print Media/Publishing:	Movies:		Equipment/Supplies:		Broadcast/Cable:		Music/Audio:		Sports/Games:	
Newspapers:	Movie Theaters:		Equipment/Supplies:	Y	Broadcast TV:	Y	Music Production:		Games/Sports:	
Magazines:	Movie Production:	Y	Gambling Equipment:		Cable TV:	Y	Retail Music:		Retail Games Stores:	
Books:	TV/Video Production:	Y	Special Services:		Satellite Broadcast:		Retail Audio Equip.:		Stadiums/Teams:	
Book Stores:	Video Rental:		Advertising Services:		Radio:		Music Print./Dist.:	Y	Gambling/Casinos:	
Distribution/Printing:	Video Distribution:		Info. Sys. Software:	Y	Online Information:		Multimedia:		Rides/Theme Parks:	Y

TYPES OF BUSINESS:

Business Leasing & Finance/Consumer Finance
Energy Systems & Consulting
Insurance Underwriting & Financial Services
Industrial & Electrical Equipment & Consumer Products
Entertainment & Broadcast Television
Real Estate Investments & Finance
Medical Equipment & Systems
Transportation, Aircraft Engines, Rail Systems & Truck Fleet Management

BRANDS/DIVISIONS/AFFILIATES:

GE Commercial Finance
GE Consumer Finance
GE Healthcare
NBC Universal, Inc.
GE Plastics
ZENON Evironmental, Inc.
GE Money

CONTACTS:
Note: Officers with more than one job title may be intentionally listed here more than once.

Jeffrey R. Immelt, CEO
Keith S. Sherin, CFO
Dan Henson, Chief Mktg. Officer/VP
William J. Conaty, Sr. VP-Corp. Human Resources
Gary M. Reiner, CIO/Sr. VP
Brackett B. Denniston, III, General Counsel/Sr. VP
Lloyd G. Trotter, Exec. VP-Oper.
Pamela Daley, Sr. VP-Corp. Bus. Dev.
Ben W. Heineman, Jr., Sr. VP-Public Affairs & Law
Keith S. Sherin, Sr. VP-Finance
Charlene Begley, CEO/Pres.-GE Plastics
Joseph M. Hogan, CEO/Pres., GE Healthcare
John Krenicki, Jr., CEO/Pres., GE Energy
Richard Laxer, CEO/Pres., GE Capital Solutions
Jeffrey R. Immelt, Chmn.
Ferdinando Beccalli-Falco, CEO/Pres., Int'l

Phone: 203-373-2211	Fax: 203-373-3131
Toll-Free:	
Address: 3135 Easton Tnpk., Fairfield, CT 06828-0001 US	

GROWTH PLANS/SPECIAL FEATURES:

General Electric Company (GE) is one of the world's largest and most diversified corporations, with six operating divisions: infrastructure, industrial, healthcare, NBC Universal, commercial finance and consumer finance. The company's products include appliances, lighting products, industrial automation products, medical imaging equipment, motors, electrical distribution and control equipment, locomotives, power generation and delivery products, nuclear power support services and fuel assemblies, jet engines, engineered materials and chemicals. The infrastructure division, the largest of the operating segments produces, sells, finances and services equipment for the air and rail transportation, water treatment and energy generation businesses. The healthcare segment develops diagnostic and therapy equipment including magnetic resonance imaging (MRI) scanners, computed tomography (CT) scanners, x-ray, nuclear imaging and ultrasound equipment. Services provided by this section include computerized data management and consumer productivity services. NBC Universal, the company's network television affiliate, is engaged in broadcasting to affiliated television stations within the U.S., the production of live and recorded television programs, operating television broadcasting stations and the production and distribution of motion pictures. The commercial finance segment offers a broad range of financial services mainly to manufacturers, distributors and end-users including loans and leases. The consumer finance segment offers credit and deposit products to consumers, retailers, banks and auto dealers in over 50 countries. In February 2006, the company announced that Canadian subsidiary GE Money will acquire the credit card and related financial services assets of Hudson's Bay Company. In March 2006, the company agreed to acquire ZENON Environmental, Inc., a leader in advanced membranes for water purification and wastewater treatment. Later in 2006, the company agreed to sell its silicone and quartz business for $3.4 billion to Apollo Management, LP. In November 2006, it agreed to combine its nuclear power business with that of Hitachi Ltd. The joint venture will have operations primarily in Japan and the U.S.

GE provides its employees with: Tuition, adoption, parenting and child care assistance; Education and career counseling; and Legal and financial information services.

FINANCIALS:
Sales and profits are in thousands of dollars—add 000 to get the full amount. 2006 Note: Financial information for 2006 was not available for all companies at press time.

2006 Sales: $	2006 Profits: $	**U.S. Stock Ticker: GE**
2005 Sales: $149,702,000	2005 Profits: $18,275,000	**Int'l Ticker:** Int'l Exchange:
2004 Sales: $134,481,000	2004 Profits: $16,285,000	Employees: 316,000
2003 Sales: $134,187,000	2003 Profits: $15,002,000	Fiscal Year Ends: 12/31
2002 Sales: $130,685,000	2002 Profits: $14,118,000	Parent Company:

SALARIES/BENEFITS:

Pension Plan:	ESOP Stock Plan:	Profit Sharing:	Top Exec. Salary: $3,225,000	Bonus: $
Savings Plan: Y	Stock Purch. Plan:		Second Exec. Salary: $2,500,000	Bonus: $6,270,000

OTHER THOUGHTS:

Apparent Women Officers or Directors: 8
Hot Spot for Advancement for Women/Minorities: Y

LOCATIONS: ("Y" = Yes)

West:	Southwest:	Midwest:	Southeast:	Northeast:	International:
Y	Y	Y	Y	Y	Y

Note: Financial information, benefits and other data can change quickly and may vary from those stated here.

GETTY IMAGES INC

www.gettyimages.com

Industry Group Code: 453990 Ranks within this company's industry group: Sales: 1   Profits: 1

Print Media/Publishing:	Movies:	Equipment/Supplies:		Broadcast/Cable:	Music/Audio:	Sports/Games:
Newspapers:	Movie Theaters:	Equipment/Supplies:		Broadcast TV:	Music Production:	Games/Sports:
Magazines:	Movie Production:	Gambling Equipment:		Cable TV:	Retail Music:	Retail Games Stores:
Books:	TV/Video Production:	Special Services:	Y	Satellite Broadcast:	Retail Audio Equip.:	Stadiums/Teams:
Book Stores:	Video Rental:	Advertising Services:	Y	Radio:	Music Print./Dist.:	Gambling/Casinos:
Distribution/Printing:	Video Distribution:	Info. Sys. Software:		Online Information:	Multimedia:	Rides/Theme Parks:

TYPES OF BUSINESS:

Imagery & Footage
Imagery Products & Services
Archival Film & Stills
Royalty-Free Visual & Audio Content
Stock Photography
Illustrations
Custom Photography

BRANDS/DIVISIONS/AFFILIATES:

Allsport Concepts
Photodisc
Photographer's Choice
Archive Films
Getty Images Editorial
Photonica
Pixel Images Holdings Limited
Stockdisc

CONTACTS: *Note: Officers with more than one job title may be intentionally listed here more than once.*

Jonathan Klein, CEO
Thomas Oberdorf, CFO/Sr. VP
Jack Sansolo, Sr. VP/Chief Mktg. Officer
Jim Gurke, Sr. VP-Human Resources
Jeff Beyle, General Counsel/Sr. VP
Michael Teaster, Sr. VP-Bus. Dev.
Nicholas Evans-Lombe, Sr. VP-Imagery & Svcs.
Linda Ranz, Sr. VP-Customer Experience
Mark Getty, Chmn.
Bo Olofsson, Sr. VP-Global Sales

Phone: 206-925-5000	Fax: 206-925-5001
Toll-Free:	
Address: 601 N. 34th St., Seattle, WA 98103 US	

GROWTH PLANS/SPECIAL FEATURES:

Getty Images, Inc. is a world-leading provider of imagery and related products and services to businesses worldwide. The firm delivers its products digitally via the Internet and CD-ROMs. In addition, products are sold through a global network of distributors serving customers in approximately 100 countries. Customers include creative professionals at advertising agencies and graphic design firms; press and editorial customers involved in newspaper, magazine, book, CD-ROM and online publishing; corporate communications departments and other business customers; and customers requiring moving imagery, such as filmmakers, television advertisers and producers of promotional videos. A variety of visual content products are offered, including stock imagery (both still and moving images), editorial photography, archival imagery (both still and moving), illustrations and related products and services. Imagery is offered to customers through the company's creative photography collections and the collections of other imagery providers, such as Digital Vision, National Geographic and Time Life Pictures. The company's subsidiaries presiding over themed image selections include Allsport Concepts, Photodisc, Photographer's Choice and Stone; those that carry film collections include Archive Films and Digital Vision; subsidiaries in editorial images include Getty Images Editorial and Hulton/Archive. In addition, Getty offers turnkey assignment services for custom photography projects such as photographing executives for annual reports, producing product shots for brochures or documenting news events. Getty operates locations in Seattle, Los Angeles, Chicago, New York, London, Paris, Hamburg, Munich, Dublin, Barcelona, Amsterdam, Sydney, Hong Kong, Singapore and Tokyo. In April 2006, the company acquired Pixel Images Holdings Limited and its Stockbyte and Stockdisc collections. In August 2006, Getty added three major film collections to its roster: American Bandstand, Discover FootageSource and AP Archive.

Getty offers its employees benefits including medical and other insurance coverage, educational assistance, incentive bonuses, tax-free reimbursement accounts and a 401(k) plan.

FINANCIALS: Sales and profits are in thousands of dollars—add 000 to get the full amount. 2006 Note: Financial information for 2006 was not available for all companies at press time.

2006 Sales: $	2006 Profits: $	U.S. Stock Ticker: GYI
2005 Sales: $733,729	2005 Profits: $149,703	Int'l Ticker: Int'l Exchange:
2004 Sales: $622,400	2004 Profits: $106,700	Employees: 1,823
2003 Sales: $523,196	2003 Profits: $64,017	Fiscal Year Ends: 12/31
2002 Sales: $463,000	2002 Profits: $21,500	Parent Company:

SALARIES/BENEFITS:

Pension Plan:	ESOP Stock Plan:	Profit Sharing:	Top Exec. Salary: $950,000	Bonus: $691,600
Savings Plan: Y	Stock Purch. Plan:		Second Exec. Salary: $392,500	Bonus: $208,000

OTHER THOUGHTS:

Apparent Women Officers or Directors: 1
Hot Spot for Advancement for Women/Minorities:

LOCATIONS: ("Y" = Yes)

West:	Southwest:	Midwest:	Southeast:	Northeast:	International:
Y		Y		Y	Y

GLU MOBILE

www.glu.com

Industry Group Code: 511208 Ranks within this company's industry group: Sales: Profits:

Print Media/Publishing:	Movies:	Equipment/Supplies:	Broadcast/Cable:	Music/Audio:	Sports/Games:	
Newspapers:	Movie Theaters:	Equipment/Supplies:	Broadcast TV:	Music Production:	Games/Sports:	Y
Magazines:	Movie Production:	Gambling Equipment:	Cable TV:	Retail Music:	Retail Games Stores:	
Books:	TV/Video Production:	Special Services:	Satellite Broadcast:	Retail Audio Equip.:	Stadiums/Teams:	
Book Stores:	Video Rental:	Advertising Services:	Radio:	Music Print./Dist.:	Gambling/Casinos:	
Distribution/Printing:	Video Distribution:	Info. Sys. Software:	Online Information:	Multimedia:	Rides/Theme Parks:	

TYPES OF BUSINESS:

Mobile Entertainment Applications
Mobile Phone Games
Ringtones

BRANDS/DIVISIONS/AFFILIATES:

Sorrent, Inc.
Macrospace, Ltd.
ProvisionX
Daily Puzzle
Fox Sports Mobile Pro
Flintstones Bedrock Bowling
World Series of Poker Texas Hold'em
iFone

CONTACTS: *Note: Officers with more than one job title may be intentionally listed here more than once.*

Greg Ballard, CEO
Greg Ballard, Pres.
Rocky Pimintel, Exec. VP/CFO
Jill Braff, Sr. VP-Worldwide Mktg.
Alex Galvagni, Chief Tech. Officer
Alex Galvagni, Sr. VP-Eng.
Paul Zuzelo, Chief Admin. Officer
Robert Hayes, VP-Corp. Dev.
Eric Ludwig, VP-Finance
Robert Nashak, Chief Creative Officer
Greg Suarez, VP-Licensing
Beth Doherty, VP-North American Sales
David Ward, Chmn.
Shukri Shammas, VP-Oper., EMEA

Phone: 650-571-1550	**Fax:** 650-571-5698
Toll-Free:	
Address: 1800 Gateway Dr., 2nd Fl., San Mateo, CA 94404 US	

GROWTH PLANS/SPECIAL FEATURES:

Glu Mobile, formed in June 2005 by the merger of Sorrent, Inc. and Macrospace, Ltd., is a developer and publisher of mobile entertainment applications, including games, ringtones, wallpapers and information apps. The company's selection of titles includes original ones and those licensed from major brands including Atari, Cartoon Network, FOX Sports Interactive, Hasbro, PopCap Games, Twentieth Century Fox and Celador International. Glu Mobile's games include Aqua Teen Hunger Force Destruc-o-Thon, The Flintstones Bedrock Bowling, Manchester United Football, Baldur's Gate and World Series of Poker Texas Hold'em. Some of GLU Mobile's other applications are its Daily Puzzle and Fox Sports Mobile Pro. The company's applications are available to over 800 million mobile subscribers through 90 international carriers. Glu offers a mobile gaming sourcing, management and delivery solution called ProvisionX, whose catalog includes over 200 titles tested for over 100 mobile devices. In April 2006, GLU Mobile acquired iFone, a wireless entertainment publisher based in Manchester, U.K. In May 2006, the company announced that it would partner with Microsoft to develop and publish a mobile edition of Project Gotham Racing.

FINANCIALS: Sales and profits are in thousands of dollars—add 000 to get the full amount. 2006 Note: Financial information for 2006 was not available for all companies at press time.

2006 Sales: $	2006 Profits: $	**U.S. Stock Ticker: Private**
2005 Sales: $	2005 Profits: $	**Int'l Ticker:** Int'l Exchange:
2004 Sales: $	2004 Profits: $	Employees:
2003 Sales: $	2003 Profits: $	Fiscal Year Ends: 12/31
2002 Sales: $	2002 Profits: $	Parent Company:

SALARIES/BENEFITS:

Pension Plan:	ESOP Stock Plan:	Profit Sharing:	Top Exec. Salary: $	Bonus: $
Savings Plan:	Stock Purch. Plan:		Second Exec. Salary: $	Bonus: $

OTHER THOUGHTS:

Apparent Women Officers or Directors: 2
Hot Spot for Advancement for Women/Minorities:

LOCATIONS: ("Y" = Yes)

West:	Southwest:	Midwest:	Southeast:	Northeast:	International:
Y					Y

GOLD'S GYM INTERNATIONAL

www.goldsgym.com

Industry Group Code: 713940 Ranks within this company's industry group: Sales: Profits:

Print Media/Publishing:	Movies:	Equipment/Supplies:	Broadcast/Cable:	Music/Audio:	Sports/Games:	
Newspapers:	Movie Theaters:	Equipment/Supplies:	Broadcast TV:	Music Production:	Games/Sports:	Y
Magazines:	Movie Production:	Gambling Equipment:	Cable TV:	Retail Music:	Retail Games Stores:	
Books:	TV/Video Production:	Special Services:	Satellite Broadcast:	Retail Audio Equip.:	Stadiums/Teams:	
Book Stores:	Video Rental:	Advertising Services:	Radio:	Music Print./Dist.:	Gambling/Casinos:	
Distribution/Printing:	Video Distribution:	Info. Sys. Software:	Online Information:	Multimedia:	Rides/Theme Parks:	

TYPES OF BUSINESS:

Fitness Centers

BRANDS/DIVISIONS/AFFILIATES:

TRT Holdings, Inc.

GROWTH PLANS/SPECIAL FEATURES:

Gold's Gym International, a subsidiary of TRT Holdings, Inc., is one of the largest co-ed gym chains in the world. With 3 million members, Gold's Gym has over 610 franchised gyms in 41 states and in 28 countries, including the U.K., Canada, Australia, Mexico, Peru, the Virgin Islands, Japan, India, Germany and Russia. Members of Gold's not only have access to what are recognized as the industry's leading gyms, but they can also work with personal trainers to devise meal plans and develop weight programs. Gold's Gym works with other companies in the health and fitness industry by offering flexible advertising campaigns, sponsorships and promotional opportunities within its gyms. Each gym offers all of the latest equipment and services, including group exercise classes, cardiovascular equipment, spinning, pilates and yoga, while maintaining its core weight lifting tradition.

CONTACTS: Note: Officers with more than one job title may be intentionally listed here more than once.

David Schnabel, CEO
Randy Schultz, CFO
Joel Tallman, VP-Oper.
Dave Reisman, Media Contact
Joel Tallman, VP-Franchising
Terrell T. Philen, Chmn.

Phone: 214-574-4653	Fax: 214-296-5000
Toll-Free: 800-457-5375	
Address: 125 E. John Carpenter FWY, Ste. 1300, Irving, TX 75062 US	

FINANCIALS: Sales and profits are in thousands of dollars—add 000 to get the full amount. 2006 Note: Financial information for 2006 was not available for all companies at press time.

2006 Sales: $	2006 Profits: $	U.S. Stock Ticker: Private
2005 Sales: $	2005 Profits: $	Int'l Ticker: Int'l Exchange:
2004 Sales: $	2004 Profits: $	Employees:
2003 Sales: $	2003 Profits: $	Fiscal Year Ends: 2/28
2002 Sales: $	2002 Profits: $	Parent Company:

SALARIES/BENEFITS:

Pension Plan:	ESOP Stock Plan:	Profit Sharing:	Top Exec. Salary: $	Bonus: $
Savings Plan:	Stock Purch. Plan:		Second Exec. Salary: $	Bonus: $

OTHER THOUGHTS:

Apparent Women Officers or Directors:
Hot Spot for Advancement for Women/Minorities:

LOCATIONS: ("Y" = Yes)

West:	Southwest:	Midwest:	Southeast:	Northeast:	International:
Y	Y	Y	Y	Y	Y

GOOGLE INC   www.google.com

Industry Group Code: 514199B **Ranks within this company's industry group:** Sales: 1   Profits: 2

Print Media/Publishing:	Movies:	Equipment/Supplies:		Broadcast/Cable:	Music/Audio:	Sports/Games:
Newspapers:	Movie Theaters:	Equipment/Supplies:		Broadcast TV:	Music Production:	Games/Sports:
Magazines:	Movie Production:	Gambling Equipment:		Cable TV:	Retail Music:	Retail Games Stores:
Books:	TV/Video Production:	Special Services:	Y	Satellite Broadcast:	Retail Audio Equip.:	Stadiums/Teams:
Book Stores:	Video Rental:	Advertising Services:	Y	Radio:	Music Print./Dist.:	Gambling/Casinos:
Distribution/Printing:	Video Distribution:	Info. Sys. Software:		Online Information:	Multimedia:	Rides/Theme Parks:

TYPES OF BUSINESS:

Search Engine-Internet
Paid Search Listing Advertising Services
News Site Search Service
Catalog Search Service
Shopping Site
Web Log Tool

BRANDS/DIVISIONS/AFFILIATES:

Google
Google AdWords
Google AdSense
Froogle
Google Earth
Google Scholar
Blogger
Gmail

CONTACTS: *Note: Officers with more than one job title may be intentionally listed here more than once.*

Eric E. Schmidt, CEO
George Reyes, CFO/Sr. VP
Omid Kordestani, Sr. VP-Worldwide Sales/Field Oper.
Alan Eustace, Sr. VP-Research
Sergey Brin, Co-Founder/Pres., Tech.
Jonathan Rosenberg, VP-Prod. Mgmt.
Alan Eustace, Sr. VP-Eng.
David C. Drummond, General Counsel/Corp. Sec.
Shona Brown, VP-Bus. Oper.
David C. Drummond, VP-Corp. Dev.
Elliot Schrage, VP-Global Comm. & Public Affairs
Larry Page, Co-Founder/Pres., Products
W. M. Coughran, Jr., VP-Eng.
Urs Holzle, Sr. VP-Oper. & Google Fellow
Jeff Huber, VP-Eng.
Eric E. Schmidt, Chmn.

Phone: 650-623-4000	Fax: 650-618-1499
Toll-Free:	
Address: 1600 Amphitheatre Pkwy., Mountain View, CA 94043 US	

GROWTH PLANS/SPECIAL FEATURES:

Google, Inc. operates Google.com, the world's largest and most used search engine. Its system indexes the content of over 8 billion pages on the World Wide Web. While Google charges nothing for its search service, it charges fees to other sites that use its search technology, and has a lucrative program that enables business clients to bid for ad space. Google has thousands of advertising clients. The Google system receives more than 200 million searches daily from consumers worldwide. More than 50% of its searches come from consumers outside the U.S., and Google provides unique web formats in 88 different languages to accommodate foreign users. The company's technology employs a unique, distributed-computing system utilizing thousands of low-end servers rather than a small number of high-powered computers. Google has teamed with the libraries of Harvard, Stanford, the Universities of Michigan and Oxford and The New York Public Library to digitally scan books in their collections in order to make them searchable online. The company also offers Google AdWords, a global advertising program enabling advertisers to present ads to customers just when they are looking for what the advertiser has to offer. Google AdSense is a program that allows web sites in the Google Network to serve targeted ads from the AdWords advertisers. In August 2006, Google won in a fierce, four-way contest for the right to provide search technology to News Corp-owned Internet mega-site MySpace.com. Under the terms of the agreement, Google promises to pay the media giant a minimum of $900 million in cash between 2007 and the second quarter of 2010.

Employee perks include employee assistance, adoption assistance, flexible hours, child care and free lunches and dinners on-site. Many Google offices have recreation facilities with workout rooms, laundry, massage rooms, video games, foosball, pianos, pool tables and ping pong.

FINANCIALS: Sales and profits are in thousands of dollars—add 000 to get the full amount. 2006 Note: Financial information for 2006 was not available for all companies at press time.

2006 Sales: $	2006 Profits: $	U.S. Stock Ticker: GOOG
2005 Sales: $6,138,560	2005 Profits: $1,465,397	Int'l Ticker: Int'l Exchange:
2004 Sales: $3,189,223	2004 Profits: $399,119	Employees: 5,000
2003 Sales: $1,465,934	2003 Profits: $105,648	Fiscal Year Ends: 12/31
2002 Sales: $347,848	2002 Profits: $99,656	Parent Company:

SALARIES/BENEFITS:

Pension Plan: Y	ESOP Stock Plan:	Profit Sharing:	Top Exec. Salary: $175,000	Bonus: $837,956
Savings Plan: Y	Stock Purch. Plan:		Second Exec. Salary: $175,000	Bonus: $772,257

OTHER THOUGHTS:

Apparent Women Officers or Directors: 1
Hot Spot for Advancement for Women/Minorities: Y

LOCATIONS: ("Y" = Yes)

West:	Southwest:	Midwest:	Southeast:	Northeast:	International:
Y	Y	Y	Y	Y	Y

Note: Financial information, benefits and other data can change quickly and may vary from those stated here.

GRANITE BROADCASTING CORP　　　www.granitetv.com

Industry Group Code: 513120 Ranks within this company's industry group: Sales: 23 Profits: 19

Print Media/Publishing:	Movies:	Equipment/Supplies:	Broadcast/Cable:		Music/Audio:	Sports/Games:
Newspapers:	Movie Theaters:	Equipment/Supplies:	Broadcast TV:	Y	Music Production:	Games/Sports:
Magazines:	Movie Production:	Gambling Equipment:	Cable TV:		Retail Music:	Retail Games Stores:
Books:	TV/Video Production:	Special Services:	Satellite Broadcast:		Retail Audio Equip.:	Stadiums/Teams:
Book Stores:	Video Rental:	Advertising Services:	Radio:		Music Print./Dist.:	Gambling/Casinos:
Distribution/Printing:	Video Distribution:	Info. Sys. Software:	Online Information:		Multimedia:	Rides/Theme Parks:

TYPES OF BUSINESS:
Television Station Owner/Operator

BRANDS/DIVISIONS/AFFILIATES:

CONTACTS: *Note: Officers with more than one job title may be intentionally listed here more than once.*
W. Don Cornwell, CEO
John Deushane, COO
Lawrence I Willis, CFO/Sr. VP
Ann Beemish, VP-Corp. Dev.
Ann Beemish, Treas.
Les Vann, Exec. VP-Central & Southern New York
Robert E. Selwyn, Jr., Sr. Oper. Advisor
W. Don Cornwell, Chmn.

Phone: 212-826-2530	**Fax:** 212-826-2858
Toll-Free:	
Address: 767 3rd Ave., 34th Fl., New York, NY 10017 US	

GROWTH PLANS/SPECIAL FEATURES:
Granite Broadcasting Corporation is a television broadcasting company specializing in developing and operating small to middle market television broadcast stations in the U.S. The company owns and operates or provides programming, sales and other services to 23 television channels in 11 markets: San Francisco, California; Detroit, Michigan; Buffalo, New York; Fresno, California; Syracuse, New York; Fort Wayne, Indiana; Peoria, Illinois; and Duluth, Minnesota-Superior, Wisconsin. All of these channels are affiliated with ABC, NBC, CBS, CW and MyNetworkTV broadcasting networks and reach approximately 6% of all U.S. television households. The company generates its revenue through its network affiliations, trading its advertising time for cash payments from the affiliated networks. Most of the television stations owned by the company are operated through separate wholly owned subsidiaries. The company's business strategy is to provide high quality local news and sports for each of the markets it serves. Granite's goal is to become the leading provider of news, weather and sports information in these markets. In recent news, the company acquired WBNG-TV, a CBS affiliate in Binghamton and Elmira, New York for $45 million in cash. In addition, the firm's WDWB (Detroit, Michigan) and KBJR-DT (Duluth, Michigan) signed on as MyNetworkTV affiliates. In 2006, the firm sold its KBWB (San Francisco, California) and WDKB (Detroit, Michigan) to DS Audible San Francisco, LLC and DS Audible Detroit, LLC, respectively. In total, the firm retained $150 million in cash for the sale of these stations. Founder, chairman and CEO Don Cornwell owns 10% of Granite Broadcasting and controls all of the company's voting stock. In late 2006, the company declared Chapter 11 bankruptcy.

FINANCIALS: Sales and profits are in thousands of dollars—add 000 to get the full amount. 2006 Note: Financial information for 2006 was not available for all companies at press time.

2006 Sales: $	2006 Profits: $	**U.S. Stock Ticker: GBTVK.OB**
2005 Sales: $86,160	2005 Profits: $-98,926	**Int'l Ticker:** Int'l Exchange:
2004 Sales: $80,500	2004 Profits: $-83,292	Employees: 749
2003 Sales: $108,544	2003 Profits: $-46,948	Fiscal Year Ends: 12/31
2002 Sales: $135,300	2002 Profits: $-79,700	Parent Company:

SALARIES/BENEFITS:

Pension Plan:	ESOP Stock Plan:	Profit Sharing:	Top Exec. Salary: $672,000	Bonus: $679,000
Savings Plan: Y	Stock Purch. Plan: Y		Second Exec. Salary: $672,000	Bonus: $480,000

OTHER THOUGHTS:
Apparent Women Officers or Directors: 1
Hot Spot for Advancement for Women/Minorities:

LOCATIONS: ("Y" = Yes)

West:	Southwest:	Midwest:	Southeast:	Northeast:	International:
Y		Y		Y	

GRAY TELEVISION INC   www.graycommunications.com

Industry Group Code: 513120 Ranks within this company's industry group: Sales: 16 Profits: 12

Print Media/Publishing:	Movies:	Equipment/Supplies:		Broadcast/Cable:		Music/Audio:	Sports/Games:
Newspapers:	Movie Theaters:	Equipment/Supplies:		Broadcast TV:	Y	Music Production:	Games/Sports:
Magazines:	Movie Production:	Gambling Equipment:		Cable TV:		Retail Music:	Retail Games Stores:
Books:	TV/Video Production:	Special Services:	Y	Satellite Broadcast:		Retail Audio Equip.:	Stadiums/Teams:
Book Stores:	Video Rental:	Advertising Services:	Y	Radio:		Music Print./Dist.:	Gambling/Casinos:
Distribution/Printing:	Video Distribution:	Info. Sys. Software:		Online Information:		Multimedia:	Rides/Theme Parks:

TYPES OF BUSINESS:
Television Station Owner/Operator

BRANDS/DIVISIONS/AFFILIATES:
Triple Crown Media

CONTACTS: *Note: Officers with more than one job title may be intentionally listed here more than once.*
J. Mack Robinson, CEO
Robert S. Prather, Jr., COO
Robert S. Prather, Jr., Pres.
James C. Ryan, CFO/Sr. VP
Robert A. Beizer, VP-Law/Sec.
Robert A. Beizer, VP-Dev.
Rich Adams, Regional VP-Texas
Frank J. Jones, Regional VP-Midwest
Wayne M. Martin, Regional VP-Television
Tracey Jones, Regional VP/Gen. Mgr.
J. Mack Robinson, Chmn.

Phone: 404-504-9828   **Fax:** 404-261-9607
Toll-Free:
Address: 4370 Peachtree Rd. NE, Atlanta, GA 30319 US

GROWTH PLANS/SPECIAL FEATURES:
Gray Television, Inc. is a communications company that provides news and entertainment services to its television stations. The firm owns 43 network-affiliated television stations in 30 markets in the U.S. Seventeen of the stations are affiliated with CBS, ten are affiliated with NBC and eight are affiliated with ABC. In addition, the firm owns 24 digital channels, the most of any communications company. In 2006, Gray Television acquired the stock of Michiana Telecasting Corp. (owner of WHDU-TV, the NBC affiliate in South Bend, Indiana) from the University of Notre Dame for $85 million in cash. Also in 2006, Gray Media spun-off Triple Crown Media. Prior to the spinoff, Gray Media contributed its Graylink Wireless Business and newspaper publishing (with a total of five newspapers) to Triple Crown Media. In connection with the spinoff, Triple Crown Media made a $40 million cash contribution to Gray. Following the spinoff, the company's business consists of one segment, television broadcasting. CEO Mack Robinson Jr. and his family own more than 30% of the firm.

FINANCIALS: Sales and profits are in thousands of dollars—add 000 to get the full amount. 2006 Note: Financial information for 2006 was not available for all companies at press time.

2006 Sales: $	2006 Profits: $	**U.S. Stock Ticker:** GTN
2005 Sales: $261,553	2005 Profits: $3,362	**Int'l Ticker:** Int'l Exchange:
2004 Sales: $293,273	2004 Profits: $44,285	Employees: 2,113
2003 Sales: $243,061	2003 Profits: $14,000	Fiscal Year Ends: 12/31
2002 Sales: $198,600	2002 Profits: $-27,900	Parent Company:

SALARIES/BENEFITS:

Pension Plan: Y	ESOP Stock Plan:	Profit Sharing:	Top Exec. Salary: $768,000	Bonus: $750,000
Savings Plan: Y	Stock Purch. Plan: Y		Second Exec. Salary: $400,000	Bonus: $

OTHER THOUGHTS:
Apparent Women Officers or Directors: 1
Hot Spot for Advancement for Women/Minorities:

LOCATIONS: ("Y" = Yes)

West:	Southwest:	Midwest:	Southeast:	Northeast:	International:
Y	Y	Y	Y	Y	

Note: Financial information, benefits and other data can change quickly and may vary from those stated here.

GRUPO RADIO CENTRO SA DE CV www.radiocentro.com.mx
Industry Group Code: 513111 Ranks within this company's industry group: Sales: 14 Profits: 9

Print Media/Publishing:	Movies:	Equipment/Supplies:	Broadcast/Cable:	Music/Audio:	Sports/Games:
Newspapers:	Movie Theaters:	Equipment/Supplies:	Broadcast TV:	Music Production: Y	Games/Sports:
Magazines:	Movie Production:	Gambling Equipment:	Cable TV:	Retail Music:	Retail Games Stores:
Books:	TV/Video Production:	Special Services:	Satellite Broadcast:	Retail Audio Equip.:	Stadiums/Teams:
Book Stores:	Video Rental:	Advertising Services: Y	Radio:	Music Print./Dist.:	Gambling/Casinos:
Distribution/Printing:	Video Distribution:	Info. Sys. Software:	Online Information:	Multimedia:	Rides/Theme Parks:

TYPES OF BUSINESS:
Radio Broadcasting
Radio Programming

BRANDS/DIVISIONS/AFFILIATES:
Organizacion Impulsora de Radio
Red FM
Alfa Radio
Universal Stereo
Stereo Joya
Formato 21
Noticentro

CONTACTS: Note: Officers with more than one job title may be intentionally listed here more than once.
Carlos Aguirre, General Dir.
Pedro N. Beltran, CFO
Gonzalo Yanez, Dir.-Mktg.
Luis Cepero, Dir.-Audio Eng.
Pedro Beltran, Dir.-Admin.
Alvaro F. De la Mora, General Counsel
Sergio Gonzales, Dir.-Oper.
Alfredo Azpeitia, Dir.-Investor Relations
Pedro N. Beltran, Dir.-Finance
Arturo Yanez, Sub-Dir.-Admin.
Eduardo Stevens, Dir.-Transmission Eng.
Luis M. Carrasco, Dir.-Commercial
Jose L. Ocampo, Dir.-Oper., Organizacion Impulsora de Radio
Francisco A. Gomez, Chmn.

Phone: 5254-063-690   **Fax:** 52-525-728-4875
Toll-Free:
Address: Constituyentes 1154, 7 Piso, Colonia Lomas Altas, Mexico City, DF 11950 Mexico

GROWTH PLANS/SPECIAL FEATURES:
Grupo Radio Centro S.A. de C.V. is Mexico's largest radio broadcaster, owning 14 radio stations. Of these, five AM and six FM stations are located in Mexico City. In addition to broadcasting, the company produces all the programming for the stations it own or operates, including musical programs, news, talk shows and special events programs. With an average audience share of 34.6% in Mexico City, Grupo Radio Centro is easily the most popular radio broadcasting company in the country's capital, which is the largest city on the continent. Its most popular stations include Red FM, Alfa Radio, Universal Stereo and Stereo Joya. Programming usually centers on contemporary music, classic rock and talk. The Noticentro news division, broadcast on the station Formato 21, broadcasts news 24 hours a day, with updates every 10 minutes. The company owns and operates 18 production studios, which produce the company's programming as well as advertisements, informational messages and promotional spots. Subsidiary Organizacion Impulsora de Radio provides sales and programming to affiliate stations; currently, it has 100 distributed transmitters in 71 important Mexican cities. Grupo Radio Centro's primary source of revenue is the sale of commercial airtime. About one third of the company's revenues are culled from its ten largest advertisers, the two most significant being Gigante, S.A. and Comercial Mexicana, S.A. de C.V. In election years, over 20% of broadcasting revenue is derived from political parties. In 2006, a presidential election year, political advertising accounted for 31% of total broadcasting revenue. Founded in 1946 by Don Francisco Aguirre, the company held its first public offering simultaneously on the Mexican Stock Exchange and the New York Stock Exchange in 1993. The Aguirre family holds 51.6% of the company's voting shares through two Mexican trusts. In mid-2006, the company paid off the remainder of its bank debt.

FINANCIALS: Sales and profits are in thousands of dollars—add 000 to get the full amount. 2006 Note: Financial information for 2006 was not available for all companies at press time.
2006 Sales: $
2005 Sales: $55,619
2004 Sales: $49,500
2003 Sales: $73,400
2002 Sales: $68,100

2006 Profits: $
2005 Profits: $6,107
2004 Profits: $1,808
2003 Profits: $5,400
2002 Profits: $ 200

U.S. Stock Ticker: RC
Int'l Ticker: RCENTROA   Int'l Exchange: Mexico City
Employees: 422
Fiscal Year Ends: 12/31
Parent Company:

SALARIES/BENEFITS:
Pension Plan: Y   ESOP Stock Plan: Profit Sharing: Y   Top Exec. Salary: $ Bonus: $
Savings Plan: Stock Purch. Plan: Second Exec. Salary: $ Bonus: $

OTHER THOUGHTS:
Apparent Women Officers or Directors: 3
Hot Spot for Advancement for Women/Minorities: Y

LOCATIONS: ("Y" = Yes)
West:	Southwest:	Midwest:	Southeast:	Northeast:	International:
					Y

GRUPO TELEVISA SA

www.televisa.com

Industry Group Code: 513120   Ranks within this company's industry group: Sales: 7   Profits: 4

Print Media/Publishing:		Movies:		Equipment/Supplies:		Broadcast/Cable:		Music/Audio:		Sports/Games:	
Newspapers:		Movie Theaters:		Equipment/Supplies:		Broadcast TV:	Y	Music Production:	Y	Games/Sports:	
Magazines:	Y	Movie Production:	Y	Gambling Equipment:		Cable TV:	Y	Retail Music:		Retail Games Stores:	
Books:		TV/Video Production:	Y	Special Services:	Y	Satellite Broadcast:		Retail Audio Equip.:		Stadiums/Teams:	Y
Book Stores:		Video Rental:		Advertising Services:	Y	Radio:		Music Print./Dist.:		Gambling/Casinos:	
Distribution/Printing:		Video Distribution:		Info. Sys. Software:		Online Information:		Multimedia:		Rides/Theme Parks:	

TYPES OF BUSINESS:

Television Station Owner
Cable Services
Satellite Services
Internet Services
Paging Services
Film & Music Production
Radio Broadcasting
Magazine Publishing

BRANDS/DIVISIONS/AFFILIATES:

Cablevision
SKY
Innova
Televisa Cinema
SkyTel
Editorial Televisa
Volaris
La Sexta

CONTACTS: *Note: Officers with more than one job title may be intentionally listed here more than once.*

Emilio A. Jean, CEO
Emilio A. Jean, Pres.
Salvi F. Viadero, CFO
Alejandro Quintero Iniguez, VP-Corp. Sales/Mktg.
Maximiliano A. Carlebach, VP-Tech. Svc.
Jorge Eduardo Murguia Orozco, VP-Production
Maximiliano A. Carlebach, VP-Oper. & TV Production
Michel Boyance, Investor Rel. Officer
Salvi Folch Viadero, VP-Finance
Bernardo G. Martinez, Exec. VP
Alexandre M. Penna, CEO-Innova
Javier Merida Guzman, CEO-Radiopolis
Eduardo T. Michelsen, CEO-Editorial
Emilio A. Jean, Chmn.

Phone: 52-55-5261-2445	Fax: 52-55-5261-2494

Toll-Free:

Address: Avenida Vasco De Quiroga No. 2000, Colonia Santa Fe, DF 01210 Mexico

GROWTH PLANS/SPECIAL FEATURES:

Mexico's Grupo Televisa S.A. is one of the largest Spanish-speaking media companies in the world and a major participant in the international entertainment industry, with properties in television, cable, satellite services, Internet service, radio broadcasting, music recording, magazine publishing, professional sports, paging services and film production. The company broadcasts programs through its networks, cable system and its own satellite services. The firm typically holds over 70% of the television audience share in Mexico through its four television networks and over 260 affiliated stations, and distributes programming throughout Latin America, Europe, Asia and Africa. It also has a 51% interest in cable joint venture Cablevision, a cable services operator whose network consists of over 50 channels, as well as a 60% interest in Innova, the operator of the SKY direct-to-home satellite system. In addition, the company owns approximately 60% of SKY. Another subsidiary, Televisa Cinema, produces Mexican motion pictures and distributes national and international films. Televisa Video produces and distributes television programming on VHS and DVD for the home entertainment market. Through subsidiary SkyTel, Televisa provides Internet service, while esmas.com manages the company's web site and other related web sites. Editorial Televisa publishes magazines for the Spanish-speaking world, with 68 magazines distributed in more than 20 countries, including Spanish versions of magazines (Cosmopolitan, Maxim and Travel & Leisure) and original magazines (TVyNovelas and Vanidades). In addition, the company owns several soccer teams and sports and entertainment venues, as well as a 50% interest in Televisa Radio, which owns and operates 17 Mexican radio stations. Recently, the firm's subsidiary, Televisa partnered with Walmart of Mexico (WALMEX) to install 15-20 LCD screens in select 300 WALMEX stores to operate its new in-store television advertising system. Televisa will invest $20 million in the project, and will share revenue with WALMEX.

FINANCIALS: Sales and profits are in thousands of dollars—add 000 to get the full amount. 2006 Note: Financial information for 2006 was not available for all companies at press time.

2006 Sales: $	2006 Profits: $	U.S. Stock Ticker: TV	
2005 Sales: $2,968,180	2005 Profits: $559,747	Int'l Ticker: TLEVISAL	Int'l Exchange: Mexico City
2004 Sales: $2,768,072	2004 Profits: $407,635	Employees: 14,100	
2003 Sales: $2,098,800	2003 Profits: $320,400	Fiscal Year Ends: 12/31	
2002 Sales: $2,075,400	2002 Profits: $71,100	Parent Company:	

SALARIES/BENEFITS:

Pension Plan: Y	ESOP Stock Plan: Y	Profit Sharing:	Top Exec. Salary: $	Bonus: $
Savings Plan:	Stock Purch. Plan:		Second Exec. Salary: $	Bonus: $

OTHER THOUGHTS:

Apparent Women Officers or Directors:
Hot Spot for Advancement for Women/Minorities:

LOCATIONS: ("Y" = Yes)

West:	Southwest:	Midwest:	Southeast:	Northeast:	International:
					Y

Note: Financial information, benefits and other data can change quickly and may vary from those stated here.

GTECH HOLDINGS CORP
www.gtech.com

Industry Group Code: 713290 Ranks within this company's industry group: Sales: 2 Profits: 2

Print Media/Publishing:	Movies:	Equipment/Supplies:		Broadcast/Cable:	Music/Audio:	Sports/Games:
Newspapers:	Movie Theaters:	Equipment/Supplies:		Broadcast TV:	Music Production:	Games/Sports:
Magazines:	Movie Production:	Gambling Equipment:	Y	Cable TV:	Retail Music:	Retail Games Stores:
Books:	TV/Video Production:	Special Services:	Y	Satellite Broadcast:	Retail Audio Equip.:	Stadiums/Teams:
Book Stores:	Video Rental:	Advertising Services:		Radio:	Music Print./Dist.:	Gambling/Casinos:
Distribution/Printing:	Video Distribution:	Info. Sys. Software:		Online Information:	Multimedia:	Rides/Theme Parks:

TYPES OF BUSINESS:

Gambling Equipment-Lottery Systems
Lottery Technology Services
Online Game Products & Services
Credit Card Processing Services
Facilities Management Services

BRANDS/DIVISIONS/AFFILIATES:

Interlott Technologies, Inc.
Aladdin
BillBird
Leeward Islands Lottery Holding Company
Spielo
Europrint
PolCard

CONTACTS: *Note: Officers with more than one job title may be intentionally listed here more than once.*

W. Bruce Turner, CEO
W. Bruce Turner, Pres.
Jaymin B.Patel, Sr. VP/CFO
Cornelia Laverty, Chief Mktg. Officer
John L. Pothin, VP-Human Resources
Walter G. DeSocio, Chief Admin. Officer
Atul Bali, Sr. VP-Corp. Dev. &Strategic Planning
Mary Norton, Dir.-Investor Rel.
Donald R. Sweitzer, Sr. VP-Global Bus. Dev. & Public Affairs
Robert M. Dewey, Jr., Chmn.

Phone: 401-392-1000	Fax: 401-392-1234
Toll-Free:	
Address: 55 Technology Way, West Greenwich, RI 02817 US	

GROWTH PLANS/SPECIAL FEATURES:

GTECH Holdings Corporation, a subsidiary of Lottomatica S.p.A., is a leading global supplier of systems and services to the lottery, gaming and entertainment industries. The company's core business is the lottery industry, in which it does business in 50 countries. The company provides integrated online lottery solutions, services and products to governmental lottery authorities and governmental licensees worldwide. GTECH offers its customers a full range of lottery technology services, including the design, assembly, installation, operation, maintenance and marketing of online lottery systems and instant ticket support systems. The firm has introduced several new online products and services, including Aladdin, a credit-card-sized lottery ticket that can be reused up to 500 times; the Extra-Online game, an online lottery game that allows players to purchase an additional game with instant-ticket features; and e-scratch, a web-based interactive suite of scratch and reveal games. The company also owns PolCard, Poland's leading debit and credit card merchant acquirer and processor, which operates more than 34,000 point-of-sale terminals throughout Poland; Europrint, which provides sophisticated promotional games; IGI, or Interactive Games International, which creates the software and content necessary for Europrint's interactive games; Spielo, a manufacturer of video lottery terminals; Leeward Islands Lottery Holding Company, which operates lotteries throughout the Caribbean; BillBird, an electronic bill payment service in Poland; and Interlott, a leading ITVM technology company.

The company offers employees educational, adoption and employee assistance programs, flexible spending accounts, a 529 College Bound fund and a 401(k) plan. GTECH also allows employees one paid day off annually to volunteer with local non-profit organizations. If an employee volunteers with an organization for 25 hours or more annually, the company will donate $250 to that organization. The Great Place to Work Institute of Ireland named GTECH Ireland Operations, Ltd., one of the 50 best places to work in Ireland.

FINANCIALS: Sales and profits are in thousands of dollars—add 000 to get the full amount. 2006 Note: Financial information for 2006 was not available for all companies at press time.

2006 Sales: $1,304,806	2006 Profits: $211,045	U.S. Stock Ticker: Subsidiary
2005 Sales: $1,257,235	2005 Profits: $196,394	Int'l Ticker: Int'l Exchange:
2004 Sales: $1,501,330	2004 Profits: $183,200	Employees: 5,300
2003 Sales: $978,800	2003 Profits: $142,000	Fiscal Year Ends: 2/23
2002 Sales: $1,009,700	2002 Profits: $83,600	Parent Company: LOTTOMATICA SPA

SALARIES/BENEFITS:

Pension Plan:	ESOP Stock Plan:	Profit Sharing:	Top Exec. Salary: $746,154	Bonus: $
Savings Plan: Y	Stock Purch. Plan: Y		Second Exec. Salary: $488,077	Bonus: $

OTHER THOUGHTS:

Apparent Women Officers or Directors: 2
Hot Spot for Advancement for Women/Minorities:

LOCATIONS: ("Y" = Yes)

West:	Southwest:	Midwest:	Southeast:	Northeast:	International:
				Y	Y

HALLMARK CARDS INC

www.hallmark.com

Industry Group Code: 511191 Ranks within this company's industry group: Sales: 1 Profits:

Print Media/Publishing:	Movies:		Equipment/Supplies:	Broadcast/Cable:		Music/Audio:		Sports/Games:	
Newspapers:	Movie Theaters:		Equipment/Supplies:	Broadcast TV:		Music Production:		Games/Sports:	
Magazines:	Movie Production:		Gambling Equipment:	Cable TV:	Y	Retail Music:		Retail Games Stores:	
Books:	TV/Video Production:	Y	Special Services:	Satellite Broadcast:		Retail Audio Equip.:		Stadiums/Teams:	
Book Stores:	Video Rental:		Advertising Services:	Radio:		Music Print./Dist.:		Gambling/Casinos:	
Distribution/Printing:	Video Distribution:		Info. Sys. Software:	Online Information:		Multimedia:		Rides/Theme Parks:	

TYPES OF BUSINESS:

Greeting Cards Publishing
Cable Television Broadcasting
Crayons & Art Products
Portrait Studios
Stationery
Television Production & Distribution

BRANDS/DIVISIONS/AFFILIATES:

Gold Crown
Keepsake Ornaments
Maxine
Crown Media Holdings
Hallmark Entertainment
Binney & Smith
Crayola
Picture People (The)

CONTACTS: Note: Officers with more than one job title may be intentionally listed here more than once.

Donald J. Hall, Jr., CEO
Donald J. Hall, Jr., Pres.
Robert J. Druten, CFO/Exec. VP
Donald J. Hall, Chmn.

Phone: 816-274-5111	Fax: 816-274-5061
Toll-Free:	
Address: 2501 McGee St., Kansas City, MO 64108 US	

GROWTH PLANS/SPECIAL FEATURES:

Hallmark Cards, Inc. markets greeting cards and other products under its Gold Crown, Keepsake Ornaments, Maxine, Shoebox, Fresh Ink, Mahogany and Tree of Life brands. The company operates wholesale and retail businesses with over 50% share in the U.S. greeting card market. The wholesale business distributes products to over 43,000 U.S. retailers and more than 100 countries, with products in more than 30 languages. As a retailer, Hallmark distributes products in over 4,000 Hallmark Gold Crown stores, with approximately 10% corporately owned and managed. The company's Crown Media Holdings subsidiary operates various cable television channels that are viewed by 73 million subscribers worldwide. The Hallmark Channel, Crown Media's most popular cable channel, licenses many programs from Hallmark Entertainment, which produces and distributes made-for-TV miniseries and movies. The firm's Binney & Smith subsidiary produces Crayola crayons, which are sold in over 80 countries. Binney & Smith also markets Liquitex fine art products, Revell-Monogram products and Silly Putty. The Picture People, another subsidiary, operates over 250 portrait studios in malls nationwide. Subsidiary William Arthur, Inc. specializes in customized holiday cards, general invitations and announcements, social and business stationery, wedding invitations and birth announcements. In November 2005, Hallmark was selected by UNICEF to be the exclusive supplier for all UNICEF fundraising cards sold in the U.S.

Hallmark has been named among the best places to work for African Americans, Hispanics and working mothers by various publications. The firm offers its employees personal and professional training and development opportunities.

FINANCIALS: Sales and profits are in thousands of dollars—add 000 to get the full amount. 2006 Note: Financial information for 2006 was not available for all companies at press time.

2006 Sales: $	2006 Profits: $	U.S. Stock Ticker: Private
2005 Sales: $4,200,000	2005 Profits: $	Int'l Ticker: Int'l Exchange:
2004 Sales: $4,400,000	2004 Profits: $	Employees: 18,000
2003 Sales: $4,300,000	2003 Profits: $	Fiscal Year Ends: 12/31
2002 Sales: $4,200,000	2002 Profits: $	Parent Company:

SALARIES/BENEFITS:

Pension Plan:	ESOP Stock Plan:	Profit Sharing:	Top Exec. Salary: $310,577	Bonus: $88,501
Savings Plan:	Stock Purch. Plan:		Second Exec. Salary: $249,615	Bonus: $66,375

OTHER THOUGHTS:

Apparent Women Officers or Directors:
Hot Spot for Advancement for Women/Minorities:

LOCATIONS: ("Y" = Yes)

West:	Southwest:	Midwest:	Southeast:	Northeast:	International:
Y	Y	Y	Y	Y	Y

HANDS-ON MOBILE

www.mforma.com

Industry Group Code: 511208 Ranks within this company's industry group: Sales: Profits:

Print Media/Publishing:	Movies:	Equipment/Supplies:	Broadcast/Cable:	Music/Audio:	Sports/Games:	
Newspapers:	Movie Theaters:	Equipment/Supplies:	Broadcast TV:	Music Production:	Games/Sports:	Y
Magazines:	Movie Production:	Gambling Equipment:	Cable TV:	Retail Music:	Retail Games Stores:	
Books:	TV/Video Production:	Special Services:	Satellite Broadcast:	Retail Audio Equip.:	Stadiums/Teams:	
Book Stores:	Video Rental:	Advertising Services:	Radio:	Music Print./Dist.:	Gambling/Casinos:	
Distribution/Printing:	Video Distribution:	Info. Sys. Software:	Online Information:	Multimedia:	Rides/Theme Parks:	

TYPES OF BUSINESS:

Mobile Media Content
Games
Information Subscription Services
Brand Management Services

BRANDS/DIVISIONS/AFFILIATES:

MFORMA Group, Inc.

CONTACTS: Note: Officers with more than one job title may be intentionally listed here more than once.

Jonathan Sacks, CEO
Jonathan Sacks, Pres.
David Oppenheimer, CFO
Robert Tercek, Chief Mktg. Officer
Eric Bilange, Chief Tech. Officer
James Brelsford, General Counsel
Lynne Crawford, Exec. VP-Oper.
Russell S. Klein, Exec. VP-Corp. Dev.
John Rousseau, Pres./General Mgr.-Americas
Eric Hobson, Pres./General Mgr.-Europe
Dave Arnold, Pres./General Mgr.-Asia
Grace Zhang, General Mgr.-Hands-On Mobile China
Daniel Kranzler, Chmn.

Phone: 415-848-0400	Fax: 415-399-1966
Toll-Free:	
Address: 580 California St., Ste. 600, San Francisco, CA 94104 US	

GROWTH PLANS/SPECIAL FEATURES:

Hands-On Mobile, formerly MFORMA Group, Inc., develops, publishes and distributes mobile content to more than 150 of the world's leading operators in 40 countries. Hands-On offers a large catalog of Java, BREW, SMS, MMS, mophun and WAP games, including X-Men Legends 2: Rise of Apocalypse, Ultimate Spider-Man, True Crime: Streets of LA, Call of Duty and World Poker Tour–Texas Hold'em. The company also offers subscription services like Fantasy Football companion by CBS SportsLine, Baseball Game Center, Billboard Mobile and Astrology Zone Mobile. Hands-On adapts games and applications from one handset standard and language into multiple thousands of different product versions. The company has headquarters in San Francisco and offices in Los Angeles, Bellevue, London, Manchester, Beijing, Shanghai, Bangalore and Seoul. Hands-On's customers include Cingular, Spring Nextel, T-Mobile, Verizon Wireless, Alltel, US Cellular and China Mobile. MFORMA Group, Inc. announced in April 2006 that it would change its name to Hands-On Mobile, effective immediately. The name change reflects the company's new alignment toward targeting mobile-media market segments. In a separate announcement the same day, Hands-On unveiled several new products, including a partnership with Lego Classics to create Lego-banded games; Daily Devotions, a product that offers daily inspirations and prayers delivered by Pat Boone; and forthcoming games and products based on the notorious rock star Tommy Lee, with whom the company has also partnered.

FINANCIALS: Sales and profits are in thousands of dollars—add 000 to get the full amount. 2006 Note: Financial information for 2006 was not available for all companies at press time.

2006 Sales: $	2006 Profits: $	U.S. Stock Ticker: Private
2005 Sales: $	2005 Profits: $	Int'l Ticker: Int'l Exchange:
2004 Sales: $	2004 Profits: $	Employees:
2003 Sales: $	2003 Profits: $	Fiscal Year Ends:
2002 Sales: $	2002 Profits: $	Parent Company:

SALARIES/BENEFITS:

Pension Plan:	ESOP Stock Plan:	Profit Sharing:	Top Exec. Salary: $	Bonus: $
Savings Plan:	Stock Purch. Plan:		Second Exec. Salary: $	Bonus: $

OTHER THOUGHTS:

Apparent Women Officers or Directors: 2
Hot Spot for Advancement for Women/Minorities:

LOCATIONS: ("Y" = Yes)

West:	Southwest:	Midwest:	Southeast:	Northeast:	International:
Y					Y

HARPERCOLLINS PUBLISHERS INC   www.harpercollins.com

Industry Group Code: 511130 Ranks within this company's industry group: Sales: Profits:

Print Media/Publishing:		Movies:	Equipment/Supplies:	Broadcast/Cable:	Music/Audio:	Sports/Games:
Newspapers:		Movie Theaters:	Equipment/Supplies:	Broadcast TV:	Music Production:	Games/Sports:
Magazines:		Movie Production:	Gambling Equipment:	Cable TV:	Retail Music:	Retail Games Stores:
Books:	Y	TV/Video Production:	Special Services:	Satellite Broadcast:	Retail Audio Equip.:	Stadiums/Teams:
Book Stores:		Video Rental:	Advertising Services:	Radio:	Music Print./Dist.:	Gambling/Casinos:
Distribution/Printing:		Video Distribution:	Info. Sys. Software:	Online Information:	Multimedia:	Rides/Theme Parks:

TYPES OF BUSINESS:

Book Publishing
Online Publishing & E-Books
Audio Books

BRANDS/DIVISIONS/AFFILIATES:

News Corporation
ecco
Fourth Estate
Regan Books
PerfectBound
Amistad
Zondervan
Rayo

CONTACTS: Note: Officers with more than one job title may be intentionally listed here more than once.

Jane Friedman, CEO
Glenn D'Agnes, Exec. VP/COO
Jane Friedman, Pres.
Rick Schwartz, CIO
Christopher Goff, VP/General Counsel
V. K. Karthika, Chief Editor-HarperCollins India
P. M. Sukumar, CEO-HarperCollins India
Krishan Chopra, Chief Editor-HarperCollins India

Phone: 212-207-7000	Fax: 212-207-7145
Toll-Free:	
Address: 10 E. 53rd St., New York, NY 10022 US	

GROWTH PLANS/SPECIAL FEATURES:

HarperCollins Publishers, Inc., a subsidiary of News Corporation, publishes books that cover a wide range of interests. The company focuses on literary and commercial fiction, business books, children's books, cookbooks, mystery, romance, reference and religious and spiritual books. The titles are released through imprints such as ecco, specializing in classic literature; Fourth Estate, focusing on edgy fiction and nonfiction; Amistad, which focuses on authors of African descent; Rayo, a publisher of books oriented towards the Latino community; and Regan Books, focusing on popular fiction and nonfiction. Zondervan publishes Christian material, including the bestselling Purpose Driven Life series, and is the leading publisher of the Bible worldwide. The company's e-books are marketed and sold through the imprint PerfectBound in Adobe, Microsoft and Mobipocket formats. Harper Children's Audio offers bestselling children's literature on CD and cassette formats. HarperKidsEntertainment specializes in movie and TV tie-ins for children and teens. HarperCollins has received substantial business from recent movie tie-ins, including Lord of the Rings, the Chronicles of Narnia, Charlie and the Chocolate Factory and Lemony Snicket's A Series of Unfortunate Events. The company's worldwide publishing is divided into the following segments: U.S. general books, U.S. children's books, U.K., Canada, Australia and India. The company's web site, harpercollins.com, provides users with author interviews, forums to discuss political or social issues and literature, and information on best-selling books and upcoming releases.

HarperCollins offers internship and rotational associate programs to students and recent graduates. Employee benefits include medical, dental, vision and prescription drug plans; retirement and savings plans; work/life opportunities; seminars; and various retail, fitness and entertainment discounts.

FINANCIALS: Sales and profits are in thousands of dollars—add 000 to get the full amount. 2006 Note: Financial information for 2006 was not available for all companies at press time.

2006 Sales: $	2006 Profits: $	U.S. Stock Ticker: Subsidiary
2005 Sales: $	2005 Profits: $	Int'l Ticker: Int'l Exchange:
2004 Sales: $	2004 Profits: $	Employees:
2003 Sales: $	2003 Profits: $	Fiscal Year Ends: 6/30
2002 Sales: $	2002 Profits: $	Parent Company: NEWS CORPORATION LIMITED (THE)

SALARIES/BENEFITS:

Pension Plan:	ESOP Stock Plan:	Profit Sharing:	Top Exec. Salary: $	Bonus: $
Savings Plan:	Stock Purch. Plan:		Second Exec. Salary: $	Bonus: $

OTHER THOUGHTS:

Apparent Women Officers or Directors: 2
Hot Spot for Advancement for Women/Minorities:

LOCATIONS: ("Y" = Yes)

West:	Southwest:	Midwest:	Southeast:	Northeast:	International:
		Y		Y	Y

HARPO INC

www.oprah.com

Industry Group Code: 512110 Ranks within this company's industry group: Sales: 15 Profits:

Print Media/Publishing:		Movies:		Equipment/Supplies:	Broadcast/Cable:		Music/Audio:	Sports/Games:
Newspapers:		Movie Theaters:		Equipment/Supplies:	Broadcast TV:	Y	Music Production:	Games/Sports:
Magazines:	Y	Movie Production:	Y	Gambling Equipment:	Cable TV:		Retail Music:	Retail Games Stores:
Books:		TV/Video Production:	Y	Special Services:	Satellite Broadcast:		Retail Audio Equip.:	Stadiums/Teams:
Book Stores:		Video Rental:		Advertising Services:	Radio:		Music Print./Dist.:	Gambling/Casinos:
Distribution/Printing:		Video Distribution:		Info. Sys. Software:	Online Information:		Multimedia:	Rides/Theme Parks:

TYPES OF BUSINESS:

Movie & Television Production
Magazine Publishing
Online Retail
Radio Production

BRANDS/DIVISIONS/AFFILIATES:

Harpo Productions, Inc.
Harpo Studios, Inc.
Harpo Films, Inc.
Harpo Print, LLC
Oprah Winfrey Show (The)
O, The Oprah Magazine
Harpo Radio, Inc.
Oprah's Book Club

CONTACTS: Note: Officers with more than one job title may be intentionally listed here more than once.

Doug Pattison, CFO
Harriet Seitler, Exec. VP-Mktg. & Dev.
Harriet Seitler, Exec. VP-Dev.
Lisa Halliday, Dir.-Media & Corp. Rel.
Oprah Winfrey, Chmn.

Phone: 312-633-1000	Fax: 312-633-1976
Toll-Free:	
Address: 110 N. Carpenter St., Chicago, IL 60607 US	

GROWTH PLANS/SPECIAL FEATURES:

Harpo, Inc. (Oprah spelled backwards) is the creation of media star Oprah Winfrey, who is also the chairman of Harpo Productions, Harpo Studios, Harpo Films, Harpo Print, LLC and Harpo Video, Inc. Through these channels, the company markets The Oprah Winfrey Show, on the air since 1986, which is consistently the highest-rated talk show on television. The show is watched by an estimated 30 million viewers per week and is broadcast in 122 countries. The company also makes feature-length movies, such as Beloved, and made-for-TV movies, such as Oprah Winfrey Presents: Tuesdays with Morrie. In addition, the company operates oprah.com, an online extension of the TV show, and an online retailer, The Oprah Boutique (set to re-launch in early 2007). In cooperation with Hearst Corporation, the company publishes O, The Oprah Magazine, which has approximately 2.7 million subscribers. The Oprah Book Club publicizes Winfrey's book recommendations online, through her television show and with Oprah's Book Club seals that are placed on certain editions of the book when they are sold through other retail outlets. It has been noted that Oprah's Book Club selections are consistently bestsellers during their spotlight. Harpo Productions, in partnership with three other companies, produces the Rachel Ray show. In 2006, Harpo Radio, Inc. and XM Satellite Radio, launched Oprah & Friends, a satellite radio channel on XM.

FINANCIALS: Sales and profits are in thousands of dollars—add 000 to get the full amount. 2006 Note: Financial information for 2006 was not available for all companies at press time.

2006 Sales: $	2006 Profits: $	U.S. Stock Ticker: Private
2005 Sales: $290,000	2005 Profits: $	Int'l Ticker: Int'l Exchange:
2004 Sales: $	2004 Profits: $	Employees: 341
2003 Sales: $275,000	2003 Profits: $	Fiscal Year Ends: 12/31
2002 Sales: $	2002 Profits: $	Parent Company:

SALARIES/BENEFITS:

Pension Plan:	ESOP Stock Plan:	Profit Sharing:	Top Exec. Salary: $	Bonus: $
Savings Plan:	Stock Purch. Plan:		Second Exec. Salary: $	Bonus: $

OTHER THOUGHTS:

Apparent Women Officers or Directors: 3
Hot Spot for Advancement for Women/Minorities: Y

LOCATIONS: ("Y" = Yes)

West:	Southwest:	Midwest:	Southeast:	Northeast:	International:
		Y			

Note: Financial information, benefits and other data can change quickly and may vary from those stated here.

HARRAH'S ENTERTAINMENT INC   www.harrahs.com

Industry Group Code: 721120 Ranks within this company's industry group: Sales: 1   Profits: 4

Print Media/Publishing:	Movies:	Equipment/Supplies:	Broadcast/Cable:	Music/Audio:	Sports/Games:	
Newspapers:	Movie Theaters:	Equipment/Supplies:	Broadcast TV:	Music Production:	Games/Sports:	
Magazines:	Movie Production:	Gambling Equipment:	Cable TV:	Retail Music:	Retail Games Stores:	
Books:	TV/Video Production:	Special Services:	Satellite Broadcast:	Retail Audio Equip.:	Stadiums/Teams:	Y
Book Stores:	Video Rental:	Advertising Services:	Radio:	Music Print./Dist.:	Gambling/Casinos:	
Distribution/Printing:	Video Distribution:	Info. Sys. Software:	Online Information:	Multimedia:	Rides/Theme Parks:	

TYPES OF BUSINESS:
Casino Hotels
Dockside & Riverboat Casinos
Racing Venues
Casino Management

BRANDS/DIVISIONS/AFFILIATES:
Harrah's Operating Company, Inc.
Horseshoe Entertainment
Total Rewards
Caesar's Entertainment, Inc.

CONTACTS: *Note: Officers with more than one job title may be intentionally listed here more than once.*
Gary Loveman, CEO
Timothy J. Wilmott, COO
Jonathan S. Halkyard, CFO
David Norton, Sr. VP-Relationship Mktg.
Mary Thomas, Sr. VP-Human Resources
Timothy S. Stanley, CIO/Sr. VP
Stephen H. Brammell, General Counsel/Sr. VP
Anthony F. Santo, Sr. VP-Oper., Prod. & Svcs.
Richard E. Mirman, Sr. VP-New Bus. Dev.
Janis L. Jones, Sr. VP-Comm. & Gov't Rel.
Jonathan S. Halkyard, Sr. VP/Treas.
Tom Jenkin, Pres., Western Div.
Anthony Sanfilippo, Pres., Central Div.
Virginia E. Shanks, Sr. VP-Brand Mgmt.
Gary Loveman, Chmn.

Phone: 702-407-6000	Fax: 702-407-6037
Toll-Free:	
Address: One Harrah's Court, Las Vegas, NV 89119 US	

GROWTH PLANS/SPECIAL FEATURES:
Harrah's Entertainment, Inc. is one of the largest gaming companies in the world, conducting business through subsidiary Harrah's Operating Company, Inc. (HOC) and through HOC's subsidiaries. Harrah's, a geographically diverse casino company, operates 39 casinos, including 11 dockside and riverboat casinos, four casinos on Indian reservations, two cruise ship casinos and two racing venues. These facilities total approximately 3 million square feet of game space and 40,000 hotel rooms. The firm operates primarily under the Harrah's, Caesars and Horseshoe brand names. The company's marketing strategy is designed to appeal primarily to those customers who are avid, experienced players, especially those who play in more than one market. Harrah's offers reward incentives for returning customers under the Total Rewards card plan, which allows holders to earn reward credits to be redeemed for prizes including vacations, event tickets and cars. The firm recently acquired Horseshoe Entertainment, adding casinos in Indiana, Mississippi and Louisiana. In July 2005, Harrah's acquired Caesars Entertainment, adding 15 casinos and 24,000 hotel rooms in Las Vegas, Atlantic City and Mississippi. The company closed four casinos in Mississippi and Louisiana in late 2005 due to damage from Hurricanes Katrina and Rita. Harrah's is currently constructing the Chester Casino & Racetrack in Pennsylvania; the facility will include a 1,500 seat grandstand, simulcasting facilities and a slot casino, and is expected to open in 2007. In 2006, Harrah's acquired London Clubs International PLC. In December 2006, Harrah's agreed to be acquired by Apollo Management and the Texas Pacific Group for $17.1 billion. Harrah's has development projects in the Bahamas, Spain, Slovenia and Biloxi, Mississippi.

The company offers its employees benefits such as educational assistance, store and room discounts and community outreach opportunities. The management structure is designed to encourage and reward employees who promote viable new ideas.

FINANCIALS: Sales and profits are in thousands of dollars—add 000 to get the full amount. 2006 Note: Financial information for 2006 was not available for all companies at press time.

2006 Sales: $	2006 Profits: $	**U.S. Stock Ticker: HET**
2005 Sales: $7,111,000	2005 Profits: $236,400	**Int'l Ticker:** Int'l Exchange:
2004 Sales: $4,548,326	2004 Profits: $367,709	Employees: 85,000
2003 Sales: $4,126,200	2003 Profits: $292,700	Fiscal Year Ends: 12/31
2002 Sales: $4,136,400	2002 Profits: $235,000	Parent Company:

SALARIES/BENEFITS:
Pension Plan:	ESOP Stock Plan:	Profit Sharing:	Top Exec. Salary: $1,688,462	Bonus: $3,650,000
Savings Plan: Y	Stock Purch. Plan:		Second Exec. Salary: $1,096,154	Bonus: $1,973,075

OTHER THOUGHTS:
Apparent Women Officers or Directors: 3
Hot Spot for Advancement for Women/Minorities: Y

LOCATIONS: ("Y" = Yes)
West:	Southwest:	Midwest:	Southeast:	Northeast:	International:
Y	Y	Y	Y	Y	Y

Note: Financial information, benefits and other data can change quickly and may vary from those stated here.

HARRIS INTERACTIVE INC
www.harrisinteractive.com

Industry Group Code: 541910 Ranks within this company's industry group: Sales: 4 Profits: 4

Print Media/Publishing:	Movies:	Equipment/Supplies:		Broadcast/Cable:	Music/Audio:	Sports/Games:
Newspapers:	Movie Theaters:	Equipment/Supplies:		Broadcast TV:	Music Production:	Games/Sports:
Magazines:	Movie Production:	Gambling Equipment:		Cable TV:	Retail Music:	Retail Games Stores:
Books:	TV/Video Production:	Special Services:	Y	Satellite Broadcast:	Retail Audio Equip.:	Stadiums/Teams:
Book Stores:	Video Rental:	Advertising Services:	Y	Radio:	Music Print./Dist.:	Gambling/Casinos:
Distribution/Printing:	Video Distribution:	Info. Sys. Software:		Online Information:	Multimedia:	Rides/Theme Parks:

TYPES OF BUSINESS:
Market Research
Internet-Based Research
Consulting Services

BRANDS/DIVISIONS/AFFILIATES:
Harris Poll
Harris Interactive Service Bureau
Wirthlin Report
HI Europe
Novatris
Wirthlin Worldwide

CONTACTS:
Note: Officers with more than one job title may be intentionally listed here more than once.

Gregory Novak, CEO
David Vaden, COO
Gregory Novak, Pres.
Ronald Salluzzo, CFO
Dennis Bhame, Exec. VP-Human Resources
Leonard Bayer, Chief Scientist/Exec. VP
Leonard Bayer, CTO
George Terhanian, Pres., Global Internet Research
Dee Allsop, Pres., US Solutions Research Groups
Arthur Coles, Pres., US Industry Research Groups
George Bell, Chmn.

Phone: 585-272-8400	Fax: 585-272-8680
Toll-Free: 800-866-7655	
Address: 135 Corporate Woods, Rochester, NY 14623 US	

GROWTH PLANS/SPECIAL FEATURES:
Harris Interactive, Inc. is a worldwide market research and consulting firm best known for the Harris Poll and for pioneering an accurate method for Internet market research. It has made significant expenditures to drive the transformation of the market research and polling industry to an Internet-based platform. The company is one of the largest Internet-based research and polling firms in the world, based on the size of its Internet panel, number of online surveys completed and the amount of revenue it derives from online research. Harris conducts research mainly for companies in the not-for-profit, public policy, advertising and public relations, automotive and transportation, consumer packaged goods, health care and pharmaceuticals, brand consulting, and technology and telecommunications industries. Harris also conducts international research through both its various U.S. offices and its foreign subsidiaries, including London-based HI Europe, Paris-based Novatris and Wirthlin Worldwide, as well as its global network of local market and opinion research firms. Harris has three main product and service categories: custom research, including Internet-based and traditional market research studies and polling conducted on specific issues for specific customers; multi-client research, including Internet-based studies conducted on general-interest issues and sold to numerous clients; and service bureau research, which consists of Internet-based data collection conducted for other market research firms by the company's Harris Interactive Service Bureau subsidiary. In 2006, the company took efforts to streamline its operations in Europe, resulting in the closing of two facilities, a reorganization of several operating and support groups, and a small reduction in force.

FINANCIALS:
Sales and profits are in thousands of dollars—add 000 to get the full amount. 2006 Note: Financial information for 2006 was not available for all companies at press time.

2006 Sales: $216,011	2006 Profits: $9,460	U.S. Stock Ticker: HPOL
2005 Sales: $196,965	2005 Profits: $1,583	Int'l Ticker: Int'l Exchange:
2004 Sales: $146,032	2004 Profits: $29,918	Employees: 1,283
2003 Sales: $130,600	2003 Profits: $11,100	Fiscal Year Ends: 6/30
2002 Sales: $100,000	2002 Profits: $-14,793	Parent Company:

SALARIES/BENEFITS:
Pension Plan:	ESOP Stock Plan:	Profit Sharing:	Top Exec. Salary: $464,038	Bonus: $210,227
Savings Plan: Y	Stock Purch. Plan: Y		Second Exec. Salary: $318,000	Bonus: $109,318

OTHER THOUGHTS:
Apparent Women Officers or Directors:
Hot Spot for Advancement for Women/Minorities:

LOCATIONS: ("Y" = Yes)
West:	Southwest:	Midwest:	Southeast:	Northeast:	International:
Y		Y		Y	Y

HARTE-HANKS INC

www.harte-hanks.com

Industry Group Code: 511110 Ranks within this company's industry group: Sales: 12   Profits: 8

Print Media/Publishing:		Movies:		Equipment/Supplies:		Broadcast/Cable:		Music/Audio:		Sports/Games:	
Newspapers:	Y	Movie Theaters:		Equipment/Supplies:		Broadcast TV:		Music Production:		Games/Sports:	
Magazines:		Movie Production:		Gambling Equipment:		Cable TV:		Retail Music:		Retail Games Stores:	
Books:		TV/Video Production:		Special Services:	Y	Satellite Broadcast:		Retail Audio Equip.:		Stadiums/Teams:	
Book Stores:		Video Rental:		Advertising Services:	Y	Radio:		Music Print./Dist.:		Gambling/Casinos:	
Distribution/Printing:		Video Distribution:		Info. Sys. Software:	Y	Online Information:		Multimedia:		Rides/Theme Parks:	

TYPES OF BUSINESS:

Shopper Newspaper Publishing
Direct Mail Services
Direct & Interactive Marketing Services
Customer Relationship Management Software
Marketing Material Printing

BRANDS/DIVISIONS/AFFILIATES:

Flyer (The)
PennySaver
Communique Direct
Global Address
Harte-Hanks Trillium Software-Germany GmbH
Aberdeen Group

CONTACTS: Note: Officers with more than one job title may be intentionally listed here more than once.

Richard M. Hochhauser, CEO
Richard M. Hochhauser, Pres.
Dean H. Blythe, CFO/Sr. VP
Kathy Calta, Sr. VP-Direct Mktg.
David Siesel, CTO
Sloane Levy, General Counsel/VP
Jessica Huff, Chief Acct. Officer/VP-Finance
Loren Dalton, VP-Shoppers
Peter E. Gorman, Exec. VP/Pres., Harte-Hanks Shoppers
Michael Ortegon, Managing Dir.-Direct Mktg., Australia
David Blythe, Sr. VP-Bus. Dev., Asia-Pacific
Larry Franklin, Chmn.

Phone: 210-829-9000	Fax: 210-829-9403
Toll-Free: 800-456-9748	
Address: 200 Concord Plaza Dr. Ste. 800, San Antonio, TX 78216 US	

GROWTH PLANS/SPECIAL FEATURES:

Harte-Hanks, Inc. is a worldwide direct and targeted marketing company that provides customer relationship management, marketing services and shopper publications to a wide range of local, regional, U.S. and international consumer and business-to-business marketers. The company operates two main businesses: shoppers and direct marketing. Harte-Hanks' shoppers division is one of North America's largest owners, operators and distributors of shopper publications with 1,047 individual shopper editions having a weekly circulation of approximately 12,000 each. The company's shopper business operates in selected local and regional markets in California with the PennySaver publication and in Florida with the Flyer. In addition, the company operates as a service bureau, preparing list selections, maximizing deliverability and reducing clients' mailing costs. The direct marketing section (with 37 facilities worldwide and accounting for approximately 61% of the company's revenue) gathers, analyzes and distributes customer and prospect data across all points of customer contact. The company helps clients to develop and execute targeted marketing communication programs through creative consultation and graphics design. Along with back-end services (printing and personalization of communication pieces) the firm uses laser printing, target mail and fulfillment, and transportation logistics to build customized marketing databases. This provides clients with easy-to-use tools to perform analysis in order to target their best customers and prospects. Recently, the company acquired StepDot Software GmbH of Germany and integrated it into its Trillium Software. The new subsidiary, Harte-Hanks Trillium Software-Germany GmbH, is utilized by the firm's direct marketing section. In 2006, the firm acquired Global Address, a U.K.-based company (with additional operations in California) that provides postal address data software and services for over 230 territories and nations worldwide. Also in 2006, the firm acquired the Aberdeen Group of Boston, Massachusetts, a provider of technology market research and intelligence.

FINANCIALS: Sales and profits are in thousands of dollars—add 000 to get the full amount. 2006 Note: Financial information for 2006 was not available for all companies at press time.

2006 Sales: $	2006 Profits: $	U.S. Stock Ticker: HHS
2005 Sales: $1,134,993	2005 Profits: $114,458	Int'l Ticker: Int'l Exchange:
2004 Sales: $1,030,461	2004 Profits: $97,568	Employees: 7,106
2003 Sales: $944,576	2003 Profits: $87,362	Fiscal Year Ends: 12/31
2002 Sales: $908,800	2002 Profits: $90,700	Parent Company:

SALARIES/BENEFITS:

Pension Plan: Y	ESOP Stock Plan:	Profit Sharing:	Top Exec. Salary: $805,000	Bonus: $807,516
Savings Plan: Y	Stock Purch. Plan:		Second Exec. Salary: $379,365	Bonus: $114,557

OTHER THOUGHTS:

Apparent Women Officers or Directors: 3
Hot Spot for Advancement for Women/Minorities: Y

LOCATIONS: ("Y" = Yes)

West:	Southwest:	Midwest:	Southeast:	Northeast:	International:
Y	Y	Y	Y	Y	Y

Note: Financial information, benefits and other data can change quickly and may vary from those stated here.

HARVEY ELECTRONICS INC   www.harveyonline.com

Industry Group Code: 443110 Ranks within this company's industry group: Sales: 7   Profits: 5

Print Media/Publishing:	Movies:	Equipment/Supplies:		Broadcast/Cable:	Music/Audio:	Sports/Games:
Newspapers:	Movie Theaters:	Equipment/Supplies:		Broadcast TV:	Music Production:	Games/Sports:
Magazines:	Movie Production:	Gambling Equipment:	Y	Cable TV:	Retail Music:	Retail Games Stores:
Books:	TV/Video Production:	Special Services:	Y	Satellite Broadcast:	Retail Audio Equip.:	Stadiums/Teams:
Book Stores:	Video Rental:	Advertising Services:		Radio:	Music Print./Dist.:	Gambling/Casinos:
Distribution/Printing:	Video Distribution:	Info. Sys. Software:		Online Information:	Multimedia:	Rides/Theme Parks:

TYPES OF BUSINESS:

Electronics Stores
High-End Electronics
Repair & Installation Services
Online Retail
Home Theatre Furniture

BRANDS/DIVISIONS/AFFILIATES:

Bang & Olufsen

CONTACTS: Note: Officers with more than one job title may be intentionally listed here more than once.

Martin McClanan, Interim CEO
Franklin C. Karp, Pres.
Joseph J. Calabrese, CFO/Exec. VP
Roland W. Hiemer, VP-Merch.
Joseph J. Calabrese, Corp. Sec.
Michael A. Beck, VP-Oper.
Michael E. Recca, Chmn.

Phone: 201-842-0078	**Fax:** 201-842-0317
Toll-Free:	
Address: 205 Chubb Ave., Lyndhurst, NJ 07071 US	

GROWTH PLANS/SPECIAL FEATURES:

Harvey Electronics, Inc. is engaged in the retail sale, service and custom installation of high-quality audio, video and home theater equipment. The equipment for sale includes high-fidelity components and systems, VCRs, DVD players, high-definition televisions, direct view projection televisions, plasma and LCD flat-panel televisions, audio/video furniture, digital satellite systems, conventional telephones, home theatre furniture, service contracts and related accessories. The company is one of the country's largest retailers of esoteric brands manufactured by Bang & Olufsen, Crestron, Lexicon, Linn, Marantz, McIntosh, NAD, Vienna Acoustics, Sonus Faber, Kef, Krell, Loewe, Martin Logan and Fujitsu. The firm currently owns eight Harvey specialty retail stores and two Bang & Olufsen stores. Most of the stores are located in the New York market, with additional stores in New Jersey and Connecticut. Audio products account for about 27% of total sales, while video products account for 46%. Harvey purchases its products from approximately 80 manufacturers, including Bang & Olufsen, Boston Acoustics, Fujitsu, Marantz, Monster Cable, Pioneer Elite, Runco, Samsung, Sharp and Sony. The company intends to maintain a strategic focus on custom installations, which account for more then half of Harvey's net sales. In mid-2006, Harvey receieved $4 million in growth capital from institutional investors led by Trinity Investment Partners LLC. At the end of 2006, Harvey's continued listing on the NASDAQ was in jeopardy due to falling below certain market thresholds. Resolution is not expected until mid-2007.

FINANCIALS: Sales and profits are in thousands of dollars—add 000 to get the full amount. 2006 Note: Financial information for 2006 was not available for all companies at press time.

2006 Sales: $	2006 Profits: $	**U.S. Stock Ticker: HRVE**
2005 Sales: $40,400	2005 Profits: $- 800	**Int'l Ticker:** Int'l Exchange:
2004 Sales: $43,198	2004 Profits: $1,274	Employees: 152
2003 Sales: $42,400	2003 Profits: $ 300	Fiscal Year Ends: 10/31
2002 Sales: $41,500	2002 Profits: $ 200	Parent Company:

SALARIES/BENEFITS:

Pension Plan: Y	ESOP Stock Plan:	Profit Sharing: Y	Top Exec. Salary: $164,000	Bonus: $54,000
Savings Plan: Y	Stock Purch. Plan:		Second Exec. Salary: $155,000	Bonus: $51,000

OTHER THOUGHTS:

Apparent Women Officers or Directors:
Hot Spot for Advancement for Women/Minorities:

LOCATIONS: ("Y" = Yes)

West:	Southwest:	Midwest:	Southeast:	Northeast:	International:
				Y	

HASTINGS ENTERTAINMENT INC   www.gohastings.com

Industry Group Code: 532230   Ranks within this company's industry group: Sales: 5   Profits: 2

Print Media/Publishing:		Movies:		Equipment/Supplies:		Broadcast/Cable:		Music/Audio:		Sports/Games:	
Newspapers:		Movie Theaters:		Equipment/Supplies:		Broadcast TV:		Music Production:		Games/Sports:	
Magazines:		Movie Production:		Gambling Equipment:		Cable TV:		Retail Music:	Y	Retail Games Stores:	Y
Books:		TV/Video Production:		Special Services:		Satellite Broadcast:		Retail Audio Equip.:		Stadiums/Teams:	
Book Stores:	Y	Video Rental:	Y	Advertising Services:		Radio:		Music Print./Dist.:		Gambling/Casinos:	
Distribution/Printing:		Video Distribution:		Info. Sys. Software:		Online Information:		Multimedia:		Rides/Theme Parks:	

TYPES OF BUSINESS:

Video & DVD Rental Stores
Book Sales
Music Sales
Software Sales
Video Game Sales
Coffee Sales
Online Sales
Used Books, Music & DVDs

BRANDS/DIVISIONS/AFFILIATES:

gohastings.com
Hard Back Cafe
Hastings Properties, Inc.
Hastings Internet, Inc.

CONTACTS: Note: Officers with more than one job title may be intentionally listed here more than once.

John H. Marmaduke, CEO
John H. Marmaduke, Pres.
Dan Crow, CFO
Kevin J. Ball, VP-Mktg.
David Moffatt, VP-Human Resources
Alan Van Ongevalle, VP-IT
Michael Rigby, Sr. VP-Merch.
Jeff Ostler, VP-Oper.
Dan Crow, VP-Finance
Phil McConnell, VP-Product
John H. Marmaduke, Chmn.
Alan Van Ongevalle, VP-Dist.

Phone: 806-351-2300	Fax: 806-351-2424
Toll-Free: 877-427-8464	
Address: 3601 Plains Blvd., Ste. 1, Amarillo, TX 79102 US	

GROWTH PLANS/SPECIAL FEATURES:

Hastings Entertainment, Inc. is a multimedia entertainment retailer that buys, sells and trades books, music, software, periodicals, videocassettes and DVDs and rents videocassettes, video games and DVDs in a superstore format. The firm has two wholly owned subsidiaries, namely Hastings Properties, Inc. and Hastings Internet, Inc. The firm also operates gohastings.com, which offers a broad selection of books, music, software, videocassettes, video games and DVDs over the Internet. Hastings targets towns with small- to medium-sized populations and currently operates over 150 stores, averaging 20,000 square feet each, in 20 states. Superstores offer an extensive product assortment, consisting of up to 73,000 books, 4,000 periodicals, 1,000 software and 28,000 video, DVD and video game titles for sale, as well as up to 20,000 videocassettes, video games and DVDs available for rental. About 47% of revenues come from videotape, video game and DVD sales and rentals, with sales of music and books accounting for approximately the same. The company's business strategy is designed to build consumer awareness of the Hastings concept and achieve high levels of customer loyalty and repeat business. Many of its stores offer such amenities as reading chairs and Hard Back Cafe full-service coffee bars. Hastings buys used CDs, video games and DVDs from customers, offering used products as a low-cost alternative. The company has also begun buying and selling used books in certain markets and may expand this practice to more of its stores if it is successful.

FINANCIALS: Sales and profits are in thousands of dollars—add 000 to get the full amount. 2006 Note: Financial information for 2006 was not available for all companies at press time.

2006 Sales: $537,931	2006 Profits: $5,695	U.S. Stock Ticker: HAST
2005 Sales: $542,016	2005 Profits: $5,809	Int'l Ticker: Int'l Exchange:
2004 Sales: $508,318	2004 Profits: $7,750	Employees: 6,344
2003 Sales: $495,400	2003 Profits: $1,900	Fiscal Year Ends: 1/31
2002 Sales: $471,800	2002 Profits: $4,000	Parent Company:

SALARIES/BENEFITS:

Pension Plan:	ESOP Stock Plan:	Profit Sharing:	Top Exec. Salary: $250,000	Bonus: $329,375
Savings Plan:	Stock Purch. Plan:		Second Exec. Salary: $137,871	Bonus: $120,934

OTHER THOUGHTS:

Apparent Women Officers or Directors:
Hot Spot for Advancement for Women/Minorities:

LOCATIONS: ("Y" = Yes)

West:	Southwest:	Midwest:	Southeast:	Northeast:	International:
Y	Y	Y	Y		

HEARST CORPORATION (THE)

www.hearstcorp.com

Industry Group Code: 511110 Ranks within this company's industry group: Sales: 4 Profits:

Print Media/Publishing:		Movies:		Equipment/Supplies:		Broadcast/Cable:		Music/Audio:		Sports/Games:	
Newspapers:	Y	Movie Theaters:		Equipment/Supplies:		Broadcast TV:	Y	Music Production:		Games/Sports:	
Magazines:	Y	Movie Production:		Gambling Equipment:		Cable TV:	Y	Retail Music:		Retail Games Stores:	
Books:		TV/Video Production:	Y	Special Services:	Y	Satellite Broadcast:		Retail Audio Equip.:		Stadiums/Teams:	
Book Stores:		Video Rental:		Advertising Services:	Y	Radio:		Music Print./Dist.:		Gambling/Casinos:	
Distribution/Printing:		Video Distribution:		Info. Sys. Software:	Y	Online Information:		Multimedia:		Rides/Theme Parks:	

TYPES OF BUSINESS:

Newspaper Publishing
Magazine Publishing
Television Broadcasting & Production
Phone Directories
Internet Businesses
Syndicated Media Content
On-Demand Cable Television
Media Industry Services

BRANDS/DIVISIONS/AFFILIATES:

Associated Publishing Company (The)
Cosmopolitan
Esquire
Hearst-Argyle
ESPN
The A&E Networks
Hearst Interactive Media
ZynexOrder

CONTACTS: *Note: Officers with more than one job title may be intentionally listed here more than once.*

Victor F. Ganzi, CEO
Victor F. Ganzi, Pres.
Ronald J. Doerfler, CFO/Sr. VP
Pamela Raley, VP-Sales, Digital Media Unit
Eve Burton, General Counsel/VP
James M. Asher, Chief Dev. Officer/Sr. VP/Chief Legal Officer
Kendra Newton, Public Relations
Thomas W. Campo, Dir.-Investor Relations, Hearst-Argyle
David J. Barrett, CEO/Pres., Hearst Television
Cathleen Black, Pres., Hearst Magazines
Richard P. Malloch, Pres., Hearst Business Media
George B. Irish, Pres., Hearst Newspapers/Sr. VP
George R. Hearst, Jr., Chmn.

Phone: 212-649-2000	Fax: 212-649-2108
Toll-Free:	
Address: 300 W. 57 St., New York, NY 10019-3791 US	

GROWTH PLANS/SPECIAL FEATURES:

The Hearst Corporation, the legacy of former media mogul William Randolph Hearst, operates newspapers, magazines, television and radio broadcasting, cable television, real estate, interactive media and business media. The company owns 20 weekly newspapers and 12 dailies, including the Houston Chronicle, San Francisco Chronicle and Seattle Post-Intelligencer. The newspaper segment also owns The Associated Publishing Company, which produces phone directories in Texas; White Directory Publishers, Inc., which produces phonebooks for areas in 11 states; and Hearst News Service, which syndicates Hearst newspaper stories. Hearst Magazines publishes 19 titles with more than 145 international editions. Its publications include Cosmopolitan, Country Living, Esquire, Good Housekeeping, Harpers BAZAAR, O, The Oprah Magazine, Popular Mechanics, Seventeen, SmartMoney and Town & Country. Subsidiary Hearst-Argyle controls the broadcasting segment and owns 28 local television stations, which reach a combined 18% of U.S. viewers. The entertainment division comprises the A&E Television Networks, the ESPN networks, the History Channel and other cable channels; as well as King Features Syndicate, a major distributor of newspaper comics, puzzles, columns and editorials; and Reed Brennan Media Associates, a provider of pagination and editing services for more than 320 newspapers. Hearst Entertainment also owns an extensive movie library, exceeding 250 films. Hearst Interactive Media owns or has an interest in Internet-related companies including MetaTV, Circles, Mobility Technologies, Drugstore.com, Genealogy.com, Handbag.com, Medscape, iVillage, Exodus Communications and XM Satellite Radio. The Business Media subsidiary provides information services to business and runs Zynex Health, which provides scientific research and best practice guidelines to health-care providers. Hearst Corporation also has interests in over 20 business-to-business companies, including Black Book Guides, MOTOR Information Systems, European Collision Database, Diversion, Electronic Engineers Master Catalog, Electronic Products Magazine, First DataBank, Floor Covering Weekly, IDG/Hearst, Stocknet and Used Car Pricing Guides. In 2006, the company opened a new headquarters, Hearst Tower.

FINANCIALS: Sales and profits are in thousands of dollars—add 000 to get the full amount. 2006 Note: Financial information for 2006 was not available for all companies at press time.

2006 Sales: $	2006 Profits: $	U.S. Stock Ticker: Private	
2005 Sales: $4,550,000	2005 Profits: $	Int'l Ticker:	Int'l Exchange:
2004 Sales: $4,000,000	2004 Profits: $	Employees: 17,016	
2003 Sales: $4,100,000	2003 Profits: $	Fiscal Year Ends: 12/31	
2002 Sales: $3,565,000	2002 Profits: $	Parent Company:	

SALARIES/BENEFITS:

Pension Plan:	ESOP Stock Plan:	Profit Sharing:	Top Exec. Salary: $	Bonus: $
Savings Plan:	Stock Purch. Plan:		Second Exec. Salary: $	Bonus: $

OTHER THOUGHTS:

Apparent Women Officers or Directors: 31
Hot Spot for Advancement for Women/Minorities: Y

LOCATIONS: ("Y" = Yes)

West:	Southwest:	Midwest:	Southeast:	Northeast:	International:
Y	Y	Y	Y	Y	Y

HEARST-ARGYLE TELEVISION INC   www.hearstargyle.com

Industry Group Code: 513120 Ranks within this company's industry group: Sales: 12   Profits: 9

Print Media/Publishing:	Movies:		Equipment/Supplies:	Broadcast/Cable:		Music/Audio:	Sports/Games:
Newspapers:	Movie Theaters:		Equipment/Supplies:	Broadcast TV:	Y	Music Production:	Games/Sports:
Magazines:	Movie Production:		Gambling Equipment:	Cable TV:		Retail Music:	Retail Games Stores:
Books:	TV/Video Production:	Y	Special Services:	Satellite Broadcast:		Retail Audio Equip.:	Stadiums/Teams:
Book Stores:	Video Rental:		Advertising Services:	Radio:		Music Print./Dist.:	Gambling/Casinos:
Distribution/Printing:	Video Distribution:		Info. Sys. Software:	Online Information:		Multimedia:	Rides/Theme Parks:

TYPES OF BUSINESS:

Broadcast Television
Radio Stations
Web Sites
Television Production

BRANDS/DIVISIONS/AFFILIATES:

Hearst Corporation
Internet Broadcasting Systems

CONTACTS: Note: Officers with more than one job title may be intentionally listed here more than once.

David J. Barrett, CEO
David J. Barrett, Pres.
Harry T. Hawks, CFO/Exec. VP
Mary Danielski, VP-Mktg. & Creative Svcs.
Alvin Lustgarten, VP-IT
Martin Faubell, VP-Eng.
Alvin Lustgarten, VP-Admin.
Jonathan Mintzer, General Counsel/VP/Corp. Sec.
Steven A. Hobbs, Exec. VP/Chief Dev. & Legal Officer
Ellen McClain, VP-Finance
Terry Mackin, Exec. VP
Kathleen Keefe, VP-Sales
Frederick I. Young, Sr. VP-News
Emerson Coleman, VP-Programming
Victor F. Ganzi, Chmn.

Phone: 212-887-6800	**Fax:** 212-887-6855
Toll-Free:	
Address: 300 West 57th Street, New York, NY 10019 US	

GROWTH PLANS/SPECIAL FEATURES:

Hearst-Argyle Television, Inc., 70% owned by publishing giant Hearst Corporation, owns 26 digital television stations that reach approximately 18% of U.S. television households. The company also manages an additional three television stations in Florida and Missouri and two radio stations in Maryland. It is one of the country's largest independent TV station groups. Each one of Hearst-Argyle's owned or managed television stations are affiliated with one of the following major networks: ABC, NBC, CBS or CW. The firm is the largest ABC affiliate group, with 12 affiliated stations, and the second-largest NBC affiliate group, with 10 affiliated stations. Of the 25 television stations Hearst-Argyle owns, 20 are in the top 50 market areas. The programming for the television stations has three main components: programs produced by the affiliated networks (e.g. ABC's Desperate Housewives or NBC's ER) and special events such as the Academy Awards and the Olympics; programs produced by the company such as local news, weather, sports and entertainment; and first-run syndicated programs acquired by the company such as The Oprah Winfrey Show, Dr. Phil and Teen Kids News. In addition, Hearst-Argyle holds equity investments in Internet Broadcasting Systems, which forms local partnerships for the development and management of local news, information and entertainment portal web sites. In 2006, the company purchased WKCF-TV in Orlando, Florida from Emmis Communications for $217.5 million.

FINANCIALS: Sales and profits are in thousands of dollars—add 000 to get the full amount. 2006 Note: Financial information for 2006 was not available for all companies at press time.

2006 Sales: $	2006 Profits: $	**U.S. Stock Ticker: HTV**
2005 Sales: $706,883	2005 Profits: $100,217	**Int'l Ticker:** Int'l Exchange:
2004 Sales: $779,879	2004 Profits: $123,942	Employees: 3,380
2003 Sales: $686,775	2003 Profits: $94,221	Fiscal Year Ends: 12/31
2002 Sales: $721,300	2002 Profits: $108,000	Parent Company:

SALARIES/BENEFITS:

Pension Plan: Y	ESOP Stock Plan:	Profit Sharing:	Top Exec. Salary: $960,000	Bonus: $200,000
Savings Plan: Y	Stock Purch. Plan:		Second Exec. Salary: $675,000	Bonus: $125,000

OTHER THOUGHTS:

Apparent Women Officers or Directors: 5
Hot Spot for Advancement for Women/Minorities: Y

LOCATIONS: ("Y" = Yes)

West:	Southwest:	Midwest:	Southeast:	Northeast:	International:
Y	Y	Y	Y	Y	

Note: Financial information, benefits and other data can change quickly and may vary from those stated here.

HERSHEY CO

www.hersheys.com

Industry Group Code: 311330 Ranks within this company's industry group: Sales: 1   Profits: 1

Print Media/Publishing:	Movies:	Equipment/Supplies:	Broadcast/Cable:	Music/Audio:	Sports/Games:	
Newspapers:	Movie Theaters:	Equipment/Supplies:	Broadcast TV:	Music Production:	Games/Sports:	
Magazines:	Movie Production:	Gambling Equipment:	Cable TV:	Retail Music:	Retail Games Stores:	
Books:	TV/Video Production:	Special Services:	Satellite Broadcast:	Retail Audio Equip.:	Stadiums/Teams:	
Book Stores:	Video Rental:	Advertising Services:	Radio:	Music Print./Dist.:	Gambling/Casinos:	
Distribution/Printing:	Video Distribution:	Info. Sys. Software:	Online Information:	Multimedia:	Rides/Theme Parks:	Y

TYPES OF BUSINESS:

Candy Manufacturing
Baking Supplies
Chocolate Products
Confectionaries & Snacks
Amusement Park

BRANDS/DIVISIONS/AFFILIATES:

Kit Kat
Reese's
Hershey International
Pelon Pelo Rico
HERSHEYPARK
Hershey Entertainment and Resorts, Co.
Dagoba Organic Chocolate, LLC
Cacao Reserve

CONTACTS: *Note: Officers with more than one job title may be intentionally listed here more than once.*

Richard H. Lenny, CEO
Richard H. Lenny, Pres.
David J. West, CFO/Sr. VP
Michele G. Buck, Sr. VP-Chief Mktg. Officer, U.S.
Marcella K. Arline, Chief People Officer/Sr. VP
Daniel Azzara, VP-Global Innovation & Quality
George F. Davis, CIO/VP
Susan M. Sinclair, VP-Continuous Improvement
Burton H. Snyder, General Counsel/Sr. VP/Corp. Sec.
Gregg Tanner, Sr. VP-Global Oper.
Bryon Klemens, VP-Bus. Dev.
John C. Long, VP-Corp. Affairs
Mark K. Pogharian, Dir.-Investor Relations
Rosa C. Stroh, Treas.
Jay A. Cooper, VP-U.S.Chocolate
Thomas K. Hernquist, Global Chief Growth Officer/Sr. VP
Bruce A. Brown, VP/Business Process Optimization
D. Michael Wege, VP-Asia
Richard H. Lenny, Chmn.
John P. Bilbrey, Sr. VP/Pres., Hershey Int'l

Phone: 717-534-6799	Fax: 717-534-6760
Toll-Free: 800-539-0261	
Address: 100 Crystal A Dr., Hershey, PA 17033-0810 US	

GROWTH PLANS/SPECIAL FEATURES:

Hershey Co. (formerly Hershey Foods Corp.) is one of the largest candy makers in the U.S., manufacturing over 50 brands, including five of the top ten chocolate brands in the country. Some of the company's best-known brands include Kit Kat, Jolly Rancher, Reese's and Hershey Bars and Kisses. The firm operates through three main divisions: the U.S. Confectionary group; the U.S. Snacks group; and Hershey International, which oversees the corporation's international interests and exports to over 60 countries worldwide. The company generates 80% of revenues from chocolate sales. Hershey's principal product groups include chocolate and non-chocolate confectionery products sold in the form of bar goods; bagged and boxed items; and grocery products in the form of baking ingredients, chocolate drink mixes, peanut butter, dessert toppings and beverages. Its products are sold primarily to grocery wholesalers, grocery stores, candy distributors, mass merchandisers, drug stores, vending companies, wholesale clubs, convenience stores, concessionaires and food distributors by full-time sales representatives, food brokers and part-time retail sales merchandisers throughout the U.S., Canada and Mexico. The firm operates in Mexico through Pelon Pelo Rico. Most company operations occur in Hershey, Pennsylvania where the company runs HERSHEYPARK, an amusement park operated by subsidiary Hershey Entertainment and Resorts Company. In 2006, Hershey acquired Dagoba Organic Chocolate, LLC, a leading producer of organic chocolate; and introduced a new product line of all-natural chocolates and drinking cocoa called Cacao Reserve. Hershey will phase out its cocoa bean and chocolate liquor processing operations during 2007. The firm is drawing up plans to enter the Indian market with dairy firm Gujarat Co-operative Milk Marketing Federation (GCMMF) or chocolate maker Campco.

Hershey's headquarters provides employees with a swimming pool and a gym. Other employee benefits include a counseling service, a casual dress code, health insurance, a 401(k) savings plan and free chocolate.

FINANCIALS: Sales and profits are in thousands of dollars—add 000 to get the full amount. 2006 Note: Financial information for 2006 was not available for all companies at press time.

2006 Sales: $	2006 Profits: $	**U.S. Stock Ticker:** HSY
2005 Sales: $4,836,000	2005 Profits: $493,200	**Int'l Ticker:** Int'l Exchange:
2004 Sales: $4,429,200	2004 Profits: $590,900	Employees: 13,750
2003 Sales: $4,172,551	2003 Profits: $457,584	Fiscal Year Ends: 12/31
2002 Sales: $4,120,300	2002 Profits: $403,600	Parent Company:

SALARIES/BENEFITS:

Pension Plan: Y	ESOP Stock Plan: Y	Profit Sharing:	Top Exec. Salary: $1,070,000	Bonus: $2,400,000
Savings Plan: Y	Stock Purch. Plan: Y		Second Exec. Salary: $450,000	Bonus: $526,680

OTHER THOUGHTS:

Apparent Women Officers or Directors: 12
Hot Spot for Advancement for Women/Minorities: Y

LOCATIONS: ("Y" = Yes)

West:	Southwest:	Midwest:	Southeast:	Northeast:	International:
Y	Y	Y	Y	Y	Y

HOLLINGER INC

www.hollinger.com

Industry Group Code: 511110 **Ranks within this company's industry group:** Sales: 19 Profits: 17

Print Media/Publishing:	Movies:	Equipment/Supplies:	Broadcast/Cable:	Music/Audio:	Sports/Games:
Newspapers: Y	Movie Theaters:	Equipment/Supplies:	Broadcast TV:	Music Production:	Games/Sports:
Magazines: Y	Movie Production:	Gambling Equipment:	Cable TV:	Retail Music:	Retail Games Stores:
Books:	TV/Video Production:	Special Services:	Satellite Broadcast:	Retail Audio Equip.:	Stadiums/Teams:
Book Stores:	Video Rental:	Advertising Services:	Radio:	Music Print./Dist.:	Gambling/Casinos:
Distribution/Printing:	Video Distribution:	Info. Sys. Software:	Online Information:	Multimedia:	Rides/Theme Parks:

TYPES OF BUSINESS:

Newspaper Publishing
Online Publishing
Magazine Publishing

BRANDS/DIVISIONS/AFFILIATES:

Chicago Sun-Times
Digital Chicago
Digital New York
Post Tribune
Daily Southtown
Hollinger, Inc.
Hollinger Canadian Publishing Holdings Co.

CONTACTS: *Note: Officers with more than one job title may be intentionally listed here more than once.*

Gordon A. Paris, CEO
John D. Cruickshank, COO
Gordon A. Paris, Pres.
Gregory A. Stoklosa, CFO/VP
James R. Van Horn, General Counsel/VP
Paul B. Healy, VP-Corp. Dev.
Paul B. Healy, VP-Investor Rel.
Tatiana Samila, Treas.
Randall C. Benson, Chief Restructuring Officer
Frederick A. Creasey, VP/Group Corp. Controller
James R. Van Horn, Corp. Sec.
Peter K. Lane, VP-Finance
Stanley Beck, Chmn.

Phone: 212-586-5666	Fax: 212-586-0010
Toll-Free:	
Address: 10 Toronto St., Toronto, ON M5C2B7 Canada	

GROWTH PLANS/SPECIAL FEATURES:

Hollinger, Inc., through subsidiaries and affiliated companies, is one of the leading publishers of English-language newspapers in the U.S. and U.K. It maintains web sites supporting each of its major newspapers and continues to develop a strategic online media presence. The 23 paid daily newspapers the firm owns or has an interest in have a worldwide daily combined circulation of about 2 million. Hollinger also owns or has an interest in over 250 non-daily newspapers, as well as magazines and other publications. The company's Chicago group consists of more than 100 papers including the Chicago Sun-Times, the fifth most read daily newspaper in the U.S.; the Post Tribune in Gary, Indiana; and the Daily Southtown. The group also publishes Digital Chicago magazine and Digital New York, which appear both on newsstands and online. Hollinger owns approximately 70.1% voting stock and 19.7% equity interest in the Sun-Times Media Group, Inc. (formerly Hollinger International, Inc.) which owns the Chicago Sun-Times and other community newspapers in and around Chicago.

FINANCIALS: Sales and profits are in thousands of dollars—add 000 to get the full amount. 2006 Note: Financial information for 2006 was not available for all companies at press time.

2006 Sales: $	2006 Profits: $	U.S. Stock Ticker: HLR
2005 Sales: $457,889	2005 Profits: $-11,969	Int'l Ticker: Int'l Exchange:
2004 Sales: $464,439	2004 Profits: $234,668	Employees: 3,079
2003 Sales: $1,061,200	2003 Profits: $-68,900	Fiscal Year Ends: 12/31
2002 Sales: $1,006,200	2002 Profits: $-238,900	Parent Company:

SALARIES/BENEFITS:

Pension Plan:	ESOP Stock Plan:	Profit Sharing:	Top Exec. Salary: $1,714,087	Bonus: $1,100,000
Savings Plan: Y	Stock Purch. Plan:		Second Exec. Salary: $373,304	Bonus: $200,603

OTHER THOUGHTS:

Apparent Women Officers or Directors: 1
Hot Spot for Advancement for Women/Minorities:

LOCATIONS: ("Y" = Yes)

West:	Southwest:	Midwest:	Southeast:	Northeast:	International:
		Y		Y	Y

Note: Financial information, benefits and other data can change quickly and may vary from those stated here.

HOLLYWOOD ENTERTAINMENT CORP
www.hollywoodvideo.com

Industry Group Code: 532230 Ranks within this company's industry group: Sales: 3   Profits:

Print Media/Publishing:	Movies:	Equipment/Supplies:	Broadcast/Cable:	Music/Audio:	Sports/Games:
Newspapers:	Movie Theaters:	Equipment/Supplies:	Broadcast TV:	Music Production:	Games/Sports:
Magazines:	Movie Production:	Gambling Equipment:	Cable TV:	Retail Music:	Retail Games Stores:
Books:	TV/Video Production: Y	Special Services:	Satellite Broadcast:	Retail Audio Equip.:	Stadiums/Teams:
Book Stores:	Video Rental: Y	Advertising Services:	Radio:	Music Print./Dist.:	Gambling/Casinos:
Distribution/Printing:	Video Distribution: Y	Info. Sys. Software:	Online Information:	Multimedia:	Rides/Theme Parks:

TYPES OF BUSINESS:
Video Rental Stores
Video Game Rentals & Sales

BRANDS/DIVISIONS/AFFILIATES:
Hollywood Video
Game Crazy
Movie Gallery, Inc.

CONTACTS: *Note: Officers with more than one job title may be intentionally listed here more than once.*
Joe T. Malugen, CEO
Timothy A. Winner, Exec. VP/COO
Joe T. Malugen, Pres.
Thomas Johnson, Sr. VP-Finance/Interim CFO
S. Page Todd, Corp. Sec./Chief Compliance Officer
S. Page Todd, Exec. VP/General Counsel
Thomas Johnson, Sr. VP-Bus. Dev.
Michelle K. Lewis, Sr. VP-Investor Rel.
Michelle K. Lewis, Treas.
Joe T. Malugen, Chmn.

Phone: 503-570-1600	Fax: 503-570-1680
Toll-Free: 877-325-8687	
Address: 9275 SW Peyton Ln., Wilsonville, OR 97070 US	

GROWTH PLANS/SPECIAL FEATURES:
Hollywood Entertainment Corp., a subsidiary of Movie Gallery, Inc., is the second-largest retailer of rental videocassettes, DVDs and video games in the U.S., owning and operating more than 2,000 Hollywood Video retail superstores in 47 states and the District of Columbia. The company's superstores typically carry over 10,000 movie and game titles on more than 25,000 videocassettes, DVDs and video games. The stores are typically located in high-traffic, high visibility, urban and suburban locations with convenient access and parking. Hollywood's goal is to offer more copies of popular new video releases and more titles than its competitors. In part because of the firm's revenue sharing arrangements with studios, Hollywood has increased the availability of most new releases and typically acquires 100 to 250 copies of hit movies for each Hollywood Video store. The company also operates Game Crazy, a store-within-a store concept through which customers sell, buy and trade new and used video games from a stock of more than 9,000 units. Hollywood currently has approximately 700 Game Crazy locations nationwide, including 20 free-standing locations. In April 2005, following an attempted unsolicited takeover by Blockbuster, Hollywood Entertainment Corp. merged with Movie Gallery in a deal valued at $1.2 billion. In 2006, Movie Gallery planned to purchase 20 Hollywood Video stores and 17 Game Crazy stores currently owned by Boards Video Company LLC.

Hollywood offers its employees benefits including flexible spending accounts, a free 24-hour nurse hotline, a 401(k) plan and discounts on rentals and product purchases from company stores as well as selected retail partners.

FINANCIALS: Sales and profits are in thousands of dollars—add 000 to get the full amount. 2006 Note: Financial information for 2006 was not available for all companies at press time.

2006 Sales: $	2006 Profits: $	U.S. Stock Ticker: Subsidiary
2005 Sales: $933,100	2005 Profits: $	Int'l Ticker: Int'l Exchange:
2004 Sales: $1,782,400	2004 Profits: $71,300	Employees: 27,900
2003 Sales: $1,682,548	2003 Profits: $82,272	Fiscal Year Ends: 12/31
2002 Sales: $1,490,100	2002 Profits: $241,900	Parent Company: MOVIE GALLERY INC

SALARIES/BENEFITS:

Pension Plan:	ESOP Stock Plan:	Profit Sharing:	Top Exec. Salary: $1,269,231		Bonus: $
Savings Plan: Y	Stock Purch. Plan:		Second Exec. Salary: $342,461		Bonus: $

OTHER THOUGHTS:
Apparent Women Officers or Directors: 1
Hot Spot for Advancement for Women/Minorities:

LOCATIONS: ("Y" = Yes)

West:	Southwest:	Midwest:	Southeast:	Northeast:	International:
Y	Y	Y	Y	Y	

HOLLYWOOD MEDIA CORP

www.hollywood.com

Industry Group Code: 514199 Ranks within this company's industry group: Sales: 4   Profits: 6

Print Media/Publishing:	Movies:	Equipment/Supplies:	Broadcast/Cable:	Music/Audio:	Sports/Games:
Newspapers:	Movie Theaters:	Equipment/Supplies:	Broadcast TV:	Music Production:	Games/Sports:
Magazines:	Movie Production:	Gambling Equipment:	Cable TV: Y	Retail Music:	Retail Games Stores:
Books: Y	TV/Video Production:	Special Services: Y	Satellite Broadcast:	Retail Audio Equip.:	Stadiums/Teams:
Book Stores:	Video Rental:	Advertising Services: Y	Radio:	Music Print./Dist.:	Gambling/Casinos:
Distribution/Printing:	Video Distribution:	Info. Sys. Software:	Online Information:	Multimedia:	Rides/Theme Parks:

TYPES OF BUSINESS:

Movie-Related Merchandise, Online Retail
Book Publishing
Entertainment-Related Web Sites
Entertainment Research Services
Online Ticket Sales
Advertising Services
Theater Marketing & Sales
Cable Television Networks

BRANDS/DIVISIONS/AFFILIATES:

Hollywood.com
CinemaSource
MovieTickets.com
EventSource
Exhibitor Ads
Broadway.com
Tekno Books
CinemasOnline

CONTACTS: Note: Officers with more than one job title may be intentionally listed here more than once.

Mitchell Rubenstein, CEO
Nicholas Hall, COO
Laurie S. Silvers, Pres.
Scott Gomez, Chief Acc. Officer
Mitchell Rubenstein, Chmn.

Phone: 561-998-8000	Fax: 561-998-2974
Toll-Free:	
Address: 2255 Glades Rd., Ste. 221 A, Boca Raton, FL 33431 US	

GROWTH PLANS/SPECIAL FEATURES:

Hollywood Media Corp. provides on-line news, information, ticketing, data and other content for the entertainment and media industries. The firm operates an entertainment-related web site that includes movie descriptions and reviews, movie trailers, photos, movie showtime listings and entertainment news. The company operates several divisions including Data Business, Broadway Ticketing, Internet Ad Sales, Cable TV, and Intellectual Properties. The company includes Hollywood.com, CinemaSource, MovieTickets.com, EventSource, ExhibitorAds, Broadway.com, Theatre.com and Theatre Direct International. Hollywood.com is a movie and entertainment web site. CinemaSource is one of the nation's largest providers of Internet-based movie showtime listings. EventSource is a nationwide online database of general events and entertainment information. ExhibitorAds creates advertisements for the movie exhibition industry. Broadway.com provides live theater information worldwide. Theatre Direct International is a live theater marketing and sales agency for domestic and international travel professionals. In 2006, the company began operating Theatre.com, a website based on the Broadway.com model and targeted at theater in the U.K. The firm also operates two cable T.V. networks: Hollywood.com Television and Broadway.com Television. The studio store features licensed movie based merchandise including toys, apparel, video games, art, collectibles and movie posters. Additionally, Hollywood Media owns 51% of the book publishing and packaging company Tekno Books and 50% of NetCo Partners, which owns Tom Clancy's Net Force. In 2006, the company sold its Baseline StudioSystems service to the New York Times Company. In addition, the company acquired CinemasOnline, a group of Internet advertising sales and data service companies which sell advertising on cinema and theatre websites throughout the U.K.

FINANCIALS: Sales and profits are in thousands of dollars—add 000 to get the full amount. 2006 Note: Financial information for 2006 was not available for all companies at press time.

2006 Sales: $	2006 Profits: $	U.S. Stock Ticker: HOLL
2005 Sales: $95,614	2005 Profits: $-8,913	Int'l Ticker: Int'l Exchange:
2004 Sales: $72,979	2004 Profits: $-11,598	Employees: 271
2003 Sales: $64,859	2003 Profits: $-7,442	Fiscal Year Ends: 12/31
2002 Sales: $58,200	2002 Profits: $-81,600	Parent Company:

SALARIES/BENEFITS:

Pension Plan:	ESOP Stock Plan:	Profit Sharing:	Top Exec. Salary: $410,800	Bonus: $100,000
Savings Plan: Y	Stock Purch. Plan:		Second Exec. Salary: $359,450	Bonus: $100,000

OTHER THOUGHTS:

Apparent Women Officers or Directors: 2
Hot Spot for Advancement for Women/Minorities: Y

LOCATIONS: ("Y" = Yes)

West:	Southwest:	Midwest:	Southeast:	Northeast:	International:
Y			Y	Y	

Note: Financial information, benefits and other data can change quickly and may vary from those stated here.

HOOVER'S INC

www.hoovers.com

Industry Group Code: 514199 Ranks within this company's industry group: Sales: 6 Profits:

Print Media/Publishing:		Movies:	Equipment/Supplies:	Broadcast/Cable:	Music/Audio:	Sports/Games:
Newspapers:		Movie Theaters:	Equipment/Supplies:	Broadcast TV:	Music Production:	Games/Sports:
Magazines:		Movie Production:	Gambling Equipment:	Cable TV:	Retail Music:	Retail Games Stores:
Books:	Y	TV/Video Production:	Special Services:	Satellite Broadcast:	Retail Audio Equip.:	Stadiums/Teams:
Book Stores:		Video Rental:	Advertising Services:	Radio:	Music Print./Dist.:	Gambling/Casinos:
Distribution/Printing:		Video Distribution:	Info. Sys. Software:	Online Information:	Multimedia:	Rides/Theme Parks:

TYPES OF BUSINESS:

Online Corporate Intelligence
Reference Books
E-Commerce
Advertising Services
Sales & Marketing Lists

BRANDS/DIVISIONS/AFFILIATES:

Dun & Bradstreet
D&B
Hoover's Handbooks
IPO Scorecard
My Hoover's

CONTACTS: Note: Officers with more than one job title may be intentionally listed here more than once.

Paul Pellman, Interim Pres.
John Lysinger, Exec. VP-Sales
Jeff Guillot, Exec. VP-Tech.
Jeff Guillot, Exec. VP-Products
Mel Yarbrough, VP-Bus. Dev.
Chuck Harvey, VP-Finance
Fred Howard, VP-Mktg.
Russell Secker, Exec. VP-Int'l

Phone: 512-374-4500	**Fax:** 512-374-4501
Toll-Free: 800-486-8666	
Address: 5800 Airport Blvd., Austin, TX 78752 US	

GROWTH PLANS/SPECIAL FEATURES:

Hoover's, Inc., a subsidiary of Dun & Bradstreet (D&B), is a provider of online company and industry information, designed to meet the diverse needs of business organizations, sales executives, investors and researchers of many types. Hoover's customers can access information for their professional endeavors, including financial and competitive research as well as marketing and job search activities, through the company's web site. Hoover's core asset is its proprietary editorial content, which includes in-depth competitive intelligence written and edited in-house on approximately 40,000 public and private enterprises. Hoover's also provides data on initial public offerings (through the IPO Scorecard pages), corporate news, executive biographical information, corporate financial data and access to such items as credit reports by D&B. While the firm's primary focus is delivery of company intelligence via the Internet, it also publishes reference books including the Hoover's Handbooks. The company partners with Air2Web, a wireless technology firm, to provide customers with the ability to tap into key content and service offerings via wireless devices. The company generates about 80% of revenue from the sale of annual subscriptions to its premium-level data services, which include Lite, Pro, Pro Plus and Pro Premium. Significant revenue is also generated from licensing fees, e-commerce and the sale of advertising.

FINANCIALS: Sales and profits are in thousands of dollars—add 000 to get the full amount. 2006 Note: Financial information for 2006 was not available for all companies at press time.

2006 Sales: $	2006 Profits: $	**U.S. Stock Ticker:** Subsidiary
2005 Sales: $70,000	2005 Profits: $	**Int'l Ticker:** Int'l Exchange:
2004 Sales: $50,000	2004 Profits: $	Employees: 231
2003 Sales: $38,000	2003 Profits: $	Fiscal Year Ends: 12/31
2002 Sales: $31,600	2002 Profits: $-11,600	Parent Company: DUN & BRADSTREET CORP (THE, D&B)

SALARIES/BENEFITS:

Pension Plan:	ESOP Stock Plan:	Profit Sharing:	Top Exec. Salary: $320,451	Bonus: $75,000
Savings Plan: Y	Stock Purch. Plan:		Second Exec. Salary: $226,813	Bonus: $25,000

OTHER THOUGHTS:

Apparent Women Officers or Directors: 2
Hot Spot for Advancement for Women/Minorities:

LOCATIONS: ("Y" = Yes)

West:	Southwest:	Midwest:	Southeast:	Northeast:	International:
	Y			Y	

HOUGHTON MIFFLIN CO

www.hmco.com

Industry Group Code: 511130 Ranks within this company's industry group: Sales: 5 Profits: 7

Print Media/Publishing:		Movies:		Equipment/Supplies:		Broadcast/Cable:		Music/Audio:		Sports/Games:	
Newspapers:		Movie Theaters:		Equipment/Supplies:		Broadcast TV:		Music Production:		Games/Sports:	
Magazines:		Movie Production:		Gambling Equipment:		Cable TV:		Retail Music:		Retail Games Stores:	
Books:	Y	TV/Video Production:		Special Services:	Y	Satellite Broadcast:		Retail Audio Equip.:		Stadiums/Teams:	
Book Stores:		Video Rental:		Advertising Services:		Radio:		Music Print./Dist.:		Gambling/Casinos:	
Distribution/Printing:		Video Distribution:		Info. Sys. Software:		Online Information:		Multimedia:		Rides/Theme Parks:	

TYPES OF BUSINESS:

Book Publishing
Educational Materials
Software, CD-ROMs & Mixed Media
Textbooks
Electronic & Multimedia Publishing
Test Design & Consulting
Reference Materials

BRANDS/DIVISIONS/AFFILIATES:

McDougal Littell, Inc.
Great Source Education Group, Inc.
Cognitive Concepts, Inc.
Riverside Publishing Company
Edusoft
American Heritage Dictionary
Peterson Field Guides
Houghton Mifflin Holdings, Inc.

CONTACTS: Note: Officers with more than one job title may be intentionally listed here more than once.

Anthony Lucki, CEO
Stephen Richards, COO/Exec. VP
Anthony Lucki, Pres.
Stephen Richards, CFO
Gerald Hughes, Sr. VP-Human Resources
Mike Quinn, CIO/VP
Clarence Thacker, VP-Manufacturing & Corp. Fulfillment Services
Paul Weaver, General Counsel/Sr. VP/Corp. Sec.
Collin Earnst, VP-Corp. Comm.
Cheryl Cramer, VP-Investor Rel.
Donna Lucki, Pres., School Div.
Rita H. Schaefer, Pres., McDougal Littell
June Smith, Pres., College Div.
Theresa Kelly, Pres., Trade & Reference Div.
Anthony Lucki, Chmn.

Phone: 617-351-5000	Fax: 617-351-1105
Toll-Free:	
Address: 222 Berkeley St., Fl. 5, Boston, MA 02116 US	

GROWTH PLANS/SPECIAL FEATURES:

Houghton Mifflin Co. and its subsidiaries publish textbooks and other educational materials and provide educational services, as well as publishing fiction, nonfiction, children's books and dictionary and reference materials. The K-12 publishing segment operates through four divisions: School Division, which focuses on kindergarten through sixth grade; McDougal Littell, Inc., which publishes educational materials for grades 6-12; Great Source Education Group, Inc., which publishes curriculum-based supplementary and alternative instructional material for the K-12 and home school markets through Cognitive Concepts, Inc., Earobics and Write Source; and the Assessment Division, which develops and markets testing technology for K-12 through the Riverside Publishing Company. Houghton Mifflin's college division publishes textbooks, study guides and technology tools for introductory level college classes. Edusoft, now operating in conjunction with Riverside Publishing, is an online assessment tool that assists school districts in tracking test results. Houghton Mifflin's trade and reference division publishes adult and children's literature and nonfiction, poetry and cookbooks, as well as reference books including American Heritage dictionaries and Peterson Field Guides. While the firm has traditionally published printed materials, it has begun to publish in other formats, including computer software, laser discs, CD-ROM and other electronic and multimedia products. Recently, the firm sold Promissor, a professional testing business, to Pearson. The company is owned through Houghton Mifflin Holdings, Inc. by a consortium of investors including Thomas H. Lee Partners, Bain Capital and The Blackstone Group. In late 2006, Houghton Mifflin Holdings signed a definitive agreement to be acquired by HM Rivergroup plc for approximately $3.4 billion in cash and debt assumption.

Houghton Mifflin offers employee benefits including health and disability insurance, life insurance, 401(k) and retirement plans, flexible spending accounts, scholarships, tuition reimbursement, employee assistance, banking and credit union services, and discounts on Houghton Mifflin books. The firm offers internships and temporary summer positions.

FINANCIALS: Sales and profits are in thousands of dollars—add 000 to get the full amount. 2006 Note: Financial information for 2006 was not available for all companies at press time.

2006 Sales: $	2006 Profits: $	U.S. Stock Ticker: Private	
2005 Sales: $1,282,100	2005 Profits: $-56,300	Int'l Ticker:	Int'l Exchange:
2004 Sales: $1,218,900	2004 Profits: $-67,200	Employees: 3,554	
2003 Sales: $1,263,500	2003 Profits: $-71,600	Fiscal Year Ends: 12/31	
2002 Sales: $1,211,000	2002 Profits: $	Parent Company:	

SALARIES/BENEFITS:

Pension Plan: Y	ESOP Stock Plan:	Profit Sharing:	Top Exec. Salary: $398,284	Bonus: $363,428
Savings Plan: Y	Stock Purch. Plan:		Second Exec. Salary: $355,054	Bonus: $331,955

OTHER THOUGHTS:

Apparent Women Officers or Directors: 5
Hot Spot for Advancement for Women/Minorities: Y

LOCATIONS: ("Y" = Yes)

West:	Southwest:	Midwest:	Southeast:	Northeast:	International:
Y	Y	Y	Y	Y	Y

Note: Financial information, benefits and other data can change quickly and may vary from those stated here.

IAC/INTERACTIVECORP

www.iac.com

Industry Group Code: 454110B Ranks within this company's industry group: Sales: 1 Profits: 1

Print Media/Publishing:	Movies:	Equipment/Supplies:	Broadcast/Cable:	Music/Audio:	Sports/Games:
Newspapers:	Movie Theaters:	Equipment/Supplies:	Broadcast TV: Y	Music Production:	Games/Sports:
Magazines:	Movie Production:	Gambling Equipment:	Cable TV: Y	Retail Music:	Retail Games Stores:
Books:	TV/Video Production: Y	Special Services:	Satellite Broadcast:	Retail Audio Equip.:	Stadiums/Teams:
Book Stores:	Video Rental:	Advertising Services: Y	Radio:	Music Print./Dist.:	Gambling/Casinos:
Distribution/Printing:	Video Distribution:	Info. Sys. Software: Y	Online Information:	Multimedia:	Rides/Theme Parks:

TYPES OF BUSINESS:

Cable Television Shopping Programs
Entertainment & Event Ticket Sales
Catalog & Online Home Products & Apparel Retailing
E-Commerce, Online Advertising & Search Engines
Online Real Estate Services, Mortgages & Loans
Online Entertainment & Shopping Directories
Online Personals & Dating Services

BRANDS/DIVISIONS/AFFILIATES:

citysearch.com
Ticketmaster
Cornerstone Brands
HSN
Ask.com
LendingTree
Connected Ventures LLC
match.com

CONTACTS: *Note: Officers with more than one job title may be intentionally listed here more than once.*

Barry Diller, CEO
Doug Lebda, COO
Doug Lebda, Pres.
Thomas J. McInerney, Exec. VP/CFO
Johnny C. Taylor, Jr., Sr. VP-Human Resources
Michael Jackson, Pres., Programming
Michael Schwerdtman, Sr. VP/Controller
Jason Stewart, Chief Admin. Officer
Greg Blatt, Exec. VP/General Counsel/Corp. Sec.
Julius Genachowski, Chief-Bus. Oper.
Shana Fisher, Sr. VP-Strategy, Mergers & Acquisitions
Edgar Bronfman, Jr., Vice-Chmn.
Greg Morrow, Sr. VP-Tax
Jay Herratti, Sr. VP-Strategic Planning
Joanne Hawkins, Sr. VP/Deputy General Counsel
Barry Diller, Chmn.

Phone: 212-314-7300	Fax: 212-314-7309
Toll-Free:	
Address: 152 W. 57th St., New York, NY 10019 US	

GROWTH PLANS/SPECIAL FEATURES:

IAC/InterActiveCorp operates leading businesses in online sectors such as entertainment ticketing, electronic retailing, financial services and real estate, media services and teleservices with offices in the U.S. as well as South America, Australia, Asia and Europe. The company's principal operating assets include Ticketmaster, the Home Shopping Network, the Internet sites citysearch.com and match.com, LendingTree, City Auction and Precision Response Corp. Additional businesses include ReserveAmerica, TicketWEb, MuseumTix, America's Store, Improvements, 9Live, RealEstate.com, GetSmart, iNest, Domania, ServiceMagic, Entertainment Publications, Evite, uDate, Access Direct and Interval International. Ticketmaster sells tickets and provides local content and transactions online and is one of the leading providers of automated ticketing services in the U.S. HSN (formerly the Home Shopping Network), HSN.com and HSE 24 sell a variety of consumer goods and services by means of live, customer-interactive electronic retail sales programs. The network operates three retail sales programs in the U.S., each available 24 hours a day in English and in Spanish. LendingTree operates as an online mortgage referral service. The largest share of the company's revenues was generated through online travel reservations with hotels.com, TravelNow, ReserveAmerica and online reservations giant Expedia, until the company spun off its travel units into a new free-standing, publicly traded company under the Expedia. In 2005, IAC acquired Ask Jeeves for $1.85 billion dollars in stock, and renamed it Ask.com, which is now the core of IAC's more than 60 online and retail brands. Recently the company acquired a majority stake in Connected Ventures LLC, a parent of leading comedy site CollegeHumor.com.

The company encourages employees to participate in community service projects through corporate initiatives, community service days and employee matching gift program. IAC also offers benefits to domestic partners and pets as well as employee discounts.

FINANCIALS: Sales and profits are in thousands of dollars—add 000 to get the full amount. 2006 Note: Financial information for 2006 was not available for all companies at press time.

2006 Sales: $	2006 Profits: $	**U.S. Stock Ticker: IACI**
2005 Sales: $5,753,700	2005 Profits: $868,200	Int'l Ticker: Int'l Exchange:
2004 Sales: $6,192,700	2004 Profits: $164,900	Employees: 28,000
2003 Sales: $6,328,100	2003 Profits: $167,400	Fiscal Year Ends: 12/31
2002 Sales: $4,621,200	2002 Profits: $1,953,100	Parent Company:

SALARIES/BENEFITS:

Pension Plan:	ESOP Stock Plan:	Profit Sharing:	Top Exec. Salary: $726,115	Bonus: $3,250,000
Savings Plan: Y	Stock Purch. Plan: Y		Second Exec. Salary: $650,000	Bonus: $3,000,000

OTHER THOUGHTS:

Apparent Women Officers or Directors: 3
Hot Spot for Advancement for Women/Minorities: Y

LOCATIONS: ("Y" = Yes)

West:	Southwest:	Midwest:	Southeast:	Northeast:	International:
Y	Y	Y	Y	Y	Y

I-CABLE COMMUNICATIONS
www.i-cablecomm.com

Industry Group Code: 513220 Ranks within this company's industry group: Sales: 20   Profits: 12

Print Media/Publishing:	Movies:		Equipment/Supplies:		Broadcast/Cable:		Music/Audio:		Sports/Games:	
Newspapers:	Movie Theaters:		Equipment/Supplies:		Broadcast TV:		Music Production:		Games/Sports:	
Magazines:	Movie Production:	Y	Gambling Equipment:		Cable TV:	Y	Retail Music:		Retail Games Stores:	
Books:	TV/Video Production:		Special Services:	Y	Satellite Broadcast:		Retail Audio Equip.:		Stadiums/Teams:	
Book Stores:	Video Rental:		Advertising Services:	Y	Radio:		Music Print./Dist.:		Gambling/Casinos:	
Distribution/Printing:	Video Distribution:		Info. Sys. Software:		Online Information:		Multimedia:		Rides/Theme Parks:	

TYPES OF BUSINESS:

Cable TV Service
Internet Service Provider
VoIP Telephony Services
Film Production
Advertising-Mass Transit

BRANDS/DIVISIONS/AFFILIATES:

Hong Kong Cable Television, Ltd.
CABLE TV
Horizon Channel
Sundream Motion Pictures, Ltd.
Newsline Express

CONTACTS: Note: Officers with more than one job title may be intentionally listed here more than once.

Stephen T. H. Ng, CEO
William Kwan, CFO
Felix W. K. Yip, VP-Human Resources
Felix W. K. Yip, VP-Admin. & Audit
Garmen K. Y. Chan, VP-External Affairs
Vincent T. Y. Lam, Exec. Dir.-HKC
Eric Lo, Exec. Dir.-Cable Subscription Svcs.
Benjamin W. S. Tong, Exec. Dir.-HKC & i-CABLE WebServe Limited
Ronald Y. C. Chiu, Exec. Dir.-News & Sports
Stephen T. H. Ng, Chmn.
Simon K. K. Yu, VP-Procurement

Phone: 852-2112-6868	**Fax:** 852-2112-7878
Toll-Free:	
Address: Cable TV Tower, 9 Hoi Shing Rd., Tsuen Wan, Hong Kong, China	

GROWTH PLANS/SPECIAL FEATURES:

I-Cable Communications is the leading cable systems operator in Hong Kong, with more than 700,000 subscribers to its pay-TV services. The Hong Kong Cable Television, or CABLE TV, subsidiary produces the majority of the company's content and currently operates 92 separate cable channels. Also offered is Horizon Channel, a satellite network with extensive presence in the mainland. I-Cable also offers dial-up Internet services, currently serving over 290,000 users. I-Cable's largest project is the expansion of its high-speed Internet access. The firm has been upgrading its network infrastructure with hybrid fiber-coaxial cable, and also intends to introduce voice-over-IP telephony services. Recently, I-Cable announced plans to produce up to 20 full-length feature films by 2007. The project will be undertaken by new subsidiary Sundream Motion Pictures, Ltd., which was officially launched in 2005. I-Cable also recently began selling advertising air on Newsline Express, a multimedia news and advertising medium broadcast to the numerous passengers of the Kowloon-Canton Railway (KCR), a mass-transit line linking Hong Kong's Kowloon peninsula with Shenzhen in the mainland.

FINANCIALS: Sales and profits are in thousands of dollars—add 000 to get the full amount. 2006 Note: Financial information for 2006 was not available for all companies at press time.

2006 Sales: $	2006 Profits: $	**U.S. Stock Ticker:** ICAB
2005 Sales: $314,799	2005 Profits: $67,988	**Int'l Ticker:** 1097 Int'l Exchange: Hong Kong
2004 Sales: $305,200	2004 Profits: $43,700	Employees: 3,275
2003 Sales: $276,000	2003 Profits: $28,400	Fiscal Year Ends: 12/31
2002 Sales: $277,100	2002 Profits: $15,100	Parent Company:

SALARIES/BENEFITS:

Pension Plan: Y	ESOP Stock Plan:	Profit Sharing:	Top Exec. Salary: $	Bonus: $
Savings Plan:	Stock Purch. Plan:		Second Exec. Salary: $	Bonus: $

OTHER THOUGHTS:

Apparent Women Officers or Directors:
Hot Spot for Advancement for Women/Minorities:

LOCATIONS: ("Y" = Yes)

West:	Southwest:	Midwest:	Southeast:	Northeast:	International:
					Y

Note: Financial information, benefits and other data can change quickly and may vary from those stated here.

IGN ENTERTAINMENT

corp.ign.com

Industry Group Code: 514199 Ranks within this company's industry group: Sales: Profits:

Print Media/Publishing:	Movies:	Equipment/Supplies:	Broadcast/Cable:	Music/Audio:	Sports/Games:	
Newspapers:	Movie Theaters:	Equipment/Supplies:	Broadcast TV:	Music Production:	Games/Sports:	Y
Magazines:	Movie Production:	Gambling Equipment:	Cable TV:	Retail Music:	Retail Games Stores:	Y
Books:	TV/Video Production:	Special Services: Y	Satellite Broadcast:	Retail Audio Equip.:	Stadiums/Teams:	
Book Stores:	Video Rental:	Advertising Services:	Radio:	Music Print./Dist.:	Gambling/Casinos:	
Distribution/Printing:	Video Distribution:	Info. Sys. Software:	Online Information:	Multimedia:	Rides/Theme Parks:	

TYPES OF BUSINESS:
Online Video Game Information
Online Software Retail & Distribution
Video Game Development Services
Online Movie Reviews
Video Game Market Statistics
Lifestyle Web Site

BRANDS/DIVISIONS/AFFILIATES:
Fox Interactive Media
IGN.com
GameSpy.com
TeemXbox.com
Voodoo Extreme
FilePlanet.com
AskMen.com
RottenTomatoes.com

CONTACTS: Note: Officers with more than one job title may be intentionally listed here more than once.
Mark Jung, CEO
Michael Sheridan, CFO
Ken Keller, CTO
Ken Keller, Exec. VP-Eng.
David Phillips, General Counsel/VP-Corp. Strategy
Richard Jalichandra, VP-Bus. Dev.
Dale Strang, Exec. VP-Media & Publishing
Jamie Berger, VP-Consumer Products
Mark Stieglitz, VP-Publisher Services
Peer Schneider, VP-Publishing

Phone: 415-508-2000	Fax: 415-508-2001
Toll-Free:	
Address: 8000 Marina Boulevard, 4th Fl., Brisbane, CA 94005 US	

GROWTH PLANS/SPECIAL FEATURES:
IGN Entertainment, a division of Fox Interactive Media, is a highly-trafficked provider of web-based video game information, software and services. Hosting a diverse network with a large variety of content, the company's online property receives over 35 million unique visits per month. IGN.com and GameSpy.com feature general information and resources, with the former boasting one of the highest visitation rates on the Internet from the 18- to 24-year-old male demographic. Other IGN web sites have more specialized content: TeemXbox.com, providing information on the Microsoft Xbox; The Vault Network, which serves players of role-playing (RPG) and massively multiplayer online (MMO) games; Planet Network, which links over 1,500 video game fan sites; and Voodoo Extreme, a frequently updated video game news source. IGN also provides software through three digital distribution sites: FilePlanet.com, featuring demos and trials of upcoming games; 3Dgamers.com, which offers a variety of files relating to 3D games; and Direct2Drive.com, an online store where customers can download PC games onto their hard drives. Further video game services include: Powered by GameSpy, offering technological services to game developers; GameStats.com, a resource for video game popularity statistics and other information; and GamerMetrics, which analyzes the traffic and buying patterns of IGN's visitors. Non-video game sites include AskMen.com, one of the leading male lifestyle web sites; and RottenTomatoes.com, a movie review and information site. Collectively, the company's sites have 35 million unique visitors per month, including 250,000 active paying subscribers. In April 2006, IGN launched Club.IGN.com, a community hub featuring blogs, interactive lists, reader reviews and FAQ submissions. The pages are fully customizable by users.

FINANCIALS: Sales and profits are in thousands of dollars—add 000 to get the full amount. 2006 Note: Financial information for 2006 was not available for all companies at press time.

2006 Sales: $	2006 Profits: $	U.S. Stock Ticker: Subsidiary
2005 Sales: $	2005 Profits: $	Int'l Ticker: Int'l Exchange:
2004 Sales: $42,900	2004 Profits: $-14,100	Employees: 313
2003 Sales: $17,500	2003 Profits: $-3,100	Fiscal Year Ends: 6/30
2002 Sales: $11,400	2002 Profits: $-11,300	Parent Company: FOX ENTERTAINMENT GROUP INC

SALARIES/BENEFITS:
Pension Plan:	ESOP Stock Plan:	Profit Sharing:	Top Exec. Salary: $	Bonus: $
Savings Plan:	Stock Purch. Plan:		Second Exec. Salary: $	Bonus: $

OTHER THOUGHTS:
Apparent Women Officers or Directors:
Hot Spot for Advancement for Women/Minorities:

LOCATIONS: ("Y" = Yes)
West:	Southwest:	Midwest:	Southeast:	Northeast:	International:
Y		Y		Y	Y

IMAX CORPORATION

www.imax.com

Industry Group Code: 512131 Ranks within this company's industry group: Sales: 5 Profits: 3

Print Media/Publishing:		Movies:		Equipment/Supplies:		Broadcast/Cable:		Music/Audio:		Sports/Games:	
Newspapers:		Movie Theaters:	Y	Equipment/Supplies:	Y	Broadcast TV:		Music Production:		Games/Sports:	
Magazines:		Movie Production:	Y	Gambling Equipment:		Cable TV:		Retail Music:		Retail Games Stores:	
Books:		TV/Video Production:		Special Services:	Y	Satellite Broadcast:		Retail Audio Equip.:		Stadiums/Teams:	
Book Stores:		Video Rental:		Advertising Services:		Radio:		Music Print./Dist.:		Gambling/Casinos:	
Distribution/Printing:		Video Distribution:		Info. Sys. Software:		Online Information:		Multimedia:		Rides/Theme Parks:	

TYPES OF BUSINESS:
Movie Theaters-Giant Screen Format
Giant-Screen Film Production & Distribution
Feature Film Reformatting
Audio & Video Technology

BRANDS/DIVISIONS/AFFILIATES:
IMAX 3D
IMAX Dome
IMAX DMR
IMAX Theater Services, Ltd.
Deep Sea 3D
Everest

CONTACTS: Note: Officers with more than one job title may be intentionally listed here more than once.
Bradley J. Wechsler, Co-CEO
Edward MacNeil, Interim-CFO
Mary C. Sullivan, Sr. VP-Human Resources
Brian Bonnick, Sr. VP-Tech.
Larry O'Reilly, Sr. VP-Theater Dev. & Film
Mary C. Sullivan, Sr. VP-Admin.
Robert D. Lister, Exec. VP-Bus. & Legal Affairs/Gen. Counsel
Mark Welton, Sr. VP-Bus. Affairs
Stephen G. Abraham, Sr. VP-Corp. Dev.
Stephen G. Abraham, Sr. VP-Investor Rel.
Richard L. Gelfond, Co-CEO/Co-Chmn.
Greg Foster, Chmn./Pres., Filmed Entertainment
David Keighley, Sr. VP/Pres., David Keighley Productions 70MM
G. Mary Ruby, Sr. VP-Legal Affairs/Corp. Sec.
Bradley J. Wechsler, Co-Chmn.

Phone: 905-403-6500	Fax: 905-403-6450

Toll-Free:

Address: 2525 Speakman Dr., Mississauga, ON L5K 1B1 Canada

GROWTH PLANS/SPECIAL FEATURES:

IMAX Corporation designs and manufactures projection and sound systems for giant-screen theaters, based on proprietary and patented technology, and is the largest producer and distributor of films for giant-screen theaters. The company leases its projection and sound systems and licenses its trademarks. Its 280 theaters (60% located in the U.S and 40% abroad) have three screen types: IMAX, IMAX 3D and IMAX Dome. The standard IMAX theater has stadium seating and a screen that is 70 feet tall and pitched between 19 and 25 degrees, allowing for the full range of peripheral vision. More than 100 theaters are equipped with IMAX 3D, which allows the projection of three-dimensional movies that make it appear that objects on the screen extend into the audience. IMAX Dome features seats that are reclined 30 degrees and a 180-degree screen projected on the domed ceiling. Currently, there are IMAX-affiliated theaters operating in 40 countries. Half of the IMAX theaters are located in institutional venues such as museums, science centers, zoos and expositions, while others are located in commercial theater complexes. In addition, the company produces adventure, science and nature films specifically for IMAX theaters. Proprietary IMAX DMR (Digital Re-Mastering) allows the company to reformat 35mm feature films to the 70mm format. In 2006, IMAX signed agreements to introduce theaters in Russia, Columbia, and the Ukraine, and to expand in India. The firm recently signed a multi-theater deal with CineMagic and a two-theater deal with Santikos Theaters. 25 theaters are scheduled to open in China, and 38 in South America by 2009. In 2006, IMAX opened its first theater in New Zealand.

IMAX offers its employees vision, health and dental benefits; life, accidental death and dismemberment insurance; tuition reimbursement; and a charitable donation matching program.

FINANCIALS: Sales and profits are in thousands of dollars—add 000 to get the full amount. 2006 Note: Financial information for 2006 was not available for all companies at press time.

2006 Sales: $		2006 Profits: $		**U.S. Stock Ticker: IMAX**	
2005 Sales: $144,930		2005 Profits: $16,598		**Int'l Ticker: IMX** Int'l Exchange: Toronto-TSX	
2004 Sales: $135,980		2004 Profits: $10,244		Employees: 376	
2003 Sales: $119,260		2003 Profits: $ 231		Fiscal Year Ends: 12/31	
2002 Sales: $130,700		2002 Profits: $12,000		Parent Company:	

SALARIES/BENEFITS:

Pension Plan: Y	ESOP Stock Plan: Y	Profit Sharing:	Top Exec. Salary: $500,000	Bonus: $250,000
Savings Plan: Y	Stock Purch. Plan:		Second Exec. Salary: $500,000	Bonus: $250,000

OTHER THOUGHTS:
Apparent Women Officers or Directors: 3
Hot Spot for Advancement for Women/Minorities: Y

LOCATIONS: ("Y" = Yes)

West:	Southwest:	Midwest:	Southeast:	Northeast:	International:
Y	Y	Y	Y	Y	Y

Note: Financial information, benefits and other data can change quickly and may vary from those stated here.

IMG WORLDWIDE INC

www.imgworld.com

Industry Group Code: 711410 Ranks within this company's industry group: Sales: Profits:

Print Media/Publishing:	Movies:		Equipment/Supplies:		Broadcast/Cable:	Music/Audio:	Sports/Games:	
Newspapers:	Movie Theaters:		Equipment/Supplies:		Broadcast TV:	Music Production:	Games/Sports:	Y
Magazines:	Movie Production:		Gambling Equipment:		Cable TV:	Retail Music:	Retail Games Stores:	
Books:	TV/Video Production:	Y	Special Services:	Y	Satellite Broadcast:	Retail Audio Equip.:	Stadiums/Teams:	
Book Stores:	Video Rental:		Advertising Services:	Y	Radio:	Music Print./Dist.:	Gambling/Casinos:	
Distribution/Printing:	Video Distribution:		Info. Sys. Software:		Online Information:	Multimedia:	Rides/Theme Parks:	

TYPES OF BUSINESS:

Agents-Athletes
Agents-Models
Agents-Writers, Artists & Musicians
Event Marketing
Corporate Marketing Consulting Services
Sports Television Programming
Sports Schools & Training

BRANDS/DIVISIONS/AFFILIATES:

IMG Golf
IMG Models
IMG Artists
IMG Consulting
Darlow Smithson Productions
Tiger Aspect Productions
Forstmann Little & Co.
Tigress

CONTACTS: *Note: Officers with more than one job title may be intentionally listed here more than once.*

Theodore J. Forstmann, CEO
Robert D. Kain, Pres.
Terri Santisi, CFO/Exec. VP
Terri Santisi, Chief Admin. Officer
Peter Lazarus, Sr. VP-Bus. Dev. & Sales, IMG Sports & Entertain.
Jane Singer, Sr. VP-Corp. Comm. & Pub. Rel.
Alastair Waddington, Exec. VP./COO-IMG Media
Robert Dalton, Chief Creative Officer
Douglas Perlman, Pres., IMG Media, North America
George Pyne, Pres., IMG Sports & Entertainment
Theodore J. Forstmann, Chmn.
Miles Palmer, Head-Audio Sales & Distrib. Worldwide

Phone: 216-522-1200	Fax: 216-522-1145
Toll-Free:	
Address: 1360 E. 9th St., Ste. 100, Cleveland, OH 44114 US	

GROWTH PLANS/SPECIAL FEATURES:

IMG Worldwide, Inc. is one of largest sports and lifestyle marketing and management agencies in the world. The company represents some of the world's top athletes, broadcasters, models, classical musicians, authors and newsmakers through 70 offices in 30 countries. The firm's sports clients include golfers Tiger Woods and Annika Sorenstam; tennis player Venus Williams; baseball player Derek Jeter; basketball player Charles Barkley; professional racecar driver Jeff Gordon; football player Peyton Manning; and hockey player Jaromir Jagr. The company pulls about 25% of its revenue from the golf unit, including fees for representing top players and income from producing events. It also represents sportscaster John Madden and other top athletic coaches through IMG Coaches. Furthermore, IMG runs a group of sports academies providing training programs in tennis, golf, baseball, basketball and other sports. Through IMG Models, an international modeling agency, the company represents Gisele and Cindy Crawford; while IMG Artists represents classical musicians such as violinist Itzhak Perlman and operatic soprano Kiri Te Kanawa. IMG promotes, manages and represents hundreds of sporting events and classical music events worldwide, including events at Wimbledon and Nobel Prize functions. IMG's content production division, made up of TWI, Darlow Smithson Productions (DSP) and Tiger Aspect Productions (TAP), is one of the world's largest independent producers and distributors of televised sports programming, managing a library of over 150,000 hours. It annually produces and distributes 6,500 hours of original programming to more than 200 countries covering 200 sports, as well as producing factual and entertainment programs. IMG is held by private-equity firm Forstmann Little & Co. In 2006, IMG Media acquired the Tiger Aspect Group, including its subsidiaries Tigress (wildlife and adventure producer), TTP (a U.S. production company) and Tiger Aspect Pictures.

The firm hires approximately 70 college interns yearly.

FINANCIALS: Sales and profits are in thousands of dollars—add 000 to get the full amount. 2006 Note: Financial information for 2006 was not available for all companies at press time.

2006 Sales: $	2006 Profits: $	U.S. Stock Ticker: Private
2005 Sales: $	2005 Profits: $	Int'l Ticker: Int'l Exchange:
2004 Sales: $	2004 Profits: $	Employees: 2,300
2003 Sales: $1,200,000	2003 Profits: $	Fiscal Year Ends: 12/31
2002 Sales: $1,300,000	2002 Profits: $	Parent Company: FORSTMANN LITTLE & CO

SALARIES/BENEFITS:

Pension Plan:	ESOP Stock Plan:	Profit Sharing:	Top Exec. Salary: $	Bonus: $
Savings Plan: Y	Stock Purch. Plan:		Second Exec. Salary: $	Bonus: $

OTHER THOUGHTS:

Apparent Women Officers or Directors: 2
Hot Spot for Advancement for Women/Minorities:

LOCATIONS: ("Y" = Yes)

West:	Southwest:	Midwest:	Southeast:	Northeast:	International:
Y		Y	Y	Y	Y

INGRAM ENTERTAINMENT HOLDINGS INC

www.ingramentertainment.com

Industry Group Code: 422921 **Ranks within this company's industry group:** Sales: 1 Profits:

Print Media/Publishing:		Movies:		Equipment/Supplies:		Broadcast/Cable:		Music/Audio:		Sports/Games:	
Newspapers:		Movie Theaters:		Equipment/Supplies:		Broadcast TV:		Music Production:		Games/Sports:	
Magazines:	Y	Movie Production:		Gambling Equipment:		Cable TV:		Retail Music:		Retail Games Stores:	
Books:		TV/Video Production:		Special Services:	Y	Satellite Broadcast:		Retail Audio Equip.:		Stadiums/Teams:	
Book Stores:		Video Rental:		Advertising Services:	Y	Radio:		Music Print./Dist.:		Gambling/Casinos:	
Distribution/Printing:		Video Distribution:		Info. Sys. Software:	Y	Online Information:		Multimedia:		Rides/Theme Parks:	

TYPES OF BUSINESS:

Digital Publication Distribution
Entertainment Product Distribution
Internet Services
Business-to-Business Sales
Marketing Services
Magazine Publishing
Graphic Design

BRANDS/DIVISIONS/AFFILIATES:

accessingram.com
myvideostore.com
Monarch Home Video
Ingram Publications
Entertainment Preview
Ingram Design Group

CONTACTS: Note: Officers with more than one job title may be intentionally listed here more than once.

David B. Ingram, Pres.
William D. Daniel, Exec. VP/CFO
Bob Geistman, Sr. VP-Mktg. & Sales
Robert W. Webb, Exec. VP-Oper.
David B. Ingram, Chmn.
Robert W. Webb, Exec. VP-Purchasing

Phone: 615-287-4000	Fax: 615-287-4982
Toll-Free:	
Address: 2 Ingram Blvd., La Vergne, TN 37089 US	

GROWTH PLANS/SPECIAL FEATURES:

Ingram Entertainment Holdings, Inc. (IEI) is a leading national distributor of home entertainment products including DVD and video hardware and software, video rental and sell-through products, video games, audio books and grocery and drug products. The company provides support services for Internet retailers, business-to-business sales through accessingram.com and creation and maintenance of customer web sites under the myvideostore.com program. Services include sell-through promotion programs, poster pack advertising programs, monthly publications that promote new and recently-released titles, audiobook rental packages, and payment plan options for buyers. Additionally, Ingram owns and operates its own proprietary line of video titles under the Monarch Home Video label. Services provided by the company include marketing and merchandising programs, publishing and Internet retail and design services. Divisions of the company include Ingram Publications, which publishes Entertainment Preview, a weekly industry magazine that keeps clients abreast of major studio news; and Ingram Design Group, which provides services that include print, illustration, editorial, PowerPoint presentations, photography, media buying, media placement and transparency creation. IEI's 2004 net sales were derived from 71% DVD, 15% VHS and 14% video games provided by services to over 10,000 retail locations including video specialty stores, Internet retailers, drugstores and supermarkets. In recent news, IEI announced plans to restructure its sales and marketing team.

FINANCIALS: Sales and profits are in thousands of dollars—add 000 to get the full amount. 2006 Note: Financial information for 2006 was not available for all companies at press time.

			U.S. Stock Ticker: Private	
2006 Sales: $	2006 Profits: $		Int'l Ticker: Int'l Exchange:	
2005 Sales: $839,000	2005 Profits: $		Employees: 747	
2004 Sales: $980,000	2004 Profits: $		Fiscal Year Ends: 12/31	
2003 Sales: $1,030,000	2003 Profits: $		Parent Company:	
2002 Sales: $	2002 Profits: $			

SALARIES/BENEFITS:

Pension Plan:	ESOP Stock Plan:	Profit Sharing:	Top Exec. Salary: $	Bonus: $
Savings Plan:	Stock Purch. Plan:		Second Exec. Salary: $	Bonus: $

OTHER THOUGHTS:

Apparent Women Officers or Directors:
Hot Spot for Advancement for Women/Minorities:

LOCATIONS: ("Y" = Yes)					
West:	Southwest:	Midwest:	Southeast:	Northeast:	International:
Y	Y	Y	Y	Y	

INSIGHT COMMUNICATIONS COMPANY INC
www.insight-com.com

Industry Group Code: 513220   Ranks within this company's industry group: Sales: 16   Profits: 18

Print Media/Publishing:	Movies:	Equipment/Supplies:		Broadcast/Cable:		Music/Audio:		Sports/Games:
Newspapers:	Movie Theaters:	Equipment/Supplies:		Broadcast TV:		Music Production:		Games/Sports:
Magazines:	Movie Production:	Gambling Equipment:		Cable TV:	Y	Retail Music:		Retail Games Stores:
Books:	TV/Video Production:	Special Services:	Y	Satellite Broadcast:		Retail Audio Equip.:		Stadiums/Teams:
Book Stores:	Video Rental:	Advertising Services:	Y	Radio:		Music Print./Dist.:		Gambling/Casinos:
Distribution/Printing:	Video Distribution:	Info. Sys. Software:		Online Information:		Multimedia:		Rides/Theme Parks:

TYPES OF BUSINESS:

Cable TV Service
Broadband Services Provider
High-Definition Television
Video-on-Demand
Digital Phone Plans
Cable Advertising
Business Services

BRANDS/DIVISIONS/AFFILIATES:

Carlyle Group
InsightBroadband
InsightDigital
InsightPhone
Insight Business
Insight Media
Insight Midwest, LP

CONTACTS: Note: Officers with more than one job title may be intentionally listed here more than once.

Michael S. Willner, CEO
Dinesh C. Jain, COO
Dinesh C. Jain, Pres.
John Abbot, CFO/Exec. VP
Jim Morgan, Sr. VP-Human Resources
Charles E. Dietz, CTO
Pamela E. Halling, Sr. VP-Prod. Dev.
Elliot Brecher, General Counsel
Christopher Slattery, Exec. VP-Oper.
Sandra D. Colony, Sr. VP-Corp. Comm.
Daniel Mannino, Controller
E. Scott Cooley, Sr. VP-Operations West Region
Kirk A. Darfler, Sr. VP-Operations South Region
Keith Hall, Sr. VP-Government Rel.
John W. Hutton, Sr. VP-Operations East Region
Sidney R. Knafel, Chmn.

Phone: 917-286-2300	Fax: 917-286-2301
Toll-Free:	
Address: 810 7th Ave., New York, NY 10019 US	

GROWTH PLANS/SPECIAL FEATURES:

Insight Communications is a leading provider of entertainment and communications services to 1.3 million customers in mid-sized communities in Indiana, Kentucky, Illinois and Ohio. Insight's lines of service include InsightDigital, a digital television provider; InsightBroadband; and InsightPhone, providing local digital telephony. Products include a variety of traditional television cable plans as well as pay-per-view movies and events and broadband Internet. In addition, Insight's broadband network also supports numerous advanced services such as high-definition television (HDTV), digital video recorders (DVR), video-on-demand (VOD), subscription video-on-demand (SVOD), digital cable programming and digital phone plans. The company's commercial services division, InsightBusiness, provides commercial customers with data, video and hosting plans and services. In addition, the company offers cable advertising and marketing assistance through Insight Media, its advertising sales division. The company's Insight Midwest, LP subsidiary, half of which is owned by an indirect subsidiary of Comcast Cable Holdings, LLC, possesses and operates systems serving the majority of Insight's customers. Insight Midwest delivers local telephone service under the AT&T Digital Phone brand. In late 2005, co-founders Sidney R. Knafel and Michael S. Willner partnered with The Carlyle Group to take the company private.

FINANCIALS: Sales and profits are in thousands of dollars—add 000 to get the full amount. 2006 Note: Financial information for 2006 was not available for all companies at press time.

2006 Sales: $	2006 Profits: $	**U.S. Stock Ticker:** Private
2005 Sales: $1,117,681	2005 Profits: $-84,929	**Int'l Ticker:** Int'l Exchange:
2004 Sales: $1,002,456	2004 Profits: $-13,799	**Employees:** 3,916
2003 Sales: $902,592	2003 Profits: $-24,544	**Fiscal Year Ends:** 12/31
2002 Sales: $807,900	2002 Profits: $-48,000	**Parent Company:**

SALARIES/BENEFITS:

Pension Plan:	ESOP Stock Plan:	Profit Sharing:	Top Exec. Salary: $635,000	Bonus: $317,500
Savings Plan:	Stock Purch. Plan:		Second Exec. Salary: $500,000	Bonus: $250,000

OTHER THOUGHTS:

Apparent Women Officers or Directors: 3
Hot Spot for Advancement for Women/Minorities: Y

LOCATIONS: ("Y" = Yes)

West:	Southwest:	Midwest:	Southeast:	Northeast:	International:
	Y	Y		Y	

INTEGRITY MEDIA INC
www.integritymusic.com

Industry Group Code: 512230 Ranks within this company's industry group: Sales: Profits:

Print Media/Publishing:	Movies:	Equipment/Supplies:	Broadcast/Cable:	Music/Audio:		Sports/Games:
Newspapers:	Movie Theaters:	Equipment/Supplies:	Broadcast TV:	Music Production:	Y	Games/Sports:
Magazines:	Movie Production:	Gambling Equipment:	Cable TV:	Retail Music:		Retail Games Stores:
Books:	TV/Video Production: Y	Special Services:	Satellite Broadcast:	Retail Audio Equip.:		Stadiums/Teams:
Book Stores:	Video Rental:	Advertising Services:	Radio:	Music Print./Dist.:	Y	Gambling/Casinos:
Distribution/Printing:	Video Distribution:	Info. Sys. Software:	Online Information:	Multimedia:		Rides/Theme Parks:

TYPES OF BUSINESS:

Christian Music Publishing
Mobile Phone Media
Music Production
Videos
Songbooks & Sheet Music
Music Club

BRANDS/DIVISIONS/AFFILIATES:

Integrity Music
Mworship
INO Records
Hosanna! Music

CONTACTS: *Note: Officers with more than one job title may be intentionally listed here more than once.*

P. Michael Coleman, CEO
Jerry W. Weimer, COO
P. Michael Coleman, Pres.
Donald S. Wllington, CFO
Shannon Walker, Public Relations
P. Lichael Coleman, Chmn.

Phone: 251-633-9000	**Fax:** 251-776-5014
Toll-Free: 800-533-6912	
Address: 1000 Cody Rd., Mobile, AL 36695 US	

GROWTH PLANS/SPECIAL FEATURES:

Integrity Media, Inc. produces and publishes Christian music, books and related products developed to facilitate worship, entertainment and education. The company currently operates through two subsidiaries: Integrity Music and INO Records. Integrity Music's product formats include cassettes, compact discs, software, videos and songbooks. The division also produces songs recorded in indigenous languages, utilizing local artists and local songs to produce the recordings. Integrity produces products in a broad range of languages, including Russian, Spanish, Mandarin Chinese, French, German, Portuguese and Indonesian. Integrity Music also operates a music club, Hosanna! Music, which sends new recordings to members in the U.S., Europe and Australia six times a year. The company offers worship leaders new worship music, worship planning resources and networking on the Internet through its Worship Leader connection. Through INO Records the company produces Christian music ranging from praise and worship music, its largest category, to other styles of adult contemporary Christian music and children's music. Products are sold primarily online and directly to consumers throughout the U.S. and in over 160 other countries worldwide. The firm operates international offices in the U.K., Australia, Singapore, and has recently expanded to South Africa. Integrity plans to expand into various markets through importers, who will sell company-provided products, or through distributors licensed to produce Integrlty products from a master recording. In late 2006, Integrity Media agreed to sell Integrity Publishing to Thomas Nelson, Inc. for an undisclosed sum. Also in late 2006, Integrity launched MWorship in partnership with Sony BMG Music; MWorship is a mobile phone service that offers text message devotions, ring tones, music news and other services.

FINANCIALS: Sales and profits are in thousands of dollars—add 000 to get the full amount. 2006 Note: Financial information for 2006 was not available for all companies at press time.

2006 Sales: $	2006 Profits: $	**U.S. Stock Ticker: Private**
2005 Sales: $	2005 Profits: $	**Int'l Ticker:** Int'l Exchange:
2004 Sales: $	2004 Profits: $	Employees: 218
2003 Sales: $74,264	2003 Profits: $1,882	Fiscal Year Ends: 12/31
2002 Sales: $66,300	2002 Profits: $2,200	Parent Company:

SALARIES/BENEFITS:

Pension Plan:	ESOP Stock Plan:	Profit Sharing:	Top Exec. Salary: $333,644	Bonus: $
Savings Plan:	Stock Purch. Plan:		Second Exec. Salary: $241,552	Bonus: $253,303

OTHER THOUGHTS:

Apparent Women Officers or Directors: 1
Hot Spot for Advancement for Women/Minorities:

LOCATIONS: ("Y" = Yes)

West:	Southwest:	Midwest:	Southeast:	Northeast:	International:
			Y		Y

INTERACTIVE DATA CORPORATION
www.interactivedatacorp.com

Industry Group Code: 514100   Ranks within this company's industry group: Sales: 3   Profits: 2

Print Media/Publishing:	Movies:	Equipment/Supplies:		Broadcast/Cable:	Music/Audio:	Sports/Games:
Newspapers:	Movie Theaters:	Equipment/Supplies:		Broadcast TV:	Music Production:	Games/Sports:
Magazines:	Movie Production:	Gambling Equipment:	Y	Cable TV:	Retail Music:	Retail Games Stores:
Books:	TV/Video Production:	Special Services:	Y	Satellite Broadcast:	Retail Audio Equip.:	Stadiums/Teams:
Book Stores:	Video Rental:	Advertising Services:	Y	Radio:	Music Print./Dist.:	Gambling/Casinos:
Distribution/Printing:	Video Distribution:	Info. Sys. Software:	Y	Online Information:	Multimedia:	Rides/Theme Parks:

TYPES OF BUSINESS:

Financial Information
Stock Market & Equities Information
Portfolio Management Software
Consulting & Valuation Services
Online Information Service

BRANDS/DIVISIONS/AFFILIATES:

FT Interactive Data
ComStock
eSignal
CMS BondEdge
Quote.com

CONTACTS: Note: Officers with more than one job title may be intentionally listed here more than once.

Stuart J. Clark, CEO
John L. King, COO
Stuart J. Clark, Pres.
Andrew Hajducky, CFO/Exec. VP
Mary Ivaliotis, Chief Mktg. Officer
Andrea H. Loew, General Counsel/VP
Raymond L. D'Arcy, Pres., Data Delivery Products, FT Interactive Data
John L. King, COO-FT Interactive Data
Mark Hepsworth, Pres., ComStock
Laurie Adami, Pres., CMS BondEdge
John C. Makinson, Chmn.

Phone: 781-687-8500	Fax: 781-687-8005
Toll-Free:	
Address: 22 Crosby Dr., Bedford, MA 01730 US	

GROWTH PLANS/SPECIAL FEATURES:

Interactive Data Corporation provides financial market data, analytics and related services to financial institutions, active traders and individual investors. Interactive Data distributes real-time, end-of-day and historically archived data to customers through a variety of products featuring Internet, dedicated line, satellite and dialup delivery protocols. Through a range of strategic alliances, it also provides links to financial service and software companies offering trading, analysis, portfolio management and valuation services. The corporation has four divisions: FT Interactive Data, ComStock, eSignal and CMS BondEdge. FT Interactive Data supplies time-sensitive pricing, corporate action and descriptive information for more than 3.5 million securities traded around the world, as well as fixed-income portfolio analytics, consulting and valuation services to institutional fixed-income portfolio managers. Moreover, the company provides index and constituent data to banks, brokerage firms, insurance companies, government agencies, stock exchanges, trading houses and fund managers worldwide. ComStock is a real-time information service that provides worldwide financial data, news, historical information and software applications covering equity, fixed-income, foreign exchange, commodities and money markets. eSignal is the retail arm of the firm. The business is a real-time streaming quote service that delivers continuously updating, time-sensitive financial data over the Internet to investors' and traders' PCs. CMS BondEdge is a leader in fixed-income analytical software, providing bond research, analytics and valuation tools for 500 of the nation's top investment management firms, insurance companies, banks and institutional brokerage houses. Interactive Data Corporation has offices located throughout North America, Europe, Asia and Australia. In 2006, the company acquired Quote.com and certain other related assets from Lycos, Inc. for approximately $30 million.

FINANCIALS: Sales and profits are in thousands of dollars—add 000 to get the full amount. 2006 Note: Financial information for 2006 was not available for all companies at press time.

2006 Sales: $	2006 Profits: $	U.S. Stock Ticker: IDC
2005 Sales: $542,867	2005 Profits: $93,864	Int'l Ticker: Int'l Exchange:
2004 Sales: $484,565	2004 Profits: $80,271	Employees: 2,100
2003 Sales: $442,690	2003 Profits: $72,200	Fiscal Year Ends: 12/31
2002 Sales: $375,000	2002 Profits: $60,700	Parent Company:

SALARIES/BENEFITS:

Pension Plan:	ESOP Stock Plan:	Profit Sharing:	Top Exec. Salary: $518,750	Bonus: $561,750
Savings Plan: Y	Stock Purch. Plan:		Second Exec. Salary: $356,000	Bonus: $304,300

OTHER THOUGHTS:

Apparent Women Officers or Directors: 3
Hot Spot for Advancement for Women/Minorities: Y

LOCATIONS: ("Y" = Yes)

West:	Southwest:	Midwest:	Southeast:	Northeast:	International:
Y		Y		Y	Y

INTERNATIONAL CREATIVE MANAGEMENT (ICM)
www.icmtalent.com
Industry Group Code: 711410 Ranks within this company's industry group: Sales: 1   Profits:

Print Media/Publishing:	Movies:	Equipment/Supplies:		Broadcast/Cable:	Music/Audio:	Sports/Games:
Newspapers:	Movie Theaters:	Equipment/Supplies:		Broadcast TV:	Music Production:	Games/Sports:
Magazines:	Movie Production:	Gambling Equipment:		Cable TV:	Retail Music:	Retail Games Stores:
Books:	TV/Video Production:	Special Services:	Y	Satellite Broadcast:	Retail Audio Equip.:	Stadiums/Teams:
Book Stores:	Video Rental:	Advertising Services:	Y	Radio:	Music Print./Dist.:	Gambling/Casinos:
Distribution/Printing:	Video Distribution:	Info. Sys. Software:		Online Information:	Multimedia:	Rides/Theme Parks:

TYPES OF BUSINESS:
Agents-Actors & Directors
Agents-Writers & Musicians
Agents-Literary
Agents-Lecture

BRANDS/DIVISIONS/AFFILIATES:
ICM Artists
Rizvi Traverse Management
Broder Webb Chervin Silbermann Agency

CONTACTS: Note: Officers with more than one job title may be intentionally listed here more than once.
Jeffrey Berg, CEO
Edward Limato, Co-Pres.
Richard B. Levy, General Counsel
Richard B. Levy, Chief Bus. Dev. Officer
Chris Silbermann, Co-Pres.
Robert Broder, Vice Chmn.
Jeffrey Berg, Chmn.

Phone: 310-550-4000	Fax: 310-550-4100
Toll-Free:	
Address: 8942 Wilshire Blvd., Beverly Hills, CA 90211-1934 US	

GROWTH PLANS/SPECIAL FEATURES:
International Creative Management, Inc. (ICM) is one of the world's largest talent and literary agencies, with offices in Beverly Hills, New York and London. The firm operates through six industry-specific departments: Film, which has six sub-departments (talent, technical services, international, film packaging, literary, and independent production and financing); Television; Commercials, which has two departments (celebrity endorsements and voiceover); Music & Performance; Literary Publications; and Lecture. These departments represent creative and technical talent such as actors, directors, musicians and writers in the fields of motion pictures, television, publishing, music, comedy, commercials, new media, public speaking and live theater. ICM's Foreign Rights department, based in London, sells ICM book and magazine products in the U.K. and other foreign countries and the Life Rights division secures the rights to newspaper and magazine articles as well as personal life stories of people who might serve as the basis for a television production. The company's music and performance subsidiary, ICM Artists, represents classical instrumentalists, vocalists and conductors, chamber ensembles, choirs and dance and opera companies, as well as other performing groups. ICM's clients include movie actors Mel Gibson, Denzel Washington and Richard Gere; movie directors Sofia Coppola and Peter Jackson; Broadway actors Eileen Atkins and Christopher Plummer; Pulitzer Prize winner Doug Wright; musical performers Usher and Britney Spears; and screenwriters Gurinder Chadha, Brian Helgeland and Tami Sagher. In late 2005, ICM sold a controlling stake to private equity firm Rizvi Traverse Management and arranged new debt financing through Merrill Lynch. In mid 2006, it acquired the Broder Webb Chervin Silbermann Agency, an agency focused on TV talent.

ICM offers employees domestic partner benefits, flexible spending accounts and an employee assistance program.

FINANCIALS: Sales and profits are in thousands of dollars—add 000 to get the full amount. 2006 Note: Financial information for 2006 was not available for all companies at press time.

2006 Sales: $	2006 Profits: $	U.S. Stock Ticker: Private
2005 Sales: $140,000	2005 Profits: $	Int'l Ticker: Int'l Exchange:
2004 Sales: $100,000	2004 Profits: $	Employees: 393
2003 Sales: $	2003 Profits: $	Fiscal Year Ends: 6/30
2002 Sales: $	2002 Profits: $	Parent Company:

SALARIES/BENEFITS:
Pension Plan:	ESOP Stock Plan:	Profit Sharing:	Top Exec. Salary: $	Bonus: $
Savings Plan: Y	Stock Purch. Plan:		Second Exec. Salary: $	Bonus: $

OTHER THOUGHTS:
Apparent Women Officers or Directors:
Hot Spot for Advancement for Women/Minorities:

LOCATIONS: ("Y" = Yes)
West:	Southwest:	Midwest:	Southeast:	Northeast:	International:
Y				Y	Y

INTERNATIONAL GAME TECHNOLOGY

www.igt.com

Industry Group Code: 713290 Ranks within this company's industry group: Sales: 1 Profits: 1

Print Media/Publishing:	Movies:	Equipment/Supplies:		Broadcast/Cable:	Music/Audio:	Sports/Games:
Newspapers:	Movie Theaters:	Equipment/Supplies:		Broadcast TV:	Music Production:	Games/Sports:
Magazines:	Movie Production:	Gambling Equipment:	Y	Cable TV:	Retail Music:	Retail Games Stores:
Books:	TV/Video Production:	Special Services:	Y	Satellite Broadcast:	Retail Audio Equip.:	Stadiums/Teams:
Book Stores:	Video Rental:	Advertising Services:		Radio:	Music Print./Dist.:	Gambling/Casinos:
Distribution/Printing:	Video Distribution:	Info. Sys. Software:	Y	Online Information:	Multimedia:	Rides/Theme Parks:

TYPES OF BUSINESS:

Gambling Equipment
Computerized Gambling Devices
Gaming Technology & Services
Gambling Software
Consulting

BRANDS/DIVISIONS/AFFILIATES:

IGT Gaming Systems
EZ-Pay
ITG Online Entertainment
Megajackpots
IGT Canada, Inc.
WagerWorks, Inc.
Venture Catalyst, Inc.

CONTACTS: *Note: Officers with more than one job title may be intentionally listed here more than once.*

Thomas J. Matthews, CEO
Thomas J. Matthews, COO
Thomas J. Matthews, Pres.
Maureen T. Mullarkey, CFO/Exec. VP
Ed Rogich, VP-Mktg.
Tami Corbin, VP-Human Resources
Robert Bittman, Exec. VP-Prod. Strategy
Jon Wade, Exec. VP-Eng.
David D. Johnson, General Counsel/Exec. VP/Corp. Sec.
Anthony Ciorciari, Exec. VP-Oper.
Richard Pennington, Exec. VP-Corp. Strategy
Maureen T. Mullarkey, Treas.
Stephen W. Morro, Pres., Gaming Div.
Toni Martinez, VP-U.S. Western Region
Mike Walsh, VP-U.S. Central Region
Tim Shortall, VP-U.S. Eastern Region Sales
Thomas J. Matthews, Chmn.
Paulus Karskens, Pres., IGT International

Phone: 775-448-7777	Fax: 775-448-0777
Toll-Free: 866-296-4232	
Address: 9295 Prototype Dr., Reno, NV 89521 US	

GROWTH PLANS/SPECIAL FEATURES:

International Game Technology (IGT) is a world leader in the development and manufacture of computerized casino gaming products. Primarily serving the casino gaming industry, the company sells its products in legalized gaming markets in the U.S., U.K., Australia, Europe, Japan, Latin America, New Zealand and South Africa. Products include traditional spinning-reel slot machines, video gaming machines, government-sponsored terminals and other gaming devices. In addition to the machines themselves, the company offers casino management software, including IGT Gaming Systems, which keep track of machine use, and the EZ-Pay system, which allows patrons to use cards with the machines instead of coins. The company operates in two business segments: the gaming division and the international division. The gaming division consists of the company's North American operations and includes North American sales, the firm's proprietary games such as Megajackpots, IGT casino management systems and solutions, and the company's North American manufacturers and distributors. The international division manages the sales, servicing and distribution centers as well as the manufacturing plants overseas. In 2006, IGT entered into an agreement with Walker Digital, LLC to develop and incorporate Walker innovations into IGT's product line with particular respect to Walker's server-based gaming platform. IGT then installed the first ever server based gaming system in the Barona Valley Ranch Resort and Casino in San Diego, California. The company also recently acquired intellectual property pertaining to roulette equipment parts from Novomatic AG for use in IGT's M-P Series station gaming products. In 2006, IGT signed a definitive agreement to acquire Venture Catalyst, Inc., a provider of consulting services and technology in the hospitality and gaming markets, as a wholly owned subsidiary.

IGT offers its employees comprehensive benefits including a prescription drug plan, adoption assistance, an employee assistance program, an onsite daycare facility, tuition reimbursement, fitness centers and employee discounts.

FINANCIALS: Sales and profits are in thousands of dollars—add 000 to get the full amount. 2006 Note: Financial information for 2006 was not available for all companies at press time.

2006 Sales: $2,511,700	2006 Profits: $473,600	**U.S. Stock Ticker:** IGT
2005 Sales: $2,379,400	2005 Profits: $436,500	**Int'l Ticker:** Int'l Exchange:
2004 Sales: $2,484,800	2004 Profits: $488,700	Employees: 5,200
2003 Sales: $2,128,100	2003 Profits: $390,700	Fiscal Year Ends: 9/30
2002 Sales: $1,847,568	2002 Profits: $271,165	Parent Company:

SALARIES/BENEFITS:

Pension Plan:	ESOP Stock Plan:	Profit Sharing: Y	Top Exec. Salary: $650,000	Bonus: $1,442,371
Savings Plan: Y	Stock Purch. Plan: Y		Second Exec. Salary: $450,000	Bonus: $756,002

OTHER THOUGHTS:

Apparent Women Officers or Directors: 4
Hot Spot for Advancement for Women/Minorities: Y

LOCATIONS: ("Y" = Yes)

West:	Southwest:	Midwest:	Southeast:	Northeast:	International:
Y		Y			Y

INTERNATIONAL LOTTERY & TOTALIZATOR SYSTEMS
www.ilts.com

Industry Group Code: 713290 Ranks within this company's industry group: Sales: 13 Profits: 11

Print Media/Publishing:	Movies:	Equipment/Supplies:		Broadcast/Cable:	Music/Audio:	Sports/Games:
Newspapers:	Movie Theaters:	Equipment/Supplies:	Y	Broadcast TV:	Music Production:	Games/Sports:
Magazines:	Movie Production:	Gambling Equipment:	Y	Cable TV:	Retail Music:	Retail Games Stores:
Books:	TV/Video Production:	Special Services:	Y	Satellite Broadcast:	Retail Audio Equip.:	Stadiums/Teams:
Book Stores:	Video Rental:	Advertising Services:		Radio:	Music Print./Dist.:	Gambling/Casinos:
Distribution/Printing:	Video Distribution:	Info. Sys. Software:	Y	Online Information:	Multimedia:	Rides/Theme Parks:

TYPES OF BUSINESS:

Software-Lottery & Racetrack Wagering
Computerized Wagering Hardware
Facilities Management Services
Ballot Counting Systems

BRANDS/DIVISIONS/AFFILIATES:

Unisyn Voting Solutions
ILTS InterTote System
Intelimark
DATAMARK
DataTrak
InkaVote
Berjaya Lottery Management

CONTACTS: Note: Officers with more than one job title may be intentionally listed here more than once.

Jeffrey M. Johnson, Acting CEO
Jeffrey M. Johnson, Acting Pres.
T. Linh Nguyen, Acting CFO
Theodore A. Johnson, Chmn.

Phone: 760-931-4000	Fax: 760-931-1789
Toll-Free:	
Address: 2131 Faraday Ave., Carlsbad, CA 92008-7297 US	

GROWTH PLANS/SPECIAL FEATURES:

International Lottery and Totalizator Systems (ILTS) designs and services computerized wagering systems and terminals for racing organizations and lotteries worldwide. ILTS provides facilities management services to organizations authorized to conduct online lotteries. The company's wagering systems include three components: the hardware and operating systems that make up a central computer (a product known as the ILTS InterTote System); the DATAMARK and Intelimark families of point-of-sale terminals; and the communication network that links all terminals to the central computer. DATAMARK technology is capable of issuing tickets both for standard betting and pool wagers used in pari-mutuel wagering. The terminals facilitate multiple bets on one ticket and multiple selections for each bet. Utilizing its DataTrak technology, the company sets up the network needed to connect the terminals. The firm's technology can also be used in other transaction processing systems, such as automated tollbooth systems for turnpikes and electronic voting. ILTS supplies government-sponsored lotteries in 11 countries and services more than 200 racetracks worldwide. Notable clients include Global Technologies, Ltd., Philippine Gaming Management and M.I. Montreal Informatica. In 2006, ILTS agreed to provide (through its subsidiary Unisyn Voting Solutions) more than 300 InkaVote Precinct Ballot Counters to Jackson County, Missouri. In addition, the Unisyn subsidiary completed a testing process for the Inka Vote Plus Precinct Ballot Counter; the device is now ready to be used in elections in the state of California. Berjaya Lottery Management, a Malaysian firm, owns more than 71% of the company's stock.

FINANCIALS: Sales and profits are in thousands of dollars—add 000 to get the full amount. 2006 Note: Financial information for 2006 was not available for all companies at press time.

2006 Sales: $3,445	2006 Profits: $-2,344	U.S. Stock Ticker: ITSI
2005 Sales: $9,666	2005 Profits: $-1,762	Int'l Ticker: Int'l Exchange:
2004 Sales: $10,777	2004 Profits: $-1,786	Employees: 37
2003 Sales: $22,800	2003 Profits: $ 800	Fiscal Year Ends: 4/30
2002 Sales: $18,200	2002 Profits: $1,300	Parent Company:

SALARIES/BENEFITS:

Pension Plan:	ESOP Stock Plan:	Profit Sharing:	Top Exec. Salary: $183,390	Bonus: $
Savings Plan: Y	Stock Purch. Plan:		Second Exec. Salary: $110,000	Bonus: $

OTHER THOUGHTS:

Apparent Women Officers or Directors:
Hot Spot for Advancement for Women/Minorities:

LOCATIONS: ("Y" = Yes)

West:	Southwest:	Midwest:	Southeast:	Northeast:	International:
Y					Y

Note: Financial information, benefits and other data can change quickly and may vary from those stated here.

INTERPUBLIC GROUP OF COMPANIES INC
www.interpublic.com

Industry Group Code: 541810 Ranks within this company's industry group: Sales: 3 Profits: 4

Print Media/Publishing:	Movies:	Equipment/Supplies:		Broadcast/Cable:	Music/Audio:	Sports/Games:
Newspapers:	Movie Theaters:	Equipment/Supplies:		Broadcast TV:	Music Production:	Games/Sports:
Magazines:	Movie Production:	Gambling Equipment:		Cable TV:	Retail Music:	Retail Games Stores:
Books:	TV/Video Production:	Special Services:		Satellite Broadcast:	Retail Audio Equip.:	Stadiums/Teams:
Book Stores:	Video Rental:	Advertising Services:	Y	Radio:	Music Print./Dist.:	Gambling/Casinos:
Distribution/Printing:	Video Distribution:	Info. Sys. Software:		Online Information:	Multimedia:	Rides/Theme Parks:

TYPES OF BUSINESS:

Advertising Services
Marketing & Branding
Market Research
Public Relations
Online Marketing
Direct Marketing
Promotions & Events
Sports & Entertainment Marketing

BRANDS/DIVISIONS/AFFILIATES:

McCann-Erickson WorldGroup
FCB Group
Lowe & Partners Worldwide
Zipatoni
Lowe Healthcare Worldwide
Bragman Nyman Cafarelli
Initiative Media
FutureBrand

CONTACTS: Note: Officers with more than one job title may be intentionally listed here more than once.

Michael I. Roth, CEO
Frank Mergenthaler, CFO/Exec. VP
Timothy A. Sompolski, Chief Human Resources Officer/Exec. VP
Joseph Farrelly, CIO
Nicholas J. Camera, General Counsel/Sr. VP/Corp. Sec.
Stephen Gatfield, Exec. VP-Strategy & Network Oper.
Bant Breen, Sr. VP/Dir.-Strategic Dev. & Innovation
Philippe Krakowsky, Exec. VP-Strategy & Corp. Rel.
Jonathan B. Burleigh, Sr. VP-Finance & Dev.
Christopher Carroll, Chief Acct. Officer/Sr. VP/Controller
Marjorie Altschuler, Chief Growth Officer/Exec. VP
Michael I. Roth, Chmn.

Phone: 212-704-1200	**Fax:** 212-704-1201
Toll-Free:	
Address: 1114 Ave. of the Americas, New York, NY 10036 US	

GROWTH PLANS/SPECIAL FEATURES:

The Interpublic Group of Companies, Inc. is a group comprising hundreds of advertising and specialized marketing and communications services companies that together represent one of the largest resources of advertising and marketing expertise in the world, with offices and affiliations in over 130 countries. The company operates in three areas: advertising, including media management; marketing communications, including direct marketing, database and customer relationship management (CRM), public relations, sales promotions, event marketing, online marketing, corporate and brand identity, brand consultancy and health care marketing; and marketing services, including sports and entertainment marketing, corporate meetings and events, retail marketing and other business services. Interpublic is organized into six operating divisions: McCann-Erickson Worldgroup, FCB Group, The Lowe Group, Draft Worldwide, the Constituent Management Group and the Interpublic Aligned Companies. Subsidiaries include Lowe & Partners Worldwide, Zipatoni, Mullen, Dailey & Associates, Lowe Healthcare Worldwide, Octagon, Motorsports and entertainment PR firms Bragman Nyman Cafarelli and PMK/HBH. In addition, Interpublic owns many leading independent agencies, including Initiative Media, Weber Shandwick, Hill Holiday, MAGNA Global, FutureBrand and Jack Morton Worldwide.

FINANCIALS: Sales and profits are in thousands of dollars—add 000 to get the full amount. 2006 Note: Financial information for 2006 was not available for all companies at press time.

2006 Sales: $	2006 Profits: $	**U.S. Stock Ticker:** IPG
2005 Sales: $6,270,000	2005 Profits: $-262,900	**Int'l Ticker:** Int'l Exchange:
2004 Sales: $6,387,000	2004 Profits: $-538,400	Employees: 43,000
2003 Sales: $6,161,700	2003 Profits: $-539,100	Fiscal Year Ends: 12/31
2002 Sales: $6,204,000	2002 Profits: $100,000	Parent Company:

SALARIES/BENEFITS:

Pension Plan:	ESOP Stock Plan:	Profit Sharing:	Top Exec. Salary: $1,250,000	Bonus: $1,000,000
Savings Plan:	Stock Purch. Plan:		Second Exec. Salary: $1,000,000	Bonus: $

OTHER THOUGHTS:

Apparent Women Officers or Directors: 3
Hot Spot for Advancement for Women/Minorities: Y

LOCATIONS: ("Y" = Yes)

West:	Southwest:	Midwest:	Southeast:	Northeast:	International:
Y	Y	Y	Y	Y	Y

Note: Financial information, benefits and other data can change quickly and may vary from those stated here.

INTERTAN CANADA LTD

www.intertan.com

Industry Group Code: 443110 Ranks within this company's industry group: Sales: 5 Profits:

Print Media/Publishing:	Movies:	Equipment/Supplies:		Broadcast/Cable:	Music/Audio:	Sports/Games:
Newspapers:	Movie Theaters:	Equipment/Supplies:	Y	Broadcast TV:	Music Production:	Games/Sports:
Magazines:	Movie Production:	Gambling Equipment:	Y	Cable TV:	Retail Music:	Retail Games Stores:
Books:	TV/Video Production:	Special Services:		Satellite Broadcast:	Retail Audio Equip.:	Stadiums/Teams:
Book Stores:	Video Rental:	Advertising Services:		Radio:	Music Print./Dist.:	Gambling/Casinos:
Distribution/Printing:	Video Distribution:	Info. Sys. Software:		Online Information:	Multimedia:	Rides/Theme Parks:

TYPES OF BUSINESS:

Electronics Stores
Online Sales
Repair Services

BRANDS/DIVISIONS/AFFILIATES:

Circuit City Stores, Inc.
Source by Circuit City (The)
Rogers Wireless
Battery Plus
THS Studio
Logitech Electronics

CONTACTS: Note: Officers with more than one job title may be intentionally listed here more than once.

Michael E. Foss, Interim CEO
James P. Maddox, CFO/VP

Phone: 705-728-1617	Fax: 705-728-7844

Toll-Free:
Address: 279 Bayview Dr., Barrie, ON L4M 4W5 Canada

GROWTH PLANS/SPECIAL FEATURES:

InterTAN Canada Ltd., the wholly owned subsidiary and Canadian arm of Circuit City Stores, Inc., sells consumer electronics products and services through company-operated retail stores and dealer outlets throughout Canada. The firm operates more than 1,000 company owned and dealer-operated retail stores under the names The Source by Circuit City, Rogers Wireless, THS Studio, Logitech Electronics and Battery Plus. The Company's stores are typically located in malls and shopping centers in order to conveniently provide products and services that meet a wide range of consumer electronic needs. Its flagship store, The Source by Circuit City operates more than 900 stores selling a range of electronic equipment such as cameras, computers, cell phones, audio/visual equipment and accessories. In addition to its merchandise, InterTAN provides after-sale services for all the products it sells during warranty periods and beyond. The company additionally offers out-of-warranty repair services. The firm was originally founded as a holding company for the international retail operations of the Tandy Corporation, which is now known as RadioShack; later, InterTAN was spun off. The company's U.K. and Australian businesses were sold, leaving only the Canadian operations, which were subsequently acquired by Circuit City in 2004. Circuit City's acquisitions subsidiary was merged into InterTAN, with the latter as the surviving entity.

FINANCIALS: Sales and profits are in thousands of dollars—add 000 to get the full amount. 2006 Note: Financial information for 2006 was not available for all companies at press time.

2006 Sales: $	2006 Profits: $	U.S. Stock Ticker: Subsidiary
2005 Sales: $454,900	2005 Profits: $	Int'l Ticker: Int'l Exchange:
2004 Sales: $	2004 Profits: $	Employees: 3,521
2003 Sales: $403,000	2003 Profits: $7,700	Fiscal Year Ends: 2/28
2002 Sales: $393,800	2002 Profits: $13,600	Parent Company: CIRCUIT CITY STORES INC

SALARIES/BENEFITS:

Pension Plan:	ESOP Stock Plan:	Profit Sharing:	Top Exec. Salary: $500,000	Bonus: $34,723
Savings Plan:	Stock Purch. Plan:		Second Exec. Salary: $141,085	Bonus: $86,556

OTHER THOUGHTS:

Apparent Women Officers or Directors:
Hot Spot for Advancement for Women/Minorities:

LOCATIONS: ("Y" = Yes)

West:	Southwest:	Midwest:	Southeast:	Northeast:	International:
					Y

INTERVIDEO INC   www.intervideo.com

Industry Group Code: 511209 Ranks within this company's industry group: Sales: 3   Profits: 3

Print Media/Publishing:	Movies:	Equipment/Supplies:		Broadcast/Cable:	Music/Audio:	Sports/Games:
Newspapers:	Movie Theaters:	Equipment/Supplies:	Y	Broadcast TV:	Music Production:	Games/Sports:
Magazines:	Movie Production:	Gambling Equipment:		Cable TV:	Retail Music:	Retail Games Stores:
Books:	TV/Video Production:	Special Services:		Satellite Broadcast:	Retail Audio Equip.:	Stadiums/Teams:
Book Stores:	Video Rental:	Advertising Services:		Radio:	Music Print./Dist.:	Gambling/Casinos:
Distribution/Printing:	Video Distribution:	Info. Sys. Software:	Y	Online Information:	Multimedia:	Rides/Theme Parks:

TYPES OF BUSINESS:
Software-Digital Video
Consumer DVD Software
Multimedia Software
Online Sales

BRANDS/DIVISIONS/AFFILIATES:
WinDVD
WinDVD Creator
InterVideo DVD Copy
InterVideo Home Theater
InstantON
Corel Corporation

CONTACTS: *Note: Officers with more than one job title may be intentionally listed here more than once.*
Steve Ro, CEO
Steve Ro, Pres.
Randall Bambrough, CFO
Steve Ro, Chmn.

Phone: 510-651-0888	**Fax:** 510-651-8808
Toll-Free:	
Address: 46430 Fremont Blvd., Fremont, CA 94538 US	

GROWTH PLANS/SPECIAL FEATURES:

InterVideo, Inc., a DVD software provider and subsidiary of Corel Corporation, offers advanced digital video and audio multimedia software products, available in up to 27 different languages. The products allow users to capture, edit, author, burn, distribute and play digital multimedia content on PCs and consumer electronics. The company markets its products through 2,200 retail stores in the U.S., PC original equipment manufacturers, consumer electronics manufacturers and directly to consumers through its web sites, which operate in 12 languages. InterVideo's software is bundled with products sold by eight of the top 10 PC manufacturers, including Dell and Hewlett-Packard. The firm also sells to consumer electronics manufacturers and PC peripherals manufacturers worldwide, including to makers of hand-held devices such as digital cameras and cellular phones. InterVideo derives nearly all of its revenue from sales of its flagship product, WinDVD, a line of DVD player software. Other products include WinDVD Creator, a video editing, DVD authoring and burning application; InterVideo DVD Copy, an application to copy and back-up DVDs and CDs; InterVideo Home Theater, a media center suite for the viewing and management of digital media content; Linux-based versions of DVD and DVR software designed for Linux-based PCs and CE devices; and InstantON multimedia software. The company has offices in Europe, Taiwan, Japan, India and China. The company recently merged its Taiwan branch, InterVideo Digital Tech, with Ulead Systems. Intervideo was acquired by Corel Corporation in December 2006.

FINANCIALS: Sales and profits are in thousands of dollars—add 000 to get the full amount. 2006 Note: Financial information for 2006 was not available for all companies at press time.

2006 Sales: $	2006 Profits: $	**U.S. Stock Ticker: Subsidiary**
2005 Sales: $109,229	2005 Profits: $3,583	**Int'l Ticker:** Int'l Exchange:
2004 Sales: $74,460	2004 Profits: $8,826	Employees: 803
2003 Sales: $57,100	2003 Profits: $7,800	Fiscal Year Ends: 12/31
2002 Sales: $45,500	2002 Profits: $7,700	Parent Company: COREL CORPORATION

SALARIES/BENEFITS:

Pension Plan:	ESOP Stock Plan:	Profit Sharing:	Top Exec. Salary: $240,000	Bonus: $84,800
Savings Plan:	Stock Purch. Plan:		Second Exec. Salary: $200,000	Bonus: $53,500

OTHER THOUGHTS:

Apparent Women Officers or Directors:
Hot Spot for Advancement for Women/Minorities:

LOCATIONS: ("Y" = Yes)

West:	Southwest:	Midwest:	Southeast:	Northeast:	International:
Y					Y

ION MEDIA NETWORKS

www.paxson.com

Industry Group Code: 513120 Ranks within this company's industry group: Sales: 17   Profits: 20

Print Media/Publishing:	Movies:		Equipment/Supplies:	Broadcast/Cable:		Music/Audio:	Sports/Games:
Newspapers:	Movie Theaters:		Equipment/Supplies:	Broadcast TV:	Y	Music Production:	Games/Sports:
Magazines:	Movie Production:		Gambling Equipment:	Cable TV:		Retail Music:	Retail Games Stores:
Books:	TV/Video Production:	Y	Special Services:	Satellite Broadcast:		Retail Audio Equip.:	Stadiums/Teams:
Book Stores:	Video Rental:		Advertising Services:	Radio:		Music Print./Dist.:	Gambling/Casinos:
Distribution/Printing:	Video Distribution:		Info. Sys. Software:	Online Information:		Multimedia:	Rides/Theme Parks:

TYPES OF BUSINESS:

Television Broadcasting
Television Production

BRANDS/DIVISIONS/AFFILIATES:

America 51, LP
i-TV
Hope Island
Chicken Soup for the Soul
Twice in a Lifetime
i: Independent Television
i-Health
Qubo

CONTACTS: *Note: Officers with more than one job title may be intentionally listed here more than once.*

R. Brandon Burgess, CEO
Richard Garcia, CFO/VP
Stephen P. Appel, Pres., Sales & Mktg.
Seth Grossman, Exec. VP/Chief Strategic Officer
Curtis L. Brandon, VP-Principal Acc. Officer
Rick Rodriguez, Pres. & Gen. Mgr.-Qubo
Douglas C. Barker, Pres., Broadcast Distribution
Steven J. Friedman, Pres., PAX Cable
Kerry J. Hughes, Sr. VP-Qubo Advertising Sales & Sponsorships
W. Lawrence Patrick, Chmn.

Phone: 561-659-4122	**Fax:** 561-659-4252
Toll-Free:	
Address: 601 Clearwater Park Rd., West Palm Beach, FL 33401 US	

GROWTH PLANS/SPECIAL FEATURES:

ION Media Networks, (formerly Paxson Communications Corp.) owns one of the largest broadcast television groups in the U.S. with over 60 stations. The company's flagship station i promotes works by independent programmers and producers and features wholesome, traditional value-based entertainment. ION broadcasts its i-TV network to about 92 million homes, reaching 83% of U.S. primetime television sets in 39 of the top 50 U.S. markets. The company's revenue comes from selling network long form paid programming (i.e. infomercials, which generate 44.2% of revenue), network spot advertising (20.7% of revenue), and station advertising (35.1% of revenue). The firm's business strategy focuses on providing quality family-oriented programming free of excessive violence, explicit sexual themes and vulgarity. The company reaches approximately 21% of U.S. prime time television households through cable and satellite distribution. In 2006, the firm announced a programming deal with Warner Bros' Domestic Cable Division that provides ION with broadcasting rights to its movies and classic television. Also in 2006, the company partnered with RHI Entertainment in a programming agreement to broadcast RHI's library of original and award-winning titles. Per the agreement, RHI will supply ION with programming for Friday, Saturday, and Sunday nights for a two-year period. Recently, ION announced a new Digital Health Network (i-Health), dedicated to consumer health care and healthy living. In addition, the company partnered with NBC Universal, Corus Entertainment, Classic Media/Big Idea and Scholastic to launch Qubo. ION owns 51% of the Qubo, which specializes in programming for children aged four to eight and broadcasts in English and Spanish on NBC and Telemundo. Also in 2006, the firm announced a programming agreement with Sony Pictures that provides Ion with the rights to broadcast television series, feature films from the Sony library on the i-TV network.

FINANCIALS: Sales and profits are in thousands of dollars—add 000 to get the full amount. 2006 Note: Financial information for 2006 was not available for all companies at press time.

2006 Sales: $	2006 Profits: $	**U.S. Stock Ticker: PAX**
2005 Sales: $254,176	2005 Profits: $-235,670	**Int'l Ticker:** Int'l Exchange:
2004 Sales: $276,630	2004 Profits: $-187,972	Employees: 483
2003 Sales: $270,939	2003 Profits: $-76,213	Fiscal Year Ends: 12/31
2002 Sales: $276,900	2002 Profits: $-303,900	Parent Company:

SALARIES/BENEFITS:

Pension Plan:	ESOP Stock Plan:	Profit Sharing:	Top Exec. Salary: $821,559	Bonus: $832,046
Savings Plan: Y	Stock Purch. Plan:		Second Exec. Salary: $613,222	Bonus: $2,478,222

OTHER THOUGHTS:

Apparent Women Officers or Directors:
Hot Spot for Advancement for Women/Minorities:

LOCATIONS: ("Y" = Yes)

West:	Southwest:	Midwest:	Southeast:	Northeast:	International:
Y	Y	Y	Y	Y	

ION MEDIA NETWORKS INC

www.ionmedia.tv

Industry Group Code: 513120 Ranks within this company's industry group: Sales: 18 Profits: 21

Print Media/Publishing:	Movies:	Equipment/Supplies:	Broadcast/Cable:		Music/Audio:	Sports/Games:
Newspapers:	Movie Theaters:	Equipment/Supplies:	Broadcast TV:	Y	Music Production:	Games/Sports:
Magazines:	Movie Production:	Gambling Equipment:	Cable TV:		Retail Music:	Retail Games Stores:
Books:	TV/Video Production: Y	Special Services:	Satellite Broadcast:		Retail Audio Equip.:	Stadiums/Teams:
Book Stores:	Video Rental:	Advertising Services: Y	Radio:		Music Print./Dist.:	Gambling/Casinos:
Distribution/Printing:	Video Distribution:	Info. Sys. Software:	Online Information:		Multimedia:	Rides/Theme Parks:

TYPES OF BUSINESS:

Television Broadcasting
Television Production
Infomercial Broadcasting

BRANDS/DIVISIONS/AFFILIATES:

Paxson Communications Corporation
i
Qubo

CONTACTS: *Note: Officers with more than one job title may be intentionally listed here more than once.*

Brandon Burgess, CEO
Richard Garcia, CFO/Sr. VP
Stephen P. Appel, Pres., Sales & Mktg.
David A. Glenn, Pres., Eng.
Adam K. Weinstein, General Counsel/Sr. VP
Richard Garcia, Investor Rel.
Steven J. Friedman, Pres., Cable
Douglas C. Barker, Pres., Broadcast Dist. & Southern Region
Adam K. Weinstein, Corp. Sec.
W. Lawrence Patrick, Chmn.

Phone: 561-659-4122	Fax: 561-659-4252
Toll-Free:	
Address: 601 Clearwater Park Rd., West Palm Beach, FL 33401 US	

GROWTH PLANS/SPECIAL FEATURES:

ION Media Networks, Inc., formerly Paxson Communications Corporation, is a network television broadcasting company with one of the largest groups of stations in the U.S. by households served. The firm owns and operates 60 broadcast stations, including stations in all of the top 20 and 39 of the top 50 U.S. markets. Together, these stations reach approximately 91 million homes, representing 83% of U.S. television households. ION has completed construction of digital broadcast facilities for 52 of its stations. The company also has distribution agreements with cable and satellite providers. ION provides network programming 24-7. This programming includes original shows, licensed syndicated programs, movies, sports broadcasts and game shows. The firm also airs infomercials and local public interest programming. The company's entertainment programs are free of excessive violence, explicit sexual themes and foul language. ION derives revenue from airing long form paid programming (informercials), network spot advertising and station advertising. ION has had a history of operating losses, and has lately undertaken financing and restructuring efforts to develop strategic alternatives. As part of this effort, the company recently rebranded its network to the name i from PAX TV. The firm changed its name to ION Media Networks in February 2006. August 2006 saw the launch of Qubo, a multi-platform children's television network broadcasting in English and Spanish. Qubo is an alliance between content providers Scholastic, Chorus Entertainment and Classic Media/Big Idea; and broadcasters ION, NBC and Telemundo. In October 2006, the company announced a programming alliance with RHI Entertainment (formerly Hallmark Entertainment) for the broadcast of RHI's library of miniseries and TV movies.

FINANCIALS: Sales and profits are in thousands of dollars—add 000 to get the full amount. 2006 Note: Financial information for 2006 was not available for all companies at press time.

2006 Sales: $	2006 Profits: $	U.S. Stock Ticker: ION
2005 Sales: $254,176	2005 Profits: $-235,670	Int'l Ticker: Int'l Exchange:
2004 Sales: $276,630	2004 Profits: $-187,972	Employees: 433
2003 Sales: $	2003 Profits: $	Fiscal Year Ends: 12/31
2002 Sales: $	2002 Profits: $	Parent Company:

SALARIES/BENEFITS:

Pension Plan:	ESOP Stock Plan:	Profit Sharing:	Top Exec. Salary: $821,559	Bonus: $832,046
Savings Plan:	Stock Purch. Plan:		Second Exec. Salary: $613,222	Bonus: $2,478,222

OTHER THOUGHTS:

Apparent Women Officers or Directors: 1
Hot Spot for Advancement for Women/Minorities:

LOCATIONS: ("Y" = Yes)

West:	Southwest:	Midwest:	Southeast:	Northeast:	International:
Y	Y	Y	Y	Y	

ISLE OF CAPRI CASINOS INC   www.isleofcapricasino.com

Industry Group Code: 713210 Ranks within this company's industry group: Sales: 3 Profits: 4

Print Media/Publishing:	Movies:	Equipment/Supplies:	Broadcast/Cable:	Music/Audio:	Sports/Games:	
Newspapers:	Movie Theaters:	Equipment/Supplies:	Broadcast TV:	Music Production:	Games/Sports:	
Magazines:	Movie Production:	Gambling Equipment:	Cable TV:	Retail Music:	Retail Games Stores:	
Books:	TV/Video Production:	Special Services:	Satellite Broadcast:	Retail Audio Equip.:	Stadiums/Teams:	
Book Stores:	Video Rental:	Advertising Services:	Radio:	Music Print./Dist.:	Gambling/Casinos:	Y
Distribution/Printing:	Video Distribution:	Info. Sys. Software:	Online Information:	Multimedia:	Rides/Theme Parks:	

TYPES OF BUSINESS:

Casinos
Horse Racing

BRANDS/DIVISIONS/AFFILIATES:

Rhythm City
IsleOne Players Club
Colorado Central Station
Blue Chip Casinos plc
Fan Club
Pompano Park Harness Racing Track
Colorado Grand Casino
Fast Track Club

CONTACTS: Note: Officers with more than one job title may be intentionally listed here more than once.

Bernard Goldstein, CEO
Timothy M. Hinkley, COO
Timothy M. Hinkley, Pres.
Donn Mitchell, CFO
Amanda Totaro, Sr. VP-Mktg.
Allan B. Solomon, Exec. VP/General Counsel
Robert Griffin, Sr. VP-Oper.
Gregory D. Guida, VP-Bus. Dev. & Legal Affairs/Corp. Sec.
Donn Mitchell, Sr. VP-Finance/Chief Acct. Officer
Darrel Kammeyer, VP-Direct Mktg. & Mktg. Tech.
Robert S. Goldstein, Exec. Vice Chmn.
John Bohannon, VP/Gen. Mgr.-Black Hawk Properties
Julia Carcamo, VP-Brand Mktg.
Bernard Goldstein, Chmn.

Phone: 228-396-7000	Fax: 228-396-2634
Toll-Free: 800-843-4753	
Address: 1641 Popps Ferry Rd., Biloxi, MS 39532 US	

GROWTH PLANS/SPECIAL FEATURES:

Isle of Capri Casinos, Inc., one of the largest publicly held gaming companies in the U.S., currently owns and operates riverboat, dockside and land-based casinos at 17 locations in Iowa, Louisiana, Mississippi, Missouri, Colorado, the Bahamas and the U.K., with more in the works overseas. The company's dockside and riverboat casinos are aggressively marketed with a Caribbean theme under the Isle of Capri name and focus on a pre-existing loyal customer base. The firm's land-based casinos include a 57% interest in two Caribbean-themed gaming facilities in Black Hawk, Colorado. Isle of Capri also operates the Pompano Park Harness Racing Track in Florida with plans to open a casino at this location in 2007. Internationally, the firm owns a casino in Freeport, Grand Bahamas and has a two-thirds ownership interest through subsidiary Blue Chip Casinos plc in casinos in Dudley, Walsall and Wolverhampton, England. The company offers customer membership rewards programs under the IsleOne Players Club, the Fan Club and the Fast Track Club brand names at the Isle of Capri properties, Rhythm City-Davenport and the Colorado Central Station-Black Hawk, respectively. Subscribing program members can use their players club card at all of the company's properties except Colorado Grand-Cripple Creek, as well as gain rewards through a partnership with Carnival Cruise Lines. The company recently announced plans to close its Isle-Our Lucaya facility. In 2006, the company sold its properties in Bossier City, Louisiana and Vicksburg, Mississippi to Legends Gaming, LLC for $240 million.

Isle of Capri offers employees incentive prizes, performance recognition awards, company picnics and celebrations, a weight loss program, tuition reimbursement, a 401(k) savings plan, various training and development opportunities and giveaways such as cars, cash and cruises.

FINANCIALS: Sales and profits are in thousands of dollars—add 000 to get the full amount. 2006 Note: Financial information for 2006 was not available for all companies at press time.

2006 Sales: $988,020	2006 Profits: $19,023	U.S. Stock Ticker: ISLE
2005 Sales: $947,572	2005 Profits: $18,038	Int'l Ticker: Int'l Exchange:
2004 Sales: $939,529	2004 Profits: $27,749	Employees: 8,516
2003 Sales: $1,265,458	2003 Profits: $-45,593	Fiscal Year Ends: 4/30
2002 Sales: $1,288,645	2002 Profits: $- 35	Parent Company:

SALARIES/BENEFITS:

Pension Plan:	ESOP Stock Plan:	Profit Sharing:	Top Exec. Salary: $550,000	Bonus: $335,866
Savings Plan: Y	Stock Purch. Plan:		Second Exec. Salary: $465,000	Bonus: $283,959

OTHER THOUGHTS:

Apparent Women Officers or Directors: 2
Hot Spot for Advancement for Women/Minorities:

LOCATIONS: ("Y" = Yes)

West:	Southwest:	Midwest:	Southeast:	Northeast:	International:
Y		Y	Y		Y

ITV PLC

www.itvplc.com

Industry Group Code: 513220 Ranks within this company's industry group: Sales: 12 Profits: 7

Print Media/Publishing:	Movies:		Equipment/Supplies:		Broadcast/Cable:		Music/Audio:	Sports/Games:	
Newspapers:	Movie Theaters:		Equipment/Supplies:		Broadcast TV:	Y	Music Production:	Games/Sports:	
Magazines:	Movie Production:		Gambling Equipment:		Cable TV:	Y	Retail Music:	Retail Games Stores:	
Books:	TV/Video Production:	Y	Special Services:		Satellite Broadcast:		Retail Audio Equip.:	Stadiums/Teams:	Y
Book Stores:	Video Rental:		Advertising Services:	Y	Radio:		Music Print./Dist.:	Gambling/Casinos:	
Distribution/Printing:	Video Distribution:		Info. Sys. Software:		Online Information:		Multimedia:	Rides/Theme Parks:	

TYPES OF BUSINESS:

Cable TV Channel
Satellite Channels
Broadcast TV
TV Production
Cinema Advertising

BRANDS/DIVISIONS/AFFILIATES:

ITV1
ITV2
ITV3
ITV4
ITV Production
Granada
Granada International
Carlton Screen Advertising

CONTACTS:
Note: Officers with more than one job title may be intentionally listed here more than once.

Michael Grade, CEO
Henry Staunton, CFO
John Cresswell, Dir.-Finance
Peter Burt, Chmn.

Phone: 44-20-7843-8000	Fax: 44-20-7261-3520
Toll-Free:	
Address: 200 Grays Inn Road, London, WC1V 8HX UK	

GROWTH PLANS/SPECIAL FEATURES:

ITV plc, a leading media company in the U.K. and the Republic of Ireland, is the result of a merger between Carlton Communications and Granada. ITV operates through ITV1, ITV2, ITV3 and ITV4. ITV1 is the largest commercial television channel in the U.K., with approximately 53% of the U.K. television advertising market. The station broadcasts to approximately 50 million people, accounting for 88% of ITV viewing and over 90% of ITV's advertising revenue. ITV2 has been one of the U.K.'s fastest-growing channels for the last two years. It is available on satellite, cable and digital terrestrial television platforms. ITV2 airs ITV1 show spin-off programs including the popular The X-Factor. The prime demographic for ITV 2 is a younger, mainly female audience. The station features a mix of drama, comedy, movies, events and extensions of ITV1 popular shows. ITV3 shows proprietary contemporary British dramas including Prime Suspect and Inspector Morse. ITV3 is broadcast to around 13 million homes. ITV4, launched in late 2005, showcases programming targeted for a male audience, with relevant shows, movies and sports content. The ITV Production division is one of the largest commercial TV producers in the U.K. It produces over 3,500 hours of original programming each year, including six of the top 10 highest-rating programs on British television that are not sports-related. Subsidiary Granada International is responsible for distribution in Britain and beyond, with footholds in the U.K., U.S., Australian and German markets. Other subsidiaries and assets include Carlton Screen Advertising, a 50% interest in Screenvision Europe and Screenvision U.S., a 16.9% interest in SMG plc, 9.99% stakes in Arsenal Football Club and Liverpool Football Club and a 40% interest in ITN.

FINANCIALS: Sales and profits are in thousands of dollars—add 000 to get the full amount. 2006 Note: Financial information for 2006 was not available for all companies at press time.

2006 Sales: $	2006 Profits: $	U.S. Stock Ticker: ITVPF
2005 Sales: $3,796,687	2005 Profits: $394,144	Int'l Ticker: ITV Int'l Exchange: London-LSE
2004 Sales: $3,580,431	2004 Profits: $249,392	Employees: 5,952
2003 Sales: $5,244,800	2003 Profits: $-419,600	Fiscal Year Ends: 12/31
2002 Sales: $2,227,700	2002 Profits: $-590,100	Parent Company:

SALARIES/BENEFITS:

Pension Plan: Y	ESOP Stock Plan:	Profit Sharing:	Top Exec. Salary: $1,767,258	Bonus: $64,998
Savings Plan:	Stock Purch. Plan:		Second Exec. Salary: $946,988	Bonus: $70,277

OTHER THOUGHTS:

Apparent Women Officers or Directors: 1
Hot Spot for Advancement for Women/Minorities: Y

LOCATIONS: ("Y" = Yes)

West:	Southwest:	Midwest:	Southeast:	Northeast:	International:
					Y

IVILLAGE INC

www.ivillage.com

Industry Group Code: 514199 **Ranks within this company's industry group:** Sales: 5 Profits: 4

Print Media/Publishing:		Movies:		Equipment/Supplies:		Broadcast/Cable:		Music/Audio:		Sports/Games:	
Newspapers:		Movie Theaters:		Equipment/Supplies:		Broadcast TV:		Music Production:		Games/Sports:	
Magazines:	Y	Movie Production:		Gambling Equipment:		Cable TV:		Retail Music:		Retail Games Stores:	
Books:	Y	TV/Video Production:		Special Services:	Y	Satellite Broadcast:		Retail Audio Equip.:		Stadiums/Teams:	
Book Stores:		Video Rental:		Advertising Services:	Y	Radio:		Music Print./Dist.:		Gambling/Casinos:	
Distribution/Printing:		Video Distribution:		Info. Sys. Software:		Online Information:		Multimedia:		Rides/Theme Parks:	

TYPES OF BUSINESS:

Online Women's Network
Educational Publishing
Online Promotions & Direct Marketing
Consulting Services

GROWTH PLANS/SPECIAL FEATURES:

iVillage, Inc., a subsidiary of NBC Universal, Inc., is a leading women's online destination that consists of several online and offline media-based properties that seek to enrich the lives of women, teenage girls and parents through offering unique content, community applications, tools and interactive features. Current subsidiaries and divisions include iVillage.com, Healthology, HealthCentersOnline, iVillage Limited, iVillage Consulting, GardenWeb.com, gURL.com, Promotions.com, Inc., Astrology.com and iVillage Integrated Properties, Inc. The company also operates internationally through its recently acquired iVillage U.K. subsidiary. In 2006, the company was acquired by NBC Universal, Inc. for approximately $600 million.

BRANDS/DIVISIONS/AFFILIATES:

NBC Universal Inc.
Healthology, Inc.
HealthCentersOnline
iVillage Consulting
iVillage Parenting Network, Inc.
GardenWeb.com
gURL.com
iVillage Integrated Properties, Inc.

CONTACTS: Note: Officers with more than one job title may be intentionally listed here more than once.

Peter R. Naylor, Sr. VP-Sales
Jennifer Salant, Exec. VP-Oper. & Strategy
Beth Comstock, Pres., NBC Universal Digital Media

Phone: 212-600-6000	Fax: 212-604-9133
Toll-Free:	
Address: 500 7th Ave. 14th Fl., New York, NY 10018 US	

FINANCIALS: Sales and profits are in thousands of dollars—add 000 to get the full amount. 2006 Note: Financial information for 2006 was not available for all companies at press time.

2006 Sales: $	2006 Profits: $	**U.S. Stock Ticker:** Subsidiary
2005 Sales: $91,061	2005 Profits: $9,456	**Int'l Ticker:** Int'l Exchange:
2004 Sales: $66,903	2004 Profits: $2,677	Employees: 278
2003 Sales: $55,221	2003 Profits: $-27,129	Fiscal Year Ends: 12/31
2002 Sales: $59,400	2002 Profits: $-34,000	Parent Company: NBC UNIVERSAL INC

SALARIES/BENEFITS:

Pension Plan:	ESOP Stock Plan:	Profit Sharing:	Top Exec. Salary: $500,000	Bonus: $
Savings Plan: Y	Stock Purch. Plan: Y		Second Exec. Salary: $327,000	Bonus: $27,500

OTHER THOUGHTS:

Apparent Women Officers or Directors: 2
Hot Spot for Advancement for Women/Minorities: Y

LOCATIONS: ("Y" = Yes)

West:	Southwest:	Midwest:	Southeast:	Northeast:	International:
				Y	

JOHN WILEY & SONS INC   www.wiley.com

Industry Group Code: 511130 Ranks within this company's industry group: Sales: 6   Profits: 3

Print Media/Publishing:		Movies:	Equipment/Supplies:	Broadcast/Cable:	Music/Audio:	Sports/Games:
Newspapers:		Movie Theaters:	Equipment/Supplies:	Broadcast TV:	Music Production:	Games/Sports:
Magazines:	Y	Movie Production:	Gambling Equipment:	Cable TV:	Retail Music:	Retail Games Stores:
Books:	Y	TV/Video Production:	Special Services:	Satellite Broadcast:	Retail Audio Equip.:	Stadiums/Teams:
Book Stores:		Video Rental:	Advertising Services:	Radio:	Music Print./Dist.:	Gambling/Casinos:
Distribution/Printing:		Video Distribution:	Info. Sys. Software:	Online Information:	Multimedia:	Rides/Theme Parks:

TYPES OF BUSINESS:

Reference Book Publishing
Trade Books
Business Books
Scientific & Technical Books
Textbooks & Educational Materials
Professional Journals
Consumer Guides
Online Information

BRANDS/DIVISIONS/AFFILIATES:

Wiley InterScience
Wiley InterScience OnlineBooks
Mount Sinai Journal of Medicine
Moody's Corporation
Blackwell Publishing (Holdings) Ltd.
HEED
Whatsonwhen
Microsoft Official Academic Curriculum

CONTACTS: *Note: Officers with more than one job title may be intentionally listed here more than once.*

William J. Pesce, CEO
Ellis E. Cousens, COO
William J. Pesce, Pres.
Ellis E. Cousens, CFO/Exec. VP
William J. Arlington, Sr. VP-Human Resources
Eric A. Swanson, Sr. VP-Scientific, Tech. & Medical Div.
Warren C. Fristensky, Sr. VP-IT/CIO
Gary M. Rinck, General Counsel/Sr. VP
Timothy B. King, Sr. VP-Planning & Dev.
Deborah E. Wiley, Sr. VP-Corp. Comm.
Edward J. Melando, Corp. Controller/Chief Acct. Officer/VP
Mark Allin, Mng. Dir.-John Wiley & Sons (Asia) Pte.Ltd.
Bill Zerter, COO-John Wiley & Sons Canada, Ltd.
Peter C. Donoughue, Mng. Dir.-John Wiley & Sons Australia, Ltd.
John Jarvis, Sr. VP-Europe/Managing Dir.-Wiley Europe, Ltd.
Peter B. Wiley, Chmn.
Steve Miron, General Mgr.-Global STM/VP-Asia
Clifford Kline, Sr. VP-Distribution & Customer Service

Phone: 201-748-6000	**Fax:** 201-748-6088
Toll-Free:	
Address: 111 River St., Hoboken, NJ 07030-5774 US	

GROWTH PLANS/SPECIAL FEATURES:

John Wiley & Sons, Inc. (Wiley) publishes books, journals and electronic products primarily for the scientific, technical and medical (STM) markets. The firm operates publishing, marketing and distribution centers in the U.S., Canada, Europe, Asia and Australia. The company produces STM journals, encyclopedias, books and online products; professional and consumer books and subscription services in print and electronic media; and textbooks and higher education materials. Its STM publications cover life and medical sciences, chemistry, statistics, mathematics, and electrical and electronics engineering. The firm's professional products serve customers in areas including business, accounting, nonprofit institution management, computers, psychology, architecture, engineering, hospitality and culinary arts. The company's educational materials are largely targeted to the science, engineering, mathematics and accounting fields, with growing positions in business, education and modern languages. Through licensing agreements, Wiley also provides academic and corporate customers with online access to STM content through Wiley InterScience, its web-based services. Wiley InterScience offers searchable access to more than 500 of the firm's STM journals and more than 1,500 titles from Wiley InterScience OnlineBooks. The collection spans over 7.5 million pages, representing more than 1.5 million articles of scientific and scholarly research dating back to 1799. Wiley recently assumed publication of Mount Sinai Journal of Medicine. In 2006, the firm announced plans to acquire Blackwell Publishing (Holdings) Ltd. Also in 2006, Wiley acquired HEED (Health Economic Evaluations Database), and Whatsonwhen (online travel content); and expanded its partnership with Skyscape, Inc. and Microsoft Learning to develop, publish and deliver Microsoft Official Academic Curriculum (MOAC) e-learning tools and textbooks to college markets.

Wiley offers its employees bereavement leave, tuition reimbursement, a matching gift program, adoption assistance, a 401(k) plan, medical benefits, life insurance and paid medical leave. In 2006, the firm was named one of FORTUNE Magazine's 100 Best Companies to Work For.

FINANCIALS: Sales and profits are in thousands of dollars—add 000 to get the full amount. 2006 Note: Financial information for 2006 was not available for all companies at press time.

2006 Sales: $1,044,185	2006 Profits: $110,329	**U.S. Stock Ticker:** JWA
2005 Sales: $974,048	2005 Profits: $83,841	**Int'l Ticker:** Int'l Exchange:
2004 Sales: $923,000	2004 Profits: $88,800	Employees: 3,600
2003 Sales: $854,000	2003 Profits: $87,300	Fiscal Year Ends: 4/30
2002 Sales: $734,400	2002 Profits: $57,300	Parent Company:

SALARIES/BENEFITS:

Pension Plan: Y	ESOP Stock Plan: Y	Profit Sharing:	Top Exec. Salary: $823,333	Bonus: $1,201,280
Savings Plan: Y	Stock Purch. Plan: Y		Second Exec. Salary: $445,000	Bonus: $493,015

OTHER THOUGHTS:

Apparent Women Officers or Directors: 4
Hot Spot for Advancement for Women/Minorities: Y

LOCATIONS: ("Y" = Yes)

West:	Southwest:	Midwest:	Southeast:	Northeast:	International:
Y		Y		Y	Y

JOHNSON PUBLISHING COMPANY INC
www.johnsonpublishing.com
Industry Group Code: 511120 Ranks within this company's industry group: Sales: 9   Profits:

Print Media/Publishing:		Movies:	Equipment/Supplies:		Broadcast/Cable:	Music/Audio:	Sports/Games:
Newspapers:		Movie Theaters:	Equipment/Supplies:		Broadcast TV:	Music Production:	Games/Sports:
Magazines:	Y	Movie Production:	Gambling Equipment:		Cable TV:	Retail Music:	Retail Games Stores:
Books:	Y	TV/Video Production:	Special Services:	Y	Satellite Broadcast:	Retail Audio Equip.:	Stadiums/Teams:
Book Stores:		Video Rental:	Advertising Services:		Radio:	Music Print./Dist.:	Gambling/Casinos:
Distribution/Printing:		Video Distribution:	Info. Sys. Software:		Online Information:	Multimedia:	Rides/Theme Parks:

TYPES OF BUSINESS:
Magazine Publishing
Book Publishing
Cosmetics & Skin Care Products
Traveling Fashion Show
Greeting Cards

BRANDS/DIVISIONS/AFFILIATES:
EBONY Magazine
JET Magazine
Fashion Fair Cosmetics
EBONY Fashion Fair
JPC Book Division
Ebony Home
The Ebony Collection
Ebony Inspirations

CONTACTS:
Note: Officers with more than one job title may be intentionally listed here more than once.
Linda J. Rice, CEO
Linda J. Rice, Pres.
Wendy Parks, Dir.-Corp.Comm.
Eunice Johnson, Treas./Corp. Sec.
Eunice Johnson, Dir.-EBONY Fashion Fair
Treka Owens, VP/Dir.-Finance
Bryan Monroe, VP/Editorial Dir.-Ebony & Jet Magazines
John H. Johnson, Chmn.

Phone: 312-322-9200	Fax: 312-322-0918
Toll-Free:	
Address: 820 S. Michigan Ave., Chicago, IL 60605 US	

GROWTH PLANS/SPECIAL FEATURES:
Johnson Publishing Company, Inc. is a major African-American-owned and-operated publishing company with businesses in publishing, cosmetics, television production and fashion. The company owns and operates both EBONY and JET magazines. With a monthly circulation around 1.5 million and a monthly readership of around 12.9 million, EBONY provides a forum to discuss issues and provide encouragement for African-Americans. JET, with a weekly circulation of over 900,000 and a weekly readership of approximately 9.5 million, specializes in covering worldwide news. Johnson Publishing's other divisions include Fashion Fair Cosmetics, a top line of makeup and skincare for women of color, sold in 2,500 stores in the U.S., Canada, Africa, England, France, Switzerland, the Bahamas, Bermuda and the Virgin Islands; as well as the EBONY Fashion Fair, a global traveling fashion show designed to raise money for scholarships and charities in cities; and a book division, which publishes books by African-American authors covering topics such as history, culture, cooking and children's books. In the past, the company has been involved in television production. During 2005, the firm celebrated the 60th anniversary of EBONY magazine. Founder John H. Johnson, who received the Presidential Medal of Freedom, Magazine Publisher's Association Publisher of the Year and Hall of Fame recognition among other awards, died in 2005. In a partnership with American Greetings, Johnson Publishing will launch the Ebony Inspirations greeting card brand. Initially, the cards will be available at approximately 900 Wal-Mart stores in celebration of Black History month, February 2007. The deal was brokered by TurnerPatteron licensing agency in partnership with Johnson Publishing's new licensing division. The division plans to introduce new brands including: Ebony Home; The Ebony Collection, apparel for women and men; and Ebony Jr.! brand.

FINANCIALS:
Sales and profits are in thousands of dollars—add 000 to get the full amount. 2006 Note: Financial information for 2006 was not available for all companies at press time.

2006 Sales: $	2006 Profits: $	U.S. Stock Ticker: Private
2005 Sales: $495,700	2005 Profits: $	Int'l Ticker: Int'l Exchange:
2004 Sales: $498,200	2004 Profits: $	Employees: 1,707
2003 Sales: $488,500	2003 Profits: $	Fiscal Year Ends: 12/31
2002 Sales: $	2002 Profits: $	Parent Company:

SALARIES/BENEFITS:
Pension Plan:	ESOP Stock Plan:	Profit Sharing:	Top Exec. Salary: $	Bonus: $
Savings Plan:	Stock Purch. Plan:		Second Exec. Salary: $	Bonus: $

OTHER THOUGHTS:
Apparent Women Officers or Directors: 3
Hot Spot for Advancement for Women/Minorities: Y

LOCATIONS: ("Y" = Yes)
West:	Southwest:	Midwest:	Southeast:	Northeast:	International:
Y		Y		Y	Y

JOURNAL COMMUNICATIONS INC

www.jc.com

Industry Group Code: 511110 Ranks within this company's industry group: Sales: 16 Profits: 11

Print Media/Publishing:		Movies:	Equipment/Supplies:		Broadcast/Cable:		Music/Audio:	Sports/Games:
Newspapers:	Y	Movie Theaters:	Equipment/Supplies:		Broadcast TV:	Y	Music Production:	Games/Sports:
Magazines:		Movie Production:	Gambling Equipment:		Cable TV:		Retail Music:	Retail Games Stores:
Books:		TV/Video Production:	Special Services:	Y	Satellite Broadcast:		Retail Audio Equip.:	Stadiums/Teams:
Book Stores:		Video Rental:	Advertising Services:	Y	Radio:		Music Print./Dist.:	Gambling/Casinos:
Distribution/Printing:		Video Distribution:	Info. Sys. Software:		Online Information:		Multimedia:	Rides/Theme Parks:

TYPES OF BUSINESS:
Newspaper Publishing
Television Broadcasting
Radio Broadcasting
Printing Services
Label Printing

BRANDS/DIVISIONS/AFFILIATES:
Milwaukee Journal Sentinal
Journal Broadcast Group
IPC Print Services, Inc.

CONTACTS: Note: Officers with more than one job title may be intentionally listed here more than once.
Steven J. Smith, CEO
Douglas G. Kiel, Pres.
Paul M. Bonaiuto, CFO/Exec. VP
Daniel L. Harmsen, VP-Human Resources
Mary H. Leahy, General Counsel/Sr. VP
Karen O. Trickle, VP/Treas.
Douglas G. Kiel, CEO-Journal Broadcasting Group
James J. Ditter, VP/Pres., Norlight Telecommunications
Elizabeth Brenner, Exec. VP/COO-Publishing Businesses
Carl D. Gardner, VP/Exec. VP-TV & Radio, Journal Broadcasting Group
Steven J. Smith, Chmn.

Phone: 414-224-2616 **Fax:** 414-224-2469
Toll-Free: 800-388-2291
Address: 333 W. State St., Milwaukee, WI 53201-0661 US

GROWTH PLANS/SPECIAL FEATURES:
Journal Communications, Inc. is a media and communications company with operations in publishing, radio and television broadcasting, telecommunications and printing services. In newspaper publishing, the company publishes the Milwaukee Journal Sentinel, which serves as the principal daily and Sunday newspaper for the greater Milwaukee area, as well as more than 90 community newspapers and shoppers in eight states. The Milwaukee Journal Sentinel has a daily circulation of approximately 250,000, and about 425,000 on Sundays. Through the Journal Broadcast Group, Journal Communications also owns and operates 37 radio stations and nine television stations in 12 states and operates two additional television stations under local marketing agreements. The company's printing services are conducted through subsidiary IPC Print Services, Inc. Services include complete production of magazines, professional journals and documentation material, with particular emphasis on scientific, medical and technical journals. The firm's other businesses consist of a label printing business and a direct market services business. The company sold its Norlight Telecommunications subsidiary in 2006 for approximately $186 million. The company also sold KBBX-FM to Connoisseur Media of Omaha, LLC for $7.5 million that same year.

Journal Communications offers its employees benefits including educational support and tuition reimbursement, an employee assistance program, bereavement leave, AAA memberships, banking benefits with preferred rates, Dell computer and fitness center discounts, Internet access, subsidized parking, an employee stock purchase plan and a 401(k) savings plan.

FINANCIALS: Sales and profits are in thousands of dollars—add 000 to get the full amount. 2006 Note: Financial information for 2006 was not available for all companies at press time.
2006 Sales: $	2006 Profits: $	U.S. Stock Ticker: JRN
2005 Sales: $764,461	2005 Profits: $66,243	Int'l Ticker: Int'l Exchange:
2004 Sales: $773,372	2004 Profits: $78,480	Employees: 5,500
2003 Sales: $798,289	2003 Profits: $66,793	Fiscal Year Ends: 12/31
2002 Sales: $801,400	2002 Profits: $57,900	Parent Company:

SALARIES/BENEFITS:
Pension Plan:	ESOP Stock Plan:	Profit Sharing:	Top Exec. Salary: $696,154	Bonus: $78,750
Savings Plan: Y	Stock Purch. Plan: Y		Second Exec. Salary: $490,308	Bonus: $55,216

OTHER THOUGHTS:
Apparent Women Officers or Directors: 4
Hot Spot for Advancement for Women/Minorities: Y

LOCATIONS: ("Y" = Yes)
West:	Southwest:	Midwest:	Southeast:	Northeast:	International:
Y	Y	Y	Y	Y	

Note: Financial information, benefits and other data can change quickly and may vary from those stated here.

JOURNAL REGISTER CO
www.journalregister.com

Industry Group Code: 511110 **Ranks within this company's industry group:** Sales: 17 Profits: 12

Print Media/Publishing:		Movies:		Equipment/Supplies:		Broadcast/Cable:		Music/Audio:		Sports/Games:	
Newspapers:	Y	Movie Theaters:		Equipment/Supplies:		Broadcast TV:		Music Production:		Games/Sports:	
Magazines:	Y	Movie Production:		Gambling Equipment:		Cable TV:		Retail Music:		Retail Games Stores:	
Books:		TV/Video Production:		Special Services:		Satellite Broadcast:		Retail Audio Equip.:		Stadiums/Teams:	
Book Stores:		Video Rental:		Advertising Services:	Y	Radio:		Music Print./Dist.:		Gambling/Casinos:	
Distribution/Printing:		Video Distribution:		Info. Sys. Software:		Online Information:		Multimedia:		Rides/Theme Parks:	

TYPES OF BUSINESS:

Newspaper & Magazine Publishing
Commercial Printing
Online Publishing

BRANDS/DIVISIONS/AFFILIATES:

New Haven Register
Litchfield County Times
Connecticut Vacation Guide
Westchester/Fairfield County Times
Connecticut Magazine
Freeman Online
Hudson Valley Guide
Suburban Lifestyles

CONTACTS: Note: Officers with more than one job title may be intentionally listed here more than once.

Robert M. Jelenic, CEO
Julie Beck, Sr. VP/CFO
Allen J. Mailman, Sr. VP-Tech.
Edward J. Yocum, Jr., VP/General Counsel
Thomas E. Rice, Sr. VP-Oper.
William J. Higginson, VP-Production
Michael Murray, VP-Circulation
Robert M. Jelenic, Chmn.

Phone: 215-504-4200	Fax: 215-504-4201
Toll-Free:	
Address: 790 Township Line Rd., Yardley, PA 19067 US	

GROWTH PLANS/SPECIAL FEATURES:

Journal Register Company is a leading U.S. newspaper publisher, with a total daily circulation of approximately 650,000. The company owns and operates 27 daily newspapers, including the New Haven Register, Connecticut's second-largest daily and Sunday newspaper. Other major publications released by the company and its subsidiaries include Connecticut Vacation Guide, Westchester/Fairfield County Times, Litchfield County Times, Connecticut Magazine, Freeman Online, County Kids and Hudson Valley Guide. Journal Register also owns 365 non-daily publications, with a total distribution of more than 5 million, in addition to several commercial printing and software development companies. The company strategically clusters its operations in seven geographic areas: Connecticut, Michigan, Philadelphia and its surrounding areas, greater Cleveland, central New England and the Capital-Saratoga and Mid-Hudson regions of New York. Journal Register also owns 222 individual web sites featuring its newspapers. The company's newspapers are characterized by an intense focus on coverage of local news and local sports and offer compelling graphic design in colorful, reader-friendly packages. The majority of the company's daily newspapers have been published for more than 100 years and are established franchises with strong identities in the communities they serve. In many cases, Journal Register's daily newspapers are the only general-circulation daily newspapers published in their respective communities. While newspaper publishing accounts for substantially all of the company's revenues, it also owns three commercial printing operations that compliment and enhance its publishing operations. In 2006, the company acquired Michigan-based Suburban Lifestyles Community Newspaper group. The company also sold two of its New England Cluster community newspapers to Gatehouse Media.

FINANCIALS: Sales and profits are in thousands of dollars—add 000 to get the full amount. 2006 Note: Financial information for 2006 was not available for all companies at press time.

2006 Sales: $	2006 Profits: $	U.S. Stock Ticker: JRC
2005 Sales: $556,629	2005 Profits: $46,868	Int'l Ticker: Int'l Exchange:
2004 Sales: $469,092	2004 Profits: $116,513	Employees: 6,000
2003 Sales: $405,986	2003 Profits: $71,990	Fiscal Year Ends: 12/31
2002 Sales: $407,800	2002 Profits: $49,200	Parent Company:

SALARIES/BENEFITS:

Pension Plan: Y	ESOP Stock Plan:	Profit Sharing:	Top Exec. Salary: $969,000	Bonus: $100,000
Savings Plan: Y	Stock Purch. Plan:		Second Exec. Salary: $591,600	Bonus: $50,000

OTHER THOUGHTS:

Apparent Women Officers or Directors: 1
Hot Spot for Advancement for Women/Minorities:

LOCATIONS: ("Y" = Yes)

West:	Southwest:	Midwest:	Southeast:	Northeast:	International:
		Y		Y	

Note: Financial information, benefits and other data can change quickly and may vary from those stated here.

JUMPTV INC

www.jumptv.com

Industry Group Code: 513120A Ranks within this company's industry group: Sales: Profits:

Print Media/Publishing:	Movies:	Equipment/Supplies:		Broadcast/Cable:		Music/Audio:		Sports/Games:
Newspapers:	Movie Theaters:	Equipment/Supplies:		Broadcast TV:		Music Production:		Games/Sports:
Magazines:	Movie Production:	Gambling Equipment:		Cable TV:	Y	Retail Music:		Retail Games Stores:
Books:	TV/Video Production:	Special Services:	Y	Satellite Broadcast:		Retail Audio Equip.:		Stadiums/Teams:
Book Stores:	Video Rental:	Advertising Services:		Radio:		Music Print./Dist.:		Gambling/Casinos:
Distribution/Printing:	Video Distribution:	Info. Sys. Software:		Online Information:		Multimedia:		Rides/Theme Parks:

TYPES OF BUSINESS:

Internet Protocol Television

BRANDS/DIVISIONS/AFFILIATES:

JumpTV International
Sports International Group
www.SportsYa.com

CONTACTS: *Note: Officers with more than one job title may be intentionally listed here more than once.*

G. Scott Paterson, CEO
Alex Blum, COO
Alex Blum, Pres.
Kriss Bush, CFO
Rodger P. Wells II, General Mngr.-Mktg.
Dan O'Hara, Tech. Fellow
Jeremy Hope, VP-Network Oper.
Jeremy Hope, VP-Network Oper.
Brad Rosenberg, Dir.-Prod. Dev.
Willem Galle, Exec. VP-Oper.
Jeff Maser, VP-Corp. Dev.
Brad Rosenberg, Dir.-Prod. Dev.
Sila Celik, COO-JumpTV Int'l FZ-LLC
Mark David, Mng. Dir.-JumpTV Int'l
Ted Steube, VP-Corp. Dev.
Thomas J. Herman, VP-Prod. Mktg.
G. Scott Paterson, Chmn.
Kaleil Isaza Tuzman, Pres., JumpTV Int'l

Phone: 416-368-0305	Fax: 416-368-6414
Toll-Free:	
Address: BCE Place, 161 Bay St., Ste. 3840, Toronto, ON M5J 2S1 Canada	

GROWTH PLANS/SPECIAL FEATURES:

JumpTV, Inc. is a leader in Internet Protocol Television (IPTV), providing access to international television streaming over the Internet. The company has offices in Toronto; New York; London; Bogota, Colombia; Amman, Jordan; Bangkok, Thailand; and Dubai, United Arab Emirates. JumpTV is partnered with over 180 television broadcasters in over 60 countries to provide live Internet streaming of broadcasters' 24-hour feeds. Currently, the firm offers channels from Europe, Asia, the Middle East and Africa. These streams are available to subscribers over a high-speed Internet connection. The channels are offered either separately or as part of a multi-channel bundle. One of the company's major programming draws is sports, particularly soccer. Sports, along with a few other shows, are available through pay-per-view and video-on-demand options. As of September, 2006, JumpTV had approximately 22,000 subscribers with 23,900 subscriptions and had signed 225 channels; it holds exclusive Internet rights to 219 of these channels. The company has added 94 channels since its IPO. JumpTV typically loses roughly 20% of its subscribers in a month; however, its base continues to grow, having nearly doubled in the last year. The majority of the firm's subscribers are located in the U.S. (53%); the next largest segment comes from Europe (22%), with Spain making up 8% of the overall subscriber base. JumpTV is available in over 80 countries. The company held its initial public offering in August 2006, and expects to begin turning a profit in 2009. In 2006, JumpTV redesigned its website and began offering social networking tools. In December 2006, the company agreed to acquire Sports International Group LLC through its subsidiary JumpTV International. Sports International Group is the owner and operator of www.SportsYa.com, a leading Spanish language sports content web site.

FINANCIALS: Sales and profits are in thousands of dollars—add 000 to get the full amount. 2006 Note: Financial information for 2006 was not available for all companies at press time.

2006 Sales: $	2006 Profits: $	**U.S. Stock Ticker:**
2005 Sales: $	2005 Profits: $	**Int'l Ticker:** JTV Int'l Exchange: Toronto-TSX
2004 Sales: $	2004 Profits: $	Employees:
2003 Sales: $	2003 Profits: $	Fiscal Year Ends: 12/31
2002 Sales: $	2002 Profits: $	Parent Company:

SALARIES/BENEFITS:

Pension Plan:	ESOP Stock Plan:	Profit Sharing:	Top Exec. Salary: $	Bonus: $
Savings Plan:	Stock Purch. Plan:		Second Exec. Salary: $	Bonus: $

OTHER THOUGHTS:

Apparent Women Officers or Directors: 3
Hot Spot for Advancement for Women/Minorities: Y

LOCATIONS: ("Y" = Yes)

West:	Southwest:	Midwest:	Southeast:	Northeast:	International:
				Y	Y

Note: Financial information, benefits and other data can change quickly and may vary from those stated here.

JUPITERMEDIA CORP

www.jupitermedia.com

Industry Group Code: 514199 Ranks within this company's industry group: Sales: 3 Profits: 1

Print Media/Publishing:	Movies:	Equipment/Supplies:		Broadcast/Cable:	Music/Audio:	Sports/Games:
Newspapers:	Movie Theaters:	Equipment/Supplies:		Broadcast TV:	Music Production:	Games/Sports:
Magazines:	Movie Production:	Gambling Equipment:		Cable TV:	Retail Music:	Retail Games Stores:
Books:	TV/Video Production:	Special Services:	Y	Satellite Broadcast:	Retail Audio Equip.:	Stadiums/Teams:
Book Stores:	Video Rental:	Advertising Services:	Y	Radio:	Music Print./Dist.:	Gambling/Casinos:
Distribution/Printing:	Video Distribution:	Info. Sys. Software:	Y	Online Information:	Multimedia:	Rides/Theme Parks:

TYPES OF BUSINESS:

Business & Technology News Portal
Online Image Library
Market Research
Trade Shows

BRANDS/DIVISIONS/AFFILIATES:

JupiterWeb
internet.com
JupiterImages
photos.com
clipart.com
Comstock Images
JupiterEvents
JupiterResearch

CONTACTS: *Note: Officers with more than one job title may be intentionally listed here more than once.*

Alan M. Meckler, CEO
Christopher S. Cardell, COO
Christopher S. Cardell, Pres.
Christopher S. Cardell, Interim CFO
Alan M. Meckler, Chmn.

Phone: 203-662-2800	Fax: 203-655-4686
Toll-Free:	
Address: 23 Old Kings Hwy. S., Darien, CT 06820 US	

GROWTH PLANS/SPECIAL FEATURES:

Jupitermedia Corp. is a leading global provider of original online information, images, research and events for information technology, business, and design and art professionals. The firm develops and disseminates original content and provides access to one of the largest online image libraries. Jupitermedia delivers its content through a number of proprietary channels, including its extensive online media networks, online image networks, proprietary research business and its various trade shows and conferences. The firm owns and operates JupiterWeb, a network of over 150 web sites, including the massive internet.com network, and more than 150 e-mail newsletters that are viewed by 20 million users and generate 300 million page views monthly. Site visitors are offered real-time Internet industry news, tutorials, training and skills development, market research, buyer's guides, product reviews, discussion forums and software downloads. As part of its ongoing international expansion, Jupitermedia has international business-to-business portals in Germany, Hong Kong, Japan, Korea, Singapore and Turkey. The company's JupiterImages division is one of the leading paid subscription-based image companies in the world, with over 7 million online images serving creative professionals. It owns and markets products that include Comstock Images, photos.com and clipart.com. JupiterResearch is a leading international research advisory organization, specializing in business and technology market research in 18 business areas and 14 vertical markets. The firm also owns JupiterEvents, which produces offline conferences and trade shows focused on IT and business-specific topics, including Wi-Fi Planet, Search Engine Strategies and Internet Planet; and JupiterWebEvents, which offer similar information on a live, electronic platform. Recent acquisitions include Workbook Stock Image Collection, IFA Bilderteam of Munich, Germany, Cover-Imagen Y Publicaciones, S.L. and a 90% stake in HAAP Media Ltd.

The firm offers its employees major medical and AD&D coverage, flexible spending accounts, tuition reimbursement, stock options and paid holidays.

FINANCIALS: Sales and profits are in thousands of dollars—add 000 to get the full amount. 2006 Note: Financial information for 2006 was not available for all companies at press time.

2006 Sales: $	2006 Profits: $	**U.S. Stock Ticker:** JUPM
2005 Sales: $124,577	2005 Profits: $78,399	**Int'l Ticker:** Int'l Exchange:
2004 Sales: $61,959	2004 Profits: $15,737	Employees: 639
2003 Sales: $38,713	2003 Profits: $1,382	Fiscal Year Ends: 12/31
2002 Sales: $40,700	2002 Profits: $- 500	Parent Company:

SALARIES/BENEFITS:

Pension Plan:	ESOP Stock Plan:	Profit Sharing:	Top Exec. Salary: $294,490	Bonus: $
Savings Plan: Y	Stock Purch. Plan:		Second Exec. Salary: $294,490	Bonus: $

OTHER THOUGHTS:

Apparent Women Officers or Directors:
Hot Spot for Advancement for Women/Minorities:

LOCATIONS: ("Y" = Yes)

West:	Southwest:	Midwest:	Southeast:	Northeast:	International:
Y				Y	Y

Note: Financial information, benefits and other data can change quickly and may vary from those stated here.

KERZNER INTERNATIONAL LIMITED
www.kerzner.com

Industry Group Code: 721120 Ranks within this company's industry group: Sales: 11 Profits: 9

Print Media/Publishing:	Movies:	Equipment/Supplies:	Broadcast/Cable:	Music/Audio:	Sports/Games:	
Newspapers:	Movie Theaters:	Equipment/Supplies:	Broadcast TV:	Music Production:	Games/Sports:	
Magazines:	Movie Production:	Gambling Equipment:	Cable TV:	Retail Music:	Retail Games Stores:	
Books:	TV/Video Production:	Special Services:	Satellite Broadcast:	Retail Audio Equip.:	Stadiums/Teams:	
Book Stores:	Video Rental:	Advertising Services:	Radio:	Music Print./Dist.:	Gambling/Casinos:	Y
Distribution/Printing:	Video Distribution:	Info. Sys. Software:	Online Information:	Multimedia:	Rides/Theme Parks:	Y

TYPES OF BUSINESS:

Casino Hotels
Luxury Resort Hotels
Resort Development

BRANDS/DIVISIONS/AFFILIATES:

Atlantis
Palm (The)
Dig (The)
One&Only
Related Companies L.P. (The)
Istithmar PJSC
Colony Capital LLC
Providence Equity Partners, Inc.

CONTACTS: Note: Officers with more than one job title may be intentionally listed here more than once.

Paul O'Neil, CEO
John R. Allison, CFO/Exec. VP
Richard M. Levine, General Counsel/Exec. VP
Solomon Kerzner, Chmn.

Phone: 242-363-6000	Fax: 242-363-5401
Toll-Free:	
Address: Atlantis, Coral Towers, Exec. Offices, Paradise Island, C5 Bahamas	

GROWTH PLANS/SPECIAL FEATURES:

Kerzner International, Ltd. (formerly Sun International Hotels) is a resort and gaming company that develops, operates and manages premier resort and casino properties. The company's flagship property is its Atlantis resort on Paradise Island, near Nassau in the Bahamas, which features the world's largest open-air aquarium and the largest hotel and casino in the Caribbean market. The 2,317-room resort features three interconnected hotel towers built around a seven-acre lagoon and a 34-acre marine environment. Kerzner International is currently expanding its Atlantis resort by 1,500 rooms and adding an 18-hole golf course on a nearby island and a water park including an area where guests can swim with dolphins. Also under development is the Palm, a joint venture with an affiliate of Nakheel, LLC. Located on one of two man-made islands shaped like date palms, the Palm will include a 1,000-room luxury hotel, an extensive water theme park and the Dig, an Atlantis-themed archeological experience. Kerzner International manages or owns interests in 10 beach resorts, six of which operate under the company's One&Only brand. In development and planning are One&Only Reethi Rah, Maldives, as well as locations in Cape Town, South Africa and Havana, Cuba. Mid-term expansion plans include a 2,000-room Atlantis casino hotel in Dubai, valued at $1.1 billion; a $230-million casino in Morocco; and three new casinos, valued at $1 billion, in the U.K. The Dubai Government is a major backer of the firm. Eventually, the company hopes to open an Atlantis casino hotel in Asia and sponsor a Native American casino in the Catskill Mountains. In March 2006, Kerzner International was acquired by an investor group consisting of Istithmar PJSC, Colony Capital LLC, Providence Equity Partners, Inc. and The Related Companies L.P. in a transaction valued at $3.6 billion.

FINANCIALS: Sales and profits are in thousands of dollars—add 000 to get the full amount. 2006 Note: Financial information for 2006 was not available for all companies at press time.

2006 Sales: $	2006 Profits: $	U.S. Stock Ticker: Private
2005 Sales: $721,524	2005 Profits: $50,648	Int'l Ticker: Int'l Exchange:
2004 Sales: $621,085	2004 Profits: $68,132	Employees: 11,870
2003 Sales: $525,292	2003 Profits: $71,572	Fiscal Year Ends: 12/31
2002 Sales: $573,700	2002 Profits: $39,603	Parent Company:

SALARIES/BENEFITS:

Pension Plan:	ESOP Stock Plan:	Profit Sharing:	Top Exec. Salary: $	Bonus: $
Savings Plan: Y	Stock Purch. Plan:		Second Exec. Salary: $	Bonus: $

OTHER THOUGHTS:

Apparent Women Officers or Directors:
Hot Spot for Advancement for Women/Minorities:

LOCATIONS: ("Y" = Yes)

West:	Southwest:	Midwest:	Southeast:	Northeast:	International:
				Y	Y

KNOLOGY INC

www.knology.com

Industry Group Code: 513220 Ranks within this company's industry group: Sales: 22 Profits: 16

Print Media/Publishing:	Movies:	Equipment/Supplies:		Broadcast/Cable:		Music/Audio:	Sports/Games:
Newspapers:	Movie Theaters:	Equipment/Supplies:		Broadcast TV:		Music Production:	Games/Sports:
Magazines:	Movie Production:	Gambling Equipment:	Y	Cable TV:	Y	Retail Music:	Retail Games Stores:
Books:	TV/Video Production:	Special Services:	Y	Satellite Broadcast:		Retail Audio Equip.:	Stadiums/Teams:
Book Stores:	Video Rental:	Advertising Services:		Radio:		Music Print./Dist.:	Gambling/Casinos:
Distribution/Printing:	Video Distribution:	Info. Sys. Software:		Online Information:		Multimedia:	Rides/Theme Parks:

TYPES OF BUSINESS:

Cable TV Service
Internet Service Provider
Local & Long-Distance Telephone Service

BRANDS/DIVISIONS/AFFILIATES:

Passive Optical Network
Managed Integrated Network Solutions

CONTACTS: *Note: Officers with more than one job title may be intentionally listed here more than once.*

Rodger L. Johnson, CEO
Rodger L. Johnson, Pres.
M. Todd Holt, CFO
Michael B. Roddy, VP-Mktg.
Rick Perkins, VP-IT & Billing
Richard Luke, Chief Tech. Officer
Chad S. Wachter, VP/General Counsel
Brett T. McCants, VP-Network Oper.
Felix L. Boccucci, VP-New Bus. Dev.
Andrew Sivell, VP-Network Oper.
Allan Goodson, VP-Regional Oper.

Phone: 706-645-8553	Fax: 706-645-0148
Toll-Free:	
Address: 1241 O. G. Skinner Dr., West Point, GA 31833 US	

GROWTH PLANS/SPECIAL FEATURES:

Knology, Inc. is a provider of digital and analog cable television, local and long-distance telephone service and high-speed Internet access to homes and businesses in metropolitan areas in the southeastern U.S. The company provides a full suite of video, voice and data services in Huntsville and Montgomery, Alabama; Panama City and Pinellas County Florida; Augusta, Columbus and West Point, Georgia; Charleston, South Carolina; and Knoxville, Tennessee. Knology provides a bundled package of television, phone and Internet service on one bill for substantially less than it would cost to pay for all three separately. The company also owns all of the networks that it uses, so it does not have to pay rent for bandwidth or rely on another company's communications lines. The firm's interactive broadband network is designed using redundant fiber-optic cables, and its fiber rings provide for rapid, automatic redirection of network traffic. The self-correcting properties of the fiber rings allow service to continue even during single-point failures. Knology's fiber-based business products include Passive Optical Network (PON), which supplies IP architecture with segmented voice and data bandwidth; and Managed Integrated Network Solutions (MATRIX), an integrated IP-based technology, which combines data and voice. The company now has an aggregate total of 443,000 operating connections.

FINANCIALS: Sales and profits are in thousands of dollars—add 000 to get the full amount. 2006 Note: Financial information for 2006 was not available for all companies at press time.

2006 Sales: $	2006 Profits: $	U.S. Stock Ticker: KNOL
2005 Sales: $230,857	2005 Profits: $-55,402	Int'l Ticker: Int'l Exchange:
2004 Sales: $211,458	2004 Profits: $-75,564	Employees: 1,386
2003 Sales: $172,938	2003 Profits: $-87,788	Fiscal Year Ends: 12/31
2002 Sales: $141,869	2002 Profits: $31,995	Parent Company:

SALARIES/BENEFITS:

Pension Plan:	ESOP Stock Plan:	Profit Sharing:	Top Exec. Salary: $393,469	Bonus: $78,185
Savings Plan: Y	Stock Purch. Plan:		Second Exec. Salary: $194,725	Bonus: $25,014

OTHER THOUGHTS:

Apparent Women Officers or Directors:
Hot Spot for Advancement for Women/Minorities:

LOCATIONS: ("Y" = Yes)

West:	Southwest:	Midwest:	Southeast:	Northeast:	International:
			Y		

LAGARDERE ACTIVE MEDIA   www.hfmus.com

Industry Group Code: 511120 Ranks within this company's industry group: Sales: Profits:

Print Media/Publishing:		Movies:		Equipment/Supplies:		Broadcast/Cable:		Music/Audio:		Sports/Games:	
Newspapers:	Y	Movie Theaters:		Equipment/Supplies:		Broadcast TV:	Y	Music Production:		Games/Sports:	
Magazines:	Y	Movie Production:		Gambling Equipment:		Cable TV:		Retail Music:		Retail Games Stores:	
Books:		TV/Video Production:	Y	Special Services:	Y	Satellite Broadcast:		Retail Audio Equip.:		Stadiums/Teams:	
Book Stores:		Video Rental:		Advertising Services:	Y	Radio:		Music Print./Dist.:		Gambling/Casinos:	
Distribution/Printing:		Video Distribution:		Info. Sys. Software:		Online Information:		Multimedia:		Rides/Theme Parks:	

TYPES OF BUSINESS:

Magazine Publishing
Photography Services
Media Buying
Newspaper Publishing
Magazine Advertising Services
Television Broadcasting & Production
Radio Broadcasting

BRANDS/DIVISIONS/AFFILIATES:

Lagardere SCA
Elle
Paris Match
Car & Driver
Hachette Rusconi
Hachette Filipacchi Photos
Lagardere Images
Lagardere Global Advertising

CONTACTS: Note: Officers with more than one job title may be intentionally listed here more than once.

Didier Quillot, CEO
Bernard Mainfroy, Exec. VP-Legal
Pascal Bellanger, Exec. VP-Finance
Jack Kliger, CEO/Pres., Hachette Filipacchi U.S., Inc.
Phillipe Guelton, COO-Hachette Filipacchi U.S., Inc.
Antoine de Noyer, CFO-Hachette Filipacchi U.S., Inc.
Gerald de Roguemaurel, Chmn.

Phone: 33-1-41-34-60-00	Fax: 33-1-41-34-77-77
Toll-Free:	
Address: 149-151 rue Anatole France, Levallois-Perret, 92300 France	

GROWTH PLANS/SPECIAL FEATURES:

Lagardere Active Media (LAM), formerly known as Hachette Filipacchi Medias (HFM), was formed when the HFM subsidiary of the French media and high-technology conglomerate Lagardere SCA merged with the Lagardere Active division. The company is one of the world's leading magazine publishers, producing approximately 260 magazines and newspapers in 41 countries on five continents. The combined circulation of its publications is over 1 billion, with more than 202 million from subscriptions. Its publications include fashion magazine Elle, the Parisian local journal Paris Match, Car & Driver, Premiere, American Photo, Cycle World and Woman's Day. The company is the largest magazine publisher in France, publishing 60 magazines.   It is focusing on international expansion, operating out of 16 international offices. Some of the firm's international ventures include: Hachette Filipacchi Media U.S., Inc., which is one of the largest magazine publishers in the U.S.; Hachette Filipacchi S.A., which is the leading magazine publisher in Spain; Hachette Rusconi, a leading magazine publisher in Italy; and Hachette Fujingaho, which is the leading publisher of high-end women's magazines in Japan. The firm also has operations in China, Russia and the U.K. LAM's images division, Hachette Filipacchi Photos, has the dual purpose of improving the quality of the pictures reproduced in magazines and of developing the photographic activity essential to its print media core business.   As part of the 2006 merger, Interdeco and Lagardere Active Publicite joined to form Lagardere Global Advertising, which is now France's second-largest advertising agency. Also as part of the merger, Lagardere Images oversees all of the group's TV production activities. The group's audiovisual arm, Lagardere Active, owns radio stations such as Europe 1, Europe 2 and RFM, and TV channels such as Canal J, Filles TV, Gulli and Tiji.

FINANCIALS: Sales and profits are in thousands of dollars—add 000 to get the full amount. 2006 Note: Financial information for 2006 was not available for all companies at press time.

2006 Sales: $	2006 Profits: $	U.S. Stock Ticker: Subsidiary
2005 Sales: $	2005 Profits: $	Int'l Ticker: Int'l Exchange:
2004 Sales: $2,819,584	2004 Profits: $	Employees:
2003 Sales: $	2003 Profits: $	Fiscal Year Ends: 12/31
2002 Sales: $	2002 Profits: $	Parent Company: LAGARDERE SCA

SALARIES/BENEFITS:

Pension Plan:	ESOP Stock Plan:	Profit Sharing:	Top Exec. Salary: $	Bonus: $
Savings Plan:	Stock Purch. Plan:		Second Exec. Salary: $	Bonus: $

OTHER THOUGHTS:

Apparent Women Officers or Directors:
Hot Spot for Advancement for Women/Minorities:

LOCATIONS: ("Y" = Yes)

West:	Southwest:	Midwest:	Southeast:	Northeast:	International:
				Y	Y

Note: Financial information, benefits and other data can change quickly and may vary from those stated here.

LAKES ENTERTAINMENT INC   www.lakesgaming.com

Industry Group Code: 713210 Ranks within this company's industry group: Sales: 11 Profits: 9

Print Media/Publishing:	Movies:		Equipment/Supplies:		Broadcast/Cable:	Music/Audio:	Sports/Games:	
Newspapers:	Movie Theaters:		Equipment/Supplies:		Broadcast TV:	Music Production:	Games/Sports:	
Magazines:	Movie Production:		Gambling Equipment:	Y	Cable TV:	Retail Music:	Retail Games Stores:	
Books:	TV/Video Production:	Y	Special Services:		Satellite Broadcast:	Retail Audio Equip.:	Stadiums/Teams:	
Book Stores:	Video Rental:		Advertising Services:		Radio:	Music Print./Dist.:	Gambling/Casinos:	Y
Distribution/Printing:	Video Distribution:		Info. Sys. Software:		Online Information:	Multimedia:	Rides/Theme Parks:	

TYPES OF BUSINESS:

Casino Management
Televised Poker Events
Gaming Systems & Technology

BRANDS/DIVISIONS/AFFILIATES:

WPT Enterprises
World Poker Tour
WPT Studios
WPT Consumer Products
US Playing Card
FourWinds Casino
WPTonline.com

CONTACTS: *Note: Officers with more than one job title may be intentionally listed here more than once.*

Lyle Berman, CEO
Joseph Galvin, Exec. VP/COO
Timothy J. Cope, Pres.
Timothy J. Cope, CFO
Robert Wyre, Sr. VP-Oper.
Richard Bienapfl, VP-Dev.
Janice Saeugling, Investor Rel.
Timothy J. Cope, Treas.
Timothy J. Cope, Sec.
Lyle Berman, Chmn.

Phone: 612-449-9092	**Fax:** 612-449-9353
Toll-Free: 800-946-9464	
Address: 130 Cheshire Ln., Minnetonka, MN 55305 US	

GROWTH PLANS/SPECIAL FEATURES:

Lakes Entertainment, Inc. is a casino development and management company that focuses on Native American-owned properties with a potential for long term development of related entertainment facilities. The company has development and management contracts with five different tribes: the Miwok Indians, the Pokagon Band of Potawatomi Indians, the Jamul Indian Village, the Pawnee Nation and the Iowa Tribe of Oklahoma. The contracts include one new casino in Michigan, two in California and three new and two existing casinos in Oklahoma. The firm also has a division dedicated to buying, patenting and licensing the rights for new table game concepts to market and distribute to casinos. The division has developed such games as: World Poker Tour; All-In Hold'Em; Rainbow Poker; Pyramid Poker; and Bonus Craps. The firm owns approximately 62% of WPT Enterprises (WPTE), a separate, publicly held media and entertainment company engaged in the development; production and marketing of gaming themed televised programming. WPTE operates through four entities: WPT Studios (generates 76% of WPTE's total revenues); WPT Consumer Products; WPT Corporate Alliance; and WPT online gaming. WPTE is the creator of the World Poker Tour television show, which is based on a series of high-stakes poker tournaments, and airs on the Travel Channel in the U.S. and nearly 140 global markets. The firm's online gaming aspect generates revenue through an agreement with WagerWorks, Inc. Per the agreement, WPT online.com features an online casino with slot machines, table games, and an online poker room. In 2006, the firm loaned $37.9 million to the Shingle Springs Tribe to be used in the development of a new casino. Also in 2006, Lakes Entertainment completed the financing for a $380 million Four Winds Casino project in Michigan on behalf of the Pokagon Band of Potawatomi Indians.

FINANCIALS: Sales and profits are in thousands of dollars—add 000 to get the full amount. 2006 Note: Financial information for 2006 was not available for all companies at press time.

2006 Sales: $	2006 Profits: $	**U.S. Stock Ticker:** LACO.PK
2005 Sales: $18,222	2005 Profits: $-11,870	**Int'l Ticker:** Int'l Exchange:
2004 Sales: $17,557	2004 Profits: $-4,041	Employees: 123
2003 Sales: $4,268	2003 Profits: $-1,769	Fiscal Year Ends: 12/31
2002 Sales: $1,502	2002 Profits: $-10,926	Parent Company:

SALARIES/BENEFITS:

Pension Plan:	ESOP Stock Plan:	Profit Sharing:	Top Exec. Salary: $500,000	Bonus: $100,000
Savings Plan: Y	Stock Purch. Plan: Y		Second Exec. Salary: $350,000	Bonus: $100,000

OTHER THOUGHTS:

Apparent Women Officers or Directors:
Hot Spot for Advancement for Women/Minorities:

LOCATIONS: ("Y" = Yes)

West:	Southwest:	Midwest:	Southeast:	Northeast:	International:
Y	Y	Y	Y		

LAMAR ADVERTISING CO

www.lamar.com

Industry Group Code: 541850 Ranks within this company's industry group: Sales: 1 Profits: 1

Print Media/Publishing:	Movies:	Equipment/Supplies:		Broadcast/Cable:	Music/Audio:	Sports/Games:
Newspapers:	Movie Theaters:	Equipment/Supplies:		Broadcast TV:	Music Production:	Games/Sports:
Magazines:	Movie Production:	Gambling Equipment:		Cable TV:	Retail Music:	Retail Games Stores:
Books:	TV/Video Production:	Special Services:	Y	Satellite Broadcast:	Retail Audio Equip.:	Stadiums/Teams:
Book Stores:	Video Rental:	Advertising Services:	Y	Radio:	Music Print./Dist.:	Gambling/Casinos:
Distribution/Printing:	Video Distribution:	Info. Sys. Software:		Online Information:	Multimedia:	Rides/Theme Parks:

TYPES OF BUSINESS:

Billboards
Highway Logo Signs
Graphic Design Services
Transit Advertising

BRANDS/DIVISIONS/AFFILIATES:

Lamar Media Corp.
Obie Media Corp.

CONTACTS: Note: Officers with more than one job title may be intentionally listed here more than once.

Kevin P. Reilly, Jr., CEO
Sean Reilly, COO
Kevin P. Reilly, Jr., Pres.
Keith A. Istre, CFO
Thomas F. Teepell, Chief Mktg. Officer
Tammy Duncan, VP-Human Resources
James R. McIlwain, General Counsel
Robert B. Switzer, VP-Oper.
Keith A. Istre, Treas.
Sean Reilly, Pres., Outdoor Div.
Tom Sirmon, Regional Mgr.-Gulf Coast Region
Everett Stewart, Pres., Interstate Logos
John M. Miller, VP-Nat'l Sales

Phone: 225-926-1000	Fax: 225-923-1005
Toll-Free:	
Address: 5551 Corporate Blvd., Ste. 2-A, Baton Rouge, LA 70808 US	

GROWTH PLANS/SPECIAL FEATURES:

Lamar Advertising Co. is the holding company for Lamar Media Corporation, one of the largest and most experienced owners and operators of outdoor advertising structures in the U.S. The firm operates 150 outdoor advertising companies in more than 40 states and is one of the U.S. leaders in the highway logo sign business, with operations in 19 of the 25 states that have privatized their logo programs as well as in the province of Ontario, Canada. Logo signs are signs located near highway exits that display brand-name information on available gas, food, lodging and camping services. Operating more than 149,000 billboards and 97,500 logo sign displays, the company earns revenue by leasing display space and, through its graphics division, designing advertisements for its clients. The company also helps with the strategic placement of advertisements throughout an advertiser's market by using software that allows it to analyze the target audience and its demographics. This amounts to a fully integrated service for advertising customers, covering their billboard display requirements from ad copy production to placement and maintenance. Moreover, Lamar has over 75 transit advertising franchises that operate transit advertising displays on bus shelters, buses and bus benches in 12 states. Over the past decade, the firm has pursued an aggressive growth strategy through strategic acquisitions of outdoor advertising assets, including outdoor advertising businesses as well as isolated purchases of outdoor advertising displays.

FINANCIALS: Sales and profits are in thousands of dollars—add 000 to get the full amount. 2006 Note: Financial information for 2006 was not available for all companies at press time.

2006 Sales: $	2006 Profits: $	U.S. Stock Ticker: LAMR
2005 Sales: $1,021,656	2005 Profits: $41,779	Int'l Ticker: Int'l Exchange:
2004 Sales: $883,510	2004 Profits: $13,155	Employees: 3,200
2003 Sales: $810,139	2003 Profits: $-46,851	Fiscal Year Ends: 12/31
2002 Sales: $775,700	2002 Profits: $-36,300	Parent Company:

SALARIES/BENEFITS:

Pension Plan: Y	ESOP Stock Plan:	Profit Sharing: Y	Top Exec. Salary: $550,000	Bonus: $300,000
Savings Plan: Y	Stock Purch. Plan: Y		Second Exec. Salary: $425,000	Bonus: $175,000

OTHER THOUGHTS:

Apparent Women Officers or Directors: 1
Hot Spot for Advancement for Women/Minorities:

LOCATIONS: ("Y" = Yes)

West:	Southwest:	Midwest:	Southeast:	Northeast:	International:
Y	Y	Y	Y	Y	Y

Note: Financial information, benefits and other data can change quickly and may vary from those stated here.

LANDMARK COMMUNICATIONS INC   www.landmarkcom.com

Industry Group Code: 511110 Ranks within this company's industry group: Sales: 9   Profits:

Print Media/Publishing:		Movies:		Equipment/Supplies:		Broadcast/Cable:		Music/Audio:		Sports/Games:	
Newspapers:	Y	Movie Theaters:		Equipment/Supplies:		Broadcast TV:	Y	Music Production:		Games/Sports:	
Magazines:	Y	Movie Production:		Gambling Equipment:		Cable TV:	Y	Retail Music:		Retail Games Stores:	
Books:		TV/Video Production:		Special Services:	Y	Satellite Broadcast:		Retail Audio Equip.:		Stadiums/Teams:	
Book Stores:		Video Rental:		Advertising Services:	Y	Radio:		Music Print./Dist.:		Gambling/Casinos:	
Distribution/Printing:		Video Distribution:		Info. Sys. Software:	Y	Online Information:		Multimedia:		Rides/Theme Parks:	

TYPES OF BUSINESS:
Newspaper Publishing
Cable TV Programming
TV Broadcasting
Education Services
Tradeshows & Events
Database Marketing
Classified Magazines
Wireless Internet Services

BRANDS/DIVISIONS/AFFILIATES:
Weather Channel (The)
Landmark Publishing
Landmark Broadcasting
Landmark Education Services, Inc.
Shorecliff Communications, LLC
Landmark Travel Channel, Ltd.
Landmark Community Newspapers, Inc.
CoolSavings, Inc.

CONTACTS: Note: Officers with more than one job title may be intentionally listed here more than once.
Frank Batten, Jr., CEO
Decker Anstrom, COO
Decker Anstrom, Pres.
Teresa F. Blevins, CFO/Exec. VP
Charlie W. Hill, VP-Human Resources
Guy Friddell, III, Corp. Counsel/Exec. VP/Corp. Sec.
Michael Alston, VP-Corp. Dev. & New Ventures
Colleen R. Pittman, VP-Finance
Dan Sykes, Pres., Landmark Education Svcs., Inc.
Max Heath, VP
R. Bruce Bradley, Exec. VP/Pres., Landmark Publishing Group
Debora Wilson, Pres., The Weather Channel
Frank Batten, Jr., Chmn.

Phone: 757-446-2000   Fax: 757-446-2983
Toll-Free: 800-446-2004
Address: 150 W. Brambleton Ave., Norfolk, VA 23510 US

GROWTH PLANS/SPECIAL FEATURES:
Landmark Communications, Inc. is a privately held media company with interests in newspapers, television broadcasting, cable TV programming and electronic publishing companies. The firm also has holdings in database marketing, career education and tradeshows. The company owns the Weather Channel networks, including The Weather Channel, Inc., Weather.com and Weather Services International. Landmark's publishing segment publishes three metro newspapers in North Carolina and Virginia: The Virginia-Pilot, News & Record and The Roanoke Times. Through Landmark Community Newspapers, Inc., the firm also publishes nearly 100 paid and free newspapers, shoppers and special-interest publications. The firm's broadcasting segment owns KLAS TV, a high-definition Las Vegas, Nevada TV channel; and the channels NewsChannel 5 and NewsChannel 5+ in Nashville, Tennessee. The company's emerging business segment includes: Shorecliff Communications, a tradeshow and conference producer for the communications and wireless infrastructure industries; Continental Broadband, Inc., which provides Internet access to business customers using fixed wireless technology; CoolSavings, Inc., an online direct marketing and media company; Landmark Travel Channel, Ltd., a U.K. company that provides travel-related broadcasting; and Landmark Education Services, which manages career schools (Certified Career Institute, Glendale Career College, Nevada Career Institute and Virginia School of Technology) focused on allied health and information technology. Landmark is also a partial owner of Trader Publishing Co., a nationwide publisher of classified magazines; Capital-Gazette Communications, Inc., which includes Washington Magazine and The Capital; Pelmorex, Inc., a company that owns English- and French- language cable networks in Canada; and Alliant Cooperative Data Solutions, a leader in market profitability databases. In late 2006, the company acquired VelocityServer, a provider of dedicated servers, colocation and virtual private servers. Also in 2006, TotalVid, a Landmark subsidiary, announced a distribution agreement with AT&T, Inc. TotalVid's video content will be delivered as part of AT&T U-verseSM TV video-on-demand lineup.

FINANCIALS: Sales and profits are in thousands of dollars—add 000 to get the full amount. 2006 Note: Financial information for 2006 was not available for all companies at press time.
2006 Sales: $	2006 Profits: $	U.S. Stock Ticker: Private
2005 Sales: $1,719,000	2005 Profits: $	Int'l Ticker: Int'l Exchange:
2004 Sales: $	2004 Profits: $	Employees: 11,750
2003 Sales: $743,000	2003 Profits: $	Fiscal Year Ends: 12/31
2002 Sales: $	2002 Profits: $	Parent Company:

SALARIES/BENEFITS:
Pension Plan:	ESOP Stock Plan:	Profit Sharing:	Top Exec. Salary: $	Bonus: $
Savings Plan:	Stock Purch. Plan:		Second Exec. Salary: $	Bonus: $

OTHER THOUGHTS:
Apparent Women Officers or Directors: 3
Hot Spot for Advancement for Women/Minorities: Y

LOCATIONS: ("Y" = Yes)
West:	Southwest:	Midwest:	Southeast:	Northeast:	International:
Y	Y	Y	Y	Y	Y

LANDRY'S RESTAURANTS INC   www.landrysrestaurants.com

Industry Group Code: 722110 Ranks within this company's industry group: Sales: 1 Profits: 1

Print Media/Publishing:	Movies:	Equipment/Supplies:	Broadcast/Cable:	Music/Audio:	Sports/Games:	
Newspapers:	Movie Theaters:	Equipment/Supplies:	Broadcast TV:	Music Production:	Games/Sports:	
Magazines:	Movie Production:	Gambling Equipment:	Cable TV:	Retail Music:	Retail Games Stores:	
Books:	TV/Video Production:	Special Services:	Satellite Broadcast:	Retail Audio Equip.:	Stadiums/Teams:	
Book Stores:	Video Rental:	Advertising Services:	Radio:	Music Print./Dist.:	Gambling/Casinos:	Y
Distribution/Printing:	Video Distribution:	Info. Sys. Software:	Online Information:	Multimedia:	Rides/Theme Parks:	

TYPES OF BUSINESS:

Casual Dining Restaurants
Entertainment Complexes
Casino Gambling

BRANDS/DIVISIONS/AFFILIATES:

Joe's Crab Shack
Landry's Seafood House
Rainforest Cafe
Chart House
Saltgrass Steak House
Aquarium: An Underwater Dining Adventure
Golden Nugget Casino
T-Rex: A Prehistoric Place To Eat, Shop & Discover

CONTACTS: *Note: Officers with more than one job title may be intentionally listed here more than once.*

Tilman J. Fertitta, CEO
Tilman J. Fertitta, Pres.
Richard H. Liem, Sr. VP-Finance/CFO
Steven L. Scheinthal, Exec. VP/General Counsel/Corp. Sec.
Richard E. Ervin, Exec. VP-Restaurant Oper.
Jeffrey L. Cantwell, Sr. VP- Dev.
Tilman J. Fertitta, Chmn.

Phone: 713-850-1010	**Fax:** 713-850-7205
Toll-Free: 800-552-6379	
Address: 1510 W. Loop S., Houston, TX 77027 US	

GROWTH PLANS/SPECIAL FEATURES:

Landry's Restaurants, Inc. operates 318 food-service restaurants, over 3,000 hotel rooms and other ventures in 35 states and 7 international locations. The company's brands include Joe's Crab Shack, Landry's Seafood House, Chart House, Saltgrass Steak House, Rainforest Cafe, Charley's Crab, Crab House and a small number of other limited-menu restaurants. Joe's Crab Shack, featuring a seafood menu with crab specialties, represents the company's primary growth vehicle. Its first international location recently opened in Cairo, Egypt. The atmosphere of a Joe's Crab Shack has a casual feel, with a decor influenced by weathered, beach-front fish shacks. Landry's Seafood House offers an extensive menu featuring fish, crustaceans, other seafood, beef and chicken in a casual atmosphere. The Rainforest Cafe restaurants offer a full menu of food and beverage items served in a simulated rainforest, complete with thunderstorms, waterfalls and active wildlife. The Crab House is a full-service seafood restaurant chain with a casual, nautical theme. The Chart House and Charley's Crab restaurants sit on prime waterfront venues. Both restaurants offer an extensive variety of more upscale seasonal fresh fish, shrimp, beef and other daily specialties. Saltgrass Steak House offers full-service casual dining in Texas-Western themed stone and wood beam ranch houses with fireplaces and saloon-style bars. Landry's has recently developed the Aquarium: An Underwater Dining Adventure concept as its newest restaurant chain. In this model patrons are surrounded by aquaria while they eat. The company is also involved in a number of complementary businesses, including the Kemah Boardwalk in Galveston, Texas; the Galveston Island Convention Center; and three Texas hotels. In addition, Landry's owns Golden Nugget Hotels & Casinos in Las Vegas and Laughlin, Nevada. The company recently acquired T-Rex: A Prehistoric Place to Eat, Shop, Explore and Discover, a theme concept with locations planned domestically and internationally.

FINANCIALS: Sales and profits are in thousands of dollars—add 000 to get the full amount. 2006 Note: Financial information for 2006 was not available for all companies at press time.

2006 Sales: $	2006 Profits: $	**U.S. Stock Ticker:** LNY
2005 Sales: $1,254,806	2005 Profits: $44,815	**Int'l Ticker:** Int'l Exchange:
2004 Sales: $1,167,475	2004 Profits: $66,522	Employees: 28,000
2003 Sales: $1,105,755	2003 Profits: $44,914	Fiscal Year Ends: 12/31
2002 Sales: $894,800	2002 Profits: $45,901	Parent Company:

SALARIES/BENEFITS:

Pension Plan:	ESOP Stock Plan:	Profit Sharing:	Top Exec. Salary: $1,350,000	Bonus: $1,650,000
Savings Plan: Y	Stock Purch. Plan:		Second Exec. Salary: $325,000	Bonus: $400,000

OTHER THOUGHTS:

Apparent Women Officers or Directors:
Hot Spot for Advancement for Women/Minorities:

LOCATIONS: ("Y" = Yes)

West:	Southwest:	Midwest:	Southeast:	Northeast:	International:
Y	Y	Y	Y	Y	Y

LAS VEGAS SANDS CORP (THE VENETIAN)
www.lasvegassands.com
Industry Group Code: 721120 Ranks within this company's industry group: Sales: 4   Profits: 2

Print Media/Publishing:	Movies:	Equipment/Supplies:	Broadcast/Cable:	Music/Audio:	Sports/Games:	
Newspapers:	Movie Theaters:	Equipment/Supplies:	Broadcast TV:	Music Production:	Games/Sports:	
Magazines:	Movie Production:	Gambling Equipment:	Cable TV:	Retail Music:	Retail Games Stores:	
Books:	TV/Video Production:	Special Services:	Satellite Broadcast:	Retail Audio Equip.:	Stadiums/Teams:	
Book Stores:	Video Rental:	Advertising Services:	Radio:	Music Print./Dist.:	Gambling/Casinos:	Y
Distribution/Printing:	Video Distribution:	Info. Sys. Software:	Online Information:	Multimedia:	Rides/Theme Parks:	

TYPES OF BUSINESS:
Hotel Casinos
Convention & Conference Centers
Shopping Center Development
Casino Property Development

BRANDS/DIVISIONS/AFFILIATES:
Venetian Resort Hotel Casino (The)
Sands Expo (The)
Palazzo Resort Hotel Casino (The)
Sands Macao Casino (The)
Venetian Macao Resort Hotel Casino (The)

CONTACTS: Note: Officers with more than one job title may be intentionally listed here more than once.
Sheldon G. Adelson, CEO
William P. Weidner, COO
William P. Weidner, Pres.
Scott A. Henry, CFO/Sr. VP
Bradley K. Serwin, General Counsel
Harry D. Miltenberger, Chief Acct. Officer/VP-Finance
Robert G. Goldstein, Sr. VP
Bradley H. Stone, Exec. VP
Sheldon G. Adelson, Treas.
Sheldon G. Adelson, Chmn.

Phone: 702-414-1000	Fax: 702-414-4884

Toll-Free:
Address: 3355 S. Las Vegas Blvd. S., Rm. 1A, Las Vegas, NV 89109 US

GROWTH PLANS/SPECIAL FEATURES:
Las Vegas Sands, Corp. (LVSI) owns and operates The Venetian Resort Hotel Casino, The Sands Expo and Convention Center in Las Vegas, Nevada and The Sands Macao Casino in Macao, China. It is in the process of developing additional casino resorts and properties in Las Vegas and Macao, including The Palazzo Resort Hotel Casino, which will be connected to The Venetian, The Venetian Macao Resort Hotel Casino and other casino properties on the Cotai Strip in Macao. It is seeking licenses to develop gaming properties in Singapore, Pennsylvania and the U.K., as well as exploring other gaming entertainment opportunities in Asia, Europe and the U.S. The Venetian, one of the world's largest and most luxurious casino resorts, is a Renaissance Venice-themed resort on the Las Vegas Strip. The Venetian is the Strip's first and only all-suites hotel, with over 4,000 suites in addition to its gaming facility. In 2003, the Venetian claimed the single greatest revenue-producing year for an individual hotel. The Venetian is connected to The Sands Expo Center, a 1.15 million square foot convention and trade show facility. The Palazzo will be a world-class luxury hotel, adjacent to the Venetian and The Sands, and will feature a 50-floor tower with 3,025 suites, a 105,000 square foot gaming facility and a 450,000-square-foot enclosed shopping, dining and entertainment complex, to be completed in summer of 2007. Also in 2007, the firm plans to open the Venetian Macao, a hotel, resort and convention complex that will feature the world's largest casino at 600,000 square feet, along with 3,000 hotel rooms and 1.2 million square feet of convention space. In June 2006, the company annouced that it will build the first casino in Singapore.

LVSI offers employees free meals, use of the Wellness Center, on-site child care, educational assistance, a concierge for personal errands, a valet that cleans employee's uniforms and credit union membership.

FINANCIALS: Sales and profits are in thousands of dollars—add 000 to get the full amount. 2006 Note: Financial information for 2006 was not available for all companies at press time.

2006 Sales: $	2006 Profits: $	U.S. Stock Ticker: LVS
2005 Sales: $1,824,225	2005 Profits: $283,686	Int'l Ticker: Int'l Exchange:
2004 Sales: $1,258,570	2004 Profits: $495,183	Employees: 12,230
2003 Sales: $641,500	2003 Profits: $37,400	Fiscal Year Ends: 12/31
2002 Sales: $571,700	2002 Profits: $-38,400	Parent Company:

SALARIES/BENEFITS:
Pension Plan:	ESOP Stock Plan:	Profit Sharing:	Top Exec. Salary: $1,557,692	Bonus: $30,000,000
Savings Plan: Y	Stock Purch. Plan:		Second Exec. Salary: $1,282,561	Bonus: $13,157,243

OTHER THOUGHTS:
Apparent Women Officers or Directors:
Hot Spot for Advancement for Women/Minorities:

LOCATIONS: ("Y" = Yes)
West:	Southwest:	Midwest:	Southeast:	Northeast:	International:
Y					Y

Note: Financial information, benefits and other data can change quickly and may vary from those stated here.

LASERPACIFIC MEDIA CORP   www.laserpacific.com

Industry Group Code: 512191 Ranks within this company's industry group: Sales: Profits:

Print Media/Publishing:	Movies:	Equipment/Supplies:	Broadcast/Cable:	Music/Audio:	Sports/Games:
Newspapers:	Movie Theaters:	Equipment/Supplies:	Broadcast TV:	Music Production:	Games/Sports:
Magazines:	Movie Production:	Gambling Equipment:	Cable TV:	Retail Music:	Retail Games Stores:
Books:	TV/Video Production:	Special Services: Y	Satellite Broadcast:	Retail Audio Equip.:	Stadiums/Teams:
Book Stores:	Video Rental:	Advertising Services:	Radio:	Music Print./Dist.:	Gambling/Casinos:
Distribution/Printing:	Video Distribution:	Info. Sys. Software:	Online Information:	Multimedia:	Rides/Theme Parks:

TYPES OF BUSINESS:

Post-Production Services-Film & Television
DVD Technology
Audio Processing Services

BRANDS/DIVISIONS/AFFILIATES:

Eastman Kodak Company
High Definition Laboratory
Electronic Laboratory
inDI

CONTACTS: *Note: Officers with more than one job title may be intentionally listed here more than once.*

Brian Burr, CEO
Jane Swearingen, COO
Leon D. Silverman, Pres.
Lisa Griffin, VP-Sales & New Bus. Dev.
Randolph D. Blim, CTO
Alex Moradian, Sr. VP-Bus. Dev.
Bill Roberts, Sr. VP-Finance
Paul Clay, Supervisor-Digital Sound Div.
Glenn Kennel, VP/General Mngr.-Motion Picture Svcs.
Bob Fernley, Dir.-Digital Intermediate Oper.
Dan Murrell, Chmn.

Phone: 323-462-6266	Fax: 323-464-3233
Toll-Free:	
Address: 809 N. Cahuenga Blvd., Hollywood, CA 90038 US	

GROWTH PLANS/SPECIAL FEATURES:

LaserPacific Media Corporation, a subsidiary of Eastman Kodak Company, specializes in post-production services for films and television programs. The company offers services that include 16 and 35 mm film processing, digital intermediates (DI), telecine transfer, color timing, insertion of digital graphics and visual effects, sound editing and mixing, digital compression service and duplication. LaserPacific encoded the first DVD ROM title, designed the first animated menus seen on a DVD for a feature film and pioneered the use of dual layer technology. Through the development of the Electronic Laboratory, the company was a leading force in the television industry's transition from analog, film-based methods to new electronic and digital post-production techniques. It has worked on a variety of television shows, including Everwood, Touched By An Angel, Diagnosis Murder, Judging Amy and The Simpsons. LaserPacific has won six Emmy Awards for outstanding achievement in television engineering development. With the opening of its High Definition Laboratory in 1998, LaserPacific became a leader in the delivery of digital high-definition sound services and currently has 24-frame progressive high-definition capabilities. Moreover, the company opened Hollywood's first Motion Picture Experts Group (MPEG) compression facility, which created some of the first DVDs. Recently, the firm began offering a complete range of audio services. These include sound editing, two mixing stages, and foley and automated dialogue replacement (ADR) recording rooms. LaserPacific also offers DI for independent filmmakers through inDI, a cost effective method that transfers dailies to high definition allowing filmmakers on a tight budget to circumvent a second scanning of the film after shooting has been completed. The inDI workflow yields results that are similar to a 2K DI scan.

FINANCIALS: Sales and profits are in thousands of dollars—add 000 to get the full amount. 2006 Note: Financial information for 2006 was not available for all companies at press time.

2006 Sales: $	2006 Profits: $	U.S. Stock Ticker: Subsidiary
2005 Sales: $	2005 Profits: $	Int'l Ticker: Int'l Exchange:
2004 Sales: $	2004 Profits: $	Employees: 226
2003 Sales: $	2003 Profits: $	Fiscal Year Ends: 12/31
2002 Sales: $31,800	2002 Profits: $1,200	Parent Company: EASTMAN KODAK CO

SALARIES/BENEFITS:

Pension Plan:	ESOP Stock Plan:	Profit Sharing:	Top Exec. Salary: $350,000	Bonus: $30,000
Savings Plan:	Stock Purch. Plan:		Second Exec. Salary: $275,004	Bonus: $30,000

OTHER THOUGHTS:

Apparent Women Officers or Directors: 2
Hot Spot for Advancement for Women/Minorities:

LOCATIONS: ("Y" = Yes)

West:	Southwest:	Midwest:	Southeast:	Northeast:	International:
Y					

LEE ENTERPRISES INC

www.lee.net

Industry Group Code: 511110 Ranks within this company's industry group: Sales: 14 Profits: 10

Print Media/Publishing:		Movies:		Equipment/Supplies:		Broadcast/Cable:		Music/Audio:		Sports/Games:	
Newspapers:	Y	Movie Theaters:		Equipment/Supplies:		Broadcast TV:		Music Production:		Games/Sports:	
Magazines:		Movie Production:		Gambling Equipment:		Cable TV:		Retail Music:		Retail Games Stores:	
Books:		TV/Video Production:		Special Services:	Y	Satellite Broadcast:		Retail Audio Equip.:		Stadiums/Teams:	
Book Stores:		Video Rental:		Advertising Services:	Y	Radio:		Music Print./Dist.:		Gambling/Casinos:	
Distribution/Printing:		Video Distribution:		Info. Sys. Software:		Online Information:		Multimedia:		Rides/Theme Parks:	

TYPES OF BUSINESS:

Newspaper Publishing
Specialty Publications
Advertising Services
Internet Publishing & Services
Commercial Printing

BRANDS/DIVISIONS/AFFILIATES:

Quad-Cities Group
William Street Press
TNI Partners
Pulitzer
Star Publishing Company
Citizen Star Publishing Company
Madison Newspapers
TownNews.com

CONTACTS: Note: Officers with more than one job title may be intentionally listed here more than once.

Mary E. Junck, CEO
Mary E. Junck, Pres.
Carl G. Schmidt, CFO/VP
Vytenis P. Kuraitis, VP-Human Resources
Brian E. Kardell, CIO/VP-Production
Karen J. Guest, Chief Legal Officer/VP
Gregory P. Schermer, VP-Interactive Media
Daniel K. Hayes, VP-Corp. Comm.
Carl G. Schmidt, Treas.
Linda Lindus, VP-Publishing
Michael R. Gulledge, VP-Publishing
Joyce Delhi, VP-News
Nancy L. Green, VP-Circulation
Mary E. Junck, Chmn.

Phone: 563-383-2100	Fax: 563-323-9608
Toll-Free: 800-468-9716	
Address: 201 N. Harrison St., Davenport, IA 52801 US	

GROWTH PLANS/SPECIAL FEATURES:

Lee Enterprises, Inc. publishes 56 daily newspapers in 23 states and nearly 300 weekly, classified and specialty publications, as well as associated online services. The company owns and operates its newspapers (with a combined circulation of 1.7 million daily and 1.9 million on Sunday) through eight publishing subsidiaries, including Madison Newspapers, Lincoln Group, Quad-Cities Group, Central Illinois Newspaper Group, River Valley Group, Missoula Group, Magic Valley Group and Mid-Valley News Group. Lee also offers commercial printing services through William Street Press; Hawkeye Printing and Trico Communications; Platen Press; Farcountry Press and Broadwater Printing; Journal Star Commercial Printing; Little Nickel Quik Print; Spokane Print and Mail; Triangle Press; and Wingra Printing. Nearly 75% of the firm's revenues come from retail, national, classified, niche publications and online advertising. Lee's Internet activities consist of web sites supporting its newspapers as well as its subsidiary, INN Partners, L.C (d.b.a TownNews.com), a provider of web infrastructure for more than 1,000 small daily and weekly newspapers and shoppers. The firm also owns a minority interest in PowerOne Media and CityXpress Corp., which provide integrated online classified solutions for the newspaper industry; integrated online editorial content; and transactional and promotional opportunities. In 2006, the firm announced that it has joined a consortium of other newspaper companies to strengthen its online sites (via combined online job listings from more than 150 newspapers) with the Yahoo Hot Jobs platform. The company also recently acquired ZWire, AdQuest and a national advertising network from PowerOne Media.

FINANCIALS: Sales and profits are in thousands of dollars—add 000 to get the full amount. 2006 Note: Financial information for 2006 was not available for all companies at press time.

2006 Sales: $1,128,648	2006 Profits: $70,832	**U.S. Stock Ticker:** LEE	
2005 Sales: $818,890	2005 Profits: $76,878	**Int'l Ticker:** Int'l Exchange:	
2004 Sales: $643,277	2004 Profits: $86,071	Employees: 9,400	
2003 Sales: $656,741	2003 Profits: $78,041	Fiscal Year Ends: 9/30	
2002 Sales: $523,656	2002 Profits: $79,830	Parent Company:	

SALARIES/BENEFITS:

Pension Plan: Y	ESOP Stock Plan:	Profit Sharing:	Top Exec. Salary: $775,000	Bonus: $1,100,000
Savings Plan: Y	Stock Purch. Plan:		Second Exec. Salary: $400,000	Bonus: $317,600

OTHER THOUGHTS:

Apparent Women Officers or Directors: 6
Hot Spot for Advancement for Women/Minorities: Y

LOCATIONS: ("Y" = Yes)

West:	Southwest:	Midwest:	Southeast:	Northeast:	International:
Y	Y	Y	Y	Y	

Note: Financial information, benefits and other data can change quickly and may vary from those stated here.

LERNER PUBLISHING GROUP

www.lernerbooks.com

Industry Group Code: 511130 Ranks within this company's industry group: Sales: Profits:

Print Media/Publishing:	Movies:	Equipment/Supplies:	Broadcast/Cable:	Music/Audio:	Sports/Games:
Newspapers:	Movie Theaters:	Equipment/Supplies:	Broadcast TV:	Music Production:	Games/Sports:
Magazines:	Movie Production:	Gambling Equipment:	Cable TV:	Retail Music:	Retail Games Stores:
Books: Y	TV/Video Production:	Special Services:	Satellite Broadcast:	Retail Audio Equip.:	Stadiums/Teams:
Book Stores:	Video Rental:	Advertising Services:	Radio:	Music Print./Dist.:	Gambling/Casinos:
Distribution/Printing:	Video Distribution:	Info. Sys. Software:	Online Information:	Multimedia:	Rides/Theme Parks:

TYPES OF BUSINESS:

Book Publishing
Educational Books
Children's Books
Online Information

BRANDS/DIVISIONS/AFFILIATES:

Lerner Publications
Carolrhoda Books, Inc.
First Avenue Editions
ediciones Lerner
Millbrook Press
Twenty-First Century Books
Kar-Ben Publishing
Visual Geography Series Online

CONTACTS:
Note: Officers with more than one job title may be intentionally listed here more than once.
Harry Lerner, CEO
Adam Lerner, Pres.
Margaret Wunderlich, CFO
Adam Lerner, Publisher

Phone: 612-332-3344	Fax: 800-332-1132
Toll-Free: 800-328-4929	
Address: 1251 Washington Ave. N, Minneapolis, MN 55401 US	

GROWTH PLANS/SPECIAL FEATURES:

Lerner Publishing Group is a publisher of both hardcover and paperback K-12 children's books for the retail, school and library markets. The company currently has more than 2,500 titles in print on a variety of subjects, most of which fall into the nonfiction category, including biographies, social studies, science, geography, sports, picture books, activity books and multicultural issues, as well as fiction. Books range from information-intensive school and library books to graphic, colorful general-interest titles. The firm publishes through eight divisions and imprints: Lerner Publications; Carolrhoda Books; First Avenue Editions; Millbrook Press; Twenty-First Century Books; ediciones Lerner; Kar-Ben Publishing; and LernerClassroom. The ediciones Lerner series offers Spanish language material. Lerner's new Kar-Ben Publishing group produces a library of Jewish children books. Lerner also publishes two free educational web sites: Visual Geography Series Online, which offers country-specific information, links and downloadable photos and maps at vgsbooks.com; and In America Books Online, which provides links and information on America's various immigrant populations at inamericabooks.com. In addition to libraries, schools and other educational organizations, the company's books are purchased by traditional book stores such as Barnes and Noble and Borders; educational stores such as the Discovery Store; and non-traditional channels such as direct sales, catalogs, book clubs and fairs and non-book retail stores, including museums, gift shops and toy stores.

FINANCIALS:
Sales and profits are in thousands of dollars—add 000 to get the full amount. 2006 Note: Financial information for 2006 was not available for all companies at press time.

2006 Sales: $	2006 Profits: $	U.S. Stock Ticker: Private
2005 Sales: $	2005 Profits: $	Int'l Ticker: Int'l Exchange:
2004 Sales: $	2004 Profits: $	Employees: 46
2003 Sales: $12,000	2003 Profits: $- 700	Fiscal Year Ends:
2002 Sales: $18,600	2002 Profits: $	Parent Company:

SALARIES/BENEFITS:

Pension Plan:	ESOP Stock Plan:	Profit Sharing:	Top Exec. Salary: $153,000	Bonus: $30,000
Savings Plan:	Stock Purch. Plan:		Second Exec. Salary: $146,000	Bonus: $15,000

OTHER THOUGHTS:

Apparent Women Officers or Directors: 1
Hot Spot for Advancement for Women/Minorities:

LOCATIONS: ("Y" = Yes)

West:	Southwest:	Midwest:	Southeast:	Northeast:	International:
		Y			

LIBERTY GLOBAL

www.lgi.com

Industry Group Code: 513220 Ranks within this company's industry group: Sales: 11 Profits: 17

Print Media/Publishing:	Movies:	Equipment/Supplies:		Broadcast/Cable:		Music/Audio:	Sports/Games:
Newspapers:	Movie Theaters:	Equipment/Supplies:		Broadcast TV:		Music Production:	Games/Sports:
Magazines:	Movie Production:	Gambling Equipment:	Y	Cable TV:	Y	Retail Music:	Retail Games Stores:
Books:	TV/Video Production:	Special Services:	Y	Satellite Broadcast:		Retail Audio Equip.:	Stadiums/Teams:
Book Stores:	Video Rental:	Advertising Services:		Radio:		Music Print./Dist.:	Gambling/Casinos:
Distribution/Printing:	Video Distribution:	Info. Sys. Software:		Online Information:		Multimedia:	Rides/Theme Parks:

TYPES OF BUSINESS:

Cable TV Service
Local & Long Distance Telephone Service
Internet Service Provider
Media & Content Services

BRANDS/DIVISIONS/AFFILIATES:

Liberty Media
Austar United Communications
VTR GlobalCom, S.A.
UGC Europe, Inc.
UPC Broadband
Liberty Media International
Jupiter Telecommunications Co.

CONTACTS: Note: Officers with more than one job title may be intentionally listed here more than once.

Michael T. Fries, CEO
Michael T. Fries, Pres.
Bernard C. Dvorak, Co-CFO
Amy M. Blair, Sr. VP-Human Resources
Anthony G. Werner, CTO
Elizabeth M .Markowski, General Counsel
Shane O'Neill, Chief Strategy Officer
Frederlck Westerman, VP-Corp. Comm.
Bernard C. Dvorak, Principal Acct. Officer
Charles H. R. Bracken, Co-CFO
Miranda Curtis, Pres., Liberty Global Japan
Mauricio Ramos, Pres., Liberty Global Latin America
Gene Musselman, Pres./CEO, UPC Broadband
John C. Malone, Chmn.

Phone: 303-220-6600	**Fax:** 303-220-6601
Toll-Free:	
Address: 12300 Liberty Blvd., Englewood, CO 80112 US	

GROWTH PLANS/SPECIAL FEATURES:

Liberty Global, Inc. is a cable television and broadband service provider. The company operates broadband distribution and content companies that do business mostly outside the continental U.S., principally in Europe, Asia, and The Americas. Its networks reach approximately 19 million subscribers in 18 countries, including 3.1 million broadband Internet subscribers and 2.1 million telephone subscribers. Liberty Global began doing business in 2005 with the merger of cable operators Liberty Media International (LMI) and UnitedGlobalCom (UGC), each of which was previously spun off from Liberty Media Corporation. UGC Europe, which evolved out of UnitedGlobalCom, is a leading pan-European broadband communications company, providing services through its UPC Broadband division, television, Internet access and telephony segments to 13 million customers in 13 countries. UGC Europe also owns interests in and develops media and content services through its chellomedia division. UGC, since 2005, owns a majority interest in Austar United Communications, a leading pay television provider in Australia offering digital satellite services to customers in regional and rural areas, dial-up Internet and mobile telephone services. The subsidiary VTR GlobalCom is the largest broadband communications provider in Chile and a growing provider of telephone services throughout the Americas. The company is active in Japan through J:COM, a subsidiary of SuperMedia of which Liberty owns 59%, providing service to about 1.7 million customers. In September 2005, Liberty Global agreed to acquire Cablecom of Switzerland for $2.1 billion dollars, making it the largest cable provider in Switzerland.

FINANCIALS: Sales and profits are in thousands of dollars—add 000 to get the full amount. 2006 Note: Financial information for 2006 was not available for all companies at press time.

2006 Sales: $	2006 Profits: $	**U.S. Stock Ticker:** LBTYA
2005 Sales: $5,151,332	2005 Profits: $-80,097	**Int'l Ticker:** Int'l Exchange:
2004 Sales: $2,531,889	2004 Profits: $-21,481	**Employees:** 21,600
2003 Sales: $108,390	2003 Profits: $20,889	**Fiscal Year Ends:** 12/31
2002 Sales: $1,515,000	2002 Profits: $-504,400	**Parent Company:**

SALARIES/BENEFITS:

Pension Plan:	ESOP Stock Plan:	Profit Sharing:	Top Exec. Salary: $738,195	Bonus: $375,000
Savings Plan: Y	Stock Purch. Plan:		Second Exec. Salary: $732,192	Bonus: $600,000

OTHER THOUGHTS:

Apparent Women Officers or Directors: 3
Hot Spot for Advancement for Women/Minorities: Y

LOCATIONS: ("Y" = Yes)

West:	Southwest:	Midwest:	Southeast:	Northeast:	International:
Y					Y

Note: Financial information, benefits and other data can change quickly and may vary from those stated here.

LIBERTY MEDIA CORP

www.libertymedia.com

Industry Group Code: 512110 Ranks within this company's industry group: Sales: 2 Profits: 9

Print Media/Publishing:	Movies:		Equipment/Supplies:		Broadcast/Cable:		Music/Audio:		Sports/Games:
Newspapers:	Movie Theaters:		Equipment/Supplies:		Broadcast TV:		Music Production:		Games/Sports:
Magazines:	Movie Production:		Gambling Equipment:		Cable TV:	Y	Retail Music:		Retail Games Stores:
Books:	TV/Video Production:	Y	Special Services:	Y	Satellite Broadcast:		Retail Audio Equip.:		Stadiums/Teams:
Book Stores:	Video Rental:		Advertising Services:		Radio:		Music Print./Dist.:		Gambling/Casinos:
Distribution/Printing:	Video Distribution:		Info. Sys. Software:		Online Information:		Multimedia:		Rides/Theme Parks:

TYPES OF BUSINESS:

Television Shopping Network
Television Production
Video Distribution
Online Retail
Satellite Television

BRANDS/DIVISIONS/AFFILIATES:

QVC, Inc.
Starz Entertainment
Provide Commerce, Inc.
FUN Technologies, Inc.
TruePosition, Inc.
BuySeasons, Inc.
DirecTV
BuySeasons Inc.

CONTACTS: Note: Officers with more than one job title may be intentionally listed here more than once.

Gregory B. Maffei, CEO
Gregory B. Maffei, Pres.
John C. Malone, Chmn.

Phone: 720-875-5400	Fax: 720-875-7469
Toll-Free:	
Address: 12300 Liberty Blvd., Englewood, CO 80112 US	

GROWTH PLANS/SPECIAL FEATURES:

Liberty Media Corp. is a holding company that, through its ownership of interests in subsidiaries and other companies, is primarily engaged in the video and on-line commerce, media, communications and entertainment industries in the U.S., Europe and Asia. The company's more significant operating subsidiaries include QVC, Inc. and Starz Entertainment. QVC markets and sells a wide variety of consumer products in the U.S. and several foreign countries, primarily by means of televised shopping programs and via the Internet through its domestic and international websites. Starz Entertainment provides video programming distributed by cable operators, direct-to-home satellite providers, other distributors and via the Internet throughout the U.S. Other consolidated subsidiaries include Provide Commerce, Inc., FUN Technologies, Inc., TruePosition, Inc., Starz Media, LLC, and BuySeasons, Inc. In May 2006, the company completed a restructuring pursuant to which Liberty was organized as a holding company. In September 2006, Liberty entered into a stock purchase agreement to sell its controlling interest in OpenTV for approximately $113 million and in December 2006 the company sold its On Command subsidiary to LodgeNet Entertainment Corporation. Recent acquisitions include Provide Commerce, BuySeasons, Inc. In December 2006, Liberty Media Corp. completed a significant $11 billion asset swap with News Corp. Under the agreement, LIberty received News Corp.'s 38.5% stake in DirecTV, $550 million in cash and three regional sports networks. News Corp. received Liberty's $11.2 billion stake in News Corp. itself. This gives Liberty controlling interest in DirecTV.

FINANCIALS: Sales and profits are in thousands of dollars—add 000 to get the full amount. 2006 Note: Financial information for 2006 was not available for all companies at press time.

2006 Sales: $	2006 Profits: $	U.S. Stock Ticker: LINTA
2005 Sales: $7,960,000	2005 Profits: $-33,000	Int'l Ticker: Int'l Exchange:
2004 Sales: $7,682,000	2004 Profits: $46,000	Employees: 13,660
2003 Sales: $4,028,000	2003 Profits: $-1,222,000	Fiscal Year Ends: 12/31
2002 Sales: $2,084,000	2002 Profits: $-5,330,000	Parent Company:

SALARIES/BENEFITS:

Pension Plan:	ESOP Stock Plan:	Profit Sharing:	Top Exec. Salary: $1,000,000	Bonus: $1,000,000
Savings Plan: Y	Stock Purch. Plan:		Second Exec. Salary: $680,000	Bonus: $

OTHER THOUGHTS:

Apparent Women Officers or Directors:
Hot Spot for Advancement for Women/Minorities:

LOCATIONS: ("Y" = Yes)

West:	Southwest:	Midwest:	Southeast:	Northeast:	International:
Y	Y	Y	Y	Y	Y

LIN TV CORP

www.lintv.com

Industry Group Code: 513120 **Ranks within this company's industry group:** Sales: 14 Profits: 16

Print Media/Publishing:	Movies:	Equipment/Supplies:	Broadcast/Cable:		Music/Audio:	Sports/Games:
Newspapers:	Movie Theaters:	Equipment/Supplies:	Broadcast TV:	Y	Music Production:	Games/Sports:
Magazines:	Movie Production:	Gambling Equipment:	Cable TV:		Retail Music:	Retail Games Stores:
Books:	TV/Video Production:	Special Services:	Satellite Broadcast:		Retail Audio Equip.:	Stadiums/Teams:
Book Stores:	Video Rental:	Advertising Services:	Radio:		Music Print./Dist.:	Gambling/Casinos:
Distribution/Printing:	Video Distribution:	Info. Sys. Software:	Online Information:		Multimedia:	Rides/Theme Parks:

TYPES OF BUSINESS:

Television Broadcasting

BRANDS/DIVISIONS/AFFILIATES:

Banks Broadcasting, Inc.
WAND (TV) Partnership

CONTACTS: Note: Officers with more than one job title may be intentionally listed here more than once.

Vincent L. Sadusky, CEO
Vincent L. Sadusky, Pres.
Bart Catalane, CFO/Sr. VP
Edward L. Munson, Jr., VP-Station Sales
Robb Richter, VP-Internet
Denise Parent, VP-General Counsel/Sec.
Robb Richter, VP-Internet
Scott Blumenthal, Exec. VP-Television
Gregory M. Schmidt, Exec. VP-Digital Media
Douglas McCormick, Chmn.

Phone: 401-454-2880	Fax: 401-454-0089
Toll-Free:	
Address: 4 Richmond Sq., Ste. 200, Providence, RI 02906 US	

GROWTH PLANS/SPECIAL FEATURES:

LIN TV Corp. owns and operates a network of approximately 30 television stations, primarily in the midwestern and northeastern regions of the U.S. These include three under local marketing agreements, three low-power networks and many low-power broadcast television stations. The company also has investments in five other stations, as well as stations in Puerto Rico. LIN's stations cover approximately 10.7% of U.S. television households including 1.3 million television households in Puerto Rico. The company generally has more than one station in the markets where it operates, and this multi-channel strategy increases its share of the TV audience. The firm operates the number-one or number-two news stations in 91% of its markets. Local advertisers account for approximately 92% of the company's revenue. All of the company's stations are affiliated with one of the national broadcasting networks: NBC, ABC, CBS, FOX, CW, Telefutura or Univision. The company has a number of proprietary interests in other television stations. The largest of these include its 33.3% interest in WAND (TV) Partnership with Block Communications, Inc., which owns and operates WAND-TV in Illinois. LIN also has a 50% interest in Banks Broadcasting, Inc., which owns and operates CW affiliates KWCV-TV in Kansas and KNIN-TV in Idaho. Recently, the firm acquired KASA, the FOX affiliate in Albuquerque, New Mexico, from Raycom Media for $55 million in cash. KASA will operate in the same multi-station sector as KRQE (local CBS affiliate), also owned by LIN. In 2006, LIN announced that it will sell its Puerto Rico operations to InterMedia Partners for $130 million in cash. Included in the sale will be the full-power independent station WJPX (branded as MTV Puerto Rico).

LIN offers a scholarship program for minorities interested in journalism and broadcasting.

FINANCIALS: Sales and profits are in thousands of dollars—add 000 to get the full amount. 2006 Note: Financial information for 2006 was not available for all companies at press time.

2006 Sales: $	2006 Profits: $	**U.S. Stock Ticker:** TVL
2005 Sales: $380,400	2005 Profits: $-24,200	**Int'l Ticker:** Int'l Exchange:
2004 Sales: $374,800	2004 Profits: $88,300	Employees: 2,414
2003 Sales: $349,500	2003 Profits: $-90,400	Fiscal Year Ends: 12/31
2002 Sales: $349,600	2002 Profits: $-47,300	Parent Company:

SALARIES/BENEFITS:

Pension Plan: Y	ESOP Stock Plan:	Profit Sharing:	Top Exec. Salary: $800,000	Bonus: $200,000
Savings Plan: Y	Stock Purch. Plan:		Second Exec. Salary: $388,000	Bonus: $193,000

OTHER THOUGHTS:

Apparent Women Officers or Directors: 1
Hot Spot for Advancement for Women/Minorities:

LOCATIONS: ("Y" = Yes)

West:	Southwest:	Midwest:	Southeast:	Northeast:	International:
Y	Y	Y	Y	Y	

Note: Financial information, benefits and other data can change quickly and may vary from those stated here.

LIONS GATE ENTERTAINMENT CORP   www.lionsgate.com

Industry Group Code: 512110 Ranks within this company's industry group: Sales: 10 Profits: 7

Print Media/Publishing:	Movies:		Equipment/Supplies:		Broadcast/Cable:	Music/Audio:	Sports/Games:
Newspapers:	Movie Theaters:		Equipment/Supplies:		Broadcast TV:	Music Production:	Games/Sports:
Magazines:	Movie Production:	Y	Gambling Equipment:		Cable TV:	Retail Music:	Retail Games Stores:
Books:	TV/Video Production:	Y	Special Services:	Y	Satellite Broadcast:	Retail Audio Equip.:	Stadiums/Teams:
Book Stores:	Video Rental:		Advertising Services:		Radio:	Music Print./Dist.:	Gambling/Casinos:
Distribution/Printing:	Video Distribution:		Info. Sys. Software:		Online Information:	Multimedia:	Rides/Theme Parks:

TYPES OF BUSINESS:
Film Production
TV Production & Distribution
Film Distribution
Video-on-Demand Services

BRANDS/DIVISIONS/AFFILIATES:
Lions Gate Films Corp.
Lions Gate Television
Lions Gate Entertainment, Inc.
CinemaNow, Inc.
Trimark
Maple Pictures Corp.
Image Entertainment, Inc.
Debmar-Mercury LLC

CONTACTS: Note: Officers with more than one job title may be intentionally listed here more than once.
Jon Feltheimer, CEO
Steven Beeks, Pres.
James Keegan, CFO
James Keegan, Chief Admin. Officer
Wayne Levin, General Counsel
Wayne Levin, Exec. VP-Corp. Oper.
Marni Wieshofer, Exec. VP-Corp. Dev.
Peter Wilkes, Investor Rel.
James Keegan, Chief Acct. Officer
Michael Burns, Vice-Chmn.
Harald Ludwig, Co-Chmn.

Phone: 604-983-5555   **Fax:** 604-983-5554

Toll-Free:

Address: 555 Brooks Bank Ave., North Vancouver, BC V7J 3S5 Canada

GROWTH PLANS/SPECIAL FEATURES:
Lions Gate Entertainment Corp. is an independent producer and distributor of motion pictures, television programming, home entertainment and video-on-demand content. The firm releases approximately 15 to 18 motion pictures and 100 hours of television programming per year. Lions Gate acquires, produces and distributes independent, mainstream commercial and star-driven blockbuster feature films and manages a library of approximately 3,000 motion pictures and 2,500 television episodes. Subsidiary Lions Gate Television (LGTV) produces movies-of-the-week, television series and miniseries for cable networks, such as The Dead Zone, Missing, Weeds, Wildfire, The Cut, and made-for-TV movies. The company owns a minority interest in CinemaNow, Inc., a provider of video-on-demand services for feature films that holds distribution rights to more than 3,000 film titles, and a minority interest in Maple Pictures Corp., a Canadian film and television distributor. In 2006, Lions Gate purchased 18% of Image Entertainment, Inc., which is a home video and television distribution company specializing in digital distribution of television programs, public domain and copyrighted feature films, and music concerts. Also in 2006, the company acquired Debmar-Mercury LLC, a top television distributor; additionally, the company sold its studio facilities in North Vancouver, British Columbia to Bosa Development Corporation for $36.1 million. Movies slated for release in 2007 include Rogue, Saw 3, Daddy's Little Girl, Delta Farce, Ivy League, Kidnapped, Stir of Echoes 2, Punisher 2 and The U.S. vs. John Lennon.

Lion's Gate provides its employees with health benefits, incentive plans, paid vacation and Blackberry e-mail devices.

FINANCIALS: Sales and profits are in thousands of dollars—add 000 to get the full amount. 2006 Note: Financial information for 2006 was not available for all companies at press time.

2006 Sales: $951,228	2006 Profits: $6,096	**U.S. Stock Ticker: LGF**
2005 Sales: $842,586	2005 Profits: $20,336	**Int'l Ticker: LGF** Int'l Exchange: Toronto-TSX
2004 Sales: $375,910	2004 Profits: $-95,157	Employees: 354
2003 Sales: $301,800	2003 Profits: $1,100	Fiscal Year Ends: 3/31
2002 Sales: $267,700	2002 Profits: $-46,200	Parent Company:

SALARIES/BENEFITS:

Pension Plan:	ESOP Stock Plan:	Profit Sharing:	Top Exec. Salary: $850,000	Bonus: $395,000
Savings Plan: Y	Stock Purch. Plan:		Second Exec. Salary: $550,000	Bonus: $293,750

OTHER THOUGHTS:
Apparent Women Officers or Directors: 1
Hot Spot for Advancement for Women/Minorities:

LOCATIONS: ("Y" = Yes)

West:	Southwest:	Midwest:	Southeast:	Northeast:	International:
Y				Y	Y

Note: Financial information, benefits and other data can change quickly and may vary from those stated here.

LIQUID DIGITAL MEDIA
www.liquidaudio.com

Industry Group Code: 451220E Ranks within this company's industry group: Sales: Profits:

Print Media/Publishing:	Movies:	Equipment/Supplies:	Broadcast/Cable:	Music/Audio:	Sports/Games:
Newspapers:	Movie Theaters:	Equipment/Supplies:	Broadcast TV:	Music Production:	Games/Sports:
Magazines:	Movie Production:	Gambling Equipment:	Cable TV:	Retail Music:	Retail Games Stores:
Books:	TV/Video Production:	Special Services: Y	Satellite Broadcast:	Retail Audio Equip.:	Stadiums/Teams:
Book Stores:	Video Rental:	Advertising Services:	Radio:	Music Print./Dist.: Y	Gambling/Casinos:
Distribution/Printing:	Video Distribution:	Info. Sys. Software:	Online Information:	Multimedia:	Rides/Theme Parks:

TYPES OF BUSINESS:
Internet-Based Music Retailing
Online Media Distribution Services

BRANDS/DIVISIONS/AFFILIATES:
Liquid Audio
Anderson Media Corporation
Geneva Media LLC
Liquid Music Mall

CONTACTS: Note: Officers with more than one job title may be intentionally listed here more than once.
J. P. Lester, CTO
Ole Olberman, VP/Gen. Mgr.

Phone: 650-549-2000	Fax: 650-549-2001

Toll-Free:
Address: 999 Main St., Redwood City, CA 94063 US

GROWTH PLANS/SPECIAL FEATURES:
Liquid Digital Media, formerly Liquid Audio, is an online digital music business that changed its name in late 2003 after being acquired by wholesaler Anderson Media Corporation through its subsidiary Geneva Media LLC. It serves as the music distributor for Wal-Mart. The company provides clients with custom solutions for Internet media delivery. Liquid Digital offers a catalogue of over 300,000 digital music tracks from all major labels, as well as from numerous independents. The Wal-Mart web site uses Liquid Digital's technology to distribute thousands of tracks of music at 88 cents per song. Liquid Digital's representatives are trained to custom-design music media solutions for clients interested in distributing music online. These services include video and audio encoding, Digital Rights Management (DRM) secure packaging, metadata management, image processing and conversion, content hosting, distribution and fulfillment, and marketing support and reporting. Clients can feature music through real-time streams, free downloads and time-limited downloads. Liquid Digital offers .erchant services including catalog distribution, download management, windows media DRM licensing, customer service, technical support, fulfillment API, reporting/reconciliation, physical/digital tie-ins, front end design and development, merchandising, and application and tool development. Liquid Digital was the first company to offer secure music online. In addition to powering Wal-Mart's music downloads, Liquid media also works with Tower Records and FYE.

FINANCIALS: Sales and profits are in thousands of dollars—add 000 to get the full amount. 2006 Note: Financial information for 2006 was not available for all companies at press time.

2006 Sales: $	2006 Profits: $	U.S. Stock Ticker: Subsidiary
2005 Sales: $	2005 Profits: $	Int'l Ticker: Int'l Exchange:
2004 Sales: $	2004 Profits: $	Employees:
2003 Sales: $	2003 Profits: $	Fiscal Year Ends: 12/31
2002 Sales: $	2002 Profits: $	Parent Company: ANDERSON MEDIA CORPORATION

SALARIES/BENEFITS:

Pension Plan:	ESOP Stock Plan:	Profit Sharing:	Top Exec. Salary: $310,198	Bonus: $
Savings Plan:	Stock Purch. Plan:		Second Exec. Salary: $235,220	Bonus: $

OTHER THOUGHTS:
Apparent Women Officers or Directors:
Hot Spot for Advancement for Women/Minorities:

LOCATIONS: ("Y" = Yes)

West:	Southwest:	Midwest:	Southeast:	Northeast:	International:
Y					

LIVE NATION INC

www.livenation.com

Industry Group Code: 711310 Ranks within this company's industry group: Sales: 1 Profits: 1

Print Media/Publishing:	Movies:	Equipment/Supplies:	Broadcast/Cable:	Music/Audio:	Sports/Games:
Newspapers:	Movie Theaters:	Equipment/Supplies:	Broadcast TV:	Music Production: Y	Games/Sports: Y
Magazines:	Movie Production:	Gambling Equipment:	Cable TV:	Retail Music:	Retail Games Stores:
Books:	TV/Video Production:	Special Services: Y	Satellite Broadcast:	Retail Audio Equip.:	Stadiums/Teams: Y
Book Stores:	Video Rental:	Advertising Services:	Radio:	Music Print./Dist.:	Gambling/Casinos:
Distribution/Printing:	Video Distribution:	Info. Sys. Software:	Online Information:	Multimedia:	Rides/Theme Parks:

TYPES OF BUSINESS:

Concerts & Events Production
Theater Production
Sports Representation
DVD Production & Distribution

BRANDS/DIVISIONS/AFFILIATES:

LiveNation.com
House of Blues
Concert Productions International

CONTACTS: Note: Officers with more than one job title may be intentionally listed here more than once.

Michael Rapino, CEO
Michael Rapino, Pres.
Alan Ridgeway, CFO
Faisel Durrani, Pres., Mktg. & Artist Mktg. Products
Michael G. Rowles, General Counsel/Exec. VP
Bryan Perez, Pres., Digital Distribution
David Ian, Chmn.-Global Theatrical
Thomas Johansson, Chmn.-Int'l Music
Carl Pernow, Pres., Int'l Music
Charlie Walker, Pres., Music
Randal T. Mays, Chmn.
Bruce Eskowitz, Pres./CEO-Global Venues & Alliances

Phone: 310-867-7000 **Fax:** 310-867-7001
Toll-Free:
Address: 9348 Civic Center Dr., Beverly Hills, CA 90210 US

GROWTH PLANS/SPECIAL FEATURES:

Live Nation, Inc. (LN) is one of the world's leading live entertainment companies. The company is a leading producer of live concerts in the world, a leading venue management company and is owner and operator of one of the most popular collections of entertainment event websites in the U.S. Formerly a division of media giant Clear Channel, Live Nation began operating as an independent company in late 2005. The company has primary operations in two segments. The Global Music segment is responsible for the promotion and production of live music shows in one of 170 venues that the company owns, operates or has the booking rights to. Through the Global Music segment, Live Nation owns or operates 119 venues worldwide. The firm annually produces, promotes or hosts over 29,500 events with total attendance of over 6 million. Live Nation's Global Theater segment presents and produces touring and other theatrical performances focusing mainly on commercially successful productions such as The Lion King and Phantom of the Opera. Additionally, Live Nation's Other segment produces and promotes specialized motor sports events such as monster truck shows and motocross racing; offers professional sports representation and management services for approximately 600 clients including Kobe Bryant and Andy Roddick; produces and distributes live concert DVDs; and produces other live entertainment events including family shows Dora the Explorer and Blue's Clues. In 2006, Live Nation sold its SFX Sports, Europe segment to Wasserman Media Group. Additionally in 2006, the company acquired House of Blues; acquired a controlling interest in the touring division of Concert Productions International (CPI); acquired a 50% interest in the Grand Entertainment division of CPI; and agreed to acquire a majority stake in Musictoday, which connects artists and fans through media such as fan clubs and websites.

FINANCIALS: Sales and profits are in thousands of dollars—add 000 to get the full amount. 2006 Note: Financial information for 2006 was not available for all companies at press time.

2006 Sales: $	2006 Profits: $	**U.S. Stock Ticker:** LYV
2005 Sales: $2,936,845	2005 Profits: $-130,619	**Int'l Ticker:** Int'l Exchange:
2004 Sales: $2,806,128	2004 Profits: $16,260	Employees: 3,000
2003 Sales: $	2003 Profits: $	Fiscal Year Ends: 12/31
2002 Sales: $	2002 Profits: $	Parent Company:

SALARIES/BENEFITS:

Pension Plan:	ESOP Stock Plan:	Profit Sharing:	Top Exec. Salary: $612,500	Bonus: $
Savings Plan:	Stock Purch. Plan:		Second Exec. Salary: $476,010	Bonus: $

OTHER THOUGHTS:

Apparent Women Officers or Directors: 2
Hot Spot for Advancement for Women/Minorities:

LOCATIONS: ("Y" = Yes)

West:	Southwest:	Midwest:	Southeast:	Northeast:	International:
Y	Y	Y	Y	Y	Y

Note: Financial information, benefits and other data can change quickly and may vary from those stated here.

LODGENET ENTERTAINMENT CORP   www.lodgenet.com

Industry Group Code: 513220 Ranks within this company's industry group: Sales: 21   Profits: 14

Print Media/Publishing:	Movies:	Equipment/Supplies:		Broadcast/Cable:		Music/Audio:	Sports/Games:
Newspapers:	Movie Theaters:	Equipment/Supplies:		Broadcast TV:		Music Production:	Games/Sports:
Magazines:	Movie Production:	Gambling Equipment:		Cable TV:	Y	Retail Music:	Retail Games Stores:
Books:	TV/Video Production:	Special Services:	Y	Satellite Broadcast:		Retail Audio Equip.:	Stadiums/Teams:
Book Stores:	Video Rental:	Advertising Services:	Y	Radio:		Music Print./Dist.:	Gambling/Casinos:
Distribution/Printing:	Video Distribution:	Info. Sys. Software:		Online Information:		Multimedia:	Rides/Theme Parks:

TYPES OF BUSINESS:

Cable TV Service-Hospitality Industry
Satellite TV Service
Broadband Internet Access
Network-Based Video Games
Video-on-Demand

BRANDS/DIVISIONS/AFFILIATES:

SigNETure HDTV
StayOnline, Inc.
Ascent Entertainment Group, Inc.
On Command Corporation

CONTACTS: *Note: Officers with more than one job title may be intentionally listed here more than once.*

Scott C. Petersen, CEO
Scott C. Petersen, Pres.
Scott E. Young, Chief Mktg. Officer
Gary H. Ritondaro, Sr. VP-Info.
David M. Bankers, Sr. VP-Tech.
David M. Bankers, Sr. VP-Products
Gary H. Ritondaro, Sr. VP-Admin.
Gary H. Ritondaro, Sr. VP-Finance
Steven D. Truckenmiller, Sr. VP-Programming & Content Mgmt.
Steven R. Pofahl, Sr. VP-Tech. Oper.
Stephen D. McCarty, Sr. VP-Hotel Rel. & Sales
Scott C. Petersen, Chmn.

Phone: 605-988-1000	**Fax:** 605-988-1511
Toll-Free: 888-563-4363	
Address: 3900 W. Innovation St., Sioux Falls, SD 57107-7002 US	

GROWTH PLANS/SPECIAL FEATURES:

LodgeNet Entertainment Corporation is one of the world's largest providers of broadband interactive television services to the hospitality industry. It is a specialized communications company that provides on-demand digital movies, digital music and music videos, video games, high-speed Internet access and other interactive television services designed to serve the needs of the lodging industry and the traveling public. The company serves more than 6,000 hotels, resorts and casinos throughout the U.S., Canada and select international markets. The firm's system architecture and technology is licensed to global firms in Latin America, Israel and Japan. LodgeNet provides both guest-pay and free-to-guest services to its clients. Guest-pay services are purchased by guests on a per-view, hourly or daily basis and include on-demand movies, network-based video games, Internet-enhanced television and high-speed Internet access. Complimentary guest services include satellite-delivered premium cable television programming and other interactive entertainment and information services that are paid for by the hotel. The company also has an agreement with DIRECTV that allows LodgeNet to provide the programming to its guests. LodgeNet's clients include hotel chains such as Sheraton, Ritz-Carlton, Harrah's Casino Hotels, La Quinta Inns, Red Roof Inns, Marriott, Holiday Inn, Hilton, Radisson, Westin, Doubletree and Embassy Suites. Recent acquisitions include StayOnline, Inc. for $15.0 million and Ascent Entertainment Group, Inc., the owner of On Command Corporation, for $380 million.

FINANCIALS: Sales and profits are in thousands of dollars—add 000 to get the full amount. 2006 Note: Financial information for 2006 was not available for all companies at press time.

2006 Sales: $	2006 Profits: $	**U.S. Stock Ticker: LNET**
2005 Sales: $275,771	2005 Profits: $-6,959	**Int'l Ticker:** Int'l Exchange:
2004 Sales: $266,441	2004 Profits: $-20,781	Employees: 809
2003 Sales: $250,100	2003 Profits: $-35,100	Fiscal Year Ends: 12/31
2002 Sales: $235,000	2002 Profits: $-29,100	Parent Company:

SALARIES/BENEFITS:

Pension Plan:	ESOP Stock Plan:	Profit Sharing:	Top Exec. Salary: $449,712	Bonus: $114,300
Savings Plan: Y	Stock Purch. Plan: Y		Second Exec. Salary: $349,712	Bonus: $70,400

OTHER THOUGHTS:

Apparent Women Officers or Directors: 1
Hot Spot for Advancement for Women/Minorities:

LOCATIONS: ("Y" = Yes)

West:	Southwest:	Midwest:	Southeast:	Northeast:	International:
Y	Y	Y	Y	Y	Y

Note: Financial information, benefits and other data can change quickly and may vary from those stated here.

LOUD TECHNOLOGIES INC   www.loud-technologies.com

Industry Group Code: 334310 Ranks within this company's industry group: Sales: 11 Profits: 9

Print Media/Publishing:	Movies:	Equipment/Supplies:		Broadcast/Cable:	Music/Audio:		Sports/Games:
Newspapers:	Movie Theaters:	Equipment/Supplies:	Y	Broadcast TV:	Music Production:		Games/Sports:
Magazines:	Movie Production:	Gambling Equipment:		Cable TV:	Retail Music:		Retail Games Stores:
Books:	TV/Video Production:	Special Services:		Satellite Broadcast:	Retail Audio Equip.:	Y	Stadiums/Teams:
Book Stores:	Video Rental:	Advertising Services:		Radio:	Music Print./Dist.:		Gambling/Casinos:
Distribution/Printing:	Video Distribution:	Info. Sys. Software:	Y	Online Information:	Multimedia:		Rides/Theme Parks:

TYPES OF BUSINESS:
Audio Equipment
Recording Equipment
Audio Software
Audio & Music Accessories

BRANDS/DIVISIONS/AFFILIATES:
Mackie Designs, Inc.
Mackie
EAW
EAW Commercial
TAPCO
SIA Software
SLM Marketplace
St. Louis Music, Inc.

CONTACTS: Note: Officers with more than one job title may be intentionally listed here more than once.
Jamie Engen, CEO
Jamie Engen, Pres.
Timothy O'Neil, Sr. VP/CFO
Ken Berger, Sr. VP-Mktg.
Gary Reilly, Sr. VP-Eng.
Shawn Powers, Sr. VP-Oper.
Michael MacDonald, Interim Sr. VP-Domestic Sales
Ted Kornblum, SR. VP-Entertainment & Artist Rel.
Jeffery Cox, VP-EAW Brand Group
Jamie T. Engen, Chmn.
Frank Loyko, Jr., Sr. VP-Int'l Sales

Phone: 425-487-4333   **Fax: 425-487-4337**
Toll-Free:
Address: 16220 Wood-Red Rd. N.E., Woodinville, WA 98072 US

GROWTH PLANS/SPECIAL FEATURES:
LOUD Technologies, Inc. (LOUD), formerly Mackie Designs, Inc., develops, manufactures, sells and supports professional audio and recording equipment under the Mackie, EAW, EAW Commercial, TAPCO and SIA Software brand names. Additionally, LOUD distributes professional audio and music accessories through its SLM Marketplace catalogue. The company's primary products include analog and digital mixers, digital and desktop recording products, hard disk recorders, amplifiers, audio systems, audio system measurement software, and loudspeakers and their components. A mixer serves as the central component of any professional audio system by electronically blending, routing and enhancing sound sources, such as voices, musical instruments, sound effects and audio tape, video tape and other pre-recorded material. The firm's products are used in a wide variety of sound applications, including home and commercial recording studios, multimedia and video production, live performances and public address systems. In the U.S., LOUD distributes its products through a network of independent representatives to over 1,500 retail dealers, including musical instrument stores, pro audio outlets and several mail-order outlets, as well as more than 500 installed sound contractors. Internationally, the firm offers its products in the U.K., Italy, Japan, and 70 other countries through subsidiaries. The company recently acquired St. Louis Music, Inc., a manufacturer, distributor and importer of musical instruments and professional audio products. In 2006, the company began trading on the NASDAQ Capital Market under the ticker LTEC. LOUD also recently implemented a new direct distribution system in North America that reduced selling costs by nearly $1 million.

FINANCIALS: Sales and profits are in thousands of dollars—add 000 to get the full amount. 2006 Note: Financial information for 2006 was not available for all companies at press time.

2006 Sales: $	2006 Profits: $	**U.S. Stock Ticker: LTEC**
2005 Sales: $204,328	2005 Profits: $3,757	**Int'l Ticker:** Int'l Exchange:
2004 Sales: $123,276	2004 Profits: $-2,291	Employees: 704
2003 Sales: $130,766	2003 Profits: $-21,795	Fiscal Year Ends: 12/31
2002 Sales: $159,362	2002 Profits: $-37,928	Parent Company:

SALARIES/BENEFITS:

Pension Plan:	ESOP Stock Plan:	Profit Sharing:	Top Exec. Salary: $325,000	Bonus: $123,567
Savings Plan: Y	Stock Purch. Plan:		Second Exec. Salary: $190,000	Bonus: $89,867

OTHER THOUGHTS:
Apparent Women Officers or Directors:
Hot Spot for Advancement for Women/Minorities:

LOCATIONS: ("Y" = Yes)

West:	Southwest:	Midwest:	Southeast:	Northeast:	International:
Y		Y		Y	Y

LUCASARTS ENTERTAINMENT COMPANY LLC
www.lucasarts.com

Industry Group Code: 511208 **Ranks within this company's industry group:** Sales: Profits:

Print Media/Publishing:	Movies:	Equipment/Supplies:	Broadcast/Cable:	Music/Audio:	Sports/Games:	
Newspapers:	Movie Theaters:	Equipment/Supplies:	Broadcast TV:	Music Production:	Games/Sports:	Y
Magazines:	Movie Production:	Gambling Equipment:	Cable TV:	Retail Music:	Retail Games Stores:	
Books:	TV/Video Production:	Special Services:	Satellite Broadcast:	Retail Audio Equip.:	Stadiums/Teams:	
Book Stores:	Video Rental:	Advertising Services:	Radio:	Music Print./Dist.:	Gambling/Casinos:	
Distribution/Printing:	Video Distribution:	Info. Sys. Software: Y	Online Information:	Multimedia:	Rides/Theme Parks:	

TYPES OF BUSINESS:
Computer Software-Games
Online Retail

BRANDS/DIVISIONS/AFFILIATES:
Lucasfilm, Ltd.
Star Wars: Knights of the Old Republic
Star Wars: Battlefront
Indiana Jones & the Emperor's Tomb
Armed and Dangerous
Wrath Unleashed
Secret Weapons Over Normandy
Letterman Digital Arts Center

CONTACTS: *Note: Officers with more than one job title may be intentionally listed here more than once.*
Jim Ward, Pres.
John Geoghegan, VP-Worldwide Sales & Mktg.
Peter Hirschmann, VP-Prod. Dev.
Mike Nelson, VP-Admin.
Kevin Weston, VP-Finance
Atsuko Matsumoto, Sr. Dir.-Production. Svcs.
George Lucas, Chmn.
Mary Bihr, VP-Global Publishing

Phone: 415-507-4545	**Fax:** 415-507-0300
Toll-Free:	
Address: 1110 Gorgas Ave., San Francisco, CA 94129 US	

GROWTH PLANS/SPECIAL FEATURES:
LucasArts Entertainment Company LLC, a subsidiary of Lucasfilm, Ltd., produces game software for PCs, Xbox and Playstation. The company was founded in 1982 by George Lucas to produce games with the Star Wars and Indiana Jones brand names. Today there are more than 50 game titles in these series. Current titles include Star Wars: Knights of the Old Republic II, Star Wars: Battlefront II and Indiana Jones and the Emperor's Tomb. The company has branched out into many other titles, including Wrath Unleashed, Armed and Dangerous and Secret Weapons Over Normandy. The company offers its games and game paraphernalia for direct sale on its web site, store.lucasarts.com. LucasArts' Star Wars franchise has been highly successful, particularly Star Wars: Knights of the Old Republic. The game won ign.com's Overall Best Game title in 2003, in addition to 34 other industry awards from other organizations. Following this success, the company released a slew of new titles in 2004 and 2005, including Republic Commando, Knights of the Old Republic II and Galaxies: Jump to Lightspeed, a multiplayer game. LucasArts entered into an agreement with Day 1 Studios in May 2006 in which the two companies will collaborate on the development of new intellectual property for release on next-generation console platforms.

LucasArts offers its employees medical, dental and life insurance, as well as fitness programs, complementary flu shots, tuition assistance, employee parties, child care, community activities, an observatory and access to the Sky Walker Ranch and company sailboat. The firm's new offices include a 350-seat theater, a 1,600-square-foot stage with 34 cameras including 3-D, a child care center, a fitness center, 15 editing suites and an ultra-fast 1-gigabyte network hookup at every desktop.

FINANCIALS: Sales and profits are in thousands of dollars—add 000 to get the full amount. 2006 Note: Financial information for 2006 was not available for all companies at press time.

2006 Sales: $	2006 Profits: $	**U.S. Stock Ticker: Subsidiary**
2005 Sales: $	2005 Profits: $	**Int'l Ticker:** Int'l Exchange:
2004 Sales: $	2004 Profits: $	Employees:
2003 Sales: $	2003 Profits: $	Fiscal Year Ends: 4/30
2002 Sales: $	2002 Profits: $	Parent Company: LUCASFILM LTD

SALARIES/BENEFITS:

Pension Plan:	ESOP Stock Plan:	Profit Sharing:	Top Exec. Salary: $	Bonus: $
Savings Plan: Y	Stock Purch. Plan:		Second Exec. Salary: $	Bonus: $

OTHER THOUGHTS:
Apparent Women Officers or Directors: 2
Hot Spot for Advancement for Women/Minorities:

LOCATIONS: ("Y" = Yes)

West:	Southwest:	Midwest:	Southeast:	Northeast:	International:
Y					

Note: Financial information, benefits and other data can change quickly and may vary from those stated here.

LUCASFILM LTD

www.lucasfilm.com

Industry Group Code: 512110 Ranks within this company's industry group: Sales: 7 Profits:

Print Media/Publishing:		Movies:		Equipment/Supplies:		Broadcast/Cable:		Music/Audio:		Sports/Games:	
Newspapers:		Movie Theaters:		Equipment/Supplies:		Broadcast TV:		Music Production:		Games/Sports:	Y
Magazines:		Movie Production:	Y	Gambling Equipment:		Cable TV:		Retail Music:		Retail Games Stores:	
Books:	Y	TV/Video Production:	Y	Special Services:	Y	Satellite Broadcast:		Retail Audio Equip.:		Stadiums/Teams:	
Book Stores:		Video Rental:		Advertising Services:		Radio:		Music Print./Dist.:		Gambling/Casinos:	
Distribution/Printing:		Video Distribution:		Info. Sys. Software:	Y	Online Information:		Multimedia:		Rides/Theme Parks:	

TYPES OF BUSINESS:

Film Production
Special Effects
Sound Effects
Digital Animation
Software & Video Games
Online Publishing
Merchandising

BRANDS/DIVISIONS/AFFILIATES:

Industrial Light & Magic
Skywalker Sound
Lucas Digital
LucasArts
Lucas Online
Indiana Jones
Star Wars
Lucasfilm Animation Singapore

CONTACTS: Note: Officers with more than one job title may be intentionally listed here more than once.

Micheline Chau, COO
Micheline Chau, Pres.
Joshua Katz, VP-Mktg.
Steve Sansweet, Head-Fan Relations
Chrissie England, Pres., Industrial Light & Magic
Glenn Kiser, VP/General Mgr.-Skywalker Sound
Howard Roffman, Pres., Lucas Licensing
Jim Ward, Sr. VP/Pres., LucasArts
George Lucas, Chmn.
Christian Kubsch, Gen. Mgr.-Lucasfilm Animation Singapore

Phone: 415-662-1800	**Fax:** 415-662-2437
Toll-Free:	
Address: P.O. Box 29901, San Francisco, CA 94129-0901 US	

GROWTH PLANS/SPECIAL FEATURES:

Lucasfilm Ltd., created by George Lucas in 1971, has produced some of the most popular films in history, including Star Wars; The Empire Strikes Back; The Return of the Jedi; Raiders of the Lost Ark; Indiana Jones and the Temple of Doom; Indiana Jones and the Last Crusade; Star Wars Episodes I-III: The Phantom Menace, Attack of the Clones and Revenge of the Sith; and American Graffiti. The company operates through seven divisions. Lucasfilm is responsible for production, promotion and strategic management of theatrical, television and entertainment properties. Industrial Light & Magic (ILM) creates digital and visual special effects for the entertainment industry and has received 31 Academy Award nominations and 14 awards. Skywalker Sound produces post-production digital sound effects, for which it has won 18 Academy Awards. LucasArts is a software company that develops computer games based on Lucas's movies. The firm's licensing division is responsible for licensing and merchandising Lucasfilm properties. Animation and Lucasfilm Animation Singapore are digital animation studios. Finally, Lucasfilm's online division produces entertainment, education, reference and e-commerce sites for Lucasfilm properties. Since 2005, the company has been operating out of the Letterman Digital Arts Center. This new center brings the entire organization together and enables units producing games and films to collaborate more closely and share technologies. In 2005, Lucasfilm established Lucasfilm Animation Singapore, a studio intended to produce films, television and games for global audiences. In 2006, the new division added the newly formed Handheld Games and Digital Artists Groups, which will work with ILM on the production of visual effects.

Lucasfilm's headquarters, the Letterman Digital Arts Center, contains a 300-seat theater, screening rooms, a 1,600-square-foot stage with 34 cameras, a childcare center, a fitness center, 15 editing suites and an ultra-fast 1-gigabyte network hookup at every desktop.

FINANCIALS: Sales and profits are in thousands of dollars—add 000 to get the full amount. 2006 Note: Financial information for 2006 was not available for all companies at press time.

2006 Sales: $	2006 Profits: $	**U.S. Stock Ticker: Private**
2005 Sales: $1,483,000	2005 Profits: $	**Int'l Ticker:** Int'l Exchange:
2004 Sales: $	2004 Profits: $	Employees: 1,500
2003 Sales: $1,200,000	2003 Profits: $	Fiscal Year Ends: 3/31
2002 Sales: $1,350,000	2002 Profits: $	Parent Company:

SALARIES/BENEFITS:

Pension Plan:	ESOP Stock Plan:	Profit Sharing:	Top Exec. Salary: $	Bonus: $
Savings Plan: Y	Stock Purch. Plan:		Second Exec. Salary: $	Bonus: $

OTHER THOUGHTS:

Apparent Women Officers or Directors: 3
Hot Spot for Advancement for Women/Minorities: Y

LOCATIONS: ("Y" = Yes)

West:	Southwest:	Midwest:	Southeast:	Northeast:	International:
Y					

MACROVISION CORP

www.macrovision.com

Industry Group Code: 511202 Ranks within this company's industry group: Sales: 1   Profits: 1

Print Media/Publishing:	Movies:	Equipment/Supplies:		Broadcast/Cable:	Music/Audio:	Sports/Games:
Newspapers:	Movie Theaters:	Equipment/Supplies:	Y	Broadcast TV:	Music Production:	Games/Sports:
Magazines:	Movie Production:	Gambling Equipment:		Cable TV:	Retail Music:	Retail Games Stores:
Books:	TV/Video Production:	Special Services:	Y	Satellite Broadcast:	Retail Audio Equip.:	Stadiums/Teams:
Book Stores:	Video Rental:	Advertising Services:		Radio:	Music Print./Dist.:	Gambling/Casinos:
Distribution/Printing:	Video Distribution:	Info. Sys. Software:	Y	Online Information:	Multimedia:	Rides/Theme Parks:

TYPES OF BUSINESS:

Software-Video Copyright Protection
Digital Rights Management Technologies

BRANDS/DIVISIONS/AFFILIATES:

SafeDisc
InstallShield Installer
FLEXnet
AdminStudio
RipGuard
Update Service
Hawkeye

CONTACTS: *Note: Officers with more than one job title may be intentionally listed here more than once.*

Alfred J. Amoroso, CEO
Alfred J. Amoroso, Pres.
James Budge, CFO/Exec. VP
Mark Bishof, Exec. VP-Sales & Service
Buff Jones, Exec. VP/General Mgr.-Products
Stephen Yu, General Counsel/Exec. VP
Jim Wickett, Exec. VP-Corp. Dev.
Loren Hillberg, Exec. VP/General Mgr.-Emerging Bus.
John O. Ryan, Chmn.
David Rowley, Sr. VP/Managing Dir.-Asia-Pacific

Phone: 408-743-8600	**Fax:** 408-743-8610
Toll-Free:	
Address: 2830 De La Cruz Blvd., Santa Clara, CA 95050 US	

GROWTH PLANS/SPECIAL FEATURES:

Macrovision Corporation provides digital product value management offerings to entertainment producers, software publishers and their customers. Services include anti-piracy technologies, embedded licensing technologies and usage monitoring for enterprises. Major customers include film studios, independent video producers, hardware and software vendors, music labels, consumer electronics manufacturers and on-demand television network operators. The company operates in two segments: Entertainment Technologies and Software Technologies. The Entertainment Technologies Group licenses technologies including copy protection and rights management software to video, music and PC games content owners. This segment manages the company's Hawkeye anti-piracy service and RipGuard content protection technologies. Macrovision's PC game protection products include integrated tools that allow video game developers and publishers to protect, distribute and promote their products securely and effectively. The Software Technologies Group develops and markets value management solutions to hardware and software vendors and their customers. The firm's InstallShield Installer, Update Service and Admin Studio products are part of the FLEXnet Publisher and FLEXnet Manager products overseen by this division. Macrovision's offerings allow software manufacturers to provide standard, seamless installation and activation of their product, simplify product marketing strategies and reduce the costs of product development, distribution and delivery, as well as lower costs associated with unpaid usage. The company generates revenues by licensing the use of its technologies and software. In 2006, the company's analog content protection technology was included as a requirement on next generation video media such as Blu-ray and HD DVD. Macrovision recently agreed to acquire eMeta Corporation, a privately held company that provides software for control and sales of digital content online.

The company offers its employees benefits including an employee stock purchase plan, a 401(k) savings plan, flexible time off, educational assistance and health club memberships.

FINANCIALS: Sales and profits are in thousands of dollars—add 000 to get the full amount. 2006 Note: Financial information for 2006 was not available for all companies at press time.

2006 Sales: $	2006 Profits: $	**U.S. Stock Ticker:** MVSN
2005 Sales: $203,230	2005 Profits: $22,115	**Int'l Ticker:** Int'l Exchange:
2004 Sales: $182,099	2004 Profits: $36,730	Employees: 692
2003 Sales: $128,346	2003 Profits: $26,941	Fiscal Year Ends: 12/31
2002 Sales: $102,262	2002 Profits: $12,089	Parent Company:

SALARIES/BENEFITS:

Pension Plan:	ESOP Stock Plan:	Profit Sharing: Y	Top Exec. Salary: $323,319	Bonus: $73,215
Savings Plan: Y	Stock Purch. Plan: Y		Second Exec. Salary: $287,041	Bonus: $75,000

OTHER THOUGHTS:

Apparent Women Officers or Directors: 1
Hot Spot for Advancement for Women/Minorities:

LOCATIONS: ("Y" = Yes)

West:	Southwest:	Midwest:	Southeast:	Northeast:	International:
Y		Y		Y	Y

MAGNA ENTERTAINMENT CORP

www.magnaent.com

Industry Group Code: 713210 Ranks within this company's industry group: Sales: 4 Profits: 10

Print Media/Publishing:	Movies:	Equipment/Supplies:		Broadcast/Cable:		Music/Audio:	Sports/Games:	
Newspapers:	Movie Theaters:	Equipment/Supplies:		Broadcast TV:		Music Production:	Games/Sports:	Y
Magazines:	Movie Production:	Gambling Equipment:		Cable TV:	Y	Retail Music:	Retail Games Stores:	
Books:	TV/Video Production:	Special Services:		Satellite Broadcast:		Retail Audio Equip.:	Stadiums/Teams:	Y
Book Stores:	Video Rental:	Advertising Services:		Radio:		Music Print./Dist.:	Gambling/Casinos:	Y
Distribution/Printing:	Video Distribution:	Info. Sys. Software:	Y	Online Information:		Multimedia:	Rides/Theme Parks:	

TYPES OF BUSINESS:

Racetracks-Horse Racing
Cable Television Network
Simulcasting
Account Wagering
Horse Bedding Products
Pari-Mutual Gambling Information Technology

BRANDS/DIVISIONS/AFFILIATES:

PariMax, Inc.
Gulfstream Park
Magna Racing
StreuFex
XpressBet
Racetrack Television Network
HorseRacing TV
AmTote

CONTACTS: Note: Officers with more than one job title may be intentionally listed here more than once.

Frank Stronach, Interim CEO
W. Thomas Hodgson, Pres.
Blake S. Tohana, CFO/Exec. VP
Jim Bromby, Sr. VP-Oper.
Blake Tohana, Investor Rel. Contact
Mary L. Seymour, Controller
Brant Latta, Sr. VP-Oper
Corey Johnsen, Pres., MEC Operations in the Southwest
Frank Stronach, Chmn.

Phone: 905-726-2462	Fax: 905-726-7164
Toll-Free:	
Address: 337 Magna Dr., Aurora, ON L4G 7K1 Canada	

GROWTH PLANS/SPECIAL FEATURES:

Magna Entertainment Corp. (MEC) is a leading North American owner and operator of thoroughbred racetracks, as well as one of the world's leading simulcast broadcasters of live racing content to inter-track, off-track and account wagering gamers. The company currently operates or manages 11 thoroughbred racetracks, one standardbred harness racing racetrack and one racetrack that runs both thoroughbred and standardbred meets. In addition to its racetracks, the firm owns and operates thoroughbred training centers situated near San Diego, California; in Palm Beach County, Florida; and in the Baltimore, Maryland area, as well as a large real estate portfolio including two golf courses with related facilities. MEC will be adding to their real estate holdings with a residential and commercial development around their Gulfstream Park racetrack. The company also owns and operates production facilities in Austria and North Carolina for StreuFex, a straw-based horse bedding product. MEC operates off-track betting facilities and a national account wagering business known as XpressBet, which permits customers to place wagers by telephone and over the Internet on horse races at more than 100 racetracks in North America and internationally and began slot operations at its Gulfstream Parks track. HorseRacing TV is MEC's television network focused exclusively on horse racing, currently available to more than 12 million cable and satellite TV customers. The firm has a minority interest in the Racetrack Television Network, which telecasts races from all of its racetracks. In 2006, one of MEC's subsidiaries acquired a 100% interest in AmTote International, a pari-mutuel wagering information technology company. In 2006, MEC formed PariMax, Inc, to oversee the development of its electronic distribution platforms, including XpressBet, HRTV, Magnabet, and AmTote International. In late 2006, MEC completed its sale of The Meadows racetrack to PA Meadows, LLC, a subsidiary of Cannery Casino Resorts, LLC.

FINANCIALS: Sales and profits are in thousands of dollars—add 000 to get the full amount. 2006 Note: Financial information for 2006 was not available for all companies at press time.

2006 Sales: $	2006 Profits: $	U.S. Stock Ticker: MECA
2005 Sales: $624,655	2005 Profits: $-105,293	Int'l Ticker: MEC Int'l Exchange: Toronto-TSX
2004 Sales: $702,473	2004 Profits: $-95,636	Employees: 5,200
2003 Sales: $686,598	2003 Profits: $-105,100	Fiscal Year Ends: 12/31
2002 Sales: $549,200	2002 Profits: $-14,400	Parent Company:

SALARIES/BENEFITS:

Pension Plan:	ESOP Stock Plan:	Profit Sharing:	Top Exec. Salary: $409,600	Bonus: $400,000
Savings Plan: Y	Stock Purch. Plan:		Second Exec. Salary: $359,600	Bonus: $350,000

OTHER THOUGHTS:

Apparent Women Officers or Directors: 1
Hot Spot for Advancement for Women/Minorities:

LOCATIONS: ("Y" = Yes)

West:	Southwest:	Midwest:	Southeast:	Northeast:	International:
Y	Y	Y	Y	Y	Y

MARKETWATCH INC   www.marketwatch.com

Industry Group Code: 514100   Ranks within this company's industry group: Sales: 5   Profits:

Print Media/Publishing:	Movies:	Equipment/Supplies:	Broadcast/Cable:	Music/Audio:	Sports/Games:
Newspapers:	Movie Theaters:	Equipment/Supplies:	Broadcast TV:	Music Production:	Games/Sports:
Magazines:	Movie Production:	Gambling Equipment:	Cable TV:	Retail Music:	Retail Games Stores:
Books:	TV/Video Production: Y	Special Services: Y	Satellite Broadcast:	Retail Audio Equip.:	Stadiums/Teams:
Book Stores:	Video Rental:	Advertising Services:	Radio:	Music Print./Dist.:	Gambling/Casinos:
Distribution/Printing:	Video Distribution:	Info. Sys. Software: Y	Online Information:	Multimedia:	Rides/Theme Parks:

TYPES OF BUSINESS:
Online Financial Information
Television & Radio Programming

BRANDS/DIVISIONS/AFFILIATES:
Dow Jones & Company, Inc.
bigcharts.com
MarketWatch Information Services
Hulbert Financial Digest
Retirement Weekly
ETF Trader
MarketWatch Weekend
MarketWatch.com Radio Network

CONTACTS: *Note: Officers with more than one job title may be intentionally listed here more than once.*
Maria Molland, General Manager
Brian Quinn, VP-Sales
Jamie Thingelstad, CTO

Phone: 415-439-6400   Fax: 415-439-6485
Toll-Free:
Address: 201 California St., 13th Fl., San Francisco, CA 94111 US

GROWTH PLANS/SPECIAL FEATURES:
MarketWatch, Inc., a wholly-owned subsidiary of Dow Jones & Company, Inc., is a leading financial media company providing comprehensive web-based, real-time business news, financial programming and analytic tools. It operates two main web sites, marketwatch.com and bigcharts.com, as well as virtualstockexchange.com, a stock market simulation web site. In addition to business and financial news, the sites offer in-depth commentary on trends and events, personal finance commentary and data, community features and other services, designed to provide a one-stop-shop for audiences. Other features include a mutual fund center, a seasonal tax guide, market advisors and research columns. Customers create personal user settings including portfolio trackers, news and quotes, custom views, allocation analysis, financials and charting. MarketWatch also delivers relevant financial news to user e-mail accounts, hosts investment discussion communities, offers personalized automatic alerts and through portfolio creation provides customers with wireless capabilities. The company's MarketWatch Information Services group is a leading licensor of market news, data, investment analysis tools and other online applications to financial services firms, media companies, wireless carriers and Internet service providers. The firm also sells subscription-based content for individual investors under the Hulbert Financial Digest, Retirement Weekly and ETF Trader brand names. MarketWatch produces the syndicated MarketWatch Weekend television program and provides business and financial news updates every 30 minutes on the MarketWatch.com Radio Network.

FINANCIALS: Sales and profits are in thousands of dollars—add 000 to get the full amount. 2006 Note: Financial information for 2006 was not available for all companies at press time.
2006 Sales: $	2006 Profits: $	U.S. Stock Ticker: Subsidiary
2005 Sales: $50,000	2005 Profits: $	Int'l Ticker: Int'l Exchange:
2004 Sales: $	2004 Profits: $	Employees: 337
2003 Sales: $47,173	2003 Profits: $2,655	Fiscal Year Ends: 12/31
2002 Sales: $44,500	2002 Profits: $-9,700	Parent Company: DOW JONES & COMPANY INC

SALARIES/BENEFITS:
Pension Plan:	ESOP Stock Plan:	Profit Sharing:	Top Exec. Salary: $315,000	Bonus: $226,686
Savings Plan: Y	Stock Purch. Plan: Y		Second Exec. Salary: $285,000	Bonus: $142,500

OTHER THOUGHTS:
Apparent Women Officers or Directors: 2
Hot Spot for Advancement for Women/Minorities:

LOCATIONS: ("Y" = Yes)
West:	Southwest:	Midwest:	Southeast:	Northeast:	International:
Y					

MARTHA STEWART LIVING OMNIMEDIA INC
www.marthastewart.com
Industry Group Code: 511120 Ranks within this company's industry group: Sales: 13   Profits: 9

Print Media/Publishing:	Movies:	Equipment/Supplies:	Broadcast/Cable:	Music/Audio:	Sports/Games:
Newspapers:	Movie Theaters:	Equipment/Supplies:	Broadcast TV:	Music Production:	Games/Sports:
Magazines: Y	Movie Production:	Gambling Equipment:	Cable TV:	Retail Music:	Retail Games Stores:
Books: Y	TV/Video Production: Y	Special Services:	Satellite Broadcast:	Retail Audio Equip.:	Stadiums/Teams:
Book Stores:	Video Rental:	Advertising Services:	Radio:	Music Print./Dist.:	Gambling/Casinos:
Distribution/Printing:	Video Distribution:	Info. Sys. Software:	Online Information:	Multimedia:	Rides/Theme Parks:

TYPES OF BUSINESS:
Magazine Publishing
Television & Video Production
Book Publishing
Home & Garden Products
Web Sites
Satellite Radio
Merchandising

BRANDS/DIVISIONS/AFFILIATES:
Martha Stewart Living
Martha Stewart Signature
Martha Stewart Weddings
Blueprint
Everyday Food
Martha Stewart: The Catalog For Living
Martha Stewart Radio
Body+Soul Magazine

CONTACTS: *Note: Officers with more than one job title may be intentionally listed here more than once.*
Susan Lyne, CEO
Susan Lyne, Pres.
Howard Hochhauser, CFO
Robin Marino, Pres.,Merchandising
John R. Cuti, General Counsel
Holly Brown, Pres., Internet
Howard Hochhauser, VP-Investor Rel.
Sheraton Kalouria, Pres., Television
Gael Towey, Chief Creative Officer
Lauren Stanich, Pres., Publishing
Christine Cook, VP-Interactive Advertising Sales
Charles Koppelman, Chmn.

Phone: 212-827-8000	Fax: 212-827-8204
Toll-Free:	
Address: 20 West 43rd St., New York, NY 10036 US	

GROWTH PLANS/SPECIAL FEATURES:
Martha Stewart Living Omnimedia, Inc. (MSL) is an integrated content and commerce company that creates how-to content and related merchandise for homemakers and other consumers. The company leverages the Martha Stewart brand name across media and retail outlets, focusing on domestic arts. Content and merchandise span eight core areas: home, cooking and entertaining, gardening, crafts, holidays, housekeeping and organizing, weddings, and baby/kids.   MSL operates through four business segments: publishing, broadcasting, merchandising and Internet. The publishing segment currently publishes five magazines, Martha Stewart Living, Everyday Food, Martha Stewart Weddings, Body + Soul and Blueprint, as well as special-interest books (51 total, 16 authored by Martha Stewart). The broadcasting segment develops television programming (featuring Everyday Food, MARTHA and the Martha Stewart Living program which airs on Style Network), theme-based DVDs (distributed with Warner Home Video) and operations of a satellite radio channel (Martha Stewart Living Radio). Merchandise is distributed under several labels, including Martha Stewart Everyday (the firm's mass-market brand label) and Martha Stewart Signature (the company's high-end brand).   MSL's Internet segment consists of Martha Stewart: The Catalog For Living; MarthaStewart.com and MarthasFlowers.com. In 2006, the firm partnered with several companies to create new lines of merchandise, including: Quality Home Brands, LLC (Martha Stewart branded ceiling fans and lighting); Safavieh (new line of area rugs); Eastman Kodak Company (Martha Stewart branded photo products); Flor, Inc. (Martha Stewart branded carpet tiles); Lowe's (Martha Stewart branded paint colors), and Macy's (Martha Stewart Collection home merchandise). Also in 2006, the company announced licensing relationship with EK Success, Ltd. and GTCR Golder Rauner, LLC to create, market and sell paper-based craft products to be sold in major craft chains and independent craft stores in the U.S.

FINANCIALS: Sales and profits are in thousands of dollars—add 000 to get the full amount. 2006 Note: Financial information for 2006 was not available for all companies at press time.

2006 Sales: $	2006 Profits: $	U.S. Stock Ticker: MSO
2005 Sales: $209,462	2005 Profits: $-75,789	Int'l Ticker: Int'l Exchange:
2004 Sales: $187,400	2004 Profits: $-59,600	Employees: 656
2003 Sales: $245,848	2003 Profits: $-2,771	Fiscal Year Ends: 12/31
2002 Sales: $295,000	2002 Profits: $7,300	Parent Company:

SALARIES/BENEFITS:

Pension Plan: Y	ESOP Stock Plan:	Profit Sharing:	Top Exec. Salary: $900,000	Bonus: $
Savings Plan: Y	Stock Purch. Plan:		Second Exec. Salary: $750,000	Bonus: $512,588

OTHER THOUGHTS:
Apparent Women Officers or Directors: 6
Hot Spot for Advancement for Women/Minorities: Y

LOCATIONS: ("Y" = Yes)

West:	Southwest:	Midwest:	Southeast:	Northeast:	International:
				Y	

Note: Financial information, benefits and other data can change quickly and may vary from those stated here.

MARVEL ENTERTAINMENT INC www.marvel.com

Industry Group Code: 511130 Ranks within this company's industry group: Sales: 7 Profits: 2

Print Media/Publishing:		Movies:		Equipment/Supplies:		Broadcast/Cable:		Music/Audio:		Sports/Games:	
Newspapers:		Movie Theaters:		Equipment/Supplies:		Broadcast TV:		Music Production:		Games/Sports:	
Magazines:	Y	Movie Production:	Y	Gambling Equipment:		Cable TV:		Retail Music:		Retail Games Stores:	
Books:	Y	TV/Video Production:		Special Services:	Y	Satellite Broadcast:		Retail Audio Equip.:		Stadiums/Teams:	
Book Stores:		Video Rental:		Advertising Services:	Y	Radio:		Music Print./Dist.:		Gambling/Casinos:	
Distribution/Printing:		Video Distribution:		Info. Sys. Software:		Online Information:		Multimedia:		Rides/Theme Parks:	

TYPES OF BUSINESS:

Comic Book Publishing
Toys
Licensing & Merchandising
Movie Production

BRANDS/DIVISIONS/AFFILIATES:

Toy Biz
Marvel Comics
Spider-Man
X-Men
Incredible Hulk
Fantastic Four
Daredevil
Ghost Rider

CONTACTS: *Note: Officers with more than one job title may be intentionally listed here more than once.*

Isaac Perlmutter, CEO
Kenneth West, Exec. VP/CFO
Alan Fine, Pres./CEO-Toy Biz
Alan Fine, Pres./CEO-Publishing
David Maisel, Exec. VP-Office of the Chief Exec.
John Turitzin, Exec. VP-Office of the Chief Exec.
Morton E. Handel, Chmn.

Phone: 212-576-4000 **Fax:** 212-576-8517
Toll-Free:
Address: 417 Fifth Ave., 11th Floor, New York, NY 10016 US

GROWTH PLANS/SPECIAL FEATURES:

Marvel Entertainment, Inc., formerly Marvel Enterprises, Inc., is one of the world's most prominent character-based entertainment companies, with a proprietary library of over 5,000 characters, mostly superheroes. The company operates in the licensing, comic book publishing and toy businesses in both domestic and international markets. Marvel's library of characters includes Spider-Man, X-Men, Fantastic Four and the Incredible Hulk. The company's business is divided into four divisions: entertainment, licensing, publishing and toys through subsidiary Toy Biz. The licensing division licenses the company's characters for use in a wide variety of products, including toys, electronic games, apparel, accessories and collectibles. This division also receives fees from the sale of licenses to a variety of media, including television and video games. The publishing segment has been in business since 1939 and publishes in many foreign countries in a variety of languages. Comic books are distributed through three channels: comic book specialty stores, traditional retail outlets and subscription sales. Toy Biz designs, develops, markets and distributes a limited line of toys worldwide. In recent years, Marvel has begun producing movies based on its characters, and by 2008 plans to have delivered up to 10 Marvel films to Paramount Pictures, which will act as the distributor. This moves Marvel well beyond being a licensor into being the actual producer. Upcoming films include Ghost Rider, Spider-Man 3, and Fantastic Four: Rise of the Silver Surfer in 2007; and The Incredible Hulk and Iron Man in 2008. In 2006, Marvel terminated its toy licensing agreement with Toy Biz and plans to transition to a Hasbro license in 2007. Also in 2006, Marvel teamed with video game developer Cryptic Studios with plans to produce the first online Marvel Super Heroes game, which will be released exclusively to Xbox 360 and Windows Vista and published by Microsoft Game Studios.

FINANCIALS: Sales and profits are in thousands of dollars—add 000 to get the full amount. 2006 Note: Financial information for 2006 was not available for all companies at press time.

2006 Sales: $	2006 Profits: $	**U.S. Stock Ticker: MVL**	
2005 Sales: $390,507	2005 Profits: $102,819	**Int'l Ticker:** Int'l Exchange:	
2004 Sales: $513,468	2004 Profits: $124,877	Employees: 253	
2003 Sales: $347,626	2003 Profits: $151,648	Fiscal Year Ends: 12/31	
2002 Sales: $299,000	2002 Profits: $31,000	Parent Company:	

SALARIES/BENEFITS:

Pension Plan:	ESOP Stock Plan:	Profit Sharing:	Top Exec. Salary: $987,981	Bonus: $1,323,520
Savings Plan: Y	Stock Purch. Plan:		Second Exec. Salary: $500,000	Bonus: $1,125,000

OTHER THOUGHTS:

Apparent Women Officers or Directors:
Hot Spot for Advancement for Women/Minorities:

LOCATIONS: ("Y" = Yes)

West:	Southwest:	Midwest:	Southeast:	Northeast:	International:
Y				Y	Y

Note: Financial information, benefits and other data can change quickly and may vary from those stated here.

MATAV-CABLE SYSTEMS MEDIA LTD　　　　www.matav.co.il

Industry Group Code: 513220 Ranks within this company's industry group: Sales:　　Profits:

Print Media/Publishing:	Movies:	Equipment/Supplies:		Broadcast/Cable:		Music/Audio:		Sports/Games:
Newspapers:	Movie Theaters:	Equipment/Supplies:		Broadcast TV:		Music Production:		Games/Sports:
Magazines:	Movie Production:	Gambling Equipment:		Cable TV:	Y	Retail Music:		Retail Games Stores:
Books:	TV/Video Production:	Special Services:	Y	Satellite Broadcast:		Retail Audio Equip.:		Stadiums/Teams:
Book Stores:	Video Rental:	Advertising Services:		Radio:		Music Print./Dist.:		Gambling/Casinos:
Distribution/Printing:	Video Distribution:	Info. Sys. Software:		Online Information:		Multimedia:		Rides/Theme Parks:

TYPES OF BUSINESS:

Cable Television Service
Broadband Internet Services
Mobile & International Phone Service

BRANDS/DIVISIONS/AFFILIATES:

Partner Communications
Barak, I.T.C.
HOT
Delek Investments Properties
Hot Telecom

CONTACTS: *Note: Officers with more than one job title may be intentionally listed here more than once.*

Meir Srebernik, CEO
Tal Peres, CFO
Ron Sharon, VP-Info. Systems
Ori Gur Arieh, General Counsel
Ayelet Shiloni, Integrated Investor Rel.
Meir Srebernik, Chmn.

Phone: 972-9-860-2160	Fax: 972-9-860-2282
Toll-Free:	
Address: 42 Pinkas St., North Industrial Area, PO Box 13600, Netanya, 42134 Israel	

GROWTH PLANS/SPECIAL FEATURES:

MATAV-Cable Systems Media Ltd. is one of three cable television operators in Israel. The firm operates digital and analog cable television systems and provides approximately 120 channels to 265,000 subscribers. In addition, the company provides cable-based high-speed Internet services with more than 126,500 subscribers. The company also holds a minority interest in Partner Communications, a company providing mobile phone service to 29% of Israeli citizens; and 10% of Barak, Ltd., a provider of international phone service. Approximately 25% of Israeli households are connected to MATAV's network, including the metropolitan areas of Bat Yam/Holon, Haifa and Netanya/Hadera and the rural areas of Kiryat Shmona, Safed, Tiberias, part of Galilee and the Golan Heights. The company, together with two additional Cable television operators, Golden Channels & Co. Group and Tevel Israel International Communications Ltd., formed the brand HOT, a nationwide cable television provider. HOT has approximately 1 million television subscribers and 450,000 Internet subscribers. The joint venture is part of an operational merger of the three cable companies that involves marketing, sales, engineering, customer service, operations and information systems, forming a monopoly of cable TV services in Israel. In addition, the company's joint venture owns Hot Telecom, a cable network fixed-line telephony service. In 2006, the firm announced plans to purchase all shares, assets and liabilities of Golden Channels & Co. Group and Tevel Israel International Communications Ltd. pending regulatory approval.

FINANCIALS: Sales and profits are in thousands of dollars—add 000 to get the full amount. 2006 Note: Financial information for 2006 was not available for all companies at press time.

2006 Sales: $	2006 Profits: $	U.S. Stock Ticker: MTA
2005 Sales: $	2005 Profits: $	Int'l Ticker: MATV　Int'l Exchange: Tel Aviv-TASE
2004 Sales: $135,700	2004 Profits: $-19,300	Employees: 826
2003 Sales: $125,100	2003 Profits: $-1,300	Fiscal Year Ends: 12/31
2002 Sales: $106,600	2002 Profits: $7,300	Parent Company:

SALARIES/BENEFITS:

Pension Plan:	ESOP Stock Plan:	Profit Sharing:	Top Exec. Salary: $	Bonus: $
Savings Plan:	Stock Purch. Plan:		Second Exec. Salary: $	Bonus: $

OTHER THOUGHTS:

Apparent Women Officers or Directors:
Hot Spot for Advancement for Women/Minorities:

LOCATIONS: ("Y" = Yes)

West:	Southwest:	Midwest:	Southeast:	Northeast:	International:
					Y

MATSUSHITA ELECTRIC INDUSTRIAL CO LTD
www.panasonic.net
Industry Group Code: 334310 Ranks within this company's industry group: Sales: 1 Profits: 4

Print Media/Publishing:	Movies:	Equipment/Supplies:	Broadcast/Cable:	Music/Audio:		Sports/Games:	
Newspapers:	Movie Theaters:	Equipment/Supplies:	Broadcast TV:	Music Production:		Games/Sports:	
Magazines:	Movie Production:	Gambling Equipment:	Cable TV:	Retail Music:		Retail Games Stores:	
Books:	TV/Video Production:	Special Services:	Satellite Broadcast:	Retail Audio Equip.:	Y	Stadiums/Teams:	
Book Stores:	Video Rental:	Advertising Services:	Radio:	Music Print./Dist.:		Gambling/Casinos:	
Distribution/Printing:	Video Distribution:	Info. Sys. Software:	Online Information:	Multimedia:		Rides/Theme Parks:	

TYPES OF BUSINESS:
Audio & Video Equipment, Manufacturing
Industrial Equipment & Machinery
Home Appliances
Electronic Components
Cellular Phones
Medical Equipment
Photovoltaic Equipment
Batteries

BRANDS/DIVISIONS/AFFILIATES:
Panasonic
Quasar
Technics
JVC
Tropian, Inc.

CONTACTS: *Note: Officers with more than one job title may be intentionally listed here more than once.*
Koshi Kitadai, Sr. Managing Exec. Officer
Fumio Ohtsubo, Pres.
Shunzo Ushimaru, Sr. Managing Dir.-Mktg.
Shinichi Fukushima, Managing Dir.-Human Resources
Takae Makita, Exec. Officer-Info. Systems & IT Innovation
Susumu Koike, Exec. VP-Tech. & Semiconductors
Takahiro Mori, Managing Dir.-Planning
Tetsuya Kawakami, Exec. VP-Finance & Acct.
Masayuki Matsushita, Vice Chmn.
Koshi Kitadai, Pres., Panasonic Electronic Devices Co., Ltd.
Yoshiaki Kushiki, Pres., Panasonic Mobile Communications Co., Ltd.
Toru Ishida, Pres., Matsushita Battery Industrial Co., Ltd.
Kunio Nakamura, Chmn.

Phone: 81-6-6908-1121	Fax: 81-6-6908-2351
Toll-Free:	
Address: 1006 Oaza Kadoma, Kadoma-shi, Osaka, 571-8501 Japan	

GROWTH PLANS/SPECIAL FEATURES:
Matsushita Electric Industrial Co., Ltd. is a global leader in electronics, with consumer products marketed under brand names including Panasonic, Quasar, Technics and JVC. The company's business areas are audio, visual and communications; home appliances; industrial equipment; and electronic components. Matsushita's principal products in the audio, visual and communications networks category include computers; monitors; optical disk drives; cell phones; copying machines and printers; TVs, VCRs, camcorders, DVD players and recorders; audio equipment; and pre-recorded audio and video software. The firm's home appliance products include refrigerators, air conditioners, washing machines, dryers, vacuum cleaners, dishwashers, microwave ovens, rice cookers and other cooking appliances, as well as kitchen fixture systems, bath and sanitary equipment, health care equipment, electric lamps, bicycles and cameras. Matsushita's industrial equipment segment encompasses factory automation equipment, welding machines, power distribution devices, ventilating and air conditioning equipment, vending machines and medical equipment. Major products in the electronics component segment include semiconductors, display devices, electric motors, photovoltaic cells, compressors and batteries. The company has emerged as an industry leader in developing semiconductors that feature system LSIs, which it targets for enhanced product lines in digital televisions, optical disk applications (DVDs and CD-ROMs), mobile communications, network-related devices, SD memory cards and CCD (charge coupled device) image sensors. In January 2006, Panasonic announced plans to build the world's largest plasma display panel plant in Japan with an annual output of over 11 million panels. The plant was designed to commence operations in July 2007. The company closed several divisions in 2006, including Panasonic AVC Networks Germany GmbH, Matsushita Air-Conditioning India Private Limited and Panasonic Electronic Devices U.K. Ltd. Panasonic also entered into a joint venture agreement with NEC and Texas Instruments Incorporated, among others, to create a company focused on hardware and software communications platforms for third generation mobile phones.

FINANCIALS: Sales and profits are in thousands of dollars—add 000 to get the full amount. 2006 Note: Financial information for 2006 was not available for all companies at press time.

2006 Sales: $75,601,800	2006 Profits: $1,312,500	U.S. Stock Ticker: MC
2005 Sales: $81,298,000	2005 Profits: $546,000	Int'l Ticker: 6752 Int'l Exchange: Tokyo-TSE
2004 Sales: $71,920,600	2004 Profits: $405,200	Employees: 334,752
2003 Sales: $61,681,000	2003 Profits: $-162,000	Fiscal Year Ends: 3/31
2002 Sales: $51,830,000	2002 Profits: $3,248,000	Parent Company:

SALARIES/BENEFITS:
Pension Plan:	ESOP Stock Plan:	Profit Sharing:	Top Exec. Salary: $	Bonus: $
Savings Plan:	Stock Purch. Plan:		Second Exec. Salary: $	Bonus: $

OTHER THOUGHTS:
Apparent Women Officers or Directors:
Hot Spot for Advancement for Women/Minorities:

LOCATIONS: ("Y" = Yes)
West:	Southwest:	Midwest:	Southeast:	Northeast:	International:
Y	Y	Y	Y	Y	Y

Note: Financial information, benefits and other data can change quickly and may vary from those stated here.

MCCLATCHY COMPANY (THE)　　　　www.mcclatchy.com

Industry Group Code: 511110 Ranks within this company's industry group: Sales: 11   Profits: 6

Print Media/Publishing:		Movies:	Equipment/Supplies:		Broadcast/Cable:	Music/Audio:	Sports/Games:
Newspapers:	Y	Movie Theaters:	Equipment/Supplies:		Broadcast TV:	Music Production:	Games/Sports:
Magazines:		Movie Production:	Gambling Equipment:		Cable TV:	Retail Music:	Retail Games Stores:
Books:		TV/Video Production:	Special Services:	Y	Satellite Broadcast:	Retail Audio Equip.:	Stadiums/Teams:
Book Stores:		Video Rental:	Advertising Services:	Y	Radio:	Music Print./Dist.:	Gambling/Casinos:
Distribution/Printing:		Video Distribution:	Info. Sys. Software:		Online Information:	Multimedia:	Rides/Theme Parks:

TYPES OF BUSINESS:

Newspaper Publishing
Online Publishing
Direct Marketing
Paper Manufacturing

BRANDS/DIVISIONS/AFFILIATES:

Sacramento Bee (The)
Star Tribune (The)
Anchorage Daily News
News & Observer (The)
RealCities.com
McClatchy Interactive
Newsprint Ventures, Inc.
Knight Ridder, Inc.

CONTACTS: Note: Officers with more than one job title may be intentionally listed here more than once.

Gary B. Pruitt, CEO
Gary B. Pruitt, Pres.
Patrick J. Talamantes, CFO/VP Finance
Heather L. Fagundes, VP-Human Resources
Karole Morgan-Prager, General Counsel/VP/Corp. Sec.
Frank Whittaker, VP-Oper
Christian A. Hendricks, VP-Interactive Media
Patrick J. Talamantes, VP-Finance
Maggie Wilderotter, Chmn./CEO Citizens Communications
Robert J. Weill, VP-Oper.
Lynn Dickerson, VP-Oper
Howard Weaver, VP-News
Gary B. Pruitt, Chmn.

Phone: 916-321-1855	Fax: 916-321-1869
Toll-Free:	
Address: 2100 Q St., Sacramento, CA 95816 US	

GROWTH PLANS/SPECIAL FEATURES:

The McClatchy Company is the second largest newspaper company in the U.S, with 32 daily and 50 community newspapers with and daily circulation of 3.3 million. The firm's portfolio of publications includes The Sacramento Bee, The News & Observer, The Fresno Bee, Anchorage Daily News, The News Tribune, Tri-City Herald, The Beaufort Gazette, The Modesto Bee, The Island Packet, The Herald and The Minneapolis Star Tribune. Advertising accounts for approximately 84% of the firm's total revenues, while circulation accounts for about 14%. Over the decades, McClatchy's newspapers have been 13 Pulitzer Prizes, three of which were gold medals for public service. The firm's largest newspaper is The Star Tribune in Minneapolis-St. Paul, Minnesota. The company's oldest and second-largest daily newspaper is The Sacramento Bee, originally published in 1857. McClatchy's core newspaper business is supplemented by a growing array of niche products and direct marketing initiatives. The company operates RealCities.com, (the largest national network of regional and city websites); McClatchy Interactive (an online publishing business that provides newspapers with content publishing tools and software development); and is part owner of Career Builder.com, the largest online classified employment listing service. The firm also operates Newsprint Ventures, Inc., which in turn operates the Ponderay newsprint mill near Spokane, Washington. In late 2006, McClatchy Co. acquired Knight Ridder, Inc., doubling its circulation and number of daily and community papers. This acquisition significantly expanded its Washington, D.C. news bureau, and added an international presence comprising 10 foreign news bureaus. Of the newspapers the firm acquired from Knight Ridder, 12 will be sold for a total of $2.078 billion. Recently, the firm sold four newspapers to MediaNews and Hearst Corporation for $1 billion. In December 2006, McClatchy agreed to sell its largest paper, the Minneapolis Star Tribune, to Avista Capital Partners, a private-equity firm, for $530 million.

FINANCIALS: Sales and profits are in thousands of dollars—add 000 to get the full amount. 2006 Note: Financial information for 2006 was not available for all companies at press time.

2006 Sales: $	2006 Profits: $	U.S. Stock Ticker: MNI
2005 Sales: $1,186,115	2005 Profits: $160,519	Int'l Ticker:　　Int'l Exchange:
2004 Sales: $1,163,400	2004 Profits: $155,900	Employees: 8,948
2003 Sales: $1,099,391	2003 Profits: $150,222	Fiscal Year Ends: 12/31
2002 Sales: $1,081,900	2002 Profits: $131,200	Parent Company:

SALARIES/BENEFITS:

Pension Plan: Y	ESOP Stock Plan:	Profit Sharing:	Top Exec. Salary: $1,000,000	Bonus: $950,000
Savings Plan: Y	Stock Purch. Plan:		Second Exec. Salary: $515,000	Bonus: $230,000

OTHER THOUGHTS:

Apparent Women Officers or Directors: 8
Hot Spot for Advancement for Women/Minorities: Y

LOCATIONS: ("Y" = Yes)

West:	Southwest:	Midwest:	Southeast:	Northeast:	International:
Y		Y	Y	Y	

Note: Financial information, benefits and other data can change quickly and may vary from those stated here.

MCGRAW HILL COS INC
www.mcgraw-hill.com

Industry Group Code: 511130 Ranks within this company's industry group: Sales: 2   Profits: 1

Print Media/Publishing:		Movies:		Equipment/Supplies:		Broadcast/Cable:		Music/Audio:		Sports/Games:	
Newspapers:		Movie Theaters:		Equipment/Supplies:		Broadcast TV:	Y	Music Production:		Games/Sports:	
Magazines:	Y	Movie Production:		Gambling Equipment:		Cable TV:		Retail Music:		Retail Games Stores:	
Books:	Y	TV/Video Production:		Special Services:	Y	Satellite Broadcast:		Retail Audio Equip.:		Stadiums/Teams:	
Book Stores:		Video Rental:		Advertising Services:	Y	Radio:		Music Print./Dist.:	Y	Gambling/Casinos:	
Distribution/Printing:		Video Distribution:		Info. Sys. Software:	Y	Online Information:		Multimedia:		Rides/Theme Parks:	

TYPES OF BUSINESS:

Book Publishing
Financial Information
Magazine Publishing
Online Data
Research Services
Television Broadcasting

BRANDS/DIVISIONS/AFFILIATES:

Standard & Poor's
S&P 500
McGraw-Hill Education
BuisinessWeek Magazine
McGraw-Hill Construction
Aviation Week
McGraw-Hill Broadcasting
J.D. Power & Associates

CONTACTS: Note: Officers with more than one job title may be intentionally listed here more than once.

Harold W. McGraw, III, CEO
William P. Kupper, Jr., Pres.
Robert J. Bahash, CFO/Exec. VP
David L. Murphy, Exec. VP-Human Resources
Bruce D. Marcus, CIO/Exec. VP
Kenneth M. Vittor, General Counsel/Exec. VP
Deven Sharma, Exec. VP-Global Strategy
Henry Hirschberg, Pres., McGraw-Hill Education
Glenn S. Goldberg, Pres., Info. & Media Svcs.
Kathleen A. Corbet, Pres., Standard & Poor's
Talia M. Griep, VP-Global Business Svcs.
Harold W. McGraw, III, Chmn.

Phone: 212-512-2000	Fax: 212-512-4502
Toll-Free:	
Address: 1221 Ave. of the Americas, New York, NY 10020 US	

GROWTH PLANS/SPECIAL FEATURES:

McGraw-Hill Companies, Inc. is a leading global information services provider focused in the financial services, education and information and media services markets. Within the financial services segment, the company operates Standard & Poor's. Standard & Poor's plays an integral role in the global financial infrastructure, providing credit ratings, independent investment information, analytical services and corporate valuations, including the S&P 1200, a global equity performance benchmark, and the S&P 500, a U.S. portfolio index. In education, McGraw-Hill Education is the leading kindergarten through 12th grade publisher in the U.S., providing traditional textbooks as well as online multimedia tools to assist students and educators. The company also offers online courses. In media services, the company operates BusinessWeek Magazine, a publication with more than 5 million readers, containing news and analysis with a global perspective on current financial, business and technology issues. Platts is a leading provider of energy information and marketing services, delivered through newsletters, Internet-based news, magazines, databases, conferences and consulting services. Platts' offerings cover the oil, natural gas, electricity, nuclear, coal, petrochemical and metals markets. Aviation Week reaches over 100,000 subscribers in 130 countries, serving technology, business, aerospace and military markets. McGraw-Hill Broadcasting encompasses four local television stations, all ABC affiliates, providing news to viewers in Denver, Colorado; Indianapolis, Indiana; and San Diego and Bakersfield, California. The company owns a total of 279 locations, 182 of which are in the U.S.

McGraw-Hill offers employee benefits including continuing development, adoption and tuition assistance, parental leave and flexible work arrangements. McGraw-Hill has been recognized for its commitment to diversity.

FINANCIALS: Sales and profits are in thousands of dollars—add 000 to get the full amount. 2006 Note: Financial information for 2006 was not available for all companies at press time.

2006 Sales: $	2006 Profits: $	U.S. Stock Ticker: MHP	
2005 Sales: $6,003,642	2005 Profits: $844,306	Int'l Ticker: Int'l Exchange:	
2004 Sales: $5,250,538	2004 Profits: $755,823	Employees: 19,600	
2003 Sales: $4,999,382	2003 Profits: $687,650	Fiscal Year Ends: 12/31	
2002 Sales: $4,787,700	2002 Profits: $576,800	Parent Company:	

SALARIES/BENEFITS:

Pension Plan:	ESOP Stock Plan:	Profit Sharing:	Top Exec. Salary: $1,172,000	Bonus: $1,827,504
Savings Plan: Y	Stock Purch. Plan:		Second Exec. Salary: $779,000	Bonus: $1,045,000

OTHER THOUGHTS:

Apparent Women Officers or Directors: 2
Hot Spot for Advancement for Women/Minorities:

LOCATIONS: ("Y" = Yes)

West:	Southwest:	Midwest:	Southeast:	Northeast:	International:
Y	Y	Y		Y	Y

Note: Financial information, benefits and other data can change quickly and may vary from those stated here.

MDI ENTERTAINMENT INC   www.mdientertainment.com

Industry Group Code: 541800 Ranks within this company's industry group: Sales: Profits:

Print Media/Publishing:	Movies:	Equipment/Supplies:		Broadcast/Cable:	Music/Audio:	Sports/Games:	
Newspapers:	Movie Theaters:	Equipment/Supplies:		Broadcast TV:	Music Production:	Games/Sports:	
Magazines:	Movie Production:	Gambling Equipment:	Y	Cable TV:	Retail Music:	Retail Games Stores:	
Books:	TV/Video Production:	Special Services:	Y	Satellite Broadcast:	Retail Audio Equip.:	Stadiums/Teams:	
Book Stores:	Video Rental:	Advertising Services:	Y	Radio:	Music Print./Dist.:	Gambling/Casinos:	Y
Distribution/Printing:	Video Distribution:	Info. Sys. Software:		Online Information:	Multimedia:	Rides/Theme Parks:	

TYPES OF BUSINESS:

Lottery-Focused Marketing
Events & Promotions
Web Design
Electronic Lottery Cards

BRANDS/DIVISIONS/AFFILIATES:

Scientific Games Corp.

CONTACTS: *Note: Officers with more than one job title may be intentionally listed here more than once.*

Anne Villa, Dir.-Oper.
Steven M. Saferin, Pres.
David Darko, Sr. Accountant
Jeff Schweig, Sr. VP-Integrated Mktg.
Don Walsh, Sr. VP-Merch. & Prod. Dev.
Kenneth M. Przysiecki, Sr. VP-Admin.
Jeff Schweig, VP-Creative Planning & Dev.
Bob Kowalczyk, VP-Internet Svcs.
Paul Guziel, VP-Creative & Client Svcs.
Charles Kline, Exec. VP
Kyle Rogers, Sr. VP/General Mgr.
Bev Opie, VP-Sales
Evelyn Yenson, Sr. VP-Int'l Sales & Mktg.
John Monaco, Mgr.-Purchasing & Fulfillment

Phone: 770-664-3700	Fax: 770-343-8798
Toll-Free:	
Address: 1500 Bluegrass Lakes Pkwy., Alpharetta, GA 30004 US	

GROWTH PLANS/SPECIAL FEATURES:

MDI Entertainment, Inc., a subsidiary of Scientific Games Corp., specializes in creating, marketing and implementing entertainment-based promotions mainly in the U.S. and Canada. Its strategic focus is to develop and market lottery ticket games based on well-known entertainment and pop cultural icon licensed properties. MDI's basic selling proposition to lotteries is that a licensed lottery game will create appeal and interest among a segment of consumers much better than a generic lottery game, which will hold no value for many potential lottery customers. The company encourages lotteries to establish a constant stream of different licensed games, about one per quarter, as part of their overall product marketing program. Beginning with brands such as Star Trek, Wheel of Fortune and Twilight Zone, the firm's licensed games division now includes over 80 brands, such as Sudoku, American Idol and Pac-Man. The company's revenue comes from two main sources: the sale of bonus prize products to lotteries using MDI-licensed games; and license/royalty fees paid by lotteries for the rights to market the games in their jurisdictions. MDI purchases prize products resold to lotteries from other licensees of a particular brand, often becoming one of the largest customers of the suppliers. Products are sold to lotteries in bulk, and then MDI fulfills prizes individually to lottery winners as designated by the lottery, which are packaged as elements of a full-service lottery promotion tied to licenses that the company acquires. The company also offers services for pre-paid phone cards and offers other services, such as web design and promotional events, to its lottery customers. In partnership with Electronic Game Card, Inc., MDI has been marketing electronic lottery cards to stores in Iowa. The new game format has been so successful that operations are expected to begin in other states.

FINANCIALS: Sales and profits are in thousands of dollars—add 000 to get the full amount. 2006 Note: Financial information for 2006 was not available for all companies at press time.

2006 Sales: $	2006 Profits: $	U.S. Stock Ticker: Subsidiary	
2005 Sales: $	2005 Profits: $	Int'l Ticker: Int'l Exchange:	
2004 Sales: $	2004 Profits: $	Employees: 22	
2003 Sales: $	2003 Profits: $	Fiscal Year Ends: 12/31	
2002 Sales: $	2002 Profits: $	Parent Company: SCIENTIFIC GAMES CORPORATION	

SALARIES/BENEFITS:

Pension Plan:	ESOP Stock Plan:	Profit Sharing:	Top Exec. Salary: $330,750	Bonus: $
Savings Plan:	Stock Purch. Plan:		Second Exec. Salary: $201,212	Bonus: $

OTHER THOUGHTS:

Apparent Women Officers or Directors: 9
Hot Spot for Advancement for Women/Minorities: Y

LOCATIONS: ("Y" = Yes)

West:	Southwest:	Midwest:	Southeast:	Northeast:	International:
			Y		

MEDIA GENERAL INC
www.media-general.com

Industry Group Code: 511110 Ranks within this company's industry group: Sales: 13   Profits: 18

Print Media/Publishing:		Movies:	Equipment/Supplies:		Broadcast/Cable:		Music/Audio:	Sports/Games:	
Newspapers:	Y	Movie Theaters:	Equipment/Supplies:		Broadcast TV:	Y	Music Production:	Games/Sports:	Y
Magazines:		Movie Production:	Gambling Equipment:		Cable TV:		Retail Music:	Retail Games Stores:	
Books:		TV/Video Production:	Special Services:	Y	Satellite Broadcast:		Retail Audio Equip.:	Stadiums/Teams:	
Book Stores:		Video Rental:	Advertising Services:	Y	Radio:		Music Print./Dist.:	Gambling/Casinos:	
Distribution/Printing:		Video Distribution:	Info. Sys. Software:		Online Information:		Multimedia:	Rides/Theme Parks:	

TYPES OF BUSINESS:

Newspaper Publishing
Broadcast Television
Interactive Media
Gaming & Advergaming

BRANDS/DIVISIONS/AFFILIATES:

Tampa Tribune (The)
Richmond Times-Dispatch
Blockdot.com
Central Virginia Gazette (The)
Winston-Salem Journal
Mechanicsville Local (The)

CONTACTS: Note: Officers with more than one job title may be intentionally listed here more than once.

Marshall N. Morton, CEO
O. Reid Ashe, Jr., COO/Exec. VP
Marshall N. Morton, Pres.
John A. Schauss, CFO
James F. Woodward, VP-Human Resources
George L. Mahoney, General Counsel/VP
Lou Anne J. Nabhan, VP-Corp. Comm.
John A. Schauss, VP-Finance
H. Graham Woodlief, Jr., VP/Pres., Publishing Div.
James A. Zimmerman, VP/Pres., Broadcasting Div.
Neal F. Fondren, VP/Pres., Interactive Media Div.
J. Stewart Bryan, III, Chmn.

Phone: 804-649-6000	Fax: 804-649-6066
Toll-Free:	
Address: 333 E. Franklin St., Richmond, VA 23219 US	

GROWTH PLANS/SPECIAL FEATURES:

Media General, Inc. is an independent communications company, situated primarily in the Southeast with interests in newspapers, television stations and interactive media. The business incorporates three different divisions: publishing (earning 50% of revenues), broadcasting (earning 50% of revenues) and the interactive media division. Its publishing division includes three metropolitan newspapers (The Tampa Tribune, the Richmond Times-Dispatch, and the Winston-Salem Journal); 25 daily community newspapers in Virginia, North Carolina, Florida, Alabama and South Carolina; and more than 100 weekly newspapers and other publications. Media General's broadcast division owns and operates 26 broadcast television stations affiliated with NBC, ABC, CBS and CW, and located primarily in the southeastern U.S. Media General's stations reach more than 30% of all television households in the Southeast and nearly 8% nationwide. The interactive media division operates more than 75 online enterprises affiliated with the company's newspapers and television stations. The division recently expanded into the gaming and advergaming (the use of interactive games to deliver advertising messages) sectors. The company's corporate strategy emphasizes convergence, meaning integration of the three divisions to create a superior information base for the consumer. An example of these efforts is the Tampa market, where The Tampa Tribune, WFLA-TV and TBO.com share the company's news center facility and work side by side to provide comprehensive news, information and entertainment. In 2006, the firm sold KWCH-TV (Kansas) to Schurtz Communications for $73 million. In addition, the company sold WDEF-TV (Tennessee) to Morris Multimedia for $22 million, as well as WIAT-TV (Alabama) and KIMT-TV (Iowa) to New Vision Television for $35 million. Also in 2006, the firm purchased four NBC stations (in North Carolina, Ohio, Alabama and Rhode Island) for $450 million.

Media General offers its employees flexible benefits including various health and welfare programs, insurance programs, tuition reimbursement and counseling assistance.

FINANCIALS: Sales and profits are in thousands of dollars—add 000 to get the full amount. 2006 Note: Financial information for 2006 was not available for all companies at press time.

2006 Sales: $	2006 Profits: $	U.S. Stock Ticker: MEG
2005 Sales: $917,937	2005 Profits: $-243,042	Int'l Ticker: Int'l Exchange:
2004 Sales: $900,400	2004 Profits: $80,200	Employees: 7,200
2003 Sales: $837,423	2003 Profits: $58,685	Fiscal Year Ends: 12/31
2002 Sales: $836,800	2002 Profits: $-72,900	Parent Company:

SALARIES/BENEFITS:

Pension Plan:	ESOP Stock Plan:	Profit Sharing:	Top Exec. Salary: $875,000	Bonus: $423,596
Savings Plan: Y	Stock Purch. Plan: Y		Second Exec. Salary: $715,000	Bonus: $346,139

OTHER THOUGHTS:

Apparent Women Officers or Directors: 1
Hot Spot for Advancement for Women/Minorities:

LOCATIONS: ("Y" = Yes)

West:	Southwest:	Midwest:	Southeast:	Northeast:	International:
		Y	Y	Y	

Note: Financial information, benefits and other data can change quickly and may vary from those stated here.

MEDIACOM COMMUNICATIONS CORP www.mediacomcc.com

Industry Group Code: 513220 Ranks within this company's industry group: Sales: 17 Profits: 19

Print Media/Publishing:	Movies:	Equipment/Supplies:		Broadcast/Cable:		Music/Audio:	Sports/Games:
Newspapers:	Movie Theaters:	Equipment/Supplies:		Broadcast TV:		Music Production:	Games/Sports:
Magazines:	Movie Production:	Gambling Equipment:	Y	Cable TV:	Y	Retail Music:	Retail Games Stores:
Books:	TV/Video Production:	Special Services:	Y	Satellite Broadcast:		Retail Audio Equip.:	Stadiums/Teams:
Book Stores:	Video Rental:	Advertising Services:		Radio:		Music Print./Dist.:	Gambling/Casinos:
Distribution/Printing:	Video Distribution:	Info. Sys. Software:		Online Information:		Multimedia:	Rides/Theme Parks:

TYPES OF BUSINESS:

Cable TV Service
Internet Service
Digital Cable
Telephone Service

BRANDS/DIVISIONS/AFFILIATES:

CONTACTS: *Note: Officers with more than one job title may be intentionally listed here more than once.*

Rocco B. Commisso, CEO
Mark E. Stephan, CFO/Exec. VP
Michael Rahimi, VP-Mktg.
Italia Commisso-Weinand, Sr. VP-Human Resources
Joseph E. Young, General Counsel/Sr. VP
John G. Pascarelli, Exec. VP-Oper.
Calvin G. Craib, Sr. VP-Bus. Dev.
Brian M. Walsh, Controller
Mark E. Stephan, Treas.
Charles J. Bartolotta, Sr. VP-Customer Oper.
Italia Commisso-Weinand, Sr. VP-Programming
Joseph E. Young, Corp. Sec.
Rocco B. Commisso, Chmn.

Phone: 845-695-2600	**Fax:** 845-695-2699
Toll-Free:	
Address: 100 Crystal Run Rd., Middletown, NY 10941 US	

GROWTH PLANS/SPECIAL FEATURES:

Mediacom Communications Corp., one of the largest cable television companies in the U.S., provides customers with a wide array of broadband products and services. Specializing in smaller cities and towns, the company serves more than 1.5 million basic subscribers 494,000 digital customers, 478,000 high-speed data customers, and 22,000 telephone customers in 23 states with networks passing approximately 2.7 million homes served. About 60% of the company's customers are located within the top 100 television markets in the country. The firm offers its customers a full array of traditional analog video services including traditional cable television services. Through these services, customers can access several digital cable programming packages that include up to 41 digital basic channels, 61 multi-channel premium services, 60 pay-per-view movie and sports channels, 45 channels of digital music and an interactive on-screen program guide to help them navigate their viewing choices. In addition, Mediacom offers advanced broadband products and services such as digital cable television and high-speed Internet access to a large portion of its customer base.

The firm offers it employees short- and long-term disability and group life coverage, in addition to tuition reimbursement.

FINANCIALS: Sales and profits are in thousands of dollars—add 000 to get the full amount. 2006 Note: Financial information for 2006 was not available for all companies at press time.

2006 Sales: $	2006 Profits: $	**U.S. Stock Ticker: MCCC**
2005 Sales: $1,098,822	2005 Profits: $-222,228	**Int'l Ticker:** Int'l Exchange:
2004 Sales: $1,057,226	2004 Profits: $13,552	Employees: 4,248
2003 Sales: $1,004,889	2003 Profits: $-62,475	Fiscal Year Ends: 12/31
2002 Sales: $923,000	2002 Profits: $-161,700	Parent Company:

SALARIES/BENEFITS:

Pension Plan:	ESOP Stock Plan:	Profit Sharing:	Top Exec. Salary: $800,000	Bonus: $425,000
Savings Plan: Y	Stock Purch. Plan:		Second Exec. Salary: $280,000	Bonus: $60,000

OTHER THOUGHTS:

Apparent Women Officers or Directors: 1
Hot Spot for Advancement for Women/Minorities:

LOCATIONS: ("Y" = Yes)

West:	Southwest:	Midwest:	Southeast:	Northeast:	International:
Y		Y	Y	Y	

MEDIANEWS GROUP INC

www.medianewsgroup.com

Industry Group Code: 511110 Ranks within this company's industry group: Sales: 15 Profits: 13

Print Media/Publishing:		Movies:		Equipment/Supplies:		Broadcast/Cable:		Music/Audio:		Sports/Games:	
Newspapers:	Y	Movie Theaters:		Equipment/Supplies:		Broadcast TV:	Y	Music Production:		Games/Sports:	
Magazines:		Movie Production:		Gambling Equipment:		Cable TV:		Retail Music:		Retail Games Stores:	
Books:		TV/Video Production:		Special Services:	Y	Satellite Broadcast:		Retail Audio Equip.:		Stadiums/Teams:	
Book Stores:		Video Rental:		Advertising Services:	Y	Radio:		Music Print./Dist.:		Gambling/Casinos:	
Distribution/Printing:		Video Distribution:		Info. Sys. Software:		Online Information:		Multimedia:		Rides/Theme Parks:	

TYPES OF BUSINESS:

Newspaper Publishing
Television Broadcasting
Radio Broadcasting
Commercial Printing
Electronic Advertising
Online Publishing
Website Development & Maintenance Services
Real Estate Marketing Services

BRANDS/DIVISIONS/AFFILIATES:

Denver Post
Salt Lake Tribune
Detroit News
MediaNews Group Interactive
Power One Media
SeeitBuyit
Rate Watch
Prairie Mountain Publishing Company

CONTACTS: Note: Officers with more than one job title may be intentionally listed here more than once.

William D. Singleton, CEO/Vice Chmn.
Steven B. Rossi, COO/Exec. VP
Jody Lodovic, IV, Pres.
Ronald A. Mayo, CFO/VP
Charles M. Kamen, VP-Human Resources
David Bessen, CIO/VP
Anthony F. Tierno, Sr. VP-Oper.
Liz Gaier, Sr. VP-New Bus. Dev.
James L. McDougald, Treas.
Eric J. Grilly, Pres., MediaNews Group Interactive
Michael J. Koren, VP/Controller
Steve Barkmeier, VP-Tax
Patricia Robinson, Corp. Sec.
Richard B. Scudder, Chmn.

Phone: 303-954-6360	Fax: 303-954-6320
Toll-Free:	
Address: 101 W. Colfax Ave., Ste. 1100, Denver, CO 80202 US	

GROWTH PLANS/SPECIAL FEATURES:

MediaNews Group, Inc. (MNG) controls 54 market-dominant daily and approximately 80 non-daily newspapers in 12 states (including suburban markets in close proximity to the San Francisco Bay area, Los Angeles, New York, and Boston). The company also owns three metropolitan daily newspapers: the Denver Post, the Salt Lake Tribune and the Detroit News (purchased in early 2005). MNG's principal sources of revenue are print advertising and circulation. Other sources of revenue include commercial printing and electronic advertising. MNG's newspapers have a combined daily and Sunday paid circulation of approximately 2.6 million and 2.9 million, respectively, as of 2006. In addition, the company owns a CBS affiliate television station in Anchorage, Alaska and four radio stations in Texas. The company also owns MediaNews Group Interactive (MNGi), which maintains 74 web sites, most affiliated with the company's newspapers. Services include providing the company's newspapers with the tools, technologies and services they require to maintain their presence as competitive web sites in each of the communities they serve. These services include hosting, online publishing/site delivery, maintenance, ongoing development, training, advertisement delivery, site analytics and business development support. 72% of the group's revenue is generated by automotive and real estate advertising. In 2007, MNGi will launch a Mobile eNewspaper in conjunction with Amazon. The company has investments in PowerOne Media, a provider of classified advertising technologies; and SeeitBuyit, incorporated as Rate Watch, a marketing and promotional services company that provides real estate industry listing and selling tools. MNG's new consolidated printing plant in Denver is expected to come online in January 2008. In 2006, the company acquired the San Jose Mercury News, California; Contra Coast Times, California; Monterey County Herald, California; and the St. Paul Pioneer press, Minnesota. Also in 2006, MNG formed the Prairie Mountain Publishing Company with E.W. Scripps Co.

FINANCIALS: Sales and profits are in thousands of dollars—add 000 to get the full amount. 2006 Note: Financial information for 2006 was not available for all companies at press time.

2006 Sales: $835,900	2006 Profits: $1,100	U.S. Stock Ticker: Private
2005 Sales: $779,300	2005 Profits: $39,900	Int'l Ticker: Int'l Exchange:
2004 Sales: $753,800	2004 Profits: $27,600	Employees: 10,100
2003 Sales: $738,598	2003 Profits: $40,828	Fiscal Year Ends: 6/30
2002 Sales: $711,130	2002 Profits: $12,365	Parent Company:

SALARIES/BENEFITS:

Pension Plan:	ESOP Stock Plan:	Profit Sharing:	Top Exec. Salary: $962,475	Bonus: $450,000
Savings Plan: Y	Stock Purch. Plan:		Second Exec. Salary: $639,600	Bonus: $400,000

OTHER THOUGHTS:

Apparent Women Officers or Directors: 2
Hot Spot for Advancement for Women/Minorities:

LOCATIONS: ("Y" = Yes)

West:	Southwest:	Midwest:	Southeast:	Northeast:	International:
Y	Y	Y		Y	

Note: Financial information, benefits and other data can change quickly and may vary from those stated here.

MEREDITH CORP

www.meredith.com

Industry Group Code: 511120 Ranks within this company's industry group: Sales: 5 Profits: 3

Print Media/Publishing:		Movies:		Equipment/Supplies:		Broadcast/Cable:		Music/Audio:		Sports/Games:	
Newspapers:		Movie Theaters:		Equipment/Supplies:		Broadcast TV:	Y	Music Production:		Games/Sports:	
Magazines:	Y	Movie Production:		Gambling Equipment:		Cable TV:		Retail Music:		Retail Games Stores:	
Books:	Y	TV/Video Production:		Special Services:		Satellite Broadcast:		Retail Audio Equip.:		Stadiums/Teams:	
Book Stores:		Video Rental:		Advertising Services:	Y	Radio:		Music Print./Dist.:		Gambling/Casinos:	
Distribution/Printing:		Video Distribution:		Info. Sys. Software:		Online Information:		Multimedia:		Rides/Theme Parks:	

TYPES OF BUSINESS:

Magazine Publishing
Television Broadcasting
Marketing Services
Book Publishing
Interactive Media

BRANDS/DIVISIONS/AFFILIATES:

Ladies' Home Journal
Better Homes and Gardens
MORE
Midwest Living
Country Home
Successful Farming
Meredith Integrated Marketing
Meredith Hispanic Ventures

CONTACTS: *Note: Officers with more than one job title may be intentionally listed here more than once.*

Stephen M. Lacy, CEO
Stephen M. Lacy, Pres.
Suku V. Radia, CFO/VP
John S. Zeiser, General Counsel
Art Slusark, VP-Corp. Comm.
Suku V. Radia, Acting Treas.
Paul Karpowicz, Pres., Broadcasting Group
Jack Griffin, Pres., Publishing Group
William T. Kerr, Chmn.

Phone: 515-284-3000	**Fax:** 515-284-2700
Toll-Free:	
Address: 1716 Locust St., Des Moines, IA 50309-3023 US	

GROWTH PLANS/SPECIAL FEATURES:

Meredith Corporation, a leading U.S. media and marketing companies, engages in magazine and book publishing, television broadcasting, integrated marketing and interactive media. Headquartered in Des Moines, Iowa, the company's publishing group features 25 magazine brands, including Better Homes and Gardens, Ladies' Home Journal, Country Home, MORE, Midwest Living, Traditional Home, WOOD, American Baby, Successful Farming and Renovation Style. Moreover, the firm has over 200 special-interest publications, roughly 350 books in print, 32 web sites and strategic alliances with leading Internet destinations. The publishing group also creates custom marketing programs through Meredith Integrated Marketing, licenses the Better Homes and Gardens brand and publishes books created and sold under the Meredith and Ortho trademarks. Meredith's most popular book is the Better Homes and Gardens New Cook Book. Meredith Hispanic Ventures publishes five Spanish-language titles, making Meredith the largest Hispanic publisher in the U.S. The company's broadcasting group owns and operates 14 television stations throughout the U.S., including FOX-, CBS- and NBC-affiliated stations and stations in top-25 markets such as Atlanta, Phoenix and Portland. The corporation has one of the largest domestic databases among media companies, with approximately 85 million consumer names, enabling advertisers to precisely target marketing campaigns. The firm's largest source of revenues is magazine and television advertising. Meredith has established marketing relationships with some of America's leading companies, including The Home Depot, DaimlerChrysler and Carnival Cruise Lines. In recent news, Meredith acquired American Baby magazine and related properties from Primedia, Inc. The company also recently expanded its international presence with multiple publication deals in Australia and China; and announced the acquisition of the station license and other assets of KSMO TV, Kansas City.

The company offers its employees several reimbursement programs, including tuition and fitness reimbursement.

FINANCIALS: Sales and profits are in thousands of dollars—add 000 to get the full amount. 2006 Note: Financial information for 2006 was not available for all companies at press time.

2006 Sales: $1,597,564	2006 Profits: $144,792	**U.S. Stock Ticker: MDP**
2005 Sales: $1,221,289	2005 Profits: $129,042	**Int'l Ticker:** Int'l Exchange:
2004 Sales: $1,161,652	2004 Profits: $110,716	Employees: 3,160
2003 Sales: $1,080,100	2003 Profits: $5,400	Fiscal Year Ends: 6/30
2002 Sales: $987,800	2002 Profits: $91,400	Parent Company:

SALARIES/BENEFITS:

Pension Plan: Y	ESOP Stock Plan:	Profit Sharing:	Top Exec. Salary: $1,000,000	Bonus: $2,500,000
Savings Plan: Y	Stock Purch. Plan:		Second Exec. Salary: $710,000	Bonus: $1,250,000

OTHER THOUGHTS:

Apparent Women Officers or Directors:
Hot Spot for Advancement for Women/Minorities:

LOCATIONS: ("Y" = Yes)

West:	Southwest:	Midwest:	Southeast:	Northeast:	International:
Y	Y	Y	Y	Y	

Note: Financial information, benefits and other data can change quickly and may vary from those stated here.

METRO INTERNATIONAL SA

www.metro.lu

Industry Group Code: 511110 Ranks within this company's industry group: Sales: 20 Profits: 16

Print Media/Publishing:		Movies:	Equipment/Supplies:		Broadcast/Cable:	Music/Audio:	Sports/Games:
Newspapers:	Y	Movie Theaters:	Equipment/Supplies:		Broadcast TV:	Music Production:	Games/Sports:
Magazines:		Movie Production:	Gambling Equipment:		Cable TV:	Retail Music:	Retail Games Stores:
Books:		TV/Video Production:	Special Services:		Satellite Broadcast:	Retail Audio Equip.:	Stadiums/Teams:
Book Stores:		Video Rental:	Advertising Services:	Y	Radio:	Music Print./Dist.:	Gambling/Casinos:
Distribution/Printing:		Video Distribution:	Info. Sys. Software:		Online Information:	Multimedia:	Rides/Theme Parks:

TYPES OF BUSINESS:

Newspaper Publishing
Free Daily Newspapers

BRANDS/DIVISIONS/AFFILIATES:

Metro Boston
Metro USA
Mempo

CONTACTS: Note: Officers with more than one job title may be intentionally listed here more than once.

Pelle Tornberg, CEO
Jens Torpe, COO/Sr. VP
Pelle Tornberg, Pres.
Robert Patterson, CFO/Sr. VP
Bill Skerrett, VP-Human Resources
Steve Nylundh, Exec. VP-Corp. Dev.
Dennis Malamatinas, Chmn.

Phone: 44-20-7016-1300	Fax: 44-20-7016-1400
Toll-Free:	
Address: Interpark House, 7 Down St., 3rd Fl., London, W1J 7AJ UK	

GROWTH PLANS/SPECIAL FEATURES:

Metro International S.A., one of the largest and fastest growing international newspapers, publishes 60 editions of a free daily newspaper in 100 major cities across Europe, North and South America and Asia, attracting about 18.5 million daily readers in 21 countries and 19 languages. It publishes newspapers on weekday mornings for distribution in high-traffic commuter zones or on public transportation networks. Weekend editions are published in Sweden, Holland and Chile on Saturdays. All Metro editions carry headline local, national and international news in a standardized, accessible format and design. The newspapers are distributed through self-service racks or by hand distributors located in or around public transport networks (such as subways, trains, buses and trams), office buildings and retail outlets; at key distribution points on busy streets; or in other high-density population areas such as college campuses. The company derives revenue solely from selling space for display or classified advertisements in its newspapers. The timing and method of Metro's distribution enables it to target a high proportion of young, professional readers who are not typically reading a daily newspaper. Metro daily readership averages 40% under the age of 30 and 70% under the age of 45, with an equal share of men and women readers. In U.S. operations, Metro distributes in New York City, and began distributing in Boston and Philadelphia in early 2006. The company sold its Finnish operations to Sanoma Corporation in 2006.

FINANCIALS: Sales and profits are in thousands of dollars—add 000 to get the full amount. 2006 Note: Financial information for 2006 was not available for all companies at press time.

2006 Sales: $	2006 Profits: $	U.S. Stock Ticker: MTOAF
2005 Sales: $359,700	2005 Profits: $-6,971	Int'l Ticker: MTRO SDB A Int'l Exchange: Stockholm-SSE
2004 Sales: $302,400	2004 Profits: $-8,689	Employees: 1,200
2003 Sales: $203,600	2003 Profits: $-6,900	Fiscal Year Ends: 12/31
2002 Sales: $142,800	2002 Profits: $-71,900	Parent Company:

SALARIES/BENEFITS:

Pension Plan:	ESOP Stock Plan:	Profit Sharing:	Top Exec. Salary: $	Bonus: $
Savings Plan:	Stock Purch. Plan:		Second Exec. Salary: $	Bonus: $

OTHER THOUGHTS:

Apparent Women Officers or Directors:
Hot Spot for Advancement for Women/Minorities:

LOCATIONS: ("Y" = Yes)

West:	Southwest:	Midwest:	Southeast:	Northeast:	International:
				Y	Y

METRO-GOLDWYN-MAYER INC (MGM)

www.mgm.com

Industry Group Code: 512110 Ranks within this company's industry group: Sales: 8   Profits:

Print Media/Publishing:	Movies:		Equipment/Supplies:	Broadcast/Cable:		Music/Audio:		Sports/Games:
Newspapers:	Movie Theaters:		Equipment/Supplies:	Broadcast TV:	Y	Music Production:	Y	Games/Sports:
Magazines:	Movie Production:	Y	Gambling Equipment:	Cable TV:	Y	Retail Music:		Retail Games Stores:
Books:	TV/Video Production:	Y	Special Services:	Satellite Broadcast:		Retail Audio Equip.:		Stadiums/Teams:
Book Stores:	Video Rental:		Advertising Services:	Radio:		Music Print./Dist.:		Gambling/Casinos:
Distribution/Printing:	Video Distribution:		Info. Sys. Software:	Online Information:		Multimedia:		Rides/Theme Parks:

TYPES OF BUSINESS:

Film Production & Distribution
Television, Video & Music Production & Distribution
Broadcast & Cable Television

BRANDS/DIVISIONS/AFFILIATES:

MGM Studios
United Artists Films
Orion Pictures
MGM Television Entertainment
MGM Networks
American Movie Classics
Independent Film Channel (The)
WE: Women's Entertainment

CONTACTS: Note: Officers with more than one job title may be intentionally listed here more than once.

Harry E. Sloan, CEO
Rick Sands, COO
Steve Shaw, Exec. VP-Human Resources
Jeff Pryor, Exec. VP-Corp. Comm.
Charles Cohen, Exec. VP
Jim Packer, Exec. VP-TV Distribution
Blake Thomas, Exec. VP-Home Entertainment
Bruce Tuchman, Exec. VP-MGM Networks
Harry E. Sloan, Chmn.

Phone: 310-449-3000	Fax: 310-449-8857
Toll-Free:	
Address: 10250 Constellation Blvd., Los Angeles, CA 90067-6421 US	

GROWTH PLANS/SPECIAL FEATURES:

Metro-Goldwyn-Mayer, Inc. (MGM) produces and distributes entertainment products worldwide, including motion pictures, television programming, home video, interactive media, music and licensed merchandise. The firm's operating units include MGM Studios, United Artists Films, Orion Pictures, MGM Television Entertainment, MGM Networks, MGM Distribution Co., MGM Worldwide Television Distribution, MGM Home Entertainment, MGM On Stage, MGM Consumer Products, MGM Music, MGM Interactive and MGM Direct. The company has accumulated a library of more than 4,000 theatrically released films and a significant television library. Films in MGM's library have won over 205 Academy Awards. The company owns 22 James Bond films, five titles in the Rocky film franchise and nine titles in the Pink Panther franchise. The library also includes over 10,400 episodes from television series previously broadcast on prime-time network television, including episodes of The Addams Family, Pink Panther and In the Heat of the Night. Television programs in the firm's library have won 87 Emmy awards and 18 Golden Globe awards. Moreover, MGM has a 20% ownership interest in Rainbow Media's national cable networks, including American Movie Classics (AMC), The Independent Film Channel (IFC) and WE: Women's Entertainment. The company's television production studio produces the current shows Stargate SG-1, Stargate Atlantis, Dead Like Me and The Outer Limits. The firm also holds equity interests in a number of international television channels. MGM is owned by a consortium led by Sony Corporation of America and its equity partners, Providence Equity Partners, Texas Pacific Group, Comcast Corporation and DLJ Merchant Banking Partners.

MGM's corporate headquarters in Santa Monica, California features restaurants, a childcare center, a health club, dry cleaners, a barbershop and a credit union, as well as basketball, volleyball and tennis courts.

FINANCIALS: Sales and profits are in thousands of dollars—add 000 to get the full amount. 2006 Note: Financial information for 2006 was not available for all companies at press time.

2006 Sales: $	2006 Profits: $	U.S. Stock Ticker: Private
2005 Sales: $1,430,000	2005 Profits: $	Int'l Ticker: Int'l Exchange:
2004 Sales: $1,724,800	2004 Profits: $-29,200	Employees: 1,440
2003 Sales: $1,883,044	2003 Profits: $-161,714	Fiscal Year Ends: 12/31
2002 Sales: $1,654,100	2002 Profits: $-142,200	Parent Company:

SALARIES/BENEFITS:

Pension Plan: Y	ESOP Stock Plan:	Profit Sharing:	Top Exec. Salary: $2,500,000	Bonus: $1,125,000
Savings Plan: Y	Stock Purch. Plan:		Second Exec. Salary: $2,300,000	Bonus: $1,035,000

OTHER THOUGHTS:

Apparent Women Officers or Directors:
Hot Spot for Advancement for Women/Minorities:

LOCATIONS: ("Y" = Yes)

West:	Southwest:	Midwest:	Southeast:	Northeast:	International:
Y				Y	Y

MGM MIRAGE   www.mgmmirage.com

Industry Group Code: 721120 Ranks within this company's industry group: Sales: 2   Profits: 1

Print Media/Publishing:	Movies:	Equipment/Supplies:	Broadcast/Cable:	Music/Audio:	Sports/Games:	
Newspapers:	Movie Theaters:	Equipment/Supplies:	Broadcast TV:	Music Production:	Games/Sports:	
Magazines:	Movie Production:	Gambling Equipment:	Cable TV:	Retail Music:	Retail Games Stores:	
Books:	TV/Video Production:	Special Services:	Satellite Broadcast:	Retail Audio Equip.:	Stadiums/Teams:	Y
Book Stores:	Video Rental:	Advertising Services:	Radio:	Music Print./Dist.:	Gambling/Casinos:	
Distribution/Printing:	Video Distribution:	Info. Sys. Software:	Online Information:	Multimedia:	Rides/Theme Parks:	

TYPES OF BUSINESS:
Casino Hotels & Resorts

BRANDS/DIVISIONS/AFFILIATES:
Bellagio
MGM Grand Las Vegas
Mandalay Bay
Mirage (The)
Luxor
Whiskey Pete's
MGM Grand Macau
Mandalay Resort Group

CONTACTS: Note: Officers with more than one job title may be intentionally listed here more than once.
J. Terrence Lanni, CEO
James J. Murren, Pres.
James J. Murren, CFO
Glenn D. Bonner, CIO/Sr. VP
Gary N. Jacobs, General Counsel/Exec. VP
James J. Murren, Treas.
John T. Redmond, CEO/Pres., MGM Grand Resorts, LLC
Robert H. Baldwin, CEO/Pres., Mirage Resorts, Inc.
Gary N. Jacobs, Corp. Sec.
J. Terrence Lanni, Chmn.
Mark Stolarczyk, Asst. VP-Corp. Purchasing

Phone: 702-693-7120	Fax: 702-693-8626
Toll-Free:	
Address: 3600 Las Vegas Blvd. S., Las Vegas, NV 89109 US	

GROWTH PLANS/SPECIAL FEATURES:

MGM Mirage, one of the world's leading hotel and gaming companies, owns and operates 26 casino resorts located in Nevada, Mississippi, Michigan and Australia, with investments in three other casino resorts in Nevada, New Jersey and Illinois. Its Las Vegas strip brands are the Bellagio, MGM Grand Las Vegas, Mandalay Bay, The Mirage, Luxor, Treasure Island, New York-New York, Excalibur, Monte Carlo and Circus Circus Las Vegas. Its other properties in Nevada include Whiskey Pete's, Buffalo Bill's, Primm Valley Resort and two championship golf courses at the California/Nevada state line; as well as two sites each in Reno, Laughlin and Jean. Its other major casinos are the MGM Grand Detroit, the Beau Rivage in Biloxi, Mississippi, the Gold Strike in Tunica, Mississippi and 50% owned locations in Atlantic City, New Jersey and Elgin Illinois. Since divesting a property in Darwin, Australia, the firm has been hoping to expand its operations abroad. It currently owns a 50% interest in MGM Grand Paradise, Ltd., a company devoted solely to develop and operate the MGM Grand Macau, a 600-room luxury hotel and casino to be located on the waterfront of the former Portuguese colony, which is currently protected by the Chinese government. It is also investigating possible expansions into the U.K. and Singapore. Almost half of the company's current revenues are derived from properties gained through the monumental $7.9 billion acquisition of Mandalay Resort Group in mid-2005. MGM Mirage is also developing Project CityCenter in Las Vegas, a $7 billion mixed-use environment to feature a 4,000-room casino hotel, two 400-room non-casino hotels, 470,000 square feet of retail, restaurant and entertainment space and 2.3 million square feet slated for residential use.

Employee benefits at MGM include employee assistance programs, tuition reimbursement, flexible spending accounts and an on-site child development program.

FINANCIALS: Sales and profits are in thousands of dollars—add 000 to get the full amount. 2006 Note: Financial information for 2006 was not available for all companies at press time.

2006 Sales: $	2006 Profits: $	U.S. Stock Ticker: MGM
2005 Sales: $6,481,967	2005 Profits: $443,256	Int'l Ticker: Int'l Exchange:
2004 Sales: $4,238,104	2004 Profits: $412,332	Employees: 66,500
2003 Sales: $3,908,800	2003 Profits: $243,700	Fiscal Year Ends: 12/31
2002 Sales: $4,031,300	2002 Profits: $292,500	Parent Company:

SALARIES/BENEFITS:

Pension Plan:	ESOP Stock Plan:	Profit Sharing:	Top Exec. Salary: $2,000,000	Bonus: $3,393,533
Savings Plan: Y	Stock Purch. Plan:		Second Exec. Salary: $1,500,000	Bonus: $2,542,327

OTHER THOUGHTS:
Apparent Women Officers or Directors: 1
Hot Spot for Advancement for Women/Minorities:

LOCATIONS: ("Y" = Yes)

West:	Southwest:	Midwest:	Southeast:	Northeast:	International:
Y		Y	Y	Y	Y

Note: Financial information, benefits and other data can change quickly and may vary from those stated here.

MGM PICTURES

www.mgm.com

Industry Group Code: 512110 Ranks within this company's industry group: Sales: Profits:

Print Media/Publishing:	Movies:		Equipment/Supplies:	Broadcast/Cable:	Music/Audio:	Sports/Games:
Newspapers:	Movie Theaters:		Equipment/Supplies:	Broadcast TV:	Music Production:	Games/Sports:
Magazines:	Movie Production:	Y	Gambling Equipment:	Cable TV:	Retail Music:	Retail Games Stores:
Books:	TV/Video Production:	Y	Special Services:	Satellite Broadcast:	Retail Audio Equip.:	Stadiums/Teams:
Book Stores:	Video Rental:		Advertising Services:	Radio:	Music Print./Dist.:	Gambling/Casinos:
Distribution/Printing:	Video Distribution:		Info. Sys. Software:	Online Information:	Multimedia:	Rides/Theme Parks:

TYPES OF BUSINESS:

Movie Production
Movie Distribution
Television Programming

BRANDS/DIVISIONS/AFFILIATES:

Metro-Goldwyn-Mayer
Sony Corporation of America
Comcast Corporation
Providence Equity Partners
Texas Pacific Group
Quadrangle Group
Stargate SG-1
Barbershop: The Series

CONTACTS: *Note: Officers with more than one job title may be intentionally listed here more than once.*

Peter Adee, Pres., Worldwide Mktg.
Toby Jaffe, Pres., Production
Harry E. Sloan, Chmn./CEO-Metro-Goldwyn-Mayer, Inc.

Phone: 310-449-3000	Fax: 310-449-8750
Toll-Free:	
Address: 10250 Constellation Blvd., Los Angeles, CA 90067 US	

GROWTH PLANS/SPECIAL FEATURES:

MGM Pictures, one of the many operating units of Metro-Goldwyn-Mayer (MGM), produces and distributes movies in a wide range of genres. Parent company MGM also operates subsidiaries including MGM Television Entertainment, MGM Networks, MGM Distribution Co., MGM Worldwide Television Distribution and MGM Home Entertainment. The company has a prodigious film library, which includes about 4,000 titles as well as 10,400 television episodes. It also produces Stargate SG-1, a leading science fiction television show, as well as the spin-off Stargate Atlantis and the shows Barbershop: The Series and The Outer Limits. It first gained recognition for musicals such as Fiddler on the Roof and West Side Story. Recent film projects include Home of the Brave, Rocky Balboa, James Bond: Casino Royale and National Lampoon's Van Wilder: The Rise of Taj. In 2005, MGM was acquired by a consortium composed of Sony Corporation of America, Comcast Corporation, Providence Equity Partners, Texas Pacific Group, DLJ Merchant Banking Partners and Quadrangle Group. Sony Pictures Entertainment will assume certain distribution responsibilities for the firm's film library, and the two companies expect to co-finance and co-produce certain pictures. In November 2005, MGM announced its support of the new high definition Blu-ray Disc DVD format. It released its first Blu-ray title, Flyboys, in January 2007.

The company offers employee benefits including dependent care plans, flexible spending accounts, domestic partner insurance, employee assistance, educational assistance, a 401(k) plan and stock options. Perks include employee screenings, health club memberships, discounts on theme park tickets and on-site amenities. MGM also offers paid and unpaid internships to students.

FINANCIALS: Sales and profits are in thousands of dollars—add 000 to get the full amount. 2006 Note: Financial information for 2006 was not available for all companies at press time.

2006 Sales: $	2006 Profits: $	U.S. Stock Ticker: Subsidiary
2005 Sales: $	2005 Profits: $	Int'l Ticker: Int'l Exchange:
2004 Sales: $	2004 Profits: $	Employees:
2003 Sales: $	2003 Profits: $	Fiscal Year Ends: 12/31
2002 Sales: $	2002 Profits: $	Parent Company: METRO-GOLDWYN-MAYER INC (MGM)

SALARIES/BENEFITS:

Pension Plan:	ESOP Stock Plan:	Profit Sharing:	Top Exec. Salary: $	Bonus: $
Savings Plan: Y	Stock Purch. Plan:		Second Exec. Salary: $	Bonus: $

OTHER THOUGHTS:

Apparent Women Officers or Directors:
Hot Spot for Advancement for Women/Minorities:

LOCATIONS: ("Y" = Yes)

West:	Southwest:	Midwest:	Southeast:	Northeast:	International:
Y					

MICROSOFT CORP

www.microsoft.com

Industry Group Code: 511204 Ranks within this company's industry group: Sales: 1 Profits: 1

Print Media/Publishing:	Movies:	Equipment/Supplies:	Broadcast/Cable:	Music/Audio:	Sports/Games:
Newspapers:	Movie Theaters:	Equipment/Supplies: Y	Broadcast TV:	Music Production:	Games/Sports: Y
Magazines:	Movie Production:	Gambling Equipment:	Cable TV: Y	Retail Music:	Retail Games Stores:
Books: Y	TV/Video Production:	Special Services: Y	Satellite Broadcast:	Retail Audio Equip.:	Stadiums/Teams:
Book Stores:	Video Rental:	Advertising Services:	Radio:	Music Print./Dist.: Y	Gambling/Casinos:
Distribution/Printing:	Video Distribution:	Info. Sys. Software: Y	Online Information:	Multimedia:	Rides/Theme Parks:

TYPES OF BUSINESS:

Computer Software-Diversified
Internet Access Provider
Online Media Portal
Book Publishing
Entertainment & Cable TV Interests
Computer Peripherals
Personal Game Players
Venture Capital

BRANDS/DIVISIONS/AFFILIATES:

Windows
Microsoft Office 12
Vista
Passport.net
Xbox 360
Zune
MSN
Hotmail

CONTACTS: *Note: Officers with more than one job title may be intentionally listed here more than once.*

Steve Ballmer, CEO
B. Kevin Turner, COO
Christopher Liddell, CFO
Joanne K. Bradford, Corp. VP-Global Sales & Mktg.
Lisa Brummel, Sr. VP-Human Resources
Daniel T. Ling, Corp. VP-Research
Stuart L. Scott, CIO/Corp. VP
Jonathan Murray, CTO/VP
Craig J. Mundie, Chief Research & Strategy Officer
Brad Smith, General Counsel/Sr. VP
Jan Muehlfeit, VP-Corp. & Gov. Strategy
Steve Berkowitz, Sr. VP-Online Services Group
, Corp. VP-Finance
Eric Boustouller, Gen. Mgr.-Microsoft France
Gerri Elliott, Corp. VP-Worldwide Public Sector
Robert J. Bach, Pres., Entertainment & Devices Div.
Olga Dergunova, Chairwoman-Microsoft Russia & CIS
William Gates, III, Chmn.
Jean-Philippe Courtois, Pres., Microsoft Int'l

Phone: 425-882-8080	**Fax:** 425-936-7329
Toll-Free: 800-642-7676	
Address: One Microsoft Way, Redmond, WA 98052-6399 US	

GROWTH PLANS/SPECIAL FEATURES:

Microsoft Corp., the world's largest software firm, develops, manufactures and supports software for businesses, government and consumers. The company offers online services; input devices; operating systems; server applications; business and consumer productivity applications; software development tools; and Internet and intranet software and technologies, including .NET for web services. The firm has three core divisions: Platform Products and Services; Business Solutions; and Entertainment and Devices. The Platform and Products division contains Windows Client, Server and Tools, and MSN, and is responsible for the Windows products line. The Servers and Tools segment develops and markets Windows Server System operating systems. MSN manages the company's online entertainment and instant messaging services. The Business Solutions division contains Information Worker and develops and delivers information software for customer relationship and supply chain management. The Microsoft Entertainment and Devices division combines the Home and Entertainment Division with the current Mobile and Embedded Devices Division to manage the development and marketing of products that extend the Windows platform to a variety of devices (mobile phones and personal digital assistants). The Home Entertainment segment includes the Xbox video game system, online games, software and TV platforms. In 2006, the firm partnered with DIRECTV to explore digital music, television and movies in portable devices. Recently, the firm introduced Windows Live and Office Live, which provide small businesses with Microsoft hosted Internet-based business services. Microsoft also recently unveiled the following new products: Windows Live Search, Windows Live Academic Search, Live SafetyCenter, Windows Live OneCare, Windows Live Mail, Windows Live Messenger and Xbox Live. The firm also created Live Labs, an applied research program that targets Internet products and services. In late 2006, Microsoft announced the 2007 version of its Office suite (Windows Vista).

Microsoft employees receive relocation expenses, health club membership, tuition reimbursement, a 24-hour health hotline and adoption assistance.

FINANCIALS: Sales and profits are in thousands of dollars—add 000 to get the full amount. 2006 Note: Financial information for 2006 was not available for all companies at press time.

2006 Sales: $44,282,000	2006 Profits: $12,599,000	**U.S. Stock Ticker: MSFT**
2005 Sales: $39,788,000	2005 Profits: $12,254,000	**Int'l Ticker:** Int'l Exchange:
2004 Sales: $36,835,000	2004 Profits: $8,168,000	Employees: 71,000
2003 Sales: $32,187,000	2003 Profits: $9,993,000	Fiscal Year Ends: 6/30
2002 Sales: $28,365,000	2002 Profits: $7,829,000	Parent Company:

SALARIES/BENEFITS:

Pension Plan:	ESOP Stock Plan:	Profit Sharing:	Top Exec. Salary: $616,667	Bonus: $350,000
Savings Plan: Y	Stock Purch. Plan: Y		Second Exec. Salary: $616,667	Bonus: $350,000

OTHER THOUGHTS:

Apparent Women Officers or Directors: 14
Hot Spot for Advancement for Women/Minorities: Y

LOCATIONS: ("Y" = Yes)

West:	Southwest:	Midwest:	Southeast:	Northeast:	International:
Y	Y	Y	Y	Y	Y

Note: Financial information, benefits and other data can change quickly and may vary from those stated here.

MIDWAY GAMES INC

www.midway.com

Industry Group Code: 511208 Ranks within this company's industry group: Sales: 8   Profits: 9

Print Media/Publishing:	Movies:	Equipment/Supplies:	Broadcast/Cable:	Music/Audio:	Sports/Games:	
Newspapers:	Movie Theaters:	Equipment/Supplies:	Broadcast TV:	Music Production:	Games/Sports:	Y
Magazines:	Movie Production:	Gambling Equipment:	Cable TV:	Retail Music:	Retail Games Stores:	
Books:	TV/Video Production:	Special Services:	Satellite Broadcast:	Retail Audio Equip.:	Stadiums/Teams:	
Book Stores:	Video Rental:	Advertising Services:	Radio:	Music Print./Dist.:	Gambling/Casinos:	
Distribution/Printing:	Video Distribution:	Info. Sys. Software:	Online Information:	Multimedia:	Rides/Theme Parks:	

TYPES OF BUSINESS:
Computer Software, Games & Entertainment

BRANDS/DIVISIONS/AFFILIATES:
Pong
Spy Hunter
Blitz
Mortal Kombat
Surreal Software, Inc.
Inevitable Entertainment, Inc.
Midway Games GmbH
Happy Feet

CONTACTS: Note: Officers with more than one job title may be intentionally listed here more than once.
David F. Zucker, CEO
David F. Zucker, Pres.
Thomas E. Powell, CFO
Steven M. Allison, Chief Mktg. Officer
Deborah K. Fulton, General Counsel/Sr. VP
Thomas E. Powell, Exec. VP-Finance/Treas.
Matthew V. Booty, Sr. VP-Worldwide Studios
Miguel Iribarren, VP-Publishing
James Boyle, VP-Finance/Controller,/Assistant Treas.
Kenneth D. Cron, Chmn.

Phone: 773-961-2222	Fax: 773-961-1099
Toll-Free:	
Address: 2704 W. Roscoe St., Chicago, IL 60618 US	

GROWTH PLANS/SPECIAL FEATURES:
Midway Games, Inc. is a leading developer and producer of gaming software for all major videogame systems, including Playstation 3 from Sony; Xbox 360 from Microsoft; Nintendo's Wii and Game Boy Advance systems; and personal computers. To date, the company has published over 400 titles. The firm's early games in the 1980s included Pong, Asteroids, Gauntlet, Defender, and Spy Hunter, while its current offerings include Blitz, Rampage, Happy Feet, The Grim Adventures of Billy & Mandy, The Ant Bully, Unreal Anthology, and the Mortal Kombat series. Mortal Kombat has been the company's most successful game, selling in excess of 20 million copies across seven different consoles as well as being licensed into other areas, such as film and television. The largest purchasers of Midway games are retailers Wal-Mart and Gamestop. Midway Games GmbH in Germany and Midway Games SAS in France are responsible for the company's German and French sales, marketing and distribution operations. Sumner Redstone, Chairman and majority shareholder of Viacom, Inc., owns 88% of Midway. In recent years, the firm has acquired five privately-held software developers: Surreal Software, Inc., Inevitable Entertainment Inc., CWS Entertainment Ltd. (d/b/a Paradox Development), Ratbag Holdings Pty Ltd. and its subsidiary companies, and The Pitbull Syndicate Ltd. Ratbag was subsequently closed due to operating and cost inefficiencies.

FINANCIALS: Sales and profits are in thousands of dollars—add 000 to get the full amount. 2006 Note: Financial information for 2006 was not available for all companies at press time.
2006 Sales: $	2006 Profits: $	U.S. Stock Ticker: MWY
2005 Sales: $150,078	2005 Profits: $-112,487	Int'l Ticker: Int'l Exchange:
2004 Sales: $161,600	2004 Profits: $-19,945	Employees: 820
2003 Sales: $92,524	2003 Profits: $-115,227	Fiscal Year Ends: 12/31
2002 Sales: $191,857	2002 Profits: $-53,823	Parent Company:

SALARIES/BENEFITS:
Pension Plan:	ESOP Stock Plan:	Profit Sharing:	Top Exec. Salary: $600,000	Bonus: $
Savings Plan:	Stock Purch. Plan:		Second Exec. Salary: $337,423	Bonus: $

OTHER THOUGHTS:
Apparent Women Officers or Directors: 2
Hot Spot for Advancement for Women/Minorities:

LOCATIONS: ("Y" = Yes)
West:	Southwest:	Midwest:	Southeast:	Northeast:	International:
Y	Y	Y			Y

Note: Financial information, benefits and other data can change quickly and may vary from those stated here.

MIRAMAX FILM CORP
www.miramax.com

Industry Group Code: 512110 Ranks within this company's industry group: Sales: Profits:

Print Media/Publishing:	Movies:		Equipment/Supplies:	Broadcast/Cable:	Music/Audio:	Sports/Games:
Newspapers:	Movie Theaters:		Equipment/Supplies:	Broadcast TV:	Music Production:	Games/Sports:
Magazines:	Movie Production:	Y	Gambling Equipment:	Cable TV:	Retail Music:	Retail Games Stores:
Books:	TV/Video Production:		Special Services:	Satellite Broadcast:	Retail Audio Equip.:	Stadiums/Teams:
Book Stores:	Video Rental:		Advertising Services:	Radio:	Music Print./Dist.:	Gambling/Casinos:
Distribution/Printing:	Video Distribution:		Info. Sys. Software:	Online Information:	Multimedia:	Rides/Theme Parks:

TYPES OF BUSINESS:
Movie Production & Distribution
Online Merchandise Retail

BRANDS/DIVISIONS/AFFILIATES:
Walt Disney Studio Entertainment
Dimension Films
Buena Vista Home Entertainment

CONTACTS: Note: Officers with more than one job title may be intentionally listed here more than once.
Daniel Battsek, Pres.
Kristin Jones, Sr. VP-Production & Acquisitions
Kristin Jones, Sr. VP-Int'l Dev.

Phone: 917-606-5500	Fax: 917-606-5535

Toll-Free:
Address: 161 Avenue of the Americas, New York, NY 10013 US

GROWTH PLANS/SPECIAL FEATURES:
Miramax Film Corp., a business segment of Walt Disney Studio Entertainment, is a producer and distributor of acclaimed and award-winning movies such as The Aviator, Gangs of New York, The Hours, Shakespeare In Love, The English Patient and Frida. Founded in 1979 by brothers Bob and Harvey Weinstein, the firm was originally known for producing small, quirky art-house pictures, but it has recently developed bigger-budget movies, such as Chicago. Miramax's Dimension Films division found success in the teen horror genre with the Scary Movie and Scream titles. It also produced the Spy Kids series. Miramax sells movie-related merchandise via its web site. Disney Studios purchased the company for $75 million in 1993. The Weinsteins recently left the company to start a new film production company called The Weinstein Company. Films under the Miramax name will continue to be released through Disney's Buena Vista Home Entertainment division. Miramax hits include Pulp Fiction, Good Will Hunting, Kill Bill 1 and 2, Garden State, Cold Mountain and Sin City.

FINANCIALS: Sales and profits are in thousands of dollars—add 000 to get the full amount. 2006 Note: Financial information for 2006 was not available for all companies at press time.
2006 Sales: $ 2006 Profits: $
2005 Sales: $ 2005 Profits: $
2004 Sales: $ 2004 Profits: $
2003 Sales: $ 2003 Profits: $
2002 Sales: $ 2002 Profits: $

U.S. Stock Ticker: Subsidiary
Int'l Ticker: Int'l Exchange:
Employees:
Fiscal Year Ends: 9/30
Parent Company: WALT DISNEY COMPANY (THE)

SALARIES/BENEFITS:
Pension Plan: ESOP Stock Plan: Profit Sharing: Top Exec. Salary: $ Bonus: $
Savings Plan: Stock Purch. Plan: Second Exec. Salary: $ Bonus: $

OTHER THOUGHTS:
Apparent Women Officers or Directors: 1
Hot Spot for Advancement for Women/Minorities:

LOCATIONS: ("Y" = Yes)
West:	Southwest:	Midwest:	Southeast:	Northeast:	International:
				Y	

Note: Financial information, benefits and other data can change quickly and may vary from those stated here.

MOBITV INC

www.mobitv.com

Industry Group Code: 513120A Ranks within this company's industry group: Sales:　Profits:

Print Media/Publishing:	Movies:	Equipment/Supplies:		Broadcast/Cable:		Music/Audio:	Sports/Games:
Newspapers:	Movie Theaters:	Equipment/Supplies:		Broadcast TV:	Y	Music Production:	Games/Sports:
Magazines:	Movie Production:	Gambling Equipment:		Cable TV:		Retail Music:	Retail Games Stores:
Books:	TV/Video Production:	Special Services:	Y	Satellite Broadcast:		Retail Audio Equip.:	Stadiums/Teams:
Book Stores:	Video Rental:	Advertising Services:		Radio:		Music Print./Dist.:	Gambling/Casinos:
Distribution/Printing:	Video Distribution:	Info. Sys. Software:		Online Information:		Multimedia:	Rides/Theme Parks:

TYPES OF BUSINESS:

Mobile Phone Media Service
Cellular Telephone Television Network
Cellular Telephone Radio Network
Cellular Telephone Sports Broadcasting

BRANDS/DIVISIONS/AFFILIATES:

MobiTV
MobiRadio
MobiMLB Gameday Audio
Idetic, Inc.

CONTACTS: Note: Officers with more than one job title may be intentionally listed here more than once.

Phillip Alvelda, CEO
Paul Scanlan, COO
Bruce Gilpin, Interim CFO
Kevin Grant, VP-Sales
Ana Recio, VP-Human Resources
Kay Johansson, Chief Tech. Officer
Domingo Mihovilovic, VP-Eng.
Andy Missan, General Counsel/VP
Bruce Gilpin, Chief Strategy Officer
Jeff Bartee, VP-Finance
Phillip Alvelda, Chmn.

Phone: 510-450-5000	**Fax:** 510-981-5001
Toll-Free:	
Address: 6425 Christie Ave, 5th Fl., Emeryville, CA 94608 US	

GROWTH PLANS/SPECIAL FEATURES:

MobiTV, Inc., formerly Idetic, Inc., is a private company that markets its mobile television and radio services to the world's mobile phone users. Launched in late 2003, MobiTV delivers live television feeds in real time over existing cellular networks, requiring no additional equipment. The subscription service is available to Sprint, Cingular, Midwest Wireless and Alltel customers and is one of the fastest-selling mobile services on the market. Users in Canada receive services from Bell Canada, Rogers and Tellus Mobility, and U.K. viewers receive them from carriers Orange UK and 3. At this time, MobiTV is also available in Brazil, Puerto Rico, the Dominican Republic, Peru and Ecuador. In addition to cell phones, the service is available to handheld Treo or Palm devices. MobiTV viewers can expect to receive MSNBC, ABC News Now, CNN, Fox News, Fox Sports, ESPN 3GTV, MLB, NBC Mobile, CNBC, CSPAN, the Discovery Channel, TLC, the Weather Channel, and a large variety of networks offering music, comedy, cartoon and regional interest programming. Cingular customers can also receive MobiRadio, which offers over 40 stations of commercial-free, digital streaming radio. In addition, the Mobi-MLB GameDay Audio service broadcasts every Major League Baseball game. In late 2005, MobiTV was awarded an Emmy for outstanding achievement in engineering development for the television industry.

The firm offers its employees competitive salaries and stock options.

FINANCIALS: Sales and profits are in thousands of dollars—add 000 to get the full amount. 2006 Note: Financial information for 2006 was not available for all companies at press time.

2006 Sales: $	2006 Profits: $	**U.S. Stock Ticker:** Private	
2005 Sales: $	2005 Profits: $	**Int'l Ticker:**　Int'l Exchange:	
2004 Sales: $	2004 Profits: $	Employees:	
2003 Sales: $	2003 Profits: $	Fiscal Year Ends:	
2002 Sales: $	2002 Profits: $	Parent Company:	

SALARIES/BENEFITS:

Pension Plan:	ESOP Stock Plan:	Profit Sharing:	Top Exec. Salary: $	Bonus: $
Savings Plan:	Stock Purch. Plan:		Second Exec. Salary: $	Bonus: $

OTHER THOUGHTS:

Apparent Women Officers or Directors: 2
Hot Spot for Advancement for Women/Minorities:

LOCATIONS: ("Y" = Yes)

West:	Southwest:	Midwest:	Southeast:	Northeast:	International:
Y				Y	Y

MODERN TIMES GROUP MTG AB

www.mtg.se

Industry Group Code: 513120 Ranks within this company's industry group: Sales: 10   Profits: 7

Print Media/Publishing:		Movies:		Equipment/Supplies:		Broadcast/Cable:		Music/Audio:		Sports/Games:	
Newspapers:		Movie Theaters:		Equipment/Supplies:		Broadcast TV:	Y	Music Production:		Games/Sports:	Y
Magazines:	Y	Movie Production:	Y	Gambling Equipment:		Cable TV:	Y	Retail Music:		Retail Games Stores:	
Books:		TV/Video Production:	Y	Special Services:		Satellite Broadcast:		Retail Audio Equip.:		Stadiums/Teams:	
Book Stores:		Video Rental:		Advertising Services:		Radio:		Music Print./Dist.:		Gambling/Casinos:	Y
Distribution/Printing:		Video Distribution:		Info. Sys. Software:		Online Information:		Multimedia:		Rides/Theme Parks:	

TYPES OF BUSINESS:

Television Broadcasting & Cable
Radio Broadcasting
Television & Film Production
Internet Businesses
Home Shopping Network
Gambling Operations
Magazine Publishing
Video Games

BRANDS/DIVISIONS/AFFILIATES:

Viasat Broadcasting
Modern Studios
TV Shop24/7
RIX FM
BET24.com
Engine
Strix
Redaktorerna

CONTACTS: Note: Officers with more than one job title may be intentionally listed here more than once.

Hans-Holger Albrecht, CEO
Andrew Barron, COO
Hans-Holger Albrecht, Pres.
Mathias Hermansson, CFO
Hasse Breitholtz, Exec. VP-MTG/Managing Dir.-Modern Studios
Anders Nilsson, Manging Dir.-Free-to-Air & Pay-TV & Radio, Sweden
Hein E. Hattestad, Managing Dir.-Free-to-Air & Pay-TV & Radio, Norway
Elvind Schackt, Managing Dir.-Home Shopping
David Chance, Chmn.

Phone: 46-8-562-000-50	Fax: 46-8-205-074
Toll-Free:	
Address: Skeppsbron 18, Box 2094, Stockholm, SE-103 13 Sweden	

GROWTH PLANS/SPECIAL FEATURES:

Modern Times Group MTG AB is a major player in European television, radio and media services. The company is organized into four divisions: Viasat Broadcasting (earning 77% of revenue), MTG radio (earning 3% of revenue), Modern Studios (earning 8% of revenue) and Home Shopping (earning 12% of revenue). Viasat Broadcasting, reaching over 86 million people in 21 countries in the Nordic region and Central and Eastern Europe, is arranged into Free-TV and Pay-TV. Free-TV consists of TV3, ZTV, TV8, TV3+, 3+, Tango TV, DTV, TV Prima and Viasat 3, reaching viewers in Sweden, Norway, Denmark, Finland, Estonia, the Czech Republic, Russia, Latvia and Lithuania. The pay-TV division owns channels that are sold in Gold and Silver packages to viewers in Sweden, Norway, Denmark, Finland, Latvia and various Eastern European countries. In addition, the company distributes about 30 third-party channels, including Viasat Sport 2, Viasat Sport 3, Viasat Sport 24, TV1000 Action, TV1000 Classic, TV1000 Nordic, TV1000 Family, Viasat History, Viasat Explorer, Toon Disney, Cartoon Network and E!Entertainment Television. MTG Radio's flagship station brand, RIX FM operates 36 of the 86 commercial stations in Sweden, including Star FM, Power Hit FM, Lugna Favoriter, NRJ, Svenska Favoriter and Bandit. Modern Studio produces television programming, videos, movies, electronic games and magazines in 72 countries, through its seven subsidiaries: Strix (TV production house), Sonet Film (film distributor), Engine (music and video), Modern TV, Brombergs Bokforlag, Redaktorema and Zoommobile. The company's Home Shopping business operates a home shopping network (CDON.com), which features TV Shop24/7 and PIN 24 and operates in more than 50 countries. MTG also owns 90% of BET24.com, a betting and gaming company. In 2006, the firm acquired rights to 40 European Tour Golf Tournaments and will launch new pay-TV station Viacast Golf.

FINANCIALS: Sales and profits are in thousands of dollars—add 000 to get the full amount. 2006 Note: Financial information for 2006 was not available for all companies at press time.

2006 Sales: $	2006 Profits: $	U.S. Stock Ticker: MTZZZ
2005 Sales: $1,036,941	2005 Profits: $160,099	Int'l Ticker: MTG B Int'l Exchange: Stockholm-SSE
2004 Sales: $880,727	2004 Profits: $87,627	Employees: 1,554
2003 Sales: $870,900	2003 Profits: $39,900	Fiscal Year Ends: 12/31
2002 Sales: $694,500	2002 Profits: $-7,700	Parent Company:

SALARIES/BENEFITS:

Pension Plan: Y	ESOP Stock Plan:	Profit Sharing:	Top Exec. Salary: $	Bonus: $
Savings Plan:	Stock Purch. Plan:		Second Exec. Salary: $	Bonus: $

OTHER THOUGHTS:

Apparent Women Officers or Directors:
Hot Spot for Advancement for Women/Minorities:

LOCATIONS: ("Y" = Yes)

West:	Southwest:	Midwest:	Southeast:	Northeast:	International: Y

Note: Financial information, benefits and other data can change quickly and may vary from those stated here.

MONARCH CASINO & RESORT INC www.monarchcasino.com

Industry Group Code: 721120 Ranks within this company's industry group: Sales: 14 Profits: 10

Print Media/Publishing:	Movies:	Equipment/Supplies:	Broadcast/Cable:	Music/Audio:	Sports/Games:	
Newspapers:	Movie Theaters:	Equipment/Supplies:	Broadcast TV:	Music Production:	Games/Sports:	
Magazines:	Movie Production:	Gambling Equipment:	Cable TV:	Retail Music:	Retail Games Stores:	
Books:	TV/Video Production:	Special Services:	Satellite Broadcast:	Retail Audio Equip.:	Stadiums/Teams:	
Book Stores:	Video Rental:	Advertising Services:	Radio:	Music Print./Dist.:	Gambling/Casinos:	Y
Distribution/Printing:	Video Distribution:	Info. Sys. Software:	Online Information:	Multimedia:	Rides/Theme Parks:	

TYPES OF BUSINESS:

Casino
Hotel
Restaurants
Sports & Race Wagering

BRANDS/DIVISIONS/AFFILIATES:

Atlantis Casino Resort
Golden Road Motor Inn, Inc.

CONTACTS: Note: Officers with more than one job title may be intentionally listed here more than once.

John Farahi, CEO
Bob Farahi, Pres.
Ron Rowan, CFO
Debra Robinson, General Counsel
Darlyne Sullivan, Exec. VP-Oper.
Bob Farahi, Interim Treas.
Bob Farahi, Co-Chmn.
Darlyne Sullivan, Gen Mgr.-Golden Road
Richard Cooley, VP-Finance, Golden Road
John Farahi, Co-Chmn.

Phone: 775-335-4600	Fax: 775-332-9171
Toll-Free: 800-723-6500	
Address: 3800 South Virginia St., Reno, NV 89502 US	

GROWTH PLANS/SPECIAL FEATURES:

Monarch Casino & Resort, Inc., through its wholly-owned subsidiary, Golden Road Motor Inn, Inc., owns and operates the Atlantis Casino Resort, a hotel/casino facility in Reno, Nevada. The Atlantis, sporting a tropical-themed atmosphere, is located in the generally more affluent southern area of Reno and features three high-rise hotel towers with an adjoining low-rise structure containing a two-story motor lodge, additional casino and public space, a sky terrace and an enclosed overhead skywalk that leads to a mostly undeveloped 16-acre plot of land. The complex has a total of 975 guest rooms. The property has over 51,000 square feet of casino space interspersed with waterfalls, giant artificial palm trees, thatched roof huts, nine food outlets, a nightclub, enclosed and outdoor pools, a health club and two retail outlets. The facility's food outlets include seafood, barbeque, Italian, sushi, pizza, a snack bar and a coffee shop, which together have over 1,370 seats. The casino features roughly 40 table games, including blackjack, craps and roulette; 1,450 slot and video poker machines; a race and sports book; keno; and a poker room. The majority of the casino's revenue comes from slot and video poker machines. Atlantis is the only hotel/casino within easy walking distance to the 570,000-square-foot Reno Sparks Convention Center, which recently underwent a $105-million renovation. Marketing is directed toward potential casino customers in three consumer groups: Reno-area residents, conventioneers and leisure travel visitors to the Reno area. In May 2006, Monarch announced plans to expand the Atlantis, including the addition of over 20,000-square-feet to the casino floor; enlarging the poker room and race and sports book; remodeling and expanding the spa and fitness center; and adding a pedestrian skywalk connecting the complex directly to the Reno-Sparks Convention Center.

FINANCIALS: Sales and profits are in thousands of dollars—add 000 to get the full amount. 2006 Note: Financial information for 2006 was not available for all companies at press time.

2006 Sales: $	2006 Profits: $	U.S. Stock Ticker: MCRI
2005 Sales: $139,785	2005 Profits: $21,035	Int'l Ticker: Int'l Exchange:
2004 Sales: $129,457	2004 Profits: $16,526	Employees: 1,850
2003 Sales: $115,951	2003 Profits: $9,606	Fiscal Year Ends: 12/31
2002 Sales: $128,413	2002 Profits: $8,603	Parent Company:

SALARIES/BENEFITS:

Pension Plan:	ESOP Stock Plan:	Profit Sharing:	Top Exec. Salary: $400,000	Bonus: $200,000
Savings Plan: Y	Stock Purch. Plan:		Second Exec. Salary: $240,000	Bonus: $50,000

OTHER THOUGHTS:

Apparent Women Officers or Directors: 1
Hot Spot for Advancement for Women/Minorities:

LOCATIONS: ("Y" = Yes)

West:	Southwest:	Midwest:	Southeast:	Northeast:	International:
Y					

MONSTER WORLDWIDE

www.monsterworldwide.com

Industry Group Code: 514199C Ranks within this company's industry group: Sales: 1 Profits: 1

Print Media/Publishing:	Movies:	Equipment/Supplies:		Broadcast/Cable:	Music/Audio:	Sports/Games:
Newspapers:	Movie Theaters:	Equipment/Supplies:		Broadcast TV:	Music Production:	Games/Sports:
Magazines:	Movie Production:	Gambling Equipment:		Cable TV:	Retail Music:	Retail Games Stores:
Books:	TV/Video Production:	Special Services:	Y	Satellite Broadcast:	Retail Audio Equip.:	Stadiums/Teams:
Book Stores:	Video Rental:	Advertising Services:	Y	Radio:	Music Print./Dist.:	Gambling/Casinos:
Distribution/Printing:	Video Distribution:	Info. Sys. Software:		Online Information:	Multimedia:	Rides/Theme Parks:

TYPES OF BUSINESS:

Advertising Services-Human Resources
Online Career Information
Recruitment Services
Online Media

BRANDS/DIVISIONS/AFFILIATES:

Monster
monster.com
Military.com
Tickle
ChinaHR.com Holdings Ltd
JobKorea

CONTACTS: Note: Officers with more than one job title may be intentionally listed here more than once.

William M. Pastore, CEO
William M. Pastore, Pres.
Lanny Baker, CFO/Sr. VP
Paul M. Camara, Exec. VP-Creative, Sales & Mktg.
Brad Baker, Pres., Product, Tech. & Service
Douglas Klinger, Pres., Monster North America
Peter Dolphin, Group Pres., Europe
Mark Stoever, Gen. Mgr.-Internet Advertising & Fees Div.
John McLaughlin, Exec. VP
Sal Iannuzzi, Chmn.
Steve Pogorzelski, Pres., Int'l

Phone: 212-351-7000	Fax: 646-658-0541
Toll-Free:	
Address: 622 3rd Ave., 39th Fl., New York, NY 10017 US	

GROWTH PLANS/SPECIAL FEATURES:

Monster Worldwide, Inc. is the parent company of Monster, a global careers web site; and TMP Worldwide Advertising and Communications, a global leader in recruitment advertising. Monster, formerly promoted as monster.com, is the company's flagship product, offering online recruitment in 24 countries and hosting over 75 million resumes and adding at a rate of approximately 50,000 resumes every day. The Monster network is global in scale, with local content and native language sites in all its countries of operation. TMP Worldwide Advertising and Communications specializes in designing global, national or local recruitment advertising campaigns for top tier Fortune 500 clients and government agencies. TMP operates by placing help wanted ads both in traditional venues such as newspapers, and through web-based recruitment solutions. Monster also owns Military.com, a web site that helps servicemembers, military families and veterans access benefits such as government programs, scholarships and discounts; and Tickle, which runs an entertainment and lifestyle web site. In 2005, Monster acquired all or parts of three foreign companies specializing in online job searching: Emailjob.com, a company based in France; ChinaHR.com Holdings Ltd. and its job search website ChinaHR.com; and JobKorea, with its jobkorea.co.kr web site. The company also won a contract for the management of the Federal Government's online job sites from the U.S. Office of Personnel Management, with four one-year renewal options. In 2006, the company announced the separate sales of the Asia Pacific, North American and European segments of TMP.

The company offers full health, vision and dental insurance, as well as life insurance and long and short term disability.

FINANCIALS: Sales and profits are in thousands of dollars—add 000 to get the full amount. 2006 Note: Financial information for 2006 was not available for all companies at press time.

2006 Sales: $	2006 Profits: $	U.S. Stock Ticker: MNST
2005 Sales: $986,900	2005 Profits: $107,500	Int'l Ticker: Int'l Exchange:
2004 Sales: $845,500	2004 Profits: $73,100	Employees: 4,800
2003 Sales: $679,640	2003 Profits: $-81,864	Fiscal Year Ends: 12/31
2002 Sales: $1,114,622	2002 Profits: $-534,896	Parent Company:

SALARIES/BENEFITS:

Pension Plan:	ESOP Stock Plan:	Profit Sharing:	Top Exec. Salary: $1,000,000	Bonus: $1,800,000
Savings Plan: Y	Stock Purch. Plan:		Second Exec. Salary: $600,000	Bonus: $1,100,000

OTHER THOUGHTS:

Apparent Women Officers or Directors: 1
Hot Spot for Advancement for Women/Minorities:

LOCATIONS: ("Y" = Yes)

West:	Southwest:	Midwest:	Southeast:	Northeast:	International:
Y	Y	Y	Y	Y	Y

Note: Financial information, benefits and other data can change quickly and may vary from those stated here.

MOODY'S CORPORATION

www.moodys.com

Industry Group Code: 561450 Ranks within this company's industry group: Sales: 1   Profits: 1

Print Media/Publishing:	Movies:		Equipment/Supplies:		Broadcast/Cable:	Music/Audio:	Sports/Games:
Newspapers:	Movie Theaters:		Equipment/Supplies:		Broadcast TV:	Music Production:	Games/Sports:
Magazines:	Movie Production:		Gambling Equipment:		Cable TV:	Retail Music:	Retail Games Stores:
Books: Y	TV/Video Production:		Special Services: Y		Satellite Broadcast:	Retail Audio Equip.:	Stadiums/Teams:
Book Stores:	Video Rental:		Advertising Services:		Radio:	Music Print./Dist.:	Gambling/Casinos:
Distribution/Printing:	Video Distribution:		Info. Sys. Software:		Online Information:	Multimedia:	Rides/Theme Parks:

TYPES OF BUSINESS:
Credit Bureau
Risk Management Products
Credit Processing Software
Credit Training Services
Credit Industry Research

BRANDS/DIVISIONS/AFFILIATES:
Moody's Investors Service
Moody's KMV
Moody's Economy.com

CONTACTS: Note: Officers with more than one job title may be intentionally listed here more than once.
Raymond W. McDaniel, CEO
Linda Huber, CFO/Exec. VP
Jennifer Eliot, Chief Human Resources Officer
John J. Goggins, General Counsel/Sr. VP
Joseph J. McCabe, Sr. VP/Corp. Controller
Jane Clark, Corp. Sec.
Jay McCabe, Corp. Controller
Jeanne Derling, Dir.-Global Regulatory Affairs & Compliance
Raymond W. McDaniel, Pres., Moody's Investor Service, Inc.
Raymond W. McDaniel, Chmn.
Chester V. A. Murray, Exec. VP-Int'l

Phone: 212-553-0300	**Fax:** 212-553-7194
Toll-Free:	
Address: 99 Church St., New York, NY 10007 US	

GROWTH PLANS/SPECIAL FEATURES:

Moody's Corporation is a provider of credit ratings, research and analysis covering fixed income securities, other debt instruments and the entities that issue such instruments in the global capital markets; it also offers credit training services and quantitative credit risk assessment products and services and credit processing software for banks, corporations and investors in credit-sensitive assets. The company maintains offices in 22 countries. Moody's operates through its two main subsidiaries: Moody's Investors Service and Moody's KMV. Moody's Investors Service publishes investor-oriented credit research on major debt issuers, industry studies, special comments and credit opinion handbooks. These services, which are available in approximately 100 countries, are designed to increase market efficiency and reduce transaction costs. The Moody's KMV business offers credit risk management products for banks and investors in credit-sensitive assets. Moody's has ratings relationships with more than 11,000 companies and more than 25,000 public finance issuers. Additionally, the company has rated more than 70,000 structured finance obligations. Ratings are disseminated via press releases to the public through a variety of print and electronic media, including the Internet and real-time information systems widely used by securities traders and investors. Beyond credit rating services for issuers, Moody's Investors Service provides research services, data and analytic tools that are utilized by institutional investors and other credit and capital markets professionals. These services cover various segments of the loan and debt capital markets, and are sold to more than 7,300 customer accounts worldwide. Within these accounts, more than 25,000 users accessed Moody's research website during calendar year 2005.

The firm compares its workplace environment to a collegial think-tank, and employs individuals from backgrounds ranging from MBAs, lawyers, CPAs, software engineers, marketing specialists and PhDs. The Moody's Foundation makes donations toward educational and health services programs.

FINANCIALS: Sales and profits are in thousands of dollars—add 000 to get the full amount. 2006 Note: Financial information for 2006 was not available for all companies at press time.

2006 Sales: $	2006 Profits: $	**U.S. Stock Ticker: MCO**
2005 Sales: $1,731,600	2005 Profits: $560,800	**Int'l Ticker:** Int'l Exchange:
2004 Sales: $1,438,300	2004 Profits: $425,100	Employees: 2,900
2003 Sales: $1,246,600	2003 Profits: $363,900	Fiscal Year Ends: 12/31
2002 Sales: $1,023,300	2002 Profits: $288,900	Parent Company:

SALARIES/BENEFITS:

Pension Plan: Y	ESOP Stock Plan:	Profit Sharing:	Top Exec. Salary: $675,000	Bonus: $1,600,000
Savings Plan:	Stock Purch. Plan:		Second Exec. Salary: $462,500	Bonus: $551,941

OTHER THOUGHTS:
Apparent Women Officers or Directors: 4
Hot Spot for Advancement for Women/Minorities: Y

LOCATIONS: ("Y" = Yes)

West:	Southwest:	Midwest:	Southeast:	Northeast:	International:
Y	Y	Y	Y	Y	Y

MORRIS COMMUNICATIONS COMPANY LLC

www.morriscomm.com

Industry Group Code: 511110 Ranks within this company's industry group: Sales: 18   Profits: 14

Print Media/Publishing:		Movies:		Equipment/Supplies:		Broadcast/Cable:		Music/Audio:		Sports/Games:	
Newspapers:	Y	Movie Theaters:		Equipment/Supplies:		Broadcast TV:		Music Production:		Games/Sports:	
Magazines:	Y	Movie Production:		Gambling Equipment:		Cable TV:		Retail Music:		Retail Games Stores:	
Books:	Y	TV/Video Production:		Special Services:		Satellite Broadcast:		Retail Audio Equip.:		Stadiums/Teams:	
Book Stores:		Video Rental:		Advertising Services:	Y	Radio:		Music Print./Dist.:		Gambling/Casinos:	
Distribution/Printing:		Video Distribution:		Info. Sys. Software:	Y	Online Information:		Multimedia:		Rides/Theme Parks:	

TYPES OF BUSINESS:

Newspaper Publishing
Radio Broadcasting
Magazine Publishing
Book Publishing
Outdoor Advertising
Online Publishing
Printing Services

BRANDS/DIVISIONS/AFFILIATES:

Morris Publishing Group, LLC
Florida Times-Union (The)
Broadcaster Press
Fairway Outdoor Advertising
Globe Pequot Press (The)
Morris Desert Radio Group
Cowboy Publishing Group (The)
Morris Digital Works

CONTACTS: Note: Officers with more than one job title may be intentionally listed here more than once.

William S. Morris, III, CEO
William S. Morris, IV, Pres.
Steve K. Stone, CFO/VP
Craig S. Mitchell, Sr. VP-Finance/Treas.
Susie Morris Baker, VP
James C. Currow, Exec. VP-Newspapers
Carl N. Cannon, Exec. VP-Newspapers
J. Tyler Morris, VP-The Cowboy Publishing Group
William S. Morris, III, Chmn.

Phone: 706-724-0851	Fax: 706-722-7125
Toll-Free: 800-622-6358	
Address: 725 Broad St., Augusta, GA 30901 US	

GROWTH PLANS/SPECIAL FEATURES:

Morris Communications Company LLC is one of the most widespread publishing groups in the U.S. With operations in almost 30 states, as well as in the U.K. and Monaco, Morris has a number of publishing activities, from its core newspaper business to magazines, book publishing, online publishing and specialty printing services, with additional business in radio broadcasting and outdoor advertising. Morris Publishing Group, LLC, the company's newspaper subsidiary, includes 27 daily, 12 non-daily and 23 free community newspapers, as well as 17 city magazines in the U.S. The Globe Pequot Press, another company subsidiary, is one of the world's leading publishers and distributors of outdoor recreation and leisure titles, with more than 2,800 travel guides for every continent and books for anglers, equestrians and other outdoor enthusiasts, notably the well-know Falcon Guides. Additionally, the company has two commercial printing operations, which produce the firm's local newspapers and shoppers, as well as business forms, business cards, letterheads, circulars, ad inserts, newsletters and catalogs. Morris's radio broadcasting operations include 34 stations and two networks operating through several radio station groups, most notably the Columbia River Media Group, the Grays Harbor Radio Group, the Morris Desert Media Radio Group and the Anchorage Media Group. Fairway Outdoor Advertising provides outdoor advertising services, including posters and bulletins in North Carolina, South Carolina, Minnesota, Alabama and Georgia. Subsidiary Morris Digital Works develops online publishing platforms and tools such as MDClassifieds and SiteWeaver. The company's recent acquisitions include Network Media, a Hawaii-based publishing and broadcast firm, and the assets of Chattanooga Outdoor Advertising.

FINANCIALS: Sales and profits are in thousands of dollars—add 000 to get the full amount. 2006 Note: Financial information for 2006 was not available for all companies at press time.

2006 Sales: $	2006 Profits: $	U.S. Stock Ticker: Private
2005 Sales: $465,100	2005 Profits: $31,300	Int'l Ticker: Int'l Exchange:
2004 Sales: $455,700	2004 Profits: $30,300	Employees: 6,000
2003 Sales: $533,000	2003 Profits: $	Fiscal Year Ends: 12/31
2002 Sales: $	2002 Profits: $	Parent Company:

SALARIES/BENEFITS:

Pension Plan:	ESOP Stock Plan:	Profit Sharing:	Top Exec. Salary: $	Bonus: $
Savings Plan: Y	Stock Purch. Plan:		Second Exec. Salary: $	Bonus: $

OTHER THOUGHTS:

Apparent Women Officers or Directors: 1
Hot Spot for Advancement for Women/Minorities:

LOCATIONS: ("Y" = Yes)

West:	Southwest:	Midwest:	Southeast:	Northeast:	International:
Y	Y	Y	Y	Y	Y

MOVIE GALLERY INC

www.moviegallery.com

Industry Group Code: 532230 Ranks within this company's industry group: Sales: 2 Profits: 3

Print Media/Publishing:	Movies:		Equipment/Supplies:	Broadcast/Cable:	Music/Audio:	Sports/Games:	
Newspapers:	Movie Theaters:		Equipment/Supplies:	Broadcast TV:	Music Production:	Games/Sports:	
Magazines:	Movie Production:		Gambling Equipment:	Cable TV:	Retail Music:	Retail Games Stores:	Y
Books:	TV/Video Production:	Y	Special Services:	Satellite Broadcast:	Retail Audio Equip.:	Stadiums/Teams:	
Book Stores:	Video Rental:	Y	Advertising Services:	Radio:	Music Print./Dist.:	Gambling/Casinos:	
Distribution/Printing:	Video Distribution:		Info. Sys. Software:	Online Information:	Multimedia:	Rides/Theme Parks:	

TYPES OF BUSINESS:

Video Rental Stores
Online Sales
Video Game Sales
DVD & VHS Sales
Game Stores

BRANDS/DIVISIONS/AFFILIATES:

Movie Gallery US, Inc.
Movie Gallery Canada, Inc.
Hollywood Entertainment Corp.
Game Crazy
VHQ Entertainment
MG Automation LLC
MGTV

CONTACTS: Note: Officers with more than one job title may be intentionally listed here more than once.

Joe T. Malugen, CEO
Jeffrey S. Stubbs, Exec. VP/COO, Movie Gallery
Joe T. Malugen, Pres.
Thomas D. Johnson, Jr., Sr. VP-Finance & Bus. Dev./Interim CFO
S. Page Todd, Corp. Sec./Chief Compliance Officer
S. Page Todd, Exec. VP/General Counsel
Mark S. Loyd, Chief Admin. Officer
Keith A. Cousins, Exec. VP-Dev.
Michelle K. Lewis, Sr. VP-Investor Rel.
Michelle K. Lewis, Treas.
H. Harrison Parrish, Sr. VP/Vice Chmn.
Timothy A. Winner, Exec. VP/COO-Hollywood Entertainment
Joe T. Malugen, Chmn.
Mark S. Loyd, Exec. VP-Product & Dist. Mgmt.

Phone: 334-677-2108	Fax: 334-677-1169
Toll-Free: 800-677-2106	
Address: 900 W. Main St., Dothan, AL 36301 US	

GROWTH PLANS/SPECIAL FEATURES:

Movie Gallery, Inc., headquartered in Dothan, Alabama, owns and operates approximately 4,500 video stores located in 50 states, Canada and Mexico, through its brands Movie Gallery and Hollywood Video. As one of the largest North American home entertainment retailers, the stores rent and sell videocassettes, DVDs and video games. Movie Gallery stores are primarily located in small towns and suburban areas and focus on rural and secondary markets, competing with independently owned stores and small regional chains. Hollywood Video stores are larger and primarily target urban centers and surrounding suburban neighborhoods. Approximately 680 Hollywood Video stores include a Game Crazy store-in-store concept where game enthusiasts can buy, sell and trade new and used video game hardware, software and accessories. Game Crazy, which typically carries 9,000 video game and hardware units, also has 20 stand alone stores. Movie Gallery maintains a flexible store format, tailoring the size, inventory and look of each store to local demographics. Movie Gallery also prepares a customized video program, MGTV, which plays on televisions in the stores. Stores offer 2,700-16,000 movie titles and 200-1,500 video games. The company's web sites hollywoodvideo.com, gamecrazy.com, reel.com and moviegallery.com sell new and used movies and used video games, as well as providing movie news, reviews and information on upcoming releases. The company acquired Canadian-based VHQ Entertainment during 2005, adding an additional 61 new stores in western Canada. Movie Gallery is currently combining employment forces, cutting costs, closing some stores and restructuring its Alabama and Oregon offices. In 2006, the firm began to restructure and downsize the leases of approximately 3,300 stores, attempting to sublease an average of 2,500 square feet square feet of retail space at each location.

Movie Gallery offers its employees flexible schedules, product discounts and performance-based salary increases.

FINANCIALS: Sales and profits are in thousands of dollars—add 000 to get the full amount. 2006 Note: Financial information for 2006 was not available for all companies at press time.

2006 Sales: $	2006 Profits: $	U.S. Stock Ticker: MOVI
2005 Sales: $1,987,327	2005 Profits: $-552,740	Int'l Ticker: Int'l Exchange:
2004 Sales: $791,177	2004 Profits: $49,488	Employees: 45,873
2003 Sales: $528,988	2003 Profits: $20,934	Fiscal Year Ends: 12/31
2002 Sales: $529,000	2002 Profits: $20,900	Parent Company:

SALARIES/BENEFITS:

Pension Plan:	ESOP Stock Plan:	Profit Sharing:	Top Exec. Salary: $1,269,231	Bonus: $
Savings Plan: Y	Stock Purch. Plan: Y		Second Exec. Salary: $342,769	Bonus: $

OTHER THOUGHTS:

Apparent Women Officers or Directors: 1
Hot Spot for Advancement for Women/Minorities:

LOCATIONS: ("Y" = Yes)

West:	Southwest:	Midwest:	Southeast:	Northeast:	International:
Y	Y	Y	Y	Y	Y

Note: Financial information, benefits and other data can change quickly and may vary from those stated here.

MP3.COM INC

www.mp3.com

Industry Group Code: 451220E Ranks within this company's industry group: Sales: Profits:

Print Media/Publishing:	Movies:	Equipment/Supplies:	Broadcast/Cable:	Music/Audio:	Sports/Games:
Newspapers:	Movie Theaters:	Equipment/Supplies:	Broadcast TV:	Music Production:	Games/Sports:
Magazines:	Movie Production:	Gambling Equipment:	Cable TV:	Retail Music:	Retail Games Stores:
Books:	TV/Video Production:	Special Services: Y	Satellite Broadcast:	Retail Audio Equip.: Y	Stadiums/Teams:
Book Stores:	Video Rental:	Advertising Services:	Radio:	Music Print./Dist.: Y	Gambling/Casinos:
Distribution/Printing:	Video Distribution:	Info. Sys. Software:	Online Information:	Multimedia:	Rides/Theme Parks:

TYPES OF BUSINESS:

Online Digital Music Sales
Audio Hosting
Digital Music Information Portal

BRANDS/DIVISIONS/AFFILIATES:

CNET Networks

CONTACTS: *Note: Officers with more than one job title may be intentionally listed here more than once.*

Vince Broady, Sr. VP-Games & Entertainment, CNET Networks
Shelby Bonnie, Chmn./CEO-CNET Networks

Phone: 415-344-2000	**Fax:** 415-395-9207
Toll-Free:	
Address: 235 2nd St., San Francisco, CA 94105 US	

GROWTH PLANS/SPECIAL FEATURES:

MP3.com, Inc., a subsidiary of CNET Networks, operates a web site offering users a wide selection of articles, reviews, free streaming music, forums information on mp3 players and a collection of millions of digital music tracks from a wide range of genres that is its primary attraction for most users. Customers can purchase and listen to music media without leaving their homes, as MP3.com offers both tracks and albums to be played on computers and digital music players. After setting up a free account, consumers can build their MP3 collections, track favorite artists and chart their own musical tastes. Users can also participate in 18 separate forums ranging from music genre specific boards, MP3 player reviews, to a forum for promoting music and a musician's lounge. The company specializes in promoting lesser-known artists, numbering some 700,000, accessible through bios, discographies, reviews, videos, photos and news. Over 6 million 30-second song clips are available on the site with links to digital-music providers where legal downloads are available. After losing millions of dollars in a copyright suit, MP3.com was purchased by Vivendi Universal in 2001. The MP3.com domain and brand was then purchased in 2003 by CNET Networks and re-launched in early 2004. In November 2006, after being a news and editorial site since their acquisition by CNET, MP3.com re-opened its servers to allow artists to upload audio files. MP3.com now offers band profiles; 100 MB of audio storage (which will hold approximately 85 songs); unlimited space for videos; and software to upload and edit music, videos and photos. Bands have the ability to see which zip codes their music is being downloaded in. The site has also added the ability to create and save play lists through its new Flash audio player.

FINANCIALS: Sales and profits are in thousands of dollars—add 000 to get the full amount. 2006 Note: Financial Information for 2006 was not available for all companies at press time.

2006 Sales: $	2006 Profits: $	**U.S. Stock Ticker: Subsidiary**
2005 Sales: $	2005 Profits: $	**Int'l Ticker:** Int'l Exchange:
2004 Sales: $	2004 Profits: $	Employees: 308
2003 Sales: $	2003 Profits: $	Fiscal Year Ends: 12/31
2002 Sales: $	2002 Profits: $	Parent Company: CNET NETWORKS INC

SALARIES/BENEFITS:

Pension Plan:	ESOP Stock Plan:	Profit Sharing:	Top Exec. Salary: $283,851	Bonus: $302,250
Savings Plan:	Stock Purch. Plan:		Second Exec. Salary: $246,160	Bonus: $302,250

OTHER THOUGHTS:

Apparent Women Officers or Directors:
Hot Spot for Advancement for Women/Minorities:

LOCATIONS: ("Y" = Yes)

West:	Southwest:	Midwest:	Southeast:	Northeast:	International:
Y					Y

MTR GAMING GROUP INC

www.mtrgaming.com

Industry Group Code: 721120 Ranks within this company's industry group: Sales: 12 Profits: 11

Print Media/Publishing:	Movies:	Equipment/Supplies:	Broadcast/Cable:	Music/Audio:	Sports/Games:	
Newspapers:	Movie Theaters:	Equipment/Supplies:	Broadcast TV:	Music Production:	Games/Sports:	Y
Magazines:	Movie Production:	Gambling Equipment:	Cable TV:	Retail Music:	Retail Games Stores:	
Books:	TV/Video Production:	Special Services:	Satellite Broadcast:	Retail Audio Equip.:	Stadiums/Teams:	Y
Book Stores:	Video Rental:	Advertising Services:	Radio:	Music Print./Dist.:	Gambling/Casinos:	
Distribution/Printing:	Video Distribution:	Info. Sys. Software:	Online Information:	Multimedia:	Rides/Theme Parks:	

TYPES OF BUSINESS:

Gaming Facilities
Horse Racing Venues
Casinos
Hotels

BRANDS/DIVISIONS/AFFILIATES:

Scioto Downs
Mountaineer Race Track and Gaming Resort
Binion's Horseshoe Hotel and Casino
Ramada Inn and Speedway Casino
Jackson Trotting Association
Jackson Harness Raceway

CONTACTS: Note: Officers with more than one job title may be intentionally listed here more than once.

Edson R. Arneault, CEO
David Hughes, COO
Edson R. Arneault, Pres.
John W. Bittner, Jr., CFO
Robert A. Blatt, VP/Asst. Corp. Sec.
Rose Mary Williams, Corp. Sec.
Edson R. Arneault, Chmn.

Phone: 304-387-5712	Fax: 304-387-2167
Toll-Free: 800-804-0468	
Address: P.O. Box 356, State Rte. 2 S., Chester, WV 26034 US	

GROWTH PLANS/SPECIAL FEATURES:

MTR Gaming Group, Inc. owns and operates unique gaming facilities throughout the U.S. The company's flagship property, Mountaineer Race Track and Gaming Resort in Chester, West Virginia recently underwent a significant expansion. The resort encompasses 3,220 slot machines, a thoroughbred racetrack, 359 hotel rooms, a spa, a fitness center, a golf course, dining and entertainment, a theater and events center and a convention center. The company also operates the Ramada Inn and Speedway Casino in North Las Vegas, Nevada, which has more than 400 slots and a 95-room hotel; Scioto Downs, a harness horse racing facility in Columbus, Ohio; as well as Binion's Horseshoe Hotel and Casino in Las Vegas, operated jointly with an affiliate of Harrah's. MTR also holds a license to build a new thoroughbred racetrack in Erie, Pennsylvania, where the company plans to finish its building by 2007; and it is currently constructing a new racetrack in Anoka County, Minnesota, 30 miles north of Minneapolis. In December 2005, the firm acquired a 90% interest in Jackson Trotting Association, which operates Jackson Harness Raceway in Michigan.

FINANCIALS: Sales and profits are in thousands of dollars—add 000 to get the full amount. 2006 Note: Financial information for 2006 was not available for all companies at press time.

2006 Sales: $	2006 Profits: $	U.S. Stock Ticker: MNTG
2005 Sales: $358,295	2005 Profits: $7,769	Int'l Ticker: Int'l Exchange:
2004 Sales: $315,222	2004 Profits: $14,455	Employees: 2,850
2003 Sales: $293,606	2003 Profits: $15,100	Fiscal Year Ends: 12/31
2002 Sales: $266,300	2002 Profits: $17,900	Parent Company:

SALARIES/BENEFITS:

Pension Plan: Y	ESOP Stock Plan:	Profit Sharing:	Top Exec. Salary: $907,607	Bonus: $100,000
Savings Plan: Y	Stock Purch. Plan:		Second Exec. Salary: $321,469	Bonus: $50,000

OTHER THOUGHTS:

Apparent Women Officers or Directors: 1
Hot Spot for Advancement for Women/Minorities:

LOCATIONS: ("Y" = Yes)

West:	Southwest:	Midwest:	Southeast:	Northeast:	International:
Y		Y		Y	

MTV NETWORKS

www.mtv.com

Industry Group Code: 513210 Ranks within this company's industry group: Sales: Profits:

Print Media/Publishing:	Movies:		Equipment/Supplies:		Broadcast/Cable:		Music/Audio:		Sports/Games:	
Newspapers:	Movie Theaters:		Equipment/Supplies:		Broadcast TV:		Music Production:	Y	Games/Sports:	
Magazines:	Movie Production:	Y	Gambling Equipment:		Cable TV:	Y	Retail Music:		Retail Games Stores:	
Books:	TV/Video Production:	Y	Special Services:		Satellite Broadcast:		Retail Audio Equip.:		Stadiums/Teams:	
Book Stores:	Video Rental:		Advertising Services:	Y	Radio:		Music Print./Dist.:		Gambling/Casinos:	
Distribution/Printing:	Video Distribution:		Info. Sys. Software:		Online Information:		Multimedia:		Rides/Theme Parks:	

TYPES OF BUSINESS:

Television Programming
Film Production
Radio
Online Portal
Recorded Music
Merchandise Sales

BRANDS/DIVISIONS/AFFILIATES:

Viacom
Nickelodeon
VH1
Punk'd
Real World (The)
Total Request Live
Atom Entertainment, Inc.
Harmonix Music Systems, Inc.

CONTACTS: Note: Officers with more than one job title may be intentionally listed here more than once.

Judy McGrath, CEO
John Cucci, CFO
Larry Divney, Pres., MTV Networks Ad Sales
Judy McGrath, Pres., MTV Networks Group
Jason Hirschhorn, Sr. VP-Digital Music & Media
Judy McGrath, Chmn.
Bob Bakish, Pres., MTV Networks Int'l

Phone: 212-258-8000	Fax: 212-258-6175
Toll-Free:	
Address: 1515 Broadway, New York, NY 10036 US	

GROWTH PLANS/SPECIAL FEATURES:

MTV Networks, a business segment of Viacom, owns and operates the MTV, VH1 and Nickelodeon television networks, as well as 35 other locally programmed channels. With more than 40 offices worldwide, MTV broadcasting alone reaches over 480 million households in 179 countries and 22 languages. The company's other holdings include 43 locally operated web sites, along with publishing, recorded music, radio, home video, licensing and merchandising and feature film divisions. The firm produces films through a close association with Paramount Pictures. On the small screen, MTV has seen success in the production of quirky shows such as The Real World, The Osbournes, Total Request Live, Cribs, Diary and Punk'd. The mtv.com site caters to an audience of music fans in their teens and 20s and provides information on show times, merchandise ordering for consumer products based on its brand names, music downloads and band information. Recent acquisitions include Atom Entertainment, Inc., four websites featuring casual games, short films and video, and Harmonix Music Systems, Inc., creator of the video game Guitar Hero.

FINANCIALS: Sales and profits are in thousands of dollars—add 000 to get the full amount. 2006 Note: Financial information for 2006 was not available for all companies at press time.

2006 Sales: $	2006 Profits: $	U.S. Stock Ticker: Subsidiary
2005 Sales: $	2005 Profits: $	Int'l Ticker: Int'l Exchange:
2004 Sales: $5,471,000	2004 Profits: $	Employees:
2003 Sales: $	2003 Profits: $	Fiscal Year Ends: 12/31
2002 Sales: $	2002 Profits: $	Parent Company: VIACOM INC

SALARIES/BENEFITS:

Pension Plan:	ESOP Stock Plan:	Profit Sharing:	Top Exec. Salary: $	Bonus: $
Savings Plan:	Stock Purch. Plan:		Second Exec. Salary: $	Bonus: $

OTHER THOUGHTS:

Apparent Women Officers or Directors: 1
Hot Spot for Advancement for Women/Minorities:

LOCATIONS: ("Y" = Yes)

West:	Southwest:	Midwest:	Southeast:	Northeast:	International:
Y				Y	Y

Note: Financial information, benefits and other data can change quickly and may vary from those stated here.

MULTIMEDIA GAMES INC   www.multimediagames.com

Industry Group Code: 713290 Ranks within this company's industry group: Sales: 7   Profits: 7

Print Media/Publishing:	Movies:	Equipment/Supplies:		Broadcast/Cable:	Music/Audio:	Sports/Games:
Newspapers:	Movie Theaters:	Equipment/Supplies:		Broadcast TV:	Music Production:	Games/Sports:
Magazines:	Movie Production:	Gambling Equipment:	Y	Cable TV:	Retail Music:	Retail Games Stores:
Books:	TV/Video Production: Y	Special Services:	Y	Satellite Broadcast:	Retail Audio Equip.:	Stadiums/Teams:
Book Stores:	Video Rental:	Advertising Services:		Radio:	Music Print./Dist.:	Gambling/Casinos:
Distribution/Printing:	Video Distribution:	Info. Sys. Software:		Online Information:	Multimedia:	Rides/Theme Parks:

TYPES OF BUSINESS:

Gambling Technology
Video Gaming Machines
Electronic Bingo Games
Bingo Television Shows

BRANDS/DIVISIONS/AFFILIATES:

BetNet
MegaMania
Flash 21
People's Choice
Meltdown
Fruit Stand
Bad Monkey
Jungle Juice

CONTACTS: *Note: Officers with more than one job title may be intentionally listed here more than once.*

Clifton E. Lind, CEO
Clifton E. Lind, Pres.
Randy S. Cieslewicz, Interim CFO
Gary Loebig, Exec. VP-Sales
Scott A. Zinnecker, VP-Human Resources
Brendan O'Connor, CTO/Exec. VP
Scott A. Zinnecker, VP-Central Oper.
P. Howard Chalmers, Sr. VP-Planning
P. Howard Chalmers, Sr. VP-Corp. Comm.
Randy S. Cieslewicz, VP-Tax, Budget, & Corp. Compliance
Robert F. Lannert, Exec. VP-Class II Gaming
Steven K. Kent, VP-Quality
James A. Bannerot, Legal Coordinator
Gordon T. Sjodin, Exec VP
Michael J. Maples, Sr., Chmn.

Phone: 512-334-7500	Fax: 512-334-7695
Toll-Free:	
Address: 206 Wild Basin Rd., Bldg. B, 4th Fl., Austin, TX 78746 US	

GROWTH PLANS/SPECIAL FEATURES:

Multimedia Games, Inc. develops and distributes electronic gaming and paper bingo systems for Native American bingo operations, charitable bingo operations and video lottery systems. In addition, the company designs and develops network systems that allow electronic gaming terminals to be linked to one another within a single facility or across multiple facilities. Multimedia Games operates its interactive bingo games on behalf of its tribal customers through a multi-channel telecommunications network called BetNet. Employing combinations of frame relay, intranets, satellite, telephone, Internet and local area networks, BetNet enables distant players to play the same game and compete for pooled prizes in a progressive jackpot game. The company also produces high-stakes TV bingo game shows that are televised live to multiple participating Native American bingo halls linked via closed-circuit satellite and broadband telephone communications networks. Proprietary games include MegaMania, Big Cash Bingo, Flash 21, People's Choice, Meltdown, Fruit Stand, Bad Monkey and Jungle Juice. In 2006, Multimedia Games was selected to provide traditional bingo gaming services, electronic bingo, technical support and related services to Apuestas Internacionales S.A. de C.V., a Mexican gaming company. Multimedia will provide these services in 65 locations throughout Mexico. In exchange for these services, Multimedia will receive a percentage of each gaming station's win.

FINANCIALS: Sales and profits are in thousands of dollars—add 000 to get the full amount. 2006 Note: Financial information for 2006 was not available for all companies at press time.

2006 Sales: $145,112	2006 Profits: $3,532	U.S. Stock Ticker: MGAM
2005 Sales: $153,216	2005 Profits: $17,643	Int'l Ticker: Int'l Exchange:
2004 Sales: $153,675	2004 Profits: $32,772	Employees: 503
2003 Sales: $368,766	2003 Profits: $31,655	Fiscal Year Ends: 9/30
2002 Sales: $291,000	2002 Profits: $25,300	Parent Company:

SALARIES/BENEFITS:

Pension Plan:	ESOP Stock Plan:	Profit Sharing:	Top Exec. Salary: $467,553	Bonus: $17,000
Savings Plan: Y	Stock Purch. Plan:		Second Exec. Salary: $220,615	Bonus: $17,000

OTHER THOUGHTS:

Apparent Women Officers or Directors: 1
Hot Spot for Advancement for Women/Minorities:

LOCATIONS: ("Y" = Yes)

West:	Southwest:	Midwest:	Southeast:	Northeast:	International:
Y	Y	Y		Y	Y

Note: Financial information, benefits and other data can change quickly and may vary from those stated here.

NAPSTER INC

www.napster.com

Industry Group Code: 451220E **Ranks within this company's industry group:** Sales: 2   Profits: 2

Print Media/Publishing:	Movies:	Equipment/Supplies:		Broadcast/Cable:	Music/Audio:		Sports/Games:
Newspapers:	Movie Theaters:	Equipment/Supplies:	Y	Broadcast TV:	Music Production:		Games/Sports:
Magazines:	Movie Production:	Gambling Equipment:		Cable TV:	Retail Music:		Retail Games Stores:
Books:	TV/Video Production:	Special Services:		Satellite Broadcast:	Retail Audio Equip.:	Y	Stadiums/Teams:
Book Stores:	Video Rental:	Advertising Services:		Radio:	Music Print./Dist.:	Y	Gambling/Casinos:
Distribution/Printing:	Video Distribution:	Info. Sys. Software:	Y	Online Information:	Multimedia:		Rides/Theme Parks:

TYPES OF BUSINESS:

Online Music Retailing
Digital Media Software
Online Radio
Online Retail-Media Hardware
Mobile Phone Media Sales

BRANDS/DIVISIONS/AFFILIATES:

Napster To Go
Napster Light
shop.napster.com
napstertones.com
NapsterLinks
Narchive
Napster UK
Free Download of the Day

CONTACTS: *Note: Officers with more than one job title may be intentionally listed here more than once.*

Chris Gorog, CEO
Laura B. Goldberg, COO
Bradford D. Duea, Pres.
Nand Gangwani, CFO
William E. Pence, CTO/Sr. VP-Tech.
Evan Cowitt, VO-Advertising Sales, Western U.S.
Mike Owen, Dir.-Advertising Sales, Eastern U.S.
William E. Growney, Jr., Corp. Sec.
Chris Gorog, Chmn.

Phone: 310-281-5000	**Fax:** 408-367-3101
Toll-Free: 866-280-7694	
Address: 9044 Melrose Ave., Los Angeles, CA 90069 US	

GROWTH PLANS/SPECIAL FEATURES:

Napster, Inc. operates an online music service with over 500,000 subscribers. The company serves markets in the U.S., Canada, the U.K., Japan, and Germany. Napster offers its customers a digital music subscription service with unlimited access to over 2 million tracks in a wide variety of music genres with both major and independent record labels. Members also have access to over 50 interactive radio stations and complete information about the music offered. The Napster To Go membership includes everything in a standard membership, plus the ability to download an unlimited amount of music onto a portable mp3 player. The company's Napster Light allows customers to purchase songs and albums individually. On its e-commerce site shop, Napster offers music devices for personal use, automobiles and living rooms; computer audio equipment; accessories; and branded merchandise. Napstertones.com sells ringtones and graphics for mobile phones. The firm expanded its mobile market by joining with Cingular and Japanese company DoCoMo to allow customers the option of sending full-length songs and ringtones over-the-air to their mobile phones. Napster recently introduced Napster 3.7 with PowerSync, an optimized sync engine for use by its paid subscribers. In 2006, Napster unveiled the upgraded Napster.com. The website now offers free listening five times per song to any song in its catalogue. Approximately 3 million unique visitors per month access the firm's two new web tools, NapsterLinks and Narchive. NapsterLinks enables users to share links to songs in the Napster catalogue through e-mails, websites, blogs and instant messages. The Narchive is a public archive of music memorabilia, photos and artist biographies. Also in 2006, Napster paired with Intel to offer Free Download of the Day. In late 2006, Napster expanded to Japan.

FINANCIALS: Sales and profits are in thousands of dollars—add 000 to get the full amount. 2006 Note: Financial information for 2006 was not available for all companies at press time.

2006 Sales: $94,691	2006 Profits: $-54,945	**U.S. Stock Ticker:** NAPS
2005 Sales: $46,729	2005 Profits: $-29,506	**Int'l Ticker:** Int'l Exchange:
2004 Sales: $99,300	2004 Profits: $44,400	Employees: 145
2003 Sales: $120,400	2003 Profits: $-9,900	Fiscal Year Ends: 3/31
2002 Sales: $142,500	2002 Profits: $2,300	Parent Company:

SALARIES/BENEFITS:

Pension Plan:	ESOP Stock Plan: Y	Profit Sharing:	Top Exec. Salary: $698,918	Bonus: $
Savings Plan:	Stock Purch. Plan: Y		Second Exec. Salary: $311,538	Bonus: $

OTHER THOUGHTS:

Apparent Women Officers or Directors: 1
Hot Spot for Advancement for Women/Minorities:

LOCATIONS: ("Y" = Yes)

West:	Southwest:	Midwest:	Southeast:	Northeast:	International:
Y				Y	Y

NASPERS LIMITED

www.naspers.co.za

Industry Group Code: 513220 Ranks within this company's industry group: Sales: 14   Profits: 6

Print Media/Publishing:		Movies:		Equipment/Supplies:		Broadcast/Cable:		Music/Audio:		Sports/Games:	
Newspapers:	Y	Movie Theaters:		Equipment/Supplies:		Broadcast TV:		Music Production:		Games/Sports:	
Magazines:	Y	Movie Production:		Gambling Equipment:		Cable TV:	Y	Retail Music:		Retail Games Stores:	
Books:	Y	TV/Video Production:		Special Services:	Y	Satellite Broadcast:		Retail Audio Equip.:		Stadiums/Teams:	
Book Stores:		Video Rental:		Advertising Services:	Y	Radio:		Music Print./Dist.:		Gambling/Casinos:	
Distribution/Printing:		Video Distribution:		Info. Sys. Software:		Online Information:		Multimedia:		Rides/Theme Parks:	

TYPES OF BUSINESS:

Cable Television
Internet Subscriber Platforms
Printing & Distribution Services
Content Protection Technology
Magazine & Book Publishing
Private Education

BRANDS/DIVISIONS/AFFILIATES:

MIH Holdings
Irdeto Access
Entriq
Media 24
Via Afrika
Educor
Tiscali
MIH Limited

CONTACTS: *Note: Officers with more than one job title may be intentionally listed here more than once.*

Koos Bekker, CEO
Giancarlo Civita, COO
Steve Pacak, Group CFO
Mark Sorour, CIO
Andre Coetzee, Group Counsel
Antonie Roux, CEO-Internet Oper.
Beverly Branford, Investor Rel.
Patricia Scholtemeyer, CEO-Media 24
Cobus Stofberg, CEO-MIH Holdings
Jim Volkwyn, CEO-Pay TV Platforms
Graham Kill, CEO-Irdeto Access
Ton Vosloo, Chmn.

Phone: 27-21-406-2121	Fax: 27-21-406-3753
Toll-Free:	
Address: 40 Heerengrarcht, Cape Town, 8001 South Africa	

GROWTH PLANS/SPECIAL FEATURES:

Naspers is a multinational media company with operations in pay television, Internet subscriber platforms, print media, book publishing, private education and technology markets. Naspers is located in South Africa, where it generates 72% of its revenues, with other operations located elsewhere in sub-Saharan Africa, Greece, Cyprus, Brazil, the Netherlands, the U.S., Thailand and China. The company's operations are divided into two business segments: electronic media (68% of total revenues) and print media. The electronic media segment offers pay television through MIH Holdings. The firm also provides content protection technologies to more than 40 countries worldwide through Irdeto Access. Irdeto's products enable pay-media operators to encrypt and decrypt their broadcast or multicast signals, while Entriq, another subsidiary, operates a media authorization network that enables content and broadband service providers to protect, track, sell and syndicate online media. Media 24, Naspers' print media segment, consists of book publishing and private education operation with approximately 35 magazine titles and 50 newspaper titles. The company's book publishing activities are conducted through Via Afrika, a leading African publisher, with an extensive portfolio of fiction, nonfiction, reference, academic, religious and illustrated books. The firm's private education business is conducted through Educor, which offers programs ranging from adult basic education and training to higher education and corporate training. In 2006, the firm sold its interest in United Broadcasting Corporation, Thailand's leading pay-television operator, and MKSC World Dot Com Co. a leading Thai ISP, for $142 million. Also in 2006, the Irdeto subsidiary acquired CryptoTec Conditional Access business from Koninklijke Philips Electronics for $31 million. In addition, Naspers acquired 30% interest in Abril S.A. for $422 million. Also in 2006, the firm's subsidiary, MIH Print Media acquired a 20.2% interest in Titan, a leading Chinese sports publishing company, for $15 million.

FINANCIALS: Sales and profits are in thousands of dollars—add 000 to get the full amount. 2006 Note: Financial information for 2006 was not available for all companies at press time.

2006 Sales: $2,128,200	2006 Profits: $341,000	**U.S. Stock Ticker: NPSN**
2005 Sales: $2,243,200	2005 Profits: $417,800	**Int'l Ticker: NPN** Int'l Exchange: Johannesburg
2004 Sales: $2,025,673	2004 Profits: $78,356	Employees: 15,710
2003 Sales: $1,396,100	2003 Profits: $40,700	Fiscal Year Ends: 3/31
2002 Sales: $	2002 Profits: $	Parent Company:

SALARIES/BENEFITS:

Pension Plan: Y	ESOP Stock Plan:	Profit Sharing:	Top Exec. Salary: $270,255	Bonus: $303,788
Savings Plan:	Stock Purch. Plan:		Second Exec. Salary: $	Bonus: $

OTHER THOUGHTS:

Apparent Women Officers or Directors: 4
Hot Spot for Advancement for Women/Minorities: Y

LOCATIONS: ("Y" = Yes)

West:	Southwest:	Midwest:	Southeast:	Northeast:	International:
					Y

NATIONAL AMUSEMENTS INC www.national-amusements.com

Industry Group Code: 512131 Ranks within this company's industry group: Sales: Profits:

Print Media/Publishing:	Movies:		Equipment/Supplies:		Broadcast/Cable:	Music/Audio:	Sports/Games:	
Newspapers:	Movie Theaters:	Y	Equipment/Supplies:		Broadcast TV:	Music Production:	Games/Sports:	Y
Magazines:	Movie Production:		Gambling Equipment:		Cable TV:	Retail Music:	Retail Games Stores:	
Books:	TV/Video Production:		Special Services:		Satellite Broadcast:	Retail Audio Equip.:	Stadiums/Teams:	
Book Stores:	Video Rental:		Advertising Services:	Y	Radio:	Music Print./Dist.:	Gambling/Casinos:	
Distribution/Printing:	Video Distribution:		Info. Sys. Software:		Online Information:	Multimedia:	Rides/Theme Parks:	

TYPES OF BUSINESS:

Movie Theaters
Online Ticketing
Video Games
Slot Machines
Advertising Services

BRANDS/DIVISIONS/AFFILIATES:

Showcase Cinemas
Multiplex Cinemas
Cinema de Lux
Viacom
Midway Games
CyGamZ
CBS

CONTACTS: *Note: Officers with more than one job title may be intentionally listed here more than once.*

Sumner M. Redstone, CEO
Shari E. Redstone, Pres.
William Towey, Sr. VP-Oper.
Wanda Whitson, Dir.-Corp. Comm.
Jerome Magner, Sr. VP-Finance/Treas.
Sumner M. Redstone, Chmn.

Phone: 781-461-1600	**Fax:** 781-407-0052
Toll-Free:	
Address: 200 Elm St., Dedham, MA 02026 US	

GROWTH PLANS/SPECIAL FEATURES:

National Amusements, Inc. (NAI) operates under the Showcase Cinemas, Multiplex Cinemas and Cinema de Lux brands, which together operate over 1,500 screens in 119 theaters across the U.S., Europe and Latin America. National Amusements is an equal partner in the online ticketing service, MovieTickets.com, and is the parent company of both Viacom and CBS Corporation. Currently the company operates 1,093 screens in 81 theaters in the U.S., 243 screens in the U.K., 210 screens in Latin America and 23 screens in Russia. NAI has among the highest per-screen revenue totals of any theatre circuit in the U.S. Features include Descriptive Video Service, which provides descriptive narration to visually impaired moviegoers over headsets, and Rear Window Captioning, which superimposes captions on movie screen by a system of reflectors. The firm offers customized advertising opportunities including onscreen slide advertising, rolling stock commercials, lobby monitor placement and web site opportunities. The company has stakes in Midway Games, a video game publisher which it will promote in conjunction with CyGamZ. In late 2006, the company launched the first location of CyGamZ, an interactive gaming venue. CyGamZ offers full-service dining, both PC and console-based games, high-tech audio and plasma screen displays. The franchise is being launched with Intel, Alienware and Pepsi. The company plans to host gaming tournaments, and the locations feature rooms equipped for parties or business meetings. In 2006, NAI opened the first IMAX theater in Argentina. The firm plans to convert several of its properties to a high-end concept called Cinema De Lux (CDL) which outfits theaters with martini bars, Starbucks coffee counters, concierge desks, private party rooms, and theaters that boast luxurious leather reclining seats which are assigned (as opposed to open seating), live performances before showings and escorted seating service.

NAI's corporate employees receive benefits including pension and 401(k) plans and movie passes. Theater staff are offered incentive programs and free movies.

FINANCIALS: Sales and profits are in thousands of dollars—add 000 to get the full amount. 2006 Note: Financial information for 2006 was not available for all companies at press time.

2006 Sales: $	2006 Profits: $	**U.S. Stock Ticker: Private**
2005 Sales: $	2005 Profits: $	**Int'l Ticker:** Int'l Exchange:
2004 Sales: $	2004 Profits: $	Employees:
2003 Sales: $	2003 Profits: $	Fiscal Year Ends: 12/31
2002 Sales: $	2002 Profits: $	Parent Company:

SALARIES/BENEFITS:

Pension Plan: Y	ESOP Stock Plan:	Profit Sharing:	Top Exec. Salary: $	Bonus: $
Savings Plan: Y	Stock Purch. Plan:		Second Exec. Salary: $	Bonus: $

OTHER THOUGHTS:

Apparent Women Officers or Directors: 2
Hot Spot for Advancement for Women/Minorities:

LOCATIONS: ("Y" = Yes)

West:	Southwest:	Midwest:	Southeast:	Northeast:	International:
Y		Y		Y	Y

Note: Financial information, benefits and other data can change quickly and may vary from those stated here.

NBC UNIVERSAL

www.nbcuni.com

Industry Group Code: 513210 Ranks within this company's industry group: Sales: 2 Profits: 1

Print Media/Publishing:	Movies:	Equipment/Supplies:	Broadcast/Cable:		Music/Audio:	Sports/Games:	
Newspapers:	Movie Theaters:	Equipment/Supplies:	Broadcast TV:	Y	Music Production:	Games/Sports:	
Magazines:	Movie Production:	Gambling Equipment:	Cable TV:	Y	Retail Music:	Retail Games Stores:	
Books:	TV/Video Production: Y	Special Services:	Satellite Broadcast:		Retail Audio Equip.:	Stadiums/Teams:	
Book Stores:	Video Rental:	Advertising Services:	Radio:		Music Print./Dist.:	Gambling/Casinos:	
Distribution/Printing:	Video Distribution:	Info. Sys. Software:	Online Information:		Multimedia:	Rides/Theme Parks:	Y

TYPES OF BUSINESS:

Television Broadcasting
Online News & Information
TV & Movie Production
Radio Broadcasting
Interactive Online Content
Cable Television Programming
Theme Parks
Film, TV & Home Video Distribution

BRANDS/DIVISIONS/AFFILIATES:

General Electric Company
Vivendi Universal Entertainment
NBC
Universal Pictures
Universal Studios
MSNBC
Universal Parks & Resorts
Telemundo

CONTACTS: Note: Officers with more than one job title may be intentionally listed here more than once.

Robert C. Wright, CEO
Lynn Calpeter, CFO/Exec. VP
Eileen Whelley, VP-Human Resources
Stacy Snider, Chmn., Universal Pictures
Rick Cotton, General Counsel/Exec. VP
Beth Comstock, Pres., Digital Media
Randy Falco, Pres., NBC Universal Television Networks Group
Jay Ireland, Pres., NBC Universal Television Stations
Bridget Baker, Pres., NBC Universal Television Networks Distrib.
Thomas L. Williams, CEO-Universal Parks & Resorts
Robert C. Wright, Chmn.
Jean-Briac Perrette, Pres., Digital Distrib.

Phone: 212-664-4444	**Fax:** 212-664-4085
Toll-Free:	
Address: 30 Rockefeller Plaza, New York, NY 10112 US	

GROWTH PLANS/SPECIAL FEATURES:

NBC Universal is a subsidiary of General Electric (GE) and the product of a 2004 merger of Vivendi Universal Entertainment with NBC (National Broadcasting Company). The company is 20%-owned by Vivendi Universal and 80%-owned by GE. Assets merged into the new organization include Universal Pictures, Universal Television and the Universal Studios theme parks. In addition, the company oversees the NBC Television Network. NBC Universal TV Stations operates 10 NBC affiliate stations and 15 Telemundo stations in major U.S. markets. The firm operates cable channels including Bravo, CNBC, MSNBC and USA Networks and holds a partial interest in A&E. NBC Internet, Inc., a wholly-owned subsidiary of NBC, operates a network of web sites centered around nbci.com and msnbc.com, integrating access across all of its major media platforms, including Internet, broadcast and cable television and radio. International assets include sales and distribution positions for video and DVD titles, television programming and feature films in more than 200 countries around the world. Universal Recreation Group brings together the operations of Universal Parks and Resorts, including wholly-owned Universal Studios Hollywood and Universal CityWalk Hollywood, and major interests in both Universal Orlando properties (including Islands of Adventure, CityWalk Orlando and Universal Studios Florida) and international locations including Universal Studios Japan and Universal Mediterranean in Spain. NBC Universal oversees a 50% stake in the Universal Orlando properties, which have been developed as a joint venture with private equity firm the Blackstone Group. In March 2006, NBC Universal agreed to acquire IVillage.com for $600 million dollars. The firm announced a restructuring and cost-reduction plan in late 2006, including the layoff of 5% of the workforce.

NBC Universal offers a large number of internships to college students and graduates each year.

FINANCIALS: Sales and profits are in thousands of dollars—add 000 to get the full amount. 2006 Note: Financial information for 2006 was not available for all companies at press time.

2006 Sales: $	2006 Profits: $	**U.S. Stock Ticker: Subsidiary**
2005 Sales: $14,689,000	2005 Profits: $3,092,000	**Int'l Ticker:** Int'l Exchange:
2004 Sales: $12,886,000	2004 Profits: $2,558,000	Employees: 16,000
2003 Sales: $6,871,000	2003 Profits: $1,998,000	Fiscal Year Ends: 12/31
2002 Sales: $7,149,000	2002 Profits: $1,658,000	Parent Company: GENERAL ELECTRIC CO (GE)

SALARIES/BENEFITS:

Pension Plan:	ESOP Stock Plan:	Profit Sharing:	Top Exec. Salary: $615,393	Bonus: $450,000
Savings Plan: Y	Stock Purch. Plan:		Second Exec. Salary: $336,549	Bonus: $367,103

OTHER THOUGHTS:

Apparent Women Officers or Directors: 7
Hot Spot for Advancement for Women/Minorities: Y

LOCATIONS: ("Y" = Yes)

West:	Southwest:	Midwest:	Southeast:	Northeast:	International:
Y		Y		Y	Y

NETFLIX
www.netflix.com

Industry Group Code: 532230 Ranks within this company's industry group: Sales: 4   Profits: 1

Print Media/Publishing:	Movies:		Equipment/Supplies:	Broadcast/Cable:	Music/Audio:	Sports/Games:
Newspapers:	Movie Theaters:		Equipment/Supplies:	Broadcast TV:	Music Production:	Games/Sports:
Magazines:	Movie Production:		Gambling Equipment:	Cable TV:	Retail Music:	Retail Games Stores:
Books:	TV/Video Production:		Special Services:	Satellite Broadcast:	Retail Audio Equip.:	Stadiums/Teams:
Book Stores:	Video Rental:	Y	Advertising Services:	Radio:	Music Print./Dist.:	Gambling/Casinos:
Distribution/Printing:	Video Distribution:		Info. Sys. Software:	Online Information:	Multimedia:	Rides/Theme Parks:

TYPES OF BUSINESS:
Online DVD Rental

BRANDS/DIVISIONS/AFFILIATES:
CineMatch
Friends
Profiles

CONTACTS:
Note: Officers with more than one job title may be intentionally listed here more than once.

Reed Hastings, CEO
William J. Henderson, COO
Barry McCarthy, CFO
Leslie Kilgore, Chief Mktg. Officer
Patty McCord, Chief Talent Officer
Neil Hunt, Chief Product Officer
Ted Sarandos, Chief Content Officer
Reed Hastings, Chmn.

Phone: 408-399-3700	**Fax:** 408-399-3737
Toll-Free:	
Address: 100 Winchester Circle, Los Gatos, CA 95032 US	

GROWTH PLANS/SPECIAL FEATURES:

Netflix is the nation's largest online DVD rental subscription service, distributing more than 1.4 million DVDs per day to over 5.7 million members. Members choose one of ten subscription plans, which set the number of movies they may have simultaneously, and which range in price from $5.99 for 1 DVD at a time to $23.99 for 4 DVDs at a time. Members log onto the Netflix web site and create a list of movies or television titles they would like to see. When a member returns a title from home, the next title in the list is automatically sent out via first class mail. Netflix maintains a prodigious inventory of DVDs covering 70,000 unique movie titles. Over 65% of the firm's rentals are generated by back-catalog titles, in contrast to the industry average of about 20%. The average customer rents five titles monthly. There is no time limit for keeping selected titles. Members are not charged for shipping, and are provided with prepaid mailers for returns. Over 90% of Netflix's subscribers enjoy one-business-day delivery. Netflix primarily uses pay-for-performance marketing programs and free trial offers to acquire new subscribers. The company operates 41 shipping centers nationwide, and mails 11,000 tons of DVDs each year. New technology is continually being developed to streamline the delivery system as the firm's consumer base continues to grow. For example, the company's CineMatch service gives personalized recommendations to customers on the web site based on movies previously rented and rated; and Friends allows subscribers to share movie recommendations. Members can also now watch previews of almost all movies before adding them to their list.

FINANCIALS:
Sales and profits are in thousands of dollars—add 000 to get the full amount. 2006 Note: Financial information for 2006 was not available for all companies at press time.

2006 Sales: $	2006 Profits: $	**U.S. Stock Ticker: NFLX**
2005 Sales: $688,000	2005 Profits: $41,900	**Int'l Ticker:** Int'l Exchange:
2004 Sales: $506,228	2004 Profits: $20,838	Employees: 1,430
2003 Sales: $272,243	2003 Profits: $6,512	Fiscal Year Ends: 12/31
2002 Sales: $152,800	2002 Profits: $-21,900	Parent Company:

SALARIES/BENEFITS:

Pension Plan:	ESOP Stock Plan:	Profit Sharing:	Top Exec. Salary: $740,000	Bonus: $
Savings Plan: Y	Stock Purch. Plan:		Second Exec. Salary: $575,000	Bonus: $

OTHER THOUGHTS:
Apparent Women Officers or Directors: 2
Hot Spot for Advancement for Women/Minorities:

LOCATIONS: ("Y" = Yes)

West:	Southwest:	Midwest:	Southeast:	Northeast:	International:
Y	Y	Y	Y	Y	

NETRATINGS INC
www.nielsen-netratings.com

Industry Group Code: 541910 Ranks within this company's industry group: Sales: 5 Profits: 5

Print Media/Publishing:	Movies:	Equipment/Supplies:		Broadcast/Cable:	Music/Audio:	Sports/Games:
Newspapers:	Movie Theaters:	Equipment/Supplies:		Broadcast TV:	Music Production:	Games/Sports:
Magazines:	Movie Production:	Gambling Equipment:		Cable TV:	Retail Music:	Retail Games Stores:
Books:	TV/Video Production:	Special Services:	Y	Satellite Broadcast:	Retail Audio Equip.:	Stadiums/Teams:
Book Stores:	Video Rental:	Advertising Services:	Y	Radio:	Music Print./Dist.:	Gambling/Casinos:
Distribution/Printing:	Video Distribution:	Info. Sys. Software:		Online Information:	Multimedia:	Rides/Theme Parks:

TYPES OF BUSINESS:
Internet Audience Information & Analysis
Marketing Services
Market Research

BRANDS/DIVISIONS/AFFILIATES:
VNU
Nielsen/NetRatings
AdRelevance
@Plan
SiteCensus
NetView
Homescan Online
A2M2

CONTACTS:
Note: Officers with more than one job title may be intentionally listed here more than once.
William Pulver, CEO
William Pulver, Pres.
Todd Sloan, CFO
George Durney, Sr. VP-Sales
John Kleine, CTO
John Kleine, Sr. VP-Eng.
Alan Shapiro, General Counsel/Sr. VP
Manish Bhatia, Exec. VP-Global Operations
Todd Sloan, Exec. VP-Corp. Dev.
Susan Hickey, Sr. VP
Forrest Didier, Managing Dir.-Asia-Pacific & Latin America
Charles Buchwalter, VP-Industry Solutions
John A. Dimling, Chmn.
David Day, Managing Dir.-Europe, Middle East & Africa

Phone: 212-703-5900	Fax: 212-703-5901
Toll-Free: 888-634-1222	
Address: 120 W. 45th St., 35th Fl., New York, NY 10036 US	

GROWTH PLANS/SPECIAL FEATURES:
NetRatings, Inc. is a leading provider of Internet audience measurement and analysis in the U.S. and globally, covering over 70% of Internet users. The company's products and services are designed to aid companies in making critical business decisions regarding Internet strategies and initiatives. The firm's primary products and services include NetView, AdRelevance, @Plan, MegaPanel, SiteCensus, WebRF, Web Intercept and Homescan Online. NetView, NetRatings' original product, provides in-depth measurement of audience behavior online and in the digital media universe, including instant messaging and media players. AdRelevance offers comprehensive and accurate information on online advertising. @Plan is a leading resource for demographic, lifestyle and product preferences that guide advertisers, agencies and web publishers in online marketing and media strategies. MegaPanel provides increased breadth and depth of Internet behavior and activity for the market research industry, including e-commerce transaction information. SiteCensus offers extensive web analytical services based on traffic flows and visitor behaviors. WebRF offers advertisers and web publishers the ability to plan and evaluate the impact of Internet advertising. WebIntercept allows clients to survey Internet users based on their real-time online behavior. Homescan Online improves the effectiveness of online marketing for the consumer packaged goods industry and web publishers. The company also provides customized research and advisory services from its industry experts. NetRatings maintains strategic relationships with Nielsen Media Research and ACNielsen (both subsidiaries of VNU), which allow it to leverage their brands, expertise and industry relationships. VNU currently owns approximately 60% of the company's outstanding common stock. The Nielsen/NetRatings brand is marketed in France by MEDIAMETRIE, in Japan by NetRatings Japan and in Latin America by IBOPE. Recently, the firm launched its new National TV/Internet Fusion database, which merges Internet and television panels (developed through Nelson's Anytime Anywhere Media Measurement initiative, or A2M2) into a single dataset.

FINANCIALS:
Sales and profits are in thousands of dollars—add 000 to get the full amount. 2006 Note: Financial information for 2006 was not available for all companies at press time.

2006 Sales: $	2006 Profits: $	U.S. Stock Ticker: NTRT
2005 Sales: $68,017	2005 Profits: $-8,395	Int'l Ticker: Int'l Exchange:
2004 Sales: $59,300	2004 Profits: $-17,419	Employees: 396
2003 Sales: $41,432	2003 Profits: $-25,135	Fiscal Year Ends: 12/31
2002 Sales: $29,700	2002 Profits: $-38,900	Parent Company:

SALARIES/BENEFITS:
Pension Plan: Y	ESOP Stock Plan:	Profit Sharing:	Top Exec. Salary: $358,333	Bonus: $280,000
Savings Plan:	Stock Purch. Plan:		Second Exec. Salary: $256,250	Bonus: $128,750

OTHER THOUGHTS:
Apparent Women Officers or Directors: 2
Hot Spot for Advancement for Women/Minorities:

LOCATIONS: ("Y" = Yes)
West:	Southwest:	Midwest:	Southeast:	Northeast:	International:
Y				Y	Y

Note: Financial information, benefits and other data can change quickly and may vary from those stated here.

NEW LINE CINEMA

www.newline.com

Industry Group Code: 512110 Ranks within this company's industry group: Sales: Profits:

Print Media/Publishing:	Movies:		Equipment/Supplies:	Broadcast/Cable:	Music/Audio:	Sports/Games:
Newspapers:	Movie Theaters:		Equipment/Supplies:	Broadcast TV:	Music Production:	Games/Sports:
Magazines:	Movie Production:	Y	Gambling Equipment:	Cable TV:	Retail Music:	Retail Games Stores:
Books:	TV/Video Production:	Y	Special Services:	Satellite Broadcast:	Retail Audio Equip.:	Stadiums/Teams:
Book Stores:	Video Rental:		Advertising Services:	Radio:	Music Print./Dist.:	Gambling/Casinos:
Distribution/Printing:	Video Distribution:		Info. Sys. Software:	Online Information:	Multimedia:	Rides/Theme Parks:

TYPES OF BUSINESS:

Movie Production
Video & DVD Distribution
Online Retail
Merchandising & Licensing

BRANDS/DIVISIONS/AFFILIATES:

Time Warner
Fine Line Features
New Line Home Video
New Line Television
New Line Theater Distribution
New Line International Releasing, Inc.
Material Entertainment
Picturehouse

CONTACTS: *Note: Officers with more than one job title may be intentionally listed here more than once.*

Robert K. Shaye, Co-CEO/Co-Chmn.
Stephen Abramson, CFO
Rolf Mittweg, Pres./COO-New Line Worldwide Dist. & Mktg.
Ben Zinkin, Sr. Exec. VP-Legal Affairs & Bus.
Elissa Greer, Sr. VP-Publicity & Promotions
Toby Emmerich, Pres., New Line Productions
Stephen Einhorn, Pres., New Line Home Video
David Tuckerman, Pres., New Line Theatrical Distribution
Jim Rosenthal, Pres., New Line Television
Michael Lynne, Co-Chmn./Co-CEO
Camela Galano, Pres., New Line Int'l. Releasing, Inc.

Phone: 212-649-4900	**Fax:** 212-649-4966
Toll-Free:	
Address: 888 7th Ave., New York, NY 10106 US	

GROWTH PLANS/SPECIAL FEATURES:

New Line Cinema Corporation, a subsidiary of Time Warner, is a leading distributor and producer of motion pictures and one of the world's oldest independent film companies. The company operates through two main film divisions: New Line Cinema (NLC) and Fine Line Features (FLF). NLC produces, markets and distributes blockbuster films such as the Lord of the Rings trilogy and the Austin Powers series. FLF produces and acquires art-house films such as Vera Drake, Maria Full of Grace and The Sea Inside. Through its other subsidiaries, the company has operations in home entertainment, television, music, theater, licensing, merchandising and international marketing and distribution. New Line Home Video distributes the company's films on video and DVD, while New Line Television licenses its movies for pay-per-view and network and cable television. New Line Theater Distribution handles the distribution of the company's movies to theaters around the country, while New Line International Releasing, Inc. sells the international distribution rights to its films by country and region. The company sells movie merchandising through its retail web site, shop.newline.com. New Line and U.K.-based Entertainment Film Distributors also operate a joint venture, Material Entertainment, a London-based production company scheduled to produce four films a year. New Line Cinema and HBO recently paired up to create Picturehouse, a specialized film company. Picturehouse released several films in 2006, including Tristram Shandy, The Notorious Bettie Page and Fur. Recent NLC releases include The Nativity Story and Snakes On A Plane. Following the enormous success of The Lord of the Rings trilogy, which earned over $5 billion worldwide, NLC is working on a new trilogy based on the fantasy novels of Philip Pullman.

FINANCIALS: Sales and profits are in thousands of dollars—add 000 to get the full amount. 2006 Note: Financial information for 2006 was not available for all companies at press time.

2006 Sales: $	2006 Profits: $	**U.S. Stock Ticker: Subsidiary**
2005 Sales: $	2005 Profits: $	**Int'l Ticker:** Int'l Exchange:
2004 Sales: $	2004 Profits: $	Employees:
2003 Sales: $	2003 Profits: $	Fiscal Year Ends: 12/31
2002 Sales: $	2002 Profits: $	Parent Company: TIME WARNER CABLE

SALARIES/BENEFITS:

Pension Plan:	ESOP Stock Plan:	Profit Sharing:	Top Exec. Salary: $	Bonus: $
Savings Plan:	Stock Purch. Plan:		Second Exec. Salary: $	Bonus: $

OTHER THOUGHTS:

Apparent Women Officers or Directors: 2
Hot Spot for Advancement for Women/Minorities:

LOCATIONS: ("Y" = Yes)

West:	Southwest:	Midwest:	Southeast:	Northeast:	International:
				Y	

Note: Financial information, benefits and other data can change quickly and may vary from those stated here.

NEW YORK TIMES CO (THE)

www.nytco.com

Industry Group Code: 511110 Ranks within this company's industry group: Sales: 6 Profits: 4

Print Media/Publishing:		Movies:		Equipment/Supplies:		Broadcast/Cable:		Music/Audio:		Sports/Games:	
Newspapers:	Y	Movie Theaters:		Equipment/Supplies:		Broadcast TV:	Y	Music Production:		Games/Sports:	
Magazines:	Y	Movie Production:		Gambling Equipment:		Cable TV:		Retail Music:		Retail Games Stores:	
Books:	Y	TV/Video Production:		Special Services:	Y	Satellite Broadcast:		Retail Audio Equip.:		Stadiums/Teams:	
Book Stores:		Video Rental:		Advertising Services:	Y	Radio:		Music Print./Dist.:		Gambling/Casinos:	
Distribution/Printing:		Video Distribution:		Info. Sys. Software:		Online Information:		Multimedia:		Rides/Theme Parks:	

TYPES OF BUSINESS:

Newspaper Publishing
Broadcast TV
Broadcast Radio
Online Publishing
Newsprint & Paper Manufacturing
Newspaper Distribution
Online Travel Bookings
News Wire & Licensing Services

BRANDS/DIVISIONS/AFFILIATES:

New York Times (The)
Boston Globe (The)
New York Times Digital
nytimes.com
International Herald Tribune
Discovery Times Channel
Worcester Telegram & Gazette
About.com

CONTACTS: Note: Officers with more than one job title may be intentionally listed here more than once.

Janet L. Robinson, CEO
Janet L. Robinson, Pres.
James M. Follo, CFO/Sr. VP
Susan Telesmanic, VP-Consumer Mktg.
David K.Norton, Sr.VP-Human Resources
Michael Zimbalist, VP-Research and Dev. Oper.
David A. Thurm, CIO/VP
Mare Frons, CTO-Digital Oper.
Stuart P. Stoller, Sr. VP-Process Eng.
Kenneth A. Richieri, Gen. Counsel/VP
James C. Lessersohn, Sr. VP-Finance & Corp. Dev.
Catherine J. Mathis, VP-Corp. Comm.
Paula Schwartz, Asst. Dir.-Investor Rel.
R. Anthony Benton, Corp. Controller/VP
Martin A. Nisenholtz, CEO, New York Times Digital/Sr. VP Digital Op.
Scott Heekin-Canedy, Pres., The New York Times
Solomon B. Watson, IV, Sr. VP/Chief Legal Officer
George A. Barrios, VP/Treas./CFO-New England Media Group
Arthur Sulzberger, Jr., Chmn./Publisher

Phone: 212-556-1234	Fax: 212-556-7389
Toll-Free:	
Address: 229 W. 43rd St., New York, NY 10036 US	

GROWTH PLANS/SPECIAL FEATURES:

The New York Times Company is a diversified global media company with operations in newspapers, television, radio and the Internet. The company operates in three primary segments: Newspapers; Broadcasting; and New York Times Digital. The newspaper group includes The New York Times, the New England Newspaper Group, the Worcester Telegram & Gazette and the regional newspaper group. Additional operations in this segment include newspaper distribution in New York City and Boston and international news wire and licensing services. The company's broadcasting group comprises nine network-affiliated TV stations in the Northeast and Midwest and two radio stations in New York, one of which it's agreed to sell to ABC for $40 million. In early 2007, the Times agree to sell its television stations to Oak Hill Capital for $575 million. New York Times Digital operates 35 web sites, including NYTimes.com, About.com and an online archive service. The New York Times Online receives an average of 17 million monthly visitors, and over 3.2 million people receive daily newsletters from NYTimes.com. The Times' joint venture with Discovery Communications produces and distributes digital cable television through the Discovery Times Channel. The firm and its journalists have been awarded 115 Pulitzer Prizes to date. In 2006, the company released the free online tool Times Reader that enhances onscreen reading experience. Recently, the firm partnered with Expedia to create an online booking engine for the NYTimes travel section. In addition, the Times partnered with Zagat Survey; readers who register for the TimesPoints program (a free reader rewards program) receive a free year's online subscription to Zagat reviews and ratings. Also in 2006, the firm launched a new mobile site, making the NYTimes accessible on mobile phones.

The Times offers its employees assistance programs for adoption, tuition and personal issues, as well as health club memberships and child care.

FINANCIALS: Sales and profits are in thousands of dollars—add 000 to get the full amount. 2006 Note: Financial information for 2006 was not available for all companies at press time.

2006 Sales: $	2006 Profits: $	**U.S. Stock Ticker:** NYT
2005 Sales: $3,372,800	2005 Profits: $259,700	**Int'l Ticker:** Int'l Exchange:
2004 Sales: $3,303,600	2004 Profits: $292,600	Employees: 11,965
2003 Sales: $3,227,200	2003 Profits: $302,700	Fiscal Year Ends: 12/31
2002 Sales: $3,079,000	2002 Profits: $299,700	Parent Company:

SALARIES/BENEFITS:

Pension Plan: Y	ESOP Stock Plan:	Profit Sharing:	Top Exec. Salary: $1,055,596	Bonus: $560,521
Savings Plan: Y	Stock Purch. Plan: Y		Second Exec. Salary: $900,000	Bonus: $477,900

OTHER THOUGHTS:

Apparent Women Officers or Directors: 16
Hot Spot for Advancement for Women/Minorities: Y

LOCATIONS: ("Y" = Yes)

West:	Southwest:	Midwest:	Southeast:	Northeast:	International:
Y	Y	Y	Y	Y	Y

Note: Financial information, benefits and other data can change quickly and may vary from those stated here.

NEWS CORPORATION LIMITED (THE)   www.newscorp.com

Industry Group Code: 513120 Ranks within this company's industry group: Sales: 1   Profits: 1

Print Media/Publishing:		Movies:		Equipment/Supplies:		Broadcast/Cable:		Music/Audio:		Sports/Games:	
Newspapers:	Y	Movie Theaters:		Equipment/Supplies:		Broadcast TV:	Y	Music Production:		Games/Sports:	Y
Magazines:	Y	Movie Production:	Y	Gambling Equipment:		Cable TV:	Y	Retail Music:		Retail Games Stores:	
Books:	Y	TV/Video Production:	Y	Special Services:	Y	Satellite Broadcast:		Retail Audio Equip.:		Stadiums/Teams:	
Book Stores:		Video Rental:		Advertising Services:	Y	Radio:		Music Print./Dist.:		Gambling/Casinos:	
Distribution/Printing:		Video Distribution:		Info. Sys. Software:		Online Information:		Multimedia:		Rides/Theme Parks:	

TYPES OF BUSINESS:

Television Broadcasting & Distribution
Film & Television Production
Newspaper Publishing
Online Media
Advertising Services
Magazine & Book Publishing
Satellite Television

BRANDS/DIVISIONS/AFFILIATES:

Fox Entertainment Group
Fox Broadcasting Company
British Sky Broadcasting
Harper Collins Publishers
20th Century Fox
New York Post (The)
TV Guide
Jamba

CONTACTS: Note: Officers with more than one job title may be intentionally listed here more than once.

Rupert Murdoch, CEO
Peter Chernin, COO
Peter Chernin, Pres.
David F. DeVoe, CFO
Roger Fishman, Exec. VP-Mktg.
Ian Moore, Exec. VP-Human Resources
Lawrence A. Jacobs, Group General Counsel
Gary Ginsberg, Exec. VP-Corp. Comm.
Gary Ginsberg, Exec. VP-Investor Rel.
Anthea Disney, Exec. VP-Content
John Nallen, Exec. VP/Deputy CFO
Genie Gavenchak, Sr. VP- Deputy General Counsel
Michael Regan, Exec. VP-Gov. Affairs
Rupert Murdoch, Chmn.

Phone: 212-852-7000	Fax: 212-852-7145
Toll-Free:	
Address: 1211 Ave. of the Americas, 8th Floor, New York, NY 10036 US	

GROWTH PLANS/SPECIAL FEATURES:

The News Corporation, Ltd. (NCL) is a diversified international communications company engaged in motion pictures and television production and distribution; television, cable broadcasting; newspaper, magazine and book publishing; producing and distributing promotional and advertising products and services; developing digital broadcasting; developing conditional access and subscriber management systems; and creating and distributing online programming. NCL's activities are conducted primarily in the U.S., the U.K., Australia and the Pacific Basin. The company's filmed entertainment segment comprises the Fox Entertainment Group, which includes 20th Century Fox, 20th Century Fox Television, Fox Searchlight, Fox Music, Fox Television Studios and others. NCL's television segment includes Fox Broadcasting Company, Fox Television Stations and Star, the leading Asian media company. The company's cable network programming segment includes the Fox News Channel and Fox Cable Networks Group, which includes the Fox Movie Channel, FX and the National Geographic Channel. NCL's direct broadcast satellite television segment includes British Sky Broadcasting, SKY Italia and others. The firm's magazine holdings include Inside Out, the Weekly Standard and TV Guide. NCL's newspapers include The Sun, The Times, The New York Post and over 100 Australian titles. The company's book publishing segment operates Harper Collins Publishers. Other assets include Broadsystem, Festival Mushroom Records, News Interactive, NDS, Sky Radio and interest in the National Rugby League. In 2006, the firm acquired two New York City neighborhood newspaper groups, TimesLedger and Courier-Life. Also in 2006, the company announced plans to pay Verisign $188 million for a controlling interest in its subsidiary Jamba. Recently, NCL announced the launch of live programming on the Panasonic Activision Screen in Times Square. Per the agreement, Fox Entertainment Group will provide at least three hours of live programming daily for ten years. In December 2006, Liberty Media Corp. completed a significant $11 billion asset swap with News Corp. Under the agreement, Liberty received News Corp.'s 38.5% stake in DirecTV, $550 million in cash and three regional sports networks. News Corp. received Liberty's $11.2 billion stake in News Corp. itself. This gives Liberty controlling interest in DirecTV.

FINANCIALS: Sales and profits are in thousands of dollars—add 000 to get the full amount. 2006 Note: Financial information for 2006 was not available for all companies at press time.

2006 Sales: $25,327,000	2006 Profits: $2,314,000	U.S. Stock Ticker: NWS
2005 Sales: $23,859,000	2005 Profits: $2,128,000	Int'l Ticker: Int'l Exchange:
2004 Sales: $20,959,000	2004 Profits: $1,647,000	Employees: 44,000
2003 Sales: $17,474,000	2003 Profits: $1,046,000	Fiscal Year Ends: 6/30
2002 Sales: $16,344,000	2002 Profits: $-6,738,000	Parent Company:

SALARIES/BENEFITS:

Pension Plan:	ESOP Stock Plan:	Profit Sharing:	Top Exec. Salary: $8,100,008	Bonus: $21,175,000
Savings Plan: Y	Stock Purch. Plan:		Second Exec. Salary: $4,508,694	Bonus: $21,175,000

OTHER THOUGHTS:

Apparent Women Officers or Directors: 2
Hot Spot for Advancement for Women/Minorities:

LOCATIONS: ("Y" = Yes)

West:	Southwest:	Midwest:	Southeast:	Northeast:	International:
Y	Y	Y	Y	Y	Y

Note: Financial information, benefits and other data can change quickly and may vary from those stated here.

NEWS WORLD COMMUNICATIONS INC www.washtimes.com

Industry Group Code: 511110 Ranks within this company's industry group: Sales: Profits:

Print Media/Publishing:	Movies:	Equipment/Supplies:	Broadcast/Cable:	Music/Audio:	Sports/Games:
Newspapers: Y	Movie Theaters:	Equipment/Supplies:	Broadcast TV:	Music Production:	Games/Sports:
Magazines: Y	Movie Production:	Gambling Equipment:	Cable TV:	Retail Music:	Retail Games Stores:
Books:	TV/Video Production:	Special Services: Y	Satellite Broadcast:	Retail Audio Equip.:	Stadiums/Teams:
Book Stores:	Video Rental:	Advertising Services:	Radio:	Music Print./Dist.:	Gambling/Casinos:
Distribution/Printing:	Video Distribution:	Info. Sys. Software:	Online Information:	Multimedia:	Rides/Theme Parks:

TYPES OF BUSINESS:

Newspaper Publication
Magazine Publication
Online News & Information
News Agency

BRANDS/DIVISIONS/AFFILIATES:

Washington Times (The)
Middle East Times
Tiempos Del Mundo
Segye Ilbo
Sekai Nippo
The World & I
Insight Magazine
United Press International

CONTACTS: Note: Officers with more than one job title may be intentionally listed here more than once.

Chung Hwan Kwak, Pres.
Keith Cooperrider, CFO/VP
Wesley Pruden, Editor-in-Chief-The Washington Times
Kenneth McIntyre, Assistant Managing Editor-The Washington Times
Chung Hwan Kwak, Chmn.

Phone: 202-636-3000	Fax: 202-269-1245
Toll-Free:	
Address: 3600 New York Ave. NE, Washington, DC 20002-1947 US	

GROWTH PLANS/SPECIAL FEATURES:

News World Communications, Inc., founded in 1982 by Reverend Sun Myung Moon, is a media company owned by the Unification Church. The company's flagship publication, The Washington Times, is a well-known yet financially insolvent newspaper based in the U.S. capital, with a readership of over 100,000. In addition to its daily and weekly issues, the Times also offers online subscriptions from its web site, washtimes.com. The other company newspapers are the Egypt-based Middle East Times and a group of internationally distributed papers, Tiempos Del Mundo, Segye Ilbo, Segye Ilbo USA and Sekai Nippo, all of whose titles can be translated as The World Times from, respectively, Spanish, Korean and Japanese. Also in the firm's portfolio are two Internet news and information sites, The World & I and the World Peace Herald, as well as Insight and Golfstyles magazines. News World also owns the United Press International (UPI) news agency, with services in English, Spanish and Arabic.

FINANCIALS: Sales and profits are in thousands of dollars—add 000 to get the full amount. 2006 Note: Financial information for 2006 was not available for all companies at press time.

2006 Sales: $	2006 Profits: $	U.S. Stock Ticker: Private
2005 Sales: $	2005 Profits: $	Int'l Ticker: Int'l Exchange:
2004 Sales: $	2004 Profits: $	Employees:
2003 Sales: $	2003 Profits: $	Fiscal Year Ends: 3/31
2002 Sales: $	2002 Profits: $	Parent Company:

SALARIES/BENEFITS:

Pension Plan:	ESOP Stock Plan:	Profit Sharing:	Top Exec. Salary: $	Bonus: $
Savings Plan:	Stock Purch. Plan:		Second Exec. Salary: $	Bonus: $

OTHER THOUGHTS:

Apparent Women Officers or Directors:
Hot Spot for Advancement for Women/Minorities:

LOCATIONS: ("Y" = Yes)

West:	Southwest:	Midwest:	Southeast:	Northeast:	International:
				Y	Y

NEXSTAR BROADCASTING GROUP INC   www.nexstar.tv

Industry Group Code: 513120 Ranks within this company's industry group: Sales: 19   Profits: 18

Print Media/Publishing:	Movies:	Equipment/Supplies:	Broadcast/Cable:		Music/Audio:	Sports/Games:
Newspapers:	Movie Theaters:	Equipment/Supplies:	Broadcast TV:	Y	Music Production:	Games/Sports:
Magazines:	Movie Production:	Gambling Equipment:	Cable TV:		Retail Music:	Retail Games Stores:
Books:	TV/Video Production:	Special Services:	Satellite Broadcast:		Retail Audio Equip.:	Stadiums/Teams:
Book Stores:	Video Rental:	Advertising Services:	Radio:		Music Print./Dist.:	Gambling/Casinos:
Distribution/Printing:	Video Distribution:	Info. Sys. Software:	Online Information:		Multimedia:	Rides/Theme Parks:

TYPES OF BUSINESS:
Television Broadcasting

BRANDS/DIVISIONS/AFFILIATES:

GROWTH PLANS/SPECIAL FEATURES:
Nexstar Broadcasting Group, Inc. is a television broadcasting company focused exclusively on the acquisition, development and operation of television stations in medium-sized markets in the U.S. The firm currently owns, operates, programs or provides sales and other services to 46 television stations covering 27 markets in the northeastern, midwestern and southwestern regions of the U.S., reaching approximately 7.4% of U.S. television households. In 16 of the 27 markets that the company serves, it owns or provides services to more than one station. The company's stations are found in Illinois, Indiana, Maryland, Missouri, Montana, Texas, Pennsylvania, Louisiana, Arkansas, Alabama and New York. Most of these stations have primary network affiliations: 12 with NBC, 13 with FOX, nine with ABC, eight with CBS and three with UPN. One is independent. In 2006, Nexstar entered into a definitive agreement to acquire WTAJ-TV, a CBS affiliate in Pennsylvania. Mission Broadcasting, Inc has agreed to acquire KFTA-TV in Arkansas for $5-6 million from Nexstar, pending government approval.

CONTACTS: Note: Officers with more than one job title may be intentionally listed here more than once.
Perry A. Sook, CEO
Duane A. Lammers, COO/Exec. VP
Perry A. Sook, Pres.
Matt Devine, CFO
Paul Greeley, VP-Mktg. & Promotions
Richard Stolpe, VP/Dir.-Eng.
Shirley E. Green, VP-Finance
Brian Jones, Sr. VP/Regional Mgr.
Timothy Busch, Sr. VP/Regional Mgr.
Chris Manson, VP-News
Perry A. Sook, Chmn.

Phone: 972-373-8800   Fax: 972-373-8888
Toll-Free:
Address: 909 Lake Carolyn Pkwy., Ste. 1450, Irving, TX 75039 US

FINANCIALS: Sales and profits are in thousands of dollars—add 000 to get the full amount. 2006 Note: Financial information for 2006 was not available for all companies at press time.
2006 Sales: $	2006 Profits: $	U.S. Stock Ticker: NXST
2005 Sales: $226,053	2005 Profits: $-48,730	Int'l Ticker: Int'l Exchange:
2004 Sales: $245,740	2004 Profits: $-20,500	Employees: 2,164
2003 Sales: $214,332	2003 Profits: $-71,799	Fiscal Year Ends: 12/31
2002 Sales: $133,839	2002 Profits: $-46,796	Parent Company:

SALARIES/BENEFITS:
Pension Plan:	ESOP Stock Plan:	Profit Sharing:	Top Exec. Salary: $650,000	Bonus: $250,000
Savings Plan: Y	Stock Purch. Plan:		Second Exec. Salary: $314,846	Bonus: $200,000

OTHER THOUGHTS:
Apparent Women Officers or Directors: 2
Hot Spot for Advancement for Women/Minorities:

LOCATIONS: ("Y" = Yes)
West:	Southwest:	Midwest:	Southeast:	Northeast:	International:
Y	Y	Y	Y	Y	

Note: Financial information, benefits and other data can change quickly and may vary from those stated here.

NINTENDO CO LTD
www.nintendo.com

Industry Group Code: 334111 Ranks within this company's industry group: Sales: 2 Profits: 2

Print Media/Publishing:	Movies:	Equipment/Supplies:		Broadcast/Cable:	Music/Audio:	Sports/Games:	
Newspapers:	Movie Theaters:	Equipment/Supplies:	Y	Broadcast TV:	Music Production:	Games/Sports:	Y
Magazines:	Movie Production:	Gambling Equipment:		Cable TV:	Retail Music:	Retail Games Stores:	
Books:	TV/Video Production:	Special Services:		Satellite Broadcast:	Retail Audio Equip.:	Stadiums/Teams:	
Book Stores:	Video Rental:	Advertising Services:		Radio:	Music Print./Dist.:	Gambling/Casinos:	
Distribution/Printing:	Video Distribution:	Info. Sys. Software:		Online Information:	Multimedia:	Rides/Theme Parks:	

TYPES OF BUSINESS:
Video Games
Video Game Hardware & Software

BRANDS/DIVISIONS/AFFILIATES:
GameCube
Nintendo DS
Game Boy Advance
Wii
Mario Brothers
Legend of Zelda (The)
Donkey Kong
Pokemon

CONTACTS: *Note: Officers with more than one job title may be intentionally listed here more than once.*
Satoru Iwata, Pres.
Yoshihiro Mori, Sr. Managing Dir.
Shinji Hatano, Sr. Managing Dir.
Genyo Takeda, Sr. Managing Dir.
Shigeru Miyamoto, Sr. Managing Dir.

Phone: 81-75-662-9600	Fax: 81-75-662-9620
Toll-Free:	
Address: 11-1 Kamitoba, Hokotate-cho, Minami-ku, Kyoto, 601-8501 Japan	

GROWTH PLANS/SPECIAL FEATURES:
Nintendo Co., Ltd. makes video game hardware and software. The company's main products are the Nintendo DS, Wii, Game Boy and GameCube video game systems and related software and merchandise. Based in Kyoto, Japan, the company also owns subsidiaries in the U.S., Australia and several countries in Europe. Nintendo has recently devoted much energy to the sale of its portable devices: the Nintendo DS and the Game Boy Advance. Game Boy Advance is essentially a portable version of home-based video consoles, while the DS sports extra features, such as a dual-screen format, an LCD touch screen, wireless connectivity and voice recognition capabilities. The GameCube video game console system, with a standard television hook-up, sells slightly behind Microsoft's Xbox and Sony's PlayStation. The company's newest console and successor to the GameCube is the Wii, which offers a unique remote resembling a TV remote. The Wii remote allows for point-and-click-style game play, and is motion-sensitive. The console offers a menu that provides users with a variety of entertainment, information and communication channels. Nintendo is also a successful producer of software, offering a large number of well-known video games, including proprietary titles Mario Brothers, Donkey Kong, Pokemon and The Legend of Zelda. Nintendo has been aware that the currently constricting market for video games largely involves, first, an over-saturated market and, second, the traditional inability of brands to market outside of the young male demographic. Therefore current marketing campaigns have been attempting to offer unique approaches to hardware and branch out into the older adult and female markets. Examples include Nintendo DS software titles such as Nintendogs and Brain Age; and the Wii system.

FINANCIALS: Sales and profits are in thousands of dollars—add 000 to get the full amount. 2006 Note: Financial information for 2006 was not available for all companies at press time.

2006 Sales: $4,327,100	2006 Profits: $836,600	U.S. Stock Ticker: NTDOY
2005 Sales: $4,788,400	2005 Profits: $812,800	Int'l Ticker: 7974 Int'l Exchange: Tokyo-TSE
2004 Sales: $4,869,400	2004 Profits: $314,200	Employees: 2,977
2003 Sales: $4,206,500	2003 Profits: $561,300	Fiscal Year Ends: 3/31
2002 Sales: $4,183,300	2002 Profits: $802,500	Parent Company:

SALARIES/BENEFITS:
Pension Plan:	ESOP Stock Plan:	Profit Sharing:	Top Exec. Salary: $	Bonus: $
Savings Plan:	Stock Purch. Plan:		Second Exec. Salary: $	Bonus: $

OTHER THOUGHTS:
Apparent Women Officers or Directors:
Hot Spot for Advancement for Women/Minorities:

LOCATIONS: ("Y" = Yes)
West:	Southwest:	Midwest:	Southeast:	Northeast:	International:
Y					Y

NTL INCORPORATED

www.ntl.com

Industry Group Code: 513220 Ranks within this company's industry group: Sales: 13   Profits: 5

Print Media/Publishing:	Movies:	Equipment/Supplies:		Broadcast/Cable:		Music/Audio:	Sports/Games:
Newspapers:	Movie Theaters:	Equipment/Supplies:	Y	Broadcast TV:		Music Production:	Games/Sports:
Magazines:	Movie Production:	Gambling Equipment:	Y	Cable TV:	Y	Retail Music:	Retail Games Stores:
Books:	TV/Video Production:	Special Services:	Y	Satellite Broadcast:		Retail Audio Equip.:	Stadiums/Teams:
Book Stores:	Video Rental:	Advertising Services:		Radio:		Music Print./Dist.:	Gambling/Casinos:
Distribution/Printing:	Video Distribution:	Info. Sys. Software:		Online Information:		Multimedia:	Rides/Theme Parks:

TYPES OF BUSINESS:

Cable TV Services
High-Speed Internet Services
Telephony Services
Television & Radio Broadcasting
Business Telecommunications
Satellite Services

BRANDS/DIVISIONS/AFFILIATES:

Eurobird
Flextech Television
Virgin Mobile
Telewest

CONTACTS: *Note: Officers with more than one job title may be intentionally listed here more than once.*

Steven Burch, CEO
Neil Berkett, COO
Steven Burch, Pres.
Jacques Kerrest, CFO
Carolyn Walker, VP-Human Resources
Phil Pavitt, CIO
Bryan Hall, General Counsel
Shai Wiess, Dir.-Oper.
Ernle Cormier, VP-Corp. Dev.
Keith Monserrat, Dir.-Comm. & Policy
Malcolm Wall, CEO-Content Div.
James F. Mooney, Chmn.

Phone: 44-1256-752-000	**Fax:** 44-1256-754-100
Toll-Free:	
Address: Bartley Wood Business Park, Bartley Way, Hook, Hampshlre R627 9UP UK	

GROWTH PLANS/SPECIAL FEATURES:

NTL Incorporated is a leading communications company in the U.K., as well as a leading provider of broadband Internet. Its residential telecommunications and television bundled services include residential telephony, cable television and Internet access services, also known as the NTL triple play package. National services include national business telecommunications, national and international carrier services, Internet services and satellite and radio communications services. NTL provides its services over local, national and international network infrastructure. The company operates advanced local broadband networks serving entire communities throughout NTL's regional franchise areas. The broadcast transmission network provides national, regional and local analog and digital transmission services to customers throughout the U.K. The company's content division, Flextech Television, provides television channels for the U.K. market with the following six channels: Livingtv, Livingtv 2, Bravo, Challenge, Trouble, Ftn and is a 50% partner in UKTV. Within the U.K., the company has 3.3 million residential customers and 1.8 million broadband customers. In March 2006, NTL completed its merger with Telewest, a leading provider of television and communications services. Shortly after, the company initiated another large scale merger, this time with Virgin Mobile. If approved, Virgin Mobile would pass over to NTL, while NTL retained use of the Virgin brand name.

FINANCIALS: Sales and profits are in thousands of dollars—add 000 to get the full amount. 2006 Note: Financial information for 2006 was not available for all companies at press time.

2006 Sales: $	2006 Profits: $	**U.S. Stock Ticker:** NTLI
2005 Sales: $3,402,304	2005 Profits: $735,411	**Int'l Ticker:** Int'l Exchange:
2004 Sales: $3,494,332	2004 Profits: $-847,033	Employees: 12,480
2003 Sales: $3,645,200	2003 Profits: $-954,200	Fiscal Year Ends: 12/31
2002 Sales: $3,265,100	2002 Profits: $-2,375,800	Parent Company:

SALARIES/BENEFITS:

Pension Plan: Y	ESOP Stock Plan:	Profit Sharing:	Top Exec. Salary: $1,166,667	Bonus: $370,000
Savings Plan:	Stock Purch. Plan:		Second Exec. Salary: $1,020,359	Bonus: $1,061,411

OTHER THOUGHTS:

Apparent Women Officers or Directors: 1
Hot Spot for Advancement for Women/Minorities:

LOCATIONS: ("Y" = Yes)

West:	Southwest:	Midwest:	Southeast:	Northeast:	International:
				Y	Y

Note: Financial information, benefits and other data can change quickly and may vary from those stated here.

NTN BUZZTIME INC

www.ntn.com

Industry Group Code: 511208 Ranks within this company's industry group: Sales: 9   Profits: 8

Print Media/Publishing:	Movies:		Equipment/Supplies:		Broadcast/Cable:		Music/Audio:	Sports/Games:	
Newspapers:	Movie Theaters:		Equipment/Supplies:	Y	Broadcast TV:		Music Production:	Games/Sports:	Y
Magazines:	Movie Production:		Gambling Equipment:		Cable TV:	Y	Retail Music:	Retail Games Stores:	
Books:	TV/Video Production:	Y	Special Services:	Y	Satellite Broadcast:		Retail Audio Equip.:	Stadiums/Teams:	
Book Stores:	Video Rental:		Advertising Services:		Radio:		Music Print./Dist.:	Gambling/Casinos:	
Distribution/Printing:	Video Distribution:		Info. Sys. Software:	Y	Online Information:		Multimedia:	Rides/Theme Parks:	

TYPES OF BUSINESS:

Interactive Sports & Trivia Games
On-Site Wireless Communications Products
Restaurant & Hospitality Software

BRANDS/DIVISIONS/AFFILIATES:

NTN Hospitality Technologies
Buzztime Entertainment, Inc.
NTN Buzztime Networks
NTN Wireless Communications, Inc.
NTN Software Solutions, Inc.
QB1
NTN Enterprise
NTN Buzztime, Inc.

CONTACTS: *Note: Officers with more than one job title may be intentionally listed here more than once.*

Dario Santana, CEO
Dario Santana, Pres.
Kendra Berger, CFO
Steve Riccabona, VP-Mktg. & Sales, NTN iTV Network
V. Tyrone Lam, Pres./COO-Buzztime Entertainment, Inc.
Michele Richards, CTO-NTN Buzztime, Inc.
John A. Boozer, Sr. VP-Global Sales
Stanley B. Kinsey, Chmn.

Phone: 760-438-7400	**Fax:** 619-438-7470
Toll-Free:	
Address: 5966 La Place Ct., Ste. 100, Carlsbad, CA 92008 US	

GROWTH PLANS/SPECIAL FEATURES:

NTN Buzztime, Inc., formerly NTN Communications, is a holding company for NTN Hospitality Technologies and its subsidiary Buzztime Entertainment, Inc. NTN Hospitality operates through NTN Interactive Entertainment Networks, NTN Wireless Communications, Inc. and NTN Software Solutions, Inc. Buzztime Entertainment produces Buzztime (an interactive trivia channel) and sports prediction games such as QB1 and Predict The Play. It also owns one of the largest trivia game libraries in the world and publishes trivia books such as Mickey Dolenz' Rock n' Rollin Trivia. NTN Buzztime is one of the world's largest home interactive entertainment networks. It delivers entertainment and sports games to more than 1.7 million players and reaches more than 6 million customers a month through approximately 3,600 restaurants, sports bars and taverns across the U.S. and the UK. NTN Wireless manufactures, sells and repairs on-site communications products (primarily guest and server paging products that tell customers when their table or food is ready) to over 3,000 restaurants, as well as providing on-site messaging solutions for hospitals, church and synagogue nurseries, salons, business offices and retail locations. NTN Software designs, develops and markets primarily Windows-based software for more than 300 restaurant and hospitality companies in more than 3,300 locations in 45 countries. Its products include NTN VISION, a point-of-sale restaurant management system; NTN Enterprise, a web-based enterprise management system; NTN ProHost, a seating management system; and NTN RSViP, a reservation management system. NTN Software also provides NTN Member Services, such as stored-value gift card and loyalty programs. In 2006, the company re-branded their NTN iTV network as the Buzztime Network. The company expanded its QB1 Predict-the-Play game to include players on advanced mobile phones and Internet-connected PCs.

FINANCIALS: Sales and profits are in thousands of dollars—add 000 to get the full amount. 2006 Note: Financial information for 2006 was not available for all companies at press time.

2006 Sales: $	2006 Profits: $	**U.S. Stock Ticker:** NTN
2005 Sales: $40,759	2005 Profits: $-2,019	**Int'l Ticker:**　Int'l Exchange:
2004 Sales: $35,655	2004 Profits: $-4,979	Employees:　216
2003 Sales: $29,489	2003 Profits: $-2,711	Fiscal Year Ends: 12/31
2002 Sales: $25,600	2002 Profits: $-2,200	Parent Company:

SALARIES/BENEFITS:

Pension Plan:	ESOP Stock Plan:	Profit Sharing:	Top Exec. Salary: $389,000	Bonus: $15,000
Savings Plan: Y	Stock Purch. Plan:		Second Exec. Salary: $283,000	Bonus: $15,000

OTHER THOUGHTS:

Apparent Women Officers or Directors: 2
Hot Spot for Advancement for Women/Minorities:

LOCATIONS: ("Y" = Yes)

West:	Southwest:	Midwest:	Southeast:	Northeast:	International:
Y	Y		Y		

OMNICOM GROUP INC
www.omnicomgroup.com

Industry Group Code: 541810   Ranks within this company's industry group: Sales: 1   Profits: 1

Print Media/Publishing:	Movies:	Equipment/Supplies:		Broadcast/Cable:	Music/Audio:	Sports/Games:
Newspapers:	Movie Theaters:	Equipment/Supplies:		Broadcast TV:	Music Production:	Games/Sports:
Magazines:	Movie Production:	Gambling Equipment:		Cable TV:	Retail Music:	Retail Games Stores:
Books:	TV/Video Production:	Special Services:	Y	Satellite Broadcast:	Retail Audio Equip.:	Stadiums/Teams:
Book Stores:	Video Rental:	Advertising Services:	Y	Radio:	Music Print./Dist.:	Gambling/Casinos:
Distribution/Printing:	Video Distribution:	Info. Sys. Software:		Online Information:	Multimedia:	Rides/Theme Parks:

TYPES OF BUSINESS:

Advertising Services
Public Relations
Market Research
Marketing & Brand Consulting
Interactive & Search Engine Marketing
Media Planning & Buying
Health Care Communications
Printing

BRANDS/DIVISIONS/AFFILIATES:

BBDO Worldwide Network
DDB Worldwide
TBWA Worldwide
Arnell Group
Goodby, Silverstein & Partners
OMD Worldwide
Ketchum
DAS

CONTACTS: Note: Officers with more than one job title may be intentionally listed here more than once.

John D. Wren, CEO
John D. Wren, Pres.
Randall J. Weisenburger, CFO/Exec. VP
Michael J. O'Brien, General Counsel/Sr. VP/Corp. Sec.
Philip J. Angelastro, VP-Finance/Controller
Michael Burkin, Vice Chmn.
Bruce Redditt, Exec. VP
Susan S. Ellis, Exec. VP
Phillp J. George, Tax Counsel
Bruce Crawford, Chmn.

Phone: 212-415-3600	Fax: 212-415-3530
Toll-Free:	
Address: 437 Madison Ave., New York, NY 10022 US	

GROWTH PLANS/SPECIAL FEATURES:

Omnicom Group, Inc. is a holding company that, through its subsidiaries, is one of the largest advertising, marketing and corporate communications companies in the world. The firm owns hundreds of subsidiary agencies operating in all major markets worldwide. Its agencies provide an extensive range of services, mainly focusing on advertising, marketing services, specialty communications, media buying, digital media and public relations. Specialty communications refers to an integration of customer relationship management services, such as sports and events marketing, non-profit marketing and branding design, promotional marketing, public relations and specialized marketing, such as healthcare, corporate and financial marketing. Other group activities of note include experiential marketing, instore design, mobile marketing, package design, custom printing, reputation consulting and search engine marketing. Omnicom's manifold agency brands include global advertisers BBDO Worldwide, DDB Worldwide and TBWA Worldwide; national advertisers Arnell Group, Goodby Silverstein & Partners; media services companies OMD Worldwide and PHD Network; public relations specialists Ketchum, Porter Novelli International, Clark & Weinstock and Cone; and specialty communications firm DAS. Recent acquisitions include majority stakes in 180 Amsterdam, Gotocustomer Services India, EVB, and Unisono Fieldmarketing International Limited. In 2006, the company also acquired Rodgers Townsend, a St. Louis-based advertising agency.

FINANCIALS: Sales and profits are in thousands of dollars—add 000 to get the full amount. 2006 Note: Financial information for 2006 was not available for all companies at press time.

2006 Sales: $	2006 Profits: $	U.S. Stock Ticker: OMC
2005 Sales: $10,481,100	2005 Profits: $790,700	Int'l Ticker: Int'l Exchange:
2004 Sales: $9,747,200	2004 Profits: $723,500	Employees: 62,000
2003 Sales: $8,621,404	2003 Profits: $675,883	Fiscal Year Ends: 12/31
2002 Sales: $7,536,000	2002 Profits: $644,000	Parent Company:

SALARIES/BENEFITS:

Pension Plan:	ESOP Stock Plan:	Profit Sharing: Y	Top Exec. Salary: $1,004,796	Bonus: $2,500,000
Savings Plan:	Stock Purch. Plan: Y		Second Exec. Salary: $1,000,000	Bonus: $4,000,000

OTHER THOUGHTS:

Apparent Women Officers or Directors: 3
Hot Spot for Advancement for Women/Minorities: Y

LOCATIONS: ("Y" = Yes)

West:	Southwest:	Midwest:	Southeast:	Northeast:	International:
Y	Y	Y	Y	Y	Y

Note: Financial information, benefits and other data can change quickly and may vary from those stated here.

OMNIVISION TECHNOLOGIES INC

www.ovt.com

Industry Group Code: 334310 Ranks within this company's industry group: Sales: 9 Profits: 5

Print Media/Publishing:	Movies:	Equipment/Supplies:		Broadcast/Cable:	Music/Audio:	Sports/Games:
Newspapers:	Movie Theaters:	Equipment/Supplies:	Y	Broadcast TV:	Music Production:	Games/Sports:
Magazines:	Movie Production:	Gambling Equipment:		Cable TV:	Retail Music:	Retail Games Stores:
Books:	TV/Video Production:	Special Services:		Satellite Broadcast:	Retail Audio Equip.:	Stadiums/Teams:
Book Stores:	Video Rental:	Advertising Services:		Radio:	Music Print./Dist.:	Gambling/Casinos:
Distribution/Printing:	Video Distribution:	Info. Sys. Software:		Online Information:	Multimedia:	Rides/Theme Parks:

TYPES OF BUSINESS:

Digital Imaging Sensors
Optical Technologies

BRANDS/DIVISIONS/AFFILIATES:

CameraChip
VisEra Technologies Company Ltd.
CDM Optics, Inc.
WaveFront

CONTACTS: *Note: Officers with more than one job title may be intentionally listed here more than once.*

Shaw Hong, CEO
James He, COO
Peter V. Leigh, CFO
Howard E. Rhodes, VP-Process Eng.
Y. Vicky Chou, VP-Legal/General Counsel
Peter V. Leigh, VP-Finance
John T. Yue, VP-Quality & Reliability
Hasan Gadjali, VP-Advanced Products Bus. Unit
Jess Lee, VP-Mainstream Products Bus. Unit

Phone: 408-542-3000	Fax: 408-542-3001
Toll-Free:	
Address: 1341 Orleans Dr., Sunnyvale, CA 94089 US	

GROWTH PLANS/SPECIAL FEATURES:

OmniVision Technologies, Inc. designs, develops and markets semiconductor image sensor devices. The company's CameraChip image sensors capture images electronically and are sold to OEMs and VARs, as well as through distributors, for use in a variety of consumer and commercial products. CameraChip sensors are predominantly single-chip CMOS (complementary metal oxide semiconductor) chips that integrate a number of distinct functions, including image capture, image processing, color processing and signal conversion. CMOS chips cost less, are smaller and consume less power than the predominant CCD (charge-coupled device) imaging chips. Products that incorporate these sensors include camera cell phones, digital still and video cameras, personal computer camera applications, toy cameras, security and surveillance products, automotive products and medical imaging devices. OmniVision's technologies include OmniPixel and OmniPixel2 architecture. The latter, introduced in late 2005, is less than half the size of OmniPixel architecture, but with improved performance. The company owns 43% of VisEra Technologies Company Ltd., a Taiwan-based joint venture with Taiwan Semiconductor Manufacturing Company provides OmniVision with manufacturing and testing services. The firm's marketing efforts comprise two departments: the Mainstream Products unit addresses camera cell phones and digital still cameras; and the Advanced Products unit addresses the security, toys and games, personal computers, interactive video, automotive and medical markets. OmniVision recently acquired CDM Optics, Inc., based in Boulder, Colorado, whose WaveFront Coding technology is expected to reduce the size and complexity of camera autofocus systems. In October 2006, OmniVision launched the world's smallest 1.3-megapixel sensor; and launched a CameraChip sensor specifically designed for automotive applications.

OmniVision offers its employees medical, dental, vision and prescription drug benefits; flexible spending accounts; various income protection plans; an employee assistance plan; pre-paid legal services; travel assistance; identity theft protection; profit sharing and bonus awards; a 401(k) plan; and an employee stock purchase plan.

FINANCIALS: Sales and profits are in thousands of dollars—add 000 to get the full amount. 2006 Note: Financial information for 2006 was not available for all companies at press time.

2006 Sales: $481,926	2006 Profits: $89,148	**U.S. Stock Ticker: OVTI**
2005 Sales: $388,062	2005 Profits: $76,387	**Int'l Ticker:** Int'l Exchange:
2004 Sales: $318,123	2004 Profits: $58,745	Employees: 1,644
2003 Sales: $108,998	2003 Profits: $15,324	Fiscal Year Ends: 4/30
2002 Sales: $46,518	2002 Profits: $-1,274	Parent Company:

SALARIES/BENEFITS:

Pension Plan:	ESOP Stock Plan:	Profit Sharing: Y	Top Exec. Salary: $404,167	Bonus: $90,000
Savings Plan: Y	Stock Purch. Plan: Y		Second Exec. Salary: $270,833	Bonus: $82,000

OTHER THOUGHTS:

Apparent Women Officers or Directors: 1
Hot Spot for Advancement for Women/Minorities: Y

LOCATIONS: ("Y" = Yes)

West:	Southwest:	Midwest:	Southeast:	Northeast:	International:
Y		Y		Y	Y

ON COMMAND CORP

www.oncommand.com

Industry Group Code: 513220 Ranks within this company's industry group: Sales: Profits:

Print Media/Publishing:		Movies:		Equipment/Supplies:		Broadcast/Cable:		Music/Audio:		Sports/Games:	
Newspapers:		Movie Theaters:		Equipment/Supplies:		Broadcast TV:		Music Production:		Games/Sports:	
Magazines:		Movie Production:		Gambling Equipment:		Cable TV:		Retail Music:		Retail Games Stores:	
Books:		TV/Video Production:		Special Services:	Y	Satellite Broadcast:		Retail Audio Equip.:		Stadiums/Teams:	
Book Stores:		Video Rental:		Advertising Services:	Y	Radio:		Music Print./Dist.:		Gambling/Casinos:	
Distribution/Printing:		Video Distribution:		Info. Sys. Software:	Y	Online Information:		Multimedia:		Rides/Theme Parks:	

TYPES OF BUSINESS:

Pay-Per-View Entertainment
Video-on-Demand
High-Speed Internet Access
Music-on-Demand
Advertising Sales

BRANDS/DIVISIONS/AFFILIATES:

@Hotel TV
@Hotel PC
OCX
Liberty Media Corporation
Hotelvision, Inc.
MiniMate

CONTACTS: *Note: Officers with more than one job title may be intentionally listed here more than once.*

Christopher Sophinos, CEO
Christopher Sophinos, Pres.
Chris O'Toole, Sr. VP/CFO
Tad Walden, Sr. VP-Mktg. & Programming
Phillip Pinon, CTO
Phillip Pinon, Group VP-Eng.
Pamela Strauss, Sr. VP/General Counsel
John Johnson, Sr. VP-Oper.
David A. Simpson, Sr. VP-Bus. Dev.
David Goldstone, Group VP-Sales
Chris Bracken, VP-Corp. Planning
Marty Sabraw, VP-Bus. Dev.

Phone: 720-873-3200	Fax: 720-873-3297

Toll-Free: 800-797-7654

Address: 4610 S. Ulster St., Tower II, 6th Fl., Denver, CO 80237 US

GROWTH PLANS/SPECIAL FEATURES:

On Command Corporation, a subsidiary of Liberty Media Corporation, is a leading provider of pay-per-view entertainment and information services to hotels and cruise ships. Its customers include more than 100 well-known hotel chains such as Four Seasons, Marriott, Hilton, Hyatt and Embassy Suites, as well as the Royal Caribbean, Costa and Carnival cruise lines. The firm and its distribution network serve more than 300 million guests annually through approximately 800,000 hotel guest rooms in the U.S., Canada, Mexico and Spain. The company's services include on-demand movies, television Internet service using high-speed broadband connections, television e-mail, Sony PlayStation video games, music-on-command through Instant Media Network and television features through its partnership with DIRECTV. The firm also offers a variety of free channels, including Disney, HBO, ESPN and Showtime as well as anywhere from 25 to 55 recently released movies for pay-per-view purposes. On Command's system allows a customer to order and view a movie instantly, without the hassle of a schedule, unlike other pay-per-view systems. On Command is also a leading provider of in-room high-speed Internet access, which it offers through packages called @Hotel TV and @Hotel PC, which enable guests to surf the web using the televisions in their rooms. The company also offers MiniMate, the video-on-demand system for small hotels. In addition, the company's high-speed, two-way digital communications capability allows video checkout, through which a customer can use the TV in their room to view their bill and check out of the hotel. The company aggressively promotes its OCX multimedia services platform, which features an improved graphical user interface for movies and games and TV-based Internet with a keyboard. In late 2006, On Command's parent company Liberty Media sold the company to LodgeNet Entertainment Corporation.

FINANCIALS: Sales and profits are in thousands of dollars—add 000 to get the full amount. 2006 Note: Financial information for 2006 was not available for all companies at press time.

2006 Sales: $	2006 Profits: $	**U.S. Stock Ticker:** Subsidiary	
2005 Sales: $	2005 Profits: $	**Int'l Ticker:** Int'l Exchange:	
2004 Sales: $	2004 Profits: $	Employees: 620	
2003 Sales: $	2003 Profits: $	Fiscal Year Ends: 12/31	
2002 Sales: $238,397	2002 Profits: $-42,607	Parent Company: LODGENET ENTERTAINMENT CORP	

SALARIES/BENEFITS:

Pension Plan:	ESOP Stock Plan:	Profit Sharing:	Top Exec. Salary: $324,989	Bonus: $50,000
Savings Plan: Y	Stock Purch. Plan: Y		Second Exec. Salary: $299,063	Bonus: $90,312

OTHER THOUGHTS:

Apparent Women Officers or Directors: 1
Hot Spot for Advancement for Women/Minorities:

LOCATIONS: ("Y" = Yes)

West:	Southwest:	Midwest:	Southeast:	Northeast:	International:
Y	Y	Y	Y	Y	Y

ON STAGE ENTERTAINMENT   www.legendsinconcert.com

Industry Group Code: 512110 Ranks within this company's industry group: Sales: Profits:

Print Media/Publishing:	Movies:	Equipment/Supplies:	Broadcast/Cable:	Music/Audio:	Sports/Games:	
Newspapers:	Movie Theaters:	Equipment/Supplies:	Broadcast TV:	Music Production:	Games/Sports:	Y
Magazines:	Movie Production:	Gambling Equipment:	Cable TV:	Retail Music:	Retail Games Stores:	
Books:	TV/Video Production:	Special Services:	Satellite Broadcast:	Retail Audio Equip.:	Stadiums/Teams:	
Book Stores:	Video Rental:	Advertising Services:	Radio:	Music Print./Dist.:	Gambling/Casinos:	
Distribution/Printing:	Video Distribution:	Info. Sys. Software:	Online Information:	Multimedia:	Rides/Theme Parks:	

TYPES OF BUSINESS:

Theatrical Productions
Dinner Theaters

BRANDS/DIVISIONS/AFFILIATES:

Legends in Concert

GROWTH PLANS/SPECIAL FEATURES:

On Stage Entertainment produces and markets theatrical productions and operates live theaters and dinner theaters. The company's flagship production, Legends in Concert, features impersonators who perform as famous performance artists, for example, Elvis Presley, the Blues Brothers, Tina Turner, Michael Jackson and Marilyn Monroe. The company markets its productions directly to audiences at theaters in resort and urban tourist locations. Although the company started in Las Vegas, it owns permanent venues in Atlantic City, New Jersey; Myrtle Beach, South Carolina; Branson, Missouri; and Hollywood, Florida. On Stage also markets its productions to commercial clients, which include casinos, corporations, fairs and expositions, theme and amusement parks and cruise lines. In addition, the company sells souvenirs, such as clothing and videotapes. The firm has performed for major corporate clients such as McDonald's, Anheuser-Busch, Hewlett Packard, IBM, Pitney Bowes, Levi Strauss and Exxon.

CONTACTS: Note: Officers with more than one job title may be intentionally listed here more than once.

Timothy J. Parrott, CEO
Jeffery Victor, COO
Jeffery Victor, Pres.
Joseph Bobowicz, CFO/VP
Timothy J. Parrott, Chmn.

Phone: 702-253-1333	Fax: 702-253-1122
Toll-Free:	
Address: 333 Orville Wright Ct., Las Vegas, NV 89119 US	

FINANCIALS: Sales and profits are in thousands of dollars—add 000 to get the full amount. 2006 Note: Financial information for 2006 was not available for all companies at press time.

2006 Sales: $	2006 Profits: $	U.S. Stock Ticker: Private
2005 Sales: $	2005 Profits: $	Int'l Ticker: Int'l Exchange:
2004 Sales: $	2004 Profits: $	Employees: 400
2003 Sales: $21,700	2003 Profits: $	Fiscal Year Ends: 12/31
2002 Sales: $22,000	2002 Profits: $	Parent Company:

SALARIES/BENEFITS:

Pension Plan:	ESOP Stock Plan:	Profit Sharing:	Top Exec. Salary: $308,333	Bonus: $87,500
Savings Plan:	Stock Purch. Plan:		Second Exec. Salary: $114,400	Bonus: $

OTHER THOUGHTS:

Apparent Women Officers or Directors:
Hot Spot for Advancement for Women/Minorities:

LOCATIONS: ("Y" = Yes)

West:	Southwest:	Midwest:	Southeast:	Northeast:	International:
Y		Y	Y	Y	

Note: Financial information, benefits and other data can change quickly and may vary from those stated here.

PALACE ENTERTAINMENT   www.palaceentertainment.com

Industry Group Code: 713110 Ranks within this company's industry group: Sales: Profits:

Print Media/Publishing:	Movies:	Equipment/Supplies:	Broadcast/Cable:	Music/Audio:	Sports/Games:	
Newspapers:	Movie Theaters:	Equipment/Supplies:	Broadcast TV:	Music Production:	Games/Sports:	Y
Magazines:	Movie Production:	Gambling Equipment:	Cable TV:	Retail Music:	Retail Games Stores:	
Books:	TV/Video Production:	Special Services:	Satellite Broadcast:	Retail Audio Equip.:	Stadiums/Teams:	
Book Stores:	Video Rental:	Advertising Services:	Radio:	Music Print./Dist.:	Gambling/Casinos:	
Distribution/Printing:	Video Distribution:	Info. Sys. Software:	Online Information:	Multimedia:	Rides/Theme Parks:	Y

TYPES OF BUSINESS:

Amusement Parks
Auto Racetracks
Water Parks

BRANDS/DIVISIONS/AFFILIATES:

Malibu Grand Prix
Mountasia
SpeedZone
Wet 'N Wild
Big Kahuna's
Mountasia
Raging Waters
MidOcean Partners

CONTACTS: *Note: Officers with more than one job title may be intentionally listed here more than once.*

John Cora, CEO
John Cora, Pres.

Phone: 949-261-0404	Fax: 949-261-1414
Toll-Free:	
Address: 4590 MacArthur Blvd., Ste. 400, Newport Beach, CA 92660 US	

GROWTH PLANS/SPECIAL FEATURES:

Palace Entertainment owns and operates multiple-attraction entertainment and amusement parks designed for families. The company operates a total of 35 parks and has well over 12 million visitors per year. Primarily, it operates facilities that feature water parks, miniature golf courses, go-karts, bumper boats, batting cages, arcades, souvenir concession stands and, in some parks, scaled grand-prix-style racetracks utilizing the company's proprietary Malibu Grand Prix race cars. Palace has also introduced a new type of entertainment center called SpeedZone, with locations in Los Angeles and Dallas. Designed for teens, these centers include the Malibu Grand Prix attraction and the new Top Eliminator high-speed racing venue along with other regular amusements. The Grand Prix and Top Eliminator attractions feature cars designed by professionals in the racing industry. The company also operates water parks, including Wet 'N Wild in Las Vegas, Nevada and Greensboro, North Carolina; Raging Waters in San Dimas and San Jose, California; Splish Splash in Riverhead, New York; Big Kahuna's in Destin, Florida; Water Country in Portsmouth, New Hampshire; Mountain Creek in Vernon, New Jersey; and Wild Waters in Ocala, Florida. Palace also owns Boomers, Castle Park, Silver Springs, Malibu Grand Prix, Mountasia and SpeedZone family entertainment parks in California, Texas, Florida, Georgia and New York. In February 2006, MidOcean Partners, a New York and London-based private investment firm, announced its acquisition of Palace Entertainment. Palace will continue all of its operations.

FINANCIALS: Sales and profits are in thousands of dollars—add 000 to get the full amount. 2006 Note: Financial information for 2006 was not available for all companies at press time.

2006 Sales: $	2006 Profits: $	**U.S. Stock Ticker: Private**
2005 Sales: $	2005 Profits: $	**Int'l Ticker:** Int'l Exchange:
2004 Sales: $	2004 Profits: $	Employees: 871
2003 Sales: $	2003 Profits: $	Fiscal Year Ends: 12/31
2002 Sales: $	2002 Profits: $	Parent Company:

SALARIES/BENEFITS:

Pension Plan:	ESOP Stock Plan:	Profit Sharing:	Top Exec. Salary: $310,577	Bonus: $317,779
Savings Plan: Y	Stock Purch. Plan:		Second Exec. Salary: $147,404	Bonus: $86,332

OTHER THOUGHTS:

Apparent Women Officers or Directors:
Hot Spot for Advancement for Women/Minorities:

LOCATIONS: ("Y" = Yes)

West:	Southwest:	Midwest:	Southeast:	Northeast:	International:
Y	Y	Y	Y	Y	

PANAMSAT CORP

www.panamsat.com

Industry Group Code: 513220 Ranks within this company's industry group: Sales: 18   Profits: 11

Print Media/Publishing:	Movies:	Equipment/Supplies:		Broadcast/Cable:	Music/Audio:	Sports/Games:
Newspapers:	Movie Theaters:	Equipment/Supplies:		Broadcast TV:	Music Production:	Games/Sports:
Magazines:	Movie Production:	Gambling Equipment:	Y	Cable TV:	Retail Music:	Retail Games Stores:
Books:	TV/Video Production:	Special Services:	Y	Satellite Broadcast:	Retail Audio Equip.:	Stadiums/Teams:
Book Stores:	Video Rental:	Advertising Services:		Radio:	Music Print./Dist.:	Gambling/Casinos:
Distribution/Printing:	Video Distribution:	Info. Sys. Software:		Online Information:	Multimedia:	Rides/Theme Parks:

TYPES OF BUSINESS:

Satellite Communications
Satellite-Based Broadcasting
Government Services
Technical Support Services
Private Satellite Communications Services

BRANDS/DIVISIONS/AFFILIATES:

PanAmSat de Mexico
PanAmSat do Brasil
PanAmSat Holding Corporation
Intelsat

CONTACTS: *Note: Officers with more than one job title may be intentionally listed here more than once.*

Joseph R. Wright, Jr., CEO
James B. Frownfelter, COO
James B. Frownfelter, Pres.
Michael Antonovich, Exec. VP-Global Sales & Mktg.
James W. Cuminale, Exec. VP/General Counsel
James W. Cuminale, Exec. VP-Corp. Dev.
Kathryn Lancioni, VP-Corp. Comm.
Thomas E. Eaton, Jr., Exec. VP/Pres., G2 Satellite Solutions
James W. Cuminale, Corp. Sec.

Phone: 203-210-8000	**Fax:** 203-210-9163
Toll-Free: 800-726-2672	
Address: 20 Westport Rd., Wilton, CT 06897 US	

GROWTH PLANS/SPECIAL FEATURES:

PanAmSat Corporation, a subsidiary of Intelsat, provides video, corporate, Internet, voice and government communications services through its fleet of 23 in-orbit satellites. It also leases transponder capacity to a variety of customers, including cable television systems, television broadcasters, direct-to-home (DTH) television systems, Internet service providers (ISPs), telecommunications companies, governments and corporations. The company serves clients in the U.S., Latin America, Africa, South Asia, Asia-Pacific, the Middle East, the Caribbean and Europe. The firm's video services provide satellite services for transmitting news, sports, entertainment and educational functions. With its 23 satellites in orbit, including two in-orbit backups, the company has the world's largest commercial geostationary satellite network, allowing it to reach 98% of the world's population. PanAmSat's customers include some of the world's largest media and communications companies, such as Time Warner, Inc. (including HBO, TBS and CNN); the BBC); The News Corporation (including the Fox family of channels and The DIRECTV Group); Sony; Viacom (including MTV and Nickelodeon); China Central Television; Doordarshan (India); Comcast; and the Walt Disney Company (including ABC and ESPN); as well as civilian and military government agencies and contractors. In August 2005, Intelsat agreed to acquire PanAmSat for $3.2 billion dollars, resulting in the creation of a new satellite company. This new entity, with a combined fleet of 53 satellites serving 220 countries and territories, will offer expanded coverage with additional back-up satellites, supporting fiber networks and enhanced operational capabilities.

PanAmSat offers a benefits package including flexible spending accounts, employee assistance, tuition reimbursement and annual incentives.

FINANCIALS: Sales and profits are in thousands of dollars—add 000 to get the full amount. 2006 Note: Financial information for 2006 was not available for all companies at press time.

2006 Sales: $	2006 Profits: $	**U.S. Stock Ticker: PA**
2005 Sales: $861,003	2005 Profits: $72,729	**Int'l Ticker:** Int'l Exchange:
2004 Sales: $827,070	2004 Profits: $-79,000	Employees: 607
2003 Sales: $831,011	2003 Profits: $99,532	Fiscal Year Ends: 12/31
2002 Sales: $812,300	2002 Profits: $85,000	Parent Company:

SALARIES/BENEFITS:

Pension Plan:	ESOP Stock Plan:	Profit Sharing:	Top Exec. Salary: $685,000	Bonus: $753,500
Savings Plan: Y	Stock Purch. Plan: Y		Second Exec. Salary: $448,000	Bonus: $492,800

OTHER THOUGHTS:

Apparent Women Officers or Directors: 1
Hot Spot for Advancement for Women/Minorities:

LOCATIONS: ("Y" = Yes)

West:	Southwest:	Midwest:	Southeast:	Northeast:	International:
Y				Y	Y

PARAMOUNT PICTURES CORP   www.paramount.com

Industry Group Code: 512110 Ranks within this company's industry group: Sales: 6   Profits:

Print Media/Publishing:	Movies:		Equipment/Supplies:		Broadcast/Cable:	Music/Audio:	Sports/Games:
Newspapers:	Movie Theaters:		Equipment/Supplies:		Broadcast TV:	Music Production:	Games/Sports:
Magazines:	Movie Production:	Y	Gambling Equipment:		Cable TV:	Retail Music:	Retail Games Stores:
Books:	TV/Video Production:	Y	Special Services:	Y	Satellite Broadcast:	Retail Audio Equip.:	Stadiums/Teams:
Book Stores:	Video Rental:		Advertising Services:		Radio:	Music Print./Dist.:	Gambling/Casinos:
Distribution/Printing:	Video Distribution:		Info. Sys. Software:		Online Information:	Multimedia:	Rides/Theme Parks:

TYPES OF BUSINESS:

Film Production & Distribution
Television Production
Post-Production Services
Home Video & DVD Production & Distribution

BRANDS/DIVISIONS/AFFILIATES:

Viacom
Paramount Pictures
Paramount Classics
Paramount Home Entertainment
Dreamworks Pictures

CONTACTS: Note: Officers with more than one job title may be intentionally listed here more than once.

Brad Gray, CEO
Frederick D. Huntsberry, COO
Gail Berman, Pres.
Mark Badagliacca, CFO/Exec. VP
Rob Moore, Pres., Mktg. & Distribution
Brad Grey, Chmn.

Phone: 323-956-5000	Fax: 323-862-1204
Toll-Free:	
Address: 5555 Melrose Ave., Hollywood, CA 90038 US	

GROWTH PLANS/SPECIAL FEATURES:

Paramount Pictures Corporation, a subsidiary of Viacom, produces and distributes feature films and television programs through Paramount Pictures, Paramount Classics and Paramount Home Entertainment. The studio's recent releases include War of the Worlds, Sky Captain and the World of Tomorrow, The Longest Yard and Mean Girls. The studio releases about a dozen films annually, many of which rank among the top grossing films for the year. Paramount also produces television shows, including J.A.G., Dr. Phil, Entertainment Tonight, the various Star Trek series and Judge Judy. Some of the studio's most successful productions include The Godfather, Grease, the Indiana Jones Trilogy and Titanic. Paramount maintains an active licensing department, as well as a comprehensive center for post-production services. In 2006, the company acquired Dreamworks Pictures.

Paramount Pictures provides its employees with benefits including medical and dental plans; spending accounts; life, accident and disability insurance; and tuition reimbursement. The company also provides paid internship opportunities to university students.

FINANCIALS: Sales and profits are in thousands of dollars—add 000 to get the full amount. 2006 Note: Financial information for 2006 was not available for all companies at press time.

2006 Sales: $	2006 Profits: $	U.S. Stock Ticker: Subsidiary
2005 Sales: $2,898,700	2005 Profits: $	Int'l Ticker: Int'l Exchange:
2004 Sales: $2,205,600	2004 Profits: $	Employees:
2003 Sales: $	2003 Profits: $	Fiscal Year Ends: 12/31
2002 Sales: $	2002 Profits: $	Parent Company: VIACOM INC

SALARIES/BENEFITS:

Pension Plan: Y	ESOP Stock Plan:	Profit Sharing:	Top Exec. Salary: $	Bonus: $
Savings Plan: Y	Stock Purch. Plan:		Second Exec. Salary: $	Bonus: $

OTHER THOUGHTS:

Apparent Women Officers or Directors: 1
Hot Spot for Advancement for Women/Minorities:

LOCATIONS: ("Y" = Yes)

West:	Southwest:	Midwest:	Southeast:	Northeast:	International:
Y					

Note: Financial information, benefits and other data can change quickly and may vary from those stated here.

PEARSON PLC

www.pearson.com

Industry Group Code: 511130 Ranks within this company's industry group: Sales: 1 Profits:

Print Media/Publishing:		Movies:		Equipment/Supplies:		Broadcast/Cable:		Music/Audio:		Sports/Games:	
Newspapers:	Y	Movie Theaters:		Equipment/Supplies:		Broadcast TV:		Music Production:		Games/Sports:	
Magazines:		Movie Production:		Gambling Equipment:		Cable TV:		Retail Music:		Retail Games Stores:	
Books:	Y	TV/Video Production:		Special Services:	Y	Satellite Broadcast:		Retail Audio Equip.:		Stadiums/Teams:	
Book Stores:		Video Rental:		Advertising Services:		Radio:		Music Print./Dist.:		Gambling/Casinos:	
Distribution/Printing:		Video Distribution:		Info. Sys. Software:		Online Information:		Multimedia:		Rides/Theme Parks:	

TYPES OF BUSINESS:

Book Publishing
Educational Products
Financial Newspaper
Online Publishing
Testing Services

BRANDS/DIVISIONS/AFFILIATES:

Penguin
Financial Times (The)
Pearson Education
Putnam
Viking
Pearson Prentice Hall
ft.com
Puffin

CONTACTS: *Note: Officers with more than one job title may be intentionally listed here more than once.*

Marjorie Scardino, CEO
Robin Freestone, CFO
David Bell, Dir.-People
Marilyn Ducksworth, Sr. VP-Corp. Comm.
John Makinson, Chmn./Chief Exec.-Penguin
Oliver Fleurot, CEO-The Financial Times
Rona Fairhead, Chief Exec.-Financial Times Group
Steve Dowling, Pres./CEO Pearson School Companies
Glen Moreno, Chmn.

Phone: 44-20-7010-2000	Fax: 44-20-7010-6060
Toll-Free: 800-269-2977	
Address: 80 Strand, London, WC2R ORL UK	

GROWTH PLANS/SPECIAL FEATURES:

Pearson plc is one of the foremost publishers in the world. The Pearson group of companies comprises the Penguin group, The Financial Times and Pearson Education. Penguin publishes several different genres of books including classics, new authors, children's books and reference books. Penguin also publishes under the Allen Lane, Avery, Berkley Books, Dutton, Hamish Hamilton, Michael Joseph, Putnam and Viking imprints, as well as children's books under the Puffin, Ladybird, BBC Children's Books and Dutton and Warne imprints. In addition, Penguin is a leading illustrated reference publisher under the Dorling Kindersley (DK) imprint. The Financial Times Group (FT) provides financial and business information through The Financial Times Newspaper and ft.com, its online partner. FT Investor, a part of ft.com, provides free, up-to-date financial and market news to European private investors. FT specializes in international and global issues; through a controlling interest in Interactive Data Corporation, it is a leading source of international securities pricing and specialist information to global institutional, professional and individual investors. In addition, the FT group owns a 50% stake in The Economist Group. Pearson Education (PE) offers textbooks, software and testing material for students in preschool through college, as well as web sites for online assessment tests and digital courseware. PE's imprints include Prentice Hall, Addison Wesley, Longman and Allyn & Bacon. Its technology and professional imprints include Addison-Wesley Professional, Peachpit Press, Que and Cisco Press. In 2006, one of the firm's subsidiaries, Pearson Government Solutions, was awarded a $440 million contract by the Centers for Medicare and Medicaid Services (CMS) to manage its Beneficiary Contact Center program. In addition, the company partnered with Amazon.co.uk to launch Search Inside platform, a search engine that allows customers to buy Penguin titles. Also in 2006, the firm acquired Mergermarket for $197 million in cash.

FINANCIALS: Sales and profits are in thousands of dollars—add 000 to get the full amount. 2006 Note: Financial information for 2006 was not available for all companies at press time.

2006 Sales: $	2006 Profits: $	U.S. Stock Ticker: PSO
2005 Sales: $7,045,000	2005 Profits: $	Int'l Ticker: PSON Int'l Exchange: London-LSE
2004 Sales: $6,357,000	2004 Profits: $169,000	Employees: 33,389
2003 Sales: $7,219,000	2003 Profits: $98,000	Fiscal Year Ends: 12/31
2002 Sales: $6,962,000	2002 Profits: $-179,000	Parent Company:

SALARIES/BENEFITS:

Pension Plan: Y	ESOP Stock Plan:	Profit Sharing: Y	Top Exec. Salary: $1,134,588	Bonus: $1,461,772
Savings Plan:	Stock Purch. Plan: Y		Second Exec. Salary: $832,031	Bonus: $1,004,415

OTHER THOUGHTS:

Apparent Women Officers or Directors: 3
Hot Spot for Advancement for Women/Minorities: Y

LOCATIONS: ("Y" = Yes)

West:	Southwest:	Midwest:	Southeast:	Northeast:	International:
Y	Y	Y		Y	Y

PENN NATIONAL GAMING INC   www.pngaming.com

Industry Group Code: 713210 Ranks within this company's industry group: Sales: 1   Profits: 1

Print Media/Publishing:	Movies:	Equipment/Supplies:	Broadcast/Cable:	Music/Audio:	Sports/Games:	
Newspapers:	Movie Theaters:	Equipment/Supplies:	Broadcast TV:	Music Production:	Games/Sports:	
Magazines:	Movie Production:	Gambling Equipment:	Cable TV:	Retail Music:	Retail Games Stores:	
Books:	TV/Video Production:	Special Services:	Satellite Broadcast:	Retail Audio Equip.:	Stadiums/Teams:	Y
Book Stores:	Video Rental:	Advertising Services:	Radio:	Music Print./Dist.:	Gambling/Casinos:	
Distribution/Printing:	Video Distribution:	Info. Sys. Software:	Online Information:	Multimedia:	Rides/Theme Parks:	

TYPES OF BUSINESS:

Horse Racetracks
Casinos

BRANDS/DIVISIONS/AFFILIATES:

Charles Town Races & Slots
Freehold Racetrack
Argosy Gaming Company

CONTACTS: Note: Officers with more than one job title may be intentionally listed here more than once.

Peter M. Carlino, CEO
William J. Clifford, CFO
Jordan B. Savitch, General Counsel/Sr. VP
Leonard M. DeAngelo, Exec. VP-Oper.
Steven T. Snyder, Sr. VP-Corp. Dev.
Robert S. Ippolito, VP/Treas.
Robert S. Ippolito, Corp. Sec.
John Finamore, Sr. VP-Regional Oper.
Peter M. Carlino, Chmn.

Phone: 610-373-2400	Fax: 610-376-2842
Toll-Free:	
Address: 825 Berkshire Blvd., Ste. 200, Wyomissing, PA 19610 US	

GROWTH PLANS/SPECIAL FEATURES:

Penn National Gaming, Inc. is a leading multi-jurisdictional owner and operator of gaming properties, horse racetracks and associated off-track wagering facilities. The company owns or operates 14 casinos, located in Canada, Colorado, Louisiana, Maine, Mississippi, Missouri, Illinois, Iowa, Indiana and West Virginia, which are focused primarily on serving customers within driving distance of the properties. The casinos total 2.1 million square feet and contain a combined 17,000 slots, 350 tables and in excess of 1000 hotel rooms. The largest of these, accounting for the most revenue, is the Charles Town Races & Slots in West Virginia. Penn also owns five racetracks: two thoroughbreds, in West Virigina and Pennsylvania; and three harness racing tracks in Maine, Ohio and New Jersey. The New Jersey track, Freehold Racetrack, is a 50%-owned joint venture. It also runs six off-track wagering facilities throughout Pennsylvania. The company intends to continue to expand its gaming operations through the implementation of a disciplined capital expenditure program at its existing properties, as well as, to the extent capital is available, the continued pursuit of strategic acquisitions of gaming properties in attractive regional markets. In recent news, Penn acquired its rival, Argosy Gaming Company in October 2005. The assets, totaling $2.3 billion, added six casino facilities and one racetrack to Penn's portfolio. The firm has already sold off one of its newly acquired casinos, and plans to sell a few more.

Penn National Gaming offers its employees flexible spending accounts, medical, dental and vision coverage, life and disability insurance and employee assistance.

FINANCIALS: Sales and profits are in thousands of dollars—add 000 to get the full amount. 2006 Note: Financial information for 2006 was not available for all companies at press time.

2006 Sales: $	2006 Profits: $	U.S. Stock Ticker: PENN
2005 Sales: $1,412,466	2005 Profits: $120,930	Int'l Ticker: Int'l Exchange:
2004 Sales: $1,139,900	2004 Profits: $71,484	Employees: 13,910
2003 Sales: $1,012,681	2003 Profits: $51,471	Fiscal Year Ends: 12/31
2002 Sales: $657,500	2002 Profits: $30,800	Parent Company:

SALARIES/BENEFITS:

Pension Plan:	ESOP Stock Plan:	Profit Sharing:	Top Exec. Salary: $842,585	Bonus: $832,000
Savings Plan: Y	Stock Purch. Plan:		Second Exec. Salary: $737,261	Bonus: $728,000

OTHER THOUGHTS:

Apparent Women Officers or Directors: 1
Hot Spot for Advancement for Women/Minorities:

LOCATIONS: ("Y" = Yes)

West:	Southwest:	Midwest:	Southeast:	Northeast:	International:
Y		Y	Y	Y	Y

Note: Financial information, benefits and other data can change quickly and may vary from those stated here.

PENTON MEDIA INC

www.penton.com

Industry Group Code: 511120 Ranks within this company's industry group: Sales: 14   Profits: 8

Print Media/Publishing:		Movies:	Equipment/Supplies:		Broadcast/Cable:	Music/Audio:	Sports/Games:
Newspapers:		Movie Theaters:	Equipment/Supplies:		Broadcast TV:	Music Production:	Games/Sports:
Magazines:	Y	Movie Production:	Gambling Equipment:		Cable TV:	Retail Music:	Retail Games Stores:
Books:		TV/Video Production:	Special Services:	Y	Satellite Broadcast:	Retail Audio Equip.:	Stadiums/Teams:
Book Stores:		Video Rental:	Advertising Services:		Radio:	Music Print./Dist.:	Gambling/Casinos:
Distribution/Printing:		Video Distribution:	Info. Sys. Software:		Online Information:	Multimedia:	Rides/Theme Parks:

TYPES OF BUSINESS:

Trade Magazine Publishing
Trade Shows & Conferences
Online Media Products
Research & Marketing
E-Commerce

BRANDS/DIVISIONS/AFFILIATES:

NPIcenter
New Hope Natural Media
Machine Design Magazine
Delicious Living
Electronic Design
IndustryWeek
Machine Design CAD Library
HVAC-Talk.com

CONTACTS: Note: Officers with more than one job title may be intentionally listed here more than once.

David B. Nussbaum, CEO
Preston L. Vice, CFO
Colleen Zelina, Sr.VP-Human Resources & Org. Effectiveness
Eric Shanfelt, Sr. VP-eMedia Strategy & Dev.
Darrell C. Denny, Exec. VP & Pres., Lifestyle Media
Michael Horgan, Editorial Dir. Penton Custom Media

Phone: 216-696-7000	Fax: 216-696-1752
Toll-Free:	
Address: 1300 E. 9th St., Cleveland, OH 44114 US	

GROWTH PLANS/SPECIAL FEATURES:

Penton Media, Inc. is a leading global business-to-business media company that publishes approximately 39 specialized trade magazines, produces more than 80 trade shows and conferences, provides 47 web sites and offers a broad range of online media products, including electronic newsletters and web conferences. About 60% of sales come from advertising in its publications. Penton is divided into four sectors: industry, technology, lifestyle and retail. The industry segment publishes magazines doveted to such subjects as manufacturing, design and engineering, mechanical systems and construction, and government and compliance. The technology segment's publications cover enterprise information technology, electronics, business technology and aviation. Penton's lifestyle segment publications cover natural food products, while its retail sector covers food and retail. The firm is especially known for its Internet World trade shows that feature Internet business summits and companies presenting a variety of online services and applications. Publications distributed by the company include: Business Finance, Delicious Living, Electronic Design, Government Product News, IndustryWeek, Medical Design, Modern Baking, New Equipment Digest, SQL Server Magazine, Welding Design & Fabrication and Windows IT Pro. In 2006, the firm acquired NPIcenter and NPIcenter.com, online information resources for nutraceutical, nutritional, dietary supplement, cosmetic, and food industry professionals. Also in 2006, the company's Machine Design Partners joined with PARTSolutions, LLC to launch Machine Design CAD Library for design engineers. Recently, Penton acquired HVAC-Talk.com, an online community and discussion forum with more than 43,000 registered members, generating over 104,000 unique visitors per month. Recently, the firm reduced its headcount by 57.9%, froze its pension plan and introduced a defined contribution plan. In 2006, the firm announced plans to be acquired by Prism Business Media for $530 million.

Employee benefits at Penton include medical and dental plans, life and accident insurance, employee assistance, transportation reimbursement and spending accounts.

FINANCIALS: Sales and profits are in thousands of dollars—add 000 to get the full amount. 2006 Note: Financial information for 2006 was not available for all companies at press time.

2006 Sales: $	2006 Profits: $	U.S. Stock Ticker: PTON.OB
2005 Sales: $192,847	2005 Profits: $-8,422	Int'l Ticker: Int'l Exchange:
2004 Sales: $194,833	2004 Profits: $-67,191	Employees: 703
2003 Sales: $188,742	2003 Profits: $-93,131	Fiscal Year Ends: 12/31
2002 Sales: $235,100	2002 Profits: $-286,300	Parent Company:

SALARIES/BENEFITS:

Pension Plan:	ESOP Stock Plan:	Profit Sharing:	Top Exec. Salary: $425,000	Bonus: $175,855
Savings Plan: Y	Stock Purch. Plan:		Second Exec. Salary: $341,250	Bonus: $133,852

OTHER THOUGHTS:

Apparent Women Officers or Directors: 1
Hot Spot for Advancement for Women/Minorities: Y

LOCATIONS: ("Y" = Yes)

West:	Southwest:	Midwest:	Southeast:	Northeast:	International:
Y		Y		Y	Y

Note: Financial information, benefits and other data can change quickly and may vary from those stated here.

PINNACLE ENTERTAINMENT INC   www.pnkinc.com

Industry Group Code: 721120 Ranks within this company's industry group: Sales: 9 Profits: 12

Print Media/Publishing:	Movies:	Equipment/Supplies:	Broadcast/Cable:	Music/Audio:	Sports/Games:	
Newspapers:	Movie Theaters:	Equipment/Supplies:	Broadcast TV:	Music Production:	Games/Sports:	Y
Magazines:	Movie Production:	Gambling Equipment:	Cable TV:	Retail Music:	Retail Games Stores:	
Books:	TV/Video Production:	Special Services:	Satellite Broadcast:	Retail Audio Equip.:	Stadiums/Teams:	
Book Stores:	Video Rental:	Advertising Services:	Radio:	Music Print./Dist.:	Gambling/Casinos:	Y
Distribution/Printing:	Video Distribution:	Info. Sys. Software:	Online Information:	Multimedia:	Rides/Theme Parks:	

TYPES OF BUSINESS:

Casinos
Riverboat Casinos
Pari-Mutuel Racing

BRANDS/DIVISIONS/AFFILIATES:

The Sands
Boomtown, Inc.
Belterra Casino Resort
Hollywood Park, Inc.
Boomtown Reno
Boomtown Bossier City
Boomtown New Orleans
Casino L'Auberge du Lac

CONTACTS: *Note: Officers with more than one job title may be intentionally listed here more than once.*

Daniel R. Lee, CEO
Alain Uboldi, COO
Wade Hundley, Pres.
Stephen H. Capp, Exec. VP/CFO
Kim Townsend, Sr. VP-Mktg.
Humberto Trueba, Sr. VP-Human Resources
Carol Pride, CIO
John A. Godfrey, Sr. VP/General Counsel
Sarah L. Tucker, VP-Oper.
Jim Barich, Sr. VP-Public Affairs
Christopher K. Plant, VP-Investor Rel.
Christopher K. Plant, Treas.
Arthur I. Goldberg, Sr. VP-Risk Mgmt. & Benefits
Clifford D. Kortman, Sr. VP-Construction & Dev.
Alice Mui, VP-Corporate Taxes
Linda A. Shaffer, VP-Corp. Acct. & Controller
Daniel R. Lee, Chmn.

Phone: 702-784-7777	**Fax:** 702-784-7778

Toll-Free:

Address: 3800 Howard Hughes Pkwy., Ste. 1800, Las Vegas, NV 89109 US

GROWTH PLANS/SPECIAL FEATURES:

Pinnacle Entertainment, Inc. is a gaming, sports and entertainment company engaged in the ownership and operation of card club casinos, pari-mutuel racing facilities and the development of other gaming, sports and entertainment businesses. Headquartered in Reno, Nevada, the company owns five gaming facilities in the U.S., located in southeastern Indiana; Reno, Nevada; and Bossier City, Lake Charles and Harvey, Louisiana. These facilities are respectively named Belterra Casino Resort, Boomtown Reno, Boomtown Bossier City, Casino L'Auberge du Lac and Boomtown New Orleans. Belterra is a 38,000-square-foot dockside riverboat casino with 1,441 slot machines, 43 table games and 850 hotel rooms. Boomtown Reno is a 318-guestroom, 45,000-square-foot, land-based facility with 1,198 slot machines and 30 table games. The Bossier City facility features a dockside riverboat casino and hotel tower with 1,138 slot machines, 36 table games and 188 hotel rooms. Casino L'Auberge du Lac, a casino resort in Lake Charles, Louisiana offers 1000 guestrooms and is the largest hotel in Louisiana outside of New Orleans. Boomtown New Orleans, located in Harvey, Louisiana, features 1,435 slot machines, a 350-seat nightclub and 200 guest rooms. In 2006, the firm purchased The Sands and Traymore in Atlantic City, New Jersey for $250 million. In addition, the company bought President Riverboat Casino-Missouri for approximately $45.7 million. Recently, Pinnacle acquired Harrah's Lake Charles Gaming assets, including two casino boats and their respective gaming licenses. Concurrent to the sale, the firm sold its Casino Magic Biloxi to a subsidiary of Harrah's, paying $25 million in total for both properties. In 2006, the firm announced a partnership with Philadelphia entrepreneur Robert L. Johnson to open a gaming facility in Philadelphia (pending a city-granted license). The firm operates casinos in Argentina, has begun construction on a casino in the Bahamas, and plans to build two casinos in Chile.

FINANCIALS: Sales and profits are in thousands of dollars—add 000 to get the full amount. 2006 Note: Financial information for 2006 was not available for all companies at press time.

2006 Sales: $	2006 Profits: $	**U.S. Stock Ticker: PNK**
2005 Sales: $725,900	2005 Profits: $6,125	**Int'l Ticker:** Int'l Exchange:
2004 Sales: $547,071	2004 Profits: $9,161	Employees: 6,716
2003 Sales: $524,162	2003 Profits: $-28,242	Fiscal Year Ends: 12/31
2002 Sales: $514,001	2002 Profits: $-69,629	Parent Company:

SALARIES/BENEFITS:

Pension Plan:	ESOP Stock Plan:	Profit Sharing:	Top Exec. Salary: $774,250	Bonus: $1,312,500
Savings Plan: Y	Stock Purch. Plan:		Second Exec. Salary: $400,000	Bonus: $440,680

OTHER THOUGHTS:

Apparent Women Officers or Directors: 5
Hot Spot for Advancement for Women/Minorities: Y

LOCATIONS: ("Y" = Yes)

West:	Southwest:	Midwest:	Southeast:	Northeast:	International:
Y		Y	Y	Y	Y

Note: Financial information, benefits and other data can change quickly and may vary from those stated here.

PIONEER CORPORATION

www.pioneer.co.jp

Industry Group Code: 334310 Ranks within this company's industry group: Sales: 6 Profits: 13

Print Media/Publishing:	Movies:	Equipment/Supplies:		Broadcast/Cable:	Music/Audio:	Sports/Games:
Newspapers:	Movie Theaters:	Equipment/Supplies:	Y	Broadcast TV:	Music Production:	Games/Sports:
Magazines:	Movie Production:	Gambling Equipment:		Cable TV:	Retail Music:	Retail Games Stores:
Books:	TV/Video Production:	Special Services:	Y	Satellite Broadcast:	Retail Audio Equip.:	Stadiums/Teams:
Book Stores:	Video Rental:	Advertising Services:		Radio:	Music Print./Dist.:	Gambling/Casinos:
Distribution/Printing:	Video Distribution:	Info. Sys. Software:	Y	Online Information:	Multimedia:	Rides/Theme Parks:

TYPES OF BUSINESS:

Consumer Electronics
Audio/Video Equipment
CD/DVD Players
Automotive Electronics
Telecommunications Equipment
Research & Development
Software Development

BRANDS/DIVISIONS/AFFILIATES:

Pioneer Electronics (USA), Inc.
Discovision Associates
Pioneer Display Products Corp.
Pioneer Home Entertainment Co.
Tohoku Pioneer Corporation
Pioneer Europe
Pioneer China Holding Co., Ltd.

CONTACTS: Note: Officers with more than one job title may be intentionally listed here more than once.

Tamihiko Sudo, CEO
Tamihiko Sudo, Pres.
Toshiyuki Ito, Exec. Officer/Gen. Mgr.-Personnel
Osamu Yamada, General Mgr.-R&D Group
Osamu Yamada, Chief Dir.-Technology Dev.
Masao Kawabata, Managing Exec. Officer/Dir.-Corp. Comm.
Akira Haeno, Gen. Mgr.-Mobile Entertainment Business Group
Koki Aizawa, Exec. Officer-RW Coordination Center
Shinji Yasuda, Chief Dir.-Home Ent. Business Group
Hajime Ishizuka, Sr. Managing Dir. & Representative Dir.
Toshiyuki Ito, Chmn.
Koichi Shimizu, Gen. Mgr.-Procurement Group

Phone: 81-3-3495-6774	Fax: 81-3-3495-4301
Toll-Free:	
Address: 1-4-1, Meguro 1-chome, Meguro-ku, Tokyo, 153-8654 Japan	

GROWTH PLANS/SPECIAL FEATURES:

Pioneer Corporation is one of the leading manufacturers of consumer electronics in the world, operating mainly in four segments: home electronics, car electronics (earning 40% of its revenue), patent licensing and others. Headquartered in Japan and originally a speaker manufacturer, Pioneer now develops, designs, and manufactures (in its 30-plus facilities worldwide) amplifiers, hi-fi stereos, car electronics, cable-TV systems, audio and video equipment, CD players, and factory automation systems and parts. Pioneer was the first company to release global positioning systems (GPS) to the consumer market. The firm also makes DVD, CD-R/RW and DVD-R/RW drives, plasma-screen TVs and OLED displays. In 2006, the firm introduced two plasma televisions to the market featuring New P.U.R.E*3 Black Panel. This new design incorporates a patented Crystal Emissive layer, which allows for blacker blacks and well-detailed dark areas. Also in 2006, the firm introduced the largest pixel plasma monitor (50-inch and 1,080 pixels) to the market. The company's subsidiaries Pioneer Display Products Corp. and Pioneer Electronics USA handle specialized operations; while Discovision Associates acquires and licenses optical disc technologies and playback equipment patents. Recently, the firm announced plans to sell its Tokorozawa and Omori plants to Haseko Corp. for approximately $133 million. Also in 2006, the firm announced its new internal DVD multi writers with ATAPI interface for Windows based PCs, utilizing the firm's new Disc Resonance Stabilizer product. Pioneer also recently introduced a new HDD/DVD recorder with a built-in record feature and digital tuner that can record up to 92 hours of high definition television. In 2006, Pioneer sold its wholly owned subsidiary, Pioneer Digital Technologies.

Pioneer is involved numerous community activities, including the sponsorship of a professional and amateur orchestras and other music groups, numerous music education programs, sports teams, international exchanges and environmental conservation efforts.

FINANCIALS: Sales and profits are in thousands of dollars—add 000 to get the full amount. 2006 Note: Financial information for 2006 was not available for all companies at press time.

2006 Sales: $6,354,100	2006 Profits: $-715,270	**U.S. Stock Ticker: PNOCF**
2005 Sales: $6,906,476	2005 Profits: $-82,140	**Int'l Ticker: 6773** Int'l Exchange: Tokyo-TSE
2004 Sales: $6,612,100	2004 Profits: $234,300	Employees: 38,826
2003 Sales: $5,935,600	2003 Profits: $134,000	Fiscal Year Ends: 3/31
2002 Sales: $5,029,300	2002 Profits: $60,500	Parent Company:

SALARIES/BENEFITS:

Pension Plan:	ESOP Stock Plan:	Profit Sharing:	Top Exec. Salary: $	Bonus: $
Savings Plan:	Stock Purch. Plan:		Second Exec. Salary: $	Bonus: $

OTHER THOUGHTS:

Apparent Women Officers or Directors:
Hot Spot for Advancement for Women/Minorities:

LOCATIONS: ("Y" = Yes)

West:	Southwest:	Midwest:	Southeast:	Northeast:	International:
Y					Y

Note: Financial information, benefits and other data can change quickly and may vary from those stated here.

PIXAR ANIMATION STUDIOS

www.pixar.com

Industry Group Code: 512110 Ranks within this company's industry group: Sales: 16 Profits: 1

Print Media/Publishing:	Movies:		Equipment/Supplies:		Broadcast/Cable:		Music/Audio:	Sports/Games:
Newspapers:	Movie Theaters:		Equipment/Supplies:		Broadcast TV:		Music Production:	Games/Sports:
Magazines:	Movie Production:	Y	Gambling Equipment:		Cable TV:		Retail Music:	Retail Games Stores:
Books:	TV/Video Production:		Special Services:		Satellite Broadcast:		Retail Audio Equip.:	Stadiums/Teams:
Book Stores:	Video Rental:		Advertising Services:		Radio:		Music Print./Dist.:	Gambling/Casinos:
Distribution/Printing:	Video Distribution:		Info. Sys. Software:	Y	Online Information:		Multimedia:	Rides/Theme Parks:

TYPES OF BUSINESS:

Computer-Animated Film Production
Special Effects Software
Video & Soundtrack Sales
Children's Merchandise

BRANDS/DIVISIONS/AFFILIATES:

Walt Disney Company (The)
Toy Story
Monsters, Inc.
Finding Nemo
Incredibles (The)
Cars
RenderMan
Ratatouille

CONTACTS: Note: Officers with more than one job title may be intentionally listed here more than once.

Steve Jobs, CEO
Edwin E. Catmull, Pres.
Simon Bax, CFO/Exec. VP/Sec.
Lois Scali, General Counsel/Exec. VP
Nils Erdmann, Dir.-Investor Rel.
John Lasseter, Chief Creative Officer
Sarah McArthur, Exec. VP-Production
Steve Jobs, Chmn.

Phone: 510-752-3000	Fax: 510-752-3151
Toll-Free:	
Address: 1200 Park Ave., Emeryville, CA 94608 US	

GROWTH PLANS/SPECIAL FEATURES:

Pixar Animation Studios, a subsidiary of The Walt Disney Company, is a pioneer in computer-animated feature films through its combination of creative, technical and production capabilities. Pixar began its productions with an agreement with the Walt Disney Company to develop up to three computer-animated feature films to be marketed and distributed by Disney. The first film produced was Toy Story, which met with wide success and established Pixar as the leader in computer-animated films. Pixar has released seven films to date: Toy Story, A Bug's Life, Toy Story 2, Monsters, Inc., Finding Nemo, The Incredibles and Cars (released in June 2006), all of which have been successful at the box office. Finding Nemo won an Academy Award for Best Animated Feature, was the highest-grossing animated film of all time and broke records in DVD sales. The firm releases a new film about every 18 months, and the average film's production budget is $90 million. Along with box office revenues, Pixar generates revenue through the sale of home videos, children's merchandise and soundtracks. The firm also makes short films, such as the Academy Award-winning For the Birds, that help the company to develop new ideas and win acclaim, further establishing the Pixar brand. The firm's RenderMan software has helped create visual special effects for films including Star Wars Episode 1: The Phantom Menace, The Matrix and Gladiator. The software's creators won an Oscar for significant advancements to the field of motion picture rendering. In 2006, Disney acquired Pixar for $7.4 billion. The firm is currently producing Ratatouille, a film about a rat who aspires to be a French chef. Ratatouille is scheduled for release in summer 2007.

Pixar offers paid technical and non-technical internships to college students. All employees are offered complete benefits, including stock options and three weeks vacation.

FINANCIALS: Sales and profits are in thousands of dollars—add 000 to get the full amount. 2006 Note: Financial information for 2006 was not available for all companies at press time.

2006 Sales: $	2006 Profits: $	U.S. Stock Ticker: Subsidiary
2005 Sales: $289,116	2005 Profits: $152,938	Int'l Ticker: Int'l Exchange:
2004 Sales: $273,472	2004 Profits: $141,722	Employees: 850
2003 Sales: $262,498	2003 Profits: $124,768	Fiscal Year Ends: 12/31
2002 Sales: $201,700	2002 Profits: $90,000	Parent Company: WALT DISNEY COMPANY (THE)

SALARIES/BENEFITS:

Pension Plan:	ESOP Stock Plan:	Profit Sharing:	Top Exec. Salary: $2,862,307	Bonus: $
Savings Plan: Y	Stock Purch. Plan:		Second Exec. Salary: $545,019	Bonus: $

OTHER THOUGHTS:

Apparent Women Officers or Directors: 3
Hot Spot for Advancement for Women/Minorities: Y

LOCATIONS: ("Y" = Yes)

West:	Southwest:	Midwest:	Southeast:	Northeast:	International:
Y					

Note: Financial information, benefits and other data can change quickly and may vary from those stated here.

PLAYBOY ENTERPRISES INC   www.playboyenterprises.com

Industry Group Code: 511120 Ranks within this company's industry group: Sales: 12   Profits: 7

Print Media/Publishing:		Movies:		Equipment/Supplies:		Broadcast/Cable:		Music/Audio:		Sports/Games:	
Newspapers:		Movie Theaters:		Equipment/Supplies:		Broadcast TV:		Music Production:		Games/Sports:	
Magazines:	Y	Movie Production:		Gambling Equipment:		Cable TV:	Y	Retail Music:		Retail Games Stores:	
Books:	Y	TV/Video Production:	Y	Special Services:		Satellite Broadcast:		Retail Audio Equip.:		Stadiums/Teams:	
Book Stores:		Video Rental:		Advertising Services:		Radio:		Music Print./Dist.:		Gambling/Casinos:	Y
Distribution/Printing:		Video Distribution:		Info. Sys. Software:		Online Information:		Multimedia:		Rides/Theme Parks:	

TYPES OF BUSINESS:
Magazine Publishing
Adult Entertainment
Movie, Video & Game Production
Internet Gaming
Online Sales & Subscriptions
Cable TV Networks

BRANDS/DIVISIONS/AFFILIATES:
Playboy Magazine
Playboy Channel (The)
Spice Entertainment
Playboy Online
Playboy Auctions
playboygaming.com
Playboy Cyber Club
Club Jenna, Inc.

CONTACTS: *Note: Officers with more than one job title may be intentionally listed here more than once.*
Christie Hefner, CEO
Linda G. Havard, CFO/Exec. VP-Finance
Michael Sprouse, Sr. VP-Mktg.
Carol A. Devine, Sr. VP-Human Resources
Mark Laudenslager, CIO/Sr. VP
Danielle Barcilon, Sr. VP/Chief Tech. Officer
Howard Shapiro, Exec. VP-Admin./Corp. Sec.
Howard Shapiro, General Counsel/Exec. VP-Law
Linda G. Havard, Exec. VP-Oper.
Robert D. Campbell, Sr. VP-Strategic Planning
Martha O. Lindeman, Sr. VP-Corp. Comm.
Martha O. Lindeman, Sr. VP-Investor Rel.
Robert D. Campbell, Treas./Asst. Sec.
Hugh M. Hefner, Editor-in-Chief/Chief Creative Officer
Bob Meyers, Exec. VP/Pres., Media
Alex Vaickus, Exec. VP/Pres., Licensing Group
Louis R. Mohn, VP/Publisher-Playboy
Christie Hefner, Chmn.
Robert F. O'Donnell, Exec. VP-Int'l Publishing

Phone: 312-751-8000	Fax: 312-751-2818
Toll-Free:	
Address: 680 N. Lake Shore Dr., Chicago, IL 60611 US	

GROWTH PLANS/SPECIAL FEATURES:
Playboy Enterprises, Inc. (PEI) is a multimedia entertainment company that was organized in 1953 to publish Playboy magazine. Today, PEI publishes Playboy Magazine worldwide, operates the Playboy and Spice television networks and distributes programming via home video and DVD. The firm has recently consolidated from three operating segments to two: Media, which oversees the publishing group and the entertainment group; and Licensing. Under Media, the entertainment group's operations include the production and marketing of adult television programming for domestic and international TV and home video products. It operates domestic TV networks, which include Playboy TV, Playboy TV en Espanol and eight Spice-branded movie networks. In addition, it operates or licenses 22 Playboy, Spice and locally branded movie networks in Europe and the Pacific Rim; distributes its original programming on DVD and VHS; and offers multiple subscription-based web sites and two online video-on-demand theaters. The publishing group consists of Playboy magazine and related publications such as calendars and special editions. Playboy magazine continues to be the best-selling monthly men's magazine in the world, based on the combined circulation of U.S. and international editions. Playboy Online, a majority-owned subsidiary, operates a network of Playboy-branded web sites including two gambling sites, PlayboyCasino.com and PlayboySportsBook.com. The licensing group licenses the firm's trademarks, images and artwork for use on more than 1,500 Playboy-related products sold in over 125 countries. Licensed product lines include men's and women's apparel, men's underwear and women's lingerie, slot machines and interactive video games. Playboy Radio, available on Sirius Satellite, was launched in early 2006 and has already hit 1 million subscribers. In 2006, the company acquired Club Jenna, Inc., which includes a film production business, a video content library, web sites and a DVD distribution deal. In 2006, after a 25-year hiatus, PEI re-launched the Playboy Club in Las Vegas.

FINANCIALS: Sales and profits are in thousands of dollars—add 000 to get the full amount. 2006 Note: Financial information for 2006 was not available for all companies at press time.
2006 Sales: $	2006 Profits: $	U.S. Stock Ticker: PLA
2005 Sales: $338,153	2005 Profits: $- 735	Int'l Ticker: Int'l Exchange:
2004 Sales: $329,376	2004 Profits: $9,989	Employees: 725
2003 Sales: $315,844	2003 Profits: $-7,557	Fiscal Year Ends: 12/31
2002 Sales: $277,600	2002 Profits: $-17,100	Parent Company:

SALARIES/BENEFITS:
Pension Plan:	ESOP Stock Plan:	Profit Sharing: Y	Top Exec. Salary: $1,000,000	Bonus: $274,554
Savings Plan: Y	Stock Purch. Plan:		Second Exec. Salary: $700,000	Bonus: $384,375

OTHER THOUGHTS:
Apparent Women Officers or Directors: 6
Hot Spot for Advancement for Women/Minorities: Y

LOCATIONS: ("Y" = Yes)
West:	Southwest:	Midwest:	Southeast:	Northeast:	International:
Y		Y		Y	Y

Note: Financial information, benefits and other data can change quickly and may vary from those stated here.

PRIMACOM AG
www.primacom.de

Industry Group Code: 513220 Ranks within this company's industry group: Sales: 23 Profits: 21

Print Media/Publishing:	Movies:	Equipment/Supplies:		Broadcast/Cable:		Music/Audio:	Sports/Games:
Newspapers:	Movie Theaters:	Equipment/Supplies:		Broadcast TV:		Music Production:	Games/Sports:
Magazines:	Movie Production:	Gambling Equipment:		Cable TV:	Y	Retail Music:	Retail Games Stores:
Books:	TV/Video Production:	Special Services:	Y	Satellite Broadcast:		Retail Audio Equip.:	Stadiums/Teams:
Book Stores:	Video Rental:	Advertising Services:		Radio:		Music Print./Dist.:	Gambling/Casinos:
Distribution/Printing:	Video Distribution:	Info. Sys. Software:		Online Information:		Multimedia:	Rides/Theme Parks:

TYPES OF BUSINESS:
Cable TV Service
Video-on-Demand
Internet Services
Telephony Services
Online Radio Broadcasting

BRANDS/DIVISIONS/AFFILIATES:
prima Kabel TV
primatv
primaspeed
Liberty Media Corporation

CONTACTS: Note: Officers with more than one job title may be intentionally listed here more than once.
Wolfgang Preuss, CEO
Jens Kircher, COO
Stefan Schwenkedel, CFO
Anthony G. Werner, Sr. VP-CTO
Elizabeth M. Markowski, Sr. VP-General Counsel
Helmut Thoma, Vice Chmn.
Peter Hinkelmann, Managing Dir./Regional Mgr.-Saxonia
Gabriele Lindemann, Managing Dir./Regional Mgr.-Berlin
Thomas Eibeck, Regional Mgr.Technology-Saxonia
Heinz R. Eble, Chmn.

Phone: 49-0-6131-944-0	**Fax:** 49-0-6131-944-501
Toll-Free:	
Address: An der Ochsenwiese 3, Mainz, 55124 Germany	

GROWTH PLANS/SPECIAL FEATURES:
PrimaCom AG is a private cable network provider with operations in Germany and the Netherlands, offering analogue television, radio and digital television service (primatv) to approximately 1.3 million subscribers. Customers have access to more than 100 television and radio programs, interactive video-on-demand, high-speed Internet and telephony. PrimaCom currently has potential access to approximately 2 million homes and serves approximately 1.3 million customers in Germany and 300,000 in the Netherlands. The firm concentrates its operations on small and rural areas of Germany, and its largest consumer base is drawn from citizens of the formerly communist eastern section of Germany. PrimaCom's networks are located primarily in small to medium-sized cities in 10 German states and in the Netherlands. Its core regions are Saxony, Saxony-Anhalt, Thuringia, Rheinland-Pfalz and the Netherlands. In 2006, the firm partnered with Unity Media to transmit a digital program package featuring German football or Bundesliga, (the Federal League) to networks in Hesse and North Rhine-Westphalia. Liberty Media Corporation owns 27% of PrimaCom.

FINANCIALS: Sales and profits are in thousands of dollars—add 000 to get the full amount. 2006 Note: Financial information for 2006 was not available for all companies at press time.

2006 Sales: $	2006 Profits: $	**U.S. Stock Ticker: PCAGY**
2005 Sales: $156,060	2005 Profits: $-316,700	**Int'l Ticker: PRC** Int'l Exchange: Frankfurt
2004 Sales: $287,400	2004 Profits: $-154,900	Employees: 495
2003 Sales: $248,500	2003 Profits: $-148,200	Fiscal Year Ends: 12/31
2002 Sales: $190,800	2002 Profits: $-145,000	Parent Company:

SALARIES/BENEFITS:

Pension Plan:	ESOP Stock Plan:	Profit Sharing:	Top Exec. Salary: $	Bonus: $
Savings Plan:	Stock Purch. Plan:		Second Exec. Salary: $	Bonus: $

OTHER THOUGHTS:
Apparent Women Officers or Directors: 2
Hot Spot for Advancement for Women/Minorities:

LOCATIONS: ("Y" = Yes)

West:	Southwest:	Midwest:	Southeast:	Northeast:	International:
					Y

PRIMEDIA INC

www.primediainc.com

Industry Group Code: 511120 Ranks within this company's industry group: Sales: 7   Profits: 2

Print Media/Publishing:		Movies:	Equipment/Supplies:	Broadcast/Cable:	Music/Audio:	Sports/Games:
Newspapers:		Movie Theaters:	Equipment/Supplies:	Broadcast TV:	Music Production:	Games/Sports:
Magazines:	Y	Movie Production:	Gambling Equipment:	Cable TV:	Retail Music:	Retail Games Stores:
Books:		TV/Video Production:	Special Services:	Satellite Broadcast:	Retail Audio Equip.:	Stadiums/Teams:
Book Stores:		Video Rental:	Advertising Services:	Radio:	Music Print./Dist.:	Gambling/Casinos:
Distribution/Printing:		Video Distribution:	Info. Sys. Software:	Online Information:	Multimedia:	Rides/Theme Parks:

TYPES OF BUSINESS:

Magazine Publishing
Business Directories
Housing Guides
Magazine Distribution
Online Media

BRANDS/DIVISIONS/AFFILIATES:

Primedia Enterprises
Apartment Publications
Surfer
Off-Road
Lowrider
Motor Trend
American Trucker
Kohlberg Kravis & Roberts Co.

CONTACTS: *Note: Officers with more than one job title may be intentionally listed here more than once.*

Dean B. Nelson, CEO
Dean B. Nelson, Pres.
Kevin Neary, CFO/Sr. VP
Michaelanne C. Discepolo, Exec. VP-Human Resources
Christopher Fraser, General Counsel
Eric M. Leeds, Sr. VP-Investor Rel.
Robert J. Sforzo, Sr. VP/Chief Acct. Officer
Judy Harris, Sr. VP/CEO-Channel One
Robert C. Metz, Exec. VP/CEO-Consumer Source, Inc.
David Crawford, Sr. VP/Pres. & COO-PRIMEDIA Consumer Guides
Carl Salas, Sr. VP/Treas.
Dean B. Nelson, Chmn.

Phone: 212-745-0100	Fax: 212-745-0121
Toll-Free:	
Address: 745 5th Ave., New York, NY 10151 US	

GROWTH PLANS/SPECIAL FEATURES:

Primedia, Inc. is one of the largest targeted media companies in the U.S., producing nearly 300 separate publications in two business segments: enthusiast media and consumer guides. The enthusiast media segment includes 98 consumer magazine titles targeted toward automotive, outdoors, action sports, home technology and lifestyles enthusiasts. The group publishes more than 50 automotive magazines, including Motor Trend, Hot Rod, Super Street and Lowrider. The consumer guides segment publishes 80 guides in 74 regional markets for apartment searching. Titles include Apartment Guide (apartmentguide.com), New Home Guide (newhomeguide.com) and Auto Guide (autoguide.com). Recently, the firm discontinued its Education segment and plans to investigate a spin-off of its Consumer Guides segment. In 2006, Primedia sold all of its hunting, fishing and shooting titles, events, web sites, TV and related radio programming to InterMedia Outdoor, Inc. for $170 million in cash. Recently, the company sold its Gems to Interweave Press, LLC. In addition, the firm sold its Crafts Group (Paper Crafts, Quilter's Newsletter, McCall's Quilting and Sew News) to Sandler Capital management for $132 million. Also in 2006, the firm sold its military history and American social history magazines and related web sites to Weider History Group. Recently, the firm's Consumer Guides segment acquired RentClicks, an online marketplace for small rental properties. In addition, the firm'partnered with BioWorld Merchandising, Inc. and OC Import to create a new accessory line under its wholly owned subsidiary, Lowrider. In 2006, the company's business development arm (Primedia Enterprises) launched a weekly podcast of motor trend.com, a four-hour weekly radio show. In addition, Primedia Enterprises announced a partnership with Thorsen Tool Company to develop and enhance an exisiting line of automobile accessories. Private equity firm Kohlberg Kravis & Roberts owns more than 50% of the company.

FINANCIALS: Sales and profits are in thousands of dollars—add 000 to get the full amount. 2006 Note: Financial information for 2006 was not available for all companies at press time.

2006 Sales: $	2006 Profits: $	**U.S. Stock Ticker:** PRM
2005 Sales: $990,500	2005 Profits: $564,600	**Int'l Ticker:** Int'l Exchange:
2004 Sales: $1,307,100	2004 Profits: $35,500	Employees: 3,200
2003 Sales: $1,345,600	2003 Profits: $38,900	Fiscal Year Ends: 12/31
2002 Sales: $1,587,600	2002 Profits: $-599,400	Parent Company:

SALARIES/BENEFITS:

Pension Plan: Y	ESOP Stock Plan: Y	Profit Sharing:	Top Exec. Salary: $798,077	Bonus: $478,846
Savings Plan: Y	Stock Purch. Plan:		Second Exec. Salary: $750,000	Bonus: $412,500

OTHER THOUGHTS:

Apparent Women Officers or Directors: 2
Hot Spot for Advancement for Women/Minorities: Y

LOCATIONS: ("Y" = Yes)

West:	Southwest:	Midwest:	Southeast:	Northeast:	International:
Y	Y	Y	Y	Y	

Note: Financial information, benefits and other data can change quickly and may vary from those stated here.

PROGRESSIVE GAMING INTERNATIONAL CORP
www.progressivegaming.net

Industry Group Code: 713290 Ranks within this company's industry group: Sales: 9 Profits: 12

Print Media/Publishing:	Movies:	Equipment/Supplies:		Broadcast/Cable:	Music/Audio:	Sports/Games:
Newspapers:	Movie Theaters:	Equipment/Supplies:		Broadcast TV:	Music Production:	Games/Sports:
Magazines:	Movie Production:	Gambling Equipment:	Y	Cable TV:	Retail Music:	Retail Games Stores:
Books:	TV/Video Production:	Special Services:	Y	Satellite Broadcast:	Retail Audio Equip.:	Stadiums/Teams:
Book Stores:	Video Rental:	Advertising Services:		Radio:	Music Print./Dist.:	Gambling/Casinos:
Distribution/Printing:	Video Distribution:	Info. Sys. Software:	Y	Online Information:	Multimedia:	Rides/Theme Parks:

TYPES OF BUSINESS:
Gambling Equipment
Slot Machines
Jackpot Systems
Gaming Software
Tracking & Accounting Systems
Casino Networking Systems

BRANDS/DIVISIONS/AFFILIATES:
Intelligent Table System
Peer to Peer Texas Hold'Em
Rapid Bet Live Wireless
Tablelink
Caribbean Stud
TableMax
VirtGame Corp.
PitTrak

CONTACTS: *Note: Officers with more than one job title may be intentionally listed here more than once.*
Russel H. McMeekin, CEO
Russel H. McMeekin, Pres.
Michael A. Sicuro, CFO/Exec. VP
Robert J. Parente, Exec. VP-Sales & Mktg.
Thomas Galanty, CTO
Robert B. Ziems, General Counsel
Robert B. Ziems, VP-Bus. Dev.
Michael A. Sicuro, Treas.
Peter G. Boynton, Chmn.

Phone: 702-896-3890	**Fax:** 702-896-2461
Toll-Free: 800-336-8449	
Address: 920 Pilot Rd., Las Vegas, NV 89119 US	

GROWTH PLANS/SPECIAL FEATURES:
Progressive Gaming International Corporation manufactures, develops, acquires and markets branded slot machines and table games, progressive jackpot systems and player tracking and accounting systems for slot machines and table games. The company's customers include casinos, other gaming suppliers, operators of wide-area gaming networks and lottery authorities. The firm's operations occur in two main business sectors: slot and table games, and systems. Slot and table games include Progressive Black Jack, Texas Hold'Em Bonus, Caribbean Stud and licensed games Garfield and KISS. The systems segment designs and develops electronic player tracking and game monitoring and accounting systems for slot and table games. These systems are sold or leased to casino operators and governmental agencies. In 2006, the firm introduced a new wireless wager device (Rapid Bet Live Wireless) at the Palms Hotel and Casino in Nevada. In addition, Progressive announced the European debut of its popular World Series of Poker and Texas Hold'Em Bonus table games via Swedish gaming operator Casino Cosmopol in Gothenburg, Stockholm and Sundsvail casinos. Also in 2006, the firm entered into a patent license with Shuffle Master, who will use Progressive's table patents in casinos in the U.S. and foreign countries. In addition, the company partnered with Ameristar Casinos to install its Intelligent Table System in four Ameristar properties in the U.S. Progressive also recently introduced the World Series of Poker(R) Peer to Peer Texas Hold'em game, which will be licensed by Harrah's Company, LLC for a six-year period. Also in 2006, the firm partnered with Galaxy's Starworld Casino in Macau to install CasinoLink Intelligence Incorporating Club; Cage and PIT, as well as its Table Management System.

FINANCIALS: Sales and profits are in thousands of dollars—add 000 to get the full amount. 2006 Note: Financial information for 2006 was not available for all companies at press time.

2006 Sales: $	2006 Profits: $	**U.S. Stock Ticker:** PGIC
2005 Sales: $78,221	2005 Profits: $-5,983	**Int'l Ticker:** Int'l Exchange:
2004 Sales: $96,374	2004 Profits: $ 259	Employees: 315
2003 Sales: $91,803	2003 Profits: $-34,216	Fiscal Year Ends: 12/31
2002 Sales: $102,600	2002 Profits: $-37,900	Parent Company:

SALARIES/BENEFITS:

Pension Plan:	ESOP Stock Plan:	Profit Sharing:	Top Exec. Salary: $426,923	Bonus: $264,000
Savings Plan: Y	Stock Purch. Plan:		Second Exec. Salary: $275,423	Bonus: $58,750

OTHER THOUGHTS:
Apparent Women Officers or Directors:
Hot Spot for Advancement for Women/Minorities:

LOCATIONS: ("Y" = Yes)

West:	Southwest:	Midwest:	Southeast:	Northeast:	International:
Y	Y	Y	Y	Y	Y

PROQUEST COMPANY
www.proquestcompany.com

Industry Group Code: 511140 Ranks within this company's industry group: Sales: Profits:

Print Media/Publishing:		Movies:		Equipment/Supplies:		Broadcast/Cable:		Music/Audio:		Sports/Games:	
Newspapers:		Movie Theaters:		Equipment/Supplies:		Broadcast TV:		Music Production:		Games/Sports:	
Magazines:		Movie Production:		Gambling Equipment:	Y	Cable TV:		Retail Music:		Retail Games Stores:	
Books:	Y	TV/Video Production:		Special Services:	Y	Satellite Broadcast:		Retail Audio Equip.:		Stadiums/Teams:	
Book Stores:		Video Rental:		Advertising Services:	Y	Radio:		Music Print./Dist.:		Gambling/Casinos:	
Distribution/Printing:		Video Distribution:		Info. Sys. Software:	Y	Online Information:		Multimedia:		Rides/Theme Parks:	

TYPES OF BUSINESS:
Digital Databases
Automotive Maintenance Information
Internet Portals-Reference & Education
Automotive Parts Databases
Educational Software
K-12 Curriculum Products

BRANDS/DIVISIONS/AFFILIATES:
ProQuest Information & Learning Co.
ProQuest Business Solutions
EEBO
ProQuest SiteBuilder
Net-Compass
Early English Books Online
Voyager Learning
Syncata

CONTACTS:
Note: Officers with more than one job title may be intentionally listed here more than once.
Alan Aldworth, CEO
Alan Aldworth, Pres.
Richard Surratt, CFO
Linda Longo-Kazanova, VP-Human Resources & Bus. Optimization
Todd W. Buchardt, General Counsel/Sr. VP/Corp. Sec.
Jennifer Chelune, Investor Rel. Mgr.
Andrew Wyszkowski, Pres., ProQuest Business Solutions
Ron Klausner, Pres., ProQuest Education Bus.
David Prichard, Pres., Higher Education & Library Bus.
Alan Aldworth, Chmn.

Phone: 734-761-4700	Fax: 734-997-4040
Toll-Free:	
Address: 777 Eisenhower Pkwy., P.O. Box 1346, Ann Arbor, MI 48106-1346 US	

GROWTH PLANS/SPECIAL FEATURES:

ProQuest Co. has operated for many years as a provider of information and content to the education, powersports and transportation industries. For several months, the firm has been faced with restatement of its profits for 2001 forward. It has been selling assets to raise cash and pay down debt. It sold the Business Solutions business (PQBS) to Snap-on, Incorporated for $527 million in November 2006. In December 2006, ProQuest announced its intent to sell its Information and Learning segment (PQIL) to Cambridge Information Group for $222 million. PQIL integrates information and learning applications from over 25,000 periodicals and newspapers, 2 million dissertations, 150,000 out-of-print books and other scholarly collections. This information can be accessed online and in other electronic media. Its products are found in over 8,000 university and college libraries worldwide. PQIL also owns bigchalk.com, an educational online reference database, and EEBO (Early English Books Online), a digital compilation of the majority of English language content from 1475 to 1700, which encompasses more than 125,000 works. PQBS has been a leader in the development and deployment of parts and service information products and dealer performance applications for the automotive market. It creates solutions in 17 languages that allow automotive dealerships to electronically access manufacturers' parts catalogs, parts and service bulletins and other reference materials, and to interface with other information systems within the dealership. The company operates online electronic parts catalogs for GM and DaimlerChrysler, as well as a parts and service information system for Stihl. In early 2005, ProQuest acquired Voyager Learning, an educational software company; ExploreLearning, an online simulation maker; and Syncata, a business consulting and systems integration firm. The firm recently signed a data access agreement with Toyota Motor Australia to publish a parts catalogue specific to Toyota Australia.

ProQuest's benefits include dependent care and health care flexible spending accounts, tuition assistance, adoption assistance and business travel insurance.

FINANCIALS:
Sales and profits are in thousands of dollars—add 000 to get the full amount. 2006 Note: Financial information for 2006 was not available for all companies at press time.

2006 Sales: $	2006 Profits: $	U.S. Stock Ticker: PQE
2005 Sales: $	2005 Profits: $	Int'l Ticker: Int'l Exchange:
2004 Sales: $462,814	2004 Profits: $	Employees: 2,414
2003 Sales: $469,651	2003 Profits: $	Fiscal Year Ends: 12/31
2002 Sales: $428,300	2002 Profits: $	Parent Company:

SALARIES/BENEFITS:
Pension Plan: Y	ESOP Stock Plan:	Profit Sharing: Y	Top Exec. Salary: $625,000	Bonus: $443,594
Savings Plan:	Stock Purch. Plan:		Second Exec. Salary: $465,000	Bonus: $175,000

OTHER THOUGHTS:
Apparent Women Officers or Directors: 2
Hot Spot for Advancement for Women/Minorities:

LOCATIONS: ("Y" = Yes)
West:	Southwest:	Midwest:	Southeast:	Northeast:	International:
Y	Y	Y	Y	Y	Y

Note: Financial information, benefits and other data can change quickly and may vary from those stated here.

R R DONNELLEY & SONS CO
www.rrdonelley.com

Industry Group Code: 323000 Ranks within this company's industry group: Sales: 1 Profits: 1

Print Media/Publishing:		Movies:	Equipment/Supplies:	Broadcast/Cable:	Music/Audio:	Sports/Games:
Newspapers:		Movie Theaters:	Equipment/Supplies:	Broadcast TV:	Music Production:	Games/Sports:
Magazines:	Y	Movie Production:	Gambling Equipment:	Cable TV:	Retail Music:	Retail Games Stores:
Books:		TV/Video Production:	Special Services:	Satellite Broadcast:	Retail Audio Equip.:	Stadiums/Teams:
Book Stores:		Video Rental:	Advertising Services:	Radio:	Music Print./Dist.:	Gambling/Casinos:
Distribution/Printing:		Video Distribution:	Info. Sys. Software:	Online Information:	Multimedia:	Rides/Theme Parks:

TYPES OF BUSINESS:

Commercial Printing
Distributors-Books, Magazines, Catalogs & Direct Mail
Digital Content Management
Creative Services
Logistics Services

BRANDS/DIVISIONS/AFFILIATES:

Momentum Logistics, Inc.
Metromail Corp.
Coris, Inc.
CTC Distribution Direct
Premedia Technologies Services
Banta Corporation
Poligrafia
OfficeTiger

CONTACTS: Note: Officers with more than one job title may be intentionally listed here more than once.

Mark A. Angelson, CEO
Thomas J. Quinlan III, Interim CFO
Kenneth E. O'Brien, CIO
Suzanne S. Bettman, General Counsel/Sr. VP
Thomas J. Quinlan III, Exec. VP-Oper.
Miles W. McHugh, Controller
Stephen M. Wolf, Chmn.

Phone: 312-326-8000	Fax: 312-326-7706
Toll-Free:	
Address: 111 S. Wacker Dr., Chicago, IL 60601-1696 US	

GROWTH PLANS/SPECIAL FEATURES:

R. R. Donnelley and Sons Company provides integrated communications services that produce, manage and deliver its customers' content, regardless of medium. It has been a leader in the printing industry for 139 years. The firm also creates content for its clients, and provides creative design services as well as digital content management, production services and distribution services. Subsidiary R. R. Donnelley Logistics delivers products and packages to the U.S. Postal Services, saving customers time and money. Through Premedia Technologies Services, the company digitally captures content, converts it to the appropriate format and channels it to multiple media. R. R. Donnelley serves end markets including magazines, catalogs and retail; telecommunications, as a leader in directory printing; books, as the leading North American print provider in the book market; premedia; financial businesses, providing customized communications solutions; direct mail, providing a range of services in direct marketing; international markets, with a presence in Latin America, Europe and Asia; and logistics. In August 2005, R. R. Donnelley acquired Poligrafia, the third largest printer of magazines, catalogs, retail inserts and books in Poland. It also acquired AdPlex-Rhodes, a provider of advertising and marketing products and services based in Indiana. In December 2005, the company sold its Peak Technologies business. R. R. Donelley's 2006 activity includes the acquisition of OfficeTiger, a provider of business process outsourcing services. In November 2006, the company announced that it has agreed to acquire Banta Corporation for about $1.3 billion.

The company offers its employees flexible spending accounts, a monthly investment plan, work/life balance programs and adoption assistance.

FINANCIALS: Sales and profits are in thousands of dollars—add 000 to get the full amount. 2006 Note: Financial information for 2006 was not available for all companies at press time.

2006 Sales: $	2006 Profits: $	U.S. Stock Ticker: RRD
2005 Sales: $8,430,200	2005 Profits: $137,100	Int'l Ticker: Int'l Exchange:
2004 Sales: $7,156,400	2004 Profits: $178,300	Employees: 50,000
2003 Sales: $4,787,162	2003 Profits: $176,509	Fiscal Year Ends: 12/31
2002 Sales: $4,754,900	2002 Profits: $142,200	Parent Company:

SALARIES/BENEFITS:

Pension Plan: Y	ESOP Stock Plan:	Profit Sharing:	Top Exec. Salary: $1,000,000	Bonus: $4,000,000
Savings Plan: Y	Stock Purch. Plan: Y		Second Exec. Salary: $500,000	Bonus: $875,000

OTHER THOUGHTS:

Apparent Women Officers or Directors: 3
Hot Spot for Advancement for Women/Minorities: Y

LOCATIONS: ("Y" = Yes)

West:	Southwest:	Midwest:	Southeast:	Northeast:	International:
Y	Y	Y	Y	Y	Y

Note: Financial information, benefits and other data can change quickly and may vary from those stated here.

RADIO ONE

www.radio-one.com

Industry Group Code: 513111 Ranks within this company's industry group: Sales: 8   Profits: 6

Print Media/Publishing:	Movies:	Equipment/Supplies:		Broadcast/Cable:		Music/Audio:	Sports/Games:
Newspapers:	Movie Theaters:	Equipment/Supplies:		Broadcast TV:	Y	Music Production:	Games/Sports:
Magazines:	Movie Production:	Gambling Equipment:		Cable TV:		Retail Music:	Retail Games Stores:
Books:	TV/Video Production:	Special Services:	Y	Satellite Broadcast:		Retail Audio Equip.:	Stadiums/Teams:
Book Stores:	Video Rental:	Advertising Services:		Radio:		Music Print./Dist.:	Gambling/Casinos:
Distribution/Printing:	Video Distribution:	Info. Sys. Software:		Online Information:		Multimedia:	Rides/Theme Parks:

TYPES OF BUSINESS:

Radio Broadcasting
Television Broadcasting
Digital Broadcasting Technology

BRANDS/DIVISIONS/AFFILIATES:

TV One
Reach Media, Inc.
iBiquity
Syndication One
BlackAmericaWeb.com

CONTACTS: *Note: Officers with more than one job title may be intentionally listed here more than once.*

Alfred C. Liggins, III, CEO
Mary C. Sneed, COO
Alfred C. Liggins, III, Pres.
Scott R. Royster, CFO/Exec. VP
Marsha D. Meadows, VP-Mktg.
Amy E. Vokes, VP-Research
Leslie C. Bauer, CIO
John W. Mathews, VP-Eng.
Linda J. E. Vilardo, Chief Admin. Officer/VP
John W. Jones, General Counsel/VP
Zemira Z. Jones, VP-Oper.
Alfred C. Liggins, III, Treas.
Catherine L. Hughes, Corp. Sec.
Deborah A. Cowan, Sr. VP-Finance
Gregory A. Bublitz, VP-Finance & Corp. Controller
Pamela B. Somers, Sr. VP-Corp. Sales
Catherine L. Hughes, Chair

Phone: 301-306-1111	Fax: 301-306-9426
Toll-Free:	
Address: 5900 Princess Garden Pkwy., 7th Fl., Lanham, MD 20706 US	

GROWTH PLANS/SPECIAL FEATURES:

Radio One, Inc. is one of the largest radio broadcasting corporations in the U.S., focusing primarily on African-American and urban audiences. The company, which mostly focuses on radio, owns 70 stations in 22 markets. 42 of these stations (33FM and 9 AM) are in 14 of the top 20 African-American markets, including Atlanta, Houston, Los Angeles, Detroit and New York. In addition to broadcast radio, the company has expanded its portfolio to include XM Satellite Radio with its XM 169 The POWER subscription station. Approximately 13 million listeners tune in to Radio One's programming every week. As part of its corporate strategy, Radio One makes acquisitions of underperforming radio stations in new and existing markets that have a significant African-American presence. The firm owns 36% of TV One, a network it created with Comcast. In addition, Radio One owns 51% of Reach Media, Inc., with its popular Tom Joyner Morning Show. The company also owns a stake in iBiquity, a developer of digital broadcast technology (in-band-on-channel). Recently, the firm partnered with Reach Media to launch a new African-American news/talk radio network with leading African-American personalities; to date, 26 stations have committed to carrying all or a portion of the network's programming. Also in 2006, the company acquired the radio station WIFE-FM and the intellectual property assets of WMOJ-FM, both of Cincinnati, Ohio. In 2006, Radio One announced the launch of Syndication One (a joint venture with Reach Media), which will feature three programs (airing in Boston, Cleveland, Washington, D.C., Detroit and Miami) targeted to the African American audience and appealing to the general market. Also in 2006, the company added BlackAmericaWeb.com to its portfolio. The firm's founder and Chairperson Catherine Hughes and her son, President and CEO Alfred Liggins, together control about 75% of the firm's voting stock.

FINANCIALS: Sales and profits are in thousands of dollars—add 000 to get the full amount. 2006 Note: Financial information for 2006 was not available for all companies at press time.

2006 Sales: $	2006 Profits: $	U.S. Stock Ticker: ROIA
2005 Sales: $371,134	2005 Profits: $50,530	Int'l Ticker: Int'l Exchange:
2004 Sales: $319,761	2004 Profits: $61,602	Employees: 1,860
2003 Sales: $303,200	2003 Profits: $53,800	Fiscal Year Ends: 12/31
2002 Sales: $295,900	2002 Profits: $7,100	Parent Company:

SALARIES/BENEFITS:

Pension Plan:	ESOP Stock Plan:	Profit Sharing:	Top Exec. Salary: $551,250	Bonus: $560,000
Savings Plan: Y	Stock Purch. Plan:		Second Exec. Salary: $413,700	Bonus: $925,000

OTHER THOUGHTS:

Apparent Women Officers or Directors: 9
Hot Spot for Advancement for Women/Minorities: Y

LOCATIONS: ("Y" = Yes)

West:	Southwest:	Midwest:	Southeast:	Northeast:	International:
Y	Y	Y	Y	Y	

Note: Financial information, benefits and other data can change quickly and may vary from those stated here.

RADIOSHACK CORPORATION

www.radioshackcorporation.com

Industry Group Code: 443110 Ranks within this company's industry group: Sales: 3 Profits: 2

Print Media/Publishing:	Movies:	Equipment/Supplies:		Broadcast/Cable:	Music/Audio:	Sports/Games:
Newspapers:	Movie Theaters:	Equipment/Supplies:	Y	Broadcast TV:	Music Production:	Games/Sports:
Magazines:	Movie Production:	Gambling Equipment:		Cable TV:	Retail Music:	Retail Games Stores:
Books:	TV/Video Production:	Special Services:		Satellite Broadcast:	Retail Audio Equip.:	Stadiums/Teams:
Book Stores:	Video Rental:	Advertising Services:		Radio:	Music Print./Dist.:	Gambling/Casinos:
Distribution/Printing:	Video Distribution:	Info. Sys. Software:		Online Information:	Multimedia:	Rides/Theme Parks:

TYPES OF BUSINESS:

Consumer Electronics Stores
Cellular Telephone Sales & Distribution
Internet Services Sales & Distribution
Audio & Video Equipment Distribution
Personal Computer Sales
Franchising
Customer Support Services
Online Retail

BRANDS/DIVISIONS/AFFILIATES:

radioshack.com
RadioShack Global Sourcing
RadioShack Customer Support

CONTACTS: Note: Officers with more than one job title may be intentionally listed here more than once.

Julian Day, CEO
James Gooch, CFO
Jim Hamilton, Exec. VP-Mktg.
Cara Kinzey, Sr. VP-IT
David P. Johnson, Controller
Jim Hamilton, Exec. VP-Merch.
Jim Fredericks, Exec. VP-Admin.
Joe Formichelli, Exec. VP-Retail Oper.
Mark C. Hill, Sr. VP/Chief Corp. Dev. Officer
David P. Johnson, Sr. VP/Chief Acct. Officer
Tori Moore-Binau, Sr. VP-Mktg.
Tom Plaskett, Presiding Dir.

Phone: 817-415-3011	Fax: 817-415-2647
Toll-Free: 800-843-7422	
Address: Riverfront Campus, 300 RadioShack Cir., Fort Worth, TX 76102-1964 US	

GROWTH PLANS/SPECIAL FEATURES:

Begun as a family leather business in Fort Worth, Texas, RadioShack Corporation has grown to be one of the most well known consumer electronics specialty retailers and a growing provider of business-to-business retail support services. RadioShack operates 4,972 stores and 1,686 dealer outlets, located throughout the U.S., Puerto Rico and the U.S. Virgin Islands. It also operates 777 kiosks, including Sam's Club locations, as well as Sprint Nextel kiosks in major shopping malls. In addition, the company has seven service centers in the U.S. and one in Puerto Rico that repair name brand and private-label products. Product lines include electronic parts, batteries and accessories; wireless and conventional telephones; audio and video equipment; direct-to-home (DTH) satellite systems; and personal computers and related products, as well as specialized products such as home air cleaners and toys. Radio Shack also provides access to third-party services such as cellular and PCS phone and DTH satellite activation, long-distance telephone service, prepaid wireless airtime and extended service plans. Products, services and information are also available through radioshack.com. RadioShack operates two manufacturing facilities in the U.S. and one overseas. RadioShack Global Sourcing, a wholly owned subsidiary, serves the company's wide-ranging international import/export, sourcing, evaluation, logistics and quality control needs. Another subsidiary, RadioShack Customer Support, provides customer support services to more than 3 million customer phone calls and e-mails annually. In February 2006, RadioShack announced a significant turnaround program, the goals of which include increasing the average unit volume of its company-operated store base, rationalizing its cost structure and growing profitable square feet in its store portfolio. The company also announced plans to close 400-700 stores in order to cut costs.

Employee benefits include tuition reimbursement, a credit union, discount programs for childcare and home insurance, merchandise discounts and paid vacations.

FINANCIALS: Sales and profits are in thousands of dollars—add 000 to get the full amount. 2006 Note: Financial information for 2006 was not available for all companies at press time.

2006 Sales: $	2006 Profits: $	U.S. Stock Ticker: RSH
2005 Sales: $5,081,700	2005 Profits: $267,000	Int'l Ticker: Int'l Exchange:
2004 Sales: $4,841,200	2004 Profits: $337,200	Employees: 47,000
2003 Sales: $4,649,300	2003 Profits: $298,500	Fiscal Year Ends: 12/31
2002 Sales: $4,577,200	2002 Profits: $263,400	Parent Company:

SALARIES/BENEFITS:

Pension Plan:	ESOP Stock Plan:	Profit Sharing:	Top Exec. Salary: $912,375	Bonus: $
Savings Plan: Y	Stock Purch. Plan:		Second Exec. Salary: $720,231	Bonus: $

OTHER THOUGHTS:

Apparent Women Officers or Directors: 3
Hot Spot for Advancement for Women/Minorities: Y

LOCATIONS: ("Y" = Yes)

West:	Southwest:	Midwest:	Southeast:	Northeast:	International:
Y	Y	Y	Y	Y	Y

Note: Financial information, benefits and other data can change quickly and may vary from those stated here.

RAINBOW MEDIA HOLDINGS LLC   www.rainbow-media.com

Industry Group Code: 513210 Ranks within this company's industry group: Sales: Profits:

Print Media/Publishing:	Movies:	Equipment/Supplies:	Broadcast/Cable:	Music/Audio:	Sports/Games:
Newspapers:	Movie Theaters:	Equipment/Supplies:	Broadcast TV:	Music Production:	Games/Sports:
Magazines:	Movie Production:	Gambling Equipment:	Cable TV: Y	Retail Music:	Retail Games Stores:
Books:	TV/Video Production: Y	Special Services: Y	Satellite Broadcast:	Retail Audio Equip.:	Stadiums/Teams: Y
Book Stores:	Video Rental:	Advertising Services: Y	Radio:	Music Print./Dist.:	Gambling/Casinos:
Distribution/Printing:	Video Distribution:	Info. Sys. Software:	Online Information:	Multimedia:	Rides/Theme Parks:

TYPES OF BUSINESS:

Cable Television Broadcasting
Local News Network
Sports Teams
Sports & Performance Venues
Advertisement Sales
Network Services

BRANDS/DIVISIONS/AFFILIATES:

Cablevision Systems Corporation
Rainbow Network Communications
Madison Square Garden LP
American Movie Classics (AMC)
fuse
Independent Film Channel (IFC)
WE
Mag Rack

CONTACTS: *Note: Officers with more than one job title may be intentionally listed here more than once.*

Joshua Sapan, CEO
Joshua Sapan, Pres.
Robert Broussard, Pres., Network Sales
Charlene Weisler, Sr. VP-Research
David R. Kline, Sr. VP-Info. Systems & Facilities Mgmt.
Steven Pontillo, Sr. VP-Tech.
David Deitch, General Counsel/Sr. VP/Pres., Bus. Affairs
Mike DiPasquale, Sr. VP-Oper.
Glenn Oakley, Sr. VP-Bus. Dev.
Ellen Kroner, Sr. VP-Corp. Comm. & Mktg.
John Huffman, Sr. VP-Finance
Rob Battles, Sr. VP-Creative Svcs.
Ed Carroll, Pres., Entertainment Svcs.
Andrea Greenberg, Pres., Rainbow Media Ventures
David L. Kline, Pres./COO-Rainbow Advertising Sales Corp.

Phone: 516-803-3000	Fax: 516-803-3003
Toll-Free:	
Address: 200 Jericho Quadrangle, Jericho, NY 11753 US	

GROWTH PLANS/SPECIAL FEATURES:

Rainbow Media Holdings, LLC, a subsidiary of the Cablevision Systems Corporation, is a producer and distributor of cable television programming. Managing a broad swath of the TV business, the company owns 18 national networks, including 10 high definition stations, three regional sports networks (covering New England, Chicago and the San Francisco Bay Area and operated in conjunction with Fox Sports) and six on-demand channels. Rainbow also has seven independent ad sales divisions and a technical services department called Rainbow Network Communications. This division both handles the technological issues of company businesses and is also hired out to work for other networks, such as Bravo. Rainbow is, additionally, the owner of Madison Square Garden, LP. Not limited to the famous sports venue in New York, this subsidiary also comprises Radio City Music Hall and its subsidiaries, the Hartford Civic Center and six local sports teams, which include the New York Knicks and New York Rangers. Highlights from Rainbow's cable media portfolio include: American Movie Classics (AMC), the company's flagship, devoted solely to classic film; fuse, an interactive music channel, sporting music videos, interviews and concerts; the Independent Film Channel (IFC) companies, which not only broadcast films from low-budget and emerging producers but also assist in their development; WE, the women's entertainment channel; and the VOOM group of high definition networks. The on-demand channels, which are available to hotel customers as well as home subscribers, offer magazine-like specialty programming (on Mag Rack), sports information (on sportskool) and selections from the fuse, IFC and WE networks. In 2006, the company began marketing its HD channels globally, with new locations currently including Hong Kong, Japan, China, India, Korea, Thailand and Singapore.

FINANCIALS: Sales and profits are in thousands of dollars—add 000 to get the full amount. 2006 Note: Financial information for 2006 was not available for all companies at press time.

2006 Sales: $	2006 Profits: $	**U.S. Stock Ticker: Subsidiary**
2005 Sales: $	2005 Profits: $	**Int'l Ticker:** Int'l Exchange:
2004 Sales: $	2004 Profits: $	Employees: 499
2003 Sales: $	2003 Profits: $	Fiscal Year Ends: 12/31
2002 Sales: $	2002 Profits: $	Parent Company: CABLEVISION SYSTEMS CORP

SALARIES/BENEFITS:

Pension Plan:	ESOP Stock Plan:	Profit Sharing:	Top Exec. Salary: $	Bonus: $
Savings Plan:	Stock Purch. Plan:		Second Exec. Salary: $	Bonus: $

OTHER THOUGHTS:

Apparent Women Officers or Directors: 4
Hot Spot for Advancement for Women/Minorities: Y

LOCATIONS: ("Y" = Yes)

West:	Southwest:	Midwest:	Southeast:	Northeast:	International:
Y		Y		Y	

RANDOM HOUSE INC

www.randomhouse.com

Industry Group Code: 511130 Ranks within this company's industry group: Sales: 3 Profits:

Print Media/Publishing:	Movies:	Equipment/Supplies:	Broadcast/Cable:	Music/Audio:	Sports/Games:
Newspapers:	Movie Theaters:	Equipment/Supplies:	Broadcast TV:	Music Production:	Games/Sports:
Magazines:	Movie Production:	Gambling Equipment:	Cable TV:	Retail Music:	Retail Games Stores:
Books: Y	TV/Video Production:	Special Services:	Satellite Broadcast:	Retail Audio Equip.:	Stadiums/Teams:
Book Stores:	Video Rental:	Advertising Services:	Radio:	Music Print./Dist.:	Gambling/Casinos:
Distribution/Printing:	Video Distribution:	Info. Sys. Software:	Online Information:	Multimedia:	Rides/Theme Parks:

TYPES OF BUSINESS:
Book Publishing

BRANDS/DIVISIONS/AFFILIATES:
Bertelsmann AG
Alfred A. Knopf
Bantam Dell
Crown
Doubleday
Broadway
Knopf
Ballantine Books

CONTACTS: Note: Officers with more than one job title may be intentionally listed here more than once.
Peter Olson, CEO
Edward Volini, CFO
Edward Volini, Chief Admin. Officer
Richard Sarnoff, Corp. Dev.-Random House Ventures
Joerg Pfuhl, Verlagsgruppe Random House
Gail Rebuck, U.K. Group
Peter Olson, Chmn.

Phone: 212-782-9000 **Fax:** 212-302-7985
Toll-Free:
Address: 1745 Broadway, New York, NY 10019 US

GROWTH PLANS/SPECIAL FEATURES:
Random House, Inc., a subsidiary of German media conglomerate Bertelsmann AG, is one of the world's leading trade book publishers. Random House includes the Bantam Dell, Crown, Doubleday, Broadway, Knopf, Random House Audio, Random House Children's Books, Random House Diversified Publishing, Random House Information Group and Random House Ventures publishing groups. All of the company's publishing houses have complete editorial freedom, and the whole company operates through a decentralized business structure, meaning that each house has the freedom to publish whatever it wants, without having to go through its parent company. Publishing under the Random House name, the company releases a broad variety of titles, including fiction, non-fiction and reference books (such as the widely popular Random House Webster's College Dictionary). Other divisions of the publishing house devote themselves to children's books, discount books, large print and audio books. Ballantine Books publishes some of the best-known writers in fiction, such as Anne Rice, John Irving and Stephen King, with other activities in the areas of health, history, psychology and biography. Bantam's author list also includes Dean Koontz, Tom Robbins and Tami Hoag. Doubleday specializes in some of the best-known authors in recent history, such as Rudyard Kipling, Aldous Huxley and Bram Stoker, as well as modern authors such as John Grisham and Margaret Atwood. Alfred A. Knopf's authors have collected more Nobel Prizes, National Book Awards, Pulitzer Prizes and National Book Critics Circle Awards than those of almost any other book publisher. In recent news, the company acquired full ownership of Random House Korea from former partner JoongAng M&B Publishers. The company also acquired Multnomah Publishers, an evangelical Christian book publishing house, in 2006.

FINANCIALS: Sales and profits are in thousands of dollars—add 000 to get the full amount. 2006 Note: Financial information for 2006 was not available for all companies at press time.
2006 Sales: $	2006 Profits: $	**U.S. Stock Ticker: Subsidiary**
2005 Sales: $2,185,200	2005 Profits: $	**Int'l Ticker:** Int'l Exchange:
2004 Sales: $2,442,900	2004 Profits: $	Employees: 5,395
2003 Sales: $2,229,200	2003 Profits: $	Fiscal Year Ends: 12/31
2002 Sales: $2,096,200	2002 Profits: $	Parent Company: BERTELSMANN AG

SALARIES/BENEFITS:
Pension Plan:	ESOP Stock Plan:	Profit Sharing:	Top Exec. Salary: $	Bonus: $
Savings Plan:	Stock Purch. Plan:		Second Exec. Salary: $	Bonus: $

OTHER THOUGHTS:
Apparent Women Officers or Directors: 1
Hot Spot for Advancement for Women/Minorities:

LOCATIONS: ("Y" = Yes)
West:	Southwest:	Midwest:	Southeast:	Northeast:	International:
Y				Y	Y

Note: Financial information, benefits and other data can change quickly and may vary from those stated here.

RANK GROUP PLC (THE)

www.rank.com

Industry Group Code: 713210 Ranks within this company's industry group: Sales: 2   Profits: 11

Print Media/Publishing:	Movies:	Equipment/Supplies:		Broadcast/Cable:	Music/Audio:	Sports/Games:	
Newspapers:	Movie Theaters:	Equipment/Supplies:		Broadcast TV:	Music Production:	Games/Sports:	
Magazines:	Movie Production:	Gambling Equipment:	Y	Cable TV:	Retail Music:	Retail Games Stores:	
Books:	TV/Video Production:	Special Services:		Satellite Broadcast:	Retail Audio Equip.:	Stadiums/Teams:	
Book Stores:	Video Rental:	Advertising Services:		Radio:	Music Print./Dist.:	Gambling/Casinos:	Y
Distribution/Printing:	Video Distribution:	Info. Sys. Software:		Online Information:	Multimedia:	Rides/Theme Parks:	

TYPES OF BUSINESS:

Gambling Resorts & Casinos
Gambling Equipment

BRANDS/DIVISIONS/AFFILIATES:

Mecca Bingo
Grosvenor Casinos
Top Rank Espana
Blue Square

CONTACTS: *Note: Officers with more than one job title may be intentionally listed here more than once.*

Ian Burke, CEO
Peter Gill, Dir.-Finance
Christine Ray, Dir.-Group Human Resources
Lesly Hughes, Head-PR
Dan Waugh, Dir.-Investor Rel.
Pamela Coles, Company Sec.
Simon Wykes, Mng. Dir.-Mecca Bingo
Cyril Drabinsky, Pres., Deluxe Film
Peter Johnson, Chmn.

Phone: 020-7706-1111	Fax: 020-7262-9886
Toll-Free:	
Address: 6 Connaught Pl., London, W2 2EZ UK	

GROWTH PLANS/SPECIAL FEATURES:

The Rank Group plc is a British holding company with interests in a variety of entertainment business. The company's main segments consist of an assortment of casinos and gaming facilities. The Rank Group owns and operates: Mecca Bingo, which is the second-largest bingo club operator in the U.K. with 114 facilities; Grosvenor Casinos, which is the second largest casino operator in the U.K., with 35 facilities including two in Belgium; Top Rank Espana, which operates 11 bingo clubs in major cities across Spain; and Blue Square, which provides on-line distribution for Rank's retail gaming businesses, and Blue Square branded poker, sports betting and casino products. In 2006, Rank sold its film replication and distribution subsidiary Deluxe Film and Media Services to DX III Holdings Corporation. In December 2006, Rank agreed to sell its Hard Rock Café segment to the Seminole Tribe of Florida for $965 million. Also in 2006, Rank agreed to sell its US Holidays division, its time-share accommodation, camping and hotels business in the Pocono Mountains, Pennsylvania.

FINANCIALS: Sales and profits are in thousands of dollars—add 000 to get the full amount. 2006 Note: Financial information for 2006 was not available for all companies at press time.

2006 Sales: $	2006 Profits: $	**U.S. Stock Ticker:**
2005 Sales: $1,408,887	2005 Profits: $-362,519	**Int'l Ticker: RNK** Int'l Exchange: London-LSE
2004 Sales: $1,369,418	2004 Profits: $-24,863	Employees: 20,000
2003 Sales: $3,434,700	2003 Profits: $181,400	Fiscal Year Ends: 12/31
2002 Sales: $2,360,200	2002 Profits: $1,990,500	Parent Company:

SALARIES/BENEFITS:

Pension Plan: Y	ESOP Stock Plan:	Profit Sharing:	Top Exec. Salary: $998,648	Bonus: $
Savings Plan:	Stock Purch. Plan:		Second Exec. Salary: $712,761	Bonus: $

OTHER THOUGHTS:

Apparent Women Officers or Directors: 4
Hot Spot for Advancement for Women/Minorities: Y

LOCATIONS: ("Y" = Yes)

West:	Southwest:	Midwest:	Southeast:	Northeast:	International:
					Y

RAYCOM MEDIA INC

www.raycommedia.com

Industry Group Code: 513120 Ranks within this company's industry group: Sales: Profits:

Print Media/Publishing:		Movies:		Equipment/Supplies:		Broadcast/Cable:		Music/Audio:		Sports/Games:	
Newspapers:		Movie Theaters:		Equipment/Supplies:		Broadcast TV:	Y	Music Production:		Games/Sports:	
Magazines:		Movie Production:		Gambling Equipment:		Cable TV:		Retail Music:		Retail Games Stores:	
Books:		TV/Video Production:		Special Services:	Y	Satellite Broadcast:		Retail Audio Equip.:		Stadiums/Teams:	Y
Book Stores:		Video Rental:		Advertising Services:	Y	Radio:		Music Print./Dist.:		Gambling/Casinos:	
Distribution/Printing:		Video Distribution:		Info. Sys. Software:		Online Information:		Multimedia:		Rides/Theme Parks:	

TYPES OF BUSINESS:

Television Broadcasting
Golf Courses
Event Management
Postproduction Services
Telecommunications

BRANDS/DIVISIONS/AFFILIATES:

Raycom Sports
Raycom Post
CableVantage
Broadview Media
Liberty Corporation

CONTACTS: Note: Officers with more than one job title may be intentionally listed here more than once.

Paul McTear, CEP
Wayne Daugherty, COO/Exec. VP
Paul McTear, Pres.
Anne Adkins, VP-Mktg.
Clyde Baucom, VP-Human Resources
Billy McDowell, VP-Research
David Folsom, CTO/VP
Rebecca Bryan, General Counsel/VP
Melissa Thurber, Controller/VP
Marty Edelman, VP-Television
Leon Long, VP-Television
Susana Schuler, VP-News
Mary C. McDonnell, Exec. VP-Programming

Phone: 334-206-1400	Fax: 334-206-1555
Toll-Free:	
Address: RSA Tower, Fl. 20, 201 Monroa St., Montgomery, AL 36104 US	

GROWTH PLANS/SPECIAL FEATURES:

Raycom Media, Inc., an employee owned company, is one of the largest broadcasters in the U.S. It owns and/or operates 37 television stations in 18 states. 15 of the firm's stations are affiliated with NBC, eight with CBS, five with ABC, five with FOX, three with MyNetwork TV and one station is affiliated with the CW. In addition to broadcasting, Raycom Media, through its subsidiary Raycom Sports, is involved in event management, information systems support and design and syndicated television programming; the subsidiary also hosts Alabama's Robert Trent Jones Golf Trail web site. Through Raycom Sports, the company owns and operates two LPGA Golf tournaments and the Continental Tire Bowl; and produces pre-season NFL football games. Raycom's subsidiary Raycom Post is a post production facility in Burbank, California. Subsidiary CableVantage is a cable advertising sales group located in Columbia, South Carolina. Finally, the company's Broadview Media subsidiary is a postproduction and telecommunications company. Through a partnership with Lincoln Financial Media, Raycom owns all marketing and television rights to Atlantic Coast Conference basketball. In early 2006, the company purchased Liberty Corporation, including eight NBC affiliated stations, five ABC affiliated stations and two CBS affiliated stations. In late 2006, Barrington Broadcasting Group acquired twelve Raycom stations for a combined price of $262 million.

Raycom Media offers its employees a 401(k) plan; flexible spending accounts; disability benefits; and medical, vision and dental insurance.

FINANCIALS: Sales and profits are in thousands of dollars—add 000 to get the full amount. 2006 Note: Financial information for 2006 was not available for all companies at press time.

2006 Sales: $	2006 Profits: $	U.S. Stock Ticker: Private			
2005 Sales: $	2005 Profits: $	Int'l Ticker:	Int'l Exchange:		
2004 Sales: $	2004 Profits: $	Employees:			
2003 Sales: $	2003 Profits: $	Fiscal Year Ends: 12/31			
2002 Sales: $	2002 Profits: $	Parent Company:			

SALARIES/BENEFITS:

Pension Plan:	ESOP Stock Plan:	Profit Sharing:	Top Exec. Salary: $	Bonus: $
Savings Plan:	Stock Purch. Plan:		Second Exec. Salary: $	Bonus: $

OTHER THOUGHTS:

Apparent Women Officers or Directors: 5
Hot Spot for Advancement for Women/Minorities: Y

LOCATIONS: ("Y" = Yes)

West:	Southwest:	Midwest:	Southeast:	Northeast:	International:
Y	Y	Y	Y		

Note: Financial information, benefits and other data can change quickly and may vary from those stated here.

RCN CORP

www.rcn.com

Industry Group Code: 513300A Ranks within this company's industry group: Sales: 3 Profits: 3

Print Media/Publishing:	Movies:	Equipment/Supplies:	Broadcast/Cable:	Music/Audio:	Sports/Games:
Newspapers:	Movie Theaters:	Equipment/Supplies:	Broadcast TV:	Music Production:	Games/Sports:
Magazines:	Movie Production:	Gambling Equipment:	Cable TV: Y	Retail Music:	Retail Games Stores:
Books:	TV/Video Production:	Special Services:	Satellite Broadcast:	Retail Audio Equip.:	Stadiums/Teams:
Book Stores:	Video Rental:	Advertising Services:	Radio:	Music Print./Dist.:	Gambling/Casinos:
Distribution/Printing:	Video Distribution:	Info. Sys. Software:	Online Information:	Multimedia:	Rides/Theme Parks:

TYPES OF BUSINESS:

Local & Long-Distance Telephone Service
High-Speed Internet Access
Cable Television Service
Home Surveillance

BRANDS/DIVISIONS/AFFILIATES:

Megaband
MegaModem
MegaModem Mach 20
WebWatch
Consolidated Edison Communications

CONTACTS: Note: Officers with more than one job title may be intentionally listed here more than once.

Peter D. Aquino, CEO
Michael T. Sicoli, Exec. VP/CFO
Timothy J. Dunne, Exec. VP/CTO
Benjamin R. Preston, Sr. VP/General Counsel
Jospeh Soresso, Sr. VP-Commercial Integration
Richard Ramlall, Sr. VP-Strategic & External Affairs
John D. Filipowicz, Sr. VP/General Mgr. Pennsylvania
P. K. Ramani, Sr. VP/General Mgr. New York City
Felipe Alvarez, Pres., RCN Business Solutions
James F. Mooney, Chmn.

Phone: 609-734-3700	Fax: 609-734-6164
Toll-Free: 800-746-4726	
Address: 196 Van Buren St., Ste. 300, Herndon, VA 20170 US	

GROWTH PLANS/SPECIAL FEATURES:

RCN Corporation is a facilities-based competitive provider of bundled cable TV, phone and high-speed Internet services delivered over the company's own advanced fiber-optic Megaband network in leading urban markets. RCN currently has more than 1 million customer connections in and around Boston, New York, Philadelphia, Chicago, Los Angeles, San Francisco and Washington, D.C. The company is unique as the only residentially focused competitive local exchange carrier (CLEC) in the industry. RCN's Megaband network provides a sophisticated broadband fiber-optic platform capable of offering an array of communications services, including voice, television, on-demand video and high-speed Internet. The network employs SONET ring backbone architecture and localized nodes to ensure RCN's fiber optics travel to within 900 feet of its customers, thereby providing lower maintenance costs than those associated with local networks. RCN is currently offering MegaModem in eight markets. MegaModem Mach 20 is a high-speed Internet service that delivers data at 20 Mbps downstream and 2Mbps upstream. The company also offers WebWatch, a wireless home surveillance system accessible via the Internet. RCN recently filed a restructuring plan with the U.S. Bankruptcy Court, outlining reduction of RCN's total debt by $1.2 billion through a debt-for-equity swap. RCN has managed to eliminate this debt through restructuring. The firm acquired Consolidated Edison Communications in March 2006.

FINANCIALS: Sales and profits are in thousands of dollars—add 000 to get the full amount. 2006 Note: Financial information for 2006 was not available for all companies at press time.

2006 Sales: $	2006 Profits: $	U.S. Stock Ticker: RCNI
2005 Sales: $560,964	2005 Profits: $-136,112	Int'l Ticker: Int'l Exchange:
2004 Sales: $486,861	2004 Profits: $1,006,156	Employees: 2,000
2003 Sales: $484,900	2003 Profits: $-499,093	Fiscal Year Ends: 12/31
2002 Sales: $457,400	2002 Profits: $-1,408,200	Parent Company:

SALARIES/BENEFITS:

Pension Plan:	ESOP Stock Plan:	Profit Sharing:	Top Exec. Salary: $540,000	Bonus: $324,000
Savings Plan: Y	Stock Purch. Plan: Y		Second Exec. Salary: $540,000	Bonus: $324,000

OTHER THOUGHTS:

Apparent Women Officers or Directors:
Hot Spot for Advancement for Women/Minorities:

LOCATIONS: ("Y" = Yes)

West:	Southwest:	Midwest:	Southeast:	Northeast:	International:
Y		Y		Y	

READER'S DIGEST ASSOCIATION INC   www.rd.com

Industry Group Code: 511120 Ranks within this company's industry group: Sales: 3   Profits: 10

Print Media/Publishing:		Movies:		Equipment/Supplies:		Broadcast/Cable:		Music/Audio:		Sports/Games:	
Newspapers:		Movie Theaters:		Equipment/Supplies:		Broadcast TV:		Music Production:		Games/Sports:	
Magazines:	Y	Movie Production:		Gambling Equipment:		Cable TV:		Retail Music:		Retail Games Stores:	
Books:	Y	TV/Video Production:	Y	Special Services:		Satellite Broadcast:		Retail Audio Equip.:		Stadiums/Teams:	
Book Stores:		Video Rental:		Advertising Services:	Y	Radio:		Music Print./Dist.:	Y	Gambling/Casinos:	
Distribution/Printing:		Video Distribution:		Info. Sys. Software:		Online Information:		Multimedia:		Rides/Theme Parks:	

TYPES OF BUSINESS:

Magazine Publishing
Book Publishing
Television & Video Production
Music Collections
Electronic Media
Direct Marketing
Online Sales

BRANDS/DIVISIONS/AFFILIATES:

Reader's Digest Magazine
QSP, Inc.
Birds & Blooms
Country Woman
American Woodworker
Family Handyman
Reader's Digest Select Editions
Allrecipes.com

CONTACTS: *Note: Officers with more than one job title may be intentionally listed here more than once.*

Eric W. Schrier, CEO
Eric W. Schrier, Pres.
Michael S. Geltzeiler, CFO/Sr. VP
Gary S. Rich, Sr. VP-Human Resources
Jeffery S. Spar, CIO/VP
Michael A. Brizel, General Counsel/Sr. VP
Albert L. Perruzza, Sr. VP-Global Oper.
Richard E. Clark, VP-Investor Rel. & Global Comm.
Eric W. Schrier, Sr. VP/Global Editor-in-Chief
Lisa Cribari, VP/Global Human Resources
Dawn M. Zier, Pres., North American Consumer Mktg.
Michael A. Brennan, Sr. VP/Pres., Latin America & Asia-Pacific
Thomas O. Ryder, Chmn.
Thomas D. Gardner, Exec. VP/Pres., Int'l

Phone: 914-238-1000	**Fax:** 914-238-4559
Toll-Free:	
Address: Reader's Digest Rd., Pleasantville, NY 10570-7000 US	

GROWTH PLANS/SPECIAL FEATURES:

Reader's Digest Association, Inc. publishes and markets magazines, books, music collections and home videos. Reader's Digest Magazine (the company's flagship monthly) consists of original and previously published articles in condensed form and condensed versions of current full-length books. Reader's Digest's worldwide circulation is 18 million, with 50 editions in 21 different languages distributed in over 60 countries (including new operations in Bulgaria, Kazakhstan, Lithuania and the U.A.E.) reaching nearly 100 million readers worldwide. The company also publishes specialty magazines (Family Handyman, American Woodworker, Taste of Home, Birds & Blooms, Farm & Ranch Living and Crafting Traditions). In addition, the firm produces and distributes Reader's Digest Select Editions (formerly Condensed Books), general books, recorded music collections and home video products. The company's general books include: reference books; cookbooks; how-to and do-it-yourself books; and children's books; as well as books on subjects such as history, travel, religion, health, nature, home, computers and puzzles. Reader's Digest's music collections include about 10,000 titles across a broad range of musical styles, released as compilations on CDs and cassettes internationally. The company also sells home video products featuring travel, natural history, history and children's animated programs. Reader's Digest conducts marketing via direct mail, direct response television, telemarketing, catalogs, retail, online, and through the Books Are Fun display marketing campaign. The company's subsidiary QSP, Inc. coordinates book sales and magazine drives as fundraisers for schools. In 2006, Reader's Digest announced a licensing agreement with Marvel Entertainment for a new line of interactive books to be distributed through Simon & Schuster. In addition, the company acquired Allrecipes.com for $66 million. In late 2006, the firm agreed to be acquired by Ripplewood Holdings LLC for $1.6 billion.

Readers Digest's employees receive health insurance, 401(k) plans, flexible spending accounts, tuition reimbursement and adoption assistance.

FINANCIALS: Sales and profits are in thousands of dollars—add 000 to get the full amount. 2006 Note: Financial information for 2006 was not available for all companies at press time.

2006 Sales: $2,386,200	2006 Profits: $-117,400	**U.S. Stock Ticker: RDA**
2005 Sales: $2,389,700	2005 Profits: $-90,900	**Int'l Ticker:** Int'l Exchange:
2004 Sales: $2,388,500	2004 Profits: $49,500	Employees: 4,200
2003 Sales: $2,474,900	2003 Profits: $61,300	Fiscal Year Ends: 6/30
2002 Sales: $2,368,600	2002 Profits: $91,200	Parent Company:

SALARIES/BENEFITS:

Pension Plan: Y	ESOP Stock Plan: Y	Profit Sharing:	Top Exec. Salary: $819,505	Bonus: $550,000
Savings Plan: Y	Stock Purch. Plan: Y		Second Exec. Salary: $611,951	Bonus: $450,000

OTHER THOUGHTS:

Apparent Women Officers or Directors: 1
Hot Spot for Advancement for Women/Minorities:

LOCATIONS: ("Y" = Yes)

West:	Southwest:	Midwest:	Southeast:	Northeast:	International:
Y	Y	Y	Y	Y	Y

Note: Financial information, benefits and other data can change quickly and may vary from those stated here.

REALNETWORKS INC
www.realnetworks.com

Industry Group Code: 511209 Ranks within this company's industry group: Sales: 2 Profits: 1

Print Media/Publishing:	Movies:	Equipment/Supplies:	Broadcast/Cable:	Music/Audio:	Sports/Games:
Newspapers:	Movie Theaters:	Equipment/Supplies:	Broadcast TV:	Music Production:	Games/Sports:	Y
Magazines:	Movie Production:	Gambling Equipment:	Cable TV:	Retail Music:	Retail Games Stores:
Books:	TV/Video Production:	Special Services:	Satellite Broadcast:	Retail Audio Equip.:	Stadiums/Teams:
Book Stores:	Video Rental:	Advertising Services: Y	Radio:	Music Print./Dist.: Y	Gambling/Casinos:
Distribution/Printing:	Video Distribution:	Info. Sys. Software: Y	Online Information:	Multimedia:	Rides/Theme Parks:

TYPES OF BUSINESS:
Digital Media Services
Computer Software-Streaming Audio & Video
Online Retail-Digital Media
Mobile Games
Mobile Music
Mobile Video

BRANDS/DIVISIONS/AFFILIATES:
RealPlayer
RealOne
Rhapsody
RadioPass
RealPlayer Music Store
Helix
Zylom Media Group B.V.
WiderThan

CONTACTS: *Note: Officers with more than one job title may be intentionally listed here more than once.*
Robert Glaser, CEO
Michael Eggers, CFO
Jackie Lang, VP-Consumer Mktg.
Savino R. Ferrales, Sr. VP-Human Resources
Edmond Mesrobian, CTO/VP
Robert Kimball, General Counsel/Sr. VP
Richard Wolpert, Chief Strategic Officer
Michael Eggers, Sr. VP-Finance
Aref Matin, VP/Carrier & System Software
Carla Stratfold, Sr. VP-North American Sales
Karim Meghji, VP-Media Properties & Video Services
Harold Zeitz, Sr. VP-Media Software & Services
Robert Glaser, Chmn.
John Giamatteo, Exec. VP-Int'l

Phone: 206-674-2700	Fax: 206-674-2699
Toll-Free:	
Address: 2601 Elliott Ave., Ste. 1000, Seattle, WA 98121 US	

GROWTH PLANS/SPECIAL FEATURES:
RealNetworks, Inc. is a leading global provider of network-delivered digital media services and technology that enables digital media creation, distribution and consumption. The company functions in three ways: as an electronic retailer of digital content to consumers; as a business-to-business services provider to third parties who wish to distribute their content to consumers over digital networks; and as a supplier of the underlying technology used by content owners and network operators to create and distribute digital content. The firm's central product is the RealPlayer media player software through which it offers a variety of subscription services. The RealOne subscription service provides consumers with programming, including content provided by abcnews.com, CNN and nascar.com. Other services include Rhapsody (digital music subscription service), Rhapsody To Go (portable digital subscription service), RadioPass (high-fidelity radio content with 3,200 worldwide broadcast stations), the RealPlayer Music Store and Rhapsody.com. The firm recently acquired Zylom Media Group B.V., an online casual games distributor in Europe. RealNetworks produces Helix-brand products, allowing content creators, web site owners and network operators to create, secure and distribute digital media content to PCs and non-PC devices. In 2006, the firm partnered with Cingular to launch video-on-demand for a Helix online platform, making Cingular the first wireless carrier to use the platform. Also in 2006, the company acquired mobile music and entertainment company WiderThan for $350 million. Recently, Real Networks partnered with Google and Mozilla to distribute Firefox Web Browser and Google toolbar with RealPlayer. In addition, the company announced an agreement with HP to provide Rhapsody to HP Pavilion, Compaq Presario and HP Pavilion Media Center TV PC product lines. Also in 2006, the company partnered with SanDisk Corporation to integrate Rhapsody DNA into Sansa MP3 players.

RealNetworks offers internships to undergraduate and post-graduate degree candidates.

FINANCIALS: Sales and profits are in thousands of dollars—add 000 to get the full amount. 2006 Note: Financial information for 2006 was not available for all companies at press time.

2006 Sales: $	2006 Profits: $	**U.S. Stock Ticker: RNWK**
2005 Sales: $325,059	2005 Profits: $312,345	**Int'l Ticker:** Int'l Exchange:
2004 Sales: $266,719	2004 Profits: $-23,000	Employees: 933
2003 Sales: $202,377	2003 Profits: $-21,500	Fiscal Year Ends: 12/31
2002 Sales: $182,700	2002 Profits: $-38,400	Parent Company:

SALARIES/BENEFITS:

Pension Plan:	ESOP Stock Plan:	Profit Sharing:	Top Exec. Salary: $400,000	Bonus: $386,000
Savings Plan: Y	Stock Purch. Plan:		Second Exec. Salary: $260,000	Bonus: $164,403

OTHER THOUGHTS:
Apparent Women Officers or Directors: 2
Hot Spot for Advancement for Women/Minorities:

LOCATIONS: ("Y" = Yes)

West:	Southwest:	Midwest:	Southeast:	Northeast:	International:
Y	Y				Y

Note: Financial information, benefits and other data can change quickly and may vary from those stated here.

REED ELSEVIER GROUP PLC   www.reed-elsevier.com

Industry Group Code: 511140 Ranks within this company's industry group: Sales: 1 Profits: 2

Print Media/Publishing:		Movies:	Equipment/Supplies:		Broadcast/Cable:	Music/Audio:	Sports/Games:
Newspapers:		Movie Theaters:	Equipment/Supplies:		Broadcast TV:	Music Production:	Games/Sports:
Magazines:	Y	Movie Production:	Gambling Equipment:		Cable TV:	Retail Music:	Retail Games Stores:
Books:	Y	TV/Video Production:	Special Services:	Y	Satellite Broadcast:	Retail Audio Equip.:	Stadiums/Teams:
Book Stores:		Video Rental:	Advertising Services:		Radio:	Music Print./Dist.:	Gambling/Casinos:
Distribution/Printing:		Video Distribution:	Info. Sys. Software:		Online Information:	Multimedia:	Rides/Theme Parks:

TYPES OF BUSINESS:

Online Information Publishing
Textbooks
Scientific Journals
Business Magazines
Legal Databases
Assessment Tests
Online Databases

BRANDS/DIVISIONS/AFFILIATES:

Elsevier Science & Technology
Elsevier Health Sciences
LexisNexis
Harcourt
BioMedNet
ChemWeb
WB Saunders
Mosby

CONTACTS: *Note: Officers with more than one job title may be intentionally listed here more than once.*

Crispin Davis, CEO
Mark Armour, CFO
Nick Baker, Chief Strategy Officer
Erik Engstrom, CEO-Elsevier
Gerard van de Aast, CEO-Reed
Andrew Prozes, CEO-LexisNexis Group
Patrick Tierney, CEO-Harcourt Education
Jan Hommen, Chmn.

Phone: 44-20-7222-8420	Fax: 44-20-7227-5799
Toll-Free:	
Address: 25 Victoria St., London, SW1H 0EX UK	

GROWTH PLANS/SPECIAL FEATURES:

Reed Elsevier Group plc provides students and professionals with valuable information in the fields of science, medicine, law, education and business, publishing more than 15,000 different journals, books and reference works. The firm publishes its material mostly online, but in some print forms as well. Elsevier Science and Technology publishes 1,200 journals, 900 books and numerous online products annually, including ScienceDirect, MDL, Academic Press, BioMedNet and ChemWeb. Elsevier Health Sciences offers a library of 8,000 clinical references and 500 journals under the Mosby, Churchill Livingstone, Harcourt and WB Saunders imprints. The LexisNexis unit maintains one of the largest databases in the world and is the leading online source for legal matters and public records, with additional resources for news and business information. This information is marketed to legal professionals, law firms, schools, corporations and governments. The education division of the company is composed of the Harcourt group, publishing textbooks and assessment tests. The Reed Business Information segment publishes business, trade, contact and other information through magazines, directories, exhibitions and other channels and holds the leading market position for business-related publishing in Europe. Reed Elsevier has been expanding its holdings and position aggressively, in both Europe and the U.S., through acquisitions of similar companies. The Reed Elsevier Group is a joint venture owned by Reed Elsevier plc and Reed Elsevier NV.

FINANCIALS: Sales and profits are in thousands of dollars—add 000 to get the full amount. 2006 Note: Financial information for 2006 was not available for all companies at press time.

2006 Sales: $	2006 Profits: $	**U.S. Stock Ticker: Joint Venture**
2005 Sales: $8,982,132	2005 Profits: $806,719	Int'l Ticker: Int'l Exchange:
2004 Sales: $8,366,240	2004 Profits: $801,459	Employees: 36,000
2003 Sales: $8,756,200	2003 Profits: $593,800	Fiscal Year Ends: 12/31
2002 Sales: $8,051,600	2002 Profits: $290,300	Parent Company:

SALARIES/BENEFITS:

Pension Plan: Y	ESOP Stock Plan:	Profit Sharing:	Top Exec. Salary: $1,650,000	Bonus: $54,000
Savings Plan:	Stock Purch. Plan:		Second Exec. Salary: $1,100,000	Bonus: $18,000

OTHER THOUGHTS:

Apparent Women Officers or Directors:
Hot Spot for Advancement for Women/Minorities:

LOCATIONS: ("Y" = Yes)

West:	Southwest:	Midwest:	Southeast:	Northeast:	International:
	Y	Y	Y	Y	Y

Note: Financial information, benefits and other data can change quickly and may vary from those stated here.

REGAL ENTERTAINMENT GROUP
www.regalcinemas.com

Industry Group Code: 512131 Ranks within this company's industry group: Sales: 1   Profits: 1

Print Media/Publishing:	Movies:		Equipment/Supplies:		Broadcast/Cable:	Music/Audio:	Sports/Games:
Newspapers:	Movie Theaters:	Y	Equipment/Supplies:		Broadcast TV:	Music Production:	Games/Sports:
Magazines:	Movie Production:		Gambling Equipment:		Cable TV:	Retail Music:	Retail Games Stores:
Books:	TV/Video Production:		Special Services:	Y	Satellite Broadcast:	Retail Audio Equip.:	Stadiums/Teams:
Book Stores:	Video Rental:		Advertising Services:	Y	Radio:	Music Print./Dist.:	Gambling/Casinos:
Distribution/Printing:	Video Distribution:		Info. Sys. Software:		Online Information:	Multimedia:	Rides/Theme Parks:

TYPES OF BUSINESS:
Movie Theaters
In-Theater Advertising
Theater Rental & Special Events

BRANDS/DIVISIONS/AFFILIATES:
Regal Cinemas
United Artists Theater Company
Hoyts Cinema
Edwards Theaters
Regal CineMedia
Signature Theatres
National CineMedia, LLC
AMC Cinemark

CONTACTS: Note: Officers with more than one job title may be intentionally listed here more than once.
Michael L. Campbell, CEO
Gregory W. Dunn, COO
Gregory W. Dunn, Pres.
Amy E. Miles, CFO/Exec.VP
Dick Westerling, Sr. VP-Mktg.
Peter B. Brandow, General Counsel/Exec.VP
Donald De Laria, VP-Investor Rel.
Amy E. Miles, Treas.
Kurt C. Hall, CEO-Regal CineMedia
Clifford Marks, Chief Mktg. Officer-Regal CineMedia
Gary W. Ferrara, CFO/Exec.VP-Regal CineMedia
Tom Galley, Chief Tech. Officer-Regal CineMedia
Michael L. Campbell, Chmn.

Phone: 865-922-1123	Fax: 865-922-3188
Toll-Free: 800-784-8477	
Address: 7132 Regal Ln., Knoxville, TN 37918 US	

GROWTH PLANS/SPECIAL FEATURES:

Regal Entertainment Group (REG), through its subsidiaries, is one of the largest motion picture exhibitors in the world. The firm's nationwide network of theaters, including Regal Cinemas, United Artists Theaters, Hoyts Cinemas and Edwards Theaters, operates 6,463 screens in 555 locations in 40 states. Recently, the firm acquired four theaters and 58 screens (in New York, Massachusetts, Texas, and Washington) from AMC Entertainment, Inc. for $34.0 million in cash and two Regal theaters (Oklahoma and Arkansas). The company's screens constitute about 18% of all screens in the U.S. (nearly twice as many as the nearest competitor) and represent over 20% of domestic box office receipts. Approximately 85% of REG's screens are located in film licensing zones in which it is the sole exhibitor, providing the firm with access to all films distributed by major distributors and eliminating its need to compete with other exhibitors for films in that zone. Furthermore, REG operates theaters in 43 of the top 50 demographic market areas, drawing over 244 million annual attendees. The company also operates Regal CineMedia, which includes divisions that focus on meetings and special productions in a theater environment, including the presentation of entertainment, sports and educational events as well as the sale of group tickets and gift certificates. In 2006, the firm launched its new product, Regal Guest response System SM, in 13 theaters (Georgia, Louisiana, Tennessee, California, Florida, Delaware and New York). This pager system alerts management of any disturbances in the auditorium. In addition, the company currently uses Real D 3D screens in 23 markets.

At the corporate level, REG offers its employees paid vacations, free movies and dental and medical insurance. Movie theater salaries vary based on location, with medical and dental insurance available for full-time salaried managers.

FINANCIALS: Sales and profits are in thousands of dollars—add 000 to get the full amount. 2006 Note: Financial information for 2006 was not available for all companies at press time.

2006 Sales: $	2006 Profits: $	U.S. Stock Ticker: RGC
2005 Sales: $2,516,700	2005 Profits: $91,800	Int'l Ticker: Int'l Exchange:
2004 Sales: $2,468,000	2004 Profits: $82,500	Employees: 24,602
2003 Sales: $2,489,900	2003 Profits: $185,400	Fiscal Year Ends: 12/31
2002 Sales: $2,140,200	2002 Profits: $120,200	Parent Company:

SALARIES/BENEFITS:

Pension Plan:	ESOP Stock Plan:	Profit Sharing:	Top Exec. Salary: $594,700	Bonus: $589,100
Savings Plan: Y	Stock Purch. Plan:		Second Exec. Salary: $403,844	Bonus: $300,000

OTHER THOUGHTS:
Apparent Women Officers or Directors: 1
Hot Spot for Advancement for Women/Minorities:

LOCATIONS: ("Y" = Yes)

West:	Southwest:	Midwest:	Southeast:	Northeast:	International:
Y	Y	Y	Y	Y	Y

Note: Financial information, benefits and other data can change quickly and may vary from those stated here.

REGENT COMMUNICATIONS   www.regentcomm.com

Industry Group Code: 513111 Ranks within this company's industry group: Sales: 13   Profits: 10

Print Media/Publishing:	Movies:	Equipment/Supplies:		Broadcast/Cable:	Music/Audio:	Sports/Games:
Newspapers:	Movie Theaters:	Equipment/Supplies:		Broadcast TV:	Music Production:	Games/Sports:
Magazines:	Movie Production:	Gambling Equipment:		Cable TV:	Retail Music:	Retail Games Stores:
Books:	TV/Video Production:	Special Services:		Satellite Broadcast:	Retail Audio Equip.:	Stadiums/Teams:
Book Stores:	Video Rental:	Advertising Services:	Y	Radio:	Music Print./Dist.:	Gambling/Casinos:
Distribution/Printing:	Video Distribution:	Info. Sys. Software:		Online Information:	Multimedia:	Rides/Theme Parks:

TYPES OF BUSINESS:
Radio Broadcasting

BRANDS/DIVISIONS/AFFILIATES:

CONTACTS: *Note: Officers with more than one job title may be intentionally listed here more than once.*
William L. Stakelin, CEO
William L. Stakelin, Pres.
Anthony Vasconcellos, CFO/Exec. VP
David J. Remund, VP-Eng.
Fred L. Murr, Sr. VP-Oper.
Robert Allen, Jr., VP-Finance & Acct.
Robert J. Ausfeld, VP-Regional
Matthew A. Yeoman, VP-Oper.
Robert A. Moody, VP-Programming
Michael J. Grimsley, VP-Regional
William P. Sutter, Jr., Chmn.

Phone: 513-651-1190	Fax: 513-651-1195
Toll-Free:	
Address: 2000 Fifth Third Center, 511 Walnut Street, Cincinnati, OH 45202 US	

GROWTH PLANS/SPECIAL FEATURES:
Regent Communications owns and operates approximately 68 radio stations in 14 markets across the U.S., including Colorado, Illinois, Indiana, Kentucky, Louisiana, Michigan, Minnesota, New York, Pennsylvania and Texas.   The company offers a variety of programming that ranges from adult contemporary music to news talk programs and country music.   Regent depends almost solely on advertising revenues, which consist of close to 90% of the firm's total revenues. Regent's primary expansion strategy is to focus on the acquisition of radio stations in small and mid-sized markets, where reduced competition facilitates the purchase of stations for sale. Ownership of multiple stations in the same market places the company in a better position to grow steadily and encompass a broader range of demographic groups, a strategy aimed at raising advertising revenues. Furthermore, this makes the firm less susceptible to economic downturns due to advertising revenues being localized. In 2006, the firm sold its 10 radio stations serving the Redding and Chico, California markets to Mapleton Communications for $17.5 million. Also in 2006, Regent sold its WYNG-FM (Evansville, Indiana) to W. Russell Withers, Jr. for $1.5 million.   Recently, the firm acquired WNYQ-FM (Albany, New York) from Vox Radio Group for $4.0 million. In addition, the company announced plans to acquire two Class B FM stations, WZPW-FM and WXMP-FM, from AAA Entertainment for approximately $12.5 million, as well as three Class A FM radio stations, WIXO-FM, WVEL-FM and WPIA-FM, for approximately $2.8 million from Independence Media. Also in 2006, the company agreed to acquire WBLK-FM, WBUF-FM, WJYE-FM, WYRK-FM and WECK-AM (Buffalo, New York) from CBS Corporation for $125.0 million. All transactions will occur pending regulatory approvals.

FINANCIALS: Sales and profits are in thousands of dollars—add 000 to get the full amount. 2006 Note: Financial information for 2006 was not available for all companies at press time.

2006 Sales: $	2006 Profits: $	**U.S. Stock Ticker: RGCI**
2005 Sales: $85,600	2005 Profits: $-6,639	**Int'l Ticker:** Int'l Exchange:
2004 Sales: $84,187	2004 Profits: $13,235	Employees: 880
2003 Sales: $80,578	2003 Profits: $5,706	Fiscal Year Ends: 12/31
2002 Sales: $70,400	2002 Profits: $-6,400	Parent Company:

SALARIES/BENEFITS:

Pension Plan: Y	ESOP Stock Plan: Y	Profit Sharing:	Top Exec. Salary: $330,457	Bonus: $115,560
Savings Plan: Y	Stock Purch. Plan:		Second Exec. Salary: $252,865	Bonus: $156,000

OTHER THOUGHTS:
Apparent Women Officers or Directors:
Hot Spot for Advancement for Women/Minorities:

LOCATIONS: ("Y" = Yes)

West:	Southwest:	Midwest:	Southeast:	Northeast:	International:
Y	Y	Y	Y	Y	

Note: Financial information, benefits and other data can change quickly and may vary from those stated here.

RENAISSANCE ENTERTAINMENT CORP　　www.recfair.com

Industry Group Code: 711310 Ranks within this company's industry group: Sales:　Profits:

Print Media/Publishing:	Movies:	Equipment/Supplies:		Broadcast/Cable:	Music/Audio:	Sports/Games:	
Newspapers:	Movie Theaters:	Equipment/Supplies:		Broadcast TV:	Music Production:	Games/Sports:	Y
Magazines:	Movie Production:	Gambling Equipment:		Cable TV:	Retail Music:	Retail Games Stores:	
Books:	TV/Video Production:	Special Services:	Y	Satellite Broadcast:	Retail Audio Equip.:	Stadiums/Teams:	
Book Stores:	Video Rental:	Advertising Services:		Radio:	Music Print./Dist.:	Gambling/Casinos:	
Distribution/Printing:	Video Distribution:	Info. Sys. Software:		Online Information:	Multimedia:	Rides/Theme Parks:	Y

TYPES OF BUSINESS:
Renaissance Entertainment Parks
Food & Beverages
Halloween Events
Skiing Facilities

BRANDS/DIVISIONS/AFFILIATES:
Bristol Renaissance Faire
Southern California Renaissance Pleasure Faire
New York Renaissance Faire
Forest of Fear
Ski Sterling Forest

CONTACTS: *Note: Officers with more than one job title may be intentionally listed here more than once.*
Charles S. Leavell, CEO
J. Stanley Gilbert, COO
J. Stanley Gilbert, Pres.
Charles S. Leavell, CFO
Sue Brophy, Controller/Chief Accounting Officer
Linda McFeters, General Mgr.-Bristol Renaissance Faire
Charles S. Leavell, Chmn.

Phone: 303-664-0300	**Fax:** 303-664-0303
Toll-Free:	
Address: 275 Century Cir., Ste. 102, Louisville, CO 80027 US	

GROWTH PLANS/SPECIAL FEATURES:

Renaissance Entertainment Corp. (REC), the only publicly traded company in the Renaissance fair industry, owns and operates Renaissance fairs in the U.S. The company's fairs include the New York Renaissance Faire; the Bristol Faire in Kenosha, Wisconsin; and the Southern California Renaissance Pleasure Faire in Irwindale, California. All of the company's Renaissance fairs are outdoor family entertainment events that romanticize the ambiance of a Renaissance-era marketplace. These marketplaces include craft shops, period food, dancers, jousters, musicians and historical characters from Elizabethan England. The fairs run from six to eight weekends, all day long, with comedies and dramas enacted on multiple stages and minstrels and troubadors that walk about singing and dancing. More than 100 foods and desserts are offered, including shepherd's pie, roasted turkey legs, crepes and strawberries and cream. Each year, the fairs bring in approximately 700,000 people. During the winter months, the firm operates a ski resort in New York called Ski Sterling Forest. For Halloween, the New York fair site is turned into the Forest of Fear, a haunted house with various Halloween-inspired games, such as an axe toss, as well as various attractions such as Circus of the Damned and the Slaughter House. The firm's major sponsors have included Anheuser-Busch, Miller Brewing Co., Aquafina Water, Hard Core Cider, Red Hook Ale, Andis Systems, Pepsi Cola Co., Grand Pacific Resorts, Canandaigua Wines, Samuel Adams and Guinness Import Co.

Renaissance Entertainment offers its employees seasonal and weekend employment opportunities with flexible schedules and complimentary tickets. Most positions require some acting skills and the willingness to dress in period clothing.

FINANCIALS: Sales and profits are in thousands of dollars—add 000 to get the full amount. 2006 Note: Financial information for 2006 was not available for all companies at press time.

2006 Sales: $	2006 Profits: $	**U.S. Stock Ticker:** Private
2005 Sales: $	2005 Profits: $	**Int'l Ticker:**　Int'l Exchange:
2004 Sales: $	2004 Profits: $	Employees:　36
2003 Sales: $	2003 Profits: $	Fiscal Year Ends: 12/31
2002 Sales: $12,000	2002 Profits: $- 500	Parent Company:

SALARIES/BENEFITS:

Pension Plan:	ESOP Stock Plan:	Profit Sharing:	Top Exec. Salary: $160,000	Bonus: $
Savings Plan:	Stock Purch. Plan:		Second Exec. Salary: $120,000	Bonus: $

OTHER THOUGHTS:
Apparent Women Officers or Directors: 2
Hot Spot for Advancement for Women/Minorities:

LOCATIONS: ("Y" = Yes)

West:	Southwest:	Midwest:	Southeast:	Northeast:	International:
Y		Y		Y	

Note: Financial information, benefits and other data can change quickly and may vary from those stated here.

RENTRAK CORPORATION

www.rentrak.com

Industry Group Code: 512110 Ranks within this company's industry group: Sales: 17   Profits: 8

Print Media/Publishing:	Movies:	Equipment/Supplies:		Broadcast/Cable:	Music/Audio:	Sports/Games:
Newspapers:	Movie Theaters:	Equipment/Supplies:		Broadcast TV:	Music Production:	Games/Sports:
Magazines:	Movie Production:	Gambling Equipment:		Cable TV:	Retail Music:	Retail Games Stores:
Books:	TV/Video Production:	Special Services:	Y	Satellite Broadcast:	Retail Audio Equip.:	Stadiums/Teams:
Book Stores:	Video Rental:	Advertising Services:	Y	Radio:	Music Print./Dist.:	Gambling/Casinos:
Distribution/Printing:	Video Distribution:	Info. Sys. Software:	Y	Online Information:	Multimedia:	Rides/Theme Parks:

TYPES OF BUSINESS:

Video Distribution
Online Services
Software Development
e-Fulfillment Services

BRANDS/DIVISIONS/AFFILIATES:

Rentrak Profit Maker
Video Retailer Essentials
formovies.com
Box Office Essentials
Home Video Essentials
OnDemand Essentials
Retail Essentials
Supply Chain Essentials

CONTACTS: *Note: Officers with more than one job title may be intentionally listed here more than once.*

Paul A. Rosenbaum, CEO
Mark Thoenes, CFO/Exec. VP
Christopher Roberts, Sr. VP-Sales & Mktg.
Amir Yazdani, CIO/Exec. VP-Info. Tech.
Craig Berardi, VP-Product Dev. Oper.
Kenneth Papagan, Exec. VP-Bus. Dev. & Strategic Planning
Timothy Erwin, VP-Sales/Customer Rel.
Ron Giambra, Sr. VP-Theatrical
Marty Graham, Pres., Rentrak PPT Div.
Cathy Hetzel, Sr. VP-OnDemand Essentials
Sandra S. Kilbridge, VP-Bus. Dev.
Paul A. Rosenbaum, Chmn.

Phone: 503-284-7581	**Fax:** 503-331-2734
Toll-Free: 800-929-8000	
Address: 7700 NE Ambassador Pl., Portland, OR 97220 US	

GROWTH PLANS/SPECIAL FEATURES:

Rentrak Corporation is a video distribution company that operates in two business divisions: Pay-Per-Transaction (PPT) and Advanced Media and Information (AMI). The PPT Division focuses on managing business operations that facilitate the delivery of home entertainment content products and related rental and sales information for that content to home video specialty stores and other retailers throughout the U.S. and Canada. Through this division, the company tracks sales and rental information of DVDs, VHS tapes and videogames which have been subleased or sublicensed to retailers. In addition, the PPT division offers retailers Rentrak Profit Maker Software and Video Retailer Essentials Software which allows retailers to order new products through Point of Sale systems. This division also operates formovies.com, a web site that helps customers find local video stores and research the titles carried by those stores. Rentrak's AMI Division concentrates on the management and growth of the Essentials Suite of business intelligence services as well as operating direct revenue sharing services and the Essentials Suite of software and services. As part of the Essentials Suite, the company offers Box Office Essentials, which reports domestic and international theatrical gross receipt ticket sales to motion picture studios and movie theater owners; and Home Video Essentials, which measures rentals from both retailers and online channels. In 2006, Rentrack unveiled OnDemand Essentials, which measures viewership of on demand content in the cable and broadband industries; and Retail Essentials, which reports DVD, VHS and video game sales. Both of these products are under the AMI division. In addition, the company developed Supply Chain Essentials, to be used by retailers for supply chain management.

FINANCIALS: Sales and profits are in thousands of dollars—add 000 to get the full amount. 2006 Note: Financial information for 2006 was not available for all companies at press time.

2006 Sales: $93,394	2006 Profits: $4,466	**U.S. Stock Ticker: RENT**
2005 Sales: $98,538	2005 Profits: $5,242	**Int'l Ticker:** Int'l Exchange:
2004 Sales: $78,132	2004 Profits: $1,310	Employees: 233
2003 Sales: $86,200	2003 Profits: $- 500	Fiscal Year Ends: 3/31
2002 Sales: $102,600	2002 Profits: $9,000	Parent Company:

SALARIES/BENEFITS:

Pension Plan:	ESOP Stock Plan:	Profit Sharing:	Top Exec. Salary: $450,000	Bonus: $
Savings Plan: Y	Stock Purch. Plan:		Second Exec. Salary: $267,500	Bonus: $50,000

OTHER THOUGHTS:

Apparent Women Officers or Directors: 2
Hot Spot for Advancement for Women/Minorities:

LOCATIONS: ("Y" = Yes)

West:	Southwest:	Midwest:	Southeast:	Northeast:	International:
Y					Y

Note: Financial information, benefits and other data can change quickly and may vary from those stated here.

REUTERS GROUP PLC

www.reuters.com

Industry Group Code: 514100 Ranks within this company's industry group: Sales: 1 Profits: 1

Print Media/Publishing:	Movies:		Equipment/Supplies:		Broadcast/Cable:	Music/Audio:	Sports/Games:
Newspapers:	Movie Theaters:		Equipment/Supplies:		Broadcast TV:	Music Production:	Games/Sports:
Magazines: Y	Movie Production:		Gambling Equipment:		Cable TV:	Retail Music:	Retail Games Stores:
Books: Y	TV/Video Production:		Special Services:		Satellite Broadcast:	Retail Audio Equip.:	Stadiums/Teams:
Book Stores:	Video Rental:		Advertising Services: Y		Radio:	Music Print./Dist.:	Gambling/Casinos:
Distribution/Printing:	Video Distribution:		Info. Sys. Software: Y		Online Information:	Multimedia:	Rides/Theme Parks:

TYPES OF BUSINESS:

Financial Information
Online Information Publishing
Online Stock Trading
Market Research Distribution
Stock Market Data
Multimedia News Agency

BRANDS/DIVISIONS/AFFILIATES:

Reuters Investor
Reuters Trade Access
Bridge Information Systems
Reuters Foundation

CONTACTS: Note: Officers with more than one job title may be intentionally listed here more than once.

Thomas Glocer, CEO
Devin Wenig, COO
David J. Grigson, CFO
Lee Ann Daly, Chief Mktg. Officer/Exec. VP
Stephen Dando, Human Resources
David Lister, CIO
Michael Sayers, Chief Tech. Officer
Rosemary Martin, General Counsel
Susan T. Martin, Dir.-Corp. Strategy
Simon Walker, Dir.-Corp. Comm./Mktg.
Graham Albutt, Pres., Bus. Programs
Geert Linnebank, Editor-in-Chief
David Wenig, Pres., Business Divisions
Christopher Hagman, Global Sales/Service Oper.
Niall FitzGerald, Chmn.

Phone: 44-20-7250-1122 **Fax:** 44-20-7542-4064
Toll-Free: 800-435-0101
Address: 85 Fleet St., 77th Fl., London, EC4P 4AJ UK

GROWTH PLANS/SPECIAL FEATURES:

Reuters Group plc provides news and business updates through a variety of media, including online forums, direct data feed, a magazine and books. It is one of the world's largest international multimedia news agencies, supplying news in the form of text, graphics, video and pictures to media organizations across the globe. The company's core product is an online financial data and tools system sold on subscription to professionals in corporate, financial and media offices. The company has approximately 328,000 of these subscriptions sold worldwide at about $545 monthly per subscription. It competes against Bloomberg in this sector. Reuters subscriptions include financial analysis tools that can assist traders and asset managers with investment decisions. Sales and trading contribute 66% of Reuters revenue. The firm's Reuters Investor unit, previously known as Multex, provides access to market research and stock analysis via online sales of individual reports. Reuters also has a hosted version of its Reuters Trade Access platform for North America, a cross-asset online portfolio valuation and interactive real-time position keeping system. The company will initially provide the platform to the hedge fund market. At one time, Reuters had a 63% interest in Instinet, an online trading network. Instinet was acquired by NASDAQ in 2005. Also in 2005, Reuters sold its subsidiary Radianz to BT Group which has renamed the service BT Radianz. In late 2006, Reuters agreed to sell its 50% stake in Factiva to joint venture partner Dow Jones for roughly $153 million to $160 million. Reuters will continue to supply Factiva with news as a paid supplier.

FINANCIALS: Sales and profits are in thousands of dollars—add 000 to get the full amount. 2006 Note: Financial information for 2006 was not available for all companies at press time.

2006 Sales: $	2006 Profits: $	**U.S. Stock Ticker: RTRSY**
2005 Sales: $4,189,700	2005 Profits: $838,391	**Int'l Ticker: RTR** Int'l Exchange: London-LSE
2004 Sales: $4,068,480	2004 Profits: $652,215	Employees: 15,000
2003 Sales: $5,683,400	2003 Profits: $87,844	Fiscal Year Ends: 12/31
2002 Sales: $6,231,360	2002 Profits: $-448,018	Parent Company:

SALARIES/BENEFITS:

Pension Plan:	ESOP Stock Plan:	Profit Sharing:	Top Exec. Salary: $1,558,070	Bonus: $1,682,347
Savings Plan:	Stock Purch. Plan:		Second Exec. Salary: $954,794	Bonus: $

OTHER THOUGHTS:

Apparent Women Officers or Directors: 3
Hot Spot for Advancement for Women/Minorities: Y

LOCATIONS: ("Y" = Yes)

West:	Southwest:	Midwest:	Southeast:	Northeast:	International:
				Y	Y

Note: Financial information, benefits and other data can change quickly and may vary from those stated here.

REX STORES CORP

www.rexstores.com

Industry Group Code: 443110 **Ranks within this company's industry group:** Sales: 6 Profits: 4

Print Media/Publishing:	Movies:	Equipment/Supplies:	Broadcast/Cable:	Music/Audio:		Sports/Games:
Newspapers:	Movie Theaters:	Equipment/Supplies:	Broadcast TV:	Music Production:		Games/Sports:
Magazines:	Movie Production:	Gambling Equipment:	Cable TV:	Retail Music:		Retail Games Stores:
Books:	TV/Video Production:	Special Services:	Satellite Broadcast:	Retail Audio Equip.:	Y	Stadiums/Teams:
Book Stores:	Video Rental:	Advertising Services:	Radio:	Music Print./Dist.:		Gambling/Casinos:
Distribution/Printing:	Video Distribution:	Info. Sys. Software:	Online Information:	Multimedia:		Rides/Theme Parks:

TYPES OF BUSINESS:

Electronics Stores
Appliances
Furniture
Online Sales
Ethanol

BRANDS/DIVISIONS/AFFILIATES:

rexstores.com
Leyelland/Hockley County Ethanol LLC
Big River Resources LLC
Millennium Ethanol LLC
Patriot Renewable Fuels LLC
One Earth Energy LLC

CONTACTS: Note: Officers with more than one job title may be intentionally listed here more than once.

Stuart A. Rose, CEO
David L. Bearden, COO
David L. Bearden, Pres.
Douglas L. Bruggeman, CFO/VP-Finance
David Fuchs, VP-MIS
Keith B. Magby, VP-Oper.
Douglas L. Bruggeman, Treas.
Philip J. Kellar, VP-Store Oper.
Zafar A. Rizvi, VP-Loss Prevention
Stuart A. Rose, Chmn.

Phone: 937-276-3931	**Fax:** 937-276-8643
Toll-Free:	
Address: 2875 Needmore Rd., Dayton, OH 45414 US	

GROWTH PLANS/SPECIAL FEATURES:

REX Stores Corporation is a specialty retailer in the consumer electronics and appliance industry. The firm operates 218 stores in 37 states, serving over 200 small- to medium-sized towns with populations between 20,000 and 300,000. REX stores offer a broad selection of brand-name products within selected major product categories, including big-screen and standard-sized televisions; audio and video equipment, such as VCRs, DVD players, stereos, camcorders and radios; ready-to-assemble furniture; and major household appliances, such as air conditioners, microwaves, washers, dryers and refrigerators. REX also provides extended service contracts. Leading brands sold by the firm include Frigidaire, Hitachi, JVC, Panasonic, Philips Magnavox, RCA, Sharp, Sony, Toshiba and Whirlpool. In total, the company sells approximately 1,200 products produced by nearly 60 manufacturers. Stores are supplied by three large regional distribution centers in Ohio, Wyoming and Florida. The company often offers customers special sales through its retail stores and e-commerce site, rexstores.com. Advertisements are primarily concentrated in newspapers, with additional television and radio marketing strategies in select markets with populations under 85,000. The firm's strategy involves continuing to open stores in small to medium-sized markets. It plans to focus on markets with a newspaper circulation that can efficiently and cost-effectively utilize print advertising materials. In 2006, REX closed its Galesburg, Illinois store. Also in 2006, Rex made a move to invest heavily in the ethanol business to diversify its earnings. The company invested enough in Leyelland/Hockley County Ethanol LLC to gain a majority ownership interest. In addition, Rex has taken a minority ownership interest in Big River Resources LLC, Millennium Ethanol LLC, Patriot Renewable Fuels LLC and One Earth Energy LLC.

FINANCIALS: Sales and profits are in thousands of dollars—add 000 to get the full amount. 2006 Note: Financial information for 2006 was not available for all companies at press time.

2006 Sales: $396,032	2006 Profits: $28,269	**U.S. Stock Ticker:** RSC
2005 Sales: $379,023	2005 Profits: $27,549	**Int'l Ticker:** Int'l Exchange:
2004 Sales: $392,476	2004 Profits: $27,440	Employees: 938
2003 Sales: $428,600	2003 Profits: $22,900	Fiscal Year Ends: 1/31
2002 Sales: $464,500	2002 Profits: $22,400	Parent Company:

SALARIES/BENEFITS:

Pension Plan:	ESOP Stock Plan:	Profit Sharing: Y	Top Exec. Salary: $212,967	Bonus: $60,180
Savings Plan: Y	Stock Purch. Plan:		Second Exec. Salary: $174,783	Bonus: $60,180

OTHER THOUGHTS:

Apparent Women Officers or Directors:
Hot Spot for Advancement for Women/Minorities:

LOCATIONS: ("Y" = Yes)

West:	Southwest:	Midwest:	Southeast:	Northeast:	International:
Y	Y	Y	Y	Y	

Note: Financial information, benefits and other data can change quickly and may vary from those stated here.

RIVIERA HOLDINGS CORP

www.theriviera.com

Industry Group Code: 721120   Ranks within this company's industry group: Sales: 13   Profits: 15

Print Media/Publishing:	Movies:	Equipment/Supplies:	Broadcast/Cable:	Music/Audio:	Sports/Games:	
Newspapers:	Movie Theaters:	Equipment/Supplies:	Broadcast TV:	Music Production:	Games/Sports:	
Magazines:	Movie Production:	Gambling Equipment:	Cable TV:	Retail Music:	Retail Games Stores:	
Books:	TV/Video Production:	Special Services:	Satellite Broadcast:	Retail Audio Equip.:	Stadiums/Teams:	Y
Book Stores:	Video Rental:	Advertising Services:	Radio:	Music Print./Dist.:	Gambling/Casinos:	
Distribution/Printing:	Video Distribution:	Info. Sys. Software:	Online Information:	Multimedia:	Rides/Theme Parks:	

TYPES OF BUSINESS:

Casino Hotel
Casino Management

BRANDS/DIVISIONS/AFFILIATES:

Riviera Hotel and Casino
Black Hawk Casino
Riviera Operating Corporation
An Evening at La Cage
Splash
Player's Club
Crazy Girls

CONTACTS: *Note: Officers with more than one job title may be intentionally listed here more than once.*

William L. Westerman, CEO
Tullio J. Marchionne, General Counsel/Corp. Sec.
Duane R. Krohn, Exec. VP-Finance/Treas.
Ronald P. Johnson, Exec. VP-Gaming, Riviera Operating Corp.
Jerome P. Grippe, Exec. VP-Oper., Riviera Oper. Corp.
Robert A. Vannucci, COO/Pres., Riviera Oper. Corp.
William L. Westerman, Chmn.

Phone: 702-734-5110	Fax: 702-794-9663
Toll-Free: 800-634-3420	
Address: 2901 Las Vegas Blvd. S., Las Vegas, NV 89109 US	

GROWTH PLANS/SPECIAL FEATURES:

Riviera Holdings Corporation, through its wholly owned subsidiary Riviera Operating Corporation, owns and operates the Riviera Hotel and Casino, located on Las Vegas Boulevard in Las Vegas, Nevada. It also owns and operates the Riviera Black Hawk Casino through its wholly owned subsidiary Riviera Black Hawk, Inc., a limited-stakes casino located in Black Hawk, Colorado. The Riviera opened in 1955 and has a reputation for delivering high-quality, traditional Las Vegas-style gaming, entertainment and other amenities. The casino has 110,000 square feet of gaming space with approximately 1,150 slot machines and 40 gaming tables, including blackjack, craps, roulette and poker. It also features 160,000 square feet of convention, meeting and banquet space. The Riviera offers live entertainment shows, such as An Evening at La Cage (a female impersonation show), Crazy Girls (an adult revue) and Splash (a variety show). Black Hawk Casino, located about 40 miles west of Denver, is one of the largest full-service casinos in Colorado. The Player's Club program, in addition to rewarding frequent players, collects data about its members, which the company uses to customize promotions to attract repeat visitors. Through the company's web site, travelers to Las Vegas can book rooms, buy souvenirs, check Player's Club point balances and make other reservations before their trip. The company continues to explore the possible of development of an approximately 60,000-square-foot entertainment complex to be constructed directly over the casino, which could contain specialty themed entertainment that would appeal to the main target audience, adults age 45 to 65. The exit of this complex would deliver patrons directly to the casino. It is also exploring several options for the development of its existing 26-acre site, including a joint venture for the development of a condominium, time-share or an additional hotel tower and parking garage.

FINANCIALS: Sales and profits are in thousands of dollars—add 000 to get the full amount. 2006 Note: Financial information for 2006 was not available for all companies at press time.

2006 Sales: $	2006 Profits: $	U.S. Stock Ticker: RIV
2005 Sales: $202,227	2005 Profits: $-3,999	Int'l Ticker: Int'l Exchange:
2004 Sales: $201,350	2004 Profits: $-2,086	Employees: 1,612
2003 Sales: $190,200	2003 Profits: $-14,453	Fiscal Year Ends: 12/31
2002 Sales: $188,300	2002 Profits: $-24,700	Parent Company:

SALARIES/BENEFITS:

Pension Plan:	ESOP Stock Plan:	Profit Sharing:	Top Exec. Salary: $1,000,000	Bonus: $
Savings Plan:	Stock Purch. Plan:		Second Exec. Salary: $300,000	Bonus: $114,000

OTHER THOUGHTS:

Apparent Women Officers or Directors:
Hot Spot for Advancement for Women/Minorities:

LOCATIONS: ("Y" = Yes)

West:	Southwest:	Midwest:	Southeast:	Northeast:	International:
Y					

RODALE INC

www.rodale.com

Industry Group Code: 511120 Ranks within this company's industry group: Sales: 8   Profits:

Print Media/Publishing:		Movies:		Equipment/Supplies:		Broadcast/Cable:		Music/Audio:		Sports/Games:	
Newspapers:		Movie Theaters:		Equipment/Supplies:		Broadcast TV:		Music Production:		Games/Sports:	
Magazines:	Y	Movie Production:		Gambling Equipment:		Cable TV:		Retail Music:		Retail Games Stores:	
Books:	Y	TV/Video Production:		Special Services:		Satellite Broadcast:		Retail Audio Equip.:		Stadiums/Teams:	
Book Stores:		Video Rental:		Advertising Services:		Radio:		Music Print./Dist.:		Gambling/Casinos:	
Distribution/Printing:		Video Distribution:		Info. Sys. Software:		Online Information:		Multimedia:		Rides/Theme Parks:	

TYPES OF BUSINESS:

Magazine Publishing
Book Publishing
Online Publishing

BRANDS/DIVISIONS/AFFILIATES:

Prevention
Men's Health
Runner's World
Organic Style
Organic Gardening
Mountain Bike
Backpacker
South Beach Diet

GROWTH PLANS/SPECIAL FEATURES:

Rodale, Inc. publishes magazines and books related to health and lifestyles. The company's portfolio of magazines includes Prevention, Men's Health, Runner's World, Organic Style, Organic Gardening, Backpacker, Bicycling, Mountain Bike and Scuba Diving. Prevention, Men's Health and Runner's World reach 40 million people in 59 countries, with Rodale magazines being published in 48 countries. The company maintains a web site for each magazine. As a major independent U.S. book publisher, the company also publishes about 100 books a year, including the popular South Beach Diet, Al Gore's An Inconvenient Truth and Martha Stewart's The Martha Rules. Rodale's book publications include memoirs, biographies, narrative nonfiction, self-help, science and nature, psychology, current events and personal finance.

Rodale offer its employees healthy meals, on-site athletic facilities and on-site day care.

CONTACTS:
Note: Officers with more than one job title may be intentionally listed here more than once.

Steven P. Murphy, CEO
Steven Kalin, COO-Exec. VP
Steven P. Murphy, Pres.
Lester Rackoff, CFO/Sr. VP
Bill Ostroff, Chief Mktg. Officer
Paul McGinley, General Counsel
Mia Carbonell, Sr. VP-Corp. Comm.
David Roberson, VP-Finance
Ben Roter, Exec. VP
Bill Ostroff, Pres., Rodale Interactive
MaryAnn Bekkedahl, Exec. VP/Group Publisher, Rodale Magazines
Maria Rodale, Vice Chmn.
Ardath Rodale, Chmn.
Gianni Crespi, Pres., Int'l

Phone: 610-967-5171	Fax: 610-967-8963
Toll-Free:	
Address: 33 E. Minor St., Emmaus, PA 18098-0099 US	

FINANCIALS:
Sales and profits are in thousands of dollars—add 000 to get the full amount. 2006 Note: Financial information for 2006 was not available for all companies at press time.

2006 Sales: $	2006 Profits: $	U.S. Stock Ticker: Private	
2005 Sales: $500,000	2005 Profits: $	Int'l Ticker: Int'l Exchange:	
2004 Sales: $	2004 Profits: $	Employees: 950	
2003 Sales: $	2003 Profits: $	Fiscal Year Ends: 12/31	
2002 Sales: $500,000	2002 Profits: $	Parent Company:	

SALARIES/BENEFITS:

Pension Plan:	ESOP Stock Plan:	Profit Sharing:	Top Exec. Salary: $	Bonus: $
Savings Plan: Y	Stock Purch. Plan:		Second Exec. Salary: $	Bonus: $

OTHER THOUGHTS:

Apparent Women Officers or Directors: 3
Hot Spot for Advancement for Women/Minorities: Y

LOCATIONS: ("Y" = Yes)

West:	Southwest:	Midwest:	Southeast:	Northeast:	International:
				Y	Y

Note: Financial information, benefits and other data can change quickly and may vary from those stated here.

ROGERS COMMUNICATIONS INC

www.rogers.com

Industry Group Code: 513220 Ranks within this company's industry group: Sales: 8 Profits: 15

Print Media/Publishing:		Movies:		Equipment/Supplies:		Broadcast/Cable:		Music/Audio:		Sports/Games:	
Newspapers:		Movie Theaters:		Equipment/Supplies:		Broadcast TV:	Y	Music Production:		Games/Sports:	
Magazines:	Y	Movie Production:		Gambling Equipment:		Cable TV:	Y	Retail Music:		Retail Games Stores:	
Books:		TV/Video Production:	Y	Special Services:	Y	Satellite Broadcast:		Retail Audio Equip.:		Stadiums/Teams:	Y
Book Stores:		Video Rental:	Y	Advertising Services:	Y	Radio:		Music Print./Dist.:		Gambling/Casinos:	
Distribution/Printing:		Video Distribution:		Info. Sys. Software:		Online Information:		Multimedia:		Rides/Theme Parks:	

TYPES OF BUSINESS:

Cable Television
Internet Service Provider
Cellular Phone Service
Video Stores
Television Broadcasting
Magazine Publishing
Radio Stations
Sports Teams & Stadiums

BRANDS/DIVISIONS/AFFILIATES:

Rogers Cable, Inc.
Rogers Wireless Communications, Inc.
Rogers Media, Inc.
Rogers Video
Shopping Channel (The)
Rogers Sportsnet
ONMI.1
ONMI.2

CONTACTS: Note: Officers with more than one job title may be intentionally listed here more than once.

Edward S. Rogers, CEO
Edward S. Rogers, Pres.
William W. Linton, CFO
Douglas Perry, VP-Sales & Distribution
Kevin P. Pennington, Sr. VP-Chief Human Res. Officer
Ronan D. McGrath, CIO
David P. Miller, VP/General Counsel
Melinda Rogers, Sr. VP-Strategy & Dev.
Jan L. Innes, VP-Comm.
Bruce Mann, VP-Investor Rel.
Sarah Burcher, Controller/VP
Alan D. Horn, Pres./CEO-Rogers Telecommunications, Ltd.
Thomas I. Hull, Chmn./CEO-The Hull Group, Inc.
M. Lorraine Daily, VP/Treas.
Nadir Mohamed, Pres./COO-Rogers Wireless Communications, Inc.
Alan D. Horn, Chmn.

Phone: 416-935-7777	Fax: 416-935-3597
Toll-Free:	
Address: 333 Bloor St. E., 10th Fl., Toronto, ON A6 M4W 1G9 Canada	

GROWTH PLANS/SPECIAL FEATURES:

Rogers Communications, Inc. is a Canadian company engaged in a wide variety of television, broadband, cellular telephone and publishing businesses. Rogers conducts business via three separate entities: Rogers Cable, Inc.; Rogers Wireless Communications, Inc.; and Rogers Media, Inc. Rogers Cable is one of the largest cable television service providers in Canada, with approximately 2.26 million customers in Ontario (90% of customers), New Brunswick, Newfoundland and Labrador. Its services include cable television, digital cable, high-definition television, video-on-demand, high-speed Internet access (through RogersYahoo!) and interactive television. The cable division also operates Rogers Video, the largest domestically owned Canadian video store chain with 300 Rogers Video stores. Rogers Wireless provides wireless voice and data communications services (digital PCS, cellular and two-way messaging services) to 6.2 million customers. Rogers Media is composed of Rogers Broadcasting and Rogers Publishing. Rogers Broadcasting operates 46 radio stations (36 FM and 10 AM) throughout Canada. Its television properties include The Shopping Channel (national television shopping network); Rogers Sportsnet (a network of five channels broadcasting regional sporting events); and ONMI.1 and OMNI.2 (multicultural television channels); as well as the management of three digital television services. In addition, the firm owns the Toronto Blue Jays baseball team, Rogers Centre (formerly SkyDome) and a 50% stake in Dome Productions, a high-definition television production and broadcasting venture. Rogers Publishing is one of Canada's largest magazine publishers, producing 70 consumer magazines and trade publications such as Maclean's, Canadian Business, Chatelaine, L'actualite, Flare, Today's Parent and MoneySense. In 2006, the firm began deploying a third generation wireless network. Recently, the firm bought 60% of The Biography Channel Canada. CEO Ted Rogers controls about 91% of the company's voting power.

Rogers offers its employees a pension plan, personal computer loans, education assistance, service recognition awards, employee and family assistance programs and product discounts.

FINANCIALS: Sales and profits are in thousands of dollars—add 000 to get the full amount. 2006 Note: Financial information for 2006 was not available for all companies at press time.

2006 Sales: $	2006 Profits: $	U.S. Stock Ticker: RG
2005 Sales: $6,389,571	2005 Profits: $-38,136	Int'l Ticker: RCI.B Int'l Exchange: Toronto-TSX
2004 Sales: $4,789,390	2004 Profits: $-57,337	Employees: 21,000
2003 Sales: $3,763,000	2003 Profits: $100,300	Fiscal Year Ends: 12/31
2002 Sales: $2,746,900	2002 Profits: $198,300	Parent Company:

SALARIES/BENEFITS:

Pension Plan: Y	ESOP Stock Plan:	Profit Sharing:	Top Exec. Salary: $	Bonus: $
Savings Plan:	Stock Purch. Plan: Y		Second Exec. Salary: $	Bonus: $

OTHER THOUGHTS:

Apparent Women Officers or Directors: 4
Hot Spot for Advancement for Women/Minorities: Y

LOCATIONS: ("Y" = Yes)

West:	Southwest:	Midwest:	Southeast:	Northeast:	International:
					Y

Note: Financial information, benefits and other data can change quickly and may vary from those stated here.

RTL GROUP SA

www.rtlgroup.com

Industry Group Code: 513120 Ranks within this company's industry group: Sales: 6 Profits: 3

Print Media/Publishing:	Movies:	Equipment/Supplies:	Broadcast/Cable:		Music/Audio:	Sports/Games:
Newspapers:	Movie Theaters:	Equipment/Supplies:	Broadcast TV:	Y	Music Production:	Games/Sports:
Magazines:	Movie Production:	Gambling Equipment:	Cable TV:	Y	Retail Music:	Retail Games Stores:
Books:	TV/Video Production:	Special Services:	Satellite Broadcast:		Retail Audio Equip.:	Stadiums/Teams:
Book Stores:	Video Rental:	Advertising Services:	Radio:		Music Print./Dist.:	Gambling/Casinos:
Distribution/Printing:	Video Distribution:	Info. Sys. Software:	Online Information:		Multimedia:	Rides/Theme Parks:

TYPES OF BUSINESS:

Television Broadcasting
Television Production
Radio Broadcasting
Web Sites

BRANDS/DIVISIONS/AFFILIATES:

VOX
M6
RTL-TVI
Club RTL
RTL Klub
Yorin
Bertelsmann AG
n-tv

CONTACTS: *Note: Officers with more than one job title may be intentionally listed here more than once.*

Gerhard Zeiler, CEO
Elmar Heggen, CFO

Phone: 352-2486-5130	Fax: 352-2486-5139
Toll-Free:	
Address: 45 Blvd. Pierre Frieden, Luxembourg, L-1543 Luxembourg	

GROWTH PLANS/SPECIAL FEATURES:

RTL Group S.A., based in Luxembourg, is the largest television and radio broadcaster in Europe, with 39 television stations and 33 radio stations in 10 countries: Germany, France, Belgium, the Netherlands, the U.K., Luxembourg, Spain, Portugal, Hungary and Croatia. The company's television segment, which reaches 250 million viewers, includes VOX in Germany, M6 in France, RTL-TVI and Club RTL in Belgium, RTL Klub in Hungary, Yorin in the Netherlands and five stations in the U.K. RTL produces approximately 8,500 hours of programming per year, shown in 40 countries. RTL also owns the rights to approximately 19,000 hours of programming in 150 countries. Additionally, the company operates about 85 web sites, most of which contain forums and schedules for television programs. RTL's long-term strategy is to increase the number of channels it offers so as to further target niche audiences; diversify into music, DVDs, magazines and other media-related businesses; and in general reduce its dependency on advertising for revenue. The company is also seeking to expand geographically, eyeing up to 10 countries for near-term expansion. RTL Group is 89.8%-owned by Bertelsmann AG, which also owns BMG and Random House. In 2006, the company sold its stake in Sportfive, a European marketer of sports rights, to Lagardere SCA. The company also recently acquired n-tv, a television news channel, from CNN.

FINANCIALS: Sales and profits are in thousands of dollars—add 000 to get the full amount. 2006 Note: Financial information for 2006 was not available for all companies at press time.

2006 Sales: $	2006 Profits: $	U.S. Stock Ticker: Foreign
2005 Sales: $6,207,333	2005 Profits: $747,621	Int'l Ticker: RTL Int'l Exchange: Luxembourg-LUX
2004 Sales: $5,919,721	2004 Profits: $524,305	Employees: 8,388
2003 Sales: $5,588,200	2003 Profits: $-58,700	Fiscal Year Ends: 12/31
2002 Sales: $4,571,800	2002 Profits: $-58,700	Parent Company:

SALARIES/BENEFITS:

Pension Plan:	ESOP Stock Plan:	Profit Sharing:	Top Exec. Salary: $	Bonus: $
Savings Plan:	Stock Purch. Plan:		Second Exec. Salary: $	Bonus: $

OTHER THOUGHTS:

Apparent Women Officers or Directors: 1
Hot Spot for Advancement for Women/Minorities:

LOCATIONS: ("Y" = Yes)

West:	Southwest:	Midwest:	Southeast:	Northeast:	International:
					Y

SAGA COMMUNICATIONS INC www.sagacommunications.com

Industry Group Code: 513120 Ranks within this company's industry group: Sales: 22 Profits: 10

Print Media/Publishing:	Movies:		Equipment/Supplies:		Broadcast/Cable:		Music/Audio:	Sports/Games:
Newspapers:	Movie Theaters:		Equipment/Supplies:		Broadcast TV:	Y	Music Production:	Games/Sports:
Magazines:	Movie Production:		Gambling Equipment:		Cable TV:		Retail Music:	Retail Games Stores:
Books:	TV/Video Production:	Y	Special Services:		Satellite Broadcast:		Retail Audio Equip.:	Stadiums/Teams:
Book Stores:	Video Rental:		Advertising Services:	Y	Radio:		Music Print./Dist.:	Gambling/Casinos:
Distribution/Printing:	Video Distribution:		Info. Sys. Software:		Online Information:		Multimedia:	Rides/Theme Parks:

TYPES OF BUSINESS:

Television Broadcasting
Radio Broadcasting
Local News Coverage

BRANDS/DIVISIONS/AFFILIATES:

GROWTH PLANS/SPECIAL FEATURES:

Saga Communications, Inc. operates radio and television stations and state radio networks in mid-sized markets. The company concentrates its broadcast operations in 23 markets across the U.S. A significant portion of its revenue depends on the sale of local advertising. Saga's portfolio currently consists of five TV stations, five state radio networks, 30 AM radio stations and 57 FM stations. The firm's radio stations play a variety of music, ranging from classical to country, and the television stations maintain affiliations with CBS, ABC, FOX, Univision, NBC, UPN and Telemundo. Saga also produces the local news shown on its affiliate stations. Saga concentrates on developing strong decentralized local management at its stations responsible for the day-to-day station operations in their market areas. The firm recognizes mergers and acquisitions as an important factor in its growth. Consequently, Saga has continued its focus on mid-sized markets with significant populations and economic growth potential.

CONTACTS: Note: Officers with more than one job title may be intentionally listed here more than once.

Edward K. Christian, CEO
Edward K. Christian, Pres.
Samuel D. Bush, CFO/Sr. VP
Marcia K. Lobaito, Dir.-Human Resources
Warren S. Lada, Sr. VP-Oper.
Marcia K. Lobaito, Dir.-Bus. Affairs/Sr. VP Corp. Sec.
Samuel D. Bush, Treas.
Steven J. Goldstein, Exec. VP/Group Dir.-Program
Catherine A. Bobinski, VP/Chief Acct. Officer
Michelle Novak, Programming Coordinator/ Research Dir.
Edward K. Christian, Chmn.

Phone: 313-886-7070	**Fax:** 313-886-7150
Toll-Free:	
Address: 73 Kercheval Ave., Ste. 201, Grosse Pointe Farms, MI 48236-3603 US	

FINANCIALS: Sales and profits are in thousands of dollars—add 000 to get the full amount. 2006 Note: Financial information for 2006 was not available for all companies at press time.

2006 Sales: $	2006 Profits: $	**U.S. Stock Ticker: SGA**
2005 Sales: $140,790	2005 Profits: $10,566	**Int'l Ticker:** Int'l Exchange:
2004 Sales: $134,644	2004 Profits: $15,842	Employees: 1,341
2003 Sales: $121,297	2003 Profits: $13,884	Fiscal Year Ends: 12/31
2002 Sales: $114,800	2002 Profits: $14,000	Parent Company:

SALARIES/BENEFITS:

Pension Plan:	ESOP Stock Plan:	Profit Sharing:	Top Exec. Salary: $530,438	Bonus: $400,000
Savings Plan: Y	Stock Purch. Plan:		Second Exec. Salary: $365,815	Bonus: $87,500

OTHER THOUGHTS:

Apparent Women Officers or Directors: 2
Hot Spot for Advancement for Women/Minorities: Y

LOCATIONS: ("Y" = Yes)

West:	Southwest:	Midwest:	Southeast:	Northeast:	International:
Y	Y	Y	Y	Y	Y

SALEM COMMUNICATIONS CORP
www.salemcommunications.com
Industry Group Code: 513111 Ranks within this company's industry group: Sales: 10   Profits: 7

Print Media/Publishing:	Movies:		Equipment/Supplies:	Broadcast/Cable:	Music/Audio:		Sports/Games:
Newspapers:	Movie Theaters:		Equipment/Supplies:	Broadcast TV:	Music Production:	Y	Games/Sports:
Magazines: Y	Movie Production:		Gambling Equipment:	Cable TV:	Retail Music:		Retail Games Stores:
Books:	TV/Video Production:		Special Services:	Satellite Broadcast:	Retail Audio Equip.:		Stadiums/Teams:
Book Stores:	Video Rental:		Advertising Services:	Radio:	Music Print./Dist.:	Y	Gambling/Casinos:
Distribution/Printing:	Video Distribution:		Info. Sys. Software:	Online Information:	Multimedia:		Rides/Theme Parks:

TYPES OF BUSINESS:
Radio Broadcasting
Religious & Family Radio
Online Christian Content & Radio Streaming
Magazine Publishing
Internet Content Provider

BRANDS/DIVISIONS/AFFILIATES:
Salem Radio Network
Salem Radio Representatives
Salem Web Network
Salem Publishing
crosswalk.com
oneplace.com
CCM Magazine
christianjobs.com

CONTACTS: *Note: Officers with more than one job title may be intentionally listed here more than once.*
Edward G. Atsinger, III, CEO
Joe D. Davis, COO/Exec. VP
Edward G. Atsinger, III, Pres.
David A.R. Evans, CFO
Christopher J. Henderson, VP-Human Resources
Russell R. Hauth, Sr. VP-Admin.
Jonathan L. Block, General Counsel
Robert C. Adair, Sr. VP-Oper.
David A. R. Evans, Exec. VP-Bus. Dev.
Russell R. Hauth, Sr. VP-Public Affairs
Evan D. Masyr, VP-Acct. & Finance
Dennis Ciapura, Sr. VP-Broadcast Dev.
Michael Reichert, VP-Oper.
Stuart W. Epperson, Chmn.

Phone: 805-987-0400	**Fax:** 805-384-4520
Toll-Free:	
Address: 4880 Santa Rosa Rd., Ste. 300, Camarillo, CA 93012 US	

GROWTH PLANS/SPECIAL FEATURES:
Salem Communications Corp. is among the largest religious- and family-themed radio broadcasting companies in the U.S., operating 104 radio stations (32 FM and 72 AM), including 66 stations in 24 of the top 25 markets nationwide. The stations are mainly divided into three segments (reaching more than four million listeners weekly): Christian talk and teaching (44 stations); conservative news/talk (34 stations); and contemporary Christian music (14 stations). The firm owns Salem Radio Network, Salem Radio Representatives, Salem Web Network and Salem Publishing and is the exclusive provider of Christian radio content for XM Satellite Radio. Salem Radio Network syndicates talk, news and music programming for 2,000 affiliated radio stations. Salem Radio Representatives is the firm's national sales and advertising force. Salem Web Network is a leading Internet provider of Christian content and online radio streaming with 69 radio station web sites (including crosswalk.com, lightsource.com, oneplace.com, christianity.com, christianjobs.com, churchstaffing.com), which generate more than two million unique visitors per month and 400 million page views annually. Salem Publishing owns and operates a number of magazine titles published in the Christian Music Industry, such as its flagship publication Contemporary Christian Music (CCM) Magazine , Youthworker, Faith Talk, Singing News and Crosswalk. In 2006, the firm launched WMCA-TV Radio with Pictures, an Internet TV station featuring on-demand videos 24 hours a day; and sold its three radio stations in Jacksonville, Florida to Chesapeake-Portsmouth for 2.8 million. The firm also recently sold WKNR SportsTalk 850 AM (Cleveland) to Good Karma Broadcasting, LLC for $7 million. In addition, Salem Communications acquired Xulon Press, a digital Christian book publisher. Also in 2006, Salem Communications acquired CrossDaily.com, an online provider of Christian content, graphics and online community resources, for $2.3 million.

FINANCIALS: Sales and profits are in thousands of dollars—add 000 to get the full amount. 2006 Note: Financial information for 2006 was not available for all companies at press time.

2006 Sales: $	2006 Profits: $	**U.S. Stock Ticker: SALM**
2005 Sales: $211,839	2005 Profits: $12,980	**Int'l Ticker:** Int'l Exchange:
2004 Sales: $195,638	2004 Profits: $7,333	Employees: 1,526
2003 Sales: $178,348	2003 Profits: $- 677	Fiscal Year Ends: 12/31
2002 Sales: $164,300	2002 Profits: $14,000	Parent Company:

SALARIES/BENEFITS:

Pension Plan:	ESOP Stock Plan:	Profit Sharing:	Top Exec. Salary: $850,000	Bonus: $501,750
Savings Plan: Y	Stock Purch. Plan:		Second Exec. Salary: $700,000	Bonus: $167,250

OTHER THOUGHTS:
Apparent Women Officers or Directors:
Hot Spot for Advancement for Women/Minorities:

LOCATIONS: ("Y" = Yes)

West:	Southwest:	Midwest:	Southeast:	Northeast:	International:
Y	Y	Y	Y	Y	

Note: Financial information, benefits and other data can change quickly and may vary from those stated here.

SALON MEDIA GROUP INC

www.salon.com

Industry Group Code: 514199 **Ranks within this company's industry group:** Sales: 7 Profits: 5

Print Media/Publishing:	Movies:	Equipment/Supplies:	Broadcast/Cable:	Music/Audio:	Sports/Games:
Newspapers:	Movie Theaters:	Equipment/Supplies:	Broadcast TV:	Music Production:	Games/Sports:
Magazines:	Movie Production:	Gambling Equipment:	Cable TV:	Retail Music:	Retail Games Stores:
Books:	TV/Video Production:	Special Services:	Satellite Broadcast:	Retail Audio Equip.:	Stadiums/Teams:
Book Stores:	Video Rental:	Advertising Services:	Radio:	Music Print./Dist.:	Gambling/Casinos:
Distribution/Printing:	Video Distribution:	Info. Sys. Software:	Online Information:	Multimedia:	Rides/Theme Parks:

TYPES OF BUSINESS:

Online News & Media
Online Communities

BRANDS/DIVISIONS/AFFILIATES:

salon.com
Table Talk
Well (The)
Salon Premium
War Room
King Kaufman's Sports Daily
Daou Report (The)
Literary Guide to the World

CONTACTS: *Note: Officers with more than one job title may be intentionally listed here more than once.*

Elizabeth Hambrecht, CEO
Elizabeth Hambrecht, Pres.
Conrad Lowry, CFO
Melissa Barron, Sr. VP-Sales
Conrad Lowry, Investor Rel.
Conrad Lowry, Controller
Christopher Neimeth, Sr. VP-Publisher
Joan Walsh, Editor-In-Chief
John E. Warnock, Chmn.

Phone: 415-645-9200	Fax: 415-625-9204
Toll-Free:	
Address: 101 Spear St., Ste. 203, San Francisco, CA 94105 US	

GROWTH PLANS/SPECIAL FEATURES:

Salon Media Group, Inc. is an Internet media company providing online news and information. Salon's ten web sites feature news, interviews and regular columnists on topics including arts and entertainment, politics, technology and business, books, sports, parenting and health, and comics. Salon Media Group's other media offerings include Table Talk, an interactive forum, and The Well, a paid subscription community. The site's online communities allow users to interact and discuss Salon content with other users and with Salon's editorial staff. The company has created a front-page roadblock and splash page through which an advertiser owns all the advertising space on Salon's home page for a given period of time and the firm provides a rapidly updated array of news, features, interviews, columnists and blogs. The company's daily reports are built around nine features: War Room; the Fix; Audiophile (downloadable music); the Daou Report (opinionated blogsphere guide); King Kaufman's Sports Daily; Since you Asked; Broadsheet (women's news digest); How the World Works (editorial blog about globalization); and Video Dog (an archive of video clips). Salon Premium, a paid subscription service, offers subscribers access to exclusive new content; the option to view Salon content without advertising banners, pop-ups or other forms of advertising; access to select unabridged content; and the ability to easily download content in text format. In 2006, the firm partnered with the Travel Channel to launch Literary Guide to the World, which features essays by writers describing their favorite domestic and international travel destinations, as well as the literature that brings these destinations to life. Salon Director John Warnock holds about 40% of the company's total voting power.

FINANCIALS: Sales and profits are in thousands of dollars—add 000 to get the full amount. 2006 Note: Financial information for 2006 was not available for all companies at press time.

2006 Sales: $6,500	2006 Profits: $-1,100	U.S. Stock Ticker: SALN.OB
2005 Sales: $6,628	2005 Profits: $- 518	Int'l Ticker: Int'l Exchange:
2004 Sales: $4,499	2004 Profits: $-6,046	Employees: 64
2003 Sales: $4,003	2003 Profits: $-5,597	Fiscal Year Ends: 3/31
2002 Sales: $3,600	2002 Profits: $-8,000	Parent Company:

SALARIES/BENEFITS:

Pension Plan: Y	ESOP Stock Plan:	Profit Sharing:	Top Exec. Salary: $159,122	Bonus: $
Savings Plan: Y	Stock Purch. Plan:		Second Exec. Salary: $130,000	Bonus: $

OTHER THOUGHTS:

Apparent Women Officers or Directors: 4
Hot Spot for Advancement for Women/Minorities: Y

LOCATIONS: ("Y" = Yes)

West:	Southwest:	Midwest:	Southeast:	Northeast:	International:
Y				Y	

SAMSUNG ELECTRONICS CO LTD

www.samsungelectronics.com

Industry Group Code: 334310 Ranks within this company's industry group: Sales: 3 Profits: 1

Print Media/Publishing:	Movies:	Equipment/Supplies:		Broadcast/Cable:	Music/Audio:		Sports/Games:	
Newspapers:	Movie Theaters:	Equipment/Supplies:	Y	Broadcast TV:	Music Production:		Games/Sports:	
Magazines:	Movie Production:	Gambling Equipment:		Cable TV:	Retail Music:		Retail Games Stores:	
Books:	TV/Video Production:	Special Services:		Satellite Broadcast:	Retail Audio Equip.:	Y	Stadiums/Teams:	
Book Stores:	Video Rental:	Advertising Services:		Radio:	Music Print./Dist.:		Gambling/Casinos:	
Distribution/Printing:	Video Distribution:	Info. Sys. Software:		Online Information:	Multimedia:		Rides/Theme Parks:	

TYPES OF BUSINESS:

Consumer Electronics
Semiconductors
Cellular Phones
Computers & Accessories
Digital Cameras
Fuel-Cell Technology
LCDs
Memory Products

BRANDS/DIVISIONS/AFFILIATES:

Samsung Group (The)
Samsung NEC Mobile Displays Co., Ltd.
Samsung Semiconductor
Women's Dream Plaza

CONTACTS: Note: Officers with more than one job title may be intentionally listed here more than once.

Jong-Yong Yun, CEO
In-Joo Kim, COO
Hak-Soo Lee, Pres.
Doh-Seok Choi, CFO
Seung-Jun Ahn, Dir.-Human Resources
Hung Song, VP-Bus. Dev.
Woosik Chu, VP-Investor Rel.
Yoon-Woo Lee, Pres., Semiconductor Bus.
Tim Baxter, Exec. VP-Sales & Mktg, Samsung Electronics America
Kun-Hee Lee, Chmn.

Phone: 82-2-727-7114	Fax: 82-2-727-7985
Toll-Free:	
Address: 250, 2-ga, Taepyung-ro, Jung-gu, Seoul, 100-742 South Korea	

GROWTH PLANS/SPECIAL FEATURES:

Samsung Electronics Co., part of The Samsung Group, is a global leader in semiconductor, telecommunications and digital convergence technology. The company maintains offices in 120 offices in 57 countries. Its five business segments include digital media, telecommunications networks, digital appliances, semiconductors and liquid crystal displays (LCDs). Samsung's digital media include laptops, digital cameras, camcorders, printers, TVs, VCRs and DVD players. The company also offers one of the largest plasma TVs in the world, a high-definition flat-screen measuring a full 80 inches across, and one of the largest LCD TVs with a 57-inch screen. The telecommunications segment manufactures mobile phones, personal digital assistants (PDAs) and telecommunications hardware. The digital appliances segment includes domestic supplies such as microwaves, refrigerators, air conditioners, air purifiers, drum washers and vacuum cleaners. The firm's semiconductor segment has dynamic random access memory (DRAM), flash memory and system-on-chip (SOC) products. Samsung Semiconductor products fall under two categories: memory, which includes components for PC platforms, mobile devices and gaming products, ranging from low-power memory to high-bandwidth memory; and system LSI, or large-scale integration, which includes SOC, system-in-package (SIP) and 90nm process technology. Samsung has strategic alliances with some of the industry's leading companies, including Sony, Dell, AOL and Intel. The company's Samsung NEC Mobile Displays Co., Ltd. subsidiary is working on organic light-emitting devices (OLEDs) to use in its screens instead of LCD displays. An OLED screen is composed of several ultra-thin films of special molecules that glow when excited by an electric current. Samsung also has operations in fuel-cell technology. For the mid term, Samsung will increase its focus on growth in its memory chip business, particularly NAND flash memory popular for use in cell phones and music players.

Samsung operates the Women's Dream Plaza, a facility specifically designed for women and their needs in the areas of maternity, health and career advancement.

FINANCIALS: Sales and profits are in thousands of dollars—add 000 to get the full amount. 2006 Note: Financial information for 2006 was not available for all companies at press time.

2006 Sales: $	2006 Profits: $	U.S. Stock Ticker: SSNLF
2005 Sales: $56,720,306	2005 Profits: $7,542,165	Int'l Ticker: 000830 Int'l Exchange: Seoul-KRX
2004 Sales: $56,892,753	2004 Profits: $10,648,314	Employees: 64,000
2003 Sales: $36,740,000	2003 Profits: $4,990,400	Fiscal Year Ends: 12/31
2002 Sales: $30,753,800	2002 Profits: $64,500	Parent Company:

SALARIES/BENEFITS:

Pension Plan:	ESOP Stock Plan:	Profit Sharing:	Top Exec. Salary: $	Bonus: $
Savings Plan:	Stock Purch. Plan:		Second Exec. Salary: $	Bonus: $

OTHER THOUGHTS:

	LOCATIONS: ("Y" = Yes)					
	West:	Southwest:	Midwest:	Southeast:	Northeast:	International:
Apparent Women Officers or Directors:	Y	Y	Y	Y	Y	Y
Hot Spot for Advancement for Women/Minorities:						

Note: Financial information, benefits and other data can change quickly and may vary from those stated here.

SANDS REGENT

www.sandsregency.com

Industry Group Code: 721120 Ranks within this company's industry group: Sales: 15 Profits: 13

Print Media/Publishing:	Movies:	Equipment/Supplies:	Broadcast/Cable:	Music/Audio:		Sports/Games:	
Newspapers:	Movie Theaters:	Equipment/Supplies:	Broadcast TV:	Music Production:	Y	Games/Sports:	
Magazines:	Movie Production:	Gambling Equipment:	Cable TV:	Retail Music:		Retail Games Stores:	
Books:	TV/Video Production:	Special Services:	Satellite Broadcast:	Retail Audio Equip.:		Stadiums/Teams:	Y
Book Stores:	Video Rental:	Advertising Services:	Radio:	Music Print./Dist.:		Gambling/Casinos:	
Distribution/Printing:	Video Distribution:	Info. Sys. Software:	Online Information:	Multimedia:		Rides/Theme Parks:	

TYPES OF BUSINESS:

Casino Hotel
Convention Center

BRANDS/DIVISIONS/AFFILIATES:

Zante, Inc.
Sands Regency Casino and Hotel
Gold Ranch Casino and RV Resort
Last Chance, Inc.
Rail City Casino
Plantation Investments
Red Hawk Sports Bar
Depot Casino

CONTACTS: *Note: Officers with more than one job title may be intentionally listed here more than once.*

Ferenc Szony, CEO
Robert Medeiros, COO
Ferenc Szony, Pres.

Phone: 775-348-2200	Fax: 775-348-6241
Toll-Free: 800-648-3553	
Address: 345 N. Arlington Ave., Reno, NV 89501 US	

GROWTH PLANS/SPECIAL FEATURES:

Sands Regent owns and operates, through its subsidiaries, three Nevada casinos and related tourist amenities. The company's marquee operation, the Sands Regency Casino and Hotel in downtown Reno, is held by subsidiary Zante, Inc. and features some 850 hotel rooms and 29,000 square feet of gaming space. While the company derives most of its revenue from its 17 gaming tables, 544 slot machines and sportsbook, it also operates a comedy club, cocktail lounges, a video arcade and a music lounge. Other services include beauty and gift shops, restaurants and fast-food eateries and a 12,000-square-foot convention and meeting center that accommodates 1,000 people. Sands Regent subsidiary Last Chance, Inc. operates the Gold Ranch Casino and RV Resort in Verdi, 12 miles west of Reno. Gold Ranch is the first casino gaming attraction that travelers encounter on Interstate 80 when entering Nevada from California, and the last when leaving. Facilities include an 8,300-square-foot casino with 243 slot machines, two restaurants, two bars, a California lottery station, an ARCO gas station and a convenience store, as well as a 105-space RV park. The company subsidiary Plantation Investments is the operator of Rail City Casino in Sparks. Rail City Casino has approximately 16,600 square feet of gaming space and features more than 650 slots, six table games, keno and a sportsbook. The casino also has a family-style restaurant and a sports bar, with a convenient off-highway location. In September 2005, the company completed its acquisition of Depot Casino and Red Hawk Sports Bar, in Dayton, Nevada.

FINANCIALS: Sales and profits are in thousands of dollars—add 000 to get the full amount. 2006 Note: Financial information for 2006 was not available for all companies at press time.

2006 Sales: $92,574	2006 Profits: $2,431	**U.S. Stock Ticker: SNDS**
2005 Sales: $81,132	2005 Profits: $3,831	**Int'l Ticker:** Int'l Exchange:
2004 Sales: $62,349	2004 Profits: $6,910	Employees: 1,239
2003 Sales: $55,700	2003 Profits: $1,900	Fiscal Year Ends: 6/30
2002 Sales: $34,100	2002 Profits: $- 200	Parent Company:

SALARIES/BENEFITS:

Pension Plan:	ESOP Stock Plan:	Profit Sharing:	Top Exec. Salary: $370,000	Bonus: $99,160
Savings Plan: Y	Stock Purch. Plan:		Second Exec. Salary: $190,000	Bonus: $50,920

OTHER THOUGHTS:

Apparent Women Officers or Directors:
Hot Spot for Advancement for Women/Minorities:

LOCATIONS: ("Y" = Yes)

West:	Southwest:	Midwest:	Southeast:	Northeast:	International:
Y					

Note: Financial information, benefits and other data can change quickly and may vary from those stated here.

SANYO ELECTRIC COMPANY LTD

www.sanyo.com

Industry Group Code: 334310 Ranks within this company's industry group: Sales: 4   Profits: 14

Print Media/Publishing:	Movies:	Equipment/Supplies:		Broadcast/Cable:	Music/Audio:	Sports/Games:
Newspapers:	Movie Theaters:	Equipment/Supplies:	Y	Broadcast TV:	Music Production:	Games/Sports:
Magazines:	Movie Production:	Gambling Equipment:		Cable TV:	Retail Music:	Retail Games Stores:
Books:	TV/Video Production:	Special Services:		Satellite Broadcast:	Retail Audio Equip.:	Stadiums/Teams:
Book Stores:	Video Rental:	Advertising Services:		Radio:	Music Print./Dist.:	Gambling/Casinos:
Distribution/Printing:	Video Distribution:	Info. Sys. Software:		Online Information:	Multimedia:	Rides/Theme Parks:

TYPES OF BUSINESS:

Consumer Electronics
Fuel-Cell Technology
Communications Equipment
Industrial Equipment
Home Appliances
Batteries & Electronic Components
Photovoltaic Technology
Research & Development

BRANDS/DIVISIONS/AFFILIATES:

Solar Ark
Katana
SANYO North America Corporation
SANYO Solar USA, LLC
HIT Power 21
SANYO Logistics Corporation
SANYO Customs Brokerage, Inc.
SANYO Fisher Service Company

CONTACTS:
Note: Officers with more than one job title may be intentionally listed here more than once.

Yukinori Kuwano, CEO
Yukinori Kuwano, COO
Yukinori Kuwano, Pres.
Yoichiro Furuse, CFO/Exec. VP
Toshimasa Iue, Chief Mktg. Officer/Exec. VP
Tadahiko Tanaka, Exec. Officer
Hiromoto Sekino, Exec. Officer
Eiji Kotobuki, Exec. Officer
Satoshi Iue, Chmn.

Phone: 619-661-1134   Fax: 619-661-6795
Toll-Free:
Address: 5-5 Keihan-Hondori 2-Chome, Moriguchi City, Osaka, 570-8677 Japan

GROWTH PLANS/SPECIAL FEATURES:

Sanyo Electric Co., Ltd. is a worldwide conglomerate with 83 manufacturing companies, 37 sales companies and 38 companies in other business sectors. Sanyo offers electronics in categories including AV/information and communications equipment, home appliances, industrial and commercial equipment, electronic devices and batteries, and others. The AV/information segment manufactures and markets electronic devices such as optical pickups, TVs, PCs, mobile phones, MP3 players and digital cameras. The home appliances segment manufactures washing machines, microwaves, refrigerators and air conditioners, as well as other home appliances. The industrial and commercial equipment segment manufactures items such as heating and air conditioning systems, security cameras, micro motors and photovoltaic modules. The electronic device segment produces and markets liquid crystal displays (LCDs), semiconductors, batteries and electronic components. Sanyo also produces miscellaneous products that account for about 4% of revenues. In addition, the firm conducts research on batteries, flash memory, semiconductors, systems-on-a-chip and photonic devices using nanotechnology. Sanyo invests heavily in research and development and is focused on becoming a world technological leader in LCDs, electronic devices and environmental technology, including a joint venture with Samsung to develop fuel-cell technology. The company built the Solar Ark, an enormous solar power demonstration project that is expected to produce 630 kilowatts of power. Sanyo recently launched a multimedia phone called Katana with Sprint that offers music, live TV, high resolution digital imaging and web browsing.

Sanyo offers its employees a 401(k) retirement plan, educational assistance, an employee assistance program and company picnics, holiday parties, and community service activities.

FINANCIALS:
Sales and profits are in thousands of dollars—add 000 to get the full amount. 2006 Note: Financial information for 2006 was not available for all companies at press time.

2006 Sales: $21,804,658	2006 Profits: $-1,757,786	U.S. Stock Ticker: SANYY.PK
2005 Sales: $24,173,700	2005 Profits: $-1,603,200	Int'l Ticker: 6764 Int'l Exchange: Tokyo-TSE
2004 Sales: $24,527,700	2004 Profits: $126,400	Employees: 106,389
2003 Sales: $18,949,000	2003 Profits: $-606,800	Fiscal Year Ends: 3/31
2002 Sales: $15,881,000	2002 Profits: $12,900	Parent Company:

SALARIES/BENEFITS:

Pension Plan:	ESOP Stock Plan:	Profit Sharing:	Top Exec. Salary: $	Bonus: $
Savings Plan: Y	Stock Purch. Plan:		Second Exec. Salary: $	Bonus: $

OTHER THOUGHTS:
Apparent Women Officers or Directors:
Hot Spot for Advancement for Women/Minorities:

LOCATIONS: ("Y" = Yes)

West:	Southwest:	Midwest:	Southeast:	Northeast:	International:
Y					Y

Note: Financial information, benefits and other data can change quickly and may vary from those stated here.

SCHOLASTIC CORP

www.scholastic.com

Industry Group Code: 511130 Ranks within this company's industry group: Sales: 4 Profits: 4

Print Media/Publishing:		Movies:		Equipment/Supplies:		Broadcast/Cable:		Music/Audio:		Sports/Games:	
Newspapers:		Movie Theaters:		Equipment/Supplies:		Broadcast TV:		Music Production:		Games/Sports:	
Magazines:	Y	Movie Production:		Gambling Equipment:		Cable TV:		Retail Music:		Retail Games Stores:	
Books:	Y	TV/Video Production:	Y	Special Services:		Satellite Broadcast:		Retail Audio Equip.:		Stadiums/Teams:	
Book Stores:		Video Rental:		Advertising Services:		Radio:		Music Print./Dist.:	Y	Gambling/Casinos:	
Distribution/Printing:		Video Distribution:		Info. Sys. Software:		Online Information:		Multimedia:		Rides/Theme Parks:	

TYPES OF BUSINESS:

Children's Book Publishing
Children's TV Programming
Educational Software
Educational Magazines
Book Fairs & Clubs
Consumer Products

BRANDS/DIVISIONS/AFFILIATES:

Babysitters' Club (The)
Clifford the Big Red Dog
Goosebumps
Harry Potter
Magic School Bus (The)
READ 180
Wiggleworks
Scholastic Reading Counts

CONTACTS: Note: Officers with more than one job title may be intentionally listed here more than once.

Richard Robinson, CEO
Richard Robinson, Pres.
Mary Winston, Exec. VP/CFO
Peter Watts, Sr. VP-Corp. Human Resources/Employee Svcs.
Beth Ford, Sr. VP-IT
Beth Ford, Sr. VP-Global Oper.
Heather J. Myers, Sr. VP-Strategic Planning & Bus. Dev.
Ernest B. Fleishman, Sr. VP-Corp. Rel.
Karen A. Maloney, Sr. VP-Finance/Chief Acct. Officer
Deborah A. Forte, Exec. VP/Pres., Scholastic Media
Lisa Holton, Exec. VP/Pres., Book Fairs & Trade
Margery W. Mayer, Exec. VP/Pres., Scholastic Education
Judith A. Newman, Sr. VP/Pres., Book Clubs & Scholastic At Home
Richard Robinson, Chmn.
Hugh Roome, Exec. VP/Pres., Scholastic Int'l

Phone: 212-343-6100	Fax: 212-343-6934
Toll-Free: 800-724-6527	
Address: 557 Broadway, New York, NY 10012 US	

GROWTH PLANS/SPECIAL FEATURES:

Scholastic Corporation is a global children's publishing and media company. Scholastic creates educational and entertaining materials and products for use in school and at home. The company categorizes its businesses into four operating segments: Children's Book Publishing and Distribution; Educational Publishing; Media, Licensing and Advertising; and International. In fiscal 2006, through the Children's Book Publishing and Distribution segment, the company's largest, the firm sold more than 400 million children's books in the U.S. This division's success is based on consumer loyalty to traditional favorites, including the Babysitters' Club and Clifford the Big Red Dog series, as well as on newcomers, most notably the wildly popular Harry Potter series. Through its Educational Publishing segment, the company specializes in materials that cover subjects such as English, math, science, social studies, current events and foreign languages. A major focus of this division is reading improvement materials and the effective use of technology to support learning. Scholastic's technology based products include READ 180, Wiggleworks and Scholastic Reading Counts. Scholastic's Media, Licensing and Advertising segment focuses on the production and/or distribution of software, programming and consumer products and the development of advertising revenue. Through this division, the company produces children's television programming, DVD's, feature films and branded websites based on many of its successful titles. Scholastic recently launched a comprehensive brand marketing campaign in conjunction with the premiere of the Maya and Miguel television program, including consumer products and publishing extension, such as television tie-in books. The firm's International segment, accounting for 18% of total revenue in 2006, publishes and distributes products and services in 16 countries including Canada, Australia, India, Argentina, Ireland, Mexico and the U.K.

Scholastic offers employees tuition reimbursement, a work/life assistance program and leave programs including child care, military and compassionate leaves.

FINANCIALS: Sales and profits are in thousands of dollars—add 000 to get the full amount. 2006 Note: Financial information for 2006 was not available for all companies at press time.

2006 Sales: $2,283,800	2006 Profits: $68,600	**U.S. Stock Ticker:** SCHL	
2005 Sales: $2,079,900	2005 Profits: $64,300	**Int'l Ticker:**	Int'l Exchange:
2004 Sales: $2,233,800	2004 Profits: $58,400	Employees: 10,400	
2003 Sales: $1,958,300	2003 Profits: $58,600	Fiscal Year Ends: 5/31	
2002 Sales: $1,917,000	2002 Profits: $93,500	Parent Company:	

SALARIES/BENEFITS:

Pension Plan: Y	ESOP Stock Plan:	Profit Sharing:	Top Exec. Salary: $861,194	Bonus: $
Savings Plan: Y	Stock Purch. Plan: Y		Second Exec. Salary: $610,056	Bonus: $65,000

OTHER THOUGHTS:

Apparent Women Officers or Directors: 8
Hot Spot for Advancement for Women/Minorities: Y

LOCATIONS: ("Y" = Yes)

West:	Southwest:	Midwest:	Southeast:	Northeast:	International:
Y	Y	Y	Y	Y	Y

Note: Financial information, benefits and other data can change quickly and may vary from those stated here.

SCIENTIFIC GAMES CORPORATION www.scientificgames.com

Industry Group Code: 713290 Ranks within this company's industry group: Sales: 4 Profits: 4

Print Media/Publishing:	Movies:	Equipment/Supplies:		Broadcast/Cable:	Music/Audio:	Sports/Games:	
Newspapers:	Movie Theaters:	Equipment/Supplies:		Broadcast TV:	Music Production:	Games/Sports:	
Magazines:	Movie Production:	Gambling Equipment:	Y	Cable TV:	Retail Music:	Retail Games Stores:	
Books:	TV/Video Production:	Special Services:		Satellite Broadcast:	Retail Audio Equip.:	Stadiums/Teams:	Y
Book Stores:	Video Rental:	Advertising Services:		Radio:	Music Print./Dist.:	Gambling/Casinos:	
Distribution/Printing:	Video Distribution:	Info. Sys. Software:		Online Information:	Multimedia:	Rides/Theme Parks:	

TYPES OF BUSINESS:

Gambling Equipment-Computer-Based Lottery Systems
Pari-Mutuel Wagering Systems
Satellite Broadcasting Services
Telecommunications Products
Off-Track Betting Facilities Management
Lottery Services
Race Simulcasting
Prepaid Phone Cards

BRANDS/DIVISIONS/AFFILIATES:

Scientific Games Latin America S.A.
Printpool Honsel GmbH
Global Draw Limited
EssNet AB

CONTACTS: Note: Officers with more than one job title may be intentionally listed here more than once.

A. Lorne Weil, CEO
Michael R. Chambrello, COO
Michael R. Chambrello, Pres.
DeWayne E. Laird, VP/CFO
Brooks Pierce, VP-Corp. Mktg.
Sally Conkright, Chief Human Resources Officer
Steven W. Beason, VP/CTO
Sally L. Conkright, VP-Admin.
Ira H. Raphaelson, VP/General Counsel/Corp. Sec.
David Pye, VP-Corp. Dev.
Lisa D. Lettieri, Dir.-Corp. Comm.
Robert C. Becker, VP/Treas.
Larry A. Potts, VP-Security & Compliance
Steven M. Saferin, VP/Pres., Properties
William J. Huntley, VP/Pres., Racing, Sports & Gaming Tech.
Cliff O. Bickell, VP/Pres., Printed Products
A. Lorne Weil, Chmn.

Phone: 212-754-2233	Fax: 212-754-2372
Toll-Free: 800-367-9345	
Address: 750 Lexington Ave., New York, NY 10022 US	

GROWTH PLANS/SPECIAL FEATURES:

Scientific Games Corp. provides systems, products and services to the instant ticket lottery and pari-mutuel wagering industries, offering some of the most technologically advanced products and services in these industries to customers in the U.S. and 60 other countries. Scientific Games operates four business segments: a lottery group, a pari-mutuel group, a venue management group and a telecommunications products group. The lottery group (75% of 2005 revenue) is a fully integrated lottery service provider, offering online lottery systems, instant tickets and related facilities management programs to lottery authorities. Its instant ticket customers include 31 out of the 42 U.S. jurisdictions that sell instant lottery tickets. The firm also provides lotteries with related value-added services such as game design, sales and marketing support, inventory management and warehousing and fulfillment services. The pari-mutuel group (10%) provides computerized wagering systems for horse and greyhound racetracks, off-track betting sites, casinos, jai alai frontons and other establishments. The group also provides ancillary services including race simulcasting, telecommunications services, video gaming terminals and telephone and Internet account wagering. The venue management group (8%) operates substantially all off-track pari-mutuel wagering facilities in Connecticut, including 6 simulcasting teletheaters, as well as telephone account wagering in 25 states. It also has the right to operate all on- and off-track pari-mutuel wagering in the Netherlands. The telecommunications products group (7%) is a leading manufacturer of prepaid phone cards in Europe and worldwide. Scientific Games recently acquired Global Draw Limited, a leading U.K. supplier of fixed odds betting terminals and systems and interactive sports betting systems. It also announced the acquisition of substantially all of the online lottery assets of the Swedish firm EssNet AB.

The company offers its employees tuition reimbursement, flexible spending accounts, child and elder care resources, leaves of absence, free parking and credit union membership.

FINANCIALS: Sales and profits are in thousands of dollars—add 000 to get the full amount. 2006 Note: Financial information for 2006 was not available for all companies at press time.

2006 Sales: $	2006 Profits: $	U.S. Stock Ticker: SGMS
2005 Sales: $781,683	2005 Profits: $75,319	Int'l Ticker: Int'l Exchange:
2004 Sales: $725,495	2004 Profits: $65,742	Employees: 4,000
2003 Sales: $560,900	2003 Profits: $52,100	Fiscal Year Ends: 12/31
2002 Sales: $455,300	2002 Profits: $52,100	Parent Company:

SALARIES/BENEFITS:

Pension Plan:	ESOP Stock Plan:	Profit Sharing:	Top Exec. Salary: $1,000,000	Bonus: $1,432,500
Savings Plan: Y	Stock Purch. Plan: Y		Second Exec. Salary: $450,000	Bonus: $282,646

OTHER THOUGHTS:

Apparent Women Officers or Directors: 3
Hot Spot for Advancement for Women/Minorities: Y

LOCATIONS: ("Y" = Yes)

West:	Southwest:	Midwest:	Southeast:	Northeast:	International:
Y	Y	Y	Y	Y	Y

Note: Financial information, benefits and other data can change quickly and may vary from those stated here.

SEGA SAMMY HOLDINGS INC www.segasammy.co.jp/english

Industry Group Code: 511208 Ranks within this company's industry group: Sales: 1 Profits: 2

Print Media/Publishing:	Movies:		Equipment/Supplies:		Broadcast/Cable:		Music/Audio:	Sports/Games:	
Newspapers:	Movie Theaters:		Equipment/Supplies:	Y	Broadcast TV:		Music Production:	Games/Sports:	Y
Magazines:	Movie Production:	Y	Gambling Equipment:	Y	Cable TV:		Retail Music:	Retail Games Stores:	Y
Books:	TV/Video Production:		Special Services:	Y	Satellite Broadcast:		Retail Audio Equip.:	Stadiums/Teams:	
Book Stores:	Video Rental:		Advertising Services:		Radio:		Music Print./Dist.:	Gambling/Casinos:	Y
Distribution/Printing:	Video Distribution:		Info. Sys. Software:		Online Information:		Multimedia:	Rides/Theme Parks:	

TYPES OF BUSINESS:

Computer Software-Games
Arcade Games
Amusement Centers
Toys
Ring Tones & Mobile Phone Media
Animation Production
Karaoke Machines
Display Design & Construction Services

BRANDS/DIVISIONS/AFFILIATES:

SEGA CORPORATION
Sammy NetWorks Co., LTD.
H-I System Corporation
NISSHO INTER LIFE CO., LTD.
SI Electronics, LTD.
TMS Entertainment, LTD.
SEGA Music Networks Co., LTD.
Ginzahanbai (Ginza) Corporation

CONTACTS: *Note: Officers with more than one job title may be intentionally listed here more than once.*

Hajime Satomi, CEO/CEO-SEGA CORPORATION
Hisao Oguchi, COO
Hajime Satomi, Pres.
Yoshii Asano, Mngr.-Mktg. Planning Dep.
Yukio Sugino, Div. Mng.-Amusement R&D
Akira Sugano, Exec. Officer/Div. Mng.-Admin. Div.
Hioyuki Soga, Gen. Mng.-Legal & Compliance
Koichi Fukazawa, Exec. Officer/Div. Mng.-Corp. Planning Div.
Hirofumi Otsuki, Corp. Comm.
Seijinn Tanno, Pres./CEO-Nissho Inter Life
Hisao Oguchi, Pres./COO-SEGA CORPORATION
Hajime Satomi, Chmn/CEO-SEGA CORPORATION
Hajime Satomi, Chmn.
Naoya Tsurumi, CEO-SEGA Holdings USA & SEGA Europe LTD.

Phone: 81-3-621-59955	Fax: 81-3-5736-7066
Toll-Free:	
Address: 21F 1-9-2 Higashi Shimbashi/Minato-ku, Tokyo, 105-0021 Japan	

GROWTH PLANS/SPECIAL FEATURES:

Sega Sammy Holdings (SSH), the product of a merger between SEGA CORPORATION and Sammy Corporation, operates amusement centers and produces game software and arcade games. The company is organized into three units: Pachislot and Pachinko Machines (PPM), Amusement Center Operations (ACO) and Consumer Business. Pachinko and Pachislot machines account for 48% of net sales. In the PPM segment, the company uses a business model called ALL. Net P-ras. Under this model, PPM sells game hardware and provides mother board and software at no cost. SSH is paid by content use. This model allows operates of amusement centers to introduce new machines with a small initial investment. At the end of fiscal 2006, The ACO segment had nearly 30,000 Pachinko and Pachislot machines installed across Japan and nearly 600 million game cards for the machines in play. The company owns and operates 462 amusement centers, including those operated by TMS entertainment. The Consumer Business segment manufactures software for home video game consoles, Internet game play, and mobile phones, as well as having operations in the traditional toy market. In 2006, the company's top game software (by unit sales) was Shadow the Hedgehog. Among the company's 58 subsidiaries and affiliates are: Sega Corporation; Sammy NetWorks Co., LTD. (ring tones and games for mobile phones); TMS Entertainment, LTD. (animation planning and production, acquired in March 2006); H-I System Corporation (makes amusement hall computers and prize POS systems); NISSHO INTER LIFE CO., LTD (engages in planning, design, management and construction of displays and commercial facilities); and SEGA Music Networks Co., Ltd. (production and sales of karaoke machines). In 2006, SSH acquired three new subsidiaries: Sports Interactive Ltd.; GINZA Co., Ltd; and Secret Level, Inc. In March 2006, SEGA launched LB Style Square, official shops for its LOVE AND BERRY Dress Up and Dance! game.

FINANCIALS: Sales and profits are in thousands of dollars—add 000 to get the full amount. 2006 Note: Financial information for 2006 was not available for all companies at press time.

2006 Sales: $4,656,310	2006 Profits: $557,350	**U.S. Stock Ticker: SGAMY**
2005 Sales: $4,340,090	2005 Profits: $425,650	**Int'l Ticker: 6460** Int'l Exchange: Tokyo-TSE
2004 Sales: $1,810,400	2004 Profits: $82,900	Employees: 6,416
2003 Sales: $1,645,600	2003 Profits: $25,500	Fiscal Year Ends: 3/31
2002 Sales: $1,555,600	2002 Profits: $-134,400	Parent Company:

SALARIES/BENEFITS:

Pension Plan: Y	ESOP Stock Plan:	Profit Sharing:	Top Exec. Salary: $	Bonus: $
Savings Plan:	Stock Purch. Plan:		Second Exec. Salary: $	Bonus: $

OTHER THOUGHTS:

Apparent Women Officers or Directors:
Hot Spot for Advancement for Women/Minorities:

LOCATIONS: ("Y" = Yes)

West:	Southwest:	Midwest:	Southeast:	Northeast:	International:
Y	Y	Y	Y	Y	Y

Note: Financial information, benefits and other data can change quickly and may vary from those stated here.

SHANDA INTERACTIVE ENTERTAINMENT LIMITED
www.snda.com/en/index.jsp

Industry Group Code: 511208 Ranks within this company's industry group: Sales: 7 Profits: 7

Print Media/Publishing:		Movies:	Equipment/Supplies:		Broadcast/Cable:	Music/Audio:	Sports/Games:	
Newspapers:		Movie Theaters:	Equipment/Supplies:		Broadcast TV:	Music Production:	Games/Sports:	Y
Magazines:	Y	Movie Production:	Gambling Equipment:		Cable TV:	Retail Music:	Retail Games Stores:	
Books:		TV/Video Production:	Special Services:		Satellite Broadcast:	Retail Audio Equip.:	Stadiums/Teams:	
Book Stores:		Video Rental:	Advertising Services:	Y	Radio:	Music Print./Dist.:	Gambling/Casinos:	
Distribution/Printing:		Video Distribution:	Info. Sys. Software:		Online Information:	Multimedia:	Rides/Theme Parks:	

TYPES OF BUSINESS:
Online Gaming

BRANDS/DIVISIONS/AFFILIATES:
EZ Pod
EZ Center
InterJoy Technology, Ltd.
Jisheng Technology
Fenglin Huoshan Technology
Actoz Soft Co., Ltd
Gametea
Shanda Networking

CONTACTS: *Note: Officers with more than one job title may be intentionally listed here more than once.*
Tianqiao Chen, CEO
Jun Tang, Pres.
Daniel Zhang, VP/CFO
Qunzhao Tan, Sr. VP/CTO
Lijun Li, Assoc. Dir-General Admin.
Gehui Zhu, Assoc. Dir.-Public Rel.
Frank Liang, Dir.-Investor Rel.
Danian Chen, Exec. VP
Haibin Qu, Exec. VP
Jingying Wang, Sr. VP
Hai Ling, Sr. VP
Tianqiao Chen, Chmn.

Phone: 021-50504740	Fax: 021-50504740-8088
Toll-Free:	

Address: No. 1 Intelligent Office Bldg., No.690 Bibo Road, Shanghai, 201203 China

GROWTH PLANS/SPECIAL FEATURES:
Shanda is one of the largest operators of online games in China, offering a portfolio of free and fee-based games including The Legend of Mir II and The World of Legend. The games fall into one of two categories: casual games (Internet based), and massively multiplayer online role-playing games (MMORPG) which allow users to connect games installed on their computers to the Internet in order to interact with other gamers. Shanda's casual games include BNB, Fortress 2 and GetAmped. The firm's fee-based MMORPG games include The Sign, The Age and The Tactical Commander. Shanda gains revenue from online advertising, staffs a research and development center to acquire game development companies and earns revenue from short messaging services (SMS) and sales of publications and other related products based on its games and characters. However, the firm's principal source of revenue consists of the fees paid by online game users. Its customers purchase pre-paid game cards (sold in both virtual and physical form) to add value to their accounts in order to play. In 2006, the firm partnered with Hewlett Packard China, who will bundle its digital home products with EZPods (Shanda's interactive entertainment / PC platforms). Also in 2006, the firm sold most of its stock in SINA Corp to Citigroup Global Markets (Citigroup). Recently, Shanda announced plans to develop, distribute, and operate an online game for the Walt Disney Entertainment Group which will feature the animated characters and worlds of Disney. Shanda partnered with NHN Games (South Korea) to exclusively operate ArchLord (a 3-D MMORPG) in China. The company's 2006 partnering with JoyChina (Beijing) allows it to be the sole global operator of 3D game Kung Fu Masters. Recently, the firm announced a partnership with Motorola to launch exclusive mobile versions of Shanda's World of Legend game on customized Motorola E680g handsets.

FINANCIALS: Sales and profits are in thousands of dollars—add 000 to get the full amount. 2006 Note: Financial information for 2006 was not available for all companies at press time.

2006 Sales: $	2006 Profits: $	**U.S. Stock Ticker: SNDA**
2005 Sales: $235,014	2005 Profits: $20,480	**Int'l Ticker:** Int'l Exchange:
2004 Sales: $156,900	2004 Profits: $73,600	Employees: 2,392
2003 Sales: $	2003 Profits: $	Fiscal Year Ends: 12/31
2002 Sales: $	2002 Profits: $	Parent Company:

SALARIES/BENEFITS:

Pension Plan: Y	ESOP Stock Plan:	Profit Sharing:	Top Exec. Salary: $	Bonus: $
Savings Plan:	Stock Purch. Plan:		Second Exec. Salary: $	Bonus: $

OTHER THOUGHTS:
Apparent Women Officers or Directors: 2
Hot Spot for Advancement for Women/Minorities: Y

LOCATIONS: ("Y" = Yes)

West:	Southwest:	Midwest:	Southeast:	Northeast:	International:
					Y

SHANGHAI MEDIA GROUP (SMG)   www.smg.sh.cn

Industry Group Code: 513120 Ranks within this company's industry group: Sales: Profits:

Print Media/Publishing:		Movies:		Equipment/Supplies:	Broadcast/Cable:		Music/Audio:	Sports/Games:
Newspapers:	Y	Movie Theaters:		Equipment/Supplies:	Broadcast TV:	Y	Music Production:	Games/Sports:
Magazines:	Y	Movie Production:		Gambling Equipment:	Cable TV:	Y	Retail Music:	Retail Games Stores:
Books:		TV/Video Production:	Y	Special Services:	Satellite Broadcast:		Retail Audio Equip.:	Stadiums/Teams:
Book Stores:		Video Rental:		Advertising Services:	Radio:		Music Print./Dist.:	Gambling/Casinos:
Distribution/Printing:		Video Distribution:		Info. Sys. Software:	Online Information:		Multimedia:	Rides/Theme Parks:

TYPES OF BUSINESS:

Television Broadcasting
TV Production
Radio Production
Radio Broadcasting
TV Broadcasting via Online
Cable TV Network
Newspaper Publishing
Magazine Publishing

BRANDS/DIVISIONS/AFFILIATES:

Radio Shanghai
Eastern Radio Shanghai
Shanghai Television
Oriental Television Station
Shanghai Cable Television
Shanghai Dragon Mobile Media Company
Oriental CJ

CONTACTS: *Note: Officers with more than one job title may be intentionally listed here more than once.*

Li Ruigang, Pres.

Phone: 86-21-6256-5899	Fax: 86-21-6256-2752
Toll-Free:	
Address: 651 W. Nanjing Rd., Shanghai, 200041 China	

GROWTH PLANS/SPECIAL FEATURES:

Shanghai Media Group (SMG) is a Chinese-language producer and provider of radio and TV entertainment. In addition, it is engaged in the performing arts, sports and technical service sectors. SMG is the result of a 2001 merger of Radio Shanghai, Eastern Radio Shanghai, Shanghai Television, Oriental Television Station and Shanghai Cable Television. As of 2005, the company was broadcasting 258 hours of TV and 214 hours of radio each day. TV and radio content produced by the firm includes news, entertainment, sports, finance, music, TV series, documentaries and animated features. SMG operates 13 analog TV channels, seven of which are cable channels that cover the Shanghai area, four are terrestrial channels for Shanghai and the surrounding areas and two are satellite channels for Chinese and overseas subscribers. Other TV interests include one broadband online TV channel, one mobile phone TV channel (through its Shanghai Dragon Mobile Media Company subsidiary) and one national IPTV service platform. The firm also operates 11 analog radio stations, 16 national digital pay channels, five newspapers and magazines and five sports clubs. Moreover, SMG partners with Korea's CJ Home Shopping to oversee Oriental CJ, a home shopping company. In early 2007, CJ Home Shopping took on another partner, Jiaxing TV, to launch the home shopping program in the province of Zhejiang. Also in 2007, the firm began providing ESPN's English League Premier soccer coverage via its IPTV platform.

FINANCIALS: Sales and profits are in thousands of dollars—add 000 to get the full amount. 2006 Note: Financial information for 2006 was not available for all companies at press time.

2006 Sales: $	2006 Profits: $	U.S. Stock Ticker: Private	
2005 Sales: $	2005 Profits: $	Int'l Ticker:	Int'l Exchange:
2004 Sales: $	2004 Profits: $	Employees:	
2003 Sales: $	2003 Profits: $	Fiscal Year Ends:	
2002 Sales: $	2002 Profits: $	Parent Company:	

SALARIES/BENEFITS:

Pension Plan:	ESOP Stock Plan:	Profit Sharing:	Top Exec. Salary: $	Bonus: $
Savings Plan:	Stock Purch. Plan:		Second Exec. Salary: $	Bonus: $

OTHER THOUGHTS:

Apparent Women Officers or Directors:
Hot Spot for Advancement for Women/Minorities:

LOCATIONS: ("Y" = Yes)

West:	Southwest:	Midwest:	Southeast:	Northeast:	International: Y

SHARP CORPORATION

sharp-world.com

Industry Group Code: 334310 Ranks within this company's industry group: Sales: 5 Profits: 3

Print Media/Publishing:	Movies:	Equipment/Supplies:		Broadcast/Cable:	Music/Audio:		Sports/Games:
Newspapers:	Movie Theaters:	Equipment/Supplies:	Y	Broadcast TV:	Music Production:		Games/Sports:
Magazines:	Movie Production:	Gambling Equipment:		Cable TV:	Retail Music:		Retail Games Stores:
Books:	TV/Video Production:	Special Services:		Satellite Broadcast:	Retail Audio Equip.:	Y	Stadiums/Teams:
Book Stores:	Video Rental:	Advertising Services:		Radio:	Music Print./Dist.:		Gambling/Casinos:
Distribution/Printing:	Video Distribution:	Info. Sys. Software:		Online Information:	Multimedia:		Rides/Theme Parks:

TYPES OF BUSINESS:

Audiovisual & Communications Equipment
Electronic Components
Solar Cells & Modules
Home Appliances
Computers & Information Equipment
Consumer Electronics
LCD Flat Panel TVs, Monitors & Displays

BRANDS/DIVISIONS/AFFILIATES:

Sharp Telecommunications of Europe, Ltd.
Sharp Laboratories of Europe, Ltd.
Sharp Laboratories of America, Inc.
Sharp Technology (Taiwan) Corp.
Sharp Software Development India Pvt., Ltd.
AQUOS
Kameyama Plant No. 2

CONTACTS: *Note: Officers with more than one job title may be intentionally listed here more than once.*

Toshihiko Fujimoto, CEO
Katsuhiko Machida, Pres.
Shigeo Nakabu, Sr. Exec. VP-Sales & Mktg.
Akihiko Kumagai, Sr. Exec. VP/General Mgr.-Human Resources
Toru Chiba, Dir./General Mgr.-Corp. R&D
Kenji Ohta, Sr. Exec. Dir./CTO
Takuji Okawara, Dir./General Mgr.-Prod. Planning
Hiroshi Saji, Sr. Exec. VP/Chief General Admin. Officer
Toshio Adachi, Sr. Exec. Dir./General Mgr.-Tokyo Branch
Toshishige Hamano, Sr. Exec. Dir.-Mgmt. Planning
Tetsuo Onishi, Dir./General Mgr.-Corp. Acct. & Control
Mikio Katayama, Sr. Exec. Dir.-A/V Systems & Large LCD Bus.
Masafumi Matsumoto, Sr. Exec. VP-Info. & Comm. Systems Bus.
Masaaki Ohtsuka, Sr. Exec. Dir.-Domestic Sales & Mktg.
Takashi Tomita, Exec. Dir.-Solar Systems
Toshihiko Fujimoto, Chmn.
Takashi Nakagawa, Exec. Dir./General Mgr.-Int'l Bus.
Takashi Okuda, Dir./General Mgr.-Corp. Procurement

Phone: 81-6-6621-1221	Fax: 81-6-6627-1759
Toll-Free:	
Address: 22-22 Nagaike-cho, Abeno-ku, Osaka, 545-8522 Japan	

GROWTH PLANS/SPECIAL FEATURES:

Sharp Corporation, with more than $22 billion in assets, designs, manufactures and distributes electronic components, audiovisual and communications equipment, home appliances, information technology and solar power generators. Its audiovisual and communications products include LCD TVs, TV/VCRs, DVD players and recorders, camcorders, fax machines, mobile phones, digital broadcast receivers and CD component systems. Sharp home appliances include electric heaters, refrigerators, microwave ovens, steam ovens, washers and dryers, vacuum cleaners, air conditioners and air purifiers. The firm's information equipment division develops PCs, PDAs, electronic cash registers, digital copiers, printers, software and data terminals, software, peripherals, copier supplies and ultrasonic cleaners. Its main electronic components include flash memory, imagers, analog ICs, microcomputers, liquid crystal display (LCD) modules, electronic tuners, satellite broadcast units, switching power supplies, laser diodes and solar cells. Sharp has 27 sales subsidiaries in 22 countries, 23 manufacturing bases in 13 countries and five research and development bases in four countries. The firm is also a leading manufacturer of solar cells. In March 2006, it was listed by PV News as the worldwide leader in total production of solar cells and modules. The company operates its own manufacturing plants for LCD TVs and makes large investments in research and development for LCD technology, recently introducing triple directional viewing technology, which allows one screen to produce three different images. Sharp recently began producing and marketing its new AQUOS line of LCD TVs, with an industry-best 2000:1 contrast ratio and available with as large as 65-inch screens. The firm's state-of-the-art Kameyama Plant No. 2 became operational in August 2006. The facility features an energy supply system based on integrating diverse power sources distributed within the plant into a single large-scale system independent of the utility power grid. These sources include the world's largest photovoltaic power system.

FINANCIALS: Sales and profits are in thousands of dollars—add 000 to get the full amount. 2006 Note: Financial information for 2006 was not available for all companies at press time.

2006 Sales: $24,113,009	2006 Profits: $764,405	U.S. Stock Ticker: SHCAY
2005 Sales: $23,960,934	2005 Profits: $724,953	Int'l Ticker: 6753 Int'l Exchange: Tokyo-TSE
2004 Sales: $21,367,300	2004 Profits: $574,700	Employees: 46,872
2003 Sales: $16,741,800	2003 Profits: $272,000	Fiscal Year Ends: 3/31
2002 Sales: $13,599,000	2002 Profits: $85,000	Parent Company:

SALARIES/BENEFITS:

Pension Plan:	ESOP Stock Plan:	Profit Sharing:	Top Exec. Salary: $	Bonus: $
Savings Plan:	Stock Purch. Plan:		Second Exec. Salary: $	Bonus: $

OTHER THOUGHTS:

Apparent Women Officers or Directors:
Hot Spot for Advancement for Women/Minorities:

LOCATIONS: ("Y" = Yes)

West:	Southwest:	Midwest:	Southeast:	Northeast:	International:
Y		Y	Y	Y	Y

Note: Financial information, benefits and other data can change quickly and may vary from those stated here.

SHAW COMMUNICATIONS INC

www.shaw.ca

Industry Group Code: 513220 Ranks within this company's industry group: Sales: 15   Profits: 9

Print Media/Publishing:	Movies:	Equipment/Supplies:		Broadcast/Cable:		Music/Audio:	Sports/Games:
Newspapers:	Movie Theaters:	Equipment/Supplies:		Broadcast TV:		Music Production:	Games/Sports:
Magazines:	Movie Production:	Gambling Equipment:	Y	Cable TV:	Y	Retail Music:	Retail Games Stores:
Books:	TV/Video Production:	Special Services:	Y	Satellite Broadcast:		Retail Audio Equip.:	Stadiums/Teams:
Book Stores:	Video Rental:	Advertising Services:		Radio:		Music Print./Dist.:	Gambling/Casinos:
Distribution/Printing:	Video Distribution:	Info. Sys. Software:		Online Information:		Multimedia:	Rides/Theme Parks:

TYPES OF BUSINESS:

Cable TV Service
Internet Services
Satellite Services
Digital Phone Services
Internet Infrastructure Services

BRANDS/DIVISIONS/AFFILIATES:

Shaw Cablesystems G.P.
Video Cablesystems, Inc.
Shaw Digital Phone
Star Choice Communications, Inc.
Big Pipe, Inc.
Monarch Cablesystems
Canadian Satellite Communications, Inc.
Shaw High-Speed Xtreme

CONTACTS: Note: Officers with more than one job title may be intentionally listed here more than once.

Jim Shaw, CEO
Peter J. Bissonette, Pres.
Steve Wilson, CFO/Sr. VP
David Taniguchi, Sr. Counsel/Asst. Corp. Sec.
Bradley S. Shaw, Sr. VP-Oper.
Michael D'Avella, Sr. VP-Planning
Ken Stein, Sr. VP-Corp. & Regulatory Affairs
Rhonda Bashnick, VP-Finance
Douglas J. Black, Corp. Sec.
J. R. Shaw, Exec. Chmn.

Phone: 403-750-4500	Fax: 403-750-4501
Toll-Free:	
Address: 630 3rd Ave. SW, Ste. 900, Calgary, AB T2P 4L4 Canada	

GROWTH PLANS/SPECIAL FEATURES:

Shaw Communications, Inc. is a diversified Canadian communications company whose core business is providing broadband cable television, high-speed Internet, digital phone, telecommunications services and satellite direct-to-home services. The company serves over 3 million customers. Shaw provides customers with high-quality entertainment, information and communications services, utilizing a variety of distribution technologies that are separated into two divisions, cable and satellite. The cable segment represents Shaw's core business. The firm is currently the second-largest cable television provider in Canada and the largest cable provider in Western Canada, serving approximately 2.1 million customers. Offerings include basic cable, digital cable, pay-per-view and video-on-demand. Through this segment, the company also provides Internet access services to residential and small-business subscribers via a cable connection and cable modem. In 2004, Shaw introduced its Shaw High-Speed Xtreme service, offering significantly increased download and upload speeds. The firm's Internet infrastructure services are offered through subsidiaries Big Pipe, Inc. and Big Pipe U.S., Inc. In addition, Shaw recently began offering the Shaw Digital Phone service employing PacketCable technology. The company's satellite segment operates through subsidiary Canadian Satellite Communications, Inc., which offers satellite-based solutions to businesses and owns Star Choice Communications, Inc., one of two licensed DTH operators in Canada. In April 2006, Shaw's video-on-demand (VOD) library expanded to over 2,000 titles through a new partnership with Warner Bros. International Television Distribution.

FINANCIALS: Sales and profits are in thousands of dollars—add 000 to get the full amount. 2006 Note: Financial information for 2006 was not available for all companies at press time.

2006 Sales: $2,122,630	2006 Profits: $395,520	U.S. Stock Ticker: SJR
2005 Sales: $1,861,800	2005 Profits: $135,300	Int'l Ticker: SJR.B Int'l Exchange: Toronto-TSX
2004 Sales: $1,585,600	2004 Profits: $69,300	Employees: 6,000
2003 Sales: $1,605,120	2003 Profits: $-36,968	Fiscal Year Ends: 8/31
2002 Sales: $1,479,623	2002 Profits: $-221,310	Parent Company:

SALARIES/BENEFITS:

Pension Plan:	ESOP Stock Plan:	Profit Sharing:	Top Exec. Salary: $721,787	Bonus: $4,958,252
Savings Plan: Y	Stock Purch. Plan:		Second Exec. Salary: $673,981	Bonus: $3,134,796

OTHER THOUGHTS:

Apparent Women Officers or Directors: 1
Hot Spot for Advancement for Women/Minorities:

LOCATIONS: ("Y" = Yes)

West:	Southwest:	Midwest:	Southeast:	Northeast:	International:
					Y

Note: Financial information, benefits and other data can change quickly and may vary from those stated here.

SHOP AT HOME NETWORK LLC   www.shopathometv.com

Industry Group Code: 454110B **Ranks within this company's industry group:** Sales: Profits:

Print Media/Publishing:	Movies:	Equipment/Supplies:	Broadcast/Cable:		Music/Audio:	Sports/Games:
Newspapers:	Movie Theaters:	Equipment/Supplies:	Broadcast TV:	Y	Music Production:	Games/Sports:
Magazines:	Movie Production:	Gambling Equipment:	Cable TV:		Retail Music:	Retail Games Stores:
Books:	TV/Video Production:	Special Services: Y	Satellite Broadcast:		Retail Audio Equip.:	Stadiums/Teams:
Book Stores:	Video Rental:	Advertising Services:	Radio:		Music Print./Dist.:	Gambling/Casinos:
Distribution/Printing:	Video Distribution:	Info. Sys. Software:	Online Information:		Multimedia:	Rides/Theme Parks:

TYPES OF BUSINESS:
Television Shopping
Online Sales
Television Stations
Satellite Television

BRANDS/DIVISIONS/AFFILIATES:
shopathometv.com
Jewelry Television

CONTACTS: *Note: Officers with more than one job title may be intentionally listed here more than once.*
Tim Engle, Pres.
Stephen R. Hanon, CFO
Andy Caldwell, VP-Affiliate Mktg.
Jeffrey Doster, CTO
Bill Christopher, Sr. VP-Customer Experience
Kelly Fletcher, VP-Public Relations
Patsy Harris, Dir.-Distribution
Harris Bagley, Exec. VP-Affiliate Distribution
Burt Bagley, VP-Cable Distribution (Eastern Region)
Ray Pearson, VP-Cable Distribution (Western Region)
Tim Engle, Chmn.

Phone: 615-263-8000	**Fax:** 615-263-8084
Toll-Free: 866-366-4010	
Address: 5388 Hickory Hollow Parkway, Nashville, TN 37013 US	

GROWTH PLANS/SPECIAL FEATURES:

Shop at Home Network LLC operates Shop At Home Network, a nationally televised home shopping channel that sells merchandise 24-hours a day through interactive electronic media, including broadcast, cable, and satellite television. Shop At Home caters to men between the ages of 30 and 50, offering primarily jewelry, entertainment memorabilia, trading cards, knives and coins, emphasizing drop shipping as opposed to in-house stocking. The firm's sports and collectible products account for about 57% of sales. Shop at Home Network's television programming is available in over 70 million households through cable. In 2006, the firm sold five Shop At Home Broadcast Stations (WSAH 43 Bridgeport and Hartford, Connecticut; WMFP Boston, Massachusetts; KCNS San Francisco, California; WRAY Raleigh, North Carolina; and WOAC Cleveland, Ohio) to Multicultural Television Broadcasting, LLC for $170 million. Additional stations affiliated with Shop At Home are: WJJA (Milwaukee, Wisconsin), WYLE (Huntsville, Alabama), KSVM-LP (Santa Barbara, California), and WJYS (Chicago, Illinois). The company also operates a web site at shopathometv.com. The company's advertisements and a show host convey information about the merchandise and demonstrate various uses for each product. Shop At Home seeks to differentiate itself from other televised shopping programmers by using an informal, personal style of presentation and by offering unique products. The firm has the studio and broadcasting capability to produce multiple live shows simultaneously, and it occasionally provides multiple broadcasts to differing viewer groups during peak viewing times. Some stations air Jewelry TV in the late morning and early afternoon. Jewelry Television acquired the company for $17 million from E.W Scripps Company in 2006.

The Shop at Home Network offers its employees a 401(k) plan, discounted stock purchase, flexible spending accounts, a pension plan and a credit union.

FINANCIALS: Sales and profits are in thousands of dollars—add 000 to get the full amount. 2006 Note: Financial information for 2006 was not available for all companies at press time.

2006 Sales: $	2006 Profits: $	**U.S. Stock Ticker:** Subsidiary
2005 Sales: $	2005 Profits: $	**Int'l Ticker:** Int'l Exchange:
2004 Sales: $	2004 Profits: $	Employees: 12
2003 Sales: $6,700	2003 Profits: $-2,500	Fiscal Year Ends: 12/31
2002 Sales: $195,800	2002 Profits: $-22,600	Parent Company: JEWELRY TELEVISION

SALARIES/BENEFITS:
Pension Plan:	ESOP Stock Plan:	Profit Sharing:	Top Exec. Salary: $200,000	Bonus: $73,050
Savings Plan: Y	Stock Purch. Plan:		Second Exec. Salary: $176,923	Bonus: $75,000

OTHER THOUGHTS:
Apparent Women Officers or Directors: 2
Hot Spot for Advancement for Women/Minorities:

LOCATIONS: ("Y" = Yes)
West:	Southwest:	Midwest:	Southeast:	Northeast:	International:
Y		Y	Y	Y	

SHUFFLE MASTER INC
www.shufflemaster.com

Industry Group Code: 713290 Ranks within this company's industry group: Sales: 8   Profits: 5

Print Media/Publishing:	Movies:	Equipment/Supplies:		Broadcast/Cable:	Music/Audio:	Sports/Games:
Newspapers:	Movie Theaters:	Equipment/Supplies:		Broadcast TV:	Music Production:	Games/Sports:
Magazines:	Movie Production:	Gambling Equipment:	Y	Cable TV:	Retail Music:	Retail Games Stores:
Books:	TV/Video Production:	Special Services:	Y	Satellite Broadcast:	Retail Audio Equip.:	Stadiums/Teams:
Book Stores:	Video Rental:	Advertising Services:		Radio:	Music Print./Dist.:	Gambling/Casinos:
Distribution/Printing:	Video Distribution:	Info. Sys. Software:		Online Information:	Multimedia:	Rides/Theme Parks:

TYPES OF BUSINESS:

Gaming Machines
Automated Card Shufflers
Table & Video Slot Games
Slot Machine Operating Systems

BRANDS/DIVISIONS/AFFILIATES:

Shuffle Master Gaming
ACE
King
QuickDraw
Deck Mate
Shuffle Up Productions, Inc.
Stargames Limited
Table Master

CONTACTS: *Note: Officers with more than one job title may be intentionally listed here more than once.*

Mark L. Yoseloff, CEO
Paul C. Meyer, COO
Paul C. Meyer, Pres.
Richard L. Baldwin, CFO/Sr. VP
Jerome R. Smith, Sr. VP/General Counsel
R. Brooke Dunn, Sr. VP
Mark L. Yoseloff, Chmn.

Phone: 702-897-7150	**Fax:** 702-897-2284
Toll-Free:	
Address: 1106 Palms Airport Dr., Las Vegas, NV 89119 US	

GROWTH PLANS/SPECIAL FEATURES:

Shuffle Master, Inc. develops, manufactures and markets automatic card shuffling and chip counting equipment as well as table and video slot machine games for use in the gaming industry. The company's shufflers are marketed under the trademarks Shuffle Master Gaming, ACE, King, MD, QuickDraw and Deck Mate. The company also produces table games including Let It Ride, Three Card Poker and Side-Bet Table System. Shuffle Master has acquired a portfolio of game theme licenses such as Let's Make a Deal, The Three Stooges, The Honeymooners, Hollywood, Rubik's Cube and the Marvel Comics library, which it has used to develop and commercialize slot games independently and cooperatively with other licensed manufacturers. The firm has installed approximately 18,600 shufflers and approximately 3,700 table games in gaming facilities. In 2005, the company formed Shuffle Up Productions, Inc. to develop live and broadcast tournament events and merchandise based on the company's gaming offerings. In 2006, Shuffle Master's subsidiary Australasia Pty. Ltd. completed its acquisition of Stargames Limited, an Australian developer, manufacturer and distributor of electronic entertainment gaming products to worldwide markets. Also in 2006, the company entered into an agreement with Sona Mobile Holdings Corp. to license, develop, and distribute WiFi gaming devices usable in casinos. In late 2006, the company entered into an agreement with Cammegh Limited, through its Austrian subsidiary CARD, naming Cammegh Shuffle Master as CARD's exclusive sales agent in the U.K. In addition, the company entered into an agreement obtaining the 'last license' rights to the portfolio of wagering hardware and method patents held by Progressive Gaming International Corporation. In 2006, the company contracted with the Delaware State Lottery to supply 54 units of the company's Table Master gaming platform in the state's three lottery venues.

FINANCIALS: Sales and profits are in thousands of dollars—add 000 to get the full amount. 2006 Note: Financial information for 2006 was not available for all companies at press time.

2006 Sales: $	2006 Profits: $	**U.S. Stock Ticker:** SHFL
2005 Sales: $112,860	2005 Profits: $29,180	**Int'l Ticker:** Int'l Exchange:
2004 Sales: $84,783	2004 Profits: $24,144	Employees: 320
2003 Sales: $67,427	2003 Profits: $16,934	Fiscal Year Ends: 10/31
2002 Sales: $56,100	2002 Profits: $14,000	Parent Company:

SALARIES/BENEFITS:

Pension Plan:	ESOP Stock Plan:	Profit Sharing:	Top Exec. Salary: $411,000	Bonus: $300,000
Savings Plan: Y	Stock Purch. Plan:		Second Exec. Salary: $296,000	Bonus: $162,000

OTHER THOUGHTS:

Apparent Women Officers or Directors:
Hot Spot for Advancement for Women/Minorities:

LOCATIONS: ("Y" = Yes)

West:	Southwest:	Midwest:	Southeast:	Northeast:	International:
Y		Y			Y

SIMEX-IWERKS
www.iwerks.com

Industry Group Code: 512131 Ranks within this company's industry group: Sales: Profits:

Print Media/Publishing:	Movies:		Equipment/Supplies:		Broadcast/Cable:	Music/Audio:	Sports/Games:	
Newspapers:	Movie Theaters:	Y	Equipment/Supplies:	Y	Broadcast TV:	Music Production:	Games/Sports:	
Magazines:	Movie Production:	Y	Gambling Equipment:		Cable TV:	Retail Music:	Retail Games Stores:	
Books:	TV/Video Production:		Special Services:	Y	Satellite Broadcast:	Retail Audio Equip.:	Stadiums/Teams:	
Book Stores:	Video Rental:		Advertising Services:		Radio:	Music Print./Dist.:	Gambling/Casinos:	
Distribution/Printing:	Video Distribution:		Info. Sys. Software:		Online Information:	Multimedia:	Rides/Theme Parks:	Y

TYPES OF BUSINESS:
Movie Theaters-3D
Ride Simulation Theaters
Equipment & Facility Leasing
Format Conversion Services

BRANDS/DIVISIONS/AFFILIATES:
Iwerks Entertainment, Inc.
Simex, Inc.
Extreme Screens

CONTACTS: Note: Officers with more than one job title may be intentionally listed here more than once.
Michael Needham, CEO
Michael Needham, Pres.
David Needham, Sr. VP-Sales
Brian Peebles, Sr. VP-Oper.
Mark Cornell, Sr. Dir.-Attractions Dev.
Shiori Sudo, Exec. VP/Head-Film Distrib.
Mike Frueh, VP & General Mgr.
Michael Needham, Chmn.

Phone: 818-841-7766   Fax: 818-840-6192
Toll-Free: 800-388-8628
Address: 4520 Valerio St., Burbank, CA 91505-1046 US

GROWTH PLANS/SPECIAL FEATURES:
SimEx-Iwerks, formed by the acquisition of Iwerks Entertainment, Inc. by SimEx, Inc., designs, engineers, manufactures, markets and services high-tech entertainment attractions that employ a variety of projection, show control, ride simulation and software technologies. The company sells and installs ride simulation attractions in specialty theaters, large-format theaters and theaters that include special 3-D effects. Its Extreme Screens brand of theatres feature 80 foot tall by 80 foot wide screens and can project 2-D and 3-D pictures. SimEx-Iwerks also licenses and distributes the films in its library to ride simulation and large-format theaters and specialty theater attractions. The company has a catalog of over 150 titles, many available in French, Spanish, Mandarin, Korean, Japanese, Portuguese and German. The firm produces and distributes films in the 8/70 and 15/70 film formats for third parties and also invests in joint ventures by contributing its ride simulation technology, design and equipment and by participating in theater profits. In addition, SimEx-Iwerks leases camera equipment and rents post-production facilities. Recently, the company's equipment was used to create Spiderman II. The primary markets for the company's attractions are theme parks, museums, movie theaters and various types of location-based entertainment centers, destination centers and special event venues. The company produces six different motion-ride simulators ranging from open platforms to enclosed cabins and having seating capacities between six and 90. SimEx-Iwerks has installed more than 250 specialty-format theater attractions in 37 countries, including 119 ride simulation theaters that the company supports with a library of 50 ride simulation films, the industry's largest premium ride simulation film library.

FINANCIALS: Sales and profits are in thousands of dollars—add 000 to get the full amount. 2006 Note: Financial information for 2006 was not available for all companies at press time.
2006 Sales: $	2006 Profits: $	U.S. Stock Ticker: Private
2005 Sales: $	2005 Profits: $	Int'l Ticker: Int'l Exchange:
2004 Sales: $	2004 Profits: $	Employees: 89
2003 Sales: $	2003 Profits: $	Fiscal Year Ends: 6/30
2002 Sales: $	2002 Profits: $	Parent Company:

SALARIES/BENEFITS:
Pension Plan:	ESOP Stock Plan:	Profit Sharing:	Top Exec. Salary: $247,373	Bonus: $
Savings Plan:	Stock Purch. Plan:		Second Exec. Salary: $140,481	Bonus: $

OTHER THOUGHTS:
Apparent Women Officers or Directors: 1
Hot Spot for Advancement for Women/Minorities:

LOCATIONS: ("Y" = Yes)
West:	Southwest:	Midwest:	Southeast:	Northeast:	International:
Y			Y		Y

SIMON & SCHUSTER INC   www.simonsays.com

Industry Group Code: 511130 Ranks within this company's industry group: Sales: Profits:

Print Media/Publishing:		Movies:	Equipment/Supplies:	Broadcast/Cable:	Music/Audio:		Sports/Games:
Newspapers:		Movie Theaters:	Equipment/Supplies:	Broadcast TV:	Music Production:	Y	Games/Sports:
Magazines:		Movie Production:	Gambling Equipment:	Cable TV:	Retail Music:		Retail Games Stores:
Books:	Y	TV/Video Production:	Special Services:	Satellite Broadcast:	Retail Audio Equip.:		Stadiums/Teams:
Book Stores:		Video Rental:	Advertising Services:	Radio:	Music Print./Dist.:	Y	Gambling/Casinos:
Distribution/Printing:		Video Distribution:	Info. Sys. Software:	Online Information:	Multimedia:		Rides/Theme Parks:

TYPES OF BUSINESS:

Book Publishing & Distribution
Online Publishing
E-Books
CDs & CD-ROMs
Audio Books
Children's Publishing

BRANDS/DIVISIONS/AFFILIATES:

CBS Corporation
Fireside
Atria
Free Press (The)
Scribner
Pocket Books
Touchstone
Aladdin

CONTACTS: *Note: Officers with more than one job title may be intentionally listed here more than once.*

Jack Romanos, CEO
Jack Romanos, Pres.
David England, Sr. VP/CFO
Larry Norton, Pres., Sales & Dist. Div.
Mark Zulli, Sr. VP-Human Resources
Anne L. Davies, Sr. VP/CIO
Stephen H. Weitzen, Sr. VP/Publisher-S&S Children's Merch. Div.
Elisa Rivlin, Sr. VP/General Counsel
Joe Bulger, VP-Client Mgmt. & Bus. Dev.
Kate Tentler, Sr. VP-Digital Media
Adam Rothberg, Sr. VP/Dir.-Comm.
Carolyn Reidy, Pres., Adult Publishing Group
Rick Richter, Pres., Children's Publishing Group
Christopher Lynch, Exec. VP/Publisher-Simon & Schuster Audio
Jon Attenborough, Managing Dir.-Simon & Schuster Australia
Ian S. Chapman, Managing Dir.-Simon & Schuster UK
Joe D'Onofrio, Sr. VP-Supply Chain Oper.

Phone: 212-698-7000	**Fax:** 212-698-7099
Toll-Free: 800-223-2336	
Address: 1230 Ave. of the Americas, New York, NY 10020 US	

GROWTH PLANS/SPECIAL FEATURES:

Simon & Schuster, Inc. (S&S), a subsidiary of CBS Corporation, publishes print titles in a wide variety of genres, as well as CDs, CD-ROMs, novelty format books and e-books. The company markets and distributes its own titles as well as many titles from other publishers, such as AAA, Reader's Digest Children's Publishing and Meadowbrook Press. S&S distributes titles in 100 countries around the world through seven main divisions: the adult publishing group, children's publishing, audio, online, U.K., Canada and Australia. The company publishes under imprints including Simon & Schuster, Scribner, Pocket Books, The Free Press, Atria, Fireside, Touchstone, Aladdin and many others. Stephen King, Dr. Phil McGraw, Stephen Ambrose and Bob Dylan have all signed contracts to have books published and marketed through S&S. The company's web site, simonsays.com, which includes sites based in the U.K., Canada and Australia, provides users with a forum to discuss books; newsletters with information on new releases; and an e-books section allowing customers to purchase books online. The Simon & Schuster Audio division publishes audio books including fiction, nonfiction and self-improvement titles, as well as Pimsleur Language Programs. The firm's children's publishing division offers acclaimed backlist titles, including famous characters such as Raggedy Ann, The Hardy Boys, Nancy Drew and Buffy the Vampire Slayer. S&S is a subsidiary of CBS Corporation. Recent news includes the acquisition of Howard Publishing, a Christian and inspirational publishing company.

S&S offers an Associates Program for recent graduates. This one-year program rotates new employees through various departments, offering broad experience in the publishing business. The firm also offers internship positions.

FINANCIALS: Sales and profits are in thousands of dollars—add 000 to get the full amount. 2006 Note: Financial information for 2006 was not available for all companies at press time.

2006 Sales: $	2006 Profits: $	**U.S. Stock Ticker: Subsidiary**
2005 Sales: $	2005 Profits: $	**Int'l Ticker:** Int'l Exchange:
2004 Sales: $796,000	2004 Profits: $	Employees:
2003 Sales: $	2003 Profits: $	Fiscal Year Ends: 12/31
2002 Sales: $	2002 Profits: $	Parent Company: CBS CORPORATION

SALARIES/BENEFITS:

Pension Plan:	ESOP Stock Plan:	Profit Sharing:	Top Exec. Salary: $	Bonus: $
Savings Plan:	Stock Purch. Plan:		Second Exec. Salary: $	Bonus: $

OTHER THOUGHTS:

Apparent Women Officers or Directors: 4
Hot Spot for Advancement for Women/Minorities: Y

LOCATIONS: ("Y" = Yes)

West:	Southwest:	Midwest:	Southeast:	Northeast:	International:
				Y	Y

SINCLAIR BROADCAST GROUP INC

www.sbgi.net

Industry Group Code: 513120 Ranks within this company's industry group: Sales: 13 Profits: 5

Print Media/Publishing:	Movies:	Equipment/Supplies:		Broadcast/Cable:		Music/Audio:	Sports/Games:
Newspapers:	Movie Theaters:	Equipment/Supplies:	Y	Broadcast TV:	Y	Music Production:	Games/Sports:
Magazines:	Movie Production:	Gambling Equipment:		Cable TV:		Retail Music:	Retail Games Stores:
Books:	TV/Video Production:	Special Services:	Y	Satellite Broadcast:		Retail Audio Equip.:	Stadiums/Teams:
Book Stores:	Video Rental:	Advertising Services:	Y	Radio:		Music Print./Dist.:	Gambling/Casinos:
Distribution/Printing:	Video Distribution:	Info. Sys. Software:		Online Information:		Multimedia:	Rides/Theme Parks:

TYPES OF BUSINESS:

Radio & TV Station Owner/Operator
Broadcasting & Programming Services
Internet Development
Web Design & e-Business Services
TV Broadcast Equipment
Venture Capital

BRANDS/DIVISIONS/AFFILIATES:

Sinclair Television Group, Inc.
Sinclair Ventures, Inc.
VisionAIR, Inc.
G1440 Holdings, Inc.
Acrodyne Communications, Inc.
AppForge, Inc.
Jadoo Power Systems
Sterling Venture Partners

CONTACTS: Note: Officers with more than one job title may be intentionally listed here more than once.

David D. Smith, CEO
Steven M. Marks, COO
David D. Smith, Pres.
David B. Amy, CFO/Exec. VP
Darren Shapiro, VP-Sales
Donald H. Thompson, VP-Human Resources
Nat S. Ostroff, VP-New Technology
Delbert R. Parks, III, VP-Eng.
Barry M. Faber, General Counsel/VP
Delbert R. Parks, III, VP-Oper.
Mark E. Hyman, VP-Corp. Rel.
Lucy A. Rutishauser, VP-Corp. Finance/Treas.
Frederick G. Smith, VP
David R. Bochenek, VP-Chief Acct. Officer
Gregg Siegel, VP-Nat'l Sales
Jeff Sleete, VP-Mktg.
David D. Smith, Chmn.

Phone: 410-568-1500	**Fax:** 410-568-1533

Toll-Free: 888-881-4447

Address: 10706 Beaver Dam Rd., Hunt Valley, MD 21030 US

GROWTH PLANS/SPECIAL FEATURES:

Sinclair Broadcast Group, Inc. owns, operates, programs and provides sales services to 60 television and radio stations in 37 markets. It reaches roughly 22% of American households, concentrated primarily in the Midwest and the Northeast. Subsidiary Sinclair Television Group, Inc. controls most of the company's broadcast assets, including its television groups (20 FOX, 17 MyTV, 10 ABC, 9 CW, 2 CBS affiliates and 2 independent stations). The company has a local news network of 36 stations that share a central news network. Through its Sinclair Ventures, Inc. subsidiary, the firm owns equity interests in several Internet-based companies (such as VisionAIR, Inc.) which design, develop and market public safety software as well as wireless and web-based enterprise applications. The firm owns almost 94% of G1440 Holdings, Inc., which provides e-business solutions including web design, web hosting and e-commerce applications. The company also owns 82% of Acrodyne Communications, Inc., a leading producer of high-quality television transmitters and television broadcast equipment. In addition, the firm owns equity interests in Jadoo Power Systems, Time Domain, Inc. and AppForge, Inc.; as well as in Sterling Venture Partners, a venture capital firm; and Allegiance Capital, LP, a private mezzanine venture capital fund. In 2006, the firm renewed its affiliation agreement with FOX Broadcasting Company for six years. Also in 2006, the company partnered with The Tube Music Network In order to distribute The Tube in digital multicasting to 28 new markets. Through this partnership, viewers will be able to access The Tube Network for free via television sets equipped with digital tuners. Recently, the firm sold its WEMT-TV (FOX 30 in the Tri-Cities market of Bristol, Virginia and Bristol, Johnson City and Kingsport, Tennessee) to Aurora Broadcasting for $7.0 million.

Sinclair offers its employees insurance plans, flexible spending accounts and educational reimbursement.

FINANCIALS: Sales and profits are in thousands of dollars—add 000 to get the full amount. 2006 Note: Financial information for 2006 was not available for all companies at press time.

2006 Sales: $	2006 Profits: $	**U.S. Stock Ticker: SBGI**
2005 Sales: $692,067	2005 Profits: $187,310	**Int'l Ticker:** Int'l Exchange:
2004 Sales: $708,279	2004 Profits: $24,022	Employees: 2,862
2003 Sales: $738,741	2003 Profits: $24,392	Fiscal Year Ends: 12/31
2002 Sales: $731,400	2002 Profits: $-564,400	Parent Company:

SALARIES/BENEFITS:

Pension Plan:	ESOP Stock Plan: Y	Profit Sharing:	Top Exec. Salary: $1,000,000	Bonus: $
Savings Plan: Y	Stock Purch. Plan: Y		Second Exec. Salary: $633,000	Bonus: $74,509

OTHER THOUGHTS:

Apparent Women Officers or Directors: 1
Hot Spot for Advancement for Women/Minorities:

LOCATIONS: ("Y" = Yes)

West:	Southwest:	Midwest:	Southeast:	Northeast:	International:
Y	Y	Y	Y	Y	

Note: Financial information, benefits and other data can change quickly and may vary from those stated here.

SIRIUS SATELLITE RADIO

www.siriusradio.com

Industry Group Code: 513111A Ranks within this company's industry group: Sales: 2 Profits: 2

Print Media/Publishing:	Movies:	Equipment/Supplies:	Broadcast/Cable:	Music/Audio:	Sports/Games:
Newspapers:	Movie Theaters:	Equipment/Supplies:	Broadcast TV:	Music Production:	Games/Sports:
Magazines:	Movie Production:	Gambling Equipment:	Cable TV:	Retail Music:	Retail Games Stores:
Books:	TV/Video Production:	Special Services:	Satellite Broadcast:	Retail Audio Equip.:	Stadiums/Teams:
Book Stores:	Video Rental:	Advertising Services:	Radio:	Music Print./Dist.:	Gambling/Casinos:
Distribution/Printing:	Video Distribution:	Info. Sys. Software:	Online Information:	Multimedia:	Rides/Theme Parks:

TYPES OF BUSINESS:

Satellite Radio Broadcasting

BRANDS/DIVISIONS/AFFILIATES:

CD Radio, Inc.
Martha Stewart Radio
Sirius Canada

CONTACTS: Note: Officers with more than one job title may be intentionally listed here more than once.

Mel Karmazin, CEO
David Frear, Exec. VP/CFO
John Schultz, Sr. VP-Human Resources
Patrick Donnelly, Exec. VP/General Counsel
James Meyer, Pres.-Oper. & Sales
Scott Greenstein, Pres., Entertainment & Sports
Joseph Clayton, Chmn.

Phone: 212-899-5000	**Fax:** 212-584-5200
Toll-Free: 888-539-7474	
Address: 1221 Ave. of the Americas, 36th Fl., New York, NY 10020 US	

GROWTH PLANS/SPECIAL FEATURES:

Sirius Satellite Radio, Inc. owns and operates a subscription-based satellite radio service featuring digital audio music and news. The company's three satellites broadcast 67 channels of commercial-free music and 64 channels of news, sports, weather, comedy, talk, public radio and children's programming. Sirius broadcasts content from other networks, such as CNN, NPR, BBC, FOX, The Weather Channel, E!, ESPN and The Discovery Channel, as well as its own original programming. As of the beginning of 2007, Sirius had 6 million subscribers. The firm has entered into agreements with consumer electronics manufacturers, including Kenwood Corporation, Sony Electronics and Visteon Automotive Systems, to market Sirius receivers for use in cars, boats and homes. Its receivers are now available at over 25,000 national and regional retailers including Best Buy and Circuit City. Small business owners can use the company's service in a commercial environment without paying royalty fees, since Sirius negotiates and pays these fees on behalf of its customers. Sirius has partnerships with manufacturers and retailers to make its hardware available as an option for car buyers, and thus far, has factory-installed its systems in 89 vehicle models. In 2005, Sirius Canada, a Canadian subsidiary corporation, along with Canadian Broadcasting Corporation and Standard Broadcasting Corporation, received a license from the Canadian Radio-Television and Telecommunications Commission (CRTC) to offer a satellite radio service in Canada. Sirius Canada has launched service in Canada with 100 channels of commercial-free music, news, sports, talk and entertainment programming, including 10 channels of Canadian content.

Sirius offers its full time employees a comprehensive benefits package. The company also offers unpaid internships for college students to earn credit.

FINANCIALS: Sales and profits are in thousands of dollars—add 000 to get the full amount. 2006 Note: Financial information for 2006 was not available for all companies at press time.

2006 Sales: $	2006 Profits: $	**U.S. Stock Ticker:** SIRI
2005 Sales: $242,245	2005 Profits: $-862,997	**Int'l Ticker:** Int'l Exchange:
2004 Sales: $66,854	2004 Profits: $-712,162	Employees: 614
2003 Sales: $12,872	2003 Profits: $-226,215	Fiscal Year Ends: 12/31
2002 Sales: $ 800	2002 Profits: $-422,500	Parent Company:

SALARIES/BENEFITS:

Pension Plan:	ESOP Stock Plan:	Profit Sharing:	Top Exec. Salary: $1,250,000	Bonus: $2,200,000
Savings Plan: Y	Stock Purch. Plan: Y		Second Exec. Salary: $602,831	Bonus: $700,000

OTHER THOUGHTS:

Apparent Women Officers or Directors: 3
Hot Spot for Advancement for Women/Minorities: Y

LOCATIONS: ("Y" = Yes)

West:	Southwest:	Midwest:	Southeast:	Northeast:	International:
				Y	

SIX FLAGS INC

www.sixflags.com

Industry Group Code: 713110 Ranks within this company's industry group: Sales: 2 Profits: 2

Print Media/Publishing:	Movies:	Equipment/Supplies:	Broadcast/Cable:	Music/Audio:	Sports/Games:	
Newspapers:	Movie Theaters:	Equipment/Supplies:	Broadcast TV:	Music Production:	Games/Sports:	
Magazines:	Movie Production:	Gambling Equipment:	Cable TV:	Retail Music:	Retail Games Stores:	
Books:	TV/Video Production:	Special Services:	Satellite Broadcast:	Retail Audio Equip.:	Stadiums/Teams:	
Book Stores:	Video Rental:	Advertising Services:	Radio:	Music Print./Dist.:	Gambling/Casinos:	Y
Distribution/Printing:	Video Distribution:	Info. Sys. Software:	Online Information:	Multimedia:	Rides/Theme Parks:	

TYPES OF BUSINESS:

Theme Parks

BRANDS/DIVISIONS/AFFILIATES:

Marine World
Six Flags Wild Safari
Six Flags Great Adventure
Magic Mountain
Hurricane Harbor
Six Flags Over Texas
Frontier City
Kingda Ka

CONTACTS: Note: Officers with more than one job title may be intentionally listed here more than once.

Mark Shapiro, CEO
Mark Shapiro, Pres.
Jeff Speed, CFO
John E. Bement, Exec. VP-Retail
James M. Coughlin, General Counsel
Mark Quenzel, VP-Park Strategy
Brian Jenkins, Sr. VP-Finance
Mike Antinoro, Exec. VP-Entertainment and Mktg.
Lou Koskovolis, Exec. VP-Corp. Alliances
Andrew Schleimer, Exec. VP-In-Park Svcs.
Daniel Snyder, Chmn.

Phone: 405-475-2500	Fax: 405-475-2555
Toll-Free:	
Address: 11501 Northeast Expy., Oklahoma City, OK 73131 US	

GROWTH PLANS/SPECIAL FEATURES:

Six Flags, Inc. is the largest regional theme park operator in the world, with 30 parks in operation in North America and a yearly attendance of about 35 million. The firm's parks include 14 of the 50 most highly attended theme parks in North America and the largest paid-admission theme park in Mexico. Six Flags parks serve 9 of the 10 largest metropolitan areas in the U.S., and offer families a selection of state-of-the-art thrill rides, water attractions, themed areas, concerts and shows, restaurants, game venues and merchandise outlets. The company offers more than 1,100 rides, including over 130 roller coasters. The company's theme parks include Six Flags Marine World (in California), which features marine mammals and exotic land animals; Six Flags Wild Safari (New Jersey), a 350 acre drive-through safari; and Six Flags Great Adventure (New Jersey), the firm's largest park and the 21st largest theme park in North America. The company holds exclusive long-term licenses for theme park usage of Warner Bros. and DC Comics characters, including Bugs Bunny, Daffy Duck, Batman and Superman. In 2005, the company opened Hurricane Harbor, a Caribbean-themed water park adjacent to the Six Flags Great America park in the Chicago area; and the Kingda Ka roller coaster in the Six Flags Great Adventure park. The ride currently holds the record for tallest and fastest roller coaster in the world, at 456 feet high and attaining 128 mph. During the course of 2006, the company sold its Oklahoma City theme park, as well as its AstroWorld park in Houston.

Six Flags offers seasonal employment targeted especially to international student workers and provides accommodations and transportation (where necessary) at all of it parks. Additional benefits include free park tickets, discounts at park stores, site-seeing trips, employee parties and a flexible work schedule.

FINANCIALS: Sales and profits are in thousands of dollars—add 000 to get the full amount. 2006 Note: Financial information for 2006 was not available for all companies at press time.

2006 Sales: $	2006 Profits: $	U.S. Stock Ticker: SIX
2005 Sales: $1,089,682	2005 Profits: $-110,938	Int'l Ticker: Int'l Exchange:
2004 Sales: $998,590	2004 Profits: $-464,800	Employees: 34,000
2003 Sales: $1,007,276	2003 Profits: $-61,700	Fiscal Year Ends: 12/31
2002 Sales: $1,037,900	2002 Profits: $-105,700	Parent Company:

SALARIES/BENEFITS:

Pension Plan: Y	ESOP Stock Plan:	Profit Sharing:	Top Exec. Salary: $1,118,654	Bonus: $2,334,000
Savings Plan: Y	Stock Purch. Plan:		Second Exec. Salary: $800,000	Bonus: $1,808,988

OTHER THOUGHTS:

Apparent Women Officers or Directors:
Hot Spot for Advancement for Women/Minorities:

LOCATIONS: ("Y" = Yes)

West:	Southwest:	Midwest:	Southeast:	Northeast:	International:
Y	Y	Y	Y	Y	Y

Note: Financial information, benefits and other data can change quickly and may vary from those stated here.

SKY NETWORK TELEVISION LIMITED   www.sky.co.nz

Industry Group Code: 513220 Ranks within this company's industry group: Sales: 19   Profits: 13

Print Media/Publishing:	Movies:	Equipment/Supplies:	Broadcast/Cable:		Music/Audio:	Sports/Games:
Newspapers:	Movie Theaters:	Equipment/Supplies:	Broadcast TV:	Y	Music Production:	Games/Sports:
Magazines:	Movie Production:	Gambling Equipment:	Cable TV:	Y	Retail Music:	Retail Games Stores:
Books:	TV/Video Production:	Special Services:	Y	Satellite Broadcast:	Retail Audio Equip.:	Stadiums/Teams:
Book Stores:	Video Rental:	Advertising Services:	Radio:		Music Print./Dist.:	Gambling/Casinos:	Y
Distribution/Printing:	Video Distribution:	Info. Sys. Software:	Online Information:		Multimedia:	Rides/Theme Parks:

TYPES OF BUSINESS:
Satellite TV
Broadcast TV
Pay Per View TV
Rugby Team
Radio Stations
Online Movie Rentals
Gambling Services

BRANDS/DIVISIONS/AFFILIATES:
SkyBet Trackside
SkyBet Sport
Independent Newspapers Limited
News Corporation

CONTACTS: *Note: Officers with more than one job title may be intentionally listed here more than once.*
John Fellet, CEO
Jason Hollingworth, CFO
Mike Watson, Dir.-Mktg.
Charles Ingley, Dir.-Tech.
Brian Green, Dir.-Eng.
Martin Wrigley, Mgr.-Oper.
Tony O'Brien, Dir.-Comm.
John Simmons, General Mgr.
Kevin Cameron, Dir.-Sport
Travis Dunbar, Dir.-Movies & Entertainment
Richard Last, Dir.-Advertising
Peter Macourt, Chmn.

Phone: 64-9-579-9999	**Fax:** 64-9-525-8324
Toll-Free:	
Address: 10 Panorama Rd., Mt. Wellington, Auckland, New Zealand	

GROWTH PLANS/SPECIAL FEATURES:
SKY Network Television Limited is the largest provider of pay-television services in New Zealand. SKY offers a range of sports, movies, music, on-demand and general content across more than 80 channels. SKY's channel line-up includes six sports channels, five movie channels, five general entertainment channels, four documentary channels, three news channels, three children's channels and other niche channels. In addition to television channels, SKY offers digital music channels and its SkyBet Trackside and SkyBet Sport services through which subscribers can place wagers on horse races and other sporting events through their cable receiver. SKY has a total subscriber base of over 667,000. The firm offers digital and UHF services. The UHF package includes four channels, which require a decoder rented from the company to view. The firm's digital services offer over 40 satellite channels available in a variety of packages. The company also owns the rights to broadcast international rugby in New Zealand, a lucrative market and a significant incentive for customers to subscribe. In 2005, SKY merged with its major shareholder, Independent Newspapers Limited to form MergeCo, which was later renamed SKY Network Television Limited. News Corporation owns 44% of the company. In 2006, SKY purchased the television broadcasting business of Prime Television New Zealand, Ltd.

FINANCIALS: Sales and profits are in thousands of dollars—add 000 to get the full amount. 2006 Note: Financial information for 2006 was not available for all companies at press time.

2006 Sales: $383,840	2006 Profits: $42,090	**U.S. Stock Ticker:**
2005 Sales: $347,306	2005 Profits: $56,002	**Int'l Ticker: SKT** Int'l Exchange: Wellington-NZX
2004 Sales: $278,200	2004 Profits: $22,300	Employees: 600
2003 Sales: $227,700	2003 Profits: $ 400	Fiscal Year Ends: 6/30
2002 Sales: $167,700	2002 Profits: $-14,700	Parent Company:

SALARIES/BENEFITS:
Pension Plan:	ESOP Stock Plan:	Profit Sharing:	Top Exec. Salary: $	Bonus: $
Savings Plan:	Stock Purch. Plan:		Second Exec. Salary: $	Bonus: $

OTHER THOUGHTS:
Apparent Women Officers or Directors:
Hot Spot for Advancement for Women/Minorities:

LOCATIONS: ("Y" = Yes)
West:	Southwest:	Midwest:	Southeast:	Northeast:	International: Y

Note: Financial information, benefits and other data can change quickly and may vary from those stated here.

SONY BMG MUSIC ENTERTAINMENT   www.sonybmg.com

Industry Group Code: 512230 Ranks within this company's industry group: Sales: 3   Profits:

Print Media/Publishing:	Movies:	Equipment/Supplies:	Broadcast/Cable:	Music/Audio:		Sports/Games:	
Newspapers:	Movie Theaters:	Equipment/Supplies:	Broadcast TV:	Music Production:	Y	Games/Sports:	
Magazines:	Movie Production:	Gambling Equipment:	Cable TV:	Retail Music:		Retail Games Stores:	
Books:	TV/Video Production:	Special Services:	Satellite Broadcast:	Retail Audio Equip.:		Stadiums/Teams:	
Book Stores:	Video Rental:	Advertising Services:	Radio:	Music Print./Dist.:		Gambling/Casinos:	
Distribution/Printing:	Video Distribution:	Info. Sys. Software:	Online Information:	Multimedia:		Rides/Theme Parks:	

TYPES OF BUSINESS:

Recorded Music Production
Record Labels

BRANDS/DIVISIONS/AFFILIATES:

Sony Music Entertainment
BMG Entertainment
Sony Corporation of America
Bertelsmann
Arista Records
Columbia Records
RCA Victor Group
Jive Records

CONTACTS: Note: Officers with more than one job title may be intentionally listed here more than once.

Rolf Schmidt-Holtz, CEO
Tim Bowen, COO
Kevin Kelleher, Exec. VP/CFO
Andrew Lack, Chmn.

Phone: 212-930-4000	Fax: 212-930-4862
Toll-Free:	
Address: 1540 Broadway, 43rd Fl., New York, NY 10036 US	

GROWTH PLANS/SPECIAL FEATURES:

Sony BMG Music Entertainment, formed in 2004 through the merger of Sony Music Entertainment and BMG Entertainment, is an international record label owner and operator. Sony Corporation of America and Bertelsmann own equal shares of the company. Sony BMG has offices in Argentina, Australia, Austria, Belgium, Brazil, Canada, Chile, China, Costa Rica, Czech Republic, Denmark, Finland, France, Germany, Greece, Hong Kong, Hungary, India, Indonesia, Ireland, Italy, Japan, Korea, Malaysia, Mexico, the Netherlands, New Zealand, Norway, the Philippines, Poland, Portugal, Russia, Singapore, South Africa, Spain, Sweden, Switzerland, Taiwan, Thailand, Turkey, the United Arab Emirates, the U.K. and the U.S. Company record labels include Arista Records, Columbia Records, Epic Records, J Records, Jive Records, LaFace Records, Legacy Recordings, Provident Music Group, RCA Records, RCA Victor Group, RLG Nashville, SONY BMG Masterworks, Sony Music Nashville, Sony Urban Music, Sony Wonder, So So Def Records and Verity Records. Artists that are featured under these labels include Buddy Guy, Foo Fighters, Jars of Clay, Britney Spears and Justin Timberlake.

FINANCIALS: Sales and profits are in thousands of dollars—add 000 to get the full amount. 2006 Note: Financial information for 2006 was not available for all companies at press time.

2006 Sales: $	2006 Profits: $	**U.S. Stock Ticker: Joint Venture**
2005 Sales: $5,000,000	2005 Profits: $	**Int'l Ticker:** Int'l Exchange:
2004 Sales: $	2004 Profits: $	Employees: 10,000
2003 Sales: $	2003 Profits: $	Fiscal Year Ends: 3/31
2002 Sales: $	2002 Profits: $	Parent Company:

SALARIES/BENEFITS:

Pension Plan:	ESOP Stock Plan:	Profit Sharing:	Top Exec. Salary: $	Bonus: $
Savings Plan:	Stock Purch. Plan:		Second Exec. Salary: $	Bonus: $

OTHER THOUGHTS:

Apparent Women Officers or Directors:
Hot Spot for Advancement for Women/Minorities:

LOCATIONS: ("Y" = Yes)

West:	Southwest:	Midwest:	Southeast:	Northeast:	International:
				Y	Y

Note: Financial information, benefits and other data can change quickly and may vary from those stated here.

SONY CORPORATION

www.sony.net

Industry Group Code: 334310 Ranks within this company's industry group: Sales: 2   Profits: 2

Print Media/Publishing:	Movies:		Equipment/Supplies:		Broadcast/Cable:	Music/Audio:		Sports/Games:	
Newspapers:	Movie Theaters:	Y	Equipment/Supplies:	Y	Broadcast TV:	Music Production:	Y	Games/Sports:	Y
Magazines:	Movie Production:	Y	Gambling Equipment:		Cable TV:	Retail Music:		Retail Games Stores:	
Books:	TV/Video Production:	Y	Special Services:	Y	Satellite Broadcast:	Retail Audio Equip.:	Y	Stadiums/Teams:	
Book Stores:	Video Rental:		Advertising Services:	Y	Radio:	Music Print./Dist.:		Gambling/Casinos:	
Distribution/Printing:	Video Distribution:		Info. Sys. Software:		Online Information:	Multimedia:		Rides/Theme Parks:	

TYPES OF BUSINESS:

Consumer Electronics Manufacturer
Film & Television Production
Music Production
Personal Computers
Semiconductors
Technology Research
Video Games
Financial Services, Banking & Insurance

BRANDS/DIVISIONS/AFFILIATES:

PlayStation
Epic Records
Columbia TriStar
Sony Music Entertainment
Sony BMG
Sony Financial Holdings
Columbia Music
Sony Pictures Entertainment

CONTACTS: Note: Officers with more than one job title may be intentionally listed here more than once.

Howard Stringer, CEO
Ryoji Chubachi, Pres.
Nobuyuki Oneda, CFO/Exec. VP
Keiji Kimura, Exec. VP- Tech. Strategies/Pres., Tech. Dev. Group
Nicole Seligman, Exec. VP/General Counsel
Yutaka Nakagawa, Exec. Dep. Pres., Semiconductor & Component Group
Ryoji Chubachi, CEO-Electronics
Katsumi Ihara, Exec. Deputy Pres., Consumer Products Group
Howard Stringer, Chmn.

Phone: 81-3-5448-2111	Fax: 81-3-5448-2244
Toll-Free:	
Address: 6-7-35 Kitashinagawa, Shinagawa-ku, Tokyo, 141-0001 Japan	

GROWTH PLANS/SPECIAL FEATURES:

Sony Corporation, among the largest consumer electronics firms worldwide, produces consumer and industrial electronic products and entertainment. The company has five business segments: electronics, games, music, movies, personal solutions and financial holdings. Sony's Retail Division, Sony Style, branded Maison Sony in Quebec, currently operates over 70 retail stores in Canada and 13 Sony Outlet stores in the U.S. The electronics segment produces computers, cameras, camcorders, MP3 players, cell phones, DVD players, PDAs and televisions. The games section manufactures, markets and publishes Sony PlayStation 1 and 2 and associated software. Sony Pictures Entertainment operations include movie production and distribution in 67 countries, television programming, home video acquisition and distribution and operation of studio facilities. Sony Pictures operates Columbia TriStar, Columbia Pictures, Sony Pictures Classics and Columbia TriStar Home Entertainment. Sony's television segment produces or distributes around 60 programs worldwide. The company's music segment produces and distributes music through Sony BMG, a joint venture with Bertelsmann AG. Sony BMG releases music under various record labels, including Columbia Records, Epic Records and RCA Records. Sony's Financial Holdings subsidiary is based in Japan and is involved in life insurance, banking and brokerage. It generates around one-third of the Sony group's total profits. Sony has plans to promote company synergy by focusing more on fusing electronics with Sony's music, films and game products. In 2006, Sony released its latest Blu-ray recorder, BRAVIA flat TVs, HD camcorder HANDYCAM, personal computer VAIO and digital SLR camera. The company also exhibited Location Free in 2006, a product that allows customers to enjoy content while outside of their living rooms. In other news, Sony's anticipated PlayStation 3 was released in November 2006.

FINANCIALS: Sales and profits are in thousands of dollars—add 000 to get the full amount. 2006 Note: Financial information for 2006 was not available for all companies at press time.

2006 Sales: $56,701,100	2006 Profits: $1,047,270	**U.S. Stock Ticker: SNE**
2005 Sales: $66,912,000	2005 Profits: $1,531,000	**Int'l Ticker: 6758** Int'l Exchange: Tokyo-TSE
2004 Sales: $71,215,714	2004 Profits: $840,854	Employees: 158,500
2003 Sales: $63,264,000	2003 Profits: $978,000	Fiscal Year Ends: 3/31
2002 Sales: $57,117,000	2002 Profits: $115,000	Parent Company:

SALARIES/BENEFITS:

Pension Plan: Y	ESOP Stock Plan:	Profit Sharing:	Top Exec. Salary: $	Bonus: $
Savings Plan:	Stock Purch. Plan:		Second Exec. Salary: $	Bonus: $

OTHER THOUGHTS:

Apparent Women Officers or Directors: 1
Hot Spot for Advancement for Women/Minorities: Y

LOCATIONS: ("Y" = Yes)

West:	Southwest:	Midwest:	Southeast:	Northeast:	International:
Y	Y	Y	Y	Y	Y

Note: Financial information, benefits and other data can change quickly and may vary from those stated here.

SONY PICTURES ENTERTAINMENT   www.spe.sony.com

Industry Group Code: 512110 Ranks within this company's industry group: Sales: 4   Profits:

Print Media/Publishing:	Movies:		Equipment/Supplies:		Broadcast/Cable:	Music/Audio:	Sports/Games:	
Newspapers:	Movie Theaters:		Equipment/Supplies:		Broadcast TV:	Music Production:	Games/Sports:	Y
Magazines:	Movie Production:	Y	Gambling Equipment:		Cable TV:	Retail Music:	Retail Games Stores:	
Books:	TV/Video Production:	Y	Special Services:	Y	Satellite Broadcast:	Retail Audio Equip.:	Stadiums/Teams:	
Book Stores:	Video Rental:		Advertising Services:	Y	Radio:	Music Print./Dist.:	Gambling/Casinos:	
Distribution/Printing:	Video Distribution:		Info. Sys. Software:		Online Information:	Multimedia:	Rides/Theme Parks:	

TYPES OF BUSINESS:

Film Production & Distribution
Television Production & Distribution
Video Distribution
Film & TV Merchandising & Licensing
Digital Animation & Visual Effects
Online Games

BRANDS/DIVISIONS/AFFILIATES:

Sony Corporation of America
Sony Pictures Classics
Columbia TriStar Motion Picture Group
Columbia Pictures
Sony Pictures Home Entertainment
Sony Pictures Television
Sony Pictures Digital
Sony Pictures Studios

CONTACTS: *Note: Officers with more than one job title may be intentionally listed here more than once.*

Michael Lynton, CEO
Bob Osher, COO
David Hendler, CFO/Exec. VP
Mitch Singer, CTO
Beth Berke, Chief Admin. Officer/Sr. Exec VP
Leah Weil, General Counsel/Exec. VP
John Calkins, Sr. VP-Corp. Dev.
Ron McNair, Sr. VP-Finance & Acct.
Amy Pascal, Co-Chmn./Chmn.-Motion Picture Group
Jeff Blake, Vice Chmn./Chmn.-Worldwide Mktg. Columbia TriStar
Yadir Landau, Vice Chmn./Pres.-Sony Pictures Digital
Michael Lynton, Chmn.

Phone: 310-244-4000	**Fax:** 310-244-2626
Toll-Free:	
Address: 10202 W. Washington Blvd., Culver City, CA 90232 US	

GROWTH PLANS/SPECIAL FEATURES:

Sony Pictures Entertainment (SPE) is the media and entertainment subsidiary of Sony Corporation of America, the U.S. branch of Tokyo-based Sony Corporation. The company produces motion pictures through Columbia TriStar Motion Picture Group, which releases approximately 22 films per year. Columbia TriStar produces and distributes movies under four labels: Columbia Pictures, which produces wide-release movies; Sony Pictures Classics, which acquires, markets and distributes prestigious foreign and American independent films; Screen Gems, which produces lower-budget films than Columbia Pictures; and TriStar Pictures, a marketing and acquisition unit focused on genre films. TriStar owns a library of more than 3,500 films. The company releases its films through two subsidiaries: Sony Pictures Releasing (U.S.) and Sony Pictures Releasing International. Combined they are responsible for the sale, distribution and marketing of all SPE films in 67 countries. Sony Pictures Home Entertainment distributes over 2,500 of the firm's own and acquired third-party movies on DVD and VHS. Sony Pictures Television Group currently produces and distributes approximately 60 programs worldwide and grants licensing rights to its library of television programs and motion pictures to U.S. network affiliates and independent stations through Sony Pictures Television and internationally through Sony Pictures Television International. Sony Pictures Consumer Products manages the licensing and merchandising opportunities for the firm's films and television programs. Sony Pictures Digital oversees Sony Pictures Animation (a computer-generated film company), Sony Pictures Imageworks (a digital animation and visual effects company) and Sony Online Entertainment (an online game developer). Sony Pictures Studios features 22 sound stages and post-production facilities. In 2006, SPE acquired Grouper, an online video sharing community. Additionally, it launched Monumental Pictures in conjunction with the Patton Media Group in order to produce and distribute Russian language films in Russia, the Commonwealth of Independent States and Mongolia.

FINANCIALS: Sales and profits are in thousands of dollars—add 000 to get the full amount. 2006 Note: Financial information for 2006 was not available for all companies at press time.

2006 Sales: $	2006 Profits: $	**U.S. Stock Ticker: Subsidiary**
2005 Sales: $6,857,000	2005 Profits: $	**Int'l Ticker:** Int'l Exchange:
2004 Sales: $	2004 Profits: $	Employees: 5,700
2003 Sales: $6,700,000	2003 Profits: $	Fiscal Year Ends: 3/31
2002 Sales: $4,781,000	2002 Profits: $	Parent Company: SONY CORPORATION

SALARIES/BENEFITS:

Pension Plan:	ESOP Stock Plan:	Profit Sharing:	Top Exec. Salary: $	Bonus: $
Savings Plan:	Stock Purch. Plan:		Second Exec. Salary: $	Bonus: $

OTHER THOUGHTS:

Apparent Women Officers or Directors: 3
Hot Spot for Advancement for Women/Minorities: Y

LOCATIONS: ("Y" = Yes)

West:	Southwest:	Midwest:	Southeast:	Northeast:	International:
Y					Y

Note: Financial information, benefits and other data can change quickly and may vary from those stated here.

SPANISH BROADCASTING SYSTEM INC
www.spanishbroadcasting.com

Industry Group Code: 513111 Ranks within this company's industry group: Sales: 11 Profits: 11

Print Media/Publishing:	Movies:	Equipment/Supplies:	Broadcast/Cable:		Music/Audio:	Sports/Games:
Newspapers:	Movie Theaters:	Equipment/Supplies:	Broadcast TV:	Y	Music Production:	Games/Sports:
Magazines:	Movie Production:	Gambling Equipment:	Cable TV:		Retail Music:	Retail Games Stores:
Books:	TV/Video Production:	Special Services:	Satellite Broadcast:		Retail Audio Equip.:	Stadiums/Teams:
Book Stores:	Video Rental:	Advertising Services:	Radio:		Music Print./Dist.:	Gambling/Casinos:
Distribution/Printing:	Video Distribution:	Info. Sys. Software:	Online Information:		Multimedia:	Rides/Theme Parks:

TYPES OF BUSINESS:
Radio Broadcasting
Spanish-Language Radio
Television Broadcasting
Online News & Entertainment

BRANDS/DIVISIONS/AFFILIATES:
LaMusica.com
Mega TV

CONTACTS: Note: Officers with more than one job title may be intentionally listed here more than once.
Raul Alarcon, Jr., CEO
Marko Radlovic, COO/Exec. VP
Raul Alarcon, Jr., Pres.
Joseph A. Garcia, CFO/Exec. VP
Joseph A. Garcia, Corp. Sec.
William Tanner, VP/Dir.-Programming
Cynthia Hudson-Fernandez, Chief Creative Officer
Raul Alarcon, Jr., Chmn.

Phone: 305-441-6901 **Fax:** 305-446-5148
Toll-Free:
Address: 2601 S. Bayshore Dr., PH2, Coconut Grove, FL 33133 US

GROWTH PLANS/SPECIAL FEATURES:
Spanish Broadcasting System, Inc. (SBS) owns and operates 20 radio stations located in massive Spanish-speaking markets, including the top five Hispanic markets in the U.S.: Los Angeles, New York, Puerto Rico, Miami and Chicago. The company is the largest Hispanic radio broadcasting company in the U.S., and recently began expanding into the broadcast television realm with the purchase of Mega TV, based in South Florida. The company also offers Latin music, entertainment, news and cultural content via its bilingual LaMusica.com website. The company's radio stations broadcast a variety of Hispanic programs from news to traditional to contemporary music. Due to the cultural diversity of the Hispanic population from region to region in the U.S., most decisions regarding day-to-day programming, sales and promotional efforts are made by local managers. This approach improves flexibility and responsiveness to changing conditions in each of the firm's markets.

FINANCIALS: Sales and profits are in thousands of dollars—add 000 to get the full amount. 2006 Note: Financial information for 2006 was not available for all companies at press time.

2006 Sales: $	2006 Profits: $	**U.S. Stock Ticker: SBSA**
2005 Sales: $169,832	2005 Profits: $-35,270	**Int'l Ticker:** Int'l Exchange:
2004 Sales: $156,443	2004 Profits: $28,018	Employees: 656
2003 Sales: $135,266	2003 Profits: $-8,750	Fiscal Year Ends: 12/31
2002 Sales: $135,688	2002 Profits: $-89,846	Parent Company:

SALARIES/BENEFITS:

Pension Plan:	ESOP Stock Plan:	Profit Sharing:	Top Exec. Salary: $1,226,888	Bonus: $710,183
Savings Plan: Y	Stock Purch. Plan:		Second Exec. Salary: $617,540	Bonus: $446,500

OTHER THOUGHTS:
Apparent Women Officers or Directors: 1
Hot Spot for Advancement for Women/Minorities:

LOCATIONS: ("Y" = Yes)

West:	Southwest:	Midwest:	Southeast:	Northeast:	International:
Y	Y	Y	Y	Y	Y

SRS LABS INC

www.srslabs.com

Industry Group Code: 334310 Ranks within this company's industry group: Sales: 15   Profits: 10

Print Media/Publishing:	Movies:	Equipment/Supplies:		Broadcast/Cable:	Music/Audio:	Sports/Games:
Newspapers:	Movie Theaters:	Equipment/Supplies:	Y	Broadcast TV:	Music Production:	Games/Sports:
Magazines:	Movie Production:	Gambling Equipment:		Cable TV:	Retail Music:	Retail Games Stores:
Books:	TV/Video Production:	Special Services:	Y	Satellite Broadcast:	Retail Audio Equip.:	Stadiums/Teams:
Book Stores:	Video Rental:	Advertising Services:		Radio:	Music Print./Dist.:	Gambling/Casinos:
Distribution/Printing:	Video Distribution:	Info. Sys. Software:		Online Information:	Multimedia:	Rides/Theme Parks:

TYPES OF BUSINESS:

Audio & Video Equipment Technology
Integrated Circuits
Audio Processing Systems
Technology Licensing

BRANDS/DIVISIONS/AFFILIATES:

CHS/SRS, LLC.
TruSurround
TruBass
FOCUS
SRSWOWcast Technologies
SRSWOW HD
Circle Surround

CONTACTS: Note: Officers with more than one job title may be intentionally listed here more than once.

Thomas C. K. Yuen, CEO
Thomas C. K. Yuen, Pres.
Ulrich Gottschling, CFO
David J. Frerichs, Exec. VP-Strategic Mktg.
Alan D. Kraemer, CTO/Exec. VP
Sarah Yang, Sr. Dir.-Software Eng.
Lionel Cheng, VP-Oper.
David J. Frerichs, Exec. VP-Corp. Dev.
Jennifer A. Drescher, VP-Corp. Comm.
Jennifer A. Drescher, Dir.-Investor Rel.
Janet M. Bisiki, Treas./VP
Michael J. Franzi, VP-Sales & Licensing
Lionel Cheng, Acting Pres., Valence Tech, Ltd.
Janet Bisiki, Treas./VP
Thomas C. K. Yuen, Chmn.

Phone: 949-442-1070	Fax: 949-852-1099
Toll-Free: 800-243-2733	
Address: 2909 Daimler St., Santa Ana, CA 92705 US	

GROWTH PLANS/SPECIAL FEATURES:

SRS Labs, Inc. is a leading developer and provider of: application-specific integrated circuits; standard integrated circuits; and audio and voice technology solutions for the home theater, portable audio, wireless, computer, game, automotive, Internet and telecommunications markets. In late 2006, SRSLabs, Inc. sold its semiconductor subsidiary, ValenceTech, Ltd. to Noblehigh Enterprises for $4.3 million. As a result, SRS Labs now focuses wholly on licensing under the subsidiary CHS/SRS, LLC. Through its wholly-owned subsidiary SRSWOWcast.com, inc. the firm develops and licenses audio, voice and surround sound technology solutions to leading original equipment manufacturers, software providers and semiconductor companies worldwide. SRS Labs' WOW playback enhancement technology improves the dynamics and bass performance of mono or stereo audio when used with smaller speakers or headphones or when the audio has been digitally compressed into formats such as MP3 or Windows Media Audio. TruSurround, the company's virtual audio solution, plays 5.1 multi-channel content over two speakers. Circle Surround, the company's encoding and decoding format, enables the distribution of up to 6.1 channels of audio over two-channel carriers such as digital media files, standard and high definition television, radio, and CDs. The firm's Voice Processing brand works with wireless technologies to increase audio integrity. Recently, the firm announced plans to partner with Sharper Image Corporation in order to feature SRS WOW technology in a new line of its audio products. In 2006, SRS labs announced a partnership with CSR to feature SRS WOW HD audio content on its BlueCore 3 Bluetooth platform. To date, SRS lab technology has been used in 600 million products. 87% of the firm's revenues are generated by Hong Kong, Japan, Korea and China.

FINANCIALS: Sales and profits are in thousands of dollars—add 000 to get the full amount. 2006 Note: Financial information for 2006 was not available for all companies at press time.

2006 Sales: $	2006 Profits: $	**U.S. Stock Ticker: SRSL**
2005 Sales: $23,228	2005 Profits: $-1,424	**Int'l Ticker:** Int'l Exchange:
2004 Sales: $21,602	2004 Profits: $1,579	Employees: 113
2003 Sales: $19,814	2003 Profits: $ 459	Fiscal Year Ends: 12/31
2002 Sales: $19,000	2002 Profits: $ 800	Parent Company:

SALARIES/BENEFITS:

Pension Plan:	ESOP Stock Plan:	Profit Sharing: Y	Top Exec. Salary: $300,000	Bonus: $58,149
Savings Plan: Y	Stock Purch. Plan:		Second Exec. Salary: $234,165	Bonus: $47,425

OTHER THOUGHTS:

Apparent Women Officers or Directors: 4
Hot Spot for Advancement for Women/Minorities: Y

LOCATIONS: ("Y" = Yes)

West:	Southwest:	Midwest:	Southeast:	Northeast:	International:
Y					Y

Note: Financial information, benefits and other data can change quickly and may vary from those stated here.

STATION CASINOS INC

www.stationcasinos.com

Industry Group Code: 721120 Ranks within this company's industry group: Sales: 5 Profits: 5

Print Media/Publishing:	Movies:	Equipment/Supplies:		Broadcast/Cable:	Music/Audio:	Sports/Games:	
Newspapers:	Movie Theaters:	Equipment/Supplies:		Broadcast TV:	Music Production:	Games/Sports:	
Magazines:	Movie Production:	Gambling Equipment:	Y	Cable TV:	Retail Music:	Retail Games Stores:	
Books:	TV/Video Production:	Special Services:	Y	Satellite Broadcast:	Retail Audio Equip.:	Stadiums/Teams:	Y
Book Stores:	Video Rental:	Advertising Services:		Radio:	Music Print./Dist.:	Gambling/Casinos:	Y
Distribution/Printing:	Video Distribution:	Info. Sys. Software:		Online Information:	Multimedia:	Rides/Theme Parks:	

TYPES OF BUSINESS:

Casino Hotel
Casino Management
Restaurants
Movie Theaters & Entertainment Venues

BRANDS/DIVISIONS/AFFILIATES:

Palace Station Hotel & Casino
Texas Station Gambling Hall & Hotel
Boulder Station Hotel & Casino
Santa Fe Station Hotel & Casino
Barley's Casino & Brewing Company
Sunset Station Hotel & Casino
Fiesta Rancho Casino Hotel
Thunder Valley Casino

CONTACTS: Note: Officers with more than one job title may be intentionally listed here more than once.

Frank J. Fertitta, III, CEO
William W. Warner, COO/Exec. VP
Lorenzo J. Fertitta, Pres.
Glenn C. Christenson, CFO/Exec. VP
Scott M. Nielson, Chief Dev. Officer/Exec. VP
Richard J. Haskins, General Counsel/Exec. VP
Glenn C. Christenson, Treas.
Mark E. Brown, Exec. VP
Frank J. Fertitta III, Chmn.

Phone: 702-367-2411 **Fax:** 702-367-2424
Toll-Free: 800-544-2411
Address: 2411 W. Sahara Ave., Las Vegas, NV 89102 US

GROWTH PLANS/SPECIAL FEATURES:

Station Casinos, Inc. is a gaming and entertainment company, concentrated in the Las Vegas area. Station's properties include eight major casino and hotel properties, six smaller casino properties, 54 restaurants, entertainment venues, 50 movie theaters, 120 bowling lanes, convention banquet space and gaming offerings such as video poker, slot machines, table games, bingo, race and sports wagering. The company owns and operates 2,200 hotel rooms within its casinos, including Palace Station, Boulder Station, Texas Station Gambling Hall & Hotel, Sunset Station, Santa Fe Station, Fiesta Rancho Casino Hotel, Fiesta Henderson Casino Hotel, Wild Wild West Gambling Hall & Hotel, Wildfire Casino, Magic Star Casino and Gold Rush Casino. The firm also owns a 50% interest in Green Valley Ranch Station Casino and Barley's Casino & Brewing Company. The casinos cater to Las Vegas residents and repeat visitors. Station's loyalty program, Boarding Pass, collects points through the company's locations and rewards members with free game play. The company is constructing the Red Rock Station casino in Summerlin, Nevada, with completion expected in mid-2006. The firm also purchased 50 acres near Las Vegas to build a regional gaming and entertainment facility. In late 2005, Station entered into an agreement with The Greenspun Corporation to build a hotel and casino in Aliante, a community in North Las Vegas. The partnership calls for 50/50 ownership of the project, dubbed Aliante Station, with Station to receive a management fee. Furthermore, Station completed a new $2 billion revolving bank facility, which refinances its $1 billion revolving credit facility.

Station Casinos offers its employees child care and on-site dentistry. The firm annually raffles off the general manager to work an employee's job for one day, and the money raised goes to various charities. In 2005, the firm was listed in Fortune Magazine's 100 best companies to work for.

FINANCIALS: Sales and profits are in thousands of dollars—add 000 to get the full amount. 2006 Note: Financial information for 2006 was not available for all companies at press time.

2006 Sales: $	2006 Profits: $	**U.S. Stock Ticker: STN**
2005 Sales: $1,108,833	2005 Profits: $161,886	**Int'l Ticker:** Int'l Exchange:
2004 Sales: $986,742	2004 Profits: $66,350	Employees: 11,500
2003 Sales: $858,100	2003 Profits: $44,343	Fiscal Year Ends: 12/31
2002 Sales: $792,900	2002 Profits: $17,900	Parent Company:

SALARIES/BENEFITS:

Pension Plan:	ESOP Stock Plan:	Profit Sharing:	Top Exec. Salary: $1,839,230	Bonus: $3,750,000
Savings Plan: Y	Stock Purch. Plan:		Second Exec. Salary: $1,414,231	Bonus: $2,175,000

OTHER THOUGHTS:

Apparent Women Officers or Directors:
Hot Spot for Advancement for Women/Minorities:

LOCATIONS: ("Y" = Yes)

West:	Southwest:	Midwest:	Southeast:	Northeast:	International:
Y	Y				

Note: Financial information, benefits and other data can change quickly and may vary from those stated here.

SUDDENLINK COMMUNICATIONS   www.suddenlink.com

Industry Group Code: 513220 Ranks within this company's industry group: Sales: Profits:

Print Media/Publishing:	Movies:	Equipment/Supplies:		Broadcast/Cable:	Music/Audio:	Sports/Games:
Newspapers:	Movie Theaters:	Equipment/Supplies:		Broadcast TV:	Music Production:	Games/Sports:
Magazines:	Movie Production:	Gambling Equipment:		Cable TV: Y	Retail Music:	Retail Games Stores:
Books:	TV/Video Production:	Special Services: Y		Satellite Broadcast:	Retail Audio Equip.:	Stadiums/Teams:
Book Stores:	Video Rental:	Advertising Services: Y		Radio:	Music Print./Dist.:	Gambling/Casinos:
Distribution/Printing:	Video Distribution:	Info. Sys. Software:		Online Information:	Multimedia:	Rides/Theme Parks:

TYPES OF BUSINESS:
Cable TV Service
High-Speed Internet Services

BRANDS/DIVISIONS/AFFILIATES:
Cebridge Connections
Classic Communications, Inc.
Cequel III, LLC

CONTACTS: *Note: Officers with more than one job title may be intentionally listed here more than once.*
Jerald L. Kent, CEO
Thomas P. McMillin, COO/Exec. VP
Mary Meduski, CFO/Exec. VP
Mary Meier, Sr. VP-Mktg.
Don R. Johnson, VP-Human Resources
Robert L. Putnam, Sr. VP-IT
Terry M. Cordova, CTO/Sr. VP
Dale R. Bennett, Sr. VP-Oper.
Gene Regan, Dir.-Corp. Comm.
Michael C. Wylie, Chief Accounting Officer/Sr. VP
Patricia L. McCaskill, Sr. VP-Programming
John R. McFerron, Sr. VP-Customer Care
Ralph G. Kelly, Treas.
Kevin Stephens, Sr. VP-Commercial & Advertising Oper.

Phone: 314-965-2020   **Fax:** 314-315-9496
Toll-Free: 800-999-6845
Address: 12444 Powerscourt Ste. 450, St. Louis, MO 63131 US

GROWTH PLANS/SPECIAL FEATURES:
Suddenlink Communications, formerly Cebridge Connections, formerly Classic Communications, Inc., owns and operates cable television systems and provides high-speed Internet services, serving smaller, rural communities in the central U.S. The firm has approximately 1.4 million customers in over 15 states. Suddenlink's business strategy combines characteristics of the non-metropolitan cable market segment with the growth opportunity of broadband services and the Internet. The company delivers digital cable and high-speed Internet access to homes and businesses, providing enhanced digital video and other special services in addition to traditional cable services. Traditional cable packages include local network, independent and educational stations, with some systems also receiving signals from distant cities or local information and public access channels, as well as optional premium programming. Suddenlink is a member of a programming consortium of small to mid-sized cable system operators that creates efficiencies in the securing and administration of programming contracts. The company derives revenues from customer fees, the sale of local spot advertising time and affiliations with home shopping services. Suddenlink retains telecommunications management firm Cequel III, LLC to provide strategic management services. Following the acquisitions of cable systems from Charter Communications and Cox Communications in 2006, Cebridge Connections changed its name to Suddenlink Communications. The acquisitions brought their customer base from approximately 400,000 customers to 1.4 million. In 2007, Suddenlink will begin offering telephone service to select markets though a partnership with Sprint Nextel.

Suddenlink offers scholarships to employees who are graduating seniors and gives customers discounts on cable bills if they make donations to the Toys for Tots foundation during December.

FINANCIALS: Sales and profits are in thousands of dollars—add 000 to get the full amount. 2006 Note: Financial information for 2006 was not available for all companies at press time.

2006 Sales: $	2006 Profits: $	**U.S. Stock Ticker: Private**
2005 Sales: $	2005 Profits: $	**Int'l Ticker:** Int'l Exchange:
2004 Sales: $	2004 Profits: $	Employees: 885
2003 Sales: $	2003 Profits: $	Fiscal Year Ends: 12/31
2002 Sales: $	2002 Profits: $	Parent Company:

SALARIES/BENEFITS:
Pension Plan:	ESOP Stock Plan:	Profit Sharing:	Top Exec. Salary: $350,000	Bonus: $150,000
Savings Plan:	Stock Purch. Plan:		Second Exec. Salary: $201,923	Bonus: $

OTHER THOUGHTS:
Apparent Women Officers or Directors: 3
Hot Spot for Advancement for Women/Minorities: Y

LOCATIONS: ("Y" = Yes)
West:	Southwest:	Midwest:	Southeast:	Northeast:	International:
Y	Y	Y	Y	Y	

Note: Financial information, benefits and other data can change quickly and may vary from those stated here.

TAKE-TWO INTERACTIVE SOFTWARE INC
www.take2games.com

Industry Group Code: 511208 Ranks within this company's industry group: Sales: 4   Profits: 6

Print Media/Publishing:	Movies:	Equipment/Supplies:	Broadcast/Cable:	Music/Audio:	Sports/Games:	
Newspapers:	Movie Theaters:	Equipment/Supplies:	Broadcast TV:	Music Production:	Games/Sports:	Y
Magazines:	Movie Production:	Gambling Equipment:	Cable TV:	Retail Music:	Retail Games Stores:	
Books:	TV/Video Production:	Special Services:	Satellite Broadcast:	Retail Audio Equip.:	Stadiums/Teams:	
Book Stores:	Video Rental:	Advertising Services:	Radio:	Music Print./Dist.:	Gambling/Casinos:	
Distribution/Printing:	Video Distribution:	Info. Sys. Software:	Online Information:	Multimedia:	Rides/Theme Parks:	

TYPES OF BUSINESS:
Computer Software-Video Games
Software Distribution

BRANDS/DIVISIONS/AFFILIATES:
Rockstar Games
Global Star
2K Games
2K Sports
Grand Theft Auto
Irrational Games
Midnight Club
Jack of All Games

CONTACTS: *Note: Officers with more than one job title may be intentionally listed here more than once.*
Paul Eibeler, CEO
Trevor Drinkwater, COO
Paul Eibeler, Pres.
Karl Winters, CFO
Terry Donovan, VP-Mktg.
Samuel A. Judd, Sr. VP-Planning/Admin.
Barry Rutcofsky, Exec. VP-Strategy, Mergers/Acquisitions
Jim Ankner, Dir. Investor/Media Rel.
Terry Donovan, CEO-Rockstar Games
Gary Lewis, Pres., Take-Two Europe
Cindi Buckwalter, Exec. VP
Susan Lewis, VP-Business Dev. 2K Games
Richard W. Roedel, Chmn.

Phone: 646-536-2842	**Fax:** 646-536-2926
Toll-Free:	
Address: 622 Broadway, New York, NY 10012 US	

GROWTH PLANS/SPECIAL FEATURES:
Take-Two Interactive Software, Inc. develops, publishes and distributes software games for personal computers and video game consoles. Take-Two publishes its products under its subsidiaries Rockstar Games, GlobalStar and Jack of All Games. Rockstar Games creates original content for mature audiences on video game console systems. It publishes The Warriors, Midnight Club racing series, Table Tennis and Grand Theft Auto game titles. Global Star publishes sports games (ESPN titles with the NHL, NBA, and NFL brands) and popular licensed titles (Charlie and The Chocolate Factory, Dora The Explorer). Jack of All Games distributes third-party software, hardware, and accessories in the U.S. to Wal-Mart, GameStop, Best Buy, Circuit City and other retailers. In addition, Take-Two publishes through labels 2K and 2K Sports. The firm has publishing and distribution operations in the U.K., France, Germany, Australia, Austria, Holland, New Zealand, Italy, Spain and Canada. Recently, the firm opened its first studio in Shanghai, China. This new location (2K Shanghai) will be a hub for product development, marketing and sales in China. The firm has license agreements with Sony, Microsoft and Nintendo and develops and publishes software in North America and Europe for the PlayStation, PlayStation 2, PSP (Play Station Portable), Xbox, Xbox 360, Game Boy Advance and Nintendo GameCube. In 2006, the firm announced plans to partner with advertising agency Double Fusion. Per the agreement, Double Fusion will be the sole representative in the North American and European markets for up to nine new titles. Also in 2006, the firm's subsidiary, Rockstar Games, partnered with Capcom Co., Ltd. for the release of its newest Grand Theft Auto title (Grand Theft Auto: San Andreas) in Japan. In addition, Take-Two acquired Irrational Games, which publishes new title Bioshock in addition to System Shock 2 and Freedom Force.

FINANCIALS: Sales and profits are in thousands of dollars—add 000 to get the full amount. 2006 Note: Financial information for 2006 was not available for all companies at press time.

2006 Sales: $	2006 Profits: $	**U.S. Stock Ticker:** TTWO
2005 Sales: $1,202,595	2005 Profits: $37,475	**Int'l Ticker:** Int'l Exchange:
2004 Sales: $1,127,751	2004 Profits: $65,378	Employees: 2,002
2003 Sales: $793,976	2003 Profits: $71,565	Fiscal Year Ends: 10/31
2002 Sales: $794,000	2002 Profits: $71,600	Parent Company:

SALARIES/BENEFITS:

Pension Plan:	ESOP Stock Plan:	Profit Sharing:	Top Exec. Salary: $752,884	Bonus: $2,909,500
Savings Plan: Y	Stock Purch. Plan:		Second Exec. Salary: $542,500	Bonus: $200,000

OTHER THOUGHTS:
Apparent Women Officers or Directors: 2
Hot Spot for Advancement for Women/Minorities:

LOCATIONS: ("Y" = Yes)

West:	Southwest:	Midwest:	Southeast:	Northeast:	International:
				Y	Y

TAYLOR NELSON SOFRES PLC (TNS)   www.tns-global.com

Industry Group Code: 541910 Ranks within this company's industry group: Sales: 2 Profits: 2

Print Media/Publishing:	Movies:	Equipment/Supplies:		Broadcast/Cable:	Music/Audio:	Sports/Games:
Newspapers:	Movie Theaters:	Equipment/Supplies:		Broadcast TV:	Music Production:	Games/Sports:
Magazines:	Movie Production:	Gambling Equipment:		Cable TV:	Retail Music:	Retail Games Stores:
Books:	TV/Video Production:	Special Services:	Y	Satellite Broadcast:	Retail Audio Equip.:	Stadiums/Teams:
Book Stores:	Video Rental:	Advertising Services:	Y	Radio:	Music Print./Dist.:	Gambling/Casinos:
Distribution/Printing:	Video Distribution:	Info. Sys. Software:	Y	Online Information:	Multimedia:	Rides/Theme Parks:

TYPES OF BUSINESS:

Market Research
Internet Market Research
Business & Advertising Software

BRANDS/DIVISIONS/AFFILIATES:

TNS
AdEval
MarketWhys
Conversion Model
NeedScope System
Optima
TNS Interactive
NFO World Group

CONTACTS: *Note: Officers with more than one job title may be intentionally listed here more than once.*

Mike Kirkham, CEO
David Lowden, COO
Andy Boland, Group Dir.-Finance
Rachel Argyle, Sr. Exec.-Public Rel.
Anthony Cowling, Chmn.

Phone: 44-20-8967-0007	**Fax:** 44-20-8967-4060
Toll-Free:	
Address: Westgate, London, W5 1UA UK	

GROWTH PLANS/SPECIAL FEATURES:

Taylor Nelson Sofres plc (TNS) is one of the largest market research conglomerates in the world, with operations serving customers in 70 countries. The company provides research in several industry sectors, including automotive, consumer purchasing and behavior, political and social polling, health care, information technology, media intelligence, telecommunications and television audience measurement. The firm's business solutions include AdEval, an advertising pre-testing system that evaluates an advertisement's performance; Conversion Model, a psychological measure of customer commitment; MarketWhys, a brand and advertising tracking system; Miriad, a data integration, analysis and delivery platform; NeedScope System, a system for measuring consumer needs and motivations; Optima, a brand portfolio management tool that analyzes how and why consumers choose the brands they do; and TRI*M, a management information system that monitors a company's shareholder relationship. Through its TNS Interactive business unit, the company also provides Internet and new media research. Another division of TNS, NFO World Group, is a leading provider of panel-based market research in the U.S.

FINANCIALS: Sales and profits are in thousands of dollars—add 000 to get the full amount. 2006 Note: Financial information for 2006 was not available for all companies at press time.

2006 Sales: $	2006 Profits: $	**U.S. Stock Ticker: TYNLY**
2005 Sales: $1,725,450	2005 Profits: $94,600	**Int'l Ticker: TNN** Int'l Exchange: London-LSE
2004 Sales: $1,788,700	2004 Profits: $38,900	Employees: 12,731
2003 Sales: $1,403,700	2003 Profits: $22,900	Fiscal Year Ends: 12/31
2002 Sales: $967,500	2002 Profits: $19,900	Parent Company:

SALARIES/BENEFITS:

Pension Plan:	ESOP Stock Plan:	Profit Sharing:	Top Exec. Salary: $	Bonus: $
Savings Plan:	Stock Purch. Plan:		Second Exec. Salary: $	Bonus: $

OTHER THOUGHTS:

Apparent Women Officers or Directors: 1
Hot Spot for Advancement for Women/Minorities:

LOCATIONS: ("Y" = Yes)

West:	Southwest:	Midwest:	Southeast:	Northeast:	International:
				Y	Y

Note: Financial information, benefits and other data can change quickly and may vary from those stated here.

TELEWEST GLOBAL INC

www.telewest.co.uk

Industry Group Code: 513220 Ranks within this company's industry group: Sales: Profits:

Print Media/Publishing:	Movies:	Equipment/Supplies:		Broadcast/Cable:		Music/Audio:	Sports/Games:
Newspapers:	Movie Theaters:	Equipment/Supplies:		Broadcast TV:		Music Production:	Games/Sports:
Magazines:	Movie Production:	Gambling Equipment:	Y	Cable TV:	Y	Retail Music:	Retail Games Stores:
Books:	TV/Video Production:	Special Services:	Y	Satellite Broadcast:		Retail Audio Equip.:	Stadiums/Teams:
Book Stores:	Video Rental:	Advertising Services:		Radio:		Music Print./Dist.:	Gambling/Casinos:
Distribution/Printing:	Video Distribution:	Info. Sys. Software:		Online Information:		Multimedia:	Rides/Theme Parks:

TYPES OF BUSINESS:

Cable TV Service
Telephony Services
High-Speed Internet Service
Video-on-Demand
Interactive Content & Services
Managed Data Networks
Virtual Private Network Service

BRANDS/DIVISIONS/AFFILIATES:

Telewest Communications plc
Flextech
UKTV
SurfUnlimited
blueyonder
Eurobell
Teleport
Evolved Ethernet

CONTACTS: Note: Officers with more than one job title may be intentionally listed here more than once.

Barry R. Elson, Acting CEO
Eric J. Tveter, COO
Eric J. Tveter, Pres.
Neil Smith, CFO/VP
Howard Watson, Managing Dir.-Networks & IT
Howard Watson, CTO
Stephen Cook, General Counsel
Stephen Cook, Dir.-Group Strategy
Richard Williams, Dir.-Investor Rel.
Stephen Beynon, Managing Dir.-Telewest Bus.
Lisa Opie, Managing Dir.-Content Div.
Anthony Stenham, Chmn.

Phone: 44-20-7299-5000	Fax: 44-20-7299-5495
Toll-Free:	
Address: 160 Great Portland St., London, W1W 5QA UK	

GROWTH PLANS/SPECIAL FEATURES:

Telewest Global Inc. owns a cable network that serves over 4.7 million homes in the U.K. The company's cable segment provides digital television, telephone and Internet services to more than 1.8 million residential customers. Telewest markets its dial-up Internet under the name SurfUnlimited and its high-speed Internet services under the brand name blueyonder, which has approximately 698,000 subscribers, 93% of whom also subscribe to the firm's telephony or television services. The cable segment's business division provides voice, data and video transmission services to business customers, including point-to-point private circuits, virtual private network services and the Enterprise Connect and Evolved Ethernet managed data network services. The company's content division, Flextech, offers entertainment, information and interactive content and services to the multi-channel television and online markets. The division's portfolio includes the Bravo, Livingtv, Trouble and Challenge TV channels. Flextech also owns 50% of the companies that comprise UKTV, a portfolio of television channels operated in partnership with the BBC. Flextech and UKTV together are Great Britain's largest providers of basic thematic channels, reaching approximately 10.7 million subscribers. The company's Eurobell subsidiary is a regional telecommunications company that supplies telephone, television, data and Internet services to residential and business customers in southern England. Telewest Global replaced Telewest Communications plc as the parent company of the Telewest group following financial restructuring in 2004. In 2005, the company launched a video-on-demand service, which allows customers to rent, watch, pause, rewind and fast-forward a movie through their existing set-top equipment. Telewest's newest offering is Teleport, a TV-on-demand service that provides movies, television reruns and special interest programming.

Telewest offers employees a benefits package that includes maternity and paternity leave, performance bonuses, a product concessions package and a 37.5 hour work week.

FINANCIALS: Sales and profits are in thousands of dollars—add 000 to get the full amount. 2006 Note: Financial information for 2006 was not available for all companies at press time.

2006 Sales: $	2006 Profits: $	U.S. Stock Ticker: Subsidiary
2005 Sales: $	2005 Profits: $	Int'l Ticker: Int'l Exchange:
2004 Sales: $1,273,000	2004 Profits: $-88,000	Employees: 8,613
2003 Sales: $2,304,000	2003 Profits: $-485,000	Fiscal Year Ends: 12/31
2002 Sales: $2,065,000	2002 Profits: $-4,468,000	Parent Company: NTL INCORPORATED

SALARIES/BENEFITS:

Pension Plan: Y	ESOP Stock Plan:	Profit Sharing:	Top Exec. Salary: $723,022	Bonus: $426,266
Savings Plan:	Stock Purch. Plan:		Second Exec. Salary: $658,783	Bonus: $360,970

OTHER THOUGHTS:

Apparent Women Officers or Directors: 1
Hot Spot for Advancement for Women/Minorities:

LOCATIONS: ("Y" = Yes)

West:	Southwest:	Midwest:	Southeast:	Northeast:	International: Y

Note: Financial information, benefits and other data can change quickly and may vary from those stated here.

THOMAS NELSON INC
www.thomasnelson.com

Industry Group Code: 511130 Ranks within this company's industry group: Sales: 8 Profits: 5

Print Media/Publishing:		Movies:	Equipment/Supplies:	Broadcast/Cable:	Music/Audio:	Sports/Games:
Newspapers:		Movie Theaters:	Equipment/Supplies:	Broadcast TV:	Music Production:	Games/Sports:
Magazines:		Movie Production:	Gambling Equipment:	Cable TV:	Retail Music:	Retail Games Stores:
Books:	Y	TV/Video Production:	Special Services:	Satellite Broadcast:	Retail Audio Equip.:	Stadiums/Teams:
Book Stores:		Video Rental:	Advertising Services:	Radio:	Music Print./Dist.:	Gambling/Casinos:
Distribution/Printing:		Video Distribution:	Info. Sys. Software:	Online Information:	Multimedia:	Rides/Theme Parks:

TYPES OF BUSINESS:
Book Publishing
Religious Publications
Gifts & Stationery
CD-ROMs

BRANDS/DIVISIONS/AFFILIATES:
Nelson Electronic and Reference
Integrity Publishers

CONTACTS: Note: Officers with more than one job title may be intentionally listed here more than once.
Michael S. Hyatt, CEO
Michael S. Hyatt, Pres.
Jerry Park, Chief Mktg. Officer
Vance Lawson, Sr. VP-Oper.
Byron Williamson, Exec. VP-Strategic Dev.
Joe L. Powers, Treas./Exec. VP/Corp. Sec.
Vance Lawson, Sr. VP-Finance
Mark Schoenwald, Exec. VP/Chief Sales Officer
Ted Squires, Exec. VP-Ministry Sales
Tamara L. Heim, Exec. VP/Chief Publishing Officer
Sam Moore, Chmn.
Ted Squires, Exec. VP-World Publishing

Phone: 615-889-9000	Fax: 615-391-5225
Toll-Free: 800-251-4000	
Address: 501 Nelson Pl., Nashville, TN 37214 US	

GROWTH PLANS/SPECIAL FEATURES:
Thomas Nelson, Inc is a leading publisher, producer and distributor of books (hardcover and paperback) emphasizing Christian, inspirational and family value themes. The firm is one of the largest publishers of Christian and inspirational books and Bibles in the U.S., distributing through Christian bookstores, mass merchandisers (Barnes & Noble, Target and Wal-Mart) and direct sales to consumers, churches and ministries. The company translates its English titles into foreign languages and distributes its products internationally in South America, Europe, Australia, New Zealand, Africa, Asia and Mexico. In addition, the company publishes speakers such as Lisa Bevere, Ted Dekker, John Eldredge and Billy Graham. The company sells previously published titles (earning 54% of the firm's publishing revenues in 2006), Bibles (2,500 copies sold in 2006), commentaries, study guides and other Bible help texts. Products range from paperbacks to deluxe leather-bound Bibles to CD-ROM to audio and video products. Authors and titles are supported through radio, television, cooperative advertising, author appearances and in-store promotions. Electronic Bibles, biblical reference books, and software for preparing Bible study lessons are published through the firm's subsidiary Nelson Electronic and Reference. Recently, after acquiring Integrity Publishers (the wholly owned publishing subsidiary of Integrity Media), Thomas Nelson sold all of its subsidiaries in order to restructure its publishing units. Per this restructuring, the firm hopes to streamline its titles, thereby eliminating overlapping imprints. In the future, all titles will be printed with only the firm's name and logo on the jacket. In 2006, Thomas Nelson became a privately held firm.

FINANCIALS: Sales and profits are in thousands of dollars—add 000 to get the full amount. 2006 Note: Financial information for 2006 was not available for all companies at press time.

2006 Sales: $253,057	2006 Profits: $20,977	U.S. Stock Ticker: Private
2005 Sales: $237,817	2005 Profits: $19,817	Int'l Ticker: Int'l Exchange:
2004 Sales: $222,619	2004 Profits: $16,165	Employees: 650
2003 Sales: $217,200	2003 Profits: $10,200	Fiscal Year Ends: 3/31
2002 Sales: $215,600	2002 Profits: $-49,500	Parent Company:

SALARIES/BENEFITS:

Pension Plan:	ESOP Stock Plan: Y	Profit Sharing: Y	Top Exec. Salary: $450,000	Bonus: $289,300
Savings Plan: Y	Stock Purch. Plan:		Second Exec. Salary: $300,000	Bonus: $161,000

OTHER THOUGHTS:
Apparent Women Officers or Directors: 2
Hot Spot for Advancement for Women/Minorities:

LOCATIONS: ("Y" = Yes)

West:	Southwest:	Midwest:	Southeast:	Northeast:	International:
Y	Y	Y	Y	Y	

Note: Financial information, benefits and other data can change quickly and may vary from those stated here.

THOMSON CORPORATION (THE)

www.thomson.com

Industry Group Code: 511140 Ranks within this company's industry group: Sales: 2 Profits: 1

Print Media/Publishing:		Movies:		Equipment/Supplies:		Broadcast/Cable:		Music/Audio:		Sports/Games:	
Newspapers:	Y	Movie Theaters:		Equipment/Supplies:		Broadcast TV:		Music Production:		Games/Sports:	
Magazines:		Movie Production:		Gambling Equipment:	Y	Cable TV:		Retail Music:		Retail Games Stores:	
Books:	Y	TV/Video Production:		Special Services:	Y	Satellite Broadcast:		Retail Audio Equip.:		Stadiums/Teams:	
Book Stores:		Video Rental:		Advertising Services:	Y	Radio:		Music Print./Dist.:		Gambling/Casinos:	
Distribution/Printing:		Video Distribution:		Info. Sys. Software:	Y	Online Information:		Multimedia:		Rides/Theme Parks:	

TYPES OF BUSINESS:

Information Services & Software
Legal & Regulatory Information Services
Financial Information & Technology
Educational Materials
Scientific Data Tools
Health Care Information Tools
News Services

BRANDS/DIVISIONS/AFFILIATES:

Gardiner-Caldwell Communications, Ltd.
NewsEdge Corp.
Gale Group
Dialog
West Publishing
Disclosure, Inc.
Thomson Scientific
Medstat

CONTACTS: *Note: Officers with more than one job title may be intentionally listed here more than once.*

Richard J. Harrington, CEO
Michael E. Wilens, COO
Richard J. Harrington, Pres.
Robert D. Daleo, CFO/Exec. VP
Robert B. Bogart, Exec. VP-Human Resources
Carl Urbania, CIO
Michael E. Wilens, CTO
Deirdre Stanley, General Counsel/Sr. VP
Richard Benson-Armer, Chief Strategy Officer
Gustav Carlson, Sr. VP-Corp. Comm.
Brian H. Hall, Pres./CEO-Legal & Regulatory Group
Robert C. Cullen, Pres./CEO-Scientific & Health Care Group
Ronald H. Schlosser, Pres./CEO-Learning Group
David H. Shaffer, Exec. VP
David K. R. Thomson, Chmn.

Phone: 416-360-8700	Fax: 416-360-8812
Toll-Free:	
Address: Toronto-Dominion Bank Tower, Ste. 2706, Toronto, ON M5K 1A1 Canada	

GROWTH PLANS/SPECIAL FEATURES:

The Thomson Corp. provides specialized information in digital and print formats through operations in 46 countries. Formerly in the newspaper business, the firm sold the majority of its 130 newspaper holdings in the early 2000s to shift to its current operations. Thomson currently operates in four global market groups serving more than 20 million information users. The legal and regulatory group operates in 24 countries, providing information and software for legal, tax, accounting, intellectual property, compliance and business professionals. This group is the firm's primary source of revenues and employs most of its workers. Through its financial group, Thomson provides integrated and individualized information and technology applications to the worldwide financial community. The learning group is among the world's largest providers of tailored learning solutions. In the academic marketplace, it serves secondary, post-secondary and graduate-level students, teachers and learning institutions in both traditional and distance-learning environments. In the professional and corporate training marketplaces, it offers adult education and certification materials for corporations, training centers and individuals. The scientific and health care group offers information and services to researchers and other professionals in the health care, academic, scientific and government marketplaces. Thomson Scientific databases assist professionals at every stage of research and development, including discovery, analysis, product development and distribution. The health care group provides drug, education and clinical information tools, primarily at the point of care. Additionally, the firm's Medstat business provides decision support to employers, health care providers, insurers and others in order to manage the cost of health care. The company's recent acquisitions include Scholar One software, a web-based workflow solution for authoring, evaluating and publishing research; AFX News; Quantitative Analytics, Inc.; and MercuryMD, Inc.

Thomson offers its employees a 401(k) plan, flex time and tuition reimbursement.

FINANCIALS: Sales and profits are in thousands of dollars—add 000 to get the full amount. 2006 Note: Financial information for 2006 was not available for all companies at press time.

2006 Sales: $	2006 Profits: $	U.S. Stock Ticker: TOC
2005 Sales: $8,703,000	2005 Profits: $934,000	Int'l Ticker: TOC Int'l Exchange: Toronto-TSX
2004 Sales: $8,098,000	2004 Profits: $1,011,000	Employees: 40,500
2003 Sales: $7,606,000	2003 Profits: $846,000	Fiscal Year Ends: 12/31
2002 Sales: $7,756,000	2002 Profits: $615,000	Parent Company:

SALARIES/BENEFITS:

Pension Plan:	ESOP Stock Plan:	Profit Sharing:	Top Exec. Salary: $1,200,000	Bonus: $1,840,800
Savings Plan: Y	Stock Purch. Plan:		Second Exec. Salary: $950,000	Bonus: $1,365,150

OTHER THOUGHTS:

Apparent Women Officers or Directors: 3
Hot Spot for Advancement for Women/Minorities: Y

LOCATIONS: ("Y" = Yes)

West:	Southwest:	Midwest:	Southeast:	Northeast:	International:
Y	Y	Y	Y	Y	Y

Note: Financial information, benefits and other data can change quickly and may vary from those stated here.

THQ INC

www.thq.com

Industry Group Code: 511208 Ranks within this company's industry group: Sales: 6 Profits: 4

Print Media/Publishing:	Movies:	Equipment/Supplies:	Broadcast/Cable:	Music/Audio:	Sports/Games:	
Newspapers:	Movie Theaters:	Equipment/Supplies:	Broadcast TV:	Music Production:	Games/Sports:	Y
Magazines:	Movie Production:	Gambling Equipment:	Cable TV:	Retail Music:	Retail Games Stores:	
Books:	TV/Video Production:	Special Services:	Satellite Broadcast:	Retail Audio Equip.:	Stadiums/Teams:	
Book Stores:	Video Rental:	Advertising Services:	Radio:	Music Print./Dist.:	Gambling/Casinos:	
Distribution/Printing:	Video Distribution:	Info. Sys. Software:	Online Information:	Multimedia:	Rides/Theme Parks:	

TYPES OF BUSINESS:

Software-Video Games
Mobile Gaming Software

BRANDS/DIVISIONS/AFFILIATES:

THQ Wireless
Studio System
Relic Entertainment
Blue Tongue Entertainment Limited
Juice Games, Ltd. (U.K.)
Vigil Games
Stuntman
Paradigm Studios

CONTACTS: Note: Officers with more than one job title may be intentionally listed here more than once.

Brian J. Farrell, CEO
Brian J. Farrell, Pres.
Edward Zinser, CFO/Exec. VP
Scott Guthrie, Sr. VP- North American Sales & Distribution
Bill Goodmen, Exec. VP-Human Resources
Clarence White, CIO/IT Sec.-U.S.Western Territory
Bill Goodmen, Exec. VP-Administration
James M. Kennedy, Exec.VP-Legal Affairs
Gary Rosenfeld, Sr. VP-Bus. Dev.
Bob Finlayson, VP-Corp. Comm.
Julie MacMedan, Dir.-Investor Relations
Jack Sorensen, Exec.VP-Worldwide Studios
Kelly Flock, Exec. VP-Worldwide Publishing
Ron Shouts, IT Sec.-U.S. Central Territory
Brian J. Farrell, Chmn.
Ian Curran, Sr. VP-Intl. Publishing, Europe, Middle East

Phone: 818-871-5000	Fax: 818-591-1615
Toll-Free:	
Address: 29903 Agoura Rd., Aguora Hills, CA 91301 US	

GROWTH PLANS/SPECIAL FEATURES:

THQ, Inc. is a worldwide publisher, marketer and developer of proprietary and licensed video game software for Sony PlayStation 2, Microsoft Xbox, Nintendo GameCube, Nintendo Game Boy Advance, PCs and mobile devices. The company develops titles both internally and under contract with independent developers, and currently has twelve internal development studios and 25 independent development teams located in the U.S., Australia, Canada and Europe. Its games are typically based on properties it licenses from third parties, including Hot Wheels, Scooby-Doo, Sonic the Hedgehog, SpongeBob SquarePants, World Wrestling Entertainment and several Disney/Pixar properties. THQ Wireless produces ringtones and videogames for mobile phones. The company's corporate strategy focuses on improving its internal development capabilities and technology base, increasing its international presence and exploring the potential of the mobile interactive entertainment segment. The company announced its new strategy called Studio System, which is designed to leverage resources across the entire organization to benefit each of the separate studios. Recently, THQ signed an agreement with Microsoft Game Studios to exclusively distribute certain Microsoft PC products throughout the U.S. until 2009. Recently, the firm announced the acquisition of Juice Games, Ltd. (U.K.) its first European studio. In addition, the firm acquired Vigil Games of Austin, Texas. In 2006, the firm partnered with Polish developer People Can Fly to release their new (untitled) game for global release; and announced a multi-title deal with Swedish SimBin Development Team. Per the agreement, the firm will distribute car racing game GTR for Microsoft's Xbox 360. Also in 2006, the firm announced the acquisition of the Stuntman franchise from Atari and the acquisition of Paradigm Studios from an undisclosed seller.

THQ employees receive health insurance, annual bonus, stock options, employer matching 401(k), and educational assistance.

FINANCIALS: Sales and profits are in thousands of dollars—add 000 to get the full amount. 2006 Note: Financial information for 2006 was not available for all companies at press time.

2006 Sales: $806,560	2006 Profits: $34,269	**U.S. Stock Ticker: THQI**
2005 Sales: $756,731	2005 Profits: $62,790	**Int'l Ticker:** Int'l Exchange:
2004 Sales: $640,846	2004 Profits: $35,839	Employees: 1,600
2003 Sales: $66,800	2003 Profits: $-7,686	Fiscal Year Ends: 3/31
2002 Sales: $480,500	2002 Profits: $13,000	Parent Company:

SALARIES/BENEFITS:

Pension Plan: Y	ESOP Stock Plan:	Profit Sharing:	Top Exec. Salary: $604,281	Bonus: $601,999
Savings Plan: Y	Stock Purch. Plan:		Second Exec. Salary: $383,670	Bonus: $261,425

OTHER THOUGHTS:

Apparent Women Officers or Directors: 2
Hot Spot for Advancement for Women/Minorities:

LOCATIONS: ("Y" = Yes)

West:	Southwest:	Midwest:	Southeast:	Northeast:	International:
Y	Y	Y		Y	Y

TICKETMASTER

www.ticketmaster.com

Industry Group Code: 454110A Ranks within this company's industry group: Sales: 1 Profits:

Print Media/Publishing:	Movies:	Equipment/Supplies:		Broadcast/Cable:	Music/Audio:	Sports/Games:
Newspapers:	Movie Theaters:	Equipment/Supplies:		Broadcast TV:	Music Production:	Games/Sports:
Magazines:	Movie Production:	Gambling Equipment:		Cable TV:	Retail Music:	Retail Games Stores:
Books:	TV/Video Production:	Special Services:	Y	Satellite Broadcast:	Retail Audio Equip.:	Stadiums/Teams:
Book Stores:	Video Rental:	Advertising Services:		Radio:	Music Print./Dist.:	Gambling/Casinos:
Distribution/Printing:	Video Distribution:	Info. Sys. Software:	Y	Online Information:	Multimedia:	Rides/Theme Parks:

TYPES OF BUSINESS:

Event Ticket Sales
Campsite Reservation
Web-Based Ticketing Software
Network Ticketing Services

BRANDS/DIVISIONS/AFFILIATES:

IAC/InterActiveCorp
ReserveAmerica
Admission
Synchro Systems Limited
TicketWeb
TicketWeb 2.0 Software
TicketAlerts
Ticketmaster Auctions

CONTACTS: *Note: Officers with more than one job title may be intentionally listed here more than once.*

John Pleasants, CEO
Sean Moriarty, COO
Sean Moriarty, Pres.
Susan Bracey, CFO/Exec. VP
Brian Pike, CTO
Edward J. Weiss, General Counsel/Exec. VP
David Goldberg, Exec. VP
Eric Korman, Exec. VP
Terry Barnes, Chmn.

Phone: 213-639-6100	Fax: 213-386-1244
Toll-Free:	
Address: 3701 Wilshire Blvd., Los Angeles, CA 90010 US	

GROWTH PLANS/SPECIAL FEATURES:

Ticketmaster, a subsidiary and operating division of IAC/InterActiveCorp, focuses on retail sales of tickets to concerts, sporting events, and other entertainment related events. Ticketmaster operates through five companies: Ticketmaster, which is responsible for ticket sales through 6,500 retail locations, 20 call centers and ticketmaster.com (which generates the main portion of the company's income); ReserveAmerica, which is the largest provider of campsite reservation in North America, providing reservations for more than 100,000 campsites in 48 states; Admission, the leading provider of computerized network ticketing services in Quebec and exclusive provider of tickets for 80% of the venues and four professional sports teams within Quebec; Synchro Systems Limited, which provides software products and services to the sports and entertainment industries in the U.K.; and TicketWeb, a provider of Internet-based box-office ticketing software and services, whose TicketWeb 2.0 Software allows clients to perform box office functions, such as ticket and seating reservation, through a standard web browser.

Ticketmaster provides its employees with benefits including medical, dental, vision and prescription drug plans.

FINANCIALS: Sales and profits are in thousands of dollars—add 000 to get the full amount. 2006 Note: Financial information for 2006 was not available for all companies at press time.

2006 Sales: $	2006 Profits: $	U.S. Stock Ticker: Subsidiary
2005 Sales: $950,200	2005 Profits: $	Int'l Ticker: Int'l Exchange:
2004 Sales: $	2004 Profits: $	Employees: 4,600
2003 Sales: $743,000	2003 Profits: $	Fiscal Year Ends: 12/31
2002 Sales: $811,200	2002 Profits: $	Parent Company: IAC/INTERACTIVECORP

SALARIES/BENEFITS:

Pension Plan:	ESOP Stock Plan:	Profit Sharing:	Top Exec. Salary: $600,000	Bonus: $250,000
Savings Plan: Y	Stock Purch. Plan:		Second Exec. Salary: $387,500	Bonus: $157,000

OTHER THOUGHTS:

Apparent Women Officers or Directors: 1
Hot Spot for Advancement for Women/Minorities:

LOCATIONS: ("Y" = Yes)

West:	Southwest:	Midwest:	Southeast:	Northeast:	International:
Y	Y	Y	Y	Y	Y

TIME INC

www.time.com

Industry Group Code: 511120 Ranks within this company's industry group: Sales: 2   Profits:

Print Media/Publishing:		Movies:		Equipment/Supplies:	Broadcast/Cable:	Music/Audio:	Sports/Games:
Newspapers:		Movie Theaters:		Equipment/Supplies:	Broadcast TV:	Music Production:	Games/Sports:
Magazines:	Y	Movie Production:		Gambling Equipment:	Cable TV:	Retail Music:	Retail Games Stores:
Books:	Y	TV/Video Production:	Y	Special Services:	Satellite Broadcast:	Retail Audio Equip.:	Stadiums/Teams:
Book Stores:		Video Rental:		Advertising Services:	Radio:	Music Print./Dist.:	Gambling/Casinos:
Distribution/Printing:		Video Distribution:		Info. Sys. Software:	Online Information:	Multimedia:	Rides/Theme Parks:

TYPES OF BUSINESS:

Magazine Publishing
TV Production
Book Publishing

BRANDS/DIVISIONS/AFFILIATES:

Essence Communications Partners
People
Sports Illustrated
Grupo Editorial Expansion
Southern Living
Fortune
Southern Progress Corporation
IPC Group, Ltd.

CONTACTS: *Note: Officers with more than one job title may be intentionally listed here more than once.*

Ann S. Moore, CEO
Nora P. McAniff, Co-COO
Richard Atkinson, CFO
Jim Kelly, Managing Editor-Times Inc.
John Huey, Editor-In-Chief-Time, Inc.
John Squires, Co-COO
Ann S. Moore, Chmn.
Richard Atkinson, CEO-Int'l

Phone: 212-522-1212	**Fax:** 212-522-0602
Toll-Free:	
Address: 1271 Ave. of the Americas, New York, NY 10020-1393 US	

GROWTH PLANS/SPECIAL FEATURES:

Time, Inc. operates the magazine publishing business unit of its parent company, Time Warner, Inc. The company publishes 150 magazines worldwide (45 in the U.S. and 105 in other countries), including: Time; People; Sports Illustrated; Entertainment Weekly; Southern Living; In Style; Fortune; Money; Real Simple; Cooking Light; and 80 magazines published by IPC Group, Ltd., a U.K. an Australia subsidiary of the company. Time magazine summarizes current news and weekly events and publishes Time for Kids, a current events magazine for children ages 5 to 13. People magazine reports on celebrities and other notable personalities and produces People en Espanol, teen People and Who Weekly in the U.K. Sports Illustrated covers sports (Sports Illustrated for Kids is geared at pre-teenagers) and Entertainment Weekly reviews and reports on entertainment. In Style magazine focuses on celebrities, beauty and fashion. Fortune reports on worldwide economic and business developments. Money reports primarily on personal finance. Real Simple focuses on lifestyle and provides solutions for simplifying various aspects of life. Real Simple launched a weekly television series on PBS in 2006. Through Southern Progress Corporation, Time, Inc. publishes eight magazines, including Southern Living, Sunset, Cooking Light and Health. IPC Group publishes What's on TV, TV Times, Woman, Marie Claire, Homes & Gardens, Horse & Hound and others. Time4 Media publishes 17 popular sport and outdoor magazines including Golf, Ski, Skiing, Field & Stream, Outdoor Life, Transworld Skateboarding, Popular Science and Yachting. Time, Inc. also publishes Parenting and This Old House magazine and produces several television series, including This Old House and Ask This Old House. In 2006, the firm sold its book publishing business, conducted by Time Warner Book Group, Inc., to Hachette for $538 million. Per the agreement, Hachette acquired Warner Books; Little, Brown and Company; and Time Warner Book Group UK.

FINANCIALS: Sales and profits are in thousands of dollars—add 000 to get the full amount. 2006 Note: Financial information for 2006 was not available for all companies at press time.

2006 Sales: $	2006 Profits: $	**U.S. Stock Ticker: Subsidiary**
2005 Sales: $5,846,000	2005 Profits: $	**Int'l Ticker:** Int'l Exchange:
2004 Sales: $	2004 Profits: $	Employees: 11,000
2003 Sales: $5,533,000	2003 Profits: $	Fiscal Year Ends: 12/31
2002 Sales: $5,400,000	2002 Profits: $	Parent Company: TIME WARNER INC

SALARIES/BENEFITS:

Pension Plan:	ESOP Stock Plan:	Profit Sharing:	Top Exec. Salary: $	Bonus: $
Savings Plan:	Stock Purch. Plan:		Second Exec. Salary: $	Bonus: $

OTHER THOUGHTS:

Apparent Women Officers or Directors: 2
Hot Spot for Advancement for Women/Minorities:

LOCATIONS: ("Y" = Yes)

West:	Southwest:	Midwest:	Southeast:	Northeast:	International:
Y	Y	Y	Y	Y	Y

TIME WARNER CABLE

www.timewarnercable.com

Industry Group Code: 513220 Ranks within this company's industry group: Sales: 4 Profits:

Print Media/Publishing:	Movies:	Equipment/Supplies:		Broadcast/Cable:		Music/Audio:	Sports/Games:
Newspapers:	Movie Theaters:	Equipment/Supplies:		Broadcast TV:		Music Production:	Games/Sports:
Magazines:	Movie Production:	Gambling Equipment:		Cable TV:	Y	Retail Music:	Retail Games Stores:
Books:	TV/Video Production:	Special Services:	Y	Satellite Broadcast:		Retail Audio Equip.:	Stadiums/Teams:
Book Stores:	Video Rental:	Advertising Services:	Y	Radio:		Music Print./Dist.:	Gambling/Casinos:
Distribution/Printing:	Video Distribution:	Info. Sys. Software:		Online Information:		Multimedia:	Rides/Theme Parks:

TYPES OF BUSINESS:

Cable Television
Internet Access
VoIP Service
Video-On-Demand Service

BRANDS/DIVISIONS/AFFILIATES:

Time Warner, Inc.
Road Runner
Digital Phone
Time Warner cable, LLC
Time Warner NY Cable Holding Inc.
Time Warner NY Cable LLC
Time Warner Entertainment Company, L.P.
Time Warner Entertainment-Advance/Newhouse Partner

CONTACTS: *Note: Officers with more than one job title may be intentionally listed here more than once.*

Glenn A. Britt, CEO
Landel C. Hobbs, COO
Glenn A. Britt, Pres.
John K. Martin, CFO
Sam Howe, Exec. VP-Chief Mktg. Officer
Tomas Mathews, VP-Human Resources
Mike L. LaJoie, Chief Tech. Officer/Exec. VP
Marc Lawrence-Apfelbaum, General Counsel/Exec. VP
William R. Goetz, Jr., Exec. VP-Oper.
Carl U. J. Rossetti, Exec. VP-Corp. Dev.
Lynne Costantini, Sr. VP/Chief Business Affairs Officer
David E. O'Hayre, VP-Investments
Melinda Witmer, Sr. VP & Chief Programming Officer
Lauren LoFrisco, Group VP-Marketing Communications
Carol Hevey, Exec. VP-Oper.
Michael Diamond, Sr. VP-Mktg. Strategy & Intelligence
Don Logan, Chmn.

Phone: 203-328-0600	Fax: 203-328-0690
Toll-Free:	
Address: 290 Harbor Dr., Stamford, CT 06902-6732 US	

GROWTH PLANS/SPECIAL FEATURES:

Time Warner Cable owns and manages clustered cable television operations within the U.S. The firm is a subsidiary of Time Warner, Inc., a global media and entertainment company with operations in entertainment, cable networks, cable TV service and sports franchises, and publishing, including magazines, books and direct marketing. Time Warner Cable is a provider of new digital technology including digital phones (with 1.6 million subscribers), digital video recorders (DVRs), high definition television (HDTV), video-on-demand (VOD) and high-speed Internet with service to approximately 11 million cable subscribers, including 7.0 million (52%) digital video customers. The firm's subscribers are typically charged monthly subscription fees based on the level of service selected and, in some cases, equipment usage fees. Time Warner Cable's systems offer basic and standard analog video service, which together provide approximately 70 channels on average, including local broadcast signals, which are available for a fixed monthly fee. Subscribers to Time Warner Cable's analog video service may purchase premium channels for an additional monthly fee, with discounts for the packages including more than one premium service. Video service revenues account for approximately 75% of the company's revenues. Through the firm's cable-based ISP Road Runner and other providers, Time Warner Cable provides Internet access to more than 3.4 million customers. The company also offers Digital Phone, a VoIP telephony service, through a partnership with Sprint. In 2006, the company and Comcast Corporation acquired substantially all of the assets of Adelphia Communications Corporation. Additionally, Comcast redeemed its ownership interest in Time Warner Cable, with the result that the firm is now about 84% owned by Time Warner, Inc. and 16% owned by Adelphia.

FINANCIALS: Sales and profits are in thousands of dollars—add 000 to get the full amount. 2006 Note: Financial information for 2006 was not available for all companies at press time.

2006 Sales: $	2006 Profits: $	**U.S. Stock Ticker: Subsidiary**
2005 Sales: $9,498,000	2005 Profits: $	**Int'l Ticker:** Int'l Exchange:
2004 Sales: $8,484,000	2004 Profits: $	Employees: 30,000
2003 Sales: $	2003 Profits: $	Fiscal Year Ends: 12/31
2002 Sales: $	2002 Profits: $	Parent Company: TIME WARNER INC

SALARIES/BENEFITS:

Pension Plan: Y	ESOP Stock Plan:	Profit Sharing:	Top Exec. Salary: $1,000,000	Bonus: $4,300,000
Savings Plan: Y	Stock Purch. Plan: Y		Second Exec. Salary: $900,000	Bonus: $2,152,000

OTHER THOUGHTS:

Apparent Women Officers or Directors: 5
Hot Spot for Advancement for Women/Minorities: Y

LOCATIONS: ("Y" = Yes)

West:	Southwest:	Midwest:	Southeast:	Northeast:	International:
Y	Y	Y	Y	Y	

TIME WARNER INC   www.timewarner.com

Industry Group Code: 513220 Ranks within this company's industry group: Sales: 1 Profits: 1

Print Media/Publishing:	Movies:		Equipment/Supplies:		Broadcast/Cable:	Music/Audio:		Sports/Games:	
Newspapers:	Movie Theaters:		Equipment/Supplies:		Broadcast TV:	Music Production:	Y	Games/Sports:	
Magazines: Y	Movie Production:	Y	Gambling Equipment:		Cable TV:	Retail Music:		Retail Games Stores:	
Books: Y	TV/Video Production:	Y	Special Services:	Y	Satellite Broadcast:	Retail Audio Equip.:	Y	Stadiums/Teams:	
Book Stores:	Video Rental:		Advertising Services:	Y	Radio:	Music Print./Dist.:		Gambling/Casinos:	Y
Distribution/Printing:	Video Distribution:		Info. Sys. Software:		Online Information:	Multimedia:		Rides/Theme Parks:	

TYPES OF BUSINESS:

Cable TV Networks
Television Production
Internet Service Provider
Magazine Publishing
Entertainment Investments
Film Production
e-Commerce
Cable TV Service

BRANDS/DIVISIONS/AFFILIATES:

America Online
Warner Bros.
New Line Cinema
Home Box Office (HBO)
Turner Broadcasting System
Time, Inc.
CNN
DC Comics

CONTACTS: *Note: Officers with more than one job title may be intentionally listed here more than once.*

Richard Parsons, CEO
Jeffrey Bewkes, COO
Jeffrey Bewkes, Pres.
Wayne Pace, CFO/Exec. VP
Patricia Fili-Krushel, Exec. VP-Admin.
Paul Cappuccio, General Counsel/Exec. VP
Edward Adler, Exec. VP-Corp. Comm.
James Burtson, VP-Investor Rel.
Carol Melton, Exec. VP-Global Public Policy
Olaf Olafsson, Exec. VP
Ana Marie Cox, Washington Editor, Time.com
Richard Parsons, Chmn.

Phone: 212-484-8000	Fax: 212-489-6183
Toll-Free:	
Address: One Time Warner Ctr., New York, NY 10019 US	

GROWTH PLANS/SPECIAL FEATURES:

Time Warner, Inc., the result of the merger of America Online (AOL) and Time Warner, is a leading global media and entertainment company. Its principal business objective is to create and distribute branded information and entertainment throughout the world. The firm's AOL subsidiary is one of the world's largest Internet service providers. Time Warner's operations also include interests in film, television production and television broadcasting; cable networks and cable TV service, including cable television programming and sports franchises; and publishing, including magazine publishing and direct marketing. With about 12 million basic and digital cable subscribers as of June 2005 (with an additional 4.8 million residential high-speed data subscribers), Time Warner Cable, Inc. is a pioneering leader in the cable industry as a provider of new digital technology and high-speed Internet service in 27 states. The segment also offers video services by which subscribers are charged monthly subscription fees based on the level of services selected, which include Movies-on-Demand, Pay-Per-View movies and special events, such as professional sports championships. The company also operates New Line Cinema, Warner Bros. Entertainment, Home Box Office (HBO), Cinemax, the Time, Inc. family of over 130 magazines, CompuServe, MapQuest, Netscape, Turner Broadcasting, CNN and DC Comics, among other businesses. In April 2005, Time Warner and Comcast agreed to jointly acquire Adelphia Communications for $17.6 billion dollars. In addition, through an exchange of cash and territory Time Warner acquired Comcast's 18% share of Time Warner Cable and both companies will consolidate key geographic territories. In February 2006, Time Warner sold its book publishing unit, Time Warner Book Group, to Lagardere SCA for $537.5 million.

FINANCIALS: Sales and profits are in thousands of dollars—add 000 to get the full amount. 2006 Note: Financial information for 2006 was not available for all companies at press time.

2006 Sales: $	2006 Profits: $	U.S. Stock Ticker: TWX
2005 Sales: $43,652,000	2005 Profits: $2,905,000	Int'l Ticker: Int'l Exchange:
2004 Sales: $42,089,000	2004 Profits: $3,364,000	Employees: 87,850
2003 Sales: $39,565,000	2003 Profits: $2,639,000	Fiscal Year Ends: 12/31
2002 Sales: $41,065,000	2002 Profits: $-98,686,000	Parent Company:

SALARIES/BENEFITS:

Pension Plan:	ESOP Stock Plan:	Profit Sharing:	Top Exec. Salary: $1,500,000	Bonus: $7,500,000
Savings Plan: Y	Stock Purch. Plan:		Second Exec. Salary: $1,000,000	Bonus: $6,000,000

OTHER THOUGHTS:

Apparent Women Officers or Directors: 5
Hot Spot for Advancement for Women/Minorities: Y

LOCATIONS: ("Y" = Yes)

West:	Southwest:	Midwest:	Southeast:	Northeast:	International:
Y	Y	Y	Y	Y	Y

Note: Financial information, benefits and other data can change quickly and may vary from those stated here.

TIVO INC

www.tivo.com

Industry Group Code: 334310 Ranks within this company's industry group: Sales: 12 Profits: 12

Print Media/Publishing:	Movies:	Equipment/Supplies:		Broadcast/Cable:	Music/Audio:	Sports/Games:
Newspapers:	Movie Theaters:	Equipment/Supplies:	Y	Broadcast TV:	Music Production:	Games/Sports:
Magazines:	Movie Production:	Gambling Equipment:		Cable TV:	Retail Music:	Retail Games Stores:
Books:	TV/Video Production:	Special Services:	Y	Satellite Broadcast:	Retail Audio Equip.:	Stadiums/Teams:
Book Stores:	Video Rental:	Advertising Services:	Y	Radio:	Music Print./Dist.:	Gambling/Casinos:
Distribution/Printing:	Video Distribution:	Info. Sys. Software:		Online Information:	Multimedia:	Rides/Theme Parks:

TYPES OF BUSINESS:

Television Home Recording Technology
Digital Video Recorders
Advertising Services

BRANDS/DIVISIONS/AFFILIATES:

TiVo Mobile
TiVoCast
KidZone

CONTACTS: Note: Officers with more than one job title may be intentionally listed here more than once.

Tom Rogers, CEO
Tom Rogers, Pres.
Steve Sordello, CFO/Sr. VP
Joshua Katz, Chief Mktg. Officer
Nancy Kato, Sr. VP-Human Resources
James Barton, Sr. VP-R&D
Mark Roberts, CIO
James Barton, Chief Tech. Officer/Sr. VP
Bruce Klein, VP-Eng.
David H. Courtney, Exec. VP-Worldwide Oper. & Admin.
Matthew Zinn, General Counsel/Sr. VP/Chief Privacy Officer
Mark Roberts, Sr. VP-Oper. & Consumer Products
Naveen Chopra, VP-Corp. Dev. & Strategy
Anna Brunelle, Controller/Treas./VP
Jeff Klugman, Sr. VP/General Mng.-Service Provider & Advertising
Margret Schmidt, VP-User Experience Design & Research
Tara Maitra, VP/General Mng.-Content Services
Davina Kent, VP-National Advertising Sales

Phone: 408-519-9100	Fax: 408-519-5330
Toll-Free:	
Address: 2160 Gold St., Alviso, CA 95002-2160 US	

GROWTH PLANS/SPECIAL FEATURES:

TiVo, Inc. offers personal television services that allow viewers to pause, rewind and play back live or recorded broadcasts as well as search for, watch and record programs. The service also provides listings, daily suggestions and special viewing packages. As part of the package, the company provides the TiVo remote control and broadcast center. About 4.4 million subscribers receive TiVo's services. The firm has integrated the RealOne Player and RealOne Music (created by RealNetworks, Inc.) into its digital video recorders, giving viewers access to music recorded by over 10,000 artists. TiVo has also paired with AT&T Broadband for digital video recording of cable. In addition, it has an online scheduling option, which allows subscribers to access their TiVo service over the Internet. Moreover, the company works with DIRECTV, which provides the services to its subscribers. In 2006, TiVo paired with Verizon Wireless to launch TiVo Mobile, which allows subscribers to schedule recordings from their Verizon phones. TiVo plans to extend its base by selling services to advertisers, such as teasers implanted in ads that might entice viewers to watch the ads rather than skip through them. It also plans to deliver enhanced services to its set-top boxes, enabling customers to receive satellite radio music channels, Adobe photo album services and more. In 2006, TiVo launched TiVoCast, which allows customers to watch Internet content on their televisions. The company also recently launched KidZone, which provides parental controls. In late 2006, TiVo held a follow-on public offering of stock.

TiVo offers its employees benefits including a 401(k) plan, incentive stock options and a casual work environment. The company conducts weekly town-hall meetings on Friday afternoons, featuring a band and an espresso machine.

FINANCIALS: Sales and profits are in thousands of dollars—add 000 to get the full amount. 2006 Note: Financial information for 2006 was not available for all companies at press time.

2006 Sales: $195,925	2006 Profits: $-34,398	U.S. Stock Ticker: TIVO
2005 Sales: $172,055	2005 Profits: $-79,842	Int'l Ticker: Int'l Exchange:
2004 Sales: $141,080	2004 Profits: $-32,018	Employees: 400
2003 Sales: $96,010	2003 Profits: $-80,596	Fiscal Year Ends: 1/31
2002 Sales: $19,397	2002 Profits: $-156,705	Parent Company:

SALARIES/BENEFITS:

Pension Plan:	ESOP Stock Plan:	Profit Sharing:	Top Exec. Salary: $504,583	Bonus: $294,521
Savings Plan: Y	Stock Purch. Plan: Y		Second Exec. Salary: $300,000	Bonus: $171,000

OTHER THOUGHTS:

Apparent Women Officers or Directors: 6
Hot Spot for Advancement for Women/Minorities: Y

LOCATIONS: ("Y" = Yes)

West:	Southwest:	Midwest:	Southeast:	Northeast:	International:
Y					Y

TRADER CLASSIFIED MEDIA NV www.trader.com

Industry Group Code: 511120 Ranks within this company's industry group: Sales: 11 Profits: 5

Print Media/Publishing:		Movies:	Equipment/Supplies:		Broadcast/Cable:	Music/Audio:	Sports/Games:
Newspapers:	Y	Movie Theaters:	Equipment/Supplies:		Broadcast TV:	Music Production:	Games/Sports:
Magazines:		Movie Production:	Gambling Equipment:		Cable TV:	Retail Music:	Retail Games Stores:
Books:		TV/Video Production:	Special Services:	Y	Satellite Broadcast:	Retail Audio Equip.:	Stadiums/Teams:
Book Stores:		Video Rental:	Advertising Services:	Y	Radio:	Music Print./Dist.:	Gambling/Casinos:
Distribution/Printing:		Video Distribution:	Info. Sys. Software:		Online Information:	Multimedia:	Rides/Theme Parks:

TYPES OF BUSINESS:
Classified Ad Publications
Web Sites
Periodical Publishing

BRANDS/DIVISIONS/AFFILIATES:
Trader.com
AutoTrader
Sports & Antiques
LaCentrale.fr
Infojobs.net
Hebdo.net
Commercial Property Guide
Homebase.ca

CONTACTS: *Note: Officers with more than one job title may be intentionally listed here more than once.*
John H. M. MacBain, CEO
Didier Breton, COO
John H. M. MacBain, Pres.
Francois Jallot, CFO
Peter Reese, VP-Mktg.
William Clark, VP-Human Resources
Zouhaire Sekkat, CIO
Elizabeth Pauchet, General Counsel
Paul Guest, VP-Oper. & Finance
Eric de Teyssonniere de Gramont, Chmn.

Phone: 31-20-575-56-00 **Fax:**
Toll-Free:
Address: Overschiestraat 61, Amsterdam, 1062 XD The Netherlands

GROWTH PLANS/SPECIAL FEATURES:
Trader Classified Media N.V., formerly Trader.com, is a publishing company that sells classified advertising services. The firm offers content in multiple categories such as jobs, personal ads, computers, production equipment and leisure, but concentrates largely on its core categories, which include real estate, automotive and general merchandise. Trader operates in 19 countries around the world and owns approximately 400 publications and 50 web sites. The firm's printed publications have more than nine million readers per week, while its web sites attract 7.3 million visitors per month. Trader's print publications range from the general to the specific and include titles such as Auto Trader, Sport & Antiques and Commercial Property Guide. The company's web sites include Hebdo.net, Homebase.ca, Lacentrale.fr and US.trader.com. The firm also has a 60% stake in a major European Internet employment web site, Infojobs.net.

FINANCIALS: Sales and profits are in thousands of dollars—add 000 to get the full amount. 2006 Note: Financial information for 2006 was not available for all companies at press time.
2006 Sales: $
2005 Sales: $372,323
2004 Sales: $319,533
2003 Sales: $494,530
2002 Sales: $464,000

2006 Profits: $
2005 Profits: $15,277
2004 Profits: $299,803
2003 Profits: $302,964
2002 Profits: $365,000

U.S. Stock Ticker: TRD
Int'l Ticker: TRD Int'l Exchange: Paris-Euronext
Employees: 3,400
Fiscal Year Ends: 12/31
Parent Company:

SALARIES/BENEFITS:
Pension Plan:	ESOP Stock Plan:	Profit Sharing:	Top Exec. Salary: $	Bonus: $
Savings Plan:	Stock Purch. Plan:		Second Exec. Salary: $	Bonus: $

OTHER THOUGHTS:
Apparent Women Officers or Directors: 1
Hot Spot for Advancement for Women/Minorities:

LOCATIONS: ("Y" = Yes)
West:	Southwest:	Midwest:	Southeast:	Northeast:	International:
					Y

TRAFFIX INC

www.traffixinc.com

Industry Group Code: 541810A **Ranks within this company's industry group:** Sales: 2   Profits: 1

Print Media/Publishing:	Movies:	Equipment/Supplies:		Broadcast/Cable:	Music/Audio:	Sports/Games:
Newspapers:	Movie Theaters:	Equipment/Supplies:		Broadcast TV:	Music Production:	Games/Sports:
Magazines:	Movie Production:	Gambling Equipment:		Cable TV:	Retail Music:	Retail Games Stores:
Books:	TV/Video Production:	Special Services:	Y	Satellite Broadcast:	Retail Audio Equip.:	Stadiums/Teams:
Book Stores:	Video Rental:	Advertising Services:	Y	Radio:	Music Print./Dist.:	Gambling/Casinos:
Distribution/Printing:	Video Distribution:	Info. Sys. Software:		Online Information:	Multimedia:	Rides/Theme Parks:

TYPES OF BUSINESS:

Online Direct Marketing
Database Marketing
Online Dating Service
Online Tech Support

BRANDS/DIVISIONS/AFFILIATES:

Traffix Performance Marketing
SendTraffic
Hot Rocket Marketing
mxFocus
RocketProfit
iMatchup.com
Q121.com
LoveFreeGames.com

CONTACTS: *Note: Officers with more than one job title may be intentionally listed here more than once.*

Jeffrey L. Schwartz, CEO
Richard Wentworth, COO
Andrew Stollman, Pres.
Daniel Harvey, CFO
Joshua B. Gillon, General Counsel/Exec. VP
Jeffrey L. Schwartz, Chmn.

Phone: 845-620-1212	**Fax:** 845-620-1717
Toll-Free:	
Address: One Blue Hill Plaza, Pearl River, NY 10965 US	

GROWTH PLANS/SPECIAL FEATURES:

Traffix, Inc. is a database marketing company that uses its online media network and proprietary ad-serving optimization technology to generate leads, customers and sales for itself and its corporate clients. The firm's marketing services for companies include the development of complete, creative promotions; broadcasting online promotions; creating and hosting customized web sites; and comprehensive results reporting for use in promotion analysis. Traffix generates revenues from direct marketing activities, as well as sales and rentals of its proprietary, profiled databases. The company operates through four business groups: Traffix Performance Marketing, which offers marketers advertising distribution through Traffix's network of websites including EZ-Tracks.com, reciperewards.com, PrizeDistributors, Inc, Music of Faith.com, AtlasCreditGroup.com, TheBargainSpot.com, AltasAutomotiveGroup.com, EZGreets.com, GameFiesta.com, PrizeAmerica.com and LoveFreeGames.com; SendTraffic, a search engine marketing firm; Hot Rocket Marketing, is an online direct response media firm; mxFocus, launched in 2006, which develops and distributes content for mobile phones and other wireless devices on every major wireless carrier. In addition, Traffix offers services in e-mail marketing, Results Analysis, and syndication of its advertising campaigns to third party media. Recently, the company has launched two new websites: iMatchup.com, and online dating program conducted over the Internet; and Q121.com, a social networking site that gives users the ability to transfer content to and from their mobile phones as well as sending text messages to individuals or groups anonymously.

FINANCIALS: Sales and profits are in thousands of dollars—add 000 to get the full amount. 2006 Note: Financial information for 2006 was not available for all companies at press time.

2006 Sales: $	2006 Profits: $	**U.S. Stock Ticker:** TRFX
2005 Sales: $62,856	2005 Profits: $2,428	**Int'l Ticker:** Int'l Exchange:
2004 Sales: $37,281	2004 Profits: $1,014	Employees: 89
2003 Sales: $32,389	2003 Profits: $ 421	Fiscal Year Ends: 11/30
2002 Sales: $44,043	2002 Profits: $2,741	Parent Company:

SALARIES/BENEFITS:

Pension Plan:	ESOP Stock Plan:	Profit Sharing:	Top Exec. Salary: $605,000	Bonus: $
Savings Plan:	Stock Purch. Plan:		Second Exec. Salary: $544,500	Bonus: $50,000

OTHER THOUGHTS:

Apparent Women Officers or Directors:
Hot Spot for Advancement for Women/Minorities:

LOCATIONS: ("Y" = Yes)

West:	Southwest:	Midwest:	Southeast:	Northeast:	International:
				Y	Y

TRANS WORLD CORP   www.transwc.com

Industry Group Code: 713210 Ranks within this company's industry group: Sales: 10   Profits: 8

Print Media/Publishing:	Movies:	Equipment/Supplies:	Broadcast/Cable:	Music/Audio:	Sports/Games:
Newspapers:	Movie Theaters:	Equipment/Supplies:	Broadcast TV:	Music Production:	Games/Sports:
Magazines:	Movie Production:	Gambling Equipment:	Cable TV:	Retail Music:	Retail Games Stores:
Books:	TV/Video Production:	Special Services:	Satellite Broadcast:	Retail Audio Equip.:	Stadiums/Teams:
Book Stores:	Video Rental:	Advertising Services:	Radio:	Music Print./Dist.:	Gambling/Casinos: Y
Distribution/Printing:	Video Distribution:	Info. Sys. Software:	Online Information:	Multimedia:	Rides/Theme Parks:

TYPES OF BUSINESS:
Casinos
Hotels & Restaurants

BRANDS/DIVISIONS/AFFILIATES:
Trans World Gaming Corp.
American Chance Casinos
Route 55
Route 59
Ceska Kubice
Dolni Dvoriste Hotel
Znojmo
Value Partners

CONTACTS: *Note: Officers with more than one job title may be intentionally listed here more than once.*
Rami S. Ramadan, CEO
Rami S. Ramadan, Pres.
Rami S. Ramadan, CFO
Roland Stamberger, Dir.-Regional Mktg. Europe
Paul Benkley, Dir.-Dev. Europe

Phone: 212-983-3355	Fax: 212-563-3380
Toll-Free:	
Address: 545 5th Ave., Ste. 940, New York, NY 10017 US	

GROWTH PLANS/SPECIAL FEATURES:

TransWorld Corporation, formerly Trans World Gaming Corp., owns and operates small-to-medium casinos and hotels in the Czech Republic. The company's European partner (branded American Chance Casinos, or ACC) operates the casino division. Each casino focuses on a different American theme including: 1920s Chicago, 1950s Miami Beach, the Pacific South Seas and the Southern Antebellum era. Built on border towns, the casinos include: Ceska Kubice (located on the Czech-German border); Trans World (located on the Czech-German border); Route 59 (located on the Czech-Austrian border); and Route 55 (located on the Czech-Austrian border). The casinos feature games including American roulette, blackjack, Red Dog, poker, automatic roulette and slot machines. Trans World plans on constructing three hotels by 2008, each located near an ACC casino. Dolni Dvoriste Hotel (near Route 55) and Folmava (near Ceska) will each feature a restaurant, spa and fitness center. Znojmo (near Route 59) will feature a restaurant, bar, night club, spa and fitness center. In addition, the firm plans on developing four-star hotels featuring 80-400 rooms in Europe. In 2006, TransWorld was awarded a contract to manage a luxury casino and nightclub at Le Meridien Lav in Split, along the coast in Croatia. Trans World Director Timothy G. Ewing controls about 45% of the company's shares through Texas-based investment firm Value Partners.

FINANCIALS: Sales and profits are in thousands of dollars—add 000 to get the full amount. 2006 Note: Financial information for 2006 was not available for all companies at press time.

2006 Sales: $	2006 Profits: $	U.S. Stock Ticker: TWOC
2005 Sales: $23,249	2005 Profits: $ 79	Int'l Ticker: Int'l Exchange:
2004 Sales: $18,938	2004 Profits: $1,247	Employees: 514
2003 Sales: $17,600	2003 Profits: $ 200	Fiscal Year Ends: 12/31
2002 Sales: $14,200	2002 Profits: $-3,300	Parent Company:

SALARIES/BENEFITS:

Pension Plan:	ESOP Stock Plan:	Profit Sharing:	Top Exec. Salary: $400,000	Bonus: $
Savings Plan:	Stock Purch. Plan: Y		Second Exec. Salary: $99,959	Bonus: $

OTHER THOUGHTS:
Apparent Women Officers or Directors: 1
Hot Spot for Advancement for Women/Minorities:

LOCATIONS: ("Y" = Yes)

West:	Southwest:	Midwest:	Southeast:	Northeast:	International:
				Y	Y

Note: Financial information, benefits and other data can change quickly and may vary from those stated here.

TRANS WORLD ENTERTAINMENT CORP   www.twec.com

Industry Group Code: 451220 Ranks within this company's industry group: Sales: 1   Profits: 1

Print Media/Publishing:	Movies:	Equipment/Supplies:	Broadcast/Cable:	Music/Audio:		Sports/Games:
Newspapers:	Movie Theaters:	Equipment/Supplies:	Broadcast TV:	Music Production:		Games/Sports:
Magazines:	Movie Production:	Gambling Equipment:	Cable TV:	Retail Music:	Y	Retail Games Stores:
Books:	TV/Video Production:	Special Services:	Satellite Broadcast:	Retail Audio Equip.:		Stadiums/Teams:
Book Stores:	Video Rental:	Advertising Services:	Radio:	Music Print./Dist.:	Y	Gambling/Casinos:
Distribution/Printing:	Video Distribution:	Info. Sys. Software:	Online Information:	Multimedia:		Rides/Theme Parks:

TYPES OF BUSINESS:
Music Stores
CDs, DVDs, Videos & Video Games
Online Sales
Digital Music Content
Used Music & Video Retail

BRANDS/DIVISIONS/AFFILIATES:
Musicland Holding Corp.
Suncoast.com
FYE (For Your Entertainment)
Coconuts Music and Movies
Strawberries Music
Wherehouse
Sam Goody
Mix & Burn, LLC

CONTACTS: Note: Officers with more than one job title may be intentionally listed here more than once.
Robert J. Higgins, CEO
James A. Litwak, COO
James A. Litwak, Pres.
John J. Sullivan, CFO/Exec. VP
John J. Sullivan, Corp. Sec.
Bruce J. Eisenberg, Exec. VP-Real Estate
Robert J. Higgins, Chmn.

Phone: 518-452-1242	Fax: 518-452-3547
Toll-Free:	
Address: 38 Corporate Circle, Albany, NY 12203 US	

GROWTH PLANS/SPECIAL FEATURES:
Trans World Entertainment Corp. (TWE) is a specialty retailer of compact discs, prerecorded audiocassettes and videocassettes, DVDs, videogames and related products in the U.S. The firm operates more than 810 mall-based and free-standing stores in all 50 states, the District of Columbia, Puerto Rico and the Virgin Islands. Trans World owns 100% of Record Town, Inc., through which it conducts most of its operations, and SecondSpin, a used CD, video and DVD retailer. Stores are divided into mall based stores, under the brand name FYE (For Your Entertainment) and freestanding stores under various names. The firm has approximately 650 FYE mall stores with an average of 5,700 square feet, which carry a full complement of entertainment products. These include 14 Superstores that offer a broader and deeper assortment, 17 Saturday Matinee movie stores and one Games store. The firm operates 249 freestanding stores under the brand names Coconuts Music and Movies, Strawberries Music, Wherehouse, CD World, Spec's and Second Spin. The stores carry a full complement of entertainment products and are designed for freestanding, strip mall and downtown locations. The freestanding stores average approximately 6,200 square feet in size. The company also operates a single Planet Music store, a 31,400-square-foot freestanding superstore in Virginia Beach, Virginia. This Planet Music store offers an extensive catalog of music, DVD and VHS video, games and related merchandise. TWE also operates a number of e-commerce websites, including www.fye.com, www.coconuts.com, www.wherehouse.com, and www.secondspin.com. In 2006, the firm acquired Mix & Burn, LLC., a provider of digital content to retailers nationwide. In addition, the firm acquired all of the assets of Musicland Holding Corp., which operates retail stores and websites under the names Sam Goody, Suncoast Motion Picture Company, On Cue and MediaPlay.com.

FINANCIALS: Sales and profits are in thousands of dollars—add 000 to get the full amount. 2006 Note: Financial information for 2006 was not available for all companies at press time.

2006 Sales: $1,238,486	2006 Profits: $ 609	**U.S. Stock Ticker:** TWMC
2005 Sales: $1,365,133	2005 Profits: $41,841	**Int'l Ticker:** Int'l Exchange:
2004 Sales: $1,330,626	2004 Profits: $23,067	Employees: 8,100
2003 Sales: $1,281,900	2003 Profits: $-45,500	Fiscal Year Ends: 1/31
2002 Sales: $1,388,000	2002 Profits: $16,800	Parent Company:

SALARIES/BENEFITS:

Pension Plan:	ESOP Stock Plan:	Profit Sharing:	Top Exec. Salary: $1,250,000	Bonus: $
Savings Plan: Y	Stock Purch. Plan:		Second Exec. Salary: $347,884	Bonus: $

OTHER THOUGHTS:
Apparent Women Officers or Directors: 1
Hot Spot for Advancement for Women/Minorities:

LOCATIONS: ("Y" = Yes)

West:	Southwest:	Midwest:	Southeast:	Northeast:	International:
Y	Y	Y	Y	Y	Y

Note: Financial information, benefits and other data can change quickly and may vary from those stated here.

TRANS-LUX CORPORATION

www.trans-lux.com

Industry Group Code: 334310 **Ranks within this company's industry group:** Sales: 14   Profits: 11

Print Media/Publishing:	Movies:		Equipment/Supplies:		Broadcast/Cable:	Music/Audio:	Sports/Games:
Newspapers:	Movie Theaters:	Y	Equipment/Supplies:	Y	Broadcast TV:	Music Production:	Games/Sports:
Magazines:	Movie Production:		Gambling Equipment:		Cable TV:	Retail Music:	Retail Games Stores:
Books:	TV/Video Production:		Special Services:		Satellite Broadcast:	Retail Audio Equip.:	Stadiums/Teams:
Book Stores:	Video Rental:		Advertising Services:		Radio:	Music Print./Dist.:	Gambling/Casinos:
Distribution/Printing:	Video Distribution:		Info. Sys. Software:		Online Information:	Multimedia:	Rides/Theme Parks:

TYPES OF BUSINESS:

Electronic Equipment-Information Displays
Movie Theaters
Data, Graphics & Picture Displays

BRANDS/DIVISIONS/AFFILIATES:

CaptiVision
CaptiVue
Trans-Lux Movies
Trans-Lux West
DataWall
RainbowWall
ProLine

CONTACTS: *Note: Officers with more than one job title may be intentionally listed here more than once.*

Thomas Brandt, Co-CEO/Exec. VP
Michael R. Mulcahy, Pres./Co-CEO
Angela D. Toppi, CFO
Thomas F. Mahoney, Sr. VP-Sales & Mktg.
Karl P. Hirschauer, Sr. VP-Eng.
Al Miller, Exec. VP-Mfg.
Angela D.Toppi, Treas.
Matthew Brandt, Exec. VP-Entertainment Subsidiaries
John A. Long, Sr. VP
Gene Jankowski, Chmn.

Phone: 203-853-4321	Fax: 203-852-0836
Toll-Free: 800-243-5544	
Address: 110 Richards Ave., Norwalk, CT 06856-5090 US	

GROWTH PLANS/SPECIAL FEATURES:

Trans-Lux Corporation manufactures, distributes and services large-scale, multi-color, real-time electronic information displays utilizing LED, plasma and LCD screens; and bulb based technologies including graphics and video displays. Its indoor and outdoor displays are used in many international industries, including brokerage firms, banks, energy companies, insurance and mutual fund companies, sports stadiums, educational institutions and outdoor advertisers. In addition, displays can be found in corporate and government communication centers, retail outlets, casinos, race tracks, train stations, bus terminals, on highways and in movie theatres. The company provides products tailored to customers (including hardware components and software) as well as on-site installation and maintenance coverage. Trans-Lux's subsidiary CaptiVue specializes in outdoor display, with the capacity to include full color and blue monochrome configurations in LED messages. Subsidiary CaptiVision specializes in jumbo full colored monitors that deliver video and animation for sports and non-sports markets. ProLine, the firm's proprietary controller software, is designed for screens that require fast-changing information and imagery, such as in sports and commercial markets, and allows live or recorded video, newswire feeds, cable TV and animations to be combined with text on a single display. GraphixWall, the firm's indoor graphic display product allows for large custom displays such as flight information and baggage claim at airports; automatic call directories at contact centers; and promoting products in financial and retail environments. Trans-Lux also owns and operates 66 theaters in 11 locations in the western mountain states.

Trans-Lux offers its employees benefits including a 401(k) plan, flexible spending accounts, auto and homeowners' insurance, job share and flex time arrangements, a credit union, tuition reimbursement, training courses, recognition programs and merchandise discounts. The company also offers preventative health programs such as stress reduction seminars, blood pressure and cholesterol screenings, flu shots and a summer walking program.

FINANCIALS: Sales and profits are in thousands of dollars—add 000 to get the full amount. 2006 Note: Financial information for 2006 was not available for all companies at press time.

2006 Sales: $	2006 Profits: $	**U.S. Stock Ticker:** TLX
2005 Sales: $54,368	2005 Profits: $-1,793	**Int'l Ticker:** Int'l Exchange:
2004 Sales: $52,579	2004 Profits: $ 539	Employees: 459
2003 Sales: $56,022	2003 Profits: $1,054	Fiscal Year Ends: 12/31
2002 Sales: $74,891	2002 Profits: $ 428	Parent Company:

SALARIES/BENEFITS:

Pension Plan:	ESOP Stock Plan:	Profit Sharing:	Top Exec. Salary: $279,733	Bonus: $
Savings Plan: Y	Stock Purch. Plan:		Second Exec. Salary: $194,853	Bonus: $

OTHER THOUGHTS:

Apparent Women Officers or Directors: 1
Hot Spot for Advancement for Women/Minorities:

LOCATIONS: ("Y" = Yes)

West:	Southwest:	Midwest:	Southeast:	Northeast:	International:
Y	Y	Y		Y	Y

TRIBUNE CO

www.tribune.com

Industry Group Code: 511110 Ranks within this company's industry group: Sales: 3   Profits: 2

Print Media/Publishing:		Movies:		Equipment/Supplies:		Broadcast/Cable:		Music/Audio:		Sports/Games:	
Newspapers:	Y	Movie Theaters:		Equipment/Supplies:		Broadcast TV:	Y	Music Production:		Games/Sports:	Y
Magazines:		Movie Production:		Gambling Equipment:		Cable TV:		Retail Music:		Retail Games Stores:	
Books:		TV/Video Production:	Y	Special Services:		Satellite Broadcast:		Retail Audio Equip.:		Stadiums/Teams:	
Book Stores:		Video Rental:		Advertising Services:		Radio:		Music Print./Dist.:		Gambling/Casinos:	
Distribution/Printing:		Video Distribution:		Info. Sys. Software:		Online Information:		Multimedia:		Rides/Theme Parks:	

TYPES OF BUSINESS:

Newspaper Publishing
Online News & Information
TV & Radio Broadcasting
TV Programming Development
Professional Sports Teams
Media Marketing

BRANDS/DIVISIONS/AFFILIATES:

Los Angeles Times
Chicago Tribune
Newsday
Superstation WGN
Chicago Cubs
Tribune Entertainment
Tribune Interactive, Inc.
Tribune Broadcasting Company

CONTACTS: Note: Officers with more than one job title may be intentionally listed here more than once.

Dennis FitzSimons, CEO
Dennis FitzSimons, Pres.
Luis Lewin, Sr. VP-Human Resources
Donald Grenesko, Sr. VP-Admin.
Crane Kenney, General Counsel/Sr. VP
Thomas Leach, VP-Dev.
Ruthellyn Musil, VP-Corp. Rel.
Donald Grenesko, Sr. VP-Finance
Scott Smith, Pres., Tribune Publishing
Crane Kenney, Corp. Sec.
John Reardon, Pres., Tribune Broadcasting
Timothy Landon, Pres., Tribune Interactive
Dennis FitzSimons, Chmn.

Phone: 312-222-9100	**Fax:** 312-222-1573
Toll-Free:	
Address: 435 N. Michigan Ave., Chicago, IL 60611 US	

GROWTH PLANS/SPECIAL FEATURES:

Tribune Company, through its subsidiaries, publishes newspapers, provides broadcast television and radio entertainment, and develops and distributes information and entertainment through the Internet. The company's primary newspapers are the Los Angeles Times, Chicago Tribune, Newsday, South Florida Sun-Sentinel, Orlando Sentinel and Baltimore Sun. Tribune also operates entertainment listings, a media marketing company and Superstation WGN on national cable, among other related businesses. The firm's broadcasting segment includes WB, FOX and ABC affiliate stations across the U.S., in addition to several radio stations, the Chicago Cubs baseball team and Tribune Entertainment, a television programming development company. The interactive segment manages the web sites of the company's daily newspapers and television stations. In late 2006, the company began a major restructuring initiative, planning to sell many of its assets in an attempt to raise at least $500 million in capital.

Tribune's employee benefits include tuition reimbursement, an employee assistance program, a group legal plan, reimbursement accounts and a gift matching program.

FINANCIALS: Sales and profits are in thousands of dollars—add 000 to get the full amount. 2006 Note: Financial information for 2006 was not available for all companies at press time.

2006 Sales: $	2006 Profits: $	**U.S. Stock Ticker:** TRB
2005 Sales: $5,595,617	2005 Profits: $534,689	**Int'l Ticker:** Int'l Exchange:
2004 Sales: $5,726,247	2004 Profits: $555,536	Employees: 22,400
2003 Sales: $5,594,800	2003 Profits: $891,400	Fiscal Year Ends: 12/31
2002 Sales: $5,384,000	2002 Profits: $443,000	Parent Company:

SALARIES/BENEFITS:

Pension Plan: Y	ESOP Stock Plan:	Profit Sharing:	Top Exec. Salary: $917,308	Bonus: $260,000
Savings Plan: Y	Stock Purch. Plan: Y		Second Exec. Salary: $615,231	Bonus: $

OTHER THOUGHTS:

Apparent Women Officers or Directors: 1
Hot Spot for Advancement for Women/Minorities:

LOCATIONS: ("Y" = Yes)

West:	Southwest:	Midwest:	Southeast:	Northeast:	International:
Y	Y	Y	Y	Y	Y

TRUMP ENTERTAINMENT RESORTS INC   www.trump.com

Industry Group Code: 721120 Ranks within this company's industry group: Sales: 6 Profits: 3

Print Media/Publishing:	Movies:	Equipment/Supplies:	Broadcast/Cable:	Music/Audio:	Sports/Games:	
Newspapers:	Movie Theaters:	Equipment/Supplies:	Broadcast TV:	Music Production:	Games/Sports:	
Magazines:	Movie Production:	Gambling Equipment:	Cable TV:	Retail Music:	Retail Games Stores:	
Books:	TV/Video Production:	Special Services:	Satellite Broadcast:	Retail Audio Equip.:	Stadiums/Teams:	
Book Stores:	Video Rental:	Advertising Services:	Radio:	Music Print./Dist.:	Gambling/Casinos:	Y
Distribution/Printing:	Video Distribution:	Info. Sys. Software:	Online Information:	Multimedia:	Rides/Theme Parks:	

TYPES OF BUSINESS:
Casino Hotels
Casino Management

BRANDS/DIVISIONS/AFFILIATES:
Trump Plaza Hotel & Casino
Trump Indiana
Trump Taj Mahal Casino Resort
Trump Marina Hotel Casino
Trump Hotels & Casino Resorts, Inc.
Diamondhead Casino Corporation

CONTACTS: *Note: Officers with more than one job title may be intentionally listed here more than once.*
James Perry, CEO
Mark Juliano, COO
James Perry, Pres.
Dale Black, CFO
Craig Keyser, VP-Human Resources
Virginia McDowell, CIO
Craig Keyser, VP-Admin.
Robert M. Pickus, General Counsel/Exec. VP
Joseph A. Fusco, Exec. VP-Gov't Rel. & Regulatory Affairs
John P. Burke, Exec. VP/Corp. Treas.
Robert M. Pickus, Corp. Sec.
Richard Santoro, Exec. VP-Asset Protection & Risk Mgmt.
Joseph Fusco, Exec. VP-Gov't Affairs
Paul Keller, Exec. VP-Design & Construction
Donald J. Trump, Chmn.

Phone: 609-449-6515   **Fax:** 609-449-6586
Toll-Free:
Address: 1000 Boardwalk, Atlantic City, NJ 08401 US

GROWTH PLANS/SPECIAL FEATURES:
Trump Entertainment Resorts, formerly Trump Hotels & Casino Resorts, Inc., operates (through its subsidiaries) three casino properties in Atlantic City, New Jersey. Its Atlantic City casinos are the Trump Plaza Hotel and Casino, the Trump Taj Mahal Casino Resort and the Trump Marina Hotel and Casino. Together, these three properties comprise approximately 330,000 square feet of gaming space, offering over 9,300 slot machines, 370 gaming tables and 2,880 hotel rooms and suites. Each property features thousands of slot machines and between 75 and 205 gaming tables. The casinos occupy about a 20% share of the gaming revenue in the city. All of the casinos also offer regular live entertainment focused on themes, as well as touring events. In late 2004, the company filed for Chapter 11 bankruptcy protection, emerging in late 2005 the firm with a new name, and following the reorganization, founder Donald J. Trump owned about 30% of the company's stock. In December 2005, the firm sold its Trump Indiana subsidiary, the operator of a riverboat casino and hotel at Buffington Harbor in Gary, Indiana, for about $253 million. In the process of reorganizing, the company also transferred its management of the Trump 29 casino back to the Luiseno Mission Indians. For 2006, the company dedicated $110 million in capital for revamping the gaming floors of its existing three casinos. In June 2006, the company signed a joint venture agreement with Diamondhead Casino Corporation to build and operate a destination casino resort in Diamondhead, Mississippi.

Workers for Trump Entertainment are given a complete benefits package, paid vacation time, uniforms and cleaning, employee parties and meals.

FINANCIALS: Sales and profits are in thousands of dollars—add 000 to get the full amount. 2006 Note: Financial information for 2006 was not available for all companies at press time.

2006 Sales: $	2006 Profits: $	**U.S. Stock Ticker: TRMP**
2005 Sales: $992,221	2005 Profits: $251,856	**Int'l Ticker:** Int'l Exchange:
2004 Sales: $10,029,380	2004 Profits: $-191,300	Employees: 7,500
2003 Sales: $1,029,110	2003 Profits: $-87,300	Fiscal Year Ends: 12/31
2002 Sales: $1,229,000	2002 Profits: $-12,000	Parent Company:

SALARIES/BENEFITS:
Pension Plan: Y	ESOP Stock Plan:	Profit Sharing:	Top Exec. Salary: $1,468,415	Bonus: $
Savings Plan: Y	Stock Purch. Plan:		Second Exec. Salary: $1,208,830	Bonus: $

OTHER THOUGHTS:
Apparent Women Officers or Directors: 1
Hot Spot for Advancement for Women/Minorities:

LOCATIONS: ("Y" = Yes)
West:	Southwest:	Midwest:	Southeast:	Northeast:	International:
		Y		Y	

Note: Financial information, benefits and other data can change quickly and may vary from those stated here.

TURNER BROADCASTING SYSTEM   www.turner.com

Industry Group Code: 513210 Ranks within this company's industry group: Sales: 3   Profits:

Print Media/Publishing:	Movies:		Equipment/Supplies:	Broadcast/Cable:		Music/Audio:	Sports/Games:	
Newspapers:	Movie Theaters:		Equipment/Supplies:	Broadcast TV:		Music Production:	Games/Sports:	
Magazines:	Movie Production:		Gambling Equipment:	Cable TV:	Y	Retail Music:	Retail Games Stores:	
Books:	TV/Video Production:	Y	Special Services:	Satellite Broadcast:		Retail Audio Equip.:	Stadiums/Teams:	Y
Book Stores:	Video Rental:		Advertising Services:	Radio:		Music Print./Dist.:	Gambling/Casinos:	
Distribution/Printing:	Video Distribution:		Info. Sys. Software:	Online Information:		Multimedia:	Rides/Theme Parks:	

TYPES OF BUSINESS:
Cable Programming
News Programs
Sports Teams

BRANDS/DIVISIONS/AFFILIATES:
CNN
TBS
TNT
CourtTV
Cartoon Network
Boomerang
TCM Latin America
Atlanta Braves

CONTACTS: *Note: Officers with more than one job title may be intentionally listed here more than once.*
Philip I. Kent, CEO
Greg D'Alba, COO
Steve Koonin, Pres.
Victoria W. Miller, CFO/Exec. VP
David R. Levy, Pres., Sales & Mktg.
Kelly Regal, VP-Human Resources
Scott Teissler, CIO
Scott Teissler, CTO/Exec. VP-Tech.
Louise Sams, General Counsel/Exec.VP
Jim McCaffrey, Exec. VP-Oper.
Jim McCaffrey, Exec. VP-Strategy
Kelly Regal, Exec. VP-Corp. Comm.
Terence F. McGuirk, Vice-Chmn/Chmn.-Atlanta Braves
Mark Lazarus, Pres., Turner Entertainment Group
Jim Walton, Pres., CNN News Group
Andrew T. Heller, Pres., Domestic Distribution
Philip I. Kent, Chmn.
Louise Sams, Pres., TBS Int'l

Phone: 404-827-1700	Fax: 404-827-2437
Toll-Free: 866-463-6899	
Address: One CNN Center, 100 International Blvd., Atlanta, GA 30303 US	

GROWTH PLANS/SPECIAL FEATURES:
Turner Broadcasting System (TBS), a Time Warner subsidiary, produces news and entertainment programming internationally, as well as basic cable programming. The company's domestic program subsidiaries include news stations CNN, CNN Headline News and CNNfn (financial news); cable broadcasting networks TBS, TNT, TCM, TNT HD, Court TV and Game Tap; and animation networks Cartoon Network, Adult Swim and Boomerang. Internationally, the firm owns CNN International and CNN Espanol in news; TNT Brazil, TNT Mexico, TNT Argentina, TCM U.K., TCM France, TCM Spain and TCM Latin America in entertainment; and versions of the Cartoon Network in Mexico, Argentina, Brazil, Chile, Venezuela, Latin America, Europe, Taiwan, India, and Japan, as well as Pogo, Boomerang U.K. and Toonami U.K. in animation. TBS also owns the Atlanta Braves baseball team and the pga.com and nascar.com sports web sites. In 2006, the firm sold its Turner South to Fox Cable Networks, which plans to convert it to a regional sports channel. In addition, the firm purchased the remaining half of Court TV from Liberty Media, thus acquiring the entire network. Also in 2006, the company agreed to acquire seven pay television networks in the Latin American market from Claxson Interactive for $235 million. Per the agreement, TBS will own the networks Fashion TV, HTV, Infinito, I.Sat, MuchMusic, Retro and Space, reaching 51 million Latin American subscribers.

TBS offers its employees domestic partner and dependent insurance, transportation reimbursement, a credit union, an on-site athletic facility, tuition reimbursement, company-wide advancement training and an employee assistance program. In addition, employees are entitled to infertility treatment benefits, adoption assistance, back-up child care reimbursement, veterinary pet insurance, free sports tickets, free admission to studio series performances, as well as discounts at the Turner Store and on Time Warner merchandise.

FINANCIALS: Sales and profits are in thousands of dollars—add 000 to get the full amount. 2006 Note: Financial information for 2006 was not available for all companies at press time.

2006 Sales: $	2006 Profits: $	**U.S. Stock Ticker: Subsidiary**
2005 Sales: $9,611,000	2005 Profits: $	**Int'l Ticker:** Int'l Exchange:
2004 Sales: $9,054,000	2004 Profits: $	Employees:
2003 Sales: $8,434,000	2003 Profits: $	Fiscal Year Ends: 12/31
2002 Sales: $7,655,000	2002 Profits: $	Parent Company: TIME WARNER INC

SALARIES/BENEFITS:

Pension Plan:	ESOP Stock Plan:	Profit Sharing:	Top Exec. Salary: $	Bonus: $
Savings Plan:	Stock Purch. Plan:		Second Exec. Salary: $	Bonus: $

OTHER THOUGHTS:
Apparent Women Officers or Directors: 3
Hot Spot for Advancement for Women/Minorities: Y

LOCATIONS: ("Y" = Yes)

West:	Southwest:	Midwest:	Southeast:	Northeast:	International:
			Y	Y	

TV AZTECA SA DE CV

www.tvazteca.com

Industry Group Code: 513120 Ranks within this company's industry group: Sales: 11 Profits: 8

Print Media/Publishing:	Movies:		Equipment/Supplies:		Broadcast/Cable:		Music/Audio:		Sports/Games:	
Newspapers:	Movie Theaters:		Equipment/Supplies:		Broadcast TV:	Y	Music Production:	Y	Games/Sports:	
Magazines:	Movie Production:		Gambling Equipment:		Cable TV:		Retail Music:		Retail Games Stores:	
Books:	TV/Video Production:	Y	Special Services:	Y	Satellite Broadcast:		Retail Audio Equip.:		Stadiums/Teams:	Y
Book Stores:	Video Rental:		Advertising Services:		Radio:		Music Print./Dist.:		Gambling/Casinos:	
Distribution/Printing:	Video Distribution:		Info. Sys. Software:		Online Information:		Multimedia:		Rides/Theme Parks:	

TYPES OF BUSINESS:

Spanish-Language Television Networks
Wireless Telephone Services
Internet Services
Soccer Team
Music Production

BRANDS/DIVISIONS/AFFILIATES:

todito.com
Unefon
Azteca America
TV Azteca 7
TV Azteca 13
Azteca Music
Monarcas Morelia

CONTACTS: Note: Officers with more than one job title may be intentionally listed here more than once.

Mario San Roman, CEO
Adrian Steckel, Pres./CEO
Carlos H. Flores, CFO
Carlos Diaz, Dir.- Sales
Tristan Canales, Dir.-Comm.
Carlos Hesles, CEO
Luis J. Echarte, Chmn.

Phone: 52-55-1720-1313 **Fax:** 52-55-1720-1418
Toll-Free:
Address: Periferico Sur 4121, Colonia Fuentes del Pedregal, Mexico City, DF 14141 Mexico

GROWTH PLANS/SPECIAL FEATURES:

TV Azteca S.A. de C.V. is one of the largest producers of Spanish-language television programming in the world. The company is diversifying its position in a variety of media, including wireless phone service and the Internet. It operates the TV Azteca 7 and TV Azteca 13 networks, and has a total of 315 owned and operated stations across Mexico. The firm's programming includes a broad selection of news, sports and entertainment programs. These consist of Spanish-language versions of programs from the U.S., such as the Spanish version of The Simpsons, Los Simpson, as well as original programming such as news programs that focus on the Latin American market. The company also controls the Azteca America network. In addition, TV Azteca has interests in mobile phone operator Unefon, soccer team Monarcas Morelia, music company Azteca Music and todito.com, a Spanish-language Internet portal. The company received permission to broadcast its Azteca 13 signal in Canada in 2006.

FINANCIALS: Sales and profits are in thousands of dollars—add 000 to get the full amount. 2006 Note: Financial information for 2006 was not available for all companies at press time.

2006 Sales: $	2006 Profits: $	U.S. Stock Ticker: Foreign
2005 Sales: $797,000	2005 Profits: $114,000	Int'l Ticker: TVAZTCACPO Int'l Exchange: Mexico City
2004 Sales: $803,000	2004 Profits: $149,000	Employees: 4,228
2003 Sales: $648,000	2003 Profits: $140,000	Fiscal Year Ends: 12/31
2002 Sales: $644,000	2002 Profits: $95,000	Parent Company:

SALARIES/BENEFITS:

Pension Plan:	ESOP Stock Plan:	Profit Sharing:	Top Exec. Salary: $	Bonus: $
Savings Plan:	Stock Purch. Plan:		Second Exec. Salary: $	Bonus: $

OTHER THOUGHTS:

Apparent Women Officers or Directors:
Hot Spot for Advancement for Women/Minorities:

LOCATIONS: ("Y" = Yes)

West:	Southwest:	Midwest:	Southeast:	Northeast:	International:
					Y

Note: Financial information, benefits and other data can change quickly and may vary from those stated here.

TWEETER HOME ENTERTAINMENT GROUP INC

www.tweeter.com

Industry Group Code: 443110 Ranks within this company's industry group: Sales: 4 Profits: 6

Print Media/Publishing:	Movies:	Equipment/Supplies:		Broadcast/Cable:	Music/Audio:	Sports/Games:	
Newspapers:	Movie Theaters:	Equipment/Supplies:	Y	Broadcast TV:	Music Production:	Games/Sports:	
Magazines:	Movie Production:	Gambling Equipment:	Y	Cable TV:	Retail Music:	Retail Games Stores:	
Books:	TV/Video Production:	Special Services:	Y	Satellite Broadcast:	Retail Audio Equip.:	Stadiums/Teams:	
Book Stores:	Video Rental:	Advertising Services:		Radio:	Music Print./Dist.:	Gambling/Casinos:	
Distribution/Printing:	Video Distribution:	Info. Sys. Software:		Online Information:	Multimedia:	Rides/Theme Parks:	

TYPES OF BUSINESS:

Audio & Video Equipment Stores
Installation Services
Consumer Electronics

BRANDS/DIVISIONS/AFFILIATES:

Tweeter
HiFi Buys
Showcase Home Entertainment
Sound Advice
Consumer Electronics (CE) Playground

CONTACTS:
Note: Officers with more than one job title may be intentionally listed here more than once.

Joseph McGuire, CEO
Joseph McGuire, Pres.
Greg Hunt, Sr. VP/CFO
Judy Quye, Sr. VP-Retail Sales
Philo Pappas, Chief Merch. Officer/Sr. VP
Judy Quye, Sr. VP- Oper.
Jeff Duhamel, Dir. Corp. Comm.
Patrick Reynolds, Chief Mktg. Officer/VP
Samuel Bloomberg, Chmn.

Phone: 781-830-3000	Fax: 781-821-9956
Toll-Free: 877-893-3837	
Address: 40 Pequot Way, Canton, MA 02021 US	

GROWTH PLANS/SPECIAL FEATURES:

Tweeter Home Entertainment Group, Inc. is a specialty retailer of mid- to high-end audio and video electronics. It owns and operates 153 stores across New England, the Mid-Atlantic, the Southeast, Texas, California, greater Chicago, Florida and Arizona under the names Tweeter, HiFi Buys, Showcase Home Entertainment and Sound Advice. All stores are serviced by 10 distribution centers. The stores feature an extensive selection of home and car audio systems and components, portable audio equipment and home video products, including large-screen plasma and LCD televisions, global positioning satellite systems, DVD players, digital satellite systems, cell phones, automobile security systems, VCRs and camcorders. The firm stocks products from Alpine, B&K, Bose, Boston Acoustics, Clarion, Denon, Mirage, Martin Logan, Mitsubishi, Monster Cable, Panasonic, Philips, Pioneer, Polk, Samsung, Sharp, Sonus Faber, Sony, Velodyne and Yamaha. Tweeter's stores display products in sound rooms architecturally and acoustically designed to simulate the customer's home or car environment. The company's Automatic Price Protection Plan automatically sends a check to a customer that purchases a product if a competitor within 25 miles of the store advertises a lower price within 30 days, without requiring the customer to request payment. The company's 24 Sound Advice stores in Florida and Arizona specialize in cutting-edge high-end products. Sound Advice provides custom installation services in homes, businesses and cars, in addition to serving as consultants to customers. Nearly a third of Tweeter's revenue is generated during the winter holiday season. In 2006, the company closed 22 stores that combined contributed less than 5% of revenue and accounted for nearly one-third of operating loss. Also in 2006, the company opened three concept stores under the name Consumer Electronics (CE) Playground and changed the name of its Hillcrest stores to Tweeter.

The firm provides employees with tuition reimbursement, merchandise discounts and free concert tickets.

FINANCIALS:
Sales and profits are in thousands of dollars—add 000 to get the full amount. 2006 Note: Financial information for 2006 was not available for all companies at press time.

2006 Sales: $775,287	2006 Profits: $-16,483	U.S. Stock Ticker: TWTR
2005 Sales: $795,090	2005 Profits: $-74,353	Int'l Ticker: Int'l Exchange:
2004 Sales: $778,200	2004 Profits: $-18,100	Employees: 3,200
2003 Sales: $786,996	2003 Profits: $-11,662	Fiscal Year Ends: 9/30
2002 Sales: $796,100	2002 Profits: $-165,100	Parent Company:

SALARIES/BENEFITS:

Pension Plan:	ESOP Stock Plan:	Profit Sharing:	Top Exec. Salary: $445,000	Bonus: $
Savings Plan: Y	Stock Purch. Plan: Y		Second Exec. Salary: $410,000	Bonus: $43,800

OTHER THOUGHTS:

Apparent Women Officers or Directors: 1
Hot Spot for Advancement for Women/Minorities:

LOCATIONS: ("Y" = Yes)

West:	Southwest:	Midwest:	Southeast:	Northeast:	International:
Y	Y	Y	Y	Y	

UNITED ARTISTS CORPORATION   www.unitedartists.com

Industry Group Code: 512110 Ranks within this company's industry group: Sales: Profits:

Print Media/Publishing:	Movies:		Equipment/Supplies:	Broadcast/Cable:	Music/Audio:	Sports/Games:
Newspapers:	Movie Theaters:		Equipment/Supplies:	Broadcast TV:	Music Production:	Games/Sports:
Magazines:	Movie Production:	Y	Gambling Equipment:	Cable TV:	Retail Music:	Retail Games Stores:
Books:	TV/Video Production:	Y	Special Services:	Satellite Broadcast:	Retail Audio Equip.:	Stadiums/Teams:
Book Stores:	Video Rental:		Advertising Services:	Radio:	Music Print./Dist.:	Gambling/Casinos:
Distribution/Printing:	Video Distribution:		Info. Sys. Software:	Online Information:	Multimedia:	Rides/Theme Parks:

TYPES OF BUSINESS:

Film Production
Television Production
Film Distribution

BRANDS/DIVISIONS/AFFILIATES:

Metro-Goldwyn-Mayer, Inc.

GROWTH PLANS/SPECIAL FEATURES:

United Artists Corporation(UA), a subsidiary of Metro-Goldwyn-Mayer, Inc. (MGM), which is in turn owned by Comcast and Sony, was founded in 1919 by Hollywood legends Charlie Chaplin, Mary Pickford, Douglas Fairbanks and D.W. Griffith with the intent to allow artists and actors to control their own work. UA produces, sells and acquires limited-release and foreign films and is branded as an art house film distributor. The firm has produced more than 1,200 films including Scarface, West Side Story, the Pink Panther, Rocky and James Bond franchises. Recent films include Capote, Art School Confidential and The Woods. UA has also produced more than 2,600 television shows, including thirtysomething, The Outer Limits and The Fugitive. In 2006, MGM announced that actor Tom Cruise and his long-time production partner Paula Wagner acquired a small stake in the studio and will control production; Paula Wagner will act as CEO and Cruise will produce and act in films.

CONTACTS: Note: Officers with more than one job title may be intentionally listed here more than once.

Paula Wagner, CEO
Danny Rosett, Pres.

Phone: 310-449-3000	Fax: 310-449-8857
Toll-Free:	
Address: 10250 Constellation Blvd., Los Angeles, CA 90067 US	

FINANCIALS: Sales and profits are in thousands of dollars—add 000 to get the full amount. 2006 Note: Financial information for 2006 was not available for all companies at press time.

2006 Sales: $	2006 Profits: $	**U.S. Stock Ticker: Subsidiary**
2005 Sales: $	2005 Profits: $	**Int'l Ticker:** Int'l Exchange:
2004 Sales: $	2004 Profits: $	Employees:
2003 Sales: $	2003 Profits: $	Fiscal Year Ends: 12/31
2002 Sales: $	2002 Profits: $	Parent Company: METRO-GOLDWYN-MAYER INC (MGM)

SALARIES/BENEFITS:

Pension Plan:	ESOP Stock Plan:	Profit Sharing:	Top Exec. Salary: $	Bonus: $
Savings Plan:	Stock Purch. Plan:		Second Exec. Salary: $	Bonus: $

OTHER THOUGHTS:

Apparent Women Officers or Directors: 1
Hot Spot for Advancement for Women/Minorities:

LOCATIONS: ("Y" = Yes)

West:	Southwest:	Midwest:	Southeast:	Northeast:	International:
Y					

Note: Financial information, benefits and other data can change quickly and may vary from those stated here.

UNITED BUSINESS MEDIA PLCwww.unitedbusinessmedia.com

Industry Group Code: 511120 Ranks within this company's industry group: Sales: 6 Profits: 1

Print Media/Publishing:		Movies:		Equipment/Supplies:		Broadcast/Cable:		Music/Audio:		Sports/Games:	
Newspapers:	Y	Movie Theaters:		Equipment/Supplies:		Broadcast TV:		Music Production:		Games/Sports:	
Magazines:	Y	Movie Production:		Gambling Equipment:		Cable TV:		Retail Music:		Retail Games Stores:	
Books:		TV/Video Production:		Special Services:	Y	Satellite Broadcast:		Retail Audio Equip.:		Stadiums/Teams:	
Book Stores:		Video Rental:		Advertising Services:	Y	Radio:		Music Print./Dist.:		Gambling/Casinos:	
Distribution/Printing:		Video Distribution:		Info. Sys. Software:		Online Information:		Multimedia:		Rides/Theme Parks:	

TYPES OF BUSINESS:

Diversified Publishing
Market Research
Press Release Distribution
Business-to-Business Publishing
Media Investments

BRANDS/DIVISIONS/AFFILIATES:

NOP World
PR Newswire
CMP Media
Roper ASW
Channel 5 Television Group
Independent Television News, Ltd.
SDN, Ltd.
Eurisko

CONTACTS: Note: Officers with more than one job title may be intentionally listed here more than once.

David Levin, CEO
Malcolm Wall, COO
Nigel Wilson, CFO
Alix Raine, Sr. VP-Communications
Catherine Southgate, Head of Investor Rel.
Charles Gregson, Exec. Dir.-Bus. Info.
Geoffrey Unwin, Chmn.

Phone: 44-20-7921-5000	**Fax:** 44-20-7928-2717
Toll-Free:	
Address: Ludgate House, 245 Blackfriars Rd., London, SE1 9UY UK	

GROWTH PLANS/SPECIAL FEATURES:

United Business Media plc (UBM) offers a range of market information services. It is a market research, news distribution and professional media company with operations primarily in the U.S. and U.K., as well as business interests in Europe, Asia Pacific and Latin America. UBM's primary business provides professional media and market information solutions to customers through NOP World, PR Newswire and CMP Media. The professional media division, which includes CMP Media, is the largest business-to-business publisher in the U.S. high-tech sector, with a market share approximately twice that of its nearest competitor. The news distribution division, which includes PR Newswire, is one of the world's leading electronic distributors of corporate news, with over 40,000 customers worldwide including over 50% of U.S. Fortune 500 companies. The market research division is the world's ninth-largest market research business, with strong positions in several key sectors of the market including media, health care, automotive, business-to-business and consumer sectors. UBM also has consumer and business-to-business publishing interests, including classified advertising periodicals. It retains a number of broadcast investments including a 35.37% stake in Channel 5 Television Group, a U.K. television broadcaster; a 20% stake in Independent Television News, Ltd.; a 33.3% stake in SDN, Ltd.; and a 20% stake in Satellite Information Systems. UBM also owns Eurisko, the largest independent market research firm in Italy.

FINANCIALS: Sales and profits are in thousands of dollars—add 000 to get the full amount. 2006 Note: Financial information for 2006 was not available for all companies at press time.

2006 Sales: $	2006 Profits: $	**U.S. Stock Ticker:** Private
2005 Sales: $1,172,006	2005 Profits: $824,641	**Int'l Ticker: UBM** Int'l Exchange: London-LSE
2004 Sales: $966,534	2004 Profits: $408,872	Employees: 5,000
2003 Sales: $1,241,600	2003 Profits: $-68,800	Fiscal Year Ends: 12/31
2002 Sales: $1,278,600	2002 Profits: $-385,100	Parent Company:

SALARIES/BENEFITS:

Pension Plan:	ESOP Stock Plan:	Profit Sharing:	Top Exec. Salary: $1,220,000	Bonus: $
Savings Plan:	Stock Purch. Plan:		Second Exec. Salary: $585,000	Bonus: $117,000

OTHER THOUGHTS:

Apparent Women Officers or Directors: 1
Hot Spot for Advancement for Women/Minorities:

LOCATIONS: ("Y" = Yes)

West:	Southwest:	Midwest:	Southeast:	Northeast:	International:
Y		Y		Y	Y

Note: Financial information, benefits and other data can change quickly and may vary from those stated here.

UNITED ONLINE INC

www.unitedonline.net

Industry Group Code: 514191 Ranks within this company's industry group: Sales: 2 Profits: 1

Print Media/Publishing:	Movies:	Equipment/Supplies:		Broadcast/Cable:	Music/Audio:	Sports/Games:	
Newspapers:	Movie Theaters:	Equipment/Supplies:		Broadcast TV:	Music Production:	Games/Sports:	
Magazines:	Movie Production:	Gambling Equipment:		Cable TV:	Retail Music:	Retail Games Stores:	
Books:	TV/Video Production:	Special Services:	Y	Satellite Broadcast:	Retail Audio Equip.:	Stadiums/Teams:	
Book Stores:	Video Rental:	Advertising Services:	Y	Radio:	Music Print./Dist.:	Gambling/Casinos:	
Distribution/Printing:	Video Distribution:	Info. Sys. Software:		Online Information:	Multimedia:	Rides/Theme Parks:	

TYPES OF BUSINESS:

Internet Service Provider
Market Research
VoIP Provider
Social Networking Web Sites
Online Loyalty Marketing

BRANDS/DIVISIONS/AFFILIATES:

Juno
NetZero
Classmates.com
MyPoints.com
PrivatePhone
Juno SpeedBand
CyberTarget
Names Database (The)

CONTACTS: *Note: Officers with more than one job title may be intentionally listed here more than once.*

Mark R. Goldston, CEO
Charles S. Hillard, Pres.
Charles S. Hilliard, CFO
Jeremy Helfand, Exec. VP-Sales/Chief Sales Officer
Gerald J. Popek, CTO/Exec. VP
Frederic A. Randall, Jr., General Counsel/Exec. VP
Theodore R. Cahall, Jr., Exec. VP- Web Services/COO-Classmates Online
Robert Taragan, Exec. VP/General Mgr.-CyberTarget
Matt Wisk, Exec. VP/Chief Marketing Officer
Mark R. Goldston, Chmn.

Phone: 818-287-3000	**Fax:** 818-287-3001
Toll-Free:	
Address: 21301 Burbank Blvd., Woodland Hills, CA 91367 US	

GROWTH PLANS/SPECIAL FEATURES:

United Online, Inc. is a nationwide provider of consumer Internet and media services. Formed from the merger of NetZero and Juno Online Services, the company offers two primary services. Its Content and Media services offer social networking through its website ClassMates.com and online loyalty marketing through recently acquired MyPoints.com. Its communication services include Internet access through NetZero and Juno, e-mail, and Voice over Internet Protocol (VoIP) through PrivatePhone and NetZero Voice. The company offers its VoIP services through Best Buy stores through an extended marketing alliance with Best Buy. United focuses on providing value-priced monthly subscription-based access, offering plans at less than half the cost of its major competitors. Through its NetZero and Juno subsidiaries, the company also offers NetZero HiSpeed and Juno SpeedBand next-generation dial-up Internet access services delivering up to five times faster web surfing. Each service works from any phone jack using a standard dial-up connection, does not require any new hardware and can be downloaded from the Internet. In 2006, the company, through an agreement with Verizon Internet Services, began offering NetZero DSL, a low cost broadband Internet service. Advertisers are provided with sophisticated market research capabilities through United's CyberTarget division. With access to millions of NetZero, Juno and BlueLight Internet users, along with the benefits provided by one of the largest Oracle data warehouses in the world, CyberTarget creates unique real-time market research in an Internet environment. In 2006, United acquired Opobox, Inc., which operates The Names Database, a service that allows members to privately contact former acquaintances around the world. In addition, United acquired MyPoints, Inc., a provider of member driven Internet direct marketing, which offers customers reward incentives for online purchases and other ecommerce related activities through its website MyPoints.com

FINANCIALS: Sales and profits are in thousands of dollars—add 000 to get the full amount. 2006 Note: Financial information for 2006 was not available for all companies at press time.

2006 Sales: $	2006 Profits: $	**U.S. Stock Ticker: UNTD**
2005 Sales: $525,100	2005 Profits: $47,100	**Int'l Ticker:** Int'l Exchange:
2004 Sales: $448,600	2004 Profits: $117,500	Employees: 900
2003 Sales: $277,295	2003 Profits: $27,792	Fiscal Year Ends: 12/31
2002 Sales: $167,515	2002 Profits: $-47,810	Parent Company:

SALARIES/BENEFITS:

Pension Plan:	ESOP Stock Plan:	Profit Sharing:	Top Exec. Salary: $800,000	Bonus: $1,000,000
Savings Plan: Y	Stock Purch. Plan: Y		Second Exec. Salary: $400,000	Bonus: $400,000

OTHER THOUGHTS:

Apparent Women Officers or Directors:
Hot Spot for Advancement for Women/Minorities:

LOCATIONS: ("Y" = Yes)

West:	Southwest:	Midwest:	Southeast:	Northeast:	International:
Y				Y	Y

Note: Financial information, benefits and other data can change quickly and may vary from those stated here.

UNITED PARAMOUNT NETWORK (UPN)　　　www.cwtv.com

Industry Group Code: 513210 Ranks within this company's industry group: Sales:　Profits:

Print Media/Publishing:	Movies:		Equipment/Supplies:	Broadcast/Cable:		Music/Audio:	Sports/Games:
Newspapers:	Movie Theaters:		Equipment/Supplies:	Broadcast TV:	Y	Music Production:	Games/Sports:
Magazines:	Movie Production:		Gambling Equipment:	Cable TV:		Retail Music:	Retail Games Stores:
Books:	TV/Video Production:	Y	Special Services:	Satellite Broadcast:		Retail Audio Equip.:	Stadiums/Teams:
Book Stores:	Video Rental:		Advertising Services:	Radio:		Music Print./Dist.:	Gambling/Casinos:
Distribution/Printing:	Video Distribution:		Info. Sys. Software:	Online Information:		Multimedia:	Rides/Theme Parks:

TYPES OF BUSINESS:
Broadcast Television
Television Production

GROWTH PLANS/SPECIAL FEATURES:
United Paramount Network (UPN), a subsidiary of Viacom through CBS, is a broadcasting network with proprietary television shows. Its shows include hour-long dramas, such as Enterprise, Keven Hill and Veronica Mars; half-hour-long comedies, such as One On One, Girlfriends, All Of Us and Eve; and reality television shows including America's Next Top Model and The Road to Stardom With Missy Elliott. Many of the firm's shows feature African-American leading actors and actresses. The firm also produces WWE Smackdown, a competition show from World Wrestling Entertainment, Inc.

BRANDS/DIVISIONS/AFFILIATES:
UPN
CBS
Viacom
WWE Smackdown
Veronica Mars
America's Next Top Model
One On One

CONTACTS:
Note: Officers with more than one job title may be intentionally listed here more than once.
Leslie Moonves, Interim CEO
Kim Fleary, Sr. VP-Comedy Dev.
Maggie Murphy, Sr. VP-Drama Dev.

Phone: 310-575-7000	**Fax:** 310-575-7220
Toll-Free:	
Address: 11800 Wilshire Blvd., Los Angeles, CA 90025 US	

FINANCIALS:
Sales and profits are in thousands of dollars—add 000 to get the full amount. 2006 Note: Financial information for 2006 was not available for all companies at press time.

2006 Sales: $	2006 Profits: $	**U.S. Stock Ticker: Subsidiary**
2005 Sales: $	2005 Profits: $	**Int'l Ticker:** Int'l Exchange:
2004 Sales: $253,000	2004 Profits: $	Employees:
2003 Sales: $	2003 Profits: $	Fiscal Year Ends: 12/31
2002 Sales: $	2002 Profits: $	Parent Company: VIACOM INC

SALARIES/BENEFITS:

Pension Plan:	ESOP Stock Plan:	Profit Sharing:	Top Exec. Salary: $	Bonus: $
Savings Plan:	Stock Purch. Plan:		Second Exec. Salary: $	Bonus: $

OTHER THOUGHTS:
Apparent Women Officers or Directors: 2
Hot Spot for Advancement for Women/Minorities:

LOCATIONS: ("Y" = Yes)

West:	Southwest:	Midwest:	Southeast:	Northeast:	International:
Y					

Note: Financial information, benefits and other data can change quickly and may vary from those stated here.

UNITED TALENT AGENCY INC

www.unitedtalent.com

Industry Group Code: 711410 Ranks within this company's industry group: Sales: Profits:

Print Media/Publishing:	Movies:	Equipment/Supplies:		Broadcast/Cable:	Music/Audio:	Sports/Games:
Newspapers:	Movie Theaters:	Equipment/Supplies:		Broadcast TV:	Music Production:	Games/Sports:
Magazines:	Movie Production:	Gambling Equipment:		Cable TV:	Retail Music:	Retail Games Stores:
Books:	TV/Video Production:	Special Services:	Y	Satellite Broadcast:	Retail Audio Equip.:	Stadiums/Teams:
Book Stores:	Video Rental:	Advertising Services:	Y	Radio:	Music Print./Dist.:	Gambling/Casinos:
Distribution/Printing:	Video Distribution:	Info. Sys. Software:		Online Information:	Multimedia:	Rides/Theme Parks:

TYPES OF BUSINESS:

Talent Agency

BRANDS/DIVISIONS/AFFILIATES:

CONTACTS: *Note: Officers with more than one job title may be intentionally listed here more than once.*

Adam Ware, Head-Bus. Dev.
Chris Day, Head- Corp. Comm.
Wayne Fitterman, Head-Production Dep.
Jim Berkus, Chmn.

Phone: 310-273-6700	Fax: 310-247-1111
Toll-Free:	
Address: 950 Wilshire Blvd., Ste. 500, Beverly Hills, CA 90212-2401 US	

GROWTH PLANS/SPECIAL FEATURES:

United Talent Agency, Inc., commonly known as UTA, is a broadly situated talent agency based out of California. It is one of the largest talent agencies in the U.S., generally counted as one of the big four. UTA represents talent in all areas of entertainment, including music, television, movies, books, commercials, licensing, live entertainment, video games and digital media. UTA also represents behind the scenes personnel such as gaffers, key grips, editors, directors of photography and art directors. The firm represents such luminaries as Johnny Depp, Harrison Ford, Ben Stiller, Sandra Oh, Kate Bosworth, the Olsen twins, Liv Tyler, Vince Vaughn and Jack Black. In 2006, UTA began searching for Internet video talent through websites such as YouTube and finding work for individuals thus discovered. The firm operates an agent training program that trains individuals interested in becoming talent agents. After completion of the highly-competitive program, trainees may be promoted to agent status within the firm. As of December 2006, the firm had 19 full partners. In 2006, UTA became carbon neutral, a feat that was accomplished by planting enough trees to outweigh the firm's CO_2 emissions for the year.

FINANCIALS: Sales and profits are in thousands of dollars—add 000 to get the full amount. 2006 Note: Financial information for 2006 was not available for all companies at press time.

2006 Sales: $	2006 Profits: $	U.S. Stock Ticker: Private	
2005 Sales: $	2005 Profits: $	Int'l Ticker: Int'l Exchange:	
2004 Sales: $	2004 Profits: $	Employees:	
2003 Sales: $	2003 Profits: $	Fiscal Year Ends:	
2002 Sales: $	2002 Profits: $	Parent Company:	

SALARIES/BENEFITS:

Pension Plan:	ESOP Stock Plan:	Profit Sharing:	Top Exec. Salary: $	Bonus: $
Savings Plan:	Stock Purch. Plan:		Second Exec. Salary: $	Bonus: $

OTHER THOUGHTS:

Apparent Women Officers or Directors: 4
Hot Spot for Advancement for Women/Minorities: Y

LOCATIONS: ("Y" = Yes)

West:	Southwest:	Midwest:	Southeast:	Northeast:	International:
Y				Y	

Note: Financial information, benefits and other data can change quickly and may vary from those stated here.

UNIVERSAL MUSIC GROUP

www.umusic.com

Industry Group Code: 512230 **Ranks within this company's industry group:** Sales: 2 Profits:

Print Media/Publishing:	Movies:	Equipment/Supplies:	Broadcast/Cable:	Music/Audio:		Sports/Games:
Newspapers:	Movie Theaters:	Equipment/Supplies:	Broadcast TV:	Music Production:	Y	Games/Sports:
Magazines:	Movie Production:	Gambling Equipment:	Cable TV:	Retail Music:		Retail Games Stores:
Books:	TV/Video Production:	Special Services:	Satellite Broadcast:	Retail Audio Equip.:		Stadiums/Teams:
Book Stores:	Video Rental:	Advertising Services:	Radio:	Music Print./Dist.:	Y	Gambling/Casinos:
Distribution/Printing:	Video Distribution:	Info. Sys. Software:	Online Information:	Multimedia:		Rides/Theme Parks:

TYPES OF BUSINESS:
Music Production & Distribution
Recorded Music Sales
Music Publishing

BRANDS/DIVISIONS/AFFILIATES:
Vivendi SA
Geffen Records
Verve Music Group
Universal Music Classics
Decca Records
Island
Deutsche Grammophon
UMe Digital

CONTACTS: Note: Officers with more than one job title may be intentionally listed here more than once.
Douglas Morris, CEO
Zach Horowitz, COO
Zach Horowitz, Pres.
Marinus N. Henny, CFO
Douglas Morris, Chmn.

Phone: 212-841-8000	**Fax:** 212-331-2580
Toll-Free:	
Address: 2220 Colorado Ave., Santa Monica, CA 90404 US	

GROWTH PLANS/SPECIAL FEATURES:

Universal Music Group (UMG), a subsidiary of Vivendi, is a leader in the music industry. The company handles all areas of music including development, marketing, sales, publishing and distribution for music in all styles and genres. Through record labels including Geffen Records, Universal Motown Records Group, and Verve Music Group, the company distributes albums that run the gamut from classical to contemporary, jazz to rock. Through its Universal Music Classics Group and Verve Music Group, UMG owns the largest music catalogues for opera and jazz music in the world. Through its Universal Music Enterprises (UMe) the company distributes the music in its catalogues to consumers purchasing songs on recorded media, such as CDs, or electronic media, such as MP3s. These are marketed in retail environments, catalogue marketing, and online through UMe Digital, the first all digital record label from a major music house. In addition, UMe markets UMG's music catalogue for use in television and films as well ad infomercials. Through its catalogue of artists and songs that contains over a million copyrights, its vast distribution network and focused marketing, UMG has become leader in global music sales with a worldwide market share of 25.6% in 2005.

FINANCIALS: Sales and profits are in thousands of dollars—add 000 to get the full amount. 2006 Note: Financial information for 2006 was not available for all companies at press time.

2006 Sales: $	2006 Profits: $	**U.S. Stock Ticker:** Subsidiary
2005 Sales: $5,794,800	2005 Profits: $	**Int'l Ticker:** Int'l Exchange:
2004 Sales: $6,810,500	2004 Profits: $	Employees: 9,661
2003 Sales: $6,243,400	2003 Profits: $	Fiscal Year Ends: 12/31
2002 Sales: $6,577,900	2002 Profits: $	Parent Company: VIVENDI SA

SALARIES/BENEFITS:

Pension Plan:	ESOP Stock Plan:	Profit Sharing:	Top Exec. Salary: $	Bonus: $
Savings Plan:	Stock Purch. Plan:		Second Exec. Salary: $	Bonus: $

OTHER THOUGHTS:

Apparent Women Officers or Directors:
Hot Spot for Advancement for Women/Minorities:

LOCATIONS: ("Y" = Yes)

West:	Southwest:	Midwest:	Southeast:	Northeast:	International:
Y	Y	Y	Y	Y	Y

Note: Financial information, benefits and other data can change quickly and may vary from those stated here.

UNIVERSAL PICTURES
www.universalpictures.com

Industry Group Code: 512110 Ranks within this company's industry group: Sales: Profits:

Print Media/Publishing:	Movies:		Equipment/Supplies:	Broadcast/Cable:	Music/Audio:	Sports/Games:	
Newspapers:	Movie Theaters:		Equipment/Supplies:	Broadcast TV:	Music Production:	Games/Sports:	
Magazines:	Movie Production:	Y	Gambling Equipment:	Cable TV:	Retail Music:	Retail Games Stores:	
Books:	TV/Video Production:		Special Services:	Satellite Broadcast:	Retail Audio Equip.:	Stadiums/Teams:	
Book Stores:	Video Rental:		Advertising Services:	Radio:	Music Print./Dist.:	Gambling/Casinos:	
Distribution/Printing:	Video Distribution:		Info. Sys. Software:	Online Information:	Multimedia:	Rides/Theme Parks:	

TYPES OF BUSINESS:
Film Production & Distribution
Online Video Distribution

BRANDS/DIVISIONS/AFFILIATES:
Universal Studios
NBC Universal
Focus Features

CONTACTS: *Note: Officers with more than one job title may be intentionally listed here more than once.*
Rick Finkelstein, COO
Rick Finkelstein, Pres.
David Linde, Co-Chmn.
Eddie Egan, Co-Pres.-Mktg.
Nikki Rocco, Pres., Universal Pictures Distribution
Mary Parent, Vice Chmn.-Worldwide Production
Marc Shmuger, Chmn.

Phone: 818-777-1000	Fax: 818-866-3600
Toll-Free:	
Address: 100 Universal City Plaza, Universal City, CA 97608-1002 US	

GROWTH PLANS/SPECIAL FEATURES:
Universal Pictures produces and distributes theatrical and non-theatrical films. The company is the main motion picture production and distribution arm of Universal Studios, a subsidiary of NBC Universal. NBC Universal is 20%-owned by Vivendi Universal and 80%-owned by General Electric. Focus Features, the specialty film unit of Universal Pictures, produces, internationally distributes and finances motion pictures. Universal Pictures produces a variety of movies, including internally developed titles, co-productions, specialty motion pictures, direct-to-video titles, specialty video, classic titles and related consumer products. Previous films have included Academy Award-winning movies such as A Beautiful Mind, The Pianist and Lost in Translation, as well as Ray, The Producers and Bruce Almighty. Recently, the firm announced an agreement that will make its movies available to ITVN (Internet Protocol Television) subscribers through an IPTV set-top box. Also in 2006, the company partnered with online rental firm Lovefilm to announce a new download feature to the U.K, download-to-own. The new product allows individuals to download movies in three formats: instant download on PC, instant download for laptop, or a DVD copy sent by mail. The download process takes 40 minutes, and costs between $17.50 and $35 U.S. dollars. Eventually, Universal Pictures will have all 6,500 movies in its catalogue available for downloading. Also in 2006, the firm partnered with Microsoft to release HD DVD titles using VC-1 (compression standard) and iHD.

Universal Pictures offers its employees medical and dental benefits, prescription coverage, 401(k) and pension plans, health club discounts, tuition reimbursement, educational loans, employee discounts and child care.

FINANCIALS: Sales and profits are in thousands of dollars—add 000 to get the full amount. 2006 Note: Financial information for 2006 was not available for all companies at press time.

2006 Sales: $	2006 Profits: $	U.S. Stock Ticker: Subsidiary
2005 Sales: $	2005 Profits: $	Int'l Ticker: Int'l Exchange:
2004 Sales: $	2004 Profits: $	Employees:
2003 Sales: $6,622,000	2003 Profits: $	Fiscal Year Ends: 12/31
2002 Sales: $6,571,600	2002 Profits: $	Parent Company: NBC UNIVERSAL

SALARIES/BENEFITS:

Pension Plan: Y	ESOP Stock Plan:	Profit Sharing:	Top Exec. Salary: $	Bonus: $
Savings Plan: Y	Stock Purch. Plan:		Second Exec. Salary: $	Bonus: $

OTHER THOUGHTS:
Apparent Women Officers or Directors: 2
Hot Spot for Advancement for Women/Minorities:

LOCATIONS: ("Y" = Yes)

West:	Southwest:	Midwest:	Southeast:	Northeast:	International:
Y			Y		

Note: Financial information, benefits and other data can change quickly and may vary from those stated here.

UNIVISION COMMUNICATIONS INC　　www.univision.com

Industry Group Code: 513120　Ranks within this company's industry group: Sales: 9　Profits: 6

Print Media/Publishing:	Movies:		Equipment/Supplies:	Broadcast/Cable:		Music/Audio:	Sports/Games:
Newspapers:	Movie Theaters:		Equipment/Supplies:	Broadcast TV:	Y	Music Production:	Games/Sports:
Magazines:	Movie Production:		Gambling Equipment:	Cable TV:		Retail Music:	Retail Games Stores:
Books:	TV/Video Production:	Y	Special Services:	Satellite Broadcast:		Retail Audio Equip.:	Stadiums/Teams:
Book Stores:	Video Rental:		Advertising Services:	Radio:		Music Print./Dist.:	Gambling/Casinos:
Distribution/Printing:	Video Distribution:		Info. Sys. Software:	Online Information:		Multimedia:	Rides/Theme Parks:

TYPES OF BUSINESS:

Spanish Television Broadcasting
Cable Television Programming
Online Portal
Music Publishing & Recording
Radio Broadcasting

BRANDS/DIVISIONS/AFFILIATES:

Univision Television Group
Galavision
TeleFutura
Univision Radio
Univision Music Group
Univision.com
Hispanic Broadcasting
Sabado Gigante

CONTACTS: *Note: Officers with more than one job title may be intentionally listed here more than once.*

A. Jerrold Perenchio, CEO
Ray Rodriguez, COO
Ray Rodriguez, Pres.
Andrew W. Hobson, Sr. Exec. VP/CFO
C. Douglas Kranwinkle, Exec. VP/General Counsel
Andrew W. Hobson, Strategic Officer
Robert V. Cahill, Vice Chmn./Corp. Sec.
McHenry T. Tichenor, Pres., Univision Radio
A. Jerrold Perenchio, Chmn.

Phone: 310-556-7676	Fax: 310-556-7615
Toll-Free:	
Address: 1999 Ave. of the Stars, Ste. 3050, Los Angeles, CA 90067 US	

GROWTH PLANS/SPECIAL FEATURES:

Univision Communications, Inc. is the leading Spanish-language broadcaster in the U.S. The company believes that the breadth and diversity of its programming provides it with a competitive advantage over both Spanish- and English-language broadcasters in appealing to the Hispanic market, which now represents 13% of the U.S. population and a potential audience of more than 35 million. The firm's Univision Network reaches 99% of all U.S. Hispanic households via broadcast and cable channels nationwide. TeleFutura is the company's 24-hour Spanish-language broadcast television network, reaching 87% of U.S. Hispanic households. The company's Galavision network is the leading Spanish-language cable television network, than 5.9 million of U.S. Hispanic cable subscribers. Broadcast is supported by the Univision Television Group, which owns and operates 18 full-power and 8 low-power Univision Network stations and one full-power UPN station. The TeleFutura Television Group owns and operates an additional 18 full-power and 15 low-power TeleFutura Network stations, with 2 full power stations in Puerto Rico. Univision's best known programming includes the variety show Sabado Gigante, hosted by Mario Kreutzberger (better known as Don Francisco) and airing every Saturday night since August 1962; popular talk show Cristina, featuring Cristina Saralegui; the Novelas series of soap operas; evening news Noticiero Univision; and Mexican league soccer coverage. Univision Radio ranks as the largest Spanish-language radio broadcaster in the U.S., owning or programming 69 radio stations in 16 of the top 25 U.S. Hispanic markets, in addition to four stations in Puerto Rico. Univision Music Group is the leading Latin music recording and publishing company in the U.S. and univision.com is the most visited Spanish-language Internet portal in America, with over 3.2 billion page views in 2005. In October 2006, Univision agreed to be acquired by a consortium of private-equity investors, led by Madison Dearborn Partners, for about $12.3 billion.

FINANCIALS: Sales and profits are in thousands of dollars—add 000 to get the full amount. 2006 Note: Financial information for 2006 was not available for all companies at press time.

2006 Sales: $	2006 Profits: $	U.S. Stock Ticker: UVN
2005 Sales: $1,952,531	2005 Profits: $187,179	Int'l Ticker:　Int'l Exchange:
2004 Sales: $1,786,935	2004 Profits: $255,883	Employees: 4,219
2003 Sales: $1,311,015	2003 Profits: $155,427	Fiscal Year Ends: 12/31
2002 Sales: $1,091,293	2002 Profits: $86,528	Parent Company:

SALARIES/BENEFITS:

Pension Plan:	ESOP Stock Plan: Y	Profit Sharing:	Top Exec. Salary: $800,000	Bonus: $1,000,000
Savings Plan: Y	Stock Purch. Plan:		Second Exec. Salary: $750,000	Bonus: $1,000,000

OTHER THOUGHTS:

Apparent Women Officers or Directors:
Hot Spot for Advancement for Women/Minorities:

LOCATIONS: ("Y" = Yes)

West:	Southwest:	Midwest:	Southeast:	Northeast:	International:
Y	Y	Y	Y	Y	Y

US NEWS AND WORLD REPORT LP   www.usnews.com

Industry Group Code: 511120 Ranks within this company's industry group: Sales: Profits:

Print Media/Publishing:		Movies:	Equipment/Supplies:	Broadcast/Cable:	Music/Audio:	Sports/Games:	
Newspapers:		Movie Theaters:	Equipment/Supplies:	Broadcast TV:	Music Production:	Games/Sports:	
Magazines:	Y	Movie Production:	Gambling Equipment:	Cable TV:	Retail Music:	Retail Games Stores:	
Books:		TV/Video Production:	Special Services:	Satellite Broadcast:	Retail Audio Equip.:	Stadiums/Teams:	
Book Stores:		Video Rental:	Advertising Services:	Radio:	Music Print./Dist.:	Gambling/Casinos:	
Distribution/Printing:		Video Distribution:	Info. Sys. Software:	Online Information:	Multimedia:	Rides/Theme Parks:	

TYPES OF BUSINESS:

Magazine Publishing
Online Media

BRANDS/DIVISIONS/AFFILIATES:

usnews.com
America's Best Colleges
America's Best Leaders
America's Best Hospitals
America's Best Graduate Schools
America's Best Health Plans

CONTACTS: Note: Officers with more than one job title may be intentionally listed here more than once.

William D. Holiber, Pres./Publisher
Thomas H. Peck, CFO
Lee Wilcox, Sr. VP-Mktg.
Cynthia Powell, Dir.-Media Relations
Fred Drasner, Co-Chmn.
Mortimer Zuckerman, Co-Chmn./Editor-in-Chief

Phone: 202-955-2000	**Fax:** 202-955-2685
Toll-Free:	
Address: 1050 Thomas Jefferson St. NW, Washington, DC 20007-3837 US	

GROWTH PLANS/SPECIAL FEATURES:

U.S. News and World Report L.P. is a publisher of periodicals and Internet content, including its flagship weekly U.S. News and World Report magazine with a circulation of over 2 million. The magazine offers news on money and business, education, health, science and technology, entertainment and politics, with well-known and widely respected contributors such as Lou Dobbs and David Gergen. U.S. News Chairman and Editor-in-Chief Mortimer Zuckerman has owned the company since 1984, and during his tenure has overseen the development of the company's interactive arm, usnews.com, and the continued expansion of the magazine's standalone special issues. U.S. News offers advertisers placement in demographically segmented editions of its weekly magazine organized by geographic region, as well as targeted editions for high income and business decision makers. The company also publishes annual reports and yearly rankings of graduate and undergraduate schools, hospitals and mutual funds. The prominence of these annual guides has greatly enhanced U.S. News' advertising profile, extending its global reach to some 11 million readers.

FINANCIALS: Sales and profits are in thousands of dollars—add 000 to get the full amount. 2006 Note: Financial information for 2006 was not available for all companies at press time.

		U.S. Stock Ticker: Private
2006 Sales: $	2006 Profits: $	**Int'l Ticker:** Int'l Exchange:
2005 Sales: $	2005 Profits: $	Employees:
2004 Sales: $	2004 Profits: $	Fiscal Year Ends: 1/31
2003 Sales: $	2003 Profits: $	Parent Company:
2002 Sales: $	2002 Profits: $	

SALARIES/BENEFITS:

Pension Plan:	ESOP Stock Plan:	Profit Sharing:	Top Exec. Salary: $	Bonus: $
Savings Plan:	Stock Purch. Plan:		Second Exec. Salary: $	Bonus: $

OTHER THOUGHTS:

Apparent Women Officers or Directors: 1
Hot Spot for Advancement for Women/Minorities:

LOCATIONS: ("Y" = Yes)

West:	Southwest:	Midwest:	Southeast:	Northeast:	International:
				Y	

VAIL RESORTS INC

www.vailresorts.com

Industry Group Code: 713920 Ranks within this company's industry group: Sales: 1 Profits: 1

Print Media/Publishing:	Movies:	Equipment/Supplies:		Broadcast/Cable:	Music/Audio:	Sports/Games:	
Newspapers:	Movie Theaters:	Equipment/Supplies:		Broadcast TV:	Music Production:	Games/Sports:	Y
Magazines:	Movie Production:	Gambling Equipment:	Y	Cable TV:	Retail Music:	Retail Games Stores:	
Books:	TV/Video Production:	Special Services:	Y	Satellite Broadcast:	Retail Audio Equip.:	Stadiums/Teams:	
Book Stores:	Video Rental:	Advertising Services:		Radio:	Music Print./Dist.:	Gambling/Casinos:	
Distribution/Printing:	Video Distribution:	Info. Sys. Software:		Online Information:	Multimedia:	Rides/Theme Parks:	

TYPES OF BUSINESS:

Ski Resorts
Luxury Hotels & Lodging
Real Estate Development

BRANDS/DIVISIONS/AFFILIATES:

RockResorts
Grand Teton Lodge Company
Vail Resorts Development Company
Vail Resorts Management Company
Vail Resorts Lodging Company
Vail Village
Breckenridge
Keystone

CONTACTS: Note: Officers with more than one job title may be intentionally listed here more than once.

Robert A. Katz, CEO
Jeffrey W. Jones, Sr. Exec. VP/CFO
Christopher E. Jarnot, Sr. VP-Mktg & Sales.
Martha D. Rehm, Exec. VP/General Counsel
Mark Schoppet, VP/Controller
William A. Jensen, Co-Pres., Mountain Division
Roger McCarthy, Co-Pres., Mountain Div.
William Hall, VP-Lodging Div.
Jack D. Hunn, Sr. VP-Design, Construction & Development
Joe R. Micheletto, Chmn.

Phone: 970-845-2500	Fax: 970-479-3002
Toll-Free: 888-222-9324	
Address: 137 Benchmark Rd., Avon, CO 81620 US	

GROWTH PLANS/SPECIAL FEATURES:

Vail Resorts, Inc. is one of the leading resort operators in North America. The company owns and operates four ski resorts in Colorado, one ski resort in Lake Tahoe and one summer resort in Grand Teton, Wyoming. It also owns a majority interest in RockResorts, which manages 9 luxury resort hotels located throughout the U.S. The firm's ski resorts include Vail, Breckenridge, Keystone, Beaver Creek and Heavenly, all of which are popular skiing and snowboarding vacation destinations. The company's five ski resorts offer over 16,700 skiable acres, constituting some of the most expansive and varied terrain of any resorts in North America. The Breckenridge resort recently opened the highest chairlift in North America, the Imperial Express SuperChair, with a peak elevation of 12,840 feet. Vail Resorts' Grand Teton Lodge Company operates the company's summer destination resort in Wyoming. The resorts and resort hotels derive revenue through a comprehensive offering of amenities, including ski lift ticket sales, ski and snowboard lesson packages, resort accommodations, retail and equipment rental outlets, dining venues, private club operations and other recreational activities such as golf, tennis, horseback riding, fishing tours, float trips and on-mountain activities centers. In addition to providing extensive guest amenities, Vail Resorts leases restaurant, retail and other commercial space, offers real estate brokerage services and participates in extensive licensing and sponsorship activities with other brand-name companies. Vail Resorts Development Company develops, buys and sells real estate in and around Vail's resort communities. In recent news, Vail Resorts is undergoing a five-year, $500-million redevelopment project in Vail Village and the neighboring LionsHead area.

The firm offers its employees free and discounted ski passes and lessons and discounts on company food, lodging, gear rental and retail, child care, airfare, fitness clubs and bus passes. Vail offers health insurance for full-time employees.

FINANCIALS: Sales and profits are in thousands of dollars—add 000 to get the full amount. 2006 Note: Financial information for 2006 was not available for all companies at press time.

2006 Sales: $838,852	2006 Profits: $45,756	U.S. Stock Ticker: MTN
2005 Sales: $809,987	2005 Profits: $23,138	Int'l Ticker: Int'l Exchange:
2004 Sales: $726,643	2004 Profits: $-5,959	Employees: 15,300
2003 Sales: $710,398	2003 Profits: $-8,527	Fiscal Year Ends: 7/31
2002 Sales: $615,300	2002 Profits: $7,600	Parent Company:

SALARIES/BENEFITS:

Pension Plan:	ESOP Stock Plan:	Profit Sharing:	Top Exec. Salary: $749,346	Bonus: $924,000
Savings Plan:	Stock Purch. Plan:		Second Exec. Salary: $402,731	Bonus: $311,250

OTHER THOUGHTS:

Apparent Women Officers or Directors: 1
Hot Spot for Advancement for Women/Minorities:

LOCATIONS: ("Y" = Yes)

West:	Southwest:	Midwest:	Southeast:	Northeast:	International:
Y	Y			Y	

Note: Financial information, benefits and other data can change quickly and may vary from those stated here.

VALUE LINE INC

www.valueline.com

Industry Group Code: 514100 Ranks within this company's industry group: Sales: 4 Profits: 3

Print Media/Publishing:		Movies:		Equipment/Supplies:		Broadcast/Cable:		Music/Audio:		Sports/Games:	
Newspapers:		Movie Theaters:		Equipment/Supplies:		Broadcast TV:		Music Production:		Games/Sports:	
Magazines:		Movie Production:		Gambling Equipment:	Y	Cable TV:		Retail Music:		Retail Games Stores:	
Books:	Y	TV/Video Production:		Special Services:	Y	Satellite Broadcast:		Retail Audio Equip.:		Stadiums/Teams:	
Book Stores:		Video Rental:		Advertising Services:	Y	Radio:		Music Print./Dist.:		Gambling/Casinos:	
Distribution/Printing:		Video Distribution:		Info. Sys. Software:		Online Information:		Multimedia:		Rides/Theme Parks:	

TYPES OF BUSINESS:

Financial Data Publishing
Financial Periodicals
Investment Management/Fund Advising
Research Services
Electronic Financial Tools
Broker-Dealer
Advertising Agency

BRANDS/DIVISIONS/AFFILIATES:

Value Line Publishing, Inc.
Value Line Investment Survey (The)
Value Line 600
Value Line Securities, Inc.
Vanderbilt Advertising Agency, Inc.
Compupower Corporation
Value Line Distribution Center, Inc.
Arnold Bernhard & Company, Inc.

CONTACTS: Note: Officers with more than one job title may be intentionally listed here more than once.

Jean B. Buttner, CEO
Jean B. Buttner, Pres.
Mitchell E. Appel, CFO
Samuel Eisenstadt, Sr. VP/Research Chmn.
Steven R. Anastasio, Treas.
Howard A. Brecher, VP/Corp. Sec.
David T. Henigson, VP
Howard A. Brecher, VP/Sec.
Jean B. Buttner, Chmn.

Phone: 212-907-1500	**Fax:** 212-818-9747
Toll-Free:	
Address: 220 E. 42nd St., New York, NY 10017-5891 US	

GROWTH PLANS/SPECIAL FEATURES:

Value Line, Inc. publishes investment-related periodicals through its wholly-owned subsidiary, Value Line Publishing, Inc. (VLP), and provides investment advisory services to mutual funds, institutions and individual clients. VLP publishes The Value Line Investment Survey, one of the nation's major periodical investment services, as well as the Value Line Investment Survey-Expanded Edition, the Value Line Investment Survey-Condensed Edition, Value Line Small Cap Plus, Value Line Select, the Value Line 600 (published monthly), the Value Line Mutual Fund Survey (published every three weeks), the Value Line No-Load Fund Advisor (published monthly), the Value Line Special Situations Service (published semi-monthly), the Value Line Options Survey (published 24 times a year) and the Value Line Convertibles Survey (published semi-monthly). In addition, the company has five electronic tools: Value Line Investment Analyzer; Value Line Mutual Fund Survey for Windows; Value Line DataFile; The Total Return Service; and The Value Line Research Center. Value Line is the investment advisor for the Value Line Family of Mutual Funds, which at the end of 2006 included 14 open-end investment companies. In addition, the company manages investments for private and institutional clients and, through VLP, provides financial database information through computer media and computer time-sharing facilities. The company's other subsidiaries include a registered broker-dealer, Value Line Securities, Inc.; and an advertising agency, Vanderbilt Advertising Agency, Inc. These subsidiaries primarily provide services used by the company in its publishing and investment management businesses. Subsidiary Compupower Corporation serves the subscription fulfillment needs of the company's publishing operations. Value Line Distribution Center, Inc. handles mailing of publications to the company's subscribers. The firm's web site offers intraday market commentary webcasts; educational programming offering video instruction on the company's products; and Value Line's Research Center, the firm's second-generation web site. Arnold Bernhard & Company, Inc. owns approximately 86.5% of Value Line's shares.

FINANCIALS: Sales and profits are in thousands of dollars—add 000 to get the full amount. 2006 Note: Financial information for 2006 was not available for all companies at press time.

2006 Sales: $85,186	2006 Profits: $23,439	**U.S. Stock Ticker: VALU**
2005 Sales: $84,478	2005 Profits: $21,318	**Int'l Ticker:** Int'l Exchange:
2004 Sales: $85,270	2004 Profits: $20,350	Employees: 228
2003 Sales: $82,100	2003 Profits: $19,987	Fiscal Year Ends: 4/30
2002 Sales: $87,443	2002 Profits: $20,323	Parent Company:

SALARIES/BENEFITS:

Pension Plan:	ESOP Stock Plan:	Profit Sharing:	Top Exec. Salary: $931,045	Bonus: $
Savings Plan: Y	Stock Purch. Plan:		Second Exec. Salary: $380,363	Bonus: $

OTHER THOUGHTS:

Apparent Women Officers or Directors: 1
Hot Spot for Advancement for Women/Minorities:

LOCATIONS: ("Y" = Yes)

West:	Southwest:	Midwest:	Southeast:	Northeast:	International:
				Y	

VALUEVISION MEDIA INC

www.shopnbc.com

Industry Group Code: 454110B   Ranks within this company's industry group: Sales: 2   Profits: 2

Print Media/Publishing:	Movies:	Equipment/Supplies:	Broadcast/Cable:		Music/Audio:	Sports/Games:
Newspapers:	Movie Theaters:	Equipment/Supplies:	Broadcast TV:		Music Production:	Games/Sports:
Magazines:	Movie Production:	Gambling Equipment:	Cable TV:	Y	Retail Music:	Retail Games Stores:
Books:	TV/Video Production:	Special Services:	Satellite Broadcast:		Retail Audio Equip.:	Stadiums/Teams:
Book Stores:	Video Rental:	Advertising Services:	Radio:		Music Print./Dist.:	Gambling/Casinos:
Distribution/Printing:	Video Distribution:	Info. Sys. Software:	Online Information:		Multimedia:	Rides/Theme Parks:

TYPES OF BUSINESS:
Television Shopping Programs
Online Sales
Fulfillment, Warehousing & Telemarketing Services
Credit Cards

BRANDS/DIVISIONS/AFFILIATES:
ValueVision Interactive, Inc.
Shop NBC
ValueVision International, Inc.
shopnbc.com
VVI Fulfillment Center, Inc.
General Electric

CONTACTS: *Note: Officers with more than one job title may be intentionally listed here more than once.*
William J. Lansing, CEO
Richard D. Barnes, COO
William J. Lansing, Pres.
Frank Elsenbast, CFO/Sr. VP
Bryan Venberg, Sr. VP-Human Resources
Steven Danker, CIO
Nathan E. Fagre, Sr. VP/General Counsel
Howard Fox, Sr. VP-Oper. & Customer Svc.
Jim Gilbertson, VP-Bus. Dev. & Dist.
Brenda Boehler, Exec. VP-TV & Internet Sales
Amy Kahlow, Dir.-Comm.
Marshall S. Geller, Chmn.

Phone: 952-943-6000	Fax: 952-943-6011
Toll-Free: 800-788-2454	
Address: 6740 Shady Oak Rd., Eden Prairie, MN 55344-3433 US	

GROWTH PLANS/SPECIAL FEATURES:
ValueVision Media, Inc. is a direct marketing company that markets its products to consumers through electronic media. The company's principal electronic media activity is its television home shopping network, which markets brand-name merchandise and proprietary and private-label consumer products at competitive or discount prices. ValueVision's live, 24-hour-a-day home shopping programming operates under the brand name Shop NBC and is distributed through cable affiliation and through its own broadcast television stations to approximately 60 million homes daily. Products sold on the network include jewelry, giftware, collectibles, apparel, electronics, housewares, seasonal items and various other merchandise items. Jewelry represents the company's largest single category of merchandise, representing 54% of television home shopping and Internet sales in fiscal 2005. The company's wholly-owned subsidiary, ValueVision Interactive, Inc., complements its television home shopping business with the sale of merchandise through its e-commerce web site, shopnbc.com. Another subsidiary, VVI Fulfillment Center, Inc., provides order fulfillment, warehousing and telemarketing services to Ralph Lauren Media, LLC, the NBC Experience Store in New York City and non-jewelry merchandise sold on the company's television home shopping program and web site. FanBuzz, Inc., formerly a subsidiary of ValueVision, was shut down in fiscal 2005 due to underpreformance.   General Electric and its NBC television subsidiary own a 40% stake in ValueVision. In late 2006, ShopNBC and GE Retail Consumer Finance launched a ShopNBC branded MasterCard as well as an improved ShopNBC private label credit card.

FINANCIALS: Sales and profits are in thousands of dollars—add 000 to get the full amount. 2006 Note: Financial information for 2006 was not available for all companies at press time.

2006 Sales: $691,851	2006 Profits: $-16,040	**U.S. Stock Ticker:** VVTV
2005 Sales: $623,634	2005 Profits: $-57,886	**Int'l Ticker:** Int'l Exchange:
2004 Sales: $591,185	2004 Profits: $-11,675	Employees: 1,110
2003 Sales: $554,900	2003 Profits: $-39,100	Fiscal Year Ends: 1/31
2002 Sales: $462,300	2002 Profits: $-9,500	Parent Company:

SALARIES/BENEFITS:

Pension Plan:	ESOP Stock Plan:	Profit Sharing:	Top Exec. Salary: $850,000	Bonus: $316,331
Savings Plan: Y	Stock Purch. Plan:		Second Exec. Salary: $356,346	Bonus: $126,388

OTHER THOUGHTS:
Apparent Women Officers or Directors: 1
Hot Spot for Advancement for Women/Minorities:

LOCATIONS: ("Y" = Yes)

West:	Southwest:	Midwest:	Southeast:	Northeast:	International:
		Y		Y	

VERIZON COMMUNICATIONS
www.verizon.com

Industry Group Code: 513300A Ranks within this company's industry group: Sales: 1 Profits: 1

Print Media/Publishing:	Movies:	Equipment/Supplies:		Broadcast/Cable:	Music/Audio:	Sports/Games:
Newspapers:	Movie Theaters:	Equipment/Supplies:	Y	Broadcast TV:	Music Production:	Games/Sports:
Magazines:	Movie Production:	Gambling Equipment:		Cable TV:	Retail Music:	Retail Games Stores:
Books:	TV/Video Production:	Special Services:	Y	Satellite Broadcast:	Retail Audio Equip.:	Stadiums/Teams:
Book Stores:	Video Rental:	Advertising Services:		Radio:	Music Print./Dist.:	Gambling/Casinos:
Distribution/Printing:	Video Distribution:	Info. Sys. Software:		Online Information:	Multimedia:	Rides/Theme Parks:

TYPES OF BUSINESS:
Local Telephone Service
Telecommunications Services
Wireless Services
Long-Distance Services
High-Speed Internet Access
Directory Publishing
e-Commerce & Online Services
Video-on-Demand Services

BRANDS/DIVISIONS/AFFILIATES:
Verizon Wireless
Verizon New York, Inc.
GTE Southwest, Inc.
Verizon New England, Inc.
Verizon South, Inc.
Qwest Wireless
MCI Communications
NextWave

CONTACTS: Note: Officers with more than one job title may be intentionally listed here more than once.
Ivan G. Seidenberg, CEO
Lawrence T. Babbio, Jr., Pres./Vice Chmn.
Doreen A. Toben, CFO/Exec. VP
Jerri DeVard, Sr. VP-Mktg. & Brand Mgmt.
Marc C. Reed, Exec. VP-Human Resources
Shaygan Kheradpir, CIO
Mark A. Wegleitner, CTO
William P. Barr, General Counsel/Exec. VP
John W. Dlercksen, Exec. VP-Strategy, Dev. & Planning
Thomas J. Tauke, Exec. VP-Public Affairs, Policy & Comm.
Ronald H. Lataille, Sr. VP-Investor Rel.
Catherine T. Webster, Sr. VP/Treas.
Dennis F. Strigl, Exec. VP/Pres., Verizon Wireless
Marianne Drost, Sr. VP/Corp. Sec.
John F. Killian, Pres., Verizon Business
Thomas A. Bartlett, Controller
Ivan G. Seidenberg, Chmn.
Dan Petri, Group Pres., Int'l
Maria D. Cruz, Dir.-Corp. Sourcing

Phone: 212-395-1000	Fax: 212-921-2721
Toll-Free: 800-621-9900	
Address: 140 West St., New York, NY 10007 US	

GROWTH PLANS/SPECIAL FEATURES:

Verizon Communications, Inc. and its subsidiaries form one of the world's leading providers of communications services, including wireline, wireless and Internet services. The firm has over 48 million access line equivalents in the U.S. and 5 million internationally; and over 51 million wireless customers. Global operations encompass over 30 countries in the Americas, Europe and Asia Pacific. Verizon operates in four segments: domestic telecommunications, domestic wireless, international and information services. The domestic telecommunications segment provides local telephone services, including voice and data transport, network access and private lines, in 28 states and Washington D.C. Domestic wireless operates as Verizon Wireless. Its offerings include cellular, PCS, paging services and equipment sales. Information services revenues amount to over $4 billion yearly, making Verizon one of the world's largest publishing and information companies. Products include print and electronic publishing, directories, Internet shopping guides and e-commerce services. One of the world's most aggressive adopters of new technologies, Verizon is in the middle of a long-term network upgrade. The firm will extend the availability of high speed fiber optic lines directly into many homes and offices. The result will be the availability of DSL at extremely high speeds of 5 to 30 megabits. These network improvements will support advanced telephone services, streaming video, and movies-on-demand, and will bring fiber optic cable to the consumers' homes. Implementation began in 2004 and will be completed in 2010 at a total cost of $23 billion. Verizon is positioning itself as more of a wireless and high speed Internet access firm than a local line provider. The company's 2005 acquisition of MCI also gave it very strong Internet backbone and data services assets.

Verizon offers employees tuition assistance, an internal training program, adoption benefits and day care services. The pension plan for managers was frozen in 2006.

FINANCIALS: Sales and profits are in thousands of dollars—add 000 to get the full amount. 2006 Note: Financial information for 2006 was not available for all companies at press time.

2006 Sales: $	2006 Profits: $	U.S. Stock Ticker: VZ
2005 Sales: $75,112,000	2005 Profits: $7,397,000	Int'l Ticker: Int'l Exchange:
2004 Sales: $71,283,000	2004 Profits: $7,831,000	Employees: 250,000
2003 Sales: $67,752,000	2003 Profits: $3,077,000	Fiscal Year Ends: 12/31
2002 Sales: $67,625,000	2002 Profits: $4,079,000	Parent Company:

SALARIES/BENEFITS:

Pension Plan:	ESOP Stock Plan:	Profit Sharing:	Top Exec. Salary: $2,100,000	Bonus: $4,147,500
Savings Plan: Y	Stock Purch. Plan:		Second Exec. Salary: $1,200,000	Bonus: $1,800,000

OTHER THOUGHTS:
Apparent Women Officers or Directors: 5
Hot Spot for Advancement for Women/Minorities: Y

LOCATIONS: ("Y" = Yes)

West:	Southwest:	Midwest:	Southeast:	Northeast:	International:
Y	Y	Y	Y	Y	Y

Note: Financial information, benefits and other data can change quickly and may vary from those stated here.

VIACOM INC

www.viacom.com

Industry Group Code: 513210 Ranks within this company's industry group: Sales: 4 Profits: 3

Print Media/Publishing:	Movies:		Equipment/Supplies:		Broadcast/Cable:		Music/Audio:		Sports/Games:	
Newspapers:	Movie Theaters:	Y	Equipment/Supplies:		Broadcast TV:		Music Production:	Y	Games/Sports:	Y
Magazines:	Movie Production:	Y	Gambling Equipment:		Cable TV:	Y	Retail Music:		Retail Games Stores:	
Books:	TV/Video Production:	Y	Special Services:	Y	Satellite Broadcast:		Retail Audio Equip.:		Stadiums/Teams:	
Book Stores:	Video Rental:		Advertising Services:		Radio:		Music Print./Dist.:	Y	Gambling/Casinos:	
Distribution/Printing:	Video Distribution:		Info. Sys. Software:		Online Information:		Multimedia:		Rides/Theme Parks:	

TYPES OF BUSINESS:

Cable TV Networks
Music Production & Distribution
Film Production
Television Production/Syndication
Video Distribution
Movie Theaters
Online Media
Video Games

BRANDS/DIVISIONS/AFFILIATES:

MTV
Comedy Central
Paramount Pictures
DreamWorks LLC
Famous Music Publishing
FLUX
Harmonix Music Systems, Inc.
National Amusement, Inc.

CONTACTS: Note: Officers with more than one job title may be intentionally listed here more than once.

Philippe Dauman, CEO
Philippe P. Dauman, Pres.
Thomas E. Dooley, CFO
JoAnne A. Griffith, Exec. VP-Human Resources
Thomas E. Dooley, Chief Admin. Officer/Sr. Exec. VP
Michael D. Fricklas, General Counsel/Exec. VP/Corp. Sec.
Wade Davis, Sr. VP-Strategy, Mergers & Acquisitions
Carl D. Folta, Exec. VP-Corp. Comm.
James Bombassei, Sr. VP-Investor Rel.
Jacques Tortoroli, Chief Acct. Officer/Corp. Controller/Sr. VP
Brad Grey, Chmn./CEO-Paramount Motion Picture Group
Debra Lee, CEO/Pres., Black Entertainment Television (BET)
Judy McGrath, Chmn./CEO-MTV Networks
Bob Bakish, Pres., MTV Networks Int'l
Sumner M. Redstone, Chmn.

Phone: 212-258-6000	Fax: 212-258-6464
Toll-Free:	
Address: 1515 Broadway, New York, NY 10036 US	

GROWTH PLANS/SPECIAL FEATURES:

Viacom, Inc. is an international media conglomerate created when it reorganized and spun off CBS, Inc. in January 2006. Viacom is composed of three main segments: cable television, motion picture production and music publishing. Its more than 130 cable networks include the MTV Network which includes MTV, MTV2, Nickelodeon, Nick at Nite, VH1, BET (Black Entertainment Television), TV Land, Comedy Central, CMT: Country Music Television and Spike TV among others. The BET network includes BET, BET Jazz, BET Gospel and BET Hip Hop. The company also operates numerous web sites and is offering television content over the Internet, with plans to offer content to mobile phones. Subsidiary Paramount Pictures produces, finances and distributes feature motion pictures. Paramount also has a film library of over 1,100 titles, which it markets on DVD and VHS through Paramount Home Entertainment. In 2006, Viacom acquired DreamWorks LLC for $1.6 billion. DreamWorks produces movies, including Gladiator and The Ring, television programming such as Spin City and Las Vegas, and also markets these properties for home entertainment. Viacom's music publishing segment is composed of Famous Music Publishing, which owns the rights to more than 125,000 musical works, mostly associated with film or TV properties. The segment also has interests in 20 movie theaters. In late 2006, Viacom sold Paramount Pictures' DreamWorks film library to Soros Strategic Partners LP and Dune Entertainment II, LLC for $900 million. Also in 2006, MTV Networks acquired Xfire, Inc., an online gaming communication and community platform, for $102 million. In late 2006, the company launched FLUX, a social networking and Internet video service, in Japan. In late 2006, MTV Networks acquired Harmonix Music Systems, Inc., maker of popular videogame title Guitar Hero, for $175 million. National Amusement, Inc., owned by the Redstone family, is the 73% majority shareholder in Viacom.

FINANCIALS: Sales and profits are in thousands of dollars—add 000 to get the full amount. 2006 Note: Financial information for 2006 was not available for all companies at press time.

2006 Sales: $	2006 Profits: $	U.S. Stock Ticker: VIA
2005 Sales: $9,609,600	2005 Profits: $1,256,900	Int'l Ticker: Int'l Exchange:
2004 Sales: $8,132,200	2004 Profits: $293,700	Employees: 32,160
2003 Sales: $7,304,400	2003 Profits: $338,500	Fiscal Year Ends: 12/31
2002 Sales: $	2002 Profits: $	Parent Company:

SALARIES/BENEFITS:

Pension Plan: Y	ESOP Stock Plan:	Profit Sharing:	Top Exec. Salary: $5,806,651	Bonus: $7,125,000
Savings Plan: Y	Stock Purch. Plan:		Second Exec. Salary: $5,306,651	Bonus: $13,000,000

OTHER THOUGHTS:

Apparent Women Officers or Directors: 6
Hot Spot for Advancement for Women/Minorities: Y

LOCATIONS: ("Y" = Yes)

West:	Southwest:	Midwest:	Southeast:	Northeast:	International:
Y		Y		Y	Y

Note: Financial information, benefits and other data can change quickly and may vary from those stated here.

VINDIGO INC

www.vindigo.com

Industry Group Code: 511208 Ranks within this company's industry group: Sales: Profits:

Print Media/Publishing:	Movies:	Equipment/Supplies:	Broadcast/Cable:	Music/Audio:	Sports/Games:	
Newspapers:	Movie Theaters:	Equipment/Supplies:	Broadcast TV:	Music Production:	Games/Sports:	Y
Magazines:	Movie Production:	Gambling Equipment:	Cable TV:	Retail Music:	Retail Games Stores:	
Books:	TV/Video Production:	Special Services:	Satellite Broadcast:	Retail Audio Equip.:	Stadiums/Teams:	
Book Stores:	Video Rental:	Advertising Services:	Radio:	Music Print./Dist.:	Gambling/Casinos:	
Distribution/Printing:	Video Distribution:	Info. Sys. Software:	Online Information:	Multimedia:	Rides/Theme Parks:	

TYPES OF BUSINESS:

Mobile Media Content
Mobile Marketing Products
Navigation Tools
Ringtones
Games

BRANDS/DIVISIONS/AFFILIATES:

Vindigo
Vindigo RingMaster
Shadowgate
Upoc
For-Side.com Co. Ltd,
waymobile.com, Inc.

CONTACTS: *Note: Officers with more than one job title may be intentionally listed here more than once.*

Jason Devitt, CEO
Samantha Saturn, VP-Mktg.
Dave Hock, VP-Research
Bob Fitterman, CTO
Tricia Han, VP-Product Dev.
Janet Kasdan, VP-Eng.
Marci Weisler, VP-Carrier Rel.
Carrie Himelfarb-Seifer, VP-Sales
Greg Genrich, VP-Design
Candace L. Martin, VP-Quality Assurance

Phone: 212-590-6900	Fax: 212-590-6999
Toll-Free:	
Address: 500 7th Ave., 17th Fl., New York, NY 10018 US	

GROWTH PLANS/SPECIAL FEATURES:

Vindigo is a mobile media company that publishes and distributes content for cell phones and other wireless personal devices through a network of partnerships. This network has a combined reach of more than 140 million mobile subscribers. Vindigo's content includes wallpaper, ringtones, local information, maps, news, entertainment and sports information. Vindigo, the service after which the company is named, is a combination navigator and city guide, with information on shopping, restaurants, museums, gas stations and many other things. Vindigo RingMaster is a ringtone shop where wireless subscribers can preview and download ringtones, exclusive celebrity audio material, chart-toppers, voicetones, sound effects, classic hits, theme songs and more. Vindigo recently launched a new fantasy adventure game, developed for QUALCOMM's BREW solution on mobile phones in North America, under the name Shadowgate. Upoc is a bulletin board service that allows instant messaging within groups created to discuss certain topics. The company has created certain marketing partnerships with over 100 advertisers, for example, Cadillac and MasterCard. Vindigo has been a subsidiary of For-Side.com Co. Ltd., one of Japan's and the world's largest mobile media companies, since August 2004. The firm, together with CTIA Wireless IT and Entertainment, owns waymobile.com, Inc., a San Diego-based developer and publisher of advanced mobile content and commerce products, including AwayAuction for eBay.

FINANCIALS: Sales and profits are in thousands of dollars—add 000 to get the full amount. 2006 Note: Financial information for 2006 was not available for all companies at press time.

2006 Sales: $	2006 Profits: $	**U.S. Stock Ticker: Subsidiary**
2005 Sales: $	2005 Profits: $	**Int'l Ticker:** Int'l Exchange:
2004 Sales: $	2004 Profits: $	Employees:
2003 Sales: $	2003 Profits: $	Fiscal Year Ends: 4/30
2002 Sales: $	2002 Profits: $	Parent Company: FOR-SIDE.COM CO LTD

SALARIES/BENEFITS:

Pension Plan:	ESOP Stock Plan:	Profit Sharing:	Top Exec. Salary: $	Bonus: $
Savings Plan:	Stock Purch. Plan:		Second Exec. Salary: $	Bonus: $

OTHER THOUGHTS:

Apparent Women Officers or Directors: 6
Hot Spot for Advancement for Women/Minorities: Y

LOCATIONS: ("Y" = Yes)

West:	Southwest:	Midwest:	Southeast:	Northeast:	International:
				Y	

Note: Financial information, benefits and other data can change quickly and may vary from those stated here.

VIVENDI GAMES

www.sierra.com

Industry Group Code: 511208 Ranks within this company's industry group: Sales: 5 Profits: 5

Print Media/Publishing:	Movies:	Equipment/Supplies:	Broadcast/Cable:	Music/Audio:	Sports/Games:	
Newspapers:	Movie Theaters:	Equipment/Supplies:	Broadcast TV:	Music Production:	Games/Sports:	Y
Magazines:	Movie Production:	Gambling Equipment:	Cable TV:	Retail Music:	Retail Games Stores:	
Books:	TV/Video Production:	Special Services:	Satellite Broadcast:	Retail Audio Equip.:	Stadiums/Teams:	
Book Stores:	Video Rental:	Advertising Services:	Radio:	Music Print./Dist.:	Gambling/Casinos:	
Distribution/Printing:	Video Distribution:	Info. Sys. Software:	Online Information:	Multimedia:	Rides/Theme Parks:	

TYPES OF BUSINESS:

Video Game Development
Online Games
Mobile Games

BRANDS/DIVISIONS/AFFILIATES:

Vivendi
Blizzard Entertainment
Sierra Entertainment
Vivendi Games Mobile
Massive Entertainment
World of Warcraft
Diablo
Scarface: The World Is Yours

CONTACTS: Note: Officers with more than one job title may be intentionally listed here more than once.

Bruce Hack, CEO
Rene Penisson, Chmn.

Phone: 310-431-4000	Fax: 310-793-0603
Toll-Free:	
Address: 6080 Center Dr., 5th Fl., Los Angeles, CA 90045 US	

GROWTH PLANS/SPECIAL FEATURES:

Vivendi Games is the interactive publishing subsidiary of Vivendi (formerly Vivendi Universal). The company creates games for the PC, console, handheld, mobile and online markets, and has 16 offices operating in 75 countries worldwide. Vivendi Games' divisions include Blizzard Entertainment, Sierra Entertainment, Vivendi Games Mobile and Sierra Online. The firm's game design studios include Swedish-based Massive Entertainment, Radical Entertainment, U.K.-based Swordfish Studios and High Moon Studios. Vivendi Games' library contains over 700 titles. Blizzard Entertainment has designed of the best-selling video games in history, including Starcraft, Diablo and the wildly-successful World of Warcraft, the world's most popular massive multi-player online role-playing game with more than 6.5 million customers as of May 2006. World of Warcraft is the only such game active in all key markets, including North America, Europe, Australia, New Zealand, South Korea, China and Taiwan. Sierra Entertainment's titles include Crash Bandicoot, Empire Earth, Leisure Suit Larry, Ground Control and 50 Cent: Bulletproof. The recently-created Vivendi Games Mobile division publishes games through mobile carriers. The firm's most recent hit is Scarface: The World Is Yours, which sold over 1 million copies worldwide in 2006.

FINANCIALS: Sales and profits are in thousands of dollars—add 000 to get the full amount. 2006 Note: Financial information for 2006 was not available for all companies at press time.

2006 Sales: $	2006 Profits: $	U.S. Stock Ticker: Subsidiary
2005 Sales: $770,688	2005 Profits: $49,295	Int'l Ticker: Int'l Exchange:
2004 Sales: $571,132	2004 Profits: $-244,084	Employees:
2003 Sales: $728,082	2003 Profits: $	Fiscal Year Ends: 12/31
2002 Sales: $800,000	2002 Profits: $	Parent Company: VIVENDI SA

SALARIES/BENEFITS:

Pension Plan:	ESOP Stock Plan:	Profit Sharing:	Top Exec. Salary: $	Bonus: $
Savings Plan:	Stock Purch. Plan:		Second Exec. Salary: $	Bonus: $

OTHER THOUGHTS:

Apparent Women Officers or Directors:
Hot Spot for Advancement for Women/Minorities:

LOCATIONS: ("Y" = Yes)

West:	Southwest:	Midwest:	Southeast:	Northeast:	International:
Y	Y	Y		Y	Y

VIVENDI SA

www.vivendi.com

Industry Group Code: 512230   **Ranks within this company's industry group:** Sales: 1   Profits: 1

Print Media/Publishing:		Movies:		Equipment/Supplies:		Broadcast/Cable:		Music/Audio:		Sports/Games:	
Newspapers:		Movie Theaters:		Equipment/Supplies:		Broadcast TV:	Y	Music Production:	Y	Games/Sports:	Y
Magazines:		Movie Production:	Y	Gambling Equipment:		Cable TV:	Y	Retail Music:		Retail Games Stores:	
Books:		TV/Video Production:	Y	Special Services:	Y	Satellite Broadcast:		Retail Audio Equip.:	Y	Stadiums/Teams:	
Book Stores:		Video Rental:		Advertising Services:		Radio:		Music Print./Dist.:	Y	Gambling/Casinos:	
Distribution/Printing:		Video Distribution:		Info. Sys. Software:		Online Information:		Multimedia:		Rides/Theme Parks:	Y

TYPES OF BUSINESS:

Music Production & Publishing
Cable & Satellite Television
Video Games & Software
Telecommunications Services
Cellular Telephone Service
Film Distribution
Theme Parks

BRANDS/DIVISIONS/AFFILIATES:

Universal Music Group
Group Canal+
StudioCanal
SFR Cegetel
Maroc Telecom
Vivendi Games
NBC Universal
BMG Music Publishing Group

CONTACTS: *Note: Officers with more than one job title may be intentionally listed here more than once.*

Jean-Bernard Levy, CEO
Jacques Espinasse, CFO
Rene Penisson, Sr. VP-Human Resources
Jean-Francois Dubos, General Counsel
Robert De Metz, Exec. VP-Strategy & Dev.
Michel Bourgeois, Exec. VP-Corp. Comm.
Daniel Scolan, Exec. VP-Investor Rel.
Regis Turrini, Exec. VP-Divestitures, Mergers & Acquisitions
Jean-Bernard Levy, Chmn.

Phone: 33-1-71-71-10-00	**Fax:** 33-1-71-71-11-79
Toll-Free:	
Address: 42 Ave. de Friedland, Paris, 75380 France	

GROWTH PLANS/SPECIAL FEATURES:

Vivendi SA, formerly Vivendi Universal, is a company focusing on the areas of music, TV, cinema, telecommunications, Internet connectivity and interactive games. The company's primary subsidiaries include Universal Music Group, a leading supplier of recorded music, music videos, DVDs and music publishing; Group Canal+, a French company offering pay-TV channels through Canal+ and CanalSat and one of the world's largest film libraries through StudioCanal; SFR Cegetel, a leading French telecommunications provider; Maroc Telecom, a Moroccan telecommunications firm; and Vivendi Games, a global developer, publisher and distributor of interactive games. In 2004, Vivendi Universal and General Electric completed the merger of Vivendi Universal Entertainment, comprising the company's film, television, theme park and related holdings, with NBC, to create NBC Universal. Today, GE holds an 80% interest in NBC Universal, with the remaining 20% controlled by Vivendi. In early 2006, the SFR unit exceeded 1 million exclusively 3G cell phone customers. In September 2006, the company acquired the BMG Music Publishing Group from Bertelsmann AG for $2.09 billion.

FINANCIALS: Sales and profits are in thousands of dollars—add 000 to get the full amount. 2006 Note: Financial information for 2006 was not available for all companies at press time.

2006 Sales: $	2006 Profits: $	**U.S. Stock Ticker:** VIV
2005 Sales: $23,059,000	2005 Profits: $3,733,000	**Int'l Ticker:** VIV Int'l Exchange: Paris-Euronext
2004 Sales: $29,026,000	2004 Profits: $1,021,000	Employees: 34,031
2003 Sales: $32,328,900	2003 Profits: $-1,437,000	Fiscal Year Ends: 12/31
2002 Sales: $61,075,000	2002 Profits: $-24,473,000	Parent Company:

SALARIES/BENEFITS:

Pension Plan:	ESOP Stock Plan:	Profit Sharing:	Top Exec. Salary: $	Bonus: $
Savings Plan:	Stock Purch. Plan:		Second Exec. Salary: $	Bonus: $

OTHER THOUGHTS:

Apparent Women Officers or Directors: 1
Hot Spot for Advancement for Women/Minorities:

LOCATIONS: ("Y" = Yes)

West:	Southwest:	Midwest:	Southeast:	Northeast:	International:
Y	Y	Y	Y	Y	Y

Note: Financial information, benefits and other data can change quickly and may vary from those stated here.

VNU NV

www.vnu.com

Industry Group Code: 541910 **Ranks within this company's industry group:** Sales: 1 Profits: 1

Print Media/Publishing:		Movies:		Equipment/Supplies:		Broadcast/Cable:		Music/Audio:		Sports/Games:	
Newspapers:		Movie Theaters:		Equipment/Supplies:		Broadcast TV:		Music Production:		Games/Sports:	
Magazines:	Y	Movie Production:		Gambling Equipment:		Cable TV:		Retail Music:		Retail Games Stores:	
Books:		TV/Video Production:		Special Services:	Y	Satellite Broadcast:		Retail Audio Equip.:		Stadiums/Teams:	
Book Stores:		Video Rental:		Advertising Services:	Y	Radio:		Music Print./Dist.:		Gambling/Casinos:	
Distribution/Printing:		Video Distribution:		Info. Sys. Software:	Y	Online Information:		Multimedia:		Rides/Theme Parks:	

TYPES OF BUSINESS:
Market Research
Magazine Publishing
Media/Entertainment Audience Research
Trade Publications
Directories
Business Consulting

BRANDS/DIVISIONS/AFFILIATES:
ACNielson
Nielson Media Research
Golden Pages
Hollywood Reporter Industries
Billboard
Global Media
Adweek
Valcon Acquisition BV

CONTACTS: *Note: Officers with more than one job title may be intentionally listed here more than once.*
David L. Calhoun, CEO
Susan Whiting, Exec. VP
J. Lancaster, Dir.-Human Resources, Europe
Susan Whiting, Exec. VP
James Cuminale, EVP, Chief Legal Off.
David Berger, Controller
Jon Mandel, CEO, NielsenConnect
John Lewis, Pres/CEO ACNielsen North America
Patt Dodd, ACNielsen Europe
Nonoy Niles, Pres.-ACNielsen Asia Pacific
David L. Calhoun, Chmn.

Phone: 31-23-546-34-63	Fax: 31-23-546-39-38
Toll-Free:	
Address: Ceylonpoort 5-25, Haarlem, 2037 AA The Netherlands	

GROWTH PLANS/SPECIAL FEATURES:
VNU NV, a market research company, publishes business and media information, trade publications and directories. The company operates in six groups: marketing, retail, film, music, marketing services and travel, and residential and commercial building design. The company has operations in over 100 countries worldwide through subsidiaries ACNielson and Nielson Media Research; periodicals Billboard, Adweek and The Hollywood Reporter; and telephone directories such as Golden Pages, Gouden Gids and Pages d'Or. The marketing services group, which includes ACNielson, provides information to approximately 9,000 clients on sales volumes, market shares, distribution, pricing, merchandising and advertising gathered from a network of more than 170,000 stores; demographic information on consumer buying habits gathered from nearly 62,000 homes; and custom research in other market areas. Nielson Media Research monitors the television viewing habits of approximately 107 million American homes as well as 85% of world spending on advertising. In 2006, VNU NV was acquired by Valcon Acquisition BV, an entity formed by several investment groups including The Blackstone Group, The Carlyle Group, and Kohlberg Kravis Roberts & Co., AlpInvest Partners N.V., Hellman & Friedman LLC, and Thomas H. Lee Partners, L.P. As part of the $9 billion acquisition, VNU NV underwent major corporate restructuring. The company became a private limited liability company in July 2006, delisting its stock later that year. In addition, the company has agreed in principle to sell its Business Media Europe group to 3i, a private-equity and venture capital company.

FINANCIALS: Sales and profits are in thousands of dollars—add 000 to get the full amount. 2006 Note: Financial information for 2006 was not available for all companies at press time.

2006 Sales: $	2006 Profits: $	U.S. Stock Ticker: Private	
2005 Sales: $4,180,121	2005 Profits: $307,738	Int'l Ticker:	Int'l Exchange:
2004 Sales: $4,009,084	2004 Profits: $295,722	Employees: 42,000	
2003 Sales: $4,872,400	2003 Profits: $163,100	Fiscal Year Ends: 12/31	
2002 Sales: $4,481,100	2002 Profits: $177,800	Parent Company:	

SALARIES/BENEFITS:

Pension Plan:	ESOP Stock Plan:	Profit Sharing:	Top Exec. Salary: $	Bonus: $
Savings Plan:	Stock Purch. Plan:		Second Exec. Salary: $	Bonus: $

OTHER THOUGHTS:
Apparent Women Officers or Directors: 1
Hot Spot for Advancement for Women/Minorities:

LOCATIONS: ("Y" = Yes)

West:	Southwest:	Midwest:	Southeast:	Northeast:	International:
Y	Y	Y	Y	Y	Y

VULCAN INC

www.vulcan.com

Industry Group Code: 551110 Ranks within this company's industry group: Sales: Profits:

Print Media/Publishing:		Movies:		Equipment/Supplies:		Broadcast/Cable:		Music/Audio:		Sports/Games:	
Newspapers:		Movie Theaters:	Y	Equipment/Supplies:		Broadcast TV:		Music Production:		Games/Sports:	
Magazines:		Movie Production:	Y	Gambling Equipment:	Y	Cable TV:		Retail Music:		Retail Games Stores:	
Books:		TV/Video Production:		Special Services:	Y	Satellite Broadcast:		Retail Audio Equip.:		Stadiums/Teams:	
Book Stores:		Video Rental:		Advertising Services:		Radio:		Music Print./Dist.:		Gambling/Casinos:	
Distribution/Printing:		Video Distribution:		Info. Sys. Software:		Online Information:		Multimedia:		Rides/Theme Parks:	

TYPES OF BUSINESS:

Company & Enterprise Management
Film Production
Entertainment Investments
Telecommunications Investments
Sports Teams
Real Estate

BRANDS/DIVISIONS/AFFILIATES:

Vulcan Capital
Vulcan Productions
Experience Music Project
Hospital (The)
Plains Resources, Inc.
Seattle Seahawks

CONTACTS: Note: Officers with more than one job title may be intentionally listed here more than once.

Jody Patton, CEO
Jody Patton, Pres.
Buster Brown, CFO
Chris Purcell, VP-Tech.
Gregory P. Landis, VP/General Counsel
Denise Wolf, VP-Oper.
Denise Wolf, VP-Corp. Dev.
Steven C. Crosby, VP-Corp. Comm.
Denise K. Fletcher, Exec. VP-Finance
Lance Conn, VP-Investment Mgmt.
Ada M. Healey, VP-Real Estate Dev.
Richard E. Hutton, VP-Media Dev.
Paul Allen, Chmn.

Phone: 206-342-2000	Fax: 206-342-3000
Toll-Free:	
Address: 505 5th Ave. S., Ste. 900, Seattle, WA 98104 US	

GROWTH PLANS/SPECIAL FEATURES:

Vulcan, Inc., founded by Microsoft co-founder Paul Allen to research and implement his investments, does everything from building museums and making original motion pictures to launching businesses developing new technologies. It primarily focuses on projects involving education, history and the arts. Though the company believes that technology can enhance these projects and deliver them to a broader audience, achieving high levels of creativity is its main objective. Its creative projects include Vulcan Productions, the Experience Music Project and The Hospital. Vulcan Productions originates, develops and finances film projects with directors and producers who have a history of success in delivering great storytelling, significant artistry and long-term commercial success. The Experience Music Project is a music museum that combines interactive and interpretive exhibits to tell the story of American popular music. The Hospital is a multi-use venue for international music and film professionals created from the derelict St. Paul's Hospital in the London borough of Camden. The firm also owns several major sports teams including the Seattle Sea Hawks, as well as various Seattle real estate properties such as 505 Union Station. Vulcan invests in companies that offer services that fit Allen's wired-world strategy and can contribute to or benefit from the technology of other companies within Vulcan's extensive investment portfolio. Vulcan has invested in telecommunications, media, retail, software, hardware and biotechnology companies such as DreamWorks SKG, Oxygen Media and RCN Corporation.

Vulcan offers its employees apartment assistance, an employee assistance plan, tuition reimbursement, up to $100 a month for transportation, credit union membership, an on-premises athletic facility and health club membership. The firm also offers insurance benefits for domestic partners.

FINANCIALS: Sales and profits are in thousands of dollars—add 000 to get the full amount. 2006 Note: Financial information for 2006 was not available for all companies at press time.

			U.S. Stock Ticker: Private
2006 Sales: $	2006 Profits: $		Int'l Ticker: Int'l Exchange:
2005 Sales: $	2005 Profits: $		Employees:
2004 Sales: $	2004 Profits: $		Fiscal Year Ends: 12/31
2003 Sales: $	2003 Profits: $		Parent Company:
2002 Sales: $	2002 Profits: $		

SALARIES/BENEFITS:

Pension Plan:	ESOP Stock Plan:	Profit Sharing:	Top Exec. Salary: $	Bonus: $
Savings Plan: Y	Stock Purch. Plan:		Second Exec. Salary: $	Bonus: $

OTHER THOUGHTS:

Apparent Women Officers or Directors: 4
Hot Spot for Advancement for Women/Minorities: Y

LOCATIONS: ("Y" = Yes)

West:	Southwest:	Midwest:	Southeast:	Northeast:	International:
Y					

WALT DISNEY COMPANY (THE)

www.disney.com

Industry Group Code: 513210 Ranks within this company's industry group: Sales: 1 Profits: 2

Print Media/Publishing:		Movies:		Equipment/Supplies:		Broadcast/Cable:		Music/Audio:		Sports/Games:	
Newspapers:		Movie Theaters:		Equipment/Supplies:		Broadcast TV:	Y	Music Production:	Y	Games/Sports:	
Magazines:		Movie Production:	Y	Gambling Equipment:		Cable TV:	Y	Retail Music:		Retail Games Stores:	
Books:	Y	TV/Video Production:	Y	Special Services:	Y	Satellite Broadcast:		Retail Audio Equip.:		Stadiums/Teams:	Y
Book Stores:		Video Rental:		Advertising Services:		Radio:		Music Print./Dist.:		Gambling/Casinos:	
Distribution/Printing:		Video Distribution:		Info. Sys. Software:		Online Information:		Multimedia:		Rides/Theme Parks:	Y

TYPES OF BUSINESS:

Cable TV Networks, Broadcasting & Entertainment
Filmed Entertainment
Professional Hockey Team
Television Networks
Music & Book Publishing
Online Entertainment Programs
Theme Parks, Resorts & Cruise Lines
Merchandising

BRANDS/DIVISIONS/AFFILIATES:

Touchstone Pictures
Hollywood Pictures
Miramax
Dimension
ABC Television Network
Disneyland
ESPN
Pixar

CONTACTS:
Note: Officers with more than one job title may be intentionally listed here more than once.

Robert A. Iger, CEO
Robert A. Iger, Pres.
Thomas O. Staggs, CFO/Sr. Exec. VP
Andy Mooney, Pres., Disney Consumer Prod.
Alan Braverman, General Counsel/Sr. Exec. VP
Kevin Mayer, Exec. VP-Corp. Strategy, Bus. Dev. & Tech. Group
Zenia Mucha, Exec. VP-Corp. Comm.
Christine M. McCarthy, Exec. VP-Corp. Finance & Real Estate
Ronald L. Iden, Sr. VP-Security
Preston Padden, Exec. VP-Government Relations
George W. Bodenheimer, Pres., ESPN, Inc. & ABC Sports
Walter C. Liss., Pres., ABC Television
George J. Mitchell, Chmn.
Andy Bird, Pres., Walt Disney International

Phone: 818-560-1000	Fax: 818-560-1930
Toll-Free:	
Address: 500 S. Buena Vista St., Burbank, CA 91521-9722 US	

GROWTH PLANS/SPECIAL FEATURES:

The Walt Disney Company is an international entertainment company operating in four major business segments: media networks, studio entertainment, consumer products, and parks and resorts. The media networks segment is the largest revenue producer at about 43% of all revenues. The segment comprises broadcast television networks, television stations, cable/satellite networks and television production and distribution in the U.S. and internationally. The company also owns and operates cable networks, including ESPN, ABC Family, the History Channel, the Biography Channel, Lifetime Television, E! Entertainment Television, Style and A&E. Through the studio entertainment section, Disney produces, acquires and distributes live action and animated motion pictures, animated direct-to-video programming, musical recordings and live stage plays. The consumer products segment sells various merchandise based on the firm's intellectual property. The parks and resorts department manages the operations of the Walt Disney World Resort and the Disney Cruise Line in Florida, the Disneyland resort in California, the Disneyland Resorts in Paris and Hong Kong and licenses the Tokyo Disney Resort in Japan. The Walt Disney World Resort includes the Magic Kingdom, Epcot, Disney-MGM Studios and Disney's Animal Kingdom; hotels; vacation ownership units; a retail, dining and entertainment complex; a sports complex; conference centers; campgrounds; golf courses; water parks and other recreational facilities. The company has a 51% ownership interest in the Disneyland Resort Paris. Disney owns its interest in Hong Kong Disneyland through Hong Kong International Theme Parks Limited, an entity in which the Hong Kong Government owns a 57% interest. In May 2006, Disney acquired Pixar, a computer animation studio. In order to catch up in the growing Indian entertainment market, in July 2006 Disney acquired Hungama, a popular Indian children's cable-TV channel for $30 million.

Disney employees receive theme park passports, educational reimbursement, access to the Walt Disney Company Foundation Scholarship Program, credit union membership, a personal assistant network and on-site child care services. In addition, the company holds employee and cast member contests.

FINANCIALS: Sales and profits are in thousands of dollars—add 000 to get the full amount. 2006 Note: Financial information for 2006 was not available for all companies at press time.

2006 Sales: $34,285,000	2006 Profits: $3,374,000	**U.S. Stock Ticker: DIS**
2005 Sales: $31,944,000	2005 Profits: $2,533,000	**Int'l Ticker:** Int'l Exchange:
2004 Sales: $30,752,000	2004 Profits: $2,345,000	Employees: 133,000
2003 Sales: $27,061,000	2003 Profits: $1,267,000	Fiscal Year Ends: 9/30
2002 Sales: $25,329,000	2002 Profits: $1,236,000	Parent Company:

SALARIES/BENEFITS:

Pension Plan: Y	ESOP Stock Plan:	Profit Sharing:	Top Exec. Salary: $1,500,000	Bonus: $7,739,941
Savings Plan: Y	Stock Purch. Plan: Y		Second Exec. Salary: $1,000,000	Bonus: $9,111,806

OTHER THOUGHTS:

Apparent Women Officers or Directors: 5
Hot Spot for Advancement for Women/Minorities: Y

LOCATIONS: ("Y" = Yes)

West:	Southwest:	Midwest:	Southeast:	Northeast:	International:
Y	Y	Y	Y	Y	Y

Note: Financial information, benefits and other data can change quickly and may vary from those stated here.

WALT DISNEY STUDIOS
disney.go.com/disneypictures

Industry Group Code: 512110 Ranks within this company's industry group: Sales: 3 Profits:

Print Media/Publishing:		Movies:		Equipment/Supplies:		Broadcast/Cable:		Music/Audio:		Sports/Games:	
Newspapers:		Movie Theaters:		Equipment/Supplies:		Broadcast TV:		Music Production:	Y	Games/Sports:	
Magazines:		Movie Production:	Y	Gambling Equipment:		Cable TV:		Retail Music:		Retail Games Stores:	
Books:		TV/Video Production:	Y	Special Services:		Satellite Broadcast:		Retail Audio Equip.:		Stadiums/Teams:	
Book Stores:		Video Rental:		Advertising Services:		Radio:		Music Print./Dist.:		Gambling/Casinos:	
Distribution/Printing:		Video Distribution:		Info. Sys. Software:		Online Information:		Multimedia:		Rides/Theme Parks:	

TYPES OF BUSINESS:
Movie Production
Animation
Music Production
DVD & Home Video
Live Entertainment

BRANDS/DIVISIONS/AFFILIATES:
Walt Disney Company (The)
Fantasia
The Chronicles of Narnia
Miramax Film Corporation

CONTACTS: Note: Officers with more than one job title may be intentionally listed here more than once.
Alan Bergman, Pres.
Oren Aviv, VP-Mktg. & Sales
Richard W. Cook, Chmn.

Phone: 818-560-1000	Fax: 818-560-1930
Toll-Free:	
Address: 500 S. Buena Vista St., Burbank, CA 91521-9722 US	

GROWTH PLANS/SPECIAL FEATURES:

Walt Disney Studios is a subsidiary of The Walt Disney Company. The firm is the motion picture operation for Disney, with operations in live action, animation, music, stage plays and entertainment. The company's recent live-action titles include The Chronicles of Narnia: The Lion, The Witch and the Wardorbe, National Treasure and Herbie: Fully Loaded. Animated films include Chicken Little, Valiant, Toy Story, Finding Nemo and A Goofy Movie. The firm is also responsible for the release of Disney classic movies including the animated Cinderella, Peter Pan, Alice in Wonderland, Winnie the Poo and Fantasia and the live action Freaky Friday, Flight of the Navigator, Ella Enchanted and Mary Poppins. Walt Disney Studio also operates through Miramax Film Corporation to acquire, produce, and distribute independent movies, and it helps finance animated movies developed in conjunction with Pixar. The firm has additional divisions devoted to home entertainment, music, and live stage plays. The company's newest releases include Glory Road, Eight Below and Roving Mars.

FINANCIALS: Sales and profits are in thousands of dollars—add 000 to get the full amount. 2006 Note: Financial information for 2006 was not available for all companies at press time.

2006 Sales: $	2006 Profits: $	**U.S. Stock Ticker: Subsidiary**		
2005 Sales: $7,587,000	2005 Profits: $	**Int'l Ticker:** Int'l Exchange:		
2004 Sales: $	2004 Profits: $	Employees:		
2003 Sales: $	2003 Profits: $	Fiscal Year Ends: 9/30		
2002 Sales: $	2002 Profits: $	Parent Company: WALT DISNEY COMPANY (THE)		

SALARIES/BENEFITS:

Pension Plan:	ESOP Stock Plan:	Profit Sharing:	Top Exec. Salary: $	Bonus: $
Savings Plan:	Stock Purch. Plan:		Second Exec. Salary: $	Bonus: $

OTHER THOUGHTS:
Apparent Women Officers or Directors:
Hot Spot for Advancement for Women/Minorities:

LOCATIONS: ("Y" = Yes)

West:	Southwest:	Midwest:	Southeast:	Northeast:	International:
Y					

Note: Financial information, benefits and other data can change quickly and may vary from those stated here.

WARNER BROS ENTERTAINMENT INC www.warnerbros.com

Industry Group Code: 512110 Ranks within this company's industry group: Sales: 1 Profits:

Print Media/Publishing:		Movies:		Equipment/Supplies:		Broadcast/Cable:		Music/Audio:		Sports/Games:	
Newspapers:		Movie Theaters:		Equipment/Supplies:		Broadcast TV:	Y	Music Production:		Games/Sports:	
Magazines:	Y	Movie Production:	Y	Gambling Equipment:		Cable TV:		Retail Music:		Retail Games Stores:	
Books:		TV/Video Production:	Y	Special Services:		Satellite Broadcast:		Retail Audio Equip.:		Stadiums/Teams:	
Book Stores:		Video Rental:		Advertising Services:		Radio:		Music Print./Dist.:		Gambling/Casinos:	
Distribution/Printing:		Video Distribution:		Info. Sys. Software:		Online Information:		Multimedia:		Rides/Theme Parks:	

TYPES OF BUSINESS:
Film Production
Television Production & Broadcasting
Video Distribution
Animation
Comic Books
Brand Licensing

BRANDS/DIVISIONS/AFFILIATES:
Time Warner
Lorimar Pictures
Warner Bros. Pictures
Warner Bros. Pictures International
Castle Rock
New Line Cinema
DC Comics
CW (The)

CONTACTS: *Note: Officers with more than one job title may be intentionally listed here more than once.*
Barry M. Meyer, CEO
Alan Horn, COO
Alan Horn, Pres.
Edward Romano, Exec. VP/CFO
Barry M. Meyer, Chmn.

Phone: 818-954-6000	**Fax:** 212-954-7667
Toll-Free:	
Address: 4000 Warner Blvd., Burbank, CA 91522 US	

GROWTH PLANS/SPECIAL FEATURES:
Warner Bros. Entertainment creates, produces, distributes, licenses and markets many forms of entertainment including films, television shows, home videos and DVDs, animation, comic books, interactive entertainment and games, product and brand licensing, international cinema and television broadcasting. The firm is a subsidiary of Time Warner, which operates in cable television programming, publishing, music, filmed entertainment, cable and digital media. In 1927, Warner Bros. was the first production house to release a synchronized-sound feature film, titled The Jazz Singer. Films are produced under the names Warner Bros. Pictures, Warner Bros. Pictures International, Village Roadshow Pictures, Gaylord Films, Alcon Entertainment, New Line Cinema, Castle Rock, Lorimar Pictures, RKO and Classic MGM. Recent hit films have included the Matrix series and part of the Harry Potter series. Television, Telepictures Productions and Warner Bros. Animation. Proprietary shows include ER, The West Wing, Friends, Extra, Tom and Jerry and Scooby-Doo. Warner Bros. also owns the marketing rights to classic movies such as Citizen Kane, Casablanca, Gone with the Wind, Wizard of Oz and Singin' in the Rain. The firm owns DC Comics, a comic book publishing house and the creator of comic book icons such as Superman, Batman and Wonder Woman. The DC Comics line also includes the revamped MAD Magazine. In 2006, the company joined forces with CBS Corporation to form a new TV network, The CW, featuring shows from the former WB and UPN networks, which both ceased operations in 2006.

FINANCIALS: Sales and profits are in thousands of dollars—add 000 to get the full amount. 2006 Note: Financial information for 2006 was not available for all companies at press time.

2006 Sales: $	2006 Profits: $	**U.S. Stock Ticker: Subsidiary**
2005 Sales: $11,850,000	2005 Profits: $	**Int'l Ticker:** Int'l Exchange:
2004 Sales: $	2004 Profits: $	Employees:
2003 Sales: $	2003 Profits: $	Fiscal Year Ends: 12/31
2002 Sales: $	2002 Profits: $	Parent Company: TIME WARNER INC

SALARIES/BENEFITS:
Pension Plan:	ESOP Stock Plan:	Profit Sharing:	Top Exec. Salary: $	Bonus: $
Savings Plan:	Stock Purch. Plan:		Second Exec. Salary: $	Bonus: $

OTHER THOUGHTS:
Apparent Women Officers or Directors:
Hot Spot for Advancement for Women/Minorities:

LOCATIONS: ("Y" = Yes)
West:	Southwest:	Midwest:	Southeast:	Northeast:	International:
Y					

WARNER MUSIC GROUP

www.wmg.com

Industry Group Code: 512230 Ranks within this company's industry group: Sales: 5 Profits: 3

Print Media/Publishing:	Movies:		Equipment/Supplies:	Broadcast/Cable:	Music/Audio:		Sports/Games:
Newspapers:	Movie Theaters:		Equipment/Supplies:	Broadcast TV:	Music Production:	Y	Games/Sports:
Magazines:	Movie Production:		Gambling Equipment:	Cable TV:	Retail Music:		Retail Games Stores:
Books:	TV/Video Production:	Y	Special Services:	Satellite Broadcast:	Retail Audio Equip.:		Stadiums/Teams:
Book Stores:	Video Rental:		Advertising Services:	Radio:	Music Print./Dist.:	Y	Gambling/Casinos:
Distribution/Printing:	Video Distribution:		Info. Sys. Software:	Online Information:	Multimedia:		Rides/Theme Parks:

TYPES OF BUSINESS:

Recorded Music Distribution
Music Production
Music Printing
Music Publishing
Soundtracks
Compilations
Digital Music Downloads
Video Production

BRANDS/DIVISIONS/AFFILIATES:

Warner Bros. Records
Atlantic Records Group (The)
Elektra Entertainment
Word Entertainment
Rhino Entertainment
Warner/Chappell Music, Inc.
Warner Music Entertainment
Rykodisc

CONTACTS: Note: Officers with more than one job title may be intentionally listed here more than once.

Edgar Bronfman, Jr., CEO
Michael D. Fleisher, CFO/Exec. VP
Maria Osherova, VP-Human Resources
Maggie Miller, CIO
David H. Johnson, General Counsel/Exec. VP
Alejandro Zubillaga, Exec. VP-Digital Strategy & Bus. Dev.
Will Tanous, Sr. VP-Corp. Comm.
Lyor Cohen, CEO-U.S. Recorded Music
Caroline Stockdale, Exec. VP-Global Human Resources
Susan Ross, Sr. VP-Compensation & Benefits
Mike Saunter, CFO-Warner Music International
Edgar Bronfman, Jr., Chmn.
Patrick Vien, CEO-Warner International

Phone: 212-484-8000	Fax: 212-333-3987
Toll-Free:	
Address: 75 Rockefeller Plaza, New York, NY 10019 US	

GROWTH PLANS/SPECIAL FEATURES:

Warner Music Group is a global company specializing in Recorded Music and Music Publishing. The recorded music business (conducted through Warner Bros. Records and The Atlantic Records Group) markets, sells and licenses recorded music CDs, cassettes, LPs, DVDs, downloads and ringtones. The firm's recording companies include Reprise Records, Maverick Records, Atlantic Group, Rykodisc, Sire, Elektra Entertainment, Word Entertainment and Warner Music International (WMI). WMI distributes international and American and artists globally, with more than 1,000 artists operating in more than 70 countries. Warner-Elektra-Atlantic Corporation (WEA Corp.) and Ryko Distribution (acquired in 2006 for 67.5 million) are independent music distributors in the U.S. Elektra Entertainment, originally a pioneer of '60s rock, includes the Elektra and East West labels. The company represents popular artists including Led Zeppelin, Neil Young, Madonna, Paul Simon, The Ramones and Fleetwood Mac. Warner/Chappell Music, a music publishing company, holds the publishing rights to more than a million songs from over 65,000 songwriters and composers, including Summertime, Happy Birthday to You, Night and Day, When a Man Loves a Woman, Winter Wonderland, Star Wars Theme and Frosty the Snowman. Warner Strategic Marketing promotes the company's catalog of music and artists, and includes Rhino Entertainment (specializing in marketing music reissuances and licensing), Rhino Home Video, Warner Special Products, Warner Music Group Soundtracks and Warner Television Marketing. In 2006, after acquiring The Rights Company, a UK-based DVD production business ,the firm merged with Warner Vision to form Warner Music Entertainment, which will oversee WMI's video entertainment segment. In addition, the firm partnered with Google to offer WMG Music Video content online for free (or for purchase) on Google Video. In late 2006, the company announced plans to acquire a 73.5% stake in Roadrunner Music Group, a hard rock and heavy metal label, for $73.5 million.

FINANCIALS: Sales and profits are in thousands of dollars—add 000 to get the full amount. 2006 Note: Financial information for 2006 was not available for all companies at press time.

2006 Sales: $3,516,000	2006 Profits: $60,000	**U.S. Stock Ticker: WMG**
2005 Sales: $3,502,000	2005 Profits: $-169,000	**Int'l Ticker:** Int'l Exchange:
2004 Sales: $2,548,000	2004 Profits: $-136,000	Employees: 4,000
2003 Sales: $3,376,000	2003 Profits: $	Fiscal Year Ends: 9/30
2002 Sales: $4,205,000	2002 Profits: $	Parent Company:

SALARIES/BENEFITS:

Pension Plan:	ESOP Stock Plan:	Profit Sharing:	Top Exec. Salary: $	Bonus: $
Savings Plan:	Stock Purch. Plan:		Second Exec. Salary: $	Bonus: $

OTHER THOUGHTS:

Apparent Women Officers or Directors: 4
Hot Spot for Advancement for Women/Minorities: Y

LOCATIONS: ("Y" = Yes)

West:	Southwest:	Midwest:	Southeast:	Northeast:	International:
Y			Y	Y	Y

WASHINGTON POST CO

www.washpostco.com

Industry Group Code: 511110 Ranks within this company's industry group: Sales: 5 Profits: 3

Print Media/Publishing:		Movies:		Equipment/Supplies:		Broadcast/Cable:		Music/Audio:		Sports/Games:	
Newspapers:	Y	Movie Theaters:		Equipment/Supplies:		Broadcast TV:	Y	Music Production:		Games/Sports:	
Magazines:	Y	Movie Production:		Gambling Equipment:		Cable TV:	Y	Retail Music:		Retail Games Stores:	
Books:		TV/Video Production:		Special Services:	Y	Satellite Broadcast:		Retail Audio Equip.:		Stadiums/Teams:	
Book Stores:		Video Rental:		Advertising Services:	Y	Radio:		Music Print./Dist.:		Gambling/Casinos:	
Distribution/Printing:		Video Distribution:		Info. Sys. Software:		Online Information:		Multimedia:		Rides/Theme Parks:	

TYPES OF BUSINESS:

Newspaper Publishing
Television Broadcasting
Cable Television Systems
Magazine Publishing
Educational Services
Internet Publishing
Printing/Distribution Services
Recycling & Used Paper Sales

BRANDS/DIVISIONS/AFFILIATES:

Washington Post (The)
Daily Herald Company (The)
Gazette Newspapers, Inc.
Newsweek
CableONE
Washingtonpost.Newsweek Interactive Co.
Slate
Kaplan, Inc.

CONTACTS: Note: Officers with more than one job title may be intentionally listed here more than once.

Donald E. Graham, CEO
John B. Morse, Jr., CFO/VP
Ann L. McDaniel, VP-Human Resources
Ralph S. Terkowitz, VP-Tech.
Veronica Dillon, General Counsel/VP
Gerald M. Rosberg, VP-Planning & Dev.
Rima Calderon, Dir.-Corp. Comm.
John B. Morse, Jr., VP-Finance
Daniel J. Lynch, Treas.
Wallace R. Cooney, Controller
Pinkie D. Mayfield, Assistant Treas.
Veronica Dillon, Corp. Sec.
Donald E. Graham, Chmn.

Phone: 202-334-6000	Fax: 202-334-4536
Toll-Free:	
Address: 1150 15th St. NW, Washington, DC 20071 US	

GROWTH PLANS/SPECIAL FEATURES:

The Washington Post Company operates in five core business segments: newspaper publishing, principally The Washington Post; magazine publishing, most notably Newsweek; television broadcasting; cable television networks; and educational services, through subsidiary Kaplan, Inc. The Washington Post is a morning and Sunday newspaper with a daily circulation of over 700,000 and a Sunday circulation of close to 1 million, distributed through newsstands and home delivery in Washington, D.C., Virginia and Maryland. The Post also operates a joint news wire service with the Los Angeles Times and publishes regional newspapers in Maryland (Gazette Newspapers, Inc.) and Everett, Washington (The Daily Herald Company). Washingtonpost.Newsweek Interactive Company (WPNI) develops news and information products for electronic distribution. This includes washingtonpost.com, which features the full editorial text of The Post as well as classified advertising, online advertising and original content; and the Newsweek website. Magazines remain a stable source of revenue for the firm, with lead imprint Newsweek maintaining news bureaus in eight U.S. and 11 foreign cities. Internationally, Newsweek is published in a Europe, Middle East and Africa edition; a Korea and Japan edition; and a Latin American edition. The company owns six VHF television-broadcasting stations in Detroit, Houston, Miami, Orlando, San Antonio and Jacksonville through its subsidiary Post-Newsweek Stations, Inc. Five of these stations are affiliated with major networks; the station in Jacksonville, Florida is an independent station. The firm's cable television operations, managed by its CableONE subsidiary, provide service to over 709,000 subscribers and digital video service to over 219,000 subscriptions. Through Kaplan, Inc., the company provides educational services such as test preparation and Federal Student Financial Aid Programs funding. The company recently sold its subsidiary Post Newsweek Tech Media (which offers national publications, web sites, trade shows and conferences for the government) to 1105 Media, Inc.

FINANCIALS: Sales and profits are in thousands of dollars—add 000 to get the full amount. 2006 Note: Financial information for 2006 was not available for all companies at press time.

2006 Sales: $	2006 Profits: $	U.S. Stock Ticker: WPO
2005 Sales: $3,553,887	2005 Profits: $314,344	Int'l Ticker: Int'l Exchange:
2004 Sales: $3,300,104	2004 Profits: $332,732	Employees: 16,400
2003 Sales: $2,838,911	2003 Profits: $241,088	Fiscal Year Ends: 12/31
2002 Sales: $2,584,200	2002 Profits: $204,300	Parent Company:

SALARIES/BENEFITS:

Pension Plan: Y	ESOP Stock Plan:	Profit Sharing:	Top Exec. Salary: $550,000	Bonus: $323,215
Savings Plan: Y	Stock Purch. Plan: Y		Second Exec. Salary: $400,000	Bonus: $

OTHER THOUGHTS:

Apparent Women Officers or Directors: 5
Hot Spot for Advancement for Women/Minorities: Y

LOCATIONS: ("Y" = Yes)

West:	Southwest:	Midwest:	Southeast:	Northeast:	International:
Y	Y	Y	Y	Y	Y

WENNER MEDIA LLC

www.rollingstone.com

Industry Group Code: 511120 Ranks within this company's industry group: Sales: Profits:

Print Media/Publishing:		Movies:	Equipment/Supplies:	Broadcast/Cable:	Music/Audio:	Sports/Games:
Newspapers:		Movie Theaters:	Equipment/Supplies:	Broadcast TV:	Music Production:	Games/Sports:
Magazines:	Y	Movie Production:	Gambling Equipment:	Cable TV:	Retail Music:	Retail Games Stores:
Books:	Y	TV/Video Production:	Special Services:	Satellite Broadcast:	Retail Audio Equip.:	Stadiums/Teams:
Book Stores:		Video Rental:	Advertising Services:	Radio:	Music Print./Dist.:	Gambling/Casinos:
Distribution/Printing:		Video Distribution:	Info. Sys. Software:	Online Information:	Multimedia:	Rides/Theme Parks:

TYPES OF BUSINESS:

Magazine Publishing
Online Media
Book Publishing

BRANDS/DIVISIONS/AFFILIATES:

Rolling Stone
Men's Journal
US Weekly
Rolling Stone Online
I'm From Rolling Stone

CONTACTS: Note: Officers with more than one job title may be intentionally listed here more than once.

John Gruber, CFO
Gary Armstrong, Chief Mktg Officer-Rolling Stone
Pamela Fox, Dir.-Human Resources
William Kwan, Dir.-IT
Dana Rosen, General Counsel
Michael Small, Rolling Stone Online
Lisa Dallos, Sr. VP-Corp. Comm.
Mark Neschis, Dir.-Publicity
Will Dana, Mng. Editor
Ed Hecht, Dir.-Advertising
Timothy Walsh, VP
Jane Wenner, VP
Jann S. Wenner, Chmn.

Phone: 212-484-1616	**Fax:** 212-484-3435
Toll-Free:	
Address: 1290 Ave. of the Americas, New York, NY 10104-0298 US	

GROWTH PLANS/SPECIAL FEATURES:

Wenner Media LLC runs all the operations for publishing three magazines: Men's Journal, Rolling Stone and US Weekly. The firm also manages websites devoted to each magazine. Rolling Stone, a media icon of the rock-and-roll scene, has a circulation of approximately 1.25 million. Rolling Stone Online offers news and information about the music world, in addition to Rolling Stone radio, personal ads, shopping and ticket sales. Men's Journal, a health, fitness and adventure magazine, has a circulation of about 2.7 million. US Weekly, owned and operated by subsidiary US Weekly LLC, is a joint venture with Walt Disney; it covers celebrity gossip and has a circulation of approximately 1.06 million. Wenner also makes books based on the subject matter of the magazines through a partnership with Hyperion printing. The firm is operated primarily by CEO, Chairman and Editor of Rolling Stone Magazine, Jann Wenner, who has edited Rolling Stone since its inception in 1967. Wenner has teamed up with MTV to launch a new reality-based TV show, I'm From Rolling Stone, in early 2007.

FINANCIALS: Sales and profits are in thousands of dollars—add 000 to get the full amount. 2006 Note: Financial information for 2006 was not available for all companies at press time.

2006 Sales: $	2006 Profits: $	**U.S. Stock Ticker:** Private
2005 Sales: $	2005 Profits: $	**Int'l Ticker:** Int'l Exchange:
2004 Sales: $	2004 Profits: $	Employees:
2003 Sales: $	2003 Profits: $	Fiscal Year Ends: 12/31
2002 Sales: $	2002 Profits: $	Parent Company:

SALARIES/BENEFITS:

Pension Plan:	ESOP Stock Plan:	Profit Sharing:	Top Exec. Salary: $	Bonus: $
Savings Plan: Y	Stock Purch. Plan:		Second Exec. Salary: $	Bonus: $

OTHER THOUGHTS:

Apparent Women Officers or Directors: 22
Hot Spot for Advancement for Women/Minorities: Y

LOCATIONS: ("Y" = Yes)

West:	Southwest:	Midwest:	Southeast:	Northeast:	International:
Y	Y	Y	Y	Y	

Note: Financial information, benefits and other data can change quickly and may vary from those stated here.

WESTWOOD ONE INC

www.westwoodone.com

Industry Group Code: 512110 Ranks within this company's industry group: Sales: 11   Profits: 3

Print Media/Publishing:	Movies:	Equipment/Supplies:		Broadcast/Cable:	Music/Audio:	Sports/Games:
Newspapers:	Movie Theaters:	Equipment/Supplies:		Broadcast TV:	Music Production:	Games/Sports:
Magazines:	Movie Production:	Gambling Equipment:		Cable TV:	Retail Music:	Retail Games Stores:
Books:	TV/Video Production:	Special Services:	Y	Satellite Broadcast:	Retail Audio Equip.:	Stadiums/Teams:
Book Stores:	Video Rental:	Advertising Services:		Radio:	Music Print./Dist.:	Gambling/Casinos:
Distribution/Printing:	Video Distribution:	Info. Sys. Software:		Online Information:	Multimedia:	Rides/Theme Parks:

TYPES OF BUSINESS:

Radio Programming Production & Distribution
Information Services

BRANDS/DIVISIONS/AFFILIATES:

Metro Networks
Shadow Broadcast Services
Infinity Broadcasting Corp.
Viacom, Inc.
Shadow Traffic
SmartRoute Systems

CONTACTS: *Note: Officers with more than one job title may be intentionally listed here more than once.*

Peter Kosann, CEO
Peter Kosann, Pres.
Andrew Zaref, CFO/Exec. VP
Roby Wiener, Chief Mktg. Officer
Carolyn Jones, VP-Human Resources
Paul Bronstein, VP-Research
Luis Rodriguez, CIO
Conrad Trautman, Sr. VP-Oper. & Eng.
David Hillman, Gen. Counsel/Exec VP-Bus. Affairs
Sal Siino, Exec. VP-Natl. Sales & Oper.
Paul Gregrey, Exec. VP-Sales
Paul Gregrey, Exec. VP-Sales
David Halberstam, Exec. VP-GM Westwood One Sports
Bart Tessler, Sr. VP-Network News/Talk
Beth Robinson, Sr. VP-Eng. & Oper.
Norman J. Pattiz, Chmn.

Phone: 212-641-2000	Fax: 212-641-2185
Toll-Free: 800-877-0007	
Address: 40 W. 57th St., 5th Fl., New York, NY 10019 US	

GROWTH PLANS/SPECIAL FEATURES:

Westwood One supplies radio and television stations with information services and programming. The company is one of the largest domestic providers of traffic reporting services and the nation's largest radio networks, producing and distributing national news, sports, talk, music and special event programs, in addition to local news, sports, weather, video news and other information programming. The company has more than 5,000 affiliates. Westwood One's principal source of revenue is the sale of commercial airtime to advertisers through its operating divisions, Metro/Shadow (which is comprised of Metro Networks and Shadow Broadcast Services) and the network division. The traffic/information division provides local traffic and information broadcast reports in over 95 metropolitan markets in the United States. The network division offers radio stations traditional news services, including CBS Radio news and CNN Radio news, in addition to seven 24-hour continuous-play music formats, weekday and weekend news and entertainment features and programs. These programs include major sporting events such as the National Football League; Notre Dame football and other college football and basketball games; the NHL; the Masters; talk shows; live concert broadcasts; countdown shows; music and interview programs; and exclusive satellite simulcasts with HBO and other cable networks. The company also offers traffic reporting to over 200 television stations. CBS Radio (formerly Infinity Broadcasting) manages Westwood One. In 2006, the firm announced plans to partner with TrafficCast in order to provide real-time traffic information for Yahoo! Maps. In addition, the firm announced a multi-year agreement with Cumulus, providing Metro Source (Westwood's newswire service) to each of Cumulus' 320 radio stations. Recently, the firm partnered with Excelsior Radio Networks. Per the agreement, Excelsior will manage all aspects of the Westwood One 24/7 Music formats through its Dial Communications Global Media division. The firm announced plans to renew its contract with NBC News Radio, which airs on 300 radio stations nationwide.

FINANCIALS: Sales and profits are in thousands of dollars—add 000 to get the full amount. 2006 Note: Financial information for 2006 was not available for all companies at press time.

2006 Sales: $	2006 Profits: $	U.S. Stock Ticker: WON
2005 Sales: $557,830	2005 Profits: $84,683	Int'l Ticker: Int'l Exchange:
2004 Sales: $562,246	2004 Profits: $95,490	Employees: 2,400
2003 Sales: $539,226	2003 Profits: $100,039	Fiscal Year Ends: 12/31
2002 Sales: $550,800	2002 Profits: $109,100	Parent Company:

SALARIES/BENEFITS:

Pension Plan:	ESOP Stock Plan:	Profit Sharing: Y	Top Exec. Salary: $475,000	Bonus: $50,000
Savings Plan: Y	Stock Purch. Plan:		Second Exec. Salary: $400,000	Bonus: $

OTHER THOUGHTS:

Apparent Women Officers or Directors: 1
Hot Spot for Advancement for Women/Minorities:

LOCATIONS: ("Y" = Yes)

West:	Southwest:	Midwest:	Southeast:	Northeast:	International:
Y				Y	

Note: Financial information, benefits and other data can change quickly and may vary from those stated here.

WHEREHOUSE ENTERTAINMENT (RECORD TOWN INC)

www.wherehousemusic.com

Industry Group Code: 451220 Ranks within this company's industry group: Sales: Profits:

Print Media/Publishing:	Movies:	Equipment/Supplies:	Broadcast/Cable:	Music/Audio:	Sports/Games:
Newspapers:	Movie Theaters:	Equipment/Supplies:	Broadcast TV:	Music Production:	Games/Sports:
Magazines:	Movie Production:	Gambling Equipment:	Cable TV:	Retail Music: Y	Retail Games Stores: Y
Books:	TV/Video Production:	Special Services:	Satellite Broadcast:	Retail Audio Equip.: Y	Stadiums/Teams:
Book Stores: Y	Video Rental:	Advertising Services:	Radio:	Music Print./Dist.:	Gambling/Casinos:
Distribution/Printing:	Video Distribution:	Info. Sys. Software:	Online Information:	Multimedia:	Rides/Theme Parks:

TYPES OF BUSINESS:

Music & Video, Retail
Online Sales
Consumer Electronics Sales
Book Sales

BRANDS/DIVISIONS/AFFILIATES:

Trans World Entertainment
Wherehouse Music
wherehouse.com
F.Y.E. (For Your Entertainment)
CD World
Second Spin
Camelot Music
Record Town USA, LLC

CONTACTS: Note: Officers with more than one job title may be intentionally listed here more than once.

John J. Sullivan, Exec. VP/CFO
Fred L. Fox, Exec. VP-Merch & Mktg
Bruce J. Eisenberg, Exec. VP-Real Estate

Phone:	Fax:
Toll-Free:	
Address: 38 Corporate Circle, Albany, NY 12203 US	

GROWTH PLANS/SPECIAL FEATURES:

Wherehouse Entertainment is a brand name of Record Town, Inc., which is the principal operating division and a wholly owned subsidiary of Trans World Entertainment Corporation. Record Town operates music, movie, video game, and other entertainment software retailers across the U.S., operating under the names Waxie Maxie, Planet Music, Camelot Music, The Wall, CD World, Disc Jockey, F.Y.E. (For Your Entertainment), F.Y.E. Games, F.Y.E. Movies, Harmony House, Streetside Records, Specs, Coconuts, Strawberries, Second Spin and Wherehouse Music. In addition, the firm operates several web sites that retail movies, music, video games and other entertainment software. The firm's web sites include fye.com, coconuts.com, wherehouse.com and secondspin.com. In addition to entertainment software, many of the retailers sell electronics ranging from digital cameras to personal stereo systems.

FINANCIALS: Sales and profits are in thousands of dollars—add 000 to get the full amount. 2006 Note: Financial information for 2006 was not available for all companies at press time.

2006 Sales: $	2006 Profits: $	U.S. Stock Ticker: Subsidiary
2005 Sales: $	2005 Profits: $	Int'l Ticker: Int'l Exchange:
2004 Sales: $	2004 Profits: $	Employees: 5,260
2003 Sales: $	2003 Profits: $	Fiscal Year Ends: 1/31
2002 Sales: $604,300	2002 Profits: $-53,700	Parent Company: TRANS WORLD ENTERTAINMENT CORP

SALARIES/BENEFITS:

Pension Plan:	ESOP Stock Plan:	Profit Sharing:	Top Exec. Salary: $347,884	Bonus: $
Savings Plan:	Stock Purch. Plan:		Second Exec. Salary: $341,250	Bonus: $

OTHER THOUGHTS:

Apparent Women Officers or Directors:	
Hot Spot for Advancement for Women/Minorities:	

LOCATIONS: ("Y" = Yes)

West:	Southwest:	Midwest:	Southeast:	Northeast:	International:
Y	Y	Y	Y	Y	

Note: Financial information, benefits and other data can change quickly and may vary from those stated here.

WILLIAM MORRIS AGENCY INC

www.wma.com

Industry Group Code: 711410 Ranks within this company's industry group: Sales: Profits:

Print Media/Publishing:	Movies:	Equipment/Supplies:	Broadcast/Cable:	Music/Audio:	Sports/Games:
Newspapers:	Movie Theaters:	Equipment/Supplies:	Broadcast TV:	Music Production:	Games/Sports:
Magazines:	Movie Production:	Gambling Equipment:	Cable TV:	Retail Music:	Retail Games Stores:
Books: Y	TV/Video Production:	Special Services: Y	Satellite Broadcast:	Retail Audio Equip.:	Stadiums/Teams:
Book Stores:	Video Rental:	Advertising Services: Y	Radio:	Music Print./Dist.:	Gambling/Casinos:
Distribution/Printing:	Video Distribution:	Info. Sys. Software:	Online Information:	Multimedia:	Rides/Theme Parks:

TYPES OF BUSINESS:

Talent Agency
Literary Agency
Sports Marketing & Agents
Media Consulting
Book Publishing

BRANDS/DIVISIONS/AFFILIATES:

William Morris Consulting

CONTACTS:
Note: Officers with more than one job title may be intentionally listed here more than once.

James A. Wiatt, CEO
Steve Kram, COO
David Wirtschafter, Pres.
Irv Weintraub, CFO
Chris Pertikin, Sr. VP-Corp. Comm.
Kevin Murray, Exec.-Consulting Dep.
Mark Itkin, Head-Syndication, Cable & Non-Fiction Programming
Raul Mateu, Sr. VP
Samuel Liff, Head-Theatre Division
Norman Brokaw, Chmn.
Cecile Ablack, Sr. VP-Global Corp. Comm.

Phone: 310-859-4000 **Fax:** 310-859-4462
Toll-Free:
Address: One William Morris Pl., Beverly Hills, CA 90212 US

GROWTH PLANS/SPECIAL FEATURES:

The William Morris Agency, Inc. (WMA) is one of the largest and oldest talent and literary agencies in the world. Founded in 1898, WMA represents clients in almost every aspect of the entertainment industry including film, television, commercials, music and theater. In addition, the company is engaged in book publishing, sports marketing and corporate consulting. WMA's book department represents established authors and accepts submissions from prospective writers. The department works closely with the motion picture and television departments to bring books to both large and small screens. The sports marketing department represents athletes both on- and off- the field, with services including contract negotiation, licensing and the pursuit of broadcasting and sponsorship opportunities. WMA's roster of clients includes athletes in sports such as tennis, figure skating, basketball and football, as well as television announcers and commentators. William Morris Consulting offers media expertise to a wide variety of industry segments, including telecommunications, technology, lodging, gaming, publishing, retail, consumer products, apparel and cosmetics. At the end of 2006, WMA began construction on its new eco-friendly headquarters; the new building is expected to open in 2009.

FINANCIALS: Sales and profits are in thousands of dollars—add 000 to get the full amount. 2006 Note: Financial information for 2006 was not available for all companies at press time.

2006 Sales: $	2006 Profits: $	U.S. Stock Ticker: Private
2005 Sales: $	2005 Profits: $	Int'l Ticker: Int'l Exchange:
2004 Sales: $	2004 Profits: $	Employees:
2003 Sales: $	2003 Profits: $	Fiscal Year Ends: 12/31
2002 Sales: $	2002 Profits: $	Parent Company:

SALARIES/BENEFITS:

Pension Plan:	ESOP Stock Plan:	Profit Sharing:	Top Exec. Salary: $	Bonus: $
Savings Plan:	Stock Purch. Plan:		Second Exec. Salary: $	Bonus: $

OTHER THOUGHTS:

Apparent Women Officers or Directors:
Hot Spot for Advancement for Women/Minorities:

LOCATIONS: ("Y" = Yes)

West:	Southwest:	Midwest:	Southeast:	Northeast:	International:
Y			Y	Y	Y

WMS INDUSTRIES INC

www.wms.com

Industry Group Code: 713290 Ranks within this company's industry group: Sales: 6 Profits: 6

Print Media/Publishing:	Movies:	Equipment/Supplies:		Broadcast/Cable:	Music/Audio:	Sports/Games:
Newspapers:	Movie Theaters:	Equipment/Supplies:		Broadcast TV:	Music Production:	Games/Sports:
Magazines:	Movie Production:	Gambling Equipment:	Y	Cable TV:	Retail Music:	Retail Games Stores:
Books:	TV/Video Production:	Special Services:	Y	Satellite Broadcast:	Retail Audio Equip.:	Stadiums/Teams:
Book Stores:	Video Rental:	Advertising Services:		Radio:	Music Print./Dist.:	Gambling/Casinos:
Distribution/Printing:	Video Distribution:	Info. Sys. Software:		Online Information:	Multimedia:	Rides/Theme Parks:

TYPES OF BUSINESS:

Slot/Video Gaming Machines
Video Lottery Terminals
Equipment Servicing

BRANDS/DIVISIONS/AFFILIATES:

WMS Gaming, Inc.
MONOPOLY
World Series of Poker
Clint Eastwood
CPU-NXT
Bluebird
Powerball
Green Acres

CONTACTS: Note: Officers with more than one job title may be intentionally listed here more than once.

Brian R. Gamache, CEO
Orrin J. Edidin, COO
Brian R. Gamache, Pres.
Scott D. Schweinfurth, CFO
Seamus M. McGill, Exec. VP-Sales & Mktg.
Patricia Barte, Sr. VP-Mfg.
Scott D. Schweinfurth, Treas.
Louis J. Nicastro, Chmn.

Phone: 847-785-3000	Fax: 847-785-3058
Toll-Free:	
Address: 800 S. Northpoint Blvd., Waukegan, IL 60085 US	

GROWTH PLANS/SPECIAL FEATURES:

WMS Industries, Inc. is the successor to Williams Electronics, incorporated in 1974 and inheriting thirty-plus years of expertise from the former company. In recent years, WMS's business has consisted exclusively in the design, manufacture and marketing of gaming machines and video lottery terminals, or VLTs. The company conducts its gaming machine business through subsidiary WMS Gaming, Inc, which markets products under the WMS Gaming trademark. WMS's original products are for Class III gaming markets and it licenses its game themes for Class II and Class III gaming. It also manufactures gaming machines under an OEM agreement with Multimedia Games, Inc., for the Class II market. Class II gaming includes bingo and related or similar games or gaming accessories; Class III encompasses all other game types, including slot machines. The company offers video and mechanical reel slots and more advanced participation games, including some that allow players to play against each other. WMS Industries holds the exclusive license to the MONOPOLY trademark for use on casino-style gaming machines, one of the most successful slot gaming titles. The company also holds the gaming rights to the Pac-Man, Hollywood Squares, Clint Eastwood and Men In Black brand names and 2006 additions the World Series of Poker and Powerball brands. Other brands in the WMS portfolio include Green Acres, Kaboom, Shop Til You Drop, You Bet Your Life, Gold Fish, Beat the Clock, Cow Tippin', Money Money Money, Robin Hood, Reels O'Dublin and Reel 'Em In Poker. In addition, the company offers service contracts to its machine customers. Recently, the company launched its latest platform, CPU-NXT, along with its new game cabinet, Bluebird, which includes the Bose Free Field directed audio system.

FINANCIALS: Sales and profits are in thousands of dollars—add 000 to get the full amount. 2006 Note: Financial information for 2006 was not available for all companies at press time.

2006 Sales: $451,200	2006 Profits: $33,300	U.S. Stock Ticker: WMS
2005 Sales: $388,400	2005 Profits: $21,200	Int'l Ticker: Int'l Exchange:
2004 Sales: $230,200	2004 Profits: $- 900	Employees: 1,250
2003 Sales: $178,700	2003 Profits: $-8,300	Fiscal Year Ends: 6/30
2002 Sales: $174,700	2002 Profits: $9,900	Parent Company:

SALARIES/BENEFITS:

Pension Plan:	ESOP Stock Plan:	Profit Sharing:	Top Exec. Salary: $662,500	Bonus: $
Savings Plan: Y	Stock Purch. Plan:		Second Exec. Salary: $425,200	Bonus: $

OTHER THOUGHTS:

Apparent Women Officers or Directors: 1
Hot Spot for Advancement for Women/Minorities:

LOCATIONS: ("Y" = Yes)

West:	Southwest:	Midwest:	Southeast:	Northeast:	International:
		Y			Y

Note: Financial information, benefits and other data can change quickly and may vary from those stated here.

WORLD WRESTLING ENTERTAINMENT INC (WWF)
corporate.wwe.com

Industry Group Code: 512110 Ranks within this company's industry group: Sales: 14   Profits: 6

Print Media/Publishing:		Movies:		Equipment/Supplies:		Broadcast/Cable:		Music/Audio:		Sports/Games:	
Newspapers:		Movie Theaters:		Equipment/Supplies:		Broadcast TV:		Music Production:	Y	Games/Sports:	Y
Magazines:	Y	Movie Production:	Y	Gambling Equipment:		Cable TV:		Retail Music:		Retail Games Stores:	
Books:		TV/Video Production:	Y	Special Services:		Satellite Broadcast:		Retail Audio Equip.:		Stadiums/Teams:	
Book Stores:		Video Rental:		Advertising Services:	Y	Radio:		Music Print./Dist.:		Gambling/Casinos:	
Distribution/Printing:		Video Distribution:		Info. Sys. Software:		Online Information:		Multimedia:		Rides/Theme Parks:	

TYPES OF BUSINESS:
Television Production
Live Theatrical Productions
Magazine Publishing
Merchandise Sales
Music Recording
Brand Licensing
Film Production
E-Commerce

BRANDS/DIVISIONS/AFFILIATES:
World Wrestling Federation (WWF)
Raw
SmackDown
Extreme Championship Wrestling
Friday Night SmackDown
A.M Raw
WWE 24/7 On Demand
WWEShop

CONTACTS: *Note: Officers with more than one job title may be intentionally listed here more than once.*
Linda E. McMahon, CEO
Michael Sileck, CFO
Kurt Schneider, Exec. VP-Mktg.
John Laurinaitis, VP-Talent Rel.
Donna Goldsmith, Exec. VP-Consumer Products
Edward L. Kaufman, General Counsel/Exec. VP
Michael Weitz, Investor Rel.
Frank G. Serpe, Sr. VP-Finance
Thomas N. Barreca, Exec. VP-WWE Enterprises
Joel Simon, Pres., WWE Films
Kevin Dunn, Exec. VP-Television Production
Shane B. McMahon, Exec. VP-Global Media
Vincent K. McMahon, Chmn.

Phone: 203-352-8600	Fax: 203-359-5151
Toll-Free:	
Address: 1241 E. Main St., Stamford, CT 06902 US	

GROWTH PLANS/SPECIAL FEATURES:
World Wrestling Entertainment, Inc. (WWE) develops, produces and markets television programming, pay-per-view programming and live events featuring the World Wrestling Federation (WWF) brand. The firm operates four segments: live and televised entertainment, consumer products, digital media and WWE Films. WWE's live events (73% of 2006 revenue) are theatrical productions involving audience participation and special effects including lighting, pyrotechnics, music and props. The firm's two established brands, Raw and SmackDown, tour independently, each typically producing three to four events per week. The company is currently in the process of launching a third brand, Extreme Championship Wrestling. It usually stages events at major arenas such as Madison Square Garden in New York City and Earls Court in London, England, performing approximately 300 live shows a year. The segment produces three television shows: Monday Night Raw; Friday Night SmackDown; and A.M Raw. This programming is distributed in over 130 countries in 16 languages. The segment also derives revenue from: venue merchandise sales; sponsorship advertising; pay-per-view programming; and WWE 24/7 On Demand, a subscription video-on-demand service. The consumer products segment (22% of revenue) comprises: licensing of the firm's marks, logos, copyrighted works and characters for toys, video games, apparel and books; music recordings; home video; and Raw and SmackDown magazines. The digital media segment (5% of revenue) includes entertainment web sit WWE.com and e-commerce storefront WWEShop. WWE Films has produced feature films See No Evil and The Marine, both released in 2006. International revenue currently accounts for approximately 24% of the firm's total. In 2006, WWE launched a web storefront for mobile phone users.

FINANCIALS: Sales and profits are in thousands of dollars—add 000 to get the full amount. 2006 Note: Financial information for 2006 was not available for all companies at press time.

2006 Sales: $400,051	2006 Profits: $47,047	U.S. Stock Ticker: WWE
2005 Sales: $366,431	2005 Profits: $39,147	Int'l Ticker: Int'l Exchange:
2004 Sales: $374,909	2004 Profits: $48,192	Employees: 460
2003 Sales: $374,300	2003 Profits: $-19,200	Fiscal Year Ends: 4/30
2002 Sales: $425,000	2002 Profits: $42,200	Parent Company:

SALARIES/BENEFITS:
Pension Plan:	ESOP Stock Plan:	Profit Sharing:	Top Exec. Salary: $593,846	Bonus: $378,000
Savings Plan:	Stock Purch. Plan:		Second Exec. Salary: $346,539	Bonus: $243,500

OTHER THOUGHTS:
Apparent Women Officers or Directors: 2
Hot Spot for Advancement for Women/Minorities:

LOCATIONS: ("Y" = Yes)
West:	Southwest:	Midwest:	Southeast:	Northeast:	International:
Y		Y		Y	Y

Note: Financial information, benefits and other data can change quickly and may vary from those stated here.

WPP GROUP PLC

www.wpp.com

Industry Group Code: 541810 **Ranks within this company's industry group:** Sales: 2 Profits: 2

Print Media/Publishing:	Movies:	Equipment/Supplies:		Broadcast/Cable:	Music/Audio:	Sports/Games:
Newspapers:	Movie Theaters:	Equipment/Supplies:		Broadcast TV:	Music Production:	Games/Sports:
Magazines:	Movie Production:	Gambling Equipment:		Cable TV:	Retail Music:	Retail Games Stores:
Books:	TV/Video Production:	Special Services:	Y	Satellite Broadcast:	Retail Audio Equip.:	Stadiums/Teams:
Book Stores:	Video Rental:	Advertising Services:	Y	Radio:	Music Print./Dist.:	Gambling/Casinos:
Distribution/Printing:	Video Distribution:	Info. Sys. Software:		Online Information:	Multimedia:	Rides/Theme Parks:

TYPES OF BUSINESS:

Advertising & Marketing Services
Communications Consulting
Human Resources Consulting
IT Consulting
Advertising Consulting
Brand Research & Tools
Public Relations

BRANDS/DIVISIONS/AFFILIATES:

Ogilvy & Mather Worldwide
BRANDZ
BrandAsset Valuator
PRecision
DSG Strategies, Inc.
Black Arc Advertising
Burson-Marsteller
Shaw Marketing Group

CONTACTS: Note: Officers with more than one job title may be intentionally listed here more than once.

Martin Sorrell, CEO
Mark Read, Dir.-Strategy
Feona McEwan, Group Dir.-Comm.
Fran Butera, Dir.-Investor Rel.
Paul Richardson, Group Dir.-Finance
Richard Oldworth, CEO-Buchanan Comm.
Jon Cook, Pres., VML/Mng. Partner
Scott McCormick, Chief Vision Officer
Eric Baumgartner, Chief Creative Officer/Mng. Partner
Philip Lader, Chmn.

Phone: 44-20-7408-2204	Fax: 44-20-7493-6819
Toll-Free:	
Address: 27 Farm St., London, W1J 5RJ UK	

GROWTH PLANS/SPECIAL FEATURES:

WPP Group plc is one of the four largest global management firms for communications consulting and advertising, with more than 2,000 offices in over 100 countries. The company's revenue is generated in a variety of industry segments, including advertising and media information; consultancy; public relations; branding and identity; healthcare communications; and direct, promotion and relationship marketing. Through its more than 70 subsidiaries, the group offers assistance in human resources, information technology, public relations, brand development, property management, procurement, practice development and knowledge sharing. Each of the company's subsidiaries is a distinct entity with capabilities and resources of its own, for which WPP provides client and employee aid. The firm serves its subsidiaries through initiatives such as a collection of proprietary products, such as BRANDZ, the world's largest brand research study; BrandAsset Valuator, a tool used for the development of brands and brand names; and PRecision, a toolkit for the measurement of media and delivery impact. In addition, the group manages the Knowledge Bank, a collection of studies, essays and analyses from members of the group. Recent acquisitions include stakes in DSG Strategies, Inc., Beijing Raynet Advertising Co., Ltd., ID Consultores, Black Arc Advertising and Shaw Marketing Group, among others.

FINANCIALS: Sales and profits are in thousands of dollars—add 000 to get the full amount. 2006 Note: Financial information for 2006 was not available for all companies at press time.

2006 Sales: $	2006 Profits: $	U.S. Stock Ticker: WPPGY
2005 Sales: $9,244,400	2005 Profits: $684,700	Int'l Ticker: WPP Int'l Exchange: London-LSE
2004 Sales: $8,243,000	2004 Profits: $560,400	Employees: 91,000
2003 Sales: $7,542,790	2003 Profits: $564,300	Fiscal Year Ends: 12/31
2002 Sales: $7,179,290	2002 Profits: $215,800	Parent Company:

SALARIES/BENEFITS:

Pension Plan:	ESOP Stock Plan:	Profit Sharing:	Top Exec. Salary: $1,334,010	Bonus: $24,000
Savings Plan:	Stock Purch. Plan:		Second Exec. Salary: $533,990	Bonus: $95,640

OTHER THOUGHTS:

Apparent Women Officers or Directors: 2
Hot Spot for Advancement for Women/Minorities: Y

LOCATIONS: ("Y" = Yes)

West:	Southwest:	Midwest:	Southeast:	Northeast:	International:
Y	Y	Y	Y	Y	Y

Note: Financial information, benefits and other data can change quickly and may vary from those stated here.

WYNN RESORTS LIMITED

www.wynnresorts.com

Industry Group Code: 721120 Ranks within this company's industry group: Sales: 10　Profits: 16

Print Media/Publishing:	Movies:	Equipment/Supplies:	Broadcast/Cable:	Music/Audio:	Sports/Games:
Newspapers:	Movie Theaters:	Equipment/Supplies:	Broadcast TV:	Music Production:	Games/Sports:
Magazines:	Movie Production:	Gambling Equipment:	Cable TV:	Retail Music:	Retail Games Stores:
Books:	TV/Video Production:	Special Services:	Satellite Broadcast:	Retail Audio Equip.:	Stadiums/Teams: Y
Book Stores:	Video Rental:	Advertising Services:	Radio:	Music Print./Dist.:	Gambling/Casinos:
Distribution/Printing:	Video Distribution:	Info. Sys. Software:	Online Information:	Multimedia:	Rides/Theme Parks:

TYPES OF BUSINESS:
Hotel Casinos

BRANDS/DIVISIONS/AFFILIATES:
Wynn Las Vegas
Wynn Macau

CONTACTS: *Note: Officers with more than one job title may be intentionally listed here more than once.*
Stephen A. Wynn, CEO
Marc D. Schorr, COO
Ronald J. Kramer, Pres.
John Strzemp, CFO/Exec. VP
Kim Sinatra, General Counsel/Sr. VP/Corp. Sec.
Matt Maddox, Sr. VP-Bus. Dev.
Matt Maddox, Treas.
Linda Chen, Pres., Wynn International Mktg., Ltd.
Grant R. Bowie, Pres., Wynn Resorts Macau
Andrew Pascal, Pres./COO-Wynn Las Vegas, LLC
Scott Peterson, CFO-Wynn Resorts Macau
Stephen A. Wynn, Chmn.

Phone: 702-733-4444	Fax: 702-733-4681
Toll-Free:	
Address: 3145 Las Vegas Blvd. S., Las Vegas, NV 89109 US	

GROWTH PLANS/SPECIAL FEATURES:

Wynn Resorts, Ltd. is a leading developer, owner and operator of destination casino resorts. It owns and operates the Wynn Las Vegas, a destination casino resort on the Strip in Las Vegas, Nevada; the company is also constructing and will operate the Wynn Macau, a casino resort development located in the Macau Special Administrative Region of China. Wynn Las Vegas offers 2,674 rooms and suites in its 45-story tower, plus 36 fairway villas and 6 private-entry villas for its premium guests. The approximately 111,000-square-foot casino features 137 table games, a baccarat salon, private VIP gaming rooms, a poker room, 1,960 slot machines, a race and sports book and a keno lounge. The resort's 22 food and beverage outlets feature six fine dining restaurants, including restaurants helmed by award winning chefs. Wynn Las Vegas also offers a nightclub, an ultra-lounge, a spa and salon, a Ferrari and Maserati automobile dealership, wedding chapels, an 18-hole golf course, approximately 223,000 square feet of meeting space and an approximately 76,000-square-foot retail promenade featuring boutiques from Chanel, Christian Dior, Graff, Manolo Blahnik, Jean-Paul Gaultier and Louis Vuitton. Wynn Las Vegas also has two showrooms, The Wynn Theater and The Broadway Theater. Since opening, Wynn Las Vegas has experienced an overall 92.1% average occupancy and $274 average daily room rate, which compares favorably to the overall 89.2% average occupancy and $103 average daily room rate of the Las Vegas Strip.

Wynn Resorts offers its employees financial assistance with continuing education, an employee assistance program, annual social events and athletic team sponsorship.

FINANCIALS: Sales and profits are in thousands of dollars—add 000 to get the full amount. 2006 Note: Financial information for 2006 was not available for all companies at press time.

2006 Sales: $	2006 Profits: $	U.S. Stock Ticker: WYNN
2005 Sales: $721,981	2005 Profits: $-90,836	Int'l Ticker:　Int'l Exchange:
2004 Sales: $ 195	2004 Profits: $-204,171	Employees: 9,500
2003 Sales: $1,018	2003 Profits: $-40,099	Fiscal Year Ends: 12/31
2002 Sales: $1,200	2002 Profits: $-31,700	Parent Company:

SALARIES/BENEFITS:

Pension Plan:	ESOP Stock Plan:	Profit Sharing:	Top Exec. Salary: $2,343,151	Bonus: $3,221,833
Savings Plan: Y	Stock Purch. Plan:		Second Exec. Salary: $1,271,538	Bonus: $1,907,307

OTHER THOUGHTS:
Apparent Women Officers or Directors: 2
Hot Spot for Advancement for Women/Minorities:

LOCATIONS: ("Y" = Yes)

West:	Southwest:	Midwest:	Southeast:	Northeast:	International:
Y					Y

XM SATELLITE RADIO HOLDINGS INC   www.xmradio.com

Industry Group Code: 513111A   Ranks within this company's industry group: Sales: 1   Profits: 1

Print Media/Publishing:	Movies:	Equipment/Supplies:	Broadcast/Cable:	Music/Audio:	Sports/Games:
Newspapers:	Movie Theaters:	Equipment/Supplies:	Broadcast TV:	Music Production:	Games/Sports:
Magazines:	Movie Production:	Gambling Equipment:	Cable TV:	Retail Music:	Retail Games Stores:
Books:	TV/Video Production:	Special Services:	Satellite Broadcast:	Retail Audio Equip.:	Stadiums/Teams:
Book Stores:	Video Rental:	Advertising Services:	Radio:	Music Print./Dist.:	Gambling/Casinos:
Distribution/Printing:	Video Distribution:	Info. Sys. Software:	Online Information:	Multimedia:	Rides/Theme Parks:

TYPES OF BUSINESS:

Satellite Radio Broadcasting
Radio Programming

BRANDS/DIVISIONS/AFFILIATES:

XM Satellite Radio, Inc.
XM Originals
XM Canada
XM Public Radio

CONTACTS: Note: Officers with more than one job title may be intentionally listed here more than once.

Hugh Panero, CEO
Nate Davis, COO
Nate Davis, Pres.
Joseph J. Euteneuer, Exec. VP/CFO
Steve Cook, Exec. VP-Sales & Mktg.
Stelios Patsiokas, Exec. VP-Tech. & Eng.
Eric Logan, Exec. VP-Programming
Joseph M. Titlebaum, General Counsel
Dara F. Altman, Exec. VP-Bus. & Legal Affairs
Gary M. Parsons, Chmn.

Phone: 202-380-4000	Fax: 202-380-4500

Toll-Free: 866-962-2557

Address: 1500 Eckington Pl. NE, Washington, DC 20002-2194 US

GROWTH PLANS/SPECIAL FEATURES:

XM Satellite Radio Holdings, Inc. is a premier nationwide provider of satellite digital radio service to vehicle, home and portable radios. It serves over 230 million vehicles and 110 million households in the U.S., to which it offers more than 170 channels of which 67 are commercial-free music channels; 34 are news, talk and entertainment channels; 39 are sports coverage channels; 21 are local traffic and weather channels; and one is an emergency alert channel. Customers pay a monthly subscription of $12.95 to have the satellite signal directed to their XM radio set. As of the beginning of 2007, the company had more than 7.6 million subscribers. Its commercial free music channels span a wide range of genres including country, pop, Christian, rock, hip-hop, jazz/blues, Latin, classical and folk/bluegrass. The sports talk and sports coverage radio channels cover college football, men's and women's basketball, tennis, NASCAR and professional golf. XM is the official satellite radio network of Major League Baseball and has recently become the exclusive satellite radio network of the National Hockey League. ESPN and FoxSports supplement the company's sports talk lineup. The talk radio channels feature programming that includes Fox News, CNN, ABC News & Talk, BBC Worldservice and C-SPAN, with business news provided by CNBC. General Motors has an exclusive contract with the company to offer factory-installed XM radios in over 55 makes and models of GM automobiles. XM radios are available at national electronics retailers under a variety of brand names including Sony, Delphi, and Alpine. Some of the newer models even have customizable stock ticker and sports features as well as an alert to let the subscriber know when a favorite song or artist is being played. In November 2005, XM Canada, the company's exclusive Canadian licensee, began its satellite radio offerings.

FINANCIALS: Sales and profits are in thousands of dollars—add 000 to get the full amount. 2006 Note: Financial information for 2006 was not available for all companies at press time.

2006 Sales: $	2006 Profits: $	U.S. Stock Ticker: XMSR
2005 Sales: $558,266	2005 Profits: $-666,715	Int'l Ticker: Int'l Exchange:
2004 Sales: $244,443	2004 Profits: $-642,368	Employees: 710
2003 Sales: $91,781	2003 Profits: $-584,535	Fiscal Year Ends: 12/31
2002 Sales: $20,200	2002 Profits: $-495,000	Parent Company:

SALARIES/BENEFITS:

Pension Plan:	ESOP Stock Plan:	Profit Sharing: Y	Top Exec. Salary: $476,854	Bonus: $575,850
Savings Plan: Y	Stock Purch. Plan: Y		Second Exec. Salary: $376,704	Bonus: $143,694

OTHER THOUGHTS:

Apparent Women Officers or Directors: 1
Hot Spot for Advancement for Women/Minorities: Y

LOCATIONS: ("Y" = Yes)

West:	Southwest:	Midwest:	Southeast:	Northeast:	International:
		Y	Y	Y	Y

Note: Financial information, benefits and other data can change quickly and may vary from those stated here.

YAHOO! INC   www.yahoo.com

Industry Group Code: 514199B   Ranks within this company's industry group: Sales: 2   Profits: 1

Print Media/Publishing:	Movies:	Equipment/Supplies:		Broadcast/Cable:	Music/Audio:	Sports/Games:
Newspapers:	Movie Theaters:	Equipment/Supplies:		Broadcast TV:	Music Production:	Games/Sports:
Magazines:	Movie Production:	Gambling Equipment:		Cable TV:	Retail Music:	Retail Games Stores:
Books:	TV/Video Production:	Special Services:	Y	Satellite Broadcast:	Retail Audio Equip.:	Stadiums/Teams:
Book Stores:	Video Rental:	Advertising Services:	Y	Radio:	Music Print./Dist.:	Gambling/Casinos:
Distribution/Printing:	Video Distribution:	Info. Sys. Software:		Online Information:	Multimedia:	Rides/Theme Parks:

TYPES OF BUSINESS:

Online Portal-Search Engine
Broadcast Media
Job Placement Services
Paid Positioning Services
Advertising Services
Online Business & Consumer Information
Search Technology Licensing
E-Commerce

BRANDS/DIVISIONS/AFFILIATES:

yahoo.com
Yahoo! Mail
Musicmatch, Inc.
HotJobs.com, Ltd.
Yahoo! Shopping
Yahoo! Finance
Yahoo! Travel
Alibaba.com

CONTACTS: *Note: Officers with more than one job title may be intentionally listed here more than once.*

Terry Semel, CEO
Susan Decker, CFO/Exec. VP
Cammie Dunaway, Chief Mktg. Officer
Libby Sartain, Chief People Officer
Lars Rabbe, CIO
Farzad Nazem, CTO/Head-Technology Group
Qi Lu, Sr. VP-Eng. Search
Michael Callahan, General Counsel/Corp. Sec.
Toby R. Coppel, Sr. VP-Corp. Dev.
Jeff Weiner, Sr. VP-Search & Marketplace
Michael Murray, Sr. VP-Finance
Susan Decker, Head-Advertiser & Publisher Group
Gregory Coleman, VP-Media & Sales
Hilary Schneider, Sr. VP-Marketplaces
Terry Semel, Chmn.

Phone: 408-731-3300	Fax: 408-731-3301
Toll-Free:	
Address: 701 First Ave., Sunnyvale, CA 94089 US	

GROWTH PLANS/SPECIAL FEATURES:

Yahoo!, Inc. is a provider of comprehensive online products and services to consumers and businesses worldwide. In December 2006, the company announced a reorganization of its structure to align itself with the demands of three key customers: audiences, advertisers and publishers. Under the realigned structure, the company has three business segments: audience group, advertiser & publisher group and technology group. The audience group focuses on growing and developing the Yahoo! Tools used by everyday consumers such as Yahoo! Mail, Yahoo! Messenger, Yahoo! Calendar, Yahoo! Chat, Yahoo! Greetings, Yahoo! Clubs and Yahoo! Photos. Commerce services include Yahoo! Shopping, Yahoo! Auctions, Yahoo! Finance and Yahoo! Travel. The advertisers and publishers group was created by combining Yahoo!'s marketing solutions, sales teams and distribution partners to streamline the firm's advertising and marketing offerings. The technology group engineers and upkeeps the advertising and internet platforms of the whole organization. Yahoo!'s global network includes 25 countries and is available in 15 languages. In addition to offering a search directory of web content, the company has entered into strategic relationships with business partners that offer content, technology and distribution capabilities, which permit the company to bring Yahoo!-branded, targeted media products to the market more quickly. The company operates as an Internet recruiter through HotJobs.com, Ltd., a leading Internet job placement and recruiting company. Recently, the company acquired a 10% stake in Gmarket Inc., an e-commerce marketplace provider in Korea. In September 2006, Yahoo! entered into an agreement with eBay to be the sole provider of graphical advertisements on the auction portal's website. In December 2006, the company announced a reorganization of its structure to align itself with the demands of three key customers: audiences, advertisers and publishers.

Yahoo! benefits package includes eight weeks of maternity leave, informal telecommuting, gym membership and up to $5,000 in tuition reimbursement per year.

FINANCIALS: Sales and profits are in thousands of dollars—add 000 to get the full amount. 2006 Note: Financial information for 2006 was not available for all companies at press time.

2006 Sales: $	2006 Profits: $	U.S. Stock Ticker: YHOO
2005 Sales: $5,258,000	2005 Profits: $1,896,000	Int'l Ticker: Int'l Exchange:
2004 Sales: $3,575,000	2004 Profits: $839,553	Employees: 9,660
2003 Sales: $1,625,097	2003 Profits: $237,879	Fiscal Year Ends: 12/31
2002 Sales: $953,100	2002 Profits: $42,800	Parent Company:

SALARIES/BENEFITS:

Pension Plan:	ESOP Stock Plan:	Profit Sharing:	Top Exec. Salary: $600,000	Bonus: $
Savings Plan: Y	Stock Purch. Plan: Y		Second Exec. Salary: $500,000	Bonus: $900,000

OTHER THOUGHTS:

Apparent Women Officers or Directors: 4
Hot Spot for Advancement for Women/Minorities: Y

LOCATIONS: ("Y" = Yes)

West:	Southwest:	Midwest:	Southeast:	Northeast:	International:
Y	Y	Y	Y	Y	Y

Note: Financial information, benefits and other data can change quickly and may vary from those stated here.

YAHOO! SEARCH MARKETING GROUP

searchmarketing.yahoo.com

Industry Group Code: 541810A Ranks within this company's industry group: Sales: Profits:

Print Media/Publishing:	Movies:	Equipment/Supplies:		Broadcast/Cable:	Music/Audio:	Sports/Games:
Newspapers:	Movie Theaters:	Equipment/Supplies:		Broadcast TV:	Music Production:	Games/Sports:
Magazines:	Movie Production:	Gambling Equipment:		Cable TV:	Retail Music:	Retail Games Stores:
Books:	TV/Video Production:	Special Services:		Satellite Broadcast:	Retail Audio Equip.:	Stadiums/Teams:
Book Stores:	Video Rental:	Advertising Services:	Y	Radio:	Music Print./Dist.:	Gambling/Casinos:
Distribution/Printing:	Video Distribution:	Info. Sys. Software:		Online Information:	Multimedia:	Rides/Theme Parks:

TYPES OF BUSINESS:

Online Marketing & Advertising

BRANDS/DIVISIONS/AFFILIATES:

goto.com
Pay-For-Performance
Yahoo!

CONTACTS: Note: Officers with more than one job title may be intentionally listed here more than once.

Steve Mitgang, Sr. VP-Mktg.
Qi Lu, Sr. VP-Eng.
Jennifer Stephens, Dir.-Corp. Comm.
Jeff Weiner, Sr. VP-Yahoo! Search

Phone: 818-524-3000	Fax: 818-524-3001

Toll-Free: 888-811-4686

Address: 3333 Empire Ave., Burbank, CA 91504 US

GROWTH PLANS/SPECIAL FEATURES:

Yahoo! Search Marketing Group (YSMG), a subsidiary of Yahoo!, offers paid search results advertising services. The company uses an online auction format, with the winners of the auction receiving the highest placement. The company boasts that it can reach 80% of all active Internet users. YSMG's Internet marketplace provides consumers with quality search results, supplies advertisers with a cost-effective advertising medium and offers its distributors a revenue-generating search capability. Its core product, Pay-For-Performance, offers a real-time marketplace where its 100,000 advertisers can bid for placement in search results that the company distributes to affiliate partners such as MSN, Yahoo! and CNN. Advertisers pay for service only when users click on their listings. YSMG is headquartered in Burbank, California, with additional offices in New York, New York; Chicago, Illinois; and Palo Alto, California; and international subsidiary offices in Europe, Asia and Australia.

YSMG offers its employees numerous on-site benefits, including a pool table, satellite TV, exercise room, yoga classes and more. Employee medical benefits include PPO and HMO plans.

FINANCIALS: Sales and profits are in thousands of dollars—add 000 to get the full amount. 2006 Note: Financial information for 2006 was not available for all companies at press time.

2006 Sales: $	2006 Profits: $	U.S. Stock Ticker: Subsidiary
2005 Sales: $	2005 Profits: $	Int'l Ticker: Int'l Exchange:
2004 Sales: $	2004 Profits: $	Employees: 876
2003 Sales: $	2003 Profits: $	Fiscal Year Ends: 12/31
2002 Sales: $667,700	2002 Profits: $73,100	Parent Company: YAHOO! INC

SALARIES/BENEFITS:

Pension Plan:	ESOP Stock Plan:	Profit Sharing:	Top Exec. Salary: $98,750	Bonus: $37,500
Savings Plan: Y	Stock Purch. Plan: Y		Second Exec. Salary: $85,000	Bonus: $

OTHER THOUGHTS:

Apparent Women Officers or Directors: 1
Hot Spot for Advancement for Women/Minorities:

LOCATIONS: ("Y" = Yes)

West:	Southwest:	Midwest:	Southeast:	Northeast:	International:
Y		Y		Y	Y

YOUBET.COM INC

www.youbet.com

Industry Group Code: 713210 Ranks within this company's industry group: Sales: 7　Profits: 5

Print Media/Publishing:	Movies:	Equipment/Supplies:	Broadcast/Cable:	Music/Audio:	Sports/Games:
Newspapers:	Movie Theaters:	Equipment/Supplies:	Broadcast TV:	Music Production:	Games/Sports:
Magazines:	Movie Production:	Gambling Equipment:	Cable TV:	Retail Music:	Retail Games Stores:
Books:	TV/Video Production:	Special Services: Y	Satellite Broadcast:	Retail Audio Equip.:	Stadiums/Teams:
Book Stores:	Video Rental:	Advertising Services:	Radio:	Music Print./Dist.:	Gambling/Casinos: Y
Distribution/Printing:	Video Distribution:	Info. Sys. Software: Y	Online Information:	Multimedia:	Rides/Theme Parks:

TYPES OF BUSINESS:

Online Gambling
Horse Racetrack Wagering
Pari-Mutuel Wagering
Horse Racing Information

BRANDS/DIVISIONS/AFFILIATES:

You Bet Network
Youbet Advantage
Youbet.com TotalAccess
Youbet Express
Players Trust
International Racing Group
United Tote

CONTACTS: *Note: Officers with more than one job title may be intentionally listed here more than once.*

Charles F. Champion, CEO
Charles F. Champion, Pres.
Gary W. Sproule, CFO
Thomas L. Levenick, VP Mktg. & Sales
Victor Gallo, VP-Bus. Dev.
Scott Soloman, Corp. Sec.
Michael L. Knapp, Dir-New Product Integration
Jeff Franklin, Pres., Youbet Online Services
Todd Galbate, VP-Client Services
Charles F. Champion, Chmn.
Louis J. Tavano, Gen. Mng.-Int'l Racing Corp.

Phone: 818-668-2100	Fax: 818-668-2101
Toll-Free: 888-968-2388	
Address: 5901 De Soto Ave., Woodland Hills, CA 91367 US	

GROWTH PLANS/SPECIAL FEATURES:

Youbet.com, Inc. is a leading brand name for online event sports entertainment, pari-mutuel wagering and other types of online gaming. Its principal product, the You Bet Network, allows subscribers to wager on live events online and on all major racetracks in 41 states. To date, the company has processed over 1 billion in wagers. Network members can watch events, access a database of handicapping information and wager on a selection of coast-to-coast thoroughbred and harness horse races via a closed-loop network. You Bet Advantage is the only player incentive program of its kind in the U.S. Virtually 100% of U.S., Canadian and Australian horse racing content is available 24 hours a day. The network is interactive and provides a real-time environment. It also features commingled track pools, live audio and video and up-to-the-minute information from the tracks. Youbet.com operates Youbet.com TotalAccess, an Oregon-based hub for the acceptance and placement of wagers. The company has also developed a web-based application, Youbet Express, to enhance and improve the network. In addition, You bet.com features Players Trust, which places players' deposits in the custody of a major U.S. financial institution. Youbet.com is the sole provider of horse racing information for CBS SportsLine.com, an official online wagering platform of Churchill Downs Incorporated and the Kentucky Derby. Customers can wager online in horse races in 41 states in the U.S. and Washington D.C., and in Australia, Canada, Hong Kong, Japan, and South Africa. Youbet.com operates its international functions through a wholly-owned subsidiary, International Racing Group (IRG). In February 2006, Youbet.com acquired United Tote from UT Group, LLC for $31.9 million and $14.7 million in acquired debt.

Youbet.com's employee benefits include credit union membership, a 401(k) plan, discounted stock options, training and development programs. a wellness program., medical and dental benefits, and flexible benefit accounts.

FINANCIALS: Sales and profits are in thousands of dollars—add 000 to get the full amount. 2006 Note: Financial information for 2006 was not available for all companies at press time.

2006 Sales: $	2006 Profits: $	U.S. Stock Ticker: UBET
2005 Sales: $88,837	2005 Profits: $5,691	Int'l Ticker:　Int'l Exchange:
2004 Sales: $65,249	2004 Profits: $4,631	Employees:　106
2003 Sales: $53,120	2003 Profits: $-4,003	Fiscal Year Ends: 12/31
2002 Sales: $25,900	2002 Profits: $-9,000	Parent Company:

SALARIES/BENEFITS:

Pension Plan: Y	ESOP Stock Plan:	Profit Sharing: Y	Top Exec. Salary: $481,684	Bonus: $233,200
Savings Plan: Y	Stock Purch. Plan: Y		Second Exec. Salary: $325,000	Bonus: $130,000

OTHER THOUGHTS:

Apparent Women Officers or Directors:
Hot Spot for Advancement for Women/Minorities:

LOCATIONS: ("Y" = Yes)

West:	Southwest:	Midwest:	Southeast:	Northeast:	International:
Y					

YOUNG BROADCASTING INC   www.youngbroadcasting.com

Industry Group Code: 513120 Ranks within this company's industry group: Sales: 20   Profits: 17

Print Media/Publishing:	Movies:	Equipment/Supplies:		Broadcast/Cable:		Music/Audio:	Sports/Games:
Newspapers:	Movie Theaters:	Equipment/Supplies:		Broadcast TV:	Y	Music Production:	Games/Sports:
Magazines:	Movie Production:	Gambling Equipment:		Cable TV:		Retail Music:	Retail Games Stores:
Books:	TV/Video Production:	Special Services:		Satellite Broadcast:		Retail Audio Equip.:	Stadiums/Teams:
Book Stores:	Video Rental:	Advertising Services:	Y	Radio:		Music Print./Dist.:	Gambling/Casinos:
Distribution/Printing:	Video Distribution:	Info. Sys. Software:		Online Information:		Multimedia:	Rides/Theme Parks:

TYPES OF BUSINESS:
Television Broadcasting
Advertising Sales

BRANDS/DIVISIONS/AFFILIATES:
Adam Young, Inc.

CONTACTS: *Note: Officers with more than one job title may be intentionally listed here more than once.*
Vincent J. Young, CEO
Deborah A. McDermott, Pres.
James A. Morgan, CFO/Exec. VP/Sec.
Daniel R. Batchelor, VP-Sales
Peter Grazioli, CIO/VP-IT
Robert Harrison, Dir.-Eng./VP
Robert Peterson, VP-Bus. Dev.
Stephen J. Baker, VP/Controller/Asst. Sec
Brian Greif, VP-News
Michael Sechrist, Regional VP
Vincent J. Young, Chmn.

Phone: 212-754-7070	Fax: 212-758-1229
Toll-Free:	
Address: 599 Lexington Ave., New York, NY 10022 US	

GROWTH PLANS/SPECIAL FEATURES:

Young Broadcasting, Inc. owns and operates 10 television stations in various parts of the country. Its stations are: WLNS-TV in Lansing, Michigan; KRON-TV in San Francisco, California; WBAY-TV in Green Bay, Wisconsin; KELO-TV in Sioux Falls, South Dakota; KLFY-TV in Lafayette, Louisiana; WTEN in Albany, New York; WRIC in Richmond, Virginia; WATE in Knoxville, Tennessee; and WKRN in Nashville, Tennessee. Five of the stations are ABC affiliates; two are CBS affiliates; two are affiliates of MyNetworkTV; the tenth is affiliated with NBC. Together these stations represent 6.02% of American television household coverage. In addition to national programming, stations owned by Young Broadcasting offer local news and sports programming. Young also owns and operates a national television sales representation firm, Adam Young, Inc. Young's corporate strategy is to acquire stations at below market prices and turn them into more profitable operations by streamlining costs and boosting advertising revenue. To spread its risk, the company has made a point of acquiring stations in geographically diverse areas. It foresees additional growth in television station acquisitions and in targeted marketing techniques. To that end, the company has focused its efforts on working closely with advertisers to target specific television audiences, and on upgrading sales staffs in its local markets. In 2006, Young reached a three year joint sales and shared services agreement with Spartan TV, LLC's WHTV-TV, a UPN affiliate operating in Jackson and Lansing, Michigan.

FINANCIALS: Sales and profits are in thousands of dollars—add 000 to get the full amount. 2006 Note: Financial information for 2006 was not available for all companies at press time.

2006 Sales: $	2006 Profits: $	U.S. Stock Ticker: YBTVA
2005 Sales: $225,524	2005 Profits: $-44,276	Int'l Ticker: Int'l Exchange:
2004 Sales: $197,478	2004 Profits: $-91,346	Employees: 1,265
2003 Sales: $132,234	2003 Profits: $-49,117	Fiscal Year Ends: 12/31
2002 Sales: $225,100	2002 Profits: $-65,600	Parent Company:

SALARIES/BENEFITS:

Pension Plan:	ESOP Stock Plan:	Profit Sharing:	Top Exec. Salary: $1,271,481	Bonus: $678,301
Savings Plan: Y	Stock Purch. Plan:		Second Exec. Salary: $668,529	Bonus: $261,551

OTHER THOUGHTS:

Apparent Women Officers or Directors: 1
Hot Spot for Advancement for Women/Minorities:

LOCATIONS: ("Y" = Yes)

West:	Southwest:	Midwest:	Southeast:	Northeast:	International:
Y		Y	Y	Y	

ZIFF DAVIS MEDIA INC

www.ziffdavis.com

Industry Group Code: 511120 Ranks within this company's industry group: Sales: 15 Profits: 11

Print Media/Publishing:		Movies:	Equipment/Supplies:		Broadcast/Cable:	Music/Audio:	Sports/Games:
Newspapers:		Movie Theaters:	Equipment/Supplies:		Broadcast TV:	Music Production:	Games/Sports:
Magazines:	Y	Movie Production:	Gambling Equipment:		Cable TV:	Retail Music:	Retail Games Stores:
Books:		TV/Video Production:	Special Services:	Y	Satellite Broadcast:	Retail Audio Equip.:	Stadiums/Teams:
Book Stores:		Video Rental:	Advertising Services:		Radio:	Music Print./Dist.:	Gambling/Casinos:
Distribution/Printing:		Video Distribution:	Info. Sys. Software:		Online Information:	Multimedia:	Rides/Theme Parks:

TYPES OF BUSINESS:

Online Content & Publishing
Computer & Technology Magazines
Conferences & Events
Custom Publishing
Research Services
Market Intelligence

BRANDS/DIVISIONS/AFFILIATES:

PC Magazine
1up.com
eWEEK
CIO Insight
MacWorld
Electronic Gaming Monthly
Baseline
Ziff Davis Holdings, Inc.

CONTACTS: Note: Officers with more than one job title may be intentionally listed here more than once.

Robert F. Callahan, CEO
Mark D. Moyer, CFO/Sr. VP
Ken Beach, Sr. VP-Corp. Sales
Beth Repeta, VP-Human Resources
Elda Vale, Sr.VP-Corp. Mktg. & Research
Jasmine Alexander, Sr. VP-Tech.
Gregory Barton, General Counsel/Exec. VP-Licensing
Priscilla Ng, VP-e-Events
Randy Zane, VP-Corp. Comm.
Martha Schwartz, Sr. VP-Custom Solutions
Scott McCarthy, Pres., Game Group
Sloan Seymour, Pres., Enterprise Group
Jason Young, Pres., Consumer/Small Business Group
Robert F. Callahan, Chmn.
Suk Park, Mng. Dir.-Ziff Davis Media Int'l

Phone: 212-503-3500	Fax: 212-503-4599
Toll-Free:	
Address: 28 E. 28th St., New York, NY 10016-7930 US	

GROWTH PLANS/SPECIAL FEATURES:

Ziff Davis Media, Inc. (ZDMI) is an integrated media company focused on the technology, video game and consumer lifestyle markets. The company is an information services provider of technology media including publications, web sites, conferences, events, e-seminars, e-newsletters, custom publishing, list rental, research and market intelligence. ZDMI's operations are organized into three operating units: Consumer/Small Business, responsible for PC Magazine; the Game Group, which includes 1up.com; and the Enterprise Group, which includes eWEEK. ZDMI licenses its content and brands in over 45 countries and in 17 languages worldwide. The firm's events business is organized under the Enterprise Group through Custom Solutions, which builds targeted events for the business and consumer technology communities. ZDMI has seven established titles and 32 web sites, which reach over 28 million people per month in conjunction with event attendees. Magazines titles include PC Magazine, eWEEK, Baseline, CIO Insight, Electronic Gaming Monthly, Official U.S. PlayStation Magazine and Computer Gaming World. The firm also has a joint venture with International Data Group to publish MacWorld, a magazine providing information about Macintosh products. ZDMI's newest publications include Expedia Travels and CIO Insight. Ziff Davis Holdings, Inc. indirectly owns 100% of ZDMI through which it conducts all of its business. In December 2006, CIO Insight was launched in China in by SEEC/Ziff Davis Media Group (China) Ltd., a joint venture partnership formed with SEEC Media Group. In late 2006, ZDMI began trying to sell two of its divisions, Consumer Small Business Group and Game Group. This news came shortly after talks to sell the Enterprise segment fell through with the Quadrangle Group. In early 2007, ZDMI discontinued publication of Official U.S. PlayStation Magazine. In 2006, ZDMI launched PC Magazine and Electronic Gaming Monthly in Turkey and EGM in Thailand.

FINANCIALS: Sales and profits are in thousands of dollars—add 000 to get the full amount. 2006 Note: Financial information for 2006 was not available for all companies at press time.

2006 Sales: $	2006 Profits: $	U.S. Stock Ticker: Subsidiary
2005 Sales: $187,611	2005 Profits: $-118,075	Int'l Ticker: Int'l Exchange:
2004 Sales: $204,477	2004 Profits: $-85,186	Employees: 460
2003 Sales: $194,107	2003 Profits: $-1,909	Fiscal Year Ends: 12/31
2002 Sales: $209,000	2002 Profits: $	Parent Company: ZIFF DAVIS HOLDINGS, INC.

SALARIES/BENEFITS:

Pension Plan:	ESOP Stock Plan: Y	Profit Sharing:	Top Exec. Salary: $1,000,000	Bonus: $1,000,000
Savings Plan:	Stock Purch. Plan:		Second Exec. Salary: $500,000	Bonus: $500,000

OTHER THOUGHTS:

Apparent Women Officers or Directors: 7
Hot Spot for Advancement for Women/Minorities: Y

LOCATIONS: ("Y" = Yes)

West:	Southwest:	Midwest:	Southeast:	Northeast:	International:
Y				Y	Y

Note: Financial information, benefits and other data can change quickly and may vary from those stated here.

ADDITIONAL INDEXES

CONTENTS:

INDEX OF FIRMS NOTED AS HOT SPOTS FOR ADVANCEMENT FOR WOMEN & MINORITIES

2929 ENTERTAINMENT
ALLIANCE ATLANTIS COMMUNICATIONS INC
AMAZON.COM INC
AMERICAN EXPRESS CO
AMERICAN GREETINGS CORP
AMERISTAR CASINOS INC
ANHEUSER BUSCH COS INC
ARBITRON INC
ARISTOCRAT LEISURE LTD
AVID TECHNOLOGY INC
BALLY TOTAL FITNESS HOLDING CORPORATION
BANTA CORPORATION
BARNES & NOBLE INC
BEASLEY BROADCAST GROUP INC
BELO CORP
BERRY COMPANY (THE)
BERTELSMANN AG
BEST BUY CO INC
BOOTH CREEK SKI HOLDINGS INC
BRITISH BROADCASTING CORPORATION (BBC)
CBS CORP
CBS RADIO
CENTRAL EUROPEAN MEDIA ENTERPRISES LTD
CHARTER COMMUNICATIONS
CHURCHILL DOWNS INC
CIRCUIT CITY STORES INC
CLEAR CHANNEL COMMUNICATIONS INC
COLUMBIA TRISTAR MOTION PICTURE GROUP
COMCAST CORP
CONDE NAST PUBLICATIONS INC
CORUS ENTERTAINMENT INC
COURIER CORP
COX COMMUNICATIONS INC
COX ENTERPRISES INC
COX RADIO INC
CW NETWORK (THE)
DELAWARE NORTH COMPANIES
DIALOG NEWSEDGE
DICK CLARK PRODUCTIONS INC
DISCOVERY COMMUNICATIONS INC
DOW JONES & COMPANY INC
DREAMWORKS ANIMATION SKG INC
DREAMWORKS LLC
DUN & BRADSTREET CORP (THE, D&B)
E W SCRIPPS CO
EMAP PLC
ENTERCOM COMMUNICATIONS CORP
FISHER COMMUNICATIONS INC
FORBES INC
FREEDOM COMMUNICATIONS INC
GAMING PARTNERS INTERNATIONAL CORP
GANNETT CO INC
GEMSTAR-TV GUIDE INTERNATIONAL INC
GENERAL ELECTRIC CO (GE)

GOOGLE INC
GRUPO RADIO CENTRO SA DE CV
HARPO INC
HARRAH'S ENTERTAINMENT INC
HARTE-HANKS INC
HEARST CORPORATION (THE)
HEARST-ARGYLE TELEVISION INC
HERSHEY CO
HOLLYWOOD MEDIA CORP
HOUGHTON MIFFLIN CO
IAC/INTERACTIVECORP
IMAX CORPORATION
INSIGHT COMMUNICATIONS COMPANY INC
INTERACTIVE DATA CORPORATION
INTERNATIONAL GAME TECHNOLOGY
INTERPUBLIC GROUP OF COMPANIES INC
ITV PLC
IVILLAGE INC
JOHN WILEY & SONS INC
JOHNSON PUBLISHING COMPANY INC
JOURNAL COMMUNICATIONS INC
JUMPTV INC
LANDMARK COMMUNICATIONS INC
LEE ENTERPRISES INC
LIBERTY GLOBAL
LUCASFILM LTD
MARTHA STEWART LIVING OMNIMEDIA INC
MCCLATCHY COMPANY (THE)
MDI ENTERTAINMENT INC
MICROSOFT CORP
MOODY'S CORPORATION
NASPERS LIMITED
NBC UNIVERSAL
NEW YORK TIMES CO (THE)
OMNICOM GROUP INC
OMNIVISION TECHNOLOGIES INC
PEARSON PLC
PENTON MEDIA INC
PINNACLE ENTERTAINMENT INC
PIXAR ANIMATION STUDIOS
PLAYBOY ENTERPRISES INC
PRIMEDIA INC
R R DONNELLEY & SONS CO
RADIO ONE
RADIOSHACK CORPORATION
RAINBOW MEDIA HOLDINGS LLC
RANK GROUP PLC (THE)
RAYCOM MEDIA INC
REUTERS GROUP PLC
RODALE INC
ROGERS COMMUNICATIONS INC
SAGA COMMUNICATIONS INC
SALON MEDIA GROUP INC
SCHOLASTIC CORP
SCIENTIFIC GAMES CORPORATION
SHANDA INTERACTIVE ENTERTAINMENT LIMITED
SIMON & SCHUSTER INC

SIRIUS SATELLITE RADIO
SONY CORPORATION
SONY PICTURES ENTERTAINMENT
SRS LABS INC
SUDDENLINK COMMUNICATIONS
THOMSON CORPORATION (THE)
TIME WARNER CABLE
TIME WARNER INC
TIVO INC
TURNER BROADCASTING SYSTEM
UNITED TALENT AGENCY INC
VERIZON COMMUNICATIONS
VIACOM INC
VINDIGO INC
VULCAN INC
WALT DISNEY COMPANY (THE)
WARNER MUSIC GROUP
WASHINGTON POST CO
WENNER MEDIA LLC
WPP GROUP PLC
XM SATELLITE RADIO HOLDINGS INC
YAHOO! INC
ZIFF DAVIS MEDIA INC

INDEX OF SUBSIDIARIES, BRAND NAMES AND AFFILIATIONS

Brand or subsidiary, followed by the name of the related corporation

INDEX OF SUBSIDIARIES, BRAND NAMES AND AFFILIATIONS, CONT.

INDEX OF SUBSIDIARIES, BRAND NAMES AND AFFILIATIONS, CONT.

INDEX OF SUBSIDIARIES, BRAND NAMES AND AFFILIATIONS, CONT.

INDEX OF SUBSIDIARIES, BRAND NAMES AND AFFILIATIONS, CONT.

Broder Webb Chervin Silbermann Agency;
**INTERNATIONAL CREATIVE MANAGEMENT
(ICM)**
Bud Jones Company (The); **GAMING PARTNERS
INTERNATIONAL CORP**
Budweiser; **ANHEUSER BUSCH COS INC**
Buena Vista Home Entertainment; **MIRAMAX FILM
CORP**
Buena Vista Television; **ABC INC**
Build Your Own Membership (BYOM); **BALLY TOTAL
FITNESS HOLDING CORPORATION**
BuisinessWeek Magazine; **MCGRAW HILL COS INC**
Burson-Marsteller; **WPP GROUP PLC**
Busch Agricultural Resources, Inc.; **ANHEUSER
BUSCH COS INC**
Busch Gardens; **ANHEUSER BUSCH COS INC**
Business Journal; **DAILY JOURNAL CORP**
BuyMagazine; **BUY.COM INC**
buymusic.com; **BUY.COM INC**
BuySeasons Inc.; **LIBERTY MEDIA CORP**
BuySeasons, Inc.; **LIBERTY MEDIA CORP**
BuyTV.com; **BUY.COM INC**
Buzztime Entertainment, Inc.; **NTN BUZZTIME INC**
CABLE TV; **I-CABLE COMMUNICATIONS**
CableONE; **WASHINGTON POST CO**
CableVantage; **RAYCOM MEDIA INC**
Cablevision; **GRUPO TELEVISA SA**
Cablevision Systems Corporation; **RAINBOW MEDIA
HOLDINGS LLC**
Cacao Reserve; **HERSHEY CO**
Cactus Pete's Resort Casino; **AMERISTAR CASINOS
INC**
Caesar's Entertainment, Inc.; **HARRAH'S
ENTERTAINMENT INC**
Caesars Palace; **CAESARS ENTERTAINMENT INC**
Caesars Palace at Sea; **CAESARS ENTERTAINMENT
INC**
Caesars Tahoe; **CAESARS ENTERTAINMENT INC**
Calder Race Course; **CHURCHILL DOWNS INC**
Caledon Casino, Hotel & Spa; **CENTURY CASINOS
INC**
California Fitness; **24 HOUR FITNESS USA**
California Hotel & Casino; **BOYD GAMING CORP**
California Real Estate Journal; **DAILY JOURNAL
CORP**
Camelot Music; **WHEREHOUSE ENTERTAINMENT
(RECORD TOWN INC)**
CameraChip; **OMNIVISION TECHNOLOGIES INC**
canada.com; **CANWEST GLOBAL
COMMUNICATIONS**
Canadian Satellite Communications, Inc.; **SHAW
COMMUNICATIONS INC**
Canterbury Card Club; **CANTERBURY PARK
HOLDING CORP**
CanWest Entertainment; **CANWEST GLOBAL
COMMUNICATIONS**

CanWest Interactive; **CANWEST GLOBAL
COMMUNICATIONS**
Canyons (The); **AMERICAN SKIING COMPANY**
Capitol; **EMI GROUP PLC**
Captivate; **GANNETT CO INC**
CaptiVision; **TRANS-LUX CORPORATION**
CaptiVue; **TRANS-LUX CORPORATION**
Car & Driver; **LAGARDERE ACTIVE MEDIA**
Caribbean Stud; **PROGRESSIVE GAMING
INTERNATIONAL CORP**
Carlton Cards; **AMERICAN GREETINGS CORP**
Carlton Screen Advertising; **ITV PLC**
Carlyle Group; **INSIGHT COMMUNICATIONS
COMPANY INC**
Carolrhoda Books, Inc.; **LERNER PUBLISHING
GROUP**
Cars; **PIXAR ANIMATION STUDIOS**
Cartoon Network; **TURNER BROADCASTING
SYSTEM**
Casino Aztar Caruthersville; **AZTAR CORP**
Casino Aztar Evansville; **AZTAR CORP**
Casino Data Systems; **ARISTOCRAT LEISURE LTD**
Casino L'Auberge du Lac; **PINNACLE
ENTERTAINMENT INC**
Casino World, Inc.; **DIAMONDHEAD CASINO
CORPORATION**
Castaway Bay; **CEDAR FAIR LP**
Castle Rock; **WARNER BROS ENTERTAINMENT
INC**
CBBC Channel; **BRITISH BROADCASTING
CORPORATION (BBC)**
Cbeebies; **BRITISH BROADCASTING
CORPORATION (BBC)**
CBS; **UNITED PARAMOUNT NETWORK (UPN)**
CBS; **NATIONAL AMUSEMENTS INC**
CBS Corp.; **CW NETWORK (THE)**
CBS Corporation; **SIMON & SCHUSTER INC**
CBS Corporation; **CBS RADIO**
CBS News; **CBS CORP**
CBS Radio Network; **CBS RADIO**
CBS Sports; **CBS CORP**
CCM Magazine; **SALEM COMMUNICATIONS CORP**
CD Exchange; **CD WAREHOUSE INC**
CD Radio, Inc.; **SIRIUS SATELLITE RADIO**
CD World; **WHEREHOUSE ENTERTAINMENT
(RECORD TOWN INC)**
CDM Optics, Inc.; **OMNIVISION TECHNOLOGIES
INC**
Cebridge Connections; **SUDDENLINK
COMMUNICATIONS**
Cellular One; **AT&T INC**
Central Virginia Gazette (The); **MEDIA GENERAL INC**
Century Casino & Hotel; **CENTURY CASINOS INC**
Century Casinos Africa (Pty) Limited; **CENTURY
CASINOS INC**

INDEX OF SUBSIDIARIES, BRAND NAMES AND AFFILIATIONS, CONT.

INDEX OF SUBSIDIARIES, BRAND NAMES AND AFFILIATIONS, CONT.

INDEX OF SUBSIDIARIES, BRAND NAMES AND AFFILIATIONS, CONT.

CTC Distribution Direct; **R R DONNELLEY & SONS CO**
Cumulus Broadcasting; **CUMULUS MEDIA INC**
Cumulus Media Partners; **CUMULUS MEDIA INC**
Curves Fitness Pedometer; **CURVES INTERNATIONAL INC**
Curves Flexibilty Mat; **CURVES INTERNATIONAL INC**
Curves Free Foods On the Go Lunchbox; **CURVES INTERNATIONAL INC**
Curves Heart Rate Monitor Watch; **CURVES INTERNATIONAL INC**
Curves Travel; **CURVES INTERNATIONAL INC**
curvestravel.com; **CURVES INTERNATIONAL INC**
CW (The); **WARNER BROS ENTERTAINMENT INC**
CyberTarget; **UNITED ONLINE INC**
CyGamZ; **NATIONAL AMUSEMENTS INC**
Cypress Mountain; **BOYNE USA RESORTS**
D&B; **DUN & BRADSTREET CORP (THE, D&B)**
D&B; **HOOVER'S INC**
D&B E-Business Solutions; **DUN & BRADSTREET CORP (THE, D&B)**
D&B Risk Management Solutions; **DUN & BRADSTREET CORP (THE, D&B)**
D&B Sales & Marketing Solutions; **DUN & BRADSTREET CORP (THE, D&B)**
D&B Supply Management Solutions; **DUN & BRADSTREET CORP (THE, D&B)**
Dagoba Organic Chocolate, LLC; **HERSHEY CO**
Daily Buzz (The); **ACME COMMUNICATIONS INC**
Daily Herald Company (The); **WASHINGTON POST CO**
Daily Puzzle; **GLU MOBILE**
Daily Recorder (The); **DAILY JOURNAL CORP**
Daily Southtown; **HOLLINGER INC**
Dallas Morning News (The); **BELO CORP**
Daou Report (The); **SALON MEDIA GROUP INC**
Daredevil; **MARVEL ENTERTAINMENT INC**
Darlow Smithson Productions; **IMG WORLDWIDE INC**
DART Enterprise; **DOUBLECLICK INC**
DART for Advertisers; **DOUBLECLICK INC**
DART Motif; **DOUBLECLICK INC**
DAS; **OMNICOM GROUP INC**
DATAMARK; **INTERNATIONAL LOTTERY & TOTALIZATOR SYSTEMS**
DataTrak; **INTERNATIONAL LOTTERY & TOTALIZATOR SYSTEMS**
DataWall; **TRANS-LUX CORPORATION**
DateWorks; **AMERICAN GREETINGS CORP**
DBBC, LLC; **CUMULUS MEDIA INC**
DC Comics; **WARNER BROS ENTERTAINMENT INC**
DC Comics; **TIME WARNER INC**
DDB Worldwide; **OMNICOM GROUP INC**
Debmar-Mercury LLC; **LIONS GATE ENTERTAINMENT CORP**

Decca Records; **UNIVERSAL MUSIC GROUP**
Decide DNA 6; **24/7 REAL MEDIA INC**
Deck Mate; **SHUFFLE MASTER INC**
Deep Sea 3D; **IMAX CORPORATION**
Deep Sky; **CORUS ENTERTAINMENT INC**
DEJ Productions; **FIRST LOOK STUDIOS INC**
Delek Investments Properties; **MATAV-CABLE SYSTEMS MEDIA LTD**
Delicious Living; **PENTON MEDIA INC**
Delta Downs Racetrack & Casino; **BOYD GAMING CORP**
Dennis Direct; **DENNIS PUBLISHING LTD**
Denton Record-Chronicle; **BELO CORP**
Dentsu 24/7 Search Holdings; **24/7 REAL MEDIA INC**
Denver Post; **MEDIANEWS GROUP INC**
Depot Casino; **SANDS REGENT**
DesignWare; **AMERICAN GREETINGS CORP**
Desperate Housewives; **ABC INC**
Details; **CONDE NAST PUBLICATIONS INC**
Detroit News; **MEDIANEWS GROUP INC**
Deutsche Grammophon; **UNIVERSAL MUSIC GROUP**
Dexter Shoe Company; **BERKSHIRE HATHAWAY INC**
DGConnect; **DG FASTCHANNEL**
Diablo; **VIVENDI GAMES**
Dialog; **DIALOG NEWSEDGE**
Dialog; **THOMSON CORPORATION (THE)**
Dialog DataStar; **DIALOG NEWSEDGE**
Dialog Intelliscope; **DIALOG NEWSEDGE**
Dialog NewsEdge; **DIALOG NEWSEDGE**
Dialog Profound; **DIALOG NEWSEDGE**
Diamond; **GAMETECH INTERNATIONAL INC**
Diamondhead Casino Corporation; **TRUMP ENTERTAINMENT RESORTS INC**
diane Magazine; **CURVES INTERNATIONAL INC**
Dick Clark Communications; **DICK CLARK PRODUCTIONS INC**
Dick Clark Corporate Productions; **DICK CLARK PRODUCTIONS INC**
Dick Clark Restaurants; **DICK CLARK PRODUCTIONS INC**
Dick Clark's American Bandstand Grill; **DICK CLARK PRODUCTIONS INC**
Dick Clark's AB Diner; **DICK CLARK PRODUCTIONS INC**
Dick Clark's AB Grill; **DICK CLARK PRODUCTIONS INC**
Dick Clark's American Bandstand Theater; **DICK CLARK PRODUCTIONS INC**
Dick Clark's Bandstand-Food, Spirits & Fun; **DICK CLARK PRODUCTIONS INC**
Dig (The); **KERZNER INTERNATIONAL LIMITED**
Digeo iTV; **DIGEO INC**
Digidesign; **AVID TECHNOLOGY INC**
Digital Chicago; **HOLLINGER INC**
Digital Generation Systems; **DG FASTCHANNEL**

INDEX OF SUBSIDIARIES, BRAND NAMES AND AFFILIATIONS, CONT.

INDEX OF SUBSIDIARIES, BRAND NAMES AND AFFILIATIONS, CONT.

INDEX OF SUBSIDIARIES, BRAND NAMES AND AFFILIATIONS, CONT.

INDEX OF SUBSIDIARIES, BRAND NAMES AND AFFILIATIONS, CONT.

INDEX OF SUBSIDIARIES, BRAND NAMES AND AFFILIATIONS, CONT.

INDEX OF SUBSIDIARIES, BRAND NAMES AND AFFILIATIONS, CONT.

INDEX OF SUBSIDIARIES, BRAND NAMES AND AFFILIATIONS, CONT.

Insight Business; **INSIGHT COMMUNICATIONS COMPANY INC**
Insight Magazine; **NEWS WORLD COMMUNICATIONS INC**
Insight Media; **INSIGHT COMMUNICATIONS COMPANY INC**
Insight Midwest, LP; **INSIGHT COMMUNICATIONS COMPANY INC**
InsightBroadband; **INSIGHT COMMUNICATIONS COMPANY INC**
InsightDigital; **INSIGHT COMMUNICATIONS COMPANY INC**
InsightPhone; **INSIGHT COMMUNICATIONS COMPANY INC**
InstallShield Installer; **MACROVISION CORP**
InstantON; **INTERVIDEO INC**
Integrity Music; **INTEGRITY MEDIA INC**
Integrity Publishers; **THOMAS NELSON INC**
Intelimark; **INTERNATIONAL LOTTERY & TOTALIZATOR SYSTEMS**
Intelligent Table System; **PROGRESSIVE GAMING INTERNATIONAL CORP**
Intelsat; **PANAMSAT CORP**
InterJoy Technology, Ltd.; **SHANDA INTERACTIVE ENTERTAINMENT LIMITED**
Interlink Companies; **ALLIANCE ENTERTAINMENT CORP**
Interlott Technologies, Inc.; **GTECH HOLDINGS CORP**
International Dairy Queen; **BERKSHIRE HATHAWAY INC**
International Herald Tribune; **NEW YORK TIMES CO (THE)**
International Racing Group; **YOUBET.COM INC**
Internet Broadcasting Systems; **HEARST-ARGYLE TELEVISION INC**
Internet Broadcasting Systems; **CANWEST GLOBAL COMMUNICATIONS**
Internet Superstore (The); **BUY.COM INC**
internet.com; **JUPITERMEDIA CORP**
InterTAN, Inc.; **CIRCUIT CITY STORES INC**
InterVideo DVD Copy; **INTERVIDEO INC**
InterVideo Home Theater; **INTERVIDEO INC**
iO Games; **CABLEVISION SYSTEMS CORP**
IPC Group, Ltd.; **TIME INC**
IPC Print Services, Inc.; **JOURNAL COMMUNICATIONS INC**
iPhone; **APPLE INC**
I-Play; **DIGITAL BRIDGES LIMITED**
IPO Scorecard; **HOOVER'S INC**
iPod; **APPLE INC**
IQ 2000; **CARMIKE CINEMAS INC**
IQ Zero; **CARMIKE CINEMAS INC**
Irdeto Access; **NASPERS LIMITED**
Irrational Games; **TAKE-TWO INTERACTIVE SOFTWARE INC**
Island; **UNIVERSAL MUSIC GROUP**

IsleOne Players Club; **ISLE OF CAPRI CASINOS INC**
Istithmar PJSC; **KERZNER INTERNATIONAL LIMITED**
ITG Online Entertainment; **INTERNATIONAL GAME TECHNOLOGY**
iTunes; **APPLE INC**
i-TV; **ION MEDIA NETWORKS**
ITV Production; **ITV PLC**
ITV1; **ITV PLC**
ITV2; **ITV PLC**
ITV3; **ITV PLC**
ITV4; **ITV PLC**
iVillage Consulting; **IVILLAGE INC**
iVillage Integrated Properties, Inc.; **IVILLAGE INC**
iVillage Parenting Network, Inc.; **IVILLAGE INC**
Iwerks Entertainment, Inc.; **SIMEX-IWERKS**
J.D. Power & Associates; **MCGRAW HILL COS INC**
Jack of All Games; **TAKE-TWO INTERACTIVE SOFTWARE INC**
Jackson Harness Raceway; **MTR GAMING GROUP INC**
Jackson Trotting Association; **MTR GAMING GROUP INC**
Jadoo Power Systems; **SINCLAIR BROADCAST GROUP INC**
Jamba; **NEWS CORPORATION LIMITED (THE)**
JET Magazine; **JOHNSON PUBLISHING COMPANY INC**
Jewel Quest; **DIGITAL BRIDGES LIMITED**
Jewelry Television; **SHOP AT HOME NETWORK LLC**
Jewish Israeli Yellow Pages (The); **DAG MEDIA INC**
Jewish Master Guide (The); **DAG MEDIA INC**
JewishMasterguide.com; **DAG MEDIA INC**
JewishYellow.com; **DAG MEDIA INC**
Jisheng Technology; **SHANDA INTERACTIVE ENTERTAINMENT LIMITED**
Jive Records; **SONY BMG MUSIC ENTERTAINMENT**
JobKorea; **MONSTER WORLDWIDE**
Joe Muggs; **BOOKS A MILLION INC**
Joe's Crab Shack; **LANDRY'S RESTAURANTS INC**
Journal Broadcast Group; **JOURNAL COMMUNICATIONS INC**
Joyride; **CLARION CO LTD**
JPC Book Division; **JOHNSON PUBLISHING COMPANY INC**
Juice Games, Ltd. (U.K.); **THQ INC**
jumptheshark.com; **GEMSTAR-TV GUIDE INTERNATIONAL INC**
JumpTV International; **JUMPTV INC**
Jungle Juice; **MULTIMEDIA GAMES INC**
Juno; **UNITED ONLINE INC**
Juno SpeedBand; **UNITED ONLINE INC**
Jupiter Telecommunications Co.; **LIBERTY GLOBAL**
JupiterEvents; **JUPITERMEDIA CORP**

INDEX OF SUBSIDIARIES, BRAND NAMES AND AFFILIATIONS, CONT.

INDEX OF SUBSIDIARIES, BRAND NAMES AND AFFILIATIONS, CONT.

INDEX OF SUBSIDIARIES, BRAND NAMES AND AFFILIATIONS, CONT.

INDEX OF SUBSIDIARIES, BRAND NAMES AND AFFILIATIONS, CONT.

INDEX OF SUBSIDIARIES, BRAND NAMES AND AFFILIATIONS, CONT.

INDEX OF SUBSIDIARIES, BRAND NAMES AND AFFILIATIONS, CONT.

INDEX OF SUBSIDIARIES, BRAND NAMES AND AFFILIATIONS, CONT.

INDEX OF SUBSIDIARIES, BRAND NAMES AND AFFILIATIONS, CONT.

INDEX OF SUBSIDIARIES, BRAND NAMES AND AFFILIATIONS, CONT.

SEGA CORPORATION; **SEGA SAMMY HOLDINGS INC**

SEGA Music Networks Co., LTD.; **SEGA SAMMY HOLDINGS INC**

Segye Ilbo; **NEWS WORLD COMMUNICATIONS INC**

Sekai Nippo; **NEWS WORLD COMMUNICATIONS INC**

SendTraffic; **TRAFFIX INC**

Seymour Distribution Ltd.; **DENNIS PUBLISHING LTD**

SFR Cegetel; **VIVENDI SA**

Shadow Broadcast Services; **WESTWOOD ONE INC**

Shadow Traffic; **WESTWOOD ONE INC**

Shadowgate; **VINDIGO INC**

Shanda Networking; **SHANDA INTERACTIVE ENTERTAINMENT LIMITED**

Shanghai Cable Television; **SHANGHAI MEDIA GROUP (SMG)**

Shanghai Dragon Mobile Media Company; **SHANGHAI MEDIA GROUP (SMG)**

Shanghai Television; **SHANGHAI MEDIA GROUP (SMG)**

Sharp Laboratories of America, Inc.; **SHARP CORPORATION**

Sharp Laboratories of Europe, Ltd.; **SHARP CORPORATION**

Sharp Software Development India Pvt., Ltd.; **SHARP CORPORATION**

Sharp Technology (Taiwan) Corp.; **SHARP CORPORATION**

Sharp Telecommunications of Europe, Ltd.; **SHARP CORPORATION**

Shaw Cablesystems G.P.; **SHAW COMMUNICATIONS INC**

Shaw Digital Phone; **SHAW COMMUNICATIONS INC**

Shaw High-Speed Xtreme; **SHAW COMMUNICATIONS INC**

Shaw Marketing Group; **WPP GROUP PLC**

Shoot Stuff; **CONCRETE SOFTWARE INC**

Shop At Home Network, LLC; **E W SCRIPPS CO**

Shop NBC; **VALUEVISION MEDIA INC**

shop.napster.com; **NAPSTER INC**

shopathometv.com; **SHOP AT HOME NETWORK LLC**

Shopbop.com; **AMAZON.COM INC**

Shopila Corporation; **DAG MEDIA INC**

shopnbc.com; **VALUEVISION MEDIA INC**

Shopping Channel (The); **ROGERS COMMUNICATIONS INC**

Shorecliff Communications, LLC; **LANDMARK COMMUNICATIONS INC**

Showcase Action; **ALLIANCE ATLANTIS COMMUNICATIONS INC**

Showcase Cinemas; **NATIONAL AMUSEMENTS INC**

Showcase Home Entertainment; **TWEETER HOME ENTERTAINMENT GROUP INC**

Showtime Network; **CBS CORP**

Shrek; **DREAMWORKS ANIMATION SKG INC**

Shuffle Master Gaming; **SHUFFLE MASTER INC**

Shuffle Up Productions, Inc.; **SHUFFLE MASTER INC**

SI Electronics, LTD.; **SEGA SAMMY HOLDINGS INC**

SIA Software; **LOUD TECHNOLOGIES INC**

Sibelius Software Ltd.; **AVID TECHNOLOGY INC**

Sierra Entertainment; **VIVENDI GAMES**

Sierra-at-Tahoe; **BOOTH CREEK SKI HOLDINGS INC**

Signature Theatres; **REGAL ENTERTAINMENT GROUP**

SigNETure HDTV; **LODGENET ENTERTAINMENT CORP**

Silver Dolphin; **ADVANCED MARKETING SERVICES INC**

Silverstar Development; **CENTURY CASINOS INC**

Simex, Inc.; **SIMEX-IWERKS**

Simon & Schuster; **CBS CORP**

Simpsons (The); **FOX BROADCASTING COMPANY**

Sims (The); **ELECTRONIC ARTS INC**

Sinclair Television Group, Inc.; **SINCLAIR BROADCAST GROUP INC**

Sinclair Ventures, Inc.; **SINCLAIR BROADCAST GROUP INC**

Sirius; **CLARION CO LTD**

Sirius Canada; **SIRIUS SATELLITE RADIO**

SiteCensus; **NETRATINGS INC**

Six Flags Great Adventure; **SIX FLAGS INC**

Six Flags Over Texas; **SIX FLAGS INC**

Six Flags Wild Safari; **SIX FLAGS INC**

Ski Sterling Forest; **RENAISSANCE ENTERTAINMENT CORP**

SKY; **GRUPO TELEVISA SA**

Sky Active; **BRITISH SKY BROADCASTING PLC**

Sky Brasil Servicos Ltda.; **DIRECTV GROUP INC (THE)**

Sky Broadband; **BRITISH SKY BROADCASTING PLC**

Sky Movies; **BRITISH SKY BROADCASTING PLC**

Sky News; **BRITISH SKY BROADCASTING PLC**

Sky One; **BRITISH SKY BROADCASTING PLC**

Sky Sports; **BRITISH SKY BROADCASTING PLC**

Sky Travel; **BRITISH SKY BROADCASTING PLC**

SkyBet Sport; **SKY NETWORK TELEVISION LIMITED**

SkyBet Trackside; **SKY NETWORK TELEVISION LIMITED**

SkyTel; **GRUPO TELEVISA SA**

Skywalker Sound; **LUCASFILM LTD**

Slate; **WASHINGTON POST CO**

SLM Marketplace; **LOUD TECHNOLOGIES INC**

SmackDown; **WORLD WRESTLING ENTERTAINMENT INC (WWF)**

Smallville; **CW NETWORK (THE)**

SmartRoute Systems; **WESTWOOD ONE INC**

INDEX OF SUBSIDIARIES, BRAND NAMES AND AFFILIATIONS, CONT.

INDEX OF SUBSIDIARIES, BRAND NAMES AND AFFILIATIONS, CONT.

INDEX OF SUBSIDIARIES, BRAND NAMES AND AFFILIATIONS, CONT.

INDEX OF SUBSIDIARIES, BRAND NAMES AND AFFILIATIONS, CONT.

INDEX OF SUBSIDIARIES, BRAND NAMES AND AFFILIATIONS, CONT.

VisionAIR, Inc.; **SINCLAIR BROADCAST GROUP INC**
Vista; **MICROSOFT CORP**
Visual Geography Series Online; **LERNER PUBLISHING GROUP**
Vivendi; **VIVENDI GAMES**
Vivendi Games; **VIVENDI SA**
Vivendi Games Mobile; **VIVENDI GAMES**
Vivendi SA; **UNIVERSAL MUSIC GROUP**
Vivendi Universal Entertainment; **NBC UNIVERSAL**
VNU; **NETRATINGS INC**
Vogue; **CONDE NAST PUBLICATIONS INC**
Vogue; **ADVANCE PUBLICATIONS INC**
Volaris; **GRUPO TELEVISA SA**
Voodoo Extreme; **IGN ENTERTAINMENT**
VOX; **RTL GROUP SA**
Voyager Learning; **PROQUEST COMPANY**
VTR GlobalCom, S.A.; **LIBERTY GLOBAL**
Vulcan Capital; **VULCAN INC**
Vulcan Productions; **VULCAN INC**
Vulcan Service; **EBSCO INDUSTRIES INC**
VVI Fulfillment Center, Inc.; **VALUEVISION MEDIA INC**
W; **CORUS ENTERTAINMENT INC**
WagerWorks, Inc.; **INTERNATIONAL GAME TECHNOLOGY**
Walden Media; **ANSCHUTZ ENTERTAINMENT GROUP**
Waldenbooks; **BORDERS GROUP INC**
Wall Street Journal (The); **DOW JONES & COMPANY INC**
Wallace & Gromit: Curse of the Were-Rabbit; **DREAMWORKS ANIMATION SKG INC**
Walt Disney Company (The); **ABC INC**
Walt Disney Company (The); **PIXAR ANIMATION STUDIOS**
Walt Disney Company (The); **WALT DISNEY STUDIOS**
Walt Disney Company (The); **EURO DISNEY SCA**
Walt Disney Studio Entertainment; **MIRAMAX FILM CORP**
Walt Disney Studios; **EURO DISNEY SCA**
WAND (TV) Partnership; **LIN TV CORP**
War Room; **SALON MEDIA GROUP INC**
Warner Bros.; **TIME WARNER INC**
Warner Bros. Pictures; **WARNER BROS ENTERTAINMENT INC**
Warner Bros. Pictures International; **WARNER BROS ENTERTAINMENT INC**
Warner Bros. Records; **WARNER MUSIC GROUP**
Warner Music Entertainment; **WARNER MUSIC GROUP**
Warner/Chappell Music, Inc.; **WARNER MUSIC GROUP**
Washington Post (The); **WASHINGTON POST CO**

Washington Times (The); **NEWS WORLD COMMUNICATIONS INC**
Washingtonpost.Newsweek Interactive Co.; **WASHINGTON POST CO**
Waterville Valley; **BOOTH CREEK SKI HOLDINGS INC**
Wave; **BOSE CORPORATION**
WaveFront; **OMNIVISION TECHNOLOGIES INC**
waymobile.com, Inc.; **VINDIGO INC**
WB; **CW NETWORK (THE)**
WB Saunders; **REED ELSEVIER GROUP PLC**
WE; **RAINBOW MEDIA HOLDINGS LLC**
WE: Women's Entertainment; **METRO-GOLDWYN-MAYER INC (MGM)**
Weather Channel (The); **LANDMARK COMMUNICATIONS INC**
Webshots; **CNET NETWORKS INC**
WebWatch; **RCN CORP**
Well (The); **SALON MEDIA GROUP INC**
West Publishing; **THOMSON CORPORATION (THE)**
Westchester/Fairfield County Times; **JOURNAL REGISTER CO**
Western International Communications; **CANWEST GLOBAL COMMUNICATIONS**
Wet 'N Wild; **PALACE ENTERTAINMENT**
What America's Reading; **BARNESANDNOBLE.COM INC**
Whatsonwhen; **JOHN WILEY & SONS INC**
Wherehouse; **TRANS WORLD ENTERTAINMENT CORP**
Wherehouse Music; **WHEREHOUSE ENTERTAINMENT (RECORD TOWN INC)**
wherehouse.com; **WHEREHOUSE ENTERTAINMENT (RECORD TOWN INC)**
whfs.com; **CBS RADIO**
Whiskey Pete's; **MGM MIRAGE**
WiderThan; **REALNETWORKS INC**
Wiggleworks; **SCHOLASTIC CORP**
Wii; **NINTENDO CO LTD**
Wildhorse Saloon; **GAYLORD ENTERTAINMENT CO**
Wildwater Kingdom; **CEDAR FAIR LP**
Wiley InterScience; **JOHN WILEY & SONS INC**
Wiley InterScience OnlineBooks; **JOHN WILEY & SONS INC**
William Morris Consulting; **WILLIAM MORRIS AGENCY INC**
William Street Press; **LEE ENTERPRISES INC**
Windows; **MICROSOFT CORP**
WinDVD; **INTERVIDEO INC**
WinDVD Creator; **INTERVIDEO INC**
Winston-Salem Journal; **MEDIA GENERAL INC**
Wired; **CONDE NAST PUBLICATIONS INC**
Wired; **ADVANCE PUBLICATIONS INC**
Wirthlin Report; **HARRIS INTERACTIVE INC**
Wirthlin Worldwide; **HARRIS INTERACTIVE INC**

INDEX OF SUBSIDIARIES, BRAND NAMES AND AFFILIATIONS, CONT.

WMS Gaming, Inc.; **WMS INDUSTRIES INC**
Womacks/Legends Casino; **CENTURY CASINOS INC**
Women's Dream Plaza; **SAMSUNG ELECTRONICS CO LTD**
Wooden Nickel Pub, Inc.; **CARMIKE CINEMAS INC**
Worcester Telegram & Gazette; **NEW YORK TIMES CO (THE)**
Word Entertainment; **WARNER MUSIC GROUP**
World of Warcraft; **VIVENDI GAMES**
World Poker Tour; **LAKES ENTERTAINMENT INC**
World Series of Poker; **WMS INDUSTRIES INC**
World Series of Poker Texas Hold'em; **GLU MOBILE**
World Wrestling Federation (WWF); **WORLD WRESTLING ENTERTAINMENT INC (WWF)**
Worlds of Fun; **CEDAR FAIR LP**
WPT Consumer Products; **LAKES ENTERTAINMENT INC**
WPT Enterprises; **LAKES ENTERTAINMENT INC**
WPT Studios; **LAKES ENTERTAINMENT INC**
WPTonline.com; **LAKES ENTERTAINMENT INC**
Wrath Unleashed; **LUCASARTS ENTERTAINMENT COMPANY LLC**
wsj.com; **DOW JONES & COMPANY INC**
WUPL-TV; **BELO CORP**
WWE 24/7 On Demand; **WORLD WRESTLING ENTERTAINMENT INC (WWF)**
WWE Smackdown; **UNITED PARAMOUNT NETWORK (UPN)**
WWEShop; **WORLD WRESTLING ENTERTAINMENT INC (WWF)**
www.SportsYa.com; **JUMPTV INC**
Wynn Las Vegas; **WYNN RESORTS LIMITED**
Wynn Macau; **WYNN RESORTS LIMITED**
Xbox 360; **MICROSOFT CORP**
XL Marketing; **COMMUNITY NEWSPAPER HOLDINGS INC**
XM Canada; **XM SATELLITE RADIO HOLDINGS INC**
XM Originals; **XM SATELLITE RADIO HOLDINGS INC**
XM Public Radio; **XM SATELLITE RADIO HOLDINGS INC**
XM Satellite Radio, Inc.; **XM SATELLITE RADIO HOLDINGS INC**
X-Men; **MARVEL ENTERTAINMENT INC**
XpressBet; **MAGNA ENTERTAINMENT CORP**
Xtra-Vision; **BLOCKBUSTER INC**
Yahoo!; **YAHOO! SEARCH MARKETING GROUP**
Yahoo! Finance; **YAHOO! INC**
Yahoo! Mail; **YAHOO! INC**
Yahoo! Shopping; **YAHOO! INC**
Yahoo! Travel; **YAHOO! INC**
yahoo.com; **YAHOO! INC**
Yorin; **RTL GROUP SA**
You Bet Network; **YOUBET.COM INC**
Youbet Advantage; **YOUBET.COM INC**

Youbet Express; **YOUBET.COM INC**
Youbet.com TotalAccess; **YOUBET.COM INC**
YTV; **CORUS ENTERTAINMENT INC**
Yub.com; **BUY.COM INC**
Yucaipa Companies; **ALLIANCE ENTERTAINMENT CORP**
Zante, Inc.; **SANDS REGENT**
ZDNet; **CNET NETWORKS INC**
ZENON Evironmental, Inc.; **GENERAL ELECTRIC CO (GE)**
Ziff Davis Holdings, Inc.; **ZIFF DAVIS MEDIA INC**
Zipatoni; **INTERPUBLIC GROUP OF COMPANIES INC**
Znojmo; **TRANS WORLD CORP**
Zondervan; **HARPERCOLLINS PUBLISHERS INC**
Zumanity; **CIRQUE DU SOLEIL INC**
Zune; **MICROSOFT CORP**
Zylom Media Group B.V.; **REALNETWORKS INC**
ZynexOrder; **HEARST CORPORATION (THE)**